DISCOVERING
ART HISTORY

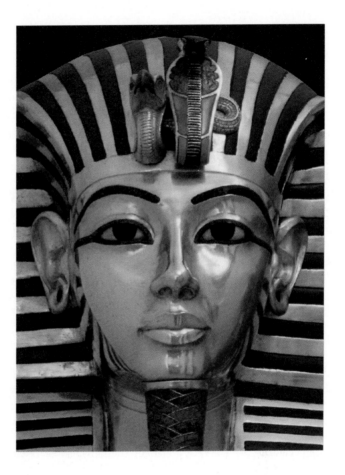

TEACHER'S EDITION

Third Edition

Davis Publications, Inc.
Worcester Massachusetts

Contributors

Author of student text
Gerald F. Brommer

Senior Contributing Editor
Helen Ronan

Contributing Editor
Virginia L. Fitzpatrick,
  Moore College of Art,
  Philadelphia, PA

Additional Contributing Editors
Sallye Mahan-Cox, *Robinson Secondary School, Fairfax, VA*
Kaye Passmore, *Notre Dame Academy, Worcester, MA*
Carolyn Peck, *Park View Junior High School, Cranston, RI*
Abby Remer, *A.R. Arts and Cultural Programs, Inc., NY*

Classroom Connections

Coordinating Editor
Nancy Bedau

Classroom Connections Consultants
William Benson, *University of Wisconsin, Eau Claire, WI*
Karen DeAmicis, *Lower Richland High School, Hopkins, SC*
Trinket Doty, *McLane High School, Fairfax, VA*
Jim Ellis, *Strath Haven High School, Wallingford, PA*
Suzy Goza, *Aztec High School, Aztec, NM*
Sandi Hammonds, *W. T. Woodson High School, Fairfax, VA*
Marsha Hogue, *Lake Highlands High School, Dallas, TX*
Susan Iovieno, *Mansfield Public Schools, Mansfield, MA*
Kathy Kalson, *Bakersfield High School, Bakersfield, CA*
Susan Klinger, *Perkiomen Valley High School, Collegeville, PA*
Barbara Levine, *Clarkstown High School North, New City, NY*
Sallye Mahan-Cox, *Robinson Secondary School, Fairfax, VA*
Joan Maresh, *John Foster Dulles High School, Stafford, TX*
Melanie Mobley, *West Potomac High School, Alexandria, VA*
Kaye Passmore, *Notre Dame Academy, Worcester, MA*
Louise Pierce, *Lower Merion High School, Ardmore, PA*
Merceda Saffron, *West Springfield High School, Springfield, VA*
Dawn Sealy, *Clarkstown High School North, New City, NY*
Roger Tomhave, *Art Curriculum Specialist,*
  Fairfax County Public Schools, VA
Paula Turner, *Eastwood High School, El Paso, TX*

Art Education Consultants

Roberta Atlas, *Marion-Franklin School, Columbus, OH*
Bruce Bishop, *Formerly of Columbus City Public Schools,*
  Columbus, OH
Charles Brunotte, *West High School, Columbus, OH*
Robert Brushwood, *Columbus City Public Schools, Columbus, OH*
Jean Clark, *Columbus City Public Schools, Columbus, OH*
Sara Chapman, *Alief Independent School District, Houston, TX*
Robin Cornover, *Atlantic City High School, Atlantic City, NJ*
Nancy Denney, *Glen Este High School, West Clermont, OH*
Jennifer Drydyk, *Amelia High School, West Clermont, OH*
Deborah Ellington, *North Harris College, Houston, TX*
Jim Ellis, *Strath Haven High School, Wallingford, PA*
Mary Helen Haines, *Richardson S.H.S., Richardson, TX*
Susan Klinger, *Perkiomen Valley High School, Collegeville, PA*
Leticia Oppelker, *Atlantic City High School, Atlantic City, NJ*
Louise Pierce, *Lower Merion High School, Ardmore, PA*
Robert Porreca, *Hilltonia Middle School, Columbus, OH*
Mark Ramsey, *Columbus Alternative High School, Columbus, OH*
Kay Savay, *Richardson Independent School District, Richardson, TX*
Connie Schalinske, *Columbus City Public Schools, Columbus, OH*
Diane Spears, *Edgewood District, San Antonio, TX*
Delores Tomkins, *Booker T. Washington High School, Dallas, TX*
Rochelle Waldman, *Linden McKinley High School, Columbus, OH*
Mark Wangberg, *Haverford Township High School, Havertown, PA*

© 1997 Davis Publications, Inc.
Worcester, Massachusetts, U.S.A.

Printed in U.S.A.
Library of Congress Catalog Card Number: 95-068098
ISBN: 87192-300-9
10 9 8 7 6 5 4 3

Managing Editor: Wyatt Wade
Production Editors: Nancy Bedau, Nancy Burnett
Production: Steven Vogelsang
Copyeditor: Lynn Simon
Editorial Assistance: Jane Boland, Heidi M. Hanson,
Holly Hanson Pearlstein, Ewa Moncure

Design: Douglass Scott, Cathleen Damplo,
Tong-Mei Chang, WGBH Design

Contents

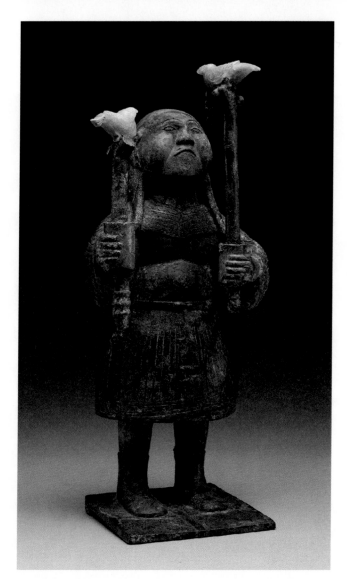

Mongolian Youth, 3rd–4th centuries BC, late Zhou period, China. Bronze figure with jade birds, 11 1/2" (29 cm) high. Museum of Fine Arts, Boston, Maria Antoinette Evens Fund.

Everything You Need to Teach

Teacher's Edition

Complete control is at hand. Create your own mix and easily manage the program as you guide students in, out and through chapters.

- Chapter organizers map out your options at a glance.

- A four-part lesson structure follows natural teaching strategies.

- Extensive supplementary information enriches student material.

- Multicultural and interdisciplinary connections expand learning.

- Points of discussion and avenues of inquiry promote further exploration.

Student Edition

A rich visual presentation and very accessible text speak directly to students.

- Vibrant maps and chapter and cultural timelines add historical and global perspective to art periods.

- Key notes, highlighted vocabulary, and built-in reviews reinforce the learning experience.

- Classroom connections and student profiles allow students to share studio experiences with peers from around the country.

Teacher's Resource Binder

Additional study and test questions and self-evaluation tools form the core of this collection of reproducible resources and supplemental information.

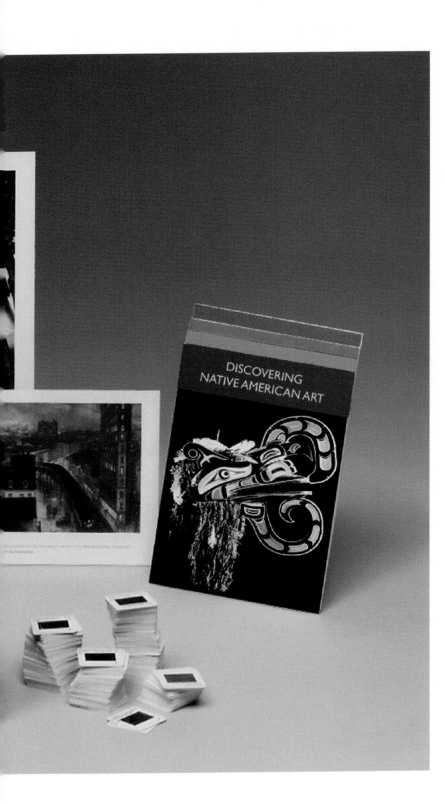

Transparencies

Twenty overhead transparencies with ten additional overlays expand important concepts and can be used for detailed analysis and comparison of art images.

Slides

Choose from a set of 125 images taken directly from the text, a set of 125 additional images that complement and correlate to the text, or the combined set of 250 for maximum instructional flexibility.

Large Reproductions

A set of thirty pivotal works of art supplement the text. These images represent major artforms, historical periods, and cultural trends.

The "Discovering" spotlight series

Expand your survey with a detailed look at the art of other cultures and their impact on world art. Examination of twelve to eighteen important works in each volume reflect cultural perspectives and can be easily integrated with the text.

- **Discovering African-American Art**

- **Discovering African Art**

- **Discovering Native American Art**

- **Discovering Oceanic Art**

Everything You Want to Teach

- A comprehensive survey of Western art
- A discipline-based approach
- A look at non-Western art
- A detailed introduction to art appreciation
- Artist profiles and primary source information

- A rich visual presentation
- Studio experiences keyed to chapter content
- Links to historical events
- Connections to performing arts and other disciplines
- Correlations to the National Visual Arts Standards

Chapter Organizers

View the entire chapter to map your teaching strategy. Teacher references and ancillaries are presented with multiple scheduling options. Objectives and activities are highlighted and correlated to the National Visual Arts Standards. A list of additional resources is also provided.

Chapter Openers

Teach only from the seventeen chapter openers and you've given students the "big picture" of art history. Two-page spreads present a snapshot of the chapter ahead in text and images.

Any Way You Want to Teach It

Select the periods, topics and extensions that match your course structure and move easily within and between chapters to suit your teaching style. You're in complete command with an array of teaching tools that provide opportunities for enrichment and further exploration.

Lesson Openers

Bring concepts into clear focus with highlighted monuments and artists that exemplify the periods. Vocabulary and key concepts are presented.

Lessons

Delve into individual lessons for the most thorough exploration of art history. Architecture, painting and sculpture, as well as sidebars and special articles, offer students different perspectives and points of exploration.

15.2 The Influence of Abstraction

IF THE ASHCAN EIGHT HAD PROBLEMS being accepted by Americans, the small group of Abstract painters had an even greater struggle. But, Abstraction persisted. In America, there was one stronghold for the young experimenters—the studio of the master photographer Alfred Stieglitz. He admired the work of Cézanne, Rodin, Brancusi and Picasso and encouraged young American Abstractionists, such as Georgia O'Keeffe and John Marin, by showing their work in his New York studio.

The 1913 New York Armory Show opened American eyes to the European art scene. American artists realized they either had to change direction or be left out. Following World War I, American artists flocked to France to study and to work. Gradually, Abstraction became an important element in American art, even though it was not yet fully accepted by the public. The American public made little attempt to understand the language and meaning of the Abstractionists. Thus, the artists worked in isolation, receiving encouragement from each other and from a small, but growing, number of patrons, museums and galleries.

Key Notes
- New York Armory Show convinces American artists that they have to change direction.
- Despite the ridicule of the public, the Abstractionists forge a new path in American art.

Vocabulary
mobiles
stabiles

Special Feature
Georgia O'Keeffe

(1887–1986)
Born and raised on a large farm in Wisconsin, Georgia O'Keeffe was an American pioneer of Abstraction. Unlike other ground-breaking artists, her training and influences were entirely American.

O'Keeffe first drew and painted representationally, but this work did not satisfy her and she began making abstract drawings of land-forms from memory. She mailed some of these charcoal drawings to a friend with express instructions not to show them to anyone else. The friend took them to Alfred Stieglitz, the famous photographer, who was running an avant-garde gallery in New York. Stieglitz loved

15–12 O'Keeffe did not study in Europe, but invented her own variety of American Abstraction based on natural forms.
Georgia O'Keeffe, *From the Plains I*, 1953. Oil on canvas, 48" x 84 1/4" (122 x 214 cm). McNay Art Institute, San Antonio, Texas.

first census counts 77 million people

...chell

...painter
...ster was born
...later moved
...nd. One of
...dence Art
...eascapes
...s life-
...genre
...5–6)
...at
...bout
...than

Notice how
...ure has been
...t to the very
...d to the
...the picture

...chell
...ewspaper
...l on can-
...76 x 63

...merican
...nd

15–7 Lewis was orphaned during her teens. She attended Oberlin College, perhaps on an Abolitionist scholarship.
Edmonia Lewis, *Hagar*, 1875. Marble, 52 5/8" x 15 1/4" x 17" (134 x 39 x 43 cm). National Museum of American Art, gift of Delta Sigma Theta Sorority, Inc., 1983.95.178.

A Look Inside

Objectives

Objectives clearly emphasize your goals.

Vocabulary Definitions

Vocabulary Definitions give you quick reference to ensure student understanding.

Teach, Evaluate and Reteach

A lesson sequence of **Teach**, **Evaluate** and **Reteach** guides you effortlessly through the complexities of presenting historical periods in art.

Materials and Techniques

Materials and Techniques provide the means to explore how works were created and how available materials influenced the final form.

Interdisciplinary Connection

Interdisciplinary Connections offer a means to link the study of art to subjects as diverse as science, mathematics, women's studies and physical education. Performing arts connections are specially highlighted and appear in every chapter.

Review Answers

Review Answers allow you to instantly gauge the level of student understanding.

Activity

Activity instruction provides objectives, preparation, materials notes and tips for classroom management and evaluation.

Introduce

The exact origins of Western art remain unclear, but cave paintings and handcrafted objects date back at least to 25,000 BC. Objects of pre-historic art, including those from Africa, Europe and Asia, demonstrate their makers' mastery of materials and keen powers of observation. The later cultures of Mesopotamia and Egypt developed magnificent art and architecture to honor their gods and rulers, and thereby reveal a great deal about these sophisticated civilizations.

Lessons at a Glance

5.1 *Earliest Beginnings*
Prehistoric cave paintings and sculptures, whose exact function remains unknown, are the earliest surviving examples of Western art.
5.2 *The Ancient Near East: Mesopotamia*
The successive cultures of Mesopotamia built great art and architecture centering around their gods and rulers.
5.3 *Egypt*
Egyptian art and architecture reflect a strong belief in the afterlife as well as illustrating the mighty power of the rulers.

Objectives

Students should be able to:

Describe the style, techniques and skills of prehistoric artists.

Explain how the art and culture of ancient Middle Eastern and Egyptian communities reflect their advanced societies.

Teach

Timeline
Challenge students to locate both Stonehenge (figs.5–c, 5–8) and the Great Sphinx (fig.5–d) on the timeline in order to understand how great monuments from different cultures were built at roughly the same time.

---

5 Beginnings of Western Art

In This Chapter...

EVER IMAGINE YOURSELF living thousands of years ago with people in a cave or along the Nile River in Ancient Egypt? Our best view of these people and what their lives were like comes from the art they created.

The earliest paintings we know of are in caves in Africa, Europe and Asia. The images say to us that these were highly skilled artists with keen powers of observation. They drew beautiful images of animals they hunted in order to survive.

Twenty-seven thousand years later, the first civilization we know of formed in Sumer, an area in Mesopotamia. The accomplishments of this first civilization were spectacular. The Sumerians designed and built huge temples called ziggurats which were the center of their cities. They invented writing, created sculptures of stone, and made beautiful musical instruments. They were highly accomplished artists who formalized the first style of art depicting the human form.

The second great civilization was Ancient Egypt. It thrived for several thousand years virtually unchanged in its isolated and fertile location along the Nile River. The Egyptian desire for stability and permanence led them to create huge monuments and tombs full of art meant to last forever. Although their glorious civilization did not last, we can still hear them, see them and learn from them through the art they created.

These early cultures of Mesopotamia and Egypt influenced later ones around the Mediterranean Sea, Europe and the United States. The art of these later cultures is what we call Western Art because it developed in Western Europe. It is the primary focus of the chapters that follow.

5–a. Tutankhamen became Pharaoh of Egypt as a young boy, but only ruled for nine years. His tomb, discovered in 1922, was filled with precious treasures.
Tutankhamen Mummy Case. 1352 BC. Gold inlaid with enamel and semiprecious stones, h. 73" (185 cm). Egyptian Museum, Cairo.

5–b The stairways of the great Persian palace at Persepolis were carved with reliefs of royal courtiers and others who served the emperor.
Audience Hall of Darius and Xerxes, detail of relief (fig.5–17).

• Approximately how many years separate the two works?

▪ Is this a short or a long time relative to all the developments depicted on the timeline of early Western art?

• To help students decide, have them calculate the number of centuries between the cave paintings at Lascaux and the Hanging Gardens of Babylon. (approximately 143 or 14,300 years)

Tell students to imagine wandering through England around 2000 BC and stumbling upon the strange boulders of Stonehenge.

• What would be their first thoughts about the function of this structure? After reading the captions, have them contemplate why ancient people might have wanted a calendar.

• What parts of their lives would have been regulated by the passing of the seasons? Can they picture rituals, plantings, harvests and feasts taking place during this ancient era?

• Are calendars as influential in contemporary Western society as during this earlier period? (Do students plan certain events, activities or vacations around particular holidays or times of the year?)

Higher-Order Thinking Skills

Thoughtful questions and ideas for discussion enable you to promote the development of critical and creative thinking.

Contextual Information

Spark discussion and encourage a more in-depth understanding with these lively and interesting facts that supplement the student text.

Truly the gods have not from the beginning revealed all things to mortals, but by long seeking mortals make progress in discovery.
Xenophanes of Colophon

Can you imagine what life in Europe might have been like before the existence of cities and countries? What kinds of climate and geographical features might be favorable for primitive civilizations?

5–c Built nearly 4000 years ago, this circle of huge stones functioned as a giant, but very accurate, calendar that was based on the movements of the sun and moon. *Stonehenge, detail (fig.5–8).*

5–d Recent findings have called into question the long-accepted dating of the Sphinx. Some scholars now believe it predates by many years the Pyramid of Cheops. Additional research is necessary before final conclusions can be drawn. *The Great Sphinx, about 2500 BC, 4th dynasty, 65' (19.8 m) high, Giza.*

3500–3000 BC Invention of the wheel, Sumeria	3300 BC Earliest known writing, Mesopotamia	2100 BC Ziggurat at Ur, Mesopotamia	1300 BC Moses receives the Ten Commandments, Mount Sinai, Egypt	
3300 BC First kilns used in Mesopotamia	2650–2575 BC Great Sphinx, Pyramids at Giza, Egypt	2000 BC Stonehenge, England		
	1530 BC Temple of Amun, Karnak	705–681 BC Height of Assyrian Empire	700 BC Hanging Gardens of Babylon	
	1352 BC Tomb of King Tutankhamen, Egypt			

Quote

Before students learn anything specific about Stonehenge or the Great Sphinx, ask them to consider how the quote relates to these two works. How much can they understand about the works just by looking? After students read the captions, ask them how long they think it has taken human beings to decide on the use and meaning of these impressive monuments.

Map

In order to illustrate what was occurring in various parts of the Western world at approximately the same period, have students locate England, where Stonehenge was built, and Egypt, the site of the Great Sphinx, on the map.

Art

Ask students to decide for whom the Tutankhamen Mummy Case (fig.5–a) and the Great Sphinx were constructed.

• Why might common citizens not have been able to commission these sorts of works?

• Could they pay for something on this scale themselves today? How much money do they estimate it might have taken to build either the enormous sculpture or the gold-covered mummy case? While ordinary people could not have afforded such art, the pharaohs did use citizens' tax money and labor to construct these stupendous testaments of their own supreme power.

Evaluate

Ask students to articulate something that is confusing about the art on pages 148–149.

• Can their classmates help them clear up any ambiguity? Can they consider the problem from another angle?

• What resources might be available to assist them?

• Encourage students to share their insights as they continue learning more about early Western art.

Reteach

Have students study both the Tutankhamen Mummy Case and Stonehenge for visual clues as to whether these works came from the same culture. (Have students check their answers by finding on the map the locations of these works.) To further their thinking, ask: "Are these two works similar in scale, material, function and intricacy of construction? For instance, are their decorations similar?" (Have them read the captions for information.)

From this experience, ask students if it is fair to make any generalizations about multiple cultures that exist at any given time. Would they consider Asian, African, American and European societies all the same today? Point out that art can often help us comprehend the distinct characteristics of a particular culture.

Introduce

You are always prepared with a concise overview of the chapter ahead and the summary in Lessons at a Glance.

Quote

Questions pertaining to the quotations used throughout the student edition turn fascinating statements into avenues of learning.

Map

Map activities provide a geographic perspective that allow you to help students pinpoint the development of art world-wide.

Multicultural Connection

You have the option to explore art from around the world with this additional information and activities suggested.

Teacher Spotlight

Share a teacher's perspective of the student work featured in the student profile.

Primary Source Connection

Background information and suggested questions assist students in understanding these direct accounts of art and history.

Scope and Sequence

National Standards Correlation

Discipline-based Content

Art History

4 Understanding visual arts in relation to history and cultures.

cultural styles / trends

setting in history (time and place)

works of artists and cultures; painting, drawing (2-D)

sculpture (3-D)

crafts, environmental art, computer art

architecture

historical events

links to other cultures

Aesthetic Perceptions/Responses

5 Reflecting upon and assessing the characteristics and merits of their work and the work of others.

Art Criticism and Evaluation

5 Reflecting upon and assessing the characteristics and merits of their work and the work of others.

description
analysis
elements (sensory properties)
principles (formal)
expressive
technical
interpretation
judgment

Creative Studio Experience

1 Understanding and applying media, techniques and processes.
2 Using knowledge of structures and functions.
3 Choosing and evaluating a range of subject matter, symbols and ideas.

art forms, media
skills, tools, processes
inspiration sources
design skills

Links to Other Disciplines

6 Making connections between visual arts and other disciplines.

careers

Chapter 1 Learning about Art	Chapter 2 Visual Communication	Chapter 3 Common Denominators
overview of world arts	universal reasons for creating art	worldwide themes definition of period style and national/
worldwide overviews	worldwide surveys, various cultures and times	regional style

similarities in various arts	drawing media: pencil, charcoal, ink, pastel
	painting media: fresco, tempera, oil, watercolor,
	  acrylic, collage
	printmaking media: woodcut, intaglio, linocut,
	  lithograph, serigraph
		individual artists' styles

	bronze, steel, wood, marble, plastic	
	fibers, glass, clay, furniture, mosaics, metalwork	
		commonalities in architecture
Louvre Palace becomes museum, 1793	watercolor and tempera used by ancient Egyptians Conté invents pencil, 1795 Picasso and Braque develop collage, 1912	
commonalities of world cultures	surveys of most world cultures	global cross-cultural influences
definition of art	visual communication of art	worldwide sense of aesthetics

process of art evaluation and study
craftsmanship
overview of aesthetic properties
  sensory properties (elements)
  formal properties (principles)
  technical properties
  expressive properties
reasons for creating art
  utility
  religion
  politics
  information/history
  aesthetics
	types of subject matter: narrative, religious,
	  literary, landscapes, cityscapes, figure,
	  historical, genre, social comment, still life,
	  animals, expression, nonobjective,
	  abstraction
	design: structure of art; elements: line,
	  shape, form, texture, space, color, value
	principles of design: symmetrical and
	  asymmetrical balance, unity, emphasis,
	  contrast, pattern, rhythm, movement
		universal commonalities
		  geometric patterns
		  animal designs
		  figure
		emotion vs. intellect
		technical style

classroom museum with found objects
archaeology poster
	paint color wheel using color theory and
	  color mixing
	poster of portraits from magazines
	  analysis of media and intentions of artists
		paint border design using repeat patterns
		paint still life considering intellect vs. emotion

archaeology, art preservation, chemistry,
  communication, dance, design, history,
  information/history, performing arts,
  science, theater, utility/religion
	communications, chemistry, dance, history,
	  performing arts, political science
		music, world social studies

National Standards Correlation	Discipline-based Content	Chapter 4 Art of the Non-Western World
	Art History	
4 Understanding visual arts in relation to history and cultures.	cultural styles / trends	most world cultures except European
	setting in history (time and place)	Asia, Oceania, Africa, Americas from prehistoric to present
	works of artists and cultures; painting, drawing (2-D)	Japanese woodcuts; Asian brush painting; Mesoamerican illustrated codices; Indian and Persian illustrations; Aborigine painting; Chinese calligraphy, ink paintings; Japanese screens, sumi-e; Native American petroglyphs
	sculpture (3-D)	statues and carvings of Africa, Oceania, India, Japan (Buddha), China (horses, soldiers), Southeast Asia, Pre-Columbia, Native America (totems)
	crafts, environmental art, computer art	weavings: Native American, Persian, Oceanic, pre-Columbian. ceramics: Native American, Chinese, pre-Columbian. jewelry: Persian, Native American. masks: African, Native American. baskets: Native American.
	architecture	pueblos; Taj Mahal, stupas, temples; Great Wall of China, Imperial Palace; pre-Columbian, Japanese and Southeast Asian temples, palaces; Islamic palaces, mosques
	historical events	Hinduism originates in India, 2000 BC Buddha lives in India, 6th century BC Great Wall of China, 3–2nd century BC Muhammad founds Islam, early 7th century AD Aztec Civilization, 1428–1519 AD Opening of Japan to West, 1868
	links to other cultures	European, relationships of these cultures to each other
	Aesthetic Perceptions/Responses	
5 Reflecting upon and assessing the characteristics and merits of their work and the work of others.		diversity of worldwide artistic expressions commonalities in subjects, designs, and materials of Non-western art cultures
	Art Criticism and Evaluation	
5 Reflecting upon and assessing the characteristics and merits of their work and the work of others.	description analysis elements (sensory properties) principles (formal) expressive technical interpretation judgment	history and culture affect art functions of art in Non-western societies influence of Hinduism and Buddhism on India's art human relationship to nature and importance of writing in Chinese art Japanese art's simplicity of form, awareness of nature Chinese and Indian traditions in Southeast Asian art Islamic elaborate, stylized ornamentation Sub-Sahara African art's fine craftsmanship, geometric abstraction, and religious orientation corbeling in pre-Columbian architecture craftsmanship, symbolism, animal forms in pre-Columbian sculpture, ceramics, metalwork, and fabrics distinct visual style of each Native American group Native American art's appreciation of nature, symbolism, and fine craftsmanship
	Creative Studio Experience	
1 Understanding and applying media, techniques and processes. **2** Using knowledge of structures and functions. **3** Choosing and evaluating a range of subject matter, symbols and ideas.	art forms, media skills, tools, processes inspiration sources design skills	clay vessels based on Native American pottery paper masks
	Links to Other Disciplines	
6 Making connections between visual arts and other disciplines.	careers	archaeology, astronomy, dance, geography, history, literature, music, natural sciences, social sciences, social studies, theater

Chapter 5 Beginnings of Western Art	Chapter 6 Greek and Roman Art	Chapter 7 Religious Conviction
Stone Age, Mesopotamian, Egyptian	Aegean, (Minoan and Mycenaean), Greek, Roman	Early Christian, Byzantine, Islamic, Early Medieval
Lascaux, Stonehenge, Mesopotamia, Egypt, 15,000–200 BC	Greece, Roman Empire, Pompeii, 1600 BC–330 AD	Rome, Ravenna, Constantinople, Venice, Near East, 4th–5th centuries
cave paintings Egyptian tomb paintings	Minoan and Roman frescoes	Roman frescoes in catacombs Islamic book illustration Medieval manuscript illumination
carvings, funeral masks, statues	Greek figures, Roman busts, statues, funeral mask	Early Christian sarcophagi, religious objects, icons, altarpieces
musical instrument (lyre)	Greek vases, Aegean vases, cup; Roman mosaics	Byzantine mosaics
ziggurat, pyramid, temple	palace at Knossos; Greek temples (Parthenon), theaters; Roman Colosseum, arch, Pantheon, baths	basilica adapted for Christian churches Byzantine Hagia Sophia, St. Mark's in Venice, Islamic Alhambra, Charlemagne's classical revival
Last Ice Age, 25,000–18,000 BC Lascaux cave paintings, 15,000 BC wheel invented, 3500–3000 BC Mesopotamian civilizations begin, 3500–3000 BC Pyramids at Giza, 2650–2575 BC Stonehenge, 2000 BC, Moses, 1300 BC	Homer, *Iliad* and *Odyssey*, 900 BC Parthenon built, 447–432 BC Alexander the Great expands Greek Empire, 356–323 BC birth of Christ, 0 AD Destruction of Pompeii, 79 AD	Constantine legalizes Christianity, 313 AD. Justinian moves Byzantine empire to East, 527 AD Charlemagne's classical revival, 8th century Islam spreads from Arabia, 7th century
African, Asian, Indian, Mediterranean, Middle Eastern, Native American, Persian, pre-Columbian,	African, Chinese, European, Indian, Native American, pre-Columbian	African, Cambodian, Chinese, modern Islamic cultures, pre-Columbian, Southwestern United States architecture
style and craftsmanship of prehistoric artists	Greek ideals of art and architecture Roman realism	stylization
rulers, gods honored in Mesopotamian art stylization of Egyptian and Prehistoric art Stone Age art more than decoration Egyptian belief in afterlife reflected in art	color on Greek statues, architecture harmony and symmetry in Greek statues and architecture to show ideals Roman building architecture reflects life-styles of civilization	small, portable medieval art geometric, abstract Islamic designs symbolism in Early Christian Art
local materials sculpture to appreciate relation of site, materials, and art presentation on ancient art	clay portrait pencil drawing of local building to consider classical architectural heritage	fresco on plaster illuminate your initials
archaeology, mathematics, music, science, social studies	engineering, geography, geology, Latin, literature, music, theater	architecture, dance, geography, geometry, history, music,

National Standards Correlation	Discipline-based Content	Chapter 8 Romanesque and Gothic Art
	Art History	
4 Understanding visual arts in relation to history and cultures.	cultural styles / trends	European Romanesque and Gothic
	setting in history (time and place)	Europe, 10th–15th centuries
	works of artists and cultures; painting, drawing (2-D)	manuscript illumination frescoes (Giotto) altarpieces (Duccio, Martini, Gentile da Fabriano)
	sculpture (3-D)	architectural figures
	crafts, environmental art, computer art	stained glass *Bayeux Tapestry*
	architecture	cathedrals
	historical events	First Crusade, 1095 Battle of Hastings, 1066 Black Death, 1346–7 Abbot Suger begins Gothic architecture , 1137 pilgrimages, powerful church growth of cities
	links to other cultures	African, Islamic, Native American, pre-Columbian
	Aesthetic Perceptions/Responses	
5 Reflecting upon and assessing the characteristics and merits of their work and the work of others.		Romanesque religious emotion unity in Gothic architecture
	Art Criticism and Evaluation	
5 Reflecting upon and assessing the characteristics and merits of their work and the work of others.	description analysis elements (sensory properties) principles (formal) expressive technical interpretation judgment	rounded Romanesque arch pointed Gothic arch cathedral floor plans architectural details transition of sculpture and painting from stylized to natural compare Romanesque and Gothic architecture analyze fresco compositions
	Creative Studio Experience	
1 Understanding and applying media, techniques and processes. **2** Using knowledge of structures and functions. **3** Choosing and evaluating a range of subject matter, symbols and ideas.	art forms, media skills, tools, processes inspiration sources design skills	narrative stitchery "stained glass" windows of cellophane
	Links to Other Disciplines	
6 Making connections between visual arts and other disciplines.	careers	construction, graphics, home economics, literature, music, physics, performing arts, political science, social studies

Chapter 9: The Italian Renaissance	Chapter 10: Renaissance in the North	Chapter 11: Baroque and Rococo
Renaissance in Italy, Mannerism	Northern European Renaissance	Baroque, Rococo
Italy, 15th–16th centuries	Low Countries, Germany England, France, Spain, 15th–16th centuries	Europe, 16th–18th centuries
frescoes Masaccio, Fra Angelico, Uccello, Piero della Francesca, Botticelli, Mantegna, Bellini, Leonardo da Vinci, Michelangelo, Raphael, Giorgione, Titian, El Greco, Rosso, Sofonisba Anguissola, Tintoretto	oils, prints Campin, van Eyck, van der Weyden, Bosch, Bruegel, Durer, Cranach, Gruenwald, Holbein, Fouquet, Clouet	ceilings Caravaggio, LaTour, Poussin, Lorrain, Leyster, Rubens, van Dyck, van Ruisdael, Hals, Vermeer, Rembrandt, Velasquez, Murillo, Zurbaran, Watteau, Boucher, Chardin, Tiepolo, Canaletto, Hogarth, Reynolds, Gainsborough, Copley, West, Stuart, Johnson
Ghiberti, Donatello, Michelangelo		Bernini's *David*
	tapestry	African-American crafts, quilts, silversmithing
Brunelleschi, dome of Florence cathedral, San Lorenzo Michelangelo's dome of St. Peter's	El Escorial, chateaux, Louvre	Bernini's and Maderno's St. Peter's, Borromini, Versailles, Wren's St. Paul's
Medici family controls Florence printing press invented, 1440 Columbus "discovers" America, 1492 sack of Rome, 1527	exploration of Americas Henry VIII, England, 1509–1547 Protestant reformation, 1517 Phillip II, Spain, 1556–1598 English defeat of Spanish Armada, 1588	Spain's "Golden Age" 1600's *Mayflower* to America, 1620 London Fire, 1666 American Revolution, 1776 French Revolution, 1793
African, Chinese, Japanese, classical Greek and Rome	African, Italy, International Style, pre-Columbian,	African, Indian, Japanese, Javanese, Native American
Renaissance classicism and order	convincing realism	exuberant Italian Baroque classical French Baroque flamboyant, ethereal Rococo
perspective chiaroscuro Renaissance mathematical proportions Renaissance classicism Mannerist expressive, personal styles compare Gothic and Renaissance architecture and art	glowing colors of oil paints details symbolic use of ordinary objects German blending of Italian Renaissance classicism with Northern realism compare Renaissance art of Northern Europe and Italy	influence of Catholic church as art patron genre, still lifes, landscapes as subjects of paintings of Protestant countries reflection of French aristocracy in early 18th-century art serious Baroque aesthetic in Italy, England, America in early 1700's compare Baroque and Rococo compare various European countries' art compare *Davids* of Bernini, Michelangelo and Donatello
sketchbook drawings stylized human figure in clay or tempera paint	symbolic colored pencil drawing fantasy triptych in colored markers	etching or drypoint portrait construction paper portrait illustrating tenebroso
history, literature, mathematics, music, performing arts, science	anatomy, biology, dance, geography, history, literature, music, performing arts	American and European history, dance, interior design, landscape design, music, physics, science, theater

National Standards Correlation	Discipline-based Content	Chapter 12 Three Opposing Views
	Art History	
4 Understanding visual arts in relation to history and cultures.	cultural styles / trends	Neoclassicism, Romanticism, Realism
	setting in history (time and place)	Europe, United States, 18th–19th centuries
	works of artists and cultures; painting, drawing (2-D)	David, Ingres, Vigee-Lebrun, Goya, Gericault, Delacroix, Constable, Turner, Cole, Bingham, Bonheur, Corot, Millet, Daumier, Courbet, Homer, Eakins, Steichen, Cameron, Muybridge
	sculpture (3-D)	Houdon's *Benjamin Franklin*
	crafts, environmental art, computer art	
	architecture	United States: Capitol, Jefferson Paris: Arc de Triomphe, Opera London: Parliament
	historical events	rapid changes in society United States Constitution adopted, 1789 Napoleon crowned, 1804 settling western United States Lincoln assassinated, 1865
	links to other cultures	classical Greek and Roman, Japanese, Native American
5 Reflecting upon and assessing the characteristics and merits of their work and the work of others.	**Aesthetic Perceptions/Responses**	severe, cool Neoclassicsm emotional Romanticism natural, everyday Realism photography as art
5 Reflecting upon and assessing the characteristics and merits of their work and the work of others.	**Art Criticism and Evaluation** description analysis elements (sensory properties) principles (formal) expressive technical interpretation judgment	rejection of Rococo frivolity and ornateness influence of Napoleon on art Neoclassical Greek and Roman references Romanticism as emotional reaction to Neoclassic restrictions Realist genre painting relation between art and photography compare Neoclassicism with Rococo, Romanticism, and Realism
1 Understanding and applying media, techniques and processes. 2 Using knowledge of structures and functions. 3 Choosing and evaluating a range of subject matter, symbols and ideas.	**Creative Studio Experience** art forms, media skills, tools, processes inspiration sources design skills	watercolor action scene using sketching and painting techniques
6 Making connections between visual arts and other disciplines.	**Links to Other Disciplines** careers	fashion design, French and United States history, Latin allegories, music, physics of photography, sports, women's studies

Chapter 13 Impressionism and Post-Impressionism	Chapter 14 A Half-Century of "Isms"	Chapter 15 American Art 1900–1950
Impressionism, Post-Impressionism, Expressionism	Expressionism, Cubism, Dada, Futurism, deStijl, Surrealism	Realism, Abstraction, Regionalism, Social Realism
France, last half of 19th century	Europe, United States, Mexico, 1900–1950	United States, 1900–1950
Monet, Manet, Pissarro, Morisot, Degas, Renior, Cassatt, Whistler, Rodin, Seurat, Cezanne, Toulouse-Lautrec, van Gogh, Gauguin, Munch, Picasso, Rousseau, Japanese prints	Rivera, Matisse, Rouault, Modersohn-Becker, Kollwitz, Kirchner, Nolde, Marc, Kandinsky, Beckman, Modigliani, Orozco, Siqueiros, Kahlo, J. Stella, Picasso, Braque, Duchamp, Boccioni, Mondrian, Chagall, De Chirico, Klee, Arp, Ernst, Schwitters, Miro, Magritte, Dali, Van der Zee, Bresson, Stieglitz, Weston, Adams, Lange	Bellows, Sargent, Inness, Bierstadt, Bannister, Tanner, Henri, Sloan, O'Keeffe, Marin, Demuth, Sheeler, Gorky, Davis, Benton, Wood, Kuhn, Hopper, Remington, Lawrence, Shahn, Marsh, Bishop, Tooker,
Rodin's *Thinker, Balzac*	Brancusi, Maillol, Giacometti, Duchamp, Barlach, Oppenheim	Lewis, Calder
United States Civil War, 1861–1865 Industrial Revolution Franco-Prussian War 1870–1871 first automobile, 1893	Zeppelin flight, 1922 Mexican Civil War,1910–15 World War I, 1914–1918 Tut's tomb found, 1922 Paris Exposition, 1937 World War II, 1939–1945	Wrights invent airplane, 1903 *Titanic* sinks, 1912 Armory Show, 1913 World War I, 1914–1918 Harlem Renaissance, 1920's Stock Market crash, 1929 World War II, 1939–1945
African, Japanese, Oceanic	African, African-American, Australian, Aztec, Mayan, Mexican, Persian	African, Chinese, European, Native American
light and color of transitory Impressionist scenes desolate emotion of early Expressionism	emotion of Expressionism dreamlike Surrealism De Stijl's bare essentials of design alienated feeling in much art	Energy of early 1900's Realism's focus on cities dehumanization of urban life in Social Realism
Impressionism evolves from Realism Impressionist use of light and color Post-Impressionism evolves from Impressionism Post-Impressionism's bold color, spontaneity, distortion, geometric structuring influence of urban life on art Gauguin's symbolism analyze Van Gogh's *Starry Night*	bright colors of Fauves motion of Futurism composition design in abstraction distortion of forms and color to express emotion simultaneity of Cubism symbolism in Picasso's *Guernica* symbolism and personal interpretation in fantasy art contrasts in Stieglitz's *Steerage*	Bierstadt romanticizes West Realists' organization of chaotic urban scenes influence of European abstraction on American art design composition and emotion in abstraction subjects of American Regionalism light in Hopper's paintings scenes from African-American experience
pastel still life pastel studies of light and atmosphere on buildings	painted wall mural surrealistic drawing	painting of city life mobile
dance, French language, geography of France and the South Pacific, graphic design, history, music, physics color theories, psychology (Freud), social science, theater (Sondheim's *Sunday in the Park with George*)	dance, European and Mexican history, journalism, literature, music, performing arts, psychology, social science, Spanish language	African-American and women's studies, American history, dance, government, history, music (jazz), performing arts, social science, sociology, theater, urban planning

National Standards Correlation	Discipline-based Content	Chapter 16 Twentieth-Century Architecture
	Art History	
4 Understanding visual arts in relation to history and cultures.	cultural styles / trends	Modernism, International Style, Post-Modernism
	setting in history (time and place)	Europe, United States, 1900–1995
	works of artists and cultures; painting, drawing (2-D)	
	sculpture (3-D)	
	crafts, environmental art, computer art	
	architecture	Mies van der Rohe, Sullivan, Harrison, Wright, Rietveld, Gropius (Bauhaus), Corbusier Bunshaft, Saarinen, Kahn, Fuller, Safdie, Piano/Rogers, Johnson/Burgee, Pei, Graves, Venturi, Jahn, Gehry, Isozaki, Pelli
	historical events	Carson Pirie Scott Dept. Store, Chicago, 1901 Bauhaus founded in Germany, 1919 Guggenheim Museum, 1943–59 geodesic dome, B. Fuller, 1967 Nat'l Gallery of Art East Wing, Washington, DC, 1978 Post-Modernism begins, 1980's
	links to other cultures	Classical Greek and Roman, Japanese, Middle Eastern, Native American
	Aesthetic Perceptions/Responses	
5 Reflecting upon and assessing the characteristics and merits of their work and the work of others.		Modernism's "Form follows function" and "Less is more." Post-Modernism's "Less is a bore."
	Art Criticism and Evaluation	
5 Reflecting upon and assessing the characteristics and merits of their work and the work of others.	description analysis elements (sensory properties) principles (formal) expressive technical interpretation judgment	Modernists' use of steel, reinforced concrete and glass Wright's harmony of structure and site Invention of steel and metal-frame construction leads to skyscrapers Modernism's insistence on essence of form as in De Stijl art Post-Modernism's rejection of steel and glass-boxes Post-Modernism mixes historical elements, symbolism, and vivid ornamentation
	Creative Studio Experience	
1 Understanding and applying media, techniques and processes. **2** Using knowledge of structures and functions. **3** Choosing and evaluating a range of subject matter, symbols and ideas.	art forms, media skills, tools, processes inspiration sources design skills	furniture design for a particular house, based on Wright's philosophies model of a community (urban planning)
	Links to Other Disciplines	
6 Making connections between visual arts and other disciplines.	careers	business, French language, geography, government (building codes, politics and architecture), history, home economics, industrial arts, math, music, science, theater

Chapter 17
Art from the Fifties to the Present

Abstract Expressionism, Op, Pop, Color Field, New Realism

United States, (New York), 1950–1995
de Kooning, Pollock, Motherwell, Hofmann, Kline, Krasner, Rothko, Diebenkorn, Rauschenberg, Johns, Lichtenstein, Warhol, Riley, Vasarely, Anuskiewicz, Davis, Frankenthaler, Albers, Newman, Noland, Kelly, F. Stella, Gottlieb, Francis, Louis, Close, Wyeth, Rosenquist, Estes, Chicago

Oldenburg, Segal, Hanson, Noguchi, Moore, Smith, Hepworth, Nevelson, Grooms

Christo and Jeanne-Claude, Umbrico, Chicago

President Kennedy assassinated, 1963
Martin Luther King assassinated, 1968
men walk on the moon, 1969
Vietnam War ends, 1973
Berlin Wall removed, 1989

Native American, European, Japanese

wide variation of individual styles
emotion of Abstract Expressionism
attitude of Pop and Op Art

Abstract Expressionism's stress of emotion
    over design
Pop and Op Art—reactions to Abstract
    Expressionism
Op Art's use of scientific principles to create
    illusion of movement
Large flat areas of color in Color Field Painting
New Realism based on 1950's Pop Art
use of new media and technology

soft sculpture based on Oldenburg
painting based on a contemporary
    artist's style

American history, computers, dance,
    ecology (environmental art), graphic design,
    home economics (sewing), math (ratios),
    music, optics, psychology, music,
    performing arts, science, women's studies

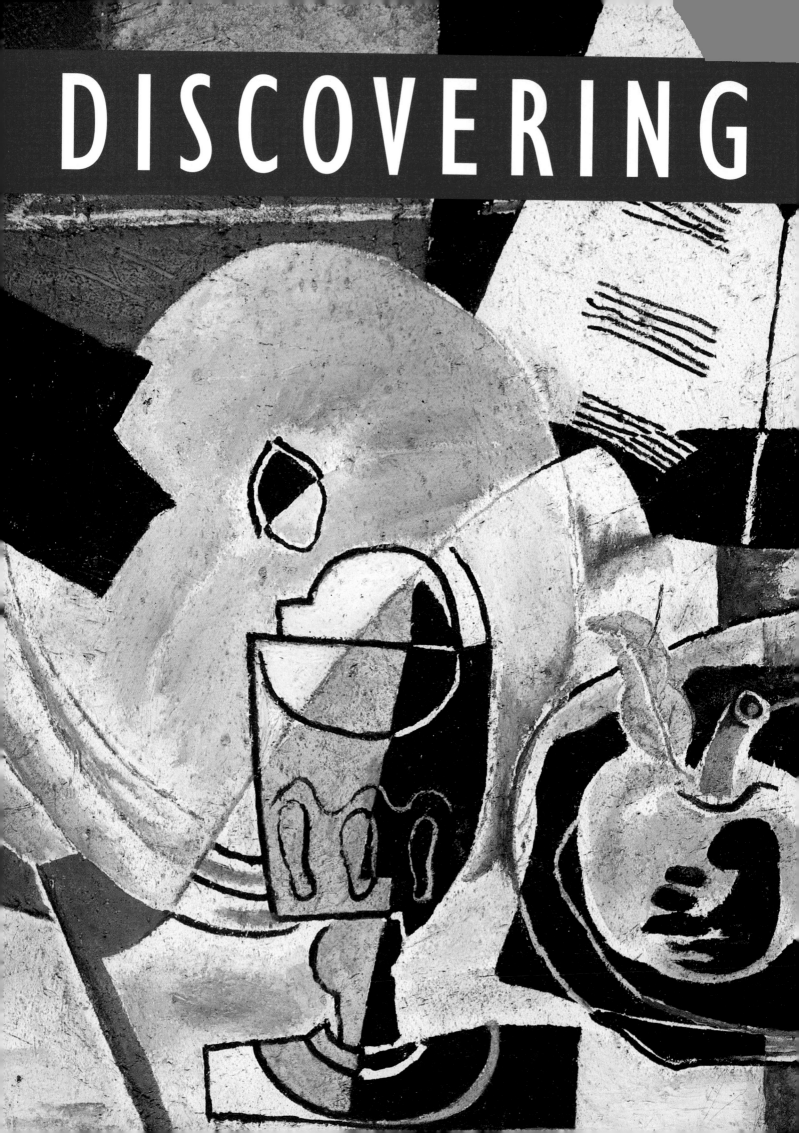

DISCOVERING

ART HISTORY

Third Edition

Gerald F. Brommer

Davis Publications, Inc.
Worcester, Massachusetts

What is Art?

"Art is like light," as a famous composer once said. "Everybody knows what it is, but few can tell you what it is."

Art *is* difficult to define. Unlike light, though, art isn't one thing or a single phenomenon. People create it, and that's enough to make it complicated and subject to many definitions.

Art can be personal, art can call for social change, and art can portray human emotions as well as evoke them. It can express harmony or disharmony, show the simple and everyday in unfamiliar ways, or be monumental, mysterious, and fantastic.

But how do we know what is good art? What makes a work good? Whatever form it takes, art is based on ideas. Art history looks at these ideas over the ages and across cultures. We learn about art objects and why they are important. We learn about artistic styles, to comprehend how style comes about through line, motion, form, texture, color and the use of space. When we read about artists, their lives, and their ideas, from century to century—how some worked in monasteries, art guilds, royal courts, and art academies, and others created art to use and wear—we can better understand the art and architecture around us.

We can discover the "good" of art when we see how new thoughts about art, new movements among artists and changes in style give us new ways of seeing the world. And that is, certainly, a kind of light.

Title page: Following spread: Georges Braque, *Still Life: The Table*, detail, 1928. Oil on canvas, 32" x 51 1/2" (81 x 130 cm). National Gallery of Art, Washington, DC. Chester Dale Collection.

Printed in U.S.A.   Library of Congress Catalog Card Number: 95-068097   ISBN: 87192-299-1   10 9 8 7 6 5 4 3 2 1

Who were the first artists?

A dog fell into a hole and some of the world's oldest known paintings were discovered. The underground paintings at Lascaux, France, have lasted more than 17,000 years. How?

Freeing figures in stone

Imagine Michelangelo. He is twenty-five. He chisels a huge block of marble and two lifelike figures emerge in one piece—a masterpiece. His art, in Italy, 1500, will influence European art *for the next three centuries!*

The mysteries of ancient art

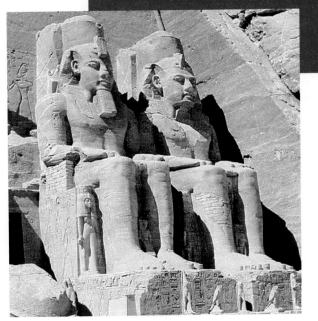

An art rescue project using computers, saws and giant cranes? Hundreds of people from many countries worked together to save the ancient Egyptian monuments at Abu Simbel. The art of Egypt fascinates people the world over. Why?

Page IV: Hans II Jordaens (figures by Cornelis Baellieur), *A Collection of Art and Rarities*, 1630. Oil on panel, 34" x 47" (86 x 120 cm). Kunsthistorisches Museum, Vienna.

Page V: (clockwise from top) *Hall of Bulls*, detail, about 15,000- 13,000 BC. Dordogne, France. *Ramses II*, about 1257, Abu Simbel. Michelangelo, *Pietà*, detail, 1499-1500. Marble, 68 1/2" high (1.74m). St. Peter's, Vatican, Rome.

Painting the real and the personal

History's first solo art show, in 1855, was opened out of spite. When the Paris art experts said "no" to Gustave Courbet's paintings about ordinary people and everyday life, he built a shed to exhibit his art anyway.

Early earth art

A hand-made mountain of art rises to the sky. Over a thousand years ago on the island of Java, Indonesia, Buddhists sculpted scenes of deities and demons along the path to the mountaintop. What were they trying to reach?

Showing the hard social truths

Paint from a local dimestore and other simple materials were the fabric of America's own Renaissance—the 1920s in Harlem. Artists like Jacob Lawrence captured the epic struggles of African Americans.

Page VI (clockwise from top left): Gustave Courbet, *Burial at Ornans*, detail, 1849-1850. Oil on canvas, 10' 3 1/2" x 21' 11" (3.15 x 6.68 m). Musée d'Orsay, Paris. *Borobudor*, about 850. Shailendra dynasty, Java. Jacob Lawrence, *One of the largest Race Riots Occurred in East St. Louis*, panel 52 from the *Migration of the Negro* series, 1940-1941. Tempera and gesso on composition board, 12" x 18" (30 x 46 cm). The Museum of Modern Art, New York, gift of Mrs. David M. Levy.

Page VII (clockwise from top left): Michael Graves, *Public Library of San Juan Capistrano*, 1983. San Juan Capistrano, California. Judy Chicago, *The Dinner Party*, 1979. Ceramic with handwoven cloth, each side 82' long (25 m). Through the Flower, Albuquerque, New Mexico. Dorothea Lange, *Migrant Mother, Nipomo California*, 1936. Photograph: Dorothea Lange Collection, The Oakland Museum.

What next?

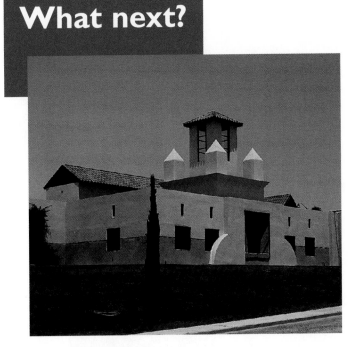

"Less is more," said Mies van der Rohe. Buildings should be simple—function comes first. "Less is a bore," said Robert Venturi years later. Great architecture can be complex. Modernism followed by Post-Modernism followed by...

Women making art

Women making art

In 1979, Judy Chicago set a place at the dinner table for each of thirty-six women whose ideas and actions changed history. Did Chicago's monument to women, "The Dinner Party," change art history?

What is context?

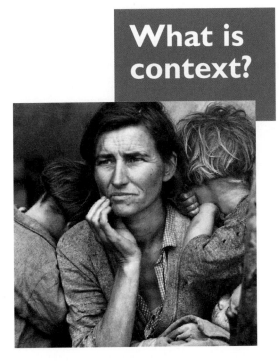

A single image that changed lives. San Franciscans opened their newspapers one day in 1935 and saw Dorothea Lange's photograph of starving migrant workers. Some readers were moved and sent the workers food—an extraordinary reaction.

Some art might make you wonder, "Why would somebody do that?" People who study art ask the same question. That question leads to others: What was life like when and where the artist lived? What did people value? Who looked at art? What materials did artists use?

Discovering Art History addresses many questions about art. It also provides opportunities to better understand art by making it yourself. Turn the page to find out more.

Your Guide to Art History

DISCOVERING ART HISTORY

GERALD BROMMER   THIRD EDITION

Get ready for an intriguing tour across centuries and into creative minds.

Visual art is a record of ideas and cross-cultural influences. It illuminates science, history and social customs of a particular time and place. *Discovering Art History* focuses mainly on Western art—the art of Europe and America. But, it makes important connections to non-Western art—the art of other cultures.

This book is organized to give you several options for a satisfying study. And there are many tools you can use to fully comprehend the long time spans and complex movements in art history.

Three Parts

Part One: The World and Work of the Artist introduces art-making. Understanding the choices among materials, techniques and subject matter will deepen your appreciation of the decisions artists make.

Part One

The World and Work of the Artist

Part Two: Trends and Influences in the World of Art shows that artists around the world often pursue similar ideas. You'll learn different perspectives, too, about Native

American art and about the art and cultures of India, China, Japan, Africa and others.

Part Three: Art in the Western World begins with the ancient world and concludes with a look at the fascinating kinds of art being made today.

Chapter Openers

Overview
Each of the book's seventeen chapters begins with a stand-alone overview. Text, images and captions combine to give you a sense of what will be covered in the chapter's lessons.

Read all seventeen chapter openers first and you'll get the "big picture" of art history.

Quotation
Sometimes a quotation sums it up well. Sometimes quotations will make you curious.

Maps
Maps help you visualize where the people lived who were making images or objects of the period.

Use the world map at the back of the book, too.

Timeline
What else is happening? The timeline points out significant European and American historical events taking place during the periods covered in the chapter. Those events can include great works of literature or music, political revolutions, inventions, or natural disasters.

Lesson Openers

Overview
The chapters are sectioned into lessons and each lesson begins with a lesson opener. Reading the lesson opener provides you with a summary of that lesson's main points and prepares you for further exploration of the topic.

Key Notes
The major concepts covered in the lesson appear as Key Notes in the lesson opener. Use these points as guides for your study, making sure you come away from the lesson with a clear understanding of each concept.

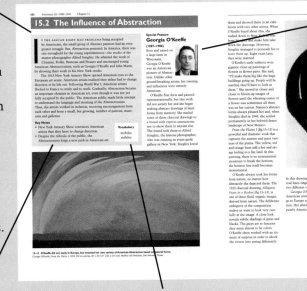

Special Feature
Here, Georgia O'Keeffe's life and work sets the foundation for understanding the shift to abstraction in American art. A practical example is provided in the opener to expand your understanding of the lesson's major concept.

Vocabulary
Important terms are listed in the opener, alerting you to the fact that they will be used in the lesson. The words are highlighted as they appear in the lesson text.

Text Features

Captions

help you understand ideas in the text or help you make comparisons between art styles. When the sizes of the original art are given, take time to imagine the work in real life. Works may be as small as a postage stamp or as large as a billboard.

World Cultural Timelines

show what's going on in cultures apart from the Western world.

Window in Time

features include some of art history's exciting events and intriguing discussions.

Text

The text is the voice of the author, explaining, defining and helping you to think.

It can point out things you might not otherwise notice, confirm conclusions you had reached on

your own and even challenge your perspective. Use the text as a starting point, and not the end point,

to your personal exploration of art history.

Sidelights

give a glimpse of important art-related topics. They help round out the historical view in the text.

Lesson Review

questions and Chapter Review questions help you recall and integrate what you've learned. Some questions and activities ask for interpretation. Analyze for yourself!

Primary Source

"More scope to the fancy..." Hogarth's words expand our sense of London in the early 1700s. A primary source is direct. We can make up our own minds about a period or an artist, based on the actual words said or written.

Other Tools for Learning

are just that. Use the timeline and

map for keener comprehension. Or tap into electronic research.

Studio Activities

Classroom Connections

Now it's your turn to be the artist! These activities help you use what you've learned from each chapter to generate new ideas and approaches to making art.

Student Profiles

Meet a fellow student. What you read may surprise you. Find out what other students have to say about making and understanding art, as they tackle a Classroom Connections activity.

Reference

Pronunciation Guide

Klee is pronounced "clay." If you've never heard someone speak of painter Paul Klee, how would you know how to pronounce his name? The Pronunciation Guide lists all the artists in the text.

Glossary

Words in lesson vocabulary lists are defined in the Glossary. Check this resource for proper names, place names, historical terms, art movements and words unfamiliar to you.

Index

The Index lists in alphabetical order the contents of *Discovering Art History* and the page number for each topic. Use it to locate artworks, artists, movements and the ideas discussed in the text.

Part One The World and Work of the Artist

Contents

Part Two Trends and Influences in the World of Art

Part Three Art in the Western World

Religious Conviction

Page 204

7

Romanesque and Gothic Art

Page 230

8

The World and Work of the Artist

Diego Rivera, *The Making of a Fresco Showing the Building of a City*, detail, April-June 1931. True fresco, 18 3/4' x 32 1/2' (9 5.68 x 9.91 m). San Francisco Art Institute.

Chapter 1 Organizer

Chapter 1 Opener: Learning About Art

Objectives

Explain how there is no single definitive definition of art.

Understand that art uses visual images to communicate.

Appreciate how learning about art is an enriching experience.

National Standards

5c Students reflect analytically on various interpretations as a means for understanding and evaluating works of visual art.

6a Students compare the materials, technologies, media, and processes of the visual arts with those of other arts disciplines as they are used in creation and types of analysis.

5c Students reflect analytically on various interpretations as a means for understanding and evaluating works of visual art.
5d Students correlate responses to works of visual art with various techniques for communicating meanings, ideas, attitudes, views, and intentions.

Teacher Edition References

Lesson 1.1 Evaluating Works of Art

Lesson 1.1 6–7
Lesson 1.1 Review 7

Contextual Info 7

HOTS 7

Lesson 1.2 Why Do People Create Art?

Lesson 1.2 10–11
Lesson 1.2 Review 11

Contextual Info 9, 10
HOTS 9, 11

Performing Arts 9, 10

Lesson 1.3 The Discovery and Preservation of Art

Lesson 1.3 14–15
Lesson 1.3 Review 15
Primary Source 15
Chapter Review 15

Contextual Info 13
HOTS 13, 14

Inquiry 13
Cooperative 15

Classroom Connections

National Standards

Studio Activity 1
Classroom Museum

5c Students reflect analytically on various interpretations as a means for understanding and evaluating works of visual art.
6a Students compare the materials, technologies, media, and processes of the visual arts with those of other arts disciplines as they are used in creation and types of analysis.

Studio Activity 2
Digging for Art

5c Students reflect analytically on various interpretations as a means for understanding and evaluating works of visual art.
6a Students compare the materials, technologies, media, and processes of the visual arts with those of other arts disciplines as they are used in creation and types of analysis.

Other Resources

Books

Adkins, Leslie, and Adkins, Roy. *Introduction to Archaeology*. Secaucus: Chartwell Books, Inc., 1989.

Belves, Pierre, and Francois Mathey. *Enjoying the World of Art*. New York: Lion Books, 1966.

Berger, John. *About Looking*. New York: Pantheon, 1980.

_____. *Ways of Seeing*. New York: Viking, 1973.

Borreson, Mary Jo. *Let's Go To An Art Museum*. New York: G.P. Putnam, 1960.

Browner, Richard. *Look Again*. New York: Atheneum, 1962.

Chase, Alice Elizabeth. *Looking at Art*. New York: Thomas Y. Crowell, 1966.

Feldman, Edmund B. *Artist*. Englewood Cliffs: Prentice-Hall, 1982.

_____. *Thinking About Art*. Englewood Cliffs: Prentice-Hall, 1985.

McIntosh, Jane. *Practical Archaeologist*. New York: Facts on File Inc., 1988.

Moore, Jane Gaylor. *The Many Ways of Seeing: An Introduction to the Pleasures of Art*. New York: Franklin Watts, 1961.

Paul, Louism. *The Way Art Happens*. New York: Ives Washburn, 1963.

Ancillaries

Slides: African, *Benin Plaque*, 29b, 52; Hopper, *Nighthawks*, 106a, 211

Teacher Edition References

Context 4
Art 5
Quote 5
Interdisciplinary 5
Performing Arts 5

Ancillaries

Slides: Terborch, *Music Lesson*, 1b, 1; Johnson, *Going to Church*, 2b, 2

Slides: Early Medieval, *Front Cover of the Binding of the Lindau Gospels*, 1a, 4; Pennsylvania German, *Chest*, 3b, 3; Chagall, *Jerusalem Windows*, 4b, 5

Overhead Transparencies: Reconstructing the Past, 1

Schedule	Materials
Give students the assignment before the studio so that they can bring in objects from home.	found objects, paper strips for labels, scissors and ruler, pencil, eraser, markers
This could be extended an extra day.	magazines, poster board, markers, glue/tape, scissors

Introduce

Throughout history, humans have communicated visually by using an unending variety of images, styles and media. Art includes not only paintings, works on paper and sculpture, but also textiles, ceramics and craft objects. Each culture applies its own exacting standards in judging the quality of a work. However, by digging beyond our first impressions, we can all become more informed viewers and thereby gain lasting satisfaction from the world's vast visual riches.

Lessons at a Glance

1.1 *Evaluating Works of Art*
Art is generally evaluated on craftsmanship, design and aesthetic qualities, as well as a work's ability to reflect the culture in which it was created.

1.2 *Why Do People Create Art?*
Throughout history, people have made art for a variety of reasons. Artists can create work that is functional, religious, political, educational or purely aesthetic, thereby representing humankind's innate desire to communicate visually.

1.3 *The Discovery and Preservation of Art*
Archaeology provides information about past cultures and often adds insight into humankind's roots. Modern museums, relatively recent institutions in Western history, offer public access to important works of art and enable scholars to carry on vital research.

Objectives

Students should be able to:

Explain how there is no single definitive definition of art.

Understand that art uses visual images to communicate.

Appreciate how learning about art is an enriching experience.

I Learning About Art

ART IS PERHAPS HUMANITY'S most essential, most universal language. While art uses visual images to communicate its messages, we use words to describe the images, reactions and feelings we have about objects of art.

All the images in this book are concerned with art. Museums around the world are filled with objects called art. Hundreds of books and magazines are filled with pictures and descriptions of fascinating objects: paintings, buildings, drawings, pottery, weavings, sculpture, prints and other things we call art. Works of art add to our enjoyment of life. And yet, some observers ask seriously, "What is so special about that chair, vase, painting or wood carving? Why is it called art?"

It is impossible to establish a definition of art that will please everyone. The term is broad; each age of humanity has different ideas about it. While we may not be able to define art to everyone's satisfaction, we can define some of the standards by which art is evaluated.

When an object is placed before a group of people, how do they come to agree it is a work of special quality? What criteria or guidelines do they use to make a judgment? And how can you learn to judge whether a work of art—your own, your peers' or a work in a museum or gallery—is good? How can you learn to think beyond "I like it" or "I don't like it" and give reasons for your preferences?

1–a Edward Hopper's painting *Early Sunday Morning* expresses some of the artist's feelings about his society. How do you respond to it? How does it make you feel? How do you think the artist created these feelings in you?
Edward Hopper, *Early Sunday Morning*, 1930. Oil on canvas, 35" x 59 3/4" (89 x 152 cm). The Whitney Museum of American Art, New York, gift of Gloria Vanderbilt Whitney.

Teach

Context

Direct students to study figs.1–a and 1–b. Ask what visual clues the pieces provide about the cultures in which they were made.

• Did Hopper paint his canvas for the same type of audience that commissioned the *Warrior and Attendants* plaque?

• Why might a king be uninterested in the subject of *Early Sunday Morning*?

• Why is it or is it not likely that a royal leader rules the town that Hopper portrays?

• What might the lives of ordinary people be like in each culture represented by the works?

• Do students think that the two cultures are located in the same part of the world? Why or why not?

• What additional observations can students make about the seventeenth-century Benin society and twentieth-century America?

• Emphasize to students that all artworks provide a lasting reflection of the cultures in which they were created.

*All art consists in bringing
something into existence.*
Aristotle

1–b This plaque containing the figures of a warrior and his helpers is from the Benin culture of Nigeria. It was designed and cast in bronze, a complex technique the Benin learned from their neighbors, the Ife people. This relief once decorated the king's palace in Benin. The king, in the center, is flanked by two soldiers and two children making music.
Warrior and Attendants plaque, late 17th century. Benin Culture, Nigeria. Bronze, 14 1/2" x 15 1/4" (37 x 39 cm). The Nelson-Atkins Museum of Art, Kansas City, Missouri, Nelson Fund.

Quote

Instruct students to find out who Aristotle was and then discuss what he might have meant by his statement. Ask how his quote relates to the images in the chapter opener.

points of agreement in each group's results. After, ask students what they found most difficult in the assignment.

• Did the variety of artwork make it more or less challenging?

• Did working with classmates make the task easier or more difficult?

Have students write police reports to a sergeant from the point of view of a police officer walking through Hopper's town in *Early Sunday Morning*. What happened on the beat that day? Require that students' stories be based on the visual information in Hopper's painting.

Performing Arts Connection

Nonverbal Communication

Ask students to name as many different ways as possible to communicate without words. Ask if students have ever played charades or watched a mime perform. How do little babies indicate that they are happy, scared, angry or tired? From infancy on, we have many ways to express ourselves without language. For instance, we use our bodies and voices to sing, dance and play instruments. We have also used drawn images since prehistoric times—as records of our lives and as prayers to the spirit world.

Interdisciplinary Connection

Science: Have students research and list different ways that animals communicate with each other, such as through actions, colors or sounds.

Art

Ask students how Hopper uses color and shape to suggest a very specific time of day. Would students know that it is early morning if this reproduction was printed in black and white?

• How does Hopper indicate the direction of the early-morning sun? What delineates the long, narrow shadows?

• What feelings, memories and sensations does his composition evoke?

• Have students use specifics from the painting to discuss how Hopper perceived small-town twentieth-century American life.

Evaluate

Ask the class if visual expressions are the same throughout the world. Tell students to choose two other images in the chapter to support their position. From their selections, what can they surmise about each society and its perception about art?

Reteach

Divide the class into small groups and assign each the task of devising a comprehensive definition of art that will encompass all the images in Chapter 1. Next, have the groups share their results and compare the similarities and differences. As a class, have students then refine a definition by sifting through the

Lesson 1.1

Art is generally evaluated on craftsmanship, design and aesthetic qualities, as well as a work's ability to reflect the culture in which it was created.

Warm-up

Ask students to select a song that they all enjoy. What makes this song preferable to another song? Have students write a list of the criteria they use to judge the work.

- How does the composition, rhythm, message and skill of the performer affect their decision? Challenge students to apply these criteria to a work of art in Lesson 1.1.

- What have they decided about the quality of the visual piece?

- Can music and art be judged by the same measures?

- What different criteria might be necessary?

Explain that Lesson 1.1 explores some of the means frequently applied to evaluating artwork.

Objective

Students should be able to:

Understand the qualities used in evaluating works of art.

Teach

Criticism: Have students identify which sense they usually employ in evaluating art. Challenge them to think of additional information they might be able to obtain by touching, hearing, tasting and smelling a work.

- What new information would they learn if they applied these senses to the ceremonial cup (fig.1–1)?

- What could its taste tell them?

- How could they learn about its texture and temperature or the way the embossed lines interact with the cup's shape?

- How could they use their hearing to understand the work?

- Now ask them how their awareness of the cup changed after considering it from these other viewpoints. Can they apply this same process to making judgments about people or situations? Do they always receive the fullest picture

1.1 Evaluating Works of Art

We generally base our evaluation of works of art on such criteria as craftsmanship, design and aesthetic properties. We also consider how well the works reflect the societies in which they were created.

Craftsmanship

A craftsperson is someone who is skilled in the use of materials and tools and produces well-made objects of above-average quality (figs.1–1, 1–2).

Aesthetic Properties

Each work of art has certain *properties* that belong to it. By analyzing them, we can understand what makes the work unique.

Sensory properties are the elements of art (see pages 41–47) that we can recognize by using our sense of sight and touch. The use of *line* is a sensory property that we can see. So are the choice and blending of *colors*, the variety of *values*, and *shapes* created by color and line. Our sense of touch helps us understand the *texture* of an object, the suggestion of *space* and the *form* or *mass* of something three-dimensional.

Formal properties are the principles of art (see pages 48–54) that help us see how artists organize the elements of art to express their ideas effectively. If we are able to analyze the *unity, balance, contrast, rhythm, pattern, emphasis* and visual *movement* in works of art, we can determine how all parts of a composition work together.

Technical properties are the media, tools and equipment used to make the work of art. For example, ceramics, oil painting, bronze casting (fig.1–b) and charcoal drawing all rely on different technical skills. Studying and working with various media and methods can help you make value judgments about the quality of artists' techniques.

Expressive properties are the characteristics of an artwork that cause us to respond to it with feeling and emotion. Paintings, for example, might express moods of tension, relaxation or sadness through color, metaphor, symbolism or design (fig.1–a). Ideas, ideals, social criticism, religion, hope and compassion can be communicated through art.

Reflection of Society. Artworks also reflect the times in which they were created. Artisans created works that often provide or confirm information about cultures. The images depicted, the materials used and the style of the piece all help place the object in a particular time and place.

1–1 This cup was made from a thin sheet of gold and the design was probably hammered from within, against a wooden mold. The gazelle is beautifully stylized and designed to fit the space comfortably. All the details are carefully planned and executed. No cracks appear, even after this tremendous length of time. All these features tell us that the piece was made with great care and a mastery of materials and tools.
Ceremonial cup, about 1000 BC. Northwest Iran. Gold, 4 1/4" (11 cm) high. Los Angeles County Museum of Art.

1–2 The weaver who created this blanket used line, shapes, color and texture. The blanket also shows an understanding of design principles, for it has pattern, unity, balance and contrast. The weaver used the elements of art and the principles of design to create an object that reflects the values of her cultural heritage.
Navajo rug, *Eye Dazzler,* 18th century. Wool. Hurst Gallery, Cambridge, Massachusetts.

if they use just a single sense? Encourage them to apply their other senses before making a snap conclusion about a new circumstance or their first meeting with someone.

Art History/Aesthetics: Have students imagine that they are archeologists who have just unearthed the drinking cup in fig.1–4.

- What might their analysis of the piece tell them about ancient Greek culture?

- What does the cup's shape indicate about the specific way it was used?

- How does the subject matter on the cup relate to its function and shape? Does the artist ignore or follow the form of the vessel?

- After students brainstorm, have them apply each of the aesthetic properties detailed in Lesson 1.1 to see what further information they can detect. Based on what they have learned, do they believe this is a quality work of art? Why?

Evaluate

Ask students if it's possible to obtain a complete picture of an artwork by looking at a single aspect of it, such as its technical or formal properties. What information might they miss, for instance, if they ignore the work's relationship to the society in which it was made?

Identifying Works of Art.
Paintings and sculptures can easily be identified as works of art. But often a bowl, blanket or other functional object is also called art. Collectors or *connoisseurs* appreciate the appearance, craftsmanship or message of such objects. If a society placed a high value on a crafted object, that object may be considered an object of art today (fig.1–3). An item is not art just because it is old, but its age is one of many factors taken into consideration.

Art historians search for pieces that are good examples of the craftsmanship, aesthetic properties and societal background of a culture. They look for certain objects that seem to reflect the highest quality

work. These objects stand out as *paradigms*, or classic examples (fig.1–4). You will encounter many paradigms in this book. Some

already will be recognizable. Others will grow in familiarity as you encounter them here and elsewhere.

1–4 This drinking cup is considered a paradigm. This work of high quality is an outstanding example from the Archaic period in Greek art.
Exekias, *Dionysus in a Boat.* Interior of an Attic black-figured kylix, about 540 BC. Diameter, 12" (30 cm). Staatliche Antikensammlungen, Munich.

1–3 This kylix, or shallow drinking cup, shows the Greek goddess of Dawn holding the body of her son, who has just been killed by Achilles. The shape of the vessel, its high quality, and the mythological scene depicted aid the viewer in identifying the piece as a product of ancient Greece.
Douris, *Eos and Memnon.* Interior of red-figured kylix, about 490–480 BC. Diameter, 10 1/2" (27 cm). The Louvre, Paris.

Lesson 1.1 Review

1 What are some of the criteria that we should consider when evaluating a piece of art?
2 List the art elements and the principles of art. What is the relationship between these sensory and formal properties of art?
3 What are the technical properties used to create art?

4 Give some examples of art media. What medium was used to create the Nigerian *Warrior and Attendant*'s plaque (fig.1–a)?
5 What are some of the factors in a piece of art that can indicate when or where it was created?
6 Define paradigm. Give an example of a paradigm from this chapter.

Lesson 1.2

Throughout history, people have made art for a variety of reasons. Artists can create work that is functional, religious, political, educational or purely aesthetic, thereby representing humankind's innate desire to communicate visually.

Warm-up

Challenge students to pretend that they are a Martian, a twenty-fifth century child, an inhabitant of a South Seas island, and a person living in prehistoric times. Have them list the reasons why each of these individuals would want to create art. Ask students to share their thoughts and discuss if these seem to be the same reasons why artists make art today.

Objectives

Students should be able to:

Explore the various reasons people create art.

Comprehend that art can serve more than one purpose at a time.

Teach

Criticism: Ask students to pretend that they are the artists of the images in Lesson 1.2. Before they look at the text or captions, have them describe their reasons for making these works. After, direct students to read the different categories outlined on pages 8 through 11 and try to apply them to each piece.

• Which works have more than one reason why someone created them? For instance, is the cover of the *Lindenau Gospels* (fig.1–7) only a religious object or does the door from the king's palace at Ikerre, Yoruba, Nigeria, (fig.1–9) express only historical information?

1.2 Why Do People Create Art?

Why do people create art? Why do they bother to carve or paint an object? There are many reasons why people have made objects of great beauty. They may include functional considerations, religion, politics, education, aesthetics and humanity's inborn desire to create.

Utility

Utility is a term that describes an object's usefulness. Nearly all societies have needed eating utensils and storage vessels, which they have formed from clay, basketry, leather or metals.

Similarly, clothing not only protects the wearer but also indicates social rank and individual taste. Architectural forms not only provide shelter. They also enclose spaces for living, worship or public assembly, and are specifically designed and decorated to enhance those functions. Functional objects from Western culture include furniture, glassware, machinery, automobiles, office buildings, airplanes, pens and lamps. Yet, all these objects have artistic qualities in addition to their functional qualities.

1–5 The storage jar of basketry created by a Western Apache artisan is meant to be utilitarian. Yet the intricate craftsmanship, the attention to ornamentation and the overall design indicate that the basket had a greater value than the simple function of storage.
Storage jar, Western Apache, Reed. Texas Memorial Museum, The University of Texas, Austin. ACC# 1074–89.

Evaluate

Ask students how the saying "The sum is greater than its parts" can apply to art. Can they identify works that are functional and also pleasing to the eye?

• What objects in their own home have more than one purpose and how does this enhance the overall piece? Do they have glass vases or decorative picture frames?

• Are all their clothes just for keeping them covered or are some outfits for special occasions?

• Are any objects in their home related to their heritage? How might they carry cultural values as well as serve some other function?

Reteach

Arrange for students to interview artists, either in the classroom or in their studios, about why they have pursued their careers. (Alternately, they can read interviews or biographies of artists in books and magazines from the library.)

• Ask students what the driving force is behind each artist's passion.

• What activity do students pursue strongly?

• Do the reasons why students themselves work at a sport, art form or other interest parallel those of professional artists?

• Can they exactly define what drives them in this love or is it partially ineffable?

1–6 The Poro Society mask was worn by dancers "possessed" by the spirit of the object. The mask is meaningless until given life by the ceremony. Then, it is no longer an inanimate object, but a real force, an abode of power and a controller of life. *Poro Society mask.* N'Gere Peoples, Ivory Coast, Africa. Wood, fiber and fur, about 18" (46 cm) high. Baltimore Museum of Art, gift of Mr. and Mrs. Leonard Whitehouse and Dr. and Mrs. Bernard Berk.

Religion

Religion has played an important role in the creation of objects. Many objects have been created to support religious beliefs and activities. In many cultures, the movement of stars and moon, the rising and setting of the sun, tidal activities, flooding rivers and the habits of animals have supernatural meanings. Worship is aided in many cultures through the use of magical designs or geometric shapes, and the creation of good-luck charms, or *fetishes*. Symbolic or ornamental containers on specially designed altars are used for ritual display. Priests and worshipers wear unique ornaments and coverings.

Objects may be made to represent a god and to remind the worshiper of that spirit's power, divinity, omniscience or humanity. Gods are often depicted in human or animal form. Many beautiful and impressive objects have been made as gifts to the gods by worshipers in cultures as diverse as *aborigines* and ancient Greeks. Structures for the worship of gods range from Neolithic circles of huge stones to elaborate cathedrals and temples.

1–7 Copies of holy writings may be elaborately printed in specially ornate script and bound or protected in cases or bindings of leather, precious metals and jeweled designs. Upper cover of binding, the *Lindenau Gospels*, about 870 AD. Gold and jewels, 13 3/4" x 10 1/2" (35 x 27 cm). The Pierpont Morgan Library, New York.

Contextual Information

Areogun

Areogun was one of the great Yoruba sculptors. He was commissioned to carve doors and pillars for several palaces of Yoruba kings. His doors for the king of Ikerre were sent to England for the British Empire Exhibition in 1924 and are now in the British Museum.

Politics

The use of art and architecture in politics goes back to ancient times. Castles and fortified cities were built to defend the people from enemies. Paintings or carvings of the ruler on walls and towers were used to perpetuate myths of the awesome power of a king. Today, political propaganda is conveyed through political cartoons, critical painting and billboard posters.

Information/History

The use of art to teach assumes great importance in societies where there is no written language or where the literacy rate is low. Paintings, sculptures, stained glass windows and symbolic abstract designs have been used to pass on a culture's history, folk tales, religious traditions, mythology and moral values. The art provides a visual record of heroes, gods, or even instructions on how to make wine or worship properly. Oral traditions are thus reinforced in a physical way.

1–8 This is a billboard poster used for political propaganda purposes in China.
Crush the Gang of Four! Political poster, 1977. About 59" x 79" (1.5 x 2 m). Guilin, China.

1–9 Some of the scenes on this door relate the visit of a British colonial official to the king. Other anecdotes of Yoruba life also are depicted.
Areogun, *Door from the king's palace at Ikerre, Yoruba, Nigeria*, about 1910. Wood, approximately 6' (1.8 m) high. The British Museum, London.

Performing Arts Connection

Information/History

Like art, songs can record and communicate history. Folk songs—those created and performed by ordinary people, or the "folk"—frequently relate personal stories. They can be about a group of people or an individual's exploits, or they can explain how things or events evolved. African-American slaves invented songs about their hardships and hopes for a better future as a means of keeping their histories alive and passing them down to younger generations. Songs of resistance came out of the early organizational efforts of labor unions,

and as recently as the 1960s, "flower children" protested the Vietnam war by singing songs about peace and love.

• Arrange students into small groups to rewrite the lyrics of a popular song so that it expresses their opinion about a current social concern—the environment, AIDS, or a local political issue. Have them rehearse and then perform the pieces for each other. Discuss what made it easy or difficult to communicate their message through music.

• Students may want to compile an illustrated book of these songs.

1–10 Robert Swain's painting may evoke many types of thoughts to viewers, regardless of their backgrounds. And, by adding a title like *Untitled*, the possible connotations are limited only by the imagination of the viewer.
Robert Swain, *Untitled*, 1968. Acrylic on cotton duck, 105 1/2" (268 cm) per side. Collection, Stephen S. Schwartz, Columbus, Ohio. Courtesy of the artist.

Aesthetics

Today we may think of art as something meant to be pleasing to the sight or touch. *Aesthetics* is the term used to sum up the search for beauty—for a feeling of balance, proportion and pleasing arrangement; for a tasteful mixture of plain surface with textured or ornamental areas; and for a conscientious use of materials to achieve good craftsmanship and permanence. Aesthetics also includes a search for subject matter that is thought-provoking.

Lesson 1.2 Review

1 List six reasons why people create art. Give an example of art created for each reason.
2 What features of the Western Apache storage jar (fig.1–5) make it not just a useful object, but a work of art?
3 Define aesthetics and use it in a sentence.

4 Explain how an automobile can be considered a work of art.
5 Write three words that come to mind as you look at Robert Swain's painting (fig.1–10).
6 Compare your terms with those of another student. Why do you think Swain did not give this painting a title?

Lesson 1.2 Review Answers

1 utility: Western Apache *Storage jar* (fig.1–5)
religion: *Poro Society mask* (fig.1–6); *Lindenau Gospels* (fig.1–7)
politics: *Crush the Gang of Four!* (fig.1–8)
information/history: Areogun's Door from the King's palace (fig.1–9)
aesthetics: Robert Swain's *Untitled* (fig.1–10)
2 The attention to ornamentation and the overall design

3 The term *aesthetics* is used to sum up the quest for beauty and thought-provoking subject matter. It is also a term that refers to our personal responses to works of art. Aesthetic qualities in an artwork might be a feeling of balance and proportion, or a pleasing mixture of smooth and textured surfaces, or a deliberate use of fine materials and technique to achieve craftsmanship and permanence.
4 A great deal of time and thought is invested in making modern cars aesthetically pleasing—from the design of the overall shape, to the selection of colors, to the craftsmanship and detail—so that contemporary cars are not only utilitarian, but pleasing to see and touch.

5 Appropriate words might be triangles, colors, inverted, rainbow and prism.
6 Swain probably wanted each viewer to have his or her own thoughts about this artwork. By leaving it untitled, the artwork itself—not a title—elicits feelings and thoughts within each viewer.

Lesson 1.3

Archaeology provides information about past cultures and often adds insight into humankind's roots. Modern museums, relatively recent institutions in Western history, offer public access to important works of art and enable scholars to carry on vital research.

Warm-up

Direct students to imagine being a nineteenth-century archaeologist who has magically traveled into the future and unearthed a large, modern department store. What would the contemporary architecture and objects tell them about how life will change for Western society in a hundred years? What are their reactions to this knowledge as someone from the past?

Objectives

Students should be able to:

Define the term *archaeology* and its importance to the study of art.

Understand the importance of archaeological remains.

Understand the role of museums in the study, preservation and appreciation of art.

Teach

Art History: Ask students to write a job description for an archaeologist, thinking carefully of all the necessary skills. Do they believe that it would be an easy task to work on a dig? Have them read the information on page 12 to see what essential talents they might have forgotten to include in the job description. Now with a clearer picture of the career, would they consider archaeology an alluring profession? Why or why not? (Students also can check college catalogs to research the courses taken by archaeology majors.)

1.3 The Discovery and Preservation of Art

Archaeology

Archaeology is the unearthing and study of evidence from past cultures which have been hidden from human eyes for centuries (fig.1–11). Much of the ancient material seen in this book, such as statues, coins and even buildings, was dug from its earthly grave and brought to society's attention by trained archaeologists. Many of these items are now preserved in museums and universities. Archaeologists also play a key role in giving people an insight into the roots of their culture.

Archaeological items are usually not discovered easily. They are located after hard, plodding detective work. Research is needed to find a probable site for some undiscovered city or culture. To determine if a site is a worthwhile place for archaeological research, cores are drilled to identify the materials under the surface. Once a likely place is found, the earth is carefully dug and removed. Nothing must be disturbed or broken. All the earth must be sifted for tiny bits of pottery or jewelry. Every item uncovered is catalogued, referenced and photographed—even broken bits of jewelry or pottery fragments. Objects are dated by scientific means (carbon-14 count) or by their historical associations.

Archaeology may seem exciting and romantic, as workers excavate sites to find buried treasure. However, it requires research, analysis and a scientific approach to cultural detective work. But there is always the chance of some extraordinary and fascinating find.

In 1977, Soviet and Afghan scientists, working a dig near Afghanistan's northern border, uncovered the grave of a nobleman covered with pieces of gold. Nearby graves revealed more gold objects:

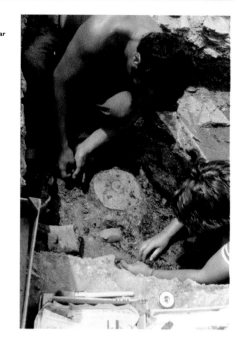

1–11 Students uncovering an *Etruscan object* near Siena, Italy. Bryn Mawr College Archives.

bracelets, beads, pins, rings, daggers, clasps and pendants. Before winter set in, they uncovered another grave with so many golden artifacts that they covered it up and returned to it the following year, after the ground had thawed. For 2000 years, these tombs had not been discovered. They date from a culture that lived there from 100 BC to 100 AD. A stunning part of the discovery is that the objects reveal the combined influences of Greek, Bactrian, Roman, Indian and Chinese cultures. It was not known before this discovery that these cultures were ever united in one place on earth. One pendant shows Bactrian rams' heads, Chinese dragons and Mesopotamian animals on the same piece of work.

Sites around the world have revealed glimpses into past great civilizations: the Ming Tombs in China, Pompeii and Herculaneum, the Athenian Acropolis, the Roman Forum, Persepolis, Niniveh, Ur, Memphis, and Monte Alban. More will be uncovered in the future. Every time a new discovery is made, our understanding of world culture is enriched.

Museums

When people want to hear good music, they go to a concert hall, and when they want to see art, they go to a museum. This seems simple enough, but it was not always so. Throughout history, artists have created their work for patrons and collectors, not for museums. Paintings and sculpture were held in the great family collections of kings and queens, nobles and wealthy families (fig.1–12). Only after the revolutions of the eighteenth and nineteenth centuries

Evaluate

Ask students whether a culture's written history is the only way to acquire information about its past. How can the images in Chapter 1 substantiate their answers? What do we learn from physical remains that cannot be learned from written or oral histories?

Reteach

Share with students that archaeologists have often discovered sites that have been robbed of some of their objects. Instruct students to play the role of the thieves explaining to the police, who have finally caught them, why they stole the items. After students review the text on pages 12 and 13, have them take on the role of one of the archaeologists who helped the police find the thieves. The archaeologist must speak before a judge about why the stolen items should be placed under the care of a museum. How can they make convincing arguments? Why is the preservation of the works so important?

tumbled the monarchies were the common people allowed to see these objects of art. The new governments opened the fabulous collections of art to the public. The Palace of the Louvre in Paris became the Museum of the Republic in 1793, and many other royal buildings in Europe followed suit. Sometimes new structures were designed to house collections.

Many collections in the United States belong to the cities (Museum of Fine Arts in Boston) or counties (Los Angeles County Museum of Art) or the nation (National Gallery in Washington, DC). These collections were built from gifts of art donated or loaned by individuals or groups of people. Some of the art was purchased with donated funds or by bequests. In this way, American collections have grown in the past century to equal many older collections around the world.

Often, owners of individual collections buy or build their own museums, fill them with their own collections, and open the doors to visitors. The Solomon R. Guggenheim Museum in New York and the

J. Paul Getty Museum in California are two examples. Asia and Europe have similar individual collections that are open to the public.

The primary function of museums is to display works of art for the enjoyment of viewers and students of art and culture. Various collections preserve artifacts of past civilizations which contribute to the public's understanding of the history and social customs of these groups. But most museums have other functions also.

Education is of great concern. Groups of schoolchildren and adults can hear lectures and see movies and television and slide programs to aid their understanding of art. Some museums even send out materials to schools and other groups.

Museums in various parts of the country and other parts of the world often work cooperatively to arrange special exhibits for their patrons. As a result of joint efforts, treasures from Mexican and Soviet museums have traveled to museums in the United States and other countries. Some large museums and collections also sponsor exhibits from

their collections that travel to smaller regional or municipal museums. In this way, the collected works of art can be enjoyed by many more people.

A program of art restoration and repair is essential to most large museums. The science of formulating pigments, matching paints and repairing canvas, bronze and marble is quite exacting. Photography is used to assure the authenticity of a work of art. Every major painting is X-rayed to record the underpainting and characteristic use of brush and pigments by the artist. This procedure aids in identification, helps prevent frauds and leads to an expanded knowledge of older painting techniques.

Museums control humidity and temperature so valuable works of art on wood or canvas do not dry out or age too rapidly. Light can also be controlled so unnecessary fading is kept to a minimum. Museums take great care to protect works of art and yet keep them on public display.

1–12 Some museum buildings are architectural works of art in themselves. The fifteenth-century Topkapi Palace in Istanbul is a magnificent structure of great historical and architectural interest. It now contains the fabulous collection of jewelry, ceramics, furniture and relics of sultans and the Ottoman Turkish Empire. Although not designed as a museum, it is a worthy setting for such a collection.
Topkapi Palace. *View of the interior,* 15th century. Istanbul.

Higher-Order Thinking Skills

Ask students to share with the class their favorite experiences with making a piece of art. Why was it special? Do they still have the work? If so, they could have a show-and-share day.

Lesson 1.3 Review Answers

1 Archeology is the finding and study of the remains of past cultures. Much of the historical art in this book was found by archeologists who give people an insight into the roots of cultures and the meanings of many of these artifacts. Art history then provides the setting and context for a work of art.

2 The Louvre was a palace until 1793.

3 Gifts of art are often donated; museums purchase art with donated funds and bequests.

4 Solomon R. Guggenheim Museum, New York; J. Paul Getty Museum, California

5 Museum restoration experts formulate pigments, match paints, and repair canvas, bronze and marble. Using photography, they authenticate work, and x-ray major paintings to record the underpainting and the artist's characteristic use of brush and pigments.

6 By producing your own work, you learn to appreciate the ability, knowledge and skill of fine artists and craftspeople. You begin to understand some of the visual and technical problems that artists solve in their work.

How We Study Art

Art covers a broad spectrum of ideas and expression. It is a beginner's attempt at watercolor; the graceful design of a table; the Statue of Liberty; a tiny piece of jewelry. Clothes, cars, textbooks and television scenery are designed by artists, and their designs affect the way you live.

Art is all around you. Do you always see it? Probably not. And you probably don't understand all of what you *do* see. But the more you learn about art, the more you'll notice. And the more you notice, the more you'll understand. Understanding things helps you enjoy them and respond to them in new ways.

To grasp the various aspects of art, we can break its study into four components: *aesthetics, history, production* and *criticism.* None of these four components stands alone. All four must be used together to fully appreciate and understand a single work of art.

Aesthetics is a term that refers to our personal responses to works of art. Why do we like some visual images and dislike others? Why do we feel more comfortable with some works than with others? We each respond differently to visual images because we each have a different set of personal experiences on which our responses are based. You say, "I like that painting because..." and your reasons will be your aesthetic response to the painting.

Art History provides the setting and context for a work of art. Artworks reflect the times and cultures of the people who produced them. Art history provides a kind of timeline that shows how art has developed from early human history to the present. It also shows how artists have been influenced by previous artistic styles, by technology

1–13 Two students study Seurat's *Sunday Afternoon on the Island of La Grande Jatte* at the Art Institute of Chicago.

1–14 Caryn Kim of West Springfield High School, Fairfax County, Virginia, sculpts her self-portrait in clay.

and social change, and how those influences show up in their artwork. Art history adds personality to works of art and helps us see artists and their times in the work they have done. We understand today's art more fully when we can trace its development through time.

Art Production is the creation of art. This process requires tools, media and technical ability. It involves learning to look carefully, use the materials you choose, make decisions, solve problems, learn about design, interpret what you see and feel, and criticize your own efforts. Through production and studio experiences, you'll learn to appreciate the ability, knowledge and skill of fine artists and craftspeople. By handling clay, mixing colors, working with composition, using brushes, carving wood or building a model, you'll enter the working world of artists and begin to understand some of the visual and technical problems they encounter daily.

Art Criticism is analysis. It is explaining and judging works of art. It is discovering how the artist used art elements such as line, color and texture. It is determining how the artist used balance, pattern, emphasis and other art principles to arrange the parts of the work. It is sensing how the artist used media and tools to create the work. It is also trying to understand what the artist might have meant to say in the work. In this way, we analyze the artwork's sensory, formal, technical and expressive qualities.

Chapter Review Answers

Review

1 Art criticism is art analysis. It involves explaining and judging artworks, discovering how artists use elements such as line, color and texture, and determining how artists use balance, pattern, emphasis and other art principles to arrange their creations. Art criticism often includes sensing how an artist used media and tools to create the work and trying to understand what the artist intended to say in the work. In art criticism, we analyze the sensory, formal, technical and expressive qualities of art.

2 Museums carefully control the humidity and temperature so that art on wood and canvas will not dry out or age too rapidly. Light must be controlled so that art will not fade.

3 Art history provides the setting and context for a work of art. It shows how artists have been influenced by previous artistic styles, technology and social change. Art history adds personality to artworks and helps us understand artists and their times.

4 First, research is done to find a probable site for an undiscovered city. Sample cores are drilled to identify materials under the surface and determine if there might be a city covered by dirt and rubble. The earth is then carefully dug and removed so as not to damage any-

Primary Source

The Artist and the Museum

Museums are not simply places that house the art of by-gone eras. They are alive with teaching and learning and inspiration. The famous nineteenth-century artist, Degas, tells us why museums were so important to him.

"The museums are there to teach the history of art and something more as well, for, if they stimulate in the weak a desire to imitate, they furnish the strong with the means of their emancipation."

"No art was ever less spontaneous than mine. What I do is the result of reflection and study of the great masters."

Edgar Degas, *Carriages at the Races*, Museum of Fine Arts, Boston. Arthur Gordon Tompkins Fund.

Chapter Review

Review
1 What are some of the processes inherent in thoughtful art criticism?
2 Why are museums concerned about controlling the humidity, temperature and light inside their buildings?
3 In studying a work of art, why is it helpful to understand the history of that piece and others like it?
4 Briefly describe the archaeological processes of unearthing an ancient city.

Interpret
1 Select a piece of art from this chapter that appeals to you. Who made it and when was it created? Describe its technical and expressive properties. Why do you think it was created? Explain why you like it.
2 What are some of the clues in the kylix (fig.1–3) that would indicate to an art historian that it was created in Greece after 500 BC?

Other Tools for Learning

Electronic Research
Videodisc player: *National Gallery of Art*
CD-ROM drive: *Microsoft Art Gallery*
1 After viewing *The History of the National Gallery of Art (Washington, DC)* on their videodisc, describe what one of the many people involved in the founding of this museum did to help create it.
2 Browse through a museum's collection, such as the *Louvre Videodisc* or the National Gallery on the *Microsoft Art Gallery* CD-ROM. Select one piece of art to describe. Who created it? When was it made? What is its medium? Describe the effect this art has on your feelings.

---

thing. The earth is sifted for tiny bits of pottery or jewelry. Each item and fragment is catalogued, referenced, photographed and dated by scientific means and historical associations.

Interpret
1 An example of a possible response is: The storage jar in fig.1–5 was made by the Western Apache (date unknown). Human figures and animals are woven in precise geometrical designs. It was probably created to hold grain or seeds. I like the texture of the surface because it seems to be so finely and carefully made.
2 Its shape, its high quality, the scene depicted on it.

Electronic Research
1 Andrew Mellon donated his art collection and money to build the first building of the National Gallery of Art. Samuel Kress, Chester Dale and Joseph Widener donated their art collections to the museum. In 1969, Paul Mellon and the Mellon Foundation bequeathed money to build the East Building which I.M. Pei designed.
2 For example, a student might choose to describe Hans Holbein's *The French Ambassadors* (fig.10–22) which was painted in oil on wood in 1533. The mood is quiet and calm. The distorted skull at the base of the picture is a morbid addition to an otherwise straightforward portrait of two gentlemen posing before green drapery on either side of a collection of their possessions.

Activity 1: Classroom Museum

Activity Objectives

Students should be able to:

• Think about what relevant facts are connected with the creation of artwork and how that information contributes to the way we perceive it.

• Verbalize how the display of art has an impact on how it is seen.

• Learn to actively read and benefit from the captions as they read the text.

• Gain an appreciation of some of the artistic relics of their own family history.

Thinking Critically

Ask aloud the questions under "Think about it." Questions not generally answered in credits might be: age or sex of the artist, what time of year the piece was created, whether the artist was familiar with the subject or materials, whether this image was taken from life or imagined, etc.

To personalize this activity, talk to students about what kinds of relics to look for at home that might reveal something about their family's history. Perhaps one of their ancestors collected old stamps, produced quilts or handmade baskets, collected interesting souvenirs or clothing from other countries, or saved antique furniture or porcelain.

Once objects are collected, ask students:

• What do you want people to notice when they look at your object?

• How can you display or present your object to show off its best features?

Preparation Ideas

• Determine where and how you want students to display their work. You may want to set up special tables (perhaps with a tablecloth) or rearrange desks or lights to create an atmosphere for display.

Notes on Materials

• Optional: use a paper cutter to cut white paper into strips for labels in order to minimize activity in the classroom and to give the students time to focus on their project.

Activity 1

Classroom Museum

Materials
found objects
paper strips for labels
scissors and ruler
pencil, eraser
markers

Take a look. Review all the artwork in Chapter 1 and read each caption carefully.

Think about it.

• The captions in this text generally have two parts. The first part asks a question or points out an interesting fact; the credits tell the title of the work, the artist's name and other information about the artwork. Does it make a difference in the way you look at an artwork to know what year it was made? In what country? What it was made of? How big it is?

• Archaeologists find and study evidence, or relics, of the past. Often, they display what they've found in exhibits that explain their discoveries. What clues might be discovered about you a few hundred years from now?

Do it. Make an arrangement of three objects, similar to a museum archaeology display.

• Be an archaeologist at home and find three objects that are clues to your family's past.

• Make labels for each object by cutting white paper into uniform strips and neatly writing out as much of the following information as possible: artist's name, title of the object, date it was made, country or state where it was made, physical description (medium, color, size), where you obtained the object, the owner.

• Consider ways of displaying your objects that will show off their best qualities. Arrange your display on your desk or a table, as indicated by your teacher.

Check it.

• Can your work be seen clearly from all angles? If not, is its "best side" facing the viewers?

• Do your labels contribute useful and interesting information to your viewers? Are they neat and easily read from about three feet away?

Helpful Hint: Write out your labels in pencil at first to determine what size, style and placement of letters is most effective. Do your final label in a color that complements your objects.

Activity 2

Digging for Art

Materials
magazines
poster board
markers
glue/tape
scissors

Take a look. Review the following artwork:

• Fig.1–1 *Ceremonial cup*, about 1000 BC.

• Fig.1–3 Douris, *Eos and Memnon.* Interior of red-figured kylix, about 490–480 BC.

• Fig.1–4 Exekias, *Dionysus in a Boat.* Interior of Attic black-figured kylix, about 540 BC.

Think about it. Art objects like these were created hundreds or thousands of years ago in early civilizations, then often lost to the world until their rediscovery centuries later. If you wanted to find ancient art, where would you look? How do you think old civilizations are found? What can we learn from discovered relics about the lives of our ancestors?

Do it. Make a display chart or poster illustrating steps that archaeologists use to find, identify and classify objects.

• Look through back issues of magazines like *National Geographic, Discover, Smithsonian, Archaeology,* etc., and clip pictures of archaeological activities, such as digging, sifting, reconstructing, photographing, drawing, plotting and so forth.

• Arrange your images on a large sheet of paper. On separate strips of paper, neatly write out labels that identify what's happening in the pictures. Before you glue everything down, do "Check it," below.

Check it. Have a friend look at your poster, and ask if he or she understands what's happening in the poster without your having to explain anything. If something is unclear, try another arrangement or new labels.

Helpful Hint: You might make up a story about the adventures of the archaeologist or the ancient artist to accompany your arrangement of images.

Additional Activities

• Art, design and visual images affect our lives in many ways every day. Make a list of things you use daily that artists have designed. Organize your list into general categories such as transportation, clothing, artwork, advertising, entertainment and others you discover.

• Research archaeology books or magazine articles that deal with parts of the world associated with your ethnic or religious roots. Write a brief report on your findings. Have many relics been discovered? Are excavations still going on? What are some theories about ancient lifestyles based on objects found?

• Optional: provide a variety of colored paper and cloth, blocks of wood or other materials to set under objects for display.

Classroom Management

Have students work individually or in groups to set up their artwork. Some possible approaches:

• Encourage each student to give a verbal presentation of their work, telling about the significance of each piece as if it were an important find in the world of art.

• Groups could come up with a name or theme for their "gallery" and choose a "tour guide" to speak about each piece.

Tips

• Ask students to imagine their art appearing in this text. How would their caption read? From what angle would they photograph their object?

• For a math correlation, have students compute the size of their object in both inches and centimeters.

• You could provide books on typefaces or calligraphy to encourage creative writing on the labels. Or, for a different approach, have students produce the labels using a computer.

• Have students photograph and write a description of each exhibit. These could be photocopied and made into books or posters to "get acquainted."

Student Profile

Kyung-Sil Chang

Age 18
West Springfield High School
Springfield, Virginia
Favorite kinds of art: painting and
sculpture
Favorite artists: Vincent van Gogh,
Pablo Picasso, Leonardo da Vinci,
Donatello, Wassily, Kandinsky
Activity 1, Classroom Museum

My first ancestor came from China to Korea about 750 years ago. Back then, a Chinese princess married a Korean prince and my ancestor had to take the princess to Korea safely. When he came to Korea, he liked it. He decided to stay and work for the Korean government. From that, my family's history started.

The portrait drawing is of my thirteenth ancestor. Back then, the king awarded him a self-portrait, drawn with rock powder so it would last forever. My ancestor's drawing is about 300 years old. One is when he was young and the other one is when he was old. All relics are so important to me, because it's about my family's history and it's about my ancestors.

My favorite subject is art and I've decided to go to an art college. My drawings are very important to me, because I put my spirit into them. If my house were to catch fire, first I would want to get my artworks. But before that, I would get my ancestors' relics, because I can't buy them and I can't make them either. Where else am I going to feel their spirit? My works I can do over, even though those were so precious to me.

I am taking art history now and learning about the history of art. I never thought about my family's history, and I think it's a shame of mine. If I don't even know mine, then how can I search for another's background? I never knew about my ancestors until we did this project in art history class.

My grandpa told me about our ancestor's history and our family tree. But, I couldn't understand the family tree that well, it was so complicated. I want my grandpa's brush for a relic, but I would like my dad and my brother to keep it, so my brother may tell his children about my grandpa. How great he was! I learned so much through this project and I had a chance to think about my family's background. I am proud of my family history!

Kyung-Sil Chang

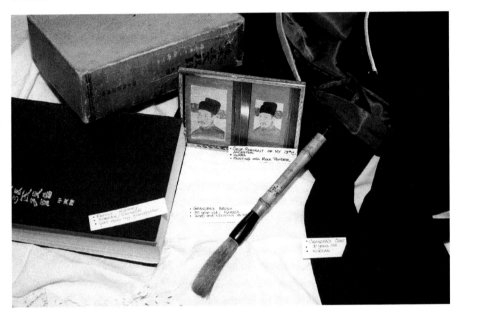

Evaluation
Review how students/groups arranged their objects.

• Does their arrangement convey a sense of awareness and pride?

• Do their credits accurately reflect the background information of each object?

Activity 2: Digging for Art

Activity Objectives
Students should be able to:

• Consider where art came from and how it was made.

• See the link between form and function.

• See how the making of art was not separate from everyday life in ancient times.

• Gain an understanding of the process of excavating art and other relics.

Thinking Critically
Art was an inseparable part of life in early cultures. Tools and clothing were art; there were no art galleries. Ask students:

• What contribution did art make to the lives of early people? How is that similar to or different from its role today?

• What kinds of things are hunted and found through archaeological excavations? (anthropological findings, dinosaurs, ancient plants)

Teacher Spotlight
Merceda Saffron
Chairperson, Fine and Practical
Arts Department
West Springfield High School

This project was extremely successful because, in this sometimes highly impersonal world, this lesson made everyone in class take time to learn something special and important about each other.

After setting up their discoveries, the class wrote a hypothesis about each other's discoveries. We found out how correct they were when they toured each other's area and heard the true story.

We have a very diverse class. Hearing about Pakistan from Ulma, Korea from Kyung, Mali from Kim, Puerto Rico from Christina, Israel from Jessica, and Ireland from Catherine and Maureen was absolutely fascinating. Customs, culture and art—all from a dig right in our homes!

• What techniques are common to both anthropology and biology? How might one area of study contribute to the other?

• What kinds of things can be learned by studying extinct species and civilizations?

Preparation Ideas
Have students flip through back issues of *National Geographic* and other magazines that regularly feature news of archaeological expeditions. Instruct students to notice the different kinds of historical objects and information that scientists are looking for and how that matches up with their own findings.

Tips
An interesting variation might be to have students design their posters with written material as if it were an article in a magazine. Have students identify and discuss what elements make a successful page design. This could lead to an appreciation of the ways typefaces, effective photography and graphic design can contribute to the presentation of information and ideas.

Chapter 2 Organizer

Chapter 2 Opener: Visual Communication

Objectives

Understand how subject matter, media, design and craftsmanship interrelate.

Understand that art communicates ideas visually.

Discuss how each era and culture uses the components of art and design in individual ways.

Discern certain evolutionary developments that have occurred over time.

National Standards

2b Students evaluate the effectiveness of artworks in terms of organizational structures and functions.
6a Students compare the materials, technologies, media, and processes of the visual arts with those of other arts disciplines as they are used in creation and types of analysis.

2a Students demonstrate the ability to form and defend judgments about the characteristics and structures to accomplish commercial, personal, communal, or other purposes of art.
3c Students describe the origins of specific images and ideas and explain why they are of value in their artwork and in the work of others.
3a Students reflect on how artworks differ visually, spatially, temporally, and functionally, and describe how these are related to history and culture.

4b Students describe the function and explore the meaning of specific art objects within varied cultures, times and places.

3a Students reflect on how artworks differ visually, spatially, temporally, and functionally, and describe how these are related to history and culture.

Teacher Edition References

1 2 ## Lesson 2.1 Subject Matter: What Is It Saying?

Lesson 2.1 20–29
Lesson 2.1 Review 29

Contextual Info 21, 22, 24, 26, 28
HOTS 21, 23, 25, 27, 29
Cooperative Learning 29

Interdisciplinary 27
Materials and Techniques 22, 28
Performing Arts 23, 24

1 2 ## Lesson 2.2 Media: Tools and Materials

Lesson 2.2 30–39
Lesson 2.2 Review 39
Primary Source 55

Contextual Info 32, 34, 36, 38
HOTS 31, 33, 35, 37, 39
Inquiry 37
Interdisciplinary 33

Materials and Techniques 31, 34
Performing Arts 31, 38

1 2 ## Lesson 2.3 Design: The Structure of Art

Lesson 2.3 40–54
Lesson 2.3 Review 54
Primary Source 55
Chapter Review 55

Contextual Info 42, 44, 46, 48, 50, 52
HOTS 41, 43, 45, 47, 49, 51, 52, 54

Materials and Techniques 50, 52
Performing Arts 42, 48, 52

1 1 1 ## Classroom Connections

National Standards

Studio Activity 1
A New Spin on Color

2a Students demonstrate the ability to form and defend judgments about the characteristics and structures to accomplish commercial, personal, communal, or other purposes of art.

Studio Activity 2
About Face

5a Students identify intentions of those creating artworks, explore the implications of various purposes, and justify their analyses of purposes in particular works.

Choose either Activity 1 or 2
Choose either Activity 1 or 2
Choose either Activity 1 or 2

2 Visual Communication

Large Reproductions:
Unicorn Tapestry
(subject matter, medium), 9;
Van Gogh, *Bedroom at Arles*
(subject matter, medium), 22

Context 18
Art 18
Quote 19
HOTS 19

Ancillaries

Slides: Bruegel, *Peasant Wedding*, 2a, 6; Greek, *Discobolus*, 3a, 7;
Chardin, *Soap Bubbles*, 5b, 8; Haverman, *Vase of Flowers*, 6b, 9

Slides: Roman, *Polyphemos and Galatea* (fresco), 7b, 10; Master of San Francesco,
Crucifixion, 4a, 11; Homer, *After the Hunt*, 5a, 12; Hiroshige, *Rain Shower on
Ohashi Bridge*, 6a, 13; Canova, *Paulina Borghese as Venus* (marble) 8b, 14;
Smith, *Cubi XII*, 7a, 15
Large Reproductions: Any of the large reproductions can be used with this lesson.

Slides: El Greco, *St. Martin and the Beggar*, 8a, 16; Rivera, *Still Life* (shape), 9b, 17;
Rubens, *Bear Hunt* (movement), 10b, 18; Duncanson, *Loch Long*, 9a, 19;
Zurbaran, *Still Life with Lemons, Oranges and a Rose*, 10a, 20; Villon, *Portrait of
Mlle. Y.D.*, 11a, 21
Overhead Transparencies: Analyzing a Work of Art, 2; Light and Form, 11

Schedule

Materials

If the color wheel shapes are simple
and small, this could be completed in
one class period. For greater depth,
allow one day to design and draw the
shapes and two days to paint.

11" x 14" white paper (or larger),
tempera, watercolor, prismacolor or
acrylic paint, brushes, surface for
mixing paint, containers of water

This activity can be completed in
one day.

magazines, 11" x 14" white paper,
scissors, glue/tape, markers

Other Resources

Books

Belves, Pierre, and Francois Mathey. *How Artists Work: An Introduction to Techniques of Art*. New York: Lion Books, 1968.

Birren, Faber. *Color and Human Response*. New York: Van Nostrand Reinhold, 1976.

Brommer, Gerald F. ed. *Concepts of Design*. Series: Books on elements of design (*Line, Color and Value, Shape and Form, Space, Texture*) and principles of design (*Balance and Unity, Contrast, Emphasis, Movement and Rythmn, Pattern*). Worcester, MA: Davis Publications, Inc., 1975.

Cheatham, Frank, Jane Cheatham and Cheryl Haler Owens. *Design Concepts and Applications*. Englewood Cliffs: Prentice-Hall, 1987

Craig, Diana. *A Miscellany of Artist's Wisdom*. Philadelphia: Running Press Book Publishers, 1993.

Collier, Graham. *Form, Space and Vision: An Introduction to Drawing and Design*. Englewood Cliffs: Prentice-Hall, 1985.

De Grandis, Luiginia. *Theory and Use of Color*. Englewood Cliffs: Prentice-Hall, 1987.

Ellinger, Richard G. *Color, Structure and Design*. New York: Van Nostrand Reinhold, 1980.

Gill, Robert W. *Basic Perspective*. London: Thames and Hudson, 1980.

Goldwater, Robert, and Treves, Marco. *Artists on Art*. New York: Pantheon Books, 1974.

Kinneir, Joan, ed. *The Artist by Himself*. New York: St. Martin's Press, 1979.

Landa, Robin. *An Introduction to Design: Basic Ideas & Appplications for Painting on the Printed Page*. Englewood Cliffs: Prentice-Hall, 1983.

Malcolm, Dorothea C. *Design: Elements and Principles*. Worcester, MA: Davis Publications, Inc., 1972.

Mayer, Ralph. *A Dictionary of Art Terms and Techniques*. New York: Crowell, 1975.

Ocvirk, Otto, et al. *Art Fundamentals Theory and Practice*. Dubuque: William C. Brown, 1985.

Pile, John F. *Design: Purpose, Form and Meaning*. New York: W.W. Norton, 1982.

Piper, David ed. *Random House Dictionary of Art and Artists*. New York: Fodor's Travel Publications Inc., 1990.

Taylor, Joshua. *Learning to Look*, 2nd ed. Chicago: University of Chicago Press, 1981.

_____. *A Visual Dictionary of Art*. Greenwich, CT: New York Graphic Society, 1974.

Zelanski, Paul, and Mary Pat Fischer. *Design Principles and Problems*. New York: Holt, Rinehart and Winston, 1983.

Introduce

Throughout history, artists have employed formal elements, principles of design and various tools to express themselves. By mastering art's visual language, we deepen our comprehension of works from all cultures, thereby fostering an appreciation for both the similarities and differences among us.

Lessons at a Glance

2.1 *Subject Matter: What Is It Saying?*
Artists represent the observable world as well as abstract ideas in their work. An artist's choice of subject, its meaning and its mode of expression are often highly personal.

2.2 *Media: Tools and Materials*
Artists rely on a wide variety of media and tools to create their work. Some materials have been used for centuries, while others are relatively new innovations.

2.3 *Design: The Structure of Art*
Artists communicate through a visual language. They string together individual elements that act as words, according to certain principles of design, that function like the rules of grammar. Artists develop their own personal style or "voice" through the individual choices they make in constructing their compositions.

2 Visual Communication

ART IS VISUAL COMMUNICATION, with a language all its own. Artists and craftspersons communicate their ideas, concepts and responses to subject matter through their artwork.

To fully understand art and the artists' communication, it is important to learn about the entire process—subjects, techniques and styles. This chapter, therefore, explores four areas: *subject matter*—what the artist is conveying; *media*—the tools and materials the artist used; *craftsmanship*—the ability to make useful objects attractive; *design*—the grammar, or structure, of visual language.

Each of these areas could be discussed in book length. However, only the major points of each area can be covered here. This brief background should make your study of art history more interesting and meaningful, and more personally satisfying. As you learn more about the history of art, you will begin to see how the artist's use of materials and approaches to subject matter have evolved. Each era has found new ways to use the elements of art and design principles to communicate its ideas and ideals.

2–a Notice how the design and placement of the subject matter, particularly the dragon, works in such harmony with the form of this jar.
Shoulder Jar. 1522–1566. Chinese, Ming dynasty. Porcelain. Ostasiatische Kunstabteilung Staatliche Museum, Berlin.

2–b The artist has used the medium of a fabric quilt to depict a series of Biblical images. Can you identify the subject matter of any of these scenes?
Harriet Powers, *Pictorial Quilt*, 1895–1898. American. Pieced and appliqued cotton embroidered with plain and metallic yarns, 69" x 105" (175 x 267 cm). Museum of Fine Arts, Boston, Bequest of Maxim Karolik.

Objectives

Students should be able to:

Understand how subject matter, media, design and craftsmanship interrelate.

Understand that art communicates ideas visually.

Discuss how each era and culture uses the components of art and design in individual ways.

Discern certain evolutionary developments that have occurred over time.

Teach

Context

Discuss with students that artists have often relied on the most readily available materials to create their work. Ask what the materials of the *Dance Mask* (fig.2–d) might indicate about the Dan tribe of Africa at the turn of the century.

• Do the materials suggest that it was a highly industrialized society?

• Where might the artist have obtained the wood, fiber and paint? Do these appear to be commercially manufactured products?

• What can students deduce about Harriet Powers' *Pictorial Quilt* (fig.2–b)? What might be the reason she did not use paints and canvas?

• Where did the fabric come from and why would Powers have chosen to use it for her artwork?

• Do students think that African-American women in late nineteenth-century America had many opportunities to study in art school? Most women in America at the time were taught the needle arts as children

as part of their training for becoming wives and mothers. Many women poured their creativity into these functional objects, infusing them with meaning and beauty.

Art

Have students draw or trace the outline of the *Shoulder Jar* (fig.2–a) onto a piece of paper. Have them imagine being the sixteenth-century artist responsible for painting its surface. Tell students to make two sketches for its design, first using only straight-edged shapes and then employing images that bend and flow. If they want to accentuate the elegant craftsmanship of the jar, ask which of their designs works better. After, direct students to observe how the painter of the jar in fig.2–a applied the animal and floral patterns.

All the arts are brothers; each one is a light to the others.

Voltaire

2–c The van Eyck brothers painted with extraordinary skill. The use of oil paint as a medium greatly expanded their ability to render textures with amazing accuracy. How many different materials and fabrics can you find in this painting? *Hubert and Jan van Eyck, Ghent Altarpiece,* detail of right wing, completed 1432. Netherlandish. Oil on panel, Cathedral of St. Bavo, Ghent, Belgium.

2–e Chardin has used the student artist as his subject. What impression is he trying to convey about this laboring student? Jean Baptiste Simeon Chardin, *Young Student Drawing,* about 1738. French. Oil on wood, 8 1/4" x 6 3/4" (21 x 17.1 cm). Kimbell Art Museum, Fort Worth, Texas.

2–d How has the artist contrasted symmetry and asymmetry in this work? Do you think the contrast is effective? *Dance Mask,* about 1900. African, Dan Tribe, Ivory Coast. Painted wood with vegetable fiber, 9 1/2" (24 cm) high. Collection of Charles W. and Janice R. Mack.

Quote

Direct students to research who Voltaire was, when he lived, and his relationship to the arts. (He was a famous French philosopher and dramatist who lived from 1694–1778.) Ask what they think he meant in his quote about the relationship between the arts.

• How can they use two or more images in the chapter opener to support his statement?

• If they extend his sentiment beyond the arts, what might it reflect about Voltaire's attitude toward people who believe in the superiority of one culture or race over another?

• How can the artwork here be used to demonstrate the concept of the "brotherhood of man"?

• If we all come from the same "family," why might it be important to open our eyes and minds to all sorts of ideas and information?

• Have students cite incidents when they have learned something from someone with a different background.

• Discuss how art offers a marvelous opportunity to explore and learn about our own history as well as that of others.

Higher-Order Thinking Skills

1 Have students use the captions to make a list of all the types of media represented on these two pages. They also should make a list of all the subjects they recognize. These can be general (e.g., singing figures, animals, flowers) or specific (e.g., the Crucifixion).

2 Have students use the captions to compare the actual size of the objects. A great deal of information can be gleaned from the captions and the color reproductions, but emphasize to students that certain information is impossible to convey without inspecting the actual object. Ask students what types of things can be better learned by seeing the object (e.g., three-dimensionality, texture).

Evaluate

Ask students to demonstrate how, despite their differences, all of the images in the chapter opener are somehow related.

• Can they illustrate how all the artists are concerned about the way in which individual elements relate to the whole? For instance, how does the length of the figures in the *Ghent Altarpiece* panel (fig.2–c) accentuate its shape? Would it look the same if the figures were sitting down?

• After, ask students what they have learned that they had not considered before. How does the information affect the way they look at and feel about art?

Reteach

Share with students that Powers' quilt was made in the tradition of women sewing together leftover scraps of material to create images that tell stories. During slavery, scenes from the Bible not only held religious associations, but also symbolized the struggle of African Americans for freedom. Before the abolition of slavery, quilts like these were sometimes hung outside homes that served as stations on the Underground Railroad. They signaled a safe house for escaped slaves to hide in as they traveled north.

• Ask how the quilt's actual function might relate to the Bible imagery. For instance, how might both the subject of the stories and the actual material offer warmth and protection?

Lesson 2.1

Artists represent the observable world as well as abstract ideas in their work. An artist's choice of subject, its meaning and its mode of expression are often highly personal.

Warm-up

Ask students to identify the subject matter of a piece of literature, a song, a play and a scientific experiment. Can they find corresponding categories in art? What might be the visual equivalent of a pastoral poem or a sea chantey?

Objective

Students should be able to:

Identify the broad range of potential subject matter.

Teach

Criticism: Write a list on the blackboard of all the general subject matter that students can think of; then add any that they may have missed from those mentioned in Lesson 2.1. Have students construct a definition for each classification. Next, instruct them to glance at all the reproductions and match them to one of the categories.

• Does everyone agree with each other's choices?

• Ask if some artworks can fit into more than a single category. For instance, how can Rubens' *Judgment of Paris* (fig.2–8) be both a narrative and a figure painting; or how can Hale Woodruff's *The Amistad Slaves on Trial at New Haven* (fig.2–11) be a narrative, a historical and a figurative scene?

• How many categories apply to Fernando Botero's *The Presidential Family* (fig.2–13)?

2.1 Subject Matter: What Is It Saying?

SUPPOSE SOMEONE HANDED YOU a pencil and told you to draw something. That *something* that you chose to draw would be the subject matter. Most artists use things as their subjects, things such as people, objects, landscape (fig.2–2) or animals. Others use ideas such as war, love, loneliness or joy. Still others are concerned with the scientific or mathematical aspects of art. Design and proportion become their subject matter.

Artists also tell something about their subject. They need a reason to paint a landscape or to sculpt a person. This reason may be as simple as liking the color of green grass or as personal as wanting to show the order and harmony of the natural world. Artists may sculpt or paint a woman because she is beautiful or because they want to show her character or her influence on her fellow humans. Throughout history, and especially in the last few decades, artists' attitudes toward subject matter have changed drastically, as you will learn in the last chapters.

Narrative Subjects

In *narrative* paintings, the artist is telling a story. The painter Pieter Brueghel of Flanders was a master storyteller. Within a large painting, he included small scenes of peasant life and little insights that can be developed into further stories. This jolly gathering is typical of his work. One can easily find the bride, but where is the groom? As Brueghel tells his own story of the wedding, he interweaves many subplots. What are they?

2–1 Pieter Brueghel, *Peasant Wedding,* 1566. Netherlandish. Oil on panel, 44 1/2" x 63 3/4" (113 x 162 cm). Kunsthistorisches Museum, Vienna.

Aesthetics/Criticism: Distribute blank sheets of drawing paper to students and ask each of them to make a quick sketch of anything they wish. Afterward, have them identify in which category their subject matter belongs, as described in Lesson 2.1.

• Ask why they decided to create this particular subject over another.

• What might have prompted the choices made by the artists of figs.2–2 and 2–3?

Evaluate

Ask students if all art depicts recognizable subject matter. Can they cite an example when it does not (e.g. fig.2–17)? What image in Lesson 2.1 demonstrate that an intangible idea or concept is also a legitimate subject (fig.2–18)?

Dürer has chosen a close-up of grass and soil as his subject matter. He presents us with a detailed view of a part of our environment that is not often subjected to careful scrutiny.

2–2 Albrecht Dürer, *The Great Piece of Turf*, 1503. German. Watercolor and tempera on paper, mounted on cardboard, 15 3/4" x 12 1/4" (40.3 x 31.1 cm). Albertina, Vienna.

Contextual Information

Peasant Wedding

Brueghel placed the scene of *Peasant Wedding* (fig.2–1) in the only large building available for peasant celebrations—a barn. Details of the event include two sheaves of wheat hanging with a rake holding them in place and a paper crown hanging above the bride's head. The workers use a door laid across two poles as a serving tray for a popular dessert of the time—rice boiled with milk and spices, sometimes colored with saffron. A contemporary practice in the sixteenth century was for the groom to wait on the bride's family. The bride's eyes are lowered, and her hands are folded in a customary pose for weddings.

During the sixteenth century, there was great interest in peasants and their lives. Brueghel was said to have disguised himself to attend their weddings. An imperial decree had limited the number of guests to 20, but peasants apparently ignored this ruling. Just as we go to country fairs and festivals today, people from the cities went to peasant weddings in Brueghel's time.

Higher-Order Thinking Skills

Have each student select a person in Brueghel's painting and write a description of the wedding from the perspective of that person.

Reteach

Have students identify other artistic expressions with subjects similar to those discussed in Lesson 2.1. For instance, can students cite examples of narrative music, religious writing, historical dance, and so forth?

Contextual Information

Hsia Kuei

The tradition of Chinese landscape painting goes back over a thousand years. Hsia Kuei was a painter-in-attendance at the Academy of Painting during the late twelfth and early thirteenth centuries. During this period, artists were respected and honored for their abilities but were not allowed to change their social status.

Hsia Kuei was unsurpassed in his lifetime in landscape painting. He was known for his details, even in the smallest, most distant objects. He created tiny scenes and forms with short lines, abstracting the essence of gesture and shape.

Only two of Hsia Kuei's handscrolls have survived, one in Taipei, the other in Kansas City. Only four of the original twelve views of the Kansas City handscroll are left; these had been at the end of the scroll.

Religious Subjects

Any religious figure from any religion can be the subject of a work of art. Biblical scenes dominate the Christian art of Europe. Buddhists and Hindus have a long tradition of sculpting and painting figures and scenes of their deities. The people of Africa, the Americas and the Pacific region have an extensive history of depicting their gods or sacred symbols. The Mayan maize god pictured here held great significance for the Mayan people. Maize was the main food staple of Mesoamerica. Can you distinguish any of the elements of a growing corn stalk in this figure?

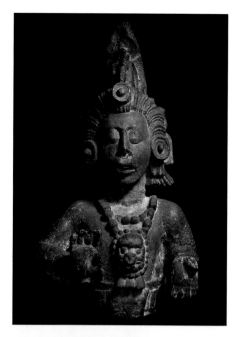

2–3 *Maize God*, from Temple 22, Maya, Copan, Honduras, about 775. Limestone, 35 1/3" x 21 1/3" (90 x 54 cm). British Museum, London.

Literary Subjects

Painters may use literary sources, such as the Bible or famous myths and legends, to get ideas for their work. This painting illustrates a scene from the famous tale of Rip Van Winkle. The legend is part of Washington Irving's *Sketch Book* and illustrates that point in the story when Rip Van Winkle has awakened from his long sleep. He is bewildered by the sight of his son who stands alone by the tree. He also confronts his fellow villagers who demand to know his name. He replies: "God knows, I'm not myself—I'm somebody else—that's me yonder—no—that's somebody else got into my shoes—I was myself last night, but I fell asleep on the mountain ..."

2–4 John Quidor, *The Return of Rip Van Winkle*, 18(4?)9. American. Oil on canvas, 39 3/4" x 49 3/4" (101 x 126.5cm). National Gallery of Art, Washington, DC, Andrew W. Mellon Collection, 1942.

Performing Arts Connection

Jewish Religious Dance

Since ancient times, Jews have used dance as an expression of joy and spirituality. The Old Testament abounds with examples. There were victory dances, usually led by women, and ecstasy dances, during which, according to the Book of Samuel, early prophets received their visions. At weddings, marriage processions were accompanied by timbrels and other instruments. The ancient Israelites also danced at harvest celebrations.

• Ask if students know any religious songs, music or dances from their own heritage. Have they changed over time? How are they passed down from one generation to the next? Will students teach them to their children? Why or why not?

Landscapes

Landscapes are paintings of the natural environment. They have been a popular subject for artists through the centuries and throughout the world. The Chinese can be considered true masters of landscape painting, which has dominated their art since the fourth century AD. Here, the artist, Hsia Kuei, is able to convey a misty, evocative view of a river and mountains with only the barest use of his brush.

2–5 Hsia Kuei, *Twelve Views from a Thatched Hut*, section of handscroll, about 1180–1230. Chinese. Ink on silk, height 11" (28 cm). The Nelson-Atkins Museum of Art, Kansas City, Missouri.

Cityscapes

Views of city streets, plazas, courtyards, buildings and activities taking place in the urban environment are called *cityscapes*. Most cityscapes have been done in the twentieth century, but Corot produced this early view of Venice in 1834. Corot, a Realist painter, portrays an authentic scene from the times. He does not tell a story nor does he reveal his feelings about Venice. He simply depicts what he saw, in about the same way a photographer would take a picture of the place to send to a friend.

2–6 Jean-Baptiste-Camille Corot, *View of Venice, the Piazzetta Seen from the Quay of the Esclavons*, 1834. French. Oil on canvas, 18 1/2" x 27 1/4" (47 x 69 cm). Norton Simon Museum, Pasadena, CA.

Higher-Order Thinking Skills

Have students compare and contrast the landscape by Hsia Kuei (fig.2–5) to the cityscape by Corot (fig.2–6). Direct students to consider the intrinsic differences between portraying a scene from nature and portraying a manufactured environment.

Materials and Techniques

The earliest ink was made in China in 251 by Wei Tan, who mixed lampblack (the black substance on the sides of an oil-lamp chimney) with water and a binder. Today's India ink is similar to Chinese ink, but a preservative has been added. Chinese and Japanese inks are dried and molded into small blocks or cakes that artists rub on special ink stones with water.

Rubens

Rubens grew up in Antwerp, then the capital of the Spanish Netherlands. Trained by local painters in a guild, he became a master himself in 1598. In Italy, he studied ancient sculpture and Renaissance paintings for eight years.

Rubens sometimes had as many as 20 assistants working with him on his commissions. The more important the commission, the more of the canvas Rubens painted.

Edward VI as a Child

Holbein's portrait of Prince Edward VI was presented to the child's father, Henry VIII, on New Year's Day, 1539. Although the prince was not yet two years old when the portrait was painted, Holbein successfully imbues the child with regal qualities. The clothing and pose of the figure help convey a formal majesty. Notice also the serious facial expression and the gaze of the eyes which falls below the viewer's eye level. The hands too are manipulated to convey the rank of the sitter. Although the pudgy nature of a toddler's hands is captured, the rattle is held as though it were a scepter. The strength of the gestures sends a subtle message of power to the viewer.

The Figure

Artists have considered the figure a supreme subject. They appreciate the human body as both an aesthetic and sensuous form. To understand this tradition, we need to recognize that artists—and their cultures—have many reasons for portraying the nude.

Ancient Greek philosophy and religion placed the human at the center of the cosmos as the "measure of all things." In their search for ideal or divine forms it was only logical for the Greeks to place the idealized, perfect human form at the top of artistic creation. Greek athletes competed in the nude because their perfectly conditioned bodies were seen as aesthetic expressions to be admired as a good painting or sculpture would be.

At times, nudity has been seen as barbaric. One statement repeatedly made by Roman historians about the ferocity of the ancient Gauls and Britons was that they fought

nude. This terrorized the Romans. During the Middle Ages, the human body was seen as corrupt and imperfect. It was not considered appropriate to portray the human body or study it.

When Renaissance artists rediscovered the Greek tradition, there was a lot of furor over the morality of portraying the nude. However, as the Western art tradition renewed its quest for naturalism, artists quickly realized that to portray people naturalistically required the study not only of the nude, but also of the cadaver. Dissection taught artists about the structure of muscles and bones.

Today, artists continue to study and portray the nude as the ultimate artistic challenge. It is a complex form that changes dramatically with the slightest shift in weight or twist in attitude. It is also capable of a tremendous range of expression and emotion.

2–7 Myron, *Discus Thrower*, Roman marble copy after Greek bronze original of about 450 BC, life-size. Museo Nazionale Romano, Rome.

2–8 Peter Paul Rubens, *Judgment of Paris*, about 1629. Flemish. Oil on panel, 57" x 76 3/4" (145 x 195 cm). National Gallery, London.

The Portrait

Portraits come in a variety of sizes and shapes, but have one thing in common—they are representations of people. The people may be alone or in groups, young or old. They may pose formally or informally and may be set against a solid background or in the natural environment. The artist may depict the full figure, from head to toe, or only the bust, the upper body. They can be painted or sculpted. Holbein, one of the world's greatest portrait artists, painted Prince Edward VI for his father, Henry VIII. The pose is rather stiff and formal, the clothes are regal, and the inscription tells Edward to emulate his father in all things. Unfortunately, Edward died before he could become England's king.

2–9 Hans Holbein, *Edward VI as a Child*, 1538. German. Oil on panel, 22 1/2" x 17 1/4" (57 x 44 cm). National Gallery of Art, Washington, DC, Andrew Mellon Collection.

Self-Portraits

Many artists make pictures of themselves, called *self-portraits*. This nineteenth-century portraitist strongly conveys her unconventional persona in a self-portrait. The cross-legged pose, beer stein and lit cigarette fly in the face of our idea of the turn-of-the-century woman. Clearly, this is a woman who does what she wants without fear of what others will say. Indeed, Frances Benjamin Johnston was a successful and prolific photographer.

2–10 Frances Benjamin Johnston, *Self-Portrait*, 1895. American. Photograph. Library of Congress, Washington, DC.

Higher-Order Thinking Skills

Have students pretend that they are planning to create a self-portrait. Ask them to describe the portrait. What features will they emphasize? Which ones will they pay less attention to? How would their self-portrait be different from one that they might commission from a professional artist?

Contextual Information
Woodruff

Hale Woodruff was born in Cairo, Illinois, in 1900. After studying art in Indianapolis and Paris, he became an art instructor at Atlanta University. Eventually, he accepted a position in the education department at New York University, where he was named professor emeritus upon his retirement.

Woodruff's work was exhibited in traveling shows sponsored by the Harmon Foundation, established in the 1920s to aid African-American artists in depicting their own lives and environment. The Harmon Foundation provided cash awards and stipends for students to attend art schools and colleges. Woodruff received an award in 1926 from the foundation, and, with the addition of a patron's gift, he went to study in Europe.

A Name, But No Details

Little is known about the Korean artist Ham Yundok, except that he was a sixteenth-century painter. This lack of information about an artist occurs with some frequency in art history. Sometimes, a signed or otherwise-documented body of work survives by a particular artist, but we know very few of the details about the artist's life. Sometimes we do not even know the artist's name, even though a coherent body of work survives. In those cases, particularly in Western art, the term "Master of . . ." is used as an identifier for the artist (see fig.2–25).

Historical Subjects

Historical subjects have often been painted on large canvases, probably to memorialize or lend importance to an event. In 1939, Hale Woodruff painted a series of murals for a library at Talladeger College, an African-American college near Atlanta. The murals tell about the Amistad Mutiny, an important chapter of African-American history. In 1839, Africans on a Portuguese slave ship bound for Havana mutinied. Led by their Sierra Leonese chief, Cinque, they ordered the ship back to Africa. They landed instead at New London, Connecticut, where a trial was held. The Africans were acquitted and freed, and allowed to return to their homeland. In this scene, Woodruff depicts the trial.

To prepare for his work, Woodruff immersed himself in the events. He traveled to New Haven, where he discovered sketches that had been drawn of the trial. The sketches depicted the Africans and the Amistad costumes and weapons of the time. These documents helped the artist bring historical accuracy to a mural painted one hundred years after the event occurred.

2–11 Hale Woodruff, *The Amistad Slaves on Trial at New Haven*, 1840. American. Oil on canvas, 12" x 40" (31 x 102 cm). Aaron Douglas Collection. Amistad Research Center at Tulane University, New Orleans.

Genre Subjects

Genre painting refers to normal, everyday activities of ordinary people. A king and queen riding in a royal carriage is not a genre subject, but a poor family riding on the local public transportation is. Farmers working in the fields, children in school, people sitting in a café, or a woman peeling potatoes are genre subjects. In this scene, the Korean painter, Ham Yundok, depicts a man on his donkey. The bent head and splayed legs of the exhausted donkey make us wonder about the nature and length of the man's journey.

2–12 Ham Yundok, *Man Riding a Donkey*, 16th century. Korean. Album leaf, ink and color on silk, 6 1/8" x 7 5/8" (15.5 x 19.4 cm). National Museum of Korea, Seoul.

Still Life

A *still life* is a painting of inanimate objects—things that cannot move. Bottles, bowls, fruit, flowers and cloth often appear in these works. The objects are usually arranged by the artist on a table top in the studio. Still-life paintings can be elaborate (fig.13–22) or extremely simple, as in this ink drawing of persimmons.

2–14 Mu-ch'i, *Six Persimmons*, 13th century. Chinese. Ink on paper. Daitoku-ji, Kyoto, Japan.

Higher-Order Thinking Skills

In the history of art, still-life and genre painting were long considered to be less important than history paintings. Ask students if they agree with that position. Have them give reasons that support their opinions.

Social Comment

Some artists want to make visual statements about their society or the world. They may criticize national leaders, churches, neighbors, wars or political oppression. Latin-American artists have a strong tradition of using their art to make pointed political statements. In this unflattering portrait of the presidential family, Botero criticized the colonial attitudes that still pervaded the upper classes.

2–13 Fernando Botero, *The Presidential Family*, 1967. Colombian. Oil on canvas, 80" x 77 1/8" (203 x 196 cm). The Museum of Modern Art, New York, gift of Warren D. Benedek, 1967.

Interdisciplinary Connection

History: Hale Woodruff took great pains to insure the historical accuracy of his painting. History paintings, however, are not always true representations of historical fact.

• Have students research the historical accuracy of a famous American history painting, such as *Washington Crossing the Delaware* or a lesser-known work that is housed in a museum or a public building in their community.

Animals

Artists are often intrigued by animals. Nearly all cultures have portrayed birds and mammals with great skill, both in realistic and stylized versions. This alpaca from the early Inca civilization is made of soldered sheet silver. The artist is careful to show the fine long hair of this wool-producing animal.

2–15 *Alpaca,* Inca. Silver, 9 1/2" x 8 1/8" x 2" (24 x 21 x 5 cm). American Museum of Natural History, New York.

Expression

While some artists paint what they see when looking at their subject matter, others, like El Greco, include their feelings about the subject. When personal and emotional feelings are added to a work, it is an *expressionist* painting. El Greco lived in Toledo, Spain. Here he paints the city from a hill on the opposite side of the river. Using greens and blues in various values and mixtures, he gives his city a distinct personality. Sparkling under a supercharged sky, the city seems vibrant and full of excitement, yet mysterious and rather lonely.

2–16 El Greco, *View of Toledo,* 1600–1610. Spanish. Oil on canvas, 47 1/2" x 42 1/2" (121 x 108 cm). The Metropolitan Museum of Art, New York, bequest of Mrs. H. O. Havemeyer.

Materials and Techniques

El Greco used a coarse hog's-hair brush in *View of Toledo* (fig.2–16). He also employed an early version of a palette knife. Hog's-hair bristles became popular because artists found that softer bristles were unsatisfactory for working on canvas.

2–17 Pablo Picasso, *The Studio*, 1927–1928. Spanish. Oil on canvas, 59" x 91" (150 x 231 cm). The Museum of Modern Art, New York, gift of Walter P. Chrysler, Jr.

2–18 Jackson Pollock, *Full Fathom Five*, 1947. American. Oil on canvas, 51" x 30 1/4" (130 x 77 cm). The Museum of Modern Art, New York, gift of Peggy Guggenheim.

Abstraction

Abstraction is the simplification of subject matter into basic and often geometric shapes. Some modern artists, such as Picasso, so simplified the objects in a painting that the simplification, not the objects, became the subject matter. Picasso here uses his studio as a starting point. He depicts a table as simplified shapes. The whitish oval on the right may be a sculpture. The two triangles in the center are a container. Pictures are on the back wall. The artist and his easel are at the left. While viewers may identify these elements, the painting is first and foremost an abstract arrangement of lines, shapes and colors. The abstracted design was far more important to Picasso than the studio objects.

Notice that the artist in the picture has three eyes. What may Picasso be suggesting about the visual awareness of artists?

Nonobjective Painting

In the late nineteenth century, artists gradually created more abstract works. However, their art, like Picasso's *The Studio*, still presented recognizable objects. Even Cézanne, who stated that the painting was more important than the subject matter, included identifiable forms. During the early twentieth century, some artists painted fully abstract works that were composed of only color, shape and line. When artists such as Jackson Pollock began a painting, they did not think of trees and people. Instead, they thought of color and line. Today, such nonobjective painting is common.

Higher-Order Thinking Skills

Ask students to explain in their own words the difference between abstract painting and nonobjective painting.

Cooperative Learning

Have students refer to Picasso's *The Studio* (fig.2–17). Provide plain white paper (for planning and drawing), markers, colored paper, scissors, glue and background paper or poster board. Divide the class into small groups, each with a different view of the classroom. On the white planning paper, ask students to draw the elements of the room as simple geometric shapes. They should give careful attention to size and proportion. Then have them use these drawings as patterns to use on the colored paper. Have them cut out the shapes and arrange and glue them on the background paper in the relationships that they observe in the room. Students should add lines with markers, as necessary for clarity or emphasis. Students can keep a journal to document this abstraction experience.

Lesson 2.1 Review Answers

1 Subject matter is what the artist is conveying. Media is the tools and materials the artist uses. Craftsmanship is the ability to make useful objects attractive. Design is the grammar, or structure, of visual language.
2 Any three of the following:
narrative subjects: Brueghel, *Peasant Wedding* (fig.2–1)
literary subjects: Quidor, *The Return of Rip Van Winkle* (fig.2–4)
religious subjects: *Maize God* (fig.2–3)
landscapes: Hsia Kuei, *Twelve Views from a Thatched Hut* (fig.2–5)
cityscapes: Corot, *View of Venice, the Piazzetta Seen from the Quay of the Esclavons* (fig.2–6)
human figures: Myron, *Discus Thrower* (fig.2–7), Rubens, *Judgment of Paris* (fig.2–8)
portraits: Holbein, *Edward VI as a Child* (fig.2–9)
self-portraits: Johnston, *Self-Portrait* (fig.2–10)
historical subjects: Woodruff, *The Amistad Slaves on Trial at New Haven* (fig.2–11)
genre subjects: Yundok, *Man Riding a Donkey* (fig.2–12)
social comment: Botero, *The Presidential Family* (fig.2–13)
still life: Mu-ch'i, *Six Persimmons* (fig.2–14)
animals: *Alpaca* (fig.2–15)
expression: El Greco, *View of Toledo* (fig.2–16)
abstraction: Picasso, *The Studio* (fig.2–17)
nonobjective: Pollock, *Full Fathom Five* (fig.2–18)
3 A representation of people
4 Ordinary people doing normal, everyday activities
5 Art in which the subject matter has been simplified into basic, often geometric, shapes

Lesson 2.2

Artists rely on a wide variety of media and tools to create their work. Some materials have been used for centuries, while others are relatively new innovations.

Warm-up

Ask students to list what materials and skills are required to play basketball and those to bake an elaborate birthday cake.

• What objects and techniques do they think artists must have in order to carry out their endeavors?

• How can they prove that mastering techniques and tools is just as important for artists as for anyone else who is trying to accomplish something?

Objective

Students should be able to:

Identify the characteristics of different media and techniques.

Teach

Criticism: Divide students into pairs and have them test each other on their knowledge of artistic media and techniques. Direct one student to read a description of a tool or a skill cited in the lesson. Have the partner search for a visual example in the textbook. Have teams check their answers by reading the information in the captions. Students should alternate roles until they have covered all the categories in Lesson 2.2.

Evaluate

Ask students if all the media and techniques outlined in Lesson 2.2 have always been available. Which do they think might not have been around before the twentieth century? Why might this have been the case?

Reteach

Ask students to bring an object from home that they have created, such as a craft, food, artwork or photograph. Ask them to select, if possible, an example that relates to their family's heritage. As students show their object to the class, have the other students guess what tools and skills were necessary to complete the work. If classmates are missing essential information, have them play a game of twenty questions with the presenter so that they arrive at the answers, rather than being told directly.

2.2 Media: Tools and Materials

Drawing Media

Pencil

The pencil has always been one of the most versatile drawing tools. The pencil dates back to the Roman stylus, a pointed tool that made delicate lines. Lead had been used to make lines, but in 1795, the French inventor Conté found a way to mix graphite and clay, and the modern pencil was born. It can be used for quick sketches and for detailed drawings. Ingres' portrait drawing of Thomas Church combines many pencil techniques in one work. There are quickly sketched lines and heavy, firm lines. The shaded areas on the body were done with broad, flat strokes while the face was finished with careful shading under great control. Ingres was a master draftsperson, and the pencil was his favorite drawing medium.

2–19 Jean-Auguste-Dominique Ingres, *Thomas Church*, 1816. French. Graphite on paper, 7 1/2" x 6 1/4" (19 x 16 cm). Los Angeles County Museum of Art, Loula D. Lasker Estate Fund.

Charcoal

The soft, grainy quality of charcoal is evident in Seurat's drawing done on textured paper. Charcoal can be compressed into sticks, like chalk, so that the ends and sides can both be used. It can also be wrapped in wood and used in pencil form. Charcoal smudges easily and is used primarily as a sketching material. Seurat used the broad side of a charcoal crayon to capture quickly the pose he wanted. Look at Seurat's painting *Sunday Afternoon on the Island of La Grande Jatte* (fig.13–19) to find this sketched figure in final form.

2–20 Georges Seurat, *Seated Woman*, about 1885. French. Charcoal on paper. The Museum of Modern Art, New York.

Ask students if the tools and materials mentioned in Lesson 2.2 are the only ones available today. Have them look through Lesson 17.6 to see what tools and materials the contemporary images required that are not listed in Lesson 2.2. For example, what media, tools and skills did Christo employ in *Running Fence* (fig.17–43) and *The Umbrellas: Japan—USA* (fig.17–44)?

Ink

When ink is applied undiluted, it makes a solid black area. When it is mixed with water, it produces a soft gray. The more water that is added, the lighter the gray. Light grays are called *washes*—a term used to describe the dilution of inks with water. For the artists of Japan and China, ink was the preferred medium, which they applied with a brush. The technique was brought to great heights throughout the history of Asian art. The exquisite skill of the Japanese artist Sesshu is demonstrated in this landscape. The washes are subtly varied, while brushed lines define buildings, vegetation and a barely defined fisherman in his boat in the foreground.

Artists often simply use brush and ink or pen and ink to make their drawings. The hard line of comic strips and cartoons is made with these techniques. Ink is often used as a sketching medium, allowing artists to explore their subjects before painting them. Diego Rivera was an exceptional draftsperson and was very confident with his application of ink to paper. This brush drawing is simple, clean and powerful. The lines have various thicknesses, which help produce a sense of form. No shading is necessary because the lines have such visual strength.

2–21 Sesshu, *Haboku Landscape*, fifteenth century. Japanese. Ink on paper, height 28 5/16" (72 cm). Cleveland Museum of Art.

Pastel

Oil pastels are a dry material, almost like colored chalk. Creating with oil pastels is halfway between drawing and painting. The final result usually looks like a colored drawing and is often called a painting. Mary Cassatt was equally adept at pastels and oil painting. Her pastel *Sleeping Baby* has delicate shading, light value colors and a sketchy, dry-textured quality—all characteristic of this soft, chalky medium. The subject matter of mother and child in a casual, loving relationship is a favorite of the artist.

2–23 Mary Cassatt, *Sleeping Baby*, about 1910. American. Pastel on paper, 25 1/2" x 20 1/2" (65 x 52 cm). Dallas Museum of Fine Arts, Munger Fund.

2–22 Diego Rivera, *Mother and Child*, 1936. Mexican. Ink on paper, 11 3/4" x 9" (30 x 23 cm). San Francisco Museum of Modern Art, gift of Albert M. Bender.

Higher-Order Thinking Skills

Divide the class into groups and set up a small still life for each group. A piece of draped fabric, fruit, and a bottle or jar will suffice. Provide paper and several drawing media, such as pencil, ink, charcoal and pastel. Have students draw the still life several times, using a different medium each time. The point is the experience of using the media, not the creation of finished drawings. They can write in their journals about the experience of using different media and their preferences for particular materials. Ask how they think an artist selects a medium for a project.

Materials and Techniques

The first charcoal was probably obtained from charred wood. Commercial-quality charcoal was originally made from charred twigs of willow or of vines; now it is made from controlled burning of hardwoods.

Pastels were first made popular in Western Europe by Venetian painter Rosalba Carriera (1675–1757), who was introduced to them by a friend. Carriera went to Paris in 1720, introduced pastel portraits there, and quickly received commissions from many important people who did not like the lengthier sittings required for oil paintings. Pastels had the added advantage of not having the odor of turpentine and varnishes.

Performing Arts Connection

The Tools of the Performing Artist

Pencils, paints, canvas, metal, clay, and so forth are the tools of the visual arts. Ask what tools musicians use. How about their bodies, instruments and sheet music? What are a dancer's tools? How do dancers hear music and see other performers on stage? Are there tools for dance other than the body? Sets, costumes and stage design are all important as well. Which tools do actors use? Are they different from or the same as those used by dancers and musicians?

• Ask students what "tools" they call upon when they are about to tackle a problem—a difficult classroom assignment, a new recipe, a home-improvement project. Besides objects, do they use advice from an expert, instruction books or their own intuition? Ask how their creative process is similar to that of artists when they approach their work.

Contextual Information

The Ajanta Frescoes

The caves of Ajanta were discovered in 1819 by an Indian army officer in the midst of a tiger hunt. The caves, or grottoes, are located in a remote region of the Northern Deccan. The caves had served as Buddhist monasteries, a destination for pilgrims since the second century BC.

The painted walls of the caves depict scenes from Buddhist mythology. At the same time the scenes provide a detailed view of life in ancient India. They are painted with remarkable skill, particularly the manner in which the figures are modeled and the way light and shade are indicated.

Although many of the frescoed scenes are rather damaged, their detail and beauty are preserved and continue to inform and delight us today.

Thomas

Alma Thomas (1891–1978) taught art at Shaw Junior High School in Washington, DC, for 45 years (1925–1960). Twelve years after her retirement, she had a solo exhibition at the Whitney Museum of American Art. This 1972 show was the first solo exhibition of works by an African-American woman ever held at that museum.

Bearden

Romare Bearden (1912–1988) began working with collage in the early 1960s. Throughout his career, he believed it was important to create art whose subject matter reflected the African-American experience. A longtime resident of Harlem, Bearden became acquainted with many of the writers and artists of the Harlem Renaissance.

Painting Media

Fresco

Fresco is one of the oldest painting media and one of the most difficult to master. Frescoes have been used in many parts of the world to decorate walls and ceilings. The most well-known fresco of the Western World is the Sistine Ceiling (*See* p.281).

In the fresco process, the surface to be painted is first covered with a coat of rough plaster, which is allowed to dry. Fresh, smooth plaster is applied only to the area to be painted that day. While the plaster is wet, pigment is brushed on. The pigment makes a permanent bond with the lime in the plaster. No changes can be made to this layer once it has dried. Paint added to the dried plaster is called *fresco secco* and does not have the permanence of the primary layer.

2–24 *Palace Scene*, 580 AD. Indian. Fresco. Ajanta, Grotto no. 17.

2–26 Peter Paul Rubens, *Garden of Love*, about 1633. Flemish. Oil on canvas, 77 1/2" x 110 1/2" (197 x 281 cm). Prado Museum, Madrid.

Tempera

Tempera is a type of paint that is similar to the poster paint used in elementary schools. As early as ancient Egypt, artists have used various forms of tempera paint. Some, such as the painter of this thirteenth-century cross, used egg yolk as the binding agent to stick the colored pigment to the wooden panel. Since egg tempera dries quickly, artists use small brushes to work on very small and detailed areas with tiny strokes. Building up layers of transparent color over each other creates a richly colored, luminous surface.

2–25 Master of San Francesco, *Crucifixion*, about 1280. Italian. Tempera and gold on wood, 74" high (1.88 m). Philadelphia Museum of Art, the Wilstach Collection.

Oil

Oil paint is a medium that came to dominate the history of European art. Oil painting became popular when artists needed to work on larger surfaces with larger brushes. Oil colors are pigments bound to a surface of wood or canvas with either linseed or poppy oil. The paint is usually thinned with turpentine to make it spreadable. Oil paint takes much longer to dry than tempera. It can be applied in thick, buttery layers (*impasto*) or in thinned washes, or *glazes*. The variety of techniques is tremendous. Peter Paul Rubens was a master of the medium. By using glazes of color mixed with varnish, he was able to make the tints of flesh and satin material glow in his paintings. When canvas became the main type of ground, oil paintings could become huge in size. Rubens took advantage of this advance in his many gigantic works. Deep darks and brilliant lights offer the ultimate range of value contrasts.

Watercolor

Used since ancient Egypt, watercolor only recently came into its own as a major painting medium. Many artists have used watercolor to make sketches before making oil paintings in their studios. Watercolor was not considered a major painting medium until Winslow Homer, an American artist, became famous. Homer thought of his watercolors as finished works instead of sketches, and exhibited them as such. The binding agent in watercolor is gum arabic, a water-soluble adhesive that sticks the pigments to paper. The colors are mostly transparent. Gouache and casein paints are opaque watercolor. Some artists prefer these paints for their excellent covering characteristics.

2–27 Winslow Homer, *After the Hunt*, 1892. American. Watercolor on paper, 18 3/4" x 24 3/4" (48 x 63 cm). Los Angeles County Museum of Art, Paul Rodman Mabury Collection.

Acrylic

In the last half of the twentieth century, acrylics became one of the most popular media. Instead of using natural materials for binders, acrylic paints use polymer emulsions that can adhere pigments to almost any surface—masonite, canvas, glass, paper, cardboard or wood. Thinned with water and easy to clean up, acrylics dry rapidly. They can be applied heavily like oils and transparently like watercolors. Their versatility has made them extremely popular.

2–28 Alma Thomas. *Iris, Tulips, Jonquils and Crocuses*, 1969. American. Acrylic on canvas, 60" x 50" (152.4 x 127 cm). National Museum of Women in the Arts, The Holladay Collection.

Collage

Collage is one the latest media to be developed. It was begun by Pablo Picasso and Georges Braque in France. In 1912, they started to embellish their canvases with glued materials. Collage involves pasting papers to a ground. (The word *collage* comes from the French term *papier collé*, meaning "pasted paper.") Artists have used all sorts of materials in collages, but paper continues to be the most popular. Romare Bearden cuts pictures with textures and colors from magazines to produce collages that make dynamic social statements. His reconstructed images always involve people. The chunky shapes in this rural scene are typical of Bearden's work. The shapes are cut from magazines and augmented with other painting media.

2–29 Romare Bearden, *Eastern Barn*, 1968. American. Collage of paper with glue, lacquer and oil on paper, 55 1/2" x 44" (141 x 112 cm). Whitney Museum of American Art, New York.

Contextual Information

Hiroshige

Hiroshige is considered one of the world's great landscapists. Famous for his many series of prints portraying scenes from throughout Japan, he was an extraordinarily prolific artist. For 33 years he designed one print every other day.

Rain Shower on Ohashi Bridge depicts citizens of Edo shielding themselves from a sudden downpour. They are crossing the Sumida River at Atake. It is interesting to note that van Gogh made a copy in oil of this print.

Catlett

Elizabeth Catlett was born in 1919, and she continues to work today in her studio in Mexico. She says that "art must be realistic for me, whether sculpture or printmaking. I have always wanted my art to service my people—to reflect us, to relate to us, to stimulate us, to make us aware of our potential."

Printmaking Media

The various printmaking techniques began as a way to furnish art to the masses at reasonable prices. Even though many copies are made by the artist, each is signed and numbered. The edition is kept to a limited number of copies, thus ensuring that the value will remain constant.

Woodcut

A woodcut is called a relief print because the image on the plate projects, or sticks up, from the surface. The artist draws on a block of wood, then cuts away the parts that will remain white. Ink is then rolled onto the remaining raised area. Then, the surface is printed to reveal a mirror image of the original cutout design. The Japanese excel at this art form. One of their most

famous artists, Ando Hiroshige, designed this scene of a rain shower. This print includes a number of colors. Each color required a separate cut block. In some Japanese prints, over fifteen separate blocks were used to achieve the final result.

2–30 Ando Hiroshige, *Rain Shower on Ohashi Bridge*, 1857. Japanese. Color woodblock print, height 13 7/8" (35 cm). Cleveland Museum of Art.

Intaglio

While woodcuts are printed from the raised surface of a block, intaglio prints are made from the lines or crevices *in* a plate. To produce the design, the printmaker makes lines and scratches in the metal plate, usually zinc or copper. The indentations can be made by applying acid (etching) or by scratching (drypoint). Indentations can also be made by engraving, or removing thin V-shaped strips with a tool called a *burin.* Ink is forced into these grooves by rubbing, and the rest of the plate is wiped clean. To transfer the image, the paper is dampened and placed against the plate in a press. Under great pressure, the dampened paper picks up the ink from the grooves and the image is made. *Intaglio* refers to the ink being transferred to paper from *below the surface.* Rembrandt's intaglio print combines etching and drypoint to produce an incredible variety of lines and dark areas.

2–31 Rembrandt van Rijn, *Christ Crucified Between the Two Thieves (The Three Crosses),* 1653. Dutch. Fourth-state etching, approx. 15 x 18" (38.1 x 45.7 cm). Metropolitan Museum of Art, New York, gift of Felix M. Warburg and his family, 1941.

Materials and Techniques

The sale of his prints provided Rembrandt with a primary source of income. The fourth-state mentioned in the caption of fig.2–31 refers to Rembrandt's practice of reworking plates to produce a new edition, or version (state). The earlier versions of this print showed much more pictorial detail. In the fourth version, Rembrandt eliminated most of the descriptive elements.

Museum of Art, Rogers Fund.

Serigraph

The newest of the printmaking media is *serigraphy*, or silkscreen printing, which developed largely in the United States. It requires a screen of silk or a similar material, stretched on a frame. A stencil is attached to the silk and ink is forced through the stencil with a rubber squeegee. The open parts of the stencil, allow the ink to pass through onto the paper or other printing surface below. Many colors can be used, but a separate stencil is needed for each one. Andy Warhol's print has been placed on canvas and is as large as one of his paintings. Each of the four colors has its own stencil, and the colors are flat and unshaded. In this print, the result seems mechanical and commercial, which is exactly the way he wanted it to appear.

2–34 Andy Warhol, *Campbell's Soup Can*, 1964. American. Silkscreen on canvas, 35 1/2" x 24" (90 x 61 cm). Leo Castelli Gallery, New York.

Linocut

Linocut is a relief printmaking medium that produces an image similar to a woodcut. This medium makes use of cutting tools and linoleum. Cuts are made into the smooth, even surface of the linoleum. Ink is rolled over the remaining surface with a brayer. Resulting prints can either be refined or jagged, depending on the artist's wishes and style. Elizabeth Catlett is a contemporary artist who uses the relief process to its best advantage. The marks of the cutting tools are evident.

2–32 Elizabeth Catlett, *The Survivor*, 1983. American. Linocut, 11" x 10 1/4" (28 x 26 cm). Courtesy Malcom Brown Gallery, Cleveland.

Lithograph

Lithographs may appear textured, flat, black-and-white or full-color. Toulouse-Lautrec made many large prints that advertised the cafés, bars and nightclubs of Paris. In this lithograph, a printmaker is making a lithographic print. The female client is checking it for accuracy. To make a lithograph or "stone writing," the artist draws a design on a limestone slab with a greasy crayon or ink. Then, water is spread over the stone. The water will adhere only where there is no greasy substance. A large brayer is then used to roll greasy ink onto the surface. Because grease will not mix with water, the ink sticks only where there is no water. Therefore, the ink sticks to places where the design was drawn. The image is now ready to be reproduced. As Toulouse-Lautrec's print shows, a sheet of paper is put over the slab and run through a lithographic press. Lithography is a difficult process to master. When several colors are used, each one has to have its own stone, and colors are printed one over the other.

2–33 Henri de Toulouse-Lautrec, *L'Estampe Originale*, 1893. French. Color lithograph, 17 3/4" x 23 3/4" (45 x 60.3 cm). The Metropolitan

Contextual Information

Maori Meeting Halls

The Maori developed a method of constructing meeting halls with very large carved beams and interior wall panels. Carved into the lintels, beams and walls were imaginary figures of former chiefs and heroes.

The buildings were large cooperative projects. A chief oversaw and organized the project; designers and builders used stone tools; mat weavers covered the floors; shell cutters made the inlays for the carvings; and wood carvers and painters provided their expertise.

Ganésa

Some Hindus believe that Ganésa is the son of the god Siva and the goddess Parvati. According to one legend, his elephant-like appearance is a result of a calamity of his infancy, in which his human head was cut off. It was replaced by the closest head at hand, which happened to be that of an elephant.

This bronze figure of Ganésa (fig.2–36) dances on a lotus platform. His trunk reaches for a *modaka,* which is held in one of his hands. The modaka is a ball of sweet rice and is said to be Ganésa's favorite food.

Sculpture Media

Sculptors work in a number of ways: by cutting away (subtractive), by putting parts together (additive), by forming with hands (modeling), and by producing from a mold (casting).

Bronze

Ancient Chinese, Egyptians, Greeks, and Ife and Benin people were expert at the complex process of casting metal. Casting is a method of reproducing a three-dimensional object by pouring a hardening liquid or molten metal into a mold bearing its impression.

In India, too, quite astonishing pieces were created. Here, the Hindu god of learning and good fortune is depicted in bronze. In temples and households, the image of Ganésa is often placed near the entrance to welcome visitors. The figure exhibits an exuberance and lightness that defies the stocky, elephantlike qualities of the god and the heaviness of the bronze.

2–36 *Dancing Ganésa,* 15th century. Indian, Karnataka. Bronze, 19 7/8" x 13" (50.3 x 32.9 cm). Los Angeles County Museum of Art, Purchase, Harry and Yvonne Lenart Funds.

Steel

Sheet steel, which can be cut and welded together, has given sculptors who enjoy the additive processes a new material to use. David Smith has produced an extensive series of sculptures by welding together flat shapes of steel into blocky forms. Because the sculptures all have cubic forms, he titled them all *Cubi,* with Roman numerals to identify each. Many of the pieces are polished to a high luster, with the machined surfaces allowed to remain scarred—a combination of industrial machinery and art. Steel can be welded into many forms and can be painted as well as polished, or allowed to rust.

2–38 David Smith, *Cubi XII,* 1963. American. Stainless steel, 109 1/2" x 32 1/4" (278 x 82 cm). Hirshhorn Museum and Sculpture Garden, Washington, DC.

Wood

Wood is a very versatile sculpture material. It can be carved and nailed, filed and drilled, sanded and glued. Artists from all over the world, from ancient times to the present, have used wood for its warm feeling, attractive color and grain. Its abundance and relative low cost have also made wood a preferred medium.

2–37 Lintel, early 18th century. Maori, New Zealand. Wood with shell, 40 1/4" (1.02 m) long. The Nelson-Atkins Museum of Art, Kansas City, Missouri.

Marble

Marble is an excellent sculptural material because it can be polished to a glasslike finish or left rough and textured. This ancient piece is from the Cyclades Islands of modern Greece. The figure and lyre have been converted into various geometric shapes (ovals, triangles and cylinders). The skillful carving of the marble, the elegance of the figure and its rather modern look make this sculpture seem very contemporary.

2–35 *Lyre Player*, from Keros, c. 2000 BC. Cycladic. Marble, 9" (22.9 cm) high. National Archaeological Museum, Athens.

Plastic

The twentieth century brought with it a bountiful array of new materials for sculptors to explore. Glass, neon lights, mirrors, plastics, acrylics and other materials have found their way into artworks. Duane Hanson combines casting techniques with plastic resins and actual clothing to produce extremely lifelike figures. The football player looks so real you might feel like talking to him. The life-size figure was cast in plastic called polyester resin, and was reinforced with fiberglass. To make molds for his sculptures, Hanson applies plaster gauze strips directly to the body of a person, whose skin and hair is heavily greased so the plaster will not stick. Then, flesh-colored resin is painted into the molds and laminated with layers of glass cloth. The hardened casts are assembled to create the finished figure. Hair and clothing are then added and painted.

2–39 Duane Hanson, *Football Player*, 1981. American. Polyvinyl, polychromed in oil with accessories, 43 1/4" x 30" x 31 1/2" (110 x 76 x 80 cm). Lowe Art Museum, University of Miami.

Higher-Order Thinking Skills

Tell students that they have been selected to decide on a sculpture for their school. Ask what medium and what subject they would be looking for in an artist's proposal. They also may want to select a site for the work.

Inquiry

Whenever possible, sculpture should be experienced with the hands as well as with the eyes. Ask a museum or local collector if it would be possible to allow students to touch and feel some of their sculptures. At the conclusion of their experience, ask students if they were particularly surprised by the tactile qualities of any of the materials used in the sculptures.

Crafts

Fibers

The early process of *twining* developed from a need for containers, clothing and household objects. Baskets and rugs were twined by many tribes of Native Americans. Later, weaving of fabrics on various types of *looms* was developed. This craft grew into today's huge fabric industry. Today, contemporary handweavers use fibers of many kinds to produce unique fabrics. The rug was woven by a Navajo craftsperson, using traditional tribal designs and colors. Contemporary fiber artists use all kinds of natural and synthetic fibers to knot, stitch, tie and weave their work. Such work is often sculptural. Tapestries, carpets, brocades, stitchery and fabrics of many kinds and of startling beauty have been created all over the world.

2–41 *Navajo rug,* 1850–1880. Native American. Wool, 78 3/4" x 49 1/4" (200 x 125 cm). The Indian Art Center of California, Studio City.

Glass

Glass is such a common item today that it is difficult to think of it as a precious material. Yet, the Egyptians used glass and precious gems in jewelry, and it was an important part of King Tutankhamen's burial mask. The glass bottle made by an Egyptian craftsperson about 3350 years ago is a beautiful example of superb craftsmanship. It probably held valuable perfume or other precious oils for a wealthy noble.

Millions of pieces of jewelry have been made by excellent craftspersons around the world. In nomadic societies, wealthy families invested in jewelry or other portable items. Nobles and rulers who acquired great wealth often had collections of jewelry. Fine jewelry and gems in some societies became synonymous with wealth. Simple jewelry, on the other hand, can be made of any material that enhances personal appearance—string, seeds or basic metals like copper. This brass and glass bead necklace was made by the Dan people of Africa.

2–43 *Necklace of glass beads with brass beads and ornaments.* Liberia, Africa. The Peabody Museum, Harvard University.

2–42 *Glass bottle shaped like a fish,* about 1370 BC. Egyptian, from el Amarna. Glass, 5 1/2" (14 cm) long. British Museum, London.

Clay

Clays of various types are dug from the earth and, when formed, dried and fired, become extremely durable. Earliest examples were *flash-fired* in open pits, but later work was heated more carefully in primitive *kilns.* Today, gas- or electric-fired kilns can be controlled carefully to create just the right temperatures, atmospheres and cooling-off times for each type of clay.

Most clay vessels are formed on a potter's wheel. Some, however, are made using the coil method. Coils of clay are added one on top of the other as the piece is slowly formed and molded by hand. Native Americans practice this technique. It is amazing to think that this was created without benefit of a wheel!

2–40 *Polacca Polychrome Style D (Sityatki Revival) jar,* 1890–1900. Hopi. Diameter 12 7/8" (32.7 cm). The Peabody Museum, Harvard University.

Furniture

Furniture, like glass, is usually taken for granted. Yet, craftspersons working with wood have produced such astounding results that they have often signed their pieces as painters and sculptors do. Like the other crafts, furniture can be as simple and stark as a Shaker chair or as elaborate as a royal throne. The commode seen here has a veneered decoration of tulipwood, burr wood and satinwood. The intricate designs are made with thin slices of wood, called veneer. When bits of veneer are cut and fitted into such designs, the craft is called *marquetry*. A fitted and shaped marble top together with gilt-bronze mounts complete this marvelous work.

2–45 Jean-Francois Oeben. *Commode*, 1761–1763. French. Veneered wood with gilt-bronze mounts, 35 3/4" (91 cm) high. The J. Paul Getty Museum, Malibu.

Mosaics

Mosaics can be made of glass, colored bits of marble, bits of ceramic tile, pieces of wood, or even seeds and paper. The walls and ceilings of early Christian churches were lined with mosaics of colored glass and even glass containing gold. Bits of glass (*tesserae*) were embedded in plaster or cement to make designs and pictures that glittered in the candlelight. Ancient Romans put thousands of incredibly small pieces of marble together to create wall decorations that were polished until smooth as glass. Often, mosaic sidewalks in front of Roman shops contained symbols or pictures of the type of business found inside.

2–44 *Apse mosaic*, c. 549. Byzantine. St. Apollinare in Classe, Ravenna.

Metalwork

Craftspersons working with metals have produced artwork for their societies ever since bronze could be worked. As with other crafts, the competence of the craftspersons provides a good indication of the sophistication of the society and its level of technology. Working in gold, silver, copper, bronze, iron, steel and aluminum, artisans have created their metal magic for centuries.

2–46 *Candlestick*, 13th century. Islamic. Engraved brass with silver and gold inlays, 9 3/8" (23.8 cm). The Nelson-Atkins Museum of Art, Kansas City, Missouri.

Lesson 2.3

Artists communicate through a visual language. They string together indivi dual elements that act as words, according to certain principles of design, that function like the rules of grammar. Artists develop their own personal style or "voice" through the individual choices they make in constructing their compositions.

Warm-up

Ask students to list special terms used in football, in mathematics and in computer technology. Could someone who is unfamiliar with these terms completely understand the areas or communicate effectively with others about them? Share that Lesson 2.3 discusses the vocabulary of art, which will help students gain a deeper understanding of what they see and provide a means of approaching any work.

Objective

Students should be able to:

Distinguish the properties of art and the elements and principles of design.

2.3 Design: The Structure of Art

VISUAL LANGUAGE, like verbal language, needs structure to make it understandable. The principles of design are the basic structure, or grammar, of visual language. These principles guide artists in their use of the elements of design—line, shape, form, texture, value, color and space. These elements of design are the vocabulary with which artists work. Artists usually use all the elements and principles in concert to produce an effective visual statement.

When studying and analyzing a work of art, ask yourself questions like the following to help you understand the work's content and properties.

Content can be determined by asking: Why has the artist made the work? What is he or she trying to tell me about the subject? What is the major theme? Are there minor themes also?

Sensory properties are the things we experience with our senses, such as line, shape, form, color, value, texture, space and light. These are the elements of art. Ask yourself: Which art element dominates the work? What kinds of line are used? How is form indicated? How is space felt? Is there texture? Are colors bright or dull? Which color dominates?

Formal properties tell us how the art elements are organized through the use of pattern, balance, movement, rhythm, unity, variety, emphasis, contrast and proportion. These are the principles of art. Ask yourself: What (if anything) is the center of interest? How does my eye move to it in the work? How did the artist establish the center of interest? Does the work have a sense of rhythm? Why? Is the composition vertical or horizontal? How is balance achieved? How is unity achieved? What shapes are repeated? Is a pattern evident? Are the figures in proportion?

Technical properties refer to the use of tools, media and techniques. Ask yourself: What materials and tools were used to make the work? Are the wood grains used effectively? What kinds of brushstrokes and pencil lines are used? Is it a finished work or a sketch for a later work? Are all parts treated with the same detail? Why or why not? Are there contrasts in value? What types of marks did the artist use? How is light indicated?

Expressive properties tell us what the work says, literally, metaphorically and symbolically. These properties are the mood language of the artist. Ask yourself: What mood does the work convey? Is the work timid or bold? Serious or comic? Does it establish a time of year? Does the work have social or religious significance? Is it a literal statement or a symbolic subject? How does the artist feel about the subject? How do I feel about the subject and its treatment?

Look at El Greco's painting of *St. Martin and the Beggar*. The subject matter is a narrative account of St. Martin, who is giving his own cloak to a naked, starving beggar. El Greco used all the elements of art in this composition. It is easy to find *line* in the work. The horse is a white *shape*. The beggar is shaded, so he seems to have three-dimensional *form*. The costume of St. Martin has a different *texture* than the horse. There are light, dark and medium *values* of color. The *colors* used (green and blues) are predominantly cool. Deep *space* is indicated by the small scale of the distant town. These elements are the vocabulary of the artist. But, what about the grammar?

When El Greco structured this composition, he had to decide where to place each part to make it most effective. The parts are in *balance* because there is just about the same visual activity and weight on both sides of the central axis. Because of the limited use of color and the elongated distortion that El Greco uses throughout, the painting has a sense of *unity*. *Emphasis* is placed on the good deed of giving to the poor and on the dominant blue-green color. There are many *contrasts*: between light and dark, textured and smooth areas, and rich and poor. The flickering light on the elongated shapes, which are repeated in the painting, forms a *pattern* of lights and darks. El Greco controls the visual *movement* so that the viewer's eyes always end at the face of St. Martin, the center of interest. The repeated vertical shapes develop a sense of *rhythm* in the painting. These principles—balance, unity, emphasis, contrast, pattern, movement and rhythm—are the grammar of the artist. They are the ways that the artist can best use the elements to create a pleasing composition.

Teach

Art History/Criticism: Challenge students to be detectives with an image from Lesson 2.3. Ask them to begin by writing down what they believe the work is about, what feelings it evokes, and how the artist has accomplished this. Next direct them to break down the piece in a more methodical way, looking at it from various angles. Have them apply the properties described on page 40. Have students use their new insights to go back and revise what they first wrote.

• Ask if the information has altered the way in which they understand the image.

• Do they feel differently about it? Why is this so? Hold a class discussion about their experiences.

• Are there similarities in what each of them has learned?

• What did they find most surprising about the activity?

2–47 El Greco. *St. Martin and the Beggar*, 1597–1599. Spanish. Oil on canvas, 76 1/2" x 40 1/2" (194 x 103 cm). National Gallery of Art, Washington, DC, Widener Collection.

Higher-Order Thinking Skills

Have students use the text to examine El Greco's painting. Then have them each select a work of art they like and describe its content, sensory properties, formal properties, technical properties and expressive properties.

Evaluate

Ask students what they think the criteria are to be visually literate. What specifically would someone need to learn to be able to converse meaningfully in the language of art?

• Do students have their own lingo that they share with one another, or one they have made up with a sibling?

• How does it feel to speak a language that is unfamiliar to others?

• How might this affect the way people react to artwork that they do not understand?

Ask students if a cursory glance at an artwork reveals everything there is to know about it. What did their experience in the Teach exercise demonstrate to them?

Reteach

Ask students to compare the language of art to written English. What in art would be the equivalent of words (line, shape, color, etc.), sentences (elements of design; that is, how the "words" are put together) and paragraphs (principles of design, or how the entire piece interrelates)?

Contextual Information

Night Rain on Kirasaki Pine

Night Rain on Kirasaki Pine is from Hiroshige's series of prints entitled *Eight Views of Lake Biwa.* The scene represents the ancient pine tree of Kirasaki which shelters a shrine beneath it.

The image is an example of Hiroshige's fascination with the forces of nature. He often depicted rain, mist and snow. These provided a sense of the spectacular to the poetic scenes he captured.

Montenegro

Roberto Montenegro started as a surrealist painter. He went to Italy to study murals but was more successful as an easel painter. In Paris, he met Picasso and Juan Gris. He returned to Mexico in 1910 for a few months but returned to Paris, where he remained for 12 years.

Before Montenegro returned to Mexico, he again studied Italian frescos. He experimented and studied in Diego Rivera's studio, following instruction written more than 400 years earlier by Cennino Cennini and Leonardo da Vinci.

The Elements of Design

Line

Lines are seen every day. They can be two-dimensional like those on a sheet of writing paper or three-dimensional like the branches of a tree.

The woodblock print by Hiroshige contains a marvelous variety of line. Some lines are thin or thick; continuous or interrupted; straight or curved; vertical, horizontal or diagonal; geometric or organic. Even *calligraphic* lines can be seen in the signature and description in the upper corners of the print. Some lines are massed together to create gray or textured areas. Other lines are used singly or in pairs. Some lines are black, while others are colored.

2–48 Ando Hiroshige, *Night Rain on Kirasaki Pine*, 1834. Japanese. Woodblock print, 9" x 14 1/4" (23 x 36 cm). Los Angeles County Museum of Art, gift of Mr. and Mrs. Nathan V. Hammer.

Shape

If a line on paper wanders around and finally crosses itself, the enclosed area is called a *shape.* Shapes have only two dimensions. They can be geometric, like a triangle, circle, square or rectangle. Or they can be organic—free form, irregular, pear-shaped or amoeba-like.

Montenegro used shape as the dominant element in his design. Some shapes are organic and others are geometric. The hard edges and sharp breaks between values and colors set off the various shapes. The elegant, flowing heads of the women contrast with the angularity of their white blouses and the houses behind them.

2–49 Roberto Montenegro, *Maya Women*, 1926. Mexican. Oil on canvas, 31 1/2" x 27 1/2" (80 x 70 cm). The Museum of Modern Art, New York, gift of Nelson A. Rockefeller, 1941.

Performing Arts Connection

Investigating Line

Ask whether there are similarities in the way "line" can be used in art, music, theater and dance. Are there times when it is used to express ideas or emotions in each format? Are there "descriptive" lines in drama, dance and music?

• Tell students to make a simple, single-line drawing that covers an entire sheet of paper. Have them reinvent this line in a performing art—choreography, theatrical dialogue or music. Exhibit students' drawings as they perform their "line" for the rest of the class.

Form

A *form* is three-dimensional and encloses volume. Like shapes, forms can be geometric (cubes, pyramids, boxlike, cones) or irregular (eggs, pears, horses, people, bottles). Form, the volume or mass of objects, is the most important art element for sculptors. While sculptors and potters work with form, painters work with shapes. Painters often use shading to make shapes look like forms.

This head from the Nok culture of western Africa shows an emphasis on simple yet full form. The pursed lips seem ready to whistle or blow out a flame.

The long, attenuated limbs of the figure by Giacometti are deflated by contrast. Yet, the near abstraction of the human form makes it very expressive and poignant.

2–50 *Head of Jemaa*, 510 BC. Nigeria, Nok Culture. Terracotta. National Museum, Lagos.

2–51 Alberto Giacometti, *Man Pointing*, 1947. Swiss. Bronze, 70 1/2" high (179 cm). The Museum of Modern Art, New York, gift of Mrs. John D. Rockefeller.

Higher-Order Thinking Skills

Ask students to choose from the textbook three works that appeal to them. Have them explain how the artists used line, shape or form in each of the three works. Is there any similarity in use of these elements in their three chosen works?

Contextual Information

Duncanson

Born in 1821, Robert Scott Duncanson was the first major African-American landscape painter. He spent the early part of his life in Canada and later moved to Cincinnati. By 1842, Duncanson was exhibiting his paintings in that city.

Early 1850s directories from Cincinnati list Duncanson as a daguerreotypist. The daguerreotype photographic process was used by landscape painters as a means of recording different views. To a certain extent, this eliminated the need for lengthy sketching sessions outdoors.

Canaletto

Copies and forgeries of Canaletto's views of Venice were made in large numbers in Italy and elsewhere, both during the artist's lifetime and throughout the nineteenth century.

These views were in high demand because wealthy tourists frequently bought them as remembrances of their travels, much as the modern traveler might buy postcards and posters.

Klimt

Klimt was trained at the School of Applied Art in Vienna. In 1898 he founded the Viennese Secession and emerged as the leading Austrian painter of Art Nouveau (or Jugend-stil, as it was called in Austria). He resigned from the Viennese Secession in 1903.

Primarily a decorator with a specialization in mural painting, Klimt also produced some works on canvas, such as *The Park*, which have achieved notable popularity in recent decades.

Texture

The surfaces of things have *texture*. Sandpaper, wool, cloth, leather and asphalt have textures. A painting may simulate textures by using color and value contrasts to make the surface *seem* textured.

Nicholas de Staël greatly simplified the landscape of Vaucluse so that only shapes and colors remain. The shapes, perhaps, remind one of cliffs and trees, sky and water, or other elements of the landscape. When the French artist put down his oil paint on canvas, he wanted to use another element of design besides color and shape—texture. One can immediately see the texture in this work. It actually exists. The paint was buttered onto the canvas with a painting knife, like a small spatula. The artist may not have used a regular brush at all on this *impasto* surface. It appears that he also added textural material like sand and sawdust to his paint. If a viewer were able to rub the surface of the painting, even with eyes closed, it would reveal the coarse textural quality.

2–52 Nicholas de Staël, *Landscape in Vaucluse, No. 2*, 1953. French. Oil on canvas, 25 1/4" x 31 3/4" (64 x 81 cm). Albright-Knox Art Gallery, Buffalo, gift of Seymour H. Knox Foundation Inc.

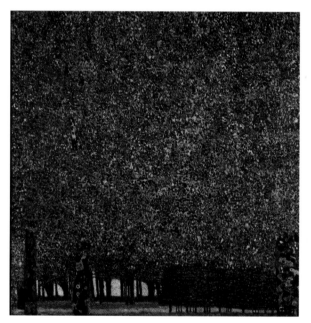

Simulated Texture

Although the surface of Gustav Klimt's painting looks more textured than de Staël's, it is not. The surface, which is painted to look like texture, in reality is relatively smooth. The textures are simulated. Klimt was a master at creating unusual and convincing textures. Flat surfaces often appear textured because of the value contrasts the artist used. Usually, paintings have a variety of simulated textures so the surface is not monotonous, but Klimt gives us little relief. The viewer is overpowered by the dense forest of uniform texture. Klimt and de Staël both enjoyed texture for its own sake. The two paintings are not representations of real textures in nature but are abstracted works which emphasize texture.

2–53 Gustav Klimt, *The Park*, before 1910. Austrian. Oil on canvas, 43 1/4" x 43 1/4" (110 x 110 cm). The Museum of Modern Art, New York, Gertrude A. Mellon Fund.

Space: Perspective

Space is where people live. Real space is three-dimensional. But space also refers to the illusion of depth in a painting or drawing. Actual space in a painting is two-dimensional. Leonardo da Vinci believed that true art makes the viewer feel three-dimensional space on a two-dimensional surface.

Artists use *perspective* to show depth or space in a painting. If two objects overlap on a flat surface, one is clearly behind and the other is in front. A sense of depth is created. Painters also use *aerial perspective* to show depth. In Duncanson's painting, the bright haze hides distant details. The

mountains are seen as being far away. The darker values are up close, and the lighter values are far away. The colors also are more intense up close, while the edges become softer farther away.

2–54 Robert Scott Duncanson, *Loch Long*, 1867. American. Oil on canvas, 7" x 12" (18 x 30 cm). National Museum of American Art, gift of Donald J. Shein, 1983.

Canaletto used *linear perspective* to help the viewer experience the space he saw at Venice. All parallel lines run toward invisible vanishing points which are off the canvas. With mathematical precision, the artist depicts the diminishing size of arches, columns and people as they recede. In both paintings, there is a strong feeling of depth or space, yet each artist used different means.

2–55 Canaletto, *The Square of St. Mark's*, about 1730. Italian. Oil on canvas, 45 1/4" x 60 1/2" (115 x 154 cm). National Gallery of Art, Washington, DC, gift of Mrs. Barbara Hutton.

Higher-Order Thinking Skills

1 Each of the paintings shown on these pages has very different surface textures. Ask students to analyze the relationship of the texture to the other elements of each painting. Which one do they prefer?

2 To reinforce their understanding, ask students to select two paintings in the text that illustrate linear perspective and two that demonstrate aerial perspective. Ask them to discuss the different effect of each type of perspective. Why might an artist choose to use one type of perspective over the other?

Color

Color is the one phase of art that is also a science. There are three terms that artists use in talking about color: hue, value and intensity. *Hue* is the name of the color. For example, yellow is a hue. *Value* is the dark or light quality of a color. Pink is a light value of red because white has been added to it. *Intensity* is the brightness or saturation of a color. The pure color is most intense; if one adds its *complement* and grays it, it is less intense. The color wheel is a good place to begin learning about color.

• *Primary hues* are red, yellow, blue. From these, all other colors can be made.

• *Secondary/Intermediate colors* are produced by mixing two primaries. For example, red and yellow make orange. If a primary and secondary color are mixed together, an intermediate color is created. Blue and green make blue-green.

• *Complementary colors* are colors directly opposite on the color wheel (yellow and violet). If they are mixed together, the original hue is grayer and less intense. A little green mixed with red will lessen the intensity of red and make it a grayed or muted color.

• *Warm colors* are hues containing red and orange. Warm colors seem to advance or come forward in a painting. Sunlight is often painted with warm colors.

• *Cool colors* are hues containing green or blue. Cool colors seem to recede or go back into a painting. Shadows are often painted with cool colors.

Painters also refer to the *local color* of objects. Local color is the color of objects when they are lit by uniform white light. If the source of light is colored, the local color will change. For example, under yellow light, objects will take on a yellowish hue. Think of how the colors in nature change when the sunset casts an orange hue over everything.

Objects also absorb colors from surrounding objects. These absorbed colors are called *reflected colors*. If two colored objects are next to each other, each will contain reflected colors as well as its own local color.

Color is the most important art element for the painter. How artists have seen color in nature has greatly determined their painting techniques and styles.

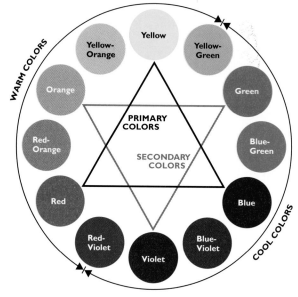

2–56 Color Wheel

Value

Value refers to the light or dark quality of a color or shape in a painting. Black is the darkest value; white is the lightest. When a basic color is mixed with white, its value is lightened; if black is added, its value is darkened. If a painting were all dark values, it would be difficult to read. Most successful paintings have a contrast of values. The stronger the contrast, the more dramatic the painting seems.

Notice the light and dark values in Zurbarán's still life. In the black-and-white print, the middle values are gray. In the color reproduction, they are variations of the dominant hues. The artist has used values to create a feeling of form, an illusion of three-dimensionality. The rounded lemons and oranges look like they have volume and take up space because of their gradual value changes from light to dark. The rims of the plates and cup have sharp edges because the value changes are sudden. The still life is dramatic because of the strong value contrasts from deepest dark to lightest light. Paintings that have mostly light values are called *high-keyed* and those of mostly dark values, *low-keyed.*

2–57 Francisco Zurbarán, *Still Life with Lemons, Oranges and a Rose,* 1633. Spanish. Oil on canvas, 23 1/4" x 41 1/4" (59 x 105 cm). The Norton Simon Foundation, Los Angeles.

Higher-Order Thinking Skills

1 When introducing color, explain intensity (dull versus bright). Use colors in the classroom as examples, such as: the green of ivy (or other plants) is more intense than the green of the chalkboard. Students sometimes enjoy comparing the shades, tints and intensities of their clothing. Look for the most intense color, the dullest color, and tints and shades of the same color. Color chips from house-painting stores can also be used to discuss color.

2 Have each student choose a painting he or she likes. Ask students to use the appropriate vocabulary to analyze the color scheme.

3 Ask students to paint and label color schemes with just a few dots of color. Or, they can make a book or poster illustrating these color schemes: analogous, warm, cool, complementary, monochromatic, triads, high intensity versus low intensity.

4 Ask students to consider the connotations of color. Have them use color to show a mood by painting a poster using only two primary colors plus black and white.

5 Have students paint a simple color wheel in a circle, then poke a pencil through the center of the wheel and spin it. The colors should swirl together. By gluing the color wheel on poster board, it can become a top.

2–58 *Raven sun clan mask with beak: transformation mask, open,* 19th century. Harbledown Island, British Columbia. Kwakiutl. The Peabody Museum, Harvard University.

Contextual Information

Degas

Throughout his career Degas returned again and again to the ballet as subject matter. Half of his mature work related to it. About 1500 drawings, pastels, paintings and sculptures survive which have ballet as their subject.

Other important themes in Degas' career were horses and riders, bathers and the theater. Asymmetry often played an important role in the construction of Degas' views of each of these subjects.

Kwakiutl Mask

Movable masks such as the one depicted in fig.2–58 were most highly developed among the Kwakiutl, although other Northwest Coast Native American groups used them. These movable masks were worn by the shaman in a variety of ceremonies. During the ceremonial dances, strings were pulled to open the outer part of the mask, revealing the inner carving. Some of the more complex masks were constructed so that three or four representations could be revealed.

Principles of Design

The principles of design describe the general ways in which artists arrange the parts of their compositions. These organizers are balance, unity, emphasis, contrast, pattern, movement and rhythm.

The principles are never used in isolation, but always in concert. A design may use balance, but it may also contrast certain areas, emphasize one part, achieve rhythm and movement, or produce an overall pattern. One principle may dominate, but when an overall unity is achieved, all the principles have probably been employed. Look again at El Greco's painting of *St. Martin and the Beggar* (fig.2–47) to see how these principles work together.

There are many ways to use the elements to achieve each design principle. However, only a few can be explored here. Readers may want to return to this section often to reinforce their understanding of design terms and dynamics.

Balance: Symmetrical

Symmetrical (or formal) balance is a roughly even distribution of visual weight or activity on each side of a central axis—like two equally sized children on a seesaw. Much art is not perfectly balanced symmetrically because one side would be a mirror image of the other. Symmetry is an integral part of the design of this mask and many other objects created by Native Americans. Colors, shapes and lines are repeated exactly. Though the creatures depicted have a potential of being frightening, the perfect symmetry, or balance, of the work has a calm, stabilizing effect.

Balance: Asymmetrical

Asymmetrical balance means that larger masses on one side of the painting may be balanced by smaller, contrasting parts on the other side. An asymmetrical painting is informally balanced and is usually more exciting than a formally balanced composition. Many of Degas' ballet paintings show an asymmetrical balance. By covering first one half and then the other half of the painting the viewer can see how different they are. It is sometimes difficult to see the balance in an asymmetrical design. However, if the overall effect is comfortable, the work is probably balanced.

2–59 Edgar Degas. *The Star,* or *Dancer on Stage,* about 1876–1877. Pastel on monotype on paper, 23 5/8" x 17 5/8" (60 x 44 cm). Musée d'Orsay, Paris.

Performing Arts Connection

Visual to Performing Arts

Ask students to select an artwork that intrigues them. Have them work either individually or in small groups to devise unusual ways to translate the work into a performing art. Ask the class how abstract art can be expressed in drama or how a narrative scene can be communicated in music.

• Ask students what it was like to use the same subject in another art form. Was it easier to express yourself in a particular form? What might you do differently next time? What part of your process was most challenging? Why?

Higher-Order Thinking Skills

Have students find one other example of both symmetry and asymmetry in the textbook. Ask them if they have a personal reaction to symmetry that is different from that to asymmetry.

Contextual Information

The Carnival

The subject of Homer's *The Carnival* has been interpreted in several ways, as depicting scenes from a Fourth of July celebration or a Mardi Gras tableau. It recently has been suggested that the scene represents an African-American family in the South preparing for a holiday known as Jonkonnu. This celebration blended African and Caribbean masquerade traditions and, before the Civil War, took place on plantations at the end of the year. On this day, slaves were permitted to go to the main house for entertainment and gifts. After the Civil War, Jonkonnu became a celebration of the freedom granted by the Emancipation Proclamation.

Vermeer

Vermeer was surrounded by artists in the early years of his professional life. Some introduced him to a light palette. Vermeer also learned from others to apply paint in small dabs. In *Officer and Laughing Girl* (fig.2–62), he used this technique for the first time.

Unity

Unity combines the principles of design and the physical aspects of a painting to create a single, harmonious work. Unity in a painting is like music played by an orchestra. All notes and chords produced by the instruments combine to make a single beautiful passage of sound. Artists can use various means to achieve unity.

Turner achieved unity in his dramatic painting of the great London fire in three ways: (1) the values are mostly high-keyed; (2) feathery brushstrokes appear throughout; and (3) all forms are rendered abstractly. The painting also has color unity. Turner used a limited palette of yellows and oranges so that all the hues are related.

2–60 Joseph Mallord William Turner, *Burning of the Houses of Parliament*, 1835. English. Oil on canvas, 36 1/4" x 48 1/2" (92 x 123 cm). Philadelphia Museum of Art, The McFadden Collection.

2–61 Winslow Homer, *The Carnival*, 1877. American. Oil on canvas, 20" x 30" (51 x 76 cm). The Metropolitan Museum of Art, New York, Lazarus Fund.

Homer's subject and methods of obtaining unity are quite different from Turner's. In *The Carnival*, Homer uses a single strong light source, entering from the left. The colors on the carnival figures are more intense than the muted background hues. The figures are, therefore, dominant while the background is subordinate. The figures also contain more detail and value contrasts than the background. The central three figures are strongest and the act of sewing up the torn costume is the center of interest. All eye movement in the painting is directed to the central figures and center of interest. A strong repetition of vertical shapes establishes a rhythm that unifies the work.

But, there is also a secondary horizontal movement, established by the fence and the ground shadows, which tie the verticals together. The little girl on the left is placed to delicately balance the asymmetrically arranged elements. Finally, the visual story, or narrative, helps to unify the subject matter and, therefore, the painting.

Materials and Techniques

Turner preferred to use pencil when he worked outdoors. When he did work on canvas, he preferred a broad underpainting of a variety of washed color, rather than the more typical monochromatic underpainting. He often used pinks, blues and yellows in his underpainting. Rather than mixing his colors on a palette, Turner overlaid his color on the canvas.

Emphasis

Emphasis is the way of developing the main theme in a work of art. It answers the question, "What is the artist trying to say?" The answers can be obvious or obscure. Artists may emphasize one or more of the art elements—such as color, line or texture—and subordinate the rest. Artists may also emphasize a particular subject or concept—symbolism, daily life, material wealth or historical fact.

Jan Vermeer emphasizes light in his work. The natural light entering from the open window floods the wall, girl and table. Vermeer also depicts the various reflected lights and different intensities of shadow. The room, officer and girl are simply props for Vermeer's beautiful study of light.

2–62 Jan Vermeer. *Officer and Laughing Girl*, 1655–1660. Dutch. Oil on canvas, 19 1/2" x 18" (50 x 46 cm). The Frick Collection, New York.

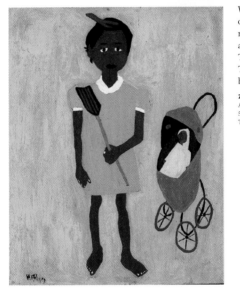

William H. Johnson placed emphasis on the little girl and her doll carriage simply by placing the figure on a plain, bright yellow background. The artist also emphasizes shape. There are very few lines, only blocks of flat, bright colors.

2–63 William H. Johnson, *Li'l Sis*, about 1944. American. Oil on canvas, 26" x 21 1/4" (66 x 54 cm). National Museum of American Art, gift of The Harmon Foundation.

Contextual Information

Tiepolo

Tiepolo painted the *Adoration of the Magi* during a three-year stay in Wurzburg, Germany. Commissioned to fresco the hall of the prince's esidence, Tiepolo found time to do some easel painting when winter came and the weather was unsuitable for fresco work.

The *Adoration of the Magi* was one of Tiepolo's most important works on canvas. He painted it for the church of the Benedictine monastery at Schwarzach in Germany. The painting is characteristic of eighteenth century depictions of religious themes. Rendered to resemble a theatrical extravaganza, the drapery is sumptuous, the colors are rich and the perspective is dramatic.

Higher-Order Thinking Skills

Ask students if there is a strong sense of rhythm in the Villon (fig.2–65) or the Tiepolo (fig.2–64). Ask them to describe the rhythm in each of the paintings.

Contrast

If all parts of a painting were alike, it would be monotonous and the viewer would lose interest quickly. To avoid monotony and to make the painting as visually interesting and exciting as possible, artists use contrasts of various kinds.

In Tiepolo's painting of the wise men visiting Mary and the Christ Child, he used many contrasts. It is easy to find contrast of light and dark values. These contrasts in values accompany the contrast in color between warms and cools. Soft, curving shapes of fabric contrast with the hard edges of the building. Small areas of light or dark contrast with large shapes. Textured areas contrast with smooth. Earthly elements contrast with heavenly; richness contrasts with poverty; youth contrasts with age. There are even ethnic contrasts in the people represented. Vertical movement contrasts with horizontal. The entire structure of the painting, which is superbly designed and painted, revolves around contrasts.

The abstract portrait by Jacques Villon is remarkably like Tiepolo's painting in design. To see this simi-larity, study both paintings with squinted eyes. Although Tiepolo's style is more representational, Villon's use of contrasting art elements is about the same. The contrast of light and dark is readily apparent. Note also the similar contrasts of size and shape in both works. Textures subtly contrast with the angular and curved shapes.

Because Villon was working solely with abstract shapes and ideas, his chief focus was on the design and arrangement of elements.

2–65 Jacques Villon, *Portrait of Mlle. Y.D.*, 1913. French. Oil on canvas, 51 1/4" x 35" (130 x 89 cm). Los Angeles County Museum of Art, gift of Anna Bing Arnold.

2–64 Giovanni Battista Tiepolo, *Adoration of the Magi*, 1753. Italian. Oil on canvas, 144" x 82 1/4" (366 x 209 cm). Alte Pinakothek, Munich.

Materials and Techniques

Because of his political and labor-union activities, Siqueiros frequently had no money. Most of the oil paintings he did in the 1930s turned black because he used cheap paints, sometimes paints he invented and mixed himself.

Siqueiros was exiled from Mexico in 1931 and went to Los Angeles, where he started a mural movement. He experimented with Duco (a nitrocellulose type of paint), Bakelite and synthetic resins. In 1934, he went to New York City and established a workshop for experimental use of Duco.

Duco is the trade name for industrial and household paint. Before the invention of acrylic paints, artists used Duco automobile lacquers.

Performing Arts Connection

The Principles of Design

After students investigate how balance, unity, emphasis, contrast, pattern, rhythm and movement work in a visual work, have them apply these principles to the performing arts. Ask in what type of dance they might see unity. In classical ballet, the corps de ballet (those who do not appear as soloists) often move together in a symmetrical pattern. What establishes the overall unity in a play? How is contrast developed in musical compositions? Have students apply the principles of design to their own artistic expressions and ask if they observed something new about their pieces that they missed before.

Chapter Review Answers

Due to space considerations and the extensive length of the answer to question 1 of Chapter Review, Interpretation (p. 55), it has been placed here.

Interpretation

1 For example, Brueghel's *Peasant Wedding* (fig.2–1) might be analyzed like this:

Content:

Why has the artist made this work? To remember a peasant wedding.
What is the artist trying to tell me about the subject? He is trying to show a typical scene in peasant life.
What is the major theme? A group of

2–67 David Alfaro Siqueiros, *Portrait of a Woman*, 1934. Mexican. Oil on masonite, 59 1/2" x 30 3/4" (151 x 78 cm). Los Angeles County Museum of Art, gift of Morton D. May.

Rhythm

Rhythm is established in a work when elements of the composition, such as curves, angles, or vertical or horizontal lines, are repeated. Repetitions can occur at either regular or irregular intervals. Rhythm and movement, like rhythm and pattern, are inseparable.

In Siqueiros' painting of the woman clasping her hands, there is strong movement up to and around her face. Her haunting eyes become the center of interest. Siqueiros repeats the gently curving shapes in regular intervals to create a strong rhythmic beat. He emphasizes the roundness of the folds so that they almost appear to be made of metal or concrete instead of cloth. Notice how the fingers and the hair repeat the rhythm established in the folds.

Pattern

Pattern can be produced by the repetition of motifs, colors, shapes or lines. Many cultures of the world rely heavily on pattern. Notice the repetition of the catlike animal motif, as well as the use of the repeated line and color in this Indonesian batik. What other elements related to pattern do you see?

2–66 *Indonesian batik*, 1980s.

Why? The eye moves through groups of overlapped figures, and along straight lines of benches and tables.
Is the composition vertical or horizontal? Horizontal
How is balance achieved? Groups of figures and space on the left balance with the larger figures on the right.
How is unity achieved? The repetition of colors and shapes and overlapping shapes
What shapes are repeated? Rounded shapes in the pots, hats, heads, pies and figures
Is pattern evident? Yes, in the way shapes are repeated.
Are figures in proportion? Yes
Technical properties:
What materials and tools were used to make the work? Brushes, oils, pigments, panel
Are the wood grains used effectively? Not applicable
What kinds of brushstrokes and pencil lines are used? Smooth and blended
Is it a finished work or a sketch for a later work? Finished
Are all parts treated with the same amount of detail? Almost
Why or why not? The people in the far back do not have as much detail as those in the foreground.
Are there contrasts in value? Yes
What types of marks did the artist use? He painted all over with smooth brushstrokes.
How is light indicated? The bodies are lightly shaded and rounded. There are shadows under the table.
Expressive properties:
What mood does the work convey? Happiness in a solemn occasion
Is the work timid or bold? Bold
Serious or comic? Serious
Does it establish a time of year? Yes, probably late fall or winter because it is indoors and all the people are dressed in warm clothes. The grain on the wall could indicate that it is near harvest.
How is loneliness expressed? It is not.
Does the work have social or religious significance? Social
Is it a literal statement or a symbolic subject? Literal
How does the artist feel about the subject? Affectionate
How do I feel about the subject and its treatment? I like it. It reminds me of contemporary gatherings of close friends and family.

ordinary people have gathered together to celebrate a special event, a peasant wedding.
What are the minor themes? There is plenty of food and drink, and small interactions between people occur within the larger group.
Sensory properties:
Which art element dominates the work? Shape
What kind of lines are used? Mostly round; some straight
How is form indicated? With rounded line and subtle shading
How is space felt? Shapes are overlapped and linear perspective is drawn in the furniture.
Is there texture? Yes

Are colors bright or dull? Mostly dull with bright spots of red
Which colors dominate? Warm golds and browns
Formal properties:
What is the center of interest? The area of the painting where the men are carrying the pies and the bride sits contrasted behind them
How does my eye move to it in the work? Lines in the benches and reaching hands lead my eye to this part of the composition.
How did the artist establish the center of interest? He made the center man larger, and made strong contrasts at that part of the composition.
Does the work have a sense of rhythm? Yes

Higher-Order Thinking Skills

Ask students to find other works that convey movement and analyze how the artist achieved the movement.

Lesson 2.3 Review Answers

1 The art principles are balance, unity, emphasis, contrast, pattern, movement, rhythm, variety and proportion. The art elements are line, shape, form, color, value, texture, space and light. Artists use art principles to arrange elements. The formal properties, or art principles, guide the artists in their use and organization of the elements.

2 Texture is the design element that refers to the quality of a surface, both tactile and visual. Texture is how the surface feels to the touch (or looks like it would feel.)

3 • Overlap objects indicating that one object is in front of the other

• Use aerial perspective—darker, brighter colors and sharper details are in the foreground while lighter, less intense colors and less distinct details are in the distance.

• Linear perspective—parallel lines run toward invisible vanishing points resulting in the appearance of smaller spaces and objects in the distance.

4 Hue is the name of the color, value is the dark or light quality of a color, and intensity is the brightness or saturation of a color.

5 Primary colors: red, yellow, blue
Secondary colors: green, violet, orange
Intermediate colors: red-violet, blue-violet, blue-green, yellow-green, red-orange, yellow-orange
Secondary colors are made by mixing two primary colors. Red and yellow make orange, red and blue make violet, and yellow and blue make green. The intermediate colors are made by mixing a primary color with one of its adjacent secondary colors. For example red and orange make red-orange or blue and green make blue-green.

6 The color of objects when they are lit by uniform white light

Movement

Movement can be conveyed in many ways. Movement in painting directs the eyes of the viewer to the center of interest. Sculpture can come alive with the infusion of movement.

The eye, moving across the surface, creates visual movement in a painting. Movement is directed by linkage or passage across like values or colors.

In sculpture, movement is directed along edges and contours to a focal area.

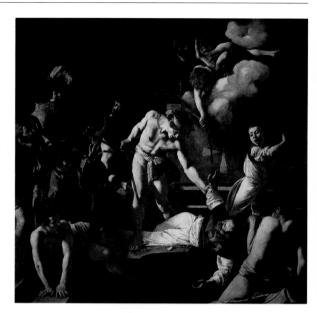

2–68 Caravaggio. *Martyrdom of St. Matthew,* 1599–1600. Approximately 10′ 9″ x 11′ 5″ (3.28 x 3.48 m). S. Luigi dei Francesi, Rome.

2–69 Niccolo dell'Arca. *The Lamentation*, detail of one of mourning figures, about 1485–1490. Italian. Terra-cotta, life-size. Santa Maria della Vita, Bologna.

Lesson 2.3 Review

1 List the art principles and elements. How are the principles of art related to the elements of design?
2 Define texture.
3 Describe three methods that artists use to show depth on a flat surface.
4 Define hue, value and intensity.
5 List the primary, secondary and intermediate colors. How are secondary and intermediate colors made?
6 What is local color?
7 What does high key and low key refer to in a painting?
8 Explain unity and emphasis in art.
9 What function does movement in a painting often play?

7 Paintings that have mostly light values are called high-keyed, and those of mostly dark values are referred to as low-keyed.

8 Unity combines the principles of design and the physical aspects of a piece of art to create a single harmonious work. The elements in an artwork together create a unified whole. Emphasis is how the artist develops the main theme in the piece. It indicates what the artist is trying to say. The artist may make one part or element of the art more important to emphasize it.

9 It directs the gaze of the viewer through the composition to the center of interest.

Chapter Review Answers

Review

1 Acrylics can adhere to almost any surface; they may be thinned with water and are therefore easy to clean up; and, they dry rapidly. They may also be applied in heavy impastos or in thin glazes.

2 In the subtractive sculptural process, material is cut away as in carving wood or marble. In the additive sculptural process, parts are put together as in welding steel or gluing together pieces of wood. Clay is often modeled, and bronze and plaster are often cast.

55

Primary Source

Artists Explain Why

Occasionally, artists tell us why they depict certain subjects or favor a particular medium. Their statements help us better understand their work and give us insight into the creative process.

Jacob Lawrence, a contemporary African-American artist who paints scenes about African-American life and history, explains why he has chosen this subject matter:

"My pictures express my life and experience. I paint the things I know about and the things I have experienced. The things I have experienced extend into my national, racial and class group. So I paint the American scene."

Louise Nevelson, a prominent woman sculptor of the twentieth century tells us why she worked so often with wood:

"I just automatically went to wood. I wanted a medium that was immediate. Wood was the thing that I could communicate with almost spontaneously and get what I was looking for...when I'm working with wood, it's very alive. The fact that it's wood means it has another life...."

Chapter Review

Review

1 What are some of the characteristics that have made acrylic paints popular with many contemporary painters? Which of the painting and drawing media have you used?

2 What is the difference between additive and subtractive sculpture processes? Name a medium that is often additive, one that is usually subtractive, one that is modeled, and one that is cast.

3 What medium is Duane Hanson's *Football Player*? How does Hanson create an exact likeness of his model?

4 How does Vermeer emphasize light in his *Officer and Laughing Girl*?

5 Describe the contrasts in Tiepolo's *Adoration of the Magi*.

Interpretation

1 Select one of the paintings in this chapter to analyze. Answer the questions about content and sensory, formal and technical properties on page 40.

2 Use hue, value and intensity to describe the colors in de Staël's *Landscape in Vancluse*.

3 Select a painting that uses mainly cool colors. Now choose another that features primarily warm hues.

4 Describe symmetrical and asymmetrical balance. Cite an example of art in this chapter with symmetrical balance and another with asymmetrical balance.

5 Take a stand. Is Mary Cassatt's *Sleeping Baby* a painting or a drawing? Explain your choice.

Other Tools for Learning
Electronic Research

CD-ROM drive: *Microsoft Art Gallery*
Videodisc player: *National Gallery of Art, Louvre Videodisc*

1 Browse through one of the gallery collections on either videodisc or CD-ROM. After viewing a number of works by one artist, analyze the style of this artist using the art elements and principles. In your review, tell what media this artist usually used.

2 Give one fact that you found interesting about pictorial composition and another fact about perspective. (Composition and Perspective Guided Tour)

---

3 *Football Player* is polyvinyl, polychromed in oil with accessories. Hanson makes molds of his models by applying plaster gauze strips directly to their bodies.

4 Vermeer paints natural light entering from the open window flooding the wall, the girl and the table. He also depicts various reflected lights and different intensities of shadow. The whole scene is a study of light.

5 There are contrasts of light and dark values, warm and cool colors, and straight and curved shapes and lines. Small areas of light and dark contrast with large shapes. Textured areas contrast with smooth areas, earthly elements with heavenly, richness with poverty, and youth with age. There are ethnic contrasts in the people.

Interpretation

1 Due to space considerations and the extensive length of the answer to this question, it has been placed on page 53.

2 Orange and yellow are the main hues. There is strong value contrast between the dark rectangles and the light sky. The orange is greater in intensity than the blue-gray shapes.

3 Possible choices for warm paintings in this chapter are Brueghel's *Peasant Wedding*, Rubens' *Judgment of Paris* and Holbein's *Edward VI as a Child*. Possible cool painting choices are Corot's *View of Venice* or El Greco's *View of Toledo*.

4 Symmetrical or formal balance is an almost even distribution of visual weight or activity on each side of a central axis. Asymmetrical or informal balance means that larger masses on

---

Primary-Source Connection

Ask several students to volunteer to write a brief statement about their personal preference for using a particular medium or for depicting a specific subject. Ask fellow students if they find that these statements help them better understand the artwork of the statement writers.

---

one side of the painting may be balanced by smaller, contrasting parts on the other side. Examples of asymmetrically balanced artworks are Brueghel's *Peasant Wedding*, Rubens' *Judgment of Paris* and Corot's *View of Venice*. Examples of symmetrically balanced artworks are Holbein's *Edward VI as a Child*, Warhol's *Campbell's Soup Can* and Oeben's *commode*.

5 Creating with oil pastels is halfway between drawing and painting. The final result usually looks like a colored drawing and is often called a painting.

Electronic Research

1 If the student chose to analyze Monet's work, for example:
Monet used much blue in his paintings. Line was not as important as color, texture and light. He used both symmetrical and asymmetrical balance in his paintings. Usually, he uses contrasting color to emphasize his center of interest.

2 Some possible facts might be:
• Piero della Francesca centered the composition of his *Baptism of Christ*. This painting has a sense of calm, partly because of the regular composition which can be evenly divided.
• Artists often organize their compositions using circular or triangular shapes. In the *Martyrdom of St. Stephen*, the artist arranged the figures in the shape of a cone.
• In the simplest form of linear perspective, the artist makes all the parallel lines that lead away from the viewer converge at a single point on the horizon line.
• In the technique known as foreshortening, the artist draws figures that seem to come out of the canvas at the viewer.
• Sometimes the perspective scheme in a painting is designed for the picture to be viewed from a certain angle, as in Holbein's *The French Ambassadors*.

Activity 1: A New Spin on Color

Activity Objectives
Students should be able to:

• Become thoroughly familiar with color vocabulary and relationships.

• Use their understanding of color to devise their own color wheel or chart (or produce an original painting demonstrating a full range of color).

Thinking Critically
Review "Think about it" questions with students to clear up any confusion about color relationships on the wheel. Define what a color diagram does and how artists use color concepts in their work. Make sure students can explain (and, when appropriate, point out on the chart):

• warm and cool colors

• primary, secondary and intermediate colors

• value, hues, tints, intensity

• complementary colors

Preparation Ideas
Show students alternative structures for color diagrams, for example, "primary" colors used when printing in ink are magenta, cyan, yellow and black.

Notes on Materials

• If using templates for color shapes, have students cut their own or provide pre-cut templates of different shapes and sizes (available in graphic design supply stores). Simple, inexpensive items can be easily traced, such as the caps from jars, square erasers and the like.

• Regarding tempera paints: as a minimum, provide the primary colors (red, yellow, blue) and allow students to mix the rest from scratch. Some tempera paints are too dark and dense for effective color mixing, so test the brand you have available. Decide whether or not you want students to include color tints and values in an expanded color wheel. If so, provide white and black paint to be used in limited quantities.

Activity 1

A New Spin on Color
Materials
11" x 14" white paper (or larger)
tempera, watercolor, prismacolor or acrylic paint
brushes
surface for mixing paint
containers of water

Take a look. Study the color wheel on page 46.

Think about it. What is the purpose of a color wheel? How is it useful in creating art? Can you think of other ways to display color relationships?

Do it. Do one or more of the following projects:
• Use tempera paints to make a color wheel that is different in design from the one on page 46. Do rough sketches of possible designs, using circles, squares or other shapes of color that you move around on a page.
• Create an original image that has twelve parts; for instance, a clown with twelve balloons. Using only primary colors, mix twelve different colors for the parts of your painting.
• Create an original image with color developed with prismacolor, using at least twelve mixed colors to complete your composition.

Check it. Are your colors clear and vibrant? Remember to rinse your brush thoroughly before switching from one color to another.

Helpful Hint: Practice mixing colors on a palette or blank sheet of paper before beginning your painting. How many shades of color can you create using just two colors at a time?

Activity 2

About Face
Materials
magazines
11" x 14" white paper
scissors
glue/tape
markers

Take a look. Review the following artwork in this chapter:
• Fig.2–9, Hans Holbein, *Edward VI as a Child*, 1538. German.
• Fig.2–10 Frances Benjamin Johnston, *Self-Portrait*, 1895. American. .
• Fig.2–19, Jean Auguste-Dominique Ingres, *Thomas Church*, 1816. French.
• Fig.2–67, David Alfaro Siqueiros, *Portrait of a Woman*, 1934. Mexican.

Think about it. Portraits have always been an important way to show how people appear to others. There are many reasons to make portraits; for instance, personal, illustration, advertising, identification, and business. What other portraits can you find in this book?

Do it.
• Clip from magazines five portraits done in each of the following ways: drawing, painting, sculpture and photography.
• You might choose portraits of people from one category for comparison, for example: sports figures, political figures, dancers or musicians. Collect both historical and contemporary examples.
• Arrange them on your paper and glue them into place. Make captions listing the probable purpose or use of each one. Tell whether you think each portrait is effective.

Check it. Do your portraits represent a range of different approaches? Are they effectively arranged on the page? Is it clear which caption goes with which image?

Helpful Hint: Consider colors, borders, type styles or other design elements you might use that would make your poster eye-catching when displayed on a wall.

Additional Activities
• Explore some of the tools and media that artists use. Find out the difference between things such as: a camel-hair and bristle brush; fine- and coarse-tooth papers; canvas and masonite; plaster and clay. In an oral presentation or video program, demonstrate such media and materials to the class.
• Nature photographers, landscape painters and landscape architects all work with nature. Write a paper describing how their work is similar and how it is different. Perhaps you can illustrate your project or present it as a videotaped documentary.
• The text identifies sixteen kinds of subject matter. Look through magazines and select advertisements, drawings or photographs that illustrate any twelve of these subjects. Label each of them and make a notebook, chart or slide/video presentation to share your findings.

Classroom Management
When using tempera paints, put together sets of just the primary colors (red, yellow and blue). Squeeze about a tablespoon of each color into plastic soufflé cups from restaurant suppliers (use lids to save leftover paint). Set paint cups on a tray (Styrofoam meat trays work well) with a brush and a plastic yogurt container of water. Another option is put the paint in egg cartons. Students can mix and test the paints on disposable pallets, white paper or scraps of posterboard.

Tips

• You could have a group-participation demonstration in color mixing, perhaps in different media. How does color mixing differ when you use paint versus pastels? Colored pencil versus layering cellophane? Encourage innovative use of bold, geometric shapes.

• Color wheels do not have to be wheels. Colors may be arranged in any shape to show the progression in a rainbow.

Evaluation

• Do the colors in color wheels move in a smooth progression from one hue to the next?

• Did students keep colors (particularly yellow) clean, so the colors are pure and intense?

• Have students compare their colors to professional color wheels.

Untitled, 1994.
Gouache, 18" x 24" (46 x 61 cm).

A Pool of Color, 1994.
Tempera paint, 8" x 8" (20 x 20 cm).

Pablo Román

Age 18
J. F. Dulles High School
Stafford, Texas
Activity 1, A New Spin on Color

This painting was my first, actually. I painted a little in junior high but never did get serious with it; I drew cartoons then.

This was a plain contour drawing of some plants I did, never supposing or planning on how I would paint it. I hadn't painted before, so I thought I would only mess it up. My teacher said it was a color assignment and that we were to experiment, using the complementary colors on the color wheel. That was a good place to start on a first painting.

Some, to look at me, might say I was slow; it's true, I did lag behind in my class. But I had a mind to work this one out with patience. I got into it. Sometimes I'd stay after school to do some extra work on it. My teacher was understanding with me, and she allowed me to go into overtime with the project. I love the patient work most of all when doing projects like these. One day I might come in and in an hour only do a few inches of detailed work. I like to take my time.

Pablo Román

Dorothea Exis

Age 15
J. F. Dulles High School
Stafford, Texas
Activity 1, A New Spin on Color

My art project is meant to express all of the basic colors of the color wheel in a creative new way. As with all my other pieces, I put a lot of care into its creation. Because of this, I value it as a carpenter would cherish a table he crafted himself.

I enjoy the ability to create something new, to take a mere thought and be able to put it on paper. This, in my opinion, is the greatest thing about art.

Dorothea Mae Exis

Teacher Spotlight
Joan Maresh
Art Instructor
John Foster Dulles High School

Teachers can do various activities when introducing color, which include: dressing in colorful outfits, showing slides of color harmonies found in nature, and showing great works of art from masters or students. You might also ask students to wear their favorite colors and then discuss why it is their favorite, followed by a discussion of the psychological effects and responses evoked with color use.

Presently my students are doing images inspired by M. C. Escher (geometric shapes or tessellations), or Bridget Riley (Op Art). They were able to choose their approach to using color harmonies with these images. Choice and decision-making are also important skills to be developed in the making of art.

produces a nice result, but is best used only in a well-ventilated area.

• Give each student an envelope in which to keep his/her clippings.

Classroom Management
Tables of four or five students would share a box of magazines. This project could easily become a cooperative project with small groups working together to produce a larger poster or mural.

Tips
• You might provide books on typefaces or calligraphy to encourage creative labeling.

• A computer could be used to produce the labels. Which font seems to go with each poster?

• If you have computer resources, students can make a color wheel using Aldus FreeHand or other graphic design software programs.

Evaluation
• Have students followed directions in finding five distinct examples of portraits?

• Was design, continuity, theme and color awareness employed in producing their poster?

Activity 2: About Face

Activity Objectives
Students should be able to:

• Notice the presence of portraits in their environment.

• Become more aware of the unique characteristics and features of the faces around them.

• Understand the purpose and value of portraits.

Thinking Critically
In reviewing portraits from this book and others, ask the students:

• What do you think is the purpose of this portrait?

• Do you think the person actually looked like this? Did the artist know the subject or did they draw from their imagination?

• Are portraits valued differently now that we can take photographs? Does photography guarantee a good likeness of a person?

Preparation Ideas
Find examples of different kinds of portraits to stimulate discussion. Help students think of places they might look for portraits they can cut out.

Notes on Materials

• For magazine collages, glue sticks are neat and easy to use, but not as permanent as Elmers glue, which can cause paper to wrinkle. Rubber cement

Part Two

Trends & Influences in the World of Art

Chapter 3 Organizer

Chapter 3 Opener: Common Denominators

Objectives

Understand that art from various cultures throughout history share certain characteristics and interests.

Explain how art demonstrates people's relationships with one another and society at large.

National Standards

4e Students analyze common characteristics of visual arts evident across time and among cultural/ethnic groups to formulate analyses, evaluations, and interpretation of meaning.

4c Students analyze relationships of works of art to one another in terms of history, aesthetics, and culture, justifying conclusions made in the analysis and using such conclusions to inform their own art making.

Teacher Edition References

Lesson 3.1 Commonalities

Lesson 3.1 62–65	Contextual Info 63, 64	Inquiry 64
Lesson 3.1 Review 65	HOTS 65	Performing Arts 64
	Cooperative 63	

Lesson 3.2 Emotion vs. Intellect

Lesson 3.2 66–69	Contextual Info 67, 68	HOTS 67, 69
Lesson 3.2 Review 69		

Lesson 3.3 Style

Lesson 3.3 70–72	Contextual Info 71, 72	HOTS 71, 73
Lesson 3.3 Review 72		
Primary-Source 73		
Chapter Review 73		

Classroom Connections

National Standards

Studio Activity 1
Over the Border

1b Students conceive and create works of visual art that demonstrate an understanding of how the communication of their ideas relates to the media, techniques, and processes they use

Studio Activity 2
Side by Side

1b Students conceive and create works of visual art that demonstrate an understanding of how the communication of their ideas relates to the media, techniques, and processes they use.
2d Students demonstrate the ability to compare two or more perspectives about the use of organizational principles and functions in artwork and to defend personal evaluations of these perspectives.

Choose either Activity I or 2
Choose either Activity I or 2
Choose either Activity I or 2

Other Resources

Books

Animals in Archaeology, ed. by
  A. Houghton Broderick. London:
  Barrie & Jenkens, 1972.
Dent, Anthony Austen. *The Horse:
  Through Fifty Centuries of Civiliza-
  tion.* London: Phaidon, 1974.
Grazca, Margaret Young, *The Bird in Art.*
  Minneapolis: Lerner Publications,
  1966.
Mackenzie, Donald A. *The Migration
  of Symbols and Their Relations
  to Beliefs and Customs.* New York:
  Alfred A. Knopf, 1926; reprint,
  Detroit: Gale Research, 1968.
Masks and the Art of Expression,
  ed. by John Mack. New York:
  Abrams, 1994.
Rawson, Jessica. *Animals in Art.* London:
  British Museum, 1977.
Shay, Rieger, *Gargoyles, Monsters,
  and Other Beasts.* New York: Lothrop,
  Lee & Shepard, 1972.
Zuelke, Ruth. *The Horse in Art.*
  Minneapolis: Lerner Publications,
  1965.

Ancillaries

Slides: Brancusi,
Blond Negress II,
12a, 22

Teacher Edition References

Context 60
Art 61
Quote 61

Ancillaries

Slides: African, *Tapestry with geometric pattern,* 11b, 23;
Pre-Columbian, *Dog,* 12b, 24; Pre-Columbian, El Castillo Pyramid Temple,
Chichen Itza, Mexico, 13a, 25
Overhead Transparencies: The Influence of Japan, 14

Overhead Transparencies: Emotion versus Intellect, 3

Slides: Rivera, *Flower Day,* 14a, 26; Harnett, *For Sunday's Dinner,* 13b, 27

Schedule	Materials
This activity can be completed in one day.	stiff paper (file folders, cardboard), 11" x 14" white paper, scissors, pencils, rulers, markers, colored pencils (optional), tempera paint, surface for mixing paint, containers of water, brushes
A day to draw. Two to three more days to paint.	8 1/2" x 11" white paper, tempera paints, brushes, surface for mixing paint, containers of water, objects to paint, such as bottles, fruit, baskets, flowers

Introduce

Art reflects both the commonalties and differences of cultures around the world. Although artists' individual approaches may differ, they often share similarities in subject matter and materials.

Lessons at a Glance

3.1 *Commonalties*
Virtually all cultures have produced art with geometric patterns, animal motifs and human figures. Each society's unique endeavors are often influenced and enriched by contact with other societies.

3.2 *Emotion vs. Intellect*
Throughout history, artists from virtually all societies have used either an emotional or an intellectual approach to their work. The swing from one tendency to another over time is evident both in the art of individuals and in entire movements.

3.3 *Style*
Individual artists, countries, regions and periods of time have specific art styles. Although some share certain elements, styles can also differ drastically from one another.

3 Common Denominators

I F YOU LOOK AT THE ART of various cultures, you soon realize that people everywhere share a sense of aesthetics. Everyone has a feel for arrangement and rhythm, color and pattern, pleasing shape and visual balance. Objects of art from around the world present a wide diversity of styles. Yet, despite this diversity, there are amazing similarities in subject matter and materials. Often, societies separated by thousands of miles have produced nearly identical art.

In a broad sense, art reveals the complexity and variety of the human personality. It demonstrates the numerous relationships individuals have with each other and with society at large. Art reflects people's responses to the environment and supernatural forces. While art forms vary stylistically from culture to culture, their general messages can be understood by all.

3–a The artist has reduced the human head to its most minimal form that blends with the carved shape of its base.
Constantin Brancusi, *Blond Negress II*, 1933. Bronze, 15 3/4" (40 cm) high, base: 71 1/4" (181 cm) high. The Museum of Modern Art, New York, The Philip L. Goodwin Collection.

3–b A few quick strokes of the brush outline the human figure in a skillful, animated manner.
Detail of lintel and pediment of a tomb, 50 BC–50 AD. Han Dynasty, Chinese. Earthenware, hollow tiles painted in ink and colors on a whitewashed background. Museum of Fine Arts, Boston, Denman Waldo Ross Collection.

Objectives

Students should be able to:

Understand that art from various cultures throughout history shares certain characteristics and interests.

Explain how art demonstrates people's relationships with one another and society at large.

Teach

Context

Ask students to detect what all the images in the chapter opener have in common. If they need guidance, ask them to consider the subject matter. Although each describes a figure, do they all portray real people? Divide the class into small groups and assign each the task of researching one of the works and then reporting to the rest of the class on the piece's meaning.

• What does the information indicate about the culture in which it was made?

• Are there parallels in the function or meaning among the images?

The world, harmoniously confused,
Where order in variety we see,
And where, tho' all things differ, all agree.
Alexander Pope

3–d Note that all the figures on pages 60 and 61 deal with the human form. The figures are from various parts of the world and span 2000 years. How are they similar? How are they different?
Sculpted figure, late 12th century, Toltec–Mayan culture. Chichen Itza, Mexico.

3–c Compare the many flourishing brushstrokes that this painter has used to create this portrait with the very few lines used in fig.3–b.
Francisco José de Goya, *Doña Isabel de Porcel*, 1806. Oil on canvas, 32" x 21 1/2" (81 x 55 cm). The National Gallery, London.

3–e Artists often use the human figure as the basis for creating religious or mythological figures.
Garuda, Cambodian, 10" (24.8 cm). The Detroit Institute of Arts, Gift of Albert Kahn.

Art

Direct students to identify the primary forms that Constantin Brancusi uses in his *Blond Negress II* (fig.3–a). Ask what other examples in the chapter opener use shape as a fundamental means of expression. Have students describe how the forms in each piece convey a sense of movement or of stasis. Are students surprised at how divergent the impact of the shapes are in each example?

Evaluate

Ask students to use reproductions from any part of the textbook except Chapter 3 to prove that people everywhere share a sense of aesthetics, even though styles may vary.

Reteach

Direct students to choose two figures from the chapter opener images and to write a letter from one to the other. They should have the two figures correspond about the interests their artists shared in terms of visual expression.

Quote

Have students use Pope's quote as a starting point for a general discussion about the commonalties and diversities that we find in world art. The images in this chapter also should be used to provide impetus to the discussion.

Lesson 3.1

Virtually all cultures have produced art with geometric patterns, animal motifs and human figures. Each society's unique endeavors are often influenced and enriched by contact with other societies.

Warm-up

Direct half the class to stand up in front of the room. Ask the remaining students to search for shared patterns, colors and images on the clothes and accessories of the standing group. Ask: "Despite the similarities, does everyone appear the same?" Explain that the students are like artwork from multiple cultures; they have commonalties and variations among them.

Objectives

Students should be able to:

Identify some of the commonalties that appear in art throughout the world.

Comprehend how cross-cultural influences enhance artistic statements.

Teach

Criticism: Instruct students to read about the common patterns in art throughout the world as described on pages 62 and 63. After they look at the reproductions on those pages, challenge students to locate additional examples throughout the book. Divide the class into small groups and have team members relate their findings to one other. Finally, direct students to use art resources from the library to find some of these same patterns in modern Western art.

3.1 Commonalities

Geometric Patterns

The use of geometric motifs is common to all societies. People the world over have had a fascination with regular, rhythmic, hard-edge patterns. For example, they have used spirals, checkerboards and wave patterns to ornament their artistic products. These designs are found in the pottery of such widely separated cultures as ancient Persia, the Indus Valley civilization, ancient Greece, Native American tribes, and the early Chinese dynasties.

Cloth woven by many cultures is often composed of colored threads woven into rhythmic patterns. From ancient civilizations of the Greeks and Romans and the Inca to the contemporary Iban tribes of Borneo, clothing has been woven with overall patterns or geometric border patterns.

3–1 Abstract geometric forms are created by Zen priests in Japanese temple grounds, where gravel is raked in patterns that aid in meditation.
Hojo Garden, Tofuku-Ji Temple, Kyoto, Japan

3–2 Animal forms are a particularly favorite motif for South American textiles.
Tabard, c. 1465. Chimú. Cotton with applied feathers, 38 1/2" x 26 3/4" (98 x 68 cm). The Textile Museum, Washington, DC.

Animal Designs

Humans have always been close to nature because they depend on plants and animals for their essential needs. Throughout history, craftspersons have used animals to represent the gods and to symbolize humans' relationship with nature. Animal designs express people's universal fascination with the animal world. Fish motifs decorate bowls of Native American, Chinese and Thai pottery. Fish are also found on the mosaic floors of early Christian basilicas and in the twentieth-century paintings of the German Expressionist Max Beckmann. In the culture of the United States, the eagle symbolizes nationalism and courage, and the bear represents strength. Wild animals, such as lions and birds, are found in the art of Persia, on ancient Greek vases, and in the weavings of North and South American tribes. Domesticated animals are used in the motifs adorning drinking vessels from Mycenae to China.

Evaluate

Ask students whether artists work in total isolation without any outside contact. How can the images in Lesson 3.1 support their answers?

• Can students cite times when they have benefited from adapting ideas from other sources?

• Did the process enrich their results? Why or why not?

Reteach

Ask students to examine figs.3–5 and 3–6 and read their captions to detect the mixing of cultures in these works. Next, ask them how they think the intermingling of influences came about. What role might war, trade, migration or colonization have played? Through additional research, students can extend their understanding of the information provided on page 64.

Human Figures

The human figure has been represented in art in just about every form imaginable. Peruvian potters created hollow clay water vessels in the form of bodies, while Michelangelo sculpted figures based on exacting anatomical precision.

Human activities of every kind have been depicted on the walls of ancient Egyptian, Indian and Mayan structures. People have carved monumental images of themselves, such as the huge likeness of the Roman Emperor Constantine or the United States presidents on Mount Rushmore. Conversely, minute images of people appear in the art of Tibetans and the miniature paintings of Islam.

Nude males and females have been used to portray the beauty of the human form or the creative power of God, as well as humanity's sensuous and sexual nature. Elaborately clothed figures depict wealth, social standing and cultural tastes. The facial portrait, which is the most highly individualized example of human design, has been executed in every conceivable material.

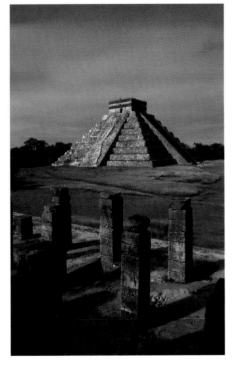

3–4 The word *pyramid* usually brings to mind the Egyptian civilization. Did you know that pyramids also were built by the Mayan culture?
Pyramid Temple, late 12th century, Toltec-Mayan culture. Chichen Itza, Mexico.

3–3 Native Americans created this vessel in the form of a human head.
Earthen Jar in Form of Human Face, painted. Fortune Mound, Poinsette County, Arkansas. 7 1/2" high (19.5 cm). Peabody Museum, Harvard University.

Architecture

Civilizations have expended tremendous energy to construct monumental architecture. The pyramids of the Egyptians, Mayans and the central Javanese were built to glorify both people and their gods. Castles of feudal Japan and Indian Hindu temples are other examples of monumental architecture.

Vertical structures have fascinated the imagination of architects throughout the world. Towers of stone have soared hundreds of feet into the sky. Ancient tribes erected enormous stones in locales as far apart as Laos and Sardinia. The ancient Egyptians carved tall needles of granite, called *obelisks,* upon which they carved historical records. The Chinese and Japanese constructed pagoda towers that function both as watch towers and Buddhist memorials. Soaring spires and towers of Gothic cathedrals testify to humankind's obsession with the vertical. Today, architects erect towers of steel and glass, perpetuating this ancient trend.

Contextual Information
Mayan Pyramids

During the first six centuries of the Christian era, the early Mayans established an empire in Mexico and Central America. They built great cities and stone-covered stepped pyramids with temples on top. Sculpture was placed along the central stairways and on the terraces of these pyramids. At some point in the seventh and eighth centuries, most of these buildings had fallen into ruins or had completely disappeared.

The Mayans wandered for a while and finally re-established themselves in the Yucatán. At Uxmal and Chichén Itzá, they again created magnificent stepped pyramids and stone buildings with complex carved decorations. They painted brightly colored frescos and intricate designs. Their new cities were composed of groups of pyramids and low buildings arranged around courts.

During the thirteenth century, the Toltec conquered the Maya and brought their own architectural ideas and religion that they combined with Mayan ideas, creating magnificently decorated buildings and large ball courts. The combined Mayan and Toltec influence lasted until the fifteenth century, when the Aztecs arrived. (For more about pre-Columbian art and architecture see Chapter 4, pages 130–135.)

Cooperative Learning

Identify buildings in your community that are of particular architectural interest. Assign a group of students to each building. The group should draw or photograph the building and research its design history as best as possible. Have the groups discuss what influences can be seen in the styles of the buildings. The groups can create a display of their work.

Contextual Information

Islamic Influence in Spain

The Alhambra in Granada, Spain, was built in the fourteenth century as a royal palace. It has large halls lavishly decorated in geometric interlacing designs in rich tiles. The courts have fountains connected by marble-lined channels leading to other important rooms and to the central fountain. (For additional information about The Alhambra see Chapter 7, pages 218–219.)

The influence of Islamic architecture was very important in Spain long after the Moslems were expelled from the country. Their use of tiles and lavish decorations came to the Western Hemisphere with the Spanish conquerors in the sixteenth century and still can be seen in Mexico and parts of South America.

Inquiry

For students to discover the areas where Moslem influence spread and how it affected the art of those areas, have them research the spread of Islam from the Mideast.

Cross-Cultural Influences

Some trends in art around the world have developed in total isolation. In many other instances, one culture has directly affected another. Cultural influence may have occurred through peaceful means, as in the Chinese and Buddhist influences upon Japanese culture. In some cases, one culture has actively sought out the aesthetic and technological expertise of another, as the Romans did when they copied Greek sculptors and techniques. The Inca had great respect for Paracas and Nazca cultures.

Ironically, military violence sometimes has been used to attain the aesthetic treasures of another society. For instance, the Japanese invaded Korea in the late sixteenth century and captured Korean potters. The Japanese transported them to the southern Japanese island of Kyushu for the crafting of tea ceremony items. The Mongols, who invaded China in the thirteenth century, did not have the artistic traditions of the Chinese. But instead of destroying Chinese art production, the Mongols encouraged Chinese potters to continue to produce the now famous blue and white ware. The Mongols then exported this ware to raise revenue throughout their far-flung empire.

Traders, missionaries, military expeditions, cultural missions and diplomatic envoys have all helped to introduce and spread the styles and motifs of one culture to another.

3–5 Osaka castle is a good example of cross-cultural influence. Chinese culture was first introduced into Japan in 552. Slowly, Chinese ideas of curved roofs and symmetrical arrangement became part of Japanese aesthetics. European traders in Japan in the 1500s taught the Japanese about fortifications built in medieval England.
Osaka Castle, late 16th century. Osaka, Japan.

3–6 The Mediterranean world changed dramatically after the rapid and militant spread of Islam in the seventh and eighth centuries. Such structures as the *Alhambra* palace in Spain reflect this radical shift in styles from a native to an imposed tradition.
The Alhambra, 13th–14th centuries. Granada, Spain.

Performing Arts Connection

Cross-Cultural Evolution—Blues Music

African Americans began performing what became known as the blues in the rural South during the late 1800s. This music had its immediate roots in the spirituals, field cries and work songs that African slaves had brought with them to the South in the seventeenth century. The music's true origins were in ancient African musical traditions that included listeners' clapping, dancing and calling out loud. Later, during the thirties and forties, African Americans brought the blues to the North, where its influence on rock 'n' roll began.

Adaptations of the European Fiddle in the Americas

Europeans introduced the violin and fiddle to the Micmac Indians of Nova Scotia, who quickly invented a new tradition by mixing Indian melodies and European harmonies. The Micmac became known as some of the best folk fiddlers of Canada for over 200 years. Much farther south, mixed-blood Cubans, or Mestizos, made three-stringed fiddles from cane stalks. In the southwestern United States, the Apache, after contact with the Spanish and Mexicans, constructed single-string fiddles from hollowed-out cactus stalks.

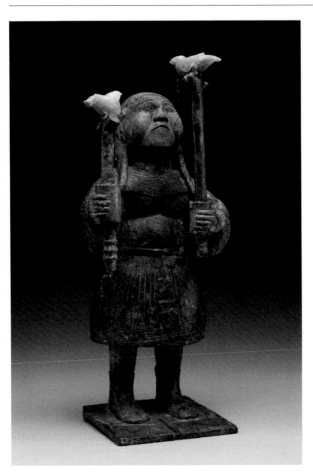

The influence of one culture upon another is usually subtle and reveals itself slowly as styles and techniques intertwine. However, aesthetic and cultural influences may also be introduced very quickly into a society. Almost overnight, styles and tastes change.

Technology has often been imported into a culture. The use of bronze suddenly appeared in China during the *Shang* dynasty. The Chinese may have gained knowledge of the lost-wax casting process from Central Asia, from the Indus Valley, or possibly from early advanced cultures in Northern Thailand.

Ideas for forms, shapes and subjects also have been borrowed. Picasso was greatly influenced by the sculpture of African tribal peoples. Gauguin went to Tahiti hoping to see the world through the eyes of its native peoples. The French Impressionists of the mid-1800s were inspired by the woodcuts of the Japanese, who depicted the world with a different use of perspective and color.

3–7 The Chinese quickly expanded the possibilities of lost-wax casting, which they learned from outsiders. The Chinese produced such excellent works as this Mongolian figure holding two birds of jade. *Mongolian Youth*, 3rd–4th centuries BC, late Zhou period, China. Bronze figure with jade birds, 11 1/2" (29 cm) high. Museum of Fine Arts, Boston, Maria Antoinette Evans Fund.

Lesson 3.1 Review

1 Name several examples of tall, vertical architectural structures built in different parts of the world.
2 How does the Osaka castle in Japan combine the architecture of different cultures?

3 What technology did the Chinese learn to use in order to produce art such as the Mongolian figure holding two birds of jade? Where might the Chinese have learned this process?
4 List three cultures whose art influenced European artists during the late nineteenth and early twentieth centuries.

Higher-Order Thinking Skills

1 Ask students what culture they would visit to inspire their art, as Gauguin was inspired by Tahiti. How would that culture influence their work?

2 Have students compare designs in the Alhambra with those in the *Lindisfarne Gospel Book* (fig.7–28) to find the similarities. (interlacing lines, intense color, outlines). What differences do they observe?

• Ask students what kind of cultural adaptations they can identify. For example, succotash, a colonial American food, was made from vegetables introduced to the settlers by the Native Americans, who had been raising the crops for generations.

Lesson 3.1 Review Answers

1 Obelisks in Egypt, pagoda towers in China and Japan, Gothic cathedral spires and towers in Europe, contemporary skyscrapers
2 The Osaka castle combines Chinese curved roofs and symmetrical arrangement with fortifications similar to those of medieval England.
3 The Chinese learned to use the lost-wax casting process from Central Asia, the Indus Valley or early advanced cultures in Northern Thailand.
4 African tribal peoples, Tahiti, Japan

Lesson 3.2

Throughout history, artists from virtually all societies have used either an emotional or an intellectual approach to their work. The swing from one tendency to another over time is evident both in the art of individuals and in entire movements.

Warm-up

Ask students to define the words *emotional* and *intellectual*. What characteristics belong to each? Have them categorize themselves as either mostly emotional or mostly intellectual. If they were to translate their personality into a work of art, how would their composition look? Explain that Lesson 3.2 investigates emotional and intellectual inclinations in art.

Objective

Students should be able to:

Decipher different cultures' intellectual and emotional approaches to art.

Teach

Aesthetics: Challenge students to write two poems, one each from the point of view of the sculptures in figs.3–8 and 3–9. As a warm-up, ask how their poems might communicate the work's distinct personality.

• Which figure appears cool and intellectual and which seems passionate and emotional?

• How do the pieces visually support their answers? Request that students recite both poems and have classmates guess which poem was written for which sculpture.

Aesthetics/Criticism: Ask students to examine the images on pages 68 and 69. Does it seem that the overall organization of the composition is more important in the emotional or in the intellectual grouping?

3.2 Emotion vs. Intellect

In all societies and at all times in history, two extremes of visual expression have been possible: a completely emotional approach and a completely intellectual approach. An emotional or romantic approach to art features an active and colorful interpretation of the subject, violent movement, distortion, bright and vivid colors, a strong interest in nature, and a personal approach to the subject. An emotional approach has little concern for design and reason.

An intellectual or classic approach features an emphasis on design and composition; a cool, analytical approach to the subject; the use of rules; and an emphasis on neat, clean arrangements and proper proportions. An intellectual approach has little room for feelings and emotions.

Compare the sculpture by Hugo Robus (fig.3–8) with the sculpture by Henry Moore (fig.3–9). Both artists used the human form as the subject, yet each treated it with a different emphasis. Although both works have similar rounded and abstract forms, the two artists had completely different purposes in mind when working. Henry Moore's sculpture demonstrates an intellectual approach to three-dimensional form. Hugo Robus' piece suggests a romantic approach.

Henry Moore abstracted the human figure until the remaining forms are merely suggestive of the human figure. This abstracting process is an intellectual one.

3–9 Henry Moore, *Reclining Nude*, 1939. Elm wood, 37" x 72" (94 x 183 cm). The Detroit Institute of Arts, Gift of Dexter M. Ferry, Jr. Trustee Corporation.

The finished product is cool and beautifully worked. There are no emotional overtones or hidden meanings. While the smooth curves may elicit a vague feeling of calm or sensuousness, they do not prompt a specific, overwhelming emotional response. The beauty of the form is appreciated chiefly for what it is, not for what it suggests.

The Hugo Robus sculpture is quite small, yet has a feeling of great size. It also has rounded forms and is somewhat abstracted. However, it has an emotional content that cannot be ignored. The title, *Despair*, adds an expressionist tag to the work. Viewers can feel the work's intended emotional content without knowing the title.

Artists generally choose the approach that best matches their interests. If artists work according to their natural feelings, they will express themselves in either one of the directions, although few can be found at either of the extremes. Most artists have had to try several approaches to visual expression before they feel comfortable working in their own natural way.

3–8 Hugo Robus, *Despair*, 1927. Bronze, 11 3/4" (30 cm) high. Whitney Museum of American Art, New York.

• In which does expressive content dominate?

• What other comparisons can students make about the use of color, shape, interest in naturalism, and distortion between the two approaches?

• Are students drawn more to one style than the other? Why? Challenge them to try to convince someone else to choose a work representing the approach that they like less. Did this exercise alter their own opinion of the approach?

Evaluate

Ask students to use images from the textbook to demonstrate how emotional and intellectual approaches to art have always existed throughout all societies. Have them examine recent art journals from the library to determine which tendency dominates the contemporary art scene.

Just as individual artists have moved between emotional and intellectual approaches, so, too, has the art of various periods. In Western art, changes between the extremes at each end of the scale seem to happen in cycles. Emotional content becomes important for a while. Then, after a time, design becomes more important than emotion. When the time is right, emotion again emerges as the dominant attitude in art and expression.

Two thousand years ago, changes in style from emotional to intellectual occurred slowly, often taking hundreds of years. Then, the time span was shortened, until, today, the two extremes tend to exist simultaneously.

Sometimes, there was a period of transition as one phase of a cycle came to an end and the other quality began to emerge. At other times, a sudden, almost physical, reaction against the waning style occurred and the succeeding style became dominant instantly.

The simplified chart illustrates the cyclical development and dominance of the intellectual or emotional approaches to art. Such a generalization is not totally accurate. However, it does help to explain why Romantic painters looked back to Baroque artists for ideas and why Neoclassic artists studied Greek and Roman art for aesthetic ideas akin to their own.

A brief look at some examples of art from different places and various periods will highlight how much the styles have in common. Emotional art is always expressionist. No matter when the work was painted and no matter what the subject, emotional art is usually a strong personal statement by an artist. Intellectual art always appears cool and carefully designed. Many of these examples may contain both qualities at the same time, but one dominates the other.

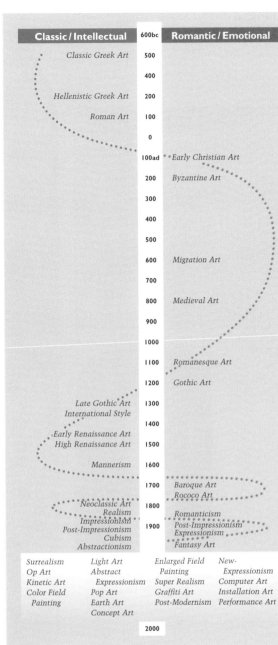

Classic / Intellectual	600bc	Romantic / Emotional
Classic Greek Art	500	
	400	
Hellenistic Greek Art	200	
Roman Art	100	
	0	
	100ad	Early Christian Art
	200	Byzantine Art
	300	
	400	
	500	
	600	Migration Art
	700	
	800	Medieval Art
	900	
	1000	
	1100	Romanesque Art
	1200	Gothic Art
Late Gothic Art International Style	1300	
	1400	
Early Renaissance Art High Renaissance Art	1500	
Mannerism	1600	
	1700	Baroque Art Rococo Art
Neoclassic Art Realism	1800	Romanticism
Impressionism Post-Impressionism	1900	Post-Impressionism Expressionism
Cubism		Fantasy Art
Abstractionism		

Surrealism	Light Art	Enlarged Field	New-
Op Art	Abstract	Painting	Expressionism
Kinetic Art	Expressionism	Super Realism	Computer Art
Color Field	Pop Art	Graffiti Art	Installation Art
Painting	Earth Art	Post-Modernism	Performance Art
	Concept Art		

2000

Contextual Information
Braque

Post-Impressionism was the first art movement to move totally away from Realism by deliberately distorting objects and figures. It was the beginning of several twentieth-century movements in which artists completely abandoned recognizable forms.

Works by Braque, Picasso, Dali, Klee and Miró depict another reality —one that is imaginary and conforms to new rules. Artists worked from logic rather than sentiment or emotion, ignoring all previous styles and inventing their own.

Braque's method of working on as many as twenty pictures at a time continued to the end of his career. André Malraux, a French writer, politician and minister of culture, visited Braque shortly before he died. Malraux cited Cézanne's remark that if he knew that every painting he created was to be destroyed and none was ever to hang in the Louvre, he would stop painting. Braque replied: "If I were certain that all my paintings would be burned, I think I'd go right on painting—yes I'd go right on painting."

Classical Intellectual

3–10 Victor Vasarely, *Edetta*, 1984. Acrylic on canvas, 39 3/4" x 39 3/4" (101 x 101 cm). Courtesy Circle Fine Arts Corporation, Chicago.

3–11 Raphael Sanzio, *The Marriage of the Virgin*, 1504. Panel, 67" x 46" (170 x 117 cm). Pinacoteca di Brera, Milan.

3–12 Jean Auguste Dominique Ingres, *Mademoiselle Caroline Riviere*. Oil on canvas, 39 1/4" x 27 1/2" (100 x 70 cm). The Louvre, Paris.

3–13 Georges Braque, *Violin and Palette*, 1909–10. Oil on canvas, 36 1/4" x 17" (92 x 43 cm). Solomon R. Guggenheim Museum, New York.

Romantic Emotional Expressionist

3–14 Käthe Kollwitz, *Bread!* 1924. Lithograph. Courtesy Galerie St. Etienne, New York.

3–15 Willem de Kooning, *Woman I*, 1950–52. 6'4" x 4'10" (193 x 147 cm). Collection, The Museum of Modern Art, New York.

3–16 El Greco, *View of Toledo*, 1600–1610. Oil on canvas, 42 1/2" x 45" (121 x 108 cm). The Metropolitan Museum of Art, New York, bequest of Mrs. H. O. Havemeyer.

3–17 Eugene Delacroix, *Arabs Skirmishing in the Mountains*, 1863. Oil on canvas, 36 3/8" x 29 1/2" (92 x 75 cm). The National Gallery of Art, Washington, DC (Chester Dale Fund).

Lesson 3.2 Review

1 What are some features usually found in emotional art and some that are in intellectual art?

2 Why do you think the transition from one art style to another has become so rapid in recent years?

3 Study the pictures on pages 68 and 69. How are the classical/ intellectual examples alike and how are the Romantic examples alike?

Lesson 3.2 Review Answers

1 Emotional art features an active and colorful interpretation of the subject, violent movement, distortion, bright and vivid colors, a strong interest in nature and a personal approach to the subject. Intellectual art features an emphasis on design and composition, a cool, analytical approach to the subject, the use of rules and an emphasis on neat, clean arrangements and proper proportions.

2 Accelerated transitions in art are probably due to easier travel and better communications. Today—with television, books, magazines, traveling art shows and computers—artists can see what other artists around the world are creating. With this rapid exchange of ideas, art and architectural styles change quickly.

3 Classical/intellectual art examples emphasize design and composition. There is a cool, analytical approach to the subject. The artists use rules of design and composition to produce neat, clean arrangements with proper proportions. Emotional/Romantic art examples are active with great movement and bright, vivid colors. The subjects are distorted by each artist's personal approach to the subject.

Lesson 3.3

Individual artists, countries, regions and periods of time have specific art styles. Although some share certain elements, styles can also differ drastically from one another.

Warm-up

Ask students what it means to say that someone "has style." Does this refer to the way a person looks, dresses, speaks, thinks or presents him- or herself? Direct students to select someone who they believe has style, and explain what it is and why they feel this way. How do the person's origins, way of life, and when, where and how they live affect their style? After, have the class compare notes. What similarities and differences can they find among their examples? Tell the class that Lesson 3.3 explores how style applies to individual artists, entire movements and also periods of time.

Objectives

Students should be able to:

Recognize that there are individual, regional, national, technical and historic styles.

Describe commonalties and differences among artistic styles that have existed throughout history and in various cultures.

Teach

Art History: Ask students to examine El Greco's painting (fig.3–18) and Jacob van Ruisdael's canvas (fig.3–19). Regardless of the subject matter, how can they define the variations in the two painting styles? Have students discuss, without looking at the captions, whether they think the artists worked in the same time period and in proximity to one another?

• Are students surprised to learn that the pieces were made only sixty years apart and that both artists lived in Western Europe?

• What does this indicate about the significance of style for both individual artists and regions or nationalities?

3.3 Style

In the history of art, there are many styles. Some are obvious while others are subtle. Although art communicates in a universal language, the styles that characterize individuals, countries, regions and periods may vary drastically. Each develops a style best suited to its needs.

Individual Style

Artists throughout history, if they have developed in an environment free of rules and directives, have worked out their own personal styles, which are as individual as their handwriting. Many of the artists illustrated in this book can be identified by characteristic features of their work. Individual style is the result of many influences. An artist's teachers, friends, environment and exposure to art of the past can all affect the artist. These influences can cause changes in methods, subject matter and approaches to art. Often, the style of an artist changes during a lifetime of such influences and during periods of experimentation. Rembrandt van Rijn, Joseph Mallord William Turner, Jean-Baptiste-Camille Corot and Pablo Picasso are some examples of artists with changing individual styles. An awareness of style and stylistic differences will help you analyze and evaluate art.

3–18 The work of El Greco is immediately recognizable because of his distinctive style— a concentration on Biblical subject matter; an elongated distortion of the figures; writhing movement; and powerful value contrasts that create flamelike lights and darks. El Greco, *Christ and the Moneychangers from the Temple*, 1600. Spanish. Oil on canvas, 41 3/4" x 51 1/4" (106 x 130 cm). The National Gallery, London.

Art History: Have students investigate what helps mold national or regional styles, as described on page 72. Ask what forms a country's culture. For instance, what makes something Korean, Greek, Canadian or Australian?

• How large a part do location, language, food, dress, social customs, architecture and artistic expression play in the process?

• What generalizations might students be able to draw about the countries of the artists in Lesson 3.3?

• How can the visual style of the artists communicate something about the societies in which they lived?

• Can students articulate how the style of objects from their own heritage reflects something about their origins?

Evaluate

Ask students whether only individual artists have a discernible style. How can the images in Lesson 3.3 demonstrate additional types of style?

Ask students if their peers in Asia, Africa or the Middle East listen to the same music, wear the same fashions or eat the same kinds of food as they do. How do the differences illustrate distinct national styles, despite the fact that they are peers living at the present time?

3–19 Jacob van Ruisdael's painting *Wheatfields* is characteristic of both the artist and the Baroque period in the Netherlands. Many Baroque artists painted such nature scenes with turbulent skies, small human figures and carefully controlled light. Jacob van Ruisdael, *Wheatfields*, about 1660. Dutch. Oil on canvas, 39" x 51" (100 x 130 cm). The Metropolitan Museum of Art, New York, bequest of Benjamin Altman.

Period Style

Art of certain periods is often alike. Egyptian art, for example, was determined by a rigid set of conventions. Images remained strikingly similar for 2500 years. While some styles lasted for centuries, others endured for only decades or less. Within one period, a dominant style may undergo subtle changes. The Italian Renaissance, for example, can be broken up into Early, High and Mannerist periods. Despite differences, these individual styles are sufficiently alike to be grouped together for study.

3–20 In the view of Vienna, the domed structure in the foreground and the towering cathedral represent two period styles. The dome and other architectural details set that building in the Baroque period. The forms, details, spires and vertical emphasis of the cathedral place it in the Gothic period. View of downtown Vienna, Austria. *St. Peter's Church* in the foreground, *St. Stephen's Cathedral* in the background.

Higher-Order Thinking Skills

Ask students what the characteristics are of the styles of art that they prefer. Ask them about subjects, design, and emotional or intellectual influences.

Contextual Information

Seventeenth Century Holland

With money from their prosperous trade, the Dutch middle class bought furniture and works of art for their homes. Realistic works were the most popular and included scenes of home interiors, landscapes, still lifes and portraits. Most of the Dutch paintings of the seventeeth century are small, but large ones were commissioned by civic associations and corporations. The middle class felt no need of the Baroque decorativeness and grand style of seventeenth-century France, Italy and Spain. Instead, they preferred the sensitive, quiet scenes of their northern European environment.

In the beginning of the seventeenth century, there was an art-buying boom. Artists in the early part of the century had had no trouble selling their work. However, a glut of paintings then appeared. With no guilds to regulate the production and no courts or state governments to regulate the market, fierce competition developed. Rembrandt, Vermeer and van Ruisdael all had financial troubles. Prices for paintings fell very low. In better times, a portrait sold for 60 guilders when the price of an ox was 90. Later, some portraits sold for 9 guilders. Rembrandt, at the height of his success, sold *The Night Watch* for 1600 guilders. Not long after, people nearly stopped commissioning him for large paintings. At the end of the century, art sold very cheaply, and artists began leaving the country to work in Flanders, France and England.

Reteach

Instruct students to analyze their own personal style. What makes them unique?

• How do they manifest their flair through dress, language, behavior, and intellectual or recreational pursuits?

• What influences them—peers, fashion, the media, public or private role models? In comparison, what impacts artists' visual styles? How are these influences similar to and different from those that affect students?

Ask the class if styles are forever the same. Have students always dressed the way they do now? Can artists also change styles? Direct students to examine numerous works by Picasso (see figs.13–33, 14–24, 14–25, 14–26, 14–27).

• How does this investigation impact their answers? Do they think artists should spend their entire careers perfecting a single approach or should they explore multiple alternatives?

• What influences their decision?

• Do they themselves like only one type of music or nationality of food?

• How can they argue that variations make life more stimulating?

Contextual Information
Rivera

Rivera was concerned that people would not understand his art. He felt that an artist's training was the first necessity, but that the artist must use forms that are comprehensible, simple, and interesting enough to engage people's attention at first glance.

Mexican artists knew that Mayan artists had been superb draftsmen who filled spaces with fantastic designs and symbols. In order to convey information to the people about their priests' teachings, these artists' works had to be clear and persuasive. The same theory would hold for Mexican muralists 300 years later. These muralists, including Rivera, felt that their mission was to call attention to the oppression of the people and their longing for relief from poverty, backbreaking work and poor living conditions.

3–21 The style of Diego Rivera is rooted in ancient Mexican styles, but has a modern feeling. The forms are rounded, monumental and simplified. Rivera's style became a Mexican national style, the foundation for several generations of Mexican and Mexican-American artists who still work in a similar manner.
Diego Rivera, *Flower Day*, 1925. Mexican. Oil on canvas, 57 3/4" x 47 1/2" (147 x 121 cm). Los Angeles County Museum of Art.

National Style and Regional Style

Sometimes a country has a national style. National style is not part of any period style, but evolves gradually over a long time. Probably arising from older forms of native culture, it often has ethnic overtones and may be part of a country's political movement.

Regional styles often evolve from the influence of a single, strong local artist or a group of people working the same locale and in similar styles and techniques.

3–22 Raphaelle Peale, an early-nineteenth-century American, painted a towel with such realism that people were tempted to pluck it from the canvas in order to see the nude figure behind it.
Raphaelle Peale, *Venus Rising from the Sea—A Deception (After the Bath)*. Oil on canvas, 29" x 24" (74 x 61 cm). The Nelson-Atkins Museum of Art, Kansas City, Missouri.

Technique Style

A certain type of painting may emerge in several periods. It may be based on a particular technique or presentation of subject matter. One of these technique styles is *trompe l'oeil*—the French term for "fool the eye." An object painted in this style is so lifelike that viewers think it is real.

There have been many trompe l'oeil painters throughout the centuries. In the late 1970s and early 1980s, a style called Super-Realism carried on this tradition. Although such technique styles appear in many periods, they are not the dominant style of the period.

Lesson 3.3 Review

1 List four major categories of styles in art.
2 What are some of the things that can influence an artist's style?

3 Which artist's painting style became a national Mexican style?
4 Define trompe l'oeil. Describe an example of trompe l'oeil.

Lesson 3.3 Review Answers

1 Individual, period, national/regional, technical
2 Teachers, friends, environment, exposure to art of the past
3 Diego Rivera
4 *Trompe l'oeil* is French for *fool the eye*. It is a type of painting that is so realistic that it looks like the actual subject rather than a painting.

Chapter Review Answers

Review

1 Possible examples of art using:
geometric patterns—
Hojo Garden (fig.3–1);
Western Apache *storage jar* (fig.1–5);
Robert Swain's *Untitled* (fig.1–10);
Picasso's *The Studio*, (fig.2–17);
animals—
ceremonial cup (fig.1–1);
Glass bottle shaped like a fish (fig.2–42);
El Greco's *St. Martin and the Beggar* (fig.2–47);
humans—Rivera's *Flower Day* (fig.3–21);
El Greco's *Christ and the Moneychangers from the Temple* (fig. 3–18);

Moore's *Reclining Nude* (fig.3–9);
Robus' *Despair* (fig. 3–8);
Raphael's *The Marriage of the Virgin* (fig. 3–11);
Brueghel's *Peasant Wedding* (fig.2–1);
Mongolian Youth (fig.3–7).

2 Roman artists copied Greek sculptors and techniques. Japanese artists captured Korean potters in the late sixteenth century to produce tea ceremony items. In the thirteenth century, Mongols invaded China and encouraged Chinese potters to continue producing blue and white ware which the Mongols sold throughout their empire. Nineteenth-century French Impressionists were inspired by Japanese woodcuts, and Picasso was influenced by the sculpture of African tribal peoples.

Primary Source

David and Kollwitz— A Contrast in Approach

Artists take a variety of approaches to art. In this chapter, two approaches, intellectual and emotional, are described and illustrated. Some artists have verbalized their thoughts on this matter. Jacques Louis David, an artist of the Classic tradition had this to say in 1796:

Jacques-Louis David, *Oath of the Horatii*, detail (fig.12–1).

"I want to work in a pure Greek style. I feed my eyes on antique statues, I even have the intention of imitating some of them. The Greeks had no scruples about imitating a composition, a gesture, a type that had already been accepted and used. They put all their art on perfecting an idea that had already been conceived."

Käthe Kollwitz, a twentieth-century artist who lived during the first half of the century, witnessed a time when Europe was torn by war and strife. Her art and words reflected the emotion she felt:

"...when I became acquainted with the difficulties and tragedies underlying proletarian life, when I met the women who came to my husband for help and so, incidentally, came to me, I was gripped by the full force of the proletarian's fate. Unsolved problems such as prostitution and unemployment grieved and tormented me, and contributed to my feeling that I must keep on with my studies of the lower classes. And portraying them again and again opened a safety valve for me; it made life bearable."

Käthe Kollwitz, *Bread!*, detail (fig.3–14).

Chapter Review

Review

1 Look through the first three chapters of this book. Select three works of art that use geometric patterns, three that portray animals, and three with human figures.

2 Describe an example of one culture influencing the art of another.

3 Why are human figures often shown nude in art? What messages can clothes convey about a figure?

Interpret

1 Compare the difference in emotional levels in Moore's *Reclining Nude* with that in Robus' *Despair*.

2 Compare El Greco's *St. Martin and the Beggar*

(fig.2–47) and *Christ Driving the Money Changers from the Temple*. What clues indicate that these pictures were painted by the same artist?

Other Tools for Learning

Electronic Research

CD-ROM drive: *Microsoft Art Gallery*

1 Look at four or five works of art by one artist. What are some of the characteristics that are shared by most of these works and indicate the artist's personal style?

2 Watch the Making Paintings Guided Tour. Describe the technique of one of the artists.

Primary-Source Connection

Have students examine the work of David (figs.12–1, 12–2) and Kollwitz (figs.14–11, 14–12). Ask them to explain why these artists' works would be considered either intellectual or emotional.

Higher-Order Thinking Skills

Have students look at last year's copies of *Artnews* and *Art in America* and compare art created in different countries. Ask if they can you tell, by looking at the art object, what country the artist is from. Ask the class if it is possible that artists' styles will tend to look even more alike in this day of transcontinental travel and the instantaneous transmission of information via computers and satellites. Is this a good thing?

---

3 Nudes have been used to portray the beauty of the human form, God's creative power, and sensuous or sexual aspects of humanity. Clothing can indicate a figure's wealth, social standing and cultural tastes.

Interpret

1 Moore's sculpture is intellectual in comparison to Robus' more emotional *Despair*. Moore's figure is cool and beautifully worked without emotional overtones. The title of Robus' work, *Despair*, adds an expressionistic tag to this sculpture. Even without the title, viewers can feel Robus' intended emotional content.

2 The figures in both are distorted and elongated. Writhing movement, powerful value contrasts that create flame-like lights and darks, and a concentration on Biblical subjects indicate that El Greco painted both scenes.

Electronic Research

1 Students might notice that one artist has painted a similar subject several times, or usually uses the same colors or type of lines, or has a particular type of brushstroke or texture.

2 The artists and pictures described in this tour are:
The Magdalen Reading by Rogier van der Weyden
The Martyrdom of St. Sebastian by Pollaiuolo

The Entombment by Michelangelo
The Cult of Cybele by Mantegna
Female Figure and St. Luke by Massys
The Adoration of the Golden Calf by Poussin
The Fighting Temeraire by Turner
The Gare St. Lazare by Monet
Bathers at Asnieres by Seurat
Students might describe the pointillism of Seurat or Monet's feathery brush-strokes or the compositional arrangement techniques of Pollaiuolo.

Activity 1: Over the Border

Activity Objectives
Students should be able to:

• Become aware of the use of geometric patterns, borders and repeated images throughout human history.

• Design an original geometric pattern or border based on their observations.

• Practice the use of templates and/or repetition to create successful patterns.

Thinking Critically
Ask students to search out examples of geometric borders and patterns in their immediate environment, in their clothing, books, posters.

• What geometric shapes are repeated in the patterns they find?

• Where else might they find patterns and borders outside of the classroom?

• What elements make a successful border?

• What are some similarities and differences between ancient and contemporary patterns?

• What shapes and patterns are characteristic of a particular culture?

Preparation Ideas

• Find (or have students find) samples of geometric borders and patterns as well as examples of their use in historical art objects. Some libraries have art posters that can be used as an additional resource for images.

• Bring in a book of Art Deco borders, and encourage students to refer to it for color and shape combination ideas.

Notes on Materials

• For a simpler, less messy activity, use markers and colored pencils instead of tempera paint.

Activity 1

Over the Border

Materials
stiff paper (file folders, cardboard)
11" x 14" white paper
scissors
pencils, rulers
markers
colored pencils (optional)
tempera paint
surface for mixing paint
containers of water
brushes

Take a look. Find examples in this book of paintings, blankets or pottery that use geometric patterns or borders.

Think about it. A border is a design or decorative strip around the edge or rim of something—a page, fabric, or a painting. Shapes are often repeated over and over. Notice how some patterns are intricate, some simple; some balanced, others chaotic. Where else in your environment can you find borders and geometric designs?

Do it. Create a border that will frame something (a photograph, a poem) or fill your page with a geometric design.
• Decide what shapes you will use in your border, such as crosses, circles, squares. You might want to select just two or three shapes to work with at different sizes.
• Will you be imitating the style of a particular culture? If so, identify characteristic elements or colors to use in your design.
• One approach would be to use a fairly stiff paper to draw and cut out your shapes. Then place them on your drawing paper and trace around them with a pencil, using some shapes repeatedly.

• When your pattern is complete, color it in with tempera paint, markers or pencils. You may want to select and repeat limited colors to enhance the repetition of the pattern.

Check it. Write down at least five words that you feel describe your border (ornate, colorful, energetic, etc.). Ask others to review your work and also write down five words. Compare and discuss the results. Are your perceptions similar?

Helpful Hint: You might want to imagine a pattern that would be effective made into cloth. What kinds of colors and patterns would you like to wear?

Activity 2

Side by Side

Materials
8 1/2" x 11" white paper
tempera paints
brushes
surface for mixing paint
containers of water
objects to paint, such as bottles, fruit, baskets, flowers

Take a look. Study the styles on pages 68 and 69 before you begin your project.

Think about it. Consider the categories called "classic/intellectual" versus "romantic/emotional." What qualities are distinctive in each? Do the paintings on pages 68 and 69 seem to strictly belong to each category or do you see "emotional" qualities in some of the "intellectual" paintings and vice versa? Why is it useful to classify paintings in this way?

Do it. Use tempera paint to create two small, simple still lifes of the same arrangement of three or four items.

• Arrange objects of varying size, color, shape and texture for the still life. If your teacher has arranged something for you, look at it from different perspectives to find an angle that interests you.
• Make one painting in a precise, carefully designed style, then set it aside.
• Now paint the same objects, same angle, same size, but in an expressionistic style.

Check it. Is it obvious to you and to others which painting is classical/intellectual and which is romantic/expressionistic? What other words might describe your work?

Helpful Hint: Instead of painting everything you see in the still life arrangement, you might try mentally "zooming in" on one interesting part and filling your page with it.

Additional Activities

• Find illustrations in magazines that demonstrate the influence of other cultures on American architecture. For example, trace the development of a style from Spain to Mexico to the United States.
• Study the illustrations on pages 68 and 69. Write a short paper discussing the general differences between classic and romantic styles. Then write a paragraph explaining which style you like better, and why.

Classroom Management
Before students begin their drawings, have them look for examples of borders, geometric designs and repeated images throughout the text. Talk with them about the different ethnic styles, colors and ideas they find. List these figures on the board and have students think of words that describe distinctive qualities of each pattern. How are they similar or different? Some possible images to discuss from early chapters are:

• Fig.1–2, Navajo blanket

• Fig.1–5, Apache storage jar

• Fig.2–41, Navajo rug

• Fig.3–1, Japanese temple grounds

• Fig.3–2, South American textile

• Fig.4–31, Chinese jar

• Fig.4–66, carved wall panels

Tips

• As you can see by the student work shown, students need not confine themselves to geometric patterns and shapes in the construction of their border. It can be a good place to start, however, in introducing a new concept. Discuss with students how a simple border can be just as effective as a more complex one.

• Students could use stencils to cut repeated shapes out of colored paper and create a cut-and-paste border as opposed to drawing one.

Seby Ravindran

Age 16
Lake Highlands High School
Dallas, Texas
Activity 1, Over the Border

My picture is of four women gazing at a beautiful sunset. I used map pencils for the women and pastels for the background. I specially liked working with the pastels because you could combine two different colors with ease. The map pencils were harder to work with because they had to be constantly sharpened and it was harder to blend two colors.

My original idea for the background was a blue sky but instead I opted to do a sunset. Growing up in India I witnessed a lot of sunsets and I was always amazed at how sunsets conveyed a beautiful and tranquil feeling as well as a beautiful moment. I chose to use pastels for my background because I wanted a smooth transition from one color to the other in the sunset. The real challenge came when I designed a border that incorporated the images in the artwork.

The result was a picture that represents the highlight of the day for four hardworking women. At the end of a long, tiring day, they take a few seconds to admire the beauty of their surroundings. I feel this is a beautiful reminder to everyone of how short but wonderful life is and to make the most of it while you can.

Seby Ravindran

Sunset, 1994. Map pencils and pastels, 18" x 24" (45.7 cm x 61 cm).

The Sound of Music, 1994. Prismacolor, 19 1/2" x 16" (49.5 x 40.6 cm).

Beth Featherstone

Age 16
Lake Highlands High School
Dallas, Texas

This piece expresses my love for the art of music and the art of drawing. When I was developing my picture, I thought of all the different ways music can flow. It can flow smooth, choppy, loud or soft. I showed this the best way I knew how in the strokes of my pencil. I prefer smooth, mellow, soothing music that's pleasing to the ears, much like I prefer smooth, mellow soothing pictures with colors pleasing to the eye.

I mostly enjoy working with colors, shading, and free strokes. It's always a relief when you come to that final stroke that jumps out at you, and you realize that you're finished!

Beth Featherstone

Teacher Spotlight
Marsha McRae Hogue
Art Department Chair
Lake Highlands High School

There were several exciting discoveries in doing the "Over the Border" activity. Earlier in the school year, my class had done an Environmental Studies drawing in a variety of media. We now experimented with some of these drawings to see if we could extend the concept by adding a border. Students were instructed to select imagery from their drawing and make a design using the same media to compliment and extend their drawing concept without sacrificing the integrity of the original concept. The students were thrilled to discover that they didn't have to come up with a new idea. They could take a piece they really liked, alter it without changing what they liked about the piece and still have it meet the "border" activity requirements. This "recycle" activity will encourage them in the future to experiment with other forms of altering and creating images on multisurfaces.

Activity 2:
Side by Side

Activity Objectives
Students should be able to:

- Understand the essential differences between classic/intellectual versus romantic/emotional styles.

- Understand why categories are useful in describing artwork.

- See that most artwork has some elements of both, but usually one is dominant.

- Accurately access these qualities in artwork.

- Produce two works of art, each exemplifying one of the two styles.

Thinking Critically
Review with students the questions in "Think about it." Ask them which style they prefer and why and/or when they might want to use one style instead of the other.

Preparation Ideas

- Gather materials for a still life or ask students to bring objects to class. Arrange a central display for everyone to paint. Keep in mind that students will probably need to work with it for more than one class and will protest if it has changed between sessions. You may want to put the arrangement on a special table that can be removed and brought back as needed.

Notes on Materials

- Objects for still life paintings should vary in size, texture, color and shape.

Tips

- As a variation you might consider having two distinctly different still lifes with class selection of objects that represent one style or the other.

Evaluation

- Has the student produced two artworks that demonstrate their understanding of the differences between classic versus romantic styles?

- Are the colors mixed well and used appropriately to emphasize each style?

1 · 1 · 1

Chapter 4 Organizer

Chapter 4 Opener: Art of the Non-Western World

Objectives

National Standards

Appreciate the diversity of artistic expressions from cultures around the globe.

4a Students differentiate among a variety of historical and cultural contexts in terms of characteristics and purposes of works of art.

Identify similarities and differences in terms of function, materials and design of the artworks from various non-Western societies.

4e Students analyze common characteristics of visual arts evident across time and among cultural/ethnic groups to formulate analyses, evaluations, and interpretation of meaning.

Teacher Edition References

Lesson 4.1 A Multitude of Perspectives

Map: World Religions 79	HOTS 79	
Remainder of Lesson 4.1 80–85 Lesson 4.1 Review 85	Contextual Info 80, 82, 84 HOTS 81, 83, 85	Materials and Techniques 80, 84

Lesson 4.2 India

Map: India 86 *Timeline:* India 86	Contextual Info 87	HOTS 87
Remainder of Lesson 4.2 88–91 Lesson 4.2 Review 91	Contextual Info 88, 90	HOTS 89, 91

Lesson 4.3 China

Map: China 93	HOTS 93	
Remainder of Lesson 4.3 94–99 Lesson 4.3 Review 9	Contextual Info 94, 96, 98 HOTS 95, 97, 99	Interdisciplinary 94, 96, 98 Materials and Techniques 97

Lesson 4.4 Japan

Map: Japan 101 *Timeline:* Japan 101	HOTS 101	
Remainder of Lesson 4.4 102–105 Lesson 4.4 Review 105	Contextual Info 102, 104 HOTS 103, 105	Interdisciplinary 103 Performing Arts 104

Lesson 4.5 Southeast Asia

Map: Southeast Asia 107 *Timeline:* Thailand, Cambodia 107	HOTS 107	
Remainder of Lesson 4.5 108–111 Lesson 4.5 Review 111	Contextual Info 108, 110 HOTS 109, 111	Conservation 109 Interdisciplinary108

Lesson 4.6 Oceania and Highland Asia

Map: Oceania and Highland Asia 113	HOTS 113	
Remainder of Lesson 4.6 115–117 Lesson 4.6 Review 117	Contextual Info 114 HOTS 117	

Lesson 4.7 The World of Islam

Map: World of Islam 119 *Timeline:* Islam 118	HOTS 119	
Remainder of Lesson 4.7 120–123 Lesson 4.7 Review 123	Contextual Info 120, 122 HOTS 121, 123	Interdisciplinary 122

Lesson 4.8 Sub-Sahara Africa

Map: Sub-Sahara Africa 124 *Timeline:* Sub-Sahara Africa 125	HOTS 125	
Remainder of Lesson 4.8 126–129 Lesson 4.8 Review 129	Contextual Info 126, 128 HOTS 127, 129	Performing Arts 126

Ancillaries

Slides: Indian, *The Descent of the River Ganges from Heaven,* Mamallapuram, India, 15a, 28; Japanese, *Jizo Bosatsu,* 16a, 29
Large Reproductions: Bali *Mask,* 1

Slides: Indian, *Shiva, Lord of the Dance, Performing the Nataraja,* 17a, 30; Indian, *Page from Bhagavata Purana,* 14b, 31

Slides: Indian, *Standing Buddha,* 15b, 32; Indian, Taj Mahal, Agra, India, 18a, 33

Slides: Chinese, *Horse,* 19a, 34; Chinese, *Red Vase,* 16b, 35

Slides: Chinese, *Bronze yu,* 17b, 36; Ma Yuan, *Scholar by a Waterfall,* 18b, 37; Chinese, Great Wall of China, 20a, 38

Slides: Koichi Takita, *Vase with plant designs,* 19b, 39

Slides: Japanese, *Haniwa figure,* 20b, 40; Hokusai, *Fuji from Hodohaya,* 21b, 41

Slides: South East Asia, Royal Palace, exterior view, Bangkok, Thailand, 21a, 42; South East Asia, Cambodia, *Dancing Aspara,* 22b, 43; South East Asia, Thailand, *Covered Box,* 23b, 44

Slides: Oceania, *Maori Panel,* 24b, 45; Oceania, *Melanesian helmet-mask,* 25b, 46

Slides: Islamic, Blue Mosque of Ahmet I, Istanbul, 22a, 47; Islamic, Mosque, mihrab vault, 26b, 48; Islamic, *Parade helmet,* 27b, 49; Persian *Bracelet,* 23a, 50

Slides: African, *Baule mask,* 28b, 51

Slides: African, *Benin plaque,* 29b, 52; African, *Bamara Antelope headdress,* 30b, 53
Overhead Transparencies: The Lost Wax Technique, 4

Other Resources

India

Coomaraswamy, Ananda K. *History of Indian and Indonesian Art.* Mineola, NY: Dover Publications Inc., 1985.
Rowland, Benjamin. *The Art and Architecture of India: Buddhist, Hindu, Jain.* Rev. ed. Baltimore: Penguin USA, 1971.

China

Blunden, Caroline, and Elvin, Mark. *Cultural Atlas of China.* Part of the *Cultural Atlas.* New York: Facts on File Inc., 1983.
De Bary, W. T., ed. *Sources of Chinese Tradition.* 2 vols. Part of the *Records of Civilization, Sources and Studies and Introduction to Oriental Classics.* New York: Columbia University Press, 1964.
Sickman, Laurence, and Soper, Alexander. *The Art and Architecture of China.* 3rd ed. New Haven: Yale University Press, 1992.
Sullivan, Michael. *The Arts of China.* 3rd ed. Berkeley: University of California Press, 1984.
The First Emperor of China, Crystal (videodisc)

Japan

Collcut, Martin, et al. *Cultural Atlas of Japan.* Part of the *Cultural Atlas.* New York: Facts on File Inc., 1988.
De Bary, W. T., ed. *Sources of Japanese Tradition.* 2 vols. Part of the *Records of Civilizations, Sources and Studies.* New York: Columbia University Press, 1964.
Paine, Robert T., and Soper, Alexander. *The Art and Architecture of Japan.* 3rd ed. New Haven: Yale University Press, 1992.

Southeast Asia

Art of Indonesia, Crystal (video)

Oceania and Highland Asia

Guiart, Jean. *The Arts of the South Pacific.* Part of the *Arts of Mankind.* New York: Golden Press, 1963.
Sutton, Peter. *Dreamings: The Art of Aboriginal Australia.* New York: George Braziller Inc., 1988.

Islam

Hoag, John. *Islamic Architecture.* Part of the *History of World Architecture.* New York: Rizzoli International Publications Inc., 1987.
Suleyman the Magnificent, Crystal (video)

Chapter 4 Organizer

4 Art of the Non-Western World

Choose either Activity 1 or 2
Choose either Activity 1 or 2
Choose either Activity 1 or 2

Teacher Edition References

Lesson 4.9 Pre-Columbian Art

Map: Pre-Columbian Art 131
Timeline: Mesoamerica, South America 131

HOTS 131

Remainder of Lesson 4.9 132–135	Contextual Info 132, 134	Interdisciplinary 133
Lesson 4.9 Review 135	HOTS 133, 135	Performing Arts 134
	Inquiry 134	

Lesson 4.10 Native America

Map: North American Tribal Areas 137
Timeline: Pre-historic Era 136

Contextual Info 137

Remainder of Lesson 4.10 138–142	Contextual Info 138, 140, 142	Cooperative 140
Lesson 4.10 Review 142	HOTS 139, 141, 143	Inquiry 140
Primary-Source 143		
Chapter Review 143		

Classroom Connections

National Standards

Studio Activity 1
Clay Vessels

1b Students conceive and create works of visual art that demonstrate an understanding of how the communication of their ideas relates to the media, techniques, and processes they use.
3b Students apply subjects, symbols, and ideas in their artworks and use the skills gained to solve problems in daily life.

Studio Activity 2
Behind the Mask

1b Students conceive and create works of visual art that demonstrate an understanding of how the communication of their ideas relates to the media, techniques, and processes they use.
3b Students apply subjects, symbols, and ideas in their artworks and use the skills gained to solve problems in daily life.

Teacher Edition References

Slides: Pre-Columbian, *Paracas mantle*, 31b, 54;

Slides: Pre-Columbian, Observatory, Chichen Itza, 32b, 55
Large Reproductions: Africa, *Power Figure*, 2

Slides: Native American, *Navajo rug*, 33b, 57

Slides: Native American Cliff dwellings, Mesa Verde, 24a, 56;
Martinez, *Jar*, 34b, 58; Native American, *Sioux Saddlebag*, 35b, 59
Large Reproductions: Cordero, *Storyteller*, 3

Schedule	Materials
Shape clay in one class. Allow another period to paint or glaze them.	newspaper or plastic cloth, containers of water, spray bottle, clay, clay tools, heavy duty plastic bags
One or two classes to form the mask. Another one or two classes to paint or embellish.	Kraft paper or brown paper bags, clear glue, toothpicks for applying glue, paper, felt, buttons, yarn, scissors, mirrors, brushes

Other Resources

Africa

Cambridge History of Africa. 8 vols. Cambridge: Cambridge University Press, 1975–86.

Chanda, Jacqueline. *African Arts and Cultures.* Worcester, MA: Davis Publications, Inc., 1993.

Gillon, Werner. *A Short History of African Art.* New York: Penguin USA, 1987.

Murray, Jocelyn, ed. *Cultural Atlas of Africa.* Part of the *Cultural Atlas.* New York: Facts on File Inc., 1981.

Vansina, Jan. *Art History in Africa.* New York: Longman Publishing Group, 1984.

Willett, Frank. *African Art.* Part of *The World of Art.* London: Thames and Hudson Inc., 1985.

African Art and Culture, NASCO (video)

Pre-Columbian

Bray, Warwick. *Everyday Life of the Aztecs.* Part of the *Everyday Life.* New York: Peter Bedrick Books Inc., 1991.

Coe, Michael D. *The Maya.* Part of the *Ancient People and Places.* 3rd ed. London: Thames and Hudson Inc., 1987.

Kubler, George. *The Art and Architecture of Ancient America.* 3rd ed. New Haven: Yale University Press, 1992.

Rome, Jesus, and Rome, Lucienne, trans. *Life of the Incas in Ancient Peru.* Part of the *Everyday Life.* Geneva: Minerva/Liber, 1987.

Soisson, Pierre, and Soisson, Janine, trans. *Life of the Aztecs in Ancient Mexico.* Part of the *Everyday Life.* Geneva: Minerva/Liber, 1987.

Stierlin, Henri, trans. *Art of the Maya: From the Olmecs to the Toltec-Maya.* New York: Rizzoli International Publications Inc., 1981.

Whitlock, Ralph. *Everyday Life of the Maya.* Part of the *Everyday Life.* London: Batsford, 1987.

Native American

Coe, Ralph T. *Lost and Found Traditions: Native American Art, 1965–1985.* Seattle: University of Washington Press, 1988.

D'Alleva, Anne. *Native American Arts and Cultures.* Worcester, MA: Davis Publications, Inc., 1993.

Feest, Christian. *Native Arts of North America.* Part of the *World of Art.* London: Thames and Hudson Inc., 1985.

Graham, Mary, and Ruppe, Carol. *Native American Artist Directory.* Phoenix: Heard Museum, 1985.

Beyond Traditon: Contemporary Indian art and its Evolution, Crystal (video)

Maria! Indian Pottery of San Ildefonso, Crystal (video)

Early Native American Art and Culture, NASCO (video)

Introduce

Non-Western cultures are those outside of the Western (European) tradition. The diversity of expressions from these great civilizations is monumental. Often, art within these societies has religious, political, functional and social aims.

Lessons at a Glance

4.1 *A Multitude of Perspectives*
Traditional non-Western art frequently contains functional, religious and decorative aims. The enormous variety of visual endeavors from cultures around the world reflects both differences and similarities among humankind.

4.2 *India*
Hinduism and Buddhism dominated Indian art for over 2500 years. At times, one religion would dominate and produce a distinct style of art and architecture. When the two coexisted, their structures and visual imagery shared visual similarities. Indian art has also adapted outside influences to its unique style.

4.3 *China*
A deep respect for nature permeates Chinese beliefs and art; this is underscored by the relatively insignificant role that human figures have in art that depicts outdoor scenes. Chinese writing has been considered an art form from its earliest beginnings as simple pictographs to later, elegant calligraphy.

4.4 *Japan*
Japan has alternated between long periods of isolation and then times of contact with outside cultures. China and Korea first influenced Japanese art in the seventh century, and the country opened to the West in 1868. Traditional Japanese art maintains a simple sense of design, sensitivity to nature and a quiet, understated style.

4.5 *Southeast Asia*
Over the centuries, various Southeast Asian cultures have either mingled with or dominated one another. Chinese and Indian art exerted the strongest influence over the region's art and government.

4.6 *Oceania and Highland Asia*
Each of the groups of disparate people in Oceania and Highland Asia developed their own unique, highly stylized visual traditions.

4 Art of the Non-Western World

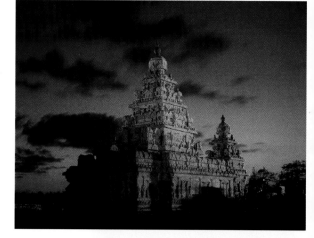

4–a Much Indian art and architecture centers around the religions of Hinduism and Buddhism. This Hindu temple complex is meant to represent the order of the universe. *Shore Temple,* 7th–8th centuries. Mamallapuram (Mahabalipuram), India. Pallava style, live rock.

4–b The cultures of ancient America are famous for their work with fabrics. This mantle is made of feathers and cotton. The feathers are striking in their color and provide a strong element of contrast to the piece. *Feather Mantle,* 13th–14th centuries. Feathers and cotton, 45 x 44 1/2" [114.3 x 113 cm]. Chimu, Peru. The Nelson-Atkins Museum of Art, Kansas City, Missouri. Purchase: Nelson Trust [60–79].

4–c This detail from a palace door of the Yoruba tribe shows genre scenes and anecdotes of tribal life. In this instance, the name of the sculptor has been recorded. It is often the case in African art, however, that we do not know the name of the artists of traditional works of art. Areogun, *Door from palace at Ikerre,* detail [fig.1–9].

4.7 *The World of Islam*
Islam, as a nation and religion, has influenced art and culture in Europe, Africa and Asia, from Spain to the Philippines. Islamic art is characterized by ornate decoration. The earliest Arab examples were small, portable objects that could be easily carried by seminomadic tribes. As Islamic architecture developed, artists extended their love of surface design from individual objects to entire environments.

4.8 *Sub-Sahara Africa*
The art of the distinctly different societies south of the Sahara are united by attention to craftsmanship, use of geometric design and religious orientation. Many of the objects were vital components of ceremonies that incorporated music, song, dance and narrative.

4.9 *Pre-Columbian Art*
Pre-Columbian art flourished in Mexico, Central America and South America long before the arrival of European invaders. Artists from these Mesoamerican and Andean regions produced architecture, sculpture, textiles and ceramics of astounding quality.

4.10 *Native America*
A diverse group of Native American peoples have created ceremonial and functional art since prehistoric times. While each nation's objects differ from one another, they share an appreciation of natural materials, a close relationship to the spiritual realm, and use of pictographic symbolism and abstract designs.

Every country nourishes the arts.
Erasmus

Non-Western areas of the world discussed in this chapter are highlighted on this map.

NATIVE NORTH AMERICA

CHINA JAPAN
HIGHLAND ASIA
WORLD OF ISLAM INDIA

Atlantic Ocean

Pacific Ocean

SOUTHEAST ASIA

OCEANIA PRE-COLUMBIA

SUB-SAHARA AFRICA

Indian Ocean

OCEANIA

Non-Western Art

4–d How would you describe the landscape depicted here? What elements of art and principles of design has the artist used to convey this effect?
Ma Yuan, *Bare Willows and Distant Mountains,* end of 12th century. Round fan mounted as album leaf, ink and light color on silk, 9 1/2" x 9 1/2" (23.8 x 23.8 cm). Museum of Fine Arts, Boston.

4–e The Japanese have created many of the world's most beautiful and skillfully made woodcuts. The subjects of these prints often focus on scenes of everyday life.
Ando Hiroshige, *Hodogaya Station* from the Tokeido Series, 1832–1834. Collection of Bertna and Mitchel Siegel, Santa Fe, New Mexico.

Quote

Ask students to define the word *nourish*. What does Erasmus mean when he uses the verb in his quote? How can the images in the chapter opener support his statement? Direct students to research who Erasmus was and why he might have written this sentence. (Erasmus was a Dutch writer and humanist. His best known work was *The Praise of Folly*.)

Map

Instruct students to locate North America and Europe on the map. Ask them to calculate how large a portion of the world these areas constitute. Were they aware of the vast number of other regions that have also made important contributions to the history of art? Inform them that although much of the textbook is devoted to the development of art in the Western tradition, all of the cultures in Chapter 4 have produced significant works as well. Ask students to consider why it is important to study non-Western contributions.

Evaluate

Ask students if only non-Western cultures create art that portrays daily life.

• What visual images in America today reveal information about people's existence?

• In addition to paintings and sculpture, where else do students see images on a daily basis?

• Would these visual forms deepen a non-Western visitor's understanding of American life?

Reteach

Challenge students to define the word *artist*; then see if they can apply the definition to the people who created the works reproduced in the chapter opener. Have students compare the roles, materials and products of artists in non-Western and Western societies. Later, tell them to alter their definition so that it encompasses artists from all cultures and times.

Objectives

Students should be able to:

Appreciate the diversity of artistic expressions from cultures around the globe.

Identify similarities and differences in terms of function, materials and design of the artworks from various non-Western societies.

Teach

Context

Direct students to carefully study figs.4–c and 1–9. Ask students what the images indicate about the tribal life of the Yoruba around 1910.

• Do the scenes describe their own experiences in modern America?

• Based on fig.1–9 and their lives today, what comparisons can they make about early twentieth-century Nigerian culture?

Art

Ask students to imagine coming upon the building in fig.4–a. Instruct them not to read the caption but speculate about the function of the structure.

• What information can they glean from its shape, size and materials in relation to the architecture?

• How might their responses change if the structure were tiny, painted red and gold, and not surrounded by the elaborate carvings? After they read the caption, direct them to Lesson 4.2 for more information about the relationship between religion and Indian art.

Lesson 4.1

Traditional non-Western art frequently contains functional, religious and decorative aims. The enormous variety of visual endeavors from cultures around the world reflects both differences and similarities among humankind.

Warm-up

Ask students to identify which of the reproductions in Lesson 4.1 they consider artworks. Why have they decided that some are and others are not art? Share that all of the images are art, but unlike most Western expressions, which are purely decorative, these objects serve a multitude of purposes.

Objectives

Students should be able to:

Comprehend the endless variety of artistic endeavors throughout the world.

Describe some of the multiple functions that art has in various non-Western civilizations.

Understand how learning about the history and culture of various peoples increases an appreciation and comprehension of their art.

4.1 A Multitude of Perspectives

ANY CULTURE THAT IS NOT RELATED TO Western civilization (the people of North America and Western Europe) is referred to as non-Western. The great civilizations of India, Asia, Islam and pre-Columbian America, and the tribal societies of Africa and North America belong to non-Western cultures.

In non-Western societies, art has many purposes, including magic, worship, status and even politics. Much of the artwork produced by these cultures features religious symbols and motifs. No understanding of art from these cultures would be complete without an understanding of their religions.

Other artwork can be understood in terms of the ways cultures have used color and perspective. But, it also helps to know something about the history and culture and people who produced it. The more you know about the experiences and attitudes that helped to shape a society, the better you can understand and appreciate its artwork.

4–2 Scholars have learned a great deal about the religious life and customs of the Mesoamerican culture by analyzing their illustrated codices.
Souche Nuttar Codex, detail (fig.4–6).

4–1 Ando Hiroshige, *Hodogaya Station*, detail (fig.4–e).

Teach

Art History: Direct students to consider what the relationship is between spirituality, history and art in America today.

• Do religions have a marked impact on shaping the nation's development? Can artistic examples support their claims?

Now ask students to examine the images and captions on pages 78 through 83 to determine if there is a difference in the correlation between religion and history in the cultures represented here. Have students read the text to understand how religions have significantly shaped the visual expressions of particular societies.

Art History/Criticism: Ask students to locate the various sacred beings in the reproductions in Lesson 4.1. Although all the figures are religious deities, do they look the same?

• Do the images have different meanings to the people of the cultures from which they came? Regardless of stylistic variations, how have all the artists created a sense of the divine?

• How do the images differ from the religious subjects in the Western, Judeo-Christian tradition? Challenge students to derive a definition of religious artwork that encompasses all cultures.

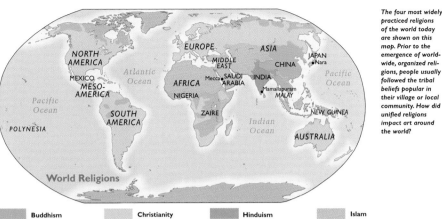

The four most widely practiced religions of the world today are shown on this map. Prior to the emergence of world-wide, organized religions, people usually followed the tribal beliefs popular in their village or local community. How did unified religions impact art around the world?

Buddhism   Christianity   Hinduism   Islam

4–3 Many ancient traditions, such as the pueblo form of architecture, are still in use today.
Pueblo, Taos, New Mexico.

4–4 Bas reliefs such as this are found throughout the temple at Borobudor. They illustrate scenes from legends.
Java, *Buddhist Borobudor*, detail (fig.4–55).

Higher-Order Thinking Skills

Have students analyze the figures in the *Souche Nuttar Codex* (fig.4–2) and the bas relief from Borobudor (fig.4–4). Then have them describe the rules, or "canon," for portraying human beings in these two works.

Evaluate

Ask whether all artwork has only a single function—such as being decorative, religious or functional. How can the images in Lesson 4.1 prove art's multiple functions? Do students prefer work that has only one purpose or are they more intrigued when it has multiple purposes? What affects their choice? Have them share their opinions with the class and see if they can examine the issue from the opposite point of view.

Reteach

Bring in sacred objects or pictures of them that represent a variety of religions. Ask students to analyze the works' materials, structure and function to discover as much as they can about the culture and beliefs of the people who made them. If some students are knowledgeable about particular religions, have them add their own information. For instance, what do the objects mean to them?

• How might they perceive the items differently than those who are unfamiliar with them? After, ask the class how their attitude toward the works changed as they learned more about them.

• What remains unanswered that they would like to know about?

• How can their classmates help them address these questions?

Contextual Information

Hinduism

Hindus believe that people are born into a caste, or certain level in society, and stay there until they die. Occupations, including that of artists, are handed down in families. The highest castes are the priests and soldiers; the lowest group is the "untouchables," who literally have no caste.

West African Reliquary Figure

The reliquary guardian figure from West Africa is one of two owned by the Peabody Museum. They probably were mounted over bark boxes that held the bones and other relics of prominent family members or defeated enemies. The boxes were kept by the heads of households in the men's council house at one end of the village. They were kept away from the sight of women and uninitiated men. (See page 126 for more about African reliquary figures.)

Souche Nuttar Codex

Like most of the extant Pre-Columbian manuscripts, the *Souche Nuttar Codex* is of Mixtec origin. These codices are not bound as pages in a book, like Western manuscripts. Instead, strips of gessoed deerskin, painted on both sides, are arranged like folding screens and protected by wooden covers. As in the Souche Nuttar Codex, the principal colors used are red, yellow, blue, green, brown and black.

Religion

Three of the world's great major religions evolved in Africa and Asia—*Hinduism, Buddhism* and *Islam.* Every civilization also developed religious practices. Many are based on the worship of nature, such as the planets, animals and fertility. These religious beliefs and values are reflected in the culture's art.

Western art depicts images of Christianity and ideas that reflect the Judeo-Christian tradition. Similarly, Asian art presents many images of Buddha, "the Enlightened One." African art presents images and symbols of its own religious traditions. The carved wooden figure shown here (fig.4–5) is from the Kuba tribe of Zaire. This male figure is the portrait of a king that "performs" a specific function.

While Hinduism, Buddhism and Islam are the three major religions, other religions have also had an impact on a culture's art. *Taoism* and *Confucianism* are important religions in China. The *Shinto* religion is the oldest in Japan. Peoples of the islands and highlands of Asia and the Pacific worship natural phenomena. Art and architecture of ancient civilizations of Mexico, Mesoamerica and South America are also founded on naturalism and mystic spiritualism. The manuscript, or codex (fig.4–6), is a strong statement about the Mixtec society of Mesoamerica. It shows their ceremonial dress and their use of the jaguar head as a religious symbol (fig.4–2). The game that is being played with a rubber ball is part of a ceremony, for their sports and games often revolved around religion.

4–5 Reliquary Guardian Figure, Cameroon or Gabon, c.1850. Wood, h. 23" (60 cm). Peabody Museum, Harvard University.

4–6 Many books of South and Central American cultures were destroyed by the Spanish conquistadors. *Souche Nuttar Codex,* one of forty-eight sheets, 14th century. Mixtec culture, Mesoamerica. Drawing and painting on deerskin, 7" x 9 3/4" (18 x 25 cm). British Museum, London.

Materials and Techniques

The reliquary guardian figure (fig.4–5) is made of blackened wood. The shiny, sticky surface is the result of steeping the figure in resin, charcoal dust and palm oil. The eyes are inlaid with metal plate or brass pegs.

At some point, the figure was removed from its bark box, and the legs were broken off at the knees. The missing legs probably were short and bulbous with inward, pointing knees.

4–8 The *Ramayana* provides us with information about the ideals, values, customs and rituals of ancient India.
Sita in the Garden of Lanka, from the *Epic of Valmaki, Ramayana.* Gold and color on paper, 22 x 31" (55.5 x 79 cm). India, Pahai, Guler School. The Cleveland Museum of Art, Gift of George P. Bickford, 66.143.

Higher-Order Thinking Skills

The subject of *Sita in the Garden of Lanka* (fig.4–8) is religious, but its subject matter can be considered narrative. Ask students what element of art the artist has used to convey the story to the viewer.

Hinduism

Hinduism, one of the world's most ancient religion, originated in ancient India about 2000 BC. Hindus believe in the gods *Brahma* the Creator, *Vishnu* the Preserver, and *Siva* the Destroyer. In artworks, Brahma appears in white robes and rides a swan. Brahma is often shown with four heads. From his four heads spring the Vedas, or sacred books, which he carries along with a scepter. Vishnu holds a discus, conch shell, mace and lotus. Siva is often entwined in snakes and wears a headdress of skulls, but, at other times, he dances in a circle of fire.

Hinduism gave order to the universe and to the structure of society. The universe was divided into three zones of earth, middle space and sky. Animals and human forms were often used to depict the powers within these three zones. In the carving *The Descent of the Ganges From Heaven* (fig.4–7), dancing and active human figures represent the source of life. The elephants in this massive work symbolize the power of nature. They have a mythological ability to call upon the clouds to produce rain. By the gigantic elephants, nature is shown as being much more powerful than human-

ity. The gods are portrayed as more important than humans. The different registers may correspond with social castes ruled over by a king with divine power.

One of the greatest Hindu writings of ancient India is the epic known as the *Ramayana.* The epic is about the legendary king *Rama,* who was unjustly deprived of his kingdom. The Hindus believe that Rama is a human form of their god Vishnu. Various episodes concern Rama's birth, his marriage to the beautiful *Sita,* her capture by the devil *Ravana,* and Rama's rescue of Sita and his land. The basic teaching of the *Ramayana* is that good prevails over evil. Rama and Sita are models that show Hindus how they should behave. Scenes from this tale are painted and sculpted on temples, shrines, palaces and courts throughout Asia (fig.4–8). The *Ramayana* was adopted by the Buddhists and, later, even became part of Islamic heritage. Each country has its own subtle version of this universal tale.

4–7 Use the text to help interpret the figures shown here.
The Descent of the River Ganges from Heaven, 10th century. Live rock carving at Mamallapuram, India.

Contextual Information

Buddhist Sculpture

The two figures found on page 82 are Japanese in origin. China and India also have very significant traditions of Buddhist art, which heavily influenced Japanese artists.

In addition to bronze and wood figures of the Buddha, the Japanese also made statues of lacquer. The lighter weight of this medium allowed the figures to be carried in religious processions.

Islamic Representational Art

Because there is no place for figural representations in the devotional art of Islam, the representational art created over the centuries was done principally in the service of rulers. The scene in fig.4–11 is a representation from the *Shah Nama*, or *Book of Kings*. The themes of power and courtly life are the most prevalent in Islamic painting.

Buddhism

Buddhism emerged in India in the sixth century BC as a Hindu reform movement. The movement was founded by Buddha, who became enlightened through years of meditation. He preached charity to all creatures, the equality of all beings, and the practice of moderation. The goal of all Buddhists is to achieve nirvana, the final state of eternal bliss. Buddha essentially reformed Hinduism without discarding the Hindu gods. However, Buddhism soon became its own strong religion and spread to other countries.

In the second century BC, a complex form of Buddhism known as *Mahayana* Buddhism developed. It preached the salvation of souls and the important role of saints, called *bodhisattvas*. These saints were believers who achieved enlightenment like Buddha, but who chose not to enter nirvana. Instead, they remained to help struggling mortals. The most popular of these bodhisattvas is *Avaloketisvara*, known in China as *Guan Yin* and, in Japan, as *Kannon*. This "goddess of mercy," with a meditative countenance and a reassuring confidence, is symbolically represented upon a lotus seat (fig.4–9). The lotus, a water lily, symbolizes purity.

Buddhism was introduced in Japan in the sixth century. There are several forms of Buddhism in Japan. The Buddhist cult of Jizo Bosatsu was introduced into Japan in the eighth century and was extremely popular from 900 to 1300. Zen Buddhism became an important cultural force in the fourteenth century.

Jizo is a compassionate deity concerned with the needs of suffering humanity and is the patron saint of children. He is usually shown as a simple monk. This carving (fig.4–10) is made of joined wood blocks. The artist used the wood grains to enhance the contours of the figure.

4–10 This monk is the patron saint of children.
Jizo Bosatsu, 12th century, late Heian period, Japan. Wood, 57 1/2" (146 cm) high. Los Angeles County Museum of Art, gift of Anna Bing Arnold.

4–9 This goddess of mercy is said to remain on earth to help people with their earthly lives.
Nyoirin-Kannon (Bodhisattva), 645–647. Nara period. Bronze. Oka-Der-a Temple, Nara, Japan.

Islam

Much of Asia is dominated by *Islam.* The religion of Islam was founded by the prophet Mohammed. In a vision, he was told that he was the messenger of Allah, the one God. Mohammed received his revelations in Mecca, a city in Saudi Arabia, during the seventh century. The spiritual writings of Mohammed are contained in the *Koran,* the sacred book of the Moslems. Mohammed preached that the way to Allah lies through learning the sacred writings and in service to him. Mohammed's followers spread his message to the Middle East, Northern Africa, China and the Malay archipelago.

Islam forbids the use of religious images of any kind. Although religious sculptures could not depict human figures, miniature paintings were allowed to include men and women as illustrations for tales about successful Islamic rulers, their loves and their adventures. This example is a single page or folio from a Shah Nama (Book of Kings), a popular illustrated history (fig.4–11).

4–11 How would you characterize the conversation in which these men are engaged? You do not know what they are saying, but do their poses give you any clues? Do other elements in the painting emphasize or repeat their poses? *Two Men Converse in a Landscape.* A folio from a Shah Nama, 16th century. Sultanate period, India. Watercolor on paper, 8 1/4" x 5 1/8" (21 x 13 cm). Los Angeles County Museum of Art, gift of Doris and Ed Wiener.

Higher-Order Thinking Skills

Have the class describe the personalities of the people portrayed in the three works on pages 82 and 83. Ask what characteristics they exhibit that seem to be valued by their cultures. Students can then do some research to verify their speculations.

Contextual Information

Hokusai

Hokusai is perhaps the most well-known Japanese artist familiar to Westerners. Unable to buckle down to the discipline of working with a single master and school, Hokusai initially had a difficult time in the world of commercial art. For a while he found himself peddling condiments and calendars in order to make ends meet.

He did eventually find success as a printmaker. His most famous series *Thirty-six Views of Mount Fuji* was a selection of images that had as their focal point Mt. Fuji, the sacred mountain of the Japanese. He represented the mountain from every possible angle, in all weather conditions and in a variety of moods.

Media

Non-Western cultures have produced artwork from materials similar to those used in the West. Materials such as stone, brick, wood, paint and clay are used. Oceanic peoples of New Guinea and Polynesia paint on bark, and the Chinese have used glass and silk as their grounds. American Indians have painted on hide, wood, stone and textiles. Lost-wax casting was used during the *Shang* dynasty of China and by the *Benin* culture of Nigeria. These cultures produced excellent metal sculptures with this technique. While bronze is permanent, non-Western art is also made from perishable items such as feathers, flowers, leather, grass, bark and shells.

Western painters tend to work within the limitations of a frame, but Chinese and Japanese painters worked on screens and scrolls. If they needed more space to tell their entire story, they added more sections to the screen or rolled the scroll out for several more feet.

4–12 Oceanic artists rely predominantly on natural materials for their artwork.
Painted Bark Cloth, 20th century. Melanesia, Lake Sentani (Irian Jaya). Bark cloth with pigment, 33 1/4" x 46 1/2" (84.4 x 118.1 cm). The Nelson-Atkins Museum, Kansas City, Missouri, gift of Mr. and Mrs. Morton I. Sosland.

Color

Over the centuries, Western artists have used color differently in their paintings. Roman and Renaissance artists used realistic colors. Impressionist painters dabbed in color as it was reflected from objects and approached it almost scientifically. Expressionists used color to symbolize feelings and emotions.

In Asian painting, color is arbitrary. Chinese painters painted their scrolls with monochromatic colors, often using color only for accents and emphasis (fig.4–27a,b). In woodcuts, colors were kept flat (fig.4–13). Color and value were not used together to describe form.

4–13 When they made their way west to Paris in the nineteenth century, prints like this had an enormous impact on Western art in the works of such artists as Gauguin.
Katsushika Hokusai, *The Great Wave* from *Thirty-six Views of Mt. Fuji*. Tokugawa period. Woodcut, 10" x 14 3/4" (25 x 37 cm). Spaulding Collection, Courtesy, Museum of Fine Arts, Boston.

Materials and Techniques

The Great Wave at Kanagawa is part of Hokusai's well-known series of prints called *Thirty-six Views of Mount Fuji*. It is interesting to note that this series is one of the first large-scale Japanese publishing ventures that extensively employed the chemical pigment Prussian Blue. In the late 1820s, the pigment became available from China at a greatly reduced price. The pigment offered artists and printers a strong dark blue which would not fade.

4–14 How does your eye move through the space in this picture?
Shen Chou, *Landscape in the Style of Ni Tsan,* 1484. Ink, 54 1/2" x 24 3/4" (138 x 62.9 cm). The Nelson-Atkins Museum of Art, Kansas City, Missouri.

Perspective

Perspective was approached differently in the East and the West. Perspective is the Western term for showing realistic spatial relationships of objects in drawing or painting. Renaissance artists discovered how to show distance by using overlapping planes and lines converging at a vanishing point. (*See* fig.9–30, for example.) In some Chinese and Japanese art, receding lines remain parallel and do not converge (fig.4–14). Thus, the eye moves back into the picture, but does not eventually meet one or two specific vanishing points.

Asian artists often depict great distance by showing three planes: a foreground, a middle distance and a far distance, each parallel to the picture plane. For example, one may see land, then water, then mountains, each painted separately, not overlapping. As the viewer's eye leaps from one distance to the next, the vastness of nature is felt. Objects are often enveloped in mist or cloud to further suggest spaciousness. Details in the background become less distinct, a technique called aerial perspective. In their monochromatic ink paintings, Chinese artists often used aerial perspective to great effect.

Some non-Western artists present the front and side view of an object simultaneously. "X-ray" views of internal parts can be seen at the same time as the exterior (fig.4–15). The artist thus depicts more than the surface of things.

4–15 Why might an artist choose to depict the exterior as well as the "interior" of an animal?
X-ray Figure of Kangaroo. Aborigine, Australia. Collection of Larry Majewski.

Higher-Order Thinking Skills

Have students analyze the Chinese preference for monochrome, their preference for ink and brush and their approach to perspective. Suggest that students use figs.4–d, 4–14 and 4–27a, b for this visual exercise. Explain that we in the Western Hemisphere tend to be trained to prefer rich color and complex media, as well as linear perspective. The analysis should help students better understand the widely varied aesthetic preferences and "ways of seeing" throughout the world.

Lesson 4.1 Review

1 When and where did Hinduism and Buddhism originate?
2 Who are Brahma, Vishnu and Siva? How are they represented in Hindu art?
3 In the carving *The Descent of the Ganges*, what do the elephants symbolize? How do we know that the artist considered nature to be more powerful than humans?
4 Who are Avaloketisvara and Jizo? How are they usually represented in Buddhist art?
5 Explain the relationship between Islam, Mohammed and the Koran.
6 Why are there no sculptures in Islamic mosques?
7 On what did traditional Chinese and Japanese artists usually paint?
8 Describe the use of color in Asian paintings.

Lesson 4.1 Review Answers

1 Hinduism originated in ancient India about 2000 BC. Buddhism originated in India in the sixth century BC.
2 Brahma is the Creator, often portrayed with four heads and clothed in white robes riding a swan. Vishnu is the Preserver who holds a discus, conch shell, mace and lotus. Siva is the Destroyer who is often entwined in snakes and wearing a headdress of skulls or dancing in a circle of fire.

3 The elephants symbolize nature's power. The artist depicts nature as more powerful than humans by making the elephants gigantic.
4 Avaloketisvara is the most popular bodhisattva in Mahayana Buddhism. This goddess of mercy is represented on a lotus seat or water lily symbolizing purity. Jizo is a compassionate deity in Japanese Buddhism who is concerned with human suffering and is the patron saint of children. He is usually shown as a simple monk.
5 The prophet Mohammed founded the religion of Islam. The Koran is the sacred book of the Moslems containing Mohammed's spiritual writings.

6 Islam forbids the use of religious images.
7 Screens and scrolls
8 In Asian painting, color is arbitrary. Chinese scrolls were painted with monochromatic colors, often using color for accents and emphasis. In woodcuts, colors were kept flat. Color and value were not used together to show form.

Lesson 4.2

Hinduism and Buddhism dominated Indian art for over 2500 years. At times, one religion would dominate and produce a distinct style of art and architecture. When the two coexisted, their structures and visual imagery shared visual similarities. Indian art has also adapted outside influences to its unique style.

Warm-up

Have students carefully examine the map on page 86. Can they determine the nations neighboring India? Have them read the caption to become aware of the predominant religion in each area.

Objectives

Students should be able to:

Describe the impact of India's rich mix of cultures.

Understand the influence of Hinduism and Buddhism on the nation's art and architecture.

Identify the effect of outside influences on Indian artwork.

Vocabulary Definitions

stupa (*stew*-pah) A reliquary structure based on the Vedic funerary mound which represents the Buddhist cosmic mountain and commemorates sacred places, events or people (especially Buddha and Buddhist monks).

harmika (har-*meek*-ah) The small railed balcony surmounting the dome of a stupa.

live rock Stone carved where it is found in nature; rock still in its original location.

gopura (go-poor-uh) Elaborate, pyramidal, tapered gateway towers typical of South Indian Hindu temple architecture.

4.2 India

INDIA WAS HOME TO ONE OF the world's oldest civilizations. Like its geography of extreme contrasts—from snow-covered mountains to steamy jungles—India has a rich mix of cultures.

Hinduism and Buddhism have dominated the art of India for over 2500 years. At times, one religion was stronger than the other, resulting in distinctly different sculpture and architecture. At other times, the two religions have co-existed, and architecture and imagery have shared similar styles. India has also received outside cultural influences at various times, but all have eventually been absorbed into the unique Indian style.

Vocabulary
stupa
harmika
live rock
gopura

4–16 This painting dates from the Mughal period, the final phase of traditional Indian art.
Rajput, Rajasthani School, *Head of Krishna.* Cartoon for mural painting, from illustration to the "Rasa Lila." Color on paper. The Metropolitan Museum of Art, New York. Rogers Fund, 1918.

The world's highest mountains, the Himalayas, effectively separate the subcontinent of India from the rest of Asia, contributing to India's unique culture. Religious differences have resulted in the formation of new political boundaries. Islamic beliefs are more prevalent in Pakistan and Bangladesh, Buddhism in Nepal and Bhutan, Hinduism in India.

	322 BC—185 BC Mauryan Empire	
c. 2500 BC—1500 BC Indus Civilization	78 AD—250 AD Gandhara Period	730 AD—1308 AD Medieval Period
India Timeline		
c. 1500 BC—400 BC Ganges Civilization c. 1500	320 AD—600 Gupta Empire 600 AD—750 AD Pallava Dynasty	846 AD—1173 AD Chola Dynasty 1206 AD—1857 AD Mughal Period

4–17 This image shows a less well-known section of the world-famous Taj Mahal. See fig.4–24 for the more familiar view.
Taj Mahal, 1632. Side building, Agra, India.

4–18 Siva often is depicted in his cosmic dance with his numerous arms rotating gracefully about his body.
Siva, Lord of the Dance, Performing the Nataraja, 10th century. Chola dynasty, India. 30" (76 cm) high. Los Angeles County Museum of Art.

Teach

Art History: Ask students to imagine being the artist of the *Colossal Head of Buddha* (fig.4–21). Have them examine examples of Greek sculpture (Chapter 6, pages 178–183) and discern what influences the Western culture's work had on the Indian carver. What did the Indian artist admire about Greek sculpture? On the other hand, what features did the artist give Buddha that do not appear in Western art? Have students read page 89 to understand the meaning of each particular symbol. After, direct students to think about how the artist might have felt about Alexander the Great's Indian campaigns.

• Might the artist have thought that something worthwhile resulted from the wars or would he be angry and feel wholly patriotic toward his homeland?

• How can students use the artist's sculpture to support their answers?

Art History/Criticism: Ask students to identify the images in Lesson 4.2 that illustrate the strong influence of Buddhism throughout the subcontinent of India. Direct small groups to research information about the life and teachings of Buddha and then relate the stories to the class as they examine the *Colossal Head of Buddha.*

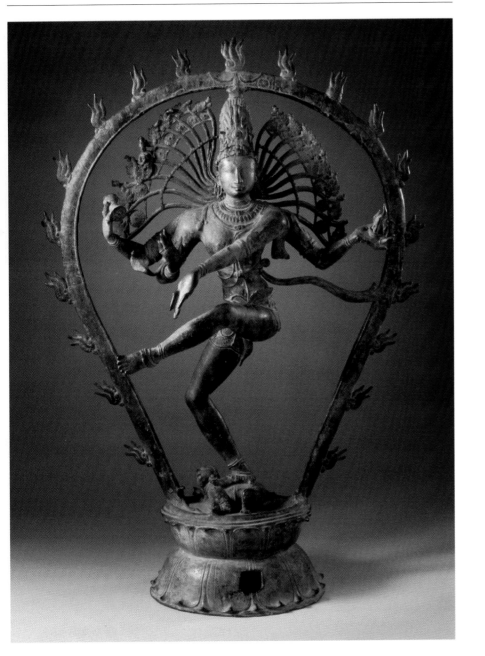

Contextual Information

Siva

Each part of the *Siva* (fig.4–18) shows opposites: his right hand creates; his left hand holds a flame with which he can destroy. The inner left hand controls progress, and the right hand creates obstructions. His face shows calm and perfect self-knowledge, which is the highest state in the Hindu religion.

Higher-Order Thinking Skills

1 The arms of *Siva* are meant to show the motion of his cosmic dance. Ask how else the artist could have depicted this motion. Have the class brainstorm as many alternatives as possible.

2 Ask students to compare and contrast the *Siva* with another Indian bronze, *Dancing Ganésa* (fig.2–36).

Evaluate

Ask students how they can prove that Indian art incorporates symbolism. If they need guidance, ask what some of the underlying meanings are of the *Shore Temple* (fig.4–a), *Stupa I* (fig.4–20) and the unusual features on Buddha's face (fig.4–21).

• What symbols in Western art can students identify?

• What does the image of a cross, a halo or white lilies signify in Christian painting and sculpture?

• Why might religions use symbols to visually communicate their message?

• How do icons work differently from spoken or written words? (Chapter 10, on Northern Renaissance art, explores the use of Christian symbols in more detail.)

Reteach

Challenge students to pretend that they are visitors from another solar system who had toured both the Indian *Stupa I* (fig.4–20) and the Roman *Pantheon* (figs.6–34 and 6–35). If they were now back on their planet showing to friends some pictures of what they saw, what might they say about the similarities and differences between the two ancient structures? Although there are visual parallels between the structures, which were constructed at approximately the same time, what would they explain about the differences between the structures regarding each culture's religion and its relationship to the building?

Contextual Information

Sanchi

Originally, the stupa was intended to resemble a bubble, an object that lives, like humans, a short time. It was not intended to be an object of worship, but to serve as a reminder of the necessity of practicing Buddhist principles.

The dome of this stupa (fig.4–20) rests on a circular pediment that represents the marriage of heaven and earth. The square section on top is the house of the gods, and the umbrellalike top represents the rule of Buddha over heaven and the world.

The Sanchi site is on a hill that rises out of a plain. There are three stupas on the hill. Stupa I also is known as the Great Stupa. Like many other stupas, it is constructed of brick and rubble, faced with gilded and white stucco.

Seals from the Indus Valley Civilization

Seals (fig.4–19) probably are the most fascinating pieces of sculpture to survive from the Indus Valley Civilization. They are made from steatite and generally range in size from 3/4" to 1 1/4" square.

The script on the seals has a distant relationship to early Sumerian and proto-Elamite symbols, but it developed separately and is, so far, indecipherable. An array of animals have been found on the seals. These include bulls, tigers, elephants, crocodiles and rhinoceroses.

Indus Valley Civilization

The earliest Indian culture is known as the *Indus Valley civilization,* a sophisticated society existing until 1500 BC. It was located along the river banks in what is modern Pakistan, stretching about two thousand kilometers, from Harappa to Mohenjo-Daro. Bronze and stone animal sculptures and small stamps, or seals, carved in stone of this culture have been discovered (fig.4–19). The seals were used to stamp signatures on official documents. The people created ceramic bowls rubbed with resin and decorated with geometric and animal motifs. They also built temples honoring popular water gods.

4–19 Scholars have been unable to decipher the script on these tiles.
Seals, from Mohenjo-Daro, Pakistan, 3000 BC. Steatite. National Museum, Delhi.

4–20 Relics of Buddha's body were placed in shrines like this, which were visited by those on pilgrimages.
Stupa I, 2nd century BC–1st century AD. Solid masonry. Sanchi, India.

Interdisciplinary Connection

Social Studies: Have students investigate several of the numerous Buddhist figures and legends that are depicted on the gateways of Stupa I at Sanchi. They also can further investigate the symbolism and use of the stupa. Students should share their findings with the class. Ask students how the additional background information helped them better understand the monument.

The Mauryan Era

A long era, known generally as the *Ganges civilization,* followed. For one thousand years there was little evidence of Indian civilization. During this era, hymns called *Vedas* were written. These Vedas marked the beginning of Hinduism. Then, in the fourth century BC, India was united under the rule of the Maurya family. The greatest of the Maurya rulers was King Asoka. Asoka was greatly influenced by Buddhism. Through these teachings, he sought to provide his people with a better way of life, one without war. By the latter half of the second century BC, Asoka had converted many subjects to Buddhism. He had large columns built and inscribed them with Buddhist teachings. The columns were topped with magnificent seated lion sculptures, which have become the mark of Asokan art.

The Mauryans constructed the first objects of Buddhist architecture—round burial mounds known as **stupas** (fig.4–20), which contained relics of Buddha's body. A stupa was surrounded by a wall. Relief carvings on the walls and gateways allowed believers on pilgrimages to read Buddhist teachings. The small railed balcony atop the structure is the **harmika**. It is topped with stylized umbrellas that symbolize the thirty-three higher heavens of Mahayana Buddhism.

The Gandhara Era

Greek armies under Alexander made conquests in Northern India and Pakistan after 326 BC. Therefore, the first significant Buddhist sculpture had a Greek influence. The first images of Buddha appeared in the Hellenistic kingdoms of Bactria and Gandhara. The sculptures were based on Greek sculptural methods and aesthetics. The sculptures had Western facial and body types. The colossal head

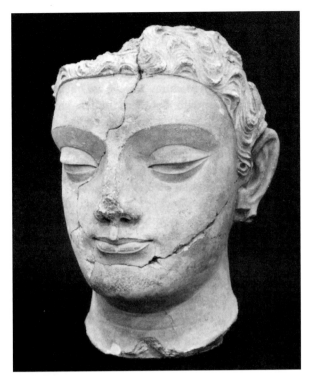

of Buddha, made of stucco, shows a Greek-style face, except for the half-closed treatment of the eyes (fig.4–21). The hair is formed in a style similar to Greek figures of Apollo. However, distinct Buddhist motifs were developed to show Buddha's sacred nature: elongated earlobes, the *ushnisha* coil of hair protruding from the back of the head, and the third eye, or *urna*, which symbolized his omniscience.

Under the Gandhara school of art, the first Indian cave temples were cut into hillsides of **live rock**. The form of these cave sanctuaries resembles earlier wooden constructions, except that they were hewn from solid rock.

4–21 The first images of Buddha were profoundly influenced by Greek ideas.
Colossal Head of Buddha, 2nd–3rd centuries. Gandhara school, India. Stucco, 27 1/2" (70 cm) high. Los Angeles County Museum of Art, Leo Meyer Collection.

The Gupta Era

Greek style in Indian art declined, and a new, distinctly Indian style emerged with the rise of the *Gupta* era in 320. The Gupta era is regarded as the golden age of Buddhist Indian art. Drama, literature, painting, sculpture and architecture flourished. Many beautiful and elaborate cave temples were carved and painted at Ajanta and Ellora. The style of temples mingles both Buddhist and Hindu designs. Distinctly Indian figures decorate these temples. The bodies are rounded and voluptuous and lack a characteristic Western look.

Higher-Order Thinking Skills

Although the tiles in fig.4–19 have not yet been deciphered, ask the class what they think the tiles mean. Students can create stories or legends to go with these images.

Students also may want to carve their own seals out of 1" x 1" x 1" gum erasers. They can use an X-acto knife or a linoleum cutter for carving. An ink pad can be used to stamp the designs on paper.

Contextual Information

The Taj Mahal

The minarets of the Taj Mahal lean slightly outward so that if they fall during an earthquake, they won't hit the main part of the building.

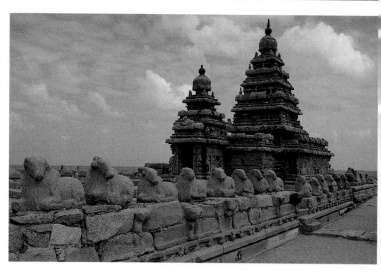

4–22 This temple was carved from some of the live rock that is found in the Mahabalipuram area.
Shore Temple. 7th–8th centuries. Mamallapuram (Mahabalipuram), India. Pallava style, live rock.

The Medieval Period

Hinduism experienced a revival toward the end of the Gupta era. From the ninth to the sixteenth centuries, a variety of kingdoms flourished simultaneously. In Southeastern India, a kingdom known as the *Pallava* produced large freestanding temples cut from live rock at Mamallapuram (fig.4–22). The monolithic structures have multistoried roofs and stone square towers developed by Hindu architects. The temple is symmetrical; the building complex is meant to represent order in the universe. Pathways are provided for worshipers and their rituals. Images of Nandi, the bull in the foreground, symbolize the god Siva.

The Pallavas also produced massive towered gateways called **gopura,** which were placed at entrances to temple complexes. The two gopura of the *Meenakshi Temple* (fig.4–23) are in the sacred southern city of Madurai. The temples are built in *Dravidian* style. This style is synonymous with Southern Indian architecture to this day. Each level of the rectangular

4–23 The poly-chromed surfaces of this temple give it a very ornate appearance.
Meenakshi Temple. 17th century. Madurai, India. Brick and stucco, painted in polychrome.

Performing Arts Connection

Siva, Lord of the Dance

Siva is a principal god in Hinduism, one of the oldest religions in the world. With his great powers, Siva destroys the world. Yet, he is also the giver of life, since the Hindu belief in the endless cycle of time means that the universe is continually recreated.

As Lord of the Dance (fig.4–18), Siva's flaming circles symbolize the forces of creation and destruction that occur during his "dance of bliss." His wild, streaming hair contains all the planets, while his lower right hand gestures "fear not." Siva's upper right hand holds a small drum that sounds out the heartbeat of the creative forces, and his upper left contains the transforming energy of fire. Siva also points down to his raised left foot to which all must bow; with the other foot, he tramples the demon of ignorance, humankind's self-centered ego that must be transcended in order to reach a full spiritual enlightenment.

and pyramidically tapered tower is filled with sculptured and painted panels from Hindu mythology.

Bronze casting in the lost-wax method was practiced by another medieval kingdom, the *Chola*. The sculpture of Siva dancing the *nataraja*, or dance of reincarnation, is rendered in minute detail (fig.4–18). Graceful movement is depicted in metal that would be impossible to portray in stone. The flame-encrusted *halo* shows a remarkable and delicate use of line and shape.

The Mughal Period

The final phase of traditional Indian art arrived with the successive waves of Moslem invasions between the twelfth and sixteenth centuries. The greatest of the *Mughal* emperors was Akbar. Akbar reunited the divided medieval kingdoms into the mighty Mughal empire. Because the Moslem religion prohibited the use of imagery, many Hindu temples and their sculptures were destroyed during the Mughal period. The Mughals replaced them with mosques and beautiful palaces of symmetrical simplicity. Mughals brought the

Persian style with them, a style mixed with Indian ideas. Mosaics of stone and ceramic decorated the floors and walls in arabesque patterns of leaves, flowers and geometric motifs. Most famous of the structures from Mughal India is the *Taj Mahal* (figs.4–17, 4–24).

Typical of Mughal art was the production of fine small objects in enamel, mother-of-pearl, glass or metalwork. Miniature paintings were made on palm leaves and paper. Here, earthly rulers (never deities) were portrayed. The faces were often in profile, and much attention was given to bodily ornament.

4–24 The Taj Mahal was built by Shah Jahan to memorialize his beloved wife. He used 20,000 workers to construct this lavish mausoleum.
Taj Mahal, 1632. Marble. Agra, India.

Lesson 4.2 Review

1 Name several types of art made by the Indus Valley civilization.
2 What are stupas and harmikas?
3 Why were the earliest Buddhist sculptures similar to classical Greek sculpture?
4 How is a temple constructed if it is carved from live rock?
5 Which era is considered the high point of Buddhist Indian art? Describe the temple art of this period.

6 Name two structures built by the Pallavas.
7 Describe the Shore Temple at Mamallapuram. What does the bull on this temple represent?
8 Who was Akbar? What was his great achievement?
9 Why did the Mughals destroy the Hindu temples and sculptures?
10 What is the most famous Mughal Indian structure?

Lesson 4.2 Review Answers

1 Bronze and stone animal sculptures, small stone stamps or seals, ceramic bowls rubbed with resin and decorated with geometric and animal motifs, temples honoring water gods
2 Stupas are round burial mounds containing relics of Buddha's body. A harmika is the small railed balcony on the top of a stupa. It is topped with stylized umbrellas symbolizing the thirty-three higher heavens of Mahayana Buddhism.

3 Alexander's armies conquered Northern India and Pakistan after 326 BC. The first images of Buddha were made in the Hellenistic kingdoms of Bactria and Gandhara. Alexander carried Greek culture into the lands that he conquered.
4 It is carved from solid rock that remains in its natural location in the earth.
5 The Gupta era is the golden age of Buddhist Indian art. Cave temples, which mingled Buddhist and Hindu designs, were elaborately carved and painted. Rounded, voluptuous, distinctly Indian figures decorate these temples.
6 The Shore Temple at Mamallapuram, India; the massive towered gateways, called gopura, on the Meenakshi Temple in Madurai.

7 This monolithic structure is carved from live rock with multistoried roofs and stone square towers. The temple is symmetrical representing order in the universe. There are pathways for worshipers and their rituals. The bull, Nandi, symbolizes the god Siva.
8 Akbar was considered the greatest of Mughal emperors who reunited the divided medieval kingdoms into the mighty Mughal empire.
9 Because the Moslem religion prohibited the use of imagery.
10 The Taj Mahal

Lesson 4.3

A deep respect for nature permeates Chinese beliefs and art; this is underscored by the relatively insignificant role that human figures have in art that depicts outdoor scenes. Chinese writing has been considered an art form from its earliest beginnings as simple pictographs to later, elegant calligraphy.

Warm-up

Ask students to find Chinese writing in some of the images in Lesson 4.3. Share that the Chinese inclusion of characters began with pictographs in ancient times (fig.4–25) and eventually evolved into the exquisite, musiclike notations represented in fig.4–27a.

Objectives

Students should be able to:

Discern some of the visual characteristics that unite the numerous discrete regions of China.

Understand how Chinese art reveals its philosophy regarding humanity's relationship to nature.

Articulate the importance of writing in traditional Chinese art.

Vocabulary Definitions

pictograph (*pik*-ta-graf) A drawing or painting stylizing or simplifying a real image; picture-writing, thus the basis of hieroglyphics and ideographs.
oracle bone (*or*-ah-kul) Large, usually flat, mammal bones or tortoise shells upon which prehistoric Chinese shamans drew picture messages. When heated, the bones cracked, revealing the response of the mystic forces, and were interpreted by the shamans who were acting as the voice of god, or oracle.
calligraphy (kah-*lig*-ra-fee) The art of beautiful writing or printing; fine lettering of elegance, often thought in the West as being similar to the grace of Oriental writing.
sprigging The attaching of pre-formed, leather-hard clay ornaments to a larger form; these ornaments are usually plant forms, human or animal bas-reliefs, or geometric bands.

pagoda (pah-*go*-dah) A circular or octagonal structure built to preserve relics, commemorate unusual acts of devotion, act as an omen of good fortune or as a water tower. Based on the Indian stupa, the form was modified when introduced to China in the third century, and again when introduced into Japan in the sixth century. Usually built of an odd number of stories.
overglaze Design or color applied onto a piece of ceramic after it has been glaze-fired, usually made permanent by firing to a low temperature.
enamel Powdered colored glass that is fused by heating to a ceramic or metal ground; a work of art created by this method. Overglaze enamels are applied over previous glazes.

4.3 China

CHINA IS OFTEN CLAIMED as the world's oldest continuing civilization. China developed first along the valley of the Yellow River and later in much of northern and eastern China. Many cultural and geographic differences between the Chinese north and south of the Yellow River were overcome by the common teachings of *Taoism* and *Buddhism*. Although the Chinese in different regions spoke different local dialects, the written language was the same.

Central to Chinese beliefs is their deep respect for nature. The ancient Chinese believed that nature was filled with spirits. Humanity did not become the conqueror of nature, but rather took its rightful place in it. In Chinese art, humans were seen as insignificant figures against the vastness of their natural surroundings.

The Chinese considered writing to be a form of art. The earliest writing appeared as *pictographs* on *oracle bones* (fig.4–25). A king would ask a question of the gods. The tribal *shaman* would heat a bone until it cracked, then interpret the fractures as the god's answer to the message. Questions and answers were often written down on the bones.

From these pictographs evolved the art of writing which is called *calligraphy*. In calligraphy, there is an evolution of rhythm, similar to that in music. In China, writing and painting are closely related. Line evolved as the dominant aspect of Chinese art.

Vocabulary
pictographs
oracle bones
calligraphy
sprigging
pagoda
overglaze
enamels

4–25 Oracle bones show early picture writing which eventually developed into modern Chinese writing. *Oracle Bones*, 1200 BC. Shang dynasty, China.

4–26 During the Tang dynasty ceramic figures of people and animals were made by the thousands for the tombs of the wealthy. *Glazed horse*, 618–906. Tang dynasty, China. Ceramic with three-color glaze, 29 1/8" (74 cm) high. Los Angeles County Museum of Art, gift of Mr. and Mrs. Felix Guggenheim.

| c.1766 BC–1027 BC Shang Dynasty | 206 BC–220 AD Han Dynasty | 960 AD–1279 AD Song Dynasty |
| 1028 BC–221 BC Zhou Dynasty | 220 AD–589 AD Six Dynasties | 1279 AD–1368 Yuan Dynasty |

Chinese Dynasty Timeline

| 221 BC–206 BC Qin Dynasty | 618 AD–907 Tang Dynasty | 1368 AD–1644 AD Ming Dynasty |
| | 907 AD–960 AD Five Dynasties | 1644 AD–1912 AD Qing Dynasty |

Teach

Art History: Instruct students to study fig.4–26. What would have been the rank of the person who had this ceramic sculpture in his tomb?

• Why would powerful and wealthy people have wanted a horse buried with them?

• What does this indicate about Chinese belief in the afterlife? Have students examine fig.4–32 and the text on page 95 for additional information.

• Were the Chinese the only people who believed in carrying objects from one life to the next? Direct students to examine Egyptian customs in Lesson 5.3.

One-fifth of today's world population lives in China. It is thought to be the oldest civilization in the world. The Great Wall, started in the third century BC, was built by southern Chinese as protection from invading neighbors to the north.

4–28 In China jade was believed to hold spiritual qualities. From very early times, Chinese artists worked with this material.
Feline Head with Bovine Horns and Elephant Trunk, about 1200 BC. Shang dynasty. Jade, 16 1/2" (42 cm) high. The Cleveland Museum of Art, Anonymous Gift, 52.573.

4–27a, b Working with a limited array of colors, this painter created an evocative, spacious landscape.
T'ao Ch'i, copy. *Peach Blossom Spring,* 7th century. Shang dynasty. Ink and color on paper. 9 7/8" high. Freer Gallery of Art, Washington, DC.

Higher-Order Thinking Skills

Students should be aware that scrolls such as *Peach Blossom Spring* (fig.4–27a, b) would not have been completely rolled out for viewing. It would have been unrolled section by section, opening out one section while rolling up the previous one. Ask students why they think the Chinese preferred to view some of their paintings in this manner. What type of viewing does this encourage? What are some of the advantages and disadvantages of viewing paintings in this way?

• If students were to include writing in their own artistic compositions, what would they say?

• How would their words relate to the images both visually and in terms of content?

Reteach

Ask students to decide how the artist of *Peach Blossom Spring* (figs.4–27a, b) created the illusion of depth in the painting.

• Does the Chinese artist use lines in the scroll the same way as the Italian Renaissance painter Raphael does in *School of Athens* (fig.9–30)?

• Do objects in the far distance of the Chinese scroll appear smaller in scale than those in front, as is the case in Raphael's work? Traditional Chinese artists often evoked a sense of deep space by overlapping and also by placing faraway objects higher up in the composition.

• Can students adjust their perceptions to this type of perspective so that they feel as though they are wandering through the Asian countryside? Explain that viewers are meant to examine long Chinese scrolls one section at a time, thereby enhancing the sense that they are literally walking in the landscape.

Criticism: Ask students to explore the relationship between the written characters and drawing style in fig.4–35.

• Is there a substantial difference between the way line is used to create Chinese characters and the way it is used to describe the subject matter? Next, ask students if written words are an important component in American art today. Direct them to Barbara Kruger's contemporary piece in Chapter 17, fig.17–50.

• Is the relationship between her words and images similar to the use of calligraphy in Chinese art? While most Western artists do not rely on words as significant components of their work, Kruger does draw inspiration from |modern advertising. She intentionally quotes the modern media's mixture of images and slogans to reflect the power of advertising. (Students may also analyze Jaune Quick-to-See Smith's use of words in fig.17–51.)

Evaluate

Ask students if Chinese artists were the only ones to incorporate writing into their work. If they need assistance, direct them to the following examples: Islamic—*The Battle of Alexander with the Dragon* (fig.4–73, page 122); Mesopotamian—*Stele of Hammurabi* (fig.5–14, page 157); Egyptian—*Greenfield Papyrus* and *Dancing Girls at a Banquet* (figs.5–28 and 5–29, both on page 166); Aztec—*The Aztec Calendar Stone* (fig.4–89, page 131).

• Do the words in the art of these cultures all serve the same purpose?

Contextual Information

Jade

Jade is a symbol of charity, wisdom and courage. It is as strong as steel. Called the "stone of Heaven," jade was used for many sacred objects as well as gifts to rulers. Musical instruments were created from small sheets of jade that were hung and then struck with a mallet.

Shang Burials

During the Shang dynasty, there were elaborate burials for the rulers. Live people were buried with them: one tomb had 24 female and 22 male skeletons; fifty male heads were buried nearby.

The Great Wall

The Great Wall was built by slave laborers who refused to change their religion (Confucianism) and others who refused to follow the conqueror and first emperor of China. These men literally were worked to death building the 1500-mile long wall that was intended to stop northern invaders.

Shang Dynasty

The bronze age in China corresponds with the *Shang* and *Zhou* periods, from about 1600 to 221 BC. The center of the Shang culture was at the walled city of Anyang. There, fine hand-built and wheel-made gray pottery was produced. Coatings of a glasslike glaze on the pottery heralded the beginnings of modern ceramics.

Sculptures were made from ivory, stone and jade. The Chinese believed that jade has spiritual and medicinal qualities. From green, brown or white jade, craftspeople carved ritual objects and ornaments (figs.4–28, 4–29). The use of jade is found continually from ancient China to the present.

Most significantly, bronze-working became very important. Bronze ritual vessels of the highest quality were made during the Shang dynasty. They were decorated with stylized linear spiral motifs and designs that symbolized clouds, thunder and fierce animal forms (fig.4–30). These bronzes were made using the piece-mold process.

4–29 Many small ancient Chinese jade sculptures have been found. They may have been used as amulets or charms. *Jade Bird*, c. 2000 BC–1500 BC. Shang dynasty. Nephrite, 1 3/4" (4.4 cm). The Nelson-Atkins Museum of Art, Kansas City, Missouri.

Ownership of bronze meant wealth and power and has been cited as one origin of the class system in Chinese history.

Zhou Dynasty

The Shang period ended around 1100 BC when the last Shang ruler was overthrown by the first Zhou king. The Zhou period marked the longest dynasty in all Chinese history, lasting until 221 BC. Pictographic symbols became more stylized and elaborate during the Zhou period. Ceramics continued to

become more sophisticated. Glasslike glazes were used to create intricate geometric designs on some ware. Glass paste was melted on the surface of porous clay bodies to form geometric patterns, as in the covered jar made of stoneware shown here (fig.4–31). The brightly colored original glass has faded to soft pastel hues.

Chinese philosophy flowered during the Zhou period. Two of China's greatest thinkers lived during this time. Lao-tzu (b. 604 BC) taught that humanity needed to exist in harmony with nature. His philosophy became known as *Tao* or "The Way," the basis of Taoism. Confucius (b. 551 BC) also taught respect for nature, as well as respect for parents, ancestors, clan, state and emperor. His ideas influenced a whole culture and were followed in China to this century.

4–30 How many animals can you distinguish on this vessel? There are three: a tiger, an owl and another, unidentified bird. *Kuang*, 12th century BC. Shang dynasty. Bronze, Freer Gallery of Art, Washington, DC.

Materials and Techniques

Jade is the name given to two minerals: nephrite and jadeite. Jadeite is found in Burma and was unknown in China until the eighteenth century. Ancient Chinese jade pieces, therefore, are made of nephrite.

Nephrite is a very hard stone. It is found in lumps or seams within larger non-precious rocks. Weathering often causes the nephrite to split from the main bulk of rock. Because the stone is so hard it must be ground with a hard

abrasive sand. Ancient Chinese jade objects often were created only after months of labor. Given the difficulty of working with this stone, it is amazing that so many ancient jade carvings were produced.

Chinese bronzes also were made in large numbers. Thousands of pieces have survived. The bronzes were cast in workshops utilizing a ceramic mold process. No single craftsperson was responsible for creating an entire vessel. Because bronzes were produced in such large quantities, the work was divided into a number of stages with model-makers, moldmakers, casters and finishers all lending their skills to create a bronze piece.

The process involved pouring alloys of copper and tin heated to a liquid state into ceramic molds. First a model for a vessel was made. A mold was created by packing clay around the model. The mold was removed in sections and fired. The mold sections then were reassembled around a core and the hot metal was poured to create a hollow vessel. (See Chapter 3, fig.3–7 for another example of an ancient Chinese Bronze.)

4–31 How has the artist used pattern to complement the shape of the jar?
Jar with cover, 5th–3rd century BC. Late Zhou dynasty. Pottery with glass paste, 4 3/4" (12 cm) high. Museum of Fine Arts, Boston, Charles B. Hoyt Collection.

4–31 How has the artist used pattern to complement the shape of the jar?
Jar with cover, 5th–3rd century BC. Late Zhou dynasty. Pottery with glass paste, 4 3/4" (12 cm) high. Museum of Fine Arts, Boston, Charles B. Hoyt Collection.

4–32 The tomb in which these figures were found is considered to be one of the greatest archaeological discoveries of modern times. An entire army of these life-sized clay figures was created to accompany the emperor into the next life.
Cavalryman and Saddle Horse, Qin dynasty (221–210 BC). Terra cotta, life-size. Xian, China. Cultural Relics Bureau PRC and The Metropolitan Museum of Art, New York.

Qin Dynasty (Ch'in)

The Chinese north of the Yang Zi (Yellow River) were united for the first time in 221 BC. The new Chinese empire was formed under the short-lived *Qin* dynasty. During this time, the system of written characters was standardized. Pottery objects were made especially for use in tombs. Burial suits of jade segments were tied together in the belief that the jade would preserve the body. In 1974, over 7000 life-size clay soldiers and horses (fig.4–32) were found in underground vaults near Xian. This clay army of imperial bodyguards was intended to serve the Qin emperor in the afterlife.

The *Great Wall* of China (fig.4–33) was also built during the Qin dynasty. The Great Wall is a massive fortification 1500 miles long, 15 to 30 feet wide and 25 feet high, designed to keep out the nomads of Mongolia and Manchuria.

4–33 The Great Wall is so enormous that it is visible to astronauts as they orbit the earth.
Great Wall of China, 3rd–2nd century BC, 1500 miles long (3971 km).

Contextual Information

Ku K'ai-chih

Ku K'ai-chih is one of the earliest known Chinese painters. We know few facts about his life except that he was born in Jiangsu Province and lived from about 344 to about 406.

He is best known as a figure painter and is the source of one of the two main styles of Chinese figure painting. The most characteristic trait of Ku K'ai-chih's style is the long lyrical lines that he used to compose his figures.

Han House Model

During the Han dynasty, replicas of buildings often were placed in tombs. The models that survive today depict buildings of various functions and they also record regional differences in architecture. These models are quite useful in informing us about the appearance of ancient Chinese architecture because no actual buildings have survived. The multistoried tower illustrated here (fig.4–34) is characteristic of the wooden and tiled buildings of northern China. This building type probably had been in existence since the Shang dynasty. It is this type of architecture that eventually dominates all later Chinese architecture.

Fig.4–34 also serves as an example of the houses of wealthy members of Han society. It is decorated with paintings on its doors and windows, as well as on its beams and capitals. Students should examine the post and lintel depicted in fig.3–b to see an example of these paintings.

Han Dynasty

The succeeding *Han* dynasty (206 BC–220 AD) was the second longest in Chinese history. Many Chinese traditions, practices and artistic motifs became established during this period. Han rulers united several territories. The "Silk Road" connected China with Syria and Rome. Toward the end of the dynasty, Buddhism was brought by missionaries from India, where it originated, and from Indo-China.

The Han period provides the first record of Chinese architecture. Clay models of actual buildings have been discovered in royal tombs. Such models show roofs with large overhanging eaves, curved and flat clay tiles, and the inward orientation of Chinese building (fig.4–34). Houses, temples and palaces all followed a similar pattern. They had one or more courtyards, with rooms facing that space.

Han culture was as sophisticated as the contemporary Romans in the West. Ceramic sculptures and functional objects were made for rituals and daily use. Potters used a technique known as **sprigging** to attach preformed clay sculptural decorations into pottery. They produced vessels ornamented with frieze panels and handles with animal forms. Using lead glazes, Chinese potters produced pottery with bright and varied colors. Cosmetic boxes, cups and many other shapes were decorated in red and black lacquer. They were often inlaid with silver or mother-of-pearl. The silk industry flourished, producing woven and embroidered cloth that was colorful, elegant in appearance, and delightfully smooth and cool to the touch. Not only popular with the wealthy in China, these items were exported to royal courts throughout Asia and the Mediterranean world.

Mural painting continued in tombs, and frescoes of scenes from daily life were created. Life-size

stone or clay figures lined the "spirit path" leading to these tombs, and more clay figures of sacrificial men and horses were placed inside.

Six Dynasties Era

Although invaders overtook the Han dynasty, the ensuing period (256–589) was one of growth and change in China. Buddhism spread with zeal, and Taoism, a strong religion based on a simplistic return to nature, grew in the south. Stupa architecture merged with local

4–34 Model houses like this one from tombs provide the first records of early Chinese architecture.
House model, 206 BC–221 AD. Han dynasty. Polychromed pottery, 52" (132 cm) high. The Nelson-Atkins Museum of Art, Kansas City, Missouri.

Chinese watchtower forms to produce the **pagoda**, a monument with an odd number of stories. The pagoda was thought to give protection to residents within its view. Cave temples and monasteries were hollowed out of rock and embellished with huge carved images of Buddha and bodhisattvas.

Interdisciplinary Connection

Astronomy: There was an avid interest in astronomy during the Han dynasty. Zhang Heng was one of the great astronomers of the period. His treatise on astronomy mentions several important findings. These include the fact that the sun is the source of the moon's light and that a solar eclipse is caused by the moon obscuring the sun.

Zhang Heng did not confine his discoveries to celestial bodies. He also is known as the inventor of the seismograph.

Paintings on scrolls of silk and paper first appeared, which enabled scholars to enjoy a long narrative without having to view the entire work at once. Figures were painted against plain backgrounds in a non-stylized naturalism, showing action and overlapping planes, as in *Instructress Writing Down Her Admonitions for the Benefit of Two Young Ladies* (fig.4–35). Note the undefined depth of the scene, emphasized by an absence of background and the lateral placement of the figures. This handscroll is one of the great examples of early Chinese figure painting.

Tang Dynasty

Chinese culture and art reached a golden age during the Tang (618–906) and Song (960–1279) dynasties. Buddhism flourished, and "paradise cults" of believers, anticipating a happy after-life, commissioned millions of images of Buddha. The development of woodblock printing would eventually lead to the printing of Buddhist scriptures and the world's first encyclopedia.

The Tang rulers established a great capital at Chang-An (modern Xian), an international metropolis of two million people. Many temples were built that followed codes of architectural principles. Proportional relationships for all parts of these wooden structures were required. Multistoried brick pagodas were constructed throughout the realm. Tang Buddhist missionaries introduced Chinese art, architecture and writing into Japan in 552.

Sculpture and ceramics flourished. Large tomb figures were manufactured in factories and sold to wealthy families. They often were in the form of a horse (fig.4–26), a symbol of wealth and loyalty to the emperor. "Three-color" glaze produced a profusion of colors on these figures. Sensitive figurines of court women and musicians were painted in subtle colors. These figures had a wonderfully calm quality.

Most Tang sculpture was religious. Buddhist images evolved into a fully "Chinese" style. However, in 845, Buddhism and other religions were banned because of their feared political and financial influence.

Life under the Tang was sophisticated, with a stress on Confucian values of education and respect for family and the growing bureaucracy. Learning centers, or academies, were established where scholars developed ideas about the aesthetics of painting. The expressive art of the beautiful written characters of calligraphy continued to evolve. Painting became the pastime of men who belonged to the social elite. Different "schools" of painting emerged. One school stressed monumental landscapes, while another favored natural still lifes of plants and animals. A third dealt with expressive images of Buddhist saints.

4–35 This is just one section of a long horizontal scroll. Scrolls in this format were meant to be viewed slowly, section by section.
Ku K'ai-chih, *Instructress Writing Down Her Admonitions for the Benefit of Two Young Ladies*. Six dynasties. Horizontal scroll, ink and colors on silk, 7 1/2" (19 cm) high. British Museum, London.

Higher-Order Thinking Skills

Many ancient objects have been found intact because they were used in burial rituals. As students read through this book, they will come across a number of works that were found in tombs and at burial sites. Using the Qin cavalryman and horse (fig.4–32) and the Han house model (fig.4–34) as examples, ask students what types of information we might be able to glean by examining burial objects. How might our view of the cultures that produced these objects be somewhat skewed by relying solely on these works for our information? (Remind students that these objects were found in tombs of important rulers and the wealthy.)

Contextual Information

Rulers of China

Kublai Khan, a Mongol, was founder of the Yuan dynasty. After his and his grandson's deaths, China became weak, and bandit warlords took over.

Return to a more stable government was lead by a Buddhist monk, Chu-Yuan-chang, who became the first Ming ruler. He tried to return China to its former Tang greatness.

Later, Yuang-le-ti, ruler of what is now Cambodia, Laos and Vietnam, developed a navy that controlled the South China Sea and the Indian Ocean. His ships explored the land all the way west to Arabia and Juddah on the Red Sea. After his death, his large navy was greatly reduced, and Chinese exploration ended. The reduced size of the navy was one reason the Chinese ports were taken over by Portuguese warriors and explorers.

Song Painting

A section of one of the most famous Song paintings, *Twelve Views from a Thatched Hut* by Hsia Kuel appears in Chapter 2, fig.2–5. Another important Song painting can be found in Chapter 2, fig.2–14.

Ming Vase

An example of a blue-and-white Ming shoulder vase can be found in Chapter 2, fig.2–a.

Song Dynasty

After the Tang empire collapsed in 906, the country was in turmoil until reunification by the Song in 960. Rulers of the Song dynasty sought to recreate the glorious politics and culture of the Tang. It was the golden age of landscape painting (fig.4–d). Painters in the north stressed bird and flower subjects while painters in the south emphasized bamboo, a plant that symbolized scholarship and wisdom.

Sculpture, while still tied to Buddhism, developed a natural appearance very different from earlier, stiff, Indian-influenced figures. The seated *Guan-Yin* (fig.4–36), the goddess of mercy, rests in a casual pose, covered with the typical elegant drapery and ornament of a bodhisattva.

Architecture of the Song period reflects the strict architectural rules developed under the Tang. Northern architecture was solid and monumental in appearance. Southern architecture evolved into a more flamboyant style with exaggerated upturned eaves.

Yuan Dynasty

The Mongols, or Yuan dynasty (1279–1368), overpowered the Song. However, the Chinese culture was so strong that, instead of imposing their own values, the Mongols supported the established culture. It was during this era that Marco Polo visited "Cathay" (his name for China) and returned to Venice to write glowing reports of Chinese urban life.

Potters, by now, had perfected the technology of porcelain that began under the Tang and, especially, the Song dynasties. Potters produced high-fired pure white ware, which was elegantly shaped and decorated. Sometimes, silver rims were added. Bold decorative floral motifs had developed under the Song, and now potters used imported Persian cobalt to create similar designs in blue. Known as *"blue-and-white,"* the objects were made for the Imperial court (fig.4–37).

4–36 Why do you suppose the pose of this figure is so casual?
Guan-Yin, about 12th century. Song dynasty. Polychromed wood, 45 1/4" (115 cm) high. Museum of Fine Arts, Boston, Henry Edward Wetzel Fund.

4–37 The Chinese for centuries have been considered masters of the art of ceramics.
Dish with flattened rim, 14th century. Yuan dynasty. Glazed porcelain, 3 1/8" x 17 7/8" (8.25 x 45 cm). Freer Gallery of Art, Washington, DC.

Interdisciplinary Inquiry

Social Science: Have students research Portuguese exploration of the Far East and how their buying of art influenced the style of Chinese art.

Ming Dynasty

When the Ming dynasty (1368–1644) came to power, it again tried to restore the glories of traditional China. The Imperial Palace in Beijing (called "The Forbidden City") was started in the early fifteenth century on the site of ancient palaces. Although it was often destroyed by fire and earthquakes, it was always rebuilt according to its original plans. Its many buildings are now open to visitors (fig.4–38).

Collecting older works of art became fashionable during the Ming dynasty, and many older art forms were imitated. In painting, nature scenes based on Song traditions were painted on both hanging and hand scrolls of paper and silk.

Ming ceramics saw an abundance of styles and techniques. Blue-and-white ware was produced in profusion for both local and overseas markets. Many white pieces were painted with colorful enamels and refired at lower temperatures to produce ***overglaze enamels*** of brilliant colors. Cloisonné enamel techniques were perfected, and enamels were applied to bronze surfaces to create exquisite decorative vessels.

Qing Dynasty

Tribes from Manchuria conquered the Ming in 1644. The Manchu, or Qing, dynasty (1644–1911) was regarded by the Chinese as barbarian. They absorbed and emulated Chinese culture, and their royal palace in Beijing imitated earlier Chinese palaces. Elaborate ornamentation, coloring and tile work are an elaborate interpretation of earlier architectural ideas. Rooftop ornaments of glazed clay showed national symbols or depicted local stories (fig.4–39).

Painting continued to be the main form of expression of the literary class (fig.4–27 a, b), and imperial kilns were revitalized.

During the middle of the twentieth century, art schools were shut down by the government to eliminate art as an anti-government threat. Artists were forced to work in communes as ordinary laborers to help produce food and needed supplies. In the 1970s, as China's borders were opened to the outside world, artists were again allowed to work and students could again attend art schools. In the 1990s, the government still had control over artistic production, but artists were beginning to express themselves more freely.

4–39 Scenes from mythology or operas first appeared on rooftops in the South of China during the Song dynasty. *Ceramic rooftop decoration (scene from a local opera), about 1820. Rooftop, Ap Lei Chao Temple, Hong Kong.*

Lesson 4.3 Review

1 What is the world's oldest continuous civilization?
2 What is calligraphy? What do music and calligraphy have in common?
3 Why were over seven thousand life-size clay soldiers and horses buried in China during the Qin dynasty?
4 Why was the Great Wall of China built?
5 Explain some of the conventions of Chinese scroll paintings as found in *Instructress Writing Down Her Admonitions for the Benefit of Two Young Ladies*.
6 Why were so many ceramic horse sculptures created during the Tang dynasty?
7 During which dynasty did Chinese landscape painting reach its high point?
8 What is the Forbidden City?
9 How did the Chinese government affect their country's art in the middle of the twentieth century?

Lesson 4.4

Japan has alternated between long periods of isolation and times of contact with outside cultures. China and Korea first influenced Japanese art in the seventh century, and the country opened to the West in 1868. Traditional Japanese art maintains a simple sense of design, sensitivity to nature and a quiet, understated style.

Warm-up

Ask students to glance at the images in the lesson opener. How do they think the Japanese artists who created these works might respond to the saying "Less is more"? Ask how the reproductions specifically substantiate their responses.

Objectives

Students should be able to:

Describe the simplicity of form, awareness of nature and the overall sense of subtlety that characterize Japanese art.

Recognize the artistic implications of exposure to outside cultures.

Vocabulary Definitions

haniwa (*hahn*-ee-wah) The late Neolithic culture of the Japanese Tumulus Age (300–700), named for the sculptured cylinder-like clay guardian figures typically found at burial sites of the period; also, the sculptures of humans, architecture and animals made during the period.

sumi-e (*soo*-mee-ay) Japanese black ink painting on white paper in the Chinese style.

ukiyo-e (oo-key-*oh*-eh) Japanese pictures of the "floating world" pleasure district of Edo. These were first made in paint, but were more commonly produced in editions of polychrome woodcuts. They are the unique creation of the Edo period.

4.4 Japan

APANESE CULTURE IS THE PRODUCT of long periods of isolation followed by eras of contact with outside cultural influences. Japanese art was influenced by China and Korea from the seventh to ninth centuries; China and Europe in the sixteenth century; and the final opening of Japan to the West following 1868.

The inherent characteristics of Japanese art are simplicity of form and design (fig.4–41), attentiveness to the beauty of nature, and subtlety. The infusions of outside cultural ideas usually stimulated a development in the arts that emphasized ornamentation and elaborate refinement. In reaction, these phases were followed by periods that stressed simplicity and renewed attentiveness to natural design.

> **Vocabulary**
> haniwa
> sumi-e
> ukiyo-e

4–40 The Japanese always seek to blend their architecture with the natural environment surrounding it. *Nagoya Temple Complex*, Japan.

4–41 This ink painting by one of Japan's greatest artists exemplifies the simplicity of form and design which are the hallmarks of Japanese art.
Katsushika Hokusai, *Flowering Squash-Vine and Bee*. Ink and tint on silk panel, 14" x 22" (35 x 55 cm). Freer Gallery of Art, Washington, DC.

Teach

Aesthetics/Criticism: Ask students to write a brief description about a stroll through the Japanese scene in Hasegawa Tohaku's *Pine Wood* (fig.4–42) and then the Chinese countryside in fig.4–27a.

• Which artist provides more visual information on which students can base their descriptions? The Japanese painting, although clearly influenced by Chinese art, is subtler and sparer in design. Now have students decide what the largest difference is in the way the Japanese and Chinese artists depict space.

• What has Tohaku done to his lines to intensify the sense that the trees are receding into the mist?

Aesthetics/Criticism: Set up a few objects in the center of the classroom and ask students to study the arrangement for eight to ten minutes. As they look, students should decide on the fewest lines they will need to use to convey the very essence of this scene. After, direct students to execute their planned composition. Does the finished work look as they had anticipated or did they make alterations? Ask them if, based on this experience, they believe it was easy for the artists of figs.4–41 and 4–42 to create such evocative scenes with a minimum of strokes. Explain that while the final marks may have been placed down in a relatively short time, the artists would have spent years learning how to look with keen vision in order to paint simple scenes that speak volumes.

Sometimes referred to as "The Land of the Rising Sun," Japan consists of four main islands and 4000 smaller islands. Two-thirds of the land is mountainous and thickly forested. The majority of Japanese people live closely packed together in coastal regions. Japan's isolation from the Asian mainland contributed to the development of a distinct culture.

4–42 The Japanese infuse the arts and design into all phases of their lives. Household screens and slide doors often are painted with eloquent scenes from nature.
Hasegawa Tohaku, *Pine Wood*, 1539–1610 (detail from a pair of six-fold screens). Ink on paper, 61" (155 cm) high. Tokyo National Museum.

Higher-Order Thinking Skills

Have students compare Hokusai's ink painting to Zurbarán's *Still Life with Lemons, Oranges and a Rose* (fig.2–57), looking especially at color and composition.

c.9000–200 BC Jomon Phase	552 AD–645 AD Asuka Period	794 AD–1185 AD Heian Period	1334 AD–1573 AD Muromachi Period	1615 AD–1868 AD Edo Period	1912 AD–1926 AD Taisho Period

Japan Timeline

200 BC–300 AD Yayoi Period	645 AD–794 AD Nara Period	1185 AD–1392 AD Kamakura Period	1573 AD–1615 AD Momoyama Period	1868 AD–1912 AD Meiji Period	1926 AD–Present Showa Period

Evaluate

Challenge students to imagine that they are environmentalists and to examine all the images in Lesson 4.3. How would they rate Japan's attitude toward nature as compared to America's? What about the images has helped them form their opinions?

Explain that Japan was not only influenced by outside cultures but exerted its own impact on others as well. Ask students to find evidence of the French Impressionists' interest in Japanese prints in a painting by Edouard Manet (fig.13–a). If they need assistance, ask how one of the prints on the wall in the painting relates to Ando Hiroshige's *Hodogaya Station* (fig.4–e)? Some French artists in the second half of the nineteenth century absorbed a sense of composition from the Japanese prints that had become widely available in Paris at the time.

Reteach

Direct students to study the Italian Renaissance artist Leonardo da Vinci's paintings in figs.9–22 and 9–24 and to read on page 277 about his use of *sfumato*. Next, have them write a critique of Tohaku's *Pine Wood* from Leonardo's point of view.

• How might Leonardo have reacted to Tohaku's depiction of space and the way he blurred the edges of his objects in order to establish the sense of receding space? Share with students that although Tohaku and Leonardo both used a similar technique to create a sense of depth, there is no evidence that they were aware of each other's work.

• Ask what this might lead us to conclude about the development of atmospheric perspective.

• Did students know that similar developments occurred in the East and West?

• Can they identify instances of similar happenstance in scientific innovations? For instance, were Europeans the only ones to invent the printing press?

Contextual Information

The Nara Period

During the Nara period, Japanese craftspeople deliberately copied Chinese art, architecture and city planning. Since wars and fires destroyed much of the seventh- and eighth-century sculpture and temples in China, the art and temples in Japan provide the only evidence we have of what China looked like during the Tang dynasty.

Kimonos

Kimonos are the national costume and traditional, robelike garment worn by the people of Japan. Kimono means "the thing worn," and to the Japanese the word simply means "clothing." Kimonos are basically the same size and shape for both men and women, with the length adjusted at the waist by the obi, or sash. The kimono has been worn by all classes and is distinguished only by color, decoration and design—elements influenced by gender, age and social status. Textile arts are highly regarded in Japan, and a variety of techniques are used to create the images on kimonos: damask weaving, paste-resist processes, stenciling, embroidery and hand-painting.

The Japanese attempted to live in harmony with their natural environment and applied to everyday life a philosophy that evolved from their early religion of Shintoism. Consequently, flowers, birds, trees, the seasons and other natural motifs had an important place in their art. However, the artists did not strive to produce a faithful and lifelike copy of nature, but a conventional, decorative effect. In this way, Japanese people wear the same patterns that decorate nature, thus reflecting their appreciation of beauty—both in nature and in the ordinary events of daily life.

Jomon and Yayoi Cultures

Little is known of Japan's early history. Its origins may date back as far as 5000 BC during the Neolithic *Jomon* culture. This culture produced simple undecorated food vessels made of red clay. By 2000 BC, colored slip was used to create animal and human abstract patterns. By 200 BC, the *Yayoi* culture from Korea and Kyushu overtook the Jomon society. This culture created clay sculptures that were set up

4–44 These buildings are reproductions of Chinese Tang architecture and are the oldest wooden structures in the world. *Horyu-ji temple complex*, begun 607. Asuka, Japan.

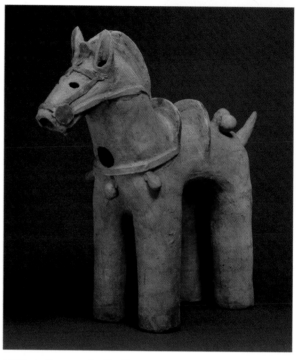

4–43 Haniwa figures were placed fencelike around burial mounds. They may have been placed there to control erosion, or perhaps to protect the dead. *Horse*, Haniwa figure, 5–6th centuries AD. Terra cotta. 23" x 26" (58.4 x 66 cm). The Cleveland Museum of Art. The Norweb Collection, 57.27.

around gigantic burial mounds. The sculptures, called **haniwa**, were pedestaled clay bowls, plates and unglazed ceramic cylinders with human or animal forms (fig.4–43) sculpted in their upper parts. In addition to these figures, the late Yayoi culture also produced bronze cast objects from about 300. The technique of bronze casting was likely imported from China sometime after the Han dynasty.

The area around present-day Kyoto came to be the center of political power. A statue of Buddha was sent to the Japanese court from Korea in 552. It was the beginning of Japan's acceptance of Buddhism and, with it, Chinese and Korean cultural influences. Although the Japanese borrowed many ideas from China and Korea, they did not copy them exactly.

Sculpted Figures of the Buddha

In ancient legends, reference is made to a portrait of the Buddha Gautama that was made of sandalwood and unpainted. A copy of it was brought from China during the Heian period. Wooden sculptures of the Buddha carved during the Heian were frequently carved from one piece of fragrant wood (sandalwood, cypress or camphor) and left unpainted.

• Have students research types of wood mentioned above to answer the following questions: What advantages do they hold for the sculptor? Do any of them have natural preservative properties? How does the fragrance of an object affect our valuing of it? Why do we use perfumes and incenses?

Asuka Period

Asuka became the Japanese capital from 538 to 645, giving its name to an era during which Buddhist missionaries, scriptures and beliefs were welcomed. Confucian ideals of government organization accompanied these Chinese and Korean imports. However, the older Japanese religion known as *Shinto*, "the way of the gods," continued to influence Japanese thought. Shinto, the oldest and still largest religion of Japan, began as a form of nature worship. The early Japanese believed that gods dwelled throughout the world of nature. Shinto later included the worship of ancestors.

Tang Chinese architecture was emulated in the building of the first Buddhist structures, the *Horyu-ji temple* at Asuka (fig.4–44). The main hall and an adjacent pagoda still exist as the oldest wooden structures in the world. These buildings are also regarded as a faithful reproduction of Chinese architecture of the Tang. The style reflects a calm and graceful atmosphere as well as a structural honesty in the exposure of beams and brackets.

Nara Period

When the capital was moved to nearby *Nara*, a new era began (646–784). Furniture, paintings, pottery and architecture were based on Chinese ideals. The court sponsored elaborate production and collection of art, including works from China and Persia. Buddhism became firmly entrenched, and huge temples and monasteries were constructed of wood in the Chinese style. Buddhist images were made of lacquer and bronze. The largest, a 70-foot-high, 700-ton, bronze *Dibutsu* (fig.4–45), is housed in the largest wooden temple in the world, the Todai-ji.

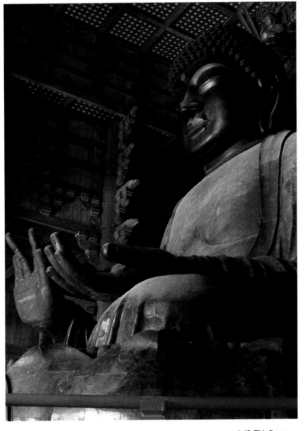

4–45 This figure is nearly six stories high.
Great Dibutsu (Buddha), 8th century. Bronze, 70'9" (21.6 m) high. Todai-ji temple, Nara, Japan.

Higher-Order Thinking Skills

Religious figures (fig.4–45) and secular sculptures sometimes are created on a very large scale. Ask the class why they think people create such large monuments. Are there any in their community?

Contextual Information

Harmony with Nature

In spite of many wars around them, artists of the Kamukura period continued working with an increasing emphasis on realism. On scrolls, they made portraits of priests, warriors and politicians. They also painted battles and historic events in bright colors.

After this difficult period of war, the Japanese developed three concepts to guide their art: the use of natural materials in natural ways, with concern for proper proportion and natural finishes; a reverence for old things, and an appreciation of sharp contrasts, which brought attention to the object. The guiding principle was harmony with nature.

Teahouses were created for each season. Natural materials were used inside, and passages in the buildings led to garden pathways and stepping stones and bridges across small ponds. Trees and bushes were trimmed to keep a set size and shape.

Flowers were planted in special patterns, with careful attention to having certain colors blooming at different times of the year. In some gardens, a moon-viewing platform was built so that visitors could view the moon's reflection on the water.

Heian Period

Heian, today the modern city of Kyoto, became the capital in 784. The Heian period marked the golden age of Japanese art and lasted until 1192. Close ties with China were broken in 898, allowing Japanese artists to create their own styles of art that differed from Chinese styles.

Yamato-e painting evolved during the later Heian period. Artists created decorative horizontal scrolls with long narratives (fig.4–46). Through these scrolls, artists expressed Japanese tastes, sentiments and nationalistic feelings.

Buddhism had split into a number of factions or sects. One of these sects, the *Shingon*, stressed the veneration of images and figures of gods with multiple heads and hands. *Amida* cult Buddhists carved peaceful images, stressing spiritual sincerity. Wooden buildings of subtle proportions were constructed in natural settings, often near water. Temples and gardens were asymmetrically arranged; buildings, ponds and rock forms signified the harmony of humanity with nature.

4–47 Compare this figure to the Khmer Buddha (fig.4–54).
Great Buddha of Kamakura, 1252. Kamakura period, Japan. Cast bronze, 42' (128 m) high.

Kamakura Period

A military government replaced the Heian government, and the capital was moved to *Kamakura* from 1192 to 1338. Many early Nara temples were restored after the civil wars. A huge bronze Buddha (fig.4–47) was cast. Fashion and taste in the new capital were at odds with the cultural heritage of Kyoto. Kamakura art was more realistic.

During the Kamakura era, *Zen Buddhism* from China gained popularity in Japan. It was to have a far-reaching cultural impact. Zen Buddhism promoted spiritual exercises, meditation and a simple monastic lifestyle. Paintings stressed portraiture, battle scenes and incidents taken from everyday life. They also depicted torments in hell, illness and suffering. Potters

4–46 This is a detail of a scroll that illustrates an eleventh-century Japanese novel by Lady Murasaki.
The Tale of Genji, detail. Late Heian period, 12th century. Scroll, color on paper, 8 1/2" x 15 3/4" (21.6 x 40 cm).

who studied Song ceramic methods established kilns in Seto and other southern centers, leading to a native Japanese ceramic tradition. The objects produced there became a mainstay in the later development of the *cha-no-yu*, the Zen-inspired tea ceremony.

Muromachi and Momoyama Periods

Kyoto was re-established as the capital in 1338, initiating the *Muromachi* era, which lasted until 1578. The warrior class patronized the arts and created an ostentatious court life. As a contrast to their incessant warfare, tranquil landscaped gardens provided respite with their peaceful arrangements of natural and architectural elements. Spiritual peace was also available in the *Noh* (dramas), *cha-no-yu* (tea ceremony) and *ikebana* (flower arranging). Individual works of art were displayed within special alcoves known as *tokonoma*.

Muromachi painting was dominated by the Chinese ink style, known also as **sumi-e**. Although usually done on absorbent rice paper (washi) in quick confident strokes, the style was used on slid-

Performing Arts Connection

Japanese Dance and Dramatic Traditions

Noh Drama: Traditional Noh theater developed in the late 1300s, blending earlier dance and theatrical forms. It was originally performed outdoors or in shrines and temples. Noh is not acted but "danced" with moments of great passion, first expressed in slow and stately movements and eventually mounting in intensity. The actors wear masks as well as rich brocade robes to indicate their characters and states of mind. The actors also distort their voices to enhance the unearthly quality of their movements. Flute, drums and chanting heighten the dance and story line. Most Noh plays revolve around a dramatic meeting between a troubled spirit (the shite) and a priest or bystander (the waki). Although the shite may find some spiritual relief, there is frequently the feeling that this haunting encounter can repeat itself.

Kabuki Theater: Kabuki theater was one of the most popular dramatic forms of entertainment during Japan's Edo period. Although the plots were initially simple, by 1680, actors were performing complex stories on lavishly designed stages with larger-than-life action and colorful costumes. Female impersonators, who wear striking make-up and perform roles of young women and courtesans, remain the cornerstone of the art form. As with Noh, Kabuki actors come mostly from theatrical families and begin their training at a very early age, mastering not only their roles but all aspects of Kabuki movement, costume and makeup.

ing door panels and screens by a family of painters named *Kano* (fig.4–48). Their style of painting was later used during the Momoyama era (1573–1615) to embellish rooms in large castles built by feudal war lords. Paintings of trees and nature scenes appear to be viewed through the pillars, adjacent to the *tatami*-matted floor.

Edo Period

Internal political turmoil caused Japanese rulers to attempt to impose order by closing Japan to the outside world. European and Christian influences were banned in 1612. The capital was moved to *Edo*, modern Tokyo (1615–1867). However, after 1868, in a period of rule called the *Meiji* Restoration, Japan again opened itself to Western influences.

In the Edo period, a unique style of genre painting evolved, known as **ukiyo-e** ("the art of the floating world"). This art was popular with the growing middle class. Ukiyo-e art features colorful images of daily life (fig.4–e), fashionable courtesans, and actors from the popular *kabuki* theater. These paintings were later adapted to the woodcut process. By the end of the era, multicolored prints were being produced by over two hundred artists and marketed to the middle class at very low prices. Among the best examples is Utagawa Hiroshige's *Night Rain on Kirasaki Pine*, part of a large series of prints (fig.2–48). These scenes provide vivid glimpses of Japanese life. They also came to be valued in the West for their bold design. Impressionist painters were particularly influenced by their aesthetic quality.

4–48 The technique of *sumi-e* involves quick, sure strokes of ink on rice paper (washi). *Kano paintings* inside audience room of Nijo Castle, Kyoto, about 1603.

Modern Period

Non-Japanese painting techniques, notably oil painting, were first introduced by the Jesuits (Catholic missionary priests) and later encouraged under the Meiji era. Ming and Qing ceramics influenced Japanese pottery production. Japanese *Imari* and *Kutani* porcelain wares are brightly surfaced and boldly colored. Contemporary artists in Japan continue to reflect their traditional heritage of simplicity and elegance, but use every medium and technique available to artists around the world. Their sculpture is admired by artists in every country, and their work has been displayed in museums around the globe.

Lesson 4.4 Review

1 Describe haniwa sculptures.
2 What are some of the beliefs of the Shinto religion?
3 What are the oldest wooden structures in the world? How old are they?
4 Where is the great Dibutsu (Buddha)? Which is taller, your school room or this statue?
5 What modern cities did the ancient cities of Heian and Edo become?
6 What is yamato-e painting? On what type of surface were these painted?
7 How was Kamakura art different from Heian art?
What were some of the subjects of Kamakura era paintings?
8 What is the Japanese term for the Zen-inspired tea ceremony? Where were the ceramics used in this ceremony first produced? Which Chinese dynasty's art influenced the production of these pieces?
9 What do Noh, ikebana and tokonoma mean?
10 What style of painting did the Kano use on the panels in the audience room of the Nijo Castle in Kyoto?

Lesson 4.5

Over the centuries, various Southeast Asian cultures have either mingled with or dominated one another. Chinese and Indian art exerted the strongest influence over the region's art and government.

Warm-up

Direct students to study the map of Southeast Asia and then locate this area on the world map at the back of the textbook. Ask what two large, nearby countries might have had the strongest impact on Southeast Asian culture. Students can check their answers in the introductory paragraph on page 106. Explain to students that artists from the region adapted rather than imitated Chinese and Indian traditions.

Objective

Students should be able to:

Identify how Southeast Asian artists assimilated Chinese and Indian traditions into their own unique style.

Vocabulary Definitions

wat (wot) A Thai or Laotian temple; a Khmer pagoda.
chedis (*jay*-dee) A tiered, pointed, spire-like Thai pagoda.
batik (bah-*teek*) A coloring or dyeing process using a wax stencil to protect design areas from coloration by dyeing of cloth or paper.

Teach

Art History/Criticism: Ask students to read about the origins of Buddhism on page 82 and examine the Indian *Colossal Head of Buddha* (fig.4–21).

• What is distinctly different about the Southeast Asian *Buddha Enthroned* (fig.4–54) as compared to the Indian *Colossal Head*?

• Can students detect its Cambodian facial features?

• What in this Cambodian work is unlike the Indonesian Buddha at Borobudor (fig.4–50) and the Japanese work in fig.4–47?

4.5 Southeast Asia

SOUTHEAST ASIA IS A GEOGRAPHIC ZONE where different cultures have mingled, coexisted or dominated each other since the days of the Roman empire. The two dominant influences have come from India and China. Southeast Asians adapted, rather than imitated, Indian and Chinese art and government to create a way of life of their own.

Several coastal areas became *Indianized* as early as the first century. Adopting Hindu and Buddhist faiths, rulers developed a form of government known as the "cult of the god-king." The king identified himself with a god, usually the Hindu gods Siva or Vishnu. The ruler became the model for society and had the blessings of the gods in his earthly rule.

Vocabulary
wat
chedis
batik

4–49 In Thailand sculpture is the predominant art form, and Buddha is one of the most popular subjects. *Royal Palace with Gold Statue,* Bangkok, Thailand.

4–50 There is a Buddha within each of the wells at the top of this monument. The figures are hidden by bell-shaped covers. *Buddha from top of Borobudor,* detail (fig.4–55).

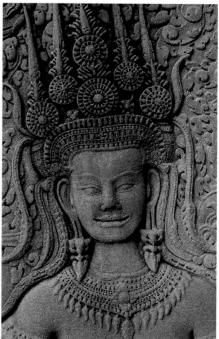

4–51 The exterior walls of many of the galleries at Angkor Wat are covered with lyrical figures. The fluid motion of this figure is characteristic of much of the relief work found at the site. Aspara, detail of bas-relief from central structure. *Angkor Wat.* See also fig.4–52.

• Is there a serpentlike creature in any of these other pieces? Is the twisting, enflamed snake actually a Buddhist deity? Have students read the text to learn about the Hindu creature *kala-makara.* How does its ability to devour and recreate time relate to Buddhism?

Aesthetics/Criticism: Ask students to pretend that they are the sculptor of the bas relief at Angkor Wat (fig.4–51). Would it have been hard to create this piece?

• How long might it have taken to carve such small, intricate figures? Now instruct students to examine the entire site in fig.4–52. Discuss what it must have been like to be part of the team that constructed this enormous complex.

• What might be the significance of all the carvings? To help students, challenge them to envision walking through the enormous structure.

• How do its size, images and materials provide information about its meaning and whom the complex was made for? Refer students to page 108 to check their answers.

• Do students feel that the temple successfully suggests a sense of the divine power that the mortal Cambodian ruler wished to embody? Why or why not?

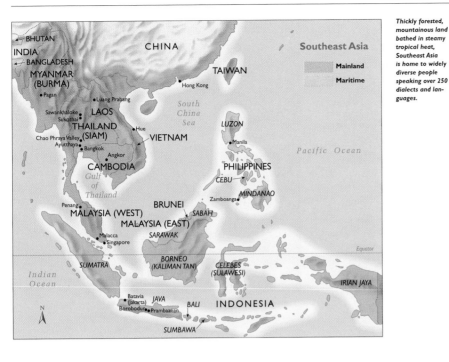

Thickly forested, mountainous land bathed in steamy tropical heat, Southeast Asia is home to widely diverse people speaking over 250 dialects and languages.

Southeast Asia

☐ Mainland

☐ Maritime

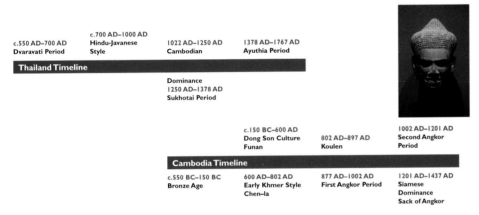

c.550 AD–700 AD	c.700 AD–1000 AD	1022 AD–1250 AD	1378 AD–1767 AD
Dvaravati Period	Hindu-Javanese Style	Cambodian	Ayuthia Period

Thailand Timeline

Dominance
1250 AD–1378 AD
Sukhotai Period

c.150 BC–600 AD	802 AD–897 AD	1002 AD–1201 AD
Dong Son Culture Funan	Koulen	Second Angkor Period

Cambodia Timeline

c.550 BC–150 BC	600 AD–802 AD	877 AD–1002 AD	1201 AD–1437 AD
Bronze Age	Early Khmer Style Chen–la	First Angkor Period	Siamese Dominance Sack of Angkor

Higher-Order Thinking Skills

Have students examine the figure and the building shown in fig.4–49. Ask how the sculptor and the architect have used line in each. Then have students compare the figure and building with the relief sculpture in fig.4–51. Do they see any similarities?

Evaluate

Ask how the images in Lesson 4.5 can prove that Hindu and Buddhist influences intermingled in Southeast Asian art.

• What might the simultaneous appearance of Buddhist and Hindu features, as in the *Buddha Enthroned*, reflect about the relationship of the two religions in this region?

Reteach

Ask students to identify other cultures in which earthly rulers associated themselves with the divine. Have them find artwork commissioned by Egyptian pharaohs (the *Tutankhamen Mummy Case*, page 148), Emperor Justinian (*Emperor Justinian and Attendants*, page 213) and King Louis XIV of France (Versailles, pages 331 and 344). Why might these rulers have associated themselves with the spiritual realm?

• Ask students to pretend to be one of their subjects; would they feel free to speak out against the laws that the rulers made?

• How does the artwork with divine implications affect their decision?

Ask students what similarities they can discern between the carvings that decorate Southeast Asian monuments and those on the Mesopotamian palace at Persepolis (page 158), the Parthenon (page 184) and the French Romanesque Church Sainte-Madeleine (page 233).

• Although the styles differ, what do these large relief sculptures share in terms of materials, scale, messages they communicate and who commissioned them?

• If students were to construct a monument commemorating their reign as supreme ruler, what would it look like? What information would they want to express?

Contextual Information

Angkor Thom

The Khmer Buddhist ruler Jayavarman VII had temples constructed in the walled city of Angkor Thom and dedicated them to the Buddhist goddess of Transcendent Wisdom, Bodhisattva Lokeshvara and Buddha. This was a change from temples created to honor rulers who thought of themselves as descended from god. Buddhists were to rely on the power of a god separate from the ruler.

Jayavarman VII also built 102 hospitals and 121 travelers' rest houses along main roads and dedicated them to the protection of Buddha. Future rulers gradually replaced Buddhism with Hinduism, and Angkor Thom was abandoned.

Cambodia

The Khmer empire had its roots in the 800s. The greatest Khmer empire was established during the twelfth and thirteenth centuries in what is now called Cambodia. Each Khmer ruler constructed his own immense national temple, or **wat**. These temples perpetuated their divine image and later served as their mausoleums.

The finest examples of god-king temples are *Angkor Wat* (fig.4–52), built about 1150, and the Bayon at Angkor Thom. The temples reflect strong Hindu influence in the tall stone towers covered with sculptures of Hindu and local religious heroes. Many walls are decorated with images from Hindu mythology (fig.4–51). Small niches inside the temples were filled with stone or bronze images of deities. The temple of Angkor Wat was dedicated to Vishnu. The Bayon features the head of King Jayavarman VII (fig.4–53). The king is depicted as the bodhisattva *Lokeshvara* on towers throughout the temple complex.

Buddhism entered Cambodia and became intermixed with older Hindu traditions. Buddhist images were cast in a unique style. Facial features were distinctly Cambodian. In the example pictured here (fig.4–54), a niche has been created for the Buddha incorporating the Hindu *kala-makara*, a serpentlike creature which devours and reproduces time. The flames, embellishments, decorations and tiny figures are part of Buddhist and Hindu iconography.

4–53 A colossal head appears on each side of the square towers at Bayon.
Tower of Bayon, Angkor Thom, 12–13th centuries, Cambodia.

4–52 Recent research indicates that the layout of Angkor Wat may have had an astronomical significance.
Angkor Wat, 12–13th centuries, Cambodia.

Indonesia

Buddhist influences most strongly affected areas of Burma, Thailand, Sumatra and Java. Sumatra and Java are the two most important islands of the country of Indonesia. Indonesia is made up of five main islands and hundreds of smaller islands. Buddhism reached its greatest political height with the *Shailendra* kingdom in ninth-century Java. There, architects created one of the seven wonders of the ancient world in the artificial cosmic-mountain known as *Borobudor*.

Borobudor is a stupa that has ten levels (fig.4–55). Bas-relief carvings on the lower six layers symbolically represent the cosmos. The lowest of

Interdisciplinary Connection

Geography: Indonesia is composed of 13,677 islands. More than half of them are uninhabitable. Today's population of 165 million people speak as many as 300 languages. Jakarta is the nation's capital and the national language is Bahasa Indonesia.

4–55 Use the text to discover more about this cosmic mountain. *Borobudor*, about 850. Shailendra dynasty. Java.

these levels represents hell and eternal torment. The images were apparently so grotesque that the Shailendras themselves covered the images with tamped earth ramparts. The next five layers represent humanity's earthly adventures. Walkways on each square level are lined with carvings of the teachings of Buddha. Sculptures show a realistic understanding of body proportion, overlapping planes to show depth, and graceful movement in the figures (fig.4–4). The sculptures provide historical records of clothing, architecture and even shipbuilding styles of the times. Four round layers finish off the top of the stupa, representing the supernatural element (fig.4–50). At the apex of Borobudor is a large solid stupa.

Buddhism declined in Java with the fall of the Shailendras in 856 but dominated the cultures of Burma, Sri Lanka, Cambodia, Thailand and Vietnam.

4–54 Hindu influences mixed with Buddhism in Cambodian portrayals of Buddha. *Buddha Enthroned*, 10th century. Khmer. Bronze. Kimbell Art Museum, Fort Worth, Texas.

Higher-Order Thinking Skills

Many ancient sites and shrines were placed in a special relationship to astronomical phenomena. Ask why ancient peoples were so concerned with their relationship to the sky. Are we as concerned today? Are our reasons similar to or different from those of ancient peoples?

Conservation Note

The world's greatest Buddhist monument, Borobudor, is said to have taken the labor of 10,000 men over the course of 100 years to build.

The structure was abandoned shortly after it was completed and was not rediscovered until 1814. After 1000 years of neglect, it was in ruins. The monument underwent a restoration between 1907–1911. More recently, UNESCO worked from the 1960s to the 1980s to restore the structure at a cost of $25 million.

Contextual Information
Identifying Southeast Asian Art

Archaeologists and art historians have had difficulties in determining where objects found in Southeast Asia were made. Because of battles, trading patterns, the general movement of people escaping conflicts, and the fact that artists used styles from across their borders, experts have found it difficult to separate objects from Thailand and Cambodia. Sometimes, they have labeled styles by the ruler of the territory in which the objects are found or by certain characteristics of the items.

Burma, Thailand

Burmese art and architecture reached a high point in the twelfth century with the construction of many bell-shaped stupa-temples in the capital city of Pagan.

Distinctive Thai art and architecture originated in the late 1200s with the formation of the first Thai kingdom at *Sukothai* in the northern Chao Phraya valley. Stupas were constructed in the style of the Ceylonese, Burmese and Khmers. Ideas about architecture and sculpture came from the Khmers and from remnants of the *Dvaravati* kingdom in far southern Thailand. Immense images of Buddha were formed in clay, brick and stucco and were often covered with gold leaf.

Thai potters for the royal courts created distinctive celadon glazes.

Thai equivalents of blue-and-white porcelain were made. The exquisite designs reflected the taste and traditions of the Thais. One such example is the *covered box* (fig.4–56) produced at the *Sawankhaloke* kilns near Sukothai about 1400.

4–57 Use the text to identify European architectural influences in the Thai palace.
Royal Palace, exterior view, 19th century. Bangkok, Thailand.

4–56 Exquisite designs cover this box from the Thai royal kilns.
Covered box. Sawankhaloke kilns, Thailand, 14–15th centuries. Stoneware with underglaze iron, 5 1/2" (14 cm) high. Los Angeles County Museum of Art.

Bangkok became the Thai capital in 1782. Its architecture blended Asian and European influences from Western trading nations. The *Royal Palace* (figs.4–49, 4–57) shows a European influence in the rusticated base, the segmentally arched portico, and the Classical columns and windows. The roof, however, is distinctly Thai and is topped with spirelike forms known as **chedis**.

Vietnam, Laos, Malaysia

Chinese culture directly influenced a small area of Southeast Asia. When Vietnam became independent from China in the tenth century, the court at Hue emulated Chinese culture in its bronze castings and in the construction of Buddhist temples. This influence carried over into areas of neighboring Laos. The resulting Buddhist architecture is a mixture of Chinese, Thai and Lao traditions. *Wat Xieng Thong* (fig.4–58) is a beautiful example of these cultural blends. The concave roof is Chinese, while the overlapping roof lines are Thai. The decorative detail reflects the local Lao style.

When Islam became established in coastal Malaysia and Indonesia between the ninth and fifteenth centuries, architects produced distinctive *mosques.* Artists produced elaborate bronze weaponry (the

4–58 Local Lao tradition combines with Chinese and Thai influences in this chapel. Can you identify them? *Wat Xieng Thong* (The Chapel). Luang Prabang, Laos.

wavy-edged *kris* dagger) and printed fabrics. The fabrics are known as **batik** and are made from wax-stencil dyeing processes. The elegant and sophisticated court life required well-crafted bronze utensils and bejeweled royal objects. Court musicians played the *gamelon,* an orchestra of drums, wooden wind instruments and sets of bronze gongs, all highly ornamented with geometric and curvilinear abstract patterns.

Portuguese, Dutch and British settlers arrived in Southeast Asia in the sixteenth century. Local peoples incorporated some Western ideas into their art and architecture. British and Dutch officials often provided financial support for local sultans in Malaysia and Indonesia. As a result, sultans devoted much time and newly acquired wealth to reviving traditional art forms and creating opulent courts.

Lesson 4.5 Review

1 In what modern country was the Khmer empire located? Why did each Khmer ruler construct a wat?
2 Describe Borobudor in Java. Why did the Shailendras cover the lower levels of this stupa with dirt ramparts?
3 List seven countries in Southeast Asia and a type of art created in each area.

4 How does the Royal Palace in Bangkok combine the architecture of Thailand and the West?
5 What is an Indonesian batik? How is it made?
6 Describe the instruments found in an Indonesian gamelon.

Lesson 4.5 Review Answers

1 The Khmer empire was located in the area that has become Cambodia. These temples perpetrated the rulers divine image and served as their mausoleums.
2 Borobudor is a ten-leveled stupa with bas-relief carvings on the lower six layers symbolically representing the cosmos. The lowest level represents hell and eternal torment, but was so grotesque that the Shailendras covered the images with tamped earth ramparts.

The next five layers show humanity's earthly adventures. Carvings of Buddha's teachings line walkways on each square level. Four round layers representing the supernatural finish off the top of the stupa. A large solid stupa is at the apex.
3 Cambodia: wat
Indonesia: stupas, artificial cosmic mountains such as Borobudor
Burma: bell-shaped stupa temples
Thailand: stupas, huge Buddha images, pottery with celadon glazes
Vietnam: bronze castings, Buddhist temples
Laos, Malaysia and Indonesia: mosques, batik, gamelon instruments

4 The Royal Palace in Bangkok shows a European influence in the rusticated base, the segmentally arched portico, and the Classical columns and windows. The roof is Thai in style, topped with spire-like forms called *chedis*.
5 A printed fabric made from a wax stencil dying process
6 Drums, wooden wind instruments and sets of turned bronze gongs, all highly ornamented with geometric and curvilinear abstract patterns.

Lesson 4.6

Each of the groups of disparate people in Oceania and Highland Asia developed their own unique, highly stylized visual traditions.

Warm-up

Ask students to pretend that they are fashion designers on a trip to gather ideas for textile designs. Which images in Lesson 4.6 inspire patterns that they would use for clothing? What adaptations might they make to the Oceanic and Highland Asian examples? What types of clothing would they create with these designs? Challenge students to think of unusual articles of clothing for special occasions as well as daily wear.

Objectives

Students should be able to:

Recognize the high degree of stylization in most Oceanic and Highland Asian art.

Comprehend that artists in this region create sculpture, fabrics, pottery and architecture.

Vocabulary Definitions

totem (*toe*-tem) An animal or natural object which symbolizes a clan or family.

Teach

Art History: Have students imagine that they are curators in an American museum and someone has brought in the *Tapa Cloth Figure* (fig.4–60) for them to examine. The visitor found the piece in an attic and would like to know what to make of it. How can they as curators begin some detective work just by handling the piece? What would holding the figure tell them about its materials?

• How might this help them determine where it came from? (Students can confirm their guesses about the object's materials in the caption information.)

• Would artists from highly industrialized nations or those in cold northern regions typically have easy access to bark and fibers?

• What types of animals could have inspired the long crooked beak and striped-head pattern? Might the artist have been familiar with tropical birds?

4.6 Oceania and Highland Asia

SOME OF THE WORLD'S most symbolic artwork has been produced in a vast area that stretches from the upper headwaters of the Mekong, Irrawaddy and Chao Phraya Rivers and south to Australia (fig.4–59) and east to Polynesia. The disparate groups of peoples throughout this area have their own traditions of sculpture (fig.4–60), fabrics (fig.4–62), architecture and pottery that are distinctive in form, style and symbolism. Many groups have had little or no contact with other cultures. They have developed artistic styles that are unique to their own cultures. Other peoples are part of larger cultural groups, most notably those within the *Oceania* area. *Oceania* is comprised of Australia, New Zealand and numerous nearby islands. Inner Pacific Islands fall into three groups: *Micronesia, Melanesia* and *Polynesia.*

Vocabulary
totem

4–60 Tapa is a beaten bark cloth made from the paper mulberry. The inner material of this figure consists of bundles of bulrushes tied with fiber bands. Only three of these tapa figures are known to exist. *Tapa Cloth Figure.* Easter Island, Polynesia. Painted mulberry bark cloth, fiber-tied bulrushes, 15 1/2" (39 cm). The Peabody Museum, Harvard University.

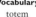

4–59 Most of the art from the Oceania region is highly stylized and symbolic. What do you think these figures represent? *Painted Bark Cloth,* detail (fig.4–12).

If so, how does this help pinpoint the origin of the piece? Next, remind students that as curators, they may not be able to tell the owner exactly what the figure means. Have them review the information in Lesson 4.6 in order to offer some possible interpretations.

• Specifically, how might the work relate to tribal religious or ancestral beliefs? Finally, have the students as curators try to convince the visitor to donate the art to the museum so that more research could be conducted.

Art History/Criticism: Direct students to study the images in Lesson 4.6 and make a list of all the different types of designs on the objects. After, have them group the designs into major categories.

• What generalizations can they make about the decorative tendencies of Oceanic and Highland Asian art?

• Do the artists try to imitate the observable world as realistically as possible? Share with students that the geometric, abstract and animal motifs frequently carry symbolic meaning.

Have students discuss how objects from their own heritage are decorated.

• Do they have symmetrical patterns, realistic images or other modes of expression?

• Are the designs purely aesthetic or are they also symbolic?

• How do they vary from or correspond to the works in Lesson 4.6?

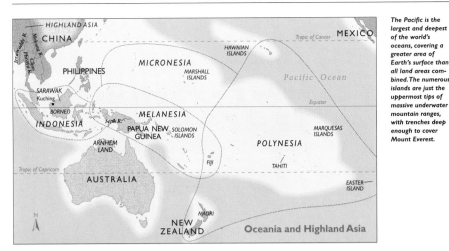

The Pacific is the largest and deepest of the world's oceans, covering a greater area of Earth's surface than all land areas combined. The numerous islands are just the uppermost tips of massive underwater mountain ranges, with trenches deep enough to cover Mount Everest.

Higher-Order Thinking Skills

1 Ask students to examine fig.4–62 and its caption. Had they ever considered feathers as a medium? Are there other materials mentioned in this chapter that they find surprising or intriguing? If students were creating a modern crested helmet to be worn by a local official, what material would they choose?

2 Have small groups of students create a story or myth for the tapa figure (fig.4–60).

4–62 The higher chiefs of Hawaii wore helmets such as this one. Lesser chiefs wore unfeathered helmets. This example probably originates from either Oahu or Maui.
Hawaiian Crested Helmet, before 1841. Red, yellow, black and white feathers on wickerwork, 22" x 15" (56 x 38 cm). The Peabody Museum, Harvard University.

4–61 When this mask was in use, ornaments filled the loops and small bamboo posts on each side of the head carried varicolored feather decorations.
Malanggan Mask. New Ireland, Melanesia. Painted, carved wood, plant pith, 23" (58 cm). The Peabody Museum, Harvard University.

Evaluate

Ask students to consider how the climate in Oceania and Highland Asia impacts its artwork. First have them determine the weather by locating the area, as detailed in the map on page 113, within the world map at the back of the text.

• How might its southern atmosphere affect the materials that artists use in this area?

• How do the materials differ from those used in the fine arts in Western societies?

• What materials would students incorporate from their surroundings to communicate the products most readily available in their locale? Would they be natural or manufactured materials?

• How do the differences between their choices and the fabrics, feathers, clay and textiles used in Oceania and Highland Asia demonstrate differences between the two cultures?

Reteach

Ask students to think of animals that are used as symbols in Christian art. For instance, what does the snake (evil) represent in the story of Adam and Eve? Who does a lamb (Jesus) symbolize? A dove (the holy spirit) flying above a religious figure?

• Why might people in cultures around the world rely on animals to relate spiritual content?

• Do students associate certain traits with particular creatures? What characteristic might they think of for a lion (courage or fierceness), lamb (gentleness), dog (loyalty) or owl (wisdom)?

Contextual Information

The Materials of Oceanic Art

There are few ancient wooden objects in Oceania because wood is highly perishable and rots within 250 years unless immersed in liquid. It can be eaten by insects and worn out by animals and humans. Wood was the most popular medium for art in this area, but shells, nephrite, walrus and whale ivory, and human bones were used for jewelry. Lava and other volcanic stones—like the monumental images at Easter Island, the Society Islands and the Marquesas—may have been carved by iron tools introduced by Westerners.

Sarawak

Many of the traditional customs and crafts of the people of Sarawak remain intact. Several different tribes live in this Malaysian state. Among the tribes are the Kenyah and the Ibanwho continue to live in traditional longhouses. These communal bamboo structures can house between 10 and 40 families under one roof.

Highland tribes of the Southeast Asian peninsula separated themselves from the mainstream of lowland cultures at various times throughout history. The various tribes have produced similar, but distinctive, art forms. Houses built on stilts with steeply sloping thatch roofs are typical throughout the region. Peoples of the highlands share many artistic similarities with Oceanic peoples of the Pacific. They created objects not simply for their aesthetic beauty, but also for their functional purposes. Many objects are primarily used for religious purposes. Painting throughout the regions features animal and geometric symbolism and symbolic pattern. Paintings, such as those inside the communal longhouses of Borneo (fig.4–63), have highly stylized curvilinear designs.

Mystic designs in Oceanic and highland art are often empowered with spiritual energy. The woven blanket shown here (fig.4–64) is filled with mystic and *totemic* symbols. (A **totem** is an animal or natural object which symbolizes a clan or family.) The alligator is a common motif in Oceanic art. However, note the bird that is illustrated in the form of an army helicopter. As the indigenous people have come into contact with modern technology, their artwork has reflected the new subject matter in their world.

Masks are an important form of Oceanic art and sculpture. Masks decorate ceremonial huts and are used as objects of worship. In rituals, the person who wears the mask loses his or her own identity and becomes the spirit of the ancestor or spirit represented by the mask. Like masks, spears, boats and eating utensils are also carved. Mystic or animal motifs carved onto these objects invest them with life and power.

Wood is the commonly used sculptural material of both highland and Oceanic peoples, although almost no sculpture is known in Micronesia. Ancient examples of sculpture are rare since the materials quickly deteriorate. Most work found today is less than one hundred years old.

4–63 Boards like this, which portray mystic forces, are a part of communal longhouses. *Gableboard painting.* Kenyah Tribe, Sarawak, Borneo. Vegetable dyes and earth colors on wood. Sarawak Museum, Kuching.

4–64 Can you find the modern helicopter which has been incorporated into this traditional totemic work? *Blanket.* Iban Tribe, Sarawak, East Malaysia. Cotton and vegetable dyes, 31 3/4" x 48 1/2" (81 x 123 cm). Collection of Mr. and Mrs. David Kohl.

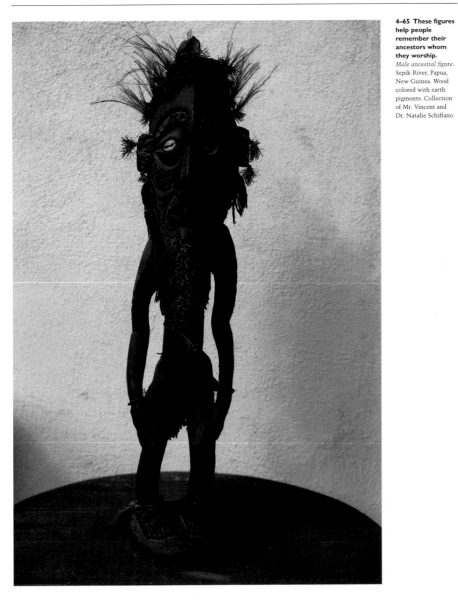

4–65 These figures help people remember their ancestors whom they worship.
Male ancestral figure. Sepik River, Papua, New Guinea. Wood colored with earth pigments. Collection of Mr. Vincent and Dr. Natalie Schiffano.

Higher-Order Thinking Skills

Ask how our society remembers ancestors. Ask students about particular customs of remembrance in their families.

4–65 These figures help people remember their ancestors whom they worship.
Male ancestral figure. Sepik River, Papua, New Guinea. Wood colored with earth pigments. Collection of Mr. Vincent and Dr. Natalie Schiffano.

Contextual Information

The Maori

The Maori were the original inhabitants of New Zealand. They migrated to New Zealand from other Pacific Islands. The last wave of immigrants arrived on the island in 1350.

Maori artists were the best stone carvers in Polynesia. They carved deep-green nephrite into ornaments, working for months with water and sand to drill sculptural images of ancestral symbols. Nephrite is a type of jade and varies in color from white to dark green. Its name comes from the Greek *nephros*, which means "kidney"; touching nephrite was thought to cure kidney diseases.

Maori arts included poetry, storytelling, music, dance and carving. The Maori chief's house and the clans' meetinghouse were decorated with carved figures and hangings that served as status symbols for the whole tribe. The chief was a direct descendant of a tribal ancestor, and his house showed a link between the past and the present. Carvings represented ancestors, and their symbolic images carved into the meetinghouse were thought to neutralize evil spirits.

Carvers were considered to be mediators between the real and otherworld spirits. They also had the practical job of carving canoes, clubs and other weapons, tool handles, musical instruments, bowls and boxes.

Maori cultural traditions are continued today in rural areas of New Zealand.

Painting is used to embellish carved wooden images and masks, especially in Melanesia. Papua, New Guinea, has one of the strongest artistic traditions in Melanesia. Objects for ancestor worship are ornamented in bright colors. *Ancestral figures* (fig.4–65) are carved from wood in sizes from three inches to three feet in height. The ancestral figure is embellished with white highlights and reddish brown paint. This brown paint represents blood and the continued existence of the soul of the deceased. *Totemism* is also common in Melanesia. Masks are considered as the permanent dwelling of spiritual forces. Masks, statues and other cult worship objects are used to identify kinship.

Native art in northern Papua reflects a broad blend of island, coastal and mountain cultures. Wood carvings show great variety in subject matter and free expression. Detailed and well-carved wooden images are embellished with shells, dogs' teeth, feathers, animal hair and paint or colored earth. Images are either ancestral masks, ceremonial masks or fertility images.

In Polynesia, masks and carvings and even boats represent sophisticated cult worship of gods and chiefs. Masks assume powerful worship force only when surrounded by ritual. In contrast to the carvings of Melanesia, Polynesian objects of worship stress the grain of the wood; stress is not placed on bright colors.

Unique in the art of Oceania, stone sculpture is found in Polynesia. On Easter Island are stunning stone carvings. These monumental ancestral images are made of volcanic rock. Other stone sculptures of stylized figures can be seen on the Marquesas Islands.

Woodcarving is common throughout Polynesia, from Hawaii to New Zealand. The houses of New Zealand's tribal *Maori* chiefs and priests contain intricately carved bas-relief panels (fig.4–66). Like the totem pole of Northwest American tribes, this wooden carving depicts a tribal ancestor as a warrior. His tongue is thrust out in defiance of his enemies. The small figure between his legs represents later tribal ancestors. Notice how only half of the figures are depicted. This is a distinctive feature of Oceanic art. The lattice panels of dyed vegetable fibers on each side of the carving are abstract representations of natural forms.

Tattoo work on the human body originated in the Marquesas. In an under-the-skin dyeing process taking years, men's bodies are covered in traditional geometric designs. These designs appear to be symbolic and mystic.

Australian aboriginal culture shares stylistic and media similarities with Oceanic and highland peoples. Aborigines have produced a tradition of painting on flattened bark. The bark is usually placed on the inside of their temporary shel-

4–66 Use the text to help identify the unique features of this wall panel from a chief's house.
Carved wall panel from Maori Meeting House, late 19th century. Dominion Museum, Wellington, New Zealand.

Higher-Order Thinking Skills

Ask students to examine fig.4–66. Have them discuss how the Maori artists have used line, color and pattern. Can they find similarities between the carved wall panel and the fabrics and objects from other cultures shown in this chapter? (Note: another Maori lintel can be found in Chapter 2, fig.2–37.)

4–67 This X-ray painting shows both a physical and spiritual understanding of the subjects.
Aboriginal rock paintings. Gunqinggu group, Western Arnhem Land, Australia.

ters. Kangaroos, birds, fish, snakes, tortoises and alligators are common subjects. An "X-ray" effect is used to depict internal organs, simultaneously showing two aspects of the same subject. Designs of humans, mammals, birds, reptiles and fish are also abraded, pecked or hammered into the surface of rock outcroppings (fig.4–67). It is common to find geometric designs carved into earth or trees as part of initiation ceremonies.

The vast heritage of this entire region has only been "discovered" in the twentieth century. So far, this art heritage has been more closely studied by anthropologists than by art historians.

Lesson 4.6 Review

1 Describe the totemic symbols in the blanket in figure 4–64. What does totemic mean? How has the artist combined contemporary culture symbols with traditional design in this blanket?

2 What does the red brown paint on New Guinea wooden ancestral figures symbolize?

3 How are Melanesian wood carvings different from Polynesian wood sculptures?

4 What type of unusual art is found on Easter Island?

5 Where did the art of body tattoo originate?

6 List some of the animals painted on bark by the Australian aborigines. How did these artists show two views of an animal at the same time?

Lesson 4.6 Review Answers

1 Totems are animals or natural objects symbolizing a clan or a family such as the alligator, fish and bird symbols in this blanket. The artist has included a contemporary symbol, the helicopter, with traditional nature symbols.

2 Blood and the continued existence of the soul of the deceased

3 Melanesian carvings are painted bright colors, while Polynesian objects stress the grain of the wood.

4 Monumental volcanic rock carvings of ancestral images

5 The Marquesas

6 Australian aborigines painted kangaroos, birds, fish, snakes, tortoises and alligators. They used an X-ray effect to show internal organs on an exterior view.

Lesson 4.7

Islam, as a nation and religion, has influenced art and culture in Europe, Africa and Asia, from Spain to the Philippines. Islamic art is characterized by ornate decoration. The earliest Arab examples were small, portable objects that could be easily carried by seminomadic tribes. As Islamic architecture developed, artists extended their love of surface design from individual objects to entire environments.

Warm-up

Ask students to envision wandering into the Topkapi Palace (fig.4–68) after coming in from a blindingly sunny day. What would it feel like to step inside? What produces the dazzling effect? Are there a lot of empty spaces for their eyes to rest? Welcome students to the world of Islam, in which every conceivable space is covered with intricate, captivating decorations.

Objectives

Students should be able to:

Discern the Islamic artistic passion for elaborate ornamentation.

Identify the stylized natural elements, abstract forms and calligraphy in Islamic art.

Articulate the extent of Islamic influence throughout the world.

Vocabulary Definitions

arabesques (*ar*-uh-besk) Intricate and fanciful surface decorations generally based on geometric patterns and using combinations of flowering vines, tendrils, etc.
mosque (mosk) An Islamic temple or place of worship.
qibla (*kee*-blah) A niche in the inner wall of a mosque, facing toward Mecca.
minaret (min-a-r*et*) A tall, slender tower attached to a mosque from which the muezzin (crier) calls people to prayer.
madrasah (mah-*drahs*-ah) A style of mosque using an enclosed courtyard, but open to the sky.
cruciform (*kroo*-sih-form) In the shape of a cross; usually a floorplan of building in such an arrangement.

4.7 The World of Islam

THE NATION AND RELIGION of Islam has directly influenced the cultures of Europe, Africa and Asia from Spain to the Philippines. Throughout all geographic areas touched by Islam, an appreciation of crafts can be seen. Ornamentation-covered carved woodwork, crystal, bronze, textiles and weaponry. All Islamic arts remained true to the philosophical foundations of the culture. The objects are a witness to the order of creation and to the believer's submission to the will of Allah.

The Arab culture, from which Islam grew, was seminomadic and, therefore, produced no monumental architecture or paintings. Instead, these peoples valued small, portable objects with rich decoration. Arabic script became highly regarded, since it was the language through which Allah had chosen to reveal his messages to the prophet Mohammed. These inspirations were written in the Koran, and devoted scribes gave great attention in recopying that sacred text. A whole style of art developed around their calligraphy.

In metalwork, pottery, carpet making and architecture, Islamic art reveals itself as an art of ornamentation. Swirling designs known as ***arabesques*** were used to ornament objects. Imaginative, stylized designs were based on *Kufic* script, flowers and leaves, and geometric patterns. These designs fill spaces on manuscript pages, copper containers, ceramic vessels and weapons. Even the walls of holy buildings, like The Dome of the Rock in Jerusalem (fig.7–24), are covered with designs. Usually, no prominent center of interest is obvious. Instead, symmetry and tranquillity seem to be the desired goal.

> **Vocabulary**
> arabesques
> mosque
> qibla
> minaret
> madrasah
> cruciform

4–68 The walls of secular and religious Islamic architecture are often covered with abstract patterns and geometric design. *Topkapi Palace*, interior view, begun 1462. Istanbul.

4–69 This detail of a Persian rug shows an incredible intricacy of design that is achieved through the painstaking technique of hand-knotting. Maqsud Kashani, *The Ardabil Carpet*, detail (fig.4–74).

622 AD Islamic Era begins	**800s–900s** Turks convert to Islam	**1031 AD** End of Caliphate of Cordoba	**1453 AD** Ottoman Conquest of Constantinople

Islam Timeline

711 AD Muslim Conquest of Spain	**c.1290 AD–1326 AD** Ottoman Empire Osman I

Teach

Criticism: Share with students that, in ballet, *arabesque* describes a position in which dancers stand on one leg and place their corresponding arm forward while bending their torsos slightly at the waist and then extending the other leg and its corresponding arm behind them. Have students try this posture. After, ask students to draw the sweeping shape their bodies made in this position. Now direct them to locate similar curving, swirling designs in the Islamic art illustrated throughout Lesson 4.7.

• What other images did they find in their search?

• What natural objects do Islamic artists incorporate into their work? Can students detect the floral and leaf patterns in *The Ardabil Carpet* (fig.4–69)?

Art History/Criticism: Challenge students to imagine being part of a nomadic Arab tribe in the early seventh century.

• What types of artistic items would they tend to create?

• Would their life style lend itself to permanent architecture and monumental paintings or sculpture?

• What would they see as the advantages of artworks such as those reproduced in figs.4–75 and 4–76?

World of Islam

The center of Islam is Mecca, the city in Saudi Arabia where the prophet Mohammed received the revelations this religion is built upon. From the Middle East, Islam spread to encompass a wide geographic area including Northern Africa, China and the Malay archipelago.

4–70 Painting did not play a part in the Arab tradition until the technique was brought from China by the Mongols in the thirteenth century.
The Battle of Alexander with the Dragon, detail (fig.4–73).

Higher-Order Thinking Skills

Ask students to explain the aspects of design that the Topkapi Palace (fig.4–68) and *The Ardabil Carpet* (fig.4–69) share.

Evaluate

Ask students how Islamic artists typically decorate surfaces. Is there a strong inclination toward naturalistic depictions? How do they most often approach empty areas? After, have students write what their thinking was like when viewing Islamic art, as compared to Japanese examples in Lesson 4.4. Was their thinking faster, quieter, slower or noisier? If they were to make sounds to correspond to their thinking in each lesson, what would they be?

Ask students to name the countries most deeply affected by Islamic culture. How far east, south, north and west did Islam reach?

Reteach

Ask students to compare the decoration on Islamic textiles, pottery, metalwork and small-scale painting to examples of the culture's architecture. What similarities can they detect in terms of decoration? (For additional information and activities on Islamic art, see Chapter 7, Lesson 3.)

Contextual Information

The Banning of Religious Images

During the eighth century, both Christians and Muslims looked for reasons to explain why their armies were losing battles. They feared it was because they had displeased God. They studied their scriptures, and both decided that it was because they allowed religious sculpture in their religious buildings, contrary to the commandment of God that they should not have carved images, bow down to them, or serve them.

In 720 AD, a calif (Muslim leader) by the name of Yazid had all images in Christian churches and mosques under his rule destroyed. In 730 AD, Christian Emperor Leo III, head of the Byzantine Empire, commanded that images be taken from churches. This ban in Byzantium lasted until 843. Many of the images taken from the churches during this period were not destroyed but were hidden or buried by those who felt that the images were holy and not evil.

The Blue Mosque

The Blue Mosque derives its name from the multitude of blue glazed tiles that covers its interior walls. The central dome of the mosque is 109 feet wide. It rests on four massive pillars which are 15 feet thick. The sunlight streams through 260 stained glass windows. (The present windows are copies of the originals which were destroyed in an earthquake.)

Topkapi Palace

Topkapi Palace (figs.1–12, 4–68, 4–72) actually consists of a number of small palaces and kiosks on a site overlooking the Bosphorus. At the height of its glory, Topkapi Palace had a royal reception room paved in gold. Its kitchens were large enough to prepare meals for 5000 people. The landscaping included a world-famous tulip garden where peacocks strutted. (Tulips were introduced to Europe when an ambassador of Louis XIV brought them back from the sultan's court. *See* sidelight on page 353.)

Architecture

The major architectural form in Islam is the **mosque**, or temple. Originally, the mosque had to have one wall facing Mecca. The wall was known as the **qibla**, and it contained a small prayer niche. A **minaret**, or prayer tower opposite the qibla, was used by a *muezzin* to call the faithful to prayer. Mosques in Spain centered on elaborately arched courtyards, with rows of columns facing the open space in front of the qibla.

The interiors of mosques are embellished with lavish designs.

A second style of mosque emerged in Turkish and Persian areas. Called a teaching mosque, or **madrasah** (also spelled *medresa*), it was still open to the sky. However, the courtyard was walled in and a large semivaulted room opened into the courtyard from each of the four surrounding walls. This created an essentially **cruciform** (cross) floor plan.

The third style of mosque, created by the Ottoman Turks, was based on the Hagia Sophia in Constantinople (fig.7–13). The style combined the madrasah cruciform plan with the domed enclosed spaces of Byzantine architecture. The domes of the *Blue Mosque* (fig.4–71) enclose a spacious interior and, at the same time, provide a sense of rhythm. Small windows in the drum of the dome allow shafts of light to enter the ceramic-tiled

4–71 Cruciform and domed, this mosque is architecturally related to the Hagia Sophia. *Blue Mosque of Ahmet I,* 1617. Istanbul.

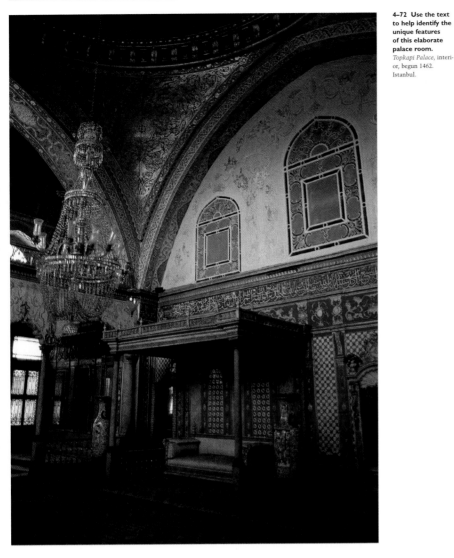

4–72 Use the text to help identify the unique features of this elaborate palace room. *Topkapi Palace*, interior, begun 1462. Istanbul.

Higher-Order Thinking Skills

Have students compare the similarities and differences between the interior of the Topkapi Palace (fig.4–72) and the audience room of Nijo Castle (fig.4–48). Students should consider form, decoration and materials.

interior, producing a mystic atmosphere.

Court palaces featured elaborately ornamented interiors. The Alhambra in Spain (fig.7–21) and *Topkapi Palace* in Turkey testify to Islamic creativity. Rooms from the

Topkapi Palace (figs.4–68, 4–72) feature Arabic calligraphy on the walls, faience wall tile, geometrically traced windows, and colorfully patterned carpets. The dais for sitting (fig.4–72) is bordered by twisted columns that support a patterned canopy.

Sculpture, particularly of humans or of God, is expressly prohibited in Islamic tradition. A few sculptured animal forms were made with an understanding that images were permitted if they were small enough so that they cast no shadows.

Contextual Information

The Evolution of Islamic Art

The first followers of Mohammed came from the Arabian peninsula. They had no strong native artistic traditions. Instead, Islamic art evolved as empires were conquered and the followers of Mohammed absorbed the art forms of their conquests. The art was modified by climate and available materials. Often, motifs from one area were adopted and became universal in the Islamic world.

Painting

Painting was not originally part of the Arab tradition. Few pictorial works appeared in Islamic courts until the *Mongol* era. During the thirteenth century, Persia was invaded by the Mongols, who brought with them the sophisticated culture of the Song. Paintings, such as *The Battle of Alexander with the Dragon* (figs.4–70, 4–73), show both a Chinese subject matter and painting technique new to the Arab world. The landscape of mountains and trees is similar to Song landscapes. The sweeping curves of the mountains seem to turn back on the scene, adding drama and power to the action. The borders are Arabic, the faces are Middle Eastern, and the compacted space is Islamic. A vast quantity of painting on palm leaves, cloth and paper was created by various Islamic dynasties throughout the realm. These paintings reflected unique regional tastes and motifs.

4–73 The Mongols brought elements of Chinese culture to Persia. Use the text to guide you in finding those influences and in identifying features that are uniquely Persian.
The Battle of Alexander with the Dragon, 14th century. Mongol period in Persia. Gouache on paper, 7" x 11 1/2" (18 x 29 cm). Museum of Fine Arts, Boston, Ross Collection.

Textiles

Unique to Central Asia is the creation of beautiful and colorful rugs, carpets and textiles of wool or silk. They are often regarded as the highest achievement of Islamic craftsmanship and design. Artisans combined painstaking knotting techniques with intricate symmetric and symbolic patterns. *The Ardabil Carpet* (figs.4–69, 4–74) may have as many as three hundred knots per square inch. The complex design of sanctuary lamps, medallion and floral motifs gave the barefooted worshiper a visual as well as tactile experience.

Pottery

Potters created elegant forms and glazes, using luster, enamels and faience techniques. They decorated ceramics with Islamic motifs, adding rich color and texture to the inexpensive base materials. Turkish potters produced drinking containers, bowls and dishes such as the Isnik platter (fig.4–75). The three peonies and two tulips in the central panel are Chinese floral designs. They are surrounded by stylized cloud patterns painted in cobalt. The designer was probably influenced by imported Chinese porcelain as seen in the lobed rim. The blue, red, green, turquoise and black colors are Turkish additions to the traditional Ming blue and white.

Metalwork

Metalworking reflects the ability of Moslem artisans to render materials into intricate forms of beauty. The Persian bracelet (fig.4–76) features rows of golden birds complete with tiny beaks, wings and feather patterns. Its rhythmic alignment is in harmony with theories of symmetry and regularity typical of Islamic culture.

Interdisciplinary Connection

Social Studies: In Islam, five daily prayers are required: before sunrise, very early afternoon, late afternoon, immediately after sunset, and before retiring (the last must be before midnight). In prayer, Muslims face toward Mecca. A prayer is composed of a series of movements combined with recitations from the Koran and other prayers. The movements consist of a standing posture, a genuflection followed by two prostrations, and a sitting position. The prayers are congregational in nature and usually take place in a mosque.

Because of the physical positions such as prostration and kneeling required for prayer, carpets are laid on mosque floors. Shoes are removed before entering a mosque. *The Ardabil Carpet* (fig.4–69) was made for a tomb-mosque in Iran.

4–75 Ming influences from China combine with traditional Turkish colors.
Dish with lobed rim and flaring body, 1550–1560. Isnik (Nicaea), Turkey. Tin-glazed faience, 13 1/4" (34 cm) diameter. Los Angeles County Museum of Art, Nasli M. Heeramaneck Collection.

4–74 Persian carpets are still excellent examples of high textile art.
Maqsud Kashani, *The Ardabil Carpet,* 1540. Safavid dynasty, Persia. Wool, 281 3/4" x 156" (716 x 396 cm). Los Angeles County Museum of Art, gift of J. Paul Getty.

4–76 Rhythm and symmetry are hallmarks of Islamic aesthetics. These tiny birds are excellent examples of fine metalsmithing.
Bracelet, 10–11th centuries. Persia. Gold, 2" x 5 1/8" (5 x 13 cm). Los Angeles County Museum of Art, Nasli M. Heeramaneck Collection.

Higher-Order Thinking Skills

1 Have students contrast the manuscript depicted in fig.4–73 to the Mesoamerican *Souche Nuttar Codex* (fig.4–2).

2 Ask students to list the characteristics of the candlestick in fig.2–46. Which of these characteristics are typical of Islamic art?

Lesson 4.7 Review

1 What is an arabesque? Give an example of arabesques in a piece of Islamic art or architecture.
2 What is a mosque, qibla, minaret and muezzin? How are these related?
3 Why were animal forms so small in Islamic architecture?

4 Describe how the art of different cultures is reflected in the Persian *Battle of Alexander with the Dragon.*
5 What form of textile art is usually regarded as the pinnacle of Islamic design and craftsmanship?

Lesson 4.7 Review Answers

1 Arabesque is intricate and fanciful surface decoration found in Islamic art. These designs are usually based on geometric patterns or Kufic script and include combinations of flowers, vines and leaves. The walls of The Dome of the Rock in Jerusalem are covered with arabesques.
2 A mosque is an Islamic temple. Early mosques were required to have one wall called a qibla, facing Mecca, which contained a small prayer niche. A minaret is a prayer tower opposite the mosque's qibla. A muezzin summons the faithful to prayer from the minaret.

3 Sculpture is prohibited in the Islamic tradition. Animal images were permitted only if they were so small that they cast no shadow.
4 This battle scene shows both a Chinese subject matter and painting technique new to the Arab world. The landscape of mountains and trees is similar to Song landscapes. The action pose of the central horse and rider resembles Chinese art. The borders are Arabic, the faces are Middle Eastern, and the compacted use of space is Islamic.
5 Colorful rugs, carpets and textiles of wool or silk

Lesson 4.8

The art of the distinctly different societies south of the Sahara are united by attention to craftsmanship, use of geometric design and religious orientation. Many of the objects were vital components of ceremonies that incorporated music, song, dance and narrative.

Warm-up

Ask students to list religious ceremonies that they have witnessed. Try to solicit those from as many cultures as possible. For each example, have students describe objects that are used in the ritual, their purpose, and what they signify. Have them investigate to find out if any of the objects endow the user with special qualities during the ceremony. Explain that spiritual rites—which combine art, music, narrative and dance—are central to traditional African culture.

Objectives

Students should be able to:

Understand that although there are three discrete categories of sub-Sahara African societies, their art shares a common interest in design, materials and function.

Discuss the relationship between spirituality and art in the societies south of the Sahara.

Vocabulary Definitions

cult figures Figures of religious devotion or ritualistic value.
fetish figures Objects to which magical powers are ascribed; good luck charms.
reliquary figures (*reh*-li-kweh-ree) Carved guardians that stand above basket receptacles for ancestral remains.

4.8 Sub-Sahara Africa

SOUTH OF THE SAHARA there are three distinct types of societies: (1) nomadic tribes in the desert and steppe regions; (2) sedentary farming cultures in the savanna and rain-forest fringe areas; and (3) ancient, sophisticated kingdoms of Nigeria and the Guinea coast. While all three have separate art traditions, their art is similar in attention to craftsmanship, use of geometric abstraction, and a religious orientation. Religion plays a dominant part in African art forms.

Ceremony dominates much of traditional Africa's life and art. Each individual is thought to have a spirit that interrelates with the spirits of all other individuals. Spirits are everywhere, uniting the whole human race in a harmonious whole with the visible and invisible universe. A strong bond unites the individual and clan with each other and with ancestors.

Vocabulary
cult figures
fetish figures
reliquary figures

4–77 Woodcarving continues to be an important medium for contemporary African artists.
Nelson Mukhuba, *Golfer*, detail (fig.4–85).

The African continent is second only to Asia in size. The Nile, the longest river in the world, is sourced halfway across the continent in Lake Victoria.

Sub-Sahara Africa

Teach

Art History: Ask students to identify masks that exist in modern society; for instance, those used in sports, at costume parties or on construction sites.

• Are these examples associated with any specific rituals?

• Do they contain underlying symbolic meaning? Now direct students to figs.4–78 and 4–79 and the information about the masks in the captions and on page 126.

• How is the role of African masks different from that of masks used in contemporary Western society?

Aesthetics/Criticism: Divide the class into small groups and have each discern the realistic and abstract elements in an artwork from Lesson 4.8. Allow teams to present and discuss any similarities among their findings, despite the varying locations from which the pieces originally came. Ask students to compare the size of the sub-Sahara region to the United States or Asia.

• Do each of these areas have cohesive artistic styles?

• Would it be accurate to say that there is only one African, Asian or American visual style? Why or why not?

• When are generalizations about art, or people, dangerous and when might they be useful?

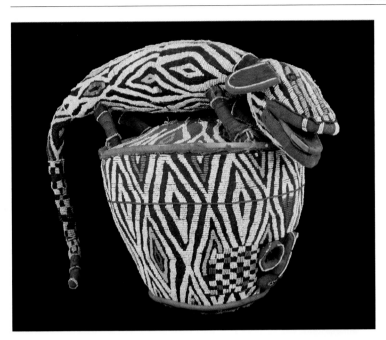

4–78 Masks are an important part of African ritual ceremonies. The multitude of materials and styles make masks one of the most exciting art forms in Africa.
Leopard Mask, Grasslands, Bamileke, Cameroon. Raffia splints, cloth, glass beads, 31" x 48" (80 x 122 cm). Collection of Charles W. and Janice R. Mack.

Higher-Order Thinking Skills

Have students choose three masks in this chapter and compare and contrast them, considering design, color, materials and function.

500 BC–200 BC Nok Culture	1235 AD–c.1464 AD Mali Empire King Sundiata	1307 AD–1332 AD Mansa Musa	1464 AD–1590 AD Songhai Empire

Sub-Sahara Africa Timeline

300 AD–1203 AD Ghana Empire	1300s –1600s AD Kongo Kingdom	1200 AD–1500 AD Ife Kingdom (Nigeria)	1500 AD–1700 AD Benin Kingdom

Evaluate

Ask students to identify the primary difference in terms of function between Picasso's *Les Demoiselles d'Avignon* (fig.14–a) and the types of masks in Lesson 4.8 that helped inspire the faces in his painting. Inquire how students feel about the way in which Picasso and many other Western artists borrowed the forms but not the content of art from another culture.

• How would they feel if someone co-opted images from their life but infused them with an entirely different meaning?

• Would they admire the artist's ingenuity? Would they be interested in seeing something familiar in a new light?

• Would they feel offended that the artist was misrepresenting something that has powerful associations for them?

• Does the artist have an obligation toward the culture from which he or she borrows visual elements? Have students discuss opposing opinions. Did their notions expand as a result of their exchange?

Reteach

Direct students to examine figs.4–84 and 4–85. Before they look at the caption, ask them when these pieces might have been created.

• What is their relationship to traditional pieces in the rest of the lesson?

• How do the images reflect the artists' concern with tradition as well as an interest in contemporary diversity? Tell students to read the text on page 129 and examine works by modern artists in Chapter 14 and Chapter 17 to help stimulate discussion.

Contextual Information

Art of the Gods and Rulers

Two different types of art, beyond decorated practical objects, are found in African cultures. Objects used in worship, such as wooden masks and objects that symbolize spirit gods and goddesses, are one type. The second type is that created by artists working for a king. These objects include sculpture that shows the ruler victorious in battle or connected to the gods or ancestors. This type of art also can serve to decorate buildings and temples as symbols of power and wealth.

The Survival of African Art

Because much African art was made of natural materials that decomposed over time, little is known about the history of art in Africa. Only pottery, stone and metals survived burial. This has left some people with the mistaken idea that sculpture, jewelry, pottery and rock paintings were the only forms of art practiced in certain cultures.

Nomadic Cultures

The wandering peoples of the semi-arid regions do not produce large sculpture, as their roaming lifestyle does not permit the accumulation of material possessions. However, they do create masks. Masks and sculpture are used in religious ceremonies. Sculpture includes ancestors or cult figures, fetishes and reliquary figures.

Sedentary Farming Cultures

A much more permanent and long-lived tradition of sculpture and masks is present among the agricultural groups of the tropical savanna regions. Masks are used in ritual ceremonies to embody spiritual forces (fig.4–78). Some are used in dance rituals, such as the wooden

4–79 A dancer puts on a mask and becomes the spirit that the mask represents.
Banda Mask, Nalu or Baga peoples, Guinea, 20th century. Wood, metal, paint. The Brooklyn Museum, New York, Caroline A. L. Pratt Fund.

one from a tribe in French Guinea (fig.4–79). The stylized geometric and naturalistic shapes combine to represent a recognizable human face. By contrast, other masks only faintly resemble natural forms. The wart-hog masks of the N'Gere people of Liberia are highly stylized representations. The N'Gere use a wide range of materials to construct the masks. Wood, paint, fabric, tin, cotton cord, fiber, cloth and woolen ornaments are combined with nails. The result is an assemblage that accentuates the mysticism of the mask (fig.1–6).

Ancestor or **cult figures** are full-body images kept in homes and shrines. As part of a ritual, individuals present offerings to them. Sometimes these figures indicate social rank or may function as fertility images (fig.4–81). Figures may be carved on the legs of a stool and support the seat. Other cult figures may be carved holding an offering bowl or as mother and child figures (fig.4–80).

Fetish figures are designed to hold ingredients that are endowed with mystical powers. The figures are human forms that are affixed with many types of material such as rope, string, feathers or shells. **Reliquary figures** are carved guardians that stand above basket receptacles for ancestral remains. In these figures, the human form has a geometric stylization. Some are concave and convex surfaces, cylinders, cubes and cones symbolize (not represent) the guardian spirits.

Performing Arts Connection

African Masks

This painted wooden mask (fig.4–79) was originally worn in special ceremonies by a man of the Simo society, a secret men's association that regulated fertility and initiation rituals within the Nalu (or Baga) culture. Ask students what animal parts they can identify. The antelope horns and crocodile jaws, combined with human facial features, reflect the interaction between the Nalu community and the environment. Ask what kinds of movement the dancer might have made when wearing this mask.

• Ask students to research mythical beings from various cultures that combine both human and animal characteristics. Have them perform the stories about these beings.

4–80 Figures of this type are removed annually from their shrines, washed, oiled and adorned with beads and cloth.
Mother and Child, Mali, Bamana People, 19–20th centuries. Wood, 48 1/2" (123.5 cm) high. The Metropolitan Museum of Art, New York. The Michael C. Rockefeller Memorial Collection, Bequest of Nelson A. Rockefeller, 1979.

4–81 Ashanti artists of the twentieth century were intrigued with the Ashanti combination of realism and geometric abstraction.
Akua 'ba doll, 19–20th centuries. Ashanti culture, Ghana. Wood, 11 3/4" (30 cm) high. British Museum, London.

Higher-Order Thinking Skills

Ask what makes the Akua 'ba doll (fig.4–81) seem to be a religious figure. Suggest that students use other religious figures to help make their points.

Contextual Information

Ife Bronzes

Art historian Werner Gillon suggests that Ife bronze heads were used at funeral ceremonies to stand in for the dead who had already been buried. Burials were done quickly because of the climate, but more time was needed for mourners to travel great distances to honor the dead, and for the collecting of food for the large and elaborate funerals. The heads also might have been used as commemorative statues in religious ceremonies.

Nigeria and the Guinea Coast

In contrast to the nomadic and sedentary agricultural tribes, the aristocratic kingdoms of Nigeria created art that reflected the tastes of the wealthy kings and courtiers, not the common people. Royal craftspersons were on the king's "staff" and produced ceremonial sculpture and household ornamental panels. They also produced artifacts used in daily living, such as bowls, stools, textiles, pottery and musical instruments.

Kingdoms flourished as early as 500 BC, when the *Nok* culture created large terra-cotta figures (fig.2–50). Nearly 2000 years later, an advanced society, known as the *Ife*, flourished in western Nigeria. Their most significant accomplishment was the production of very

4–82 This expert metalwork in a realistic portrait tradition can be compared to the tradition of ancient Greece.
Oni (King) of Ife, 12–14th centuries. Bronze, 14 1/2" (37 cm) high (life-size). British Museum, London.

4–83 This bronze sculpture was made by a master metalsmith.
Flute player, 15–16 centuries. Benin culture, Nigeria. Engraved bronze, 24 1/2" (62 cm) high. British Museum, London.

naturalistic human sculptures, which were cast in bronze by the lost-wax method. The bronze sculpture of the head of the king, or *oni,* is an excellent example (fig.4–82). All facial features in Ife sculpture are anatomically accurate, even to the bone structure beneath the skin. Holes allowed the application of real hair to give the original an even more lifelike appearance. Many experts once thought that Ife artists learned their sculptural naturalism and technology from the Egyptians or Greeks. Now, however, most scholars agree that Ife sculpture represents the culmination of the aristocratic style, not an outside influence.

Ife craftspeople taught artisans of the neighboring Benin kingdom the techniques of bronze casting in the fifteenth century. Figures such as the *flute player* (fig.4–83) show the Ife and Benin use of a head-to-body proportional ratio of one to four. Massive and realistic feet and legs contrast with the delicacy of the textures of cloth and helmet.

Contemporary African Art

Contemporary African art was "discovered" by Westerners near the end of the last century. Picasso, Matisse and other artists were influenced by the geometric qualities and abstract forms of African sculpture. These traditions continue to develop today. The vibrancy of the stone sculpture of the Shona people in Zimbabwe is remarkable for its extremely simple forms and quiet emotion (fig.4–84). In South Africa, artists work in a variety of styles and media (fig.4–85). Spontaneity is a hallmark of their work. The art of the African continent reflects its historic and contemporary diversity and complexity.

4–84 This Shona sculptor has used simplicity of form in a strikingly expressive manner. *Shona sculpture*, Richard Chirambadare, "Mweyo Mwando." Stone, h. 28" (71 cm). Gallery St. Helena, Santa Rosa, CA.

4–85 The sculptor of this piece was also a musician and a dancer. He lived in Tshakhuma Village in the Transvaal. Nelson Mukhuba, *Golfer*, Velvet corkwood, 1985. Transvaal, South Africa. Collection of Paul Stopforth and Carol Marshall.

Lesson 4.8 Review

1 What three types of societies live south of the Sahara Desert in Africa? How is their art alike?
2 What type of art do the nomadic tribes of the semi-arid regions create?
3 How are masks used in southern Africa?
4 Of what materials do the N'Gere construct their masks?

5 For which class of people was the art of the nomadic and agriculture tribes and the kingdoms of Nigeria created?
6 Who were the Nok and Ife cultures? What type of art did each group produce?
7 Measure the head of the Benin flute player. How many heads tall is he? How does this proportion compare with that of most people?

Higher-Order Thinking Skills

1 After students have read Lesson 4.8, have them select one reproduced object and then research its relationship to its culture's spiritual beliefs. Ask students to consider the major differences between their chosen work and those made in the Western art tradition.

• Can most non-Western art be wholly understood without knowing the context in which it functioned?

2 Compared to the abstract styles we often associate with African art, the Ife tradition is very naturalistic. Ask students if they were surprised to find this more realistic tradition in Africa. Have them compare the Ife bronze (fig.4–82) with works from Classical Greece and Rome.

3 Have students compare the Benin *Flute Player* (fig.4–83) and *Warrior and Attendants* (fig.1–b). What stylistic characteristics allow us to conclude that they both are from the same culture and date from approximately the same time period?

Lesson 4.8 Review Answers

1 The nomadic tribes in the desert and steppe regions, the sedentary farming cultures in the savanna and rain-forest fringe areas, and the ancient sophisticated kingdoms of Nigeria and the Guinea coast all pay careful attention to craftsmanship, use geometric abstraction, and have a religious orientation.
2 Masks and sculptures used in religious ceremonies that include ancestors or cult figures, fetishes and reliquary figures
3 In ritual ceremonies and dances to embody spiritual forces

4 Nails, wood, paint, fabric, tin, cotton cord, fiber, cloth and woolen ornaments
5 Wealthy kings and courtiers
6 The Nok and Ife cultures are ancient Nigerian cultures. The Nok flourished in 500 BC and made large terra cotta figures. In about 1500 AD, the Ife culture produced naturalistic human sculptures cast in bronze using the lost-wax process.
7 The Benin flute player is four heads tall. Most adults are six to eight heads tall.

Lesson 4.9

Pre-Columbian art flourished in Mexico, Central America and South America long before the arrival of European invaders. Artists from these Mesoamerican and Andean regions produced architecture, sculpture, textiles and ceramics of astounding quality.

Warm-up

Ask students to guess what culture developed the 365-day calendar that they use today. Direct them to fig.4–89, its caption and the information on page 134. Ask if they had been aware of the sophistication of pre-Columbian astrology and mathematics. Have students compare the timeline on page 131 to the timelines of Western cultures in order to increase their sensitivity to the major developments that occurred simultaneously throughout the world.

Objectives

Students should be able to:

Discuss the types of art made by pre-Columbian civilizations.

Understand that pre-Columbian works differ from those in the Western European tradition.

Vocabulary Definitions

corbel (*kore*-bell) An overlapping arrangement of stones, each layer projecting a bit beyond the row beneath it; also, a bracket of stone, wood or brick projecting from the face of a wall which may support a cornice or arch.

codex (*ko*-decks) A manuscript in book form, often with pages arranged in an accordion-fold, as distinguished from a scroll.

4.9 Pre-Columbian Art

CIVILIZATIONS IN THE AMERICAS flourished long before the arrival of Columbus and the conquest of the Spanish. The civilizations that flourished in Mexico, Central America and South America can be distinguished by two geographic regions: (1) *Mesoamerica*, or the areas of Mexico and the northern countries of Central America and (2) *Andean*, or the coastal and highland areas of Peru and adjacent areas in South America. Here people produced architecture, sculpture, weaving and ceramics of exceptional quality. All were technically and stylistically very different from Western traditions.

Vocabulary
corbeling
codices

4–86 The extraordinary quality of textiles from Paracas suggests that these were the pre-eminent art form of the society. Mantle, known as *The Paracas Textile*, detail (fig.4–93).

4–88 This garment has a checkerboard of different motifs on each of its sides. *Shirt,* or *poncho,* Inca. Interlocked tapestry, cotton and wool, 35 3/4" x 30" (91 x 76.5 cm). Dumbarton Oaks, Washington, DC.

4–87 Little is known of the origins or history of the Olmec culture. *Jadeite Mask,* Olmec. 8" x 7" (21 x 18 cm). Dumbarton Oaks, Washington, DC.

Teach

Criticism: Ask students to examine figs.4–86 and 4–88 and try to count the number of designs woven into each one.

• Do they think that these textiles were easy to make? Why or why not? Ask students who know how to sew, knit or needlepoint to explain the labor required for these crafts. From their experiences, how complicated do they believe it was for artists to create the pre-Columbian examples?

Art History: Have students discern which images in Lesson 4.9 are related to spiritual life.

• Are they surprised that even some ceramic vessels (fig.4–91), textiles (fig.4–86) and depictions of games (fig.4–95) had ceremonial associations?

• Is this true for corresponding art forms in modern American society?

• What does the prevalence of religious connotations indicate about pre-Columbian societies?

• How is the melding of daily and spiritual life similar to the traditional cultures of North America's first peoples? (See Lesson 4.10 for details.)

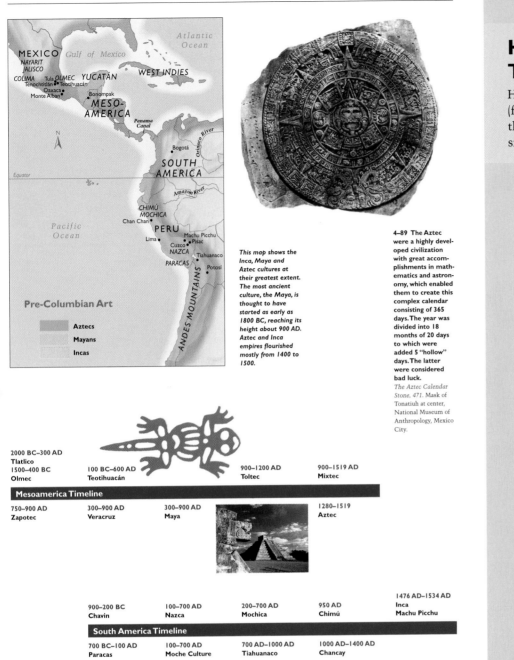

This map shows the Inca, Maya and Aztec cultures at their greatest extent. The most ancient culture, the Maya, is thought to have started as early as 1800 BC, reaching its height about 900 AD. Aztec and Inca empires flourished mostly from 1400 to 1500.

4–89 The Aztec were a highly developed civilization with great accomplishments in mathematics and astronomy, which enabled them to create this complex calendar consisting of 365 days. The year was divided into 18 months of 20 days to which were added 5 "hollow" days. The latter were considered bad luck. *The Aztec Calendar Stone,* 471. Mask of Tonatiuh at center, National Museum of Anthropology, Mexico City.

2000 BC–300 AD			
Tlatlico			
1500–400 BC	100 BC–600 AD	900–1200 AD	900–1519 AD
Olmec	**Teotihuacán**	**Toltec**	**Mixtec**

Mesoamerica Timeline

750–900 AD	300–900 AD	300–900 AD		1280–1519
Zapotec	**Veracruz**	**Maya**		**Aztec**

				1476 AD–1534 AD
				Inca
900–200 BC	100–700 AD	200–700 AD	950 AD	**Machu Picchu**
Chavin	**Nazca**	**Mochica**	**Chimú**	

South America Timeline

700 BC–100 AD	100–700 AD	700 AD–1000 AD	1000 AD–1400 AD
Paracas	**Moche Culture**	**Tiahuanaco**	**Chancay**

Evaluate

Ask students if the art of Mesoamerican and Andean civilizations was strongly influenced by Western European traditions. How can the reproductions in Lesson 4.9 substantiate their answers?

Ask students why Spanish is spoken today in many of the cultures covered in this lesson.

• Why are the languages and traditions of the original inhabitants no longer prevalent?

• How does this parallel what occurred to the indigenous peoples of North America?

• How would students feel about the invasion of European culture if they descended from the original inhabitants of the land?

Reteach

Divide the class into three groups. Have one research American quilts (fig.2–b); another, pre-Columbian textiles, as illustrated in Lesson 4.9; and the third, American Indian Navajo blankets (fig.4–107). Request that they make presentations to the class about the origins, techniques, styles and functions of these garments. After, have students discuss differences and similarities that they discovered. How does each culture's work reflect something unique about the society in which it was made?

Contextual Information

The Earliest Inhabitants of the Americas

Most archaeologists and historians have concluded that people came to what is now Canada, the United States, Mexico, and Central and South America from Asia along a land bridge about 4000 BC. They could have been looking for food or land for an enlarging population, or they could have been exploring. Some of them settled, planted crops and developed civilizations. In their exploration of the earliest cultures in Mexico and Central America, archaeologists have found sculpture made of basalt and jadeite, with designs similar to those found in Asia.

An Early Twist-off

A one-stirrup pot made about 500 AD and found in Guatemala in 1984 has a lid that can be twisted off—a unique invention in the history of ceramics.

Paracas

In 1925, a Peruvian archaeologist, Julio Tello, discovered hundreds of burials at a site he called Necropolis (City of the Dead) on the Paracas peninsula. Each burial included a body wrapped with successive layers of cloth. Some of the cloths were plain, but others were extremely colorful and were lavishly decorated with embroidery. Food, gold, ceramics and other objects were found among the wrappings. The quantity and quality of the cloths indicate that textiles were the most important of the arts in this society.

Ninety separate figures form the border around *The Paracas Textile* (fig.4–93). Most of the costumes and jewelry that appear on the border figures can be related directly to objects found in the burials. The border figures, therefore, provide us with a colorful portrayal of life in this Paracas area 2000 years ago.

Architecture

In architecture, there was no knowledge of the true arch, so openings were created by **corbeling.** A corbeled arch cannot span a wide area. Therefore, no large openings and interior spaces are found in pre-Columbian architecture. Earthquake-proof temples and palaces were made of fitted polygonal stones that were locked and bonded into massive walls (fig.4–90). Temples were pyramidal in shape, often built of earthen mounds faced with finely fit stone or sculptured *adobe.* One or more sides of these temples were fitted with an immense stairway. Carved mythological heads depicting deities such as *Quetzalcóatl,* the feathered serpent of *Teotihuacán,* were cut and fit into the slopes.

Sculpture

Sculpture throughout the Americas was often ceremonial, with heads or full figures of gods carved in low or high relief. Very often, human or animal forms became highly stylized. Animal-human gods were carved with the type of symbolism seen on the Temple of Quetzalcóatl or in the clay funeral urn made by the *Zapotec* people of Oaxaca (fig.4–91).

4–90 The precipitous stairways of these temples seem to reach into the sky. Climbing them requires endurance. Descending them needs careful stepping and concentration.
Temple of Quetzalcóatl, 500–900. Teotihuacán, Mexico.

Ceramics

Ceramics were a significant product of nearly all American cultures. No pottery was hand-thrown, because potters did not possess knowledge of the wheel. However, their hand-made work was technically excellent, with thinly made walls and surfaces painted with colored clay slips. Terra-cotta clays were *burnished* with polished wooden cylinders to produce shiny nonglazed wares. *Chimú* potters of Peru produced black wares by firing with an oxygen-deficient reduction atmosphere in the kiln. Typically, pottery

4–91 Fierce faces with glaring eyes and bared teeth are a common theme in Central American sculpture.
Funeral urn, 600–800. Teotihuacán, Mexico. Painted clay, 23 1/2" (60 cm) high. National Museum of Anthropology, Mexico City.

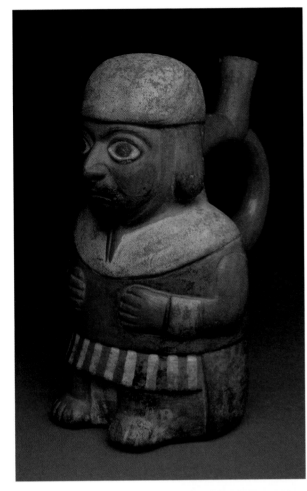

Metalwork

Metalworking originated with the early cultures, which excelled at working metals such as gold and silver. Gold was associated with the sun and silver, with the moon. Tin, copper, lead and alloys were also used to make jewelry, death masks, whistles and ritual objects. Smiths hammered, shaped, soldered, inlaid, filigreed and cast these materials with lost-wax and in open molds.

Fabrics

Fabrics of cotton, wool, feathers or strips of hide and fur were produced throughout ancient America. Weaving traditions date back to at least 1500 BC in coastal Peru, where the *Paracas* culture produced the finest of all ancient American fabrics. The example shown here (figs.4–86, 4–93) was woven of cotton and wool and includes stylized figures and animal motifs worked into geometric patterns and a repeated design. This burial mantle is an excellent example of the weaver's craft.

4–92 Pots such as this have also been found in many animal forms.
Stirrup vessel, about 500–600 AD. Mochica culture.

was made for use in ritual and burial. Pots were often broken to "release" the spirit when buried with the dead. The interesting *"stirrup"-shaped vessels* (fig.4–92) have handles that bridge both sides of the pot. The handles are hollow to form a spout through which liquids were poured. Shapes included human heads, a variety of animal forms and even fish.

4–93 This mantle probably was included in a mummy bundle. It may have been used in important ceremonies during the life of the deceased.
Mantle, known as *The Paracas Textile*, 300–100 BC. Cotton and wool, 25" x 59" (63.5 x 150 cm). The Brooklyn Museum, New York. J. T. Underwood Memorial Fund.

Higher-Order Thinking Skills

Pre-Columbian ceramics were produced without a potter's wheel. Using figs.4–91 and 4–92 as examples, have students analyze how the pots were made. Ask what elements were emphasized. How do these works differ from the ceramics that were produced by the Chinese?

Interdisciplinary Connection

Social Sciences: Inform students that the pre-Columbian world practiced mummification, even though we most often associate it with the Egyptian civilization.

• Have students choose two cultures mentioned in this chapter and research the funerary and burial customs of that culture. Their research should answer the following: Are there any similarities between the customs of the two cultures? What are the differences? How do the researched customs differ from those most commonly practiced in American contemporary life? Do we have any art forms today that we associate with death or burial?

Mesoamerica

The most ancient culture in Meso-america is the *Olmec* culture. The Olmec lived along the Gulf of Mexico from as early as 1500 BC to about 200 AD. The Olmec affected the religion, politics and art throughout the region. They carved huge monolithic basalt sculptures of faces (fig.4–94) that mixed human and catlike creatures. The jaguar became symbolic of the gods and was pictured in various forms of art.

Other ancient Mexican cultures included the *Nayarit* and *Colima* on the west coast. Their ceramic sculptures provide information about daily life. The example shown (fig.4–95) illustrates a ceremonial rubber-ball game played in a clay court. These games must have had religious significance because courts are found connected with the temples of later Mesoamerican cultures.

"Classical" Mesoamerican civilization dates from about 200 to 900. During this era, the *Teotihuacáns* built a huge stone temple-city for the use of pilgrims. *Mayan* civilization also emerged during this period, and they constructed similar pyramidal temples throughout Yucatán and much of Middle America. Frescoes were painted at Bonompak depicting life-size human figures involved in ceremonies and processions. *Zapotec* culture, noted for its ornamental

4–94
Archaeologists are not sure whether the colossal heads of the Olmec are gods or rulers.
Colossal head, Olmec. 1500–300 BC. Basalt.

clay funerary urns and incense burners, also flourished at this time.

The post-Classical era saw the rise of imperial states. First the *Toltec*, then the *Aztec* nations controlled Middle America. At Tula, the Toltec built one of the few temples to use columns, which were carved in the form of warriors and spear throwers. The Aztec reached their pinnacle of power in the later 1400s. The Aztec centered their empire at Tenochtitlán, continuing the artistic traditions of the Mixtec and Toltec. Aztec sculptors produced bas-relief calendar stones (fig.4–89) that illustrated the days of the week as well as Aztec history. Unique to this era is the development of **codices**, or illuminated manuscripts, painted on bark paper or deerskin parchment (figs.4–2, 4–6).

Andean

Andean civilizations trace their common origins to the *Chavin* culture of the Peruvian highlands. The stylized image of the jaguar that is featured in Andean art originated with the Chavin culture. The

4–95 Ball courts have been found in the ruins of later Mesoamerican temples.
Ceremonial ball game, 100–300. Nayarit culture. Ceramic, white on red slip, 13" x 7 3/4" (33 x 20 cm). Los Angeles County Museum of Art, Proctor Stafford Collection.

jaguar, which was both worshiped and feared, was one of the most powerful symbols in Andean art. Stirrup-shaped pottery vessels found in later Peruvian cultures (fig.4–92) were first made here, as were early examples of well-fitted stonework architecture.

After the Chavin era, about 500 BC, geometric decorations were used in pottery and weaving. The south coast *Paracas* culture flourished, producing thin, sculptured pottery vessels in the stirrup tradition. The pottery was covered with thick resin pigments. The Paracas culture was famous for its textiles. As mentioned, the weavings of the Paracas were the finest of all ancient American fabric art (figs.4–86, 4–93). Other coastal cultures, such as the *Mochica* and *Chimú*, constructed large pyramidal temples of adobe during this era.

From about 100 to 900, pottery production in coastal areas reached a high point in quality. Mochica potters produced naturalistic animal-shaped vessels. The vessels featured incised designs, appliquéd and pressed ornaments, and painted patterns. South coast *Nazca* potters used polychromatic decorations of bold design and color to ornament their thin, highly polished wares.

From 900 to 1200, Andean artists produced well-fitted masonry gateways covered with stylized anthropomorphic bas-reliefs. The urban Chimú kingdom reached its peak of power about 1200. Chimú goldsmiths produced fine silver and gold cups, masks, and other objects. The Chimú were also skilled architects and built urban centers organized on a grid plan. Their adobe-faced temples were ornamented with naturalistic birds, fish and geometric abstract motifs. They were also noted for their pottery, which reflected a Mochican influence.

About 1440, the *Inca* conquered the region, creating the final "imperialist" period. The Inca utilized the artistic achievements of former kingdoms for its own purposes, much as the Romans did in Europe. They were active in a number of art forms (figs.4–88, 4–96) but excelled in architecture and dry-masonry techniques. The capital at Cuzco and other cities were well-planned communities based on grid patterns. Central plazas contained public buildings and temples. Late in the Inca era, walled fortresses were built near centers like Pisac and *Machu Picchu* (fig.4–97). Despite hasty construction, huge stone blocks were expertly fitted and locked into structures that have withstood invasions and earthquakes. They stand today as a testimony to the engineering skill of the Andean civilization.

4–96 Several sets of these birds have survived, but their use is unknown. *Seven Sea Birds*, Inca, 15th century. Cut and hammered gold, 2" x 10 1/4" (5 x 26 cm). American Museum of Natural History, New York.

4–97 Huge stones were cut and fitted without masonry to build this city high in the mountains. *Machu Picchu*. Overall view, late 15th century. Inca culture, Peru.

Lesson 4.9 Review

1 What is corbeling? Which civilizations used this building technique and what is its limitation?
2 What shape were pre-Columbian temples? Describe the temple of Quetzalcóatl. Who was Quetzalcóatl?
3 Which pre-Columbian culture was renowned for its fine weaving?
4 List some of the metals used by pre-Columbian sculptors. What did they make with these metals?
5 What is the oldest Mesoamerican culture? What type of sculptures did they carve?
6 When was the classical Mesoamerican civilization? Which cultures were important in Mesoamerica during this classical time?
7 Which two cultures controlled the lands of Mesoamerica during the post-Classical era? What type of art did these cultures produce?
8 What animal was one of the most powerful symbols of Andean art?
9 For what type of textile art was the Paracas culture most famous?
10 What techniques did the Mochica potters use to decorate their pots?

Higher-Order Thinking Skills

1 Fig.4–97 shows Machu Picchu's foundations and some walls, but there are no roofs. Have students imagine what the city looked like when it was occupied and then draw a section of it as it would have been.

2 Other examples of pre-Columbian art and architecture appear in Chapter 2, figs.2–3, 2–15 and Chapter 3, figs.3–d, 3–2, 3–4. Ask students what they have found most interesting and surprising about pre-Columbian art and architecture. Had they had any preconceptions about art from that period or that region of the world. Were these preconceptions validated or proven incorrect?

Lesson 4.9 Review Answers

1 Corbeling is an overlapping arrangement of stones with each layer projecting slightly beyond the row beneath it. This technique was used for building architectural openings by pre-Columbian civilizations. Since a corbeled arch cannot span a wide area, there were no large openings or interior spaces in pre-Columbian architecture.
2 Pre-Columbian temples were pyramidal. The temple of Quetzalcóatl was pyramidal with an immense stairway and carved mythological heads depicting the deity Quetzalcóatl—the feathered serpent of Teotihuacán.
3 Paracas
4 Jewelry, death masks, whistles and ritual objects from gold, tin, copper, lead and alloys.
5 The Olmec, the oldest Mesoamerican culture, carved huge monolithic basalt sculptures of faces combining human and catlike creatures.
6 The Zapotec, Teotihuacán and Mayan cultures were important from 200 to 900 AD, the classical period of Mesoamerica.
7 The Toltec and Aztec nations controlled Mesoamerica during the post-Classical era. The Toltecs built temples with columns carved in the form of warriors and spear throwers. The Aztecs carved bas-relief calendar stones and codices (illuminated manuscripts) on bark paper and deerskin parchment.
8 The jaguar
9 Weavings
10 Incised designs, appliquéd and pressed ornaments, painted patterns

Lesson 4.10

A diverse group of Native American peoples have created ceremonial and functional art since prehistoric times. While each nation's objects differ from one another, they share an appreciation of natural materials, a close relationship to the spiritual realm, and use of pictographic symbolism and abstract designs.

Warm-up

Ask students to glance at the images in Lesson 4.10 and compare them to those in Lesson 4.2. Why are the original inhabitants of North America referred to as Indians? What might be a more accurate name for the first peoples of the American continent? Share that people from each of the approximately 350 or more nations in the United States alone identify themselves by their tribe's name—such as Lenni Lenape, Lakota, Pauite and Kiowa.

Objectives

Students should be able to:

Understand that each Native American nation has its own distinct culture and visual style.

Discuss the common respect for nature, the connection to the spirit world and the proclivity toward the use of natural materials in Native American art.

Vocabulary Definitions

mound builders Early Native Americans of the Middle West and Southeast who formed large earthen burial mounds and fortifications thus creating the first earth works in America (100–1000).

kiva (*kee*-vah) A subterranean chamber ceremonially used by Southwestern Native Americans as a worship center; kivas were square in early phases of Pueblo culture and round during the Great Pueblo era. Roofs are low and slightly domed.

adobe (a-*doh*-bee) A clay brick made of sun-dried earth used as a building material. Any structure made of adobe bricks.

Pueblo (*pweb*-lo) A communal dwelling consisting of groups of continuous flat-roofed stone or adobe houses; the Native American culture of the South-western United States typified by its

---

4.10 Native America

NORTH AMERICA SUPPORTED a diverse population of Native Americans. The groups had different customs and beliefs, although all practiced a form of nature worship. Native Americans have created ceremonial and functional objects of high craftsmanship and symbolic beauty since Neolithic times. Crafts made of bark, skin (fig.4–100), wood and beads, and fine pottery and basketwork (fig.4–98) were important traditions in Native American groups. These works share several characteristics. They reflect an appreciation for the materials of nature, a close relationship with the spirit world, pictographic symbolism, and an advanced level of craftsmanship.

Vocabulary
mound builders
kivas
adobe
pueblo
tipi
petroglyphs
totem poles

4–99 The Haida people of the Northwest Coast excelled at carving wood and argillate, a black shale stone.
Haida Box. Wool. Hurst Gallery, Cambridge, MA.

4–98 Native Americans in California have a strong tradition of basketweaving. The art flourished particularly in the late nineteenth century. The tradition continues today with women passing the techniques from one generation to the next.
Feather basket, Pomo, California. Fiber, buttons, quail topknots, 12" (30.48 cm). Hurst Gallery, Cambridge, MA.

c.1000 BC–300 BC **Adena-Hopewell**	c.1000 AD–c.1200 AD **Mesa Verde**	c.1200 AD–1300 AD **Mimbres**	1300 AD–1500 AD **Kuaua Pueblo**

Pre-historic Era Timeline

300 AD–c.1000 AD **Ipiutak**		1200 AD–1500 AD **Mississippian**	1700s–present **Navajo Hopi Chilkat, Haida, Kwkiutl, Tlingit Iroquois Crow Mandan**

---

use of such dwellings, and artistically noted for its excellent slip-painted pottery, loom-woven clothing and blankets, and kachinas.

tipi (*tee*-pee) A conical, rawhide dwelling consisting of groups of buffalo hides stretched over a framework of poles, its base diameter ranging from 12 to 30 feet. Characteristic dwelling of the Plains Indians of America.

petroglyph (*pet*-row-glif) A carving on rock, usually of a stylized image or message in such images.

totem pole A tall post or pillar carved with the heredity marks, emblems or badges of a tribe or clan, functioning as a type of family tree.

Teach

Criticism: Divide students into pairs and ask them to carefully examine the images in Lesson 4.10. After they discern the materials from which each one is made, challenge them to decide which area of the country could provide these natural elements. When they narrow down their choices, have them check their answers with the information in the captions and then find the tribe's location on the map. Discuss the visual differences among the artworks of the various nations and their relationship to the environment.

• What attitude do students think traditional Indian societies hold toward nature? Share that traditional cultures share a common view that each thing, from inanimate objects such as rocks

North American Tribal Areas

Native North American people achieved a wide cultural diversity, their tribes fanning out all over the continent. Think of the different accents, attitudes and cultures among Americans today in different parts of the country. How might geography have contributed to these differences?

4–100 Men of the Plains tribes often painted hides as a means of recording important hunts and battles. *Buffalo skin robe* with painted detail representing battle fought in 1797 between the Sioux and Attikara against the Mandon and Hidatsa. Peabody Museum, Harvard University.

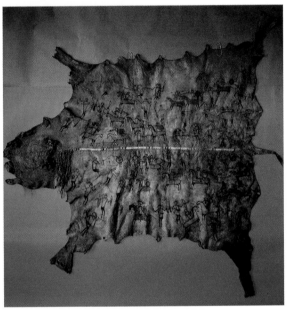

4–101 Some contemporary Native American artists choose to work with traditional materials and subjects. Others make their statements about Native American life in nontraditional ways. Compare this painting with fig.17–51.
Jon Lightfoot, *Women of Cougar Clan*, 1989. Oil on canvas, 36 x 48" (91 x 122 cm). Courtesy of the artist and the Suzanne Brown Gallery. Scottsdale, Arizona.

Contextual Information
Pomo Baskets

People of the Pomo tribe in California have traditionally used baskets as ceremonial objects, hats, cooking vessels, carrying vessels and storage containers. They still produce some of the finest baskets in the world (fig.4–98), prized by collectors of today as high-quality works of art.

Good quality materials, which include willow root, bear grass, spruce root and sedge, are essential to a successful basket. Pomo weavers do not leave finding these materials to chance, but cultivate the plants that provide what they need. These are then gathered at the right times of the year, split, trimmed and stored in coiled bundles. Thus a Native American's knowledge of the earth and its rhythms are an inherent part of the art of basket-making.

Reteach

Explain to the class that most Native American art traditions were passed down within the family from one generation to the next over many centuries. Boys and girls would learn particular skills from their relatives and then teach these to their own offspring. Ask students to compare this manner of education to the medieval European guild system and the Renaissance studios run by masters. Direct them to discover who the students were in these Western European systems.

• Would females or poor children be likely to acquire apprenticeships?

• Did everyone in Europe participate in some artistic activity or did only those with perceived talent receive art instruction?

• How might the differences between the two modes of learning reflect the Native American conception of art and life as being inseparable?

and rivers to invisible elements such as the wind or the four directions, is endowed with its own spirit.

Art History: Tell students that there is no separate word for *art* in Native American languages as conceived in Western European culture. Instruct students to examine the reproductions throughout the lesson and discuss why this might be so. Have them decide if the objects are purely decorative and meant only to be observed or if they all perform some other purpose in addition to their aesthetic qualities. Point out that each contains spiritual associations, through its symbolic content, its ceremonial function, or the fact that the spirit of the materials resides within the item after it is completed.

Evaluate

Ask students to name materials used in historic Native American art and explain what they reflect about traditional Native people's relationship to the environment.

• Why might traditional Native cultures conceive of the land and its bounties as sacred?

• How would students feel toward their own surroundings if many generations of their ancestors had been rooted in a particular place?

• Would it feel important to remain in this area? How would they feel if the government forced them to move to another location against their will? What would they do?

Architecture

The **mound builders** of eastern America created huge earthen platforms by carrying earth in baskets and tamping it into flattened terraces. One of the largest of these is at Cahokia, Illinois, a complex of eighty-five mounds. The area is over 30 meters high, 300 meters long and over 200 meters wide.

The Anasazi people were the ancestors of the Pueblo peoples in the Southwest. They built communal apartment houses under the protecting ledges of massive cliffs. The Anasazi built *cliff dwellings at Mesa Verde* (fig.4–102) in Chaco Canyon, New Mexico, and remains are still standing. The settlement of Mesa Verde has over two hundred rooms and twenty-three meeting rooms called **kivas**. Kivas were used as sacred worship centers. The interiors were painted with ceremonial designs.

Later, Pueblo Indians used stone and **adobe** (sun-dried bricks) to build square dwellings like apartment houses. They made the rooms in terraces so that the roofs of the lower rooms formed the terraces for those above. The buildings had only a few windows or T-shaped doorways high up on the walls. The openings were accessible only by retractable ladders. Thus, the **pueblo** could be defended, much like a fort. Round towers aided in this function. Contemporary pueblos continue the tradition in the Southwest (figs.4–3, 4–103).

Hunters of the Plains region relied on the portability of the **tipi**, a dwelling of rawhide stretched over a conical framework of long poles. Decoration was significant, and painting on the hide included designs representing the forces of nature. Sun, rain, animals, spirits and *mandala* patterns were all rendered with earth colors and animal dyes.

4–103 Pueblo construction continues to be used today by Native Americans of the Southwest. *Pueblo*, Taos, New Mexico.

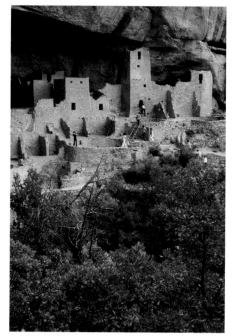

4–102 This building complex is situated on a ledge above a valley floor. This location provided shelter and protection. *Cliff dwelling*, Mesa Verde National Park, Colorado, about 1100.

4–104 In order to be successful, this intricate design must take into account the shape of the pot.
Acoma vase. Bird design. Polychrome pottery, 14 1/4" (36 cm) high. The Indian Art Center of California, Studio City.

Pottery

Pottery traditions of Native American peoples are exceptional for their fine craftsmanship and design. The earliest North American pottery was created by Eastern peoples about 2200 BC. The potter's wheel was not used. Instead, clay was slowly formed into symmetrical shapes using the coil method of building the form up ring by ring. Paddles were sometimes used to enlarge and shape the forms. No glaze was used, but pots were partially waterproofed by burnishing. Burnishing is a process of polishing a pot with smooth rocks or wood before the pot is completely dry. Decorations were stamped, incised or engraved into the surface. Often slip of various colors was painted onto the leather-hard clay.

Most Native American pottery was used as containers for food storage or for cooking. Its organic patterns and bird motif accent the form of the vase.

In New Mexico, in 1919, Maria Martinez with her husband, Julian, began the production of black polished pottery (fig.4–105). This pottery is made of clay that fires to a black finish. Before it is fired, it is burnished until it shines. No glazes are used in this process. Designs are then painted, or sometimes carved, on the elegant forms after polishing.

The painted areas appear dull black on the polished surface and create a striking effect. Note this interaction on the upper body of this vase. Women make the basic ware; then men paint it, an unusual departure from the common Indian practice in which women make the pot from start to finish.

4–106 Petroglyphs such as these can be found on rocks throughout the American Southwest.
Petroglyphs, Arizona.

Painting

Painting can be traced to ancient rock carvings called **petroglyphs**, found in at least forty-three states. Some petroglyphs are 5000 years old. The designs were scraped into the rock (fig.4–106), probably as part of ritual puberty, hunting, fertility or worship practices. Images of puma, serpents, bighorn owls, whales and human figures are stylized in what seem to be the beginnings of a written language. Carved patterns were often highlighted with color from clay, minerals, charred bone or plant pigments. Traditional designs are still found today in sand paintings, pottery decoration and kivas.

4–105 The matte portions of the pattern come from painting water on the burnished surface of the pot before it is fired.
Maria Martinez and Julian Martinez, *Black vase,* 1929. Polished pottery, 6" (15 cm) high. Collection of Gilbert Davis, Worcester, MA.

Higher-Order Thinking Skills

1 Have students consider how art and life interact in contemporary urban culture. Is there a separation between the two realms?

• Where is art made and exhibited? Who is involved in its creation?

• What specifically have students learned from Lesson 4.10 about the ways in which art and life are intimately intertwined in traditional Native American societies?

• How might students integrate art more strongly into their own daily lives? Might a keener awareness of their environment, the aesthetic qualities of common objects, or trying their hand at various artistic endeavors alter their experience of the world?

• Do students believe that only those with rare talents are qualified for instruction or should art be part of every person's life? How would they propose to integrate art into the experience of everyone?

2 Have the class compare and contrast the Han house model (fig.4–34) to the pueblo from Taos, New Mexico (fig.4–103). Ask students which house they would prefer to live in. What reasons do they have for their choice?

3 The cliff dwelling shown in fig.4–102 is well suited to its site. Have students select a site in their area and design a building that is suited to that site and takes advantage of its unique features.

4 Ask students to compare pieces of Native American pottery (figs.2–40, 4–104, 4–105) to those from China. Ask whether they think that the potters of these cultures would have admired or disliked each other's work.

Weaving and Basketry

Southwestern weaving traces its unique use of the *loom* back to Cochise and Mogollon cultures, about 300 BC. Clothing and blankets are created by innovative weave patterns known as the basket, tapestry, diagonal twill or diamond twill weaves. The Navajo rug of wool (fig.4–107) has distinct designs that represent both the tribe and the individual woman who wove it.

Related to textile weaving is the more ancient craft of basketry, first practiced about 9000 years ago. One of three methods is used in their manufacture—plaiting, twining or coiling. The fibers of grass, bark, root or hemp are woven into fine, often watertight containers. Dyed or naturally colored strands are incorporated to create rhythmical geometric patterns and representations of animals like the thunderbird. Each region has produced fine work, but the outstanding baskets of the California *Hupa* and *Pomo* peoples (fig.4–108) are regarded as some of the most excellent in both craftsmanship and decoration.

4–108 Consider how the artist has combined rhythm, shape and pattern in this basket's design.
Tray, 19th century. Hupa, Northern California. Fiber, 16 1/2 x 4" (41.9 x 10.1 cm). The Nelson-Atkins Museum of Art, Kansas City, Missouri.

4–107 Compare these designs and colors to those in the *Ardabil Carpet* (fig.4–69).
Navajo rug, 1850–1880. Wool. The Indian Art Center of California, Studio City.

Inquiry

Have students research the Native American peoples that were indigenous to their local area or state. What types of architecture did they use? What types of crafts and artistic traditions were they noted for?

Cooperative Learning

Have each student select a work of art from Chapter 4 to "own." They then draw the image and write a description of the work and their reasons for acquiring it. Have students use a bulletin board or other display space for putting together a show of their treasures. They will need to consider what the curator of such a far-reaching show takes into account—sequence, placement, information to be conveyed to the viewer. When the show is complete, the students can write a review such as one an art critic might write for a national newspaper.

4–109 This elegant hand is very expressive in its simplicity. *Human Hand,* Hopewell Mound, Ohio, 1000–1300. Cut sheet mica, 13" (33 cm) long. The Field Museum, Chicago, IL.

Metalworking

Metalworking has been practiced in copper since 3000 BC. By 1200, southeastern peoples made ceremonial plaques of eagles and costumed dancing warriors. The mound builders of Ohio hammered copper ornaments into snake heads, birds, fish and headdresses. They also fashioned mica into forms such as hands (fig.4–109). Silver was introduced by Europeans and was beaten into jewelry by the *Iroquois, Oneida* and others in the early nineteenth century. *Cheyenne* and *Sioux* created hair-plates, buckles, armbands and harness trappings during the same period. The *Navajo,* destined to become the finest of all American silversmiths, learned smithing from the Mexicans. Old silver dollars were hammered into squash-blossom necklaces and hollow beads or cast into jewelry forms (fig.4–110). *Zuni* specialized in beautiful settings for clusters of turquoise, while *Hopi* silversmiths created new techniques by adding shell and coral to their pieces.

4–110 The Navajo are the premiere American silversmiths, and they often use turquoise as an inset. *Silver bracelets,* 1920–30. Navajo. The Brooklyn Museum, New York.

Six Dynasties Era 220–589 AD
pagodas, rock cave temples and monasteries with carved Buddha and bodhisattvas images
Song Dynasty 960–1279 AD
landscape painting, natural appearing sculpture
Yuan Dynasty 1279–1368 AD
high-fired white and blue and white porcelain
Japan
Jomon Phase 9000–200 BC
red clay food vessels later with slip decoration
Yaoi Period 200 BC–200 AD
haniwa sculptures
Asuka Period 552–645 AD
wooden Horyu-ji temple at Asuka
Nara Period 645–794 AD
lacquer and bronze Buddhist images
Heian Period 794–1185 AD
Yamatoe-e painting on scrolls, architecture and landscape design stressing harmony with nature
Kamakura Period 1185–1333 AD
huge bronze Buddha, realistic paintings, tea ceremony ceramics
Muromachi and Momoyama Periods 1334–1615 AD
tranquil gardens, flower arranging, sumi-e painting on rice washi paper and on panels and screens
Edo Period 1615–1868 AD
ukiyo-e painting, woodcuts
Modern Period 1868 AD–present
art reflecting traditional heritage of simplicity and elegance

Chapter Review Answers

Due to space considerations and the extensive length of the answer to the timeline question in Chapter Review (p. 143), it has been placed here.

 Timeline
India
Indus Valley Civilization 2500–1500 BC
bronze and stone animal sculptures, seals
The Mauryan Empire 322–185 BC
columns topped with lion sculptures, stupas
The Gandhara Era 78–250AD
Greek style Buddhist sculpture
The Gupta Era 320–600AD
Buddhist Indian art, cave temples

The Medieval Period 730–1308 AD
freestanding temples cut from live rock (or 9th–16th centuries)
China
Shang Dynasty 1766–1027 BC
glazed hand-built and wheel-made gray pottery; ivory, stone, and jade sculptures; bronze vessels
Zhou Dynasty 1028–221 BC
glazed ceramics
Qin Dynasty (Chin) 221–206 BC
burial pottery and suits of jade segments, army of clay soldiers and horses, Great Wall of China
Han Dynasty 206 BC–220 AD
clay models of buildings, glazed ceramics, lacquer boxes, silk, mural painting in tombs, life-size stone and clay burial figures

Contextual Information

Totem Poles

Northwest Coast totem poles were status symbols and contained carved animals and mythological creatures. These are animals that are symbols of clans and record their activities.

Lesson 4.10 Review Answers

1 The Anasazi were the ancestors of the Pueblo in the Southwest. They built communal apartment houses under the protecting ledges of massive cliffs. They used kivas as sacred meeting rooms or worship centers.

2 The tipi was ideal for the roaming hunters because it was portable. Designs representing the forces of nature—suns, rain, animals, spirits and mandala patterns—were painted on tipis with earth colors and animal dyes.

3 In the East about 2200 BC

4 Native Americans partially waterproofed their pots by burnishing, and polishing the pot with smooth rocks or wood before the pot was completely dry.

5 Black polished pottery

6 Petroglyphs are ancient rock carvings showing images of puma, serpents, bighorn, owls, whales and stylized human figures are found in petroglyphs.

7 Basketry

8 The Navajo learned European metal-working techniques from the Mexicans. They hammered silver dollars into squash-blossom necklaces and hollow beads, and cast jewelry forms.

9 The Tlingit, Haida and Kwakiutl created sculptures in wood.

10 Supernatural and legendary characters and animals associated with certain groups or clans

Chapter Review Answers

1 India, China, Japan, Southeast Asia, Oceania, Highland Asia, Islamic cultures, Sub-Sahara Africa, pre-Columbia, Native America

2 Hinduism, Buddhism, Islam began in Africa and Asia.

3 The Judeo-Christian religion is usually reflected in Western religious art.

Woodworking

While most of the creative energy of Native Americans went into functional objects, the wood sculpture of the Northwest Coast Indians represents a contrast. The Northwest Coast is made up of the Indian tribes of the Tlingit, Haida and Kwakiutl. Carvings of the Northwest Coast represent some of the finest sculpture created by Native Americans. The *totem poles* and house posts of the Haida (fig.4-111) depict supernatural and legendary characters and animals associated with certain groups or clans. These poles stood in front of houses as signs of prestige and to showcase the family's

4-111 Compare these stylized figures to those on the East Malayasian gable-board painting. *Haida totem pole.* Tlingit Indians of Southeast Alaska.

4-112 Masks such as this one were carved for use in ceremonies of healing and cleansing. Elon Webster, *False Face Mask,* 1937. Iroquois. Wood. Cranbrook Institute of Science, Bloomfield Hills, Michigan.

totems, the animals that symbolized the family. Other Native Americans sculpted ritual masks (fig.4-112), effigy figures and utensils.

Contemporary Native American artists continue to paint, sculpt and craft in traditional fashions. Many artists also have combined tradition with modern styles (fig.4-101, 17-51).

Lesson 4.10 Review

1 Who were the Anasazi? Describe their dwellings. Why did they build kivas?

2 Why was the tipi an ideal living structure for the hunters of the American Plains? Name several designs that were painted on these rawhide tipis.

3 When and where was the earliest North American pottery made?

4 Describe the process that Native Americans used to make their pottery partially waterproof.

5 For what type of pottery was Maria Martinez and her family famous?

6 What is a petroglyph? What images are found in petroglyphs?

7 Which craft was practiced first in the Southwest, basketry or textile weaving?

8 How did European metal-working techniques influence Native American jewelry?

9 Name three Pacific Northwest Coast Indian tribes. In what medium did they create most of their great art?

10 What subjects did the Haida carve on their totem poles?

---

4 These sculptures were made of wood which deteriorates rapidly.

5 The Persian bracelet (fig.4-76), for example, features rows of golden birds with tiny beaks, wings and feather patterns. The artist created a rhythmic alignment with symmetry and regularity typical of Islamic culture.

6 Aztecs and Incas

7 Inca cities were planned on a grid pattern. Central plazas contained public buildings and temples.

8 Native American crafts reflect an appreciation for natural materials, show a close relationship with the spirit world, use pictographic symbolism, and achieve an advanced level of craftsmanship.

Interpret

1 Western artists often show distance with overlapping planes and lines converging to a vanishing point. Usually in Asian art receding lines remain parallel and do not converge. Asian artists usually depict great distance with three planes: a foreground, middle distance and far distance. Both Asian and Western artists use aerial perspective to show distance.

2 The Chinese used lead glazes in bright colors while Native American potters burnished their pots instead of using glaze. Asian potters used the wheel to form their vessels. They also used sprigging to attach pre-formed clay sculptural decorations onto pottery. Their vessels were ornamented with

Primary Source

Seeing What Is Not There

Chinese painting is in many ways very subtle. The viewer is frequently called upon to see what is not literally in the painting. Here the Chinese historian of art, Chang Yen-yuan, gives us a sense of the Chinese concept of color:

"Grasses and trees may display their glory without the use of reds and greens; clouds and snow may swirl and float aloft without the use of white color; mountains may show greenness without the use of the five colors. For this reason, a painter may use ink alone and, yet, all five colors may seem present in his painting."

Hsia Kuei, *Twelve Views of Landscape*, detail (fig.2–5).

Primary-Source Connection

Have students use the detail illustrated here or in another Chinese painting in the text to explain Chang Yen-yuan's statement. Ask how we can characterize the Chinese concept of color in relation to the European view of color.

Chapter Review

Review

1 Name six non-Western cultures discussed in this chapter.
2 List the three major religions that began in Africa and Asia.
3 Which religious traditions are usually reflected in Western religious art?
4 Why are there so few examples of ancient Micronesian sculptures?
5 Describe a piece of Islamic art. What was the artist trying to achieve in this art?
6 Which cultures were in power in Mesoamerica and in the Andean region when Europeans explored these lands in the sixteenth century?
7 Describe the architectural planning of Inca cities.
8 What are four characteristics common to the crafts of the various populations of Native Americans?

Interpret

1 Contrast the methods that Western and Asian artists use to indicate distance in their paintings.
2 In 200 BC, the Chinese and the Native Americans used very different methods for forming their pottery. Contrast these two methods. How did each culture decorate and glaze their pots?
3 What are the basic characteristics of Japanese art? Select one Japanese art piece in this chapter and explain how it exemplifies these characteristics.
4 Name two European artists influenced by African art. What features of African sculpture were appreciated by these European artists?
5 Rank the illustrations of Sub-Sahara African art pictured in this chapter from realistic to abstract.

Other Tools for Learning

Maps
1 What countries would a land trade route cross to connect China with Rome?
2 Find the Yellow River where Chinese culture first developed. What cities are located in this area now?
3 Find the Mekong, Irrawaddy and Chao Phraya Rivers on a map. Through which countries do these rivers flow?
4 Name three countries in Mesoamerica and three countries in the Andean region.
5 Select a culture near an ocean or in the middle of a continent. How do you think this proximity or distance from water affected this culture's art? Give an example to support your theory.

Timeline
Make a chart listing the Chinese, Indian and Japanese dynasties or cultural eras. Give an approximate date for each era and an example of art created in each time period.

Electronic Research
CD-ROM drive: Electronic Encyclopedia (e.g., *New Grolier Multimedia* or *Microsoft Encarta*)
Research the architecture of one of the cultures in this chapter further. Look it up in one of the encyclopedias. Either get a print out or draw a structure from this culture. Why was it built?

Higher-Order Thinking Skills

Totem poles depict symbolic images. Have the class design a totem pole for their school. They can include the school mascot and symbolic portrayals of important school and local figures. Provide a long roll of paper for students to make the pole for display.

Persian Gulf, then through Pakistan and India to China.
2 The cities of Lanzhou and Kaifeng are located on the banks of the Yellow River (Huang He or Hwang Ho.)
3 Mekong: China, Laos, Thailand, Cambodia, South Vietnam
Irrawaddy: China, Burma
Chao Phraya: China, Thailand, Laos
4 Mesoamerica: Mexico, Guatemala, El Salvador, Honduras, Nicaragua
Andean region: Peru, Chili, Bolivia, Ecuador
5 Cultures such as Northwest-Coast Native American groups lives centered around fishing. Many of their totem figures were sea animals which they carved and painted on their boats, homes and clothing. An inland culture such as the Pueblo used colored sand to create sand paintings.

Timeline
Due to space considerations and the extensive length of the answer to this question, it has been placed on page 141.

Electronic Research
One possibility would be for students to investigate the architecture of China, using the Hall of Supreme Harmony in Beijing as an example. Or they could investigate the Inca civilization and learn more about Machu Picchu.

---

frieze panels and handles with animal forms. Native American potters built their pots with coils instead of using a wheel. Decorations were stamped, incised or engraved into the surface and decorated with slip.
3 Characteristics common to Japanese art are simplicity of form and design, attentiveness to the beauty of nature and subtlety. For example, Hokusai's *Flowering Squash-Vine and Bee* (fig.4–41), shows simplicity of design and form. The artist was attentive to the beauty of this natural plant.
4 Picasso and Matisse were influenced by the geometric qualities and abstract forms of African sculpture.
5 Students may rank these in a slightly different order. Realistic to abstract:
Oni (King) of Ife (fig.4–82)
Flute player (fig.4–83)

Akua 'ba doll (fig.4–81)
Golfer (fig.4–85)
Mother and Child (fig.4–80)
Leopard Mask (fig.4–78)
Banda Mask (fig.4–79)
Shona sculpture (fig.4–84)

 Maps
1 Students may consider mountain ranges, large bodies of water, and how much of the route would be on land. The ancient Silk Road ran from China across central Asia (Russia) to the Caspian Sea and the Black Sea to Byzantium (Istanbul, Turkey) where the route usually continued by sea to Rome. From Istanbul, however, the route could continue overland through Bulgaria, Macedonia, Greece, Bosnia, Croatia, Slovenia and Italy. Another route might be through Turkey, Syria, Iraq to the

Activity 1: Clay Vessels

Activity Objectives

Students should be able to:

• Distinguish similarities and differences in the pottery of different historical cultures.

• Observe form/function relationships in pottery design.

• Formulate ideas that will work three-dimensionally.

• Relate to the experience of ancient cultures in constructing a functional object in clay.

Thinking Critically

While reviewing pottery pieces from the book, review "Think about it" questions. Ask students:

• How important is balance when designing pottery? Are these pots symmetrically balanced? How can you incorporate balance as you create a shape in clay?

Preparation Ideas

• Find pottery examples to bring to class, including actual pottery that students can hold in their hands. Different textures, shapes and sizes are desirable.

• Invite a local pottery craftsperson to visit your class with sample work and to demonstrate his/her approach.

Notes on Materials

• If there is no kiln available at your school, use self-hardening clay and paint the finished pots with either acrylic paints or watercolors. Seal the colors with an acrylic spray, which should only be used outdoors or in a well-ventilated area, as fumes can be harmful.

• Professional clay tools are nice, but aluminum can lids may be used as scrapers and pieces of wood lattice, old rulers or fat butter knives may be used as paddles to pat the pot into shape. Another alternative would be to use stones and sticks from nature to shape the clay, to recreate the sense of primitive times.

Classroom Management

• Cover tables with newspaper, plastic cloth or large tarps available in many hardware or camping supply stores. Each table needs a container or spray bottle of water to keep the pottery damp, as

Activity 1

Clay Vessels

Materials
newspaper or plastic cloth
containers of water
spray bottle
clay
clay tools
heavy duty plastic bags

Take a look. Look through this chapter and others for clay pots, bowls and vases found in archaeological sites.

Think about it. What similarities and differences do you see between the pottery of different cultures? How do you think each of these vessels were used by the people who made them? In what ways does the shape of a container dictate its use?

Do it. Make a clay pot, jar or bowl that you could imagine being discovered at an archaeological site.
• Roll a flat piece of clay for the base and use slip (clay thinned with water) as binding material.
• Roll the clay into long coils and place them on top of each other to shape your vessel.
• Smooth the surface with a stick or flat stone. Allow the piece to dry slowly. When "leather hard," trim it and carve designs into the surface.
• Ask your teacher for help with glazes, engobes and decorative techniques, as well as the firing process.

Check it. Is your vessel well-balanced and stable? Can others guess how you intended it to be used? Does it have the distinctive look of an ancient culture?

Helpful Hint: In a rough sketch, outline the shape of several pottery pieces found in this chapter. Try out some shapes of your own design on paper before beginning your pot.

Activity 2

Behind the Mask

Materials
Kraft paper or brown paper bags
clear glue
toothpicks for applying glue
paper, felt, buttons, yarn, etc.,
    for decoration
scissors
mirrors
brushes

Take a look. Review the following masks in this chapter. Look for other examples.
• 4–79 *Tribal mask*, French Guinea.
• 4–112 Elon Webster, *False Face Mask*, 1937.

Think about it. Masks have been used for more than 30,000 years, on six continents. Study several kinds of masks made by native people of different cultures. Try to understand why they were made and how they were used.

Do it. Make a stylized mask that will fit your face. Work with a partner or in front of a mirror.
• Start with 1/2"-wide torn strips of Kraft paper or paper torn from heavy brown paper bags. Wrap a strip around your forehead and join (with a drop of glue) at the back, like a headband.
• Attach the next strip of paper to either side of the band, over your head, like a close-fitting hat.
• Attach two other strips to the headband on either side and join them under your chin. A narrow vertical strip covering the bridge of your nose completes the basic framework of the headband mask.
• Using your head as a mold, attach strips of torn paper to this framework. Gradually interlace more strips of paper until the mask fits your face and is strong enough to remove.

• Stuff the mask with newspaper to keep the form intact, then decide on the shape you want for eyes and other features.
• Cut with scissors to adjust the mask and/or add laminated paper strips to the basic form until it is rigid and holds its shape well. Then add paint and any other decorations.

Check it. Is your mask sturdy; does it hold together well? Ask classmates for their reaction to your mask. Do their comments match up with the effect you intended?

Helpful Hint: Wear a bandanna or stocking cap on your head to keep your hair out of the way while you work.

Additional Activities

• Use tempera paint and/or watercolor to make a design (on paper) for a blanket or rug in one of the cultural styles described in this chapter (Islamic, Navajo, etc.). Research other books or encyclopedias for examples.
• Research and write a one-page paper discussing one of the following: the effects of colonization on the arts of Asia and the Americas; the importance of masks in tribal use in Africa; the shaman's influence on the cultures of Asian or African peoples; or several ways in which Western and non-Western art seem to differ.

---

well as plastic bags for each student to store his/her work.

• Use a piano string or other wire to cut blocks of moist clay into portions for each student. Give them each about a pound of clay—the size of a large orange. You may want to provide cardboard scraps (about 6" x 6") for students to build on, making it easier to carry work-in-progress from the worktable to storage.

• As for cleanup, a bucket of water next to the sink for a preliminary rinse of hands and equipment helps to keep clay out of the drain. Let the water run for a few minutes to flush out the pipes.

Tips

Wide coils build up faster than skinny ones. If coils are too thin, the pot will

collapse. Sometimes students keep pinching the clay until it cracks. Pots may be smoothed with a damp finger, but if the pot gets too wet, it will begin to collapse. Wadded-up newspaper, stuffed inside, will support a slumping, fragile form.

Evaluation

Students and teacher may rate the overall shape and the surface decoration (glaze, color or texture) for craftsmanship and creativity.

• Does the pot have unity?

• Does the surface decoration coordinate with the shape?

• Ask students what they would do differently if they could make another pot.

Student Profile

Marcia A. Williams

Age 16
Notre Dame Academy
Worcester, Massachusetts
Favorite kinds of art: Modern,
Impressionist, Cubism
Favorite artists: Monet, Picasso,
Haring, Gauguin, Escher
Activity 1, Clay Vessels

My art project is a clay pot. I made it from loops of clay that were smoothed together to form a pot. It represents a lot of creativity and hard work on my part. It took a while to think of the designs that I put on it.

While I was making this pot, I mostly thought about the composition of it. I thought about making the pot round and whether or not I would even put a neck on it. Once I decided on the neck, I had a hard time trying to keep the neck from caving in. After it was fired, I then had to think about how I wanted to do the glazing. I put all of the detail in with a watercolor-like underglaze and then covered the whole thing with clear gloss glaze. This way I was able to do very small details.

Before I did this project, I went to the Worcester Art Museum to see the display on Indian Art. I think that the pots that I saw there influenced the shape and design of my pot. It was meant to look like a water jug, although I'm not quite sure if I actually succeeded!

I think that I most enjoyed glazing the pot. I love painting, and putting the glaze on was very similar to that. It was relaxing but I still had to think about what I was doing and how I was going to accomplish it.

Other students who want to make things definitely need patience. To make something that you can truly appreciate, you have to work hard. You cannot expect to whip off a masterpiece in an hour, because it just won't happen. Also, you will appreciate something that you put a lot of time into more than something that you did in a few moments. I would say that my own personal philosophy is that if you work as hard as you can and do your best, you are bound to create something that you are proud of.

Marcia A. Williams

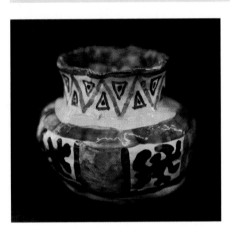

Pot, 1994. Clay,
4 1/2" x 4 1/2" (11.4 x
11.4 cm)

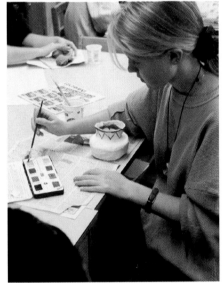

Working carefully, Marcia applies underglaze to create a colorful design on her pot.

Teacher Spotlight
Kaye Passmore, Ed.D.
Art Teacher
Notre Dame Academy

An excellent resource to show before students begin making their pots is the National Park Service film/video *Maria—Indian Pottery Maker of San Ildefonso.* This 27-minute video costs less than twenty dollars and shows Maria Martinez forming a pot using the same methods described in this activity, then firing it in cow dung and dirt.

This year's pottery unit in my art appreciation course was very successful because students went to the Worcester Art Museum for a special exhibit of Native American arts, called *Heritage of the Land,* just before beginning their own pots. After seeing these actual Native American pieces, the designs on their own work was much more interesting and creative than in past classes.

Notes on Materials

• Paper strips can be held together with tiny dots of white (Elmer's) glue.

• Papier-mâché and plaster gauze strips are good alternatives. If using plaster gauze strips, remember to grease the subject's face well with petroleum jelly or liquid soap before beginning. Hair dryers can hasten the drying process.

Classroom Management

• Have students work in pairs. Each can help construct the basic framework on their partner before removing the mask and working individually.

Tips

• Have students use the same materials for Activity 1 to form a mask out of clay designed to fit the face or hang on a wall as artwork.

• For other ideas, refer to *Maskmaking* by Carole Sivin (1986, Davis Publications).

Evaluation

First the student and then the teacher may rate the mask on creativity of shape, paint job and other surface decoration. They can also evaluate the mask in terms of craftsmanship.

Activity 2:
Behind the Mask

Activity Objectives
Students should be able to:

• Consider what masks signified in ancient cultures.

• Become acquainted with the styles of various cultures and notice similarities and differences.

• Visualize a mask that signifies personal meaning.

• Make a wearable mask that holds together and fits the face.

Thinking Critically
Lead a discussion with students on the different kinds of masks made by cultures all over the world and what their uses might be. Ask them:

• Why do you think animal images were commonly used in ancient masks? What qualities might different animals signify?

• What similarities do you see between masks of different cultures? What qualities make each one distinctly different?

• How might wearing a mask change the way you feel about yourself? What personal quality would you like to strengthen in yourself? How would you represent that in a mask?

Preparation Ideas
If you're not familiar with maskmaking, practice the method described here until you are comfortable with it.

Part Three

Art in the Western World

Giovanni Paolo Panini,
*Interior of the Pantheon,
Rome*, detail, c. 1734.
Oil on canvas, 50 1/2" x 39"
(128 x 99 cm). National Gallery
of Art, Washington, DC,
Samuel H. Kress Collection.

Chapter 5 Organizer

	Days	8 Week	1 Semester	2 Semester

Chapter 5 Opener: Beginnings of Western Art

| 1 | 1 | 1 |

Objectives

Describe the style, techniques and skills of prehistoric artists.

Explain how the art and culture of ancient Middle Eastern and Egyptian communities reflect their advanced societies.

National Standards

3a Students reflect on how artworks differ visually, spatially, temporally, and functionally, and describe how these are related to history and culture.

4e Students analyze common characteristics of visual arts evident across time and among cultural/ethnic groups to formulate analyses evaluations, and interpretation of meaning.

Teacher Edition References

Lesson 5.1 Earliest Beginnings

| 1 | 1 |

Special Feature:
The Caves at Lascaux 150–151

Contextual Info 150

HOTS 151

| 1 |

Remainder of Lesson 5.1 152–153
World Cultural Timeline 152
Lesson 5.1 Review 153

Contextual Info 152
HOTS 153

Multicultural 152

Lesson 5.2 The Ancient Near East: Mesopotamia

| 1 | 1 |

Special Feature:
The City of Ur 154–155

Contextual Info 154
HOTS 154

Performing Arts 155

| 1 |

Remainder of Lesson 5.2 156–59
Map: Ancient Near East 156
World Cultural Timeline 156, 158
Lesson 5.2 Review 159

Contextual Info 156, 158
HOTS 157, 159

Interdisciplinary 157
Multicultural 156, 158

Lesson 5.3 Egypt

| 1 | 1 |

Special Feature:
The Great Pyramids 160–161
Map: Egypt 161

HOTS 160

Materials and Techniques 161

| 2 |

Remainder of Lesson 5.3 162–168
Dynasty Timeline 162
World Cultural Timeline 164
Lesson 5.3 Review 168
Primary-Source 169
Chapter Review 168

Contextual Info 162, 165, 166
HOTS 163, 164, 167, 168
Interdisciplinary 165

Materials and Techniques 167
Multicultural 164
Performing Arts 166

Classroom Connections

| 1 | 1 | 1 |

National Standards

Studio Activity 1
Home Town Sculpture

1b Students conceive and create works of visual art that demonstrate an understanding of how the communication of their ideas relates to the media, techniques, and processes they use.

Studio Activity 2
Weathering Time

6c Students synthesize the creative and analytical principles and techniques of the visual arts and selected other arts disciplines, the humanities, or the sciences.

Choose either Activity 1 or 2

Choose either Activity 1 or 2

Choose either Activity 1 or 2

Ancillaries

Teacher Edition References

Map: Beginnings of Western Art 149
Timeline: Beginnings of Western Art 149
Context 148
Art 148
Quote 149

Ancillaries

Large Reproductions: Cave Painting

Slides: Sumerian, *Votive figure*, 36b, 60

Slides: Persian, Hall of Darius, Persepolis, 25a, 63; Sumerian, *Gudea*, 37b, 61;
Assyrian, *Gateway figure* 38b, 62
Overhead Transparencies: Mythical Creatures, 5

Slides: Imhotep, Step Pyramid of King Zoser, Sakkara, 26a, 64

Slides: Egyptian, *Mycerinus and His Queen Kah-merer*, 27a, 65;
Egyptian, South Temple, Ramses II, Abu Simbel, 28a, 68;
Egyptian, Middle Kingdom, *Mentuhotep*, 39b, 66; Eyptian, New Kingdom,
Fishing Scene, 40b, 67
Large Reproductions: Egyptian, Treasure from King Tutankhamun's Tomb, 5

Schedule	**Materials**
A glued assemblage might take one day. Possibly five days to carve wood.	locally available material, could be: clay, wood, rock, scrap metal or wire, cardboard optional: modeling clay
Preparation: Assign prior to class so students may do research. One day for presentation.	(presentation)

Other Resources

Books

Andrews, Carol. *Egyptian Mummies.* Part of *Roman Art from the Republic to Constantine.* Cambridge: Harvard University Press, 1984.

Egyptian Painting and Drawing. Part of *Roman Art from the Republic to Constantine.* Cambridge: Harvard University Press, 1985.

Ghirshman, Roman. *Persian Art: The Parthian and Sasanian Dynasties 249 BC–AD 651.* Part of *Arts of Mankind.* New York: George Braziller Inc., Odyssey Press Inc., and Golden Press, 1962.

———.*The Arts of Ancient Iran: From Its Origins to the Time of Alexander the Great.* Part of *Arts of Mankind.* New York: George Braziller Inc., Odyssey Press Inc., and Golden Press, 1964.

James, T. G. H., and Davies, W. V. *Egyptian Sculpture.* Part of *Roman Art from the Republic to Constantine.* Cambridge: Harvard University Press, 1983.

Malraux, Andre, and Salles, Georges, general eds. *Arts of Mankind.* New York: George Braziller Inc., Odyssey Press Inc., and Golden Press, 1961–1973.

Parrot, Andre. *Sumer: The Dawn of Art.* Part of *Arts of Mankind.* New York: George Braziller Inc., Odyssey Press Inc., and Golden Press, 1961.

———. *Arts of Assyria.* Part of *Arts of Mankind.* New York: George Braziller Inc., Odyssey Press Inc., and Golden Press, 1961.

Pevsner, Nikolaus, and Nairn, Judy, joint eds. *Pelican History of Art.* Baltimore: Penguin USA, 1953+.

Reade, Julian *Assyrian Sculpture.* Part of *Roman Art from the Republic to Constantine.* Cambridge: Harvard University Press, 1983.

Sandars, Nancy K. *Prehistoric Art in Europe.* 2nd ed. New Haven: Yale University Press, 1992.

Smith, W. Stevenson. *Art and Architecture of Ancient Egypt.* Rev. ed., 1981.

Stead, Miriam. *Egyptian Life.* Part of *Roman Art From the Republic to Constantine.* Cambridge: Harvard University Press, 1986.

Videodiscs

Ancient Egypt, Crystal

Videos

King Tut: Tomb of Treasure, Crystal, 1992
Lascaux Revisited, Crystal
The Pyramids and the Cities of the Pharaohs, Crystal
Pyramids. Unicorn, 1988.
Stonehenge. Horizon, 1989.

Introduce

The exact origins of Western art remain unclear, but cave paintings and handcrafted objects date back at least to 25,000 BC. Objects of prehistoric art, including those from Africa, Europe and Asia, demonstrate their makers' mastery of materials and keen powers of observation. The later cultures of Mesopotamia and Egypt developed magnificent art and architecture to honor their gods and rulers, and thereby reveal a great deal about these sophisticated civilizations.

Lessons at a Glance

5.1 *Earliest Beginnings*
Prehistoric cave paintings and sculptures, whose exact function remains unknown, are the earliest surviving examples of Western art.

5.2 *The Ancient Near East: Mesopotamia*
The successive cultures of Mesopotamia built great art and architecture centering around their gods and rulers.

5.3 *Egypt*
Egyptian art and architecture reflect a strong belief in the afterlife as well as illustrating the mighty power of the rulers.

5 Beginnings of Western Art

EVER IMAGINE YOURSELF living thousands of years ago with people in a cave or along the Nile River in Ancient Egypt? Our best view of these people and what their lives were like comes from the art they created.

The earliest paintings we know of are in caves in Africa, Europe and Asia. The images say to us that these were highly skilled artists with keen powers of observation. They drew beautiful images of animals they hunted in order to survive.

Twenty-seven thousand years later, the first civilization we know of formed in Sumer, an area in Mesopotamia. The accomplishments of this first civilization were spectacular. The Sumerians designed and built huge temples called ziggurats which were the center of their cities. They invented writing, created sculptures of stone, and made beautiful musical instruments. They were highly accomplished artists who formalized the first style of art depicting the human form.

The second great civilization was Ancient Egypt. It thrived for several thousand years virtually unchanged in its isolated and fertile location along the Nile River. The Egyptian desire for stability and permanence led them to create huge monuments and tombs full of art meant to last forever. Although their glorious civilization did not last, we can still hear them, see them and learn from them through the art they created.

These early cultures of Mesopotamia and Egypt influenced later ones around the Mediterranean Sea, Europe and the United States. The art of these later cultures is what we call Western Art because it developed in Western Europe. It is the primary focus of the chapters that follow.

5–a Tutankhamen became Pharaoh of Egypt as a young boy, but only ruled for nine years. His tomb, discovered in 1922, was filled with precious treasures.
Tutankhamen Mummy Case, 1352 BC. Gold inlaid with enamel and semiprecious stones, h. 73" (185 cm). Egyptian Museum, Cairo.

5–b The stairways of the great Persian palace at Persepolis were carved with reliefs of royal courtiers and others who served the emperor.
Audience Hall of Darius and Xerxes, detail of relief (fig.5–17).

Objectives

Students should be able to:

Describe the style, techniques and skills of prehistoric artists.

Explain how the art and culture of ancient Middle Eastern and Egyptian communities reflect their advanced societies.

Teach

Timeline

Challenge students to locate both Stonehenge (figs.5–c, 5–8) and the Great Sphinx (fig.5–d) on the timeline in order to understand how great monuments from different cultures were built at roughly the same time.

• Approximately how many years separate the two works?

• Is this a short or a long time relative to all the developments depicted on the timeline of early Western art?

• To help students decide, have them calculate the number of centuries between the cave paintings at Lascaux and the Hanging Gardens of Babylon. (approximately 143 or 14,300 years)

Tell students to imagine wandering through England around 2000 BC and stumbling upon the strange boulders of Stonehenge.

• What would be their first thoughts about the function of this structure? After reading the captions, have them contemplate why ancient people might have wanted a calendar.

• What parts of their lives would have been regulated by the passing of the seasons? Can they picture rituals, plantings, harvests and feasts taking place during this ancient era?

• Are calendars as influential in contemporary Western society as during this earlier period? (Do students plan certain events, activities or vacations around particular holidays or times of the year?)

Can you imagine what life in Europe might have been like before the existence of cities and countries? What kinds of climate and geographical features might be favorable for primitive civilizations?

5–c Built nearly 4000 years ago, this circle of huge stones functioned as a giant, but very accurate, calendar that was based on the movements of the sun and moon. *Stonehenge*, detail (fig.5–8).

5–d Recent findings have called into question the long-accepted dating of the Sphinx. Some scholars now believe it predates by many years the Pyramid of Cheops. Additional research is necessary before final conclusions can be drawn. *The Great Sphinx*, about 2500 BC, 4th dynasty, 65' (19.8 m) high, Giza.

Quote

Before students learn anything specific about Stonehenge or the Great Sphinx, ask them to consider how the quote relates to these two works. How much can they understand about the works just by looking? After students read the captions, ask them how long they think it has taken human beings to decide on the use and meaning of these impressive monuments.

Map

In order to illustrate what was occurring in various parts of the Western world at approximately the same period, have students locate England, where Stonehenge was built, and Egypt, the site of the Great Sphinx, on the map.

25000–18000 BC
Last Ice Age

3500–3000 BC Invention of the wheel, Sumeria
3300 BC First kilns used in Mesopotamia

3300 BC Earliest known writing, Mesopotamia
2650–2575 BC Great Sphinx, Pyramids at Giza, Egypt

2100 BC Ziggurat at Ur, Mesopotamia
2000 BC Stonehenge, England

1300 BC Moses receives the Ten Commandments, Mount Sinai, Egypt

Beginnings of Western Art

15000 BC Cave Paintings at Altamira, Spain, and Lascaux, France

1530 BC Temple of Amun, Karnak
1352 BC Tomb of King Tutankhamen, Egypt

705–681 BC Height of Assyrian Empire

700 BC Hanging Gardens of Babylon

Art

Ask students to decide for whom the Tutankhamen Mummy Case (fig.5–a) and the Great Sphinx were constructed.

• Why might common citizens not have been able to commission these sorts of works?

• Could they pay for something on this scale themselves today? How much money do they estimate it might have taken to build either the enormous sculpture or the gold-covered mummy case? While ordinary people could not have afforded such art, the pharaohs did use citizens' tax money and labor to construct these stupendous testaments of their own supreme power.

Evaluate

Ask students to articulate something that is confusing about the art on pages 148–149.

• Can their classmates help them clear up any ambiguity? Can they consider the problem from another angle?

• What resources might be available to assist them?

• Encourage students to share their insights as they continue learning more about early Western art.

Reteach

Have students study both the Tutankhamen Mummy Case and Stonehenge for visual clues as to whether these works

came from the same culture. (Have students check their answers by finding on the map the locations of these works.) To further their thinking, ask: "Are these two works similar in scale, material, function and intricacy of construction? For instance, are their decorations similar?" (Have them read the captions for information.)

From this experience, ask students if it is fair to make any generalizations about multiple cultures that exist at any given time. Would they consider Asian, African, American and European societies all the same today? Point out that art can often help us comprehend the distinct characteristics of a particular culture.

Lesson 5.1

The earliest known prehistoric art in the West demonstrates artists' skillful use of materials and ability to reproduce lifelike images. The exact function of these surviving sculptures and paintings is mysterious, but they help evoke the world before recorded time.

Warm-up

Have students guess when the first known artworks were created. As a group, choose the earliest event they recall in history, then compare its date to the *Venus of Willendorf* (fig.5–4), made about 25,000 BC, and the Lascaux caves (figs.5–1, 5–2), painted about 15,000 BC. Did students think humans had been making art for so long? These works show a sophisticated use of materials and the ways artists chose to represent nature.

Objectives

Students should be able to:

Explain that the exact use of Old Stone Age art is unclear, but that the works served as more than mere decoration.

Describe how prehistoric artists deliberately stylized their work to evoke the natural world.

Vocabulary Definitions

stylization The simplification or generalization of forms found in nature to present a personal and more decorative feeling in a work of art or lettering.

cromlech A circle of monoliths, usually enclosing a type of altar.

lintel Horizontal structure that spans an opening between two walls or posts.

Teach

Art History: Have students measure the dimensions of the 16-foot animals depicted in the Hall of the Bulls (fig.5–1) along the classroom wall.

• Challenge them to consider the obstacles faced by the artists painting these creatures in the low, dark caves.

• From what angles did they paint? How could they see?

• What materials did they use?

• Remind students that tools like the wheel had not been invented yet and would not be for another 12,000 years.

5.1 Earliest Beginnings

CAN WE PINPOINT the beginning of art? Are its origins in the cave paintings of Africa, Spain or France? Are they still to be discovered? Or have they been lost forever? We may never know. What we do know is that the earliest known people had two recognized occupations: hunter and artist.

Hunters of the Paleolithic era (Old Stone Age, 33,000–10,000 BC) lived in the hill country of what is now Western Europe. They hunted for bison, bear, deer, reindeer, mammoth and other wild creatures. Artists drew, painted and even carved images of these animals with startling realism and vigor. We may never know why they created these pictures. Perhaps they were a means of artistic expression. The drawings may have been used in magic rituals for hunting and fertility. Perhaps they documented major hunting expeditions. Over the years there has been much argument about their actual function. But today the emphasis is on a diversity of explanations rather than on one specific answer. What is clear is that these images had a far more serious purpose than mere decoration. Whatever the reasons for their existence, the drawings, highly ***stylized*** and very simply done, are breathtakingly beautiful.

The first cave paintings were discovered in 1870 by a small girl who was exploring a cavern at Altamira in Spain. She had been taken to the cave by her father, an amateur archaeologist. Because she was so small she was able to easily look up at the ceiling. Imagine her surprise when she saw a herd of bison stampeding across it. In 1940, several small boys discovered similar paintings in a cave at Lascaux in central France, when their dog fell into a hole that led to the underground chamber.

Key Notes
• Origins of Western art are unclear.
• Earliest forms of art focussed around caves.
• Stone Age art had serious purpose and may have served several functions.

Vocabulary
stylized
cromlech
lintels

Special Feature
The Caves at Lascaux

The earliest paintings in the most famous of the caves, Lascaux, date from about 15,000 BC (figs.5–1, 5–2). The technology was crude and the working conditions were extremely difficult. Nevertheless, these first artists produced stunning work. For sheer vitality, freedom of expression and sureness of touch, these paintings have rarely been equaled. Most cave art consisted of simple outlines. The polychrome paintings of animals at Lascaux and Altamira are in fact very unusual. The colors were made from various earth hues (red, yellow, brown, violet) and lampblack (soot) from the lamps used in the cave. The pigments were ground to powder and applied directly on to the damp limestone walls and ceilings of the caves. They were probably applied with mats of moss or hair. Some colors were sprayed through tubular bones onto the walls.

In some caves, wooden scaffolding was used to enable the artists to

5–2 Most of the paintings at Lascaux are on walls far from the entrance to the caves. Some areas can only be reached by crawling on hands and knees. Because the animals could not have been in the caves, artists must have painted from memory. *Hall of Bulls*, Lascaux, detail.

Direct them to compare their answers to the text on pages 150–151.

Criticism/Aesthetics: Have students describe the similarities in style between the *Bison* (fig.5–5) and the Lascaux caves.

• Would they conjecture that the works were made within a short time of each other? Have them check the information in the captions.

• Were they surprised that, even though the art is similar in their simple but expressive use of line, these two examples were created approximately 3000 to 5000 years apart?

• Which appeals to them more?

• What specifically about the works has influenced their choices?

Evaluate

Ask students to list some of the possible uses for prehistoric art.

• How might these early cultures' primary concern with daily survival needs have influenced the art's meaning?

• How come no one knows exactly what the function of these works was?

Reteach

Dim the lights in the classroom and ask students how it would have felt to be the children who found the caves of Lascaux. Why was their discovery so important to the history of Western art?

reach high walls and ceilings. In the Lascaux Cave, the sockets for a platform of posts survive in one passage. The interior of the cave would have been lit by torches and by burning animal fat placed on flat or dished stones. Some beautifully carved lamps have been found at Lascaux (fig.5–3), but they are extremely rare.

Artists often took advantage of the natural formation of the cave surfaces. In an unusually large chamber at Lascaux, artists painted huge bulls, each sixteen feet long. Sometimes the natural formation of the rock-face suggested to the artist the form of animal depicted. The animals are rendered with amazing fidelity to how they actually looked. They are so lifelike that one can almost hear the thunder of the bulls' hooves as they stampede across the ceiling of the "great hall" at Lascaux.

The paintings had been sealed in the dry air of the caves for over fifteen thousand years. When the caves were opened to the public, air

was let into them. The humidity, particularly from the breath of many thousands of visitors, resulted in the rapid deterioration of the paintings. The caves have been closed to the general public since 1963.

Discoveries about humankind's earliest masterpieces continue to be made. In December 1994, more cave paintings were found. These paintings are said to date from 20,000 to

5–1 Many artists worked here over a long period of time. **Do you think they had any plan or composition in mind for their animal images?**
Hall of Bulls, Lascaux, about 15,000–13,000 BC. Dordogne, France.

17,000 BC and include the first known prehistoric portrayals of a panther and an owl. They were found near the town of Vallon-Port-d'Arc in France.

5–3 Find a picture of a modern lamp. Compare it to this one. Which do you prefer? Why?
Decorated lamp, Lascaux. Musée des Antiquités Nationale, St. Germain-en-Laye, France.

Higher-Order Thinking Skills

Paleolithic hunters had no cameras, so they had to remember the animals and visualize them when they painted them in the caves. Put pictures of animals in the room or in the hall and have students draw one in a location where they cannot see the pictures. They may look all they wish and draw all they want, but they cannot do the two in the same place. They will be surprised at how intense their observation must be in order even to attempt a realistic image from memory.

You may have students either interview each other or keep a journal about the experience. Use the same technique with verbal descriptions of complex photographs of activities or landscapes. Practice over time creates dramatic improvements in students' skill.

These visualization skills are essential to creative problem solving. Have students practice with an emphasis on either verbal skills or studio skills. The point is not how well they draw but what they learn about visualization.

Contextual Information

Jericho

In 7500 BC, Jericho had a population of more than 1000. The city was surrounded by a ditch and a 33-foot–high wall that was 2100 feet long. The city is thought to have been one of the oldest in the world and was about a mile from the modern town of Jericho.

The hot, dry climate of Jericho was perfect for preserving the provisions left in tombs. Furniture, pottery bowls, wooden boxes, alabaster flasks, wooden combs and some textile fragments date from ca. 1700 BC, and other objects date from before 7000 BC. In contrast, megalithic stone structures, some engraved with designs, have been found across Western and Northern Europe and date from ca. 4000 BC.

Stonehenge

Over the centuries people have had different theories about the origin and purpose of Stonehenge. Geoffrey of Monmouth, in his *Histories of the Kings of Britain*, expressed the thought that giants from Africa had first brought the huge stones to Ireland and then that Merlin the wizard and the British King Ambrosius Aurelianus fought the Irish for the stones.

Edmund Spenser, in his poem *The Faerie Queene*, thought that Stonehenge was a monument to the dead. Others thought—and still think so today—that it is a Druid temple. By the seventeenth century Dr. Walter Charleton, after comparing Stonehenge to monuments in Denmark, gave credit for it to the Danes. He thought it was "designed to be a Court Royal, or place for the Election and Inauguration of their Kings." By 1854 a man named Henry Browne thought that the entire construction was dropped on the Salisbury Plain during the Biblical flood.

By the nineteenth century Stonehenge was a popular spot for travelers. Chips of the stones were sold and hammers rented by nearby farmers for the travelers to take home souvenirs of the structure.

Discussion

• What do you think might explain the presence of these stones in England?

• Why do we take objects from places we visit? Where do you think the chips collected by visitors to Stonehenge are today? Do you think it really makes any difference to the site that these pieces were taken?

Carvings of the Paleolithic Era

Carvings, not ancient cave paintings, may be the oldest forms of art. Carvings of female figures have been discovered in many places in Europe and western Asia. The round and bulging stone carving called the *Venus of Willendorf* (fig.5–4) was found in Austria and is considered to be 25,000 years old. This small bulbous figure suggests abundant fertility and a plentiful supply of food—the two all-important needs of any society. The name of "Venus" was given by modern discoverers and does not have any connection with the later Roman goddess.

The sculptor who carved the bison (fig.5–5) out of a reindeer antler used the natural form of the found material. The turned-back head makes elegant use of the antler's existing contours. Because the piece is broken off, its original use cannot be determined.

Architecture of the Neolithic Era

Architecture became a vital concern to ancient peoples of the Neolithic era (New Stone Age, 8000–3000 BC). Humans left their caves and began to form communities. They herded cattle and raised simple crops. They lived in simple structures of grass, mud-bricks and even stone. Protection from enemies was often provided by walls around the settlement. Recent excavations have uncovered a town of mud-brick at Jericho in southern Israel, that dates from 8000 BC (fig.5–6). A rough stone wall, surrounding the village, has been dated at 7500 BC. The walls are twelve feet high and a stone tower reaches to thirty feet—the world's earliest stone fortification.

Among the ruins of Jericho, archaeologists found a group of fascinating sculpted heads (fig.5–7) dated about 7000 BC. The heads are actual human skulls with plaster applied to reconstruct the facial features. Each head is different, as though it were meant to be an actual likeness of a person. The purpose of the heads is not known. They may have had a religious function. The excavations have

5–4 Many figures like this have been found. People may have "planted" them in the ground in an effort to guarantee a good supply of food.
Venus of Willendorf, about 25,000 BC. Limestone, 4 3/8" (11 cm) high. Naturhistorisches Museum, Vienna.

5–5 Examine carefully the artist's expert use of curved lines.
Bison, about 10,000 BC. Reindeer antler, about 4" (10.15) cm long. Musée des Antiquités Nationales, St. Germain-en-Laye, France.

30,000 BC Native Americans migrate from Asia to North America	12,000 BC World's first known domesticated dogs		

World Cultural Timeline

25,000 BC Cave Painting, Namibia	9000 BC World's first known pottery vessels, Japan		6500 BC Farming and animal domestication begins, India

Multicultural Connection

North America's First Settlers

The earliest settlers to North America are believed to have come from Asia about 30,000 years ago. These immigrants crossed the Bering Strait at the close of the Ice Age and slowly moved from Alaska to the tip of South America. They came to an uninhabited land and evolved traditions, languages, arts and ways of life that reflected their new environments. Many of the groups became isolated and developed distinct cultures. Their descendants are called Native Americans (also called American Indians). The Native Americans of the Arctic region of Canada call themselves the Inuit; in Alaska they are known as the Eskimo.

revealed that there was a thriving civilization in Jericho nearly 9000 years ago.

Several huge stone monuments have survived from the Neolithic era. *Stonehenge*, on the Salisbury Plain in England, was constructed about 2000 BC (fig.5–8). Stonehenge is a round grouping or **cromlech** of gigantic stones, some weighing fifty tons. The stones were dragged for more than twenty miles to be trimmed and stood on end. The **lintels**, or horizontal elements, were curved slightly to fit the circular plan (fig.5–c). Apparently a ritual site, Stonehenge was constructed to indicate the solstices and equinoxes of the calendar year, and probably the times for planting, harvest and religious ceremonies.

5–7 Family and community activities and stories help us remember our ancestors. This skull may have been decorated and cared for to help keep alive the memory of the person. **How do modern people remember their ancestors?** *Neolithic plastered skull*, about 7000 BC. Life-size, from Jericho. Archaeological Museum, Amman, Jordan.

5–6 This early town with its stone walls and tower is a forerunner of medieval castles. *Fortifications and circular tower*, about 7500 BC. Jericho, Israel.

5–8 Standing to the east of the circle of stones is the "heel-stone." If someone in the center of the circle looked outward, the heel-stone marked the point at which the sun rose during the midsummer solstice. *Stonehenge*, about 2000 BC. Height about 13 1/2' (4.1 m). Salisbury Plain, England.

Lesson 5.1 Review

1 Describe the tools and materials used by the artists who worked at Lascaux.
2 Why have the caves at Lascaux been closed to the public since 1963?
3 How did the earliest sculptors use the shapes found in natural materials to their advantage?
4 Where is the earliest known stone fortification located? Why did architecture gain importance during the Neolithic era?
5 Define the word "cromlech." Why was Stonehenge constructed?

• Have students locate the Bering land bridge that connected Siberia and Alaska.

• Ask students how isolation of groups of people can contribute to the formation of cultures similar to, yet unique from, the original culture.

The Earliest Pottery Vessels

The earliest known culture in Japan is called *Jomon*. It is named for the twisted rope decorations on earthenware pots made by a people who lived from about 10,000 to 300 BC. The Jomon people were nomadic hunter-gatherers and crafted handmade pottery vessels and clay figurines called *dogu*.

The skill of forming vessels out of clay appeared as early as the Neolithic period in Japan. The simplest method of forming a clay vessel was by a tech-nique called a pinch pot. However, the Neolithic cultures of Jomon employed more sophisticated techniques by using a paddle or beater to draw up the clay and achieve the desired thickness of the vessel. The Yayoi people, who arrived in Japan about 300 BC, brought their knowledge of wheel-thrown, kiln-fired ceramics. Japanese ceramics include the earliest known artifacts of their culture and are among the finest in the world.

• Discuss with students the meaning of artifacts.

• Note that earthenware is a pottery made of clay that remains unfused after firing and is therefore porous and fragile.

(For more about the Jomom and Yayoi cultures see Chapter 4, page 102.)

Higher-Order Thinking Skills

As a remembrance of their deceased ancestors, the people of Jericho may have decorated the skulls of the dead and placed them in shrines. Ask the class how people today remember their ancestors. Students can interview family members, school personnel or community leaders and then report their findings in a written or oral report, panel discussion, photo essay or any other approved form. As an extension, students could first cite and then evaluate the effectiveness of other works in this chapter that were intended to preserve the memory of a person.

Lesson 5.1 Review Answers

1 Ground earth (minerals, mud, rocks, clays) and lampblack were used to make pigments; paint was applied with mats of moss or hair or blown through tubular bones. Wooden scaffolding, torches and stone lamps were used.
2 Humidity, particularly from the breath of thousands of viewers, caused the paintings to deteriorate rapidly.
3 They would often use the natural form of a material to suggest the shape of their subject. For example, in fig.5–5 the bison's head is turned to take advantage of the natural shape of the antler. In the Lascaux caves the shape of the underlying rock sometimes suggested the animal form depicted.
4 Jericho. As Neolithic peoples left the safety of their caves, they built simple living structures and walls around their settlements for protection from their enemies.
5 A cromlech is a circle of monoliths, usually enclosing a type of altar. Stonehenge was constructed probably as a ritual site to indicate the solstices and equinoxes of the calendar year, which determined when to plant, harvest and conduct religious ceremonies.

Lesson 5.2

The successive cultures of Mesopotamia built great art and architecture centering around their gods and rulers.

Warm-up

Share with students that it is believed that prehistoric peoples, those who created the art shown in Lesson 5.1, were mostly nomadic hunters and gatherers. Have students glance at the images on pages 154–155. Ask them to describe what life might have been like for children in the Mesopotamian cultures versus in prehistoric times. How might daily chores, festivals, and religious rites have been different? Would the permanence and complexity of Mesopotamian societies have affected these activities? In which era would students have preferred to live? Why?

Objectives

Students should be able to:

Identify the art of a succession of sophisticated civilizations that ruled the fertile lands of Mesopotamia starting somewhere between 3500 and 3000 BC.

Analyze how Mesopotamian art honored both the rulers and the gods.

Vocabulary Definitions

ziggurat (zig-oo-rat) The high temple platform, built of mud brick, of Sumerian and Assyrian architecture. Usually built in the form of a truncated stepped pyramid with ramplike stairways leading to the sanctuary at the top.
cella (sell-ah) The main rectangular room of a temple containing the image of a god, goddess or cult deity.
stele (stee-lee) An upright slab, bearing sculptured or painted designs or inscriptions. From the Greek for "standing block."
low relief A surface that has only slight variations between the highest and lowest parts. Bas-relief is sculpture of low relief on a wall, and a coelanoglyph is a sculpture of low relief carved into a wall surface.

Teach

Criticism: Ask the class to define *sculpture* while they look at the *Praying Nobleman* (fig.5–12). Have them check

5.2 The Ancient Near East: Mesopotamia

BETWEEN 3500 AND 3000 BC a great civilization arose in Mesopotamia, the flat and fertile land which lay between the Tigris and Euphrates rivers. Here a group of people called Sumerians established their first city-states. Cuneiform writing, schools, democracy, and the use of the vault and arch all originated in Sumer. For well over one thousand years the Sumerians dominated Mesopotamia. Eventually, however, the Babylonians, the Assyrians and, finally, the Persians ruled the region.

Unfortunately, little remains of the Sumerian civilization. They did not leave behind numerous tombs, like the Egyptians did, although several rich tombs have been found in the city of Ur. Also, because building stone was not available in Mesopotamia, Sumerians used mainly mud-brick. Nothing is left of their structures except the foundations.

We know that the Sumerians worshipped gods. Every city-state had its own god and human ruler who led the populace in serving the deity. Because there were no hills on which to build temples, the Sumerians constructed huge mountains of earth faced with mud-brick and sometimes fired brick. These mammoth structures were called **ziggurats**. The ziggurat, or temple, was the center of both spiritual and city life. Everything else in the city clustered around its base. The most famous of the ziggurats, the biblical Tower of Babel, has been completely destroyed but others have survived at Warka and Ur.

Sumerians and the later inhabitants of Mesopotamia have left us numerous examples of their stone sculpture and metalwork. Early on, the Sumerians established conventions for the depiction of the human figure. With this development, art had begun to be formalized.

Key Notes
- A great civilization is born in Mesopotamia.
- Gods and rulers become central to the creation of art.
- Sumerians formalize the depiction of the human form.

Vocabulary
ziggurat
cella
stele
low relief

Special Feature
The City of Ur

Several of the ruined cities of Sumer today still are dominated by one of the most important of Sumerian art forms, the ziggurat. Ziggurat complexes were designed to make the worshiper go around as many corners as possible before reaching the *cella*, or main room. Sacrifices were offered in the cella.

Perhaps the most interesting of all Mesopotamian ziggurats was built at Ur about 2100–2000 BC (fig.5–9). The royal architects who designed the ziggurat at Ur included stepped levels, dramatic staircases and subtly curved lines. This ziggurat also had more than the usual single staircase. There were three, and they converged at an impressive gate tower, topped perhaps by a dome. The structure's facing has withstood floods and weathering so well that it is the best preserved ziggurat in southern Mesopotamia.

The function of the ziggurat was to bridge the gap between human and divine, the earth below and the spirit world above. This explains

5–9 Keep in mind that this structure would have been part of a vast complex of other buildings that have not survived. *Ziggurat at Ur*, about 2100–2000 BC. Iraq.

their definition against the one in the glossary. Now have them study the stairways of the Persian palace at Persepolis (fig.5-b). (They can note its placement within the larger palace complex in fig.5–17.)

- Is the stairway panel a sculpture?

- Does all sculpture have to be carved in the round?

- Although sculpted on a long shallow surface, how does the piece evoke a sense of depth?

- Is there a feeling that certain objects are in front of others? For example, can the soldiers' bodies be seen behind their shields?

- Can students imagine the figures extending back into the background space?

Challenge students to find the similarities in style between the *Praying Nobleman* (fig.5–12) and the figures in the Ur standard (fig.5–10). Ask them to quickly list their observations. Next, give them three minutes to study the figures again. Remind them that careful looking takes time. Afterward, have them fill in their new findings on their lists.

- Did they notice how the figures share the use of simplified forms to create static and stylized shapes?

- Did they observe the correlation between the shapes of the heads, roundness of the bodies and stationary poses?

- Finally, ask students to discuss what they discovered about the process of reexamining the artworks. Had their

5–10 This section of the standard depicts the results of a Sumerian military battle. Prisoners and servants carry booty. How is the king celebrating his victory?
Standard of Ur: Peace, about 2685–2645 BC, Sumerian. Mosaic panel of shell and colored stones, 19" (48 cm) long, Royal Cemetery at Ur. British Museum, London.

why they went up as high as was humanly possible.

Some of the finest works of art from the Sumerian period were discovered in the royal cemetery at Ur. Archaeologists unearthed statues, panels and other artifacts. Look carefully at the *Standard of Ur: Peace* (fig.5-10). The work is a

5–11 This instrument was buried with its owner to provide music for him in the afterlife. It is related to the modern guitar.
Lyre, about 2600 BC, Sumerian. Wood, overlaid with silver, shell and colored stones, 38 1/2" (98 cm) high, Royal Cemetery at Ur. British Museum, London.

mosaic-like panel of shell and colored stones. Notice the carefully spaced figures. This is very different from the haphazard placement of figures in Paleolithic art.

Sumerian kings and queens were buried in the tombs in all their finery, together with their servants (who were killed so they could accompany their royal masters into the next world) and their palace or temple furnishings. Some of these objects show marvelous workmanship. Among them is an exquisite lyre made of wood overlaid with silver, shell and colored stone (fig.5-11).

Though not found at Ur, the *Praying Nobleman* (fig.5-12) typifies the Sumerian depiction of the human form. Cut from a solid block, the figure is cylindrical and very simplified. Arms and legs have the roundness of pipes. The long skirt is straight. Notice the overly large eyes, which Sumerians believed were the windows to the soul. We are reminded of how humans have always perceived the power of the eye. Even today we are told to respect people who "look you straight in the eye" and to be wary of people with "shifty eyes."

5–12 The form of this figure is simplified and based on the cylinder.
Praying Nobleman, about 2600 BC, Sumerian. Alabaster, 14 1/4" (36 cm) high. The Nelson-Atkins Museum of Art, Kansas City, Missouri.

initial observations been as thorough as the second look?

Evaluate

Direct students to observe the environment around the Ur ziggurat (fig.5-9). What kind of natural materials would have been available for building this structure? Are there forests for wood or mines for metal? What was the climate like in the desert? The mammoth ziggurat was constructed on a huge mountain of earth covered with mud-brick and fired clay. Ask the class what they believe these buildings were used for. Why would they have been built on high mounds? How does the temple's location affect its function as both the physical and spiritual center of the city? Can they think of any central

building in their own community around which other structures cluster, such as a courthouse, religious site or commercial center? Does its relationship to other buildings around it influence the way they perceive its importance or impact?

Reteach

Ask students what their thinking was when they were comparing the *Praying Nobleman* (fig.5-12) with the figures in the Ur standard (fig.5-10).

• How would they describe their thinking during their initial observations and when they were asked to look again?

• Was their thinking more or less concentrated?

• How might they apply what they have learned in this process to other areas of their lives?

Contextual Information
The Babylonians

• During the sixth century BC, King Nebuchadnezzar II built Babylon, a walled city with a 300-foot ziggurat. Babylon became wealthy because it was in command of the trading routes in the Mideast. Already known as a center of learning because of its vast library, the city grew even more famous as Nebuchadnezzar added silver and gold furnishings and "the products of the mountains, the treasures of the seas" to make Babylon the greatest city in his part of the world.

The Cultural Evolution of Mesopotamia

In about 2300 BC, a Semitic-speaking people, the Akkadians, moved in from the north and conquered the Sumerians. Although they tried to dominate the entire world, their rule was not long-lasting, and the Sumerians gradually regained their self-rule. The most important of the New Sumerian rulers was *Gudea of Lagash.* Many statues of Gudea still survive. The one shown here (fig.5–13) is carved in diorite, a very hard, imported black stone. The pose is relaxed and worshipful. The muscles and facial features are sculpted carefully.

After several centuries of warfare, the Babylonians emerged in 1700 BC

5–13 About twenty statues of Gudea have been found. They depict him seated or standing with hands tightly clasped. This fragment probably was part of a standing figure.
Gudea of Lagash, about 2255 BC, Neo-Sumerian. Diorite with traces of gilt, 29 1/2" (74 cm) high. British Museum, London.

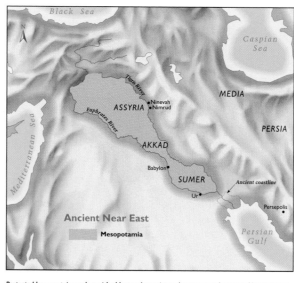

Protected by mountains and nourished by two large rivers, the area once known as Mesopotamia provided an ideal environment for a thriving culture. Why do you suppose the coastline of the Persian Gulf has changed over the years?

5–15 The Assyrians and the Sumerians had very different ideas about how to portray people. Compare this low relief sculpture to the *Praying Nobleman.*
Winged Genius, about 875 BC, Assyrian. Alabaster, 7' 9" (236 cm) high, The Palace of Ashurnasirpal II. Los Angeles County Museum of Art, gift of Anna Bing Arnold.

6000 BC Fishing with harpoons in the Nile and East African lakes

4000 BC Village planning begins, China

World Cultural Timeline

5000 BC Rice cultivation established, China

3300 BC Chili peppers domesticated, Mexico

Interdisciplinary Connection

Science: Mesopotamia has yielded the oldest written records of early scientific investigations. Cuneiform characters on clay tablets have been found with lists of astronomical observations, chemical substances, and disease symptoms as well as mathematical tables.

Mathematics: The Babylonians developed a sexagesimal (based on the number 60) system of measurement from which modern time and angle units are derived. Have students explain how a unit of 60 is the basis for timekeeping and the measurement of circles and angles.

5–14 Although these figures are in relief, the cylindrical forms seem to have great volume.
Stele of Hammurabi (upper part), about 1760 BC. Basalt, approx. 28" (71 cm) high, from Susa. Louvre, Paris.

Sidelight

Hanging Gardens of Babylon

Picture it: A splendid kingdom with a huge ziggurat at its center and a royal palace overhung with luxuriant gardens. This was the fabulous city of Babylon, capital of Babylonia. It was ruled between 604–562 BC by King Nebuchadnezzar II, the greatest ruler of the late Babylonian empire.

Nebuchadnezzar II is most often remembered as the builder of The Hanging Gardens of Babylon, one of the Seven Wonders of the World. Built within the walls of the royal palace, the gardens did not actually "hang." Instead they rose into the air in a series of terraced roof gardens filled with flowers, shrubs and trees. They appeared as a miracle of greenery within a desert city. The terraces were irrigated by water pumped from the Euphrates River. It is believed that King Nebuchadnezzar II built the gardens to console his wife, Amytis, because she missed the mountains and greenery of her homeland, Media, in Persia. Babylon itself was flat and sunbaked.

Greek and Roman writers described how the terraces were lined with reeds, bitumen and lead so that there would be no seepage. The historian Diodorus Siculus wrote about the gardens in the first century BC and described them in the following manner: "This garden was 400 feet square, and the ascent up to it was as to the top of a mountain."

Higher-Order Thinking Skills

The Assyrians and the Sumerians had very different ideas about how to portray people, and their ideas differed from those of the Egyptians. Break the class into groups and assign each one a portrayal of a human figure, such as *Winged Genius* (fig.5–15) and *Gudea of Lagash* (fig.5–13). By developing a careful description of the assigned figure, each group should arrive at the characteristics that the society that created their figure emphasized and valued in the image of a person. Have each group present its findings to the class and/or have the groups create a display that shows the comparisons and contrasts.

as the masters of Mesopotamia. Their first leader was *Hammurabi*, a powerful figure, who composed a generally humane code of laws. The code of Hammurabi was inscribed on a black basalt **stele**, or upright slab. Above the code is a relief sculpture of Hammurabi before the seated sun god (fig.5–14). It is clear that this encounter must relate to the creation of the code of laws.

The Hittites defeated the Babylonians in 1595 BC and, in turn, were overrun by a succession of warring peoples. About 900 BC, Mesopotamia was overwhelmed by the powerful Assyrians who descended on the plains from the north. They expanded their control as far away as Egypt and built marvelous palaces in the northern parts of the plain. Stone from nearby mountains was used to line these huge structures. The walls, carved in **low relief**, showed mythical figures and the exploits of the kings (fig.5–15). The sculptors were superb craftspeople who could create a feeling of depth on a very shallow surface (fig. 5–16).

Contextual Information

Persians

Persepolis was built on a high plateau between 520 and 460 BC by Darius and Xerxes I and was destroyed by Alexander the Great in 331 BC. The palace stood on a high, wide platform surrounded by courts. The most outstanding building was the audience hall containing thirty-six 40-foot columns with capitals of the foreparts of bulls or lions.

The Persian Empire was founded by Cyrus the Great and was one of the greatest empires, rivaling that of Greece and Rome. Its most renowned leader was Darius I (521–486 BC), a great military leader and administrator. Xerxes, Darius' son and successor, was conquered by the Greeks in the Persian Wars. Ultimately, Alexander the Great conquered the Persian Empire.

5–17 Stone was used for the gateways, stairs, large columns and platforms. Small columns and the roof were made of wood. The walls were constructed of brick.
Audience Hall of Darius and Xerxes, about 500 BC. Persepolis, Iran.

In 539 BC, the Persians brought an end to the Assyrian empire. Under King Darius, they built huge palaces such as the one at Persepolis (fig.5–17, 5–b). Huge, magnificent spaces had wooden ceilings supported by great columns. Atop each of the one hundred columns in a huge central room was a pair of sculpted bulls, the symbol of power (fig.5–18).

Although carved from limestone, the bulls were probably covered with silver, gold leaf and lapis lazuli.

The Persians remained dominant in this area until Alexander the Great toppled them in 331 BC, thus uniting the Greek culture with the one that had slowly developed in the land between two rivers—Mesopotamia.

3000 BC
Silk first produced, China

2500–1500 BC
Grid pattern city built at Mohenjo-Daro, Indus Valley

2000 BC
Ice cream invented, China

World Cultural Timeline

3000 BC
Mummification practiced in S. America and Africa

2000 BC
First temple-pyramids built, Peru

Multicultural Connection

Silk

Silk is one of the oldest known textile fibers. For over 3000 years the gathering and weaving of silk remained a secret process known only to the Chinese. According to tradition, Hsi-ling-shi, the fourteen-year-old bride of the Emperor Huang Ti, discovered the potential of the cocoon spun by the silkworm.

In ancient Persia workers in the courts unraveled and rewove Chinese silks into Persian designs. When Alexander defeated the Persians, Persia's king, Darius III, was dressed in such silken splendor that Alexander was overshadowed. As a result the Greek demanded the equivalent of $7 million in silk as spoils of war.

Mohenjo-Daro

The excavated city of Mohenjo-Daro, northeast of present-day Karachi, Pakistan had blocks of mud-brick buildings separated by streets. Large public buildings dominated the city, but archaeologists are not certain of the exact function of the buildings. Sometime after 2000 BC major ecological changes took place in the Indus Valley region. These changes forced the abandonment of many settlements and altered the basic characteristics of the civilization. Small farming villages became the norm during the later Indus Valley culture.

(For more information about the Indus Valley Civilization see Chapter 4, page 88.)

Pyramids in the Americas

Pyramids in the Americas served as platforms for temples and palaces. Archaeologists call them temple-mounds or platform mounds. Emphasize to students that pyramids in the Americas are four-sided, flat-topped polyhedrons, or rectangular pyramids, rather than the typical triangular pyramid shape we associate with Egypt. Point out that because both structures are called pyramids, many people incorrectly assume that the Egyptians had an influence on the rise of civilization in the Americas.

(For more information on early architecture in the Americas see Chapter 4, pages 132 and 138.)

5–16 The Assyrians depicted the hunting of big animals, especially lions, to show the power they and their kings had over nature. *Dying Lioness*, about 650 BC. Limestone, height of lion 13 3/4" (35 cm), from Nineveh (Assyria). British Museum, London.

5–18 Two of these bulls facing opposite directions formed the capital of a Persian column. *Bull capital*, about 518–460 BC, Persian. Bituminous limestone, 28" x 30" x 12" (71.1 x 76.2 x 30.5 cm) high, Persepolis. The Nelson-Atkins Museum of Art, Kansas City, Missouri (Purchase: Nelson Trust) 50–14.

Lesson 5.2 Review

1 Why does so little remain of Sumerian architecture?
2 How was the function of a ziggurat reflected in its appearance?
3 Where were some of the finest works of art from the Sumerian period found? Describe the types of objects discovered.

4 Describe the palaces built by the Assyrians.
5 Re-read the description of the Persian palace at Persepolis on page 158. Imagine, or even sketch out, how it might have looked. What impression would the central room have made on a visitor?

Lesson 5.2 Review Answers

1 Because building stone was not available in Mesopotamia, the Sumerians constructed with mud-brick, which deteriorated. Therefore, only the foundations of their buildings have survived.
2 Since the function of the ziggurats was to bridge the gap between human and divine, or the earth below and the spirit world above, the Sumerians built their ziggurats as tall as they could.
3 In the royal cemetery at Ur, statues and panels such as the Ur standard, a mosaiclike panel of shell and colored stones with carefully spaced figures, were found there along with other artifacts, like the lyre in fig.5–11, which was made of wood overlaid with silver, shell and colored stone.

4 The Assyrian palaces were huge structures lined with stone from nearby mountains. Mythical figures and the exploits of kings were carved in low relief on the walls.
5 The Persian palace at Persepolis had huge magnificent spaces with wooden ceilings supported by great columns. In the large central room each of the one hundred columns was topped with a pair of bulls carved from limestone and covered with silver, gold leaf and lapis lazuli. The room would have been sumptuous and rich, symbolizing the power, wealth and might of King Darius and his Persian Empire. The effect likely awed and impressed the viewer.

Higher-Order Thinking Skills

Your students are studying art to understand its history and also to gain an aesthetic and critical appreciation of it. Students, however, should be aware that not only art historians and artists research and study art. Scholars from a vast variety of fields view art as visual documents that offer as much as, and sometimes more than, written documents. Ask students to take a careful look at the images in this chapter and to list other fields (such as history, law, theater, language, weaponry, navigation and religion) that might use these objects as documents.

Cooperative Learning

Ask students to carefully study the *Peace Standard of Ur* (Fig.5–10) and try to develop a storyline to explain what is happening in the *Standard*. Have them select a ritual that takes place in your school or community that involves crowds, procession and presentation such as Homecoming. Discuss the characters at such an event being sure to talk about costume, poses, and location. Give each student a piece of paper and instruct them to create a figure to represent themselves at your chosen ritual. Symbolism is very important in such events, so ask them to emphasize the symbolic aspects of their figures. Each figure should fill the page so that all are the same size. Use a roll of brown package paper as a base and decorate it with paint or other media to create registers for the figures to stand in as in the *Standard*. Display your standard and ask the students to write an evaluation of it.

Lesson 5.3

Egyptian art and architecture reflect a strong belief in the afterlife as well as the illustration of the mighty power of the rulers.

Warm-up

Ask students to consider how we have come to know so much about Egyptian culture. Tell them to review the images in Lesson 5.1 and then examine the illustrations in Lesson 5.3 and ask, as a group, which ones give a clearer picture of the culture. The multitude of surviving Egyptian works has enabled historians to piece together a sense of life centuries ago. Before providing more information, have students make a collaborative list of possible interpretations about Egyptian culture based solely on the images in the chapter. At the end of the lesson, have them compare their conclusions with what they have learned. Explore what was unexpected and new. Ask if more careful looking might have revealed beforehand some of the information they now know.

Objectives

Students should be able to:

Identify the factors that provided the necessary stability for Egypt's culture to thrive for several thousands of years.

Explain why a strong belief in the afterlife was an essential ingredient in Egyptian art and culture.

Vocabulary Definitions

mastaba (mah-*stah*-bah) A rectangular Egyptian tomb of mud brick and masonry with sloping sides and a flat top. It covered the burial chamber.
step pyramid A solid stone structure built of six huge steps and used as a tomb for an Egyptian Pharaoh.
frontal A pose in figure drawing or sculpture in which figures face forward.
pylon (*pie*-lahn) The huge entrance structure for an Egyptian freestanding temple, formed by a pair of square tapering piers with a flat top and no connecting lintel. From the Greek word for "gateway." Also significant pillars in contemporary architecture.

hypostyle (*hip*-oh-stile) A building having a roof or ceiling supported by rows of columns; used to describe a hall constructed of many columns; also, a row of columns.
register One of a series of horizontal bands which are placed one above the other, usually a format for painting. Commonly used in Egyptian tomb painting, medieval church sculpture, Aztec codices and manuscript illumination.
descriptive perspective shows more important objects larger than less important objects.

5.3 Egypt

EGYPT, WITH ITS extraordinarily rich history, its glorious Nile River and its gigantic monuments to eternal life, has always been a source of fascination. Imagine living in an environment both protected from your enemies and fertile enough to produce a surplus of food. This was the situation in early Egypt.

Because of the extra food not everyone had to be a hunter or farmer and the small scattered communities living along the Nile River gradually developed into complex cultures. They learned to make bricks, to use sails on the water and wheels on land. There were many different kinds of professions available in the fast-growing cities and people became soldiers, judges, priests, scribes, engineers, merchants, laborers and, naturally, artists. From the earliest times (in the Pre-Dynastic period), Egyptian craftspeople were honored and their products admired.

In their protected environment, separated from the rest of the developing world, the Egyptians evolved a unique way of life and a style of art that remained almost unaffected for several thousand years.

The Egyptians enjoyed living in their Nile-centered homeland so much that they wished to live forever. This desire for a happy eternity (afterlife) led to a prolific development of tomb art and architecture. Historians owe much of their knowledge of Egyptian society to these monuments and their contents. The god-king (Pharaoh) was buried in his tomb along with food, servants, art and equipment to accompany him in his second life. Unlike humankind of today the early Egyptians believed with great conviction that you can take it with you.

Key Notes
- Geographic isolation allows Egyptian art and culture to remain constant for several thousand years.
- Strongly held belief in afterlife helps stimulate growth of all art forms.
- Pyramid evolves as elaborate tomb for Pharaohs.

Vocabulary
mastaba
step pyramid
frontal
pylon
hypostyle hall
register
descriptive perspective

Special Feature
The Great Pyramids

The first pyramids were constructed as successors to the low rectangular tombs, called *mastabas*, built for the Pre-Dynastic kings. King Zoser, the most important ruler of the Third Dynasty, built the first pyramid. The king asked the architect Imhotep to build his memorial tomb on a rock ledge at Sakkara, west of Memphis. Imhotep, the first artist in history whose name is known, built a solid stone structure of six huge steps rising over twenty stories in the desert air. This *step pyramid* at Sakkara (fig.5-20) was the first huge stone structure built on earth, and the architect Imhotep was deified for his work. The time was about 2600 BC.

During the Fourth Dynasty, pyramid building reached a climax in the three Great Pyramids at Giza (fig.5-19). Hundreds of thousands of men, many of whom died in the effort, constructed these pyramids. The stones (some weighing over forty tons!) were floated on rafts across the Nile valley during flooding season and hauled to the edge

5-20 This pyramid began as a large mastaba. It was enlarged twice before taking its final stepped form. Imhotep, *Step pyramid of King Zoser*, about 2600 BC, 3rd dynasty. Sakkara.

Teach

Aesthetics/Art History: Ask students to imagine what it would feel like to stand at the very foot of the Great Sphinx (fig.5-d) and the Great Pyramids (fig.5-19).

- What adjectives come to mind to describe how they feel in relationship to these enormous structures?

- The largest central pyramid covers about 13 acres, is nearly 911 feet on each side of its base, and is over 55 stories high. Have they ever stood below anything this tall, such as a skyscraper? Ask: "If you were a subject of the pharaohs, would it feel safe to rebel against their rule? How does the image support your answer?" Share that the pharaohs were god-kings who built

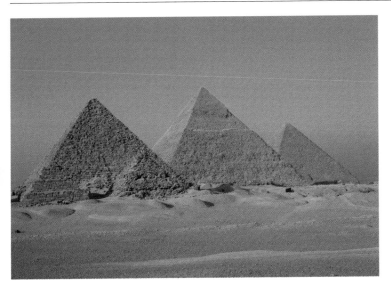

5–19 Note the last remains of an outer layer of polished limestone at the top of the Pyramid of Chefren. *The Great Pyramids,* about 2530–2470 BC, 4th dynasty. Giza.

Higher-Order Thinking Skills

Make available to the class as many photographs or slides of Stonehenge and the Great Pyramids as you can to show many points of view and relationships. Have students write a comparison of and then discuss the two types of structures. Ask them to consider form, construction techniques and function or purpose. They can differentiate what is known about the structures and what is speculative.

Egypt

Mediterranean Sea

LOWER EGYPT

Giza • Sakkara • • Memphis

Tell el-Amarna •

Red Sea

Nile River

EGYPT

Deir el-Bahari • • Karnak
Thebes • • Luxor

• Aswan

N

UPPER EGYPT

Abu Simbel •

NUBIA

Flanked by desert to the left and mountains to the right, early Egyptian civilizations flourished on the banks of the longest river in the world.

of the desert. Only levers and rollers were employed by the workers, who constructed huge earthen ramps on which to raise the stones. This mammoth undertaking required tremendous organization and planning.

The largest of the Great Pyramids was built for Cheops about 2530 BC. It covers about 13 acres and is nearly 911 feet on each side of the base. It is over 55 stories high and was the tallest structure in the world, until modern skyscrapers pierced the skies some 4500 years later. Cheops' pyramid contains over two million blocks of limestone, most weighing over two-and-a-half tons. Originally it was faced with polished limestone to reflect the sun. The glare must have dazzled Egyptians for many miles around. The stones were cut so accurately that, even today, it is difficult to find a place where a knife blade can be forced between two surfaces. The burial chamber

for the mummy of Cheops is located in the heart of the pyramid.

Besides all the possessions belonging to the dead that went into the tombs, the walls were covered with painted relief sculptures showing various activities of the persons buried there, as well as workers and relatives. The artist crammed every available space from floor to ceiling with some kind of sculpture, drawing or painting.

Two other pyramids were constructed at the same site as the Pyramid of Cheops, one for Chefren (2500 BC) and one for Mycerinus (2470 BC). Many smaller pyramids surrounded the three Great Pyramids. The Great Pyramids were all guarded by the Great Sphinx, a figure 240 feet in length, carved from the rocky ledge (fig.5–d). With the body of a lion and head of Chefren, it sat with great majesty for centuries, only to be damaged by vandalism and the sandblasting winds of the Sahara.

their conclusions. What might any variances indicate about the way we interpret the history of past civilizations?

Reteach

Challenge students to make a list of the similarities and differences between the Great Pyramids and Philip Johnson and John Burgee's *Pennzoil Place* (fig.16-19).

- What concepts do you think these architects borrowed from the ancient Egyptians? Have students compare the shapes, materials and sizes.
- What material originally covered the pyramids that would have reflected the sun in the same manner as the surface of Johnson and Burgee's twentieth-century skyscraper?

tremendous monuments to convey their divine power.

Criticism/Art History: Ask the class to consider if everyone in Egypt would have liked the pyramids.

- Who might not have been enthusiastic about them? As a clue, ask who and how many people might have been involved in building these monuments.

- Do they think people willingly hauled the stones, some weighing over forty tons, without any mechanical equipment through the desert and up huge earthen ramps?

- Have them write a description of their attitude toward the pyramids from the role of a pharaoh, a supervisor at the site and one of the laborers.

Evaluate

Have students discuss how the *Tutankhamen Mummy Case* (fig.5–a), the Great Pyramids (fig.5–19) and the *Funerary Barge* (fig.5–25) relate to the Egyptian concept of eternal life.

Divide the class into two groups. Ask one to make a list of the most significant American artifacts from today's world and, on a separate paper, have them write down what they think future historians will deduce from these items about modern America life. Give the second group only the list of artifacts. Ask this team what they would deduce about late twentieth-century culture if they were archeologists coming upon these objects 2000 years from now. Have students compare

Materials and Techniques

Research geologists, while surveying ancient Egyptian stone quarries, discovered a seven-and-one-half-mile paved road made of sandstone and limestone slabs. The road leads from a nearby quarry to a lake—which led to the Nile during the summer flood season—that no longer exists. There are no grooves or other marks to indicate that heavy stones were once dragged across the stones.

The road has a width of about six feet and was probably used for the transport of basalt, a black stone, used for temple floors at Giza and for royal sarcophagi. An unusual aspect of this discovery is that Egyptians did not use wheeled wagons until about 100 BC.

Contextual Information

Preservation

Several practical considerations have led archaeologists to rely heavily on the tombs and temples of ancient Egypt for information about the civilization. Most of the sites of ancient towns are still occupied, so excavation is either difficult or impossible. Also, the structures were built in the desert, not along the more humid river valleys. The dry desert heat helped preserve the buildings far longer and in much better condition than would have been likely in a more humid environment. Further, the Egyptians believed in the afterlife, and as a result, their tombs are filled with objects and images that provide an exceptional understanding of ancient Egypt.

Egyptian Sculpture

Ancient portrait sculptures for common people were made in wood, clay and bronze. Those used for royal portraits were of limestone and slate from Nile cliffs, granite from the Upper Nile and diorite from the desert.

Middle Kingdom proportions for sculptures of figures were determined by units on a grid. The head was 1 unit, across the shoulders was 2 1/2 units, the distance between the shoulder and the hem was 5 units, from the hem to the ground was 3 units, and from the ground to the hip was 4 1/2 units.

5–21 Mycerinus built the third and smallest of the Great Pyramids at Giza.
Mycerinus and His Queen, about 2470 BC, 4th dynasty. Slate, 56" (142 cm) high, Giza. Museum of Fine Arts, Boston

Old Kingdom

The statues unearthed in and near the great pyramids are of three types: standing, seated and sitting on the floor. The carving of the standing figures of *Mycerinus and His Queen* (fig.5–21) was cut from a single block of slate. To create the statue, the artist first drew the standing couple on all four sides of the block and then began carving toward the center. The resulting figures have a stylized and formal appearance. Arms are rigid, faces look straight ahead, and each left foot is slightly forward. There are no open spaces piercing the block; arms and legs are attached, or engaged to adjoining surfaces. Their pose is called **frontal** because both figures are facing and looking straight ahead. Although the faces are sculpted to describe some of the individual features of the king and queen, the bodies are stylized. They are ideal bodies and not accurate depictions of the king and queen.

The seated sculpture of *Katep and His Wife* (fig.5–22) was carved from limestone. Like other sculpture of its type, it was painted for added realism. Few Egyptian sculptures have survived with their paint intact. Here, too, the poses are frontal and the figures are stylized. Frontality and stylization are characteristics found in most Egyptian art. Katep was a nobleman, not a king, and the sculpture is an example of non-official art. The eyes are painted on, whereas the eyes of

Pharaohs often contain stones or inlaid quartz.

The *Seated Scribe* (fig.5–23) sits cross-legged on the floor and is ready and eager to transcribe a message. The pose is idealized but the face is carved to appear realistic. Like artists and craftspeople, scribes who could write the language held honored positions in Egypt.

Middle Kingdom

The Old Kingdom was a period of anarchy and divided rule, in which various powerful lords controlled Egypt. In the Middle Kingdom, the princes of Thebes finally grew powerful enough to establish a comparatively peaceful rule that lasted for two dynasties (Eleventh and Twelfth).

5–22 The Egyptians painted their sculptures but little of the paint has survived. They favored realistic colors which came from colored earth.
Katep and His Wife, about 2563 BC, 4th dynasty. Painted limestone, 18 1/2" (47 cm) high, found near Memphis. British Museum, London.

Early Dynastic Period 3100–2686 BC 1st and 2nd Dynasties	First Intermediate Period 2150–2100 BC 7th–10th Dynasties	Second Intermediate Period 1700–1500 BC 14th–17th Dynasties

Dynasty Timeline

Old Kingdom 2686–2150 BC 3rd–6th Dynasties	Middle Kingdom 2100–1700 BC 11th–13th Dynasties	New Kingdom c. 1500–1085 BC 18th–20th Dynasties

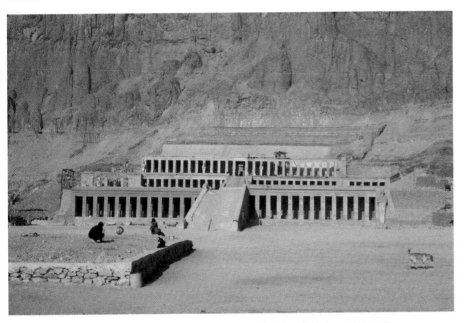

5–24 What characteristics does this temple have in common with a ziggurat and the Audience Hall at Persepolis (fig.5–17)?
Funerary Temple of Queen Hatshepsut, at Deir el-Bahari, about 1480 BC, 18th dynasty.

Higher-Order Thinking Skills

The Funerary Temple of Queen Hatshepsut, the Ur ziggurat, Stonehenge, Abu Simbel and the Great Pyramids were influenced by and have certain relationships to the landscapes in which they were constructed. Have students analyze these relationships for location, materials, visual impact and purpose. They can then pick the two that they consider the most effective and compare and contrast them. You may have the class analyze local important buildings for the same considerations.

Architecture shifted from pyramids to the construction of funerary temples built near Thebes. These were designed to hold the mummies of the rulers and were constructed so that part was cut into the cliff and part was built outside. The temple built by Queen Hatshepsut (fig.5–24), although constructed later, was built according to these Middle Kingdom architectural styles.

Art continued to flourish in the Middle Kingdom, with craftspeople still holding an honored position in society. Many models carved throughout the country's history provide an excellent idea of Egyptian life and culture. Craftspeople carved wood into figures, boats, weapons and other items. The carvings were painted to create an illusion of reality. The wooden funerary barge (fig.5–25) is typical of boats that were buried with the dead, to be used as transportation in the afterlife. The mummy, which lies beneath the canopy, is accompanied by two women mourners, a priest and the helmsman. The painted eye at the front of the barge would help guide the craft without mishap.

The Second Intermediate Period followed the Middle Kingdom. Egypt was invaded and ruled by outsiders for 150 years. During this time, there was no harmony in the land. These outside rulers, however, did introduce Egypt to such things as the horse, chariots, wheels and weapons of war.

5–23 The Egyptians honored craftspersons and held those who could write in high esteem. At first the position of scribe was held only by the sons of Pharaohs.
Seated Scribe, about 2400 BC, 5th dynasty. Painted limestone, 21" (53 cm) high, Sakkara. The Louvre, Paris.

5–25 This barge was put in a tomb to provide its owner with transportation in the afterlife. What is happening on the barge?
Funerary Barge, about 1800 BC, 12th dynasty. Polychromed wood, 31" (79 cm) long. British Museum, London.

Higher-Order Thinking Skills

Artists, craftsmen and scribes were honored in Egypt. Have the class create a list of occupations that our society honors. Have each student choose one of the occupations to develop a paper, display or work of art, such as a drawing, that identifies the characteristics of that occupation. Students might explore the interrelationships of the occupations by identifying what they have in common. Or they might make comparisons between some current, popular occupations and those of the ancient Egyptians.

New Kingdom

About 1567 BC the princes of Thebes overthrew these invaders and established the New Kingdom. The New Kingdom, which began with the Eighteenth Dynasty, was a golden age in Egypt's history. More powerful than ever, Egypt became an empire and controlled lands far beyond its own borders. Not only did the kingdom flourish, but artists and architects grew in skill and creative expression. This revival in art covers a vast range of styles, from rigid and traditional approaches to brilliant inventiveness. Huge monuments were built, but tiny decorative figures also were carved.

One of the outstanding architectural works to survive is the funerary temple of Queen Hatshepsut

(fig.5–24). As mentioned, the temple was built according to an architectural style first developed during the Middle Kingdom. Erected in 1480 BC the temple is partially cut into the cliffs at Deir el Bahari. Made of terraced walls, colonnades, sculptured reliefs, passageways and large open terraces, it blends harmoniously with the towering cliffs above. Egyptian rulers began constructing their tombs as soon as they were crowned, and Hatshepsut was no different. The Queen spent much of her reign constructing the temple, often strapping a false beard to her chin and wearing men's clothing when she visited the site.

All the great Egyptian structures we have examined so far have been associated with tombs and burial.

But during the Eighteenth Dynasty, temples were created specifically for the worship of gods and the homes of priests. Among the greatest was the Temple of Amun at Karnak (figs.5–26, 5–27). Here a huge complex of buildings included **pylons**, or entranceways, courtyards, a hypostyle hall and minor halls, chambers and passages.

The **hypostyle hall** was the most dramatic structure, consisting of 135 columns that created a forest-like feeling. There were 16 rows across the front alone. The central columns were about 69 feet high and were capped with open-flower capitals. The other capitals were in the shape of lotus buds. The columns were carved from top to bottom with relief sculptures and then painted. Stone lintels were placed atop the columns to create a sheltering roof. The higher central columns made it possible to include windows that flooded the interior with light. Because the lintel stones were of such great weight, the columns needed to be kept close together to prevent the stone slabs from breaking. Any such structure, with many columns supporting the roof (and not much open space inside), is called a hypostyle hall.

2000 BC	900 BC
Iron first used for tools and weapons in the Middle East	Chavin-style artwork produced, Peru

World Cultural Timeline

1876 BC	500–200 BC
First recorded eclipse, China	Earliest known sub-Saharan sculpture created, Nok culture, Africa

Multicultural Connection

African Art and Culture

Vocabulary is particularly important in a discussion of the continent of Africa and its people. A glossary of terms, some of them African, could be useful for students before beginning a unit on African art or before taking students to view an exhibition of African art. A review of words such as *primitive* and *tribe* could also be helpful. Although these words and others are frequently used when referring to Africa, often the reference is without a clear understanding of their definitions. Consequently, they are interpreted negatively when

used to describe non-Western people, or the art and artifacts representative of non-Western cultures. They should be avoided. Other terms can be used; for example, *nonindustrialized* or *traditional* instead of *primitive*, or *civilization* or *people* instead of *tribe*. A classroom discussion or a dictionary assignment focusing on such words will expand students' vocabulary and increase their sensitivity to the uses of language. The discussion might also increase sensitivity to other cultures and the values of those cultures.

The African continent is divided among deserts, highlands, savannas and river forests. As a result, the many African cultures are divided among nomadic tribes, farming villages and

great kingdoms, each with its own language. Therefore, for instance, carved wooden sculptures were not made in all parts of Africa but mostly in the west and central parts of sub-Saharan Africa, Africa south of the Sahara. African art, which was created for use in everyday life and rituals, covers many centuries, but the representational sculptures modeled by the Nok artists are among the most ancient. The Nok created highly simplified and stylized terracotta heads and figures (some of them almost life-size). The Nok culture flourished in northern Nigeria from about 500 BC to 200 AD. (For additional information about the Nok culture see Chapter 4, page 128.)

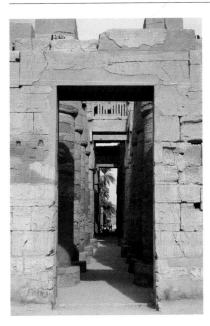

5–26 The hypostyle hall has a forest of columns. Compare it to the Audience Hall at Persepolis (fig.5–17). *Temple of Amun*, Karnak, about 1530 BC.

5–27 The Egyptians used no cement. This detail shows how the huge stones were stacked one on top of the other to create a column. *Temple of Amun*, Karnak, about 1530 BC, detail (fig.5–17).

Sidelight

Mummification

Because the ancient Egyptians believed that the dead lived on in the next world, they needed a way to preserve their bodies. A system of embalming was developed to help retain forever the form a body had in life. A mummy is an embalmed body that has been preserved for thousands of years. The process varied through the ages, but it always involved removing the internal organs, treating the body with resin, and wrapping it in linen bandages. In a later period the internal organs were treated and replaced inside the body.

According to ancient texts, it took seventy days to embalm and mummify a body. First, a hook was used to remove the brain through a nostril. The internal organs, except the heart and kidneys, were taken out through an incision in the side of the body. Then the body was coated in a salt-like chemical compound of sodium carbonate called natron. The natron drew out moisture and dried out the tissues in about forty days. Then the empty abdomen was packed with linen pads and sometimes with sawdust. The entire body was rubbed with spices and resin. Finally, the body was carefully wrapped in many layers of tightly wound linen bandages. It may have taken as long as fifteen days to wrap the body. Then the mummy was placed in a coffin.

Contextual Information

Egyptian Embalming

The practice of embalming spread from the Egyptians to other ancient peoples. It is interesting to note that the Egyptians used balsams and aromatic substances for embalming. Sometimes when experts open a mummy case and unravel the cloth that surrounds the body, the pleasant aroma of these ancient substances wafts to their noses. The Assyrians used honey in embalming; the Persians used wax; and the Jews used spices and aloes.

Ask students to speculate why aromatic substances were used in embalming.

What burial customs do we follow today? Encourage students to mention customs that might be particular to their cultural or ethnic group.

Egyptian Artists

Priests and rulers were the first known employers of artists, but not all artists were free to produce what they desired. In fact, in Egypt some were slaves. At best, artists were to execute serious, respectful and flattering representations of their employers and in a style predetermined by their employers.

Ancient writings speak of the mechanical nature of painters and sculptors. By the New Kingdom though, artists belonged to the higher classes and therefore had more autonomy. Training workshops for artists were held in temples, palaces, private estates and marketplaces.

Egyptian Glass

Students can turn to fig.2–42 to see how Egyptians worked in another medium, glass.

Interdisciplinary Connection

Social Studies: Ask students if they recall from their social studies classes the important role the Rosetta Stone played in unraveling the writing system of the Egyptians.

For centuries scholars struggled to decipher Egyptian hieroglyphics without success. In 1799 a soldier serving in Napoleon's Egyptian campaign discovered the Rosetta Stone, a trilingual stele that included the same inscription in Greek, in hieroglyphic Egyptian, and in the demotic (a simplified form of the hieroglyphs). The stele was the long-sought key to the writing system of ancient Egypt.

Contextual Information

Egyptian Burial

The burial of the dead was one of the utmost religious concerns for the Egyptians. Their funerary rituals and tomb furnishings are the most elaborate the world has known. The Egyptians believed in the ka, a duplicate of the body that departed the body after death to join the kingdom of the dead. The ka, however, could not exist without the body. This is why every effort was made to preserve the body after death. Often a wooden replica of the body was placed in a person's tomb. If anything did happen to the body, it was believed that this replica could take its place.

Akhenaten

In the fourteenth century BC Akhenaten reigned over lands from the Greek islands to Asia Minor and the upper Euphrates to the southern Nile. He declared himself son and prophet of Aten and the only one who could reveal Aten's wishes. His hymn to Aten includes: "Thou art in my heart./There is no other that knoweth thee,/Save thy son Akhenaten./Thou didst establish the world,/And raise them up for thy son,/Who came forth from thy limbs,/The king of Upper and Lower Egypt . . ."

5–28 Identify the characters in this manuscript. Is there a relationship to line drawings you saw earlier, such as those at Lascaux?
Greenfield Papyrus, about 1080 BC, 21st dynasty. 19" (49 cm) high, British Museum, London.

Many huge temples and complexes were built during the New Kingdom. But other arts also flourished. The *Greenfield Papyrus* (fig.5–28) is a painted papyrus that reveals some important characteristics of Egyptian art in all ages. In the center, Shu (god of atmosphere) raises the body of Nut (goddess of sky). His arms are supported by two ram-headed gods, while Geb (god of earth) lies on the ground. In the lower right corner is the daughter of a high priest and her soul (human-headed bird). This papyrus was drawn specially for the high priest's daughter.

The drawing is sensitive and beautifully done. The figures are placed in **registers** (layers). Many of the gods are in the form of animals. Notice that the figures are shown so the legs, arms and faces are in profile, but the upper body is turned toward the viewer. The face is in profile, but the eye is looking directly at the viewer. **Descriptive perspective** also is used. This means that the more important figures are shown larger than the less important ones. The careful design and placement of figures to fill almost all available space is also characteristic of Egyptian painting and wall sculpture.

The tomb painting of a banquet scene (fig.5–29) shows guests being entertained by two female dancers, a musician, and three singers who are clapping in rhythm. The words of the song are shown directly above the singers. The guests are painted in the register directly above. (Only their feet and legs can been seen.) Is there something in this painting that is very un-Egyptian? Several figures are shown facing frontward. They are not shown in profile. The artist was attempting to paint realistically, rather than stylistically. Usually the artists worked with formulas that they knew very well, and did not depict people as they actually looked.

Stylization characterizes most of Egypt's art. However, there was a time during the reign of Akhenaton (Eighteenth Dynasty) when realism became dominant. Akhenaton stressed a realistic approach to art. The sculpture of his wife, Nefertiti, is a superb example (fig.5–30). The portrait is delicate and sensitive and shows a marvelous knowledge of the structure of the human head. In fact, Akhenaton 's artists took molds from human faces and bodies to study the structure and create carvings of anatomical perfection. The sculpture of Nefertiti, a most beautiful woman, was left abandoned in the artist's studio after the death of the king.

Akhenaton built the largest private home in the world at that time at Tel el Amarna. He changed his name and declared a single new supreme god in Aten, the sun. Most importantly, he declared himself Aten's representative on earth and a god himself. Akhenaton's successor was his nine-year-old relative, Tutankhaten. The young king was guided by advisers to move the capital back to Thebes, to reinstate the worship of Amen, and to change his name to Tutankhamen. Although

5–29 You are familiar with how the Egyptians usually depicted people. How are these figures different?
Dancing Girls at a Banquet, about 1400 BC, 18th dynasty. Wall painting, portion shown is 24" (61 cm) high, Thebes. British Museum, London.

Performing Arts Connection

Entertainment in Ancient Egypt

The tomb painting *Dancing Girls at a Banquet* (fig.5–29) shows dancers and female musicians performing a song in praise of nature. Although we do not know exactly what Egyptian music sounded like, a small orchestra at a banquet would typically have had string, wind and percussion sections. The woman playing a double flute and the others clapping out the rhythm all wear cones of scented fat on top of their wigs. Music, singing, and dancing were among the few professional options for Egyptian women, but they probably held a low social status as entertainers.

Party scenes painted on tomb walls, songs inscribed on papyri and surviving musical instruments indicate that Egyptian life was filled with the arts. Thousands of spectators were entertained with songs and flutes, harps and castanets at great public festivals. Dancers and acrobats also performed routines alongside processions that led to temples for feasts and ritual celebrations.

Music was also an integral part of daily life. Men clapped rhythm sticks together while vintners pressed grapes for wine; farm workers sang to their oxen as these beasts threshed corn with their hooves; and a princess might have played the harp while her husband relaxed on a divan.

Window in Time

The Search for the Tomb of Tutankhamen

Obsessed with finding the tomb of Tutankhamen, who had reigned more than 3,200 years before, archaeologist Howard Carter began excavating in the Valley of Kings in Egypt in the early 1900s. Thirty-three royal tombs had already been discovered in the Valley, but every one of them had been ransacked by robbers. Most experts believed that the Valley had yielded all its secrets. But Carter disagreed.

Carter believed that the tomb was located in one small area of the Valley that was filled with rubble from the excavations of other tombs. Archaeologists had not bothered to dig beneath this rubble. But even though the area was small, the task was still daunting. Just to reach the floor of the Valley, men would have to remove tens of thousands of tons of rock and sand.

After years of searching Carter had still not found anything. His patron, Lord Carnarvon, informed Carter that he would no longer renew the excavation concession from the Egyptian government. With time running out Carter decided to dig around a line of workers' huts that stood near the entrance to the tomb of Ramses VI.

By the beginning of November in 1922, the trench had been dug to bedrock. On November 4, the beginning of a staircase was discovered. At the bottom of the staircase was a door and on the door were affixed the seals of the royal necropolis—the jackal god Anubis above nine defeated foes. Carter filled in the stairway again and cabled Carnarvon in London.

Within three weeks Carnarvon arrived and the real discovery could begin. But once the door was fully uncovered the telltale marks of holes cut by thieves were revealed in the upper part of the door. The door gave onto a rubble-filled tunnel. At the end of the tunnel was another door, again marred by thieves' holes. Carter drilled a hole into the door himself and by candlelight peered in. To his great excitement, Carter was looking at the Antechamber of Tutankhamen's tomb. Robbers had indeed been there but fortunately the tomb had not been ransacked.

All the treasures, everything the eighteen-year-old king might have needed on his journey to the other world, were inside the Antechamber. The room was heaped with statues, thrones, chairs, boxes, ornaments and chests. Gold was everywhere. Clothes,

Mask of King Tutankhamen, 1352 BC, 18th dynasty. Gold with precious stones and glass, life-size, Thebes. Egyptian Museum, Cairo.

bottles and paintings were also found.

Some months later Carter was ready to open the Burial Chamber. As soon as he had made a large enough hole he inserted an electric torch. A wall of solid gold greeted his astonished eyes. It was one side of a shrine covering Tutankhamen's sarcophagus. The great carved stone sarcophagus in the Burial Chamber rested inside a series of four nested wooden cases covered with gold leaf. Three mummy-shaped coffins nested inside the rectangular stone coffin. The innermost coffin was solid gold. Inside was the extraordinary polished gold funerary mask covering Tutankhamen's head and shoulders.

But only Carter saw the magnificent mask. Lord Carnarvon had died in Cairo less than five months after the tomb was opened. He died of blood poisoning from a mosquito bite that had become infected. This only confirmed the rumors that an ancient curse would fall upon anyone who disturbed a Pharaoh's resting place. However, Carter, the real "disturber," died peacefully at home in England at age sixty-five.

Higher-Order Thinking Skills

Egyptian wall paintings (murals) in tombs told allegorical narratives, mythological stories that explained everyday life. Students can work individually or in groups to create scenes (written or visual) of everyday life in your school or community that could be used by future generations to understand your life and times. The final product may be a book, mural, art show, or publication.

Materials and Techniques

Papyrus is a marsh grass that grows by the Nile. To form sheets of papyrus, the bark was peeled off and the inner stems cut to about 20 inches and laid out on fabric in adjacent rows. The stems were then pounded until the fibers softened and released a gluelike fluid, which was pressed out. These sheets were weighted down with cloth and heavy blocks until more fluid was pressed out. The sheets were then dried. Longer pieces were made by gluing the pieces together with a flour-and-water paste.

Higher-Order Thinking Skills

The statues of Ramses II at Abu Simbel (fig.5–31) are only four of the many colossal statues of himself that Ramses placed all over his kingdom. Each statue is 69 1/3 feet high. Provide rulers, yardsticks or tape-measures and masking tape for students to measure and mark that dimension so they really understand and experience its huge size. By comparison the *Venus of Willendorf* (fig.5–4) is only 4 3/8 inches tall. Have them measure that dimension. Ask students to look at the photographs of these two sculptures and discuss what happens to your impression of their size as they are portrayed in the book. Take students through the illustrations in the chapter asking them to determine whether each work is larger or smaller than the Ramses or the Venus. Help them develop the habit of checking the caption for the size of the work and compare it to others to form a realistic sense of scale.

5–30 Ideas of beauty change with time. Compare this woman to the *Venus of Willendorf* (fig.5–4).
Queen Nefertiti, about 1360 BC, 18th dynasty. Painted limestone, 20" (51 cm) high, El Amarna. Agyptische Museum, Berlin.

5–31 Ramses II erected colossal statues of himself all over his kingdom. These are carved from living rock.
Ramses II, about 1257 BC, 19th dynasty. Sculpted from cliff, each about 69 1/3' (21 m) high, Abu Simbel, Egypt.

he ruled for only nine years, he is Egypt's most famous king because of the wealth of art objects found in his tomb (fig.5–a). Over the years, Egypt's kings realized that the large burial structures only invited thievery of their buried treasures—crimes that had been going on for centuries. Now the rulers were secretly cutting their burial chambers into rock cliffs and disguising the entrances. Even these were found and rifled—all except one: that of Tutankhamen, whose tomb

entrance was hidden by the debris from a later tomb.

With the end of the Eighteenth Dynasty, art again returned to traditional stylization. Ramses II (Nineteenth Dynasty) ruled for sixty-seven years and had a multitude of statues of himself placed throughout the land. His temple at Abu Simbel is the most famous (fig.5–31). Four figures of Ramses are carved directly out of the standing cliff. The temple itself recedes into the stone wall. Descriptive per-

spective is used to express the size, and corresponding importance, of the queen and other relatives.

The construction of the Aswan Dam in recent years caused this site to be flooded permanently. To preserve it, the entire temple and the four mammoth sculptures were cut apart, lifted to the plain above and reassembled under the direction of American engineers. Such an effort clearly shows the importance the rest of the world places on the art of ancient Egypt.

Lesson 5.3 Review

1 Explain how the Nile River influenced the development of Egyptian culture.
2 Who was Imhotep? What is his importance in the history of art?
3 Why do we know so much about Egyptian society and art?
4 Select an example of Old Kingdom sculpture illustrated in this chapter. How is it typical of the sculpture created during that period?

5 Examine the funerary barge illustrated in fig.5–25. What does it tell us about Egyptian life at that time?
6 What were the two most important types of Egyptian architecture? How were they similar? How did they differ?

Lesson 5.3 Review Answers

1 The Nile River provided moist fertile soil that allowed the Egyptians to produce an abundance of food. This meant that the entire population did not need to be preoccupied with food gathering. Various professions were available, and some people became artists whose products were admired.
2 Imhotep built the step pyramid at Sakkara, which was the first huge stone structure built on earth. He is the first known artist.
3 The Egyptians depicted their lifestyle in their tomb art and filled their tombs with their possessions. The contents of the tombs and the monuments that the Egyptians built have given historians much information about Egyptian art and society.
4 Possible examples are *Mycerinus and His Queen*, *Katep and His Wife*, and the *Seated Scribe*. All of these have a stylized appearance with frontal poses staring straight ahead and faces carved and painted to appear realistic. *Mycerinus and His Queen* and *Katep and His Wife* have rigid arms with no spaces between the body, arms and legs.

The left foot of both Mycerinus and his queen is slightly forward, a traditional stance.
5 We can see that people dressed in white cotton dresses, how their hair was arranged, how a funerary barge was constructed, and what their pottery looked like. We also learn some of their burial customs, such as how the body was displayed, transported and attended.
6 Pyramids and temples. The pyramids were associated with tombs and burial, but the temples were created for the worship of gods and the homes of priests. They were both huge stone structures fit together without mortar. Both temples and pyramids had interior passages and chambers covered with paintings and low reliefs. The pyramids had their distinctive shape of triangular sides covered with polished limestone.

The temples had hypostyle halls with huge columns and high windows to light the interior, but the pyramids were dark inside.

Chapter Review Answers

Review

1 The children were small enough to gain entry to the caves and to easily look up at the ceiling.
2 Red, yellow, brown, violet and black
3 A horizontal structural member that spans an opening between two walls or posts
4 Large eyes, because the Sumerians believed that the eyes were the windows to the soul
5 About 4530 years ago

Primary Source

The Code of Hammurabi King of Babylon, c.1770 BC.

The Code of Hammurabi King of Babylon was written about 1770 BC. In it we find rules about what kinds of punishment were to be given for injuries suffered by innocent victims.

#188 If an artisan takes a son for adoption and teaches him his handicraft, one may not bring claim for him.

#189 If he does not teach him his handicraft, that adopted son may return to his father's house.

#195 If a son strikes his father, they shall cut off his fingers.

#200 If a man knocks out a tooth of a man of his own rank, they shall knock out his tooth.

#202 If a man strikes the person of a man who is his superior, he shall receive sixty strokes with an ox-tail whip in public.

#209 If a man strikes a man's daughter and brings about a miscarriage, he shall pay ten shekels of silver for her miscarriage.

#213 If he strikes the female slave of a man and brings about a miscarriage, he shall pay two shekels of silver.

#218 If a physician operates on a man for a severe wound with a

bronze lancet and causes the man's death; or opens an abscess (in the eye) of a man with a bronze lancet and destroys the man's eye, they shall cut off his fingers.

#228 If a builder builds a house for a man and completes it, (that man) shall give him two shekels of silver per SAR (a measurement) of the house as his wage.

#233 If a builder builds a house for a man and does not make its construction meet the requirements and a wall falls in, that builder shall strengthen that wall at his own expense.

Chapter Review

Review

1 Why is it that children were the first modern persons to encounter the cave paintings at Lascaux and Altamira?
2 What color pigments were used by the artists at Lascaux?
3 What is a lintel?
4 What human feature dominates Sumerian figure sculpture? Why?
5 How many years ago was the Pyramid of Cheops built?

Interpret

1 Compare the arrangement of figures on the Standard of Ur (figs.5–10) with the placement of figures on the walls of Lascaux (fig.5–1).
2 The art of Egypt is often described as stylized. There is a period during the 18th Dynasty, however, when the king, Akhenaton, encouraged realism in art. Compare the portrait of Akhenaton's wife, Nefertiti (fig.5–30) with the figures of Mycerinus and his queen (fig.5–21). Keep in mind the working methods of the artist of each work.
3 You have been introduced to a number of architectural monuments. Select three and describe how they relate to their environment.

Other Tools for Learning

Maps
Note the clustering of towns and cities on the maps of the ancient Near East and Egypt. Discuss the reasons for these clusters.

Timelines
The timelines within this chapter cover 25,000 years—an enormous span of time. They include events that happened all over the world. List three of the most interesting or surprising pieces of information that you can find on the timelines. Explain why you have chosen them.

Electronic Research
CD-ROM drive: Electronic Encyclopedia (e.g., *New Grolier Multimedia* and *Microsoft Encarta*)
Explore further one of the many ancient sites introduced in this chapter. Make an effort to find more information about how it was used and who used it. Also note any differences in dates that you come across. Very often scholars disagree on the precise dating of sites as old as those discussed in this chapter.

Primary-Source Connection

The Code of Hammurabi King of Babylon was written about 1770 BC. In it we find rules about what kinds of punishment were to be given for injuries suffered by innocent victims. Hammurabi's laws concerned punishment for crimes, payment for injuries, and wages for jobs completed and those not completed properly. Compensation varied according to social status.

As students read these few excerpts, ask them to think about the culture and people of this period, the economics of the community, the types of tools available, the education of craftspeople and how having these laws helped develop the skills of craftspeople.

Maps
The availability of water played a key factor in determining where clusters of early settlements would develop in the Near East. Towns would cluster along the rivers, which also became trade routes.

Timelines
There are many possible responses. For example a student might be surprised or interested that people were writing in Mesopotamia before Stonehenge was built, because Stonehenge might seem very primitive; the Japanese, not the Egyptians, created the first pottery vessels, in 10,500 BC; mummification was practiced in South America and Africa as well as Egypt.

Electronic Media
Students can research any number of places including Jericho, Ur, Perspepolis, Giza. They will find some slight discrepancies in the dating of these ancient sites. They also will find that the manner in which a date is presented can vary. For example, one source may indicate that the walls of Jericho were built in about 7000 BC, while another may say they were built in the 8th millennium BC. Students will have to think carefully to determine if these are different or basically the same.

Interpret

1 On the Ur standard the figures are carefully spaced and arranged in straight rows. On the Lascaux walls the figures have a haphazard placement, even overlapping in places.
2 The realistic sculpture of Nefertiti is delicate and sensitive, showing that the artist knew the structure of the human head. Akhenaton's artists had made molds of human faces and bodies in order to understand human anatomy and carve it perfectly.

In the stylized carving of Mycerinus and his queen, the bodies are stiff, formal traditional ideals, not copied from life, although the faces probably are likenesses of the two figures. The sculptor drew the composition on each

side of the stone and carved inward, leaving the original shape of block still visible.
3 Possible responses are:

Stonehenge rises in a circle over 13 feet from the Salisbury Plain in England. The positions of its stones are aligned with the sun to indicate solstices and equinoxes.

The Pyramid of Chefren rose like a shining mountain from the desert floor. The polished limestone reflecting the desert sun would have been brilliant.

The Funerary Temple of Queen Hatshepsut was cut back into the cliff. Its shape echoes the shape of the surrounding cliffs.

Activity 1:
Home Town Sculpture

Activity Objectives
Students should be able to:

• Understand what stylization means.

• Make connections between the art of the region and the materials that are readily available.

• Appreciate the beauty inherent in different types of sculpture media, including form, surface texture and color.

• Gain studio skills by working with a specific sculptural material and the related tools.

• Become aware of natural resources in their immediate environment.

Thinking Critically
The concept of stylization is mentioned throughout the chapter. Students can make many comparisons as they study the sculptures from the Paleolithic era, Sumeria and Egypt. They can also make connections to the types of sculpture materials used and the size of the individual pieces.

Preparation Ideas
The challenge of this activity is to work with materials common in your local area.

• You could assign the search for materials as homework, then in class have students present what they've found. Discuss where the materials came from, how they might be used and which are appropriate for development. In the next class, have necessary sculpting tools on hand.

• Another approach would be to decide ahead of time what local material is most appropriate and have students bring in samples. Then you would know what tools to have available. For instance, a class in Georgia might gather red clay and store it in plastic to prevent it from drying. You would provide newspaper or plastic to protect the work surface, water and sculpting tools.

• If wood and stone are the predominant local materials, carving is not recommended because of the expense of proper tools, possible danger to students and the need for close supervision. You could have students investigate wood or stone artwork for ideas and then substitute clay, soapstone, plaster,

Activity 1

Home Town Sculpture

Materials
locally available material, could be:
clay
wood
rock
scrap metal or wire
cardboard
optional: modeling clay

Take a look. Review the following artwork in this book:
• Fig. 5–4, *Venus of Willendorf*, about 25,000 BC. Limestone.
• Fig. 5–5, *Bison*, about 10,000 BC. Reindeer antler.
• Fig. 5–12, *Praying Nobleman*, about 2600 BC, Sumerian. Wood.
• Fig. 5–13, *Gudea of Lagash*, about 2255 BC, Neo-Sumerian. Diorite.
• Fig. 5–21, *Mycerinus and His Queen*, about 2470 BC, 4th dynasty. Slate.

Think about it. The size of sculpture often is determined by the materials artists have on hand. Mesopotamia lacked a ready supply of stone and artists worked on small pieces. Egypt, on the other hand, had an unlimited supply, and its artists carved gigantic figures. Is this still true in our contemporary world? What sculptural materials are readily available where you live?

Do it.
• Locate a material in your local area that is suitable for sculpture.
• Examine the material carefully. What form from nature comes to mind? Perhaps you imagine an animal like the *Bison* (fig.5–5) or a figure like the *Praying Nobleman* (fig.5–12). As you study the material, consider its surface texture and natural form.
• Do a few sketches of the image you would like to sculpt. It might be appropriate to sculpt a down-sized model in clay before tackling the image at full size.

• With your teacher's guidance, create your sculpture using the necessary tools. *Stylize* the form by simplifying it and eliminating detail while retaining the beauty of the material from which it is made.

Check it.
• Does the subject you chose suit the material you used?
• Have you simplified the image but still captured the spirit of it?
• Have you taken time to finish the surface in a way that communicates good craftsmanship?

Helpful Hint: As you work, continually view the piece from all angles.

Activity 2

Weathering Time

Take a look. Look for artwork dating any time before the birth of Christ (BC) in the early chapters of this book. Note what materials they are made from and where they were found.

Think about it.
• How has climate helped to preserve ancient works of art for long periods of time?
• Would these ancient objects have endured to the present if the original cultures had been located in tropical jungles? Support your answer.
• Which climates are most favorable for the preservation of art and where in the world do they occur?
• Where have some of the more successful archaeological discoveries been made?

Do it.
Choose an area of the world which has a climate that would have preserved its ancient works.
• Research this region to find examples of pieces dating from 4000 BC to 500 BC.

• Prepare a presentation to your class, which could include photographs, samples or sketches.
• Be ready to draw comparisons between the culture you have studied and those in this chapter.

Check it.
• Did you find and use relevant examples of work that supported your ideas?
• Have you listed your sources in a bibliography?

Helpful Hint: Refer often to a good map! Become familiar with key places where art has been found around the world.

Additional Activities

• Write an essay discussing the importance of art in the development of the Egyptian civilization. Include ideas such as historical documentation, visual history, art as decoration, art as writing, celebration, family history, cultural documentation, symbolism, religion, life after death. Why were artists considered essential to Egyptian culture and life?

• Find a large open area where you can mark off the dimensions of Cheops' pyramid. Outline the shape with string, or position classmates along the edges. Make a sketch to show its size in comparison to your school campus. Ask teachers of computer technology or industrial design (or local architects) about software programs that would allow you to do this activity on the computer.

vermiculite or other poured and set materials that are easily carved.

Notes on Materials
Materials and tools used will be determined by what is available in your local area.

• Students in an urban location may find a plentiful supply of cardboard boxes which can be laminated, glued together or torn into interesting shapes.

• In Southern rural areas, salt blocks are a possibility for carving.

• You may want to provide modeling clay so students can make a down-sized prototype before they begin sculpting. This gives them a chance to zero in on their ideas and adapt two-dimensional images (from their sketches) to three-dimensional form.

Classroom Management

• To promote safety, discuss (and if necessary, demonstrate) proper use of tools.

• Limiting the number of materials to be sculpted makes the project more manageable.

• Students work on individual sculptures, but it's a good idea to stop the work periodically for critiques of work in progress. Organize small groups wherein students can present or discuss where they are headed in the development of their work. This gives each student a chance to problem solve and incorporate constructive suggestions along the way.

Student Profile

Jason Panneton

Age 17
W. T. Woodson High School
Annandale, Virginia
Favorite kinds of art: large, graffiti art; abstract
Favorite artists: Robert Rauschenberg, Hex, Al Held, any artist who sparks inspiration in me!

Activity 1, Home Town Sculpture

These pieces deal with creating a sculpture out of objects or junk or whatever else I found lying around. I was lucky enough to find a bag of blocks lying around in my garage. They were the perfect thing for me to use in doing a figurative series of sculptures.

I did a piece relating to human body parts. I wanted to do more with that idea, so I created three sculptures. The sculptures are a three-dimensional interpretation of the drawing.

I like the idea of creating sculpture from found objects. I have studied a lot of art where the art was done from things that the artist found. I am very influenced by the sculpture being done by students at art colleges around the country. It is all so fascinating to me to see how some junk lying around could be crafted into a beautiful inspiring piece of art. Reading about how artists have thought so much about how to express a message and achieve a goal, and talking to my art teacher has moved me to push myself to the limits and beyond.

I love the act of making the art. I love having my hands and mind work together. There is nothing like the little spark of happiness I feel when I draw a line that is just right or when I do a self-portrait that really expresses a feeling. So to all you young artists out there, my advice is to push yourself beyond the easy stuff, stay true to yourself as an artist, and WORK HARD!

After constructing a figure from wooden blocks found in his environment, Jason adds bands of color.

Posing Figures, 1994. Wood, cardboard and paint, 17" high (43 cm). Also *Body Parts* oil pastel with *Body Parts* sculptures.

Tips

• Students should include slides of their three-dimensional work in their portfolios.

• Discuss the "finishing" of a work. Point out that rough or coarse surfaces should be intentional and add to the overall impact.

Evaluation

Grades can be based on:

• ingenuity in locating materials

• preliminary drawings/clay models

• design of the object, including the suitability of the form to the material

• success in giving and receiving constructive criticism in small groups

• craftsmanship

Activity 2: Weathering Time

Activity Objectives

Students should understand that:

• Egyptian, Mesopotamian, Chinese and Indian cultures developed simultaneously.

• Motifs, symbols and ideas have been common to many cultures.

• Climate has an impact on the preservation of an artifact.

Thinking Critically

• Have students imagine that a denim jacket will be found in the future. What might still be left, and how might someone come across it?

Teacher Spotlight

Sandi Hammonds

Fine and Performing Arts Chair
W. T. Woodson High School

Jason has been exploring the human figure in art and his own interpretations. He originally did the oil pastel drawing shown in the background for an assignment that required him to combine perspective and the human body. Jason became fascinated with the idea that "junk" could become art, so we deviated from the original concept of "carving." He then took his drawing into a three-dimensional version using plaster-soaked gauze strips, bricks and acrylic paint. This then led to the final pieces—the figures he did for the chapter assignment. The concept of stylization was key to the success of Jason's understanding of the chapter.

Preparation Ideas

• Bring in a guest speaker (a local historian or an archaeologist) to get students excited about the activity.

• Flip through back issues of *National Geographic* and other magazines that regularly feature news of archaeological expeditions. Tag examples of digs in different countries to show in class. Include objects found in shipwrecks as examples of art that has weathered a different kind of environment.

Notes on Materials

• A world map showing deserts and mountains would support a better understanding of climate differences.

Classroom Management

This would be an appropriate group project. Divide students into groups of three, four or five and have each group focus on a different culture. One student could do the visuals, and another could create handouts. The members of each group could then all work together to give a final presentation to the class.

Evaluation

Grade students on:

• accuracy of information presented in their reports;

• clarity of their presentation to the class (or to the teacher, if it's written);

• effective use of visuals.

Chapter 6 Organizer

	Days	8 Week	1 Semester	2 Semester	

Chapter 6 Opener: Greek and Roman Art

| | | 1 | 1 | 1 | |

Objectives

National Standards

Objectives	National Standards
Understand that civilizations along the Aegean existed simultaneously with Mesopotamian and Egyptian cultures.	**4c** Students analyze relationships of works of art to one another in terms of history, aesthetics, and culture, justifying conclusions made in the analysis and using such conclusions to inform their own art making.
Understand that Aegean cultures were the forebears of Greek society.	**4e** Students analyze common characteristics of visual arts evident across time and among cultural/ethnic groups to formulate analyses, evaluations, and interpretation of meaning.
Identify how the Greeks used harmony and unity to portray the human form in an idealized manner.	**2b** Students evaluate the effectiveness of artworks in terms of organizational structures and functions.
Explain how Roman art and architecture adopted aspects of the cultures the empire conquered, particularly the Greeks.	**3c** Students describe the origins of specific images and ideas and explain why they are of value in their artwork and in the work of others. **4d** Students analyze and interpret artworks for relationships among form, context, purposes, and critical models, showing understanding of the work of critics, historians, aestheticians, and artists.

Teacher Edition References

Lesson 6.1 Aegean Art

| | 1 | 1 | | | |

	Teacher Edition References	
Special Feature: Bull Dance Fresco 174–175	HOTS 175	
Remainder of Lesson 6.1 176–177 World Cultural Timeline 176 Lesson 6.1 Review 177	Contextual Info 176 HOTS 177	Interdisciplinary 176 Multicultural 176

Lesson 6.2 Greek Art

| | 1 | 1 | | | |

Special Feature: The Kritios Boy 178–179 *Timeline:* Major Periods in Greek Art 178	Contextual Info 179	HOTS 179
Remainder of Lesson 6.2 180–189 Lesson 6.2 Review 189 World Cultural Timeline 180,188	Contextual Info 180, 182, 184, 186, 188 HOTS 181, 183, 185, 187, 189 Conservation Note 186 Cooperative 183	Inquiry 185 Interdisciplinary 182, 189 Multicultural 180, 188 Performing Arts 187

Lesson 6.3 Roman Art

Special Feature: The Colosseum 190–191 *Map:* The Roman Empire 190	Contextual Info 191 HOTS 191	Inquiry 191
Remainder of Lesson 6.3 192–200 Lesson 6.3 Review 200 World Cultural Timeline 194 Primary Source 201 Chapter Review 201	Contextual Info 192, 194, 197, 198, 200 HOTS 193, 195, 196, 199 Conservation 196 Interdisciplinary 199	Multicultural 194 Performing Arts 198

Classroom Connections

National Standards

	National Standards
Studio Activity 1 Immortalized in Clay	**1a** Students apply media, techniques, and processes with sufficient skill, confidence, and sensitivity that their intentions are carried out in their artworks.
Studio Activity 2 Ancient Legacy	**3c** Students describe the origins of specific images and ideas and explain why they are of value in their artwork and in the work of others.

Choose either Activity 1 or 2 Choose either Activity 1 or 2 Choose either Activity 1 or 2

Slides: Roman, Column of Trajan, an overall view, 29a, 76; Roman, Column of Trajan, a detail, 30a, 77

Timeline: Greek and Roman Art 172
Map: Ancient Greece and Rome 173
Context 172
Art 173
Quote 173

Ancillaries

Slides: Mycenaean, *Funeral mask* 41b, 69

Overhead Transparencies: The Standing Figure Evolves, 6

Slides: Greek, *Kouros,* 31a, 70; Greek, *Procession, North Frieze of the Parthenon,* 32a, 71; Greek, *Dying Warrior,* 33a, 73; Greek, *Three Graces,* 42b, 72; Greek, Orders, 43b, 74; Greek, *Discobolus,* 3a, 7
Large Reproductions: *Geometric Krater,* 6

Slides: Roman, Column of Trajan, an overall view, 29a, 76; Roman, Column of Trajan, a detail, 30a, 77; Roman Arch of Constantine, Rome, 34a, 78; Roman, *Head of Constantine the Great,* 35a, 79; Etruscan, *She-wolf,* 44b, 75; Roman, *Wall mosaic,* 45b, 80; Roman, *Polyphemos and Galatea,* 7b, 10
Large Reproductions: Roman, *Architectural View,* 7

Schedule

Materials

Two days for a small sculpture. Larger sculptures will take longer.

for preliminary drawings:
Mirrors or photographs, soft lead pencils (#2 or 4B, 6B), 12" x 18" white drawing paper
for sculpture:
newspaper or plastic cloth, containers of water, spray bottle, terra cotta clay, clay tools, heavy duty plastic bags

One day to make a small pencil sketch. Could spend five days rendering a finished, shaded drawing.

12" x 18" white drawing paper or larger, drawing pencils (2H,4H, 6H,HB), rulers, kneaded erasers, drawing board (optional)

Other Resources

Books

Aries, Phillip, ed., trans. *A History of Private Life. Volume I: From Pagan Rome to Byzantium.* Cambridge: Belknap Press, 1987.

Bandinelli, Ranuccio Bianchi. *Rome: The Center of Power, 500 BC to AD 200.* Part of *Arts of Mankind.* New York: George Braziller Inc., Odyssey Press Inc. and Golden Press,1970.

———. *Rome : The Late Empire, AD 200–400.* Part of *Arts of Mankind.* New York: George Braziller Inc., Odyssey Press Inc. and Golden Press, 1971.

Boardman, John. *Greek Art.* Rev. ed. New York: Thames and Hudson Inc., 1985.

Boethius, Axel. *Etruscan and Roman Architecture.* New Haven: Yale University Press, 1992.

Brendel, Otto J. *Etruscan Art.* Baltimore: Penguin USA, 1979.

Cook, B. F. *The Elgin Marbles.* Cambridge: Harvard University Press, 1984.

Demargne, Pierre. *The Birth of Greek Art.* Part of *Arts of Mankind.* New York: George Braziller Inc., Odyssey Press Inc. and Golden Press, 1964.

Hood, Sinclair. *Arts in Prehistoric Greece.* New Haven: Yale University Press, 1992.

Jenkens, Ian. *Greek and Roman Life.* Cambridge: Harvard University Press, 1986.

Pevsner, Nikolaus, and Nairn, Judy, joint eds.*Pelican History of Art.* Baltimore: Penguin USA, 1953.

Pollitt, Jerry Jordan. *Art of Greece: 1400–31 BC.* Part of *Sources and Documents in the History of Art.* Englewood Cliffs: Prentice Hall, 1965.

———. *Art of Rome: 753 BC–337 AD.* Part of *Sources and Documents in the History of Art.* New York: Cambridge University Press, 1983.

Richter, Gisela. *A Handbook of Greek Art.* 9th ed. Jersey City: DaCapo Press, 1987.

Roux, Georges. *Ancient Iraq.* rev ed. Baltimore: Penguin USA, 1976.

Strong, Donald. *Roman Art.* New Haven: Yale University Press, 1992.

Ward-Perkins, John B. *Roman Imperial Architecture.* 2nd ed. New Haven: Yale University Press, 1992.

Williams, Dyfri. *Greek Vases.* Part of British Museum Cambridge: Harvard University Press, 1985.

Video

Ancient Lives, Humanities. 1980s.
Athens and Ancient Greece, Crystal
Crete and Mycenae. Museum Without Walls. Kartes, 1986.
Greek Temple. Museum Without Walls, Kartes, 1986.
Heritage of the Pharaohs. International Adventure Video, 1983.
In Search of the Trojan War. BBC, 1985.
Light of Gods, Crystal

Introduce

While Egypt and Mesopotamia thrived, along the Aegean emerged two distinct cultures whose rich artistic heritage provided the foundation for the great Greek civilization. The Greeks themselves developed an unsurpassed standard of beauty based on the idealized human form. By the early eighth century BC, the Romans influenced the art and architecture of the societies that the empire had conquered. Much of Western culture had its roots in Greek and Roman art.

Lessons at a Glance

6.1 *Aegean Art*
The rich Minoan and Mycenaean cultures along the Aegean were the forerunners of ancient Greek civilization.

6.2 *Greek Art*
Greek art and architecture reflected the culture's admiration of balance, harmony and idealized beauty, all of which stressed the supremacy of the human intellect.

6.3 *Roman Art*
Starting in the eighth century, Roman art and architecture adopted aspects of the cultures the empire came to rule while also making important contributions of its own.

---

6 Greek and Roman Art

WHILE THE MESOPOTAMIAN and Egyptian cultures prospered, two distinct cultures, the Minoans and the Mycenaeans, emerged along the Aegean Sea. The Minoans, who made their home on the island of Crete, created art that portrayed a relaxed life of luxury. On the mainland of Greece, the Mycenaeans fought to survive and left behind fortresses and monuments as proof of their struggle.

These Aegean cultures vanished, but they influenced the emergence of a great new culture in Greece which became the foundation of Western civilization. The Greeks strove for harmony and unity and placed human beings at the center of their culture. Much of their art focused on the idealized human form. It was in this form that the Greeks found the ultimate expression of beauty and harmony.

In the early 700s BC, the first Roman city-state began. It would grow to become the most powerful civilization in the Western world. The Romans created an empire which even today stands as a pinnacle of power and might.

Influenced greatly by the Greeks, the Romans made some of their greatest contributions in architecture. They were highly sophisticated, even by modern standards. They had fantastic public baths, luxurious houses, aqueducts that carried water all over the city, gigantic public arenas and marvelous bridges.

Greece and Rome provided the foundation upon which much of the art and architecture of the Western world is built. With every new generation, artists look back to see what lessons they can learn from the ancients.

6–a The Greeks often painted their sculpture, although little of the color remains today. Traces of paint can be seen on the hair of this figure.
Peplos Kore, about 530 BC. Marble, 4' (122 cm) high. Acropolis Museum, Athens.

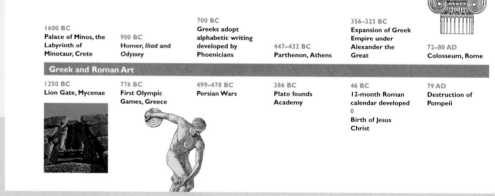

| 1600 BC Palace of Minos, the Labyrinth of Minotaur, Crete | 900 BC Homer, *Iliad* and *Odyssey* | 700 BC Greeks adopt alphabetic writing developed by Phoenicians | 447–432 BC Parthenon, Athens | 356–323 BC Expansion of Greek Empire under Alexander the Great | 72–80 AD Colosseum, Rome |

Greek and Roman Art

| 1250 BC Lion Gate, Mycenae | 776 BC First Olympic Games, Greece | 499–478 BC Persian Wars | 386 BC Plato founds Academy | 46 BC 12-month Roman calendar developed 0 Birth of Jesus Christ | 79 AD Destruction of Pompeii |

Objectives

Students should be able to:

Understand that civilizations along the Aegean existed simultaneously with Mesopotamian and Egyptian cultures.

Understand that Aegean cultures were the forebears of Greek society.

Identify how the Greeks used harmony and unity to portray the human form in an idealized manner.

Explain how Roman art and architecture adopted aspects of the cultures the empire conquered, particularly the Greeks.

Teach

Timeline

Have students review the timeline in Chapter 5 and find the notations for the tomb of King Tutankhamen (1352 BC), the Hanging Gardens of Babylon (700 BC), and the height of the Assyrian Empire (705–681 BC). Tell them to compare those notations with the ones on the timeline in Chapter 6. Now ask them if the cultures from Mesopotamia and Egypt were active at the same time as the Aegean, Greek and Roman. Share that Chapter 6 examines art that is the foundation for much of what follows in Western history.

Context

After students examine the *Column of Trajan* (figs.6–c, 6–43), ask them why they think this monument was built.

• Whom might the column have been made for? (The figure at the top of the column is St. Peter, but originally it was the emperor, Trajan.)

• What events might the 700-foot spiral relief describe? (The relief tells of the emperor's great military campaigns.)

• Since the scenes describe Trajan's war victories, what can students deduce about the importance of military supremacy to the Romans? Introduce the idea that the Roman's ability to win on the battlefield led them to become the strongest power in the West, starting in the eighth century.

Our love of what is beautiful does not lead to extravagance; our love of things of the mind does not make us soft.

Thucydides, Book II

Ancient Greece and Rome

The countries of Italy and Greece did not exist at the time of ancient Greece and Rome. They are shown on this map to provide points of reference.

6–b The Mycenaens excelled at the art of metalwork.
Vaphio Cup, one of two, see also fig.6–9.

6–d Many Greek works of art were destroyed. A great deal is known about them, however, through Roman copies. This is a detail of a Roman copy (in mosaic) of a Greek painting.
Head of Alexander the Great, *The Battle of Issus*, detail (fig.6–29).

6–c The Roman emperors frequently commissioned sculptural and architectural monuments to glorify their power and celebrate their victories.
Column of Trajan, detail (fig.6–43).

Quote

After reading the quote, ask students what beliefs the Greeks might have held about the concept of beauty and the importance of the human intellect. Review the quote again after students have completed the chapter to see if their interpretation of the quote has changed.

Map

Have students examine the map in the chapter opener and ask them to guess which culture would most likely have influenced the Romans when they began their campaigns in the eighth century BC. Students can observe Greece's proximity by referring to the contemporary world map at the back of the book.

Art

Direct students to the head of Alexander the Great. (Fig.6–29 shows the entire mosaic.)

• How many colors has the artist used to portray the image in intricate detail?

• Are students surprised that there are only four (yellow, red, white and black)?

• How are the colors used to create shadows and the illusion of three-dimensional depth? (The darker tones recede and the lighter ones project forward, enabling the artist to describe the battle in a vivid realism that is characteristic of late Hellenistic painting.)

• Students may be interested to know that the artist credited with having painted the original work on which this mosaic is based was a fourth-century Greek woman named Helena. Had they assumed that the artist was male? Ask them to consider that even though there are few recorded female painters in early Western art, it is possible that some of the countless anonymous creators might have been women.

Evaluate

Have students compare the head of Alexander the Great (fig.6–d) to the *Tutankhamen Mummy Case* (fig.5–a).

• Do students have a clearer sense of what Tutankhamen or Alexander the Great actually looked like?

• Which artwork seems to capture the person more naturalistically?

• What observation can be made about how artists in Egypt versus those in Greece treated the human figure?

• Although the mosaic appears more realistic, both portrayals are in fact idealized. Why might this be so? Ask: "If you were a ruler, would you want your blemishes to be immortalized for future generations or would you prefer to be shown without any human flaws?"

Reteach

Ask students to use the text, captions and images on pages 172 and 173 to help them deduce two or three characteristics of each of the cultures mentioned: Aegean, Greek and Roman.

Lesson 6.1

The rich Minoan and Mycenaean cultures along the Aegean were the forerunners of ancient Greek civilization.

Warm-up

Share with students some of the most essential aspects of Minoan culture—its vitality and how comfort and decoration were equally important to the people who lived on the beautiful, peaceful island of Crete. (Bring in a travel book about Crete or show students posters of the island to give them a sense of the environment.)

• Have students guess what images, architecture, colors, forms and styles might flow from such a civilization.

• Afterward, direct them to glance quickly at the Minoan images in Lesson 6.1. Do any of these, which brim with life and energy, correlate to their answers?

• Point out that for centuries previous to archaeological finds, this spirited culture was considered to be mythological, known only through Homer's *Iliad*, an epic poem developed out of older, legendary matter.

Objectives

Students should be able to:

Understand that two distinct cultures, Minoan and Mycenaean, emerged along the Aegean while the civilizations of Egypt and Mesopotamia still flourished.

Understand that the luxurious, relaxed life on Crete, where the Minoans flourished, generated a graceful and delightful style of art and architecture.

Describe the differences between the Mycenaeans, who built fortresses that reflected their warrior society, and the Minoans, who built pleasure palaces, reflecting the fact that they were mainly traders.

Vocabulary Definitions

fresco A method of painting in which pigments suspended in water are applied to a thin layer of wet plaster so that the plaster absorbs the color and the painting becomes part of the wall.

6.1 Aegean Art

WHILE THE CIVILIZATIONS in Egypt and Mesopotamia were flourishing, two distinct cultures developed along the Aegean Sea. One was on the island of Crete and is termed Minoan (after Minos, the Cretan king). The other was on the mainland of Greece at the city of Mycenae. For a long time both civilizations were considered mythological. They were known only through the *Iliad* by Homer. It was not until the late nineteenth century that these cities and their art were unearthed by archaeologists. These Aegean civilizations were the forerunners of Greek culture.

The Minoans were by far the richest of the Aegean civilizations. Bounded by the sea, the Cretans created a luxurious, relaxed way of life quite distinct from any other. Several "palace" centers developed on the island of Crete. The most important center was the huge complex at Knossos, called the Palace of Minos. The sprawling palace (fig.6–1) contained many rooms, running water, a sewage system, theater, storerooms (fig.6–2), terraces and elaborately decorated quarters for the rulers. Many *frescoes* (plaster wall paintings) decorated the interior of the palace. These frescoes provide a good idea of how these people lived.

The Mycenaeans were warriors instead of traders. They built citadels rather than pleasure palaces. Their hilltop fortresses were surrounded by walls of enormous stone blocks. The blocks were so large that later Greeks thought they were the work of the Cyclopes, a mythical race of one-eyed giants.

Key Notes
• Two distinct cultures, Minoan and Mycenaean, develop in the Aegean region.
• Minoan art is marked by a graceful ease and a delight in all forms of life.
• Mycenaean monuments reflect a protected and fortified environment.

Vocabulary
fresco

6–2. Storerooms housed jars of wine, grain, oil and honey.
View of jars in storeroom, Palace at Knossos, Crete.

Special Feature
Bull Dance Fresco

The Minoans and Mycenaeans appear to have had very different lifestyles. There is no specific historic reference that ties the two groups together. Both brought a remarkable vibrancy and extraordinary sense of beauty to their art.

These attributes are present in the *Bull Dance* (fig.6–3) fresco from the Minoan Palace of Knossos. It is the largest Minoan wall painting discovered so far. The fresco shows a ritual game in which the participants energetically vault over the bull's back. Two of the slim-waisted athletes are girls, denoted by their

Teach

Criticism/Aesthetics: Have students imagine coming upon remains of Minoan society such as the *Palace at Knossos*, (fig.6–1) the *Bull Dance* fresco (fig.6–3), the *Snake Goddess* (fig.6–4) and the *Octopus Jar* (fig.6–5).

• Ask them to describe how these objects differ in style from the Mycenaean works of the *Vaphio Cup* (fig.6–9), the *Funeral mask* (fig.6–8), and the *Lion Gate at Mycenae* (fig.6–7).

• Is there an equal sense of spontaneity and liveliness in their style? The realistic though heavier style of the Mycenaeans appears to reflect their status as warriors inhabiting the mainland as opposed to the Minoans, who were

primarily traders living on the island of Crete, which was naturally protected by the surrounding seas.

Art History: Tell students to compare the Palace at Knossos to the *Lion Gate at Mycenae* (fig.6–7) and to decide which would have been located on the mainland and which one on an isolated island protected by the surrounding waters. The Mycenaeans built citadels with thick protective walls in an effort to ward off their enemies. Nonetheless, their culture ended abruptly around 1100 BC, when they were invaded.

lighter skin color. There are so many depictions of bulls in Minoan painting and sculpture that the bull undoubtedly was a sacred animal. It is clear that bull-vaulting had something to do with a religious custom. We see an echo of this custom in the Greek legend of the youths and maidens sacrificed to the minotaur.

There is a certain ambiguity to the fresco that prevents us from understanding exactly what is going on here. The artist has idealized the ritual by stressing its harmonious, playful aspect rather than trying to provide the viewer with a factual representation of the event.

No temple architecture has been found on Crete or in Mycenae. Objects related in some way to religion (such as the *Bull Dance* fresco) have been found. Often, however, these objects raise more questions than they answer.

6–1 The plan of this palace is so complex that it survived in Greek legend as the labyrinth of the Minotaur.
Palace at Knossos, Crete, about 1600–1400 BC.

6–3 The young vaulters in this mural may have been Minoan gymnasts.
Bull Dance, from the Palace at Knossos, about 1500 BC. Fresco, 31 1/2" (80 cm) high, including border. Archaeological Museum, Heraklion, Crete.

Higher-Order Thinking Skills

The *Bull Dance* fresco may portray a religious ritual or a game. Ask students to choose either the ritual or the game as a basis for a description of the painting. Those who select the game option should also come up with the objective and rules of competition. Then have students compare their descriptions. How does the purpose of a work affect the way in which we describe it? Does not knowing the purpose hinder our ·descriptive efforts?

Evaluate

Assign students a portion of the *Iliad.* Challenge them to illustrate their section, keeping in mind what they have learned about the Aegean cultures from this lesson. However, encourage them not to imitate Minoan or Mycenaean styles but rather to develop their own visual expressions that will relate the essence of the story. Afterward, have students examine each other's work and discuss how it communicates the spirit of the Aegean civilizations. Can they find similarities and differences among the styles, colors or compositions that they used?

Reteach

Have students find the similarities and differences in how women are depicted in the Minoan fresco of the *Bull Dance* and the Egyptian works of *Mycerinus and His Queen* (fig.5–21) and *Katep and His Wife* (fig.5–22). If they need guidance, ask how the artists used color to provide a clue to the gender of the figures.

• Did they notice that the women in both cultures are depicted in lighter skin tones? Women were supposed to stay indoors, out of the sun, and thereby not be tanned like the men.

• Do the female figures in the Egyptian works or in the Minoan works seem more real? Actually, although the Minoan fresco is playful in comparison to the austere Egyptian double portraits, the women in both cultures are idealized rather than represented factually.

Contextual Information

Predecessors of the Minoans and Mycenaeans

Students can turn to fig.2–35 to view the work of the inhabitants of the Aegean during the Early Bronze Age. The *Lyre Player* is a fine example of Cycladic art. It predates by 500 years the Minoan and Mycenaean work shown here.

The Unearthing of Mycenae and Knossos

Heinrich Schliemann was an early archaeologist who selected his digging sites based on Homer's writings. For twenty years this amateur German archaeologist uncovered cities—Troy, Mycenae, Orchomenos and Tiryns—that Homer had written about.

In 1870 Schliemann dug into a large mound in Greece and found layers of fortified cities built on top of one another. At Mycenae he found massive fortress-palaces, rich tombs with large quantities of gold jewelry, cups, ornaments and inlaid weapons.

In 1900 archaeologist Sir Arthur Evans went to Crete looking for what many thought was Homer's mythological city of Minos. On the island of Crete at the site of Knossos he uncovered the palaces of the sea-kings.

6–4 This poised young woman controls the snakes in what may have been a religious ritual.
Snake Goddess, about 1550 BC. Ivory and gold, 6" (16 cm) high, from Knossos. Museum of Fine Arts, Boston, gift of Mrs. W. Scott Fitz.

6–6 The artist of this relief has chosen to depict a joyous aspect of the human character.
Harvester Vase, about 1500 BC. Steatite, 4 1/2" (11 cm) wide, from Haiga Triada. Archaeological Museum, Herakleion.

Minoan Art

Comfort and decoration were equally important in Minoan life. The facades of buildings appear to have been brightly colored. The plastered walls inside were painted red, yellow or blue. In the more important rooms there were figurative paintings and occasionally stucco reliefs. Unfortunately, only fragments of these works remain, but they clearly show the vigor and spontaneity of Minoan art. Minoan culture and art was greatly influenced by the sea. Minoan frescoes were characterized by lightness and freely shaped forms. The forms had a rhythmic quality inspired by the sea.

The lively spontaneity of Minoan art, so representative of their style of life, is portrayed beautifully in the Queen's Megaron in the palace of Knossos. Here, the elaborate frescoes painted on the plastered walls depict many aspects of Cretan life. There are processions and ceremonies. Images from nature appear, such as birds, animals and flowers. The sea and its creatures, such as dolphins, are also featured.

Minoan sculpture was small and, like the frescoes, probably decorated the living quarters of merchant rulers. The *Snake Goddess* (fig.6–4), carved from ivory and decorated with gold bands, may be the goddess of an unknown religion or simply a daring young woman playing with snakes.

Minoan pottery often was decorated with designs of plant and animal life. In the illustrated example, the octopus (fig.6–5) conforms so wonderfully with the contours of the vase that it seems to be floating in the open sea rather than painted on a hard, curving surface. The relief on the *Harvester Vase* (fig.6–6) brims with energy and life. Muscular men with scythes and rakes appear to be celebrating a harvest festival. Three singers, led by a fourth, have burst into song. So great is their enthusiasm that the leader's chest is swelled enough to show his ribs.

The Minoan civilization came to an abrupt halt. The people disappeared and no one really knows what happened. Perhaps future archaeologists will answer this question.

6–5 Why do you think marine life was a favorite subject of Minoan artists?
Octopus Jar, about 1500 BC. 11" (28 cm) high, from Palaikastro. Archaeological Museum, Herakleion.

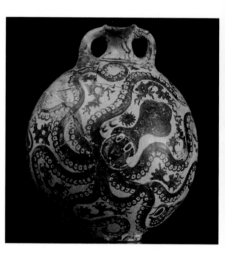

1150 BC
Colossal basalt sculptures of human heads, Olmec Civilization, Mexico

1600 BC
Colonization of the Pacific Islands

1500 BC
Spun cotton invented, India

World Cultural Timeline

1200 BC
Pictograph writing system develops in China

Interdisciplinary Connection

Literature: Heinrich Schliemann (1822–1890) was considered unreasonable for basing his excavations on the writings of Homer. Was he? What did Homer write that directed Schliemann's work? (the *Odyssey*)

Multicultural Connection

The Olmec Civilization

The Olmec were one of the earliest civilizations that flourished along the tropical central coast of the Gulf of Mexico. Between 1500 and 200 BC they built major ceremonial centers at La Venta, Tres Zapotes and San Lorenzo, and in the rain forests of the Mexican states of Veracruz and Tabasco. Some Olmec artifacts from sites in the Valley of Mexico and the distant highlands suggest that they traded with other societies over a wide area.

The Olmec, considered to be the "mother culture" of Mesoamerican civilizations, developed planned cities, hieroglyphic writing and a calendar. They were the first of the Mesoamericans to use stone for architecture and for sculpture. The stone used for their sculptures had to be quarried and transported from the Tuxtla Mountains, sixty miles to the west.

The Olmec religious centers, built on top of high hills, contained large pyramids surrounded by altars, where rituals were performed to please their gods. It is here that a number of very impressive colossal stone heads of males have been found, buried under the ceremonial pavement.

Mycenaean Art

The outer gateway of the citadel at Mycenae is called the *Lion Gate* (fig.6–7). It is topped by a huge, triangular-shaped, carved stone slab. Depicted on the stone are two majestic standing lions flanking a Minoan-type column. Notice the massive stone block that acts as a lintel over the opening. The other large blocks are cut to fit exactly together.

In 1876, excavations at Mycenae uncovered beehive tombs of massive proportions and sunken royal graves. The graves contained a dazzling display of objects in gold, silver and other metals. The *Funeral Mask* (fig.6–8) is a thin sheet of beaten gold. It was probably intended to cover the face of a deceased ruler of about 1500 BC.

The *Vaphio Cups* (figs.6–9, 6–b) from a grave in Laconia are some of the most famous gold pieces found at Mycenae. The lively reliefs on these beautifully crafted works illustrate several ways the Mycenaeans captured wild bulls.

Recently, several ivory sculptures and some paintings have been uncovered. Still, little is known of the development of Mycenaean culture. Mycenaean history abruptly ended about 1100 BC when the Dorians invaded from the north.

By 1110 BC, the Bronze Age culture on the Greek mainland, attacked by various catastrophes, had collapsed. For the next four hundred years a dreary and subdued era swept Greece. Archaeological evidence for this period suggests material poverty and social insecurity on a grand scale. Gone was the joyful expression of the Minoans and the realistic art of the Mycenaeans.

6–7 These two lions flank a column which may represent the power of the Mycenaean king. Although the stone has been eroded with time, the straining muscles of the lions are still evident.

Lion Gate at Mycenae, about 1250 BC. Limestone relief sculpture, about 9 1/2' (3 m) high.

6–9 How does the artist make use of light and shadow to bring the relief to life? *Vaphio Cup,* about 1500 BC. Gold, about 3 1/2" (9 cm) high, from Laconia. National Archaeological Museum, Athens.

6–8 At one time this mask was thought to be the death mask of King Agamemnon from Homer's *Iliad.*
Funeral mask, about 1500 BC. Beaten gold, about 12" (30 cm) high, from Royal Tombs, Mycenae. National Archaeological Museum, Athens.

Lesson 6.1 Review

1 Why did people suspect that the Minoan and Mycenaean civilizations had existed even before archaeologists discovered their ruins?
2 Describe the Palace of Knossos.
3 What is happening in the *Bull Dance* fresco?

Of which contemporary Spanish sport does this remind you?
4 List some characteristics of Minoan frescoes.
5 Draw a sketch of the *Lion Gate at Mycenae.* Identify the lintel on your sketch.

These artifacts, carved with stone tools and weighing up to 20 tons, are believed by some to be portrait carvings of actual Olmec rulers. After their mysterious decline, the Olmec continued to influence later civilizations in Mexico and Central America.

• How do you think the Olmec transported the stone from the mountains?

• What evidence do we have that the Olmec were an organized society?

(See Chapter 4, page 134 for more information about the Olmec and other Mesoamerican civilizations.)

Lesson 6.1 Review Answers

1 Homer told of them in the *Iliad*.
2 This sprawling palace had many rooms, running water, a sewage system, a theater, storerooms, terraces and elaborately decorated quarters for the rulers. The interior walls were painted with frescoes which give us clues about how the inhabitants lived.
3 Two slim-waisted girls vault over a bull's back in a ritual game. Although this is not a bullfight; it might be an ancestor to Spanish bullfights.

4 Lightness, freely shaped forms with a rhythmic quality inspired by the sea, vigor and spontaneity
5 Lintel (See illustration below.)

Lesson 6.2

Greek art and architecture reflected the culture's admiration of balance, harmony and idealized beauty, all of which stressed the supremacy of the human intellect and power of the mind.

Warm-up

Ask students whether they can name any buildings in the their community that combine art and architecture. Share with them that the ancient Greeks included a great deal of sculpture on their architecture. Have them read the captions for the *Three Goddesses* (fig.6–14) and the *Mounted Procession* (fig.6–15) in order to figure out where these works were originally installed on *The Parthenon*. (See fig.6–22.) (Note how the shape of these sculptural groups corresponds to their initial location on the building. See pages 181–182 for specific information.)

Objectives

Students should be able to:

Understand that Greek artists used harmony and symmetry to express the idealized human form, which was central to their culture.

Describe how concepts of proportion, balance and unity were the driving force behind Greek achievements in architecture, mathematics, science, philosophy, literature and sports.

Vocabulary Definitions

contrapposto (kon-tra-*pohs*-toh) Technique of sculpting a human figure in a pose that shows the weight of the body in balance. With weight on one leg, the shoulders and hips counterbalance each other in a natural way so that the figure does not fall over.

frieze (freeze) Any horizontal band, decorated with moldings or patterns, either painted or carved, usually at the upper end of a wall; specifically in Greek architecture, the middle layer (plain or carved) of an entablature.

pediment The triangular area over the entablature in Classical Greek architecture, formed by the ends of a sloping roof and the cornice.

architrave (*arch*-i-trave) The main horizontal beam at the bottom of an entablature, resting on the capitals of columns. Often made of several lintels to stretch the length of the building.

6.2 Greek Art

HUMAN BEINGS were central to the Greek culture. They gave their gods human form. The Greek ideal was to create the perfect individual. This would be accomplished by achieving a perfect balance of intellectual and physical discipline. The Greeks considered the human body beautiful, perfectly balanced and harmonious. They made it the focal point of most of their painting and sculpture.

The key concepts of proportion, balance and unity were the driving force of many of the Greeks' achievements in architecture, mathematics, science, philosophy, poetry and architecture. Everything had its ideal form.

Greek artists worked in a cultural environment that encouraged art of all types. They were free to experiment as long as they worked toward the common goal of beauty and harmony. They even signed their works.

Key Notes

- The human being was placed at the center of Greek culture.
- The Greeks encouraged all forms of art.
- Proportion, balance and unity were key Greek ideals.
- The human body was considered beautiful and perfectly proportioned.

Vocabulary

contrapposto
frieze
pediment
architrave
cornice
metope
triglyph
entasis
caryatids
encaustic
amphora
hydria

600–480 BC
The Archaic period

323–150 BC
Hellenistic period

Major Periods in Greek Art

480–323 BC
The Classic Period

Special Feature
The Kritios Boy

The development of Greek art is easily seen in its sculpture. Like Egyptian sculptures, early Greek figures were stylized. There is one sculpture that survives today, however, which shows us how artists began to move away from this rather restricted way of depicting the human form. The figure has been attributed to the Athenian sculptor Kritios and has come to be known as the *Kritios Boy* (figs.6–10, 6–11). The first important point about the *Kritios Boy* is that he really stands. His back leg is not bound to a block for balance. Openings are seen between arms and side. Previously, the figure was supported by part of the original stone block. The *Kritios Boy* stands free.

Notice how the right hip drops down and inward. The knee of the forward leg is lower than that of the other leg. The weight rests mainly on the left leg. The faint S-curve of the body causes a subtle sense of movement. The artist had grasped the concept of weight shift. Thus, the *Kritios Boy* stands in a relaxed, natural stance—as we would in the same pose.

The Italian word, **contrapposto** (counterpose), is used to describe this position where the engaged leg is in the forward position. Showing a truly relaxed body was a very important discovery. For only when the Greek sculptor had mastered the relaxed body could he begin to show the body in motion. Movement existed in Greek art prior to this, but it was very mechanical and inflexible. The *Kritios Boy* gives us a sense of the vitality that infuses our own bodies. The sculpture truly has come to life.

---

cornice (*kor*-niss) Any projecting ornamental molding along the top of a building, wall, arch, etc.; also, the topmost projecting part of an entablature in a Classical Greek building.

metope (*met*-oh-pee) The carved or plain areas between the triglyphs in the frieze of a Doric building.

triglyph (*try*-glif) A group of three vertical ridges alternating with a plain metope in the frieze of a Doric Greek building.

entasis (*en*-tah-sis) The subtle convex swelling of a Classical Greek column shaft.

caryatid (care-ee-*ah*-tid) A support or column in the form of a human figure, usually female. See *atlantes*.

encaustic (en-*koz*-tik) A method of painting on a ground, with colors dissolved in hot wax; also, a work of art produced by this technique.

amphora (am-*for*-ah) A storage jar having an egg-shaped body, a foot and two handles, each attached at the neck and shoulders of the jar.

hydria (hi-dree-ah) A large jug used to carry water.

Teach

Criticism: Ask students to suggest adjectives that describe both the *Kritios Boy* (figs.6–10, 6–11) and *The Parthenon* (fig.6–22). Would they say that these works are wild, chaotic and emotional?

- Challenge them to analyze the composition of the works to find evidence

6–10 To better understand the distribution of weight represented in this figure, stand up and mimic its pose.
Kritios Boy, about 480 BC. Marble, 34" (86 cm) high. Acropolis Museum, Athens.

6–11 This sculpture was found amid the rubble on the Acropolis.
Kritios Boy, front view.

Contextual Information
The Greeks and the Human Form

In the pre-Greek world nudity was sometimes a sign of slavery. The Greeks, however, viewed the human body as the epitome of perfection. The conventions of the pre-Greek world must have inhibited the careful study of the human body, but the shift in attitude with the evolution of Greek culture meant that the human form became a focal point for artists. The result was a rapid and dramatic development in the Greek's ability to portray the human body with great confidence and accuracy. (It might be useful now to review with students the discussion of the nude on page 24.)

Higher-Order Thinking Skills

There are stances that are typical of different periods of art. Some are physically plausible; some are not. Have students try the typical Egyptian stance of feet and head in profile and torso frontal; they can then try the stance of the *Kritios Boy*. What evolved in the portrayal of the human figure?

of the Greek's fascination with harmony, grace, balance and precision. For instance, if they drew a vertical line directly down the center of either work, would the halves be perfectly balanced?

• How do both the figure's pose and the regular repetition of the Doric columns around the Parthenon evoke a sense of grace?

• How does precision come into play in both?

• What might the Greek artistic style tell us about the types of human characteristics that the culture honored?

• Ask: "How can the artwork support your answers?"

Evaluate

Direct students to look back at the Egyptian *Greenfield Papyrus* (fig.5–28) and to compare it to the *Red-Figured Hydria* (fig.6–28).

• In which work do the figures appear more realistic?

• How does the Greek artist Meidias evoke an active sense of movement?

• Compare the poses and the use of line in the two works. Which do students prefer? They should use the art to support their decisions.

Reteach

The Greeks greatly honored the human body and power of the human intellect. What values does American culture

consider important today? Direct students to look for visual clues in media images. Hold a debate on the various possibilities.

Although the Greeks idolized the human body, presenting it in perfect balance and harmony, is anyone truly without some physical, mental or emotional flaw? If all people were perfect, how would we define individuality—or humanness—which depends on our unique qualities? Divide the class in half and have one group prepare a defense supporting the perfection of all human beings and the other arguing for the individuality that comes from our variations. Ask students to think about how these arguments might be extended to thinking about tolerance for people from different religious, cultural, political or ethnic backgrounds.

Contextual Information

Charioteer of Delphi

The *Charioteer of Delphi* (fig.6–13) originally was accompanied by a chariot and horses. The charioteer represents the driver of King Polyzalos of Gela. Ask students to try to imagine the charioteer as part of its original grouping. How would our impression of the figure change if we were to see it as it was originally meant to be seen?

Sculpture

The sculpted predecessors of the *Kritios Boy* were limited to rigid standing figures of young men and women. The sculpture of a young man was called a *Kouros* (fig.6–12). The life-size nude youth represented either Apollo or an ideal athlete. The figures were stylized and did not represent real people. The figures face toward the front. In this 600 BC example, the left foot is slightly forward. Both arms are held stiffly at their sides. Kneecaps are slightly curved. The hair is stylized into small ringlets that fall in a blocky mass to the shoulders. The mouth is set in a faint smile. In fact, the smile is so characteristic of the figures sculpted at this time, it has been termed an Archaic smile, after the name given to the period.

Over the course of the next seventy-five years, this stylization changed to a more natural and realistic representation of the human figure. Greek artists began sculpting what they saw and observed rather than creating idealized forms from memory.

The female figure, or *Kore* (fig.6–a), was a freestanding clothed figure of an idealized young girl. The clothing varied, depending upon the regions where the sculptors worked. The Kore figures were painted, as were most Greek sculptures, to appear more natural. Notice the folds of cloth, the long braided hair, the traces of color left on the work, and the hint of an Archaic smile.

The Archaic period comes to a close in about 480 BC. The *Kritios Boy* dates from this time and, as we have seen, it marks a change in how the Greeks depict the human form.

The Classic period began after 480 BC, when the Greeks defeated the Persian fleet at Salamis. In the early part of the Classic period, the Greeks enjoyed a period of peace in which the arts flourished. Individualism of ideas, thoughts and artistic representation was honored.

The *Charioteer of Delphi* (fig.6–13) is typical of the changes that took place. The figure is cast in bronze and is the earliest of the few remaining Greek bronzes. The rest were destroyed, lost or melted down for later ammunition or weapons of war. The charioteer was originally

6–12 Note that this figure is free standing. *Statue of a Youth, Kouros,* about 600 BC. Marble, 76" (193 cm) high. The Metropolitan Museum of Art, New York, Fletcher Fund, 1932.

6–13 This figure originally stood on a chariot drawn by four horses. *Charioteer of Delphi,* about 470 BC. Bronze, 71" (180 cm) high. Archaeological Museum, Delphi.

750 BC
First goldworking in S. America

563 BC
Birth of Buddha, India

World Cultural Timeline

750 BC
Kingdom of Nubia founded, Africa

551 BC
Confucius born, China

Multicultural Connection

The Kingdom of Nubia

The Kingdom of Nubia, in Africa, existed between 725 BC and 350 AD, in what is now Sudan, a country of more than 100 ethnic tribal groups from many regions. To the ancient Egyptians, the land was called Kush. To the Greeks, it was part of Abyssinia, a place whose name some believe came from an Arabic word meaning "mixed," a reference to the many ethnic groups that lived in the region. To the Romans, it was Nubia (from *nub,* which meant "slave" in a local language). And to the Arabs, it was *bilad as sudan* (land of the blacks).

The Nuba people lived in farming villages in the northeast Nuba Mountains. The young men decorated themselves with red ocher and simple hairstyles, gradually adding more color and more elaborate hairstyles as they grew older and their tribal status increased.

Sometime after 2600 BC, Egypt conquered the settlements along the upper Nile, called the land Kush and developed a new civilization that was greatly influenced by Egyptian culture. The Kushites adopted the Egyptian idea of a god-king, learned to write in hieroglyphics and imitated the Egyptian style of pyramid building. The Kushites in turn conquered Egypt in 750 BC and controlled it for about eighty years. Kush became an early center of iron

working, an activity that brought economic prosperity through trade. Kush itself existed as an independent kingdom several times, until it collapsed about 350 AD.

Confucius

Confucius, a Chinese philosopher, was one of the most influential figures in Chinese history. Confucius, whose original name was K'ung Ch'iu, or Master K'ung, was born about 551 BC to an upper-class family. *Confucius* is a Latinized version of his name. He founded Confucianism, one of the traditional philosophies of China, based upon goodness for its own sake.

6–14 Sculptors dampened the drapery of their models in order to get every fold just right to portray the form of the model.
Three Goddesses, about 435 BC. Marble, over life-size, east pediment of the Parthenon. British Museum, London.

polished. The eyes were made of glass paste, and lips and eyelashes were made of inlaid copper. In most later bronzes of Greece and Rome, these features are now missing and dark holes remain for the lost eyes. The cloth folds, muscles and facial features are natural. The Archaic smile is replaced by a look of calm and self-control, which symbolizes a classic balance of emotion, personality and physical ability. The features and pose remain a bit rigid and severe.

The Age of Pericles was the culmination of the Classic period in Greek sculpture and architecture. Athens was safe and prosperous, and the arts were admired and loved as never before and seldom since. The Athenians decorated the most prominent building in their city, the Parthenon, in their most ambitious sculptural undertaking. Both the east and west ends of the building were filled with statues that were larger than life. A continuous *frieze* (or sculpted band) ran for 525 feet around the top of the wall of the cella, which contained a huge statue of Athena. All the sculptures were produced in a period of twelve years by a team of sculptors under the direction of Phidias. Many of the works were later destroyed. In 1801,

Lord Elgin collected most of what remained and sent them back to England for safekeeping.

Some of the sculptures were designed to fit exactly into the **pediment**, or flat triangular area, at each end of the Parthenon. The *Three Goddesses* (from the east pediment) have remained as a group (fig.6–14). The fascinating drapery is startling in the way it seems to cling to the bodies. The clothing is no longer stylized or severe, but falls in natural folds and creases. These folds create visual movement. They lead the viewer's eye over the bodies and to the central event in the pediment composition, the birth of Athena.

The frieze around the inner wall depicts a procession, occurring once every four years, in which the youth of Athens pay tribute to Athena. The relief sculpture shows a multitude of figures and horses. One of the most impressive sections (fig.6–15) depicts horses and riders, sometimes four abreast. To sculpt this much depth in the shallow space of a few inches took great skill on the part of the Classical Greek sculptors. Anatomy, movement, rhythm and a convincing suggestion of space are all handled with superb control. The figures closest to the viewer are the most round. The second and third layers are

6–15 The parade of riders is part of a relief that continues around the entire inner wall of the Parthenon. The sculptor makes masterful use of a number of the elements of art and principles of design. Can you name at least three?
Mounted Procession (detail), 432 BC. Marble, 42" (106 cm) high, north frieze of the Parthenon. British Museum, London.

Higher-Order Thinking Skills

1 Use tracing paper and colored pencils to speculate about the original painted colors of the *Kouros* (fig.6–12) and the *Peplos Kore* (fig.6–a). Put colored tracings on the bulletin board to share and discuss. What difference does color make?

2 Have students set up a three-way comparison with the *Peplos Kore,* the *Kouros,* and the *Kritios Boy* (figs.6–10, 6–11). Direct them to analyze the poses and the details of each carving to determine which two were created around the same time and which sculpture was made during a later period. If they need a clue, explain that early Greek sculpture, like Egyptian art, was rather stylized. However, later Greek artists eventually moved away from static, restricted forms toward showing figures in a natural mode, as though taken directly from real life. Have students write a list of all the aspects of the *Kritios Boy* that make it seem more real than the highly stylized, earlier *Kore* and *Kouros.*

Following the death of his parents, poverty compelled him to go into government service for the chief of the district in which he lived. Meanwhile, he began his career as a teacher, traveling about and gaining disciples. The principles of Confucius' philosophy were not put into writing until much later but were handed down through the generations by his disciples.

During the second half of the Zhou dynasty (ca. 1028–221 BC), feudalism, disorder, corruption and unrest were rampant in China. Because Confucius believed that social order and good government could be restored in China, he sought a position as an administrator, whereby he could put his theories into practice and establish reforms. However, he was unsuccessful in achieving the position.

• The Chinese believed that a just ruler had divine authority and approval known as the mandate of heaven. How were the teachings of Confucius linked to this belief?

• Confucius said that five basic relationships—between ruler and subject, father and son, husband and wife, older brother and younger brother, and friend and friend—could restore China's society. What did he mean by this?

(For more information about Chinese life and art during the Zhou dynasty, see Chapter 4, page 94.)

Contextual Information

The Greeks and Sports

Greeks of the Classic period had a keen interest in sports. Earlier, in the eighth century BC, the Olympic games began as a part of thanksgiving festivals. The games were later held every four years in honor of Zeus, chief of the Greek gods.

So important were these games that all wars were suspended while they were being held. Winners of the games were given special honors; poems were written about them; and statues were dedicated to them. Winners in Olympia also received crowns of olive leaves cut with a gold sickle from a sacred tree near the Temple of Zeus. Other cities gave different prizes, including a celery wreath at Nemea, shields at Argos and pine-needle wreaths at Isthmia.

Only men took part in the Olympic games; women were not permitted on the grounds at festival time. The men were trained for the games in gymnasiums, sometimes to music. Have students turn to fig.2–7 to see the well-known sculpture, *Discobolus*, which depicts a man throwing a discus. (This figure is also known as the *Discus Thrower*.)

6–17 Most Greek bronzes are only known to us through Roman copies in marble such as this one.
Dying Gaul, about 230–220 BC. Roman, marble copy of bronze original, life-size, Pergamon. Capitoline Museum, Rome.

6–16 This figure only recently came to light. There may be other Greek bronzes waiting to be discovered.
Lysippus, *Statue of a Victorious Athlete (The Getty Bronze),* about 330 BC. Bronze, life-size. The J. Paul Getty Museum, Malibu.

shallower, and the background is flat. Originally, the frieze, like other parts of the Parthenon, was brightly painted.

The Peloponnesian War disrupted the glory of Classical Greece. The fourth century saw a subtle change in the sculpture. A bronze figure, attributed to the Greek artist Lysippus, recently has been found in the Mediterranean Sea. Known as *The Getty Bronze* (fig.6–16), it is a victorious athlete crowning himself with a laurel wreath. Lysippus made the heads of figures slightly smaller and the bodies more slender. Notice the slight S-curve of the body caused by the centering of weight on the figure's right leg. The left leg is relaxed and does not support the weight of the body. The figure has a natural feeling. Facial features, hands and muscles are exact in their detail. The hair seems unruly and natural for an athlete. Lysippus

became the official sculptor of Alexander the Great and his court.

Greek conquest of the Near East and Egypt and the spread of its civilization to the borders of India resulted in the mingling of Eastern and Western ideas. The art of this period, called Hellenistic, became more concerned with action and emotion. In art of the Classic period, these elements would have been kept under complete control.

The *Dying Gaul* (fig.6–17) is a Roman copy in marble of a Greek bronze of this time. It is life-size and shows the struggle of a wounded man about to die. The sculptor captured the ethnic features of face and hair that characterized the Gauls. The figure leans heavily on his arms because his legs no longer can help him move. There is agony in the pose and in the face of the warrior. Death seems very real and not as heroic as it might have been shown several centuries earlier.

Interdisciplinary Connection

Geography: Very early in recorded history, countries were trading among themselves over vast distances. Traders recognized that two things were essential to successful and prosperous trade: safe travel through hostile territory and maps that would make travel as quick as possible.

The earliest map that has been preserved is a Babylonian clay tablet from the sixth century BC. The first Greek mapmakers were geometers and astronomers who did a great deal of

speculating rather than on-site observation. Greek maps were drawn on tablets of wood or metal. The ancient Egyptians, ca. 1320 BC, drew their maps of the location of gold mines on papyrus.

In the second century AD Ptolemy wrote the *Guide to Geography,* which contained 26 maps of various countries. Rediscovery of Ptolemy's work in the fifteenth century—at the time that Portuguese and Spanish explorers were looking for routes to India—played a major role in the redrawing and printing of more accurate maps.

6–18 Powerful and just touching down to land, this Nike once overlooked the harbor at Samothrace.
Nike of Samothrace, about 190 BC. Marble, 8' (244 cm) high. The Louvre, Paris.

6–19 How has the artist used movement and line to convey the age and weariness of this woman?
Old Market Woman, 2nd century BC. Marble, 49 1/2" (126 cm) high. The Metropolitan Museum of Art, Rogers Fund, 1909.

Nike of Samothrace (fig.6–18) is perhaps one of the greatest of Hellenistic sculptures. Carved about 200 BC, it is the symbol of Winged Victory, her great wings spread wide as she lands on the prow of a ship. The force of the wind whips the drapery into wonderfully animated folds. Because of this effect, the space around the Nike, in front and behind her, become important parts of the sculpture itself—a concept that will not be used again for many centuries.

In contrast to the sweeping and energetic forward movement of the Nike is the bent and almost dragging motion of the *Old Market Woman* (fig.6–19). Here the artist's interest is in the realistic, rather painful portrayal of a tired, burdened woman. The sole focus of Greek art is no longer perfectly beautiful and ideal beings.

Higher-Order Thinking Skills

1 Ask students to discuss how the viewer is required to become emotionally involved when encountering the Hellenistic sculptures on these pages (*Dying Gaul, Nike of Samothrace, Old Market Woman*). How does this contrast with Classical figures such as the Getty bronze (fig.6–16)?

2 Stimulate a discussion with the following: In ancient Greece, for the first time in Western history, artists began to sign their works. Since artists had not previously laid claim to their creations, could this new occurrence have signaled a change in social status for Greek artists? Artists were no longer anonymous craftspeople but were unique individuals producing works distinct from that of others. What ramifications might this change in status have had? For instance, do you tend to give more serious consideration to artwork made by someone whose name is highly recognized as opposed to work by an unknown artist? Discuss your point of view with a classmate who has the opposite viewpoint.

Cooperative Learning

Many parts of the Parthenon frieze are in the British Museum and are known as the Elgin Marbles. Lord Elgin said that he removed them from Greece to preserve them from the violence in that country in the early nineteenth century. Greece would like to have the works back, but they are a major attraction for the London museum. Have students argue for one side or the other in the dispute, perhaps using information researched at the school or public library.

Formal statements of position give each person in a group the opportunity to voice an opinion and to hear that of others. Because such statements are usually subject to time limits, it is important to be succinct.

When each has a position about the marbles, with supporting data, ideas about rightful ownership, and so on, pair off the students to hear each other's position and make suggestions for improvement. Set a time limit for each presentation so each listener can time the presenter. After time to make changes and improvements, pair off students again to make their practice presentation to a different listener. Again, suggestions should be made. It is the listener's job to make his or her partner's presentation as good as possible. Students then make their position statements to the class. You may grade the presentations and terminate the activity here with a tally of the positions, or committees can be formed to develop plans of action, which can then be presented to the class. Videotaping each position statement and presentation can help students develop a sense of how they convey their ideas to an audience.

Contextual Information

Pericles

Athenians fled their cities just before the Persians invaded the peninsula in 480 BC. The Greeks regrouped and within a year drove out the Persian army. The Athenians also liberated other Greek cities and together they formed the Delian League in 478 BC.

With the enthusiasm of victory and the financial support of the league, the Greeks started on reconstruction of the cities that had been badly damaged during the wars. When Pericles became ruler in 461 BC, Athens had a population of approximately 230,000. He ruled until 429 BC and encouraged building projects and the arts as a way to occupy the people in a productive manner and to increase the beauty of the cities. It was at this time that a number of the buildings on the Acropolis were built.

Plutarch in *Pericles* said that when Pericles was criticized for "gilding and beautifying...and adorning [Athens] with precious marbles, and statues, and temples, worth a thousand talents," he replied that "after the city had provided all that was necessary for war, it should devote its surplus money to the erection of buildings which would be a glory to it for all ages."

Plutarch (ca. 46–ca. 120 AD) comments on the speed with which these buildings were erected. "This makes Pericles' work all the more wonderful, because it was built in a short time, and yet has lasted for ages...even at the present day the work looks as fresh as ever...."

Architecture

Greek architecture developed from a heavy and ponderous appearance in the Archaic period to a light and airy feel in the Classic period. Most Greek architectural construction was focused around temples. Because the public generally was not allowed into the temples, architects designed impressive exteriors.

The concern of the Greeks for harmony and proportion is evident in their architecture. They saw public buildings as organic units that must be organized into orderly arrangements of parts. This attitude led to definite systems of construction that were called "the orders" (fig.6–20). The *Doric order* developed in mainland areas. The *Ionic order* evolved in the islands and the coast of Asia Minor. The *Corinthian order* was used in Hellenistic times and later in Roman civilization. The orders consisted of detailed rules for construction, based on proportions and an integration of the parts of the buildings. They were a means of breaking down complex forms into simple units that made up the whole.

In the Doric order, for example, the shaft of the column rests on the topmost step. It tapers toward the top in a slightly swelling curve. Atop the shaft is the capital, which has a round cushion-like molding capped by a square block. Resting on the capitals are the **architrave**, frieze and **cornice**. The architrave is the lintel that stretches horizontally above the columns. The frieze consists of oblong panels (**metopes**, often carved) and square blocks with upright channels (**triglyphs**). The crowning member of the superstructure is the cornice. The wide flat band of the cornice casts a shadow on the frieze below. The flat triangular space under the cornice is the pediment, which was often filled with sculpture.

Archaic Doric temples were powerful structures, and heavy in appearance. The *Temple of Hera* (called "The Basilica") at Paestum (fig.6–21) was built about 550 BC. The temple has very heavy columns that bulge and taper toward the top. The capitals are huge and flat.

The Doric style reached maturity during the Classic period in the

6–21 Look at the drums of the columns. What order is the temple? "The Basilica" (*Temple of Hera*), about 550 BC. Paestum, Italy.

6–22 The Athenians' celebration of their patron goddess Athena focused on ceremonies held here. Iktinos and Kallikrates, *The Parthenon*, 448–432 BC. The Acropolis, Athens.

The Parthenon

Phidias was in charge of the building of the Parthenon, which was dedicated to the goddess of Athens and its people. The object deemed most holy in the city was an image of Athena, which legend said was dropped from heaven.

The statue of Athena was wrapped in gold in such a way that it could be taken off and weighed to ensure the honesty of the workers. This aspect of the design was useful to Phidias when he was accused of stealing gold from the sculpture.

6–20 While the idea of an organized system is the same for all three orders, the particular details differ from one order to another.
Doric, Ionic and Corinthian orders. Reproduced by permission of Harcourt Brace Jovanovich, Inc., from *Art in Perspective: A Brief History* by Henri Dorra.

Higher-Order Thinking Skills

Help students use the chart to identify the orders on each of the buildings and to note any deviation from the ideal of the form. They should form the habit of identifying the orders of new buildings they see.

Parthenon (fig.6–22) in Athens. The architects Iktinus and Kallikrates built it from 448 to 432 BC, a short time for so huge a project. It is the central building of the Athenian Acropolis, which contains several other temples and Classic structures. Compare it with the *Temple of Hera* at Paestum. It is larger, but seems less massive. Proportions have been carefully readjusted. The columns are more slender, and the space between columns is wider. The slightly curved tapering (or **entasis**) of the columns is less pronounced. Capitals are smaller and less flaring, and the cornice projects less. The columns lean slightly inward, and the corner columns are closer to their neighbors than the rest of the columns. All these visual refinements help give the structure a feeling of great harmony, balance and organic unity.

Although the ruins of the building are clean marble, originally many areas were painted, especially where sculptures were present. The cella contained a huge statue of Athena.

6–23 This small Ionic temple is very well preserved. Most temples are now only ruins.
Kallikrates, *Temple of Athena Nike*, about 425 BC. The Acropolis, Athens.

Inquiry

There are many books and articles about the Parthenon and its original appearance. At least three topics could be the focus of student inquiry: (1) its original appearance and surroundings; (2) the damage it has sustained in wars and how tourism and pollution are now affecting it; and (3) the study of the myths depicted in the sculpture.

Contextual Information

Proportion

Greek artists worked according to rules of proportion that they felt led to objects of real beauty.

Polykleitos developed proportion rules that include the statement that beauty lies in the "proportions of all the fingers to the palm and the wrist, and of these to the forearm, and of the forearm to the upper arm and of all the other parts to each other...."

In architecture, too, the Greeks had rules. The Parthenon, with its Doric columns, adheres to the building designs of the Greeks. The Doric plan has three "rules." (1) a triglyph must be exactly over the center of each column; (2) a triglyph must be over the center of each space between the columns; and (3) triglyphs on the frieze must meet exactly at the corners.

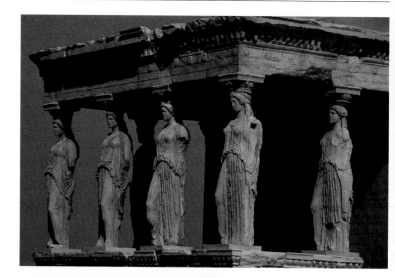

6–24 Notice how the sculptor has created figures which have a feeling of rigidity appropriate to their function as columns, yet they also have a sense of life.
The Porch of the Maidens, the Erechtheum, about 421–405 BC. The Acropolis, Athens.

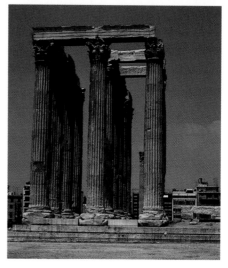

6–25 The Greeks began construction of this temple, but the Romans completed it.
Cossutius, *Temple of the Olympian Zeus,* about 174 BC–2nd century AD. Athens.

The Ionic order is much lighter and more delicate than the Doric. The columns are set on a base and are more slender. The capitals are decorated with a spiral motif. The frieze is continuous, and the super-structure is lighter in appearance.

Most Ionic temples were built away from the mainland of Greece. However, the Acropolis in Athens contains several excellent ones. The *Temple of Athena Nike* (fig.6–23), built from 427 to 424 BC, is a fine example of a small Ionic building. The *Erechtheum* (421–405 BC) is a large and more complex structure. Columns are quite thin, tall and delicate in appearance, and have scroll-like capitals. *The Porch of the Maidens* (fig.6–24) uses six female figures (**caryatids**) instead of columns to support the architrave.

All of these temples, many of which are still standing in part, were constructed without mortar or cement. The stones were cut so exactly that they fit together precisely. Sometimes, metal rods were

Conservation Note

The caryatid figures now in place on the Erechtheum are replicas of the originals. The originals are kept in a carefully controlled environment at the Acropolis Museum. The caryatids were becoming more and more damaged by the highly corrosive pollutants (primarily auto emissions) that fill the air in Athens. Sometimes, conditions in the city get so dangerous that officials announce a pollution emergency during which all driving is banned until the air clears and pollutants go below danger levels.

used as dowels to hold one block in place above another. The columns were built up of several drums and had flutes cut in after they were erected.

Corinthian columns were used in the *Temple of the Olympian Zeus* (fig. 6–25) in Athens. The temple was begun in 174 BC and completed in the second century under the Roman emperor Hadrian. The towering columns are crowned with decorative capitals of acanthus leaves. Only a small portion of the huge temple remains today.

The Greeks were also interested in drama and music, and constructed theaters in the larger cities. These were open-air, rounded structures that were placed into the sloping sides of hills. Theaters were constructed of carefully tiered stone seats with aisles and walkways. Theaters had a round stage area called the orchestra, where the action took place. Behind the orchestra was a low building that formed the backdrop and supported the scenery. All these features can be seen in *The Theater at Epidaurus*

Sidelight

A Touch of Color

Because the remains of Greek statues and architecture have lost their color over the centuries, we tend to think that much of Greek art was white. This, however, is far from the truth. In early periods, bright, even garish, colors were applied to statues, judging from the scraps of original paint that have been found. Coloring grew more restrained in the Classic period but it was still used to suggest actual colors, especially in lips, hair and eyes.

A painting technique called **encaustic** was used on the figures. This method involved mixing the pigment with wax and applying it to the surface when hot. Colors on some of the early statues have been

Benoit, *The Parthenon*, 1879–1881. Ecole Nationale Superieure des Beaux-Arts, Paris.

preserved. One reason for this is that the Athenians used fragments of broken figures as rubble fill when rebuilding the temples on the Acropolis after the Persian destruction of the fifth century BC.

Color also was used in architecture. In regions where marble was not available, limestone or sandstone temples were tinted to resemble marble. In all temples, including the marble ones, capitals and other architectural details were brightly painted. The Greeks tried always to achieve harmony in everything they did, and color was essential to the overall effect of sculpture and architecture.

(fig.6–26) which still is used for dramatic productions today.

6–26 Although they are outdoors, Greek theaters had excellent acoustics. Plays are still performed here.
The Theater at Epidaurus, about 350 BC, Greece.

Higher-Order Thinking Skills

1 Male figures were occasionally used in Greek architecture, although the female caryatids were more common. The male figures are called atlantids. Students can design buildings using well-known contemporary people as columns. Are some figures more successful than others?

2 Did the students believe that Greek works were always bright white? Are they surprised that Greek statues and architecture were originally painted with strong colors? How do they feel about this? Do they prefer Greek art as they are used to seeing it or as it was first intended? Why might the Greeks have painted their buildings and sculptures? (Since much of the art was seen from afar, the colors helped convey a sense of grandeur.)

Performing Arts Connection

The Theater at Epidaurus

Prior to the early fifth century BC, Greek dramatic festivals were presented in the marketplace, with a cart as a background. The first Greek theaters, large enough to hold nearly a whole city's population, were built around the end of the fourth century BC, just as the era of religious spectacles declined.

In Greek drama, individual actors wearing masks and costumes spoke the story line from the balcony of a building that faced a horseshoe-shaped amphitheater. The Greek chorus paraded in the orchestra or dance floor below, singing the details of the action, emotion or moral of the drama.

• Ancient Greek theater combined music, dance, song and dialogue. Have students select a myth from any culture and translate it into a complete performance using these elements of Greek theater.

Contextual Information

Alexander the Great

In the southeast corner of Asia Minor was Issus, where Alexander the Great defeated Darius III in 333 BC. This victory over the Persians and the capture of the royal family made Alexander king over all of Persia.

When he was 20 years old, Alexander the Great was the ruler of the largest empire known up to that time. He became king of Macedonia in 336 BC. During the next 13 years, he conquered an area as large as the United States—from Greece and Egypt to beyond the Indus River, where his soldiers refused to go further. In 323 BC he died of a fever in Babylon, and his large kingdom was divided among his generals.

Alexander the Great encouraged scientific studies. For instance, during his reign, measurements were made of the silt deposits from the Euphrates and Tigris rivers at the Persian Gulf. It was determined that 40 lineal yards of land were added every year. If we assume that as an average amount, we can date cities and artifacts from the depth of silt.

One result of the conquests of Alexander the Great was the immense amount of valuable gold, silver and bronze that his troops collected from those they conquered. The metals were melted down to make coins, jewelry and dinnerware.

Painting

The Greeks were proud of the large and colorful paintings decorating their walls, but not even one exists today. Only the paintings on their vases remain. Early vases of the Archaic period are of red clay and have black figures and decorations painted on them. The **amphora** (fig.6–27) from Attica—a large storage jar with two handles—was signed by Exekias. He considered it one of his finest works. The inscription reads, *Exekias painted and made me*, indicating that he both formed and painted the amphora. Two events are shown on the vase.

6–27 Greek vase painters often signed their work. In the case of this piece, the same artist both made the vase and painted it.
Exekias, *Black-Figured Amphora*, about 530 BC. 24" (61 cm) high. The Vatican Museum.

6–28 Greek vase painters portrayed stories from their mythology and history.
Meidias, *Red-Figured Hydria*, about 410 BC. 20 1/2" (52 cm) high. British Museum, The Hamilton Collection, London.

The one seen here shows Pollux (with the dog) and Castor (with the horse) being honored by Leda and Tyndareos. All are identified and named on the painted vase. This outstanding example of Greek vase painting represents the most refined phase of Attic black-figure ware. The figures and animals are beautifully designed, and executed with exquisite technique.

The **hydria** (fig.6–28)—a large jug for carrying water from the community fountain—is from 410 BC. It shows a great change in technique and style. The background is now painted black and brush lines can be drawn freely on the red figures to show exacting detail and a variety of lines. A kind of perspective is shown by having some figures higher than others. Two scenes of familiar stories are painted by the artist/potter Meidias, who signed

400 BC Earliest known calendar used in Mexico	200 BC Irrigation systems developed in N. America
World Cultural Timeline	
400 BC Chopsticks first used in China	105 BC Paper invented, China

Multicultural Connection

Earliest Calendar in Mexico

Another great civilization, that of the Maya, began in Mesoamerica about 500 BC. They lived in small farming villages within the low-lying rain forests of Central America. The Maya reached a sophisticated level of architecture, mathematics and astronomy. One of their greatest accomplishments was the calendar, which was based on that of the Olmec. It was the first seasonal and agricultural calendar produced in America.

The Maya used a 365-day cycle, the *haab*. The haab consisted of 18 months of 20 days each, making 360 days in all. To make the year 365 days, they added

five "unlucky" days. Each month had its own name, and the days were numbered from 0 to 19. The calendar was probably used for farming because the names of the months and the symbols associated with them seem to define activities such as planting and harvesting. The Maya were quite concerned with time, which they thought repeated itself in cycles.

• During the eighth and early ninth centuries, the Maya culture collapsed. Have students brainstorm the possible reasons. Was the collapse due to environmental degradation, to overpopulation, to epidemics or to the rapid rise and fall of ruling kingdoms? Were the Maya tired of working so hard to keep the priests and gods happy?

(For more information about the Mayan civilization, see Chapter 4, page 134.)

The Invention of Paper

As with most cultures, writing systems were developed long before people knew how to make paper. Materials such as tree bark, ivory, bone clay tablets, animal hides and papyrus were used for writing. The Chinese made use of slips of bamboo. These were placed vertically, side by side, and joined together by a cord to form a flat sheet that could be rolled up for storage.

Although the Japanese ultimately perfected the craft of papermaking, paper was invented in China about 200 BC. Paper was in widespread use there six centuries before it was known in the vase. The upper register shows the rape, or carrying away, of the daughters of Leucippus. The lower register shows Heracles in the garden of the Hesperides. Traces of white, brown and gold have been added to suggest form and depth on this red-figured hydria.

The sophistication of later Greek painting is revealed in *The Battle of Issus* (fig.6–29), a Roman mosaic of marble chips. The mosaic is a copy of a Hellenistic wall painting of about 315 BC. Only four colors—red, yellow, white and black—are used in the mosaic. (Quite likely the original painting was painted with the same limited palette.) The

subject is the victory of Alexander the Great over Darius and the Persian army. Alexander, on the left, is partly obliterated because many of the stone tesserae are lost (fig. 6-d). Note the accurate anatomy of both horses and men. The overlapping figures, the rounded forms created by shading, the foreshortening, the complicated composition, and the marvelous detail are exciting and advanced achievements in visual presentation. Later Hellenistic painting retained the natural appearance of people and animals which characterized the Classic period, but added excitement, action and emotion.

6–29 The Romans copied many Greek statues and paintings like this one. The painting has been lost, but the mosaic survives. *The Battle of Issus*, about 100 BC. Marble mosaic, length 16'9" (5 m). Roman copy of Greek painting, from Pompeii. National Museum, Naples.

Lesson 6.2 Review

1 How did the Greek artist create a sense of movement in the *Kritios Boy*?
2 Why have so few original bronze Greek statues survived?
3 Between the Archaic and Classical Greek periods, how did Greek artists change the way they conceived a sculpture?
4 How is it that we have some idea of what Greek wall painting looked like although no example has survived?
5 How did the sculptor show depth in the Parthenon frieze?

6 Compare the *Dying Gaul* to the *Charioteer of Delphi*. What are the differences between this Classical Greek statue and this Hellenistic sculpture? Which is more emotional?
7 What art principle is most important in the *Nike of Samothrace*?
8 Draw the column capitals of the three Greek orders of architecture. Which order has the heaviest look? Which order seems tallest and most slender?
9 During which period of Greek art was the Parthenon built?
10 How were Attic black-figured ware and red-figured ware different? Which style was older?

---

the Middle East and a thousand years before its appearance in Europe.

For the Chinese in particular, the written language was very important in unifying a large and diverse land. Paper also served as an important material for the Chinese art forms of painting, printmaking and calligraphy.

- Why did it take so long for the outside world to learn about paper?

- Have students research the process of papermaking.

(See Chapter 4, page 92 for more information about early Chinese writing. For more details about Chinese art during the period when paper was created there, see page 96.)

Interdisciplinary Connection

Literature: Have students read the Greek myths that tell the stories of the abduction of the daughters of Leucippus and of Heracles in the garden of the Hesperides. The first story concerns the abduction of two beautiful young mortals by the gods Castor and Pollux. The second concerns one of Heracles' (Hercules') twelve labors.

Lesson 6.2 Review Answers

1 By shifting the boy's weight to one leg, the artist produced a faint S-curve in the body creating a subtle sense of movement.

2 Many were melted down for ammunition or war weapons. Some were lost or destroyed in other ways.
3 The Classical Greek artists began sculpting what they saw and observed rather than creating idealized forms from memory.
4 Because Roman copies have survived. (Example: *The Battle of Issus*, fig.6–29.)
5 The artist carved the figures closest to the viewer most round, in the highest relief. He made the second and third layers shallower and the background flat.
6 Although the Charioteer has realistic cloth folds, muscles and facial features, it is slightly rigid, calm and serene. This contrasts with the dramatic, highly emotional realism in *The Dying Gaul*. The clothed charioteer is bronze, and the nude Gaul is a Roman marble copy of a Greek bronze.
7 Movement, created by folds in the drapery and the upswept wings which enclose the space around the sculpture.
8 See fig.6–20. The Doric looks heaviest. Greek architecture progressed from heavy and ponderous in the Archaic period to light, airy and refined in the Classic period. The Corinthian seems tallest and most slender.
9 The Classical period
10 Black-figured ware is older. The figures were painted in black with details scratched into the paint. In red-figured vases the background is black, leaving red clay exposed inside the figures, and exacting details and fine lines were brushed on. The red figures were more realistic than those on the black-figured ware. (You might want to take the review of these two pottery types a step further by asking students to look at figs.1–3 and 1–4. They should be able to identify which one is black-figured and which is red-figured.)

Lesson 6.3

Starting in the eighth century BC, Roman art and architecture adapted aspects of the cultures that the empire came to rule while also making important contributions of its own.

Warm-up

Ask students to explore what it would feel like to be forced to give up a way of life that they and their ancestors had known for centuries and be forced suddenly to adapt the laws, religion and customs of an invading culture. Who might gain from this occurrence? While people of the civilizations that the empire conquered may have suffered, Romans themselves benefited from the these various traditions that enriched their culture. Can students identify other instances in history when conquerors have absorbed aspects of the cultures they vanquished?

Objectives

Students should be able to:

Identify Roman architectural feats such as complex public baths, luxurious villas, effective aqueducts, gigantic public arenas and impressive bridges.

Understand that Roman painting and sculpture demonstrated a deep admiration of Greek art.

Vocabulary Definitions

arch An architectural construction (semi-circular or pointed) built of wedge-shaped blocks (voussoirs) to span an opening and usually supported by columns or piers. A corbeled arch is made by overlapping layers of stones, each one projecting slightly farther over the opening than the one below it. A building dependent upon arches for its structure is said to be "arculated."
vault (vawlt) An arched roof or covering made of brick stone or concrete. A barrel vault or tunnel vault is semi-circular. A corbelled vault is made by having each course protrude a little beyond the course below it until the two sides meet. See *groined vault.*
velarium An awning at the top of the Colosseum in Rome that protected spectators from sun and rain.
coffer In architecture, a square, rectangular or polygonal recess in a ceiling to reduce the weight of the structure.

oculus (*ah*-cue-lus) A circular opening in a wall or in the top of a dome, from the Latin for "eye."
basilica (bah-*sill*-ee-ka) Roman civic building of rectangular form whose ground plan was divided into nave, side aisles and apse, and was approached through a narthex. In Christian architecture, a church building similar in shape was the major worship form from the third to eighth centuries.
forum A central gathering place for the people of a town, particularly of ancient Rome. A place for judicial and public business.

6.3 Roman Art

THE ROMAN CITY-STATE had its first beginnings in the eighth century BC. It grew to a magnitude of unbelievable proportions. The Romans expanded their control in every direction. Eventually they dominated the Western world. To these places the Romans took their laws, religion, customs, their extraordinary ability to organize, and the Latin language. From their conquered peoples, they absorbed the cultures to make up the complex structure of Roman culture and art.

The Romans greatly admired Greek sculpture and brought back many pieces to decorate their villas. Whatever they did not import, they had copied by either Greek artists or their own Roman artists. The Romans made their greatest contribution to art in architecture—the area in which their influence is most strongly seen. They used the arch, vault and concrete to far greater advantage than previous cultures. Their architecture was a creative achievement of the highest order. In construction, planning and engineering they had no peers.

Key Notes

• Roman civilization came to dominate the Western world.
• The Romans excelled in the art of architecture.
• In painting and sculpture, the Romans often borrowed from and imitated the Greeks.

Vocabulary
arch
vault
velarium
coffered
oculus
basilica
forum

The Roman Empire eventually encompassed most of Europe. The gray boundary lines shown in this map reflect today's countries.

Special Feature
The Colosseum

Possibly the grandest of all Roman structures is *The Colosseum* (figs.6–30, 6–31). Three emperors were involved in its construction: Vespasian, Titus and Domitian. The Colosseum was originally designed for the staging of lavish spectacles, most particularly for battles between animals and gladiators. Fifty thousand Romans could be held in the marble-seated interior.

Concrete arches, walls and vaults, covered with marble or decorative plaster, made up several kilometers of passageways. The **arch** and **vault** were essential parts of monumental Roman architecture. The arch is a curved architectural element used to span an opening. The vault is an arched roof or covering made of brick, stone or concrete.

The outer wall of the Colosseum is as high as a modern sixteen-story building. This wall went completely around the structure and supported poles from which an awning could be stretched to protect spectators from sun or rain. At least 1000 men were needed to raise or lower the awning, or **velarium**.

The exterior wall is divided into four horizontal bands, with large, arched openings piercing the lower three. The arches are framed in the standard Roman sequence for multi-storied buildings: Doric–Ionic–Corinthian, from the ground up.

Map

At its height, the Roman Empire was as big as Australia (2.5 million square miles). Romans spoke of their city as *Roma eterna* (the eternal Rome) and of the Mediterranean as *mare nostrum* (our sea).

6–30 Roman amphitheaters are the models for modern sports fields. Tickets were required for entrance to the Colosseum. Each of its 76 entryways had a number carved over the arch.
The Colosseum, 72–80 AD. Rome.

Statues filled the arched niches around the outside and a heavy wooden floor covered layers of cells below in which gladiators and animals were held. An amazing system of winches and lifting tackle brought the beasts from their dens into the arena. In addition, the floor area (almost 100 meters long) could be flooded and used as a shallow lake for mock naval battles.

The Colosseum is not just an architectural masterpiece. In terms of planning, engineering and organization it ranks as one of the most astonishing achievements of antiquity. Unfortunately, the Colosseum was damaged by later citizens and architects who used it as an instant quarry for marble when constructing other buildings. But other amphitheaters were constructed in every major city of the empire. Many are still in such excellent condition that they are used today as stadiums for big events.

6–31 Notice the gouged areas which are the result of centuries of pilfering by builders who took the facing stone for later constructions.
The Colosseum, detail.

Higher-Order Thinking Skills

Provide a map of a local or regional sports facility for students to use to compare to the Colosseum. Use the comparison as a springboard to a discussion of modern and ancient athletic games. Include the Olympics in the discussion.

Contextual Information
The Colosseum

The Colosseum is one of the best-known structures in Rome. It was built by war prisoners from 72 to 80 AD. The seats in the structure were allotted according to social rank—the lower seats were reserved for the higher classes and were made of marble. The spectators here were protected from danger by wire screens. The higher seats, for the lower classes, were made of wood.

After the fall of Rome, the building fell into ruins. To obtain much-needed iron during the Middle Ages, people carved the metal fittings from the joints that held the stones. Today, damage from automobile traffic vibration and exhaust are causing further damage to the stones.

• Have students locate information about the original purpose of the Colosseum. How did it change over time? Why was the building abandoned? What efforts are being made to restore the structure?

Teach

Art History/Criticism: Direct students to examine the following Roman works: the *Colosseum* (figs.6–30, 6–31), the *Arch of Constantine* (fig.6–38), the *Equestrian Statue of Marcus Aurelius* (fig.6–44), the *Column of Trajan* (figs.6–c, 6–43), and *Constantine the Great* (fig.6–45).

• Using only visual clues, what conclusions can they draw about the Roman Empire?

• If they were rulers of small neighboring civilizations, would they pit their armies against those of the emperor? How do these artworks communicate the glory and grandeur of Rome?

• Encourage students to examine the materials, scale, function and decoration of the pieces. What type of art would they have built for their small nation if they had had to face Roman aggression? What message would they have wanted their artwork to communicate to the emperor?

Evaluate

Ask the class how it came to pass that examples of Greek sculpture ended up in Roman villas. Point out that besides bringing the art home as the spoils of war, Romans also commissioned artists to copy existing Greek works to decorate their homes. In fact, many original Greek artworks have been lost but remain known to us through their Roman copies, as seen in *The Battle of Issus* (figs.6–d, 6–29) and the *Dying Gaul* (fig.6–17).

Reteach

Just as the Romans borrowed from the Greeks, American culture has taken from the Romans. Can students identify one very common architectural structure that has Roman origins that appears in many cities across the United States? Tell students to look again through the images in Lesson 6.3 for clues, and direct them to the image of the Colosseum if they need more guidance. In ancient times, Roman amphitheaters existed in every major city of the empire, and many are still used today as stadiums for big events.

Contextual Information

The Etruscans

No one is really sure where the first Etruscans came from, but they ruled over central Italy for many years and were known for their skill on the sea, including their activities as pirates.

A contemporary writer, Diodorus, said that the Etruscans invented porticoes, a type of porch, for their houses in order "to avoid the trouble and noise of a crowd of servants and other hangers-on."

The Etruscans were comparatively wealthy, having an "abundance of all sorts of fruits, not only for necessary food, but for pleasure and delight. They have their tables spread twice a day, furnished with every variety of food, even to luxury and excess."

The Emperor Nero

The July 18, 64 AD, fire that destroyed almost half of Rome spread from building to building, across the wooden roofs. It was blamed by many to be the fault of the Emperor Nero, who was disliked by most of the citizens because of his spending, extravagant lifestyle and violent disposition. He in turn blamed the fire on the Christians.

Some of Nero's positive contributions to Rome were made after the fire, when he instituted fire codes and city designs with height restrictions for buildings, planned for broad streets, improved the water supply, required fire walls between buildings, and had people keep containers of water in the open for putting out fires. Builders were forced to use concrete and bricks in rounded vaults so that roofs could be made of fireproof materials.

After Nero died, succeeding emperors tried to erase his memory. Trajan built public baths on top of Nero's gilded palace, and another ruler built a center for stores over the former porticoes of the palace.

Roman Predecessors: Etruscan Art

If we step back several centuries from the Romans we find that much of central Italy was dominated by the Etruscans. The origins of these people are shrouded in mystery. But we have been told by ancient Roman writers that the Etruscans were master architectural engineers and town planners. The Romans must have learned a great deal from Etruscan construction. Although little remains of Etruscan architecture, a fortified city gate (fig.6–32) in the Italian city of Perugia does survive. It shows a masterful use of the arch and masonry techniques. One reason for the lack of evidence from the Etruscan culture is that their towns are buried under present-day cities and are extremely difficult to excavate.

We also know that the Etruscan use of bronze in sculpture and other decorative items was much admired, even by the Greeks. *Statuette of a Rider* (fig.6–33) is a small, solid cast bronze sculpture. The horse is missing. Like most other Etruscan sculpture, it probably was modeled after a Greek original. The rider sits stiffly upright and wears a short toga which the Romans later adopted. A considerable understanding of anatomy was necessary for the artist to sculpt a figure with such convincingly realistic features.

6–32 This is one of very few surviving Etruscan architectural monuments.
Porta Augusta, 2nd century BC. Perugia.

Architecture

The Romans learned many lessons from the Etruscans and, as we have seen in the example of the Colosseum, the Romans advanced architecture to unrivaled heights. They constructed buildings and public works in all corners of their empire. Arenas, huge public baths and public forums were built. The Romans erected the first structures in history with vast interior spaces. These buildings are impressive because of size and practicality rather than aesthetic feeling.

One of the most astounding examples is *The Pantheon* (figs.6–34, 6–35) which was built to honor all the gods. A huge dome (an

6–33 The Etruscans were master metal workers who made statues and jewelry too.
Statuette of a Rider, about 450–425 BC. Bronze, 11" (27 cm) high, Etruscan, found at Comacchio, Italy. Detroit Institute of Arts.

6–34 The portico (porch) partly hides the Pantheon's basic geometry. What forms can you identify here?
The Pantheon, about 118–125 AD. Rome.

6–34a Plan of the Pantheon
Reproduced by permission of Harcourt Brace Jovanovich, Inc., from *Art in Perspective* by Henri Dorra.

exact hemisphere on the inside) rests on a mammoth drum, creating an interior space that is overwhelming to experience. The floor space is 144 feet in diameter, and the top of the dome is 144 feet above the floor. The concrete dome is thin at the top and thickens as it meets the walls. The dome is *coffered*, or decorated, with a series of recessed rectangular panels. The walls of the building are over 20 feet thick and massive enough to support the tremendous weight of the dome. The only source of light is a single round, eye-like opening (*oculus*) at the top. This opening is 30 feet in diameter. Any rain that falls through it is carried away by an elaborate underground drainage system. The interior of the drum area is covered with marble columns and decorations.

Some of Italy's great artists and composers were later buried at the Pantheon. The once-gilded, huge bronze doors on gigantic hinges are the original doors. A colonnade of Corinthian columns, carved from

6–35 Light from the oculus in the coffered dome lights up the interior of this big enclosed space.
Giovanni Paolo Panini, *Interior of the Pantheon*, about 1750. Oil on canvas, 50 1/2" x 39" (128 x 99 cm) National Gallery of Art, Washington DC, Samuel H. Kress Collection.

Higher-Order Thinking Skills

1 The Pantheon is an example of geometric forms in perfect relationships as a basis for architecture. The dome is a hemisphere that could be rotated to fit into the drum of the cylindrical walls. Have students analyze what they can and cannot determine about the building from the floor plan and from the photographs. Models for buildings based on this premise of ideal forms and relationships can be created from Styrofoam forms and foam core board. Students can work alone, or they can work in pairs, with one partner making a floor plan and the other executing the plan into the actual model.

2 It is extremely difficult to convey a sense of the interior of the Pantheon through photographs. Its round, high-domed interior makes an overall view impossible to capture on film. This is why Panini's painting of the interior is often used instead of a photograph. The painting provides a view that can be duplicated only by actually standing inside the Pantheon and absorbing its entirety. Acquaint students with this situation. Have them discuss the advantages and disadvantages of using Panini's painting rather than a photograph as visual documentation of the building's interior.

Contextual Information

The Baths of Caracalla

The ruins of the Baths of Caracalla are presently being used as outdoor theater and musical backgrounds. At the time of their construction, however, the magnificence of the baths was well known.

Seneca, a writer of the first century, said of the Romans and the baths: "We think ourselves poor and mean if our walls are not resplendent with large and costly mirrors; if our marbles from Alexandria are not set off by mosaics of Numidian stone... if our vaulted ceilings are not buried in glass.... What a vast number of statues, of columns that support nothing, but are built for decoration, merely in order to spend money! And what masses of water that fall crashing from level to level!"

Between 27 BC and 500 AD, the number of baths in Rome increased from 170 to 900. The baths had cold, warm and hot water. Steam, air and sun baths were available; and there were places to talk, exercise, play games and get massages. There were also libraries and museums, and the baths were surrounded by parks and gardens.

People paid a small charge for the baths, and they purchased body oil for cleaning. All but the poorest could attend with some frequency. For social climbers, the baths were the place to be seen and to meet business contacts.

single blocks of stone, dominates the entrance and is topped by a Greek-style pediment. The dome originally was covered with gilded bronze plates.

The Romans also built gigantic structures to house their baths. *The Baths of Caracalla* (fig.6–36) contained several pools of various temperatures, libraries, offices, meeting rooms, conversation areas and spaces for recreation. The interior of the concrete structure was roofed with vaults that spanned enormous spaces.

Large meeting halls, called **basilicas**, were part of the civic center in each city. Many were later converted into churches. This building type will be discussed at greater length in Chapter 7.

6–36 Roman baths included pools, shops, lecture halls, libraries and running tracks.
The Baths of Caracalla, about 215 AD. Rome.

6–37 This theater was once roofed with cedar wood.
Theater of Herodes Atticus, 2nd century AD. Athens.

50 AD–500 AD		
Aksum Kingdom (Ancient Ethiopia), Africa	**100 AD Mound builders, Ohio**	**132 AD Seismograph invented, China**

World Cultural Timeline

50 AD	100 AD	271 AD
Stupa at Sanchi, India	**Insecticide developed from powdered dried chrysanthemum flowers, China**	**Directional compass invented, China**

6–39 Romans met here and at other forums to shop and catch up on the news.
Forum Romanum. Rome.

Multicultural Connection

The Mound Builders

There are many different groups of American Indians, descendants of those who first crossed the Bering Strait. One of those groups lived along the Ohio and Mississippi rivers and built thousands of earth mounds over the graves of their dead. They were called the Hopewell Indians, after the man on whose land some of their remains were discovered. These mounds—some shaped like cones, some in geometric or animal shapes, and others like pyramids—were part of elaborate religious ceremonies. Individual framed graves, along with all the possessions of the dead person, were assembled within larger frames. Elaborate works of art have been found in some of the graves, suggesting that these artifacts may have served as a form of status symbol. The mounds were created with stones and earth that covered these frames. The Serpent Mound, over 600 feet long, was built in the form of a sinuous serpent. Hopewell religious and political leaders used the serpent as a symbol of power.

This culture in southern Ohio built permanent settlements, developed an intensive agricultural system and carried on trade for exotic artifacts and materials. In addition, the Hopewell Indians were skilled craftsmen. Out of black stone called obsidian they produced beautiful figurines and pipes shaped like animals. They hammered sheets of copper into eagles and created abstract patterns on pottery.

Roman theaters differed slightly from those of the Greeks. The Romans partially cut the round Greek orchestra and constructed a raised stage area behind it. The performance was given from the stage, and important spectators were seated in the orchestra. The seating was in a semicircle rather than in the two-thirds circle of the Greeks. Theaters were often freestanding rather than placed in a concave hillside. The 5000-seat Roman *Theater of Herodes Atticus* (fig.6–37) was built on the side of the Acropolis in Athens. It is still in use today.

Several emperors built large triumphal arches to commemorate their greatest achievements. The *Arch of Constantine* (fig.6–38) celebrates Constantine's assumption of power. It is actually a large building with three arches through it. Many of the statues on it came from other monuments in Rome.

Romans loved to discuss things—politics, the weather, battles, history, art, trade business or gossip. Their *forums* provided a space in their cities for these discussions. The *Forum Romanum* (fig.6–39),

one of many in Rome, contained temples, state buildings, open spaces, basilicas and monuments. The Via Sacra (Sacred Way) passed through it. At a later time it became a valley full of rubble from the ruins and a garbage dump for the citizens, but was later cleared and excavated.

City planning was another phase of civic engineering at which the Romans excelled. Cities were equipped with sewers, running water, city squares, shopping streets, residential areas, paved streets and warehouses.

Homes were often two stories high. They were built around atriums and contained gardens and fountains. Pompeii and Herculaneum, which were covered with volcanic ash and mud from Mt. Vesuvius in 79 AD, have been excavated to reveal urban centers of great sophistication and careful planning. Similar cities were built in nearly every corner of the Roman empire. Many European, North African and Near Eastern countries have marvelous excavations and ancient ruins where Roman civic engineering can be studied firsthand.

Marvels of Engineering

Roman bridges, roads and aqueducts spread from one end of the Roman Empire to the other. The roads that tied the empire together were masterpieces of engineering and are still visible in parts of Europe. Some aqueducts, partially ruined, still extend for miles outside of Rome.

The Romans were well aware that concrete is affected adversely by extremes of temperature. Repairs on aqueducts were permitted only between April 1 and November 1. *Pont du Gard*, **first century BC. Near Nîmes, France.**

The aqueducts, composed basically of arches and vaults, are an extraordinary example of Roman practicality on the largest scale imaginable. Rome had 11 aqueducts supplying 350 million gallons of water a day from distant mountains. Quite a feat! The oldest aqueduct dates from 312 BC, but aqueducts were constructed all over the Roman Empire, wherever water had to be brought across valleys and into cities.

The *Pont du Gard* near Nîmes, France, is a triple-storied aqueduct built of stone (without mortar) that bridges the gorge of the Gard River. The aqueduct ran for about 30 miles and supplied Nîmes daily with 22,000 tons of water.

6–38 The Romans commemorated victories and important people in public monuments. *The Arch of Constantine*, about 312–315 AD. Rome.

(See Chapter 4, page 138 for more information about the Mound Builders.)

• What evidence do we have that suggests the Hopewell Indians were a well-organized, cooperative society?

• How do you think the Hopewell Indians were able to bury so many bodies at one time?

The Stupa at Sanchi

Religious temples are among the earliest examples of the art of India that remains today. Historically important, religion—particularly Buddhism, Hinduism and Islam—influenced Indian architecture, sculpture, painting and dance. Stupas are large stone mounds that house Buddhist holy objects. The Stupa at Sanchi, a site in Madhya Pradish state, India, is an example of an early Buddhist shrine or reliquary. It was probably begun in the third century BC by the emperor Asoka, a converted Buddhist, who erected numerous monasteries and stupas. It is enclosed by a stone railing with four richly carved gateways erected in the first century AD. The sculpture depicts animal life, grotesques and brackets in the form of female tree spirits and the previous lives of the Buddha.

(See Chapter 4, pages 88 and 89 for more information about the Stupa at Sanchi.)

Higher-Order Thinking Skills

1 Like the Romans, we also build structures to commemorate important events, like that marked by the Arch of Constantine. Have students sketch or photograph the monuments in your community and write a narrative that tells what the monument commemorates. They also should indicate why they believe the monument is important to the community. The narratives and the photos or drawings could be combined into a book for the school or community library. Students could also design a commemorative monument for the school or community.

2 Ask students to identify two connected architectural elements that were perfected by the Romans and appear in the *Colosseum* (figs.6–30, 6–31), the *Pantheon* (fig.6–34), the *Baths of Caracalla* (fig.6–36), the *Theater of Herodes Atticus* (fig.6–37), and the *Arch of Constantine* (fig.6–38).

• Are there any structures within your community that also use the arch and vault? (If there are none, direct students to look at the adaptation of the arch and vault in succeeding periods of art illustrated in the textbook.)

• What effect does the use of the arch and vault have on the building? Does it feel grand, sturdy and imposing, or minute and insubstantial? Point out that while the Romans demonstrated great mastery, predecessors such as the Etruscans had already employed the arch and vault.

Higher-Order Thinking Skills

1 The *Equestrian Statue of Marcus Aurelius* (fig.6–44) is about 1800 years old and is the only such ancient bronze to survive in good condition. Ask students to pick one monument from contemporary culture that they feel will survive well into the future. (You can set parameters for the monument's location, such as in your community, or leave the choice open.) Have students write about the commemorated event and detail their reasons for thinking that it has staying power.

2 Direct students to compare the Roman portrait sculptures *Portrait of a Lady* (fig.6–41), *The Roman Legislator* (fig.6–42), and the head of Augustus (fig.6–40) to the Greek *Peplos Kore* (fig.6–a) and *Kouros* (fig.6–12).

• Ask the class which sculptures capture the personality of the sitters most closely. Which ones seem like living individuals?

• Do they believe it was Greek or Roman artists who wanted to convey the likenesses of the models more accurately? Although the Romans borrowed heavily from Greeks, they developed a style of portrait sculpture that preserved individual features and now provide us with an interesting glimpse into ancient Roman life.

3 Challenge students to try to determine the personality of one of the people in the late Roman portrait sculptures in Lesson 6.3 by looking carefully at the information the artists have provided about their personalities in these carvings. Have students write a letter from the role of the sitter to someone living in the twentieth century about what the person's daily life might have been

Sculpture

Although the Romans borrowed heavily from Greek sculpture, they used original portrait sculpture to honor their emperors. These portraits helped preserve the features of the emperors and emphasized their greatness. The Roman interest in portrait sculpture, especially the bust (head and upper torso), is an important contribution to world art. Unfortunately, most of the work prior to the first century BC has been lost.

The *Head of Augustus* (fig.6–40) was part of a large full-length figure. It was probably sculpted in Alexandria, Egypt. It is cast in bronze and has eyes of glass paste. The sculpture is striking in its realistic appearance and individualized expression. It is certainly not an idealized figure. These sculptures allowed Roman subjects throughout the vast empire to know what their rulers looked like. Today a camera would assume that job.

Portrait busts of Roman people of a later date are quite realistic. *Portrait of a Lady* (fig.6–41) is

carved in marble and probably was done as a commission to decorate the home of the subject. Notice the style of the coiffure and the acanthus leaf ornament at the base. Features such as these help archaeologists date such works. The bust of the *Roman Legislator* (fig.6–42) illustrates the importance placed on realism in the later Roman style. The artist makes no attempt to minimize the wrinkled and sagging skin of the aging legislator.

Relief sculptures were used to record important events in the lives of Roman emperors. The *Column of Trajan* (fig.6–43) is a splendid marble cylinder that rises to a height of over 130 feet, including the pedestal. It was originally topped by a bronze statue of Trajan; it now holds a statue of St. Peter. The base of the column is carved into a giant laurel wreath. In a spiral relief some 700 feet long, the exploits of Trajan's Dacian campaigns are carved as a narrative history in stone (fig.6–c). The column is hollow and originally contained an urn with the ashes of the emperor.

6–42 How does this figure differ from the Greek sculpture you have studied?
The Roman Legislator, about 125 AD. Marble, 16 1/2" (42 cm) high. Nelson-Atkins Museum of Art, Kansas City.

In the piazza (square) atop the Capitoline Hill, once the center of Roman government, once stood a bronze statue of one of Rome's most notable emperors. The *Equestrian Statue of Marcus Aurelius* (fig.6–44) is the only well-preserved equestrian statue (horse and rider) from antiquity to survive and has been imitated often. Michelangelo, who designed the piazza and the surrounding buildings in the Renaissance, placed the statue here at the request of the Pope, who thought it was of Constantine, the first Christian emperor. The size of the figure is large in comparison to the horse, a characteristic of such Roman works. The bearded emperor looks out on the world, his right arm in a typical Roman oratorical gesture. The horse is superbly sculpted, showing that the artist had immense knowledge of the bone and muscle structure of horses. The balance is superb, with all the weight of the cast bronze evenly distributed over the three supporting legs.

The head of *Constantine the Great* (fig.6–45) is part of an enormous sculpture that once was

6–40 Many, many statues were made of the emperors so that their subjects in all parts of the empire would know what their ruler looked like.
Head of Augustus, 27 BC–14 AD. Bronze, 18 1/2" (47 cm) high, found at Meroe, Sudan in 1910. British Museum, London.

6–41 The realism in portraits like this one was valued in a society which revered its ancestors and tried to be accurate about its history.
Portrait of a Lady, 69 AD. Marble, 25 1/2" (64 cm) high. Nelson-Atkins Museum of Art, Kansas City.

like. Tell students to recall what they have learned throughout the lesson to help describe the activities their models might have been involved in, where they might have gone for entertainment and for religious observances, and the types of houses in which they might have lived.

Conservation Note

The *Equestrian Statue of Marcus Aurelius* is another in a continuing series of historically important sculptures that have been removed from their original outdoor location to the safety of a climatically controlled museum.

6–43 Trajan's ashes were buried in this column whose relief sculpture tells the story of his conquests.
Column of Trajan, 106–113 AD. Marble, over 130' (40 m) high. Rome.

6–45 This head was part of a seated figure of the emperor that was 30 feet high. The head alone weighs over 8 tons.
Constantine the Great, about 330 AD. Marble, head about 8 1/4' (2.5 m) high. Palace of the Conservatory, Rome.

6–44 There were many statues of mounted riders in ancient Rome. This is the only one that has survived in good condition.
Equestrian Statue of Marcus Aurelius, 161–180 AD. Bronze, over life-size. Shown in the Piazza del Campidoglio, Rome.

placed in his basilica. Head, arms, hands, legs and feet were of marble. The drapery was probably of bronze plates over a masonry frame. The colossal head and neck are superbly modeled, but the eyes, which seem to be fixed on some spot above our heads (perhaps on eternity), seem overly large. Such large eyes are common in the art of the early Christian period. The eyes of such late Roman sculptures were carved so that shadows, not paint, provided the definition of iris and pupil.

Contextual Information

The Column of Trajan

Students may wonder how the multitude of small figures on the *Column of Trajan* (fig.6–43) would have been visible to the Roman passerby. There are 150 separate episodes of Trajan's campaigns depicted, and thousands of figures are shown in relief. The sculptors made some adjustments for better visibility from the ground: The width of the relief band increases as it winds its way up the column. In addition, the figures would have been highlighted with some color, thus making them more distinguishable. The column was placed in the forum that Trajan built and was flanked by two two-story libraries. The column could have been viewed at closer range from the roofs of the libraries.

The Emperor Augustus

Note that the dating for the *Head of Augustus* (fig.6–40) spans 41 years (27 BC–14 AD), the years of his reign. Even as Augustus aged, his official portraits presented him as a young man. This makes precise dating of portraits of the emperor very difficult. The subjects of the vast Roman Empire consequently knew what the emperor looked like when he was a virile young man, but not as an older man. (Augustus died when he was 76.)

• Have students speculate why Augustus and other rulers would have preferred to have people think of them as eternally young and healthy. Ask students if they can cite other instances when leaders have refused or hesitated to make the citizenry aware of their short-comings or mishaps. (Illness is often downplayed. For instance, American president, Franklin Delano Roosevelt, who was crippled by polio, never permitted photographs of himself when he was walking with crutches. He allowed photographs of himself seated only if his wheelchair was covered or hidden.)

Contextual Information

Writing in Ancient Rome

In ancient Rome, casual writing and school exercises often were done with pointed styluses, made of metal or bone, on small, wax-coated wooden tablets. Letters were scratched on the surface with the point of a stylus. Erasures could be made with the blunt end of the stylus.

Pompeii

More than 25 percent of Pompeii still remains to be excavated. Much of it lies beneath the rubble of earlier excavations.

Painting

Both the Etruscans and the Greeks made paintings which the early Romans copied. Because none of the Greek and only a few of the Etruscan paintings have survived, the extent of their influence on Roman artists cannot be determined. The Romans used paintings to decorate and color the interiors of houses. Still lifes, portraits, landscapes and mythological subjects are found on walls in Pompeii, Herculaneum and other excavated cities. Often landscapes and architectural scenes were painted to serve as "open windows" to provide a feeling of greater space in small rooms. Portraits were sometimes painted on walls to record how members of the family looked.

All Roman wall paintings were done in fresco, a method of painting wet plaster with pigment. Entire plaster-covered walls were frescoed to look like marble and wood paneling, or were gaily decorated with flowers and vines, almost like wallpaper. The *Woman Playing the Cithara* (fig.6–46) is a decorative wall fresco. The woman and child have a feeling of individuality, yet seem slightly idealized. They may be portraits. The poses are casual and intimate. The figures are shaded to create a comfortable feeling of depth. Roman painters had mastered several types of perspective to create the illusion of depth in a painting.

The girl in *Portrait of a Young Girl* (fig.6–47) is from a wall in a Pompeian house. She holds a stylus

6–47 What do you think she is going to write?
Portrait of a Young Girl, before 79 AD. Fresco, 10" (25 cm) high, from Pompeii. National Museum, Naples.

to her lips as if thinking about what to write. The painting may be a commemorative portrait of a girl who died young and whose family wished to remember her.

6–46 These figures are life-sized, which could create the feeling that they were really in the room.
Woman Playing a Cithara, before 79 AD. Fresco, 6 1/2' (2 m) high, from Boscoreale. The Metropolitan Museum of Art, New York, Rogers Fund.

Performing Arts Connection

Woman Playing a Cithara

Scholars speculate that this lovely woman represents a Macedonian queen and her daughter or a maidservant. The small, plucked ancient Greek instrument recalls today's harp.

This painting was part of a series that adorned the walls of a late Roman Republic country villa belonging to P. Fannius Synistor of Boscoreale, an area approximately one mile north of Pompeii. The work seems to have been part of the dining room. Its artistic style evokes the late Classical and Hellenistic Greek period—a time in which wealthy men were commonly entertained at mealtime with music played by women. The allusion to the past era was meant to signify the owner's cultivated tastes.

Pompeii:
A City Frozen in Time

On the morning of August 24 in AD 79, a light dusting of ash from the volcano Mt. Vesuvius began falling on the prosperous city of Pompeii. But it was not until around 1:00 p.m. that, with a tremendous explosion, Vesuvius erupted, spewing out volcanic ash, great bombs of pumice and molten lava. A giant cloud of volcanic dust rose twelve miles into the sky and completely blotted out the sun. Within two to three hours Pompeii was over a foot deep in pumice and stone. All through the afternoon and evening the volcano continued to belch forth its contents. Pumice and volcanic debris accumulated at the rate of six inches every hour.

During the early hours of the outburst most of Pompeii's 20,000 inhabitants fled the city. But at least 2000 people chose to seek shelter within the

View of Mt. Vesuvius from Pompeii.

town, either too terrified to leave or unwilling to abandon their homes and possessions. All who remained behind were overcome by the poisonous gases and hot ashes that clogged their lungs.

When the sky cleared three days later the once thriving port had been transformed into a huge grave, sealed beneath some 25 feet of rock and ash.

Pompeii lay locked in the earth and forgotten for many centuries. It wasn't until 1748 that serious attempts to excavate Pompeii began. In the 1860s, the archaeologist and historian Giuseppe Fiorelli, in charge of the dig from 1860–1875, began to use scientific methods to excavate Pompeii. He divided the city into regions, assigning a number to every block and every doorway. His excavation uncovered a unique view of private and public life in the Roman world. Unique because everything in Pompeii had been preserved just as it was, including its inhabitants.

Fiorelli knew that the volcanic ash had turned to mud and hardened around the fallen figures. The corpses inside the hardened mud eventually disintegrated, but left behind were molds that faithfully preserved the victims' final gestures and postures. When a workman carelessly swung his pickax and accidentally made a hole in a mold at the site, Fiorelli poured liquid plaster of Paris into the cavity. After the plaster had solidified, the cocoon of ash was removed and an uncanny lifelike figure was revealed. With the aid of the casts the last moments of the Pompeians were fixed forever: A woman falls with a baby in her arms; a man collapses as he pulls his goat along; a young man and woman are stopped in their tracks as they attempt to flee.

Just as the Pompeians had been preserved in their last living moments, so too was their city and way of life. Bakeries, inns, tanneries and wool-working shops emerged intact, providing an accurate picture of how they functioned. The food people ate was recovered. In one house, eggs and fish were found lying on a dining table. Plants, too, left cavities in the hardened lava. The archaeologist Wilhelmina Jashemski used Fiorelli's method of making casts to determine the types of plants that grew in the gardens of Pompeii.

Gloriously colored paintings and mosaics found on the walls and floors of most houses testified to the Pompeians' love of art and give tantalizing glimpses of cultural and religious life. Even information about city politics and elections could be read on the graffiti-covered walls of Pompeii.

By sealing off the area so completely, Vesuvius in effect stopped time. No one who sees these visions of the dead can fail to sense the anguish of that time.

Higher-Order Thinking Skills

Ask students to tell the story of the young girl who is shown with her stylus (fig.6–47). Who is she? What is her family like? What is she writing? Encourage speculation and elaboration.

Interdisciplinary Connection

Geology: Vesuvius is the only active volcano on the European mainland. In this century a violent eruption occurred in April 1906 and lasted for ten days. It caused great destruction and 2000 lives were lost. Since then, smaller eruptions of Vesuvius have occurred in 1913, 1926, 1929 and 1944.

Contextual Information

Mosaics

Most of the Roman mosaics were made with shading and perspective as in paintings. In time, mosaics were placed on walls, where precious stones, glass and enameled pieces could be used.

Lesson 6.3 Review Answers

1 The Etruscans

2 Possible answers include the *Colosseum*, aqueducts, *Pont du Gard*, *Theater of Herodes Atticus*, *The Pantheon*, *The Baths of Caracalla*, *The Roman Forum (Forum Romanum)* and *The Arch of Constantine.*

3

4 *The Pantheon* was built to honor all the gods. The roof is a huge dome that is exactly a hemisphere on the inside with an oculus at its center. The dome is concrete, coffered and thinner at the top. Any rain that falls through the oculus is carried away by an elaborate underground drainage system.

5 Both Roman and modern cities have sewers, running water, city squares, shopping streets, residential areas, public baths (swimming pools), gymnasiums, sports arenas, theaters, temples, paved streets, warehouses and beautiful homes. Roman cities were walled. Romans also did not have modern conveniences such as electricity.

6 Both relate a story sequentially in a strip or register.

7 They thought it was a statue of Constantine, the first Christian emperor.

8 The head of Constantine is 2.5 meters or 8.2 feet tall. (1 meter = 39.37 inches or a little over three feet). The feet are about six feet long. Students should compare the relative sizes of feet to faces.

9 They were covered by ash when Mt. Vesuvius exploded in 79 AD.

Mosaics

Although the Greeks had used colored stones to create mosaic designs, the Romans excelled in this art. Small bits of marble were cut, polished and fitted together to make an image. Floor mosaics were made of pieces one to two centimeters across. The owner of a villa in Sicily was a Roman of extraordinary wealth. The villa boasted 7000 square feet of floor mosaics. One of the scenes (fig.6–48) depicts a group of women engaged in vigorous exercise. They almost seem to be involved in an ancient aerobic class or gym workout.

Wall mosaics were done with even more precision. Much smaller stones were used. Many stones were less than a millimeter in diameter. When done, the entire surface was polished to feel like a smooth sheet of glass. The artist of the wall mosaic *Doves* (fig.6–49) reveals an incomplete knowledge of space perception. While his shading of values is excellent, his perspective drawing is not precisely accurate. The frame and border also are done in the same mosaic techniques. Here, the stones are so tiny that 150 are used in every square centimeter.

The Battle of Issus (fig.6–29) is a mosaic from the House of the Faun in Pompeii. Huge in size for a mosaic, it is a brilliant example of this art form. Its subject matter and execution are extremely complex. The grading of colors and values to create rounded forms is difficult when the colors and values must be found in natural stones.

6–49 This whole picture is made up of tiny stones. In the space of a square centimeter, a Roman mosaicist might use 100 pieces.
Doves, 2nd century AD. Mosaic, 33 1/2" (85 cm) high, from villa of Emperor Hadrian at Tivoli. Capitoline Museum, Rome.

6–48 What details in this image remind you of life today?
Young Women Exercising, early 4th century AD. Mosaic, from the Roman villa at Piazza Armerina.

Lesson 6.3 Review

1 Who inhabited the land that became Rome before the Romans took it over?

2 Name several Roman architectural masterpieces.

3 Both *The Baths of Caracalla* and *The Pantheon* have domed roofs. Draw several arches that cross at the center to explain how a series of arches can be joined to form a dome.

4 Why was *The Pantheon* built? Describe its roof. What happens to rain water that falls into *The Pantheon*?

5 How were Roman cities similar to modern cities?

How were they different?

6 How is the *Column of Trajan* like a comic strip?

7 The early Christians destroyed many of the Roman statues. Why did they preserve the statue of Marcus Aurelius?

8 Compare your height to that of the head of *Constantine the Great*. How tall are you? How tall is the head of Constantine? Guess the size of one of the feet of this statue.

9 Why are so many Roman wall paintings preserved in Pompeii and Herculaneum?

Chapter Review Answers

Review

1 Human beings, the human figure in particular

2 Beauty and harmony, the ideal form of each subject

3 A procession or parade that happened every four years to honor Athena

4 Architecture

5 The eyes in Greek sculptures had either painted or inlaid glass. In *Constantine the Great*, as in many late Roman sculptures, the eyes were carved so that shadows provide the definition of iris and pupil. The eyes of *Constantine the Great* are overly large, a preview of early Christian art.

Interpret

1 All three have a great deal of energy in their forms, the rhythm and movement in each composition is more important than the precise representation of objects, and each shows a lively, almost humorous spontaneity.

2 Both stone statues are stylized, smiling slightly, and facing front with the left feet slightly forward. Both show arms held rigidly at their sides with clenched fists. The main difference is that the *Kouros* is standing free from the stone block, with the marble between his legs and between his arms and body removed. The Egyptians are clothed and the Greek is not.

3 The British Museum in London. Today countries are more protective of their national art; so, it would probably be preserved in a Greek museum.

Primary Source

Vitruvius, Roman Master Builder

Vitruvius was a Roman master builder and author of volumes about standards for architecture. Because of his writings we know a great many details about Roman architecture. In this selection from Vitruvius' *Ten Books on Architecture*, he tells us how he learned from Greek literature that the Doric column was to be based on the proportion of a man's foot and height:

"Wishing to set up columns in that temple, but not having rules for their symmetry, and being in search of some way by which they could render them fit to bear a load and also of a satisfactory beauty of appearance, they

measured the imprint of a man's foot and compared this with his height. On finding that, in a man, the foot was one-sixth of the height, they applied the same principle to the column, and reared the shaft, including the capital, to a height six times its thickness at its base. Thus the Doric column, as used in buildings, began to exhibit the proportions, strength, and beauty of the body of a man."

In this passage from Vitruvius' writings we learn why the caryatid figure (fig.6–24) was created:

"The Greeks...made common cause and declared war against the people of Caryae [who had sided

with the Persian enemies of Greece]. They took the town, killed the men, abandoned the State to desolation, and carried off their wives into slavery, without permitting them, however, to lay aside the long robes and other marks of their rank as married women...to appear forever after as a type of slavery, burdened with the weight of their shame and so making atonement for their State. Hence, the architects of the time designed for public buildings the statues of these women, placed so as to carry a load, in order that the sin and the punishment of the people of Caryae might be known and handed down even to posterity."

Chapter Review

Review

1 What subject was central to Greek art and culture?
2 What qualities were the Greeks trying to achieve in their paintings and sculptures?
3 What was the subject of the Parthenon frieze?
4 In what area of art did the Romans make their greatest contribution?
5 How are the eyes of *Constantine the Great* (fig.6–45) different from the eyes of most of the classical Greek sculptures?

Interpret

1 Compare three Minoan works of art: the *Bull Dance* (fig.6–3), the *Octopus Jar* (fig.6–5), and the *Harvester Vase* (fig.6–6). What characteristics are common to all three?
2 How is the *Kouros* (fig.6–12) similar to *Mycerinus and His Queen* (fig.5–21). How is it different?
3 Where is most of the Parthenon sculpture now? If the Parthenon were discovered today, where do you think the art would be kept?
4 Describe a Greek theater. How did it vary from the theaters that the Romans built?
5 Analyze the difference between the types of people that the Greeks and Romans sculpted.

Other Tools for Learning

Maps
1 Notice how Greek cities are spread out over a series of islands in the Mediterranean Sea. How do you think this separation affected their government and art?
2 Find Pompeii and Rome on a map. Imagine what a southern resort town like Pompeii might have been like before Vesuvius covered it with ashes.

Timelines
During the more than 1000 years that the Greek and then the Roman civilizations developed, other world cultures were equally active and inventive. Using the timelines in this chapter, determine what events were happening simultaneously throughout the world.

Electronic Media
CD-ROM drive: Electronic Encyclopedia (e.g., *New Grolier Multimedia* or *Microsoft Encarta*)
Research one of the historic or mythological figures depicted on an object in this chapter. Which characteristics of the individual is the artist trying to emphasize? If the artist is representing a specific moment in this personality's life, is it accurately portrayed?

Primary-Source Connection

Emphasize to students the importance of primary sources to the study of art. Documents from a period provide us with a fuller picture of the function and meaning of art and architecture. Have students consider how their understanding of the caryatid figure was enriched by this excerpt from Vitruvius. Historians often would be at a loss without documents that supplement the information provided by the work of art itself. Have students ponder the questions that would arise in the minds of historians 1000 years from now if there were no written information available to them when encountering the Statue of Liberty, the Washington Monument or the St. Louis arch. Suppose the monument's inscription or dedication had been lost. Where would the historians go to learn more about the purpose of these monuments?

paved with decorative mosaics, bubbling fountains and beautiful gardens. Civic life centered around a forum with a temple. As in contemporary resorts, people relaxed and played.

Timelines
Among the many possible responses are:

- Buddha was born in India and Confucius in China during the Greek Archaic period. (600–480 BC)

- The earliest known calendar was used in Mexico, chopsticks were first commonly used in China, and the Parthenon was built—all within a hundred years of each other (400 BC).

- Native Americans built mounds in Ohio, insecticide made from chrysanthemums was developed in China, and the Roman Colosseum was built during 1–100 AD. (Note: Make sure students do not scramble events occurring in 100 BC with those in 100 AD.)

Electronic Media
Possible subjects to research might be Marcus Aurelius, Constantine the Great, Trajan, Athena, Castor and Pollux, Alexander the Great or Augustus.

---

4 Greek theaters were open-air, rounded structures built into the sloping sides of a hill. They had tiered stone seats with aisles and walkways. The action happened on a round stage called the *orchestra*. A low building behind the orchestra formed the backdrop and supported the scenery. In Roman theaters, the round orchestra was partially cut with a raised stage behind it. The performance took place on stage, not in the orchestra where important spectators sat. The seating formed a semicircle, rather than the two-thirds circle of Greek theaters. Roman theaters were often freestanding rather than cut into a concave hillside.

5 Romans sculpted realistic images of their emperors and important citizens. The Greeks more often carved gods and goddesses, and idealized athletes.

Maps
1 Greek city-states were separated by water, as well as by mountainous terrain, making them fiercely independent, self-governed entities. There were constant tensions and wars between them. Only occasionally did they draw together to fight off a common enemy: the Persians. Each city developed its own style of art and architecture. Vase paintings from each city have their own particular style. Each Greek architectural order originated in one city-state, and was gradually introduced to the rest of the Greek world.
2 Students should consider contemporary southern resorts with which they might be familiar, such as Miami or San Diego. There were palm trees, citrus groves, a nearby port, an amphitheater, homes with open courtyards—often

Activity 1: Immortalized in Clay

Activity Objectives
Students should be able to:

- Learn the correct proportions of the human face.

- Discover how to create a terra-cotta clay sculpture.

- Better understand the properties of clay.

Thinking Critically
A contributing reason for the development of Roman portrait sculpture was the Roman practice of ancestor worship. Ask students what images of ancestors their family has and why they value them. Discuss the historical role that the artist and the photographer have had in regard to portraiture.

- Who would have his/her portrait done today? Why?

- What is meant by an idealized portrait? A realistic portrait?

Preparation Ideas

- Show slides of various portrait sculpture. Ask students to discuss stylistic differences through the ages.

- Read Shelley's "Ode on a Grecian Urn" and ask students to discuss whether beauty is truth or truth is beauty.

Notes on Materials
Cover tables with the newspaper or plastic cloth. Students should have a cup of water, a sponge and a spray bottle of water to keep the sculpture damp. Each student also needs an assortment of clay tools and a plastic bag to store his/her sculpture. It is important to keep the work securely covered in storage between sessions.

Classroom Management
Each student can work independently on his/her self-portrait. Demonstrate proper clay-building techniques, such as wedging of clay, scoring, using slip when adding clay and using proper drying procedures (the thicker the clay piece, the longer it should be allowed to dry), as well as proper cleanup.

Tips

- If students are making a life-size work, have them each construct a sim-

ple wooden armature using a 10" piece of wood, 2" x 2" in width, nailed to a 1/4" plywood base cut to 9" x 12" (approximate measurements). Students should make sure the base of the work is thick enough to support the weight of the head. Remove the armature when the sculpture is complete and leather-hard.

- Work that is to be fired needs to be hollowed out and allowed to dry very slowly. Fire to proper cone temperature.

Evaluation
Possible criteria for evaluation:

- correct handling of clay

- use of correct facial proportions

- expressed creativity

Activity 1

Immortalized in Clay
Materials
for preliminary drawings:
mirrors or photographs
soft lead pencils (#2 or 4B, 6B)
12" x 18" white drawing paper
for sculpture:
newspaper or plastic cloth
containers of water
spray bottle
terra cotta clay
clay tools
heavy duty plastic bags

Take a look.
- Fig.6–40, *Head of Augustus,* 27 BC–14 AD. Bronze.
- Fig.6–41, *Portrait of a Lady,* 69 AD. Marble.
- Fig.6–42, *The Roman Legislator,* about 125 AD. Marble.

Think about it. Study the ways in which these portraits reflect the individuals which they represented. Compare and contrast Greek and Roman sculpture. Study the way the Romans handled individual characteristics such as hair, clothing and facial features in their portrait sculptures.

Do it. Use terra cotta to create a miniature or lifesize self-portrait sculpture. As an option, you could portray a well-known character in literature, theater or television.
- If doing a self-portrait, use a mirror to make several drawings of yourself to record individual aspects. You may choose to portray yourself as you would have looked in Roman times.
- If choosing a living character, find photographs of him or her from different angles and do a number of sketches. To bring an imaginary character to life, make sketches from photographs and people around you to develop distinctive facial characteristics.

Check it. Turn your sculpture as you work to look at it from all sides. You may need to make adjustments to keep the proportions realistic in three dimensions.

Helpful Hint: In your preliminary sketches, draw yourself or your subject from a variety of angles.

Activity 2

Ancient Legacy
Materials
12" x 18" white drawing paper or larger
drawing pencils (2H, 4H, 6H, HB)
rulers
kneaded erasers
drawing board (optional)

Take a look. Review the following artwork in this book:
- Fig.6–22, Iktinos and Kallikrates, *The Parthenon,* 447–432 BC.
- Fig.6–34, *The Pantheon,* about 118–125.

Think about it. The Doric style temple reached maturity during the Greek Classic period with the Parthenon, the central building of the Acropolis. The Romans built the Pantheon, a structure that honored the gods. It boasts a huge dome and a colonnade of Corinthian columns, carved from single blocks of stone.

Do it. Locate buildings in your community which use ideas and forms from ancient Greece and Rome. Look for large public buildings such as a stadium or meeting hall, or construction techniques such as domes, barrel vaults or cement construction. Do one or more of the following:
- Document the use of classical concepts in drawings, paintings or photographs.
- Do a pencil drawing of one of the buildings in your community.

- Make a drawing that incorporates the characteristics of Greek and Roman architecture to redesign a selected building. You may include pediments, friezes, columns, arches, domes and vaults.

Check it. Trade work with a friend and talk about what you've discovered and what your drawings represent. What insights can you offer to others who selected the same building(s)?

Helpful Hint: Do the front (facade) of the building only as a flat surface (don't worry about perspective).

Additional Activities

- Read Plato's and Aristotle's thoughts about beauty in *Philosophies of Art and Beauty.* Then write your own criteria of beauty (addressing how you know that something is beautiful).
- Roman artists were masters of the mosaic medium. Experiment with this technique by using small color chips (tesserae) to make a design or picture. Make these by cutting colored construction paper or magazine colors into 1 cm squares or irregular chips. Draw the outline of your subject on a large piece of chip board or corrugated cardboard. Glue the tesserae in place.
- Design Greek-style vase paintings of American mythology, depicting folk tales such as Paul Bunyan or Big Foot, or the story of Betsy Ross or other American heroes and heroines. Paint these stylized scenes on such typical twentieth century containers as plastic bottles, gallon wine jugs, etc. Acrylic paint will stick to most surfaces.

Activity 2: Ancient Legacy

Activity Objectives
Students should be able to:

- Gain a better understanding of how ancient civilizations have influenced their own.

- Learn characteristics of Greek and Roman architecture and locate examples in their environment.

- Study and practice line drawings of buildings.

Aysha Venjara

Age 17
Clarkstown High School North
New City, New York
Activity 1, Immortalized in Clay

Favorite kinds of art: pencil
sketching, sculpture, watercolor
Favorite artists: van Gogh, Michelangelo, Seurat

The human face is one of the most captivating and challenging objects to render. Sculpting it makes the challenge all the more difficult; however, the experience can be one of the most rewarding you have ever had. I believe sculpting my head has been one of my greatest learning experiences.

While developing the bust, my mind was most intensely concentrated on the intricate structure of the face—its raised and lowered areas, the specific turn of the nostrils, the curve of the mouth, and every little fold of skin that formed the eye. As the bust developed, I began to concentrate not as much on every little detail, but on the overall picture, how each part of the face related to all the other parts.

Upon learning about art history in school, my view of art began to change. It is most likely a habit of mine to look at everything close up and in detail. Learning about art history taught me that great artists not only had beautiful little details, but also had beautiful pieces of art on the whole. Art history helped me in taking a step back once in a while, to take the whole piece into account. Take, for example,

Michelangelo's *David*; it has the most minute details, down to every little fold in the eye, every curl in the lovely locks of hair, all the details that I admire; however, those details are just that. They supplement the entire piece, the whole. It is the whole piece, not just the details that make an impact.

Art and its influences have always been an important part of my life. My art has been an escape from everything around me, a haven. I can be in another world while I'm working on a piece and it relaxes me thus. The whole process of sculpting the bust was ever so soothing: feeling the wet clay in my hands and between my fingers, smoothing it onto the armature, using the weight of my body to sculpt it into the shape I wanted. It is a peaceful and calming process that lets you see the results of all the built-up energy inside you.

Anyone who has even the slightest bit of creativity and imagination can create beautiful and meaningful art. It simply takes some determination to see the project through. Many times, patience is the key. If an idea or method doesn't work, try again. If it doesn't work a second time, try looking at it from a different perspective. Just keep trying, never give in. And if it gets frustrating, take a step back; maybe you'll see things in terms of the whole picture, not just little details.

Aysha Venjara

Aysha, 1994. Terra cotta, height 10" (25 cm).

With a mirror for reference, Aysha works diligently on her own likeness in clay.

Teacher Spotlight
Dawn Sealy
Art Teacher
Clarkstown High School North

My best advice for students and teachers who are going to attempt the terra-cotta clay portrait is to review facial proportions first. Look at various sculpted portraits from the Egyptian, Greek and Roman periods, as well as more expressive attempts of artists like Brancusi, Matisse and Picasso. Remember that not all students will be comfortable sculpting their own face, so allow the students to be creative and to choose to sculpt a caricature, a friend or perhaps themselves as they might look in twenty years. Your students can also add an extra element to their work by sculpting themselves with a hat, headdress or clothing. Again, refer to art history for ideas. I motivated my students by showing them slides and work done by other students. Whether they sculpted themselves or a caricature, the results were pleasing.

Thinking Critically

• Are some more than other areas of your community influenced by Classical ideas?

• What are some of the interesting facts that you know about archaeology?

• Sometime during the construction or renovation of a building, evidence of prior influences comes to light. Are there renovation projects in your community that reveal previously undetected Classical influences?

Preparation Ideas
Obtain and display a map of your community. Have each student locate his/her home on the map. Together locate all the public buildings.

Notes on Materials
You may want to check with teachers of industrial design or technical drawing for ideas and the availability of appropriate tools.

Classroom Management
Each student can work independently on his/her drawing.

Tips

• Invite experts—architects, historians and historic preservationists—to speak to the class about architecture in your community.

• Make a video tour of sites of Classical influences in your community.

Evaluation
Possible criteria for evaluation:

• Can students demonstrate that they understand the connection between the Classical world and their community?

• Have students successfully located plausible modern examples of Greek and Roman architecture?

• Do student sketches contain recognizable elements of Greek and Roman design?

7 Religious Conviction

Chapter 7 Organizer

Chapter 7 Opener: Religious Conviction

Objectives	National Standards
Explain why during the Christian era, art shifts from earlier Greek and Roman traditions of realism toward a strong use of symbols.	**3d** Students evaluate and defend the validity of sources for content and the manner in which subject matter, symbols, and images are used in the student's works and in significant works by others.
Understand that under Justinian, the Byzantine Empire moved to the East in 527 AD and that the emperor was extremely influential in fostering the art of his reign.	**5a** Students identify intentions of those creating artworks, explore the implications of various purposes, and justify their analyses of purposes in particular works.
Comprehend that during the seventh century, the rival faith of Islam, which began in Arabia, spread rapidly to the Near East and the southern Mediterranean.	**4a** Students differentiate among a variety of historical and cultural contexts in terms of characteristics and purposes of works of art.
Describe Islamic art and explain why it relied heavily on geometric and abstract forms.	**3c** Students describe the origins of specific images and ideas and explain why they are of value in their artwork and in the work of others.
Understand that early medieval art was made largely by nomadic tribes until Charlemagne fostered a revival of Classical culture in the late eighth and early ninth centuries.	**3a** Students reflect on how artworks differ visually, spatially, temporally, and functionally, and describe how these are related to history and culture.

Lesson 7.1 Early Christian Art

	Teacher Edition References	
Special Feature: The Archangel Michael 206–207	Contextual Info 207	HOTS 207
Remainder of Lesson 7.1 208–211 Lesson 7.1 Review 211	Contextual Info 208, 210	HOTS 209, 211

Lesson 7.2 Byzantine Art: A Shift to the East

Special Feature: The Justinian and Theodora Mosaics 212–213	Contextual Info 213	HOTS 213
Remainder of Lesson 7.2 214–217 World Cultural Timeline 214 Lesson 7.2 Review 217	Contextual Info 214, 216 HOTS 215, 217	Conservation 216 Multicultural 214

Lesson 7.3 Islamic Faith and Art

Special Feature: The Alhambra 218–219	Contextual Info 219	HOTS 219
Remainder of Lesson 7.3 220–221 Lesson 7.3 Review 221	Contextual Info 220 HOTS 221	Multicultural 220 Performing Arts 220

Lesson 7.4 Early Medieval Art

Special Feature: The *Lindisfarne Gospel* Book 222–223	Contextual Info 224 HOTS 223	Cooperative 224 Multicultural 224
Remainder of Lesson 7.4 224–226 Lesson 7.4 Review 226 World Cultural Timeline 224 Primary-Source 227 Chapter Review 226	Contextual Info 226 HOTS 225	Performing Arts 225

Classroom Connections

	National Standards
Studio Activity 1 Family Fresco	**1b** Students conceive and create works of visual art that demonstrate an understanding of how the communication of their ideas relates to the media, techniques, and processes they use.
Studio Activity 2 Illuminate Your Initials	**3b** Students apply subjects, symbols, and ideas in their artworks and use the skills gained to solve problems in daily life.

1 Choose either Activity 1 or 2
1 Choose either Activity 1 or 2
1 Choose either Activity 1 or 2

Slides: Byzantine,
St. Apollinare in Classe,
Ravenna, interior,
36a, 82

Timeline: Early Christian, Byzantine,
Islamic and Early Medieval 204
Map: Byzantine and Islamic Empires 205
Context 205
Art 205
Quote 205

Other Resources

Books

Aries, Phillip, ed., trans. *A History of Private Life. Volume I: From Pagan Rome to Byzantium.* Cambridge: Belknap Press, 1987.

Beckwith, John. *Early Christian and Byzantine Art.* 2nd ed. New Haven: Yale University Press, 1992.

Conant, Kenneth John. *Carolingian and Romanesque Architecture: 800–1200.* 4th. ed., New Haven: Yale University Press, 1992.

Davis-Weyer, Caecilia. *Early Medieval Art: 300–1150.* Part of *Sources and Documents in the History of Art.* Toronto: University of Toronto Press Inc., reprint 1986.

Dodwell, Charles. *Painting in Europe 800–1200.* New Haven: Yale University Press, 1971.

Grabar, Andre. *The Golden Age of Justinian: From the Death of Theodosius to the Rise of Islam.* Part of *Arts of Mankind.* New York: George Braziller Inc., Odyssey Press Inc., and Golden Press, 1967.

————. *Early Christian Art: From the Rise of Christianity to the Death of Theodosius.* Part of *Arts of Mankind.* New York: George Braziller Inc., Odyssey Press Inc., and Golden Press, 1969.

Hubert, Jean, Porcher, Jean, and Volbach, W. F. *Europe of the Invasions.* Part of *Arts of Mankind.* New York: George Braziller Inc., Odyssey Press Inc., and Golden Press,1969.

————. *The Carolingian Renaissance.* Part of *Arts of Mankind.* New York: George Braziller Inc., Odyssey Press Inc., and Golden Press, 1970.

Krautheimer, Richard. *Early Christian and Byzantine Architecture.* 4th ed. New Haven: Yale University Press, 1992.

Lasko, Peter. *Ars Sacra 800–1200.* Baltimore: Penguin USA, 1972.

Mango, Cyril A. *Art of the Byzantine Empire, 312–1453.* Part of *Sources and Documents in the History of Art.* Toronto: University of Toronto Press Inc., 1986.

Snyder, James. *Medieval Art: Painting, Sculpture, Architecture, 4–14th Century.* Englewood Cliffs: Prentice Hall, 1989.

Slides: Early Medieval, *Fibulae*, 51b, 92

Slides: Byzantine, St. Apollinare in Classe, 470 AD, Ravenna, exterior, 37a, 83;
Early Christian, *Gospel Cover*, 46b, 81

Slides: Byzantine, *Emperor Justinian and Attendants*, San Vitale, Ravenna, 38a, 85;
Byzantine, *Empress Theodora*, San Vitale, Ravenna, 39a, 86;
Byzantine, Exterior of San Vitale, 47b, 84

Slides: Byzantine, *St. Mark's Exterior*, Venice, 40a, 87;
Byzantine, *Cyprus Plate*, 48b, 88

Slides: Islamic, *Dome of the Rock*, Jerusalem, 41a, 89; Islamic, *Koran page*, 49b, 90;
Islamic, *Koran title page*, 50b, 91 **Overhead Transparencies:** Supporting a Dome, 7
Large Reproductions: Interior of mosque, Cordoba, 8

Slides: Early Medieval, *Fibulae*, 51b, 92; Early Medieval, *Front Cover of the Binding of the Lindau Gospels*, 1a, 4

One day to pour plaster. (This project could be done in one day if the plaster were poured and allowed to harden before the studio.) One to three days to draw and paint.

styrofoam platter, tempera paint or watercolors, plaster of Paris, bucket, water, assorted brushes, terry-cloth towel, vine charcoal, newspapers, paper clips

This activity can be completed in one day.

white drawing paper, no larger than 4"x6" or 6"x 9", pencil, #3 or 4H, kneaded eraser, assorted fine-tipped markers

Introduce

All four periods of art discussed in this chapter had religious conviction as a driving force behind their development. Sometimes the creative momentum was carried primarily by religious fervor, as in the case of early Christian, Islamic and early medieval monastic art. Byzantine art under Justinian and early medieval art under Charlemagne flourished because of imperial patronage and religious power and often aggrandized the role of the emperor.

Lessons at a Glance

7.1 *Early Christian Art*
Early Christian art relied on figures and objects as symbols to communicate religious thoughts and ideas.

7.2 *Byzantine Art: A Shift to the East*
Byzantine art reached its golden age in Constantinople under Emperor Justinian. The style, lasting hundreds of years, spread throughout the Eastern Empire to Russia.

7.3 *Islamic Faith and Art*
Islamic religion and culture spread rapidly across the Near East and the southern Mediterranean in the seventh century, introducing a style of art that was based on complex geometric and abstract designs.

7.4 *Early Medieval Art*
In the early medieval era, Christian and pagan nomadic tribes made small, portable art objects that could be carried as they migrated throughout Europe. Under Charlemagne, a renewed interest in Classical culture influenced the art and architecture of the late eighth and early ninth centuries.

---

7 Religious Conviction

7–a This clasp would have been used to fasten a cloak or other exterior garment. *Fibula*, 6th century, silver. Archaeological Museum, Udine, Italy.

WITH THE EMERGENCE OF Christianity on the European continent, there was a change in the kind of art produced. During the Greek and Roman period before the birth of Christ, art had been realistic. But, the early Christians were more concerned with symbolic representation.

When the Christian religion first began, it was outlawed in the Roman Empire. These early Christians worshipped and buried their dead in tunnels called catacombs where they created frescoes on the walls and ceilings.

Christianity eventually became the official religion of the Roman Empire in 313 AD. Once this happened, a church-building campaign began that would last for centuries. The earliest churches were built like the Roman civic buildings called basilicas. These churches were plain on the outside and decorated on the inside.

In 337, the Roman Empire split into two parts. The Western Empire declined, but the Eastern Empire, with its capital in Constantinople, flourished. In 527, Justinian became emperor and began the period known as the Golden Age of Byzantium. During this period, many gorgeous churches were built which had extraordinary interiors of glass mosaics. Byzantine architecture spread all over Eastern Europe all the way into what is now Russia.

Then, in the seventh century, another faith, which was to rival Christianity, started in Arabia. This was Islam (its practioners are Muslims) and it spread rapidly into the Near East and the southern Mediterranean. The Islamic religion forbade the use of the human figure in its religious artwork, so its artists turned to a more abstract form of expression.

Early medieval art began the period known as the Middle Ages. This early part of the Middle Ages lasted from the 400s to the 900s. After the collapse of the Roman Empire, various European tribes moved through Europe looking for a place to settle. They created small works of art that were portable, such as weapons or ornaments. These were decorated with geometric designs and animal motifs influenced by both Christian and Islamic art.

			750 Gregorian chant music, England, France and Germany		**1453** Constantinople conquered by Ottoman Turks
331 Seat of Roman Empire moves to Constantinople	**570** Mohammed, founder of Islam, born	**698–721** *Lindisfarne Gospel*, England		**1286** Spectacles invented	

Early Christian, Byzantine, Islamic and Early Medieval

| **532–537** Hagia Sophia, Constantinople | **643** Dome of the Rock begun, Jerusalem | **700** Easter eggs come into use among Christians | **800** Charlemagne crowned Holy Roman Emperor c. 980 Vikings discover Greenland | **1334–1391** The Alhambra palace, Spain | **1554–1566** Cathedral of St. Basil, Moscow |

Objectives

Students should be able to:

Explain why during the Christian era, art shifts from earlier Greek and Roman traditions of realism toward a strong use of symbols.

Understand that under Justinian, the Byzantine Empire moved to the East in 527 AD and that the emperor was extremely influential in fostering the art of his reign.

Comprehend that during the seventh century, the rival faith of Islam, which began in Arabia, spread rapidly to the Near East and the southern Mediterranean.

Describe Islamic art and explain why it relied heavily on geometric and abstract forms.

Understand that early medieval art was made largely by nomadic tribes until Charlemagne fostered a revival of Classical culture in the late eighth and early ninth centuries.

> Faith is the substance of things hoped for, the evidence of things not seen.
>
> Hebrews, xi, i

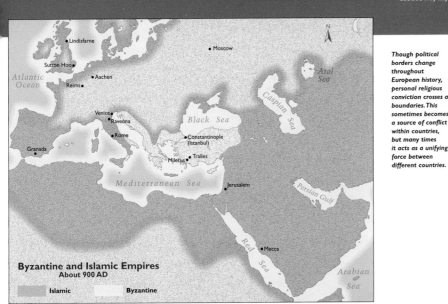

Though political borders change throughout European history, personal religious conviction crosses all boundaries. This sometimes becomes a source of conflict within countries, but many times it acts as a unifying force between different countries.

Byzantine and Islamic Empires
About 900 AD

Islamic   Byzantine

7–b Islamic monuments are decorated with abstract motifs. Human figures are prohibited in religious art and architecture.
Dome of the Rock, Jerusalem, Israel detail (fig.7–24).

7–c Can you name at least three different materials that were used to construct and decorate the interior of this church?
St. Apollinare in Classe, Ravenna, 533–549. Interior view.

Quote
Have students read the quote. Ask them if they think that spiritual faith can be made visible through art. Next, have students respond from the point of view of an ordinary citizen, a religious leader, a politician and a scientist. How and why might their opinions change with each role?

Map
Have students identify the modern countries that were influenced by the Islamic faith by comparing the chapter map to the contemporary world map at the back of the book. Ask in what present-day country is the city that was once called Constantinople.

Evaluate
Ask students what change occurred in art with the emergence of Christianity and Islam. Using the fibula and view of the Dome of the Rock, have students explain how the art of this period differed from the that of the Greeks and Romans.

Reteach
Ask students to find images in Chapter 7 that illustrate how art was used to influence people's religious beliefs.

• Are students familiar with any spiritual objects from their own heritage?

• Can they identify any similarities or differences to the ones in the book?

Ask students whether art can ever truly capture discernible, objective qualities of the divine.

• What does spiritual truth actually look like?

• Since human beings are limited by their experiences on earth, can we know?

• Share that symbols can be powerful representations for something in both the physical world and tangible realm.

Teach
Timeline
To demonstrate how both the Christian and Islamic traditions existed at the same time, have students find the notation for the Dome of the Rock on the timeline and then plot a notation for St. Apollinare in Classe (fig.7–c), using the date in the caption.

Context
Ask students to pretend that they are creatures from outer space walking into St. Apollinare in Classe during the sixth century.

• What might it feel like to stand within this resplendent building?

• What do you think Christian worshipers might have felt about the holy figure (St. Apollinare) in the center of the apse?

• What in the image helped you form your opinion?

Art
Tell students to compare the decorations in fig.7–b and fig.7–c.

• Which one is Islamic and which one is early Christian?

• Are there any figures depicted in fig.7–b?

• What symbols indicate that fig.7–c is part of an early Christian church?

Lesson 7.1

Early Christian art relied on figures and objects as symbols to communicate religious thoughts and ideas.

Warm-up

Make simple line drawings on the blackboard of a heart, a flower and a house. Ask students to divide a piece of notebook paper in half. On the left, have them write the name of the three drawn objects. On the right, tell them to list what each image means or represents to them. Afterward, discuss how a visual image can describe something in the real world and also be symbolic, communicating a meaning outside of itself. Introduce the idea that early Christian art used recognizable images as a symbolic language or code to express religious concepts.

Objectives

Students should be able to:

Explain why early Christian art used figures and images symbolically.

Understand that before Emperor Constantine made Christianity the state religion in 313 AD, frescoes of Christian subjects were painted on the ceilings and walls of secret, underground tunnel-like catacombs.

Comprehend that the legalization of Christianity gave rise to new architecture and highly crafted objects.

Describe the typical plan of an early Christian church and understand its origins in Roman basilicas.

Understand that the T-shaped basilica plan became the general basis for European churches for many centuries.

Vocabulary Definitions

diptych (*dip*-tik) A pair of wood, ivory or metal panels (large or small) usually hinged together, with painting or carving on the inside surfaces. Usually placed over an altar.
catacombs (*kat*-i-komz) Underground burial places made up of passageways and niches for holding the sarcophagi. Some catacombs contained chapels and meeting rooms of the early Christians.
atrium (*ay*-tree-um) The inner court of a Roman house, open to the sky. Also, the enclosed (but open to the sky) courtyard in front of the main doors of a basilica or church.

7.1 Early Christian Art

BEFORE THE SPREAD OF Christianity, Romans had painted figures and scenes that were natural and realistic. The followers of Christianity, however, developed a new type of art based on their new religion. Their paintings were *symbolic*. Figures and objects suggest people and events of religious importance. Realism was not the goal of these artists. Instead, they wanted to communicate a religious thought or idea. This concept changed the course of art for several centuries.

At first, Christian artists borrowed symbols from the Romans around them. Juno's peacock became the symbol for immortality. The phoenix became the symbol for Christ's resurrection. Although first shunned as evil and deathly, the cross later became the dominant Christian symbol.

Christianity gained broad acceptance in the fourth century when the Emperor Constantine made it the state religion. This meant that the religion and its art were officially sanctioned. Large building campaigns were undertaken. The interior decoration of churches and the creation of highly crafted objects for the Christian liturgy would occupy hundreds of artists and artisans for centuries.

Key Notes
- Early Christian art was symbolic.
- Earliest surviving Christian art is found on frescoed walls of catacombs outside Rome.
- Acceptance of Christianity as state religion created a need for new architecture.

Vocabulary
diptych
catacombs
atrium
nave
apse
baldachin
transept
crypts
rotunda
sarcophagus

7–2 The creator of this ivory diptych was not interested in depicting real space. The niche and stairs are simply ornamental.
The Archangel Michael, detail.

The Archangel Michael

During the early Christian period, large sculptures were not made. However, artists did produce small pieces of exquisite craftsmanship. Artists sculpted relief carvings on sarcophagi (stone coffins), ivory panels, metalwork, church furniture and accessories, and book covers.

All art was religious and symbolic in nature, but these works also reflected the Classical ideals of beauty. Human figures were idealized, not realistic. A particularly fine example of the blend of Classical style and Christian beliefs is an ivory panel called *The Archangel Michael* (fig.7–1). The ivory panel is one half of a hinged *diptych* (two pieces).

In Western religions, archangels represent aspects of the divine energy. Compare this majestic archangel with a winged Victory from Greek or Roman art. The flowing folds of the robe are Classical yet naturalistic. The delicately incised wings, the features and the way the hair is styled are of the pre-Christian tradition. However, the Archangel Michael heralds a power that comes from God, not mortals. He does not inhabit an earthly space. Notice how his feet seem to hover above the stairs (fig.7–2). Clearly, Michael is not really standing on the step. The architectural setting behind him is symbolic and ornamental, not three-dimensional. The disembodied quality of the sculpture conveys the sense that Archangel Michael is a divine messenger.

nave The central section of a church where the congregation assembles. In a basilica plan, the space extends from the main entrance to the apse or the crossing. Usually, the nave is flanked by side aisles.
apse A large semicircular (or polygonal) area at the choir end of a church. Usually contains the altar. May also be found at the ends of transepts or at the ends of smaller chapels.
baldachin (bal-dah-*cheen*) A fixed canopy of wood, stone, fabric, etc., over an altar, throne or doorway. Sometimes portable, as when it is over a movable statue during a parade or procession.
transept The part of a cross-shaped church at right angles to the long nave, usually with one arm on each side of the crossing.

crypt (kript) A vaulted space below ground level, usually beneath the raised choir or apse of a church, or under a temple or shrine.
rotunda (ro-*tun*-dah) A round building or interior hall, topped by a dome.
sarcophagus (sar-*koff*-ah-gus) A stone coffin, often elaborately carved.

Teach

Art History: Explain how early Christian art blended the Classical emphasis on the idealized human body with the use of Christian symbols that expressed religious concepts. Have students study the Greek statue of the *Kritios Boy* (fig.6–10, fig.6–11) and then compare it to *The Archangel Michael* (fig.7–1).

- How is early Christian ivory carving different from the Greek sculpture?

7–1 What aspects of this work are naturalistic? Which are stylized?

The Archangel Michael, 5th century. Part of ivory diptych, 16 1/2" (42 cm) high. British Museum, London.

Thinking Like a Conservator

Faced with the task of preserving works of art, a conservator is rigorously trained in chemistry, physics and the technical aspects of treating and repairing art. The conservator also needs to know the process by which an object is made. To make an ivory relief such as the *Archangel Michael* (fig.7–1), rectangles are sawed out of the walls of a tusk. These reliefs are seldom more than 12 inches in length. The *Archangel Michael*, nearly 50% larger, is exceptional. This relief must have been a rare and expensive item when it was created.

The conservator, very aware of the relief's uniqueness and its increasing fragility, must keep it in an optimal environment. As with most works of art, the regulation of humidity and temperature is critical. Excessive dryness causes ivory to crack. Too much moisture makes it warp. Elevated temperatures can result in color changes. Ideal conditions for the storage and display of ivory are 45% to 55% relative humidity and 65 to 72 degrees Fahrenheit. Light levels need to be kept at a minimum.

The next time you walk into a room in a museum that is a little bit chilly and rather dimly lit, keep in mind that this environment was created for a reason. The hope is that objects displayed there will be preserved for generations to come.

Contextual Information
Romans and Christians

Group worship was not a part of most Roman religious practices, which were based on giving offerings to appease the gods, who took the forms of winds, rain and trees. With the emergence of Christianity, and its code of ethics that stressed love, forgiveness and eternal life in heaven, Roman emperors began persecuting its followers because the emperors considered themselves to be gods and wanted no competition from the God of Christians. The persecution of Christians began with Nero in 64 AD and lasted nearly 300 years.

Higher-Order Thinking Skills

Refer to images in chapters 5 and 6 to help students identify naturalistic and stylized elements of this ivory. Particularly look at the images of *Gudea of Lagash* (fig.5–13) from Sumeria, *The Winged Genius* (fig.5–15) from Assyria, and the *Charioteer of Delphi* (fig.6–13) and the *Mounted Procession from the Parthenon* (fig.6–15) from Greece. Ask students to name other images that would be helpful for identification of these elements.

• What parts are not highly realistic? Have students note how the robe falls and how the Archangel stands on the stairs.

• Is there a sense that this figure is an actual person?

Criticism: Ask students to examine the exterior of an early Christian church (fig.7–6) and imagine that they are about to enter the building to worship during the late fifth century. After they view the facade, have them describe what the inside of this building might look like—its walls, floor and ceiling.

• What images, colors and forms might they see? Since there is no electricity, where will the light come from? After they have brainstormed possibilities, have them study fig.7–5, an etching that depicts the inside of an early Christian church.

• What surprised them and what did they find that they expected to see?

• How might the glittering mosaics that covered every available surface have made them feel?

• Does this type of interior, typical of Early Christian churches, evoke an otherworldly spiritual atmosphere? (The glittering reflections symbolize the ethereal light of God's kingdom and power.)

Evaluate

Ask students to draw a diagram of a Christian cross, the central symbol of the Christian religion. Ask them to describe any similarities to the shape of the basilica plan in fig.7–4. Students should see that the church buildings themselves were symbols since they resembled the cross, signifying Christ's sacrifice.

Reteach

Ask students to consider the following: Early Christian art was symbolic rather than realistic.

• Are there times when your thinking is symbolic instead of literal?

• How about when you dream or tell stories that are meant to make a point? Help students to name other forms of art that can be symbolic. Discuss examples in dance, music and poetry.

Contextual Information

Catacombs

Catacombs were first only hollows in hillsides but became intricate underground tombs cut in rock. Because Roman law forbade burial within the city, these tunnels—and churches such as St. Paul Outside the Walls—are all found outside the old city walls. The use of the catacombs was abandoned after Christianity became the official religion, but they were uncovered in 1578 during excavations of Rome. Catacombs were constructed not just by Romans, and have been found in Malta, Sicily, Egypt and what was the ancient land of Palestine.

The Contributions of Constantine

The Edict of Milan allowed the practice of Christianity and also restored to Christians all money, property and possessions taken from them during their persecution. Through his edict, Constantine hoped also to restore public order.

Constantine ordered the construction of what became Old St. Peter's on the site thought to be St. Peter's burial spot. The church, 850 feet long and 300 feet wide with a walkway around the sacred plot, could accommodate thousands of pilgrims and became a clear statement of Rome's new religion and Constantine's greatness. Constantine ordered the building of many churches that used the basilica plan, a design well suited not only to government functions but also to decoration in marble, paint and fresco. Incorporated into these churches, partly because of the speed of their construction, were columns, capitals and some ornaments from earlier Roman temples.

7–3 The catacombs functioned primarily as cemeteries. There may have been as many as four million bodies buried in the catacombs of Rome.
The Good Shepherd. Ceiling fresco, early 4th century. Catacomb of Saints Peter and Marcellinus, Rome.

Early Christian Frescoes

In Italy, Rome became the center of Christian activities, although Roman religion and traditions continued to be practiced. For a time, before the era of Constantine, the Christian religion was outlawed. Believers were persecuted and blamed for many of the troubles in the empire. In order to escape torture and death, they often inhabited the tunnel-like *catacombs* outside Rome. Here they met for worship, buried their dead and even lived at times in complete protection.

The earliest surviving Christian art known are frescoes that decorate the ceilings and walls of chapels within the catacombs. The ceiling fresco in the Catacomb of Saints Peter and Marcellinus shows Christ as *The Good Shepherd* (fig.7–3) in the center. (Christ had often spoken of himself as the good shepherd who gives his life for his sheep.) As in other very early Christian art, he is shown as a beardless Roman youth.

In the half-circles are several parts of the story of Jonah, an Old Testament prophet. Jonah was a significant symbol for early Christians, and his story was often used in their art. At the left, Jonah is thrown from the ship. On the right, he emerges from the whale, and, at the bottom, he is safe again on dry land. Perhaps the missing section showed him in the belly of the whale. The story was a great comfort to the Christians because it showed God's protection, care and

deliverance. The standing figures with their hands raised are symbols of church members in attitudes of prayer. The circle itself represents the dome of heaven. Notice the cross formed by the bands used as connecting lines.

The Beginnings of Christian Churches

The Emperor Constantine issued the Edict of Milan in 313 AD, which made Christianity the official religion. Until his edict, worshipers had met secretly in small houses. Now, a new architecture was needed for large numbers of worshipers. The Roman basilicas (civic buildings) seemed to fit the requirements. The basilica plan seemed ideally suited for Christian worship.

The early Christian basilica (fig.7–4) was a long brick building with a timber roof. Connected to the front of the structure was an *atrium* (a courtyard) with a covered walkway around it. Entrances were at the rear of the atrium on the corners. Worshipers stood in the *nave*, or central part of the basilica. On each side of the nave were side aisles. The side aisles were separated by a row of columns, usually taken from pagan temples.

7–4 Typical basilica plan.
Upper diagram reproduced by permission of Harcourt Brace Jovanovich, Inc., from *Art in Perspective* by Henri Dorra.

7–6 The plain exterior of this church contrasts with its rich and colorful interior (fig.7–c).
St. Apollinare in Classe. Exterior view, 533–549. Ravenna.

7–5 The long nave with its rows of columns leads the eye to the altar, the focal point of the church.
Giovanni Battista Piranesi, *St. Paul Outside the Walls.* Etching, 1749. Rome.

Higher-Order Thinking Skills

Use the plan and diagram of a basilica along with the text's description to help students identify the parts of a basilica shown in the etching of *St. Paul Outside the Walls* (fig.7–5) and both views of *St. Apollinare in Classe* (figs.7–c, 7–6). Students may have trouble seeing the relationship between the segments shown in the photographs to the whole shown by plans and diagrams. Understanding these relationships will increase students' ability to visualize and imagine an experience of the building.

or **baldachin**, over it. This was made of carved and painted wood or stone.

A triumphal arch, so-called because it symbolized the victory of Christ over eternal death, separated the nave from the apse. Later basilicas had **transepts** (fig.7–4) that added interior space to accommodate larger crowds and a greater number of clergy. **Crypts** were sometimes placed under the raised apse to provide burial space for bishops or church leaders. The general plan, enlarged and elaborated as time passed, became the basis for European cathedrals of later centuries. About forty of the original three hundred basilicas are still standing.

Windows were located above the columns to flood the interior with light. The **apse** was a semicircular area at the front of the nave. Above the apse was a half-dome. The altar was placed on the raised portion of the apse and always had a canopy,

Contextual Information

Christian Persecution

Because of the persecution of the Christians before the Edict of Milan in 313, they did not create much sculpture because they could not provide for its safekeeping. Also because of the persecution, Christians found that the use of symbols rather than any obvious Christian references in their art was a safer means of expression. Stories from the Bible could be told through art by the use of symbols for Christ and the early saints. One such symbol was the god Orpheus as the good shepherd Christ.

7–7 Early Christians identified themselves as the sheep of the Church's flock and Christ as their shepherd.
The Good Shepherd, 3rd century. Marble, half life-size. Lateran Museum, Rome.

7–8 Early Christian art uses symbols to stand for stories, people and ideas.
Chalice of Antioch. 350–500. Silver and gilt, 7 1/2" (19 cm) high, from Syria. Cloisters Collection, Metropolitan Museum of Art, New York.

The greatest basilica was Old St. Peter's in Rome. It was torn down during the Renaissance to make way for the current huge basilica of St. Peter's in the Vatican. Slightly later, *St. Paul Outside the Walls* (fig.7–5) was erected. It was destroyed by fire but was rebuilt according to old plans, paintings and drawings. Like all Christian basilicas, the interior was highly decorated. Mosaics of colored glass and gold cover the walls, creating a shimmering and sparkling surface. Even the floor is decorated with inlaid marble designs. Eighty granite columns in four rows direct the view toward the triumphal arch (also covered with mosaics) and toward the apse and altar.

In direct contrast to the glittering interiors, which symbolized the richness of spirit, the exteriors were plain brick. The exterior of *The Basilica of St. Apollinare in Classe* (fig.7–6) in Ravenna gives no hint of the mosaic-covered walls inside (fig.7–c).

Although the basilica plan was used most often in early Christian churches, it is important to note that some churches followed a central, or ***rotunda***, plan.

Sculpture and Other Metalwork

Little sculpture was produced in the early Christian church, and much of it has been destroyed. *The Good Shepherd* (fig.7–7) is a freestanding sculpture in the Roman style. It is one of the last Christian works that adheres to naturalism rather than stressing the symbolic nature of its subject. Christ is depicted as a Roman youth with his feet firmly planted on the ground. With the evolution of early Christian art, figures became more ethereal or otherworldly, as we have seen in *The Archangel Michael* (fig.7–1).

The Chalice of Antioch (fig.7–8) is an example of the metalwork produced during this period. Its inner, plain silver cup is set into an ornately carved silver and gilt openwork shell. The carved and footed shell has a figure of Christ depicted on each side. One is youthful and the other is more mature. Apostles, animals and birds are woven into a network of vines, branches, leaves and grapes—all symbolic of Christ

and his work. The eagle on one side and the rosettes at the top are signs of immortality.

Coffin-like boxes made of stone, called *sarcophagi* (one is a **sarcophagus**) were carved completely in relief. The sarcophagi were used as caskets for burial. The carved sarcophagus was a Roman development, but the subject matter on the Christian sarcophagi was religious (fig.7–9).

7–9 Can you identify any of the biblical scenes depicted on this sarcophagus?
Sarcophagus of Junius Bassus, about 359. Marble, 3' 10 1/2" x 8' (1.2 x 2.4 m). Museo Petriano, St. Peter's, Rome.

Lesson 7.1 Review

1 Name an early Christian symbol and tell what it represented.
2 Where were the earliest Christian frescoes painted?
3 What is a diptych?
4 What type of Roman buildings did the early Christians adapt to become churches?

5 How were basilicas decorated on the inside? Contrast this to their exterior appearance.
6 What was the purpose of a sarcophagus?
7 Describe how Christ was usually portrayed in the earliest Christian art.

Lesson 7.1 Review Answers

1 Possible answers include:
peacock = immortality
phoenix = Christ's resurrection
Good Shepherd = Christ
cross = Christ
2 On the walls of the catacombs outside Rome
3 A diptych is a pair of painted or carved panels, usually hinged together.
4 Basilicas

5 The interiors were highly decorated to symbolize the richness of the inner Christian spirit. Shimmering, sparkling mosaics of colored glass and gold covered the walls. Floors were decorated with inlaid marble designs. In contrast, the exteriors were plain brick.
6 A casket for burial
7 As a Roman youth

Lesson 7.2

Byzantine art reached its golden age in Constantinople under Emperor Justinian. The style, lasting hundreds of years, spread throughout the Eastern Empire to Russia.

Warm-up

Pose this question to students: "If you wanted to create a shimmering, heavenly light inside a church, what materials would you use?" If they need a hint, give them a choice between thick, opaque paint or small bits of reflective glass set close together at varying angles within a bed of cement. Share with them that Byzantine mosaics with messages of salvation covered every available surface so that the entire building glittered with a celestial glow.

Objectives

Students should be able to:

Understand that the Roman Empire was divided into two after the death of Constantine in 337, and Constantinople became the powerful seat of the Eastern sphere.

Describe the Golden Age of Byzantine art and culture that began under the emperor Justinian.

Describe how Byzantine art stresses symbolism over naturalism as a means of communicating spiritual ideas.

Explain that Byzantine architecture and mosaic decoration spread throughout Eastern Europe and eventually to Russia.

Comprehend that in the early eighth century, a controversy disrupted the development of Byzantine culture for over 100 years as iconoclasts, who wanted to destroy religious images, fought those who felt it important to keep religious depictions.

Explain that Byzantine icons (religious images) were painted on wood panels and were used both in worship centers at home and in church interiors.

Vocabulary Definitions

tessera (*tess*-ah-rah) (pl. tesserae [*tess*-ah-ree]) Bits of colored glass or stone used in making mosaics.
pendentive (*pen*-den-tiv) A triangular piece of vaulting springing from the corner of a rectangular area to support

7.2 Byzantine Art: A Shift to the East

AFTER THE DEATH of Constantine in 337, the Roman Empire was split into Eastern and Western Empires. The West went into a steady decline. Rome lost its power and was sacked by Germanic tribes. The Eastern Empire, with its capital in Constantinople, gained great political strength. In 527, Justinian ascended the throne of the Eastern Roman, or Byzantine, Empire. He recaptured most of southern Italy and established Ravenna on the east coast as the new center of power.

Justinian's reign began the so-called Golden Age of Byzantine culture and art. The number of important and beautiful church buildings constructed in Ravenna and Constantinople in the fifth and sixth centuries is amazing. Many are plain brick on the outside and look rather ordinary at first (fig.7–10). However, inside they are sumptuously encrusted with brilliant Byzantine mosaics.

Byzantine architecture spread over Eastern Europe. Gradually the exterior as well as the interior became highly imaginative, as seen in the onion-shaped domes of Russian churches.

The Byzantine tradition of art and architecture extended for centuries. For well over 1000 years artists worked to produce masterpieces of heavenly, glimmering beauty.

Key Notes

- Center of power moves to the east with Constantinople as its capital.
- First Golden Age of Byzantine begins with the reign of the Emperor Justinian.
- Mosaics made of glass become the primary means of wall decoration and completely cover the interiors of churches.

Vocabulary
tesserae
pendentives
piers
icons
iconostasis
triptych

Special Feature
The Justinian and Theodora Mosaics

Artists of the early Christian and Byzantine churches conveyed their message of salvation through mosaics. They achieved an incredible degree of expressiveness in this medium. Roman mosaics had been of polished, colored stone, but Byzantine mosaics were made of brightly colored glass (**tesserae**) pressed into wet plaster. Glass increased the color range and could be made to reflect the light. The pieces were set at a slight angle to the surface to create a shimmering effect.

One of the most striking mosaics is found in the church of San Vitale in Ravenna. The building and the mosaics inside it are extraordinary achievements of Byzantine art.

The mosaics cover almost every available surface. They sparkle with color. Green and gold are used most often, but there are also scarlets, purples and blues. Images and sym-

7–10 This building is based on the central, or rotunda, plan.
San Vitale. Interior, about 525–547. Ravenna.

a round or polygonal dome. Usually four pendentives spring from the four corners of a crossing to support the dome.
pier (peer) A massive vertical masonry pillar that supports an arch, a vault or another kind of roof. Also used under pendentives to support a dome. A square area in a Gothic church marked by a pier at each corner is known as a "bay."
icon (*eye*-kon) A religious image or likeness; in the Eastern Orthodox religion, usually a panel painting of a saint or of Christ.
iconostasis (eye-kon-*ah*-stah-sis) A decorated screen (often of icons) in Eastern Orthodox churches, separating the main part of the church from the sanctuary.

triptych (*trip*-tik) An altarpiece consisting of three panels joined together. Often, the two outer panels are hinged to close over the central panel.

Teach

Art History: Emperor Justinian heralded in the Golden Age of Byzantine art. Have students examine fig.7–11 and search for ways that the artist equates the emperor with divine power.

- Where is Justinian located within the mosaic?

- What surrounds his crowned head? Halos of radiant light are symbols that express the virtue and holiness of saints.

7–11 Notice that the name of the bishop of Ravenna, Maximianus, is written above his head. The bishop played an important role in building the church, and he dedicated it in 547. *Emperor Justinian and Attendants*, about 547. Mosaic, nearly life-size figures. San Vitale, Ravenna.

bols covering the entire sanctuary illustrate primarily Biblical subjects.

There are two mosaics flanking the altar which depict contemporary figures. *Emperor Justinian and Attendants* (fig.7–11) is on one wall, and the *Empress Theodora and Attendants* (fig.7–12) is on the other. Justinian and Theodora are participating in a church service. The bread and wine of the Eucharist are being presented. Justinian carries a vessel containing the bread, and Theodora carries the golden cup containing the wine.

The emperor, with a halo around his head, is showing everyone that he is God's holy representative on earth and is therefore holy himself. Justinian is exactly at the center. The positions of the figures are very important and denote their rank. Justinian is flanked by his sources of power—court officials and the military on his right, the priesthood on his left.

The figures are generally stylized. Several of the faces are quite individualistic and are probably por-

7–12 Analyze how the artist has placed these figures in a particular place, yet at the same time, has negated any sense of real space. *Empress Theodora and Attendants*, about 547. Mosaic, nearly life-size figures. San Vitale, Ravenna.

traits. The bodies of these tall, slim figures disappear under flat, decorative costumes. Large eyes stare from small, almond-shaped faces. Their feet do not seem to touch the ground as they look directly ahead. They look as though they are posing rather stiffly for a photographer.

Note the monogram of Christ on the shield at left. The monogram consists of the superimposed Greek letters X and P (chi and rho) which are the first two letters of the Greek word for Christ. This symbol serves

to further emphasize the divine protection the emperor believed God bestowed on his reign.

All of the figures sparkle today as they did in the sixth century. The background of gold glass tesserae (gold leaf embedded in glass) in the Justinian mosaic symbolizes the holiness and perfection of heaven and eliminates any specific spatial reference. The use of gold for this symbolic purpose was typical of Byzantine art.

• What color dominates the scene? The sparkling gold leaf represents the heavenly spiritual realm. Have students read pages 212–213 for further information on how Justinian is shown as God's representative on earth and is therefore holy himself.

Art History: Why might the artist of fig.7–12 have decided that the illusion of a real place was not important in describing Empress Theodora and her attendants? What qualities in the mosaic indicate that she, like her husband, is directly connected to God? In addition to the impressive symbols and colors, the ruling couple are shown participating in a Mass, an important church ceremony.

Evaluate

Art and architecture have created evocative sacred settings for centuries. Divide the class into teams and assign each the task of planning the design and decoration of a contemporary structure that evokes a sense of divine power. How would they use shapes, colors, forms, materials and scale to create the effects they wanted?

Reteach

Byzantine architecture spread throughout Europe but also reflected distinct characteristics of its locations. For example, have students compare the exteriors of *St. Mark's* in Venice (fig.7–17), the *Cathedral of St. Basil* in Moscow (fig.7–18) and *Hagia Sophia* in Constantinople (fig.7–13). Ask students

Contextual Information

The Emperor Justinian

In *Emperor Justinian and Attendants* (fig.7–11), the emperor is wearing imperial purple, a color reserved for royalty, and his head is surrounded by a halo—a design from ancient Persia that signified connection to the sun god, or a supreme being. At his left is Bishop Maximianus, who was responsible for the completion of San Vitale and its consecration in 547. His name is over his head to show his importance. Between the bishop and the emperor is Julius Argentarius, the principal benefactor of the church. The men in the mosaic are divided into three groups: the emperor and his staff, the clergy, and the army, which bears the *chi-rho* shield.

Justinian was responsible for simplifying Roman law from 2000 law books to 100. He wanted to reduce the number of lawsuits, which were based on thousands of existing rules. It took six years for seventeen lawyers to write the new law, *Corpus Juris Civilis*, in Latin.

Higher-Order Thinking Skills

The mosaics of Justinian and Theodora can be compared to *Doves* (fig.6–49), from Rome, for stylistic and representational characteristics. By analyzing the mosaics for composition and spatial placement, the discussion of symbolism can move into ideas about the relationship of the emperor and empress to the saints and to God. This tie between ruler and God became the Christian basis for the long-standing concept known in Europe as the Divine Right of Kings, which held that royalty ruled by the express will of God and possessed a particular connection to heaven. Works of art portrayed that concept extensively and validated its practice.

to pretend they are a priest and to choose in which building they would want to conduct services. Have them explain what specifically in the images influenced their choice.

Contextual Information

Hagia Sophia

Hagia Sophia, the Church of the Holy Wisdom, was built on the site of earlier temples that were destroyed by fire and war. Thousands of workmen from all parts of the empire came to build it.

The church is made of multicolored stone and marble and of brick. The stones were held together with iron clamps. Liquid lead was poured into the spaces between the stones.

Hagia Sophia has been damaged by earthquakes and wars. It was stripped of the original gold and silver ornaments, icons and crosses by Crusaders in 1204 and Muslims in 1453. The Muslims covered the walls with plaster and then painted them with calligraphy in praise of Allah and the Koran. Minarets were added when the church became a mosque. In 1935 Hagia Sophia was made a museum.

Architecture

The sixth century is known as the First Golden Age of Byzantine Art. Under the reign of Justinian, the large basilica called *Hagia Sophia* (Church of the Holy Wisdom) was built in Constantinople in 532–537 (fig.7–13). Hagia Sophia is a monumental structure of completely original design. It was created by the two architects Anthemius of Tralles and Isidorus of Miletos. The unique design (fig.7–13a) combines a long open space (like a basilica) and a centralized dome (like a rotunda). The structural challenge was to place a huge round dome on square supporting walls. The diagram (fig.7–13b) shows how the problem

7–13 Compare the plan of this church to the plan of the Pantheon (fig.6–34a).
Anthemius of Tralles and Isidorus of Miletos, *Hagia Sophia*, about 532–537. Istanbul.

7–13a Plan of the Hagia Sophia

WINDOW WALL

HALF DOME — GREAT DOME — HALF DOME

PENDENTIVE

PIER

π

190 AD	400–1240 AD	450 AD
π (3.14) calculated, China	Kingdom of Ghana at its peak	Japanese Empire founded

World Cultural Timeline

300 AD	651 AD
First court ball-games played in Mesoamerica	Koran written

7–14 Notice the location of the windows and compare them to the oculus of the Pantheon (fig.6–35).
Hagia Sophia, interior.

Multicultural Connection

Mesoamerican Ball games

Today we consider ball games an all-American pastime and invention. In fact, ancient artifacts confirm that ceremonial ball games originated in Mesoamerica and played an important part in Mayan and other, later civilizations. Varying versions of a ball game spread across Mesoamerica, each region apparently developing special rules and costumes. Evidence of the ritual and the political importance of the events comes from surviving courts, sculpture and ceramics, as well as from deciphered text.

The ceremonial ball games were played in the alleyways of special stone courts. Small teams of players, wearing heavy protective gear, attempted to hit a rubber ball—another Native-American innovation—across the field. The players, forbidden to use their hands, struck the ball with their bodies, making it bounce off the sloping surfaces around the court. If the ball dropped to the paved floor, it was "dead," and so too may have been the team at fault.

Have students do research to answer the following:

• Were the games played for recreation or for the pleasure of the nobility?

• Who were the players of these games?

• Were sacrifices made to appease the gods?

(See Chapter 4, fig.4–87 for an image depicting a Mesoamerican ball game.)

was solved. Four concave spherical triangles, called **pendentives**, are supported by four **piers**. These units form four arches on the walls and create a continuous circle at their top edge, on which the dome rests.

The pendentives provide a graceful transition from square base to round dome. With the four piers carrying the weight, the pendentives allow the walls to remain open under the arches. The dome seems to float above the arches. Pendentive and dome construction became a characteristic construction technique of later Byzantine churches, Renaissance domed buildings and domed structures in America and the rest of the world. This mammoth work was completed in less than six years—an incredible feat, considering the new type of construction, the gigantic size and the lack of modern machinery.

From the outside, Hagia Sophia seems to be a mountain of masonry that reaches its apex at the top of the flat dome, about 200 feet above the city. The minarets were added in 1453 when the Moslems conquered Constantinople and changed the church to a mosque. (To see how it originally looked, cover the minarets.)

The exterior of the Hagia Sophia does not prepare one for what will be seen and felt inside. The space is overpowering: 65 feet long and 130 feet wide. The inside of the dome is almost 165 feet above the floor. On either end of the dome rest two half-domes, which make the nave a long oval. The church was the largest interior space in the world at that time. Arcades and galleries open onto the main space on two levels, adding to the feeling of enormous space. Light floods the interior from many windows, although more existed in the original structure.

Originally, the interior walls (fig.7–14) were completely covered with Byzantine mosaics of brilliant

DOME
SUPPORT FOR DOME
PENDENTIVES
ARCH
PIERS

7–13b If a round dome is placed on a square base (as at left), only a small part of the dome will be supported by the existing walls. If arches are placed in the four walls (as at right) and the circle of the dome rests on the four arches, a pendentive is formed in the four corners. The massive weight of the dome is supported by this spherical triangle, which transfers the thrust to the four huge piers that support it.

7–15 The gold glass makes this mosaic shimmer. Compare it to earlier Roman mosaics. *Christ between the Virgin and Saint John the Baptist* (detail), 1261. Mosaic, southern gallery, Hagia Sophia, Istanbul.

colors and gold. As in Ravenna, the glass tesserae are placed irregularly and create a glittering visual sensation. Eyewitnesses tell of a feeling that the entire golden dome was hanging from heaven by a chain. As they walked past the sparkling mosaics, they felt they were walking the very streets of heaven.

When the Moslems converted the church to a mosque, they scraped the mosaics from the walls or covered them with plaster because their religion did not permit any likenesses of people. Geometric

designs were painted over the plaster, completely changing the character of the interior space. Skilled workers have recently uncovered many of the mosaics.

In 1933, one of the last mosaics completed in Hagia Sophia was uncovered. It features Christ placed between John the Baptist and the Virgin Mary (fig.7–15). Christ previously often had been shown as a stern judge, but here he has a compassionate and loving look. His face is rather realistic, although his robes are stylized. Today, Hagia

The Kingdom of Ghana

Ghana was one of several large trading kingdoms that prospered in the savanna region of West Africa from 300 to 1076 AD. The gold-salt trade, which Ghana controlled until 900, encouraged the establishment of kingdoms and empires and provided them with a source of wealth and power. Salt from the Sahara was brought by caravans to the savanna and traded to the Ghanian merchants for gold from the mines between the Niger and Senegal rivers.

It is believed that these merchants used a unique method of trading called silent bartering. The Ghanians would leave salt at a site on the ground and beat drums to signal the gold miners. The gold miners would appear, leaving the gold. If the Ghanians thought they had received enough gold, they would take it and leave. If not, they would withdraw and wait for more. Only gold dust could be used in trade. Nuggets became the property of the king, who controlled the economy. Dwindling gold supplies and Muslim warfare ended Ghana's age of glory.

Contextual Information

Byzantine Icons

A popular type of painting in Byzantine churches and homes was the icon. Icons were portraits of saints, Christ and Mary, painted on wood and gilded with gold. They were carried on trips and in parades, and placed in special places in churches. Because candles were burned in front of them, their surfaces became blackened. The icons were then overpainted occasionally by less-talented painters.

Conservation Note

The four bronze horses from the facade of Saint Mark's have been replaced by replicas and are now housed in a nearby museum. Many sculptures originally located on the exteriors of historic Italian buildings have been removed to protect them from the corrosive properties of modern-day pollution. Some works that had endured the weathering of centuries have been irreparably damaged within only a few decades.

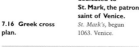

7-17 This church is dedicated to St. Mark, the patron saint of Venice.
St. Mark's, begun 1063. Venice.

7.16 Greek cross plan.

7-18 Analyze the many decorative elements for their geometric shapes.
Cathedral of St. Basil, 1554–1566. Moscow.

Sophia is not used for worship, but is a huge museum of Byzantine art.

The Iconoclastic Controversy disrupted the growth of Byzantine culture after 726 and caused a split in the church. On one side were iconoclasts, who wanted to destroy religious images, or **icons**. On the other side of the controversy were those who wanted to keep images in the church. Much of what had been created earlier was destroyed. No art was produced for over a hundred years.

The year 843 heralded the Second Golden Age of Byzantium, or the Byzantine Renaissance. No Byzantine structure rivaled Hagia Sophia in any way, although smaller churches used many of the features developed in its construction. The plan of an Eastern European church usually was of a Greek cross (four arms of equal length) contained in a square (fig.7–16). The apse was in one of the arms. A central dome rested on a square base. Often the dome was set on a cylindrical drum that raised it high above the roof line.

The largest and most lavishly decorated church of the Second Golden Age is St. Mark's in Venice (fig.7–17). The church was begun in 1063 and built to hold the body of St. Mark, brought from Alexandria.

It has the typical Greek cross plan. But in addition to the usual central dome, each arm has a dome of its own. The exterior has many mosaics and 2643 colored marble columns brought from Constantinople by Crusaders. The interior is completely covered with brilliant mosaics of both Byzantine and Venetian glass.

Four horses formerly stood above the main entrance. They also were brought from Constantinople. They are probably original Greek bronzes from about 300 BC.

Byzantine architecture, like the Eastern Orthodox faith, spread over Eastern Europe and into the center of Russia. Often churches were constructed of wood rather than brick, but the interiors still glowed with mosaics and paintings of saints and apostles. The most famous of the Russian churches is the Cathedral of St. Basil (fig.7–18) located across Red Square from the Kremlin. While Moscow contains many Byzantine-style buildings and churches, St. Basil's is unique and fantastic. Built during the rule of Ivan the Terrible, it has a large number of onion-shaped domes surrounding a central tentlike structure. The brilliantly painted domes and walls create a fairy-tale appearance that is both joyful and impressive.

Painting and Sculpture

We have seen how Byzantine artists excelled in the art of mosaics. They also had a very strong tradition of painting. Most paintings were icons (religious images) painted on wooden panels. Icons were often used as worship centers in homes. The interiors of the churches also were decorated with icons. A large screen of images (**iconostasis**) separated the sanctuary from the nave of the Byzantine church.

Byzantine painting was colorful and emotional. Artists used egg tempera as their medium. Figures were painted against a brilliant gold background. The *Enthroned Madonna and Child* (fig.7–19) is typical of the Byzantine style of

work. The Madonna floats rather than sits on her throne. The Christ Child seems to be resting securely on her arm, but on closer examination the figure actually hovers in front of the elaborate design of the Virgin's garment. Indeed, the fabric of her robe takes on an abstract life of its own. The folds resemble sunbursts. The artist makes no attempt to place the figures firmly in space. The beauty of the image and emotion conveyed by the figures are the essence of this representation. The artist has adhered to the Byzantine tradition. Meaning and emotion take precedence over the depiction of reality. Icon painting continued to be important for centuries in all areas where the Eastern Orthodox church was present.

Craftspersons often decorated churches and the objects used in worship. Brilliantly colored enamels were fused to metal surfaces on crosses, boxes and chalices used in various rites. Ivory panels also were carved.

The *Harbaville Triptych* (fig.17–20), displays a series of saints with Christ enthroned at the top center between St. John and the Virgin. The **triptych** (three hinged pieces) is an example of the portable nature of many works of Byzantine art. Small objects like this ivory often were transported to faraway lands as gifts or as plunder. Consequently, Byzantine art and its style became known throughout Europe.

7–19 An icon's meaning is more important than an accurate depiction of reality. *Enthroned Madonna and Child*, 13th century. Egg tempera on panel, 51 5/8" x 30 1/4" (131 x 77) cm. National Gallery of Art, Washington DC, gift of Mrs. Otto H. Kahn.

7–20 The hinged wings of this piece fold in on the central panel and add to its compact, portable nature. *Harbaville Triptych (Christ Enthroned with Saints)*, c. 950. Ivory, central panel 9 1/2" x 5 1/2" (24 x 14 cm). Louvre, Paris.

Lesson 7.2 Review

1 How are the figures stylized in *Emperor Justinian and Attendants*?
2 Analyze how the artist has made Theodora the center of attention in the mosaic *Empress Theodora and Attendants*.
3 Where is *Hagia Sophia* located? What was extraordinary about its construction?
4 What did the iconoclasts want to destroy?
5 Name the largest, most ornate church of the Second Golden Age of Byzantium.
6 From where did the horses over the entrance of St. Mark's cathedral in Venice come?
7 Describe the roof of the Cathedral of St. Basil in Moscow.
8 What is an icon?

Lesson 7.3

Islamic religion and culture spread rapidly across the Near East and the southern Mediterranean in the seventh century, introducing a style of art that was based on complex geometric and abstract designs.

Warm-up

Tell students to fill an entire sheet of paper with images except those describing human figures. Display their results and point out any geometric and abstract patterns. Afterward, have them compare their choice of decorations to those in the Alhambra (figs. 7–21, 7–22). Explain that the Islamic religion did not allow artists to describe human beings or the Moslem god, Allah, in religious art and architecture. Instead, they created resplendent environments solely from nonfigurative forms.

Objectives

Students should be able to:

Describe how Islam began in Arabia during the seventh century and quickly swept across the Near East and the southern Mediterranean, India and the southern portion of Western Europe.

Comprehend that Islamic culture rivaled Christianity and influenced medieval Europe.

Understand that Islamic art is based primarily on ornate abstract and geometric designs.

Explain that as the Islamic faith spread, architects built new structures and also converted old Christian basilicas and churches for use as mosques.

Vocabulary Definitions

arabesque (*ar*-uh-besk) Intricate and fanciful surface decoration generally based on geometric patterns and using combinations of flowering vines, tendrils, and so on.
stucco (*stuk*-oh) Any of several types of plaster used for decorative cornices, moldings or ceilings; also, a cement coating for the exterior of a building.
mosque (mosk) An Islamic temple or place of worship.

minaret (min-ar-*et*) A tall, slender tower attached to a mosque, from which the muezzin calls people to prayer.
miniature (*min*-ee-a-choor) A small painting executed with great detail; a small portrait, picture or decorative letter on an illuminated manuscript.

7.3 Islamic Faith and Art

ISLAM REFERS TO BOTH the religion of the Moslems and the nations that follow the religion. In the seventh century, Islam began in Arabia and swept across the Near East and the southern Mediterranean with astonishing speed. By 732, only 100 years after the death of its founder, Mohammed, the Moslems had reached India in the east, and Spain, Portugal and southwestern France in the west. Islam created a civilization that rivaled Christianity and had a far-ranging influence in medieval Europe.

The Moslem religion prohibited the use of human figures in religious art. Therefore, artists developed elaborate geometric and abstract designs. The term **arabesque**, which means "in the Arab style," was coined to describe their complex designs.

Islamic architecture, like Western architecture, used arches, columns and vaults. However, Islamic architects created a unique style and richly decorated their buildings with stucco reliefs.

In addition to the inventive designs and architecture, Islam developed Arabic numerals and led the way in government, philosophy, science and medicine. The splendor of the Islamic heritage, particularly its architecture, left a lasting impression on the European imagination.

Key Notes
- Islam spread rapidly in the seventh century across the Near East and the Mediterranean.
- Islamic design is complex, geometric and abstract.
- Islamic architecture is outstanding for its splendor and imaginativeness.

Vocabulary
arabesque
stucco
mosque
minarets
miniature

7–23 Stucco relief is an inexpensive means of creating elaborate architectural elements. *Court of the Lions, the Alhambra,* detail of stucco work.

Special Feature
The Alhambra

Some of the most splendid Moslem architecture was built in Spain. The Alhambra Palace in Granada is an outstanding example of Islamic arch construction. *The Alhambra* (fig. 7–21) is a sprawling palace with royal residential quarters, court complexes and offices, a bath and a mosque.

The most famous feature of the Alhambra are the courtyards. Within the courtyards are fountains and light-reflecting water basins. The courtyards are surrounded by slender columns with decorated arches.

The most famous of the courtyards of the Alhambra is the *Court of the Lions* (fig. 7–22). The courtyard is framed by rhythmically spaced single, double and triple columns. The arches above the columns are heavily decorated with **stucco** reliefs (fig. 7–23). Stucco (wet plaster) is extremely flexible and the architecture it decorates can be made to appear very free flowing and organic. The delicate reliefs in the Court of the Lions give the building an airy, almost floating appearance. The arches themselves seem to hang from, rather than support, the ceiling. Even with the elaborate stucco work, there is a wonderful symmetry and rhythm that prevails throughout the building. Like the wonderful stories from *The Thousand and One Nights,* Islamic architecture and decoration evoke a sense of wonder and romance.

Teach

Criticism: Have students describe how architects developed a sense of rhythm and symmetry in the Alhambra.

- Ask what structural and decorative elements are repeated and how are they balanced against one another. The delicate arched walkway of 124 marble columns recalls similar ones in monasteries throughout Western Europe.

- Ask students to read page 218 for more information on the use of columns, arches and stucco relief to evoke an inspiring and enchanting environment. Since there are so many open courtyards in the royal palace, what do they think the climate is like in this part of Spain?

7–21 The Alhambra is a large complex that includes a variety of buildings.
The Alhambra, Granada, Spain. Overall view.

7–22 This courtyard contains some of the finest examples of stucco decoration produced in the Moslem world.
Court of the Lions, the Alhambra, 1354–1391. Granada, Spain.

Contextual Information
Granada

Granada was founded in the eighth century by the Moors. Between 1036 and 1232, it was part of Moorish Spain. By the first half of the thirteenth century, the Moorish possessions in Spain had diminished, and Granada replaced Córdoba as the capital of the remaining Moorish territory. The city flourished during this period and became a wealthy trading center and a center for art, literature and science. It was during this period that the Alhambra was built as the fortress-palace of the Moorish rulers.

Higher-Order Thinking Skills

Many comparisons can be made between the Alhambra and other architecture of this time, such as San Vitale, St. Mark's and Hagia Sophia, as well as Classical buildings such as the Baths of Caracalla. The lions can also be compared to those on *The Lion Gate at Mycenae* (fig.6–7) and to portrayals such as the *Dying Lioness* from Assyria (fig.5–16). Ask students to compare the symbolism of the lion in each of these or other works.

Art History: Ask students to examine figs.7–24 and 7–25, and discuss the similarities and differences between the two buildings. (Both are mosques, and mosques were built wherever the Islamic faith flourished.) Have them read the information on the locations of these buildings in the captions under the images and then use the map at the back of the book to find the countries in which the mosques are located.

Evaluate

Ask how Islamic religious art differs from Christian art. How widespread was the influence of the Islamic faith? (Students should review the map on p.205 to answer this question.)

Reteach

Ask students to compare the book illustration in fig.7–27 to the interiors of Islamic mosques and palaces in this lesson. What parallels can they find? Does the painting reveal the same love for rich decorative effects as seen in the buildings?

Contextual Information

Mosques

The earliest followers of Mohammed worshipped in his domestic compound. Of interest is that all mosques repeat the plan of Mohammed's house. They generally are composed of an enclosed courtyard, a building at one end for prayer, and arcades on the sides.

Performing Arts Connection

Islamic Dance

One of the most important Turkish Islamic sects is Mawlawiya, founded in the thirteenth century by Jalal al-Din Rumi, long regarded as the greatest mystic poet of Islam. Rumi experienced a great spiritual transformation when he met the wandering holy man Shams al-Din, in whom he saw the "perfect image of the Divine Beloved." When Shams al-Din disappeared, Rumi invented the wild, whirling dance that characterizes his Mawlawiya order and symbolizes the search for his lost beloved. The dance, which is performed in several Central Asian and North African orders, involves a circular anti-clockwise rotation that balloons participants' simple belted robes.

Continuity in Islamic Art

The *Koran*, sacred book of Islam, contains both spiritual and social law. The Koran regulates not only the religion of Islam, but also acts of daily life, like brushing teeth, saying hello and eating a meal. All followers of Islam, whether they lived in Spain or Arabia, were governed by the same religious and social rules. This consistency in religious and social life was mirrored in the uniformity of Islamic art. There were certain rules that Islamic art had to follow, whatever part of Islam it may have come from. Artists in Islamic countries adhered to a single style that had been sanctioned by time and convention.

Page from the Koran.

Islamic artists are forbidden to represent humans or the Moslem god, Allah, in their art. Calligraphy, the noblest and most continuous of the arts, owes its supreme status to the fact that it transmits the Koran. Therefore, Arabic script serves as the basis for many designs.

Islamic Architecture

The Islamic architectural heritage is especially evident in the places of worship, called **mosques**. Islamic architects constructed new buildings and also made old Christian basilicas and churches into mosques. Moslems from many countries built *The Dome of the Rock* (fig.7–24) in Jerusalem. The site of the dome marks the place where Mohammed was said to have left this earth. The dome also covers the top of the rock mountain on which Abraham attempted to sacrifice his son Isaac. This oldest Islamic monument (begun about 643) has an octagonal base. Many columns inside support the golden dome. The building is Byzantine in its rotunda form and was designed for this one particular spot. The slightly pointed dome of wood was overlaid with lead and gilded with gold, but today it reflects the brilliant sun from an anodized aluminum surface (fig. 7–b). The exterior of the mosque is covered with brightly glazed ceramic tiles. Originally, it contained mosaics of Byzantine glass.

The earliest, huge Moslem building for congregational purposes is *The Great Mosque at Damascus* (fig.7–25), built from 705 to 711. It made use of existing Christian and

7–24 Moslems from many countries built this monument.
Dome of the Rock, late 7th century. Jerusalem, Israel.

Roman structures. The existing square towers were turned into the first Moslem **minarets**. From these minarets, people were called to prayer several times a day. The huge sanctuary has many columns to support the roof. It measures about 525 feet by 328 feet. It still contains some of the original mosaic decoration. Other early Islamic mosques can be found in North Africa, Iraq, Turkey, Mesopotamia, Egypt and Spain.

7–25 This mosque was built within the enclosure of a Roman sanctuary.
Great Mosque, 706–715. Damascus, Syria.

Multicultural Connection

Calligraphy

Have students compare the similarities and differences in the calligraphy in the Koran to examples of Chinese calligraphy. Can they name other cultures in which writing is practiced as an art form?

Islamic Book Illustration

Islamic artists greatly advanced the art of book illustration. Islamic decorative style featured elaborate geometric designs and complex patterns of intertwining lines and shapes. The use of abstract designs was highly developed because artists were forbidden to use human figures in religious art. In the page from a book shown here, a Turkish calligrapher used a lavish and inventive design to write the single word Allah (fig.7–26).

Laila and Majnun (fig.7–27) is an example of a **miniature** (small picture) from a manuscript. It illustrates a romantic poem. The scene is two-dimensional with little shading or perspective. The colors are bright and clear. The intertwining patterns of leaves and flowers are purely Islamic.

7–27 What elements of art and principles of design dominate this painting? How is depth of space shown?
Laila and Majnun at School, miniature from a manuscript of the Khamsa of Nizami, 1524–1525. Ink, colors and gold on paper. The Metropolitan Museum of Art, New York, gift of Alexander Smith Cochran, 1913.

7–26 This page has a very modern look. How would you describe it?
Calligraphic page, from the *Album of the Conqueror*, 15th century, Turkish. Topkapi Palace Museum, Istanbul.

Lesson 7.3 Review

1 Define arabesque.
2 Describe the Alhambra. What part of the Alhambra's architecture is most famous?
3 What is a mosque?
4 Why is the *Dome of the Rock* in Jerusalem important to both Christians and Moslems?
5 What were some of the characteristics of Islamic book illustration?
6 Describe the Great Mosque of Damascus.

Higher-Order Thinking Skills

1 Like most buildings, the *Dome of the Rock* (fig.7–24) has similarities to other buildings, both contemporary and older. Based on information that students have about other buildings (diagrams, plans, elevations), ask them to speculate about the interior plan and decoration of this building and to attempt to verify their ideas through research at the library.

2 The term *arabesque*, which means "in the Arab style," was coined to describe the elaborate geometric and abstract designs in Islamic art. Challenge students to find examples of this style in the miniature (fig.7–27), which is an illustration for a Romantic poem.

• Besides the intertwining patterns of leaves and flowers, how else has the artist avoided the illusion of three-dimensional space? (Have students pay particular attention to the relationship between the characters and the large rectangular carpet, and also the two running figures on the brick pavement.)

• Ask students why there are human figures in this Islamic work. (The Turkish artist was illustrating a secular poem, not creating a religious piece of art.)

3 Have students share with each other what they find most interesting about the differences and/or similarities among the cultures covered in Chapter 7. Afterward, ask them to discuss if they believe that religion and culture in contemporary America are as closely linked as in Europe during these earlier periods. What evidence from life today can they use to support their opinions?

Lesson 7.3 Review Answers

1 Arabesque means "in the Arab style" and is used to describe intricate, fanciful designs based on geometric patterns, and the use of intertwining combinations of forms such as flowering vines and tendrils.
2 The Alhambra is a sprawling palace with residential quarters, court complexes, offices, a bath and a mosque. The most famous architectural features are the courtyards with fountains and water basins. Slender columns topped by arches decorated with stucco reliefs surround the courtyards, giving the building an airy appearance. The Court of the Lion is the Alhambra's most famous courtyard.
3 An Islamic temple or place of worship
4 The dome is on the place where Mohammed is said to have left this earth, and where Abraham attempted to sacrifice his son Isaac.
5 Elaborate geometric designs and complex patterns of intertwining lines and shapes; two-dimensional illustrations with little shading; and clear bright colors
6 Existing Christian and Roman structures were incorporated into the design of the Great Mosque. The Moslem minarets were made from existing square towers. Many columns support the ceiling of the huge sanctuary, which contains some original mosaic decoration and a monument to St. John the Baptist.

Lesson 7.4

In the early medieval era, Christian and pagan nomadic tribes made small, portable art objects that could be easily carried as they migrated throughout Europe. Under Charlemagne, a renewed interest in Classical culture influenced the art and architecture of the late eighth and early ninth centuries.

Warm-up

Ask the class to imagine roaming throughout Europe during the fifth or sixth centuries in search of a permanent home. As a group, have them list types of artworks they would make that would express their religious convictions but could also be easily transported from one place to another. Afterward, have them glance at the images in Lesson 7.4 and compare their list to these examples of early medieval art objects.

Objectives

Students should be able to:

Explain that between the fifth and seventh centuries, various Christian and pagan European tribes carried small, portable art treasures with them as they searched for permanent homes after the collapse of the Roman Empire.

Describe the geometric designs and animal motifs that were popular elements of pagan art.

Comprehend that elegant and delicate manuscript illumination became an important art form as Christian missionaries tried to establish their religion among the nomadic groups.

Describe how the arts prospered in the late eighth and early ninth centuries under Charlemagne, who brought stability to the north.

Understand that Charlemagne stimulated a revival of Classical art, studies and language.

Vocabulary Definitions

illumination (i-*loo*-mi-*nay*-shun) Colored illustrations, often containing gold and silver, that decorated manuscripts in medieval times in Europe. ***vellum*** A fine parchment made from calfskin and used for writing, manuscript illumination and book binding.

7.4 Early Medieval Art

T HE MIDDLE AGES is a period that spans over 1000 years. The first half of the medieval era was a time of much turmoil and change. The Roman empire had collapsed, having been overrun by the Visigoths, the Huns and the Vandals. Because the Roman empire no longer put up a defense against European tribes, these tribes were able to move through Europe to look for permanent homes. In this Migration period (400–600), few paintings or large buildings were produced. Tribes needed to carry their art and treasures with them. Therefore, artwork was entirely confined to portable objects such as ornaments, weapons and objects for daily use.

Most medieval tribes were Christian, but they also had a pagan tradition. Dreadful monsters and dragons were featured in their songs and epics. Animal motifs were common in their decoration and design.

Manuscript ***illumination*** became an important art form. Not only could books be easily carried, they were of great use to missionaries. Christian missionaries tried to establish the authority of the Church among the wandering tribes and bring stability. Illuminated manuscripts were drawn by monks in secluded monasteries throughout Europe.

Key Notes
- The early Middle Ages was a time of unrest as tribes moved through Europe.
- Most early medieval art was portable.
- Geometric designs and animal motifs were favored as decorative elements.
- Manuscript illumination became an important art form and reached a high point in its development.

Vocabulary
illumination
vellum

7–29 Can your eye follow the looping and curving lines of this intricate design?
Lindisfarne Gospel Book, detail of fig.7–28.

Special Feature

The *Lindisfarne Gospel Book*

Artists of the early period were influenced by Christian art of the Mediterranean. But they also were fascinated with the tribal (or barbaric) tradition of geometric motifs and interlaced designs of letters, flowers and animals. Monks in secluded monasteries spent their lifetimes illustrating pages of scripture with fantastic animals, intricate designs and infinite detail. For these artists, ornamentation represented everything that was rich and beautiful. They believed that by illustrating the holy word in this manner, they were paying tribute to the glory of God.

The *Lindisfarne Gospel Book* (fig.7–28), illustrated between 698 and 721 in Christianized Great Britain, is a volume of many **vellum** (parchment) pages. The page shown here is the beginning of the Gospel of St. Matthew. The X–P (chi-rho), a contraction of the Greek name for Christ, is rendered with incredible intricacy (fig.7–29) and pulsates with a life of its own. It is a fitting way for the gospel to begin. The illustration is beautifully interlaced with abstract and geometric designs of minute detail. Hidden in the curves and swirls are serpents, dragons and other fantastic animals.

7–28 This manuscript is made of a superior type of parchment (bleached animal skin) called vellum. Vellum is made of calfskin.
X-P (Chi-Rho) Page, from *Lindisfarne Gospel Book*, 698–721. Miniature on parchment, 9 1/2" x 8" (24 x 20 cm), Lindisfarne, England. British Library, London.

Teach

Aesthetics: Explain to students that in the *Lindisfarne Gospel Book* (figs.7–28, fig.7–29) the large letters X and P are a contraction of the Greek name for Christ. Ask them to search the illumination for the influence of tribal art traditions, which included the use of geometric motifs, interlaced designs, flowers and animals. Remind them to look long enough to locate the tiny painted creatures.

Art History: Have students write their initials in large block letters on a small piece of paper and then fill in all the available space with designs and small images. Have them compare the intricacy of their work to the Lindisfarne example (fig.7–28). Calling on their own experiences, how long do they think it took to complete each page of these manuscripts? Monks, and sometimes nuns, devoted their whole life to working in secluded monasteries or convents, carefully illustrating the scriptures as a sign of their devotion to God.

Criticism/Art History: Share with students that most early Medieval art contained intricate interweaving designs. Ask them to compare the fibula (fig.7–a) to the Lindisfarne illumination.

- What is similar about the way the shapes of the pin and the large X and P are treated?

Higher-Order Thinking Skills

The decoration of the *X-P Page* (fig.7–28) is clearly related to the decoration of the *Chalice of Antioch* (fig.7–8). Ask students to find similarities. They can compare *St. Matthew the Evangelist* (fig.7–32) to the *Seated Scribe* (fig.5–23) from Egypt. Images of people writing are still created today. Ask students to find or create such images and to discuss their meaning. Ideas about the importance and power of literacy, communication with those at a distance from us, and writing as a personal, private act should come out in the discussion. Note that although Charlemagne was illiterate, he so valued literacy that he established schools.

Contextual Information

Manuscript Covers

Extremely elaborate covers often were created for important illuminated manuscripts. See fig.1–7 for one of the finest medieval manuscript covers to have survived.

• Are the patterns chaotic or do they fit snugly within the forms?

• While the two works share an avoidance of empty space, they ultimately served two separate purposes. Discuss the sacred use of the Gospel book versus the secular function of the clasp.

• Can students name objects from home that are ornately decorated but have ordinary functions, such as antique picture frames, painted teapots, filigree silverware or fancy serving dishes?

Evaluate

Ask why handmade manuscripts were so important during this period. Have students discuss how the introduction of the printing press in the fifteenth century would change this tradition. Pose the following questions to students:

• What was your thinking like when you were filling in the piece of paper with your initials?

• Did your thoughts become little and intricate or did you have broad, sweeping ideas? What activities make your thinking small and delicate and what ones stimulate huge, grand thoughts? Share your experiences with your classmates.

Reteach

Ask students why most early medieval art tended to be small in size. Why were there no magnificent churches built during this time?

Have students share what was new to them about manuscript illumination. Do they remember who made them, how long it took and why they were created? Have students work with partners to stimulate their memories as they reexamine some of the examples in Lesson 7.4.

Contextual Information

Life in the Time of Charlemagne

The ninth-century rule of Charlemagne was also the time of the beginning of the feudal system and knighthood in the western realm. Strong suits of protective armor covered the bodies of men and their expensive horses. The invention of stirrups allowed archers and lancers more accuracy.

Charlemagne was born in the land of the barbarians, but by the ninth century these people had been assimilated into the Roman culture. After Charlemagne's death the land was again invaded by a variety of armies. The church, which had developed hierarchical systems within abbeys and monasteries and extended its authority to the lands adjacent to their buildings, became the only source of stability.

Cooperative Learning

This activity builds on the preceding activity. Grade each student's biography presentation and list of objects. Ask the class to identify groups to which their famous personages could belong—performers, politicians, artists and so forth. Write that notation on their paper. Students can form committees based on those groups to create presentations, displays, videos or written articles that can be submitted to school publications. Set a date for the completed project and help students to identify what tasks need to be accomplished and to create a timeline for the work. Each student in the group should have an assigned task for which he/she is responsible. Students can then help to create an evaluation sheet to be used by themselves and you to grade their finished work individually and as a group.

Migration Art

Artists of the barbaric tribes crafted ornate metalwork. Pins used to fasten garments (fig.7–a) were often inlaid with precious or semiprecious stones.

A powerful ruler probably once owned the *Purse Cover* (fig.7–30). The piece makes use of garnets, glass, enamel and gold. The lid is mounted on a slab of ivory. In 1939, it was excavated in England as part of the Sutton Hoo ship-burial. The decorations at the top are geometric and have a heavily interlaced design. The two outside groups show a man between two beasts. The inner groups show two eagles seizing two ducks.

The Classical Revival under Charlemagne

Charlemagne, the Frankish king (786–814) and emperor of the West (800–814), brought a period of stability to the north. His reign provided an opportunity for the arts to flourish. He was directly responsible for a short revival of interest in Classical studies, art and language.

Under his direction, the Palatine Chapel (fig.7–31) was built in Aachen, Germany. The Palatine Chapel, designed by the architect Odo of Metz, is the greatest surviving monument of the Carolingian era. Built from 792–805, the chapel was meant to symbolize the religious and political power of

7–31 The interior of this chapel is heavy and massive in appearance compared to early Christian and Byzantine churches. *Palatine Chapel of Charlemagne*, 792–805, interior view. Aachen, Germany.

7–30 This piece was found at the burial site of a king. *Purse Cover*, first half of 7th century. Gold, garnets, glass and enamel, 7 1/2" (19 cm) long, from Sutton Hoo, England. British Museum, London.

600 AD
Concept of zero invented in India

800 AD
Beginning of Inca Empire; Machu Picchu built using passive-solar energy designs

845 AD
Paper money in China leads to inflation and state bankruptcy

1000 AD
Stone quarried for first Easter Island monoliths

World Cultural Timeline

800–1200 AD
The Temple of Angkor Wat built, Cambodia

1312 AD
The Mali Empire reaches its height

Multicultural Connection

The Mali Empire

The Mali Empire, which lasted from about 1240 to 1500, was the wealthiest and most powerful state in West Africa. Its capital, the city of Timbuktu, was said to have had about 6000 houses. Mali cities were centers of the caravan trade and controlled the gold trade. Influenced by Arab traders, the Mali kings converted to Islam and were highly revered by their subjects.

Under the rule of Mansa Musa, a wealthy and powerful Muslim ruler, Mali became an Islamic empire and was known as a great center of learning. Scholars came from many lands to live and study in its large commercial areas.

The kingdom grew so large that it became hard to rule. In the 1400s, civil wars began to weaken Mali. The West African kingdom of Songhai soon took its place.

• Have students research the geographical and political features that made it possible for this culture to create more permanent art objects to keep in their homes and at religious shrines.

The Temple of Angkor Wat

Angkor was an early Khmer civilization that flourished in northwestern Cambodia from the early 800s to the 1400s. Its capital, also called Angkor, meant "city" or "capital." The Khmer kingdom included the lands of present-day Thailand, Cambodia, the southern part of Vietnam and parts of Laos.

Charlemagne. Charlemagne wanted a chapel that would rival the churches of Rome and Byzantium.

The chapel is shaped like an octagon. It was the model for several later German churches. The chapel

is 105 feet high inside and is over 49 feet in diameter. The sense of space is increased by the wide walkway,

Window in Time

Monastic Life

Monasticism developed during the early Christian era, when Christians devoted themselves to solitary meditation and prayer. The earliest monks lived in small communities, each in a separate hut or cell, or in complete solitude in remote places. This hermit style of monasticism was particularly widespread in the eastern Mediterranean.

Eventually, however, some monks came together to form communities headed by an abbot. They still spent most of their time alone, but they prayed together and obeyed certain rules. This style of monastic life eventually spread into southern Europe.

In 440, St. Patrick brought the monastic tradition to Ireland, which became a refuge for Christians who fled Britain and Gaul. The site of Skellig Michael on an island off the western coast of Ireland was one of the first monastic communities. The monks lived in remote stone humps perched on steep precipices overlooking the sea. The humps were constructed from flat, unworked fieldstone and clustered around a small oratory (place for prayer) also made of stone. When not praying, the monks grew what they could in the rocky soil and supplemented their diets with any fish they could catch.

Monasteries in Ireland and Scotland became important centers of learning and the arts. In scriptoria, or writing workshops, monks produced and illuminated many Gospels and other books of sacred writings.

Following in the footsteps of St. Patrick, the Irish became fervent missionaries of their Celtic Christianity. They founded numerous important monastic communities in England, at Lindisfarne, and on the Continent, at Luxeuil in France, Saint Gall in Switzerland and Bobbio in Italy.

But it was a more regulated, less austere kind of monasticism that ultimately became most popular throughout Europe. It was established by St. Benedict of Nursia (c. 480–543) who around 529 founded a monastery at Monte Cassino in Italy. St. Benedict formulated a Benedictine Rule, which detailed how the community would be organized and how it would work. Vows were taken regarding poverty, chastity, obedience and *stabilitas loci*, which meant promising to not leave the monastery. It was important that monks stayed within the community, for sharing the

manual work that made the monastery self-sufficient was of vital importance to its continued existence. St. Benedict visualized a monastery with everything the monks might need within its walls so that they would never have occasion to leave.

A plan for a medieval monastery drawn up around 820 by Abbot Heito of Reichenau is preserved in the Chapter Library at Saint Gall in Switzerland. This plan was the model used for such monasteries throughout the Middle Ages. This unique document that has survived through the centuries clearly reflects St. Benedict's wishes.

Looking at the plan we can see how every facet of life was taken care of within the monastery walls. The church is the largest structure. Close to the church were other important buildings: the dormitory, the refectory or eating hall, the kitchen and the scriptorium where manuscripts were copied. These buildings were grouped around a square courtyard or cloister. A covered walk around the four sides functioned as a sheltered walkway between essential buildings. There were various barns for livestock, workshops, a mill, a wine press and storage areas. Behind the church were an infirmary and a novitiate where young boys were trained to be monks. To the left of the church the abbot had his quarters and in front of that was a guest house for important visitors and a hostel to accommodate travelers and pilgrims.

Plan of Saint Gall.

Angkor Wat, one of the world's largest religious structures, was begun in the reign of Suryavarman II and was to be his dynastic temple and mortuary shrine. It was at that time and has continued to be the supreme example of the Khmer concept of the temple as sacred mountain. Dedicated to the Hindu god Vishnu, Angkor Wat dominates the city with its complex of pyramidal stone temples, gold-topped towers and moats, all of which occupy more than a half mile. Staircases and terraces lead to the highest tower.

The galleries that surround the central pyramid are richly decorated with carved scenes of Khmer history, with images from Hindu mythology and with scenes of everyday life. Moats (representing the ocean that the Khmer

believed lay around Earth) still surround Angkor Wat and are even now regarded with religious reverence.

The Angkor Empire began to decline after the 1100s and fell in 1450 to Thais from China's borderland. Looters overran the remaining temples, and years of forest growth and rain destroyed many of the beautiful sandstone carvings and statues.

• Be sensitive to the fact that some of the Khmer political history may be unpleasant to some Southeast Asian students.

• Have students look at figs.4–51 and 4–52 for other views of Angkor Wat.

7–32 This painting reflects the strong interest in Roman civilization prevalent during Charlemagne's time.
St. Matthew the Evangelist, about 800, from the *Gospel Book*, Rhineland. Miniature on parchment, 14" x 9 1/2" (36 x 24 cm). British Museum, London.

7–33 What elements has the artist used to give this work its extraordinary energy?
St. Matthew the Evangelist, about 816–835, from the *Gospel Book of Archbishop Ebbo of Reims*. Approximately 10" x 8" (25 x 20 cm), Hautvilliers near Reims. Bibliothèque Nationale, Paris.

Contextual Information

Carolingian Script

The period of Charlemagne's reign is often referred to as "Carolingian." Charlemagne was a great admirer of all forms of learning, as well as the arts. At his palace, he established a school with its own scriptorium (a room in which manuscripts were written and stored). One of the projects on which scholars under his patronage labored was the correction of the script used by scribes. Over the centuries, it had become nearly illegible. The lettering that we use today is the descendant of the clear, crisp system of lettering devised by Charlemagne's scribes.

Lesson Review 7.4 Answers

1 The Medieval period began in the third century and lasted for more than 1000 years.

2 Since the Roman Empire had collapsed, there was not a strong army to defend against European tribes looking for permanent homes.

3 Ornaments, weapons and objects for daily use were some of the small, portable art produced. Manuscript illustration became an important art form.

4 Charlemagne

5 Both are decorated with geometric and swirling interlaced designs of fantastic animals and vines. The ornamentation on both is rich and beautiful.

6 The Palatine Chapel in Aachen, Germany

7 This book is 12" x 9" (27.5 x 22 cm). *St. Matthew the Evangelist* from the *Gospel Book*, Rhineland, is 14" x 9 1/2" (36 x 24 cm), so it is a little larger than this book. *St. Matthew the Evangelist* from the *Gospel Book of Archbishop Ebbo of Reims* is about 10" x 8" (25 x 20 cm), making it slightly smaller than this book.

Chapter Review Answers

Review

1 Early Christian basilicas were long, brick buildings with timber roofs. At the front was an atrium surrounded by a covered walkway. Entrances were at the rear corners of the atrium. Worshipers stood in the nave, or central

or ambulatory. The interior dome was originally covered with mosaics of reflecting glass tesserae. The chapel still holds the remains of Charlemagne.

Under Charlemagne's rule, monasteries were constructed to preserve the learning of the past. Monks spent their lives copying scripture and other important writings from the past. The art of manuscript illumination was very active during the Carolingian era. While some pages of these manuscripts contained no illustrations, others

were filled with designs and figures. These images, or miniatures, often illustrated or embellished the written text.

St. Matthew the Evangelist was painted during Charlemagne's reign in Rhineland (now Germany). St. Matthew is writing his Gospel as he works in a Classical setting. The painting reflects the Carolingian interest in classical mathematics, architecture and perspective drawing. The canopy and building are similar to the central plan structure of both San Vitale in Ravenna and Charlemagne's Palatine Chapel.

Compare *St. Matthew the Evangelist* (fig.7–32) with another *St. Matthew* from a gospel book made for Archbishop Ebbo of Reims (fig.7–33). The first is Classical and calm; the saint is intent on setting down his own thoughts. The second is extremely expressive and is filled with energy as St. Matthew hurries to write his Gospel. He appears to be seized with divine inspiration. The contrast between these two styles shows the wide range in style that existed in the ninth century.

> **Lesson 7.4 Review**
>
> 1 When was the Medieval period?
> 2 Why were nomadic tribes able to move so freely through Europe during the Middle Ages?
> 3 Name the main types of art produced during the Middle Ages.
> 4 Which medieval king revived an interest in Greek and Roman art?
>
> 5 How are the *Lindisfarne Gospel* and the Sutton Hoo purse cover similar?
> 6 What was the name of Charlemagne's chapel? What city is it in?
> 7 Compare the size of both *St. Matthew* illuminations to the size of this book. Which is larger?

part of the basilica. Rows of columns separated the side aisles from the nave. At the front of the nave, the altar—covered by a baldachin—was located in a semicircular apse with a half-domed ceiling. A triumphal arch separated the nave from the apse. Burial crypts were under the raised apse. The interiors were highly decorated with mosaics on the walls and inlaid marble on the floors.

See fig.7–4 for the basilica floor plan. Many European and American churches were derived from the basilica plan. Students may be reminded of a local church with a long narrow nave and a raised altar at the front.

2 The floor plan was a Greek cross. The apse was in one of the arms, and a central dome, usually raised on a cylindrical drum, rested on a square base.

The interior of the dome often contained a figure of Christ on a gold background. The interiors were usually covered with mosaics.

3 Roman mosaics were made of polished colored stone; Byzantine mosaics were made of brightly colored glass pressed into wet plaster.

4 Egg tempera as the medium; gold used in the background; symbolic poses; flat, two-dimensional robes.

5 They destroyed much of the art that had been produced before, and broke the continuous development of art for over a hundred years.

6 A pendentive is a triangular piece of vaulting springing from the corner of a rectangular area to support a round or polygonal dome. See fig.7–13a for the diagram.

7 Stucco

Hagia Sophia

In the sixth century, the historian, Procopius, described Hagia Sophia (Church of the Holy Wisdom). The building was surfaced with marbles of many colors: black and white, green, silver-flecked, red and white, and yellow. Columns were gilded with gold. Brass chains from the ceiling held silver oil lamps. In the sanctuary there was a gold-plated screen with religious images. Around the altar there was a brilliant red curtain embroidered in gold.

The church was finished in less than six years by a team of ten thousand workmen gathered from all the surrounding areas. It was dedicated by the Emperor Justinian, who supplied 1006 oxen, 6000 sheep, 600 stags, 1000 swine and 10,000 birds and fowl plus 30,000 bushels of meal for the gigantic thanksgiving celebration and dedication. In his book, *On the Buildings*, Procopius describes the amazement of his contemporaries upon viewing the interior of the huge domed structure:

"So the church has become a spectacle of marvelous beauty, overwhelming to those who see it, but to those who know it by hearsay altogether incredible....Yet it seems not to rest upon solid masonry, but to cover the space with its golden dome suspended from Heaven...though they turn their attention to every side, and look with contracted brows upon every detail, observers are still unable to understand the skillful craftsmanship, but they always depart from there overwhelmed by the sight...It was by many skillful devices that the Emperor Justinian and the master-builder Anthemius and Isidorus secured the stability of the church, hanging, as it does, in mid-air."

Review

1 Describe the early Christian basilicas. Draw a basilica floor plan. Do you know a contemporary church that has a similar floor plan?

2 Describe a typical Eastern European church built during the Second Golden Age of Byzantium.

3 Name one way that Roman and Byzantine mosaics differ.

4 List several characteristics of Byzantine painting as exemplified in *Enthroned Madonna and Child*.

5 How did the iconoclasts change the development of Byzantine art?

6 What is a pendentive? Include a diagram in your explanation.

7 What material did Islamic artists use to decorate the arches in the Court of the Lion at the Alhambra?

Interpret

1 List several ways that early Christian art differed from classical Greek art.

2 How did the Edict of Milan affect architecture?

3 Compare the Roman copy of the Greek painting, *The Battle of Issus*, to *Emperor Justinian and Attendants*. Discuss medium, location and style.

4 Five illuminated manuscript pages are illustrated in this chapter. All are considered masterpieces. Which do you prefer? Why?

Other Tools for Learning

 Maps

1 Look at the location of Ravenna on a map. On what sea is it located? It was surrounded by marshes and a shallow bay. Why do you think it was an important city within the Byzantine Empire?

2 Why do you think Constantinople's location has made it so important throughout history?

Timelines

1 Which is older, Dome of the Rock in Jerusalem or Hagia Sophia in Constantinople?

2 How old was Hagia Sophia when Constantinople was conquered by the Turks?

3 Name a piece of art that was made within 200 years before or after the coronation of Charlemagne.

Electronic Media

CD-ROM drive: *Microsoft Art Gallery*

1 Research illuminated manuscripts. Copy an illuminated capital letter.

CD-ROM drive: Electronic Encyclopedia (e.g., *New Grolier Multimedia* or *Microsoft Encarta*)

1 Discover why Charlemagne established monasteries. How did his love of the Classics influence art and architecture?

Primary-Source Connection

The interior of Hagia Sophia with its extraordinary "floating" dome leaves today's visitor awestruck. Have students use Procopius' description to speculate about how much more amazing the building must have been to his contemporaries. How would the response of his contemporaries have differed from ours today? Have students consider in their response what machinery and technology was not yet available at the time Hagia Sophia was built.

 Maps

1 An acceptable answer is the Mediterranean Sea. Because Ravenna had the natural defenses of water and marshes, it could withstand barbarian assault. *Note:* direct students to the map on page 173. The body of water to the right of Italy is actually the Adriatic Sea (there are many "seas" in the Mediterranean).

2 Constantinople sits between the Black Sea and other waterways leading to the Mediterranean Sea. This spot controls ocean access to Eastern Europe from Asia. Because of this strategic location, the Turks were able to control trade routes to Asia for hundreds of years.

Timelines

1 Hagia Sophia is older, built in 532–537. Construction of the Dome of the Rock began about 643.

2 About 916 years old, in 1453.

3 Charlemagne's coronation was in 800; therefore, any art that was made between 600 and 1000 would be a correct answer: the *Lindisfarne Gospel Book* (698) the Sutton Hoo purse lock (seventh century), *St. Matthew the Evangelist,* from either the *Gospel Book*, Rhineland (800) or the *Gospel Book of Archbishop Ebbo of Reims* (816–835).

Electronic Media

Electronic Encyclopedia: Learning was kept alive in the monasteries established by Charlemagne. Monks copied the Bible, creating illuminated manuscripts. Charlemagne visited Italy five times and brought back the influence of Classical Roman architecture to buildings he commissioned in Europe.

Interpret

1 Classical Greek (and Roman) art was realistic. Christian art was symbolic. The religious thought or idea rather than realism was important to Christian artists.

2 Before the Edict of Milan, which made Christianity the official religion, Christians met secretly in small houses. After, larger spaces for public worship spaces were needed for great numbers of new Christians, and the Roman basilica plan was adapted to meet this need.

3 Both *The Battle of Issus* and the *Emperor Justinian and Attendants* are mosaics. *The Battle of Issus*, a copy of a Greek painting, has much more motion and realism than the stiff, stylized, symbolic Byzantine *Emperor Justinian and Attendants. The Battle of Issus* is on the floor in a Pompeian house, and the *Emperor Justinian and Attendants* is high on the wall of San Vitale in Ravenna.

4 Possible choices are:

• The calligraphic page from the *Album of the Conqueror*, fig.7–26

• *X-P (Chi-Rho) Page*, from *Lindisfarne Gospel Book*, fig.7–28

• *St. Matthew the Evangelist* from the *Gospel Book*, Rhineland, fig.7–32

• *St. Matthew the Evangelist* from the *Gospel Book of Archbishop Ebbo of Reims*, fig.7–33

• *Laila and Majnun at School*, miniature, fig.7–27

Activity 1: Family Fresco

Activity Objectives

Students should be able to:

- Experience working with frescoes, to learn the properties of plaster.

- Gain appreciation for artists who have painted successful frescoes.

- Practice mixing clear, clean colors successfully.

- Produce a balanced composition with a center of interest.

- Make good decisions regarding how much detail to include in their fresco.

Thinking Critically

Focus on the last "Think about it" question to assist students in choosing their subject. Encourage them to select something they're comfortable with or excited about. Suggest that they use a familiar, simple image as they work with this new, challenging medium. Spend ample time in the questioning/sketching process until you feel students are confident about what they want to paint. In particular, focus on planning colors ahead of time and on an awareness of strong composition with a center of interest and good use of space.

Preparation Ideas

- Ahead of time, do a test run to determine how much plaster you will need to fill platters for each student in your class. You may need to mix more than one batch.

- During your test, try different ways of inserting the paper clip into the plaster for hanging. You can set one clip in the middle or try one on each side, attaching string between the two.

- You may want to spend one entire class in preparation, asking questions and allowing time for students to develop sketches for their fresco.

Notes on Materials

- Use shallow, rectangular styrofoam platters, the kind that supermarkets use for meat. Have students bring these from home, if possible, along with a terry-cloth towel.

- For brushes, use rounds: sizes 2, 7, 10, and 12.

- Cover the tables with newspaper for the fresco painting.

Activity 1

Family Fresco

Materials
Styrofoam platter
tempera paint or watercolors
plaster of Paris
bucket, water
assorted brushes
terry cloth towel
vine charcoal
newspapers
paper clips

Take a look.
- Fig.7-3, *The Good Shepherd*. Ceiling fresco, early 4th century.

Think about it. Among the first Christian art known to exist are the frescoes that decorate the ceilings and walls of the catacombs. (See page 32 to refresh your memory on fresco technique). Study the fresco, *The Good Shepherd*.
- What story does this fresco tell?
- Note the simplification of the figures, animals and clothing.
- Think about yourself and your experiences with your family, school and community. What events are vivid in your mind?

Do it.
- Make a list of personal experiences that are important to you and prioritize them. Choose one of your top three as the foundation for your fresco. Do several preliminary drawings.
- Follow instructions for mixing plaster into Styrofoam platters. The side facing out will be the back of your fresco. Bend a paper clip and place it in the center of the plaster (to be used for hanging once the plaster is dry).
- After the plaster has set, remove it from the platter and turn it over. You should find a smooth surface with curved edges. Use the vine

charcoal to draw your idea. You can "erase" by blotting the surface gently with a damp cloth.
- Use watercolor or tempera to paint your fresco. Place a damp terry cloth towel around the platter for storage.

Check it. As you work, keep these questions in mind:
- Does your fresco have a center of interest? Does it have a theme? Is your composition balanced?
- Have you planned your use of color? Are your colors mixed well (not muddy)?

Helpful Hint: You may use figures or symbols in your fresco.

Activity 2

Illuminate Your Initials

Materials
White drawing paper, no larger than 4" x 6" or 6" x 9"
pencil, #3 or 4H
kneaded eraser
assorted fine-tipped markers

Take a look.
- Fig.7–28, *X-P (Chi-Rho) Page*, from *Lindisfarne Gospel Book*, 698–721.

Think about it. Whenever Islamic and European cultures clashed there were fascinating changes. The arabesques and geometric decorations of Islam contributed to manuscript illumination.
- What is the meaning of *arabesque* and *illumination*?
- Think about some characteristics of a line: its direction, curves, thickness or thinness. Does it taper at one or both ends?
- Consider the motifs and their forms. Do they repeat to create a pattern and design?

Do it.
- Visualize your initials or name. How would you illuminate them? What colors and patterns would best reflect your personality?

- Lightly sketch your initials onto a small piece of paper. Use a minimum of lines to lay out your sketch, as too many pencil marks will muddy your colors.
- Use a variety of lines to develop your design with markers. Make it look like an ancient, medieval illumination—or you may give it a more contemporary look. As you proceed, gently erase any original pencil marks when you no longer need them.

Check it. Do your letters and design elements complement each other? Do your color combinations work well together? Are there any original pencil lines showing?

Helpful Hint: Work on a small scale since this is an intricate and exacting art. After completion, laminate your illumination to intensify the color.

Additional Activities

- Perhaps there is an area in the school that would be appropriate for a mosaic. Have a school-wide design contest. Several classes could participate in the layout and development of the mural.
- Design a mural that reflects the art and cultures the class has studied. You can use icons, flags or symbols to represent each culture.
- Write an essay about famous individuals in a hypothetical situation. Use information from this and other chapters to justify your work. For example: Charlemagne and King Tutankhamen Debating _____ (you insert the topic)

Classroom Management

- To start the fresco, have all the students ready, with platter and paper clip in hand. Remind them that the surface facing out will be the back of the fresco. Talk about the best way to attach their paper clip.

- Measure out how much plaster you will need. Fill the bucket with the required amount of water and pour plaster into the water. The plaster should form a little peak above the water level.

- Stir until evenly mixed and there are no lumps. Work quickly.

- Have students approach you with their platters. Pour plaster into each one.

- After the plaster has set, have students carefully remove it from the platter. They should sketch lightly on the surface with vine charcoal before beginning their painting.

- If the painting is not finished by the end of class and will be worked on at a later time, have students place a damp terry-cloth towel around the plaster for storage.

Evaluation

- Evaluate the work habits of the students, such as how well they followed instruction, gathered and organized materials, and worked with procedures.

- Has the student met the objectives of creating a successful composition with a center of interest, mixing clean colors, and making good use of detail?

Angela McPherson

Age 17
Lower Richland High School
Hopkins, South Carolina
Favorite kinds of art:
Abstract/realism
Favorite artist: Dali

Activity 2, Illuminate Your Initials

My art project symbolizes the blacks' faith in God
as they struggled through slavery, hoping to one
day be free. The Egyptian sign of life symbolizes
freedom. The black man in chains symbolizes slavery. The Star of David symbolizes religion and
belief in God. The scales symbolize the weight of
the world that was against blacks.

*What was your thought process when you were
creating and developing your project?*
What part of my history could I use to symbolize
what happened, using my initials.

*What have you read, seen or learned about the
history of art that has influenced your approach
to art?*
Watching cartoons got me interested in art. At first
I wanted to be a cartoonist. Now I want to go into
advertising design.

*What do you enjoy most about the artistic
process?*
Being able to create the impossible or unimagin-
able. A purple sky, a horse with wings, whatever
you desire.

*What advice do you have for other students who
enjoy creating art?*
To keep doing it. You'll always find a career that
involves what you enjoy best.

Angela (far left) and her classmates work on their drawings in
Ad Design class.

Illustrated ASM, 1994. Colored pencil and felt-tip pens,
6" x 9" (15.2 x 22.8 cm).

Teacher Spotlight

Karen DeAmicis

Art Teacher
Lower Richland High School

We had previously studied various
kinds of lettering and did a unit on
calligraphy with a project on Italic
lettering with an illustrated border.
For this project, we studied a variety
of resources on illuminated manuscripts. [*See* list below.] We discussed
family shields and the significance
of symbols. We used markers and
colored pencils to achieve more color
variety and to have the metallic gold
look which is not achievable with
markers. The students really seemed
to enjoy this project.

Alexander, J. J., Ed. *The Decorated Letter,*
New York: George Braziller, Inc., 1978.
Backhouse, Janet. *The Illuminated
Manuscript,* Kent City County, UK:
Phaidon, 1990.
Calkins, Robert G. *Illuminated Books
of the Middle Ages,* Ithaca: Cornell
University Press, 1983.
Child, Heather. *Calligraphy Today:
Twentieth Century Tradition and
Practice,* New York: Taplinger Publish-
ing Co., Inc. 1988.
Gutmann, Joseph. *Hebrew Manuscript
Painting,* New York: George Braziller,
Inc., 1978.
Mütherisch, Florentine and Joachim E.
Gaehde. *Carolingian Painting,* New
York: George Braziller, Inc., 1977.

(e.g., Old English, Chaucerian). You can
find many examples in magazines and
especially in advertisements.

Notes on Materials

• Students can also use watercolor to
do the illumination. After the watercolor is dry, they can outline with India
ink and pen or colored markers.

Classroom Management

• Students can work in groups of
four per work area to share fine-tipped
markers for their illumination.

Tips

• Provide a variety of books on styles
of lettering.

• Invite calligraphers or local craftspeople in the art of cloisonné to give a
discussion and demonstration about
the art.

Activity 2:
Illuminate Your Initials

Activity Objectives
Students should be able to:

• Experiment with creative use of line.

• Explore effective use of lettering.

• Gain insight into the precision of
detail employed by early artists producing illuminated manuscripts.

Thinking Critically
Ask students to think about the most
important thing they own. What is it?
(You will get all kinds of answers!) Lead
students to an awareness that *their
name* is perhaps the most important
thing they own. Refer them to the *X-P*

(Chi-Rho) Page on page 223 and initiate
a discussion.

• What is the meaning of illumination?
Arabesque?

• Explain to the students that a pattern
is repetition of line, shape and color.
Ask them to find examples of pattern.

• What style of lettering best reflects
each student's personality and his/her
name? Delicate? Bold? Curvy? Print?
Script? Have each student select a style
of lettering for his/her initial or name.

Preparation Ideas

• Find other examples of illuminated
manuscripts to stimulate ideas.

• Introduce a variety of styles of lettering. Show students several examples

Chapter 8 Organizer

Chapter 8 Opener: Romanesque and Gothic

Objectives

Understand that the Church gained tremendous power in medieval Europe and initiated artistic endeavors to demonstrate its powerful role as political, religious and cultural leader of the West.

Understand how Romanesque art was designed to evoke powerful responses through its spirited and emotional style.

Explain how Gothic art, particularly sacred architecture, communicated the unity between exterior and inner spaces and, hence, the connection between God and humankind.

National Standards

4b Students describe the function and explore the meaning of specific art objects within varied cultures, times and places.

5d Students correlate responses to works of visual art with various techniques for communicating meanings, ideas, attitudes, views, and intentions.

2a Students demonstrate the ability to form and defend judgments about the characteristics and structures to accomplish commercial, personal, communal, or other purposes of art.

Teacher Edition References

Lesson 8.1 Romanesque Art

Special Feature:
Sainte-Madeleine Tympanum 232–233

HOTS 233

Remainder of Lesson 8.1 234–239
World Cultural Timeline 234, 238
Lesson 8.1 Review 239

Contextual Info 234, 236, 238
HOTS 235, 237, 239
Inquiry 236

Interdisciplinary 237
Multicultural 234, 238
Performing Arts 236

Lesson 8.2 Gothic Art

Special Feature:
Chartres Cathedral 240–241

Contextual Info 241

HOTS 241

Remainder of Lesson 8.2 242–256
World Cultural Timeline 244, 248
Lesson 8.2 Review 256
Primary Source 257
Chapter Review 257

Contextual Info 242, 244, 246, 248, 250, 252, 254, 256
HOTS 243, 245, 247, 249, 251, 253, 255
Conservation 245
Cooperative 243

Inquiry 252
Interdisciplinary 244, 246
Materials and Techniques 254
Multicultural 244, 248, 250
Performing Arts 242, 247

Classroom Connections

National Standards

Studio Activity 1
The News in Stitches

1b Students conceive and create works of visual art that demonstrate an understanding of how the communication of their ideas relates to the media, techniques, and processes they use.

Studio Activity 2
Stained Glass Windows

3b Students apply subjects, symbols, and ideas in their artworks and use the skills gained to solve problems in daily life.
1a Students apply media, techniques, and processes with sufficient skill, confidence, and sensitivity that their intentions are carried out in their artworks.

Ancillaries

Timeline: Romanesque and
Gothic Art 230
Map: Romanesque and Gothic Art 231
Context 230
Art 231
Quote 231

Ancillaries

Slides: Romanesque, *Christ Figure from the tympanum*, Sainte Madeleine, Vezelay, 42a, 93; Romanesque, *The Mission of the Apostles from the tympanum*, Sainte Madeleine, Vezelay, 43a, 94

Slides: Romanesque, Interior of Saint-Sernin, 52b, 95; Romanesque, Worms Cathedral, Germany, 44a, 96; Romanesque, *Christ in Majesty*, Saint-Sernin, 53b, 97; Romanesque, *The Prophet Jeremiah from the south portal*, St. Pierre, Mossaic, 45a, 98

Overhead Transparencies: Reaching for the Sky, 8

Slides: Gothic, Cross vaults, Cathedral of Amiens, 46a, 99; Gothic, Interior of nave, Cathedral of Amiens, 47a, 100; Gothic, Exterior of Ste-Chapelle, 54b, 101; Gothic, Interior of Salisbury, 55b, 102; Gothic, Fan Vaulting, Chapter House, Wells Cathedral, 48a, 103; Gothic, *Four Ancestors of Christ*, jamb statues, Cathedral of Chartres, 49a, 104; Riemenschneider, *Group of Three Saints* (*St. Christopher, St. Eustace and St. Erasmus*), 50a, 105; Sluter, *Moses with Two Prophets*, Cartusian Monastery of Champol, 51a, 106
Large Reproductions: *Unicorn Tapestry* 9, *Gargoyle* from Notre Dame, Paris, 10

Schedule

One day to draw the small group designs. One day to arrange the small designs and transfer them to fabric. Two to six days to stitch. Smaller pieces take less time.

One day to draw design on board and cut it. One day to paste on cellophane. Small, simple designs or collaborative projects may take less time.

Materials

embroidery floss, embroidery needles, scissors, drawing paper, heavyweight tracing paper, embroidery transfer paper, loosely woven cotton, wool, burlap or muslin, optional: iron, ironing board, wooden hoops

gray chipboard, white paper, black markers, black railroad board, colored cellophane, glue, mat knife, scissors

Other Resources

Books

Conant, Kenneth John. *Carolingian and Romanesque Architecture: 800–1200.* 4th ed., New Haven: Yale University Press, 1992.

Dodwell, Charles. *Painting in Europe 800–1200.* New Haven: Yale University Press, 1971.

Duby, Georges, ed. *A History of Private Life. Volume II: Revelations of the Medieval World.* Cambridge: Harvard University Press, 1988.

Frankl, Paul. *Gothic Architecture.* Baltimore: Penguin USA, 1963.

Frisch, Teresa. *Gothic Art: 1140–c. 1450.* 2nd ed. Toronto: University of Toronto Press Inc., reprint 1987.

Holt, Elizabeth Gilmore, ed. *A Documentary History of Art. Volume I: The Middle Ages and Renaissance.* Princeton: Princeton University Press, 1981.

Lasko, Peter. *Ars Sacra 800–1200.* Baltimore: Penguin USA, 1972.

Snyder, James. *Medieval Art: Painting, Sculpture, Architecture, 4–14th Century.* Englewood Cliffs: Prentice Hall, 1989.

Stoddard, Whitney S. *Art and Architecture in Medieval France.* New York: HarperCollins, 1972.

Stokstad, Marilyn. *Medieval Art.* New York: HarperCollins, 1986.

White, John. *Art and Architecture in Italy: 1250–1400.* 2nd ed., New Haven: Yale University Press, 1992.

Zarnecki, George. *Art of the Medieval World: Architecture, Sculpture, Painting, The Sacred Arts.* Englewood Cliffs: Prentice Hall, 1975.

Video

Castles. Unicorn, 1985.
Cloisters, The Glories of Medieval Art, Crystal

Music

Perotin–*Alleluia*
Machaut–*Agnus Dei*
Trouvere Song–*Or La Triux*
Dufay– *Kyrie* from *Mass Se La Face Ay Pale*
School of Notre Dame–*Motet "En Non Diu! Quant Voi"*

These and other pieces can be found on *Haydn Society, Masterpieces of Music Before 1750.* Other Gothic music can be found on R.C.A., *History of Music in Sound* and also on Decca, *Archives Productions.*

Introduce

In the eleventh century, Christianity triumphed throughout Europe. As people wandered across the land on pilgrimages and as a result of the Crusades, they brought various traditions to bear on the primarily sacred art of the Romanesque period. In the twelfth and thirteenth centuries, the church's influence increased to such an extent that it dominated the social, political and religious realms of the Western world and became the principal sponsor of art.

Lessons at a Glance

8.1 *Romanesque Art*
Virtually all Romanesque art was sacred, and its highly expressive and emotional style was influenced by the past traditions of ancient Roman, early Christian, and Byzantine art.

8.2 *Gothic Art*
In the twelfth and thirteenth centuries, form, function and style united in Gothic art and architecture. Magnificent Gothic buildings, with their corresponding interior and outer spaces and interwoven sculpture and painting decoration, visually symbolized the unity between God and humankind.

Objectives

Students should be able to:

Understand that the Church gained tremendous power in medieval Europe and initiated artistic endeavors to demonstrate its powerful role as political, religious and cultural leader of the West.

Understand how Romanesque art was designed to evoke powerful responses through its spirited and emotional style.

Explain how Gothic art, particularly sacred architecture, communicated the unity between exterior and inner spaces and, hence, the connection between God and humankind.

Teach

Timeline

Share with students that the Romanesque period of the eleventh century was followed by the Gothic era

8 Romanesque and Gothic Art

In This Chapter...

THE ELEVENTH CENTURY began the period of medieval art called Romanesque. Christianity was triumphing in Europe and the Church was gaining tremendous power. The Crusades were initiated to take back the Holy Land from the Moslems. As a result, many people moved back and forth across great land areas, creating an exchange of ideas and artistic styles.

Romanesque art had influences from ancient Roman, Early Christian and Byzantine times. Its expressive and emotional style was mainly religious in theme. It was designed to evoke powerful responses in the viewer. Great building campaigns started. Churches and their decoration were the primary means of employment for artists and builders.

Large population shifts also occurred in the 1100s and 1200s. During the Gothic period, people moved from country to city. Christianity continued to grow in popularity. The Church became the social, political and religious leader of the Western world. Monasteries were replaced by church-sponsored schools and universities as centers of learning. This led to new energy and freedoms.

Architecture was the principal means of artistic expression during this time. The unity between outer and inner spaces, and between God and humankind, became a central goal. The buildings of the Gothic period soar to the heavens in celebration of this ideal.

8–a This drawing is from the sketchbook of a medieval architect who visited many of the new cathedrals built during the Gothic period. He recorded architectural innovations and stylistic variations.
Villard de Honnecourt, *Sketch of flying buttresses on apse of Cathèdral of Reims*. Bibliothèque Nationale, Paris.

| | | | 1298 First documented use of spinning wheel in Europe | | |
| 1053–1272 Pisa Cathedral 1095 First Crusade | 1130–1330 Great advances in stained glass manufacture | 1142 Cathedral of Chartres, France | 1305 Giotto advances use of pictorial space in Western painting | 1387–1400 Chaucer, *Canterbury Tales* | 1428 Joan of Arc leads French armies against England |

Romanesque and Gothic Art

| 1120–1132 *The Mission of the Apostles*, tympanum of Sainte-Madeleine | 1137 Abbot Suger helps develop Gothic architecture | 1220 Climax of Gothic architecture, Amiens Cathedral, France | 1347 Black Death devastates Europe | 1413 Limbourg Brothers, *Book of Hours* | 1465 First printed music |

in the twelfth and thirteenth centuries. Next have them study the figures in *The Battle of Hastings* (fig.8–c) and compare them to the ones in Duccio's *Christ Raising Lazarus from the Dead* (figs.8–d, 8–44). Ask students to decide which image is an example of Gothic art (which strove to present figures in realistic space) and which one typifies the earlier, less naturalistic style of the Romanesque. Have them check their answers by plotting the dates of the works on the timeline, informing them that *The Battle of Hastings* was created from about 1073 to 1083 and that Duccio was active between 1278 and 1319. Based on what they have learned, when do they think *Moses* (figs.8–b, 8–37) was made, during the earlier Romanesque or the later Gothic period? (Again, have students see if their visual

analysis corresponds to what they find by plotting the date of the work, carved between 1395 and 1404, on the timeline.)

Context

Have students examine *Moses, Christ Raising Lazarus from the Dead* and the sketch of flying buttresses at the cathedral of Reims (fig.8–a). Ask them what theme or idea unites the three images. Are these scenes of daily life? To help them understand how each work is religious in nature, guide them with the following types of questions:

• What significant piece of literature do *Moses* and *Christ Raising Lazarus from the Dead* come from?

• What type of building is described by the sketch in fig.8–a?

The church shines with its middle part brightened.
For bright is that which is brightly coupled with the bright,
And bright is the noble edifice which is pervaded by the new light.

Abbot Suger

The development of Romanesque and Gothic
art included nearly all of Western Europe.

8–b During the medieval era there was extensive sculptural activity. Over the centuries, medieval sculptors became more and more interested in carving realistic figures.
Claus Sluter, *Moses*, detail from the *Well of Moses* (fig.8–37).

8–c This tapestry is unique in Romanesque art because it depicts in detail a contemporary event shortly after it occurred.
The Battle of Hastings, detail of *Bayeux Tapestry* (fig. 8–13).

8–d Paintings on wood panels grow in popularity during the thirteenth and fourteenth centuries. Artists used gold leaf and brilliant colors to depict religious scenes that begin to show human emotion.
Duccio, *Christ Raising Lazarus from the Dead*, detail (fig.8–44).

• What sorts of activities occur within the building? Since all the works here, which represent the times, are related to religion, what can you conclude about the importance and power of Christianity during the medieval period?

Art

Ask students to describe how the architect of the cathedral of Reims (figs.8–a, 8–20) planned to create a bright, vertical, ethereal structure. This sketch of flying buttresses shows tall, narrow towers and very thin, elegant arches spreading between. Flying buttresses helped hold up the outside high, slim walls of Gothic churches.

• Can students detect how the elongated columns that decorate the towers add to the sweeping upward movement?

• What has the architect placed on top of the towers?

• How would the lower towers look without the trio of small towers on top? (Students can cover this area with their fingers for a comparison.)

Evaluate

Ask students who the guiding force was behind art in the Middle Ages. If they need guidance, ask them who would have commissioned the works in figs.8–a, 8–b and 8–d (the Christian Church).

Quote

Ask students what they think Abbot Suger, who was responsible for the quote, meant in the line "For bright is that which is brightly coupled with the bright"? Is he referring to literal light only? If students need guidance, have them think about the function of the building. Can they make a connection between light and divinity?

Map

After students study the map of Romanesque and Gothic art, ask them in which countries these styles flourished. According to the map, do they believe that Islamic or Asian cultures significantly influenced Romanesque and Gothic art and architecture?

Reteach

Ask students to decide if religion is a typical subject of art in America today.

• Ask why they think that sacred art is not as popular in contemporary times as it was during the medieval period.

Deepen students' thinking by asking: "Does any single religion exert as much power in the United States as Christianity did in Western Europe in the Middle Ages? What might contemporary life be like if America were controlled by a single religious order?" (Students might want to research and compare daily life, religious and political freedom and cultural diversity in the United States to that in Moslem countries.)

Have students discuss if they would have enjoyed life during the medieval period.

• What in the artworks within the chapter opener and throughout Lesson 8.1 and Lesson 8.2 have influenced their opinions? (At the end of the lessons, you may wish to ask students if, after learning more about life in the eleventh through thirteenth centuries, they have changed their minds, and, if so, why.)

Lesson 8.1

Virtually all Romanesque art was sacred, and its highly expressive, emotional style was influenced by the past traditions of ancient Roman, early Christian and Byzantine art.

Warm-up

Explain to the class that a religious intensity infused Western Europe during the Middle Ages. In addition to religious pilgrimages to holy sites, the church instigated the Crusades, wars fought to regain the Holy Land from the Moslems. If students had lived in medieval times, would they have felt inspired to join the Crusades after worshiping in Sainte-Madeleine (figs.8–1, 8–2)? Point out that the sculpture over the doorway depicts Christ sending his disciples out to preach during his era, not the time of the Crusades.

Objectives

Students should be able to:

Understand that the intermingling of cultural tradition as a result of the Crusades, pilgrimages and the church's patronage contributed to the vitality of Romanesque art and architecture.

Understand that *Romanesque* was a nineteenth-century term coined to describe art from Roman times until the Gothic period.

Explain how Romanesque art expressed the religious fervor of the era.

Understand that church architecture and its accompanying sculptural decorations were the primary artistic expressions.

Vocabulary Definitions

tympanum (*tim*-pa-num) A carved or decorated space over the door and under the arch of a Romanesque or Gothic church facade.
narthex A porch or vestibule, sometimes enclosed, preceding the main entrance of a church.
mandorla An almond-shaped outline enclosing the full figure of a person endowed with divine light, usually Christ.

8.1 Romanesque Art

THE NAME ROMANESQUE was coined in the nineteenth century to cover all art from Roman times until the Gothic period. Today, the term applies to the eleventh and twelfth centuries in western Europe.

A variety of factors contributed to the growth and development of Romanesque art. The threat of Islam had waned, the barbarian raids from the north had subsided, the eastern tribes were held in check, and Christianity was triumphing everywhere in Europe. Monasteries began to exert influence in business and the social services. There was a growing spirit of religious fervor. More and more people were undertaking pilgrimages to holy sites. Then along came the Crusades, a bloody movement organized to liberate the Holy Land from the Moslems and recapture it for Christendom. The Crusades moved huge numbers of people back and forth across Europe. This resulted in a great mingling of cultures and ideas.

All of these factors produced a new phenomenon. We now encounter a period in art and architecture when certain traits, or characteristic features, appear throughout what we today call Europe. This happened without the backing or influence of any one particular political ruler, as was the case, for instance, during the Roman Empire. It was the movement of people and artists and the influence of the Church that provided the opportunity for artistic ideas and innovations to travel great distances.

Building campaigns were undertaken everywhere. Major efforts were directed toward constructing churches and carving sculpture to decorate them. Romanesque art reflected the activity and religious enthusiasm that characterized medieval life from about 1050 to 1200.

Key Notes

- The movement of people across Europe because of pilgrimages and the Crusades resulted in an exchange of ideas and styles.
- Church building and sculptural decoration were the principal activities of artists during the Romanesque period.
- Romanesque art is characterized by its expressive nature and by the religious fervor it represents.

Vocabulary
tympanum
narthex
mandorla
crossings
lantern
ambulatory
buttresses
choir
abbey
cloister
cathedra
campanile

Special Feature
Sainte-Madeleine Tympanum

Sculpture, like all Romanesque art, most often was associated with the church. It was intended to help the people of the faith understand the teachings of the church. Sculptures appeared on capitals of columns and around portals. They were placed in niches both inside and outside the church. The exterior of Romanesque churches provided many areas for sculptures. The doorways were important focal points. The *tympanum*, or arched area below the arch and above the lintel of a doorway, was a large space that could be filled with a scene sculpted in relief. Anyone entering the church would notice its decoration.

One of the most beautiful of all Romanesque churches is Sainte-Madeleine in Vezelay. Its crowning glory is a set of three sculptured portals opening into the nave and side aisles from the *narthex*, or vestibule. The central tympanum contains *The Mission of the Apostles* (fig.8–1). Here Christ is shown sending his disciples to preach to the entire world. This was a fitting subject for a church from which many Crusades departed. The huge figure of Christ is placed in an almond-shaped form, or *mandorla*, his knees turned in a zig-zag position. From the hands (one is missing) of the majestic Christ, we see the rays of the Holy Spirit pouring down upon the apostles. The apostles, who are all equipped with copies of the Gospels, are receiving their assignments, or missions.

crossing The area of a church where the transept intersects the nave. Sometimes a dome or tower is built over this area, further emphasizing it as the focal area of the worship space.
lantern A small dome, usually with windows around its drum, built atop a larger dome or on a roof to allow light to enter the structure.
ambulatory (*am*-byoo-lah-tor-ee) Any passageway around a central space. A place for walking around the apse of a church, often a continuation of the side aisles; also, a covered walkway around a cloister.
buttress A massive support built against a wall to receive the lateral thrust (pressure) exerted by a vault, roof or arch.

choir (kwire) The part of the church in which the service is sung, usually the apse; also, a group of trained singers.
abbey A complex of buildings comprised of a monastery and a church.
cloister (kloy-stur) A covered walkway or ambulatory around an open court or garden. Usually, a colonnade faces the garden, allowing light to enter.
cathedra The chair or throne of a bishop.
campanile (camp-uh-*neel*-ee) A bell-tower either attached to a church or freestanding nearby.
tracery Ornamental stonework in a decorative pattern with a lace-like effect; a decorative interlacing of lines suggestive of such stonework.

The lintel and the compartments around the central group are filled with grotesque people (fig.8–2). They represent the heathen, or unconverted, from many lands. There are people with dog heads, people with enormous ears, others are covered in hair, some have snoutlike noses and some are so small they have to use a ladder to mount a horse. There are also the blind, the lame, mutes and hunchbacks. All of them are awaiting conversion, which the Christians believed would bring them salvation. The arch framing the tympanum contains the signs of the zodiac and the labors for each month of the year. The whole composition is crowded and agitated, a common feature of Romanesque relief sculpture.

Relief work dominated Romanesque sculpture. At Vezelay the figures are in such high relief that many of them are carved almost in the round. The Christ also is an outstanding example of the Romanesque skill with decorative line. At Vezelay we can see how the technical expertise of centuries of working with small portable art is beautifully translated by Romanesque artists into a monumental scale.

8–2 The title of this relief refers to the Christian belief that the apostles and all the faithful are obligated to spread the Gospel to all nations.
The Mission of the Apostles, detail (fig.8–1).

8–1 Vezelay was the church most closely associated with the crusades. The Third Crusade left from here. *The Mission of the Apostles.* Tympanum of the central portal of the narthex, 1120–1132. Sainte-Madeleine, Vezelay, France.

Higher-Order Thinking Skills

Provide a photocopied photograph of a school event, club or activity that shows at least several people. The yearbook or school newspaper may be a good source. Ask students to identify the importance of each person relative to each other and to the event. Students can draw or photocopy the image to enlarge it several times so that they have each person in a size relative to his or her importance. Students can then reconstruct the scene, showing the weighted importance of the figures.

Have students describe how art from about 1050 to 1200 reflects the religious enthusiasm of the Romanesque period. How do the images support their answers?

Ask why most Romanesque sculpture was carved in relief rather than fully in the round. (For a hint, direct students to review the locations of the sculptures illustrated in Lesson 8.1. Could anyone have seen the sculpture from the back?)

Reteach

Have students ponder why church officials would have wanted stories from the Bible illustrated in their buildings.

• Do students think that most people during this period were educated and knew how to read?

• Since most of the population was illiterate and only those in religious orders and the wealthy class were educated, what purpose would the sculpted and painted narratives have served?

• Can you imagine how it might have felt to follow portions of the Scriptures by looking at the art around you as the clergy read aloud? Would these images have helped fire your imagination or would they have stifled it?

Teach

Criticism: Ask students to compare the carving in *The Mission of the Apostles* (figs.8–1, 8–2) to that in *The Archangel Michael* (fig.7–1).

• Can they find any similarities between the two divine figures?

• How about in the folds of their clothing and also the use of symbols?

• Can they identify the major differences in style?

• Which sculpture appears more lifelike? Which one is more stylized?

• How does the depth of the actual carving differ in the works?

• What in the scene of Christ communicates the Romanesque interest in evoking a sense of religious passion rather than describing the natural world? (The image's agitated surface, tightly squeezed composition and stylized patterns increase the intensity of its impact.)

Evaluate

Ask the class why the Crusades and long pilgrimages were so critical in enriching Romanesque art.

• How were visual traditions shared in an era before television, publications, satellites and computers?

• Who helped transport images from one part of Europe to another during this time?

Contextual Information

Romanesque Churches

There were a number of factors that led to the tremendous boom in the construction of churches beginning in the eleventh century. One of the more interesting reasons is related to the passing of the millennium. In the years leading to 1000 AD, people's fears and anticipation grew because there was a widespread belief that the millennium would bring an end to the world. When this did not occur, there was tremendous relief and thankful celebration. This fervent drive resulted in the construction of numerous churches.

A more practical reason for the widespread building was that hundreds of churches, especially in France and Italy, had been burned and destroyed during the raids of the Norse and Magyars. The churches needed to be rebuilt, and they needed to be fireproof. The wooden roofs of earlier churches were eschewed in favor of stone construction. Structural elements had to be devised to hold up the heavy masonry. It is this practical concern that accounts for the heavy, blocky look of Romanesque churches.

8–3 Common vaulting systems.

Romanesque Architecture

The number of Romanesque churches still standing after almost a thousand years is remarkable. They are scattered all over western Europe but most are in France, Germany and Italy. The churches were built of carefully cut local stone, which varied in color and texture from place to place. The entrances were usually at the west end. Worshipers faced toward the east (and symbolically toward Jerusalem). The **crossings**, or the place where nave and transept intersect, are often topped with towers,

or domes with **lanterns**. These intersecting spaces produced the shape of a Latin cross with one arm longer than the other three.

Ambulatories, or walkways, were built around the apse to allow for large processions. Often small chapels were added to the outside of these ambulatories to hold relics of saints brought back in the Crusades. Interior columns separated the nave from side aisles. The columns divided the side walls into a series of rectangular units that created a strong feeling of rhythm as one looked down the nave.

The wooden roofs of previous ages were replaced by masonry barrel vaults (fig.8–3). These vaults eliminated the danger of fire and produced better acoustics. The stone vaults, similar to those used by the Romans, were extremely heavy. They spanned the naves and produced tremendous outward thrust, requiring massive exterior **buttresses** and thick walls for support. Groin vaults (cross vaults) were often used to stabilize the naves or to add strength over the side aisles (fig.8–3). Interior space could never attain great height because the problem of weight and thrust was simply too difficult to overcome with existing engineering skills. Windows were kept small so as not to weaken the walls. Therefore, interiors were quite dark and had a rather heavy feeling.

Rounded arches, also a Roman feature, were used over windows and over niches that contained sculpture. They also appeared in

arcades, supports and side aisles.

To accommodate a larger clergy and more ritual, the apse area was greatly enlarged. The apse included a **choir**, a raised area for the singing clergy. Large crypts were built under the choir to hold the remains of high-ranking clergy and other important personages.

When a monastery accompanied a church, the complex of buildings was called an **abbey**. A **cloister**, or open courtyard, with an arcaded ambulatory usually connected the church with the living quarters of the monks. The home church of a bishop always contained a special chair or throne for him. The chair was called a **cathedra**. It is from this term that the word cathedral is derived. Churches that do not contain such chairs cannot be correctly called cathedrals, no matter how beautiful or large the building.

Romanesque architecture was a dynamic art form. It was always changing to meet new situations and to solve new problems in construction. Often different architects worked on successive phases of a project and brought completely new ideas. A few examples will provide a

8–4 These towers are closely related to the towers of castles.
Worms Cathedral, about 1016–1181. Worms, Germany.

| 900–1300 | 1000 |
| **5000 temples built in Burma** | **Lady Murasaki Shikibu, *Tales of Genji*** |

World Cultural Timeline

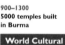

| 1000 | 1009 |
| **Zimbabwe culture; with the walled city of Great Zimbabwe at its center, dominant in Africa.** | **First illustrated book written in Iran** |

Multicultural Connection

The Zimbabwe Culture

As trading kingdoms in West Africa prospered and grew, so did its population. As a result, many of its people were forced to migrate to the East in search of new homelands. The Shona settled in Zimbabwe, in East Africa, about 700 AD and developed one of the best-known trading kingdoms in this area. Zimbabwe's inland location provided protection from Muslim influence and provided a place for exchange, which was overseen by kings who taxed and controlled the trade. Its people traded gold, copper, iron and ivory from the interior to merchants

from cities along Africa's east coast. From these cities, trade was carried on with Arabia, Persia, India and China.

Bantu is the language of the Shona. The name *zimbabwe* is derived from a Bantu phrase meaning either "stone enclosure" or "dwelling of the chief." The Shona built towns with houses, markets, warehouses, a fort, the royal court and religious shrines, all by using fitted, mortarless stones. Shona rulers built an impressive residence known as the Great Zimbabwe, which included a mortarless stone conical tower 30 feet high and a surrounding wall, also more than 30 feet high and measuring 800 feet around. In the 1500s, Zimbabwe's trade declined because of European invasions in East Africa.

8–5a Diagram of Sainte-Sernin. Toulouse, France.

8–5 This church was designed with a long nave and transept to accommodate vast numbers of pilgrims. *Saint-Sernin*, about 1080–1120. Toulouse, France.

8–6 Locate the clerestory windows. How do they make the interior different from most Romanesque churches? Interior, *Sainte-Madeleine*, about 1104–1132. Vezelay, France.

Higher-Order Thinking Skills

1 Have the class create models of vaulting systems by using cardboard tubes cut in half to form barrel, groin and ribbed vaults. Students can then analyze the way each system responds to weight placed above it (as a roof would bring to bear) and identify the stress points.

2 Tell students to read the glossary for the definitions of the following architectural terms pertaining to the Romanesque period: apse, nave, choir, barrel vault, flying buttress, rounded arch. Ask students to identify examples of each of these terms in the images on pages 234–235. Have them review the Colosseum (figs.6–30, 6–31) to determine which of these elements had Roman roots. (The rounded arches and stone vaults, typical of Romanesque architecture, stemmed from ancient times.)

basic understanding of this architecture—its variety and characteristic features.

Worms Cathedral (fig.8–4) typifies Romanesque architecture in Germany. Based on earlier structures built during the reigns of Charlemagne and Otto the Great, it is heavy and fortress-like, with strong geometric forms. The church has an apse on each end. The towers resemble the turrets used in castles and are repeated at the other end of the building.

The exterior view of *Saint-Sernin* in Toulouse, France (fig.8–5), shows a huge tower over the crossing and an exterior view of one arm of the large transept. This structure was a pilgrimage church. That is, it was built to hold multitudes of travelers on their way to sacred shrines. A large apse and ambulatory, many small chapels, and double side aisles helped control the crowds that moved through the church (fig.8–5a).

The interior of *Sainte-Madeleine* at Vezelay (fig.8–6) exhibits some expected Romanesque features as well as some surprises. Instead of using single barrel vaults, the architect used groin vaults. With these vaults, the architect was able to open large windows in the upper level, allowing light to flood the interior. Even with the added strength of the groin vaults, the church had to be reinforced from the outside in the following centuries. The compound piers (many columns massed together) have sculpted capitals of white limestone. Soft golden limestone and light pink granite blocks were used in the piers. The striking two-color effect created by these blocks is a direct influence of the Islamic mosques built in Spain. The brightly lit choir is a later renovation.

Notre-Dame-la-Grande in Poitiers, France, is a low and wide church (fig.8–7). The barrel-vaulted interior has small windows, and is

• The African continent is divided into five major regions. Have students locate and identify the geographic characteristics of each.

• The Shona viewed their chief as a god-king. It was particularly important to the kings to impress their power on the people they ruled. Have students analyze how the building of the Great Zimbabwe expressed this concept.

• Have students compare and contrast the Ghana, Mali and Zimbabwe empires.

• What are some reasons that people today move from one geographical area to another?

(Students can view an example of contemporary Shona art by turning to Chapter 4, fig.4–84.)

Burma

The early Southeast Asian kingdom of Burma was bordered by India, Vietnam and the Khmer Empire. Although Indian traders and Buddhist missionaries helped to spread Indian culture into Burma, art in Burma, for the most part, means Buddhist art.

In 1044, a Burmese ruler named Anawrahta united the region and founded a kingdom that lasted nearly 250 years. Anawrahta set up his state religion as a unifying force in opposition to earlier forms of Buddhism and so-called "nature religion." He controlled the strategic city of Pagan, which stood on the Irrawaddy River in central Burma and became the center of great art and architecture. Hundreds of gilded Buddhist shrines and pagodas were built in the capital city of Pagan.

The temples were richly decorated in stucco. Glazed tiles, including reliefs depicting Buddhist stories, adorned the exterior and played an important part of Pagan architecture. Beautiful mural paintings were on the interior walls. In 1287, Burma was invaded by Mongols led by Kublai Khan, and building activity at Pagan all but ceased.

• How did the temples of Burma help to unify the diverse religious groups?

(For more on Burmese art, see Chapter 4, pages 110 and 111.)

Contextual Information

Castles

The design of castles changed to reflect the development and use of new weapons. The height of castle walls was increased with the invention of towers on wheels, which served as covered ladders for the soldiers. Moats were added when tunnels were dug under walls for protection. Castle walls were built thicker when the cannon and the catapult were designed.

To withstand sieges, castles were stocked with food and water. People crowded inside the walled perimeter for safety and even began to establish businesses there. As a result, castle walls were expanded, and soon these areas became fortified cities.

Pilgrims

After people made the journey to any of the three major pilgrimage sites (Santiago at Compostela, St. Peter's in Rome, the Holy Land) they were permitted to wear a symbol that indicated that they had made the pilgrimage. If they had journeyed to Compostela, they wore a scallop shell. If they had reached Rome, a cross was their symbol. The sign of a successfully completed pilgrimage to the Holy Land was a palm leaf.

Sidelight

Pilgrimage Roads

During the Middle Ages, Christians in search of salvation made pilgrimages to important shrines. Although there were many shrines that people traveled to, three destinations were the most important: St. Peter's Church in Rome; the Holy Land; and the shrine of Santiago, or St. James, at Compostela in northwest Spain. The "Way of St. James" was a challenging journey to the major Romanesque churches in France and northern Spain with the shrine of St. James as a final destination.

A pilgrimage could mean a dangerous trip of hundreds, or even thousands, of miles. The trek could take many months or sometimes years. Pilgrims from many different ranks in life traveled in groups along established routes, stopping at inns along the way. They traveled on horseback or on foot, and were often prey to bandits and the forces of nature. The monks at the monastery of St. Bernard, with the help of their famous dogs, saved countless pilgrims caught in the treacherous snows of the Alpine pass.

Pilgrims traveled to churches to see the relics, or remnants of a saint's clothing, hair or bones, which they believed had the power to cure disease, forgive sins and perform miracles. Like tourist centers today, people in the various towns where shrines were located made their living from the tourist trade and sold souvenirs and fake relics to the weary pilgrims.

8–7 The helmet roofs on the towers were added after the church was finished. Do you think they are a positive addition?
Notre-Dame-la-Grande, about 1162–1271. Poitiers, France.

heavy and dark. The exterior has more sculpture than many Romanesque churches. The west facade contains fourteen large sculpted figures in niches formed by round arches and stumpy columns. Directly above the entrance is a frieze of many figures illustrating scenes from the life of Christ. Taller columns are bunched at the corners and lead upward to cone-shaped helmets. The helmets were added at a later time and do not seem to belong to the rest of the church. A heavy tower sits on the roof at the crossing. It, too, is capped with a cone-shaped top. The church is smaller than many others of the time and has only one portal, or

grand entrance. The flanking arches are decorative and not functional.

Italian Romanesque architecture was brighter, more colorful and more highly decorated than contemporary buildings north of the Alps. The grandest in central Italy is the complex at Pisa, made up of the cathedral, the baptistry (not shown) and the *campanile*, or bell tower (fig.8–8). All are built of white marble with horizontal bands of inlaid green marble. They are set off by the huge green lawn that surrounds them. The campanile—the famous Leaning Tower—started leaning during early construction. Efforts were made, unsuccessfully, to straighten it. Settling causes further tilting each year. Even extreme efforts have not stopped its continued leaning toward eventual destruction.

The cathedral is built on a Latin cross plan with an apse at each end of the transept and a pointed dome crowning the crossing. The facade consists of tiers of superimposed arcades. The interior has been strongly influenced by Early Christian basilicas, with rows of columns and a wooden roof. The baptistry is a freestanding building that was completed in the late thirteenth century.

Most Romanesque construction effort was spent on cathedrals. Much of the labor was donated by pious Christians from every level of society, who were eager to help earn

8–8 The tower keeps leaning more and more and may collapse despite efforts to reinforce it. Tourists are no longer permitted to climb to the top of this famous landmark.
Cathedral (begun 1063) *and Campanile* (begun 1174). Pisa, Italy.

Performing Arts Connections

Roving Entertainers

Itinerant dancers in medieval Europe performed from town to town as early as the sixth century AD. Acrobats, jugglers, buffoons, wrestlers, animal trainers with monkeys, dancing dogs and bears wandered throughout the land. Roving minstrels, or "jongleurs," came to town fairs to recount comic tales in rollicking couplets. The characters in these verses were typically peasants, sacrilegious clerics and feeble-minded knights. The audience loved the jokes and language that revolved around greed, hypocrisy and stupidity.

Inquiry

Have students research the history of American vaudeville and examine some of the similarities between this public entertainment tradition and its earlier, European antecedents. Is there entertainment today that has broad mass appeal?

8–9 Romanesque castles and churches shared many features of form and detail. What similarities do you see?
Marksburg Castle, 12th century. Braubach, Germany.

their way into heaven. However, powerful secular rulers constructed strong fortresses for themselves and their knights in France, Germany, England, Italy and Spain. The majestic *Marksburg Castle* (fig.8–9) is typical of twelfth-century fortifications in Germany. The castle stands on a cliff 495 feet above the Rhine River. Its main tower reaches another 130 feet into the air. Still intact, the castle resembles churches of the period in its towers, cones, thick walls, stone materials and small windows.

Romanesque Sculpture

As we already have seen at Vezelay, sculpture during the Romanesque period was primarily large in scale and attached to architecture. It was expressive in nature and placed an emphasis on evoking an emotional response from the viewer.

The Abbey Church of Saint-Pierre at Moissac provides an outstanding example of Romanesque sculpture. On the central support of the south portal are interlaced lions and lionesses. Such intertwined animals

reflect barbaric influences as well as the style of Islamic art. Wedged against the side of these animals is the prophet Jeremiah (fig.8–10). The figure of the prophet is thin and elongated. His legs are crossed beneath garments that fall in complex patterns. His hair and beard are long and flowing. A mustache sweeps across his face. Jeremiah's head is turned to the side; the prophet seems lost in thought. The stretched limbs and piety of the figure produce a direct emotional response from us. The sculptor has taken the problem of decorating this narrow, vertical architectural element and solved it in a way that gives perfect expression to the religious fervor of the time.

Another landmark of Romanesque sculpture is on the tympanum of the church of St. Lazare at Autun (fig.8–11). It is a carving of *The Last Judgment*, the moment at the end of the world when Christians believe all of humankind will rise from the dead. Each will be judged worthy of Heaven, or condemned forever to Hell. In the relief, the dead are shown rising up from their graves. Demons grab those that have been sent to Hell by the central figure of Christ, the Divine Judge. Angels lift the blessed into Heaven. Many of the scenes are

horrific and appalling. Those who passed beneath the tympanum as they entered the church could not help but be reminded of the fate that would await them should they stray from the path of strong faith and a good life.

The tympanum at Autun also has a feature that rarely is encountered in medieval art. It is one of the earliest surviving figurative sculptures that is signed by the artist who sculpted it. An inscription runs across the top of the lintel. It includes the words GISLEBERTUS HOC FECIT (Gislebertus made this).

8–10 One of the great achievements of Romanesque artists was reviving the technique of carving large-scale stone sculptures.
The Prophet Jeremiah, 1115–1135. South portal, St. Pierre. Moissac, France.

8–11 The tympanum of the central portal of most Romanesque churches had a large figure of Christ at the center of the composition.
Giselbertus, *The Last Judgment*, about 1130. West tympanum, St. Lazare. Autun, France.

Higher-Order Thinking Skills

The Bayeaux Tapestry is a visual, continuous narrative, a story of an important contemporary event. Ask students to identify contemporary visual narratives of important events in various formats, such as the news, documentaries, paintings and cartoons. Individuals or the class can create a visual narrative of a contemporary event in a mural, video, stitchery or painting. Students can also write about the purposes for the creation of such narratives, such as historical awareness and propaganda.

8–13 This famous work of art was embroidered by women.
The Battle of Hastings, detail of *The Bayeux Tapestry*, about 1073–1083. Wool embroidery on linen, 20" (51 cm) high. Town Hall, Bayeux, France.

Romanesque Painting and Crafts

Painting took on added importance during the Romanesque period as the fresco technique gained in popularity. Frescoes were used to decorate some interior spaces, especially in Spain and Italy. Churches in the north did not have frescoes because the interiors were too dark and the weather was too damp to use the fresco technique effectively.

Although many of the frescoes have been destroyed, some remain in excellent condition. *Virgin and Child Enthroned* (fig.8–12) was painted by the Master of Pedret (an unknown artist) in a small church in the Pyrenees Mountains of Spain. The Virgin and Child are rendered symbolically. They are placed in a mandorla to signify heaven. The archangels Michael and Gabriel are

8–12 Although this fresco is currently in a museum, it originally was painted on the wall of a now demolished church in Spain.
Master of Pedret, *Virgin and Child Enthroned*, about 1130. Fresco, 125" (318 cm) high at center. The Metropolitan Museum of Art, New York, The Cloisters Collection, 1950.

standing to their sides. The painting was originally on the half-dome of the apse. Modern techniques were used to remove the entire fresco and place it on a flat surface prior to the destruction of the church.

One of the most important historic events that occurred during the Romanesque period was the Battle of Hastings. It inspired the creation of a famous work in fabric.

Soon after the Battle of Hastings, Bishop Odo of Bayeux, France, commissioned the marvelous illustration of William the Conqueror's invasion of England in 1066. The wool embroidered frieze, which is 230 feet long and 20 inches high, decorated the Bayeux Cathedral. It is a documentation of the battle, with soldiers, horses, weapons, shields, towns, animals, invasion fleets and even a running commentary in Latin. It is called *The Bayeux Tapestry*, but is really a richly embroidered panel and not a true tapestry.

This small section (fig.8–13, 8–c) shows the variety of weapons used as the men ferociously fight one another: battle axes, javelins, hurling spears and crossbows. The bor-

1050	1100–1400
Foot binding first used in China	**Lost-wax metal castings, Ife, Nigeria**

World Cultural Timeline

1227	1185–1867
Genghis Khan's empire is divided among his four sons	**Shoguns rule Japan with Emperor**

Multicultural Connection

Ife Bronzes

Items made of bronze were produced in Africa as early as 2500 BC. The aristocratic Ife society (centered around Ife, Nigeria) flourished from the 1100s to the 1300s and created lifelike bronze portraits made by the lost-wax method (see Glossary) of casting. Kings were regarded as gods, and the portraits may have been commemorative of them. The figures' dimensions are nearly life-size and symmetrical; the features are anatomically correct and realistic. However, on some, the whole facial area is patterned with close parallel,

vertical lines. These lines were probably meant to symbolize the beaded veil used to protect the king from the gaze of his subjects or may represent body marks of some kind. On other bronze portraits, irregularly placed holes surround the mouth, the lower jaw and the top of the head. The artists, outstanding for their skill in carving and restrained naturalism, may have influenced the later Benin bronzes. Although Ife art was believed to have been created independent of outside influences, comparisons have been made to works produced in ancient Egypt, Classical Greece and Renaissance Italy.

(Students can turn to fig.4–82 for an example of an Ife bronze.)

• The lost-wax method of casting is one method of making sculpture. Ask students to describe other basic methods.

• Have students analyze the similarities and differences between Greek and Ife sculpture and explain what visual elements are favored in the works.

8–14 The Abbot had this cup made from an ancient Roman cup. French kings continued to use it for several centuries.
Chalice of Abbot Suger of Saint-Denis, about 1140. Sardonyx cup with gilded silver mounting, adorned with filigrees set with stones, pearls, glass insets and opaque white glass pearls, 7 1/2" (19 cm) high. National Gallery of Art, Washington DC, Widener Collection.

der above the scene is purely decorative while the one below shows dead soldiers, animals and discarded weapons, all part of the story.

Many works were crafted in the service of the church. The *Chalice of Abbot Suger* (fig.8–14) is created from an ancient Roman cup that was carved from a single piece of sardonyx. The twelfth-century gilt silver mounting is studded with precious stones and pearls. The chalice has a beauty and technical expertise that resembles the craftsmanship of the barbarian peoples of earlier years. It was made for Abbot Suger of Saint-Denis in Paris, one of the originators of the Gothic style. He wished to use only the best, most precious and most beautiful things in the service of God. The chalice was admired so much that it was used by French kings for three hundred years.

Lesson 8.1 Review

1 What is happening in the scene of *The Mission of the Apostles* in the tympanum at Sainte-Madeleine in Vezelay? Why is this subject appropriate for this particular church?
2 Describe a typical Romanesque church. Include these terms in your description: ambulatory, crossings, nave, transept and apse.
3 What was the purpose of an ambulatory?
4 Name two advantages of the masonry barrel vaulted roofs found in most Romanesque churches over the wooden roofs of earlier churches.
5 Draw a Romanesque arch. Which ancient culture used this same type of arch extensively in their architecture?
6 List three characteristics of Romanesque sculpture.
7 Where is a tympanum found in a Romanesque church?
8 Why did northern European churches not have frescoes painted on their walls?
9 What event is depicted in *The Bayeux Tapestry*?
10 Who was Abbot Suger? What was his philosophy concerning objects used in the church worship service?

Lesson 8.1 Review Answers

1 Christ is sending his disciples to preach to the entire world. Because many Crusades departed from this church, this is a fitting subject for this tympanum.
2 Romanesque churches were built of stone with the entrances usually facing west so worshipers would face east, toward Jerusalem. The place where the nave and the transept joined was called the *crossing* and was often topped with a tower or lantern. This floor plan resembled a Latin cross.

Ambulatories were walkways built around the apse and perimeter of the nave. Columns separated the nave from the side aisles. Thick walls and buttresses held up barrel-vaulted and groin-vaulted stone roofs. Rounded Roman arches were used over small windows, sculpture niches, supports and arcades. Towers were often at the front corners and crossings and sometimes freestanding on the roof. The apse area was enlarged to include a choir. Large crypts were under the raised apse.
3 Originally, an ambulatory was meant for large processions. It also provided small worship areas. Today it is used to funnel tourists around the worship in the central part of the nave. In medieval times it provided a similar function with pilgrims.
4 Masonry vaults eliminated the danger of fire and produced better acoustics.

5 The Romans used this same type of arch.

6 Intertwined animals; sometimes reflected barbaric and Islamic influences
7 Above the door
8 The interiors were too dark and the weather was too damp to use the fresco technique effectively.
9 The Battle of Hastings
10 Suger was abbot of Saint-Denis in Paris, and one of the originators of the Gothic style. He believed that the most precious and beautiful things should be used in the service of God.

Lesson 8.2

In the twelfth and thirteenth centuries, form, function and style united within Gothic art and architecture. Magnificent Gothic buildings, with their corresponding interior and outer spaces and interwoven sculpture and painting decoration, visually symbolized the unity between God and humankind.

Warm-up

Have students glance briefly at the images of *Chartres Cathedral* (figs.8–15, 8–16, 8–17). Ask them to find examples of the pointed arches, thin spires and sense of verticality that typifies Gothic architecture. Why would Grant Wood, a painter in America during the first half of the twentieth century, have titled his painting *American Gothic* (fig.15–23). What is similar in both form and feeling about the two works? (Clue students to the pointed pitchfork and solid verticality of the stoic couple.)

Objectives

Students should be able to:

Understand that cathedrals became religious, cultural and social centers of Europe as the population shifted from the countryside into towns during the twelfth and thirteenth centuries.

Explain how Gothic art and architecture encompassed new ideas and technological advances, thereby representing the unparalleled achievements and power of unified Christendom.

Understand that unity is the guiding principle behind Gothic architecture, epitomized by the correlation between interior and exterior spaces and the accompanying sculptural and painting decorations.

Vocabulary Definitions

flying buttress A supportive structure consisting of a tower buttress and a flying arch which spans the side aisles and supports the upper wall of the nave of a Gothic church.
clerestory (*clear*-story) The upper section of a wall (windowed or open) used for lighting and ventilation; also, the upper story of the nave of a church building.
rose window A circular window with stone tracery radiating from the center

8.2 Gothic Art

THE TWELFTH AND THIRTEENTH centuries saw a massive shift in the population of Europe. People moved from the countryside into towns, which grew in size to become cities. Cathedrals became the religious, cultural and social centers of the growing cities. Cathedral schools and universities replaced the monasteries as learning centers. The thirteenth century represents the summit of achievement for unified Christendom. It was a time of fresh ideas and technical knowledge. From this newly found freedom emerged Gothic art and, more particularly, Gothic architecture.

Gothic was first used as a term of ridicule by Renaissance critics because the style did not conform to the standards of Classical Greece and Rome. Today, however, Gothic art is synonymous with the new energy and dynamic style of the period.

Unity is the key word in Gothic architecture. Interiors and exteriors belong together and are similarly decorated. For the first time in history, they received equal emphasis. Structure, aesthetics, purpose and meaning are fused together to present an organic whole or a unified structure. This unity was sometimes an astonishing feat considering that the buildings often took several generations to complete, required the services of several architects, and were never completed according to their original design.

Key Notes

- Cities grow during the Gothic period and cathedral building flourishes.
- The church becomes the most important influence in art and in daily life.
- Unity is the key concept in Gothic architecture.

Vocabulary

flying buttresses
clerestory
rose window
tracery
fan vaulting
cartoon

8–17 Scenes from the life of Christ surround the west portal of Chartres.
West portal, *Cathedral of Chartres*, about 1145–1170. France.

Special Feature
Chartres Cathedral

One of the best remaining examples of Gothic construction is *Chartres Cathedral* (fig.8–15). Because the basic design is so unified, it seems that it must have been planned by a single master builder. However, the construction proceeded through four centuries and was never completely finished. For this reason, the cathedral incorporates a harmony that evolved over time rather than being planned in every detail from the beginning. For instance, the west towers, though similar, are not identical. They were built fifty years apart, the plainer one first and the more elaborate one later. Their spires can be seen for miles around.

You can see by the photograph how huge Chartres is and thereby how important it was to the community. Its shadow fell over everything. It represented the group effort of all who gave their labor, skill and money to build it.

Chartres incorporated many new ideas (fig.8–16). The use of *flying buttresses* (flying arches combined with tower buttresses) eliminated the need for heavy, solid Romanesque walls and allowed for the construction of a self-supporting skeletal structure. This, in turn, permitted huge window walls of stained glass, which today remain virtually intact. Although the windows admit far less light than one would expect, the colored light

and a characteristic feature of Gothic church architecture.
fan vault A complex vault with radiating ribs, characteristic of late English Gothic (perpendicular) architecture.
cartoon A full-scale drawing from which a painting or fresco is made. Also, a simplified humorous drawing.

Teach

Criticism: Have students compare the exterior of Chartres Cathedral (fig.8–15) to that of Saint-Sernin (fig.8–5) and Notre-Dame-la-Grande (fig.8–7).

- What is the most noticeable structural distinction between the Gothic cathedral of Chartres and the two earlier, Romanesque buildings?

- What holds up the walls at Chartres? Are the walls the same height and thickness as those in the Romanesque examples?

- Direct students to read about flying buttresses on pages 240–241 to understand why this architectural development was so important in allowing Gothic builders to create taller, thinner walls with many more windows.

Aesthetics/Criticsm: Direct students to compare the interior of the Gothic Chartres Cathedral (fig.8–16) to a Romanesque church interior, such as that of Sainte-Madeleine (fig.8–6).

- How did the architects of Chartres emphasize its soaring height and fine, internal articulation?

streaming down from the upper level, or **clerestory**, produces a magical effect.

Like the revolutionary changes in Gothic architecture, there were changes in sculpture. Gothic sculpture faced the outside world, where it clustered around and over the porches and entrance portals (fig.8–17). The exterior of Chartres boasts more than two thousand carved figures. You would think that the profusion of sculpture could lead to considerable confusion. This is prevented by the close relationship of the sculptured forms to the architectural framework. The figures look as if they are enjoying their position in a perfect system.

8–15 Name three features of Chartres that make it Gothic in style.
Cathedral of Chartres, about 1194. France.

8–16 How does this interior differ from the interior of a Romanesque church?
Interior, *Cathedral of Chartres.* France.

Contextual Information
Chartres

Chartres Cathedral was built after a fire destroyed an earlier church. Chartres is 121 feet tall and has 126 windows, most of which still have their original glass. The original wooden roof was destroyed by a fire in 1836 and was replaced with a copper roof.

Higher-Order Thinking Skills

Help students learn to assemble and integrate information that is not grouped in the text. Take them through the chapter to locate all of the images related to Chartres Cathedral—exterior, stained glass, sculptures. Have students use appropriate vocabulary to identify structural components and artistic characteristics.

• How might this feeling of ultimate oneness between God and human beings affect worshipers in the Middle Ages?

• How might you have felt about Christianity when attending services in these churches?

• What sort of architecture and decoration would you design in order to impress your followers if you had been a religious leader in the Middle Ages?

• Describe the size, scale, colors, decoration and forms of your building. Compare your proposal to that of others in class to explore your various approaches.

Ask students to extend their thinking by finding a similarity between human anatomy and Gothic architecture, with its delineated structural support. (See fig.8–16 as an example.)

• What does the architectural term *ribbed* (as in ribbed vault) remind them of?

• Can they see how Gothic architects made the "skeletal" structure of the church visible whereas human skeletons remain hidden within our bodies?

• Have students look at the arches; the number of stories; the use, location and quantity of windows; and the width and height of the ribs in the columns and arches. Which building seems to bring the grandeur and heavenly light of God's kingdom into the earthly realm?

Evaluate

Have students name the single exterior architectural innovation that helped Gothic churches to increase the sense of verticality, lightness and ethereal atmosphere. (A clue is in fig.8–a.) Could architects have achieved this result without the ability to build tall, thin walls that also reveal the church's skeletal structure?

Remind students that unity is the guiding force behind the Gothic style.

• How does this principle exist in the more than two thousand carved figures on the exterior of Chartres Cathedral?

• Can they determine a logical visual and thematic design for the figures? The thoughtful relationship among the placement, forms and narrative of the sculpture and architecture prevents the decoration from exploding into chaos. (See page 241 for details.)

Reteach

Ask why the church would want its art and architecture to reflect an overall sense of unity.

Contextual Information

Abbot Suger

Before he began the redesign of his church, Abbot Suger described the great crowd of pilgrims, in addition to the usual worshipers, as becoming jammed at the doors and totally blocking other people from entering. Women were pushed "as in a wine-press." Many screamed in terror, and some were trampled. Monks, who served as guides, on occasion had to climb out windows, relics in tow, to escape the crowds. Consequently, one of Suger's first priorities became the enlargement of the entrances and side aisles.

Gothic Architecture

The Gothic style of architecture began at the royal abbey of Saint-Denis, outside Paris, in 1140, when Abbot Suger started to enlarge and redesign his small church to accommodate the many pilgrims who were visiting the chapel. (Today, little remains of its original Gothic appearance.)

Abbot Suger wished to construct a church that was as beautiful and richly decorated as possible because anything less would be unsuitable for God's house. His main concern was light because it symbolized the presence of God. He greatly enlarged the apse of his church, providing an ambulatory for the pilgrims. He designed huge windows that let in great quantities of light through stained glass. He was instrumental in developing this architecture of supports rather than walls. Columns and piers supported the vault. As we have seen at Chartres, windows replaced walls. Heavy Roman-type vaults and massive post-and-lintel construction were suddenly obsolete.

There are several features that characterize Gothic construction. There is an overall feeling of verticality as master builders tried to make the interiors as high as possible, as if reaching toward heaven. Ribbed cross vaults of several types added stability and strength and allowed for huge glass windows at the clerestory level, over the side aisles. Pointed arches provided greater height and more open area. The height-to-width ratio in round arches is about 2 to 1, but in pointed arches can be 3 to 1. The pointed arches also changed the thrust of the vault to a more vertical direction. With the addition of flying buttresses (fig.8–a), the thrust of the vault was transferred, not to the walls, but to the massive towers outside the structure, thereby eliminating the need for solid, thick

walls. The arches of the flying buttresses reached over the side aisles and allowed light to enter unhindered through the clerestory windows. A Gothic church has at least three (sometimes five) portals in the facade. A huge round window (or **rose window**) often was placed over the main portal or at the ends of the transept.

From Saint-Denis, the Gothic architectural style moved to Chartres, Paris and the rest of northern France. It spread to England, Germany and all of northern Europe. Finally it filtered into Italy, where it inspired a tremendous building boom.

On a small island in the heart of Paris is perhaps one of the best

8–18 The multitude of windows flood the nave with colored light to create an otherworldly affect in the nave.
Nave, *Notre Dame*, about 1163–1250. Paris, France.

8–19 Locate the flying buttresses which help to hold up the walls and make possible so many windows.
Exterior, *Notre Dame*. Paris, France.

Performing Arts Connection

Church-Sponsored Music

From the twelfth to the thirteenth centuries, French composers at Notre Dame Cathedral dominated the music world. They wrote the first motets, choral liturgical works in Latin or French that borrowed from secular music of the time.

known of all Gothic cathedrals, *Notre Dame.* Construction began in 1163 and continued for about a hundred years, but was never completed. The two square towers at the front were originally to be the bases for impressive spires. The interior view (fig.8–18) from the transept shows the use of the pointed arch and ribbed vaults. The clerestory windows are huge and reach up to the roof, allowing light to flood the vault itself. Over both double side aisles is a gallery through which monks, nuns and priests walked while in prayer. The heavy, rounded columns seem Romanesque, but are well integrated into the overall construction. The thin, engaged columns extending to the vault add a feeling of lightness and help develop a visual rhythm on the side walls.

Remarkably, the openings in the galleries, the huge windows and the lower openings between the columns leave little bearing wall to hold up the great weight of the massive stone vault. By looking at the exterior view (fig.8–19), one can see how this is possible. Reaching over the side aisles and over the ambulatory of the choir and apse, flying buttresses lean against the walls at a point between the windows where the vault starts on the inside. The thrust of the vault is absorbed by the arches and buttresses. The result is functional as well as aesthetic. The exterior view also shows the huge rose window at the end of the transept and the immense choir, used for all the clergy and the pageantry of the Paris cathedral. The delicate tower over the crossing was added at a later date.

Reims Cathedral has an interior arrangement similar to Notre Dame in Paris. An immense choir takes up about half the length of the building. Because the kings of France were often crowned here, an

8–20 The rose window has replaced the usual carved tympanum. Stone was carved to hold the glass in place.
West facade, *Cathedral of Reims,* about 1225–1299. France.

extremely large space was needed for the pageantry.

The west facade of the *Reims Cathedral* (fig.8–20) is fascinating. Solidity and heaviness have been replaced by openings and lightness. You can actually see through the facade (on the second level over the outside portals) to the flying buttresses of the nave. The towers are not solid at all but are carved stone openings of delicate *tracery.* Over each portal, the usual carved tympanum is replaced by a window, also with stone tracery. Only at the third level is the facade solid and here it is full of carved niches holding full-figure, sculpted portraits of French kings. The rest of the facade is filled with sculpture: in the portals, over the portals, in other niches and on

platforms. Each pinnacle is carved with knobs and protrusions to create a delicate and airy feeling. The towers were designed to hold huge spires, which were never built. The human figure at the bottom creates a sense of scale for the size of the cathedral.

Gothic architectural style reached its climax in *Amiens Cathedral* (fig.8–21). With a nave over 137 feet high, the soaring effect of its interior is dramatically overpowering. The ribbed columns, rising uninterrupted from floor to vault, seem much too slender and graceful to hold up the heavy stone vault. The clerestory windows are immense. They are separated only by the thin columns. The vault seems to float without support above the glass. These windows, the tracery openings of the middle level gallery and the large arched spaces below almost eliminate the feeling of any walls at all. This sense of openness was the ultimate goal of Abbot Suger when he started to work on his church in Saint-Denis.

The interior view is from the choir toward the entrance with the rose window (40 feet in diameter) above the main portal. By looking at the ribs in the vault, one can see where the transept crosses the nave. A view directly up at the cross vaults (fig.8–22) reveals the incredible amount of glass and the small visible columns that support the stone vault.

In Germany, the cathedral erected at Cologne (fig.8–23) is the largest in the country. Built on the site of an old Roman town on the Rhine River, the cathedral followed the plan of French cathedrals. The French plan was not a popular design in Germany. Later builders designed churches with high side aisles and wide interior spaces called *hallenkirche* or hall churches.

The ring of flying buttresses surrounding the choir appears to be a forest of stone. Notice the height of the towers and the mass of the structure when compared with the large buildings around the cathedral.

8–21 Locate the rose window, transept crossing, columns and windows. Interior of nave, *Cathedral of Amiens,* begun about 1220. France.

8–22 The effect of lightness and effortlessness in this structure belies its heavy stone building material. Interior, *Cathedral of Amiens.* France.

Across the channel in England, the Gothic style spread rapidly. The countryside was dotted with structures that combined French ideas and Norman influences. Compared with French cathedrals, the *Salisbury Cathedral* is low and wide (fig.8–24) because the builders did not desire a soaring effect. Sculptures fill the horizontal bands of the screen-like facade. Only a few flying buttresses can be seen. The tower over the crossing is Salisbury's crowning achievement. It reaches over 400 feet into the English sky. However, it is solid and not highly sculptured such as those in France.

A beautiful cloister (fig.8–25) is attached to the Salisbury Cathedral. The garden is visible to strollers through the carved tracery arches of the covered walkway.

1300 Anasazi abandon Canyon de Chelly National Monument, modern New Mexico	**1325** Ibn Battuta journeys from North Africa to Indonesia and China

World Cultural Timeline

1325 Aztecs found Tenochtitlán	**1350** Chocolate drinking popular with Aztecs

Multicultural Connection

The Anasazi

The Anasazi, or "Ancient Ones," lived in the valleys and canyons of the American Southwest between 600 and 1200 AD. The Anasazi were farmers and gatherers whose main food supply was corn. They built square, flat-roofed homes (called "pueblos") of sun-baked earthen bricks or stone that dotted the Chaco Canyon in northwestern New Mexico. They often built clusters of dwellings right into the walls of the canyon.

Relying on human labor to quarry sandstone from the canyon walls and to move it to their building sites, the

Anasazi constructed cube-shaped homes and endlessly combined them into new forms. These complexes varied in height from one to five stories and included ceremonial rooms called *kivas*. The kivas were round and were often built half underground. The entire complex was usually grouped around a plaza or arranged to face an open space where religious ceremonies were held.

Pueblo Bonito, meaning "beautiful village," was built around 1000 AD and is the largest pueblo in Chaco Canyon, containing more than 800 rooms and kivas. Around 1200 AD, when a prolonged drought threatened their food supply, the Anasazi abandoned their pueblos and vanished mysteriously.

Massed columns and ribbed cross vaults are characteristic features of the early Gothic style in England. In later English Gothic architecture, the ribbing becomes extremely decorative, as in the vault of the Chapter House of the Cathedral at Wells (fig.8–26). Here small clustered columns seem to be transformed into ribs for the vault and create a feature called *fan vaulting*. So elaborate was the rib work done at a later time that the final style of Gothic art in England is called *Flamboyant Gothic*.

8–24 This church is surrounded by an open, grassy area.
Exterior, *Salisbury Cathedral*, begun in 1220. England.

8–25 A cloister is a covered walkway which allowed people to walk around the garden when the weather was bad.
Cloister, *Salisbury Cathedral*. England.

8–26 This elaborate vaulting system is called fan vaulting because it has the appearance of giant open fans.
Fan vaulting. Chapter House, *Wells Cathedral*, early 14th century. England.

8–23 The modern city of Cologne is dominated by its cathedral.
Cathedral of Cologne, begun 1248. Germany.

- How did the Anasazi adapt their architecture to the geographical and environmental conditions?

- What evidence do we have that the Anasazi were a well-organized, cooperative society?

- How did the location of these settlements contribute to their permanency?

(See Chapter 4, page 138 for more information and images relating to the Anasazi.)

Chocolate

Cacao, or chocolate, is said to have originated in the Amazon or the Orinoco basin at least 4000 years ago. Cacao ranked among the items prized by the Mayas. From cacao came chocolate, a drink of the upper classes, which was harvested from plantations controlled by nobles. The Aztec used this once bitter, watery drink, called *xocoatl*, as a ritual beverage to seal Mixtec marriages. Considered the "food of the gods," this liquid was so valued that it was often served in golden goblets that were thrown away after one use. Ceramic vessels unearthed from royal tombs bear the glyph for "chocolate" and have provided us with a clue to the product's importance. In fact, cacao beans were also used as Aztec currency.

- Have students research the meaning of *glyph* and find examples of Aztec glyphs. Then have them create designs based on the Aztec glyphs.

Contextual Information

Italian churches

Churches in Italy did not have great numbers of windows because the Italian sunlight is strong and summers are hot. Fewer windows meant that wall space could be reserved for frescoes.

The Doge's Palace

The Doge's Palace was the seat of government for the republic of Venice, an oligarchy with an elected duke (doge). Venice is the only state in Western Europe that survived from ancient to modern times without conquest. Napoleon put an end to the republic in 1792.

8–27 Compare this Italian Gothic cathedral to the Cathedral of Reims. What similarities and differences do you see?
Cathedral of Siena, begun about 1284. Italy.

8–28 The lacy screen of the triforium on the second level adds lightness to the design.
Palazzo Ducale, 1340–1424. Venice, Italy.

Performing Arts Connection

Medieval Christian Music, Dance and Drama

Medieval cathedrals, with their resounding acoustics and abundant light, were inspiring locales for church performances. These liturgical dramas combined dialogue, action and song to tell stories from the Bible about the Resurrection, the Nativity, and the miracles of the saints and prophets.

From the fourteenth to the sixteenth centuries, liturgical dramas came to be sponsored by municipalities rather than the church. These mystery plays (*mystery* meaning "religious rite or ceremony") and pastorales (dramatic performances or operas based on rural themes) were community sponsored and incorporated the use of local guild members. The dramas were performed on large outdoor stages in the town square. Music accompanied the secular comic interludes. A great deal of ingenuity and labor went into producing special effects, including ascensions into heaven and falling into the flaming jaws of hell.

In Italy, *Siena Cathedral* is a zebra-striped marble church (fig.8–27). Its elaborate facade is covered with statuary and mosaics. A dome and lantern stand over the crossing. The campanile pierces the sky. The striping continues on the interior of the church. Except for the time in history and the builders' desire to construct beautiful sanctuaries for the glory of God, most Italian Gothic churches have little in common with the French Gothic style to the north.

Although the construction of cathedrals dominated the building activity of the Gothic period, municipal buildings also were erected in major cities all over Europe. Some have the appearance of churches while others have used the features of Gothic construction in different ways. Like the cathedrals, all the buildings shown here are still in use after six hundred years or more, attesting to the skill of the architects, engineers and masons.

In Venice, the *Palazzo Ducale* (Doge's Palace) is a lacy network of marble (fig.8–28). A large arcade is on the first level and an open gallery, or triforium, is on the second level. This is similar to the interior wall plan of a French Gothic cathedral. The windows on the top story are small, but the colored pattern in marble keeps this level from seeming too heavy. The lower columns seem to be sunk in the ground, but they were not always so. The three steps on which they rest have now sunk with the subsiding Venetian ground level. The building has a very unified feeling. Light and color are reflected from its surface. These two elements would continue to fascinate Venetian artists for centuries.

In northern Europe, municipal buildings compete with cathedrals for ornateness and beauty. The town hall of Louvain, Belgium (fig.8–29), is built in the flamboyant Gothic style of the fifteenth century. It has an elaborate surface that sparkles with reflected light. There is hardly a square foot of uncarved or undecorated surface. The incredible amount of stone tracery produces a lace-like feeling in many places.

The belfry in Bruges, Belgium (fig.8–30), is an enormous brick and stone tower begun in 1376. It was completed in 1482 when the octagonal top portion was added. It dominates the small city which contains many other Gothic buildings, and its carillon of 47 bells can be heard for miles around.

8–29 In northern Europe, municipal buildings became as ornate as cathedrals.
Town Hall. 15th century. Louvain, Belgium.

8–30 The bells in this huge tower weigh a total of 27 tons.
Belfry of the City Hall. 1376–1482. Bruges, Belgium.

Higher-Order Thinking Skills

Ask students to select three or four architectural examples to trace the development of the Christian church from early Christian times. What characteristics identify each as a new development?

Interdisciplinary Connection

Political Science: Have students research the types of governments that were responsible for running Louvain and Bruges in the fourteenth and fifteenth century when these civic buildings were constructed.

Contextual Information

Guilds and Master Artists

During the medieval period, guilds, which represented various crafts and merchants, were formed. The guilds were thought to be under the protection of saints.

Secrets of the various trades were kept within the guilds, and guild members, not knowing how to read and write, passed on their secret methods through apprenticeship programs. Guilds established prices and parceled out contracts for work.

In a typical medieval guild, the master would simply conceive the design for a work. His workshop would then set about executing the sculpture or painting. Sometimes the master did not set his hand to the work at all. In other cases, he would work on the most important aspects of the piece (for example, the faces of the key figures). Explain to students that the role of the medieval artist, therefore, was quite different from that of artists today.

Numerous artists worked on the altarpiece at Toledo (fig.8–34). Because it was an extraordinarily large commission, one master designed it and many worked on its execution. Often, in the interest of time, two or three masters and their shops would collaborate on large commissions.

8–31 These figures seem very much a part of the architecture.
Four Ancestors of Christ. Jamb statues, about 1150. Stone. Cathedral of Chartres, France.

8–32 These three figures have individual expressions on their faces and gesture freely.
St. Stephen, Empress Kunigunde and Emperor Henry II. Jamb statues, about 1235–1240. Sandstone. Bamburg Cathedral, Germany.

Sculpture

The revolutionary changes in Gothic architecture were duplicated in the evolution of sculpture. The change was slow but constant. Interest in the Classic sculptural tradition was revitalized. The symbolism of Romanesque sculpture gave way to a new awareness of the natural world. Artists began to work again with increasingly natural human, animal and plant forms.

The earliest existing examples of Gothic sculpture are on the west facade of Chartres, done about 1150. The three portals are filled with sculpture on the tympanums, in the archivolts and on the door jambs. The *Four Ancestors of Christ* (fig.8–31) are from the central door jamb. The figures are extremely elongated. The drapery is still stylized and flat, often just chiseled lines. The statues appear to be part

of the columns. Like Romanesque sculpture, the statues lack a sense of movement. In spite of the early date, there is some individualization of the faces. The feet seem to be floating over the sloping platforms instead of resting on them.

The figures on the door jamb of the Bamberg Cathedral (fig.8–32) illustrate the change that had occurred by the late Gothic period. Carved in sandstone about 1235, the figures are almost casual in their stance. They seem to be free of the columns and are sculpted in the round. Their faces are individual, each having a different expression. The drapery is loose and the folds are fully carved. Real bodies seem to exist beneath the garments. The figures are naturally proportioned and almost seem capable of movement. Their feet rest naturally on flat pedestals.

Not all sculpture in churches was religious in subject matter. Contemporary people and events often shared space with saints. The man with a toothache (fig.8–33) is from the capital of a column in the transept of the cathedral in Wells, England.

The highest Gothic expression in Spain occurred in magnificent altarpieces. The altarpieces were really

1350
Maori migrate from the Marquesas to New Zealand

1400
Incas develop an accounting system

1400–1591
Songhai Kingdom, Africa

World Cultural Timeline

1400
Blue and white Ming ware popular in China

Multicultural Connection

The Inca Empire

In 1438, the Inca (ruler) Pachacuti conquered and founded the Inca Empire, which stretched over 2500 miles along the western coast of South America. The Inca called the empire Tahuantinsuyo, meaning "the four quarters." The king claimed to be a descendant of Inti, the sun god, and possessed absolute authority. The rulers called themselves "children of the sun."

In order to control this vast empire of twelve million people, the Inca built 10,000 miles of stone highway, similar to one the Romans had built. Four main roads led from Cuzco, their splendid capital high in the Andes, to the four regions of the empire. The Inca rulers, unlike the Aztec, were able to maintain control over their vast empire by collecting tribute from those they conquered and by treating their subjects well.

8–34 The elaborate carvings tell the story of the life of Christ.
High altar, *Cathedral of Toledo*, about 1498–1504. Wood, paint and gold. Toledo, Spain.

carved screens that separated the altars from the windows behind them. The incredible detail in the *Toledo Cathedral* altarpiece (fig.8–34) was designed by Peti Juan, but carved in wood by artists from Holland, France, Germany and Spain. The figures illustrate fifteen events in the life of Christ and are painted in brilliant color. There is a multitude of other painted figures. The entire altar is woven together with incredibly detailed carvings of Gothic spires, needles, platforms and canopies that are covered with gold. It is an elaborate and decorative way of presenting the New Testament happenings to Toledo's churchgoers.

Virgin and Child (fig.8–35) is from the private chapel of a castle near Rouen, France. The sculpture is carved from limestone and was originally painted. The figures are carved completely in the round so that they can be viewed from all sides. They stand on their own as a work of art, not as part of a cathedral, chapel or column. The pose and the drapery are natural. There is a delightful interplay between the child and mother, something that is quite human.

While many artists and craftspeople of the Middle Ages worked anonymously, several became well known because of their extremely fine work. Among them are Tilman Riemenschneider of Germany (1460–1531) and Claus Sluter of Holland (active 1380–1406). Riemenschneider was the last of the great altarpiece carvers of Germany. He specialized in elaborate and detailed wood sculpture. *Group of Three Saints* (fig.8–36) is a carving of Sts. Christopher, Eustace and Erasmus. The three saints are part of a larger group of fourteen saints carved for a church altar in Würzburg, Germany. People turned to these saints for help in times of pestilence, tragedy, storm, sickness and travel. Such saints were easily identified by medieval people because the symbolism was well known. St. Christopher carries Christ on his shoulders. (Christ's head and hand, unfortunately, are missing.) St. Eustace was recognized by his knightly attire. St. Erasmus was believed to have been martyred by disembowelment, and so carries a spindle around which his entrails are wrapped.

8–33 Contemporary people and common-place events often were portrayed on column capitals.
Toothache. Capital from south transept, Wells Cathedral, about 1250. Stone. Wells, England.

Higher-Order Thinking Skills

Before students read the text, have them compare the jamb statues of Chartres (fig.8–31) and Bamburg (fig.8–32). Then have them compare their impressions with the information in the text. Students also can compare these Gothic jamb figures to the caryatids of the Athenian Erechtheum (fig.6–24). Students should explore the idea of how these figures function on their respective buildings.

Unlike the Maya and the Aztec, the Inca lacked a written language and consequently found that communication between rulers and subjects was difficult. They did, however, use the *quipu* to record messages and to tally births, crops, herds and deaths. The quipu was a series of color-coded knotted strings that could be deciphered by highly trained specialists.

• How did the environment of the Inca make the building of roads difficult?

• Have students compare the status of the Inca rulers with that of the Egyptian pharaohs.

(For more information about the Inca, see Chapter 4, page 135.)

Contextual Information

The Black Death

One result of the Black Death was the raising of wages for those who survived. However, there were few goods to buy. Even priests' wages went up because so few of the clergy had survived the plague. The English king tried unsuccessfully to put a cap on wages.

Tilman Riemenschneider

Tilman Riemenschneider used linden wood, which has a tremendous natural beauty, for a number of his sculptures. Unlike other sculptors, Riemenschneider preferred to leave the linden wood unpainted. The sculptures were finished with a brown glaze rather than polychromed.

Riemenschneider had a very large workshop that produced numerous sculptures in Würzburg from 1485 to the 1520s.

Identifying Saints

As the repertoire of Christian saints became larger and larger, it became more and more important to distinguish among them. Attributes provided a means for accomplishing this goal. Each saint carries an object, wears particular clothes or has particular facial or body features. For example, St. Christopher carries the Christ child on his shoulder; St. Peter is dark-haired, bearded and carries a key; Mary Magdalene is usually dressed in red, has long flowing red or blonde hair and often carries an ointment jar. (Students might enjoy reading the life of a saint to discover why a certain attribute identifies a particular saint.)

8–35 The Virgin and Child was an extremely popular subject during the Middle Ages. As in the case of this group, the artist often tried to convey the tender feeling between a mother and child.
Virgin and Child, about 1475. Limestone with traces of polychrome, 3' (90 cm) high. From castle of Gisors, near Rouen. The Nelson-Atkins Museum of Art, Kansas City.

8–36 Saints usually were depicted carrying or wearing certain objects so that they could be easily identified. These objects are known as the saints' attributes.
Hans Tilman Riemenschneider, *Group of Three Saints (St. Christopher, St. Eustace and St. Erasmus),* 15th century. Lindenwood, 21" (53 cm) high. The Metropolitan Museum of Art, New York, The Cloisters Collection, 1961.

8–37 How has the sculptor used the element of texture to enhance this figure?
Claus Sluter, *Moses with Two Prophets,* 1395–1404. Marble figures about 6 1/2' (2 m) high. From the *Well of Moses.* Carthusian Monastery of Champmol, Dijon, France.

The compact group is carved in linden wood and is unpainted. The complex interweaving of line and form in the folds of cloth and the placement of the figures are characteristic of the artist's work. It creates a rather restless feeling that is repeated in the expressive, somber faces and the long hands and fingers. Although done about 1494 while the Renaissance was exploding in Italy, it is Gothic in form and content. Northern Europe followed the Gothic style far longer than Italy.

Claus Sluter was born in Holland. His greatest work, however, was done in France, particularly at Dijon for the Duke of Burgundy. Sluter brought new zest and ultimate realism into Gothic sculpture. His work is so strong and his style so individualistic that it could be placed in

the Renaissance period. *Moses with Two Prophets* (fig.8–37) is a masterful statement in marble. The facial expression is intense and powerful—more than merely natural (fig. 8–b). Moses has returned from Mt. Sinai with the tablets of the law in his right hand. The horns on his head had become a traditional symbol for the prophet as he returned from facing God. (This symbol came from an incorrect translation of the Old Testament story.) His full, parted beard and the lush, flowing robes create a dynamic rhythm and visual movement that leads up to the expressive face. The sculpture was part of a large carved monument, much of which has been lost. Because only the fountain part remains, it is known as the *Well of Moses.*

Multicultural Connection

Religious Imagery

Many religions and cultures portray their deities and other holy figures in their art. Have students review the images in Chapters 1–4 (particularly 3 and 4) for examples of religious art from other cultures.

• Do many of the cultures use the human form for their deities?

• What other forms does religious art take?

Black Death

Sometime during 1346, word reached Europe that a terrible plague was rife in the East. Rumors abounded and it was said that Tartary, Mesopotamia, Syria and Armenia were covered with dead bodies. By 1347 the plague, called the Black Death because blotches of blood turned black under the skin, spread to Europe.

According to an account by an Italian writer of the period, Gabriel de Mussis, the plague began in 1346 in the Tartar lands of Asia Minor. One report indicates that 80,000 people died in the Crimea alone.

One of the principal ways the plague spread was along the major trade routes from Eastern ports to the Mediterranean. Ships from plague-stricken cities in the East would dock in European ports. Sometimes these ships were quarantined and their crews forbidden to disembark. This proved to be a futile measure because, as soon as the ship's ropes were tied to a dock, infected rats carrying fleas scurried ashore. Within days the fleas would transmit the disease to the population of the city and countryside.

The Black Death, a combination of bubonic, pneumonic and septicemic plague strains, spread horror and death wherever it went. Between 1347 to 1351, it raged over the Western world, killing from 25 to 50 percent of Europe's population.

In the Italian city of Florence, more than half the population died between April and October 1348. The famous Florentine writer, Giovanni Boccaccio, places the recitation of his tales of the *Decameron* against the backdrop of the plague. He chronicles the effect of the disease on his native city and describes the physical appearance of the plague's victims for us. "...At the onset of the disease both men and women were afflicted by a sort of swelling in the groin and under the armpits which sometimes attained the size of a common apple or egg...Afterwards, the manifestation of the disease changed into black or livid spots on the arms, thighs and the whole person." These latter symptoms were an indication of certain death.

No country was spared. The plague spread from Italy to France, then to England and Germany, and then along the northward sea route to Denmark, Norway and Sweden.

Fear of the disease took many forms. Some people fled while others threw themselves into frenzies of religious excess. The Flagellants whipped themselves until they drew blood, hoping in this way to stem the pestilence. Jews were accused of spreading the Black Death by poisoning wells, and many were massacred in the Rhineland and Switzerland. Charges of sorcery and witchcraft were rife. But none of this had any effect on the disease. Rich or poor, religious or heathen, peasant or aristocrat, child or grandmother, the Black Death spared no one.

For at least a century after 1350, there were cyclical recurrences of the plague and the European population continued to decline. The population would only stabilize again in the fifteenth century.

This is a contemporary depiction of the effect of the plague that ravaged Italy in the forteenth century.
Giovanni Serambi, *The Plague*, 14th century. State Archives, Lucca.

Higher-Order Thinking Skills

Have students compare and contrast *Moses with Two Prophets* (fig.8–37) to the early Christian ivory of *The Archangel Michael* (fig.7–1). Suggest that they pay special attention to issues of naturalism and symbolism and the figures' relationship to their architectural space.

Contextual Information

Manuscript Illumination

Illuminated manuscripts painted and signed by women artists have been dated to the eighth century. Typically, only nuns had the money to buy parchment and inks, and the time, opportunity and encouragement to do the tedious work. In the tenth century, Prior Petrus said that the "terrible ordeal" of writing and illustrating manuscripts adversely affected one's eyesight and caused backaches due to the position of the illuminator in dimly lit halls.

By the thirteenth century, women were working in professional bookmaking shops known as scriptoria, which were dedicated to illuminated manuscripts. By the fourteenth century, women could join the Confraternity of St. Luke, a painting guild.

Illumination work in nunneries continued for years after the printing press was invented. Women worked as teachers of bookmaking and signed their names as miniaturists and illuminators.

Stained Glass

The smaller stained glass windows at Chartres were donated by the various guilds in the town. These guilds included the carpenters, wheelwrights, wine merchants, clothiers, bakers and blacksmiths.

More than three quarters of the structure of Sainte-Chapelle is glass. The windows in the chapel are 49 feet high and 15 feet wide.

8–38 Chartres is the only major Gothic cathedral that retains much of its original stained glass.
Rose window and lancets, 13th century. Stained glass, 42'7" (13 m) diameter. Cathedral of Chartres, France.

8–39 Jean-Clement was the donor of this window. St. Denis is giving his banner to him.
St. Denis and Jean-Clement, 12th century. Stained glass. Cathedral of Chartres, France.

Stained Glass

Abbot Suger would have been pleased to think of twelfth- and thirteenth-century cathedrals as frameworks to hold stained glass. The techniques of producing glass sheets with brilliant color began during the Romanesque period, but they reached their peak in the magnificent windows of Gothic structures. The colors glow when light passes through the glass. The glass could be cut to fit the shapes the artist required. A full-scale line drawing (called a **cartoon**) was first put on a large board. Then sheets of glass were placed over it and cut according to the lines. These pieces were then put together like a giant jigsaw puzzle, and later soldered in place with I-shaped lead strips. Carved stone tracery or iron bars were used as supports to hold the entire window flat so that it could be set upright in place. Before assembly, paint was applied in certain places to create shading, lines and details. The individual pieces were fired in a kiln to harden the pigment.

Reds and blues dominated Gothic color schemes, although many other colors also were used. These deep hues darkened the interiors of churches, causing the windows to glow like huge jewels. Much original glass has been destroyed, but the remains indicate that the windows were brilliantly colored visual teaching aids for the church.

A huge rose window (nearly 43 feet in diameter) and lancet windows are found on the end wall of the south transept of Chartres Cathedral (fig.8–38). One of four rose windows in the church, this one features Christ at the center. The lancets symbolize the evangelists, or writers, of the New Testament. The dark spaces between the medallions that make up the rose window are carved stone that appear as silhouettes from the inside.

The single large window from Chartres (fig.8–39) is from the upper level. It shows St. Denis presenting his red banner to the knight who donated the window to the church. This interesting custom of showing the donors in the work they contributed was used in forty windows at Chartres. Donors appear with saints, Christ or the Virgin Mary. This custom also occurred in many paintings of the period and continued into the Renaissance. In this window, some of the lines and shading that were painted onto the glass can be seen. However, it is often hard to distinguish the painted lines from the lead lines.

Inquiry

Have students study stained glass in local places of worship. Discuss colors, types of glass, subject matter, date and artist, if known. Students also might want to visit the studio of a stained glass artist and discuss the technique. Has the technique changed very much since medieval times?

The incredibly complex windows in *Sainte-Chapelle* in Paris (fig.8–40) are the ultimate in Gothic architectural decoration. Built by Louis IX (later known as St. Louis) in 1243, the small chapel has no side aisles and no flying buttresses—but the windows are magnificent. They are huge for the size of the small chapel. Single panels of glass extend from several feet above the ground all the way to the vault. Nowhere else is the feeling so strong that glass is holding up the vault. The columns between the windows seem incredibly thin and fragile. The pieces of glass are cut very small and illustrate Bible stories in the medallions. Those at the top are so small that viewers have difficulty reading the detailed pictures. In sunlight, all details are blurred by the brightness and the entire chapel seems to glow with brilliant color.

Late Gothic Painting

Because the huge stained glass pictures successfully illustrated the Bible in northern European cathedrals, architectural painting was kept to a minimum. Some altarpieces were painted, but most French religious painting was restricted to manuscript illumination. In *The Annunciation* page (fig.8–41) from the French *Book of Hours* (1440), the angel Gabriel is telling the Virgin Mary that she will be the mother of Christ. In the single illustration is a tiny landscape outside and a cathedral-like setting inside. God the Father (at the top) presides over all the events. The words are Mary's response to the angel. Surrounding the scene is an extremely complex and interwoven decoration of angels playing instruments. The fantastic border includes flowers, leaves, scrolls, birds and fanciful designs.

The page from a manuscript (fig.8–42) was painted in tempera and gold leaf by Goffredo da Viterbo in Italy. Many late Gothic illustrators were not monks or nuns but talented lay people working in studios such as Goffredo in Viterbo. They also illustrated nonreligious and civic books.

8–41 Manuscript painting was the dominant form of painting in Gothic France.
The Annunciation page from French *Book of Hours*, 1440. Tempera and gold on parchment. Huntington Art Gallery, Pasadena.

8–42 Many late Gothic illustrators were lay people in an occupation traditionally done by members of religious orders.
Goffredo da Viterbo, *detail from a manuscript*, 1331. Bibliothèque Nationale, Paris.

8–40 Describe how you think it must feel standing in the center of Sainte-Chapelle.
Interior, *Sainte-Chapelle*, 1243–1248. Paris, France.

Contextual Information

Giotto

Giotto was considered the greatest painter of his day. There is a legend that states that the pope, planning to decorate St. Peter's and having heard of Giotto's great reputation, wanted to see evidence of Giotto's talent. He sent a messenger to the artist to request proof of his ability. Entering Giotto's shop, the messenger explained the pope's request and asked the artist for a small drawing to bring back to Rome. Giotto took paper and pencil and—without a compass and without moving his arm away from his side—drew a perfect circle. The messenger was perplexed but nonetheless delivered the drawing to the pope. He told the pope how the artist had executed the drawing without a compass and without moving his arm. From this the pope recognized Giotto's astonishing talent.

An exciting departure in Italian painting took place in the thirteenth century because of a change in the religious ceremony of the church. Until then the mass had been celebrated with the priest behind the altar, facing the people (as it is done again now). Then the priest's position was changed so that he faced the altar from the front. This freed the space behind and above the altar for large paintings on wood panels. Like the manuscript illuminations, these works were painted with egg tempera.

Giotto
(about 1267–1337)

According to legend, when Giotto was a boy of ten, he drew pictures of his father's sheep that he was tending. He was seen by Cimabue, one of the most respected painters in Florence from 1272 to 1302. Cimabue went to Giotto's father to ask permission to make the boy one of his apprentices. Florence, soon to become a leading center of the Renaissance, was already vigorous, dynamic and experimental. Here, Giotto became recognized in his own day as one of the great men of Florence. He revolutionized painting by reviving the art of working from nature. Giotto's paintings may not seem revolutionary today, but since Roman times, few artists had been interested in painting from nature because an emphasis had been placed on the symbolic.

Giotto's masterpiece is a series of frescoes that decorate the walls of a small chapel. Working between 1305 and 1306 in the Arena Chapel in Padua, not far from Venice, Giotto illustrated the lives of Christ and the Virgin. He used the fresco technique to fill the walls of the chapel with three powerful bands of paint. The *Lamentation* (fig.8–43) is one painting in the series. The scene appears to be played out by a group of real people. The figures are in active, natural poses: leaning, holding, sitting and bending. They are monumental and solid. The large folds in their robes suggest weight and mass. Notice how the shading creates a sense of roundness and natural light coming from above. Finally, a hint of natural landscape and sky (not a gold background) enhances the reality of the event.

The center of interest in the painting is Christ, who has been taken down from the cross and is being held by several figures. His mother Mary grieves as she searches his lifeless face. Sorrow is expressed on every face.

8–43 Note how Giotto has used the large figures seated at the front edge of the scene to draw the viewer right into the picture. Giotto, *Lamentation*, 1305–1306. Fresco. Arena Chapel, Padua.

8–44 What details has Duccio used to make the scene seem more human and believable? Duccio, *Christ Raising Lazarus from the Dead*, 1309–1311. Tempera on panel, 17" x 18" (43 x 46 cm). Kimbell Art Museum, Fort Worth.

Materials and Techniques

Gold leaf was applied to paintings for use as background, for haloes and for highlighting drapery. In most cases, it was applied only to those areas that were meant to be gold in color. Sienese painters, such as Duccio and Simone Martini, first applied gold to the entire surface of a painting. They then painted over the gold in the areas meant to have color. The result is a shimmering and luminous quality caused by light hitting the panel, going through the color and then bouncing back some of the light from the gold underneath.

The composition of *Lamentation* is asymmetrically balanced. A huge rock form leads the viewer's eyes diagonally across the painting directly to Christ's face. There are many other shapes and lines that also lead there. The bare tree in the upper right, separated from the figures, helps create a feeling of desolation. It also recalls a legend known by all at the time: the Tree of Knowledge in Eden withered when Adam and Eve sinned, and would come back to life when Christ fulfilled his work of redeeming humanity.

Giotto's students continued his techniques, but with less power and waning conviction. Giotto's spirit and ideas on painting would normally place him in the Renaissance, but it was almost a century before that searching and dynamic era would begin.

Duccio

(active 1278–1319)

The town of Siena was a short distance from Florence. Here, the Byzantine tradition remained a strong influence into the fourteenth century, although some drastic changes were made. Duccio was asked to paint a large altarpiece for the cathedral of Siena. He worked on it for three years. When it was finished, a holiday was declared. The artist and his masterpiece were paraded through the city, from his studio to the cathedral, accompanied by the ringing of church bells and the blare of trumpets. The altarpiece, called the *Maesta* (*Madonna in Majesty*), was freestanding, about 13 feet wide, and painted on both sides. The front contained Mary and the Christ Child as large central figures, surrounded by dozens of apostles, prophets and saints. Each figure is individualized to a great degree. Such a work had never been

8–45 Paintings are often re-framed hundreds of years after they were created. This frame is from the nineteenth century.
Simone Martini, *Annunciation*, 1333. Tempera and gold on panel, 10' 1" x 8' 8 3/4" (270 x 300 cm). Uffizi Gallery, Florence.

seen before. The back side was covered with panels that illustrated the life of Christ. Painted in tempera, they were much more detailed than Giotto's large frescoes at Padua.

In the panel called *Christ Raising Lazarus from the Dead* (fig.8–44), a crowd of people surround Christ. Faces are individualized and the overlapping bodies suggest spatial depth. Although there seems to be a single light source to create the forms of faces and figures, there are no shadows cast on the ground. They are not as massive as Giotto's and yet they seem to have weight. Small brushes were used in the tempera technique, allowing Duccio to create great detail in such small works. He acquired this technique while painting miniatures in his earlier years. Many of his paintings contain part of the Sienese landscape and the city itself—a delightful mixing of time and place.

Simone Martini

(about 1284–1344)

Duccio's pupil, Simone Martini, made a further break with Byzantine tradition. While working in Naples for the French king, he picked up some ideas, techniques and styles from the French Gothic painters. *Annunciation* (fig.8–45) is a panel painting over ten feet wide. The angel Gabriel is dressed in a magnificent gold brocade robe. The Virgin's blue mantle has a deep gold border. This concern for fabric detail and beautifully drawn line is a direct influence of Simone's contact with French artists of the time. Byzantine art portrayed spiritual beauty rather than such material magnificence. The angel's message, "Hail thou that art highly favored, the Lord is with thee," appears on the burnished gold background. Mary recoils from the unexpected message in a coy and graceful way.

Higher-Order Thinking Skills

Have students compare Giotto's *Lamentation* (fig.8–43) to the Byzantine *Enthroned Madonna and Child* (fig.7–19). Have them note especially the differences in anatomy and the portrayal of drapery. Remind students to consider that both are religious images. What is the difference in their emotional reaction to each?

Students should come to the conclusion that there had been a change in the presentation of these religious figures. The Byzantine Madonna is aloof, far removed from the human world. Giotto's figures show tremendous human emotion, allowing us to identify more closely with them.

Contextual Information

Paintings and Location

So many paintings hang in museums today that we often forget that these works were originally intended to be placed in a far different environment. The Duccio *Maesta*, of which *Christ Raising Lazarus* (fig.8–44) was a piece, originally was placed on the main altar of the cathedral of Siena. The *Annunciation* (fig.8–45) by Simone Martini was originally placed on an altar adjacent to the main altar in the same cathedral. These two paintings, therefore, would have been part of the same decoration plan.

Remind students that these works would have been seen only by candlelight and whatever natural light entered the church. They also would have been seen at a much greater distance than our often "nose-to-nose" vantage point in a museum.

Lesson 8.2 Review Answers

1 *Gothic* was first used as a term of ridicule by Renaissance critics because the style did not conform to the standards of Classical Greece and Rome which were admired by Renaissance people.

2 Unity

3 1140 at the royal abbey of Saint Denis, outside of Paris

4 Cathedral of Cologne

5 The tower over the crossing

6 Moses has an intense and powerful facial expression. Because he has just returned from Mt. Sinai, he is holding the tablets of the law in his right hand. He has horns on his head, a full parted beard and lush flowing robes which create a dynamic rhythm and visual movement leading up to his expressive face.

7 Sheets of colored glass, mostly red and blue, were cut to fit the shapes of a full-size cartoon. Paint was applied in some places for shading and details. The individual pieces were fired in a kiln to harden the pigment. The glass pieces were fit together and soldered in place with I-shaped lead strips. Carved stone tracery or iron bars supported the window and kept it flat as it was installed.

Gentile da Fabriano

(1370–1427)

There seems to have been a steady exchange of ideas, themes and techniques between the artists of Tuscany and those of central France. By the end of the fourteenth century, French and Italian Gothic styles had merged into an International style. Claus Sluter was the foremost sculptor in this style (see p.250).

The greatest Italian painter of the International style was Gentile da Fabriano who, like Simone Martini, exchanged ideas with French artists. Gentile's tempera painting, *The Adoration of the Magi* (fig.8–46), is a superb example of the style. The richly colored and patterned fabrics are skillfully rendered. Gentile took care with natural details. The animals, for instance, are rendered in a convincing manner. There is weight in the figures, yet great attention is paid to pattern and decoration.

The world was still one step from the Renaissance—one step from a true three-dimensional feeling in painting.

8–46 The gold-leafed frame on this painting is original. The owner paid more for it than he paid for the painting itself.
Gentile da Fabriano, *The Adoration of the Magi,* 1423. Tempera on panel, 9' 11" x 9' 3" (300 x 280 cm). Uffizi Gallery, Florence.

Lesson 8.2 Review

1 How did the term *Gothic* originate?
2 What is the most important art principle in Gothic architecture?
3 When and where did the Gothic style begin?
4 What is the largest Gothic cathedral in Germany?
5 What is the most memorable architectural feature of Salisbury Cathedral?
6 Describe Moses on Sluter's *Well of Moses.*
7 Explain the process of making a stained glass window. What two colors were used most often in Gothic stained glass windows?
8 Describe the body language of the figures, particularly the angels, in Giotto's *Lamentation.*

8 The angels contort in agony. One stretches out its arms and throws back its head and moans. Another covers its face with its robe and several of them wring their hands in despair. Mary rounds her shoulders as she bends over Christ, intently searching his lifeless face. John throws back his arms. One woman raises her hand while the woman next to her rests her cheek on her hands in sadness.

Chapter Review Answers

Review

1 *Romanesque* describes the art and architecture of the eleventh and twelfth centuries in western Europe.

2 *Romanesque:* Worms Cathedral, Worms, Germany; Cathedral of Pisa, Italy. *Gothic:* Cathedral of Siena, Italy; Salisbury Cathedral, England.

3 To let in great quantities of light which symbolized the presence of God.

4 Sculpture changed from Romanesque rigid symbolism to increasingly realistic forms drawn from nature in the Gothic period.

5 Tilman Riemenschneider—*Group of Three Saints;*
Claus Sluter—*Moses with Two Prophets* or *Well of Moses*

Interpret

1 Probably—it is 70 meters long, designed to fit around the inside of a small nave.

The Abbey at Cluny

Monks at the Abbey of Cluny, in France, were expected to read books daily. There was a lending library within the monastery. All of these books were handwritten and, when worn out, they were copied again by hand.

Copyists were given special privileges such as exemption from church services, special foods and opportunities to stay near fires to dry their manuscripts as well as to get warm.

The following is an excerpt from the Benedictine Rule regarding copyists in the monastery:

"Artificers, if there be any in the monastery, shall practise their special arts with all humility, if the abbot permit. But if any one of them be exalted on account of his knowledge of his art, to the extent that he seems to be conferring something on the monastery, then such a one shall be deprived of his art, and shall not again return to it, unless it hap that the abbot again order it, he being humiliated."

Peter the Venerable, a Cluniac monk, described the copying of books in the following manner:

"It is more noble to set one's hand to the pen than to the plough, to trace divine letters upon the page than furrows upon the fields. Sow on the page the seed of the word of God, and when the harvest is ripe, when your books are finished, the hungry readers shall be satisfied by an abundant harvest."

Review
1 Define the term *Romanesque*.
2 Name two Romanesque churches and two Gothic churches in Europe.
3 Why did Abbot Suger incorporate so many windows in his remodeling of the Cathedral of St.-Denis?
4 How did sculpture change from the Romanesque to the Gothic period?
5 Name two known Gothic sculptors. Name one sculpture that each one carved.

Interpret
1 Imagine that *The Bayeux Tapestry* was hung near the ceiling of your classroom. Would it be long enough to fit around the perimeter of the room?
2 In a chart, compare the arches, windows, wall decoration, walls and floor plans of Byzantine, Romanesque and Gothic churches.
3 Analyze the composition of Giotto's *Lamentation*. What is the center of interest? How has Giotto directed the viewers attention to this?

Other Tools for Learning

 Maps
1 Find Vezelay on the map. What country is it in today?
2 Why would the art of Venice be more closely aligned with that of northern Europe than the rest of Italy?

 Timelines
1 Select a discovery or invention from the 12th through the 16th centuries that has influenced your own life. Explain why you chose it.
2 How many years elapsed between the building of the first Gothic cathedral and Chaucer's writing of *The Canterbury Tales*? What styles would the churches have been that Chaucer's pilgrims visited on their trip?

Electronic Media
CD-ROM drive: *Microsoft Art Gallery*
1 Find a copy of one of John Constable's paintings of the Salisbury Cathedral. How does it compare with the photograph of the cathedral in this chapter?
2 Describe Duccio's *Maesta* altarpiece before it was disassembled. How large was it? Find another panel, other than the one in this book, from the *Maesta* and describe its subject matter.

CD-ROM drive: Electronic Encyclopedia (e.g., *New Grolier Multimedia* or *Microsoft Encarta*, etc.)
1 Why is the Tower of Pisa leaning? What is being done to stabilize it?

Primary-Source Connection

Those charged with the task of copying manuscripts were given certain privileges because of the importance of their work, yet they also were cautioned to maintain their humility. Ask students why their role in medieval society was so important. What were they helping to preserve? How would the printing press change this situation? Who or what plays the role of preserving humankind's knowledge today? (e.g., government via the Library of Congress)

– In 1400, blue Ming ware was developed. My favorite restaurant serves soup in bowls that look very similar to blue Ming ware.
2 When Chaucer began to write *The Canterbury Tales* in 1387, 250 years had elapsed since the Gothic remodeling of St.-Denis in 1137. Therefore, most of the churches the pilgrims visited would have been Gothic, although they would also have seen some older Romanesque-style churches.

Electronic Media
Microsoft Art Gallery
1 Whichever Constable painting is found will probably show the *Salisbury Cathedral* at a great distance surrounded by rolling landscape.
2 The *Maesta* altarpiece was 13' high and 14' wide (nearly 5 meters square) with more than 40 individual panels on its front and back painted in brilliant colors and gold leaf. On the front was a 7' panel with a monumental painting of the *Madonna* seated on a throne surrounded by angels, prophets, apostles. Small panels depicted scenes from her life and her son's life. Small panels painted in a narrative style depicting events in Christ's life were on the back. These paintings include: *The Betrayal of Jesus*, *The Transfiguration*, *The Annunciation*, *Entry into Jerusalem* and *The Crucifixion*.

Electronic Encyclopedia
1 The foundation began to settle soon after it was built. In 1995, it remained closed to visitors as engineers began work on renovations to stop the settling before it toppled over.

2

Byzantine	Romanesque	Gothic
arches		
rounded	rounded	pointed
windows		
small	small	large, stained glass
wall decor		
mosaics	some mosaics, frescoes in Italy	frescoes in Italy
walls		
thick	thick	thinner, supported by flying buttresses
floorplans		
basilica or Greek cross	Latin cross	Latin cross

3 Christ is the center of interest, and all of the figures look toward him. A huge rock directs the viewer's attention diagonally across the painting to Christ's face which is placed off center, on the left side of the picture plane, creating an asymmetrically balanced composition.

Maps
1 France
2 Because Venice is in the northern part of Italy, much closer to northern Europe than Rome.

Timelines
1 Examples of possible answers:
– Drinking chocolate became popular with the Aztecs in 1350 AD. If it had not been for the chocolate milkshake my father served my mother, I doubt that I would be here today.

Activity 1:
The News in Stitches

Activity Objectives
Students should be able to:

• Learn a variety of stitches.

• Relate individual work to a whole finished piece.

• Work cooperatively.

Thinking Critically
As students brainstorm ideas for their tapestry, remind them that the narrative potential of a tapestry can link well with other subjects, as follows:

• English: Feature characters and events from literature or folk stories.

• History: Select important figures and events in history.

• Health and Science: Illustrate important discoveries, advancements or inventions.

Preparation Ideas

• Prepare handouts with visual diagrams and written directions for several embroidery stitches, such as running stitch, outline/stem stitch, couching, buttonhole, chain stitch, satin stitch and French knot.

• Have the students use embroidery floss to create a sampler of these stitches on felt. As they complete one practice row, they should label the name of each stitch learned.

• Show small groups of students how to create stitches so that they can see close up exactly how to make the stitch. Also, show students how to use the diagrams. When some students understand quickly, encourage them to show other students what to do. This helps students get the individualized instruction they need while developing cooperative learning skills.

Notes on Materials
There are a number of ways to frame the finished tapestry. One way is to stretch it over foam core, tacking or taping it to the back. Another possibility is to use canvas stretchers (either one big one or a series of "panels"). Or, if you have a large bulletin board, tack the finished tapestry to the wall.

Classroom Management

• Discuss significant topics and write them on the board.

Activity 1

The News in Stitches

Materials
embroidery floss
embroidery needles
scissors
drawing paper
heavyweight tracing paper
embroidery transfer paper
loosely woven cotton, wool,
    burlap or muslin
optional: iron, ironing board,
    wooden hoops

Take a look.
• Fig.8–13, *The Battle of Hastings*, detail of *The Bayeux Tapestry*, about 1073–1083. Wool embroidery on linen.

Think about it. *The Bayeux Tapestry* is a narrative of the invasion of England by William the Conqueror from Normandy, France. The lively action of the piece gives a sense of the crowded battlefield and the ferocity of the fighting.
The embroidery uses line to define the figures. Notice the way borders are created at the top and bottom of the work.

Do it.
• With your classmates, select a current event or a happening from everyday life in your school or community.
• Divide the event into parts or scenes and decide how to make one relate to the next. Individuals or groups may be responsible for different scenes.
• Use contour lines to draw the figures in your narrative, noting their relationship to other figures. Classmates can pose as models.
• Once the action is drawn, put all of the scenes together on a piece of paper representing the intended size of the tapestry. Plan out any panels, check for continuity and consider the use of borders.

• Transfer the drawings to fabric. Use a variety of yarns, threads and stitches to create an embroidered tapestry.
• Assemble the narrative. Mount and stretch the completed tapestry for display.

Check it. Throughout the project, check that your scene, choice of colors and design works with those of your classmates.

Helpful Hint: Practice several different kinds of stitches using both yarn and embroidery floss. Notice how each gives a different effect and texture on the cloth.

Activity 2

Stained Glass Windows

Materials
gray chipboard
white paper
black markers
black railroad board
colored cellophane
glue
mat knife
scissors

Take a look.
• Fig.8–18, Notre Dame, nave.
• Fig.8–38, Rose windows and lancets.
• Fig.8–39, *St. Denis and Jean-Clement.*
• Fig.8–40, Interior, *Sainte-Chapelle.*

Think about it. Study the Gothic Cathedrals of England, France and Italy.
• Notice the shape and size of the windows, as well as similarities and differences.
• How is tracery (ornamental stonework) used in all these cathedrals?

Do it.
• Select and measure a window to be redesigned as a stained glass window. Use gray chipboard to create a "stone" frame to enclose your design.

• Create the stained glass design using a broad marker or heavy line to emphasize the linear quality of the drawing.
• Transfer the drawing to black railroad board and cut out the enclosed shapes, leaving black lines. Use colored cellophane to fill in the open areas.
• Put your "stained glass" windows over your selected window.

Check it. Write about the effect the colored light has on the atmosphere of the room. What kind of mood does it create?

Helpful Hint: Think of the figures in the stained glass windows you have seen. How complex or simple are these figures?

Additional Activities
• Research the shapes and materials used by various cultures for ceremonial cups (see the *Chalice of Abbot Suger*, fig.8–14). Write about the particular ceremony in which it is used.
• Arrange a print or slide show that illustrates the changing concepts in figure painting (or sculpture) from Greek to Gothic times. Cite dates and describe stylistic changes.
• The dimensions of many Gothic cathedrals are overwhelming. The German cathedral at Cologne has a nave 151' (46 m) high and towers 498' 8" (152 m) high. Devise a visual presentation that will compare the size of several buildings in your community with this gigantic Gothic structure. Research the length and width of several cathedrals (from the encyclopedia) and plot them in your neighborhood or on school grounds.

• Divide the class into groups. Then, from the many suggestions, choose the same number of topics as you have groups.

• Have each group decide which topic to illustrate. Then have them complete at least two designs.

• To ensure that everyone participates, have each student demonstrate a particular stitch. Encourage students to invent stitches of their own.

Tips

• Have needlepoint or embroidery books and/or samples on hand to give examples of various kinds of stitches.

Evaluation
Each student is responsible for some portion of the tapestry and receives a grade for it along with a group grade for combined work. For example, if a student is responsible for a house in a scene of a neighborhood, the grade for the house is 75 percent of the total grade, and the scene of the entire neighborhood is 25 percent of the total grade. Points to consider:

• Did each student in the group do his/her share of the work?

• Did all students develop a vocabulary of stitches? Were they able to use those stitches appropriately?

• Did the students work cooperatively, helping each other learn how to do the stitches?

• Did the finished artwork make a statement?

From left to right, Eve Binder, Deborah Cambetas, Tina Greenberg and Michele Wang display their completed tapestry.

Diversity, 1995. Embroidery floss on cotton cloth, 27 1/2" x 12" (70 x 30.5 cm)

Four students from:

Clarkstown High School North
New City, New York
Activity I, The News in Stitches

Eve Binder *Age 17*

We made a tapestry with a theme that was related to the area that we live in. After brainstorming for a while we came up with many different ideas for our theme, but we settled on diversity. We chose this particular theme because all of us working on the project came from different backgrounds. There is also a wide variety of cultures in our school.

By making squares of different cultures, sewing them all together, and giving them a common border—American symbols—we demonstrate our hope for unity in our country as well as the world.

I hope that people will look at our tapestry and understand that we are all put here as equals. We all live in the same country and no problems will be solved until we work together. *(Eve stitched the Native American panel.)*

Debora Cambetas *Age 18*

For my part of this project I chose to embroider the Statue of Liberty, which represents freedom and liberty for all peoples. I appreciate its value, being an immigrant to this country.

The part I liked most about this project was the fact that there are many different stitches I could use in order to signify shadowing and texture. I believe that if anyone is really dedicated to accomplishing a project she should follow her heart and the project will be her best ever.

Tina Greenberg *Age 15*

In this art project, my responsibility was to embroider a drawing of a woman in India. I have learned about Indian culture and I have expanded my horizons. While I was creating my tapestry I attempted to depict Indian customs correctly. I used proper colors and patterns.

Michele Wang *Age 15*

This project meant a great deal to me. I had the privilege of doing my own culture—China. When I was doing this, I was captivated by the dragon. The dragon had an interesting form to it that really captured my thoughts.

This project helped me to explore deep into my culture. It made me realize how important it was for me to accept other people even though it was very difficult. It's very difficult for me because in the past I wasn't accepted by people in this country. People laughed and scorned me for my culture and my skin. I used to hate myself mostly being Chinese. Now, I realize that being Chinese is what makes me special.

Teacher Spotlight
Barbara Levine
Art Department Chairperson/Art Teacher

This hardworking, select group of students spent many hours planning and stitching the group project entitled *Diversity*. Because of the time element, the project could not be tried in a regular classroom situation. Students met a few times a week after school and worked on their individual pieces at home. Stitchery is very labor intensive, requiring many more hours than drawing. The four students who completed the cooperative artwork demonstrated dedication, patience and good skills working within a group.

The students discussed the project together, sought advice from and offered suggestions to each other. Although the students were not classmates, spanning tenth to twelfth grade, they respected each other's art abilities, complimenting and appreciating everyone's part of the project. They were surprised and excited to see that the finished piece, once sewn together, was even nicer than they had anticipated.

where you plan to put them. You may want to have each art class cooperatively design and produce one window in your room, or you may have one class do a whole set of windows with an individual or group responsible for separate panels. If there are no appropriate windows in your classroom, request permission to construct a window in the school hallway, lobby or cafeteria.

Tips

• Check places of worship in your city or town for interesting stained glass windows. Go together as a class or send individuals or small groups to investigate. Have students do rough sketches of designs that interest them.

• Invite craftspeople trained in stained glass techniques to give a demonstration.

Evaluation

Each student is responsible for some portion of the design and receives a grade for it, along with a group grade for combined work.

Activity 2: Stained Glass Window

Activity Objectives
Students should be able to:

• Practice and explore contour drawing.

• Work with transferring drawings into a structural creation (glass window design).

Thinking Critically
Compare the exteriors and interiors of Gothic and Romanesque cathedrals. Ask the students to describe a rose window.

• Where is the window usually located?

• What might be some difficulties in making a stained glass window?

• What do you think the limitations would be in creating figures in the stained glass?

Preparation Ideas
Check with numerous sources for slides of stained glass windows to show in class; for example, local libraries or art galleries, or perhaps a parent or traveler in the local community.

Notes on Materials
The backs of sketch pads are a source for gray chipboard.

Classroom Management
The scope of the project and the number of windows to make depends on

Chapter 9 Organizer

Days	8 Week	I Semester	2 Semester
	1	1	1

Chapter 9 Opener: The Italian Renaissance

Objectives	National Standards
Identify Florence as the birthplace of the Italian Renaissance.	**4a** Students differentiate among a variety of historical and cultural contexts in terms of characteristics and purposes of works of art.
Understand that powerful merchant families now commissioned art along with aristocratic, royal and church patrons.	**4b** Students describe the function and explore the meaning of specific art objects within varied cultures, times and places.
Articulate the significant visual developments of Italian Renaissance painting and their long-range impact on Western art.	**3c** Students describe the origins of specific images and ideas and explain why they are of value in their artwork and in the work of others.
Comprehend that the Renaissance gave rise to the idea of artists as divinely inspired geniuses	**5d** Students correlate responses to works of visual art with various techniques for communicating meanings, ideas, attitudes, views, and intentions.
Explain that Mannerist artists shared an interest in expressive, highly personal compositions rather than in a unified style.	**2b** Students evaluate the effectiveness of artworks in terms of organizational structures and functions.

Lesson 9.1 Early Renaissance

Teacher Edition References

Special Feature: Filippo Brunelleschi 262–263	Contextual Info 263 · HOTS 263
Remainder of Lesson 9.1 264–275 World Cultural Timeline 272 Lesson 9.1 Review 275	Contextual Info 264, 266, 268, 270, 272, 274 HOTS 265, 267, 269, 271, 273, 275 Conservation 265, 268 Inquiry 264, 274 · Interdisciplinary 266 Materials and Techniques 271 Multicultural 272 Performing Arts 270

Lesson 9.2 High Renaissance

Special Feature: Leonardo da Vinci 276–277	Contextual Info 277 · HOTS 277
Remainder of Lesson 9.2 278–287 World Cultural Timeline 280, 284 Lesson 9.2 Review 287	Contextual Info 278, 280, 282, 284, 286 HOTS 279, 281, 283, 285, 287 Interdisciplinary 279 · Multicultural 280, 284 Performing Arts 283

Lesson 9.3 Mannerism

Special Feature: El Greco 288–289	Contextual Info 289 · HOTS 289
Remainder of Lesson 9.3 290–298 World Cultural Timeline 292 Lesson 9.3 Review 298 Primary-Source 299 Chapter Review 299	Contextual Info 290, 292, 294, 296 HOTS 291, 293, 295, 297, 299 Collaborative 293 Inquiry 291 · Interdisciplinary 297 Multicultural 292 Performing Arts 296

Classroom Connections

	National Standards
Studio Activity 1 Leonardo's Sketchbook	**1a** Students apply media, techniques, and processes with sufficient skill, confidence, and sensitivity that their intentions are carried out in their artworks.
Studio Activity 2 Stretching the Truth	**1b** Students conceive and create works of visual art that demonstrate an understanding of how the communication of their ideas relates to the media, techniques, and processes they use.

Choose either Activity I or 2   Choose either Activity I or 2   Choose either Activity I or 2

Other Resources

Books

Chartier, Roger, ed., trans. *A History of Private Life.*, Vol.3: *Passions of the Renaissance.* Cambridge: Harvard University Press, 1989.

Cole, B. *Italian Art, 1250–1550: The Relation of Art to Life and Society.* New York: HarperCollins, 1987.

———. *Renaissance Artist at Work: From Pisano to Titian.* New York: Harper-Collins, 1984.

Gilbert, Creighton. *Italian Art 1400–1500.* Part of *Sources and Documents in the History of Art.* Evanston, IL: Northwestern University Press, 1991.

Hale, J.R. *A Concise Encyclopedia of the Italian Renaissance.* New York: Oxford University Press, 1981.

Heydenreich, Ludwig, and Lotz, Wolfgang. *Architecture in Italy: 1400–1600.* Baltimore: Penguin USA, 1974.

Holt, Elizabeth Gilmore, ed. *A Documentary History of Art.* Vol.1: *The Middle Ages and Renaissance.* Princeton: Princeton University Press, 1981.

———. *A Documentary History of Art. Volume II: Michelangelo and the Mannerists–The Baroque and the Eighteenth Century.* Princeton: Princeton University Press, 1983.

Klein, Robert, and Zerner, Henri. *Italian Art: 1500–1600.* Part of *Sources and Documents in the History of Art.* Evanston, IL: Northwestern University Press, 1989.

Leonardo: To Know How to See. National Gallery of Art, 1972.

Levey, Michael. *Early Renaissance.* Baltimore MD: Penguin USA, 1978.

———. *High Renaissance.* Baltimore MD: Penguin USA, 1978.

Seymour, Jr. Charles. *Sculpture in Italy: 1400–1500.* New Haven: Yale University Press, 1992.

Vasari, Giorgio, trans. *Lives of the Most Eminent Painters, Sculptors, and Architects.* 10 vols. Repr. of 1915 ed. New York: AMS Press Inc.

Videodisc

Michelangelo: Self-Portrait, Crystal

Video

The First Modern Sculptor, Donatello, Crystal
The Life of Leonardo da Vinci, Crystal
Raphael, Crystal
Return to Glory: Michelangelo Revealed, Crystal
Tintoretto, Crystal

Music

Renaissance Musical Examples from Italy.
Marenzio—*S'io Parto, l'Moro*
Orlandus Lassus— *Motet, Tristis Est Amima Mea*
Palestrina— *Agnus Dei* from *Veni Sponsa Christi*
(these examples can be fournd in Haydn Society, Masterpieces of Music before 1750.)

Ancillaries

Large Reproductions: Michelangelo, *The Creation of Adam*, 12

Teacher Edition References

Timeline: The Italian Renaissance 260
Map: The Italian Renaissance 261
Context 260
Art 260
Quote 261

Ancillaries

Slides: Brunelleschi, Dome of Cathedral of Florence, 52a, 107; Brunelleschi, Ospedale degli Innocenti, 56b, 108; Alberti, Palazzo Rucellai, 57b, 109

Slides: Donatello, *David*, 53a, 110; Donatello, *Gattamelata*, Padua, 54a, 111; Fra Angelico, *The Annunciation*, 55a, 112; Mantegna, St. Sebastian 58b, 113
Overhead Transparencies: The Development of Linear Perspective, 9
Large Reproductions: Botticelli, *La Primavera (Spring)*, 11

Slides: Michelangelo, *David*, 56a, 114; Michelangelo, *Tomb of Lorenzo de'Medici*, 59b, 115; Michelangelo, *Dome of St. Peters*, Rome, 57a, 116; Raphael, *Baldassare Castiglione*, 58a, 117; Titian, *Gypsy Madonna*, 60b, 118
Large Reproductions: Michelangelo, *The Creation of Adam*, 12

Slides: El Greco, *Fray Paravicino*, 61b, 119; El Greco, *St. Martin and the Beggar*, 8a, 16

Slides: Tintoretto, *Carrying the Body of St. Mark*, 62b, 120; Palladio, Villa Capra (Villa Rotunda), Vicenza, Italy, 59a, 121

Schedule

Students might begin their sketchbook in the studio and continue drawing in it outside of class.

Varies depending on the medium. A small sculpture might take one class and a detailed tempera painting might require five days.

Materials

drawing pencils or charcoal, 12" x 18" white drawing paper or sketchbook, optional: colored pencil, pen and ink, conte crayon

for sculpture
plasticine clay, newspaper or plastic, clay tools (optional), newspaper
for painting
white paper, 12" x 18" or larger, tempera paints, containers to mix paint, container of water, paint brushes

Introduce

The Italian Renaissance originated in Florence during the early fifteenth century. Individual wealthy families, the nobility and royal courts now joined the church as patrons of art. By the sixteenth century, the art capital shifted to Rome. During the Renaissance, for the first time, artists were perceived as brilliant individuals with tremendous talents rather than as mere craftspeople. Mannerism, the period between the High Renaissance, and the Baroque, encompassed highly personal styles that did not solidify into a single movement.

Lessons at a Glance

9.1 *Early Renaissance*
The early Renaissance of the fifteenth century began in Florence. Scientific and mathematic advances, inspired by serious study of ancient Greek and Roman culture, became tools that artists used in their work.

9.2 *The High Renaissance*
During the High Renaissance, Rome became the art capital of Italy, and great artists throughout Europe were summoned by the pope to complete splendid commissions that glorified the papal state.

9.3 *Mannerism*
Mannerism occurred in Western Europe from about 1525 to 1600, roughly spanning the years between the end of the High Renaissance and the beginning of the Baroque era. Mannerism was not a unified movement but was instead enriched by various unique modes of visual expression.

Objectives

Students should be able to:

Identify Florence as the birthplace of the Italian Renaissance.

Understand that powerful merchant families now commissioned art along with aristocratic, royal and church patrons.

Articulate the significant developments of Italian Renaissance painting and their long-range impact on Western art.

Comprehend that the Renaissance gave rise to the idea of artists as divinely inspired geniuses.

9 The Italian Renaissance

R ENAISSANCE MEANS REBIRTH. In the early 1400s, a cultural rebirth created a period of intense artistic activity throughout Europe that would last for 200 years.

Leaders in this artistic flowering lived in the city of Florence which was dominated by the Medici, a powerful family who were great patrons of the arts. The Florentine artists, fueled by a renewed interest in the ancient Romans and Greeks as well as in science and math, created a city of extraordinary beauty. Though magnificent sculpture and architecture were produced, painting dominated the art of the Renaissance.

The High Renaissance was a very short period in Rome and Venice. The primary center was Rome where popes commissioned artists, like Michelangelo, who were considered geniuses. Their work was more expressive than the earlier Renaissance artists and is probably some of the most well known in the world.

The last period to be discussed in this chapter is Mannerism, a transitional period which fell between the end of the High Renaissance and the beginning of the Baroque period. Mannerism is more a grouping of various individual artists' styles than a single style.

9–a Leonardo da Vinci was the quintessential Renaissance individual. He was knowledgeable not only in the arts, but also was an expert in many of the technical and natural sciences. He left behind ten thousand pages of drawings, sketches and notes.
Leonardo da Vinci, *Five Heads*. Department of Drawings and Prints, Uffizi Gallery, Florence.

1401
Baptistry door competition, Florence

1492
Death of Lorenzo de Medici

1498
da Vinci, *The Last Supper*

1517
Protestant Reformation begun by Martin Luther

1527
The sack of Rome by Emperor Charles V

1536–1541
Michelangelo, *Last Judgment*, Sistine Chapel

1586
El Greco, *The Burial of Count Orgaz*

The Italian Renaissance

1420–1436
Donatello, *David*
1440
Gutenberg invents printing press with movable type

1492
Columbus arrives on the island of San Salvador

1516
Titian succeeds Bellini as official painter to Venetian Republic

1527
Center of art shifts to Venice

1575
Beginning of modern botany

1600
Wigs and dress trains become fashionable

Explain that Mannerist artists shared an interest in expressive, highly personal compositions rather than in a unified style.

Teach

Timeline

Have students mark a place on the timeline for Paolo Uccello's *Battle of San Romano* (fig.9–45, 9–15), at 1445, and one for Paolo Veronese's *Christ in the House of Levi* (fig.9–45), at 1573. Now that they know which work was painted first, what observations can they make, from looking at the images, about the advancement of realism from early to late Renaissance art? Suggest that they make a list and periodically check it as they complete the lessons in Chapter 9.

Context

Ask students: "Since the person and his/her mind became central concerns during the Renaissance, what types of intellectual studies might have become important?" The great thinkers of the day looked back to the Classical period, devouring the mathematics, science, philosophy, art and culture of ancient times. The Greek and Roman past became the basis for many innovations that would transform Western culture for centuries.

Art

Direct students to discover the techniques Paolo Uccello used in *Battle of San Romano* to evoke a sense of depth.

• What colors seem to move toward the viewer and which ones recede into the background?

Men can do all things if they will.
Leon Battista Alberti

9–b Science and mathematics became tools for artists in the early Renaissance. There was a strong interest in the use of linear perspective.
Paolo Uccello, *Battle of San Romano,* detail (fig.9–15).

The Italian Renaissance

During the 15th and 16th centuries, a creative force rippled across the Italian peninsula and produced the Renaissance. What Italian cities do we most often associate with the Renaissance?

9–c This is a detail of one of the most well known works of art from the Renaissance. It is a symbol of the enduring beauty and appeal of the period.
Michelangelo, *Pietà,* detail (fig.9–25).

Quote

After students have read the quote, ask them if they agree with Leon Battista Alberti's assumption about human beings. Is there anything they can imagine that humankind cannot do? Share that Renaissance philosophers proposed that humans, particularly men, could do anything they set their minds to. Do students think that this new attitude toward man's intellectual abilities altered their feelings about God and religion? Compared to the Middle Ages, a great deal more art that was unconnected to Christianity was created for the comfort and glorification of wealthy individuals.

Map

Ask students to examine the map and find the city of Florence where the Renaissance began. To which cities did the movement spread?

and the illusion of three-dimensional space.

• Do their conclusions hold true for other Gothic and Renaissance paintings in the textbook?

• Ask students to give reasons why the Gothic and Renaissance portrayals of biblical scenes were different. They should consider not only the artistic changes that took place in the intervening centuries, but also should comment on how the beliefs and philosophies of each period would have affected the art.

Reteach

If America adopted a state religion, how might this affect the types of art that the government would support? How much freedom do you think artists would have in their range of expression, materials and subject matter?

Discuss how Italian culture continues to exert a discernible influence on contemporary society. How many Italian expressions do students use in everyday conversations? (e.g., ciao, mangia, buono, bravo, presto, bella) What Italian foods do they eat regularly? Are they familiar with any Italian clothing designers?

• Are all the figures and objects on the same flat plane? Uccello overlaps his figures so that the ones behind are partially covered by those in front. He also arranges swords and armor in a linear pattern that suggests deep space.

• From what angle or perspective did Uccello paint the breastplate under the rearing horse? The metal shield (and the fallen soldier seen in the full painting) are foreshortened; that is, the nearer parts are drawn larger than the sections that should be perceived as farther away.

• Italian Renaissance artists perfected all these techniques, which continue to be used today in realistic paintings.

Evaluate

Ask students if Gothic or Renaissance paintings appear more realistic by having them compare the late Renaissance work *Christ in the House of Levi* by Veronese to Duccio's *Christ Raising Lazarus from the Dead* (figs.8–d, 8–44) from the Gothic period.

• Did either artist actually see these scenes occur?

• Although both artists painted imaginary views of Biblical stories, which one makes the viewer feel able to walk into the image?

• Have students make observations about the artists' use of color, naturalistic poses, degree of individualization in the faces, realism of the background

Lesson 9.1

The early Renaissance of the fifteenth century began in Florence, which initiated impressive building campaigns to demonstrate the city's new role as the intellectual and political leader of Italy. Scientific and mathematic advances, inspired by serious study of ancient Greek and Roman culture, became tools that artists used in their work.

Warm-up

Ask students if they have ever heard the term *Renaissance*. Direct them to glance quickly at the images in Chapter 9 to determine what earlier cultures were being "reborn" in fifteenth-century art. Classical Greece and Rome inspired the Renaissance as well as later periods such as Neoclassicism (see Chapter 12). These influences were also evident in early medieval art and architecture of the late eighth and early ninth centuries.

Objectives

Students should be able to:

Identify Florence as the city in which the Italian Renaissance began.

Analyze Florence's major building campaign, which helped demonstrate its political and intellectual leadership in Italy.

Comprehend how ancient Greek and Roman sources profoundly influenced Renaissance art.

Understand how Renaissance artists incorporated knowledge of science and mathematics into their works.

Vocabulary

cupola (*coop*-oh-lah) A rounded convex roof on a circular base; a dome of small size.
tondo A round-shaped painting.
foreshortening A method of applying perspective to an object or figure so that it seems to recede in space by shortening the depth dimension, making the form appear three-dimensional.

Teach

Criticism/Art History: Explain to students that Filippo Brunelleschi discovered scientific perspective, a way of accurately illustrating three-dimensional objects on a flat surface. He, like many other Renaissance

9.1 Early Renaissance

WHEN WE LOOK AT WORKS from the early Renaissance, they appear so calm and harmonious that we might be fooled into thinking that they were a reflection of the period. This is far from the truth. Like so many other creative periods, the early Renaissance was an era of extreme stress and conflict.

The city of Florence became the political and intellectual leader among Italian cities—a "new Athens." It was the epicenter of a tremendous creative force that swept the Italian peninsula. Nevertheless, the city was still a beleaguered place. Led by the Medici family, Florence warded off conquering armies from the north and south of Italy in the early fifteenth century. Only in their great monuments and works of art did the Florentines achieve the harmony and serenity they so desired.

Despite threats to the city's safety, the people embarked on programs to finish the cathedral, build beautiful doors for their baptistry, line the streets with magnificent homes and plan a city of extraordinary beauty. The Florentines took tremendous pride in the advances made by their native artists. They were well aware of the great beauty of their city, which remains timeless and breathtaking even today.

Key Notes
- Florence is the birthplace of the Renaissance.
- Science and mathematics become tools for artists.
- Ancient Rome and Greece are sources of inspiration for artists.

Vocabulary
cupola
tondo
foreshortening

Special Feature
Filippo Brunelleschi
(1377–1446)

The crowning jewel of the Florentine cityscape is the *cupola*, or dome, of its cathedral (fig.9–1). Designed by Filippo Brunelleschi (1377–1466), the dome is an architectural and engineering wonder.

Typical of the artistic genius of the Renaissance, Brunelleschi was a goldsmith, sculptor, mathematician, clock builder and architect. (His death mask is pictured above.) Trained as a sculptor, he discovered scientific perspective, a way of accurately showing three-dimensional buildings or objects on a flat sheet of paper. His greatest achievement, however, was in architecture, where he initiated a new style of building.

9–1 The transept was so huge that it could not be domed by any known system so Brunelleschi had to invent a new way to construct the dome.
Filippo Brunelleschi. Dome, *Cathedral of Florence*, 1420–1436. Florence.

artists, was fascinated with mathematics. Ask the class to identify all the geometric shapes he incorporated into his architecture (figs.9–1, 9–2). Have them study pages 262 and 263 to identify what Brunelleschi learned about Classical architecture and mathematics on his visit to Rome.

Criticism/Aesthetics: Have students study Brunelleschi's dome for the *Cathedral of Florence* (fig.9–1) and the interior of *San Lorenzo* (fig.9–2). Have them compare the Renaissance buildings to the Gothic exterior of the *Cathedral of Chartres* (fig.8–15). Ask them to hum a tune that corresponds to Chartres' complex decoration and architectural forms and then create one for Brunelleschi's architecture.

- What adjectives would they use to describe their musical compositions?

- Which one sounds more passionate?

- Is the tune for Brunelleschi's architecture more balanced and repetitive?

- Are there more variations in the composition for Chartres?

The immediate visual logic of Brunelleschi's designs communicates the respect Renaissance society placed on the power of the human rational mind, which, in this case, was used to honor God. Ask students which architecture they feel more successfully creates a reverent atmosphere. Have students with opposing views try to convince each other of their decisions.

9–2 Compare this interior to that of Notre Dame in Paris (fig.8–18). Look for similarities as well as differences.
Filippo Brunelleschi. Nave and choir, *San Lorenzo*, 1421–1469. Florence.

At some time between 1402 and the beginning of his architectural career, Brunelleschi had gone to Rome to study and accurately measure the remains of ancient Roman buildings. He came back to Florence with his own ideas about how ancient elements could be utilized. In 1418, he won a competition to design the mammoth dome over the cathedral.

The dome was built as two shells, one inside the other. The shells were ingeniously linked with ribs and supports so that each helped support the other. The dome is enormous. It is 140 feet in diameter and rises 300 feet above the floor.

Usually ramps were used to lift building materials to such height, but Brunelleschi designed a system of hoists that eliminated the need for ramps and scaffolding. He showed succeeding generations of architects that technical problems can be solved with scientific approaches. This was a new concept in the building trades. Previously, builders had looked at earlier structures for help in solving problems.

Brunelleschi, like the Greeks and Romans, used basic geometrical shapes and simple proportions. While Gothic interiors had become decorative and elaborate, Brunelleschi simplified. In the Church of San Lorenzo, built for the

Medici family, he went back to the basilica plan for a simple framework (fig.9–2). Lines are clean and walls are uncluttered. Brunelleschi's work is in dramatic contrast to previous Gothic detail and movement. His work tends toward cool and static perfection—a drastic change. His experience in measuring the ancient Roman buildings helped him arrive at his concept of architectural design. Brunelleschi concluded that discipline of thought, clarity of design, the proportion of one part to another and a constant awareness of regular visual rhythm are essential to fine architecture.

Contextual Information

Brunelleschi's Death Mask

At one time it was fairly common practice to make a plaster mold of someone's face after death, particularly if he or she was a prominent person of the day. Research could uncover a photograph of Napoleon's death mask, for instance. Nowadays we can take photographs to remember what people looked like when they were alive.

Higher-Order Thinking Skills

CAD (Computer Assisted Design) is used extensively by modern architects to test their designs and ideas. In Brunelleschi's time, a complex system of schooling for architects through lengthy apprenticeship programs handed the knowledge of builders from one generation to the next. There was a strong element of experimentation as designers sought to push the limits. Sometimes, as in the case of the Cathedral of Florence, the architects exceeded the limits. For instance, only because of Brunelleschi's ingenious design solution were the Florentines able to put a dome on their cathedral. See if your school or community has a CAD system that your students could see or work with. Are CAD results always correct? Does CAD aid in the search for ingenious solutions or does it restrict an architect's options?

Evaluate

Have students explain how Brunelleschi's architecture demonstrates an interest in science and mathematics. Would his buildings look as ordered and logical without the incorporation of scientific perspective and mathematical geometry?

Ask students how Florence demonstrated its civic pride in being the political and intellectual leader of Italy during the fifteenth century. How did the city's buildings and their accompanying sculptural decoration symbolize its desire to become a splendid and imposing urban center?

Reteach

Ask students to find interior images of sacred architecture from the past in the textbook (for instance, Egyptian in fig.5–27, Roman in fig.6–35, Byzantine in fig.7–14 and Gothic in fig. 8–16.). Despite the variations in physical structure, is there any feeling common to all the examples of what it must be like to step inside these buildings?

- In each case, how has the architect aroused a sense of spiritual awe?

- How do examples of contemporary architecture use decoration, light, height and structure to create inspiring secular environments? (Students may wish to consider skyscrapers, shopping malls, movie complexes or apartment-building lobbies.)

Is there a "renaissance" of interest in any previous period in modern American culture? What fashions, hairstyles, music, foods or forms of entertainment from the past have gained popularity once again?

Direct students to research the Harlem Renaissance of approximately 1922 to 1931. What cultures were being "reborn" during this period? If students were to revive an earlier era, which one would they use to generate exciting new modes of artistic expression?

Contextual Information

Gates of Paradise

Ghiberti's bronze doors (*Gates of Paradise*) cost 22,000 florins in the fifteenth century. A person living in a nice house with servants and a horse could live on 200 florins a year.

According to legend, Michelangelo gave the name *Gates of Paradise* to Ghiberti's second set of doors. The name derives from the fact that the doors open to the area between a baptistry and the entrance to its cathedral. This area is called "paradiso" in Italian. Michelangelo, playing on this word, is believed to have said that the doors were worthy of being the gates of Paradise.

Ghiberti included a self-portrait on the *Gates of Paradise*. His bust-length figure can be found in a medallion just outside the lower right of the Jacob and Esau panel.

9–3 Brunelleschi did not win the competition for the Baptistry doors with this panel. Can you "read" the story from this panel by studying it? What clues do you find?
Filippo Brunelleschi, *Sacrifice of Isaac*, 1401–1402. Gilt bronze relief, 21" x 17" (53 x 43 cm). National Museum, Florence.

9–4 Compare this to Brunelleschi's panel which tells the same story. Which do you prefer?
Lorenzo Ghiberti, *Sacrifice of Isaac*, 1401–1402. Gilt bronze relief, 21" x 17" (53 x 43 cm). National Museum, Florence.

Sculpture

The Classical tradition inspired not only Brunelleschi and his new architecture. Sculptors in the early part of the fifteenth century also learned many lessons from ancient Rome. When they looked at Roman sculpture they found a realism and spirit that reflected their own interest in humans and their achievements. Sculptures from antiquity were large and lifelike, celebrating the beauty, harmony and proportions of the human figure. In the early fifteenth century, sculptors once again began to place an emphasis on these values. They were commissioned to create works for public buildings, homes, palaces and churches.

Lorenzo Ghiberti
(1381–1455)

We encounter Brunelleschi at an earlier point in his career when, in 1401, a competition was held for the design and sculpting of the north doors of the baptistry of Florence. Lorenzo Ghiberti, Brunelleschi and many other artists competed intensely for this commission. The seven final contestants were assigned to sculpt the sacrifice of Isaac. Only the panels by Brunelleschi and Ghiberti have survived.

9–5 These panels are designed to work with light to help create the sense of three-dimensional space. Can you explain how Ghiberti did that?
Lorenzo Ghiberti, *Gates of Paradise*, 1425–1452. Gilt bronze relief, 15' (4.57 m). Baptistry, Florence.

Inquiry

Important commissions are often awarded by means of a competition. Have students research a community monument or building that was built by the winner of a competition. If there are no local competitions for students to investigate, have them research the competition that was held for the design of the Vietnam Veterans Memorial, in Washington, DC.

9–6 Locate this panel on the illustration of the complete door. How does it relate to the other panels? Compare it to the relief sculptures from the Parthenon.
Lorenzo Ghiberti, *The Story of Jacob and Esau* (detail, baptistry doors), 1425–1452. Gilt bronze relief, 31 1/2" x 31 1/2" (80 x 80 cm). Florence.

Higher-Order Thinking Skills

Have students compare and contrast Brunelleschi's and Ghiberti's solution to the same artistic problem in the competition for the baptistry doors. Then select a story or myth for students to illustrate in painting, drawing, collage or other media. Hold a discussion to critique and compare their solutions. Have students hold a secret ballot to choose the work they consider to be the most effective.

Brunelleschi's panel (fig.9–3) is filled with energy and high drama. The angel rushes in and grabs Abraham's arm just as he is about to plunge the knife into his son's neck. Daring and original, it lacks the Renaissance qualities of harmony and balance—qualities Brunelleschi particularly expressed in his architecture. Ghiberti's panel (fig.9–4) is perhaps less dramatic, but more unified. Abraham's knife is poised to strike but does not touch Isaac. Figures are classical. The nude Isaac is beautifully proportioned, like the sculptures of ancient Greece.

The twenty-one-year-old Ghiberti won the competition. The two doors took more than twenty years to complete. The twenty-eight panels illustrate stories from the New Testament as well as other figures. They were received so well that Ghiberti was commissioned to do the final set of doors on the east side of the baptisty. These doors (fig.9–5) were to become his masterpiece. Later called *The Gates of Paradise* by Florentines, they were very different from the previous work. Instead of so many small panels, Ghiberti divided the space into ten large, square panels. He used pictorial space and one-point perspective (originated by Brunelleschi) to produce convincing depths on relief surfaces.

Look particularly at the panel *The Story of Jacob and Esau* (fig.9–6). Notice how the space creates an illusion of reality. The figures diminish in size as they recede in space. Parallel lines lead to a single vanishing point, and detail becomes simpler as it gets farther away. Several of the closer figures seem to project out in space in front of the panel. While his first doors contained remnants of Gothic sculpture, these doors are truly works of Renaissance art and thinking. The doors are cast in bronze, covered with gold. Said Ghiberti, "I did my best to observe the correct proportions, and endeavored to imitate nature as much as possible."

Conservation Note

A result of the devastating flood of 1966 in Florence was the uncovering of the beautiful gilding of the *Gates of Paradise*. Many of the panels were knocked off the door with the force of the floodwaters. Covered with dirt and grime, the panels received a cleaning that they had not had for many, many years; and experts thus uncovered Ghiberti's original gilded finish.

Many of today's restoration techniques were a direct result of the work that was done in Florence after the ruinous flood of 1966, when floodwaters in some sections of the city rose to just over 19 feet. The extensive repair work that was done following the flood led to significant advances in the restoration of paintings and frescoes.

Contextual Information

Donatello

Donatello left Florence to work in the northern Italian city of Padua for ten years and thereby had a strong impact on the painting and sculpture of the area. Giotto, the groundbreaking artist of the fourteenth century, also worked in Padua in the Arena Chapel (fig. 8–43). Though they worked 100 years apart, both of these artists sought to bring a greater realism and a sense of human emotion to their work.

Donatello's life in Florence was closely intertwined with the Medici family. The sculptor continued to be a favorite of Cosimo Medici after his return from Padua, and received a pension from him in his old age. When the elder Medici died, his son Piero continued to assist Donatello financially, providing him with a farm in a town outside of Florence. The artist, however, found that the running of the farm interfered with his work and asked Piero to take it back. Piero obliged and instead provided him with a stipend equal to the income of the farm.

Donatello took his close association with the Medici all the way to the grave. He is buried in a sarcophagus with Cosimo and Cosimo's brother, Lorenzo, in the floor just before the main altar in the church of San Lorenzo.

9–7 Compare this statue with the Greek sculpture, the *Kritios Boy* (fig.6–10). How are they similar? How do they differ?
Donatello, *David*, 1430–1432. Bronze, 62 1/4" (159 cm) high. National Museum, Florence.

9–9 Donatello never met Gattamelata. This is an idealized portrait of a military leader. What characteristics has the sculptor tried to portray in the face of the figure?
Donatello, *Gattamelata*, detail of head.

Donatello

(1386–1466)

In a city where competition was keen among the artists, Donatello emerged as the greatest sculptor of his time and as one of the greatest ever to live. His work was a combination of Classic style and Renaissance expression. He used the contraposto of the Greeks to suggest action. His figures seem capable of movement. The facial expressions provide images of pride, dignity and self-reliance—attitudes that were a part of the Renaissance. Although most were sculpted to stand in niches, they are no longer a part of the architecture. Many of Donatello's figures, sculpted in either marble or bronze, looked out over the daily life of the Florentines.

Among his outstanding later works, his bronze *David* (fig.9–7) is unique. It was the first life-size, freestanding nude statue since ancient times. It must have seemed

Interdisciplinary Connection

History: The Medici gained their power and wealth by becoming bankers to all of Europe. In the early fifteenth century Giovanni de Medici established the family fortune. Cosimo, Giovanni's son, established the first public library since ancient Roman times. Lorenzo, the grandson, built another library. The Laurentian Library—designed by Michelangelo and filled with hundreds of important books, manuscripts and documents—still stands in Florence, adjacent to the Medici family church of San Lorenzo.

9–8 Gattamelata requested in his will that this monument be built. His family had to get a waiver from the Venetian State in order to commission the work. **Previously this type of monument had been reserved for rulers.**

Donatello, *Gattamelata,* Equestrian Statue of Erasmo da Narni, about 1445–1450. Bronze, approximately 11' x 13' (3.4 x 4 m). Piazza del Santo, Padua.

Sidelight

Medici Patronage

The competition among artists of the early Renaissance was no less intense than the competition among wealthy Florentine leaders for political power. The Medici family emerged as the clear victor for political control of Florence. They were also highly important patrons of the arts. Three generations of Medici "princes"—Giovanni, Cosimo and Lorenzo—commissioned sculptures and architecture that turned Florence into a city of unsurpassed beauty. Their commissions provided artists with the income and freedom they needed to create some of the greatest works the world has known.

To be favored by the Medici assured success for any artist in Florence. In 1491, Giovanni commissioned Brunelleschi to design a parish church and sacristy space near the family home to honor the Medici patron saint, San Lorenzo. Donatello designed the sculpted ornament for the sacristy and also supplied a bronze pulpit.

In mid-century, political power passed to Giovanni's son, Cosimo de Medici. Cosimo continued the building and decoration of San Lorenzo (fig.9–2). In addition, Cosimo undertook the construction of a massive urban palace nearby.

Cosimo's grandson, Lorenzo the Magnificent, became the greatest patron, encouraging Michelangelo and Botticelli. During his rule, Florence flowered. When Lorenzo died in 1492, the greatest period in Renaissance art was also ending.

Higher-Order Thinking Skills

Ask students to compare *Gattamelata* (fig.9–9) to the *Equestrian Statue of Marcus Aurelius* (fig.6–44) from ancient Rome. Have students locate any equestrian statues in your community and find what they commemorate.

Consider the difficulties an artist might encounter in designing an equestrian statue. Focus particularly on the balance of size, power and control that must be achieved between the horse and rider.

revolutionary. It stands in a classic contraposto, its body in a slight S-curve with its weight firmly carried by the right leg. The youth's relaxed left foot toys with the severed head of Goliath. The body of the young David is wiry and smooth. Its gently swelling muscles contrast vividly with the crisp, straight edge of the sword and the shaggy head below. Donatello's faces are usually very expressive, but David's face seems calm and serene—almost Classical—while the face of Goliath is horrifying.

Commissioned by Cosimo de Medici, *David* was designed to be viewed from all angles and to stand free of any wall or niche. David's head is crowned with contemporary fighting headgear and a laurel wreath—another combination of ancient and contemporary traditions. Throughout the Middle Ages, David's victory over Goliath was symbolic of Christ's victory over sin and death. Yet, to the Florentines, it became symbolic of the victory of the small and self-sufficient over the brute force of much larger opponents.

In 1443, Donatello was commissioned to sculpt a huge equestrian statue to place before the Basilica in Padua, where it still stands (fig.9–8). The subject was a Venetian general, nicknamed *Gattamelata* ("Honeyed Cat"), who had died before the artist arrived in Padua. Donatello undoubtedly drew his ideas from the Classic statue of Marcus Aurelius in Rome. Donatello's bronze creation is huge in size and mounted on a high pedestal. The horse is gigantic, but is controlled by the domineering will of its rider. The rider's face (fig.9–9) is a powerful and idealized portrait of the general. The visual rhythms are beautifully coordinated, from the arched tail to the arched flank to the arched neck. It was the first large equestrian statue of the Renaissance and the first larger-than-life horse and rider since ancient Rome.

Contextual Information

The Church of San Marco

Between 1438 and 1445 Fra Angelico and his assistants painted a series of frescoes in the monks' cells at the monastery of San Marco, Florence. These paintings were a series of devotional images created for the purpose of meditation. The fresco of *The Annunciation* at San Marco (fig.9–12) was painted a bit later than the monks' cells.

Cosimo de Medici was the principal patron of the church of San Marco. He provided funds to extend the monastery around the church. In 1437 work began on the new monastery and library. Fra Angelico's fresco decoration was a part of this building campaign. Rooms were built around three sides of a cloister. A guest hospice, chapter house and refectory (dining room) also were built.

In 1444 Cosimo donated over 400 Greek and Latin manuscripts to the library, which became a vital component of the building complex. With his donation, San Marco became one of the largest and most important of the early public libraries in Italy.

San Marco housed the Dominican order of monks, which emphasized learning and study. The privacy of the individual monks' cells and the resources of the library of San Marco helped the monks in the fulfillment of these goals.

Painting

Almost a hundred years had passed since Giotto painted his magnificent and daring frescoes on the chapel walls in Padua. Gentile da Fabriano had brought a new realism in painting to Florence with his International style, which blended French and Italian Gothic style. It was only when a young man named Masaccio painted a chapel wall in Florence that Renaissance painting began. Painting would soon become the dominant art form of the Renaissance.

Masaccio

(1401–1428)

Masaccio revolutionized the art of painting when he was in his mid-twenties. He studied the International style of Gentile da Fabriano and combined visual perspective and fascination with texture with the monumental forms of Giotto to initiate Renaissance painting in Florence.

Tribute Money (fig.9–10), a fresco in the church of Santa Maria del Carmine, is one of only several paintings done by the young genius before his death at the age of twenty-seven. The New Testament illustration depicts three succeeding events at the same time. In the cen-

9–10 This painting shows three scenes from the biblical story of the Tribute Money. Can you identify them? Masaccio, *Tribute Money*, about 1427. Fresco. Brancacci Chapel, Santa Maria del Carmine, Florence.

9–11 How has Masaccio used light to give the figures such a strong sense of realism? Masaccio, *Tribute Money*, detail of figures.

tral group of figures (fig.9–11), Christ and his disciples are confronted by a Roman tax collector and asked to pay tribute to Caesar. Christ sends Peter to the Sea of Galilee where he finds the tribute money in the mouth of a fish (at the left). Peter is seen paying the tax collector (at the right).

Masaccio used light as never before seen in a painting. There is a single source of light coming from the right side. Notice how it brightens the right part of most of the figures and casts a dark shadow on the left sides. It appears to make the rounded legs, massive folds, expressive faces and three-dimensional bodies occupy real space.

No longer is there any indication of flatness or invented light.

Masaccio used atmospheric perspective to add to the sense of depth. Adding to the appearance of reality, the figures appear to be illuminated by the very real light coming from a window just to the right of where the fresco was painted.

Giotto's paintings had an illusionary depth of only a few feet, but Masaccio's depth seems endless. Look past the figures to the lake and the diminishing trees. The parallel lines of the building converge to a single vanishing point above the head of Christ. Christ's face was used as a model by painters for many years.

The halos still persist, but the bodies are no longer of the Middle Ages. They are solid and sculptural, convincing and natural under the folds of the cloaks.

Fra Angelico

(1400–1455)

Before Guido di Piero entered the Dominican order and changed his name to Fra Angelico ("Fra" means "Brother"), he was already a painter in the Late Gothic tradition. He became a prior, or high ranking administrator, of the Monastery of San Marco in Florence and filled its walls with lyrical frescoes, such as *The Annunciation* (fig.9–12). Unlike the powerful work of Masaccio or Giotto, the figures of the angel Gabriel and the Virgin Mary seem tender and frail. They are placed in an arched and vaulted porch that is painted in careful perspective.

Fra Angelico was the Florentine master of landscape painting, as seen in the *Adoration of the Magi* (fig.9–13), a **tondo** (a painting round in shape) painted in tempera on wood. It is the work of both Fra Angelico and Fra Filippo Lippi, a Florentine contemporary who finished it when Fra Angelico went to Rome. It reflects the past in its decorative color and line, but also

9–13 During the Renaissance, artists frequently collaborated on commissions. Fra Angelico and Fra Filippo Lippi, *Adoration of the Magi*. Tempera on wood, 54" (137 cm) diameter. National Gallery of Art, Washington DC, Samuel H. Kress Collection.

foretells the future of Renaissance painting. Mary and the Christ Child are the focal point. A richly dressed group of wise men, together with hordes of other figures in fine clothing, are paying them homage. Although the perspective is not accurate in every way, it shows great depth of space. The introduction of nearly naked figures of boys

watching the procession hints at the future Florentine fascination with figure painting. The animals and people in the stable foretell the painting of common, everyday subjects. The landscape elements of flowers, trees, mountains and sky indicate the Renaissance interest in nature.

9–12 Can you identify the two types of Classical capitals the artist has placed atop the columns? Fra Angelico, *The Annunciation*, 1440–1450. Fresco. Monastery of San Marco, Florence.

Contextual Information

Uccello

The three panels of the *Battle of San Romano* are housed in the Uffizi Gallery, Florence; the Louvre, Paris; and the National Gallery, London. They originally decorated a bed-chamber in the Medici Palace. They were placed just above a wooden wainscoting and originally measured more than 34 feet in length.

Paolo Uccello

(1397–1475)

Perspective was of such great concern to Paolo Uccello that he once made a linear diagram of a seventy-two-sided polyhedron. Here, we see a perspective drawing of a chalice that Uccello made in pen and ink (fig.9–14).

His fascination with this scientific aspect of painting is seen in *The Battle of San Romano* (fig.9–15). This complex composition is one part of a three-panel painting now in three separate museums. It was once a continuous work in the Medici Palace. *The Battle of San Romano* is a study in pattern, contrasting values and perspective (fig.9–b). The foreground becomes a stage for the main action. Riders joust with each other—left and right, into the picture plane and out. The horses are plump and artificial-looking as they prance on the stage. The landscape near San Romano in the Arno Valley is distant and contains many small figures. The fallen warrior is also in perspective. Here, Uccello has used *foreshortening* to create the feeling of the body pointing toward the viewer.

9–14 Today, wire frame models similar to this are generated by computer.
Paolo Uccello, *Perspective Study of a Chalice*, 1430–1440. Pen and ink, 13 3/8" x 9 1/2" (34 x 24 cm). Department of Drawings and Prints, Uffizi Gallery, Florence.

9–15 Does this battle scene seem real? Why or why not?
Paolo Uccello, *Battle of San Romano*, 1445. Tempera on panel, 6' x 10' 5 3/4" (1.82 x 3.2 m). National Gallery, London.

Performing Arts Connection

Renaissance Instrumental Music

Renaissance music, from about the fifteenth to the early seventeenth century, burst its sacred bonds as secular city guilds and imperial courts competed for the finest entertainment to demonstrate their cultivated tastes. Instrumental music—such as suites (works in several sections, each based on a dance) and compositions for the organ, harpsichord, clavichord, spinet and virginal—separated from vocal forms.

During the Renaissance, the church, nobility and royalty paid for all the music that was written and performed. Ask students why they think this was so.

• What might these individuals have wished the music to reflect about their tastes?

• How much individual freedom of expression do students think composers and performers had?

• Are there forms of music today that symbolize the character of a person, country or group?

• How do students feel when they listen to band marches, national anthems, gospel, soul, rap or jazz?

• Do these forms express something about the people who wrote and/or perform them?

Piero della Francesca

(1420–1492)

Piero spent several years around 1439 studying in Florence. He was an apt student. From Masaccio's paintings, he learned about form. From Fra Angelico, he learned about light. From Brunelleschi, he learned scientific perspective. In fact, Piero also wrote an extensive book describing methods of working with perspective and proving its geometric exactness.

His painting has a cool and severe character, almost like the classical severity of Greek sculpture. Piero used mathematics to design his pictorial space effectively.

In his emphasis on mathematical precision, he is closely related to many of today's contemporary abstract artists. His figures are scientifically accurate, but are unemotional and possess no warmth. The poses and facial expressions produce a "frozen-in-action" feeling. The light in his paintings seems to be at a low angle, like early morning, and produces solid and rounded forms.

Piero della Francesca's masterpiece is the huge wall of the Church of San Francesco in Arezzo. Several tiers of paintings relate the entire story of *The Legend of the True Cross.* In the scene reproduced here (fig.9–16), Piero depicts the actual

discovery and proving of the True Cross. On the left side, the cross of Christ is found by Helena, the mother of Constantine the Great. On the right side, it is proved the True Cross by the miracles of healing it causes. Even though such a discovery would normally cause tremendous joy and excitement, Piero's figures are cool and calm. In this fresco, you can see how interested Piero was in light and how he used it to create solid geometric forms. With accurate perspective, both linear and aerial, the artist also produces a feeling of great depth in space.

9–16 Describe the narrative (story) the artist has depicted.
Piero della Francesca, *The Discovery and Proving of the True Cross,* about 1453–1454. Fresco. Church of San Francesco, Arezzo.

Contextual Information

Botticelli

Botticelli had such a great reputation as an artist in Florence that Pope Sixtus IV in Rome asked him to be superintendent of paintings for his new chapel (the Sistine). Botticelli painted several paintings there with other leading painters and earned a "considerable sum of money," according to Vasari. In the sixteenth century Pope Julius II would commission Michelangelo to paint the ceiling and altar wall of the same chapel.

Humanism and Neoplatonism

Two words that arise in discussions of the early Renaissance are *humanism* and *Neoplatonism*. Humanism is centered around human abilities and potential. In the visual arts, humanists found inspiration in the art of ancient Greece and Rome, where the human form was held to be the epitome of perfection. Neoplatonism sprang from the beliefs and teachings of the Platonic Academy that formed within the courts of Lorenzo de Medici. The Neoplatonists struggled to reconcile Classical philosophies with the Christian religion. Botticelli was the leading painter in this group, and his work has been interpreted through the writings of the Florentine Neoplatonists, particularly Marselio Ficino, who spent much of his life translating and writing commentaries on the works of Plato.

Sandro Botticelli

(1445–1510)

In the last third of the fifteenth century, few of the founders of the Renaissance were still living. The Florentine struggle for survival had eased, and the patricians lived lives of luxury. Artists continued to explore the Renaissance scientific appreciation of nature and the human body. They also often used the poetic and unreal subject matter of allegories and myths.

Botticelli's huge painting of the *Birth of Venus* (fig.9–17) is an example of a scene based on traditional mythology. Venus, the goddess of love, rises from the sea and emerges from a shell. On the left, West Winds, looking like puffing angels, push her toward land. The figure on the right is Spring, ready to toss a robe around Venus's unclothed body.

Often mythological and allegorical scenes were considered metaphors for Christian ideas. In this case, Venus, the water and Spring could symbolize Christ, baptism and John the Baptist. Baptism, like the birth of the celestial Venus, signifies the rebirth of humanity.

Botticelli was a master of delicate lines. His figures and fabrics are beautifully drawn. The figures seem outlined with an extremely fine line. The pale colors and the floating appearance of the figures add to the unreality of the subject. Notice the stylized waves in the sea and the spring flowers blown by the wind. It is one of the first Italian works on canvas instead of wood panel. Botticelli used gold to heighten the color of hair and robes and to add a feeling of elegant refinement.

Botticelli's *The Adoration of the Magi* (fig.9–18) reveals another characteristic of some late-fifteenth-century painting. The wise men and many others who have come to see the Holy Family are actually portraits of Italian contemporaries. Each is painted with very individualized features. Notice the figure on the far right of the painting that gazes directly at us. It is believed that this is a self-portrait of the

9–17 Use the text to identify the characters here. What elements are classical?
Sandro Botticelli, *Birth of Venus*, after 1482. Tempera on canvas, 5' 8 7/8" x 9' (1.75 x 2.8 m). Uffizi Gallery, Florence.

1400s
Tea ceremony, Japan

1409
First book printed with metal type, Korea

World Cultural Timeline

1403
22,937 volume encyclopedia written in China

1440–1550
The Book of the Thousand and One Nights written in Arabic

Multicultural Connection

The Tea Ceremony

Sado (cha-no-yu) is the Japanese term given to the tea ceremony that started in China and was brought to Japan by merchants and scholars who had visited China. Tea, the Japanese believed, cleansed the body, purified the mind and encouraged thinking and meditation.

A separate house or a room in the main house, often surrounded by a garden, was set aside for the tea ceremony. The room usually had low doors so that a person had to stoop to a humble position in order to enter. Depending on the season, there were specific times of the day most suitable for holding the ceremony, and the number of guests was usually limited to five.

Every step of the ceremony, even the order in which people entered, took place in a prescribed manner. Conversation was limited to the subjects of art, music and poetry. Pots and cups in this ceremony revealed that beauty can be found in simple objects. Skillfully hand-modeled, the cups, boxes and jars used in the tea ceremony were deliberately uneven in shape and often showed marks of the potter's hands. The tea bowls were cylindrical.

• Have students discuss and compare the similarities of the tea ceremony with the artistic values of Italian artists of the High Renaissance period.

artist. The arrangement of the figures is quite complex. The composition is calm at the center and active at the outside. Botticelli presents the serene Italian countryside in the background. Botticelli's scene is elegant and luxurious, especially when compared with Masaccio's and Giotto's treatments or to the events as they took place in the Bible.

Botticelli was not alone in his painting activity at the end of the century. Florence, Rome and other Italian cities enjoyed the works of artists such as Ghirlandaio, Perugino and Signorelli.

9–19 Artists sometimes placed themselves in their own paintings. These self-portraits often look out toward the viewer.
Sandro Botticelli, *The Adoration of the Magi*. detail of self-portrait.

9–18 Botticelli painted this popular subject seven times during the course of his career.
Sandro Botticelli, *The Adoration of the Magi*. early 1470s. Tempera on panel, 27 1/2" x 41" (70 x 104 cm). Uffizi Gallery, Florence.

Higher-Order Thinking Skills

Neoplatonists were able to "read" *Birth of Venus* as a naturalistic allegory for its hidden meaning. The text on page 272 explains some of the imagery, and more can be found in other sources. One had to be "in the know" to fully understand such paintings. What contemporary visual allegories can students document and explain? (Hint: Commercials and music videos.) Ask them to discuss what viewers in the future will have to know to interpret these works.

The Thousand and One Nights
Islamic writers produced a great variety of literature. Arabs had a strong tradition of oral storytelling that has survived in the form of about two hundred stories, fairy tales, anecdotes and fables. Eventually more stories were added to bring the total up to 1001. This collection included such Persian, Arabian and Indian tales as "Ali Baba and the Forty Thieves," "Aladdin and His Magic Lamp," and "Sinbad the Sailor." Each story is characterized by the use of a frame story, a narrative device that gives the collection continuity.

The *Arabian Nights*, or "The Thousand and One Nights," is a collection of these stories set within the framework of the romance of King Shahriyar and his wife Scheherazade. This book tells how she saved her life by entertaining her husband every night with ongoing fairy tales.

• Fairy tales come from many different parts of the world. Have students select and identify the origins of some well-known fairy tales.

• *Arabian Nights* was used to entertain the king. Have students research the oral traditions of Native American and African cultures.

Contextual Information

Mantegna

Mantegna, like many other artists, learned his skills by drawing from casts of antique statues and copying paintings that his teacher brought from Florence and Rome. Later, as a result of criticism that his figures were too rigid, he began to paint from life.

9–20 What effect does the artist's use of extreme foreshortening have on you, the viewer?
Andrea Mategna, *Dead Christ*, after 1466. Canvas, 26 3/4" x 31 7/8" (68 x 81 cm). Brera Gallery, Milan.

Venice and Northern Italy

During the early fifteenth century in northern Italy, Venice became a dominant economic and political power. Its art remained a blend of Byzantine and Gothic styles. Gentile Fabriano and Uccello visited Venice and worked there for short periods. They influenced native Venetian artists to a small extent.

It was Donatello's eleven-year stay in Padua, however, that revolutionized Venetian art. He brought the Florentine interest in perspective, form, anatomy and the classic tradition. The Venetians quickly combined these with their fascina-tion for color and texture. Venetian artists developed a dynamic and exciting style that finally outshone Florence in its richness of expression.

Andrea Mantegna
(1431–1506)

Born in northern Italy, near Padua, Mantegna was already a polished artist by the time he was seventeen. He learned much from the Florentine artists who visited the north. He soon mastered form and anatomy. He excelled in working with perspective, especially fore-shortening.

In his painting *Dead Christ* (fig.9–20), Mantegna used extreme foreshortening. The body of Christ lies on a slab of marble. The viewer can look directly into the face of Christ and at the same time see the nail holes in Christ's hands and feet.

The strong realism combined with the unusual perspective makes this image fascinating, yet unset-tling, to the modern viewer. To the devout fifteenth-century Italian, however, it was an image that aided meditation. This painting, in fact, originally may have been placed outside the bedroom of a northern Italian noblewoman.

Giovanni Bellini

(1431–1516)

The master painter of Venice in the last part of the fifteenth century was Giovanni Bellini. His entire family was very artistic, and his sister married Mantegna. Bellini was greatly influenced by his brother-in-law in his early years of painting. Then with the arrival of the oil painting technique in Italy, he developed a richness of color and depth of value unequaled in Italy at the time.

In his portrait of *The Doge Leonardo Loredan* (fig.9–21), Bellini concentrated on the facial features of the Doge. The Doge was elected at age sixty-five to be the leader of the Venetian Republic. The sensitive face is beautifully captured by the artist. The light from the left softly models the forms. The extreme detail and the use of oil paints show the influence of contemporary painters in Flanders in northern Europe. Undoubtedly, works by these painters were brought to Venice at the time. Like Flemish artists, Bellini has superbly painted the luxurious brocade cloth of the Doge and contrasted the softly lit figure with the darkened and flat background. The artist signed his name as though it were on a bit of paper stuck on a piece of frame.

9–21 Locate the light source for this portrait.
Giovanni Bellini, *The Doge Leonardo Loredan*, 1502. Oil on panel, 24" x 17 1/2" (61 x 45 cm). National Gallery, London.

Higher-Order Thinking Skills

While the *Dead Christ* is considered an excellent example of extreme foreshortening, Mantegna made some adjustments to what would actually be seen in such a view to achieve the effect that he wanted. A student can model this pose, and others in the class can use the artist's vantage point to assess where Mantegna deviated from what he actually saw. Let students discover that, when seen from that vantage point, the feet will hide the rest of the body.

Lesson 9.1 Review

1 Which family ruled Florence during most of the fifteenth century?

2 Who designed the dome of the Florence cathedral?

3 Tell the story of the competition to select an artist to design the Florence baptistry doors. Describe Brunelleschi's and Ghiberti's panels for the competition.

4 What statue was the first life-size, freestanding nude made since those of classical Rome?

5 Which Roman statue was probably the inspiration for Donatello's equestrian statue of Gattamelata in Padua?

6 In what art principle was Uccello most interested in his *The Battle of San Romano*?

7 What is the subject of Piero della Francesca's frescoes in the Church of San Francisco in Arezzo, Italy?

8 Describe Botticelli's *The Adoration of the Magi*. Whose portraits were painted as the faces of the guests?

9 What means did Mantegna use to dramatize his painting of the *Dead Christ*?

10 From what city was Bellini? What characteristics in his paintings demonstrate the influence of Northern European painters?

Lesson 9.1 Review Answers

1 The Medici family

2 Filippo Brunelleschi

3 Seven final contestants carved panels depicting the sacrifice of Isaac. Brunelleschi's panel is very dramatic with the angel grabbing Abraham's arm just before he slits Isaac's neck. Ghiberti's panel is more unified, harmonious and balanced, but not as violent or dramatic. In Ghiberti's panel, Abraham's raised knife does not touch Isaac and the figures, particularly Isaac, look like classical Greek sculptures.

4 Donatello's bronze *David*

5 The classic statue of Marcus Aurelius in Rome

6 Depth or perspective, which is technically an art element—*The Battle of San Romano* is a study in pattern, contrasting values and perspective.

7 *The Legend of the True Cross*

8 The wise men and guests visiting Mary and the baby Jesus are detailed portraits of Botticelli's Italian contemporaries. The rhythm moves from the center of the composition outward to the edges. The center is calm with more activity on the outside. A serene Italian countryside forms the background. The linear perspective of the stable directs the eye to the center of this elegant and luxurious scene.

9 Extreme foreshortening

10 Bellini was from Venice. Like northern European painters he used extreme (fine) detail and oil paints.

Lesson 9.2

During the High Renaissance, Rome became the art capital of Italy, and great artists throughout Europe were summoned by the pope to complete splendid commissions that glorified the papal state.

Warm-up

Direct students to draw a single horizontal line across a blank sheet of paper. Tell them to place a dot somewhere along the line. Next have them draw two straight lines veering out diagonally from this point to form an upside-down V. Finally, ask them to sketch simple forms along these diagonal lines, decreasing their size as they move back toward the horizontal line. Explore if their drawings suggest a sense of depth. Explain to the class that they have just demonstrated single-point perspective, a technique developed in the Renaissance and used throughout Western art history to evoke the illusion of space. Can students identify the use of single-point perspective in Raphael's *School of Athens* (fig.9–30) and how it gives order and a central focus to the composition?

Objectives

Students should be able to:

Identify Rome as the art center of Western Europe during the High Renaissance.

Understand the importance of the pope's role in commissioning art to glorify the church.

Vocabulary Definitions

chiaroscuro (key-ah-ross-*kyoo*-roh) A technique for modeling forms in painting by which the lighted parts seem to emerge from surrounding dark areas. Strong contrast of dark and light values in painting.

sfumato (sfoo-*mah*-toh) A slight blurring of the edges of figures and objects in a painting, creating a hazy feeling and aerial perspective.

painterly style or ***painterly quality*** A technique of painting in which forms are depicted by patches of color rather than by hard and precise edges. Brush-strokes are left visible as part of the surface of the painting.

9.2 High Renaissance

BETWEEN ABOUT 1495 AND 1527, a series of powerful and ambitious popes created a new force in Italy—a papal state, with Rome as its capital. Rome eventually took the lead from Florence and became the art capital of Europe.

The popes, living splendidly and luxuriously themselves, embellished the city with great works of art. They invited artists from all over Italy to Rome and provided them with challenging and exciting commissions. The High Renaissance lasted a very short time—a mere twenty or so years. But, during this period, artists in Rome and Venice produced great works that would influence European art for at least three centuries.

During the High Renaissance, artists began to be viewed as geniuses rather than craftspersons. It was widely believed that artists, like poets, created their work under divine inspiration. Artists of the Early Renaissance had relied on formulas, scientific perspective, ratios and proportions to structure their work. Now, the artists of the High Renaissance often disregarded those rules and let their feelings dictate their styles. Painters, sculptors and architects created works that were more expressive than those of their predecessors. Some of the most well-known artists in the history of the world worked at this time. Their achievements were so great that today we know them simply by their first names: Michelangelo, Raphael, Leonardo.

Key Notes
- Rome becomes the art center of Europe.
- The notion of artist as genius is born.
- Venetian artists make dramatic innovations in painting.

Vocabulary
chiaroscuro
sfumato
painterly

Special Feature
Leonardo da Vinci
(1452–1519)

If the ideal "Renaissance man" was to be knowledgeable in all things, then Leonardo was it! This artist-genius was ahead of his time not only in painting, sculpture and architecture, but in engineering, military science, botany, anatomy, geology, aerodynamics and optics, to mention only a few of the areas in which he made original contributions. Not only was he interested in these fields, he was considered an expert in all of them. He left *ten thousand* pages of drawing, ideas, sketches and notes, all written left-handed in reverse, or mirror, images.

Although he left only a dozen or so works, Leonardo considered painting the supreme form of art. To sculpt, he said, was simply to copy nature. To paint was to be "Lord and God" of the subject and

9–23 This painting is undergoing a long-term restoration. It is a slow, inch-by-inch process because the condition of the work is so poor. Always an experimenter, Leonardo painted on dry plaster with an oil and tempera mixture. Unfortunately, it began peeling almost immediately.
Leonardo da Vinci, *The Last Supper*, c. 1495–1498. Tempera wall mural, 15' 2" x 28' 10" (4.6 x 8.8 m). Santa Maria della Grazie, Milan.

Teach

Art History/Aesthetics: Ask students if they know anyone who is an expert at painting, sculpture, architecture, engineering, military science, botany, anatomy, geology, aerodynamics and optics.

- Is it possible to be thoroughly knowledgeable about all these fields? Direct them to read on pages 276 and 277 about Leonardo da Vinci's astounding achievements.

- By looking at figs.9–22, 9–23 and 9–24, do students think Leonardo's multifaceted abilities detracted from his artistic talent?

- Leonardo's *Mona Lisa* (fig.9–24) remains one of the best-recognized artworks in the Western world. Instead of

linear perspective, how did Leonardo use color in a new way to create the illusion of depth in his painting? Have students review the text to understand how Leonardo's invention of *chiaroscuro* and *sfumato* helped make his paintings different from those of any previous artist.

Art History: Although the idea of the artist as genius was generated in the Renaissance, would students wish to have been one of these great masters? Share with the class that the pope, who was the most powerful man in all of Italy during the High Renaissance, would summon artists from around Europe to come and work in Rome on exciting commissions. However, how much freedom do students think these honored artists had to create what, how

9–22 Use the text to identify the characters and the action in this painting.
Leonardo da Vinci, *Virgin of the Rocks*, about 1485. Oil on panel (transferred to canvas), 75" x 43 1/2" (190 x 110 cm). The Louvre, Paris.

9–24 How does Leonardo use chiaroscuro and sfumato in this work?
Leonardo da Vinci, *Mona Lisa*, 1503–1506. Oil on panel, 30 1/4" x 21" (77 x 53 cm). The Louvre, Paris.

art, a point on which he and Michelangelo never agreed.

Though trained in Florence, Leonardo created most of his works away from that city. *The Virgin of the Rocks* (fig.9–22) was painted in Milan. The figures in *The Virgin of the Rocks* are joined together in a triangular composition. The angel points to the infant John the Baptist, who is blessed by the Christ Child and sheltered by the Virgin's loving hand. Leonardo leads the viewer from one figure to another, but the viewer's eyes finally come to rest on the face of the Virgin. Light forms emerge from the background to create a dramatic contrast

of values. This extreme contrast of dark and light values is called *chiaroscuro*.

The Last Supper (fig.9–23) was painted on the wall of the dining hall of the monastery of Santa Maria della Grazie in Milan. Despite its ruined state, the painting is extraordinarily impressive in both form and emotion. Christ and the apostles are celebrating Passover. Suddenly a horrible announcement is made. Christ, with outstretched hands, has just said, "One of you will betray me." A shudder passes through the group as they ask themselves, "Is it I?" The intense shock and amazement is clearly visible.

The Last Supper is one of the Western world's most well-known paintings. Leonardo also painted the world's most famous portrait, the *Mona Lisa* (fig.9–24). The woman sits in a relaxed position in front of a typical Leonardo landscape. The distant hills and mountains are partially obscured by a light haze, or *sfumato*, an effect that allowed Leonardo to create a feeling of enormous depth.

The *Mona Lisa*'s "smile" and her identity have been the subject of endless speculation. We do know that painting must have been a particular favorite of Leonardo's. The artist carried it with him until he died.

and when they wanted? As an example, explain that Pope Julius II commanded Michelangelo to paint the Sistine Chapel (page 281) and continually rushed him so that it would be complete before the pope's death. Julius II was impervious to Michelangelo's physical exhaustion and the injury he sustained from painting on a six-story-high scaffolding in a prone position for over four years and five months.

Evaluate

Ask students what the position was of artists in Renaissance society. Were they viewed as mere craftspeople? Had artists been perceived as celebrities in previous generations? Have students come up with a list of today's creative "geniuses" in the arts whose names are

as immediately recognizable as those of Leonardo, Michelangelo, Raphael and Titian.

Reteach

Ask students whom they would label as a "renaissance" person in today's society.

• How about professional athletes who are successful in multiple sports?

• Would single mothers—raising large families on a small income, attending school, holding a job and providing a warm and stimulating home environment—be candidates for "renaissance woman" status?

• Are students themselves proficient and interested in more than one area?

• What types of characteristics are common to "renaissance" people?

• What traits can students add to a list that might include energetic, innovative, curious and persistent?

• What are the disadvantages of being good at and interested in many things simultaneously?

• Is there ever a time when it is better to be singly focused?

Ask students to consider what their thinking was like when they were creating a composition with single-point perspective in the warm-up exercise.

• Did their thoughts change in size, speed or mood over the course of the activity?

Contextual Information

Michelangelo

Florence in 1475, the year of Michelangelo's birth, had approximately 70,000 citizens. Located on the banks of the Arno River, the city was then surrounded by five miles of walls. It had 100 monasteries and convents, 4 hospitals, 66 doctors and more than 60 palaces. Hospitals and doctors treated sicknesses caused by lack of sewers, the plague, battles and fires.

While studying in the court of Lorenzo de Medici, Michelangelo was influenced by Neoplatonist thought. At the same time the Neoplatonists were flourishing, a Dominican monk from the Church of San Marco in Florence was condemning the Medici and Neoplatonist way of thinking. The monk's name was Savonarola, who preached a series of sermons in the Cathedral of Florence. He denounced the sins and worldliness of Renaissance Florence with such force that his listeners wept and repented. Michelangelo heard these thunderous sermons, and the moral conflict between his love of human beauty and anatomy and his fear of God's punishment for sin was to haunt him for the rest of his life.

David

It is said that Michelangelo would look at a block of stone in front of him and envision a figure inside. As he carved, he felt as though he were releasing it from a prison of stone. The stone from which *David* was carved had been lying on the grounds of the Florence cathedral for a number of years. During the 1460s it had been cut into, but no one was able to work with it because it was very long (approximately 15 feet) and thin. Michelangelo was commissioned to sculpt a figure of David from it.

The sculpture of David was seriously damaged in a fight after the expulsion of the Medicis from Florence in 1527. Vasari and a friend went to the piazza, picked up pieces of the broken arm and saved the work from further harm.

Michelangelo Buonarroti

(1475–1564)

Recognized by his contemporaries as "the greatest man ever known to the arts," Michelangelo dominated the High Renaissance. His artistic genius influenced the Late Renaissance and beyond. Born of a poor family, he knew at an early age that he wanted to be an artist. When he was thirteen, his father finally allowed him to study with the Florentine artist, Ghirlandaio, where he learned the art of fresco painting. After a short time, Michelangelo was accepted by Lorenzo de Medici into his school for sculptors and was treated as a son in the Medici household. Here, he studied with Bertoldo, a pupil of Donatello, and developed an intense interest in Greek and Roman culture.

His earliest masterpiece, the *Pietà* (fig.9–25), was done in Rome about 1500. It is a work of profound Christian feeling. Mary holds the almost nude body of Christ on her lap. She does not grieve sorrowfully over her son, but accepts his death as the necessary fulfillment of humanity's salvation. The folds of drapery and the feeling of flesh are superbly handled. The seated mother of Christ is overly large when compared with the body of her son. Michelangelo was concerned with the overall appearance and visual effect of the pyramidal composition rather than with exact proportions.

The work was carved from a single block of marble. The sculpture is polished completely in the style of the Early Renaissance. In his later works, parts are often left in roughly chiseled condition that contrasted with polished areas. Michelangelo signed the work on the band across Mary's chest.

Michelangelo's heroic *David* (fig.9–26) goes far beyond imitating nature. It is huge in size and superhuman in its muscular perfection. The young boy of the Bible has a manly body and an expression that is angry and defiant. The empty sling drapes over his left shoulder and a round stone is cradled in his huge right hand. He stands relaxed, but ever alert—a god-like being, half Apollo and half Hercules. It expresses Michelangelo's belief that human beauty is the outward indication of divine spirit. At only twenty-nine, Michelangelo was declared the greatest sculptor in Italy.

9–25 Michelangelo made many adjustments in the anatomy of these figures to enhance the composition of the whole.
Michelangelo, *Pietà*, 1499–1500. Marble, 68 1/2" (1.74 m) high. St. Peter's, Vatican, Rome.

When finished, *David* was placed in the main square in front of the Florentine town hall, or Palazzo Vecchio. The original work is now protected indoors at the Academy in Florence. A duplicate stands in the original location in the piazza.

In 1505, Pope Julius II called Michelangelo to Rome to design his monumental tomb. The pope wanted forty over-life-size figures to be placed in St. Peter's, which was then being built. Because of innumerable interruptions, including the painting of the Sistine Chapel, the work was scaled down until only

three sculptures were made, and the tomb was placed in a small church in Rome. The sculpture of *Moses* (fig.9–27) is now the dominant feature of the tomb, although it was carved to be on the second level in the original design. An incredibly powerful figure, Moses seems ready to burst into action from his seated position. The tablets of the law are only a prop as Michelangelo awes the viewer with the rippling muscles and stern glare of the prophet. Hair, beard and cloth are all deeply carved. The figure, with its dynamic power and intensity, seems ready to

battle the world in defense of God's newly given law. Michelangelo had studied many ancient sculptures. From them, he gained knowledge of Classical sculpture techniques and the powerful representation of human forms.

In 1546, the seventy-one-year-old artist was in poor health. Yet, he accepted without salary the commission to finish the construction of St. Peter's. Donato Bramante, the original architect, had died while construction was underway. The huge basilica was untouched for so long that trees were growing from

9–26 The figure still holds the stone which will kill the giant, Goliath, in his hand. What moment has Michelangelo chosen to portray in the story of David and Goliath? Michelangelo, *David*, 1501–1504. Marble, about 13' 5" (4.08 m) high. Gallery of the Academy, Florence.

9–27 This figure was meant to be placed on the second story of the tomb of Pope Julius II. The plan for the tomb was changed and cut back in size. As a result, this figure was placed on the floor where it loses the impact that Michelangelo intended. Michelangelo, *Moses*, about 1513–1515. Marble, 7' 8 1/2" (2.35 m) high. San Pietro in Vincoli, Rome.

Interdisciplinary Connection

History: The Age of Exploration and the Renaissance were contemporaneous. What did they have in common? How might we compare the explorer Columbus and the artist Michelangelo? Was Italy (as a country) involved in exploration and colonization? Why or why not?

Higher-Order Thinking Skills

1 Have students compare and contrast Michelangelo's *Moses* (fig.9–27) with Claus Sluter's *Moses with Two Prophets* (fig.8–37). Then ask students to compare and contrast Donatello's *David* (fig.9–7) with that of Michelangelo's (fig.9–26), paying special attention to what they think were the personalities of the two Davids, who are about the same age as high-school students. Ask if the figures seem older, younger or the same age as typical high-school students. Why?

2 Explore with the class how art can often persuade viewers to accept an idea or a point of view. For instance, during the European Renaissance, the papacy and courts used art and architecture (as well as music, dance and drama) to impress others with their power and prestige. Have students look at Michelangelo's *David* and also note the height of the figure. Ask them to describe how gazing up at this enormous man might make them feel. What do they think David might have felt about fighting the giant Goliath? The figure's exquisite beauty and serene confidence instilled the Florentine people with courage to fight the armies of Milan. How are images in contemporary American society used to persuade us of things? Have students examine a number of visual images, perhaps on CD covers or magazine advertisements, and analyze how the artists have used these images to create desire, understanding or rejection of an idea or a product.

Contextual Information

Sistine Chapel

The chapel is named after Pope Sixtus IV for whom it was constructed in 1477–1480 to serve as the papal palace chapel. The chapel is lit by twelve windows, six on each side. Sixtus called on painters from Umbria and Florence to decorate the walls. His nephew, Pope Julius II (1503–1513) commissioned Michelangelo to redecorate the ceiling. The original ceiling had a starry sky depicted on it. Twenty years later Michelangelo was called upon by Clement VII and Paul III to paint the wall behind the altar with a scene of the Last Judgment. It is interesting to note that the chapel's measurements (132 feet long, 44 feet wide and 68 feet high) are exactly the same as those given in the Bible for Solomon's Temple.

The chapel is the official private chapel of the pope and is used for the conclaves held for the election of a new pope.

the huge arches. Michelangelo went to work immediately on the basilica. He slightly altered Bramante's plan. Although he retained the shape of the Greek cross, he redesigned the exterior, built the rear of the church, and designed the enormous dome (fig.9–28) which was completed after his death.

The exterior walls took on a sculptural quality that produces an upward thrust toward the dome. The hemispherical dome of Bramante's design was replaced by a high, pointed, double-shelled dome (like Brunelleschi's) placed on a tall drum. The heavily sculpted lantern completes the upward visual movement of the walls, drum and dome. The lantern is crowned by a large cross. The dome, the largest in the world, rests on four pendentives and four huge piers inside the church. Although the nave was lengthened later and a new facade was added, the imprint of Michelangelo can be easily detected in the present basilica.

Working on sculptures until six days before he died, Michelangelo said on his deathbed, "I regret that I am dying just as I am beginning to learn the alphabet of my profession."

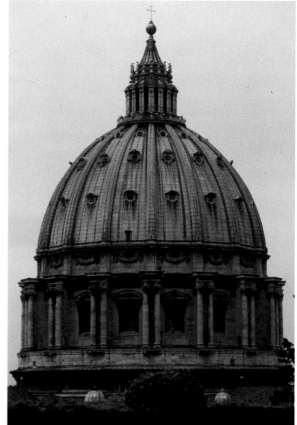

9–28 Compare this dome to Brunelleschi's for the Cathedral of Florence.
Michelangelo. *Dome of St. Peter's*, 1546–1564. The Vatican, Rome.

1450 **Great Mosque at Kilwa built, East Africa**	1457 **City of Edo (now Tokyo), Japan is founded**

World Cultural Timeline

1453 **Shin Sawba, Burma's first woman ruler, takes throne**	1470 **Road systems begun, Inca Empire**

Multicultural Connection

Kilwa

Beginning around 1100 along the coast of East Africa, a series of city-states developed. These port cities became independent states that included the city itself and its surrounding territory. Kilwa, the southernmost port in the Indian Ocean trade route, was the most prosperous of these city-states. The Great Mosque at Kilwa was built in the mid-1400s. At that time Kilwa also had a large palace, irrigated gardens and multistoried stone houses.

• Have students use the timelines in Chapter 4 to determine what other cultures were thriving at the time Kilwa flourished.

Window in Time

The Sistine Ceiling and Its Restoration

The painting of the Sistine Chapel ceiling was a monumental undertaking that took Michelangelo four years and five months to complete. It contains four large and five smaller Old Testament scenes. In addition, there are over 400 figures on the ceiling that fill the architectural elements and separate the main scenes.

To paint the gigantic *Last Judgment* on the end wall of the Sistine Chapel, Michelangelo had to climb between six and seven levels of scaffolding every day. Once he fell, badly injuring a leg. Between 1536 and 1541, he labored on the wall, producing an incredible work of the horror of hell and the reward of eternal life in heaven. When the *Last Judgment* was unveiled in 1541, Pope Paul III was so overcome he fell to his knees in prayer.

The Sistine Chapel ceiling and the wall with the *Last Judgment* were filled with dark tortured figures commonly believed to express the tortured genius of their creator. However, some of the darkness was due to the grime that had accumulated on the ceiling. At every papal Mass, oil lamps, incense and hundreds of candles were burned and their combined soot had collected on the ceiling. The roof also leaked and salts washed through. Attempts to undo the damage only made it worse.

The *Last Judgment*, being more accessible than the ceiling, fell more frequently into the hands of early restorers. A common fault was coating the frescoes with animal glue, or *size*. At first the glue, acting like varnish, enhanced the fresco's colors, but eventually it darkened. Then someone would add another coat of size. More torches. Candles. Salt stains. Glue, torches, candles, glue. Eventually the dark skin on the fresco was thicker than the paint beneath it.

Finally, in 1979, four hundred years after its completion, restorers began to clean the paintings of the Sistine Chapel, this time correctly. It took much experimentation and argument, but eventually a method was agreed upon. The team of experts who restored the Sistine Chapel took ten years to clean what took Michelangelo four years to paint. Using sponges soaked in a special mixture of chemicals and pure water, they carefully removed the layers of grime to reveal the original bright colors underneath. At last, the scaffolding and safety netting, which had obscured the frescoes in the Sistine Chapel for fourteen years, were removed.

Everyone, including scholars, were stunned by the results of the restoration. In place of the dark, often foreboding, colors were brilliantly rich and sparkling bright hues. Most were thrilled with the new Sistine ceiling and *Last Judgment*. Some experts, however, believed that the restoration was inaccurate and that touches of paint added by Michelangelo after the plaster had dried were removed by restorers. The controversy raged rather hotly for a while with scholars taking sides and battling with a barrage of articles and interviews.

No doubt, for as long as the frescoes exist, there will be heated arguments over how they should really look. However, the Vatican has insured that the paintings will not again suffer damage. They have installed a climate control system that filters dust and chemical pollution from the air and monitors the temperature and humidity so that no moisture can collect on the frescoes. This is a major concern in a room that receives up to 19,000 visitors a day.

Overall view of Sistine Chapel.

Higher-Order Thinking Skills

Ask what Michelangelo learned from Brunelleschi's doming of the Cathedral of Florence. Use models and drawings to help students understand how pendentives and piers were used to support this huge dome.

Contextual Information

The *School of Athens*

Many art historians would agree that the *School of Athens* (fig.9–30) is the culmination of the High Renaissance ideal of formal and spatial unity. The figure sitting in the central foreground of the fresco and leaning against a block of marble has been identified as Michelangelo. Dressed in the garb of a sixteenth-century stonecutter, the rather forlorn figure is not in the extant cartoon that Raphael executed for the fresco. It is believed that the figure was added after Raphael visited the Sistine Chapel ceiling with the rest of Rome when it opened in August of 1511. The prominence of the Michelangelo figure in the *School of Athens* can be viewed as a tribute from the younger master to the older one. In fact, the figure is reminiscent of the powerful figures that populate the Sistine Chapel ceiling.

The *Alba Madonna* and Its Provenance

Art historians are often fascinated with the history of the ownership of a great work of art. This is known as tracing a work's *provenanc*e.

Raphael's *Alba Madonna*, for example, was originally located in the Church of Monteoliveto in the town of Nocera di Pagani near Naples. At the end of the seventeenth century the painting was taken to Spain by the Spanish viceroy in Naples, Don Gaspar de Guzmán. It soon entered the collection of the Duchess of Alba and remained there for more than one hundred years. It is from this collection that the painting acquired its name.

Charles IV of Spain coerced the Albas into giving the painting to Don Manuel Godoy, who eventually became Prime Minister of Spain. When Napoleon's armies entered Spain, Godoy's collection was confiscated. The Albas attempted to recover the painting through a lawsuit, but they failed.

Raphael Sanzio

(1483–1520)

The spirit of the High Renaissance reached its peak in the work of Raphael. Raphael's paintings are masterpieces of balance and harmony. They combine the sculptural quality of Michelangelo, the grace and feeling of Leonardo and the detail and light of Perugino, who was Raphael's first teacher. While Michelangelo was a solitary genius with nothing to live for but art, Raphael (several years younger) enjoyed the social whirl of Rome and the adulation of many admirers. After working in Urbino with Perugino for several years, Raphael came to Florence in 1505, where Michelangelo and Leonardo had already established the foundations of the High Renaissance. They were too busy with large commissions to satisfy the wants of the merchants, and Raphael happily filled the gap. For eager patrons, he painted popular Madonnas and numerous flatter-

9–29 A good friend of Raphael's, Castiglione wrote a book of manners and proper behavior. Raphael, *Baldassare Castiglione*, about 1515. Canvas, 32 1/4" x 26 1/2" (82 x 67 cm). The Louvre, Paris.

9–30 Describe how Raphael has mastered the art of perspective in this fresco. Raphael, *School of Athens*, 1510–1511. Fresco. Stanza della Segnatura, Vatican, Rome.

The work was sold to the Danish ambassador in Madrid, Count de Bourke. The count took it to London and sold it at auction for £4000 to W. G. Coesvelt. Coesvelt held onto the painting for a few years while its value increased, then sold the Madonna to the Hermitage Gallery in Leningrad for £14,000.

One hundred years passed. In 1937 Andrew Mellon bought the work for £233,000. It is Mellon's collection that forms the core of the National Gallery's collection. The *Alba Madonna* currently rests on a wall in the National Gallery in Washington.

ing portraits, such as the portrait of *Baldassare Castiglione* (fig.9–29).

Raphael went to Rome in 1508 at the invitation of the pope and immediately became a popular figure. Raphael was court painter in the Vatican until his early death at thirty-seven.

At the bequest of Pope Julius II, Raphael worked from 1509 to 1511 on large frescoes in the Stanza della Segnatura (Room of Signatures, where official papers were signed). The four subjects on the four walls are: *The Disputation over the Sacrament; The School of Athens; Parnassus;* and *Prudence, Force and Moderation.*

The School of Athens (fig.9–30) is probably his masterpiece. It embodies perfectly the spirit of the High Renaissance. The painting is Raphael's superb way of balancing pagan Classicism and Renaissance Christianity in one monumental work. All the masters of Classical Greek thought, science and art are in animated conversations. The two main figures, Plato and Aristotle, are deep in conversation. The figures of Socrates, Pythagoras and Euclid are actually portraits of contemporary persons. Bramante, Michelangelo and Leonardo (Plato) are included, as are many others. Raphael includes himself as a bystander.

The sculptural quality, the individual poses and the grouping of the figures in an architectural setting are influences of Michelangelo, who was painting his ceiling only a few yards away. Yet, the balance and composition are reminiscent of Leonardo's *Last Supper.* The result is a synthesis that is Raphael at his best. The architectural setting suggests the interior of the incomplete St. Peter's. The setting is dramatic and in harmony with the number and placement of the figures. The architectural perspective leads the viewer's eyes to a vanishing point between the heads of Plato and Aristotle.

The Alba Madonna (so named because it was in the collection of the Duke of Alba in Spain) was painted in 1510 and reflects the influence of Michelangelo (fig.9–31). Tondo paintings require extremely fine balance in order to keep them from seeming to roll like a wheel. Raphael used the most stable composition available, the triangle. The three solid forms of Mary, John the Baptist and the Christ Child are firmly resting on the ground. Yet, they are related to the surrounding landscape, which has a feeling of great depth. Raphael guides the viewer's eyes easily around the balanced composition, from Mary's leg, her left arm, shoulder and face, which looks at the cross and at the Baptist. The artist uses many devices (value contrast, direction of eyes and composition) so that visual

movement is directed to come to rest on the cross.

Leonardo's sfumato can be detected in the portrayal of deep space, clear light and the Italian landscape. The foreshortened leg of Mary, her pose and the sculptural quality of her robes are reminiscent of Michelangelo. But the sensitive faces, graceful gestures and the balance of all elements are Raphael's.

After his early death in 1520, at the age of thirty-seven, Raphael was buried in the Pantheon in Rome. The era of the High Renaissance, which began with Leonardo's *Last Supper* twenty-five years earlier, came to an end. Although Michelangelo and Leonardo were the geniuses of the High Renaissance, it was the balance brought about by Raphael that was imitated and admired by artists in succeeding generations.

9–31 Compare this painting to Leonardo's *Virgin of the Rocks.*
Raphael, *The Alba Madonna*, c. 1510. Oil on wood panel, transferred to canvas, 37 1/5" (94 cm) diameter. The National Gallery of Art, Washington DC, Andrew W. Mellon Collection.

Performing Arts Connection

Ancient and Contemporary Love Songs

Madrigals (unaccompanied vocal compositions for two or three voices in simple harmony with a strict poetic form) were the primary secular vocal style in Renaissance Italy from the fourteenth to the sixteenth century. Have students compare a Renaissance madrigal to their favorite contemporary love song. Are there any similarities in style, sentiment, words or musical themes? Have students try to compose their own madrigal about a modern love story.

Contextual Information

Italian Artists and Their Names

Students may notice that many artists of the early Renaissance and some from the High Renaissance are known by their first name. This is because the second part of their name denotes the place of their birth or the name of their father (Giorgione da Castelfranco, Leonardo da Vinci, Donatello di Niccolò Bardi). The term *da* in Italian means "from" ("Leonardo from Vinci"). The term *di* means "of" ("Donatello, son of Niccolò Bardi").

9–32 Can you identify Giorgione's techniques for handling light to make a unified composition?
Giorgione, *The Adoration of the Shepherds*, about 1505. Oil on panel, 35 4/5" x 43 4/5" (91 x 111 cm). National Gallery of Art, Washington DC, Samuel H. Kress Collection, 1939.

1500
Aztecs play early form of basketball, Mexico

1525
Raku-ware, Japan

World Cultural Timeline

1521
Aztec Empire ends

1526
Babar founds Mogul Empire

Northern Italian Art

After the death of Raphael, the sixteenth century saw a shift in the dominance in art from Florence and Rome to Venice in northern Italy. The one exception was Michelangelo, who remained the solitary genius in central Italy until his death in 1564. But Venice gradually took over the leadership in painting, building on the foundation laid down by Giovanni Bellini and benefiting from the discovery of flexible resins that made painting on canvas possible.

Multicultural Connection

Raku-ware

Raku-ware, a type of Japanese pottery, was invented in Kyoto in the sixteenth century, specifically for the tea ceremony. Raku-ware was highly regarded for its "natural" hand-modeled shapes; for its lightweight, low-fired, iron-rich body; and for its beauty of color and texture. Raku vessels were made of lead-glazed earthenware and fired in small single-chamber kilns. Colors of the glazes included red, black, green or, on occasion, cream. A seal bearing the word *raku* (meaning "enjoyment" or "felicity") was impressed on many early examples of this pottery.

• Japanese potters have often been influenced and stimulated by Chinese and Korean ceramics, but have ignored the perfection typical of Chinese ceramics and emphasized instead the hand-made quality that expresses the individual personality of the artist. Have students analyze why the Japanese preferred hand-modeled vessels over wheel-thrown vessels.

• What other cultures produced vessels for specific purposes? Who made them? How were they decorated?

Giorgione da Castelfranco

(1478–1510)

Giorgione lived and worked only a very short lifetime and left only a relatively small number of paintings. However, he made some dramatic innovations in painting that pushed Venetian art to the forefront in Europe. Early Renaissance artists had thought of painting as colored drawings with definite contours. Forms were modeled in light and shade to suggest relief. Fifteenth-century painters realized that individual figures and objects are not seen separately, but together. The artists created interesting groupings that react with their surroundings. Yet, each part was shown as crystal clear, such as in Botticelli's *Adoration of the Magi.*

Giorgione changed this bright light that picks up all details to a soft, misty sunlight. This light helps blend all parts of a composition together to create a strong visual unity. In *The Adoration of the Shepherds* (fig.9–32), colors and values are muted for a more unifying

effect. Two shepherds have come to the stable-cave to worship the Christ Child lying before Mary and Joseph. While a fairly bright light brings out the details in the principal figures, Giorgione used chiaroscuro in the cave and a soft golden light to illuminate the middle and far distance. He loved to paint landscapes. The upper left portion of the painting (fig.9–33) is not only an environment for the subject, but a jewel of a landscape painting in itself. Notice the overcast sky, which softens the light and eliminates harsh contrasts and sharp shadows. Notice, also, how the dark shadows on Mary and Joseph blend into the darks of the cave. The middle values of the shepherds blend into the middle gray values around them. By squinting, one can see how the figures seem to melt into the values around them. With these techniques, Giorgione conveyed his special feelings or moods about his subjects. While Michelangelo and Raphael excelled in creating form, Giorgione mastered mood in painting.

9–33 This detail of *The Adoration* clearly illustrates Giorgione's love for painting landscapes. Although it is only a small part of the whole, when isolated, it takes on a life of its own.
Giorgione, *The Adoration of the Shepherds,* detail.

Is Venice Sinking?

When the Roman empire fell in the fifth century, a group of Roman citizens fled to the safety of some muddy islands at the head of the Adriatic Sea. So began one of the greatest Italian cities: Venice. Venice is a city quite unlike any other in the world. More than 400 bridges span the network of canals that crisscross it. Boats, gondolas and barges remain, to this day, the only source of transport.

Throughout its long history, the islands comprising Venice have been threatened by high waters and flooding. The flooding occurs partly because Venice's only outlets to the sea are three large openings between the islands. The winter winds, called *sirocco*, drive huge tidal waves through these three openings into the lagoon, causing enormously high water pressure. The water that comes rushing in must drain away quickly to prevent a dramatic rise in the water level. But, this quick draining of the lagoon is no longer possible because of high industrial pollution. Another problem has been caused by the draining away of underground water reserves. As a result, the floor of the lagoon has sunk markedly and Venice risks being destroyed.

In 1966, the flooding reached critical levels when a southeasterly sirocco blowing at gale force prevented the morning tide from flowing out of the lagoon. On this occasion, the water in Venice rose to almost six and one-half feet above sea level.

Higher-Order Thinking Skills

Have students compare and contrast *The Adoration of the Shepherds* work (fig.9–32) to *The Adoration of the Magi* (fig.9–18) by Botticelli, paying particular attention to the mood created by the lighting, the setting, the casts of characters and the social classes portrayed.

Contextual Information

Titian

Contemporaries of Titian relate how he would turn his paintings to the wall for months after first working on them. When he approached them again, he could better judge his works, often with a severely critical eye. He then usually added new layers of paint and glazes.

Madonna with Members of the Pesaro Family

The *Madonna with Members of the Pesaro Family* (fig.9–34) is in its original location. The work includes depictions of six Pesaro family members. Jacopo, the donor, kneels in the left foreground. The five other members are kneeling at the right. Of note is that these figures are less animated than the other figures in the scene.

Titian

(1490–1576)

The artistic giant of Venice, comparable to Michelangelo in Florence and Rome, was Tiziano Vecellio, known as Titian. Like Giovanni Bellini and Giorgione, he believed that color and mood were more important in painting than line and scientific accuracy. His painting methods were innovative. He often painted his figures in bright colors over a red-painted background, which added a warmth to the entire work. After it was dry, the surface was painted with as many as thirty or forty glazes. The glazes, transparent mixtures of color and medium, toned down the bright colors and unified the surface. Preferring not to smooth out the surface paint, he allowed brushstrokes to remain visible and let the soft edges of his figures blend into the background. In his later work, no outlines or hard edges are visible at all. Color blends into color to create form. Detail was often ignored in order to emphasize the color and movement created by rapid and powerful brushstrokes. The brushstrokes created a textured surface quality that is called *painterly*.

Three subjects dominated Titian's imagination: events from pagan mythology, especially those involving Venus; portraits of important people and rulers from all over Europe; and religious subjects that called for great emotion, mood or physical activity.

The architectural setting of the *Madonna with Members of the Pesaro Family* (fig.9–34) is characteristic of the High Renaissance. However, unlike Leonardo's *Last Supper* or Raphael's *The School of Athens*, the composition is not symmetrical and horizontal. Instead, the composition has a drama and power that comes from the use of diagonals, angles and triangular arrangements. The Madonna, which is the focus of the composition, is placed to the right, not the center. Except for the kneeling figures, all the figures are in motion.

The figures in Titian's portraits almost always seem to have superhuman power. The *Doge Andrea Gritti* (fig.9–35) was a ruthless maritime ruler. His Venetian fleets dominated the shipping lanes of the trading world and made Venice a feared power. Yet, he also was a patron of the arts and commissioned many religious, historical and allegorical paintings from Titian.

Compare Titian's *Doge* to Bellini's (fig.9–21). Although the same robes and caps are worn by both men, Titian disregards detail and uses slashing brushstrokes to characterize the physical strength of his subject. Edges are soft, suggesting movement. A swirling motion is evident, even though the figure is sitting still. Both brushstrokes and the turn of the head contribute to this feeling. The powerful hand that holds the robes is similar to the

9–34 Jacopo Pesaro presented this painting to the Church as a thanksgiving offering for his successful expedition during a war between the Venetians and the Turks.
Titian, *Madonna with Members of the Pesaro Family*, 1526. Oil on canvas, 16' x 8' 10" (4.9 x 2.7 m). Santa Maria del Gloriosa dei Frari, Venice.

Lesson 9.2 Review Answers

1 Between 1495 and 1527

2 Artists began to be viewed as geniuses rather than as craftspersons.

3 Engineering, military science, botany, anatomy, geology, aerodynamics, optics

4 Four figures, Mary, an angel and two infants (John the Baptist and Jesus), form a triangular composition in a rocky grotto. There is a warmth and intimacy to the scene as the angel points to John the Baptist who is being blessed by the Christ Child. Mary reaches out a protective hand toward her son.

5 A young woman with a hint of a smile sits in a relaxed position in front of a landscape of distant hills and mountains partially obscured by a light haze. This technique of using a hazed background, called *sfumato* in Italian, allowed Leonardo to create a feeling of enormous depth.

6 Lorenzo de Medici's school for sculptors in the Medici household

7 The statue of Moses was created to be a part of Pope Julius II's proposed monumental tomb.

8 Chiaroscuro is a technique for modeling forms in painting by which the lighted parts seem to emerge from surrounding dark areas. Chiaroscuro is also an extreme contrast of dark and light values in a painting.

9–35 Artists often use hands to provide insight into the character of the figures they portray. Gritti's hands are quite powerful. Find two other figures in this chapter that have hands that give a clue to their personality. Titian, *Doge Andrea Gritti*, about 1540. Oil on canvas, 52 1/2" x 40 1/2" (133 x 103 cm). National Gallery of Art, Washington DC, Samuel H. Kress Collection, 1961.

Higher-Order Thinking Skills

Compare Titian's portrayal of Venus (fig.9–36) to that in the *Birth of Venus* (fig.9–17) by Botticelli. How is the Venetian ideal of beauty different from that of Botticelli?

Have students analyze how Titian extends the scene of the *Madonna with Members of the Pesaro Family* beyond the boundaries of the canvas.

sculpted hand of Michelangelo's *Moses*. Bellini's fabrics and textures are very realistic. But, Titian relies on brushstrokes, deep values and vivid colors to create a robust and individualistic figure rather than simply a likeness of the Doge.

The painting of *Venus with a Mirror* (fig.9–36) was one of Titian's favorites. Painted when he was seventy-eight, the work was not easy for him to design. X-rays show that it was painted over two previous compositions; the first was horizontal with two figures and the second was of Venus with two cupids. The face and pose of the second were used in this final version. Again, the rich and glowing colors emerge from deep shadows as two cherubs are seen with the goddess of love. The figures crowd the composition as if ready to burst out of

the frame. The painting expresses Titian's ideal of feminine beauty—a concept that changes throughout history.

Titian received honors from many parts of Europe in his long and productive life. Like Michelangelo and Raphael, he was quite wealthy when he died. His work was as popular in Spain and Germany as it was in Italy, making him the most sought-after artist of his time. Titian's later work, like that of Michelangelo, moved him into the trends of Mannerism and on the verge of Baroque painting.

9–36 Titian painted his idea of the perfect woman. **Compare her to beautiful women from other times.** Titian, *Venus with a Mirror*, 1555. Oil on canvas, 48 4/5" x 41" (124 x 105 cm). National Gallery of Art, Washington DC, Andrew W. Mellon Collection.

Lesson 9.2 Review

1 When was the High Renaissance in Italy?
2 How did most people's perception of painters and sculptors change during the Renaissance?
3 Name four fields of knowledge other than art in which Leonardo da Vinci was an expert.
4 Describe Leonardo da Vinci's *Virgin of the Rocks*. What type of composition has he used? Who are the people in this painting?
5 Describe the *Mona Lisa*. What technique did Leonardo use to show distance in the background?

6 As a teenager where did Michelangelo study sculpture?
7 Why did Michelangelo carve the huge statue of *Moses*?
8 Define *chiaroscuro*.
9 Describe Titian's painting technique.
10 Compare Titian's *Doge Andrea Gritti* to Bellini's *Doge Leonardo Loredan*.

9 Titian usually painted his figures in bright colors over a red-painted background. After the background dried, he would add as many as thirty or forty layers of transparent oil-paint glazes. He allowed his brushstrokes to show, and let the soft edges of his figures blend into the background. In his later work, there are no hard edges or outlines. He used swift, strong brushstrokes to emphasize color and movement, which resulted in a textured surface quality called *painterly*.

10 Both men are wearing the same type of robe and cap. Bellini's *Doge Leonardo Loredan* has a calm, sensitive, clean-shaven face with soft lighting and careful attention to details in the luxurious brocade robe. With slashing brushstrokes Titian shows the physical strength of *Doge Andrea Gritti*. Titian disregards detail, keeps edges soft, and suggests movement in this seated, bearded figure who clutches his robe with one hand.

Lesson 9.3

Mannerism occurred in Western Europe from about 1525 to 1600, roughly spanning the years between the end of the High Renaissance and the beginning of the Baroque era. Mannerism was not a unified movement but was instead enriched by various unique modes of visual expression.

Warm-up

Ask students to glance through Chapter 17 and examine examples of the most recent trends in late twentieth-century art. Can they name any single theme, style or image that unites them all? Explain that Mannerism, a period between approximately 1525 and 1600 in Western Europe, similarly had no codified approach to art.

Objectives

Students should be able to:

Define Mannerism as the period between the end of the High Renaissance and the beginning of the Baroque period in Europe.

Understand that Mannerism included a number of individual styles rather than a united approach to art.

Describe Mannerism's features, including distorted forms and perspectives, crisp and static shapes, attenuated anatomy, expressive color and unique approaches to subject matter.

Vocabulary Definitions

genre (*zhahn*-ra) Referring to the common, ordinary; also, a type of localized art.

Teach

Art History/Criticism: Have students study El Greco's *The Burial of Count Orgaz* (fig.9–37) and *Resurrection* (fig.9–38). As students dictate to you, write on the blackboard a list of adjectives that describe his use of color, realism of his compositions, naturalism of the figures and the overall mood.

• How does El Greco's work differ from the refined, cool, ordered paintings of Raphael (figs. 9–29, 9–30, 9–31), a High Renaissance master?

9.3 Mannerism

THE TERM *Mannerism* REFERS TO the period between the end of the High Renaissance and the beginning of the Baroque period (from 1525 to 1600). Mannerism was originally a derogatory term applied to painters who had a formal, mannered style that imitated various aspects of Raphael's and Michelangelo's works.

Included in the Mannerist style are such features as crisp and frozen shapes, elongated bodies, distorted forms and peculiar perspective views. The artists had very individual and expressionistic approaches to subject matter. Instead of a single dominant style, there was a mix of styles that were extensions of the Renaissance. Mannerism, therefore, was not a unified approach by several artists, but stressed unique approaches. Mannerism could be compared to the present-day art scene, in which there is a great variety of visual expression.

Key Notes
• Mannerism has strong ties to the High Renaissance, but rejects many of its conventions.
• Mannerism does not refer to a single style, rather to a variety of styles.

Vocabulary
genre

9–37 Note that the black-clad figures behind the burial seem to be individualized portraits of important Spanish contemporaries. El Greco, *The Burial of Count Orgaz*, 1586. Oil on canvas, 16' x 12' (490 x 360 cm). San Tomé, Toledo, Spain.

Special Feature
El Greco
(1541–1614)

Domenikos Theotocopoulos was born in Crete but emigrated to Italy as a young man. He studied in Venice with Tintoretto and knew Titian and his work. But, when he went to Rome, he fell under the spell of Raphael, Michelangelo and the central Italian Mannerists. By 1577, he had left for Spain and settled in Toledo where he would spend the rest of his life. He was nicknamed El Greco (the Greek) there. El Greco never forgot his Byzantine heritage and continued to sign his name in Greek.

El Greco's strong personal style developed from the blending of his Byzantine background with the influence of Venetian painting and Italian Mannerist elements. His paintings are intensely emotional, which greatly appealed to the religious fervor of the Spanish. Form is often dematerialized. Color is very important and there is a strong sense of movement. His paintings featured elongated distortion and a flickering light that is much more personal than realistic. However, El Greco's style was not fully appreciated until the latter part of the nineteenth century.

Generally considered the artist's masterpiece, *The Burial of Count Orgaz* (fig.9–37) was painted in 1586 for the church of San Tomé in Toledo. The theme illustrates the legend of the Count of Orgaz. The Count, who had died some two centuries before, had been so saintly that Saints Stephen and Augustine had miraculously descended from heaven to help bury him.

The work is divided into two sections. The lower part is sixteenth century on earth, the upper is eter-

Tell students to read El Greco's biographical profile on pages 288 and 289. Next divide the class into pairs. One partner writes an article from the role of a contemporary art reporter criticizing El Greco's work, and the other partner responds from the artist's position, writing a letter that defends his innovative and unique contributions to art history.

Criticism: Direct students to compare El Greco's *The Burial of Count Orgaz* and *Resurrection* to Sofonisba Anguissola's works (figs.9–40, 9–41).

• Did the two artists paint in a similar manner? Have students read the text about both artists to find out whom they worked for. Although their styles differed greatly, both were patronized by royalty and wealthy individuals. Share that during the Renaissance, the church lost its role as the sole patron of the arts, although it remained a significant player for some centuries.

Evaluate

Ask students if there was a single unified Mannerist style. Ask how the artworks in Lesson 9.3 support their answers.

nal and in heaven. The faces of the noblemen in attendance on the lower half of the painting are portraits of El Greco's friends in Toledo. He even included himself in the group and his son in the foreground. The angel bearing Orgaz's soul to heaven (his soul looks like a small doll in the center) unites the lower part of the painting with the upper. The upward gaze of the priest at the right also makes us look up. The celestial beings in the upper half of the picture are painted differently from the lower half. The figures on earth are represented rather realistically. The heavenly figures are elongated, with fluttering draperies and on giant swirls of clouds.

El Greco painted many religious works for churches and hospitals in and around Toledo. One of the finest examples of his later mystical style is the *Resurrection* (fig.9–38). Christ soars effortlessly toward heaven, carrying the victory banner with him. He calmly observes the scene below where soldiers seem to be flung apart by the explosive power of His resurrection. The writhing movement and flickering lights and darks create a powerful and unified statement. Notice how the elongated figures and thin arms, hands and legs fill most of the available space. They draw the viewer's eyes up to the Christ figure with unrelenting magnetic force. The artist has made a personal statement powerfully expressive. Physical reality does not exist in this late work.

El Greco was concerned primarily with emotion and with the effort to express his own religious fervor. To accomplish this he, like other Mannerist painters, bent the rules of Renaissance painting to create very powerful and unique visual expressions.

9–38 Can you identify two Mannerist features in this painting?
El Greco, *Resurrection*, about 1597–1604. Oil on canvas, 9' x 4'10" (275 x 146 cm). Prado Museum, Madrid.

Contextual Information
El Greco
El Greco's rebellion against the Renaissance style and the lack of approval of his Mannerist style prompted him to move to Spain, where he thought independence of thought would be prized. However, King Philip II refused to accept a work he commissioned from El Greco because it was so different from the work of his favored artists.

The portrait of El Greco pictured here is not a universally accepted self-portrait. The Metropolitan Museum, where the work is housed, has changed its title to *Portrait of a Man*.

Higher-Order Thinking Skills

1 Use the text to help students identify the characters in *The Burial of Count Orgaz*. What makes this a Mannerist painting? Can students identify various historical influences?

2 El Greco's painting of *St. Martin and the Beggar* can be found on page 41 (fig.2–47) of the text. Ask students to compare it to El Greco's *Resurrection*. What stylistic similarities can they find that would identify the painting of St. Martin as a work by El Greco? (Point out to students that the two paintings also were created at about the same time in El Greco's career.)

Reteach
Tell students to look briefly at the subject of El Greco's *The Burial of Count Orgaz*, Sofonisba Anguissola's *Self-Portrait* (fig.9–41) and Benvenuto Cellini's *The Saltcellar of Francis I* (p.296).

• Do they think the Christian Church commissioned these works?

• What about their subject matter indicates that art during and after the Renaissance began to be made for royalty, nobles and wealthy individuals as well as for the church?

Remind students that *Mannerism* was initially a negative term applied to painters who had a formal, mannered style that imitated various aspects of the High Renaissance. The term *Gothic* was originally used by Renaissance critics to ridicule the twelfth- and thirteenth-century style because it did not conform to Classical Greek and Roman standards. In the eighteenth century, the word *Baroque* (meaning "pebbly ground," "rough pearl," or "a convoluted argument in logic") was applied derogatorily to seventeenth-century art.

• Can students identify the French late-nineteenth-century art style whose name was also initially meant as a negative term?

• Why might critics have used words like *Impressionism, Gothic, Mannerism,* and *Baroque* in disparaging ways about art that we consider important today?

• What does the continual reevaluation of the past tell us about the objectivity and stability of the study and understanding of history?

• Is there one absolute, immutable standard for valuing art for all time?

Contextual Information

Rosso Fiorentino

Giovanni Battista di Jacopo was nicknamed Rosso Fiorentino, which can be translated as "the red-headed Florentine." Rosso apparently was a practical joker. He owned a mischievous monkey whom he adored and regarded as a child. Rosso was not beyond letting the monkey loose among the clergy of a Florentine church.

Women Artists

In the fifteenth and early sixteenth centuries students of art would study cadavers and then live models. Artists began to study anatomy routinely, leading to increased realism of the human figure. However, the opportunity to study dead bodies or live male models was not available to women. In earlier times, women who did become artists were nuns who were taught to read and write and paint illuminated manuscripts in convents. By the sixteenth century, girls were encouraged to read, learn to play musical instruments, write and become fine artists. Unless they were from wealthy families, however, they did not have time to attend classes or to paint. Also, girls were expected to marry by the time they were 14 or 15.

Sofanisba Anguissola

Sofanisba Anguissola signed her works with Latin inscriptions and twice painted herself playing a musical instrument, possibly to show her "feminine" skills as well as her ability to paint. Sofonisba sent a portrait of the queen of Spain to Pope Pius IV with an accompanying letter stating: "If the brush could repeat the beauties of the queen's soul to your eyes, they would be marvelous. However, I have used the utmost diligence to present what art can show, to tell your holiness the truth." What do students think Sofonisba's view was on the importance of adhering to observable reality? Because women were not allowed to draw from male nude models, female artists such as Sofonisba excelled in works that did not require complicated full-figure compositions, such as portraiture and still lifes. Even so, Sofonisba is the first known female Renaissance artist to have achieved international acclaim and patronage.

Rosso Fiorentino

(1494–1540)

Some of the earliest Mannerist work can be found in central Italy. About 1520, a group of Florentine painters led by Rosso shocked their fellow artists and the citizens of central Italy with works like *The Descent from the Cross* (fig.9–39). Rejecting many of the conventions of Renaissance painting, Rosso crowds figures into a tight composition with open space in the center. The impact of such spidery forms spread out against a dark sky was shocking to his contemporary Italians. The figures are agitated, yet rigid, as if quick-frozen in time and space. The acid colors and peculiar light produce a brilliant, but unreal, sensation—almost with a nightmarish quality. Rosso's mystifying work went against the Classical tradition of Renaissance painting, which emphasized balance and harmony.

9–39 How has the artist purposely avoided balance and harmony in this work?
Rosso Fiorentino, *The Descent from the Cross*, 1521. Oil on panel, 11' x 6' 5 1/2" (334 x 196 cm). Pinacoteca, Volterra.

Sofonisba Anguissola

(1535–1625)

Sofonisba was the oldest child of a wealthy family in Cremona. She was a widely recognized artist in her own long lifetime. A child prodigy, she received the attention of Michelangelo. Her paintings are charming and informal, almost like affectionate family photographs instead of formal portraits. Poses are natural. Some of her work capture small moments in everyday life, such as *Boy Pinched by a Crayfish* (fig.9–40). This lively drawing clearly conveys the small boy's painful surprise at having his finger pinched by the crayfish. The comforting

9–40 This artist delighted in capturing everyday activities. Though drawn more than 350 years ago, the reaction and response of the figures seem very familiar to us.
Sofonisba Anguissola, *Boy Pinched by a Crayfish*. Museo e Gallerie di Capidimonte, Naples.

older child provides a warmth and intimacy that is typical of the artist's work. The drawing, which she gave to Michelangelo, was so popular that other artists made copies of it.

In 1559, she became court painter to Philip II of Spain. She remained in Spain for twenty years, where she was a popular portrait artist. Her self-portraits (fig.9–41), in which she often showed herself playing the spinet, were also in demand. She is credited with introducing **genre**, or everyday activity, into formal portraiture.

9–41 Sofonisba was considered a child prodigy. Her career was quite long. She lived over 80 years.
Sofonisba Anguissola, *Self-Portrait*. Pinacoteca di Brera, Milan.

Higher-Order Thinking Skills

Explain that during the Renaissance, artists commonly created self-portraits, either as singular studies or as part of larger compositions. Have students examine the self-portraits in Chapter 9 (Leonardo's appears on page 276, Boticelli's in fig.9–19, Raphael's in fig.9–30, El Greco's in fig.9–37 and Sofonisba's in fig.9–41). Direct students to read the accompanying text to help identify the artists in each example. Ask students to consider what the phenomenon of self-portraits reveals about these artists' status within Renaissance society. Have students seen self-portraits in earlier periods?

Inquiry

Have students interview women artists about their art training and ask if they had difficulties that they feel men did not have in becoming artists. Have students discuss their findings.

Contextual Information

Tintoretto

Tintoretto painted a great many canvases with the help of his workshop, which included his two sons, Domenico and Marco, and his daughter Marietta. Their painting skills were so good and similar to their father's that it is difficult to tell where Tintoretto's work stopped and their painting began. Marietta's paintings brought her independent commissions, but her father never let her leave his workshop to work on her own.

• Ask students to offer reasons why Tintoretto might have wanted to keep Marietta at home.

Tintoretto

(1518–1594)

About the middle of the sixteenth century, two Venetian painters began to crowd into Titian's dominance: Jacopo Robusti, called Tintoretto, and Paolo Caliari, called Veronese. The name Tintoretto means "Little Dyer," which was his father's occupation. Tintoretto became the most dramatic painter of the sixteenth century. He filled huge walls with canvases of soaring and hurtling figures. His subjects were mostly religious and sprang from a strong faith.

Tintoretto would arrange small models on stages and even suspend some from wires to set the composition and see the foreshortening as it should be. He made small drawings of these arrangements and enlarged them enormously on his huge canvases. Tintoretto would first paint the bright colors. Then he would add intense darks and highlights, producing the effect of a night scene illuminated with flashes of light. His brushstrokes were less controlled than Titian's, causing the nineteenth-century critic John Ruskin to accuse him of painting

9–42 Peter leaves the boat to try to walk to Christ over the surface of the water. How does Tintoretto make you feel the emotion of the moment?

Tintoretto, *Christ at the Sea of Galilee,* about 1580. Oil on canvas, 46" x 66 1/2" (117 x 169 cm). National Gallery of Art, Washington DC, Samuel H. Kress Collection.

with a broom. Although he painted constantly, he did much of his work for charity houses at a small salary. He died almost penniless.

Christ at the Sea of Galilee (fig.9–42) presents a Biblical narrative through the eyes of Tintoretto. Christ's disciples were in a boat on the Sea of Galilee when a sudden storm arose. As the boat was being tossed about, the men saw Christ walking toward them on the water. They were astounded and afraid, but Peter asked if he could walk to Christ on the water. Christ invited him and Peter stepped from the boat. Tintoretto shows this moment of psychological tension in his painting. The artist has created a powerful composition, placing

1540 Horses introduced to the Americas from Europe	1593 The *bunraku,* a Japanese theater form using marionettes, first introduced
World Cultural Timeline	
1571 Manila, The Philippines, founded	1603 Japanese Shinto priestess develops *Kabuki* theater

Multicultural Connection

Kabuki

The most popular form of traditional Japanese theater is *kabuki*. It was well-established in Japan by the mid-seventeenth century. Kabuki tends to be a spectacle rather than a drama. The acting, music and dancing are remarkable, as are the brilliantly colored sets.

Kabuki music includes instrumentalists and singers. Most of the musicians sit at the back of the stage; the others are offstage and provide sound effects and special incidental music. Kabuki continues to be an extremely popular form of theater today and is often performed in the United States.

Christ against the left edge of the canvas. Although Christ is important in the design, the center of interest is Peter. The viewer wonders, "Will he make it? If not, why not?" The dominant hues of bluish-green are favorites of Tintoretto. The elongated figures and flickering lights are features of much of his work.

Tintoretto's masterpiece is the magnificent series of over fifty canvases in the School of San Rocco in Venice. Here, he labored for twenty-three years for a small yearly salary. He produced a monument that rivals Giotto's Arena Chapel and Michelangelo's Sistine Chapel in visual impact and sustained creative intensity. The largest canvas is the *Crucifixion* (fig.9–43) (40 feet long) which is overpowering in its visual effect. The foreground figures are over-life-size. The upward thrust of the cross seems to crush Christ against the top border. Groups of soldiers, horses, disciples and Mary are visually interlocked by their overlapping forms and the dramatic light which seems to emanate from the head of Christ. Tintoretto calls even more attention to Christ by having a great number of lines and shapes direct the visual movement toward the top center of the canvas. The use of unreal light counteracted the natural light used by Renaissance painters.

Thinking like a Museum Curator

A museum curator is responsible for the proper care, display, research, cataloging and publication of the objects in a collection. A "good eye" and an excellent visual memory are two of the most important qualifications that an individual must bring to the job. A good eye means that the curator is able to determine the quality, condition and authenticity of a work of art. A curator also needs to have an extensive knowledge of the history of art.

Cataloging is one of the most interesting, but often most difficult, of a curator's duties. Cataloging includes the proper documentation of an object's physical state. Cataloging also requires that the curator try to determine the artist, title and date of an object. In some cases attributing a work to an artist is quite simple because the work is signed and even dated. In many instances, however, a work of art is not signed and the curator must make a decision based on factors such as style, comparisons, surviving documents and the opinions of other scholars.

Consider the painting *Christ at the Sea of Galilee* (fig.9–42). It is usually attributed to Tintoretto,

as it is here. It is not signed and no documents (such as papers commissioning Tintoretto to paint this subject) have been found. The assignment of this work to Tintoretto, therefore, has to be made purely on the basis of "eye." Is its style and technique similar to other paintings the artist executed? Is the treatment of the subject similar to any other works by Tintoretto?

The answer to the latter question is no. It is the only painting attributed to Tintoretto in which water takes up so much of the canvas. Style and technique, therefore, become the primary means of judging the work. Brushstroke, the treatment of the sky, the small figures in the boat all point to Tintoretto. But the opinions are not unanimous.

Some have suggested that the work is by El Greco. The intense blues favored by El Greco play a strong role in the painting. The elongation of the figure of Christ also recalls El Greco.

The curator at the National Gallery has weighed the opinions, carefully scrutinized the painting and made an attribution: the style and brushstroke indicate Tintoretto. What do you think?

9–43 The figures in the foreground are larger than life. The unnatural light emphasizes the importance of the event.
Tintoretto, *Crucifixion*, 1565. Oil on canvas, 17 1/2' x 40' (5.3 x 12.2 m). End wall, Sala dell'Albergo, School of San Rocco, Venice.

Contextual Information

Veronese

Because Veronese included animals, dwarfs and soldiers in his religious paintings, he was tried by the Inquisition because religious leaders wanted images of only sacred objects and saints in religious paintings. (An account of Veronese's 1573 trial is in the second volume of Elizabeth Holt's *A Documentary History of Art*.)

Veronese frequently painted on a huge scale and received a number of commissions to paint the refectories of wealthy monasteries. He painted *Christ in the House of Levi* (fig.9–45) for the refectory (dining room) of the monastery of Santi Giovanni e Paolo in Venice. Have students read the Biblical passage from Luke 5:29–31, which relates the story of Christ in the house of Levi. What aspects of the passage has Veronese depicted? To leave no doubt in the minds of his audience as to what the painting depicted, Veronese inscribed "LUCAE CAP V" in the balustrade, thus pointing the viewer to Chapter 5 of Luke.

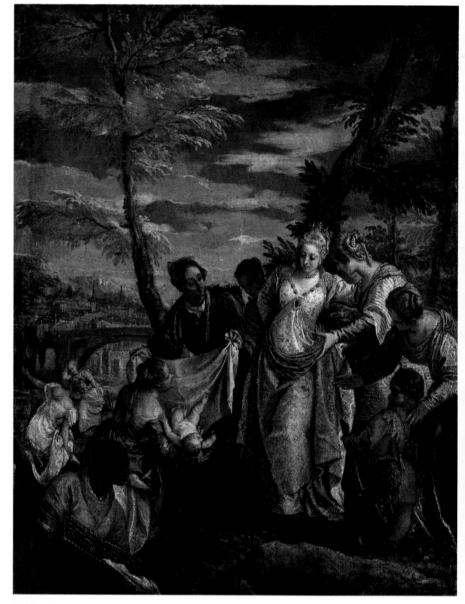

9–44 How does the artist make the princess the central focus of the composition?
Paolo Veronese, *The Finding of Moses*, c. 1570. Oil on canvas, 22 4/5" x 17 1/2" (58 x 44 cm). National Gallery of Art, Washington DC, Andrew W. Mellon Collection.

Veronese

(1528–1588)

Paolo Caliari was called Veronese because he came from Verona, some distance west of Venice. Tintoretto was concerned with turbulent and swirling light and action in religious scenes. Veronese emphasized the material beauty of marble, gold, textiles and other materials of superb quality and great expense. Like other Mannerist painters, he was adept at using perspective to create startling effects—such as looking straight up at figures on a ceiling or looking upward or downward diagonally. He was so skilled at foreshortening that he had no trouble portraying figures in any conceivable location and position.

His interest in the luxurious quality of fabrics can be seen in *The Finding of Moses* (fig.9–44).

Although the event happened in Egypt over three thousand years earlier, Veronese placed the scene in northern Italy—the Alps and a Tyrolian town are in the background—and peopled it with a sixteenth-century princess and her court. The basis for the painting is the hiding of Moses by his mother when all first-born sons of Israel were to be put to death by the Egyptian Pharaoh. The princess, out on her daily walk, finds Moses in a basket in the reeds by the river bank. The flowing colors and spiraling, twisting figures are designed to lead the viewer's eyes to the face of the princess, even though the baby Moses is the reason for the painting. While Veronese leads the viewer's eyes along many paths, they always return to the face of the princess. Her light complexion is set off by

the dark foliage behind her. The arbitrary use of light, placed just where the artist wants it, is contradictory to the use of natural light so admired by Renaissance artists.

Christ in the House of Levi (fig.9–45), like High Renaissance paintings, is symmetrically balanced. The figures, which are full of action and motion, are placed in a Classical architectural setting. Christ is seated in the center and surrounded by men of high station and their servants. The painting was originally titled *The Last Supper*. However, the Inquisition charged Veronese with impiety for including drunkards and dwarfs in such a solemn occasion. Rather than make changes in his painting, Veronese simply changed the title to one with less religious significance.

9–45 **Compare this work to Leonardo's *Last Supper*.**
Paolo Veronese, *Christ in the House of Levi*, c. 1573. Oil on canvas, 18' 2" x 42' (5.5 x 12.8 m). Academy, Venice.

Higher-Order Thinking Skills

The portrayal of Biblical characters in clothing contemporary to the artist's time is an old tradition; however, with the Renaissance there came a distinctive modern-world look. Have students work in groups to make collages of the Moses story. They can present the figures in clothing that signifies different times, including modern. Discuss what students and their peers might be wearing in such a scene. Are historical stories that are set with figures in contemporary clothing and location as effective as those set in other times?

Contextual Information

Abduction of the Sabine Women

The exact subject of Giovanni Bologna's figure group (fig.9–47) mattered little to the sculptor. Proposed earlier versions had been presented as Paris and Helen, Pluto and Proserpina, and Phineus and Andromeda. The sculptor's main interest was in portraying the vitality and spiraling movement of the figures. Its current title, *Abduction of the Sabine Woman*, was given to the group after it was placed in the Piazza della Signoria.

Cellini's Saltcellar

Benvenuto Cellini was a sculptor and craftsman in metals who was born in Florence in the sixteenth century. He also wrote a famous autobiography that has made his life as familiar to many modern readers as his artwork. Virtuosity characterized both the art and the flamboyant life of Cellini.

Like many Florentine artists, Cellini spent much of his time away from his hometown and by 1540 went to the royal court of France at Fontainebleau. Eventually, Cellini was commissioned as goldsmith to the king. Before he left France in 1545, Cellini completed a magnificent table ornament in gold and enamel for Francis I: a *saltcellar*.

The forms of the gilded figures and the basic allegorical concept of the saltcellar derive directly from Michelangelo's work in the Medici Chapel. For the salt from the sea, Cellini provided a male Neptune (Water) figure with a trident and an accompanying ship that held the spice. Opposite him lay a reclining female Ceres (Earth), whose adjacent temple held pepper. Each of the figures is set against a field of colored enamel that includes appropriate animal companions (sea horses, dolphins and an elephant). On the ebony base, gold reliefs of the winds or seasons were depicted, as well as the times of day.

Benvenuto Cellini, *The Saltcellar of Francis I,* **1539–1543. Gold with ebony base, 10 1/4" x 13 1/8" (26 x 33.6 cm). Kunsthistorisches Museum, Vienna.**

Sculpture and Architecture

Although painting was the most important medium during the late sixteenth century, several sculptors made excellent contributions to the art of the period. A slight change in style and an emphasis on luxurious elegance were characteristics of the work produced.

Benvenuto Cellini
(1500–1571)

Cellini's *Autobiography* is a book that gives us a vivid picture of life in sixteenth-century Italy. Besides being an author, Cellini was an excellent goldsmith and a sculptor in bronze. His *Perseus and Medusa*

9–46 It took Cellini nine years to devise a technique that would allow him to cast a bronze figure this size.
Benvenuto Cellini, *Perseus and Medusa,* 1545–1554. Bronze, 18' (5 1/2 m) high with base. Piazza della Signoria, Florence.

Performing Arts Connection

The Birth of Opera

Opera as we know it today began at the end of the sixteenth century in Florence, Italy, when amateur musicians began changing the way musical stories were told. They wanted each singer's words to be clearly understood. At first, actors partly sang and partly spoke their text (recitative) while the singers performed offstage. Gradually, solo singers and choruses moved on-stage too, wearing costumes and performing among stage sets of houses, streets or the countryside that indicated the story's location.

Initially, dramatic themes centered around ancient Greek mythology and glories of past epochs. Operas were hours long; some even took days to perform. The nobility would often sponsor lavish balls, presenting acts of an opera on consecutive nights along with other forms of entertainment.

(fig.9–46) stands in the Piazza della Signoria in Florence in an honored location. The heavily muscled figure of Perseus reminds one of Michelangelo's many powerful bodies. Perseus holds the severed head of Medusa, whose blood is turning to precious coral strands as it pours from body and head. These ornamental strands and the highly decorated pedestal add the luxurious touch to a Mannerist sculpture.

Giovanni Bologna
(1529–1608)
Coming to Italy from northern Europe, Jean Boulogne (renamed Giovanni Bologna in Italy) was the most original sculptor between Michelangelo and Bernini, thus bridging the time span between the Renaissance and the Baroque. His powerfully designed *Abduction of the Sabine Woman* (fig.9–47) was carved from a single block of marble. The muscular central figure carries away the Sabine woman as her father crouches in defeat. The three figures are interwoven in a spiraling composition that seems as difficult to unravel as the groupings in many of the Mannerist paintings. All sculpture until this time was made to be viewed from front, back and profile, but Bologna's work has no front or back and viewers must constantly move around it to see the complete work. Parts of arms, legs and heads seem to flail outward at various angles, creating a feeling of violent action and tension. The monumental sculpture displays all of Bologna's considerable skills and stands close to Cellini's *Perseus* in the Palazza della Signoria in Florence.

9–47 This statue is meant to be viewed from multiple angles.
Giovanni Bologna, *Abduction of the Sabine Woman*, 1583. Marble, 13' (4 m) high. Piazza della Signoria, Florence.

Higher-Order Thinking Skills
Ask students to analyze the differences between the portrayal of the human figure in Greek Hellenistic sculpture (p.182–183) and the two Mannerist sculptures shown here and on the previous page. Emotion plays an important role in each period, but the sculptures from each period handled their task very differently.

Interdisciplinary Connection

Literature: Ask students to study *Perseus and Medusa* (fig.9–46) and record their impressions. Next have them research the myth of these two figures and then return to Cellini's image. Did their impression of the piece change after they had become familiar with the legend? Explore with students how background in other disciplines can greatly enrich their appreciation of art.

Lesson 9.3 Review Answers

1 Spain
2 Contemporary Italians were jarred by the impact of spidery figures against a dark sky and the unreal, almost nightmarish, quality Rosso produced with acid colors and peculiar light. Rosso's work did not emphasize the Classical balance and harmony of the Renaissance.
3 Sofonisba Anguissola
4 Peter is the center of interest. Peter has just stepped from the boat carrying the other disciples in an attempt to walk across the water to Christ who is walking on the stormy sea of Galilee.
5 The luxurious fabrics worn by the figures in *The Finding of Moses*

Chapter Review Answers

Review

1 Contrapposto
2 Masaccio creates an illusion of depth in his background with atmospheric perspective. His figures appear three-dimensional with expressive faces, and he uses a realistic light source. His rounded bodies occupy real space.
3 *Renaissance* means a revival or rebirth of cultural awareness and learning.
4 Michelangelo's *David* is 4.8 meters or about 16 feet high; so, it is probably about three times the height of most students.

Interpret

1 In Brunelleschi's Church of San Lorenzo, lines are clean and walls are uncluttered as compared to the ornate carvings on Gothic churches. Brunelleschi's cool, static perfection, with each part a proportion of another, contrasts dramatically with the Gothic flamboyance and movement.
2 Michelangelo's *David* is much larger, more mature, and more muscular than Donatello's. Michelangelo shows an intelligent David sizing up the giant before he kills him. He cradles a rock in one huge hand and drapes a slingshot on his other shoulder. Donatello depicts David after the killing, wearing a hat, holding a sword in one hand, and his foot on Goliath's head. Both Davids rest their weight on one foot, creating a slight S-curve to their bodies. Donatello's *David* is relaxed and graceful. Michelangelo's is relaxed but alert.

9–48 Palladian architecture continues to influence the design of buildings today.
Andrea Palladio, *Villa Capra (Villa Rotunda)*, begun 1550. Vicenza, Italy.

Andrea Palladio

(1508–1580)

The only northern Italian architect that ranks with Bramante and Michelangelo was Andrea Palladio from Vicenza. Many of the buildings in his hometown (palaces, town hall and theater) were designed and built by him. Many structures in Venice, Padua and other nearby cities also were his, but none are more influential than his villas or large country homes. The *Villa Capra* (fig.9–48) (called the *Villa Rotunda* because of its dome and central plan) uses Classic forms such as a flat dome like that of the Pantheon, Ionic columns, pediments and arches. The large central cube has porches on four sides that enlarge the form to a more horizontal feeling of grace and stability. The building has the quiet elegance of Mannerism rather than the severe discipline of Renaissance architecture. In 1570, Palladio wrote and illustrated a book that contained his thoughts and ideas on architecture based on Classic ideals: a set of rules by which to build. It became the international guide for many builders up to the eighteenth century, including British and American architects, among them Thomas Jefferson (*see* p. 388). Some of the buildings seen in the next several chapters will illustrate the influence of Palladio on world architecture and the emergence of a style that bears his name—Palladian.

Lesson 9.3 Review

1 In what country did El Greco make most of his paintings?
2 Name two elements in Rosso Fiorentino's *The Descent from the Cross* that jarred most sixteenth-century viewers.
3 Which artist is credited with introducing common, everyday activities into formal portraiture?
4 Study Tintoretto's *Christ at the Sea of Galilee.* Who has Tintoretto put as the center of interest? What is happening in this picture?
5 Give an example of Veronese's art that demonstrates his love of opulent fabrics.

3 Leonardo created depth by using linear perspective in the architecture, overlapping figures and aerial perspective in the landscape background through the windows behind Christ. This painting is symmetrically balanced with Christ at the center. Leonardo directs our gaze with the linear perspective lines in the architecture which converge at a point near Christ's head.
4 Plato and Aristotle converse in the center of this gathering of the masters of Classical Greek thought, science and art. Socrates, Pythagoras, Euclid, Bramante, Michelangelo, Raphael and Leonardo as Plato are included. This painting embodies the spirit of the Renaissance by showing Classical Greek subjects in a setting with Greek sculptures, rounded Classical Roman arches and linear perspective. It blends pagan Classicism and Renaissance Christianity. The composition is symmetrically balanced with the architectural lines converging at the two main figures, near the center of the painting.
5 In the lower center of the painting, Saints Stephen and Augustine are helping bury Count Orgaz. They are surrounded by noblemen, a monk and a priest. An angel carries Orgaz's soul to heaven, uniting the upper and lower parts of the painting. A celestial crowd of elongated figures and fluttering draperies fills the top part of the picture. Indications that this is a Mannerist painting are the elongated bodies and high drama of the scene.

Michelangelo and the Sistine Ceiling

The Sistine ceiling took Michelangelo four years to complete. He built his own scaffolding and hired five painters from Florence to help, but their work did not meet his standards so he continued with a few assistants to mix plaster and grind colors. Day after day for four years, he stood with his face up, painting over his head. Michelangelo's friend and biographer, Condivi, says that for a time after he finished the ceiling, Michelangelo was unable to read except by holding paper over his head.

This sonnet written by Michelangelo, describes the strain and pain he suffered:

I've grown a goiter by dwelling in this den–
  As cats from stagnant streams in Lombardy,
  Or in what other land they hap to be–
  Which drives the belly close beneath the chin;
My beard turns up to heaven; my nape falls in,
  Fixed on my spine: my breast-bone visibly
  Grows like a harp: a rich embroidery
  Bedews my face from brush drops thick and thin.
My loins into my paunch like levers grind:
  My buttock like a crupper bears my weight;
  My feet unguided wander to and fro;
In front my skin grows loose and long; behind,
  By bending it becomes more taut and strait;
  Crosswise I strain me like a Syrian bow:
  Whence false and quaint, I know,
  Must be the fruit of squinting brain and eye;
  For ill can aim the gun that bends awry.
    Come then Giovanni, try
  To succor my dead pictures and my fame,
  Since foul I fare and painting is my shame.

Review

1 What stance, developed by the Greeks, did Donatello use in his *David* to indicate motion?
2 List three ways Masaccio's *Tribute Money* was different from Gothic paintings.
3 Define the term *renaissance*.
4 How many times larger than you is Michelangelo's *David*?

Interpret

1 How is Brunelleschi's Church of San Lorenzo different from Gothic churches?
2 Compare Donatello's bronze *David* to Michelangelo's marble *David*.
3 Analyze the composition in Leonard da Vinci's *Last Supper*. What techniques did he use to show depth in this painting? What type of compositional balance did he use? What is the center of interest? How did he direct the viewer's gaze toward this focal point?
4 Describe Raphael's *School of Athens*. Explain why this painting is such a good example of Renaissance art. Analyze its composition. Who are the central figures in this painting?
5 Describe El Greco's *Burial of Count Orgaz*. What are some indications that this is a Mannerist painting?

Other Tools for Learning

Maps
Choose five cities from the map on p. 261. List one famous work of art or architecture that is located in each city.

Timelines
1 What were the French doing to Rome around the time that Michelangelo painted *Last Judgment*? How do you think this might have influenced the mood of this painting?
2 As Leonardo da Vinci painted *The Last Supper*, do you think he had heard about Columbus's discovery of America? Why or why not?
3 Which event was probably most significant to your ancestors? Explain why.

Electronic Research
CD-ROM drive: *Microsoft Art Gallery* (Composition and Perspective Guided Tour)
1 Select an individual object from Paolo Uccello's *The Battle of San Romano*. Describe how Uccello painted this object to give it depth or perspective.
2 Explain how Piero della Francesca directs the viewers eyes through the composition in his *Baptism of Christ*.

Higher-Order Thinking Skills

An understanding of the *Villa Rotunda* is important for students because of Palladio's significant influence on succeeding generations of architects. Ask students to identify those elements of the structure that are Classical and those that are Palladian. Remind students that the building is a villa, a home.

Primary-Source Connection

Many Renaissance primary sources have survived, including the tax records that the Florentines started keeping in the early fifteenth century, autobiographies, the notebooks of Leonardo and the sonnets and letters of Michelangelo. Have students review this chapter and list any primary sources that are cited or alluded to. How do personal documents such as this sonnet by Michelangelo shed light on the personality and work of the artist?

3 Depending on the students' ethnic heritages, a wide variety of responses is possible.

Maps
Milan: Leonardo's *The Last Supper*
Venice: Tintoretto's *Crucifixion* in the School of San Rocco
Florence: Brunelleschi's dome on the Cathedral of Florence; Donatello's *David* and Michelangelo's *David*; Ghiberti's *The Gates of Paradise*; Masaccio's *Tribute Money*; Fra Angelico's *The Annunciation*; Botticelli's Birth of Venus; Bologna's *Abduction of the Sabine Woman*
Arezzo: Piero della Francesca's *The Discovery and Proving of the True Cross*
Rome: Michelangelo's *Pietà*, *Last Judgment* and *Creation* in the Sistine Chapel and St. Peter's; Raphael's *School of Athens*

Timelines
1 The French had sacked Rome prior to Michelangelo's painting *Last Judgment*. The mood was turbulent. The peaceful stability found in the Renaissance compositions was replaced with swirling menacing figures inflicting torture and suffering, as many Romans had suffered at the hands of the French.
2 Leonardo painted *The Last Supper* in 1495–1498; Columbus discovered America in 1492. Leonardo had probably heard about the Columbus' discovery. Soon after Columbus returned to Spain from his first voyage, pamphlets were printed describing Columbus' journey—one in Italian—and widely circulated in Europe. Note, however, that Columbus thought he had landed in the East Indies.

Electronic Research
1 Uccello painted a dead knight lying on the ground in the midst of the battle. He used foreshortening, vanishing the shape to a single point. He painted horses, swords and men in perspective.
2 Piero della Francesca used regular circles to lead the eye through the picture. Notice how the tree arches over Christ's head, directing the viewer back down to Christ and John. Another circle is formed with John's arms. He designed his composition so that it may be subdivided into thirds or halves both horizontally and vertically. For example, John's body and the tree on the left both fall at equal thirds in this painting.

Activity 1: Leonardo's Sketchbook

Activity Objectives

Students should be able to:

• Practice realistic sketches of inanimate objects or objects from nature.

• Closely observe and render detail.

• Study and learn from the sketches of Leonardo da Vinci.

Thinking Critically

Ask students: "What is the difference between a study and a still life? How are they similar?" Some distinctions might be:

• A still life is an arrangement of several inanimate objects; a study usually focuses on one object or a part of a whole (e.g., a study of eyes).

• A still life can be a long-term investigation (i.e., a painting that takes weeks or more to complete); a study is usually a short-term investigation.

• A still life is more likely to produce a single, finished work; a study is a series of sketches in preparation for a finished work.

Preparation Ideas

Check available libraries for slides, books and videos that contain some of Leonardo's sketches. You could engage students in a comparison between his sketches (studies) and his finished works.

Notes on Materials

Each year of study should be a balance between using familiar media and making an effort to learn new materials. You could have students do studies of the same subject in all three media to experience different effects.

• Charcoal is considered by many to be very messy, but it can produce great results. Use fixatives in well-ventilated areas.

• The wax content in Conté crayon makes this medium less likely to smear. You may wish to restrict use of color at first to keep attention on line and detail.

• Pencil is cheap and easy to transport. You can introduce a range of soft to hard leads, kneaded erasers, tools for smudging, and so on.

Activity 1

Leonardo's Sketchbook

Materials
drawing pencils or charcoal
12" x 18" white drawing paper or sketchbook
optional: colored pencil, pen and ink, conte crayon

Take a look.
• Fig.9–a, Leonardo da Vinci, *Five Heads.*
• Fig.9–22, Leonardo da Vinci, *Virgin of the Rocks.*
• Fig.9–23, Leonardo da Vinci, *The Last Supper.*
• Fig 9–24, Leonardo da Vinci, *Mona Lisa.*

Think about it. Leonardo da Vinci investigated many aspects of life in hundreds of pages in his sketchbook and journals. He would sketch his subject, then write notes in "mirror writing." This was "study" in the true sense of the word, a way of learning about life through close observation.

Do it. Find one or more subjects from life and draw them in a sketchbook or journal. Choose anything from human anatomy to objects found in nature or your everyday environment. Surround your sketches with notes and thoughts. An interesting option would be to work in a brown (burnt sienna) medium.

Check it. Do your sketches capture the essence of your subject? Try zooming in on details one at a time and drawing them separately. Ask a friend to identify the object by looking only at the details.

Helpful Hint: Find examples of Leonardo's sketches in your school or local library. Notice how he would sometimes draw an object from several angles to better understand its construction.

Activity 2

Stretching the Truth

Materials
for sculpture:
plasticine clay
newspaper or plastic
clay tools (optional)
newspaper
for painting:
white paper, 12" x 18" or larger
tempera paints
containers to mix paint
container of water
paint brushes

Take a look.
• Fig.9–37, El Greco, *The Burial of Count Orgaz*

Think about it. Research Michelangelo's late works. How did his elongated bodies and expressionistic approaches to subject matter influence visual expression? El Greco took the distortion effect even further, exemplifying the style we call Mannerism.

Do it. Represent a stylized human figure in clay or in tempera painting based on the Mannerist style. Emphasize certain features of the individual or distort the figure through elongation.
• Select a subject to work with: family member, classmate, fairy tale figure, political figure, media celebrity or yourself. Consider the direction you have in mind and what emotion or mood you wish to express.
• If working in clay, plan your figure to be no larger than 18" or 24"—do preliminary sketches if you wish. Don't try to make things "look real."

• If painting, consider what elements you will include, such as people, a particular setting, animals, trees. Whatever you include, distort all the elements to work together in your composition. Identify what colors El Greco used to enhance his expression; plan what colors will work best to express your idea.

Check it. Does your painting reflect the Manneristic style? What primary emotion or mood is being expressed?

Helpful Hint: Be expressive! Think of people who move dramatically, such as dancers, symphony conductors or rock stars. Bring the spirit of movement and drama to your work.

Additional Activities

• Write an essay on "Why I Want to Be an Apprentice to..." (insert a Renaissance artist's name).
• Renaissance artists used the human body to show perfection by stressing muscular development, sensuality, proportion and pose. Take photographs (or do drawings) of students in gym classes or other sports activities to be labeled and used as illustrations for such concepts as loneliness, strength, thought, action, determination, dismay, exhaustion and exhilaration. Think of faces, legs, torso, hands, arms and backs as expressions of the feelings and tensions of the mind as well as the body.

• As your budget allows, try to provide high-quality paper at least occasionally (perhaps after a series of sketches on cheaper paper) so that students can experience the difference it makes.

Warm-up Exercise

To zero in on detail, have right-handed students sketch their left hand in various positions (vice versa for left-handed students). Or, have students draw just ears or eyes.

Tips

• Bring in a skeleton from biology class and have students sketch details such as the finger bones, vertebrae, kneecap, and so forth.

• If school surroundings are suitable, take the class outside to a field, courtyard or atrium to draw items from nature. Or, have students do studies of items in someone's locker. Decide where you're going, make up a list of materials students will need to take with them, and discuss ground rules before leaving the classroom.

Evaluation

Points to consider:

• Did the student record representational drawings of objects?

• Did the student see and record details and have the drawing reflect his or her powers of observation?

• Did the student execute the medium in a way that enhances the object?

Zuzana Zborilová

Age 18
J.F. Dulles High School
Stafford, Texas
Activity 1, Leonardo's Sketchbook

This is a picture which I like most from all of my work. I really like working with black pencil and doing all of the details and shadows of my shoes. Before I started with the drawing I found a contour drawing from the beginning of the year and I wanted to develop it. I drew the shoe below at first and situated it in an easier position, but I love the shoe on the left side which looks like it's kicked into the air.

What do I enjoy about the artistic process? I never know at the beginning how the picture will look like finished. I every time find new ideas during creating. I like doing art during listening to some mystical music and thinking about my dreams. I can relax and forget about the busy world around me.

Zuzana Zborilová

Rich Koehler

Age: 18
J.F. Dulles High School
Stafford, Texas
Activity 2, Stretching the Truth

I enjoy doing contour lines and expanding the body parts. In this picture, I tried to expand many of the features of his body, such as his feet, and shrink his face. When I was working, I was concentrating on the lines in his clothes. I tried to put every crinkle in his clothes. When I was coloring him, I was attempting to make his clothes look real and actually folding around his body parts.

The one thing I have heard is that you cannot mess up in art. For me that statement is hard to believe, but it is true. No matter how bad I mess up it can be fixed somehow. I have also learned that not every drawing has to be life-like. Many of the famous artists did not do life-like pictures and painting.

Richard Koehler

Zuzana Zborilová, *Shoes*, 1994. Pencil, 18" x 24" (46 x 61 cm).

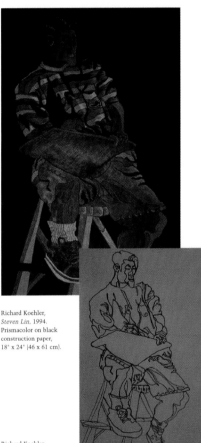

Richard Koehler,
Steven Lin, 1994.
Prismacolor on black
construction paper,
18" x 24" (46 x 61 cm).

Richard Koehler,
Steven Lin, 1994 sketch

Teacher Spotlight
Joan Maresh
Art/Technology Teacher
J.F. Dulles High School

I enjoy allowing the students to discover how to look at the world in new ways, or how to interpret a subject in ways similar to that of the masters: using thick paint in the manner of van Gogh, or filling up sketchbooks with drawings from life, as Leonardo did. It all comes to life for the students when they see that these great artists had a unique way of expressing themselves in the art world and in doing so had artistic breakthroughs to another level of expression. The students begin to see that with persistence and practice, they too will rise to another level of expressing themselves.

Classroom Management
Sculpture:

• Each student works independently and, if necessary, gets additional clay from the supply table. Protect work areas with newspaper or plastic.

Painting:

• Cover work areas with newspaper. This serves to protect the area and to allow students to stroke their wet brushes to rid them of excess water.

• Arrange five containers of paint (black, white, red, blue, yellow) per work station. Violet, green and brown are optional colors. Each student should have his or her own container of water.

Tips
Sometimes a trip to other classes can be a refreshing change of pace. Students could draw athletes in gym class, dancers in dance class or musicians in band practice.

Evaluation
Evaluate students on a variety of criteria. Points to consider:

• Did the student participate in the activity in a positive and responsible manner?

• Could the student supporting his or her decisions (e.g., " I chose these colors because . . ." or "The arms in my sculpture are emphasized or distorted because . . .")?

Activity 2:
Stretching the Truth

Activity Objectives
Students should be able to:

• Understand how distortion and elongation were used by Michelangelo and Mannerist artists.

• Successfully use stylization in a painting or sculpture.

Thinking Critically
Have students study El Greco's *The Burial of Count Orgaz.* Ask them to describe the colors in this painting.

• How does color affect the mood of a painting?

Have students consider the properties of the two art materials by asking:

• How does it feel to manipulate these materials? Can one of these materials express how you feel better than the other?

Preparation Ideas
Find a copy of Michelangelo's Rondanini Pietà in Milan, the last Pietà he sculpted. Have students compare the Mannerist style of this late work to the Pietà featured in the text.

Notes on Materials
If using plasticine clay, you may need two to four sticks per student. These sticks can also serve as structural support inside of softer clay (e.g., as the spine of a small figure). Also useful for support are toothpicks or soda straws.

Chapter 10 Organizer

Chapter 10 Opener: Renaissance in the North

Objectives	National Standards
Discern the difference between the convincing realism of Northern Renaissance painting and the Classical allusions permeating Italian Renaissance art.	**4a** Students differentiate among a variety of historical and cultural contexts in terms of characteristics and purposes of works of art.
Understand that Northern Renaissance artists used ordinary objects as symbols to communicate religious meaning.	**3d** Students evaluate and defend the validity of sources for content and the manner in which subject matter, symbols, and images are used in the student's works and in significant works by others.
Explain how the artistic medium of oil paint assisted Northern Renaissance artists in describing scenes in great detail.	**5b** Students describe meanings of artworks by analyzing how specific works are created and how they relate to historical and cultural contexts.
Comprehend that Renaissance architecture flourished in France while painting remained tied to the earlier International style.	**3a** Students reflect on how artworks differ visually, spatially, temporally, and functionally, and describe how these are related to history and culture.
Articulate how Philip II used the wealth of the Hapsburg Empire to build impressive monuments illustrating Spain's growth as a significant world power.	**4a** Students differentiate among a variety of historical and cultural contexts in terms of characteristics and purposes of works of art.

Teacher Edition References

Lesson 10.1 The Low Countries

Special Feature: The Master of Flémalle 304–305	Contextual Info 306 HOTS 305	Performing Arts 306
Remainder of Lesson 10.1 306–313 World Cultural Timeline 310 Lesson 10.1 Review 313	Contextual Info 308, 310, 312 HOTS 307, 309, 311, 313 Interdisciplinary 309	Materials and Techniques 307, 3(Multicultural 310

Lesson 10.2 Germany

Special Feature: Albrecht Dürer 314–315	Contextual Info 315	HOTS 315
Remainder of Lesson 10.2 316–321 World Cultural Timeline 318 Lesson 10.2 Review 321	Contextual Info 316, 318, 320 HOTS 317, 319, 321 Interdisciplinary 320	Materials and Techniques 316 Multicultural 317, 318

Lesson 10.3 England, France and Spain

Special Feature: El Escorial 322–323	HOTS 323	Performing Arts 323
Remainder of Lesson 10.3 324–326 World Cultural Timeline 324 Lesson 10.3 Review 326 Primary-Source 327 Chapter Review 326	Contextual Info 324, 326 HOTS 325 Cooperative 325	Multicultural 324 Performing Arts 325

Classroom Connections

	National Standards
Studio Activity 1 Symbols, Detail and Light	**1b** Students conceive and create works of visual art that demonstrate an understanding of how the communication of their ideas relates to the media, techniques, and processes they use. **3b** Students apply subjects, symbols, and ideas in their artworks and use the skills gained to solve problems in daily life.
Studio Activity 2 Fantasy World Triptych	**1b** Students conceive and create works of visual art that demonstrate an understanding of how the communication of their ideas relates to the media, techniques, and processes they use. **3b** Students apply subjects, symbols, and ideas in their artworks and use the skills gained to solve problems in daily life.

Other Resources

Books

Chartier, Roger, ed., trans. *A History of Private Life. Vol.3: Passions of the Renaissance.* Cambridge, Harvard University Press, 1989.

Cutler, Charles D. *Northern Painting From Pucelle to Bruegel: 14th, 15th and 16th Centuries.* Orlando: Harcourt Brace Jovanovich, 1973.

Muller, Theodor. *Sculpture in the Netherlands, Germany, France, and Spain: 1400–1500.* New Haven: Yale University Press, 1992.

Snyder, James. *Northern Renaissance Art: Painting, Sculpture, The Graphic Arts from 1350 to 1575.* New York: Harry N. Abrams Inc., 1985.

Stechow, Wolfgang. *Northern Renaissance Art: 1400–1600.* Part of *Sources and Documents in the History of Art.* Evanston: Northwestern University Press, 1989.

von der Osten, Gert, and Vey, Horst. *Painting and Sculpture in Germany and the Netherlands: 1500–1600.* New Haven: Yale University Press, 1992.

Music

Josquin des Pres—*Ave Maria*
Crequillon—*Pour Ung Plaisir*
Bennet—*Thyrsis, Sleepest Thou?*
(these examples can be found in Hadyn Society, Masterpieces of Music Before 1750.)

Ancillaries

Slides: van der Weyden, *Portrait of a Lady*, 60a, 122; Grünewald, *Meeting of Saints Erasmus and Maurice*, 64b, 126

Teacher Edition References

Timeline: Renaissance in the North 302
Map: Northern Renaissance 303
Context 302
Art 302
Quote 303

Ancillaries

Slides: van der Weyden, *Portrait of a Lady*, 60a, 122; van der Weyden, *Annunciation*, 63b, 123; Bruegel, *Return from the Hunt (Winter)*, 61a, 124; *Peasant Wedding* 2a, 6

Large Reproductions: Dürer, *The Four Horsemen of the Apocalypse*, 13

Slides: Dürer, *Knight, Death and the Devil*, 62a, 125; Grünewald, *Meeting of Saints Erasmus and Maurice*, 64b, 126; Holbein, *Edward VI*, 65b, 127
Overhead Transparencies: The Art of the Print, 10
Large Reproductions: Dürer, *The Four Horsemen of the Apocalypse*, 13

Slides: Juan Bautista, El Escorial, Spain, 63a, 128

Slides: Nepveu, Chateau of Chambord, France, 64a, 129; Nepveu, Chateaux of Chambord, bedroom, 66b, 130

Schedule

One day for a small drawing, up to five days for a larger more finished rendering.

Materials

11" x 14" or 12" x 18" white drawing paper, assorted colored pencils

One day for a small drawing, up to five days for a larger more finished rendering.

11" x 14" paper, assorted fine-line colored markers, optional: colored pencils, oil pastels or watercolors

Introduce

Artists in the Low Countries (Holland and Belgium) were the first to capitalize on the new medium of oil paint, which enabled them to capture the minute nuances of the observable world. Northern Renaissance artists used ordinary objects in their compositions to communicate religious content. While English and French artists continued to paint in the older International style, French architects excelled in designing elaborate palaces and châteaux that populated the Loire River valley. To embellish his court, Philip II of Spain used the wealth and prestige of the Hapsburg Empire to draw artists from all over Europe.

Lessons at a Glance

10.1 *The Low Countries*
Artists in Belgium and Holland, the Low Countries, were the first to develop the extensive potential of oil paint. The common objects within their compositions symbolically communicated religious messages.

10.2 *Germany*
Germany became the art center of northern Europe in the sixteenth century. Its artists absorbed influences from Italy and blended them with the northern tendency toward extreme realism.

10.3 *England, France and Spain*
During the sixteenth century, England contributed to the advancement of music and literature, but it was France that excelled in architecture. Philip II summoned leading artists from across Europe to help build an impressive capital to symbolize the great wealth and increasing strength of the Spanish Hapsburg Empire.

Objectives

Students should be able to:

Discern the difference between the convincing realism of Northern Renaissance painting and the Classical allusions permeating Italian Renaissance art.

Understand that Northern Renaissance artists used ordinary objects as symbols to communicate religious meaning.

Explain how the artistic medium of oil paint assisted Northern Renaissance artists in describing scenes in great detail.

302

10 Renaissance in the North

THE RENAISSANCE THAT HAD SO INSPIRED Italian painters occurred not only in Italy, but in all of Europe. In Northern Europe however, the style of the Renaissance painters was rather different from their Italian counterparts.

Northern artists, especially those from Belgium and Holland (the Low Countries), used ordinary everyday objects to render their highly symbolic religious subject matter. There was great attention to detail. But the innovation that had the greatest impact during this period was oil paint. The new medium tremendously expanded the use of color and light and Northern Renaissance artists used it to its full advantage.

In the sixteenth century, Germany became the art center of Northern Europe. German artists were strongly individualistic, much like their contemporaries in Italy.

In England and France, painters preferred to continue with the International style that had its roots in the Gothic era. Renaissance architecture did flourish in France with the construction of many châteaux.

The great wealth of Spain drew many artists to its court. Philip II built monuments and commissioned works in a manner similar to the Medici and the popes in Italy.

10–a Northern Renaissance artists became masters of the oil painting technique. This new medium produced incredible color and permitted artists to paint with unsurpassed attention to detail.
Hans Holbein, *Sir Thomas More*, detail (fig.10–21).

| 1425–1426 Master of Flémalle (Robert Campin), *Mérode Altarpiece* | 1480 Leonardo invents the parachute and helicopter | 1497 The Cabots reach the east coast of North America | 1527 Holbein, *Sir Thomas More* | 1551 Breugel becomes a master in the Antwerp painters' guild / 1564 Galileo Galilei born | 1594 Shakespeare, *Romeo and Juliet* |

Renaissance in the North

| 1436 van der Weyden becomes official painter to Brussels | 1480 Arrival of oil painting technique in Italy | 1519 Château of Chambord begun | 1543 Copernicus' planetary theory | 1588 Spanish Armada defeated by the English |

Comprehend that Renaissance architecture flourished in France while painting remained tied to the earlier International style.

Articulate how Philip II used the wealth of the Hapsburg Empire to build impressive monuments illustrating Spain's growth as a world power.

Teach
Timeline

Instruct students to superimpose the dates and events of the Northern Renaissance timeline over the one for Italy in Chapter 9. Ask if the two periods occurred sequentially or simultaneously. Why might it be important to understand that art developed in northern and southern Europe at the same time?

Context

Ask students to decide who the art patrons were in the Northern Renaissance by looking at fig.10–a (detail of fig.10–21) and fig.10–b (detail of fig.10–6). Do the patrons shown in the images look like kings, queens and religious leaders? Share that the increasingly affluent middle class began to commission and purchase art.
Ask students how the role of painters in the North changed as the wealthy middle class joined royalty and nobility as art patrons.

• Did artists have to be as concerned about gaining court appointments?

• How might the emergence of new middle-class patrons affect the amount of freedom artists had over their styles and subject matter?

What beauty is I know not, though it adheres to many things...As what all the world prizes as right we hold to be right, so what all the world esteems to be beautiful that will we also hold for beautiful and strive to produce.

Albrecht Dürer

10–b Realism is an important element of Northern Renaissance art. This is a small detail from a painting that documents a wedding. The ceremony between Giovanni Arnolfini and Jeanne Cenami is witnessed by the artist and another individual. The witnesses are reflected in this mirror.
Jan van Eyck, detail of *Arnolfini Wedding*, (fig. 10–6).

The Renaissance soon found its way north where it impacted the artwork and architecture of Flanders, Holland, Germany, England and France. It also moved westward to Spain (see map on page 331).

10–c The facade of this Renaissance addition to the Louvre includes a profusion of sculptured figures on the top story. The facade is considered by some to be the best example of French Renaissance architecture.
Pierre Lescot, *Square Court of the Louvre*, detail (fig. 10–28).

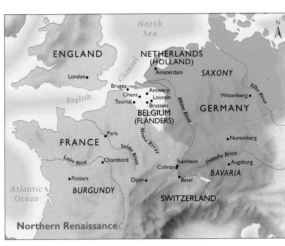

Quote

Ask students what Dürer's statement reveals about his view of the role of an artist in society. Does it allow very much room for the notion of artist as free-thinker or bohemian? Remind students that the concept of artist as someone going against the grain or creating an individual expression of beauty is a very modern idea that has its roots in the nineteenth century.

Map

After students review the map, ask them why this period is referred to as the Northern Renaissance. Although the Low Countries (Belgium and Holland), England, France and Spain were north of Italy, they were not completely isolated from its culture, since artists and their work traveled back and forth across Europe.

• Ask if they feel it is easier to understand history when it is taught simultaneously or sequentially.

• How does knowing that the Renaissance flourished in many locations at the same time affect their thinking?

Reteach

Remind students that for centuries only aristocrats, royalty and the church could afford to commission art. But now have students imagine that they and their families have recently become wealthy.

• Ask: "How would you choose to make others aware of your new-found wealth? What painted images would you want to decorate your home? How does it feel to be able to commission artists?"

• Ask the class what medium we usually use today to document special events or important people in our lives.

• Were there disadvantages to this new patronage?

• For whom would students have preferred to work if they had been artists during this period?

Art

Have students examine the painting by Hans Holbein and the one by Jan van Eyck.

• How would they describe the Northern Renaissance style; for instance, its color, the edges of the forms and the tendency toward realism? Share with students that the new medium of oil paint greatly enhanced artists' ability to meticulously represent the physical world. The medium was slow-drying and therefore allowed artists to pay increasing attention to fine details. (See

the texture of Sir Thomas More's clothing in fig. 10–a and the accurate description of the scene reflected in the small mirror of *Arnolfini Wedding* in fig. 10–b.)

Evaluate

Ask students how oil paint revolutionized painting in the North. What are its advantages over tempera? To check their answers, guide them to the discussion of the two media in Lesson 2.2.

Did the Northern Renaissance occur after the Italian Renaissance? Have students recheck their timelines to understand that developments occurred in the North at the same time as those in Italy. Remind them not to be misled by the fact that the two areas are covered in separate chapters in the textbook.

Lesson 10.1

Artists in Belgium and Holland, the Low Countries, were the first to develop the extensive potential of oil paint. They used the new medium to describe scenes in microscopic detail, capturing the radiant colors, light and textures of the tangible world. The common objects within their compositions symbolically communicated religious messages.

Warm-up

Instruct students to pretend that they are mice in the house, workshop and garden of the *Mérode Altarpiece* (figs.10–1, 10–2, 10–3). Can they find many places to hide and objects to run around? Share that Northern Renaissance artists were more interested in articulating the natural world than in presenting an idealized beauty, which characterized the Italian Renaissance style.

Objectives

Students should be able to:

Differentiate between the references to Classical antiquity in Italian Renaissance art and the accurate portrayal of the visible world in Northern Renaissance art.

Understand that painters in the Low Countries were the first to master the medium of oil paint and the dramatic effect the medium had on their style.

Describe how Northern Renaissance painters incorporated everyday objects as religious symbols.

Vocabulary Definitions

realism A mid-nineteenth-century style of art based on the belief that the subject matter should be shown true to life, without any stylization or idealization. By extension it can refer to realistically painted work of any time.

symbol A form, image, sign or subject representing a meaning other than its outward appearance.

Teach

Criticism: Direct students to study the Flemish room in the center of fig.10–1 (detail in fig.10–2).

10.1 The Low Countries

THE GOTHIC STYLE OF ARCHITECTURE dominated northern Europe into the early sixteenth century. In painting, however, the Northern Renaissance painters moved in a different direction from Italian Renaissance styles. As we have seen, many Italian painters had returned to the aesthetics and ideals of Classical antiquity. Northern Renaissance artists began to direct their attention to creating works with a powerful sense of realism.

The painters of the Low Countries (Belgium and Holland) were the first to master the new medium of oil paint. With the new medium, painters were able to create richer colors than before. As a result, painting of the Low Countries in the fifteenth century is characterized by glowing colors that appear to be lit from within. This new medium revolutionized painting and allowed artists to work with an unlimited range of values and colors. Colors could be blended to produce the delicately shaded folds in cloth and the carefully observed changes in light intensity.

Painters aimed at clear, hard-edged detail in their representation of objects. Their realism was one of radiant decorative color rather than sculptural form.

All Renaissance artists tried to reconcile religious subjects with scenes and objects from everyday life. Artists in Northern Europe, particularly the Low Countries, accomplished this by using symbolism.

As had happened in Italy, the Northern painters also found a new prestige and place in society. Some women are also recorded as belonging to the art guilds of Flemish cities. To pursue a craft, individuals had to belong to the guild that controlled that craft.

Key Notes

- Northern Renaissance art is powerfully realistic.
- Oil paint, the new medium, produces marvelous color.
- Ordinary objects are used to symbolize religious subjects.

Vocabulary
realism
symbolism

Special Feature
The Master of Flémalle
Robert Campin (about 1378–1444)

Attention to detail, extreme *realism* and the use of commonplace settings is perfectly illustrated by the work of the Master of Flémalle. Most art historians believe that the Master of Flémalle was Robert Campin, the leading painter of the city of Tournai in Flanders (Belgium). Unfortunately, early Renaissance paintings in the Low Countries were not signed by the artist. Without signatures, names have been lost. Although there might be some doubt as to the name of the artist, there is no doubt that the *Mérode Altarpiece* (fig.10–1) is an early Renaissance masterpiece.

10–1 Notice how the top of the table is tipped up so that the viewer can clearly see everything that is on it. The Master of Flémalle (Robert Campin), *Mérode Altarpiece*, about 1425–1426. Oil on panel, center: 25″ x 25″ (64 x 64 cm). The Metropolitan Museum of Art, New York, The Cloisters Collection.

10–2 Oil painting revolutionized art. It allowed artists to work with a range of values and colors and to use detail in a way not possible with tempera or fresco. The Master of Flémalle (Robert Campin), *Mérode Altarpiece*, detail of central panel.

- How does it differ from the interior of the same subject in Fra Angelico's *The Annunciation* (fig.9–12)?

- Does the Flemish or the Italian artist include more details and individual objects?

- Explain that Flemish artists concentrated on describing the physical world in the most realistic manner possible and used familiar elements symbolically to communicate religious messages.

Art History: Ask students to guess what the individual objects in the *Mérode Altarpiece* (fig.10–1) are meant to signify about the Virgin. The lilies symbolize her chastity; the rosebush, her charity; and the violets, her humility. The water basin, although an ordinary household item, is also an emblem of Mary as the "vessel most clean" and the "well of living waters." Although their disguised references are a mystery to many people today, during the Renaissance many viewers would have readily understood their implications. Have students discuss if and how knowing what these items represent changes their attitude toward the painting.

Evaluate

Ask students how Northern Renaissance artists used everyday objects in their paintings.

- Do most contemporary artists communicate with universally understood symbols?

So named because it was in the Mérode family for many years, the *Mérode Altarpiece* is a triptych. From left to right, the three panels contain the kneeling donors of the altarpiece, an Annunciation scene with the Virgin Mary and the angel Gabriel, and Joseph in his carpenter's shop in the last panel. The *Mérode Altarpiece* belongs within the tradition of the International style yet it contains a new pictorial experience. One of the new elements is the setting of a typical contemporary Flemish dwelling. This is, in fact, the earliest Annunciation panel painting that takes place in a completely domestic interior.

The donors, a soberly dressed man and wife belonging to the middle-class, kneel in a little courtyard. The man peers through the door at the Annunciation taking place in the central panel. The donors set the tone of the painting. Discreetly set apart from the sacred

scene, they take it in as a fact, as reality. They draw the viewer into looking, too. We see a very proper middle-class Mary surrounded by all the domestic details of a typical Flemish household (fig.10–2). The items are also symbols. The spotless room and the vase of lilies on the table symbolize the Virgin's purity. In the right panel, Joseph has made a mousetrap (fig.10–3). It symbolizes Christ's appearance in the world in human form as a means of fooling (baiting) and catching the Devil. So close are the sacred personages to real people that they are represented without halos.

The tonality of the painting is also different from earlier panel paintings. The color scheme is far less decorative. The artist uses subdued hues. All these effects, part of the realistic style of the Master of Flémalle, were made possible by the use of oil paint. The Master of Flémalle was among the first painters to exploit this new medium.

10–3 What is Joseph building? Why did the artist show him with that project?
The Master of Flémalle (Robert Campin), *Mérode Altarpiece*, detail of St. Joseph.

• Twentieth-century artists frequently use personal symbols to explore a vast variety of ideas and emotions. However, what symbols can students name within modern society that are readily understood by the majority of people? (for example, a heart, a green light or a cigarette in a large circle with a diagonal line through the image)

• Explore how visual symbols within modern culture are often secular, as compared to the religious implications of those in Northern Renaissance paintings.

Remind students that the new medium of oil paint dried more slowly than the tempera mixtures used previously.

• How would artists' ability to work more slowly have affected their style?

• Could they have paid as much attention to fine details and realism if they had to work quickly or could not go back and make changes?

Reteach

Ask students if they would describe Northern Renaissance style as realistic.

• What can the images on these pages tell us about the time period and culture?

• Do students tend to accept Northern Renaissance paintings as truthful visual documents?

• How do these images differ from photographs?

• Can both photographers and painters alter their works in order to imbue them with a particular interpretation?

Ask students to glance at the twentieth-century painting *Drugstore* by Richard Estes (fig.17–35) and note one strong similarity to the *Mérode Altarpiece*.

• Although the subjects are vastly different, what ties the two images together? If students need help, have them consider the style and media in both paintings.

• Do the artists appear equally concerned with capturing every nuance of light and color in their work?

10–5 Contrast this Annunciation to the one done by Fra Angelico (fig.9–12). Which do you prefer?
Jan van Eyck, *The Annunciation*, 1434–1436. Oil on wood, transferred to canvas. 35 3/8" x 13 7/8" (90 x 35 cm). National Gallery of Art, Washington DC, Andrew W. Mellon Collection.

Jan van Eyck

(about 1390–1441)

No painter could equal the color and light of Jan van Eyck. Like other northern European Renaissance painters, he had a fascination with detail. Yet, areas of his paintings are subordinated in order to direct attention to the most important parts. His understanding of light was far greater than that of his Italian contemporaries. Van Eyck excelled at portraying direct and diffused light, shadows falling on a variety of surfaces, and light's effect on the illusion of distance.

Philip the Good, Duke of Burgundy, considered van Eyck the world's greatest artist. Van Eyck traveled for the Duke and even went to Italy where he met Masaccio and other Florentine artists. He finally settled in Bruges in Flanders in 1430 and began to sign and date his works for the first time.

The greatest early Flemish masterpiece was *The Ghent Altarpiece* (fig.10–4). It was begun by Hubert van Eyck in 1425 and finished by his brother Jan seven years later. Art historians have spent much time trying to determine which

10–4 Compare the nude figures here to sculptures from ancient Greece.
Hubert and Jan van Eyck, *Ghent Altarpiece* (open), completed 1432. Oil on panel, 11 1/2' x 15' (3.5 x 4.6 m). Cathedral of St. Bavo, Ghent, Belgium.

parts were done by each, but the work largely reveals Jan's genius. The entire altarpiece is about 16 1/2 feet wide when the triptych is opened. The two wings are painted on both sides so that even when closed the altarpiece is decorative.

When the altarpiece is opened, the entire bottom section across five panels tells the story *The Adoration of the Lamb* from the Book of Revelations. Marvelous landscapes, animals, trees, people, fabrics, light and air are handled with meticulous detail, as if each part were to be studied separately. Using the new oil medium, van Eyck presents in glowing color a scene in Paradise (with Flemish buildings). The dove of the Holy Spirit sheds light on the enthroned Mystic Lamb (a symbol of Christ). The Fountain of Life pours its water into an octagonal basin and, from there, into a river in which jewels are seen. Prophets, patriarchs and kings of the Old Testament are grouped on the left, while apostles and saints are on the right.

Adam and Eve and singing angels appear in the top side panels of the altarpiece. The figures of Adam and Eve are the first almost-life-size nudes done in northern Europe. In the incredibly detailed central panel is God the Father flanked by Mary and John the Baptist.

In van Eyck's painting *The Annunciation* (fig.10–5), the angel Gabriel announces the birth of Christ to Mary. The event takes place in a fifteenth-century Gothic church. The setting could almost be the set of a play that the viewer is watching. Words coming from Gabriel's mouth ("Ave Maria...") are answered by Mary's words, which are upside down—to be read by God. Robes, building, windows, faces and the floor are painstakingly detailed. Jewels in Gabriel's crown and robe reflect the light with amazing accuracy. The panel is filled with **symbolism**. The lilies symbolize Mary's purity and her gesture is one of submission to the will of God. Lilies on the angel's robe again symbolize Mary while pomegranates signify Christ's resurrection. From the top of the painting, the dove of the Holy Spirit descends to Mary on rays of light. Floor panels illustrate Old Testament events: David killing Goliath, Samson destroying the temple, and so on.

One of van Eyck's best-known paintings is the *Arnolfini Wedding* (fig.10–6), a work of marvelous reality and unity. Meticulous detail and incredibly realistic light share importance in the painting. Light enters at the left and softly illuminates the metal chandelier, hard walls, soft fabrics and flesh. All the detailed objects in the room have symbolic significance. The raised right hand and the little dog are symbols of fidelity. The clogs, cast aside, indicate that the couple stands on holy ground. The peaches ripening on the chest are a sign of fertility.

Jan van Eyck witnessed the ceremony, and so signed his name on the wall above the mirror with words meaning "Jan van Eyck was here in 1434." A miniature composition can be seen in the convex enlarging mirror (fig.10–b). The mirror shows not only the backs of the couple but also the front view of Jan and another person.

10–6 This painting has been described as a visual marriage license. Can you explain that description?
Jan van Eyck, *Arnolfini Wedding*, 1434. Oil on panel, 32" x 23" (82 x 59 cm). National Gallery, London.

Higher-Order Thinking Skills

The *Arnolfini Wedding* (fig.10–6) can be considered a wedding certificate. Have students use the text to identify the symbolism of the various items included in the painting.

Materials and Techniques

The *Arnolfini Wedding* is painted on a panel made of two pieces of oak with the grain running vertically. An animal skin glue and chalk ground, called gesso, was applied in a uniform layer. It then was polished. The ground totally obscures the wood grain and provides a fine, smooth surface upon which to paint.

Contextual Information

Van der Weyden

Rogier van der Weyden's *Portrait of a Lady* (fig.10–8) has been tentatively identified as Marie de Valengin, daughter of Philip the Good, Duke of Burgundy. Van der Weyden was ranked as one of the foremost portraitists of his time.

10–8 Compare this portrait to the *Mona Lisa* (fig.9–24). Rogier van der Weyden, *Portrait of a Lady*, about 1455. Oil on panel, 14 1/2" x 10 1/2" (37 x 27 cm). National Gallery of Art, Washington DC, Andrew Mellon Collection.

Materials and Techniques

The new medium of oil painting involved the following process: Over an underpainting of grayish tempera that was really a value drawing in darks and lights, oil colors were brushed in thin, transparent, colored layers, one over the other until the desired richness was achieved. Because oil paints did not dry as rapidly as tempera, colors could be blended to produce the delicately shaded folds in cloth and the carefully observed changes in light intensity. This new medium revolutionized painting and allowed artists to work with an unlimited range of values and colors and to use detail in a way not possible with tempera or fresco.

Rogier van der Weyden

(1399–1464)

The third great artist of early Flemish painting was Rogier van der Weyden. Rogier van der Weyden became the official painter for the city of Brussels in 1435 and had a strong influence on countless artists that followed. He worked on larger surfaces than van Eyck and infused his detailed religious works with drama and emotion.

The large *Descent from the Cross* (probably part of a triptych) was painted for a church in Louvain in 1435 (fig.10–7). The setting (what one can see of it) is symbolic, taking place inside the sepulcher and not on a hill outside Jerusalem. Rather than use the natural light of van Eyck, Rogier lights each part carefully so that every wrinkle, tear and detail can be seen. This lighting is much like the evenly lighted treatment in the Master of Flémalle's work. The crisp folds so noticeable in the Master of Flémalle's paintings are again evident in Rogier's work. The twisted and bending bod-ies emphasize the strong emotional feeling expressed in each face. Notice how the limp S-curve of Christ's body is repeated in Mary's body in the foreground. Her hand almost touches the skull of Adam, which, according to legend, was discovered when the hole was dug for the cross. The entire complex composition is balanced beautifully. The figures are grouped carefully, and the almost horizontal body of Christ ties the parts together.

Jan van Eyck had been one of the first northern European artists to paint portraits. But, equally impressive are those by Rogier van der Weyden. His *Portrait of a Lady* (fig.10–8) is an excellent example. Exquisite line and delicate shading form the face. The face is set off by the beautiful white coif placed against a dark background. The folded hands are a familiar gesture in such paintings. The only bit of bright color is in the red belt, which seems much too small for the figure. The stark, simple and cool design is emphasized by the woman's aloof expression.

10–7 The twisting, turning bodies emphasize the powerful emotions of the scene.
Rogier van der Weyden, *Descent from the Cross*, about 1435. Oil on panel, 7' 2 5/8" x 8' 7 1/8" (217 x 260 cm). The Prado Museum, Madrid.

Tapestry

In the Middle Ages, tapestry and embroidery were widely appreciated as an art form, and women were instrumental in their making. Tapestry, which is extremely time-consuming, was a serious occupation for women. During the Middle Ages, many women used their embroidery skills to fashion some of the most significant works of their epoch. Richly colored tapestries featured scenes from history or favorite romances of the times.

Tapestries continued to be made in the Renaissance. Flemish tapestry reached a height of excellence between 1480 and 1520 that has never been equaled in Europe. Women were primarily responsible for the weaving of these masterpieces.

Tapestries had advantages over wall paintings in that they were portable and could be taken down to be rehung elsewhere. They added warmth to cold castle walls and helped reduce echoes in stone-walled halls. The materials, dyed wools and silks, and even gold and silver threads, added luxurious textures and colors to building interiors.

The process of Flemish tapestry making was long and costly. After producing a sketch, the artist would create a full-size painting on paper (cartoon). The highly skilled weavers would work from the cartoon. The entire tapestry was woven on a huge loom, thread by thread. These tapestries were found in every castle and palace in Europe.

Higher-Order Thinking Skills

Have students compare the lighting in *Descent from the Cross* (fig.10–7) to that in the *Mérode Altarpiece* (fig.10–1) or the *Arnolfini Wedding* (fig.10–6).

Interdisciplinary Connection

Geography: In the fifteenth and six-teenth centuries, what routes would have been taken by people traveling between the Netherlands and Italy? By what means did people travel those distances?

Contextual Information

Bosch

Hieronymus Bosch came from a family of many painters. These included his father, his sister, a brother, four uncles and his grandfather, Jan. Born Jheronimous Anthonissen van Aken, the multitude of family artists might have prompted him to call himself Hieronymus Bosch after his hometown, 's-Hertogenbosch, in order to distinguish himself from the rest of the family. Little is known about Bosch's childhood, but it is assumed that he enjoyed a middle-class upbringing.

Hans Memling

(about 1440–1494)

Born in Germany, Hans Memling (also written as Memlinc) became a citizen of Bruges and probably studied under Rogier van der Weyden for a time. Memling's work was quiet and serene, and was sometimes confused with that of Jan van Eyck.

His *Madonna and Child with Angels* (fig.10–9) is similar in theme to many works of this time. His technique is superior. The composition is symmetrically balanced. On each side of Mary and the Christ Child are two angels with musical instruments. One angel plays with the child, offering an orange. The child reaches with one hand for the orange while ruffling the pages of the book with the other, both very natural movements for a child. Notice the textural detail of the various fabrics. Some are rich brocades, others are plain and smooth. Gothic sculptures flank a rounded arch. In the distance is a medieval landscape with a castle and distant church. Every corner of the painting is carefully done. The light on each material (stone, wood, cloth, carpet, skin) is painted with knowledge and great skill.

10–9 Memling's work was sometimes confused with the work of Jan van Eyck. What similarities do you see?
Hans Memling, *Madonna and Child with Angels*, about 1480. Oil on panel, 22 5/8" x 19" (57.5 x 48 cm). National Gallery of Art, Washington DC, Andrew Mellon Collection.

Hieronymus Bosch

(about 1450–1516)

A Dutch painter with an incredible imagination, Hieronymus Bosch presents a world full of weird images and puzzling symbols. His work is usually packed with tiny people, mostly naked, who are engaged in dozens of activities. It is almost as if ten or more paintings were crammed into a single frame.

Probably the most complex of his busy works is the strangely wonderful *Garden of Delights* (fig.10–10), a huge triptych. The symbolism, complexity and incredible detail of the three-part story take a long time to read. The left panel is *The Garden of Eden*. Here, amid exotic animals, plants and landscape, God is introducing Adam to Eve. The

1400
Chan Chan, the largest known adobe city, built in Peru

1405
Cheng Ho begins exploration to Southeast Asia, India and Africa

World Cultural Timeline

400–1600
Kongo Kingdom

1421
Chinese emperors occupy Forbidden City, Peking, China

Multicultural Connection

The Kongo Kingdom

The Kongo kingdom, which flourished during the sixteenth century, was in present-day Zaire. One of the world's largest and thickest rain forests covers most of the country's northern region, and the mighty Congo River (also known as the Zaire River) flows through the country and is part of the boundary between the Congo and Zaire. As a navigable route to the interior, the river figured prominently in the subsequent colonization of Central Africa. It is believed that at its height the Kongo kingdom extended from present-day Angola to Gabon.

In 1482, Portuguese navigator Diogo Cam made contact with the Kongo people along the Congolese coast. The Kongo king subsequently signed a cultural exchange treaty with Portugal in

10–10 Many twentieth century artists have been influenced by Bosch's work.
Hieronymus Bosch, *Garden of Delights*, about 1505–1510. Triptych, oil on panel, center panel 86 1/4" x 76 3/4" (219 x 195 cm), each wing 86 1/2" x 38" (219 x 97 cm). The Prado Museum, Madrid.

10–11 This painting could be explored inch by inch. It is crammed with fantastic figures, forms and landscapes.
Hieronymus Bosch, *Garden of Delights*, detail of central panel.

right panel, *The Garden of Satan*, is a nightmare of indescribable tortures. It portrays Bosch's idea of Hell. Hundreds of figures are being tortured. The eggshell-human-tree trunk figure of Satan in the center supervises the scene. Across the River Styx, a city burns with fire and dense smoke. The huge central panel, the *Garden of Delights*, is also a huge question mark. What does it all mean? The fantastic landscape is filled with hundreds of light-pink, naked figures. They are innocently parading, riding on various beasts, sitting on giant birds, swimming, bathing, and crawling in and out of gigantic eggs and other equally amazing forms (fig.10–11).

If one reads the entire story together, Bosch is revealed as a moralist. The left panel shows God's beautiful creation. The middle panel depicts humanity's constant search to satisfy its earthly desires with overindulgence and sin. This eventually leads to Hell, shown on the right. Although it is called a *Garden of Delights*, Bosch's work is a pessimistic look at humanity. No chance of salvation is shown.

Higher-Order Thinking Skills

1 Have students compare and contrast Memling's *Madonna and Child with Angels* (fig.10–9) and *The Alba Madonna* (fig.9–31) by Raphael. Ask what makes each especially representative of the Northern Renaissance or the Italian Renaissance, respectively.

2 The imagination of Hieronymus Bosch may provide some ideas for students to depict their own ideas. Have students select a title for a composition (e.g., "Stones in the Closet," "Garden of Electronics," "The Weird World of _____") and create a collage or drawing of the wildest combinations they can imagine. Suggest that they study Bosch's work to note his characteristics. The final result may be a humorous, critical or serious statement.

the late 1400s and began welcoming Franciscan missionaries. The king converted to Christianity, but his attempts to impose the religion on his people provoked violent opposition. In the early 1500s, his successor also made attempts to Christianize the country. He adopted the Portuguese model for his government and built many churches. Despite these developments, thousands of Africans in the area were enslaved and sold to the Portuguese and other Europeans. The kingdom declined and so did all possibilities of its becoming a Christianized country.

• Have students research the tribal arts of the Pende, Bakuba and Bakele tribes of Zaire.

Contextual Information

Bruegel

On his travels across the Alps to Rome and Sicily, Bruegel sketched people and landscapes and later used them in his paintings. Many other artists went to Rome to see collections and to receive their training. Many came back and painted in the Italian style, but others, like Bruegel, went to Italy and studied with artists there but never copied their style.

Pieter Bruegel

(about 1525–1569)

Religious wars wracked the Low Countries during the early sixteenth century. Amid this unsettling environment, Low Country painting began to discard the detail and reality of van Eyck and Rogier and to absorb the influence of Italian art.

Pieter Bruegel was the most highly acclaimed Low Country master of the sixteenth century. Born near Bosch's hometown in what is now Holland, his early work was greatly influenced by Bosch. A four-year trip to Italy changed his outlook on painting. His later work contains larger figures that often have the monumentality of Giotto or Masaccio.

Bruegel filled his painting of the *Tower of Babel* (fig.10–12) with hundreds of tiny figures that contrast with the mammoth structure set into a far-reaching landscape. According to the Old Testament, the people of Mesopotamia attempted to build a tower that reached to heaven. However, the pride of the people became so great that God could not tolerate it and confused their languages. The people could not communicate and work had to stop.

Bruegel had no knowledge of the squarish ziggurats of the Sumerians. Instead he invented a huge round structure somewhat like the Roman Colosseum. Boats and barges unload materials, which are carried up ladders and ramps to the work sites. As the mountainous structure rises into the clouds, more stone is being cut in the foreground. Bruegel emphasizes the work process, the huge scale of the tower, and the inevitable failure of the impossible task.

Very few artists have captured the silent, cold crispness of winter the way Pieter Bruegel has in *The Return of the Hunters* (fig.10–13). The painting is one of a series depicting the seasons of the year. He loved to paint peasants in their daily activities as well as at their special festivals. The world here is covered with snow. The weary hunters trudge homeward, their dogs following dejectedly behind. The hunt has been hard work, not a jolly sport, but is part of the seasonal struggle of the peasants. Below the village on the hillside, skaters frolic on the frozen ponds. Alpine peaks, which Bruegel observed on his Italian trip, are shown in the

10–12 What construction activities can you identify in this painting?
Pieter Bruegel, *The Tower of Babel*, 1563.
Oil on oakwood, 44 1/2" x 61" (113 x 155 cm).
Kunsthistoriches Museum, Vienna.

distance. The depth is felt more strongly because of the birds flying in the intervening space. The leafless trees march down the hill and help unite the foreground with the middle distance. Simple human activities and ordinary landscapes receive extreme importance and dignity in Bruegel's treatment. Humans and nature are bound together as a working unit.

10–13 Paintings of common, everyday activities were unusual in Bruegel's time. Did the hunters have a successful day?
Pieter Bruegel, *The Return of the Hunters*, 1565. Oil and tempera on panel, 46 1/2" x 63 3/4" (117 x161 cm). Kunsthistorisches Museum, Vienna.

Higher-Order Thinking Skills

1 Ask students to create oral or written anecdotes about the people in the town of Bruegel's *The Return of the Hunters* (fig.10–13). They can start with a character sketch and then add an incident that involved the character. Discuss elements of good storytelling with the class.

2 Another work by Bruegel, *Peasant Wedding* (fig.2–1), appears in Chapter 2. Ask students to turn to that image and describe the scene. Then have them indicate what about the work's style and subject matter might identify it as a painting by Bruegel.

Lesson 10.1 Review

1 What were two advantages of oil paint over tempera paint?

2 List several features of Robert Campin's *Mérode Altarpiece* that are often found in Northern European Renaissance paintings.

3 Explain the symbolism of two objects in the *Mérode Altarpiece*.

4 Which art element did Jan van Eyck understand and paint better than most of his contemporary artists?

5 Explain the symbolism of three objects in one of Jan van Eyck's paintings.

6 Describe the composition of Rogier van der Weyden's *Descent from the Cross*. How has he created unity and directed the viewer's gaze through his painting?

7 How has Bruegel created depth in *The Return of the Hunters*?

Lesson 10.1 Review Answers

1 Oil paints may be mixed to create an unlimited range of values and colors richer than the range that can be created by tempera. Oil paints are easier to blend than tempera, which dries faster than oil paint.

2 Attention to detail, extreme realism, use of commonplace settings, symbolism and the use of oil paints

3 The spotless room and the vase of lilies on the table symbolize Mary's purity. The mousetrap represents Christ's appearance in human form as bait set in a trap to catch the Devil.

4 Light

5 In *The Annunciation*: Lilies symbolize Mary's purity and her gesture represents submission to the will of God. The lilies on the angel's robe also symbolize Mary's purity, and the pomegranates signify Christ's resurrection. The dove is the Holy Spirit.

In *Arnolfini Wedding*: The raised right hand and dog represent fidelity. The cast-aside clogs signify that the couple is standing on holy ground. The ripening peaches symbolize fertility.

6 The whole composition is symmetrically balanced with the figures closely grouped around the almost horizontal body of Christ, which ties the picture together. Van der Weyden leads the eye through the limp S-curve of Christ's body. He repeats this curve in Mary's body.

7 Bruegel created depth by making the figures and trees in the foreground much larger than the objects in the background. He created even greater depth by painting birds flying in the intervening space. The line of trees marching down the hill unites the foreground with the middle distance and the distant Alpine peaks.

Lesson 10.2

Germany became the art center of northern Europe in the sixteenth century. Its artists absorbed influences from Italy and blended them with the northern tendency toward extreme realism.

Warm-up

Ask students to take a close look at one of their hands and forearms. Tell them to list exactly what they see, pores, hairs, lines and so forth. Afterward, ask what they noticed about their hand and arm that they had not observed before. Are they often this careful in their looking? What does the exercise have in common with what Dürer would have done to create his *Self-Portrait* (fig.10–14)? How long do they believe Dürer studied himself in order to render his own likeness?

Objectives

Students should be able to:

• identify Germany as the leader of art in northern Europe during the early 1500s

• comprehend that German artists blended Italian High Renaissance characteristics with northern techniques and styles

Vocabulary Definitions

polyptych (pah-*lip*-tik) An altarpiece or devotional painting consisting of more than three panels joined together.

Teach

Criticism: Have students compare Dürer's *Self-Portrait* to Italian Renaissance portraits in Chapter 9, such as Leonardo's *Mona Lisa* (fig.9–24) and Raphael's *Baldassare Castiglione* (fig.9–29). Ask what visual clues indicate that Dürer assimilated lessons from Italian art during his travels through Italy as a young man.

• Are there any similarities in the poses or backgrounds?

• How has Dürer mingled these Italian aspects with a northern concern for precise observation?

• Is Dürer's painting more or less informative about his appearance and inner personality than the Italian portraits seem to be about their subjects?

10.2 Germany

EARLY FIFTEENTH-CENTURY GERMAN ART was part of the International style. The German tradition lay in medieval expressionism and the use of line. The Italian use of nude figures and monumental forms, based on Classical Greek and Roman art, was very strange to these northern European artists. So, instead of looking to Italy for inspiration, they looked to Flanders. Van Eyck and van der Weyden were strong influences. But, the German artists did not attain the heights, in style or technique, of Flemish artists.

However, this was to change in the early sixteenth century as German art moved to the forefront of northern Europe. Now, we start to find some artists who shared the free, individualistic spirit of Italian Renaissance artists. In southern Germany, there were painters of great originality, imagination and strong individual character. Among them were artists like Albrecht Dürer from Nuremberg, Matthias Grünewald, who worked in Mainz and other centers, and Hans Holbein the Younger, who worked in Switzerland and England.

Key Notes

• In the early 1500s, Germany becomes the leader in art in northern Europe.

• German artists absorb the influence of the Italian High Renaissance and blend it with northern technique and style.

Vocabulary

polyptych

10–14 Using this painting as a guide, how would you describe Dürer's personality?
Albrecht Dürer, *Self-Portrait*. 1498. Oil on panel, 20" x 16 1/5" (51 x 41 cm). The Prado Museum, Madrid.

Special Feature
Albrecht Dürer

(1471–1528)
Albrecht Dürer was the leader of the German High Renaissance. Unlike many of his colleagues, Dürer had a strong sense of being an artist, not a craftsperson. Dürer admired the princely lifestyle enjoyed by Titian and other Italian artists. He attempted to raise the status of art in Germany and the rest of northern Europe to an equally high level. This awareness led him to date his works and sign them—a fairly unusual practice at the time. Fascinated with Classical ideas used by Italian Renaissance artists, he was the first Northern artist to travel to Italy expressly to study Italian art. He agreed strongly with Leonardo that sight is our most important faculty. He believed that through looking, truth is revealed. Dürer was also the first artist outside of Italy to become internationally acclaimed.

He was also the first Northern artist to very consciously document himself in a series of self-portraits. One of his best self-portraits was painted in 1498 (fig.10–14). Dürer is elegantly dressed. His face bears a serious, searching expression that reflects the seriousness with which he regarded his mission as an artistic reformer. The influence of Italian portraiture appears in the pose and the landscape through the window. Although the pose is Italian, the line is still German and distinctively Dürer's. Hair is not treated as a mass but as individual lines—hundreds of them. Line is also evident in the clothes, the crisp folds and edges, and the faint outlines of hands and face.

• Have students note the intensity of Dürer's gaze and the use of lines to describe each physical nuance. (Have students read Dürer's biographic profile on pages 314 and 315 for further information.)

Art History: Ask students to compare Dürer's *Self-Portrait* and the man (believed to be the artist Jan van Eyck) observing the ceremony in the mirror of *Arnolfini Wedding* (figs.10–b, 10–6).

• What do these paintings have in common with Italian Renaissance self-portraits such as Leonardo's (p.276), Botticelli's (fig.9–19), Raphael's (fig.9–30), El Greco's (fig.9–37) and Sofonisba Anguissola's (fig.9–41). (Students can read the accompanying text to identify the artist in each example.)

• What is similar about the way artists presented themselves in both the northern and the southern countries?

• Do they seem to be anonymous craftspeople or esteemed intellectuals?

• How does the conception of an artist as a unique, gifted individual differ from earlier periods? As a clue, ask students to name who painted the *Mérode Altarpiece* (fig.10–1). Ask why the artist is referred to only as the Master of Flémalle.

Evaluate

Instruct students to pretend that they are art students of Albrecht Dürer during the late fifteenth and early sixteenth centuries.

Albrecht Dürer loved animals and used them in many of his prints and paintings. In his *Young Hare* (fig.10–15), a watercolor sketch, he applied line with tender care to produce a feeling of soft fur. Dürer was a master of watercolor, a medium that, at the time, was used mostly for preliminary studies that were often discarded.

Dürer's masterpiece is the powerful oil painting of *The Four Apostles* (fig.10–16), a diptych meant as the side wings of a large triptych. The apostles John and Peter on the left with Mark and Paul on the right. The solidness and weight of these figures are more Italian influenced than any of Dürer's other works. Each part could easily stand alone. But, the two parts together produce a balanced composition of powerful expression and sculpturesque forms. The figures are crowded into the space, creating tension and a feeling of explosive energy, as if they are ready to burst from the frame and proclaim their message.

10–16 Compare the apostles above to the figures in Masaccio's *Tribute Money* (fig.9–10). Albrecht Dürer, *Four Apostles*, about 1526. Oil on panel, each part 84 3/4" x 30" (215 x 76 cm). Alte Pinakothek, Munich.

10–15 Do you think this young rabbit might have been a pet of Dürer's? Albrecht Dürer, *Young Hare*, 1502. Watercolor with opaque white, 9 7/8" x 9" (25 x 23 cm). The Albertina Museum, Vienna.

Contextual Information
Dürer

During his travels in Holland, Dürer experienced the Dutch culture and saw some of the treasures, such as silver and gold from the New World, brought back to Holland by Dutch seamen. Because he was impressed by these treasures, Dürer wrote extensively of them in his diary and sketched many of the objects. He also sketched the animals in private zoos of the wealthy Dutch and Flemish merchants and later used these animals in woodcuts, etchings and drawings.

Higher-Order Thinking Skills

Have students use the self-portrait of Albrecht Dürer to write a description of him. They might also use the text for images in order to create a newspaper-style review of a show of Dürer's work. Reviews by critics appear in major newspapers and may be used as examples. To expand the assignment, suggest that students find other images of Dürer's in the library.

Reteach

Ask students to bring photographs of themselves to class. Display the pictures and then have students compare them to Dürer's *Self-Portrait*.

• Which would they say is more accurate?

• What can each medium do that the other cannot?

• Do photographs or paintings have more flexibility in interpreting physical reality?

• Although Dürer and other Northern Renaissance artists were dedicated to visual honesty, how could they manipulate the oil paints, poses, compositions and choice of backgrounds to present a specific impression?

• If students were creating their own self-portraits, which medium would they choose and why?

• What do they think he might stress in creating art?

• Which of the five senses would Dürer consider most vital for artists to cultivate?

• Ask what in Dürer's artwork supports their opinions. Have them reread the primary source material on page 327 to deepen their conclusions.

• Do students think it would have been easy to study with Dürer? Why or why not?

Ask students what southern culture had an impact on Dürer's art.

• What cross-cultural influences occur within modern American society?

• What evidence is there of Italian, Japanese, Chinese, African, Indian, Scandinavian, French, German and Russian culture in the United States?

• Suggest that students think in terms of language, arts, food, fashion, manufacturing and celebrations.

• Would students prefer to live in an isolated community or one in which various cultures intermingle?

Ask students to think back to the warm-up activity and name a significant quality that realist artists must have. (As a clue, have students describe what they learned about the amount of time and the quality of their looking during the exercise.)

Contextual Information

Cranach

Cranach's paintings were so popular that he became very wealthy. His workshop assistants even made copies of his most sought-after paintings. His son Lucas the Younger (1515–1586) imitated his father's painting style so well that it has been difficult for scholars to tell their work apart.

Window in Time

Dürer and Printmaking

The first artist to emerge from medieval anonymity with a distinct personality, was Albrecht Dürer (1471–1528). Dürer was the third of eighteen children and, after he had completed elementary school, he was taken on as apprentice to his goldsmith father. Dürer's thorough grounding in the goldsmith's art explains the accuracy he later displayed as an artist.

By the time he had finished his apprenticeship, Dürer had decided he was more interested in being an artist than a goldsmith. His father was not too happy about this at first, but he eventually agreed to let Dürer do another apprenticeship, this time under an artist.

Dürer proved to be extraordinarily talented in both woodcut and copper engraving. He was one of the first artists in the Western world to turn to woodcut as a major medium and, from the start, it was obvious that his technique was very original. His style was extremely precise and demanded incredible skill in cutting into the wood. In 1498, he finished a series of fifteen woodcuts illustrating events from the *Apocalypse*, the Book of Revelation (last book in the Bible) which reveals the visions of St. John. They are extremely detailed and, where other printmakers worked with single lines, Dürer massed fine lines together to produce gray-valued areas that give his prints depth and shading. The cut lines are unbeliev-

ably fine for the woodcut medium and give the appearance of being pen and ink drawings.

These cut blocks could be inked and printed in presses (Gutenberg had already invented movable type in 1446) and sold for much more modest prices than Dürer's paintings. The market for these works was huge and Dürer became a wealthy artist and honored citizen in his home town of Nuremberg. As well as writing what today we would call memoirs, he wrote a family chronicle based on the diaries of his parents. He also signed his work with an A-D monogram. Dürer was very ambitious and aimed from early on in his career for fame.

Prints like his *Four Horsemen of the Apocalypse* (one of the finest woodcuts ever made) were used as wall decorations and above altars in middle-class homes or were pasted inside trunks and travel cases as worship aids for travelers. The four horsemen seen by St. John (war, pestilence, famine and death) ride recklessly over helpless humanity. It is absolutely amazing how much detail Dürer manages to include in so small a woodcut (9 3/4" x 7 3/8"). He uses his lines to give form to the figures and horses as well as to outline, shade and indicate hair.

Another printmaking medium at which Dürer excelled was copper engraving. *Knight, Death and the Devil* is a master print made by Dürer in 1513. The subject is a knight, which symbolizes the Christian warrior, sitting astride a magnificently drawn horse. In this engraving, Dürer's comprehensive knowledge of animals and their forms is clearly demonstrated. The brave knight fears no evil and rides gallantly ahead without paying attention to Death (who holds an hourglass) or the Devil (a monster of hideous form). Dürer used incised line to outline as well as crosshatch, creating a fantastic variety of darks which appear to be solid grays rather than linear pattern. He achieved a chiaroscuro with line comparable to what the Italians did with paint.

As Dürer grew older he devoted more and more of his time to writing and teaching. He thought hard about the development and welfare of the arts and interested himself, more than any other artist of his time, in the grounding of young artists. This can be seen by the way in which he describes a little work he intended to publish as "something for budding artists to get their teeth into."

Albrecht Dürer, *Knight, Death and the Devil*, 1513. Engraving, 9 3/4" x 7 3/8" (24.8 x 18.7 cm). Graphic Arts Council Fund, 1970, Los Angeles County Museum of Art.

Materials and Techniques

A discussion of terminology is particularly important in a study of printmaking. Like drawings, prints are produced on paper, but with an important difference. A print can be reproduced several times by transferring an inked image from one prepared surface (plate) to another (usually paper). The three basic printmaking steps are making the printing plate, inking the plate and transferring the image.

The four main methods for making prints are relief printing, intaglio, lithography and screen printing. In relief methods (for example, woodcut or linoleum cut), the parts that are to print black are left in relief, and the other

parts are cut away. In intaglio methods (for example, etching or engraving), the principle is the reverse; the ink is held in lines incised into the plate. In lithography, or surface or planographic methods, the design is printed from a flat surface; the inked and non-inked areas are created by the repulsion of grease and water. In screen printing, also known as serigraphy, the principle involved is of using a squeegee to force color through the open parts of a stencil and onto paper or another printing surface beneath. (See Chapter 2, pages 34–35 for additional information and examples of printmaking.)

• Explain that monoprinting is a printmaking technique in which the image to be printed is put on the plate with ink or paint and then transferred to paper by pressing or hand-rubbing. A monoprint plate can be used only once. Have students research the Japanese art of making monoprints, called *gyotaku*, directly from fish.

• Ask the class who likely benefited from the use of prints. Ask students to speculate about why prints originated in the North rather than in Italy. Why were the media of woodcut and intaglio more fitting to the working styles of the northern artists?

10–17 This painting is a documentary work. It illustrates a contemporary event, and might be compared with today's photographs of hunting parties and their catches.

Lucas Cranach, *Hunting Party in Honor of Charles V at the Castle of Torgau*, 1545. Oil on panel, 43 3/5" x 68 7/8" (111 x 175 cm). The Prado Museum, Madrid.

10–18 Notice that women took an active role in the hunt.

Lucas Cranach, *Hunting Party in Honor of Charles V at the Castle of Torgau*, detail.

Lucas Cranach

(1472–1553)

Lucas Cranach (the Elder) was a Protestant painter and architect. A friend of Martin Luther, he painted several portraits of the leader of the Reformation. Cranach became official painter for the Elector of Saxony at Wittenberg, where he and his two sons, Hans and Lucas (the Younger), were responsible for dozens of paintings. Cranach painted many nudes of Adam, Eve and various gods from ancient mythology. However, he painted them as German folk posed in rugged outdoor settings rather than as Classic figures of Greek and Roman times.

His work includes a number of hunting scenes such as *Hunting Party in Honor of Charles V at the Castle of Torgau* (figs.10–17, 10–18). The painting documents a hunting event of the time. The composition is extremely complex. Assistants and dogs are driving the stags into the open and to the pond in the foreground. In the lower left, the Duke of Saxony, Emperor Charles V and a knight are waiting for the kill with their crossbows and spears. Bears are being hunted in the upper left and upper right, and above all towers the Castle of Torgau. Cranach has combined architecture, landscape, animals and people in a writhing composition. The viewer's eyes are constantly moving from one area to another, seeking a place to pause.

Contextual Information

The *Isenheim Altarpiece*

Disease and healing are primary themes in the *Isenheim Altarpiece* (figs.10–19, 10–20), a work commissioned for the monastic hospital of St. Anthony of Isenheim. When the altarpiece is closed, St. Anthony is seen on the right and St. Sebastian on the left. St. Anthony was the patron saint of the monastic order and was identified with miraculous cures. It was believed that the intercession of St. Sebastian could ward off disease, especially the plague.

The condition known as ergotism, also called St. Anthony's fire, was treated at the monastic hospital. However, the cause of this condition (eating grain infected with ergot fungus) was not discovered until the early seventeenth century. Its known, dreaded symptoms were gangrene and convulsions, and the gangrene often resulted in amputation. The theme of amputation in the altarpiece has been noted by scholars. Two of the movable sections of the altarpiece cause Christ's limbs to be separated when they are moved apart. This is true of the lower section of the altarpiece (called the predella), where Christ is about to be laid into his tomb. Both legs are "cut" by the split in the panel. Christ's arm is "severed" from his body when the Crucifixion scene in the center panel opens.

10–19 Grünewald reached back to Byzantine and Gothic ideas to help him portray this scene with great spiritual power.
Matthias Grünewald, *Isenheim Altarpiece*, (closed), about 1512–1515. Oil on panel, center panel, 8' 10" x 11' 2 1/2" (2.69 x 3.4 m). Unterlinden Museum, Colmar, France.

1484
Sugar cane cultivated, Canary Islands

1518
Traders begin sending shiploads of African slaves to the West Indies

World Cultural Timeline

1490
Toothbrush invented, China

1510
Major hospitals appear in Indian cities and offer free treatment

Multicultural Connection

Slave Trade

Beginning in the fifteenth century, the European Age of Discovery, exploration and colonization provided the impetus for the modern slave trade. The Portuguese, exploring and raiding the coasts of Africa, discovered a labor force of young, healthy, strong black Africans who could cultivate their crops of tobacco, rice and sugarcane in the colonies and in the New World. Thus began the importation of black Africans, a slave trade that the Portuguese virtually monopolized for more than a century. The increasing demands for slaves by the British, French and Dutch, as well as the Spanish and Portuguese, stimulated a systematized traffic in slaves called the triangle trade. The English would first trade goods with west-coast Africans for black African slaves. The next stop was either the West Indies or the English Colonies, where the slaves would be exchanged for spices or sugar. The ships would then return to England with a valuable cargo of goods, completing the triangle. Thus the slave trade in the New World, with its ever-increasing markets, rapidly expanded into an enormous and highly lucrative industry.

• Discuss how slaves were used in ancient Egypt, Greece and Rome.

Matthias Grünewald
(about 1480–1528)

Although he was an excellent artist, Dürer's greatest contemporary was not a well-known figure. In fact, the real name of Matthias Grünewald (Mathis Niethardt Gothardt) was not known until this century. Grünewald was the last and most powerful of the expressive Gothic artists. He painted only a limited number of works but his single greatest masterpiece is the *Isenheim Altarpiece* (figs.10–19, 10–20). This altarpiece was done for the Hospital of St. Anthony in Isenheim, a small town now part of France. The painting is a complex **polyptych**, made of many opening panels and wings. The polyptych was hung in two sets of paintings in front of a carved shrine to St. Anthony. When closed, the *Crucifixion* is seen, as in the illustration. As these panels are opened there are scenes of the *Annunciation*, the *Nativity*, the *Resurrection* and various saints.

The saints are painted in bright orange, red, gold and blue. Finally, the carved and gilded shrine to St. Anthony appears.

The *Crucifixion* is the most dramatically powerful work ever done on the subject of Christ's suffering and death. The cross, placed slightly off-center to add to the tension, is seen as the cruelest means of death. The scarred body of the beaten Christ hangs as a broken figure, dangling from cross arms that are bent under the weight of the body and the world's sin. The pull of gravity is so strong that the fingers and hands are almost pulled apart. The bent head, bloody with the crown of thorns, seems ready to take its last breath. The drama is intensified by the black sky that adds to the feeling of death, gloom and sorrow.

On the left, St. John is consoling Mary, according to one of Christ's last wishes. Mary Magdalene shows her grief with raised clasped hands. John the Baptist is pointing to Christ as the Savior of the world. The symbolic lamb with a cross is bleeding into the chalice. The lamb was often used as a symbol of Christ and his suffering and death. The two figures standing in the side panels are St. Sebastian on the left and St. Anthony on the right. Below the central panel, under a ledge, is a horizontal composition of the *Pietà*. Christ's body has been taken down from the cross and will soon be placed in the open sarcophagus.

The entire cycle of the altarpiece is a marvel of organization. It reaches its climax in the resurrection scene in the second set of panels. Christ bursts from the tomb with the energy of an explosion. While his crucifixion is awesome, Grünewald's resurrection is the most astonishing ever painted.

10–20 Consider how the artist has used color to give this work its dynamism and supernatural qualities.
Matthias Grünewald, *Isenheim Altarpiece*, (open), about 1512–1515. Oil on panel, Unterlinden Museum, Colmar, France.

Higher-Order Thinking Skills

1 Help students to use the text to follow the story through the altarpiece. They can take turns talking each other through the complexities of the work to help themselves better understand it and identify the characters and symbols.

2 Have students discuss how Northern Renaissance painters might have responded to the saying "It is important to tell the truth, the whole truth, and nothing but the truth." Direct students to glance through Chapter 10 to find images by artists who might not have adhered to this dictum. (If students need help, refer them to Bosch's figs.10–10 and 10–11 and Bruegel's fig.10–12.) How might subject matter affect the artists' decision to paint in a realistic or in a fantastic style? Does truth always refer to observable reality?

Contextual Information

Holbein

In Basel, Switzerland, Holbein formed a friendship with Erasmus, the Dutch scholar. The artist provided a series of woodcuts for an edition of Erasmus' *The Praise of Folly*. Holbein was invited to England by Erasmus, who had many friends among the wealthy English political leaders. Erasmus introduced Holbein to Sir Thomas More, an English statesman and scholar whose portrait Holbein later painted. More wrote *Utopia*, a fictional story about an ideal country that he compared to England. In Utopia, people would live by just laws and care for one another under a representative government that cared for everyone.

10–21 Holbein was recommended to Thomas More by the famous author Erasmus. More was the Chancellor of England under Henry VIII.
Hans Holbein, *Sir Thomas More*, 1527. Oil on panel, 29 1/2" x 23 1/5" (75 x 59 cm). The Frick Collection, New York.

10–22 The text will help you identify the objects which make a visual list of the sitters' interests. Can you see the skull?
Hans Holbein, *The French Ambassadors*, 1533. Oil on panel, 6' 8" x 6' 9 1/2" (206 x 208 cm). The National Gallery, London.

Hans Holbein

(1497–1543)

One of the finest portrait painters of all times, Hans Holbein (the Younger) was born in Germany but moved to Basel, Switzerland, when he was about thirteen and stayed there for eleven years. He enjoyed great popularity in Basel where people appreciated his paintings, prints, murals, jewelry and architectural designs. In the mid-1520s, Holbein went to England where he became court painter to Henry VIII. He painted many portraits of royalty and English contemporaries. Holbein's work provides a realistic look at sixteenth-century clothing, hair styles and general appearance.

Portraits were Holbein's strength and the source of a very handsome income. His style is characterized by extreme detail and an objective likeness of his sitters. He had a wonderful ability to describe fabrics with his brushes. Holbein painted a remarkable portrait of Sir Thomas More, the witty author and statesman (fig.10–21). No one has painted velvet or fur more convincingly (fig.10–a). More's face is beautifully rendered. Set against a green drape and dark hat, the modeling of the features is brilliant, particularly the treatment of the eyes. The face is determined and dignified. One can almost sense that this man who wrote *Utopia* could not compromise his ideals—a quality that led to his clash with Henry VIII and his beheading.

One of Holbein's greatest achievements is his double portrait, *The French Ambassadors* (fig.10–22). The French Ambassador to England, Jean de Dinteville, is on the left in a casual pose. With him is his friend, Bishop Georges de Selve. While both men are portrayed with Holbein's usual care and detail, the array of objects in the painting is fascinating. The objects are a virtual catalog of the two men's interests: eye glass, lute, celestial globe, Lutheran hymnbook, compasses, flutes, sundial, crucifix and books.

The most astounding feature is the shape that seems to grow out of the frame at the lower left in the foreground. It is impossible to tell what it is until one looks at it from below, near the left corner of the painting. Hold the book at a flat angle and view the object from the lower left to see it. Viewed from the correct angle, a skull appears. The painting was perhaps made to hang over a doorway so that when people looked up, they saw a skull.

Although England had not produced any painters of international stature, Holbein showed the world how the English looked. He established a trend in portraiture that would be long-lasting in the British empire.

Interdisciplinary Connection

History: The Protestant Reformation began in Germany in 1517 when Martin Luther published his 95 theses, which challenged the church's practice of selling indulgences. Church authorities ordered Luther to retract his statement, but he refused.

Luther, who urged that religion should be based on individual faith guided by the Bible, found great favor in much of northern Europe. Tremendous upheaval resulted as the reformists and the church engaged in bitter debate and battle.

• Have students research more information about the Protestant Reformation. Students should consider what role artists might have played in the movement. How would the movement have affected their work?

Window in Time

Art and Anatomy

Artists, physicians and butchers all come under the guardianship of the same patron saint, the evangelist St. Luke. According to legend, St. Luke was both a physician and a painter.

Physicians, artists and butchers also hold in common their interest in dissecting bodies. In ancient times, people believed that the human body was sacred and to dissect it was a serious crime.

Accidents and battle wounds gave physicians information about the internal organs of human beings, but they had very little knowledge of how various organs related to each other. Pictures illustrated the internal workings of the body, but without any emphasis on showing an anatomically correct body. The more involved physicians and artists became with the workings of the human body, the more extensive became their knowledge of anatomy. For the most part, this knowledge was to come from the process of dissection. What better vehicle could there be to reveal the relationship of organs, muscles and bones than an opened corpse?

The ancient Greeks were the first people to become involved in anatomical dissections of the human body. By the third century BC, the Greeks permitted some dissections of human corpses. After the Greek civilization declined, a medical center in Alexandria, Egypt, flourished for several hundred years. It is said that, here, criminals who had been condemned to die were dissected alive. They justified this dreadful act by saying that surgeons could better understand how organs worked if they were still functioning.

In the Middle Ages, monasteries became great centers of medicine. It has been erroneously believed that in the Middle Ages and into the Renaissance the Church banned dissections. But, Leonardo da Vinci conducted dissections on as many as fifty cadavers at the ecclesiastical hospital of Santa Maria Nuova. Michelangelo was provided with corpses for anatomical study by the prior of the monastery hospital of Santo Spirito. There, he learned about the workings of the human body and its muscles, organs and skeleton. His understanding of anatomy is evident in all of his works.

If anatomical discoveries were to reach a wide audience, the anatomist had to work closely with an expert artist. The first physician to realize this was the remarkable Andreas Vesalius. In the 1500s, Vesalius revolutionized the study of anatomy. His masterwork, the *Fabrica*, became the standard anatomical textbook in use throughout Europe. The illustrations, probably done by John Stephen of Calcar, a Flemish artist, are startlingly good. The drawings of the human skeleton even include a detailed background landscape. The skeleton or "muscleman" is a standing male figure with skin, fat, connective tissue and blood vessels removed. The muscles combine beautifully with the skeleton. The posture is relaxed and "alive."

Andreas Vesalius, *Untitled*, 1555. Woodcut from *De humani corporis fabrica libri septem*, 2nd Ed. Royal College of Surgeons in Ireland, Dublin.

Lesson 10.2 Review

1 Which German Renaissance artist became a celebrity and painted many self-portraits?
2 What are two of the events happening at the *Hunting Party in Honor of Charles V* painted by Lucas Cranach?
3 Describe one of the bodies in Grünewald's *Crucifixion* from the *Isenheim Altarpiece*.

4 Which German Renaissance artist was the court painter for the English King Henry VIII?
5 What are some of the hobbies and interests of the French ambassadors displayed in Holbein's portrait of them?
6 Analyze the Italian influence found in Dürer's *Four Apostles*. Refer to paintings by Italian masters to illustrate your points.

Higher-Order Thinking Skills

1 Go over the text's description of the articles in *The French Ambassadors* (fig.10–22) that represent the personal interests of the figures. Have each student create a list of objects that he or she would want an artist to use to describe his or her interests in a portrait. Form pairs of students and, without sharing the first list, have each partner create a similar list for his or her partner. The pairs can then compare their lists to see how well they know each other's interests.

2 Holbein's delightful portrait of Edward VI as a child can be found in Chapter 2 (fig.2–9). Ask students to compare it to the artist's portrait of Thomas More (fig.10–21). How are the two portraits similar? How are they different?

Lesson 10.2 Review Answers:

1 Albrecht Dürer
2 Assistants and dogs drive the stags into the open and to the pond. The Duke of Saxony, Emperor Charles V and a knight wait for the kill with their crossbows and spears. Bear are being hunted.
3 The scarred body of Christ with a bent, bloody head dangles from the cross with fingers and hands that seem to be almost pulled apart by the weight of gravity. John holds Mary, consoling her. Mary Magdelan kneels with upraised folded hands. John the Baptist, wearing a rough robe, holds an open book and points to Christ with a long finger.

4 Hans Holbein
5 Holbein shows an eye glass, lute, celestial globe, Lutheran hymnbook, compasses, flutes, sundial, crucifix and books which represent the ambassadors' religion and their interest in music, travel and learning.
6 The figures in Dürer's *Four Apostles* are large with intense expressions and clothing shaded in a manner reminiscent of Masaccio's *Tribute Money* and Michelangelo's *Sistine Chapel Ceiling*. With their classical dress and open books the apostles seem to be related to the figures in Raphael's *School of Athens*.

Lesson 10.3

During the sixteenth century, England contributed to the advancement of music and literature, but it was France that excelled in architecture. Philip II summoned leading artists from across Europe to help build an impressive capital to symbolize the great wealth and increasing strength of the Spanish Hapsburg Empire.

Warm-up

Direct students to imagine being locked up after dark in *El Escorial* (figs.10–23, 10–24). Ask the class what it would feel like to wander around this vast complex that combined a palace, court and church. Is Philip II, who commissioned El Escorial, someone with whom you would like to sit down and share a meal? How does the building specifically affect your thinking?

Objectives

Students should be able to:

Explain that French architecture flourished under Francis I as he and the aristocracy built opulent châteaux and palaces throughout the Loire River valley.

Comprehend that Philip II used the increasing wealth of Spain to summon leading European masters to help build his grand Hapsburg capital.

Vocabulary Definitions

château (shat-*oh*) A French castle or large country house. (plural=chateaux)

10.3 England, France and Spain

THE RENAISSANCE IN ENGLAND brought the flowering of the English language and literature in works by Shakespeare and other writers. However, the flourishing of literature and music was not matched in the visual arts.

In France, the International style, which originated in Burgundy, continued to set the tone in painting. Two important French artists of this period were Jean Fouquet and Jean Clouet. In architecture, sixteenth-century France enjoyed a period of exceptional growth. Francis I and the French aristocracy built a group of opulent **châteaux** in the Loire River valley. The Square Court of the Louvre in Paris, designed as a grand palace for Francis I, was the first truly French Renaissance building.

Spain was extremely wealthy at the time. With the riches of the Old World and the unlimited resources of the New World at his command, Philip II summoned the leading artists of Europe to help build and embellish his chosen capital. His single greatest monument was the magnificent El Escorial.

Key Notes

• Music and literature were more dominant than art in England.
• In France, architecture experiences tremendous growth.
• The great wealth of Hapsburg Spain attracts artists and Philip II builds his greatest monument, El Escorial.

Vocabulary

châteaux

Special Feature

El Escorial

In the sixteenth century, Spain, under the Hapsburg Empire, was a dominant force in Europe. It ruled much of Europe and claimed vast areas of land in the Americas. With the great wealth accumulated by the Hapsburgs, the arts flourished.

The Spanish disdained the Classical ideals of purity and proportion. The need of Spanish architects to do something different with Italian form is never more magnificently visible than in *El Escorial* (fig.10–23), constructed for Philip II of Hapsburg. The main architect for this project was Juan de Herrera but the king had a lot to do with the design. Philip insisted on the right to judge the suitability of every public building undertaken during his

Teach

Art History: Ask students to consider what Philip II might have wanted people to perceive about him and his Spanish kingdom when he combined a palace, court and church into his massive monument El Escorial.

• How might Philip have felt about religion?

• What might he have been implying about the relationship between church and state?

• What does the size and style of the enormous structure suggest about Philip's pride and also the sense of Spain's growing role in world politics? Direct students to the text on pages 322 and 323 for more information.

Criticism: Have students determine what traditions the Italian architects brought with them when they helped build El Escorial by comparing the complex to Filippo Brunelleschi's dome for the *Cathedral of Florence* (fig.9–1) and the interior of *San Lorenzo* (fig.9–2). Tell students to draw parallels between the size, regularity of design, sense of grandeur, scale and function of the buildings.

• What about El Escorial looks most different from the Italian buildings?

• Despite its large scale, is El Escorial as decorative?

• What might the austerity of its design indicate about the personality of Philip II?

10–24 Note the simplicity of the facade and the use of horizontal elements which give the building its ponderous appearance. Juan Bautista De Toledo, *El Escorial*, detail.

reign. El Escorial is a vast building complex combining a palace and court with a church. It expressed the unified Catholic spirit in Spain. The huge structure is an apt expression of Philip's passionate Catholicism, his pride in his dynasty, as well as the austerity that seems to have been very much a part of his character.

The site chosen was at the foothills of the bleak Guadarrama Mountains about thirty miles from Madrid near the village of Escorial. El Escorial is a huge square grid of corridors and courtyards with an austere basilica at its center. Beneath the high altar lie eleven Spanish kings, including Philip II. The return to Classic simplicity,

the visual balance and the mathematical proportions put the stamp of Renaissance planning on the complex. It was called by Philip's contemporaries "the eighth wonder of the world."

El Escorial is gloomily grand and austerely magnificent. These characteristics perfectly represent the somber personality of Philip II. El Escorial is not a place to be trapped in alone after dark. The main entrance is built in the strict Doric order. Only the royal coat of arms and a gigantic statue of St. Lawrence holding his gridiron relieve the general starkness.

Like the whole complex of buildings, the domed church is constructed of granite. The horizontal

elements used by the architect on the church facade and other buildings create the feeling of ponderous weight and mass (fig.10–24). The plainness of the facades reinforce this effect and convey a sense of starkness and severity. This contrasts sharply with the graceful elegance of Italian Renaissance architecture. (See the map on page 331 for the location of Escorial, Spain.)

10–23 The palace, court and church are combined for a completely integrated church and state that reflected the power of an absolute monarchy. Juan Bautista De Toledo, *El Escorial*, c.1563–1584, near Madrid.

Higher-Order Thinking Skills

Have students compare El Escorial to Marksburg Castle (fig.8–9). What makes each identifiable as belonging to its particular period?

Performing Arts Connection

Globe Theater

Before 1576, London had no proper theater, and plays were performed in the courtyards of inns. One of the earliest theaters was the Globe, which opened in 1599. Many of Shakespeare's plays were first staged here, and the actors, including Shakespeare himself, were the Lord Chamberlain's men, later known as the King's men.

• In Shakespeare's acting company, all the roles were performed by men. Ask students to play a character of the opposite sex in a scene from one of Shakespeare's plays. Ask them beforehand what they might do to convey their role's gender. How might they use gestures, clothes and their voices to help them? Afterwards, ask what they found most challenging about the performance. Did they experience anything unexpected?

• Does the plainness of the facade seem to convey a sense of the king as a frivolous or as a severe person?

Criticism: Direct students to compare El Escorial to French Renaissance architecture (figs.10–c, 10–28). Ask which is more restrained. Have them describe ways in which the facade of the *Square Court of the Louvre* is opulent and full of life.

• Can they identify the Classical elements? (Refer them to Greek architecture in Chapter 6, particularly the information about columns in fig.6–20.)

• If they were kings or queens, which style of architecture would they prefer?

• Why does one suit their needs and personality more than the other?

Evaluate

Ask students if they believe Philip II of Spain was an ambitious man. What in El Escorial supports their conclusions?

Reteach

Remind students that the sixteenth century was an age of exploration, both visually and physically.

• What locations did Spain explore in order to expand its rule?

• What lands did Cortés, Balboa, Pizarro and Coronado invade?

• What did they accomplish on their journeys?

• How did their activities aid Spain's expansion of power in Europe?

Contextual Information

King Francis I

King Francis I wanted to establish a center of Renaissance art and architecture to rival that of the Medicis of Florence. He began his work at Fontainebleau, using Italian master artists and builders who had flooded into France in part to escape the battles in their own country and in part to take advantage of the jobs and money offered to those who could create art and build Renaissance-style homes. Rich nobles, following the example of their king, built classically styled châteaux up and down the Loire River valley.

• Ask students to research King Francis I to find what political events his reign is most noted for.

1520
**Chocolate intro-
duced to Spain
from the Aztec
Empire**

1571
**Bornu Empire in
Sudan reaches its
height**

World Cultural Timeline

1538
**First plays pro-
duced in Mexico**

1585
**Toyotami Hideyomi
becomes Japan's
military ruler**

**10–25 The artist
spent two years
in Italy and combines
that influence
with Flemish
characteristics.**
Jean Fouquet, *Etienne
Chevalier and St.
Stephen*, c. 1450. From
a diptych now divided.
Tempera on wood,
36 1/2" x 33 1/2" (93 x
85 cm). Staatliche
Museen zu Berlin
Preussischer
Kulturbesitz
Gemäldegalerie, Berlin.

Multicultural Connection

Cacao Bean

In March 1519, Spanish explorer and conqueror Hernán Cortés landed in Mexico. Once there he learned of the Aztec Empire and its ruler, Montezuma II. Prior to his conquest of the Aztec Empire, Cortés was introduced by the Aztec people to the use of cacao (chocolate) as a beverage. Cortés also learned that cacao beans were used as Aztec currency (about a hundred beans would buy a slave). When the Spaniards left to return to Spain, they took cacao beans to plant on Trinidad, Haiti and the West African island of Fernando Po, now Bioko. (Inform students that cacao trees thrive only twenty degrees above and below the equator, in moist tropical climates.) This action later gave imperial Spain a virtual monopoly on the cacao bean market for almost a century. When Cortés finally arrived in Spain in 1528, he introduced the cacao bean to his king, Charles V. Its use gradually spread from Spain through Europe and into England.

• Ask why spices had enormous value to Europeans.

French Painting

Jean Fouquet (about 1420–1481), the most important French artist of the fifteenth century, painted portraits and religious scenes and worked on manuscript illuminations. The clear details in *Etienne Chevalier and St. Stephen* (fig.10–25) reflect the Flemish influence. Fouquet was also influenced by Italian art, as can be seen in the architectural setting. Although the donor is seen with his patron, St. Stephen, the painting is more secular than religious in nature.

Jean Clouet (about 1485–1541) painted portraits, such as *Francis I* (fig.10–26). Equal emphasis is given to the face and expression and the rich brocades and silks of the king's clothing. Clouet, however, failed to reach a stature of major importance.

10–26 Note the stiff frontal pose of the king and the way his sleeves push out beyond the border of the painting.
Jean Clouet, *Francis I*, c.1525–1530. Tempera and oil on wood, approx. 38" x 29" (96 x 74 cm). The Louvre, Paris.

French Architecture

The *Château of Chambord* (fig.10–27) is an excellent example of the French architecture of the sixteenth century. Started in 1519, it has a large central block that contains numerous apartments. On each corner is a rounded tower. Wings on each side contain simple hallways that terminate in huge rounded fortress-like structures with conical roofs. Viewed from afar, the entire structure has a horizontal feeling. From close up, however, the Gothic-style roof towers and the vertical elements on the exterior walls produce a vertical pull on the viewer's senses. Inside the central block is a marvelously intertwined stairway to the various apartments. It is constructed so that a person walking up the spiraling stairs can hear, but cannot see, persons coming down. The entire

10–27 Compare this chateau to the castle at Marksburg (fig.8–9).
Pierre Nepveu, *Chateau of Chambord*, begun 1519.

Compare this chateau to the castle at Marksburg (fig.8–9).

Higher-Order Thinking Skills

The image of *Chambord* (fig.10–27) shows how landscaping was used and considered for the building of the château. With the Renaissance's interest in nature also came the study of botany and biology, and the foundations were laid for what is now known as nature illustration. Have the class use this image and others to discuss what landscaping can contribute to architecture. Discuss local examples.

Cooperative Learning

Divide the class into groups, either randomly or by student interest. Ask each group to design a castle or large home that uses particular styles with which they are familiar. Discuss floor plans and elevations. Students should be ready to explain why they feel their particular style is effective and what its shortcomings are.

Performing Arts Connection

Renaissance Court Dance

While there had been dancing in ancient Greek festivals and the orchestra of the Greek drama, it was the Renaissance that gave birth to ballet. (The word *ballet* is from the Italian word *balletti*, meaning "a figured dance.") These spectacles developed in Italian courts around the fifteenth century and were designed to glorify the image of the monarch as a quasi-divine ruler.

When court ballet spread to France, it incorporated social dances of the day along with dialogue, music, song and staging machines (whereby divinities could be lowered from heights to be among the mortals). The ballets were not performed on stages but in the central space of large halls with the audience seated above or around the edges in order to observe the elaborate floor patterns. The cumbersome fashions of the times demanded an emphasis on complex footwork, and hence a dancer's precision, memory, grace and ease of execution were most admired.

• Discuss with students how individual dukedoms used the arts to vie with one another for power and prestige. Then divide the class into small groups and have each devise a dance that is meant to dazzle others. Afterward, have the class examine the similarities and differences in the steps each group felt would be impressive. Were there any parallels among their choices of movements?

Contextual Information

Louvre

Until 1682 the Louvre was a residence of the kings of France. It is one of the largest palaces in the world and is built on the site of a thirteenth-century fortress. Begun during the Renaissance by Francis I under the direction of the architect Pierre Lescot, the Louvre was added to throughout the centuries. Its most recent addition was in 1989. (See fig.16–22.)

• The Louvre is now one of the largest museums in the world. Students can get a sense of the scope of the museum's collection by going through the textbook and listing all the works that are located in the Louvre.

10–28 Use the text to help you identify the features of this palace which is now part of a famous museum.

Pierre Lescot, *Square Court of the Louvre*, 1546. Paris.

structure is a remarkable combination of styles. The bottom three stories are coolly Renaissance while the roof is flamboyant Gothic. To see this dramatic contrast, cover the roof, then the lower three stories with a piece of paper.

The *Square Court of the Louvre* in Paris (fig.10–28) is the first truly French Renaissance building. It was designed by Pierre Lescot and Jean Goujon. Goujon also furnished the structure with sculptures and fine reliefs (fig.10–c). A three-story block, its large windows and steeply sloping roof are French additions to an Italian Renaissance idea. The sculptural details contrast with the Classical forms to produce a carefully balanced facade, both rich in detail, yet more restrained than Gothic flamboyance. The windows on each floor receive different treatment, yet the stories are visually tied together with vertical pilasters and Corinthian columns. Originally part of the royal palace in Paris, it is today part of the magnificent museum of the Louvre.

Lesson 10.3 Review

1 What was the El Escorial? Who built it? Where is it? Where did the funds come from to build it?

2 Who was the most important French artist during the 1400s?

3 Describe how two architectural styles are combined in the chateau of Chambord?

4 What was the first French Renaissance building in Paris?

Lesson 10.3 Review Answers

1 El Escorial is a vast building complex that combines a palace and court with a church. It was built by architect Juan de Herrera for Philip II of Spain near the village of Escorial about thirty miles from Madrid. Spain was wealthy at this time commanding the riches of the Old World and importing gold from its colonies in the Americas.

2 Jean Fouquet

3 The bottom three stories are Renaissance in style, while the roof is Gothic in style.

4 The *Square Court of the Louvre* was the first truly Renaissance building.

Chapter Review Answers

Review

1 Italian painters were influenced by the aesthetics and ideals of Classical Greek and Roman art, while Northern European artists were inspired by the realism of the International style. Italian artists used fresco and tempera paint as the Northern Europeans began painting with oils. The Northern Europeans were more concerned than the Italians with creating hard-edged details in their painting. The Northern paintings were usually smaller than the massive Italian Renaissance murals.

2 Albrecht Dürer, Jan van Eyck and Pieter Bruegel were interested in learning to draw perspective using the scientific techniques developed by Brunelleschi and Alberti. They also wanted to see the classical, monumental figures created by Masaccio and Michelangelo.

3 The paintings of both Bruegel and Bosch are symbolic, filled with many small figures and were painted with oils.

Interpret

1 The ziggurats created by the Sumerians were usually squarish structures, not the round Colosseum-type building painted by Bruegel.

2 Some of the choices might be the thin veil in van der Weyden's *Portrait of a Lady*, the fur hat or fur-trimmed robe of Giovanni Arnolfini or the green dress of his bride in van Eyck's *Arnolfini Wedding*, or Dürer's soft-striped cap in his *Self-Portrait*.

Primary Source

Albrecht Dürer

Albrecht Dürer was impressed by the scientific methods and natural proportions used by Italian artists. He observed these methods on a trip to Venice. As a result, he wrote a number of books including *The Teaching of Measurements* (1525), *Fortifications of Towns, Castles, and Places* (1527) and *Four Books of Human Proportions* (1528). Dürer said that the purpose of his books was to teach Italian methods to students in his own country.

Dürer suggested that they should practice drawing many different kinds of people from life. This would eventually enable them to draw accurately proportioned figures from memory. This selection is from *Four Books on Human Proportion*, Book III, "Aesthetic Excursus:"

"...if a man accurately follows life in his imitation so that his work resembles life and is like unto nature, and especially if the thing imitated is beautiful, the work is held to be artistic, and, as it deserves, it is highly praised."

"Wherefore it follows that no powerful artist should abandon himself to one manner only; but he should be practiced in several styles and in many kinds, and should have understanding therein. Then he will be able to make whatever sort of picture is required of him."

"Therefore let no one put too much belief in himself, lest he err in his work and fail. It is very needful for one who busies himself about these things to see many good figures and especially such as have been made by the famous good masters, and that he hear them discourse therof. Howbeit you must ever observe their faults and consider how they might be bettered."

Chapter Review

Review

1 Describe three differences between Renaissance painting of Northern Europe and that of Italy.
2 Name three Northern European Renaissance artists who traveled to Italy to study Italian art. Why do you think they were interested in Italian art?
3 Discuss how the paintings of Bruegel and Bosch are alike.

Interpret

1 Explain how Bruegel's imagined *Tower of Babel* is different from the actual tower of Babel, a Sumerian ziggurat?
2 Describe a piece of clothing that seems unusual to you in one of the paintings in this chapter. Can you identify any of the fabrics from which it was made?
3 Compare El Escorial with an Italian Renaissance building you have studied.

Other Tools for Learning

Maps
1 What present-day countries make up the low countries? Why do you think they were called low? Name two towns in the low countries.
2 Notice the great rivers that the Northern European towns cluster on and around. Why do you think towns would be built near these rivers? Name a town on or near the Loire River, the Seine River and the Rhine River.

Timelines

1 The Renaissance is also known as an age of exploration. People were beginning to trade with other cultures and explore parts of the world far from their own homes. What foods or objects from non-European cultures were eagerly accepted by the sixteenth-century Europeans?
2 The Renaissance was a time of political unrest. List three wars or revolts that happened during the fifteenth and sixteenth centuries.

Electronic Research
CD-ROM drive: *Microsoft Art Gallery*
1 Explain how the distorted skull in the lower left of Holbein's *The French Ambassadors* is meant to be seen. (Composition and Perspective Guided Tour)
2 How did Jan van Eyck modify the *Arnolfini Wedding* as he painted it? (Beneath the Varnish Guided Tour)
3 Fold a piece of paper to demonstrate how triptych altarpieces such as the *Mérode* and the *Ghent Altarpiece* fold. (Look at the animation sequence in the Paintings as Objects Guided Tour to understand how this works.)

Primary-Source Connection

Ask students to reword Dürer's writing into more contemporary language as though they themselves were providing some advice to young artists. Do they think Dürer offers good advice?

Electronic Research
1 If the painting were high on a staircase wall, viewers would see the skull as they stood at the bottom of the stairs to the left of the painting. As they climbed the stairs toward the picture, the skull would become distorted.
2 Van Eyck moved Arnolfini's hands: He made Arnolfini's left hand hold his wife's hand more closely and placed Arnolfini's right hand farther to the left.
3 The two side panels were folded in toward the center panel.

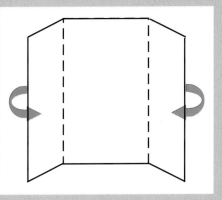

3 El Escorial can be compared to San Lorenzo designed by Brunelleschi. The two buildings have Classic simplicity, as well as the visual balance and the mathematical proportions of the Renaissance. However, the massive facade of El Escorial's church seems to have an overwhelming strength and weight that is different from the grace and elegance of Italian Renaissance architecture.

Maps
1 Present-day Luxemburg, Belgium and the Netherlands make up the low countries. Their flat plains are low in elevation and close to sea level. Cities in this area are Luxemburg, Amsterdam, The Hague, Brussels, Antwerp, Ghent, Haarlem, Bruges, Louvaine and Rotterdam.

2 Navigable rivers were important trade routes with cities forming on their banks. Falls and rapids also provided water power to run mills. Paris is on the Seine River. Chambord is near the Loire River. Isenheim, Colmar, and Basel are near the Rhine River.

Timelines
1 Gold, tobacco, potatoes, chocolate, coffee, silk, tea, sugar and slaves
2 The Hundred Years' War between France and England occurred between 1337 and 1453; the Dutch Revolt against Spain began in 1566, the Spanish Armada was defeated by the English in 1588, and the Spanish conquest of the Aztec empire began in 1519.

Activity 1: Symbols, Detail and Light

Activity Objectives

Students should be able to:

• interpret and discuss the use of symbolism in a work of art

• demonstrate their observations of symbolism and soft lighting in a colored-pencil drawing

Thinking Critically

Discuss symbolism as it relates to particular historical time periods, perhaps using the *Mérode Altarpiece* (figs.10–1, 10–2, 10–3) as an example. Have students list all the symbols they know. Then ask the following questions:

• Which symbols are from the past? Which are from the present?

• What do the symbols mean? In what context (e.g., religious, secular) are these symbols used?

• Do you see symbolism in your everyday life? What symbols are important to you? Why?

• Invent a symbol. What would it be and what would its purpose be?

Discuss how color can create a mood or an atmosphere.

• What colors do you associate with specific human feelings, certain religious events, public ceremonies and so forth?

• Have the students examine the reasons they make associations with certain colors. (For example, ask: "What is your favorite color? How does it make you feel?")

Preparation Ideas

Bring in resources on the interpretation of symbols, such as the *Dictionary of Subjects and Symbols in Art,* by James Hall, Harper and Row Publishers, New York, 1979. Other ideas might be generated by a discussion of Carl Jung's *Man and His Symbols,* or other books on the interpretation of dreams.

Notes on Materials

The success of any colored-pencil drawing depends on the quality of the pencil. If possible, try different brands before buying. As an option, students could use oil pastels.

Activity 1

Symbols, Detail and Light

Materials
11" x 14" or 12" x 18" white drawing paper
assorted colored pencils

Take a look.
• Fig.10–6, Jan van Eyck, *Arnolfini Wedding,* 1434. Oil on panel.

Think about it. Northern Renaissance painters moved in a different direction from that of their Italian counterparts. Symbolism, the fascination with detail, and realistic light all share importance in *Arnolfini Wedding,* a painting by the Northern Renaissance painter Jan van Eyck. (Refer to Chapter 9 to compare and contrast the two Renaissance trends.)
• Study the detailed objects in the room and explain their significance. What might they symbolize?
• Observe how the light softly illuminates the variety of textures—skin, flesh, metal and fabrics.
• How do all of these create unity in the painting?

Do it. Using colored pencil, illustrate an important event or ceremony in your life. Incorporate symbolism, soft lighting and detail to make your composition portray the mood of the event.

Check it. Have a friend describe what he or she sees in your artwork. Is your friend's interpretation close to what you had in mind? Do the same with your friend's work. Discuss how easy or difficult it is to convey a mood or idea in images.

Helpful Hint: Make a list of symbols and their meanings.

Activity 2

Fantasy World Triptych

Materials
11" x 14" paper
assorted fine-line colored markers
optional: colored pencils, oil pastels or watercolors

Take a look.
• Fig.10–10, Hieronymus Bosch, *Garden of Delights.,* triptych, about 1505–1510.

Think about it. Hieronymus Bosch, a Dutch painter, presented a world of weird sights, fanciful images and puzzling symbols. His triptych, *Garden of Delights,* is a strange story filled with incredible detail. Bosch's painting, packed with tiny people set in a fantastic landscape, shows a pessimistic look at humanity.

Do it. Visualize your own world of fantasy and miniature images. Using fine-line colored markers, create a triptych which tells the story of your fantasy world. Make your drawing very detailed.

Check it. As you work, consider the way images, ideas and colors interact between your panels.

Helpful Hint: Relax and doodle first.

Additional Activities

• Read excerpts from Sir Thomas More's *Utopia* (1516). Create a collage showing your own personal utopia. Use photographs, illustrations and drawings. Write an essay predicting the success of your utopia.

• Using tempera, paint a picture of your favorite outdoor winter activity. Paint it in flat colors, similar to the style of Bruegel (see *The Return of the Hunters,* fig.10–13.)

• Pieter Bruegel's paintings of the four seasons are known as a cycle. He painted his Flemish community in four settings (spring, summer, autumn and winter). You (and several classmates) could depict your own community, neighborhood or school in a series of four drawings, paintings, sculptures or photographs.

• Northern European artists imitated nature by painting miniature worlds of their own. Using watercolor or colored pencils, make a tiny painting, no more than 4" wide. Work from nature (grass, flowers) or from a still life, and keep everything in proportion. Try painting with egg tempera on a wooden panel or a piece of illustration board. Use egg yolk, water and powdered pigments as your medium, and the smallest brush you can find. (Then, imagine using this exacting technique on a large altarpiece.)

• Do a miniature pen and ink line drawing of a landscape or your favorite animal. If your school has a badge-maker, turn your miniature into an art history button.

Classroom Management

This could be done with the classroom as a whole or in small groups with questions written on the board.

• Share a special event in your life.

• Why the event was special?

• Did anyone else participate or share in this special occasion?

• Was special clothing required? Describe in detail what you wore.

After class discussion, have the students create their own artwork that relates a personal event or their participation in a ceremony.

Tips

Have students bring in their family photos of special occasions. Encourage the students to talk about the traditions and customs surrounding these events.

Evaluation

• Has the student creatively rendered an event in his or her life in artistic, symbolic language?

• Is attention to soft lighting apparent in the work? Does the source of light appear to be consistent?

• Does the work show thoughtful use of media?

Steve Meneely

Age 17
Lower Merion High School
Ardmore, Pennsylvania
Favorite artists: Dürer, Poussin,
Ingres
Activity 2,
Fantasy World Triptych

When I was a young child, I lived in a small bush village in Zaire, Africa. I can remember pausing our soccer games to chase the small whirlwinds that swept across the hard, cracked field. The tornado in the left portion of my triptych is much larger and more destructive than the ones we tried to run into.

One of the major themes in this piece is time. Time has turned what was once an unreal reality into a warm memory that slowly fades away with time. Time goes by very quickly, I am learning, and is a division, much like the cliffs and the fault line in the center piece. In all three panels, there are the two figures with torches, life and death, who are hand in hand. My fantasy is to be ruler over time, and to be with those who have vanished from my life.

To me art depends on the world surrounding us, and the inspirations and ideas of other artists. The more and more I look at art, the more I learn about what has been done, and the messages artists have conveyed in their work. This becomes a stepping block, to go on to discover new things for myself.

You should explore, expanding your horizons and your understanding. Stay away from the comforts you can create for yourself, and don't end up in a rut. Keep your eyes open at all times, be aware of the things that pass the majority by. Always improve what you do by seeing what others have done. And good luck!

Steve Meneely

Untitled, 1994. Watercolor, 30" x 42" (76 x 107 cm).

Activity 2: Fantasy World Triptych

Activity Objectives
Students should be able to:

• design an original triptych

• generate a creative fantasy world from their imagination

• effectively use the medium of their choice in rendering their work

Thinking Critically
Have the class look at the painting *Garden of Delights* (fig.10–10) and ask:

• What is a three-paneled painting called?

• What elements does the artist use to create such a "busy" painting?

• How does the color influence the mood?

Preparation Ideas
To spark ideas, locate other examples of Bosch's work, as well as contemporary fantasy art that will interest students.

Notes on Materials
Have a minimum of six colored markers, colored pencils or oil pastels per student. Encourage students to use what they have to blend new colors.

Tips
• Stimulate the students' imagination by doing a mind map on the chalkboard (sometimes called "bubbling"). Begin

Teacher Spotlight
Louise Pierce
Art Teacher
Lower Merion High School

I showed my students examples of Bosch's work other than the *Garden of Delights*. I knew the students would love his creatures and characters, and I felt it would flesh out the historic reference. The kids were really surprised at how long ago he worked, and they found his work to be quite modern. I guess most of the old masters they have looked at have been very realistic. I also tried to leave the definition of a triptych fairly open because I wanted to afford the students the opportunity to put their own stamp on it rather than having to work in a traditional format. Some of the students worked vertically or in a triangular mode, and I liked that.

For materials, I allowed the students to choose from markers, colored pencil, oil pastel and watercolors. I also allowed them to work in any size they wished, the smallest being 12" x 16". I thought by opening up the size and materials a bit, I would get more professional results because, to me, "small" and "in markers" usually means "cartoon."

with a single word or theme. The student elaborates and makes connections until an idea forms. He or she continues to develop the idea until ready to create the drawing.

• Have students read fables. Then ask them to write and illustrate their own fable.

• Students may find the specific size of paper suggested for the activity too confining. Allow students to choose the size and shape of their paper.

Evaluation

• Has the student created a triptych?

• Does the work express a theme? Do the panels relate to one another?

• Does the subject matter clearly show a fantasy world derived from imagination?

• Does the work show skillful use of media?

Chapter 11 Organizer

Chapter 11 Opener: Baroque and Rococo

Objectives

Understand how Rome briefly reemerged as the center of the Western art world during the early Baroque period.

Identify the church as the major art patron in Italy.

Recognize the exuberant and emotional characteristics of the Baroque style.

Comprehend the differences and similarities of Baroque art in Italy, Austria, Germany, France, Spain, Flanders and Holland.

Articulate the contrast between the charming and ethereal Rococo art of the eighteenth century and its Baroque antecedents.

National Standards

4a Students differentiate among a variety of historical and cultural contexts in terms of characteristics and purposes of works of art.

5a Students identify intentions of those creating artworks, explore the implications of various purposes, and justify their analyses of purposes in particular works.

5d Students correlate responses to works of visual art with various techniques for communicating meanings, ideas, attitudes, views, and intentions.

4c Students analyze relationships of works of art to one another in terms of history, aesthetics, and culture, justifying conclusions made in the analysis and using such conclusions to inform their own art making.

3a Students reflect on how artworks differ visually, spatially, temporally, and functionally, and describe how these are related to history and culture.

Teacher Edition References

Lesson 11.1 The Baroque in Italy and Germany

	Teacher Edition References	
Special Feature: Gianlorenzo Bernini 332–333	Contextual Info 333	Performing Arts 333
Remainder of Lesson 11.1 334–339 World Cultural Timeline 336 Lesson 11.1 Review 339	Contextual Info 334, 336, 338 HOTS 335, 337, 339 Collaborative 338	Interdisciplinary 337 Multicultural 336 Performing Arts 338

Lesson 11.2 The Baroque in France

Special Feature: Georges de La Tour 340–341	HOTS 341	
Remainder of Lesson 11.2 342–345 World Cultural Timeline 342 Lesson 11.2 Review 345	Contextual Info 342, 344 HOTS 343, 345 Inquiry 342	Multicultural 342 Performing Arts 344

Lesson 11.3 The Baroque in Flanders and Holland

Special Feature: Judith Leyster 346–347	Contextual Info 347 HOTS 347	Performing Arts 347
Remainder of Lesson 11.3 348–359 World Cultural Timeline 348 Lesson 11.3 Review 359	Contextual Info 348, 350, 352, 354, 356, 358 HOTS 349, 351, 353, 355, 357, 359	Conservation 357 Interdisciplinary 350, 354 Multicultural 348

Lesson 11.4 The Baroque in Spain

Special Feature: Diego Rodriguez de Silva y Velazquez 360–361	Contextual Info 361	HOTS 361
Remainder of Lesson 11.4 362–363 World Cultural Timeline 362 Lesson 11.4 Review 363	Contextual Info 362 HOTS 363	Multicultural 362

Lesson 11.5 The Early Eighteenth Century

Special Feature: Antoine Watteau 364–365	HOTS 365	Performing Arts 365
Remainder of Lesson 11.5 366–376 World Cultural Timeline 368, 372 Lesson 11.5 Review 376 Primary Source, Chapter Review 377	Contextual Info 366, 368, 370, 372, 374, 376 HOTS 367, 369, 371, 373, 375	Interdisciplinary 370 Multicultural 362, 368, 372

Classroom Connections

National Standards

Studio Activity 1
Learning from Rembrandt

1a Students apply media, techniques, and processes with sufficient skill, confidence, and sensitivity that their intentions are carried out in their artworks.
4c Students analyze relationships of works of art to one another in terms of history, aesthetics, and culture, justifying conclusions made in the analysis and using such conclusions to inform their own art making.

Studio Activity 2
Light and Contrast

Other Resources

Books

Blunt, Anthony. *Art and Architecture in France: 1500–1700.* New Haven: Yale University Press, 1992.

Boime, Albert. *Art in an Age of Revolution, 1750–1800.* Chicago: University of Chicago Press, 1987.

Eighteenth-Century Women. Metropolitan Museum of Art, 1982.

Enggass, Robert, and Brown, Jonathan. *Italy and Spain: 1600–1750.* Part of *Sources and Documents in the History of Art.* Englewood Cliffs: Prentice Hall, 1970.

Gerson, Horst, and Ter Kuile, E. H. *Art and Architecture in Belgium: 1600–1800.* 3rd ed., Baltimore: Penguin USA, 1960.

Held, Julius S., and Posner, Donald. *17th and 18th Century Art: Baroque Painting, Sculpture, and Architecture.* Englewood Cliffs: Prentice Hall, 1972.

Hempel, Eberhard. *Baroque Art and Architecture in Central Europe.* Baltimore: Penguin USA, 1965.

Holt, Elizabeth Gilmore, ed. *A Documentary History of Art. Volume II: Michelangelo and the Mannerists: The Baroque and the Eighteenth Century.* Princeton: Princeton University Press, 1983.

Kalnein, Wend G., and Levey, Michael. *Art and Architecture of the Eighteenth Century in France.* Baltimore: Penguin USA, 1973.

Martin, John. *Baroque.* Part of *Style and Civilization.* New York: HarperCollins, 1977.

Plumb, John Harold. *England in the Eighteenth Century.* Baltimore: Penguin USA, 1951.

Rembrandt and Velaszuez: Two Faces of the Seventeenth Century. Metropolitan Museum of Art, 1986.

Rosenberg, Jakob, Seymour, Slive and Ter Kuile, E.H. *Dutch Art and Architecture: 1600–1800.* 3rd ed., New Haven: Yale University Press, 1992.

Whinney, Margaret D. *Sculpture in Britain: 1530–1830.* 2nd ed., New Haven: Yale University Press, 1992.

Waterhouse, Ellis K. *Painting in Britain: 1530–1790.* 4th ed. New Haven: Yale University Press, 1992.

Wittkower, Rudolf. *Art and Architecture in Italy: 1600–1750.* 3rd ed., New Haven: Yale University Press, 1992.

Video

Joshua Reynolds. Home Video, 1987.
Rembrandt, Crystal

Music

Monteverdi—*Orfeo*
Giovanni Gabrieli—*Sacrae Symphoniae*
Vivaldi—*Concerti Crossi*
Bach—*Passacaglia and Fugue in C Minor*
Christ Lay in the Bonds of Death
Brandenburg Concerti
Handel—*Messiah*
Concerti Grossi

Ancillaries

Slides: Le Vau/Mansart, Versailles, 69a, 137; Hardouin-Mansart, Royal Chapel, Versailles, 69b, 138

Teacher Edition References

Timeline: Baroque and Rococo 330
Map: Baroque and Rococo 331
Context 330
Art 331
Quote 331

Ancillaries

Slides: Bernini, *David*, 65a, 131
Overhead Transparencies: Baroque Illusions, 12

Slides: Caravaggio, *Bachus*, 67b, 132; Maderno, St. Peter's Facade, Rome, 66a, 133; Borromini, *St. Ivo*, 68b, 134; Zimmermann, Interior of Die Wies, Upper Bavaria, 67a, 135

Slides: Poussin, *Holy Family on the Steps*, 68a, 136; Le Vau/Mansart, Versailles, 69a, 137; Hardouin-Mansart, Royal Chapel, Versailles, 69b, 138; Hardouin-Mansart, Church of the Invalides, Paris, 70a, 139

Slides: Hals, *Young Man and Woman in an Inn, (Yonker Ramp and His Sweetheart)*, 71a, 140; Vermeer, *Allegory of the Art of Painting*, 72a, 141; Ruisdael, *Sluice Gate*, 70b, 142; Steen, *Twelfth Night*, 71b, 143; Rembrandt, *Descent from the Cross*, 72b, 144
Overhead Transparencies: Light and Form, 11

Slides: Velasquez, *The Jester Calabazos*, 73b, 145
Large Reproductions: Velasquez, *Surrender of Breda*, 14

Slides: Zurbaran, *Still Life with Lemons, Oranges and a Rose*, 10a, 20

Large Reproductions: Watteau, *Embarkation to Cythera*, 15

Slides: Chardin, *Grace at Table*, 74b, 146; Reynolds, *Sarah Bunbury Sacrificing to the Graces*, 73a, 147; Stuart, *George Washington*, 75b, 148
Large Reproductions: Johnson, *The Westwood Children*, 16

Schedule

One day each to sketch, engrave, and print.

One day to sketch and another to cut and paste the collage. To shorten the class time needed for this, cut down on the number of preliminary quick sketches or have students complete the collage outside of class.

Materials

pencils, drawing paper, etching supplies

pencils, drawing paper for sketching, construction paper: white, yellow, gray, black, glue

Introduce

Seventeenth-century Baroque art was far more emotional and exuberant than Renaissance art. The style was followed in parts of Western Europe by the lighthearted Rococo movement, although English and American artists preferred the less frivolous Baroque manner.

Lessons at a Glance

11.1 *The Baroque in Italy and Germany*
Baroque art was born in Italy, and its variations spread to Germany and Austria.

11.2 *The Baroque in France*
France was the most powerful nation in Europe after the mid-seventeenth century and emerged as the art capital of the Western world. Under the reign of Louis XIV, the "Sun King," the country set the standards for art and culture.

11.3 *The Baroque in Flanders and Holland*
During the seventeenth century, Flanders remained under the rule of Catholic Spain, although its art was influenced by Italy and the Netherlands. After Holland broke free from the Hapsburg Empire, middle-class citizens who grew wealthy from the country's international trade yearned for familiar images of their everyday life.

11.4 *The Baroque in Spain*
The Golden Age of Spanish art began in the early seventeenth century when the country's artists came into their own after absorbing lessons from their peers in Italy and the Netherlands.

11.5 *The Early Eighteenth Century*
In the eighteenth century, the French aristocracy commissioned art in the light and playful Rococo style, while those living in England and America remained loyal to the more serious Baroque aesthetic.

11

Baroque and Rococo

IT WAS ABOUT 1600 when Rome emerged again as the center of the art world. The church remained all-powerful, continuing to patronize art and commission artists from all over Italy. From this hotbed of creative talent, the exuberant, emotional Baroque style was born and spread through Europe.

Throughout the 1600s, Europe was filled with an energy that inspired the production of hundreds of great paintings and sculptures and scores of architectural masterpieces. From the magnificent palace at Versailles to the world-famous canvases of Rembrandt and Rubens, Europe has seldom seen a century of such intense and widespread activity.

In the 1700s, Rococo made its first appearance in France. Its charm and lightheartedness contrasted with the power and seriousness of the Baroque. This new style was not popular in all of Europe. The English and their American colonies preferred the more serious nature of the Baroque and extended the life of that style into the later 1700s.

The late 1700s was a time of great change in Europe and America. The beginning of the industrial revolution, along with the democratic revolutions in France and America, would begin the period we consider the modern world.

11–a Part of Gianlorenzo Bernini's contribution to Baroque art in Rome was the installation of magnificent sculpted fountains. This is a detail of one of the most spectacular fountains designed during the Baroque period. It reflects the Baroque fascination with drama and emotion.
Gianlorenzo Bernini, *Fountain of the Four Rivers*, 1648–1651. Travertine and marble. Piazza Navona, Rome.

1632
van Dyck becomes court painter to Charles I
1642

1602–1604
Caravaggio, *Deposition of Christ*
1618
30 Years War begins

1642
Rembrandt, *The Night Watch*
1656
Velazquez, *The Maids of Honor*

1666
Great Fire and Plague of London

1768–1770
Copley, *Paul Revere*
1789–1802
French Revolution
1793
The Louvre becomes a national art gallery, Paris

Baroque and Rococo

1620
The Mayflower sails to New Plymouth, Massachusetts

1675–1710
Wren, Saint Paul's Cathedral

1717–1719
Watteau, *Embarkation for Cythera*
1719
Defoe, *Robinson Crusoe*

1730
Rococo at its peak
1768
Mozart produces first opera at age 12

Objectives

Students should be able to:

Understand how Rome briefly reemerged as the center of the Western art world during the early Baroque period.

Identify the church as the major art patron in Italy.

Recognize the exuberant and emotional characteristics of the Baroque style.

Comprehend the differences and similarities of Baroque art in Italy, Austria, Germany, France, Spain, Flanders and Holland.

Articulate the contrast between the charming and ethereal Rococo art of the eighteenth century and its Baroque antecedents.

Teach

Timeline
Have students identify the countries in which the events on the timeline occurred. Ask them if the Baroque and Rococo flowered only in one country at a time or somewhat simultaneously throughout much of Western Europe.

Context
Have students examine figs.11–a and 11–c. Ask what message the papacy and the French monarchy wished to convey about themselves through their artworks.

• How was most of Western Europe ruled during the Baroque era?

Nature is nearly always feeble and puny, so that if their [students'] imaginations are filled only with natural forms, they never will be able to produce anything beautiful and grand, for these qualities are not to be found in nature.

Gianlorenzo Bernini

11–c The Hall of Mirrors at Versailles is considered one of the most splendid rooms in all of Europe. Seventeen arched windows admit abundant sunlight that is reflected from seventeen mammoth mirrors.
Jules Hardouin-Mansart and Charles Lebrun, Hall of Mirrors, *Palace of Versailles*, begun 1678.

11–b In the eighteenth century wealthy travelers often purchased paintings of the cities they visited to bring home as souvenirs. This is a detail from a painting of Venice. It depicts the city in the midst of a celebration and is filled with rich and exacting details.
Antonio Canaletto, *The Basin of San Marco on Ascension Day*, detail (fig.11–48).

Baroque and Rococo

The widespread Baroque movement was influential in all of Europe.

Quote

Ask students if Gianlorenzo Bernini's quote indicates that he was satisfied with accurately duplicating the visual world. What in fig.11–a supports their conclusions? Do they think Bernini would have gotten along with the French painter Jean-Baptiste-Simeon Chardin, who said: "The eye must be taught to look at nature; and how many have never seen and will never see it!" (See pages 366 and 367 for information on and images by Chardin.)

Map

Ask students to examine the map and decide if the Baroque, which began in Rome, was confined to a single country. Where else did the style spread to in Europe?

Reteach

Have students stand in the pose of Bernini's personification of a river (fig.11–a).

• Is this pose passive or full of life? Is this pose easy to hold?

• How might Bernini's choice of pose affect the way viewers react to his work?

• As a comparison, have students sit perfectly upright on chairs, with their legs together, feet planted flat on the ground and hands in their laps. Does this pose emit the same kind of dynamism as that in Bernini's figure?

• He further enhanced the sense of motion by incorporating water that dribbles, spills, spouts, ribbons and jets throughout the marble and glistens in the surrounding light.

Challenge students to think of TV-show parallels for Renaissance and Baroque art. If an educational program on public television could symbolize the Renaissance, what type of program might represent the extreme theatricality of Baroque art?

• Would this type of art be commissioned by democratic countries today? Why or why not? (Have the class compare figs.11–a and 11–c to images of the United States Capitol or national monuments.)

Art

Ask students how the Hall of Mirrors (fig.11–c) at the *Palace of Versailles* represents the splendid, sumptuous quality of the Baroque. Have them consider the room's scale, design, light and materials.

• How do they think it would have felt to minuet down the hall in elaborate court outfits during the seventeenth century?

• Would they have preferred to live at court, with all its rules, etiquette and dangerous politics, or to have been a peasant residing in the countryside and living off the land?

Evaluate

Ask students what was more important in Baroque art, the Classical ideals of antiquity; or passion, emotion and drama? Have them use specific artworks to support their observations.

Pose the following questions: "Were art and politics completely independent of one another during the Western European Baroque and Rococo period? Why or why not? What is the arts-politics situation like today in America? Do you think it should change? What influences your opinion?"

Lesson 11.1

Baroque art was born in Italy, and its variations spread to Germany and Austria.

Warm-up

Have students examine figs.11–1, 11–2, 11–4 and 11–5. Ask them to imagine worshipping in a large church during the seventeenth century and encountering these works firsthand. Ask: "How do these make you feel? Relaxed? Excited? Bored? Tired?" Have students brainstorm a list of adjectives that apply to each piece. Then have them discuss the similarities in the words they chose.

Objectives

Students should be able to:

Identify early seventeenth-century Rome as the birthplace of Baroque art.

Understand how the Catholic Church, Italy's major art patron, commissioned works to glorify its own power and wealth.

Comprehend how German and Austrian artists and architects infused their work with a sense of light, air and motion.

Vocabulary Definitions

tenebrism A late-sixteenth-century Italian painting technique which exaggerated strong contrasts of light and dark.
baldachin (bal-dah-*cheen*) A fixed canopy of wood, stone, fabric, etc., over an altar, throne or doorway. Sometimes portable, as when it is over a movable statue during a parade or procession.
stucco (*stuk*-oh) Any of several types of plaster used for decorative cornices, moldings or ceilings; also, a cement coating for the exterior of a building.

Teach

Art History: Ask the class who paid for the art that they viewed in the warm-up activity.

• Was Italian Baroque art made for ordinary people or for wealthy church officials, royalty and nobility?

• Could average citizens today afford to commission such work? Explain how the Catholic Church paid artists from all across Europe to come and create

11.1 The Baroque in Italy and Germany

THE TRANSFORMATION from Mannerism to Baroque took place in Rome near the end of the sixteenth century and gradually spread throughout Europe. Artists of this period were highly competent at drawing and painting the human figure from every possible angle. They reproduced the most complicated perspective and used color and value contrasts with ease. The Baroque was filled with a dynamism and opulence that contrasts with the Renaissance. Artists delighted in the theatrical and extravagant and showed incredible versatility in their work.

Around 1600, Rome became the birthplace of Baroque art, as it had been the center of the High Renaissance a century before. Artists from many regions gathered in Rome to receive challenging papal commissions. These ambitious young artists, attracted by the great activity in Rome, created the new style.

In Germany, the southern region in particular looked to Italy as its model. The leading figures of the time were architects. Though Italy was the source for many building plans, the interiors of German Baroque churches show a lavish exuberance and airiness that is a departure from Italian Baroque ideals.

Key Notes

• The Baroque is born in Italy under the patronage of the Catholic Church.
• A papal program to beautify Rome draws artists from all regions of Italy.
• The German Baroque, as seen in its churches, is exuberant and festive.

Vocabulary
tenebrism
baldachin
stucco

11–1 This enormous piazza is frequently jammed with thousands of worshipers and tourists.
Gianlorenzo Bernini. *Piazza and colonnade of St. Peter's*, Rome, designed 1657.

Special Feature
Gianlorenzo Bernini

(1598–1680)

One of the most influential and fiery artists of the Baroque period was Gianlorenzo Bernini. Too late to belong to the Renaissance period, Bernini was nevertheless a Renaissance man: sculptor, painter, architect, stage designer, dramatist and composer.

It is impossible to look at or visit St. Peter's in Rome without thinking of Bernini. Inside and out his imprint is evident. Under his supervision, thirty-nine artists carried out his sculptural plans during several years of intense activity. Bernini's largest and most impressive project was the design for a magnificent piazza in front of *St. Peter's* (fig.11–1). It begins with a trapezoidal plaza in front of the basilica's facade and opens out into a huge oval area framed by massive

---

impressive masterpieces that would extol its power.

Criticism: Have students study Michelangelo's Renaissance sculpture of *David* (fig.9–26) and then pretend that they are a Baroque artist devoted to grandiose emotions and actions. How would they alter this composition of the young man? After students have articulated their ideas, have them compare their answers to Bernini's choices in his *David* (fig.11–3).

• Does his sculpture look anything like what students proposed?

• Does Michelangelo's Renaissance work or Bernini's Baroque piece feel more exciting to view? Why?

• How do the figures' poses affect their answers?

• What words would they use to differentiate the older Renaissance style from that of the Baroque?

Evaluate

Question students about what they think the relationship was between artists and their patrons in the Baroque era.

• Could artists choose whatever style and subject matter they wished?

• Why might artists in the seventeenth century have had so little freedom?

• How was Europe ruled then in comparison to the United States today?

11–2 The artist used a hidden window to enhance the effect of light in this sculpture.
Gianlorenzo Bernini, *Ecstasy of Saint Theresa*, 1645–1652. Marble, about 11 1/2' (3.5 m) high. Cornaro Chapel, Santa Maria della Vittoria, Rome.

11–3 Notice how Bernini chose to portray the moment just before the stone is released from the sling. The viewer is forced to imagine how the action will be completed.
Gianlorenzo Bernini, *David*, 1623. Marble, 67" (170 cm) high. Galleria Borghese, Rome.

Doric colonnades. An Egyptian obelisk stands in the center flanked by two magnificent fountains. Although grandly Classic in its style, the curves of the piazza are Baroque.

The *Ecstasy of Saint Theresa* (fig.11–2) is the work in which Bernini most completely captures the Baroque spirit. The sculpture commemorates a mystical event involving Saint Theresa, a Carmelite nun. She believed that a pain in her side was caused by an angel of God stabbing her repeatedly with a fire-tipped arrow. Her face in Bernini's sculpture shows the ecstasy of the combined pain and pleasure while her body swoons. According to her vision, the pain

was dreadful, yet so sweet she wanted it to continue forever. Saint Theresa floats on a marble cloud that seems suspended in air. Rays of glimmering bronze shower down on the figures from the painted ceiling of the chapel. Bernini enhanced this sensation of light by including a hidden window to let in real light.

Bernini's *David* (fig.11–3) also expresses the Baroque spirit to perfection. It is expansive, dramatic and energetic. We see David at the beginning of the powerful pivoting motion that will propel the stone out of his sling. The space around the sculpture seems to be part of it. Viewers do not stand for long in the path of the about-to-be-hurled stone.

Discuss what it might mean to have a Baroque personality. Have students describe someone they know or an imaginary person who exemplifies the grandeur, pomp and circumstance of the term "Baroque personality."

Performing Arts Connection

Baroque Music (ca. 1600–1750)

The Baroque period gave rise to the modern orchestra and the development of opera, as well as new compositional forms such as the concerto (a composition for an orchestra and one or more solo instruments) and the symphony (an extended orchestral piece in three or more movements). Opera *buffa*, or Italian comic opera, evolved in the early eighteenth century. Light and frivolous, opera buffa often parodied current political or social events.

• Mostly everything about the Baroque age was fancy and complex. Have students examine the architecture of churches and palaces from the period while listening to compositions by Johann Sebastian Bach, such as the *Brandenburg Concertos*. Ask how both creative forms communicate the pomp and circumstance of the era.

• Ask students: "If you had lived in the seventeenth century, would you have agreed readily to create artwork solely to meet the desires of the person who was paying you?" Have students defend their point of view in a class discussion.

Direct students to study figs.11–1 and 11–2. Ask what image about itself the papacy wished to project with its commissioned art. If students had been the leader of a different religious group or a ruler from a nearby country, would they have wanted to tangle with the powers behind the church? Why or why not? Have students use the artwork to support their answer.

Reteach

Share with the class that during the earlier period of the Italian Renaissance, artists had learned how to use color, contrast and single-point perspective to suggest the illusion of three-dimensional reality.

• Ask students if Baroque art imitates life as closely as Renaissance painting does?

• What did Baroque artists add to Renaissance techniques that made their work appear more dramatic?

• Direct students' thinking by asking them which style affects them more deeply and immediately, and also by having them study fig.11–a and its caption.

Contextual Information

Caravaggio

When styles in art change, artists of the old style are sometimes ignored or criticized. Caravaggio is an example. One of the results of the Counter-Reformation was a reexamination of art. Paintings and sculpture were to show good conduct, contemplation of good actions and religious scenes. Paintings, such as those by Caravaggio, that included ordinary people among saints were criticized. Emphasis was to be placed on important religious figures as ideal examples.

Gentileschi

Gentileschi, whose preferred subjects were the Biblical heroines Judith, Bathsheba, Esther and Susanna, was one of many women painters in the Baroque era. Many of these artists were taught and encouraged by family members, but it was difficult for women to travel to see other artists' works. They could use only female models, and many stopped painting when they married and had children.

11–4 Caravaggio's dramatic use of light combined with naturalism influenced many other artists.
Caravaggio, *The Supper at Emmaus*, 1597. Oil on canvas, 54 1/4" x 76 1/2" (138 x 194 cm). National Gallery, London.

Caravaggio
(1571–1610)

Working about twenty-five years earlier than Bernini, Michelangelo Merisi, called Caravaggio (after his hometown) was the first giant of the Baroque. He was considered a rebel against conventional society and met an early death at thirty-seven while running from the law.

Unlike Bernini who worked as painter, sculptor and architect, Caravaggio focused solely on painting. He often tried to shock his patrons by placing his religious figures in very common, earthly settings. Figures were frequently shown barefoot, with the dirty soles of their feet presented directly to the viewer. For this reason and the fact that he used everyday citizens and common people as models, churches sometimes refused his commissioned work.

Caravaggio's work featured extreme naturalism, intense value contrasts and a hard-edged painting style. His ability to use these three elements to create intense drama strongly influenced many artists. His large paintings on canvas had a significant impact on northern European art where naturalism was already accepted.

The subjects in Caravaggio's *The Supper at Emmaus* (fig.11–4) are brilliantly lit by a single source of light. The scene is taken from the Biblical account of Easter Sunday evening. Christ had appeared and walked with two of his followers to their home at Emmaus. When Christ blessed the food on the table, the followers suddenly knew who he was—their risen Lord. Caravaggio captures them at the moment of recognition. With Christ's hand over the meal in blessing, the man on the right throws out his arms in amazement. The man on the left shoves his chair away from the table in utter astonishment. Their servant looks on in disbelief.

Set against a solid wall of dark values, the figures seem lit with a floodlight as they surround the table, acting out the drama. They are nearly life-size. Each has facial expressions and hand gestures that intensify the dramatic impact. Caravaggio is a master of foreshortening, color, light, drama and still lifes. Notice the exquisite basket of fruit, the roast chicken, the bread and the dishes on the table. All receive the same dramatic treatment as the human figures.

Caravaggio was one of the earliest artists to paint still-life subjects with such naturalism, even including rotten spots on the apples.

In his painting, *Deposition of Christ* (bringing Christ down from the cross), Caravaggio has an ideal subject for his dramatic technique (fig.11–5). The tightly composed group is made up of three women, Joseph of Arimathea and the Apostle John. They ease the lifeless body onto a huge stone slab projecting out from the canvas. Christ's limp hand and the corner of the winding cloth touch the slab, uniting it with the group of figures.

Caravaggio places the eye level right at the top of the slab so that all the action takes place above the viewer, adding to the stagelike feeling. The black background intensifies the drama. The deep shadows eat into the group of figures, making the lighter values even more powerful by contrast. The nearly nude figure of Christ contrasts with the various cloth textures. Light contrasts with dark; life with death; hunched figures with erect; and horizontal direction with vertical and diagonal.

The light plays most directly on Christ's body and highlights the faces of John and Joseph. The faces of Christ's mother and Mary Magdalene are darkened in shadow. The light again strikes the face and uplifted hands of the third Mary at the top of the composition. The exaggerated contrast of darks and lights, called **tenebrism**, together with the naturalistic style of Caravaggio creates an overpowering work. Since the figures are slightly over life-size, viewers feel that they are watching the event take place before their eyes.

Artemisia Gentileschi

(1593–1653)

Caravaggio's followers used his dramatic staging of events set against a plain dark background as part of their own style. Among his followers was Artemisia Gentileschi. She helped spread Caravaggio's style to Florence, Genoa and Naples. By 1615, Gentileschi was a well-known artist in Florence. She moved to Rome in 1620 and painted *Judith and Maidservant with the Head of Holofernes* (fig.11–6). The story centers around the Hebrew heroine, Judith. The Babylonian army was besieging a Hebrew city when Judith surrendered herself to the enemy. Once in camp, she and her servant found and beheaded the general, Holofernes, causing the Babylonian army to retreat and lift the siege.

Instead of focusing on the violence of the killing, Gentileschi dramatizes the start of the escape from the enemy camp. The maidservant is stuffing the head of Holofernes into a sack at the bottom of the painting. Using a candle as the single light source, the artist emphasizes deep shadows and brilliant lights. The tenebrism effect highlights the forms of the figures and the satiny gold material in Judith's robe. The blacks from the background infringe on the dark shadows of the figures. The foreshortening of the figures is handled beautifully as they are shown rushing to get their work done before they are detected.

11–6 One of the first known important women painters who was important in her own right, Gentileschi was a student of her father's and of other important artists of her time.
Artemisia Gentileschi, *Judith and Maidservant with the Head of Holofernes*, about 1625. Oil on canvas, 72 3/4" x 56" (185 x 142 cm). The Detroit Institute of Arts.

11–5 Can you identify the elements of the story and the techniques used to emphasize them?
Caravaggio, *Deposition of Christ*, 1602–1604. Oil on canvas, 117 1/4" x 79 1/2" (298 x 202 cm). Vatican Museums, Rome.

Higher-Order Thinking Skills

1 Ask students to compare *The Supper at Emmaus* (fig.11–4) to Leonardo's *The Last Supper* (fig.9–23), paying particular attention to the mood and expressions of each of the participants.

2 Ask the class to consider whether there is a difference in the way men and women paint and sculpt. Are there features of Artemisia Gentileschi's painting that they would consider feminine or done from a woman's point of view?

Contextual Information

Time of Change

As reforms in the Catholic Church began, church officials worked to make Rome once again a great city. They employed artists to decorate their buildings. Another change in Italy during this period included the start of an art school in Bologna. Young people could then attend art school instead of serving years as apprentices in a guild.

Baroque Sound

Sound was a very important component of the Baroque experience. Churches were designed with exceptional acoustics. The churchgoer, surrounded by beautiful church music and gazing up at ceiling frescoes that seemed to extend to infinity, could not help but be moved by the experience. Sound also was taken into careful consideration when fountains were designed. Factors such as height and water flow were adjusted so that the sound of the water moving through the fountain was appealing and musical.

The Counter-Reformation

The Counter-Reformation was a sixteenth- and seventeenth-century movement within the Roman Catholic Church to revitalize the church and to oppose Protestantism. As part of this revitalization effort, the Church called upon artists to design and decorate a new kind of place of worship, a structure that would illustrate the joy, light, energy and vigor of the new power of the church. Expressions of this were church interiors filled with elaborate decoration and ceilings that became visions of the glory of heaven.

11–7 The basilica of St. Peter's is an extraordinary blending of Renaissance and Baroque elements that combine to create the most impressive building in Christendom.
Carlo Maderno. *Facade of St. Peter's*, Rome, 1606–1612.

Carlo Maderno

(1556–1629)

Carlo Maderno made important contributions to the style of Baroque architecture. His work on St. Peter's in Rome brought him much fame. In 1606 Pope Paul V commissioned Maderno to add a nave to Michelangelo's building and provide a facade. Maderno moved the new facade far forward, reducing the importance of Michelangelo's dome. The dome now cannot be seen except from a distance or from the papal gardens in the rear of the basilica. The new facade (fig.11–7) has a heavy horizontal look because huge corner structures were added. Each, pierced with an arch and crowned with a clock, is a gateway to the Vatican properties behind. Maderno intended them to be the basis for massive towers. The towers were never built because the foundations were not strong enough.

The windows, five doors, columns and statues of the facade are enormous in size. But because of the careful scale and design, they work together beautifully and do not seem excessively large. Only when comparing them to a person standing by a column does one realize the massive size of the parts and the whole.

A painting by Giovanni Panini (done about 1750) shows the decoration and size of the interior of *St. Peter's* (fig.11–8). Baroque decoration can be seen in the richly gilded, coffered ceiling, the piers of colored marble and the huge sculptural monuments. Huge clear windows allow sunlight to flood the interior. Compared with the somber majesty of earlier Gothic cathedrals, the interior is startling in its brightness.

The scale is hard to believe. The parts fit together beautifully. Sizes are so carefully interrelated that, at first glance, the basilica does not seem large at all, but many steps must be taken before one reaches the high altar. The interior, from entrance to the end of the apse, is 632 feet long—longer than two football fields. Notice the size of the people in comparison with the sculpture or the thickness of the piers. To bring the scale into concrete dimensions, look at the **baldachin** (Bernini's creation) over the high altar, under Michelangelo's dome. It is 93 feet high or about the height of a 10-story building. Yet it is dwarfed by the hugeness of the open spaces and the massive size of the structure.

Francesco Borromini

(1599–1667)

Borromini was a seventeenth-century Italian architect who strongly influenced succeeding generations. His buildings are marvels of Baroque feeling and are noted for their facades. The facades move in and out in great swags as though made of a plastic material. Borromini's design for Sant' Agnese in Rome (fig.11–9) combines Classic, Renaissance and Baroque styles into a unified design. This design was adopted in other parts of Europe and even Mexico. The convex sculptural quality of the dome, which rests on a high drum, is repeated in convex features of the two corner towers. The concave surface of the central part of the facade provides a gentle contrast to the dome. Notice the many places where features project out from or recede into the facade. The two corner towers are similar to those Maderno planned for St. Peter's, which were never built.

1600 Chinese tea becomes popular in Europe	1624 First theater in Tokyo, Japan, established

World Cultural Timeline

1600 Oyo Kingdom of Nigeria at height of power	1601 First strike of textile workers in China

Multicultural Connection

Japanese Theater

Masks are worn by the main characters in the Japanese Noh theater. The masks, usually white with painted features, have frozen expressions of one emotion and are specific to the characters. They can show nobility, youth, old age, sadness, joy, serenity, fear, beauty and pain. Monster masks can have fangs, exaggerated eyes and noses, horns and frightening expressions.

The actors, who stare at the masks in deep concentration before they put them on, consider them to be sacred. Once the masks are fixed in place, the actors feel that they are no longer themselves but have become their character. Only the actors' movements and words show change.

• Have students research or contribute what they know about the use of masks in other cultures. Discuss any similarities and differences.

• Discuss the use of masks today.

Baroque Ceilings in Rome

During the middle of the seventeenth century, several artists created illusionary paintings of tremendous complexity on the ceilings of some Baroque churches in Rome. The paintings are filled with figures that appear to be floating and soaring into infinity, like large balloons cut loose to float heavenward. A mark on the floor indicated the exact spot from which the perspective could be viewed most accurately. Several ceilings, like the barrel vault of the church of Il Gesu, contained *stucco* (plaster) figures in addition to the painting (fig.11–10). The reliefs gave the added illusion of figures tumbling out of the picture and into the realm of three-dimensional reality.

Painted by Giovanni Battista Gaulli (1639–1709) with sculpture by Antonio Raggi (1624–1686) and directed by Bernini, the ceiling of Il Gesu is highly gilded with a painted oval opening to the sky. Through this window one can look into heaven and see various Jesuit saints. (Il Gesu is the burial place of Ignatius Loyola, founder of the Jesuit order.) The same power that draws the faithful into heaven also casts out the unbelievers. The unbelievers tumble through the frame and seem ready to crash to the floor. The three-dimensional illusion is enhanced by the sculptures, which cast shadows on the sloping vault ceiling.

11–9 The famous *Fountain of the Four Rivers* by Bernini stands in front of Borromini's church in the Piazza Navona.
Francesco Borromini. *Facade of Sant' Agnese.* Rome, 1653–1666.

11–8 Compare this to the interior of Notre Dame in Paris. Do you see a difference in the light?
Giovanni Paolo Panini, *Interior of St. Peter's, Rome.* 1746–1754. Oil on canvas, 60 3/4" x 77 1/2" (154 x 197 cm). National Gallery of Art, Washington DC, Ailsa Mellon Bruce Fund.

11–10 Can you find the parts that are sculpture and the ones that are painted?
Giovanni Battista Gaulli and Antonio Raggi, *Triumph of the Sacred Name of Jesus.* Ceiling fresco, 1676–1679. Il Gesu, Rome.

Contextual Information

Die Wies

The exterior of Die Wies is white-washed like a simple village church. The interior explodes with gold and elaborate decoration.

• Have students imagine the contrast between the exterior and interior. Ask them to describe the impact the interior might have had on the viewer.

The Baroque in Germany and Austria

While the Baroque style was developing in Italy, central Europe was engaged in the devastating Thirty Years War, which ended in 1648. Not until the eighteenth century were Austria and Germany able to begin building projects of any great size. But when they started, the activity was tremendous. Architects filled the cities and countryside of Austria and southern Germany with structures that had exteriors of stately elegance and interiors of gilded light and swirling movement.

Jacob Prandtauer
(1660–1726)

Prandtauer chose a rocky cliff above the Danube River on which to erect the *Benedictine Abbey* at Melk (fig.11–11). The imposing structure is dominated by an ornate dome and two magnificent bell towers. Each tower is topped with an onion dome so familiar in the southern German and Austrian countryside. The exterior presents a powerful appearance with curved surfaces and superb detail. The interior (fig.11–12) is filled with gilded surfaces that allow little chance for eyes to rest. Light streams into the vast space from windows in the dome. Painted areas, gilded statues and carved surfaces are all intricately woven into a huge work of art alive with swirling visual activity.

Dominikus Zimmerman
(1685–1766)

Dominikus Zimmerman created one of the finest spatial designs of the German Baroque—the Bavarian pilgrimage church called *Die Wies*. The exterior is serenely plain and was influenced by contemporary Italian building. But the interior (fig.11–13) is a sudden burst of heavenly energy. Color and light are combined with swirling decoration to create an unbelievable eruption of visual movement. Natural light from many large windows floods the interior. Marble sculptures seem to float. The pulpit appears to defy gravity. The white walls and gold decoration seem to reflect the bril-

11–11 The location of this church on a cliff above the Danube River adds to its monumentality.
Jacob Prandtauer. *Benedictine Abbey*, begun 1702. Melk, Austria.

11–12 Compare this interior with an early Renaissance church interior. Which do you prefer?
Jacob Prandtauer. Interior, *Benedictine Abbey*, begun 1702. Melk, Austria.

Performing Arts Connection

Northern Music

During the Baroque era, music filled the palaces, gardens and churches and even spilled out into the streets of major Austrian cities, so it became an integral part of daily life. Later, Vienna gave rise to the Classical period (1760–1830), which included the great composers Bach, Handel, Haydn, Mozart and Beethoven.

Cooperative Learning

Have students work with music-class students to present an Italian or German Baroque multimedia event. Art students will be responsible for the art component of the program. They can utilize slides, overhead transparencies, video clips or prints. The music students will develop the audio portion of the program. The objective of the event is to provide a more complete vision of the Baroque age and to learn how music and art enhanced each other.

liance of the sun. As glorious as it appears, the interior of Die Wies is typical of hundreds of similar churches in Bavaria and Austria. While Baroque in its structure, the interior decoration of Die Wies exhibits the lavishness and gaiety

of an extension of the Baroque, called Rococo, that becomes popular in northern Europe during the eighteenth century.

11–13 The plan of this church is oval in shape.
Dominikus Zimmerman. Interior, *Die Wies*, 1746–1754. Upper Bavaria.

Higher-Order Thinking Skills

1 Light has a lot to do with the way that people perceive architecture. Have the class design ways, which they may actually carry out, to influence the light in the classroom. Have students analyze the ways that changes of light influence their perceptions of the room. Suggest that they consider color, light sources, brightness and direction.

2 Instruct students to compare the stately, airy elegance of German and Austrian Baroque architecture (figs.11–11, 11–12, 11–13) to the bombastic opulence of its Italian predecessors (figs.11–1, 11–7, 11–8). Ask students to determine the lessons that the northern architects learned from Italian Baroque buildings. Help students sharpen their observations by having them list the similarities and differences of the buildings in the two regions.

Lesson 11.1 Review

1 At the beginning of the seventeenth century, which city became the major center of Baroque art?
2 What was Bernini's most important architectural project?
3 Describe Bernini's *Ecstasy of St. Theresa*. How does this sculpture exemplify Baroque art?
4 In your own words, what would you call a contemporary person with Caravaggio's personality?
5 If the *Deposition of Christ* by Caravaggio were on a stage, where on the stage would all the action be happening? Describe the light and motion in this painting.

6 Define *tenebrism*. Name a Baroque painting that is a good example of tenebrism.
7 Name an Italian Baroque artist who helped spread Caravaggio's style of painting to Florence, Genoa and Naples.
8 How did Giovanni Battista Gaulli and Antonio Raggi create a feeling of depth and space in the ceiling fresco, *Triumph of the Sacred Name of Jesus*?
9 Describe the interior of the Bavarian church, Die Wies.

Lesson 11.1 Review Answers

1 Rome, Italy
2 The design for the monumental piazza in front of St. Peter's in Rome
3 Bernini's *Ecstasy of St. Theresa* exemplifies the Baroque spirit in its uncontrollable passion and theatrical drama. St. Theresa is swooning from the pain and pleasure caused by an angel of God who has stabbed her with an arrow. She floats on a marble cloud lit from a hidden window. Rays of glimmering bronze shower down on the figures beneath the painted ceiling of the chapel.
4 Caravaggio might be described as a thug, hood, rogue, rebel or ruffian.

5 The figures would be close to the front edge of the stage, above the audience members who would look up at the scene. Strong light on the main figures contrasts dramatically with the dark background. Christ's body has the most light on it, with highlights on the faces of John and Joseph and the uplifted hands and face of the third Mary at the top of the painting. Caravaggio leads the viewer's gaze through a series of curves from the lower arm of Christ along his body, to the arms and bodies of those holding him and up to the outstretched arms of Mary.
6 *Tenebrism* is the exaggerated contrast of light and dark. Caravaggio's *Deposition of Christ* is an excellent example of this technique.
7 Artemisia Gentileschi

8 Gaulli and Raggi painted the ceiling so that parts of the church seemed to extend up into the ceiling or space. The painted figures float and seem to soar into infinity, while plaster figures cast shadows on the sloped ceiling, combining to create an additional feeling of depth.
9 The interior of Die Wies is lavish, joyful Rococo. Large windows flood the swirling decoration of marble sculptures, white walls and gold with natural light creating an astonishing effect of visual movement.

Lesson 11.2

France was the most powerful nation in Europe after the mid-seventeenth century and emerged as the art capital of the Western world. Under the reign of Louis XIV, the "Sun King," the country set the standards for art and culture.

Warm-up

Have students guess why the ordinary-looking woman in Georges de La Tour's painting (fig.11–14) holds a skull and stares at a candle. Is this an everyday scene or does La Tour want us to understand a subtler, deeper message? Share that the young woman is Mary Magdalen, a symbol in the Catholic doctrine of forgiveness of sins through penance. She personifies a life of contemplation and devotion to God. Does the painting have the same exuberance as Bernini's *Ecstasy of Saint Theresa* (fig.11–2)? La Tour's quieter composition is more emblematic of French Baroque art, although both works share an equal sense of piety.

Objectives

Students should be able to:

Identify France as the center of the art world starting in the second half of the seventeenth century.

Understand that Louis XIV established the tone for art and culture throughout Western Europe.

Describe the Classical and balanced qualities of French art and architecture as opposed to the extreme expressionism characteristic of the Italian Baroque.

Articulate how Louis XIV increased control over French art by establishing the government-controlled Royal Academy of Painting and Sculpture.

Vocabulary Definitions

pavilions (pah-*vill*-yens) Protrusions of central entrance and corner sections from the facade of a building.

11.2 The Baroque in France

I N THE SECOND HALF of the seventeenth century, France became the most powerful nation of Europe. Rome had been the world capital of the arts for centuries but now Paris began to take over that position. (Paris remained the center of the art world until World War II, after which the center shifted to New York.) The French regard the seventy-two-year reign of the "Sun King," Louis XIV, as their golden age. During this time, French art, fashion and etiquette were held as the standard. It was also during this period that French became the language of diplomacy. French political and cultural power reached great heights. France's influence over taste can still be felt today.

Art and architecture began to serve the king as they had once served the church. Vast projects glorifying the king's reign were embarked upon. Although the influence of Caravaggio and Bernini was felt in France, the French were not entirely comfortable with their extreme expression and enthusiasm. The French favored a more rational and balanced Classicism. The unity of style found in the art and architecture of the time is the result of the taste of Louis XIV. This taste was imposed on the whole nation through the academies that Colbert, Louis' minister, set up to regularize style in all the arts. Even though we find much that is Baroque in the "Classical" art produced in the time of the Sun King, the French preferred to call their more restrained style the Style of Louis XIV, and they continue to do so.

Key Notes

- Louis XIV sets the tone for the arts in France and, eventually, Europe.
- Paris takes over from Rome as art center of the world.
- The French favor a more balanced and Classical Baroque style.

Vocabulary

pavilions

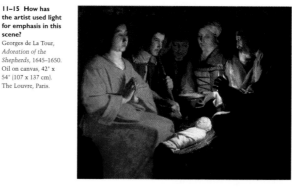

11–15 How has the artist used light for emphasis in this scene?
Georges de La Tour, *Adoration of the Shepherds*, 1645–1650. Oil on canvas, 42" x 54" (107 x 137 cm). The Louvre, Paris.

Georges de La Tour

(1593–1652)

During the early part of the seventeenth century, France remained under the influence of Italy and Flanders. However, some artists of originality emerged. Among them was Georges de La Tour. The influence of Caravaggio is unmistakable in his tenebrism and realism, but La Tour developed a style that was entirely his own. La Tour was well known in his own time, but then he was completely forgotten until fairly recently. Only forty of his paintings are known to exist, yet he is now considered one of the important figures in French painting.

Often using a candle as the only source of light, La Tour built dramatic nighttime compositions. The feeling in these paintings is very intense. At first glance, the painting seems to show a genre subject, or a narrative of some happening from peasant life. However, the subject becomes charged with emotion and takes on aspects of reverence in La Tour's silent but powerful treatment. His *Magdalen with the Smoking Flame* (fig.11–14) is one of four paintings he did of this subject. Set against a flat, dark background and using a candle as the single light source, La Tour builds a striking composition in which the forms are simple and monumental. Mary Magdalen was a symbol of the Catholic doctrine of the forgiveness of sins through penance, but this picture is more than just a picture of the saint. The figure personifies a life of contemplation and

Teach

Criticism: Challenge students to discover how Georges de La Tour creates drama in his painting *Magdalen with the Smoking Flame* (fig.11–4). Have them compare her pose and the objects around her to Bernini's *Ecstasy of Saint Theresa*.

- If Bernini's main device is the highly theatrical pose, what is it that La Tour uses to enhance the emotions of his canvas?

- What would the scene look like if it took place during the day, in diffused sunlight? Although both the French and Italian artists share a sense of spiritual drama, they used different means of expressing their message.

Aesthetics/Criticism: Direct students to study the Hall of Mirrors (fig.11–c) at the Palace of Versailles.

- Ask what in this structure illustrates the French preference for balance and rational Classicism. For instance, what form is repeated throughout? (The huge rounded windows recall ancient Roman arches.)

- What else unites the entire space? What is the purpose of the gilt ceiling and the sense of light that suffuses the entire hall?

- Would you like to live in a palace decorated like this? Why or why not?

mortification, devoted to the love of God. This painting was discovered and identified in 1972.

La Tour's *Adoration of the Shepherds* (fig.11–15) again shows us one of the night settings that he so favored. The painting is of a group of humbly clad men and women gathered around the Christ Child. Once again a sacred event is depicted in an ordinary, everyday way. There is little in the painting that hints at the holy nature of the scene. The figures do not have halos. There are no angels or other heavenly signs. The light that infuses the scene is natural. It comes from a candle. However, there is a reverence in the way these ordinary people contemplate the candlelit infant that tells us that the scene is holy. The great calm that pervades this picture is characteristic of La Tour's work.

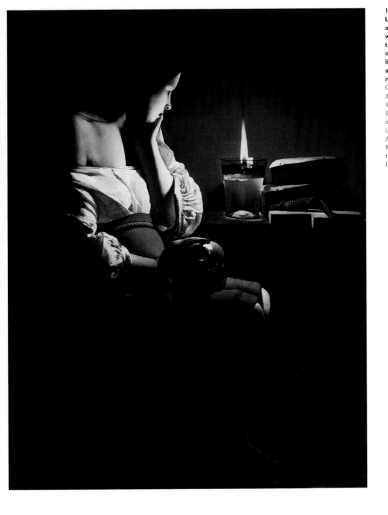

11–14 Very few of La Tour's paintings are known, but he was a master of tenebrism who often used unusual light sources such as candles and moonlight.
Georges de La Tour, *Magdalen with the Smoking Flame*, about 1630–1635. Oil on canvas, 46" x 36 1/4" (117 x 92 cm). Los Angeles County Museum of Art, gift of the Ahmanson Foundation.

Higher-Order Thinking Skills

Artists who work with special lighting effects sometimes exaggerate or emphasize the light for the effect that they want to achieve. Ask the class if one candle would really provide the light that La Tour shows in *Magdalen with the Smoking Flame*.

Evaluate

Ask students who the most important patron of art in France was after the mid-seventeenth century.

• How might the arts in America today be affected if only the government commissioned works?

• Do students think there would be much diversity? Why or why not?

Have students determine what natural element is an integral part of the Hall of Mirrors at Versailles. As a hint, remind them of the name King Louis XIV adopted.

• What physical materials in the hall increase the impact of the sun?

• What would happen when daylight hit the gold ceilings or rows of tall mirrors?

• For good measure, the long room was also illuminated with 3000 candles. What must it have felt like to walk into this glittering passage?

• Would it make you feel awe or disdain toward the monarchy?

Reteach

Ask students which artwork conveys the sense of religious passion more effectively, Bernini's Italian *Ecstasy of Saint Theresa* or La Tour's *Magdalen with the Smoking Flame*. Designate teams to debate the issue.

Contextual Information

Poussin

To meet his expenses early in his career, Poussin worked as a draftsman, painted decorations in the Louvre and drew designs for tapestries and illustrations for books. All of this work taught him the value of practice and how to use a variety of methods to form composition and create expression.

Claude

Claude Lorrain started as an apprentice pastry cook in the Roman household of the painter Agostino Tassi. However, Claude soon changed his occupational training to become a studio assistant in Tassi's workshop. His paintings became the favorite of seventeenth- and eighteenth-century collectors and inspired landscape architecture designs in Europe.

Because his works were so admired, artists painted in his style and forged his name to their work so that they could earn more money. To stop this, in 1635 Claude wrote a book called *The Book of Truth*, which contains sketches of almost all his paintings created after that date. The book, which is now in the British Museum, offers documentation of his paintings to art historians.

Claude was said to have used a small black convex glass (called a Claude glass) to reflect landscapes in miniature without distracting details or color. The glass became a popular tool of artists in the seventeenth and eighteenth centuries.

Inquiry

Have students research the early professional years of an artist to learn how difficult that time can be and what the artist did to overcome the problems.

Nicolas Poussin

(1593/94–1665)

Even though he was the most important painter of France in the late seventeenth century, Nicolas Poussin spent most of his productive years in Rome. Poussin used the colored glazes of Titian, but employed the simplified sculptural quality of Raphael. He stressed the elimination of unnecessary detail and put emphasis on composition, balance and other qualities of Classical art which he loved. He often constructed a model stage filled with wax figures so he could obtain the best balance and movement in his painting. But, at other times, as in the *Rape of the Sabine Women* (fig.11–16), he filled his paintings with swirling activity and strong brushwork.

To Poussin, subject matter was of great importance in painting. He felt that it should be grand, heroic or divine. His *Holy Family on the Steps* (fig.11–17) illustrates his theories of painting. The theme or subject matter is divine, with Mary, Joseph, the Christ Child, Elizabeth and John the Baptist. The setting is Classical. The composition is triangular, and the design is perfectly calculated. Poussin also includes some subtle symbolism. He places Joseph and his carpentry tools, which represent the working life, in the shadow of Mary and the Christ

11–16 Consider how Poussin has used diagonals to give this painting its incredible motion. Nicolas Poussin, *Rape of the Sabine Women*, about 1634. Oil on canvas, 61" x 82 1/2" (155 x 209 cm). The Metropolitan Museum of Art, New York, Harris Brisbane Dick Fund, 1946.

11–17 Compare this to Raphael's *School of Athens* (fig.9–30). Also use the text to discover Poussin's composition technique. Nicolas Poussin, *Holy Family on the Steps*, 1648. Oil on canvas, 27 1/4" x 38 1/2" (69 x 98 cm). National Gallery of Art, Washington DC, Samuel H. Kress Collection.

Child, who represent the spiritual life. Asymmetrical balance is worked out carefully. Joseph's small highlighted foot balances the larger light-valued masses of Saint Elizabeth and her son John. The still-life items on the lower step are also asymmetrically balanced. Every part is considered carefully and placed to attain a perfectly balanced composition. If any part were changed in value or moved to some extent, the feeling of comfortable balance would be destroyed. With all this attention on composition, Poussin is still able to subordinate Elizabeth, John and Joseph with shadows and to center the visual emphasis on Mary and the Christ Child.

1630	1631
Bhutan becomes independent from Tibet	**Shah Jahan begins construction of Taj Mahal, Agra, India**

World Cultural Timeline

1637	1644
Emperor Iemitsu forbids subjects to leave Japan	**The Ming dynasty, the last native Chinese line of Emperors, ends**

Multicultural Connection

The Taj Mahal

During the rule of the Moguls, Islam influenced the arts of India. Muslims introduced new styles of architecture; the rich and powerful Mogul rulers built mosques and other buildings of marble that had domes and minarets. Since the Muslims were forbidden by their religion to carve the human figure, they decorated their buildings with elaborate designs that were often inlaid in white marble with semi-precious stones.

One of the best examples of Muslim art and architecture in India is the Taj Mahal (1632–1653), in Agra, commissioned by Shah Jahan as a mausoleum, or tomb, for his wife, Mumtaz Mahal. As with Mogul painting, there is a strong Persian influence in the building, but its sheer perfection of proportion and detail contributed to its uniqueness. (A photograph of the Taj Mahal, as well as additional information, is in Chapter 4, page 91.)

• Have students examine visuals of the Taj Mahal and discuss how it is similar to and different from other architectural styles of this period.

Claude Lorrain

(1600–1682)

Like Poussin, Claude Lorrain went to Rome; however, he remained there and never returned to France. He spent much time in the Italian countryside making hundreds of ink and wash sketches that he later used as subjects for studio paintings.

Claude composed his landscapes as carefully as Poussin designed his figure paintings. In *The Marriage of Isaac and Rebecca* (fig.11–18) he placed large trees in the foreground at right. These trees move in an arc to several more trees in the middle ground at the left, and then back into a spacious, sunlit countryside. The soft light creates the dreamy mood found in many of his landscapes. Claude did not enjoy painting figures and often paid fellow artists to paint them for him. Yet, the figures are important to the paintings because they provide a scale by which to see the huge size of the trees and the vastness of the landscape. The painting has also been called *The Mill* because of the buildings in the middle ground. The figures could be any group of people enjoying a party in the Italian countryside. Claude gave the work a Biblical title even though he was only interested in the landscape.

11–18 Claude Lorrain was so famous for his landscapes that compositional arrangements he used are named after him. This is a typical *Claudian* composition.
Claude Lorrain, *The Marriage of Isaac and Rebecca* (*The Mill*), about 1648. Oil on canvas, 58 3/4" x 77 1/2" (149 x 197 cm). The National Gallery, London.

The French Royal Academy of Painting and Sculpture

Throughout antiquity and the Middle Ages, artists had been trained by apprenticeship. They learned their techniques under the personal direction and in the studio of an older and well-established master. But, as painting, sculpture and architecture gained the status of liberal arts, artists needed to supplement their "practical" training with theoretical knowledge.

In France, the history of official art is also a history of the transition from the guild-controlled arts sanctioned by the church to an academic system sponsored by the state. When Louis XIV, the "Sun King," took control of the French government in 1661, he claimed that, as the state and the king were one, all art should glorify him. Thus, the Royal Academy of Painting and Sculpture in Paris was opened to train young artists in the correct style. Instruction was based on a system of rules and formulas, with the official style being the only acceptable approach. Not surprisingly, this strict and controlling system produced no significant artists.

The French Royal Academy did set the pattern for all later academies, including their modern successors, the art schools of today. Over the centuries, there has been much change in emphasis. Today, art schools attempt to recognize all the various artistic styles and techniques connected to the making of artwork.

Higher-Order Thinking Skills

1 In the seventeenth century, landscape became an important subject in itself and not simply a backdrop. People respond differently to landscape types. Discuss with students what they find beautiful. Would landscape play an important part in where they would choose to live?

2 Ask: "If all art in France was made to glorify the king, why did Louis XIV establish a school? Would he have more or less control over subjects and styles in a government-run academy?" Direct students to read about the emergence of the French Royal Academy of Painting and Sculpture on page 343 to understand its long-term influence and its part in supporting the king and state.

The Fall of the Ming Dynasty

Unlike Europe during the Renaissance, China's culture and learning did not advance significantly during this time. It wasn't until 1644, when the Ming dynasty was overthrown by the Manchus, that Chinese culture begin to thrive. Manchu rulers established the Ch'ing dynasty, and Chinese artists began to create exquisite paintings, jade carvings and fine porcelain vases.

The high output of painting and pottery was enhanced by new porcelain techniques, notably blue underglaze painting and the use of enamel colors over the glazing. Outstanding skill was also shown in ivory and jade carving and in cloisonné enamel. (See Chapter 4, page 99 for more about the art of the Ming dynasty.)

• Remind students that the Chinese saw history as cyclical, not linear. Discuss what this view of history implies about progress.

Contextual Information

French Baroque Architecture

During the seventeenth century, theatrical extravaganzas, large dinner groups, crowds of people in costumes and little or no privacy were common for kings. By the eighteenth century, before the death of Louis XIV, even the rich and noble had had enough court drama and wanted moments of privacy. They therefore built smaller homes, called châteaux, away from the cities. Even at Versailles, the king had smaller buildings designed as hideaways from the crowds. Churches were also made smaller so that people could better listen to and see the services.

A proponent of constructing buildings that served their intended purpose, Perrault, architect of the east front of the Louvre, wrote *On the Orders of Architecture*, in which he criticized academy architectural theories and stated that real beauty resulted from proper construction, size and materials as determined by custom and usage. These ideas were the forerunner of "form follows function."

Versailles

The gardens at Versailles show human power over nature, bending natural growth to the plans of rulers, architects and gardeners. Le Notre, the landscape architect of Versailles, caused plants and trees to grow in predetermined ways through pruning and careful placement. His landscape design is meant to direct visitors along a route from the city of Versailles, through the center portion of the palace and the Hall of Mirrors and to the gardens on the other side where a planned view leads from the gardens to the grand canal and up to the sky.

Window in Time

Versailles

On the site of his father's small hunting lodge, Louis XIV, the Sun King, built Versailles, Europe's greatest palace. Building began in 1661 and continued through the reigns of Louis XV and Louis XVI. Versailles, originally a symbol of the glory of the king, later became a symbol of the excesses of the monarchy and helped to bring about the French Revolution.

Although the architect, Louis Le Vau, began work on Versailles, it was Jules-Hardouin Mansart who gave Versailles its present appearance. He was responsible for designing the *Hall of Mirrors* (fig.11–c), the Chapel and the North and South Wings. The Opera House, built by Jean-Ange Gabriel under the reign of Louis XV, vies with the white and gold Chapel for theatricality.

The palace was built by an army of architects, landscape designers, sculptors, stonecutters and decorators. During the peak of construction, more than 30,000 men and 6,000 horses were needed. In today's money, Versailles would cost $10 billion.

At first, Versailles was home to the king and his court. Later, it was made the seat of government and enlarged to hold 20,000 people. Versailles was a separate world; indeed, the courtiers of Versailles always referred to it as *ce pays-ci*—"this country of ours."

From the marble courtyard can be seen the gilded balcony where the king greeted noble visitors. Inside the Grand Apartments behind the balcony are a series of six rooms where Louis XIV held court. The architecture was artfully designed to follow the movement of the sun, so that the king could move from room to room bathed in the glow of sunlight.

The Hall of Mirrors has seventeen large windows overlooking the park. The view of the park is reflected by seventeen tall mirrors on the wall opposite. The ceiling, too, sparkles with light reflected off the elaborate gold decoration. In its days of glory, the Hall was lit by 3000 candles to form a brilliant setting for ceremonies.

The palace is surrounded by formal gardens spread out over 250 acres. The Classic landscaping includes a mile-long Grand Canal. A river was even diverted to keep the 600 fountains flowing.

Two small palaces, The Grand Trianon and The Petit Trianon, housed the favorite court ladies of Louis XIV and Louis XV. On the grounds as well is Le Hameau, Marie Antoinette's model farm, where she and her companions played at being shepherds in an arcadian setting.

Louis Le Vau and Jules Hardouin-Mansart. *Palace of Versailles*, garden view, 1669–1685.

• Have students look at images of Versailles, the king's royal residence and capital of France in the late seventeenth century. Ask how many and what types of people they think were needed to build this enormous complex. How do students think average French citizens, whose money helped build Versailles, felt when the palace became the seat of government?

Performing Arts Connection

Baroque Ballet

Prior to the Baroque period, Classical ballet was performed by the lords and ladies of the courts. However, a division arose between amateurs and professionals when Louis XIV himself retired from performing in 1670 and established a school for dance training. The onset of professionalization meant that star status would now be achieved through skill rather than social position.

At this point, ballet was largely a male profession. Women's heavily draped costumes, based on contemporary social dress, were too cumbersome to allow any grand movements, and, hence, the dazzling sequences went to men.

11–19 What classical elements are used here?
Claude Perrault. *East Facade of the Louvre*, 1667–1670. Paris.

11–20 Compare this dome to the one on the Cathedral of Florence. Use the text to identify all of the elements of this church.
Jules Hardouin-Mansart. Facade, *Church of the Invalides*, 1676–1706. Paris.

Architecture

The ultimate expression of the French Baroque (they called it Classic style) was the Palace of Versailles, but several major developments preceded it. The building of châteaux, begun during the Renaissance, continued and, under excellent architects, became larger and more impressively grand. In 1665, Louis XIV wanted to finish the east facade of the Louvre. The king called the Italian master Bernini to design it. But Bernini's ambitious plans were too majestic for the French. Bernini returned to Rome and the commission was turned over to Claude Perrault (1613–1688), Charles Le Brun (1619–1690) and Louis Le Vau (1612–1670), with Perrault getting most of the credit.

Often called The Colonnade, it marks a distinct victory of French Classicism over Italian Baroque (fig.11–19). The Corinthian columns, arches, pediments and low severe lines are Classic features. They are relieved somewhat by the French technique of protruding the central entrance and corner sections slightly from the facade. Such protrusions are called **pavilions**. The ground floor is treated as a podium upon which the columns rest. Although some columns are engaged and others are freestanding, the design of the facade is simple, elegant and completely unified. It became the model for French architects for many years.

Among the most impressive Baroque buildings in Paris is the *Church of the Invalides* (fig.11–20), built by Jules Hardouin-Mansart.

The vertical emphasis topped by a soaring dome is wonderfully French Baroque. The two-storied facade has graceful Corinthian columns that lead the viewer's eyes upward. The small pediment at the center is emphasized because of the treatment of the doorways below it and the drum of the dome behind it. The drum has paired columns, like St. Peter's. However, the two columns immediately behind the pediment are recessed slightly. The dome itself is highly decorated, unlike previous domes, and is topped by a square lantern, another first. Although it has no concave-convex features like those the Italians were using, the facade has a pavilion similar to some other French buildings and an unmistakable French Baroque feeling.

Lesson 11.2 Review

1 After 1650, which country became the world center for art?
2 Who was the French Sun King? What style of art did he prefer?
3 What type of setting did La Tour favor for his painted scenes?
4 Describe the subject matter, setting and composition of Poussin's *Holy Family on the Steps*.
5 What subjects did Claude Lorrain enjoy painting?
6 Describe the east facade of the Louvre.

Lesson 11.3

During the seventeenth century, Flanders remained under the rule of Catholic Spain, although its art was influenced by Italy and the Netherlands. After Holland broke free from the Hapsburg Empire, middle-class citizens who grew wealthy from the country's international trade yearned for familiar images of their everyday life.

Warm-up

Share with the class that during the seventeenth century in Holland, the Calvinist Protestant religion forbade the use of art in churches and the democratic country had no courts or nobility. Discuss who might therefore have taken the place of the church and state as art patrons.

Objectives

Students should be able to:

Understand that Flanders remained Catholic and under Spanish Hapsburg domination.

Learn that the Flemish artist Peter Paul Rubens brought the Italian Baroque style to his home country.

Explain that Holland gained its independence from the Hapsburg Empire and became Protestant, and thereby prohibited artwork in the churches.

Describe the vital impact that new middle-class art patrons had on the range of Dutch subject matter.

Vocabulary Definitions

camera obscura (ob-*skyoor*-ah) A box with a small opening on one side through which an image was transferred in reverse onto the opposite wall of the box; similar to a modern camera.

Teach

Criticism/Aesthetics: Explain to students that a growing middle class, prosperous from the country's lucrative international trade, emerged as Holland's new art buyers.

• Ask students that if they had been one of these individuals, what paintings would they have wanted to see adorn their homes? Would religious subjects, historical scenes or familiar images from their daily life be most appealing?

11.3 The Baroque in Flanders and Holland

URING THE SEVENTEENTH CENTURY, Flanders, comprising the southern part of the Low Country provinces, was Catholic and under Hapsburg and Spanish domination. Although they shared a common history and culture with the Dutch, the Flemish were separated from their northern neighbors by religion and economic and social structure. There was little large-scale construction, so Baroque architecture is not very visible in today's Belgium. But painting and, most particularly, the work of Peter Paul Rubens is another story.

Holland, the northern part of the Low Country provinces, had gained independence from Spain and had become Protestant and democratic. This produced significant changes, notably that three of the usual art patrons—the church, the court, and the nobility—were absent. Calvinist Protestantism forbade the use of art in churches. Artists were thrust into the open market, which completely revolutionized the role of art and the artist in the community. Holland, a wealthy country with new colonies and expanding commerce, developed a large middle class who wanted to buy paintings for their homes. The open-market system of artists selling their work to individual patrons led to trade in art, a method of merchandising paintings through galleries, dealers and fairs. So, artists began painting subjects that were in demand, such as landscapes, cityscapes, ideal country scenes, parties, still lifes and portraits. There are obvious parallels, here, with the modern art world.

Key Notes

• Flanders remains Catholic and is ruled by the Hapsburgs. Painting, led by Peter Paul Rubens, is dominant.

• Painting in democratic Holland becomes a commodity sought by the middle class.

Vocabulary

camera obscura

11–21 Can you detect the influence of Caravaggio in this portrait?
Judith Leyster, *Boy with Flute*, about 1635. Oil on canvas, 28 3/4" x 24 1/2" (73 x 62 cm). National Museum, Stockholm.

Special Feature
Judith Leyster
(1609–1660)

As you have seen, there has been very little reference to female artists, particularly to women who became famous. However, the Dutch artist, Judith Leyster, was probably the best-known female painter of the seventeenth century. While many women artists until this time had the advantage of having artist fathers from whom to learn, Judith Leyster's father owned a brewery and she developed her very own style. Although influenced by some artists in Utrecht who worked in the style of Caravaggio and by Frans Hals whom she knew, her style is distinctive. Leyster made her reputation as a genre painter, and she was one of the first artists to paint intimate genre scenes in Holland.

One of Leyster's freshest and most original works, *Boy with Flute* (fig.11–21), is a portrait of a young boy playing his flute. Intent on his instrument, the boy is completely self-absorbed. The composition of the painting is carefully balanced. The instruments on the wall are a counterweight to the boy sitting on the chair. An unseen window on the left provides a controlled light and is a vital part of the painting.

In Leyster's well-known *Self-Portrait* (fig.11–22), which hangs in the National Gallery in Washington, our attention is immediately caught by the ease of her pose and her obvious pleasure in her task. She is painting a violinist and the animation of both of these cheerful figures is remarkable.

Although after her death her works were often attributed to other Dutch painters, Judith Leyster's work has since gained new recognition.

• Have students look at the Dutch art in Lesson 11.3 to help guide their thinking. Can they find examples of portraiture, still lifes, genre (everyday scenes) and landscapes that articulated the everyday world with which the Dutch burghers were familiar?

Art History: Ask students how a market system instead of royal or church commissions affected artists' choice of subject matter. If they needed to vie with one another for customers, might artists paint whatever they wished or scenes that they knew would be appealing to potential buyers? Explain that many Dutch seventeenth-century artists specialized in a particular subject once they found it sold well.

Evaluate

Tell students to list the types of subject matter that were painted in Holland in the seventeenth century. Then have them look through contemporary art magazines and museum or auction catalogs to find what categories are popular today. Ask them what new subjects have appeared in addition to portraits, still lifes, genre scenes and landscapes.

• Have students discuss why there were no religious pictures painted for church interiors after Holland broke away from Spain in the seventeenth century.

• Ask who replaced the church, nobility and courts as art patrons in Holland in the seventeenth century.

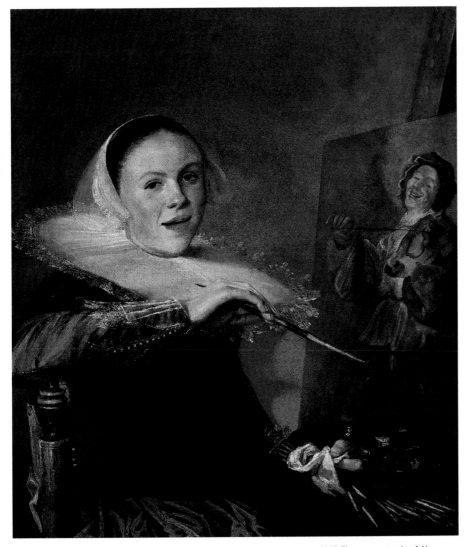

11–22 The great spontaneity of this self-portrait is due in part to the pose of the artist.
Judith Leyster, *Self-Portrait*, 1630. Oil on canvas, 29" x 26" (74 x 66 cm). National Gallery of Art, Washington, DC. Gift of Mr. and Mrs. Robert Woods Bliss.

Contextual Information

Leyster

Leyster was a member of the Haarlem guild of painters at the age of 24 and had her own pupils in 1635. Frans Hals persuaded one of her pupils to leave her studio for his, but Leyster successfully sued Hals for the money she lost as a result.

In 1636 Leyster married a fellow artist and former pupil of Hals and the next year moved to the capital, Amsterdam. Her paintings were so like Hals' that people forged his signature on her paintings in later years to be able to sell them for higher prices.

Until 1893 there was little information available on Leyster. Illustrating that point is the story of a painting acquired by the Louvre and assumed to be a Frans Hals. After the work had been cleaned, Leyster's signature was visible.

• Ask students to explain why a valuable painting thought to be by Hals decreased in value when the Louvre discovered that it was by Leyster.

Higher-Order Thinking Skills

Ask students to discuss what they would want to emphasize about themselves in a self-portrait. Is realism always the artist's goal?

Reteach

What do students think it might have been like to be a female artist in Holland during the seventeenth century? What might it have felt like to have worked in such a male-dominated field? Have students examine Judith Leyster's work (figs.11–21, 11–22) as well as that of Rachel Ruysch (p.353 and fig.11–28) and read their biographies. How could the Dutch lack of interest in grand historical, Biblical and mythological scenes have affected women's ability to succeed as artists? (The still lifes, portraits and genre scenes—subjects in which women had always excelled and were associated with the domestic realm—became popular throughout Holland during the century.)

Performing Arts Connection

Boy with Flute, Judith Leyster

Paintings of ordinary people playing music were quite popular in seventeenth-century Holland. On the one hand, these depictions demonstrated a fondness for pleasurable entertainment. Yet, the scenes simultaneously carried subtle moral messages warning against the temporary nature of earthly pleasures.

• Ask students how Leyster communicates the high, melodious sounds of the flute in *Boy with Flute* (fig.11–21). In which direction does the young boy gaze? (Despite the realism of her image, the heavenly illumination adds an ethereal quality.)

Peter Paul Rubens

(1577–1640)

While Bernini was filling Baroque Rome with sculpture, Peter Paul Rubens was flooding Flanders and the rest of Europe with magnificent Baroque paintings. Possessing enormous intelligence and an unending capacity for work, he produced over 2000 paintings. The earlier Flemish painters had specialized in detail and a cool detachment from their subjects. However, Rubens disregarded them and turned to Italy for his inspiration. He spent eight years studying the masterworks of Classic Rome, the Renaissance, Mannerism and the Baroque.

When he returned to Antwerp, he set up a painting workshop to keep up with his numerous commissions. He hired assistants (many of whom were established painters) to paint in still-life objects, flowers

11–23 Lions were exotic and rare in Ruben's time. He used lions in private zoos for models and combined drawings from many subjects to put this painting together.
Peter Paul Rubens, *Lion Hunt*, 1616. Oil on panel, 97" x 146" (246 x 372 cm). Alte Pinakotek, Munich.

and landscapes. He generally painted the figures himself, but even these were often started by assistants. He would paint small studies on wooden panels. From these, his helpers painted their sections on the large canvas or wooden panels. Meanwhile, from a large balcony in the studio, Rubens directed all of their work simultaneously. He often put the finishing glazes on the works and added his characteristic brushstrokes—if the price was right. The amount he charged his patrons was in proportion to how much work he did himself.

Rubens often picked up new patrons on his travels to other countries. He also studied the work of other artists on these trips. When he first went to Italy, he met Velazquez

1644
Potala Palace built, Tibet

1674
Last description of live dodo, a native of Mauritius

World Cultural Timeline

1650
Ukiyo-e school of art begins to flourish in Japan

1660
Bambara Kingdom of the upper Niger begins to flourish

1680
Rise of the Ashanti Kingdom, West Africa

Multicultural Connection

Ukiyo-e

The Japanese school of art best known in the West is that of the Ukiyo-e ("the art of the floating world") paintings and woodblock prints. Ukiyo-e prints began to be produced in the mid-seventeenth century and used themes from everyday life. Favorite subjects were theater scenes and bathhouse women catering to the tastes of the merchant class.

The medium of woodblock printing, introduced to Japan during the eighth century, was favored because multiple images could be mass-produced. Prints from these carved woodblocks were made by a team of distinguished artists, engravers and printers. The works entered Europe not as works of art but as wrapping and packaging on other, more expensive goods. During the 1800s, Ukiyo-e prints came to be valued in the West for their aesthetic virtues, influencing Impressionist and Post-Impressionist European artists. (For additional information on Ukiyo-e, see Chapter 4, page 105.)

• Have students research how religion in Japan at this time influenced the aesthetic values of Ukiyo-e woodblock printing.

• Discuss the flat patterns, linear qualities and asymmetrical design qualities characteristic of Ukiyo-e prints.

from Spain. He also made sketches and small paintings of works by Leonardo, Raphael, Titian, Tintoretto, Veronese, Mantegna and Caravaggio, among others. He even had assistants make sketches for him, so that when he returned to Antwerp he had a collection of thousands of ideas from which he would develop his personal style. His style was one of swirling physical movement, marvelous color and energetic brushwork—the epitome of Baroque painting.

From 1616 to 1618, Rubens painted a number of huge works about hunting exotic animals. Europeans were fascinated by lions, tigers, leopards, elephants and crocodiles. Many noblemen had examples in their private zoos. Whenever Rubens got the chance, he would sketch them for future use in his hunting scenes. *Lion Hunt* (fig.11–23) is typical of this phase of Rubens' painting. It boils with violent activity as turning and twisting bodies of horses, lions and humans are intertwined in a complicated knot. Rubens uses the straight lances and swords to stabilize the writhing composition and to lead the viewer's eyes back to the central area. The low eye level increases

the dramatic upward thrust of the action. The confrontation would explode out of the frame if the curved necks, arms and heads did not direct the movement back to the center of the canvas. Each detail is charged with tension. The foreshortening is handled with mastery. Never before had an artist used swirling action, color and light with such complete authority and seeming ease.

In his later years, after a second stay in Madrid, Rubens' subjects became more serene and calm. Titian, whose work was much admired and abundant in the Spanish palace, became a strong influence. In his *Garden of Love* (fig.2–26), Rubens pays a superb tribute to the joy of life and love. As a widower, he had recently married the young and beautiful Helena Fourment. He and his bride are shown on the left. Four of Helena's sisters are shown also, some with their husbands. The setting is partly from Rubens' elaborate home in Antwerp and partly imaginative. Chubby cupids flit about the scene. Controlled light strikes only where the artist wants it. Yet even in a scene in which all the people are stationary and there is no evident

action, Rubens still creates energetic visual movement. Light plays over and reflects from the crinkled satin gowns and translucent flesh. The painting is a portrait of happiness. The combination of reality, Classical mythology and Baroque material elegance is Rubens at his finest.

The *Castle of Steen* (fig.11–24) was a favorite painting of Rubens and one he kept until his death. After he returned from Madrid, he moved to this country estate. With tender care, he portrays the Belgian landscape with its broad receding spaces flooded with afternoon light. His earlier landscapes had been turbulent and depicted nature's violence. But, in his later years, Rubens chose to represent the quiet atmosphere surrounding his own country house. A hunter, wagon master and castle occupy the shadowy lower-left part of the scene. However, the emphasis easily shifts to the vast expanse of fields and trees that seem to reach into infinity, finally uniting with the high-keyed sky.

11–24 This is Rubens' own home. How do you think he felt about it? Peter Paul Rubens, *Castle of Steen*, 1635. Oil on panel, 51" x 90" (131 x 230 cm). National Gallery, London.

Higher-Order Thinking Skills

1 Rubens carefully chose the composition, colors and images for the *Castle of Steen* (fig.11–24), a portrait of his home. Have students work from drawings or photographs as references to create portraits of their homes with carefully chosen compositions, color and images. They can then discuss how the portraits "read" in relationship to how they feel about their homes.

2 Direct students to compare Judith Leyster's works (figs.11–21, 11–22) to Peter Paul Rubens' *Lion Hunt* (fig.11–23). Ask if the two are similar. Why not? Have students cite reasons why Rubens' painting has more in common with Bernini's Italian work (figs.11–2, 11–3) than the style adopted by nearby Holland. (Instruct students to read on page 348 about the influence of Rubens' trip to Italy.)

3 In the swirling visual movement of Rubens' gigantic paintings, the Baroque reaches its ultimate statement. Project one of Rubens' complicated compositions onto a chalkboard and have students trace the various movements with chalk. Remove the slide and have students study the movements that remain. Guide them to see the interlocking action, counterthrusting movement, use of diagonals and other devices for expressing action.

Ashanti Weaving

Cloth weaving has always been a part of African life, practiced by both men and women in some regions and by only men in others. The weaving techniques varied from one region to another. Kente cloth is a style of weaving done by the Ashanti men of Ghana, highly skilled craftsmen who passed the craft down from father to son. The cloth is woven on narrow strip looms and then sewn together to form large pieces of fabric. Traditionally worn by the royal family and advisors, kente cloth was made by reweaving imported silk cloth that had been unraveled. The strip cloth was valued for its rich designs

and named patterns that specified rank and social status. Eventually, kente cloth became the national dress of Ghana and is still worn on special occasions today.

• Have students study examples of kente cloth and then design and weave narrow strips on cardboard looms.

• Ask the class what items of clothing in our culture have been assigned significant meaning or status.

Anthony van Dyck
(1599–1641)

Among the fine artists who painted for Rubens in his Antwerp workshop was Anthony van Dyck. Van Dyck was already an accomplished painter when only seventeen. His early work was influenced greatly by Rubens, but when he went to Italy he fell under the spell of the work of Titian, Tintoretto and Veronese.

Anthony van Dyck excelled at portraiture and worked as official court painter for Charles I of England, just as Holbein had done for Henry VIII. Van Dyck flattered his subjects, endowing them with aristocratic refinement, delicacy and elegance. It is no wonder that he became a favorite of English noblemen. In his *Portrait of Charles I in Hunting Dress* (fig.11–25), he creates the impression of regal splendor and dignity. Charles is posed dramatically with his horse and servant in an outdoor setting. With apparent ease, van Dyck accents the shimmering mane of the horse and the satin shirt of the king. They glisten with light amid the shadows of the scene. In reality the king was short and lacked a handsome appearance, but one would never suspect it after looking at van Dyck's official portrait.

Van Dyck typically placed his figures in an outdoor setting with large shaded trees, distant landscape and cloudy sky. This setting became a standard treatment for portrait paintings in England. Although a Flemish painter, van Dyck did much of his work in service of the English king and, when he died in London, he was buried there.

11–25 Van Dyck flattered his sitters. What do you think he has done here to flatter Charles I?
Anthony van Dyck, *Portrait of Charles I in Hunting Dress*, 1635. Oil on canvas, 8' 11" x 6' 11 1/2" (271 x 213 cm). The Louvre, Paris.

Jacob van Ruisdael
(1629–1682)

In Holland, Jacob van Ruisdael was a master at portraying the Dutch landscape and the drama of the sky, with its ever-changing and powerful clouds. Because Holland is so very flat, van Ruisdael places the horizon line low in the painting. The emphasis naturally is forced to the huge sky, which van Ruisdael fills with superb cumulus clouds. As in *The Mill at Wijk by Durstede* (fig.11–26), the light and dark values of the clouds lead to brightly lit highlights on the ground. These highlights contrast sharply with the dark shadowed areas. The mill is emphasized against the turbulent sky. The mill and boats pause as if held in time for the viewer to see. Even the river runs smoothly and quietly in contrast to the active sky. To drive or walk through the Dutch countryside is to experience the reality of van Ruisdael's painting.

Jan Steen
(1625–1679)

While the Dutch are noted for the immaculate order of the interiors of their homes, Jan Steen shows another side: chaos, clutter and humor. He enjoyed the unexpected and often crammed his canvases full with children, animals, drunken

11–26 The sky is the focus of the activity while the water remains calm.
Jacob van Ruisdael, *The Mill at Wijk by Durstede*, not dated. 32 1/4" x 40 1/4" (82 x 102 cm). The Rijksmuseum, Amsterdam.

Higher-Order Thinking Skills

1 The relationship between a portrait artist and a sitter can be quite complex. Issues of vanity, self-expression, observation and personality can create disputes. What would students want a portrait artist to emphasize about them in a portrait? What would they want minimized or left out?

2 Have students write a brief narrative of the family celebration depicted in Steen's *The Feast of St. Nicholas* (fig.11–27).

folk and upset baskets. In *The Feast of St. Nicholas* (fig.11–27), Steen weaves a tender narrative of a children's festival for the viewer to enjoy. Some children are happy, having been given candy and toys. Another is crying because others are making fun of him. But, the child clutching the statue of a saint and her grandmother receive the most light and the most attention. Steen loved to portray older folks enjoying the pleasure of small children. The loose shoe and spilled fruit are almost trademarks of the clutter in his paintings. Much family interplay is taking place in the warm room. A whole story could be written about the actions and appearances of all the family members and of their relationships to each other and to the scene.

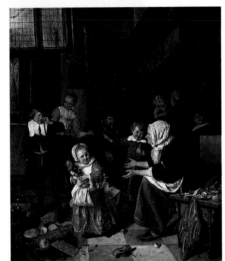

11–27 In contrast to the traditional portrayal of immaculate Dutch interiors, Steen often shows family life in action complete with clutter.
Jan Steen, *The Feast of St. Nicholas*, about 1660–1665. Oil on canvas, 32 1/4" x 27 1/2" (82 x 70 cm). Rijksmuseum, Amsterdam.

Contextual Information

Ruysch

Ruysch's father, a professor of anatomy and botany, collected specimens of shells, fossils, skeletons and rare plants. Examples of some of these specimens can be seen in her paintings.

Still Lifes

After the Reformation, when religious paintings were seldom done in the Protestant northern countries, still lifes became popular, particularly those of the *Vanitas* type, which included objects that symbolized the shortness of life. Such objects were hourglasses, skulls, mirrors, butterflies and flowers.

• Ask students to find a book on Dutch seventeenth- and eighteenth-century painting to see examples of *Vanitas* objects.

Rachel Ruysch

(1664–1750)

The daughter of an amateur painter, Ruysch became one of Holland's foremost painters of still lifes with flowers. She studied under a local artist named William van Aelst for a time before she went on to develop her own distinctive style. Her settings were not limited to a vase of flowers on a table. Instead, she often placed the flowers in a woodland setting complete with various inhabitants like mice, snails and grasshoppers. *Flower Still Life* (fig.11–28) is an excellent example of Ruysch's carefully detailed, delicate style. Each flower is rendered realistically. The flowers are asymmetrically arranged, something she learned from van Aelst. This S-curve arrangement would later be a standard for eighteenth-century flower painters.

Ruysch married Juriaen Pool, a portrait painter, and together they were appointed court painters of the Elector Palatine in Düsseldorf. She reared ten children while still devoting time to her painting. She was widely admired, and her paintings earned her from 750 to 1250 guilders each. Compare this with Rembrandt's compensation, which was seldom more than 500 guilders per painting for his later work.

11–28 The Dutch were, and still are, avid horticulturists. Can you identify some of the varieties of flowers in this vase?
Rachel Ruysch, *Flower Still Life*, c. 1782. Oil on canvas, 27" x 25" (68 x 64 cm). Academy, Vienna.

Frans Hals

(about 1580–1666)

Frans Hals was brilliantly adept at portraiture. Developing a technique using slashing brushstrokes, he captured the momentary smile and the twinkle of an eye with unerring accuracy. Although his painterly brushstrokes remain visible and his paintings appear to have been done in minutes, Hals spent much time on them to get just the right instantaneous quality. This loose feeling is completely different from the tight and exact features in the portraits of Leonardo, Holbein or Dürer.

Hals enjoyed painting the common people, especially his good friends. In *Yonker Ramp and His Sweetheart* (fig.11–29), Hals shows his friend, whom he painted often, in a happy scene at the local tavern in Haarlem. Hoisting his glass in a toast, the man is obviously enjoying his evening. His girlfriend cuddles as close as the broadbrimmed hat will allow, as if trying to get into the picture. The dashing brushstrokes add to the feeling of spontaneity and vibrant action. It is obvious that Hals enjoyed making this painting.

Although he sold many paintings and enjoyed excellent success as a portrait painter, Hals died penniless in a poorhouse. His career almost parallels the artistic development of his country. He flourished when Holland was growing and expanding her trade. However, in the second half of the seventeenth century, French painting became more in demand in Holland. Hals and many of his contemporary artist friends could find little work. After his death, agents were not able to sell his work at all, yet today there is a Frans Hals Museum in Haarlem that honors him and his vigorous painting.

11–29 Describe this occasion and the relationship of these two people.
Frans Hals, *Yonker Ramp and His Sweetheart*, not dated. Oil on canvas, 41 1/4" x 31" (105 x 79 cm). The Metropolitan Museum of Art, New York, bequest of Benjamin Altman, 1913.

Sidelight

Tulips from Amsterdam

Many people think of tulips when they think of Holland. Indeed, bulbs, not only tulip bulbs, have been a specialty of Holland since the sixteenth century. Imagine a single tulip bulb selling for $1500. This was the case during a tulip mania that rocked Europe from 1634–37. One bulb, a *Semper Augustus*, sold for $2000 plus a coach and four. Rich nobles in many lands courted bankruptcy in their eagerness to gamble on the Amsterdam tulip *bourse* (stock market) and many of them were ruined. Everyone was investing in tulips, even the poor, and sometimes life savings were lost in one season. In fact, things got so out of hand that the Netherlands government finally had to stop the madness by decree in 1637.

Rachel Ruysch, *Flower Still Life*, detail.

How did the tulip first come to Holland? Austria's ambassador to Turkey brought the first bulbs to Europe in 1554. The word *tulipa* was derived from the Turkish word for turban and is plainly descriptive. Another reason that Holland became the bulb capital of the world has to do with Holland's canal system. The canals make it possible to maintain a constant water level two and a half feet below the planted bulbs, regardless of whether droughts or floods occur.

The tulip is still in high demand and some two thousand varieties are grown in Holland today on twenty thousand acres of soil.

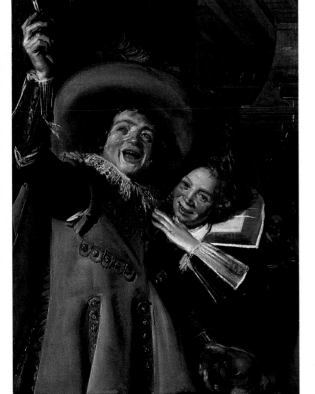

Higher-Order Thinking Skills

1 Ask students if they would like to have *Flower Still Life* (fig.11–28) for their home. Ask what other paintings or works of art would likely be in a home that had this type of still life. Students can select examples from the text or from other sources of reproductions.

2 Have students review the biographical profiles of Judith Leyster (p.346) and Rachel Ruysch (p.352). Direct them to compare the women's experiences to those of Joshua Johnson, the first African-American artist to gain prominence in the United States (page 376).

• What was similar and also vastly different about the obstacles that the women and Johnson faced?

• Have students consider artistic training, family support, societal recognition and cultural prejudice. Ask if students have ever attempted to pursue something that was unusual for someone their age, gender, temperament, race, family background or education. How did it feel to follow this desire anyway?

• Have students discuss what their feelings toward their careers might have been as a Dutch seventeenth-century woman artist and as a free African-American painter in the United States during the time of slavery.

Jan Vermeer

(1632–1675)

Even in his own day, Jan Vermeer of Delft was not well known, and after his death his name practically disappeared. In the eighteenth century, Sir Joshua Reynolds, a painter from England, saw a Vermeer painting in Holland and proclaimed it one of the greatest he had seen. Only during and after the nineteenth century was his work fully appreciated. Today he is considered one of the finest Dutch painters. All that is known of him is found in the few luminous, tranquil paintings that exist. He worked in a slow and painstaking way. Until now, only thirty-eight paintings have been attributed to him. Three of these are outdoor works; the rest are portraits or interior views. But, what views they are. Carefully designed with figures and furniture, they feature light and realistic color.

Perhaps no artist until Vermeer's time perceived natural light and color with such awareness. It is thought that he used a *camera obscura* to achieve this absolute realism. This device, similar to a modern camera, was a box with a small opening on one side. The image seen through the opening was transferred to the back wall of the box, in reverse of the actual scene. With a mirror and lens attachment, the user could reverse the image and focus it. With such a device, Vermeer could observe that everything in an interior scene is not on the same plane or in equal focus. He also noticed that colors from one object or area are reflected in other parts of the room. Most Northern artists had painted each object in absolute focus and disregarded reflected colors as they painted each part precisely and individually. Look back at the work of van Eyck as an example.

Woman Holding a Balance (fig.11–30) illustrates many of Vermeer's characteristics. The design of the elements is carefully planned. Vermeer often used a map or painting to back up his figures and provide a colored shape on the wall. The foreground objects—here, a large rumpled cloth—are somewhat out of focus as the viewer's steady gaze centers on the woman.

The quiet interior is lit by a window on the left. A soft light illuminates the figure and touches other objects with varying intensity. Notice the quality of the light that brushes the wall and how carefully Vermeer has observed it. The light bouncing off the clothing of the pregnant woman illuminates the objects on the table and reflects off the glass in the frame at the left. Notice how the light from the translucent window bounces off the pearls on the table and creates soft shadows elsewhere. The grays are beautifully composed through a wide range of values. No other artist had used the tones of color with such subtle distinction, or been able to indicate the light source and depth of the objects in the painting. The chiaroscuro of the Italian Renaissance is fully realized in Vermeer's work.

This simple scene also functions on a symbolic level. Notice the painting on the wall. This scene of Christ on Judgment Day, weighing the souls of humanity, makes the weighing of pearls and gold in real life take on another meaning. The pearls represent earthly possessions that account for nothing in the end.

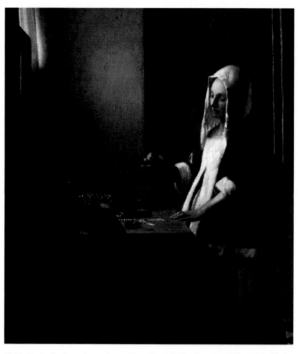

11–30 Two levels of meaning can be read into this work. Use the text to help you identify the composition, light and symbolism of this seemingly simple genre scene.
Jan Vermeer, *Woman Holding a Balance*, about 1664. Oil on canvas, 16 3/4" x 15" (42 x 38 cm). National Gallery of Art, Washington, DC, Widener Collection.

11–31 The artist's intent in this work is not known, but there are many interpretations of it. What do you think the artist intended?

Jan Vermeer, *Allegory of the Art of Painting,* about 1665–1672. Oil on panel, 47 1/4" x 39 1/4" (120 x 100 cm). Kunsthistorisches Museum, Gemaeldagalerie, Vienna.

Higher-Order Thinking Skills

Ask the class to speculate about the artist's intent for creating *Allegory of the Art of Painting.* Is there any agreement? Ask if it is important to know an artist's purpose in creating a work. If so, why?

But Vermeer's woman is pregnant, about to bring new life into the world. In relation to the painting, her condition is a celebration of life. Most of Vermeer's seemingly simple paintings can be viewed on two such levels.

This double significance also is true of Vermeer's later painting (fig.11–31) *Allegory of the Art of Painting* (also called *Allegory of Fame* and, at one time, *The Artist and His Studio*). The titles, none given by the artist, depend on one's interpretation of the symbolism, also not provided by the artist. It is now thought that the model represents Clio, the Muse of history, looking at a table full of objects that symbolize other Muses. The artist in a sixteenth-century costume cannot be Vermeer... or is he? The map of Holland on the wall, surrounded by pictures of twenty cities, could symbolize that Holland is the center of world art and that the painter is the greatest creator. Whatever the meanings, this is a fine painting, again organized beautifully. Light is the most important ingredient. An unseen window on the left illuminates the model and the deep space in the work. Another source highlights the drapery in the foreground. The artist is in focus, but the foreground, the model and her space are slightly out of focus. The colors that are closest to the light source are most intense. Even with all the complex elements Vermeer uses, the painting is still clear, cool and orderly.

Contextual Information

Rembrandt

Rembrandt was unwilling to marry Hendrickje Stoffels because of a clause in his deceased wife's will that stated he would lose all further income from her estate if he remarried. Though his huge debts eventually forced him to sell all his possessions and his house, Rembrandt was still in demand as a portrait artist. His son and Hendrickje set up an art firm that employed Rembrandt so that he could get some relief from his creditors.

One of the problems in ascribing a painting to the correct artist is the fact that painters who were teachers frequently had pupils as talented, or nearly so, as they themselves. Some of Rembrandt's students painted in his style and because his name brought higher prices, his name was put on their work. Only by studying a painting for such things as the way a particular feature, such as a hand, has been painted or the liveliness of a figure's eyes or the colors used can art historians come to a decision about the authenticity of the work. It takes many years of studying one artist's work before a historian can ascribe the work correctly.

Window in Time

The Art of Forgery

Can an art forger ever be good enough to fool even the greatest expert? In the case of the artist Hans van Meegeren, the answer is yes.

Van Meegeren was born in Holland in 1889 and had achieved some success as a painter by 1932, when he decided on a new course for his career. Van Meegeren thought himself exceptionally talented, and he was unhappy with the response of the art world to his work. He decided to take revenge on the art critics. He would forge works by old masters and see if the art experts could detect the forgeries.

He tried his hand at various Dutch masters, but eventually he decided on Jan Vermeer. Vermeer, a seventeenth-century artist, had left behind only about three dozen paintings. A discovery of a new Vermeer would bring fabulous riches. So van Meegeren set out to produce this "new" Vermeer.

First, he had to find a way to ensure that the painting he painted would look like it was three hundred years old. He knew that the paint and canvas would be subjected to thorough testing. To get an authentic canvas, he bought a painting by a minor artist of that period, then carefully scraped and rubbed all the paint off it. Next, he experimented with various paints and techniques until he was satisfied. For subject matter, he painted a religious theme because Vermeer as a young man had been interested in such themes. Not only would he paint in the style of Vermeer, he would paint a subject that Vermeer himself might have chosen.

The actual painting took van Meegeren about six months. When the painting was completed, he invented a way to dry the paint to the requisite hardness. Normally, it takes half a century for paint to dry so that there is no trace of oil.

After completing the painting, he devised a story to explain its existence. According to his story, a family that he knew wished to sell the painting and had appointed him their agent. Just as he had planned, the painting, *Christ at Emmaus*, was acclaimed a masterpiece. The painting passed all tests of authenticity. There were many bidders for the painting, but eventually van Meegeren sold it to the Boymans Museum in Rotterdam for $285,000.

Although van Meegeren originally planned to expose his forgery and ridicule the art experts, he reconsidered his scheme after realizing how much he could earn by selling his forgeries. He continued to produce forgeries and eventually painted a series of six "Vermeers." By 1945, he was a very wealthy man.

During World War II, one of the fake Vermeers, *Christ and the Adulteress*, was acquired by Hermann Goering, Hitler's deputy. When Allied investigators found it in his collection in 1945, the Dutch members of the commission were anxious to learn how a national treasure had fallen into the enemy's hands. Their investigation led them to van Meegeren, who was charged with collaboration. Van Meegeren was subjected to some hard questioning and eventually he blurted out the truth.

But, ironically, nobody believed him. To prove he was telling the truth, van Meegeren had to paint a "Vermeer" while the experts watched. In 1947, he was tried for forgery and found guilty. He died of a heart attack before he could serve his one-year sentence.

Hans van Meegeren

11–32 Looking into a mirror, Rembrandt painted this image of himself when he was about thirty years old.
Rembrandt van Rijn, *Self-Portrait*, about 1636. Oil on canvas, 25" x 20" (64 x 51 cm). The Norton Simon Museum, Pasadena.

11–33 For this group portrait, each person paid an equal amount to the artist. Some of those who ended up in the background were not happy.
Rembrandt van Rijn, *The Shooting Company of Captain Frans Banning Cocq* (*The Night Watch*), 1642. Oil on canvas, 11 1/2' x 14 1/4' (3.5 x 4.37 m). Rijksmuseum, Amsterdam.

Rembrandt van Rijn
(1606–1669)

Rembrandt van Rijn was the greatest of Dutch painters and one of the great geniuses of the art world. He was the son of a miller, whose business was located on the Rijn (Rhine) River in Holland. When Rembrandt moved from Leiden to Amsterdam in 1632, he was already a competent artist. His early portraits provided him with an excellent income. When he married and bought a large house, he was seemingly well off. After several years, his wife died; he managed his income so poorly that his wealth declined and commissions dropped off. His style of painting changed and became more personal and expressionistic, which further alienated him from the public. His son and his mistress took over his business affairs as he

became bankrupt. Yet, through all this adversity, his work became stronger and more powerful. He left over 600 paintings, 300 etchings and over 2000 drawings for the world to enjoy.

Rembrandt, like many other Baroque artists, painted many self-portraits. One can actually note the progress and decline of Rembrandt's fortunes by analyzing his clothes and facial expressions in dozens of such works. Using a mirror to view himself, Rembrandt would often put on one of the costumes he loved to collect, so that he could create a special mood.

The *Self-Portrait* (fig.11–32) was done in the late 1630s when the artist was just over thirty years old. His painting style was already well established, and he shows himself as successful and well dressed. The light is carefully controlled to highlight the face and collar and to shade the rest of the figure. Rembrandt used a heavy white impasto in the brightest areas. He then applied glazes over them and in the deep shadows to obtain the golden tones he desired. These

light-valued passages emerge from the dark brown shadows as a brilliant use of chiaroscuro. Notice how the highlights on beads, buttons and the band of the beret help direct attention to the face. The eyes, which are always important to Rembrandt in expressing the inner feeling of the sitter, hold one's attention. Here they look confidently at the viewer and hide nothing.

A popular type of painting in Holland at this time was the group portrait, usually consisting of a number of people posed in a row or some other formal arrangement. Rembrandt accepted a commission to paint *The Shooting Company of Captain Frans Banning Cocq* (fig.11–33) and revolutionized the concept of group portrait painting. The huge painting is 11 1/2 feet high with foreground figures about life-size. He accepted equal payment from each member of the company, who expected to receive equal treatment. Rembrandt wished to make a fine painting, not produce a stereotyped group portrait. He placed Captain Cocq (in black) in a

Contextual Information

Rembrandt and Printmaking

Rembrandt was not only one of the greatest painters in the art world, but he was also a master of printmaking. During the height of his fame, he produced hundreds of etchings that explored the chiaroscuro technique. By the 1600s, woodcutting had become obsolete, but Rembrandt originated a technique of etching by which he coated copper plates with a wax substance, drew into the wax with a fine point and burned the lines into the copper with acid. He began using cross-hatching in etchings such as *St. Jerome in an Italian Landscape* to create the darks and shadows similar to the depth of feeling and humanistic moods evoked in his paintings. (For another example of an etching by Rembrandt, see fig.2–31.)

• Ask the class how Rembrandt's subject matter differed from that of his fellow Dutch artists. Ask students to give reasons for why Rembrandt's work was not appreciated in his lifetime as much as it is now.

11–35 This print combines etching and drypoint to produce an incredible variety of lines and dark areas. Rembrandt van Rijn, *St. Jerome in an Italian Landscape*, 1653. Etching and drypoint, 10" x 8 1/4" (26 x 21 cm). Los Angeles County Museum of Art.

central position and put his lieutenant at his side. He placed the rest of the men at random to simulate natural action, as if they were preparing for a parade. Some are in shadow and some in light. Some are almost completely hidden. A little girl (who looks amazingly like the artist's wife Saskia) runs among the men and receives an ample dose of Rembrandt's mysterious light. He produced a superb painting. But, naturally, some of the men were disappointed in their portrayal, especially the man who could only see his eyes and the top of his head.

The painting at one time was brighter in color. However, oxidation of the colors and layers of soot have turned all the values darker, so it is now often called *The Night Watch*. After World War II, it was cleaned to reveal much richer color and detail, but the name remained.

The painting originally was larger. When it was moved to a new location, someone cut three feet off the left side and about a foot off the right, so it could fit between two doors. The major alteration has drastically changed the composition and balance of the work.

However, it remains a powerful, dramatic and popular painting. The pulsating light bounces off several faces and provides a number of minor centers of interest. These areas lead the viewer to the two major figures in the foreground who seem to be stepping off the stage into the viewer's presence.

The Mill (fig.11–34) is Rembrandt's greatest landscape painting. He completed it about 1650 at the height of his fame. It is a melancholy work with a mood of extreme sadness and loneliness. Details are nonexistent because a powerful chiaroscuro eliminates them. Large shapes dominate, but there are things happening in subtle ways in the shadows. Rembrandt has used the mill as the focus of a dramatic visual statement. The painting greatly influenced later English artists, who considered it a masterwork. They admired it for the artist's handling of light, its dramatic mood and its simple, powerful arrangement of elements. Design, subject, mood, spirit and technique are completely integrated in a single statement.

Even in his etchings, of which he did hundreds, Rembrandt used his favorite chiaroscuro. In *St. Jerome*

11–34 How would you describe the mood of this painting? Rembrandt van Rijn, *The Mill*, 1650. Oil on canvas, 35" x 42" (88 x 106 cm). National Gallery of Art, Washington DC, Widener Collection.

Lesson 11.3 Review Answers

1 Holland gained independence from Spain and became Protestant and democratic in the seventeenth century. There was no longer a church, court or nobility to buy art. Therefore, Dutch artists painted landscapes, cityscapes, ideal country scenes, parties, still lifes and portraits to sell to the middle class.

2 Judith Leyster made her reputation as a genre painter, and was one of the first artists to paint genre scenes in Holland.

3 Rubens hired assistants to paint in the still-life objects, flowers and landscapes in his paintings.

4 *The Lion Hunt* swirls with physical movement, marvelous color and energetic brushwork. Horses, lions and humans intertwine in a knot of twisting bodies. The straight lances and sword stabilize the writhing composition and focus the attention back to the central area.

5 In reality, Charles I was short and not very handsome. Van Dyck makes Charles seem taller as he strikes an elegant pose, endowing the king with regal splendor and dignity.

6 The Dutch landscape under a dramatic sky

11–36 Although they are all in similar costume, each of the sitters is shown with a unique personality.
Rembrandt van Rijn, *The Syndics of the Cloth Guild*, 1662. Oil on canvas, 75 1/4" x 109 3/4" (191 x 279 cm). Rijksmuseum, Amsterdam.

Higher-Order Thinking Skills

Have students compare *The Syndics of the Cloth* (fig.11–36) to *The Night Watch* (fig.11–33). Have them debate the success of each as a group portrait. Have students also consider comparisons to class pictures and yearbook photos.

in an Italian Landscape (fig.11–35), Rembrandt combines etching and drypoint to produce a print of rich value contrasts and excellent design. He has massed lines together to produce gray-valued passages from which St. Jerome emerges as a glistening white figure. The brightness is intensified by leaving lines broken and obliterated, suggesting a glare that eliminates detail. St. Jerome's lion stands in the shadow of the huge tree while a bridge, several tiny figures, and two marvelously drawn buildings make up the setting. But Rembrandt clearly leads the viewer's eyes back to the glowing figure of St. Jerome. During his bad years, when he lost his house and art collection to his creditors, Rembrandt produced and sold many editions of such etchings at small prices for income.

In Rembrandt's late years, his work increased in power and personal expression. Sometimes, he painted friends who posed as Biblical figures. But, at the urging of close friends, he accepted one last group portrait commission. He handled this commission beautifully. *The Syndics of the Cloth Guild* (fig.11–36) is portraiture at its best— six times. The five seated figures were the officers of a trade union in Amsterdam. The bare-headed man in the background was their favorite steward whom they included at no cost to him. All faces are treated with individuality. Rembrandt interprets the inner character of each, especially in the eyes. The life-size figures are posed in a casual way. The man on the right even fondles a tiny dog. Yet, all are dignified and at ease. The controlled light makes the book and the carpet on the table seem to glow with an internal light.

Each of the five men who paid for the work received equal treatment. None is hidden as in *The Night Watch*. Here, Rembrandt conformed to tradition and the desires of the group. Yet, he produced an exceptional painting. The eye level is kept very low because the painting was meant to hang over a large fireplace, above the viewer's eyes. The viewer is immediately drawn into the work. It is as if the noise of opening the door made the syndics stop and look up. Are they pleased or dismayed? Do all handle the intrusion in the same way? In a moment, they will look down and continue their meeting, but for now Rembrandt has frozen them in time and space in his ever-glowing light.

Lesson 11.3 Review

1 What factors led to art being sold as a commodity in Holland during the seventeenth century? What subjects did the Dutch artists begin to paint as a result of having to sell their art to the middle class?
2 Who was the most famous Dutch woman artist of the seventeenth century? What type of art did she paint that established her reputation?
3 How was Rubens able to paint so many huge paintings in only one lifetime?
4 Describe Rubens' brushwork, movement and color in the *Lion Hunt*.
5 How do you think van Dyck flattered Charles I of England?

6 What subject did van Ruisdael usually paint?
7 What was a *camera obscura*? How would it have helped Vermeer make his paintings realistic?
8 Describe the light in Vermeer's *Allegory of the Art of Painting*.
9 Describe one of Rembrandt's group portraits. Who paid for this painting? Who are the people in the portrait? How are group portraits usually produced today?
10 What elements contribute to a sad, lonely mood in Rembrandt's *The Mill*?

---

7 Similar to a modern camera, a camera obscura was a box with a small hole on one side. The image seen through this hole is reversed on the back wall of the box. The user could reverse and focus the image with a mirror and lens attachment. Vermeer used this device to paint a more realistic picture by noticing that objects are on different planes in a room, in different degrees of focus, and that colors from one object or area are reflected in other parts of the room.
8 The light comes from an unseen window on the left, illuminating the model and deep space. The foreground drapery is lit by another light source.

9 *The Shooting Company of Captain Frans Banning Cocq* was paid for by the members of the company portrayed. The foreground figures in this huge oil painting are about life size. Captain Cocq and his lieutenant are center front with the rest of the men randomly placed to create a natural scene. A small girl, who looks like Rembrandt's wife Saskia, is lit among the group of men. Lances crisscross in the background. Strong contrasts of light and dark make this a dramatic composition.

The figures in the *Syndics of the Cloth Guild* are also about life size, and this painting was also commissioned by the subjects portrayed. The six men gather around an open book. Their white collars, the book, and the highlights on the faces contrast with the darker background.

Today most group portraits are photographs.
10 The windmill sits isolated on a hill, contrasted against a sky partially filled with threatening dark clouds. Powerful chiaroscuro eliminates details. The colors are somber browns.

Lesson 11.4

The Golden Age of Spanish art began in the early seventeenth century when the country's artists came into their own after absorbing lessons from their peers in Italy and the Netherlands.

Warm-up

Share with students that Diego Velazquez's painting *Las Meninas* (figs.11–37, 11–38) is an informal portrait of the royal family. Have students locate the king and queen of Spain. (Since they were the most powerful people in the country, where would Velazquez have placed them in the composition?) Divide students in teams of two to role-play what the royal parents might be saying to each other as they look out over this scene. How does the action in the painting support their dialogue?

Objectives

Students should be able to:

Describe how Spain's close contact with Italy and the Netherlands during the sixteenth century influenced its Baroque artists of the next generation.

Explain that Spain's "Golden Age" began shortly after 1600.

Teach

Art History/Criticism: Have students carefully study Velazquez's *Las Meninas* for five minutes in silence to try to determine its exact story. Is the five-year-old princess posing for Velazquez? If so, why does she have her back to him? Maybe she has turned to address her parents, who appear in the doorway, as seen in the mirror's reflection. Possibly Velazquez is painting the king and queen, and the princess has just run in and her attendants have followed in order to prevent her from disrupting the royal sitting. Can students devise other interpretations? Afterward, ask the class to describe the scene from the role of the princess, the mysterious officer in the background and the sleeping dog. Does the story change from each perspective? Discuss the various results.

11.4 The Baroque in Spain

SPANISH BAROQUE CANNOT BE fully understood without some knowledge of what was happening artistically in Italy and the Netherlands. Because of Spain's close contacts with Italy and the Netherlands during the sixteenth century, Spanish painters were familiar with the main trends in European art. Developments in Venice were particularly influential.

The "Golden Age" of Spanish art began shortly after 1600, when the nation's power was already beginning to decline. It was during the Baroque period that Spanish artists really seemed to come into their own. There was activity in all the visual arts of Spain during the seventeenth century, but painting dominated.

Key Notes

- The Spanish Baroque is based on developments in Italy and the Netherlands.
- The 17th century is the "Golden Age" of Spanish painting.

11–38 Notice how Velazquez avoided the use of line in his work. Color and light are used to build forms.
Diego Velazquez, *Las Meninas (The Maids of Honor)*, detail.

Special Feature

Diego Rodriguez de Silva y Velazquez

(1599–1660)

One of Spain's great artists of the Baroque period was undoubtedly Velazquez. Velazquez, who trained in Seville, came to the attention of King Philip IV as a young man, and was appointed court painter in Madrid. For more than thirty years, he painted the family and court of King Philip IV. He worked on a few religious subjects and several landscapes, but his main concentration was on portraiture. Unlike many of his Baroque contemporaries, Velazquez was interested in what was real far more than what was not.

An extraordinary example of his mastery of optical realism is his recognized masterpiece *Las Meninas (The Maids of Honor)*. Velazquez combines the formality of a royal group portrait with the informality of a more casual genre scene in his studio (fig.11–37). The painter represents himself in his studio standing in front of a very large canvas. He may be painting this very picture or perhaps the portraits of the king and queen, reflected in the mirror on the far wall. In the foreground is the five-year-old princess (fig.11–38) with her two ladies-in-waiting, her favorite dwarfs and a large dog. One of the dwarfs is poking the sleepy dog with his foot. In the middle ground are two adult chaperones. In the background, a gentleman is framed in a brightly lit open doorway.

The artist's aim is to show the movement of light and the countless ways it can be reflected. Notice

Criticism: Ask students to determine how many ways Velazquez plays with reality in his painting.

- What is he painting on his huge canvas?

- Whom is he looking at? The king and queen? Himself in a mirror in order to include his self-portrait in the scene? Or us as viewers?

- How many rooms does Velazquez describe? There are at least two: the one in which the major group stands and the one behind the distant soldier. But are the king and queen in the main room or in a third space?

Evaluate

Have the class compare the models in Velazquez's painting *Las Meninas* to the sitters in the Dutch Baroque portraits throughout Lesson 11.3. Ask whether the art patrons for these works are from the same social and economic class in both countries.

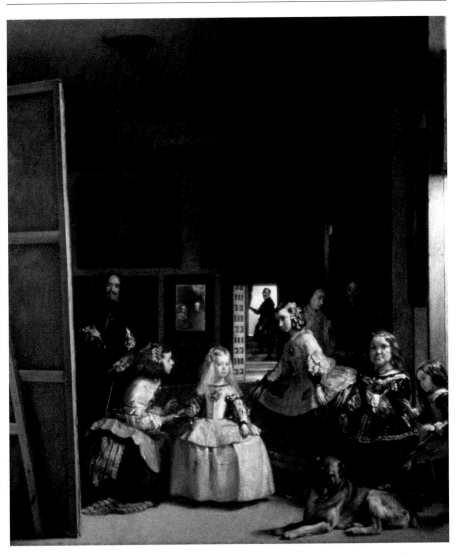

the effect of light on form and color in the painting. The indirect light in the spacious studio contrasts with the direct light that strikes the figures in the foreground and bounces and reflects from a variety of materials. Like Vermeer, Velazquez was fascinated by the quality

of light and the way it interacts with the eye to create the visible world. Spots, patches of color, and light are used to define the forms. Line was seldom used by Velazquez in his work. For this reason, the closer you get to one of his canvases, the less solid are the forms.

11–37 Velazquez has been an important influence on many modern artists.
Diego Velazquez, *Las Meninas* (*The Maids of Honor*), 1656. Oil on canvas, 124 3/4" x 107 3/4" (317 x 274 cm). Prado Museum, Madrid.

Contextual Information
Velazquez

When Velazquez was 18, he became a master painter. Five years later, he became the exclusive painter of King Philip IV, who sent Velazquez to Italy to buy paintings and sculpture for the royal collections.

The cross on Velazquez's chest in *Las Meninas* was painted there after the artist's death to show that in his lifetime he had received the high honor of being named a knight of the Order of Santiago for his paintings and contributions to the king.

Higher-Order Thinking Skills

The room in *Las Meninas* is part of the castle that is the home of the little princess. Have students describe what they imagine it would be like to have lived in that castle. What would a typical day have been like?

Reteach

Ask students what their very first impression was of Velazquez's *Las Meninas*.

• Did their opinions about it change as they explored it more thoroughly? How?

• Did their thinking change as they tried to figure out the story?

• Were their thought processes faster, slower, deeper, longer, tougher? Have them describe their experiences.

Instruct students to find the similar visual device that gives us another perspective of the room in Velazquez's *Las Meninas* and Jan van Eyck's *Arnolfini Wedding* (figs.10–b, 10–6).

• Do they think it was possible that Velazquez saw how van Eyck used the mirror in his painting, which was part of the royal art collection of Spain during Velazquez's employment at court?

• Direct students to research Velazquez's biography in an encyclopedia to understand his thirst to learn from many cultures and artists.

Contextual Information

Zurbarán

Note that Zurbarán signed and dated *St. Francis in Meditation* (fig.11–39) in the lower right-hand corner. The inscription reads *Franco Dezurbara/faciebat/1639* (Francesco de Zurbarán made this in 1639).

Bartolomé Estaban Murillo

(1617–1682)

The last great painter of Spain's Golden Age was Bartolomé Estaban Murillo of Seville. Although he was influenced by Zurbarán and Velazquez, he developed his own warm, coloristic style. He painted relaxed and sentimentalized scenes of street urchins and flower girls in addition to religious subjects, such as the *Immaculate Conception* (fig.11–40). He painted this subject about fifteen times. The emotional quality of this painting is similar to the Flemish and Italian Baroque styles. The Virgin has a sweetness and prettiness that is especially engaging. The charm and immediacy of his style made Murillo very popular.

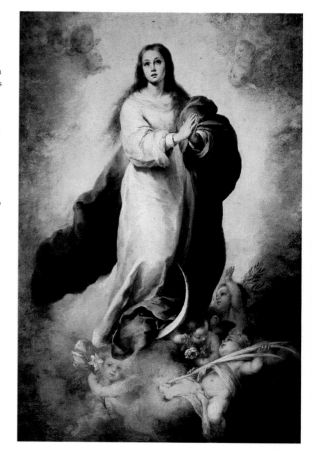

11–40 Murillo became famous for painting this subject. He did many versions of it during his career. Bartolomé Murillo, *Immaculate Conception*, c.1666–1670. Oil on canvas, 6'9" x 4' 8" (2.06 x 1.42 m). Prado Museum, Madrid.

1687 Lima, Peru destroyed by earthquake

1691 Juana Ines de la Cruz writes *Reply to Sister Philotea* advocating expanded rights for women, Mexico

1700 Bantu Kingdom of Buganda develops, East Africa

World Cultural Timeline

1696 Coffee growing introduced into Java from India

Multicultural Connection

Bantu Kingdom of Buganda

Buganda was a kingdom located on the western shore of Lake Victoria in what is now Uganda. Today the Bantu are a linguistically related group of about 60 million people living in equatorial and southern Africa.

- Many of the ancient kingdoms of Africa are unfamiliar to us. Have students cull the names of African kingdoms mentioned in the cultural timelines in Chapters 5–17 and make an African-kingdom timeline. They then can juxtapose major events from European history on the timeline so that they can get a better sense of the simultaneity of historical events in the West and in Africa.

Francisco de Zurbarán

(1598–1664)

Working in Seville, Francisco de Zurbarán developed a style reminiscent of Caravaggio and La Tour. He often placed single figures against a solid, dark background, then lit them from a single source. This produced dramatic cross lighting and emphasized the simple, basic forms. *St. Francis in Meditation* (fig.11–39) is a powerful statement with Caravaggio-like tenebrism. From the black background emerges the simple sculptural form of the saint, kneeling in prayer. The strong diagonal movement is balanced by the landscape background, the skull, the book and gesturing hand, and the white paper in the foreground on which Zurbarán signed his name. All of these elements are used to stop the rushing diagonal movement and to contain it in the painting. Like Caravaggio, he also produced several still life paintings with the same dramatic light treatment. *Still Life with Lemons, Oranges and a Rose* (fig.2–57) is a beautifully designed still life by Zurbarán.

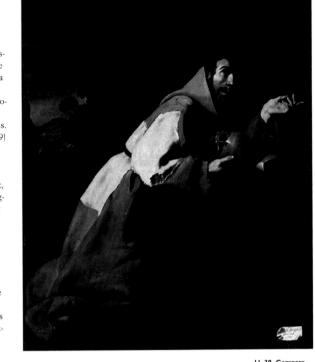

11–39 Compare this dramatically lit subject with La Tour's *Magdalen with the Smoking Flame.*
Francisco de Zurbarán, *St. Francis in Meditation,* 1639. Oil on canvas, 75 1/4" x 54 1/4" (191 x 138 cm). The National Gallery, London.

Higher-Order Thinking Skills

Have students compare *St. Francis in Meditation* to La Tour's *Magdalen with the Smoking Flame* (fig.11–14), paying close attention to color, composition, mood and the direction of the light.

Lesson 11.4 Review

1 When did the Golden Age of Spanish art begin?
2 Describe the scene in Velazquez's *Las Meninas*. Who are the main characters and who is reflected in the mirror?
3 Name three Spanish Baroque painters and a painting by each.

4 Against what type of background did Zurbarán usually set his figures? Describe the lighting that he usually used in his portraits.
5 Which religious subject did Murillo paint many times?

Lesson 11.4 Review Answers

1 Shortly after 1600
2 In this portrait of the Spanish royal family, Velazquez painted himself in his studio in front of a large canvas. The five-year-old princess, two ladies in waiting, a dwarf and a dog are in the foreground being watched by two adult chaperones behind them. The king and the queen are reflected in a mirror on the back wall. A man stands in a lit doorway in the background.

3 Diego Velazquez—*Las Meninas*; Francisco de Zurbarán—*St. Francis in Meditation*; Bartolomé Estaban Murillo—*Immaculate Conception*
4 Zurbarán usually set his figures against a solid, dark background with a single light source.
5 The Immaculate Conception

Lesson 11.5

In the eighteenth century, the French aristocracy commissioned art in the light and playful Rococo style, while those living in England and America remained loyal to the more serious Baroque aesthetic.

Warm-up

Explain to the class that the word *Rococo* comes from the French *rocaille*, meaning "a fanciful design derived from the twists and turns of seashells and tiny pebbles." Ask students why they think Rococo is applied to eighteenth-century French art, such as fig.11–41.

Objectives

Students should be able to:

Understand how the powerful European aristocracy during the first half of the eighteenth century continued to commission art that reflected their wealth and social status.

Comprehend that the second half of the eighteenth century was a time of great change in Europe.

Locate the initiation of the flamboyant Rococo style in eighteenth-century France.

Identify the perpetuation of the more serious Baroque aesthetic in Italy, England and America during the early eighteenth century.

Vocabulary Definitions

fête galante Elegant entertainment.
view painting An eighteenth-century style of painting depicting city views with incredible accuracy.
limners Early American artists who painted portraits without faces and later found patrons who wanted their faces filled in.

11.5 The Early Eighteenth Century

THE EIGHTEENTH CENTURY was a time of great changes in every phase of European society. Industrialism was beginning, and established society was being challenged by ideas such as the rights and the dignity of the common people. Revolutions in America and France heralded the birth of modern democracy. However, during the first half of the century, the members of the European aristocracy still held much economic and social power. They continued to commission works of art that reflected their wealth and social position.

Artists and their art reflected the confusion and complexity of the times, but no artistic giants emerged to equal the Baroque standardbearers: Caravaggio, Bernini, Rubens and Rembrandt. Instead, musical giants such as Bach, Handel, Vivaldi, Haydn and Mozart were the creative geniuses. The only new element to emerge in the visual arts was the Rococo style, which centered in France. An extension of the Baroque period, the Rococo substituted gaiety, charm and wit for Baroque grandeur. However, Classicism and Realism were not dead. It would only be a matter of time before they would appear again to dominate the art of the latter half of the century. Italy, England and America were not enticed by Rococo lavishness. These countries preferred a more dignified and serious extension of the Baroque.

Key Notes

- The eighteenth century is an age of change in Europe.
- A new style, the Rococo, emerges and is centered in France. The Baroque continues in some countries.

Vocabulary
fête galante
view painting
limners

Special Feature
Antoine Watteau
(1684–1721)

The painter above all others whom we associate with the French Rococo was Antoine Watteau. He was actually born in Flanders shortly after it was annexed by Louis XIV. Influenced by the colorism of his countryman, Rubens, Watteau created shimmering surfaces that sparkle with life and gaiety and capture the essence of the *fête galante* (elegant entertainment). His work in general shows scenes of elegant society or comedic actors in parklike settings.

His technique involved underpainting the canvas with a pearly color that combined white, pale blue and rose. When this dried, he would rapidly brush in the trees and background with thin washes of color. Then, he would add the important figures in impastos of jewel-like colors, again featuring rose, pale blue, pink, yellow and white hues. Glazes would then be added over these to create a warm, atmospheric effect through which the earlier colors gleamed with sparkling richness. His technique faithfully captures the sheen of wrinkled satin and silk, favorite materials of the French aristocracy.

In *The Gamut of Love* (fig.11–41), Watteau possibly sets before us a small theatrical piece of the successive stages of love: courtship, marriage and children. He has set on

11–42 This detail shows the magnificent jewel-like colors Watteau created with his brush and palette.
Antoine Watteau, *The Gamut of Love*, detail.

Teach

Art History: Ask students if they believe the figures in Antoine Watteau's *The Gamut of Love* (figs.11–41, 11–42) are to appear as real people. Have they ever seen anyone involved in these activities? During the reign of Louis XV of France, the wealthy nobility loved to dress up and play at rural life. (For example, have the class review the information on page 344 about Marie Antoinette and her companions pretending to be shepherds on a model farm at Versailles.)

- Why do students think the aristocracy wanted to indulge in make-believe lives?

- Would students themselves have liked to have participated in courtly, romantic outdoor picnics such as the one in Watteau's painting?

Criticism/Aesthetics: Tell students to identify the three different stages of life Watteau depicts in *The Gamut of Love*. To help them determine the first, ask what kind of feelings and activities they associate with the music the man is playing for the woman. Then ask if there is a depiction of the couple as a united pair. Finally, ask what happens to the couple after marriage. (Direct students to pages 364 and 365 for further information.)

11–41 This painting is symmetrically balanced. There also are strong diagonal movements from one corner of the canvas to the other.
Antoine Watteau, *The Gamut of Love*, 1717. Oil on canvas, 20" x 23 1/4" (51 x 59 cm). The National Gallery, London.

Higher-Order Thinking Skills

Ask students to explain how *The Gamut of Love* differs in tone and subject matter from what they have seen in Baroque painting.

canvas the glittering and fanciful lives of his Parisian patrons. The delicately lit scene and the shimmering surfaces are typical of Watteau's skillful handling of his subject matter and of his painting technique. Poetic and playful courtship is the main theme as a costumed gentleman of the comedic theater strums a few bars for his lady love (fig.11–42). To the right and in the distance, the viewer sees the same couple walking off together into the forest (marriage) and then again with several children (family). This is only one of several interpretations of the painting. What else do you think it could represent?

Watteau also is considered one of the world's great draughtsmen. He continually drew from life and left behind many figurative sketches.

11–43 How has the artist incorporated a sense of movement in these figures?
Antoine Watteau, *Six Figures*. Chalk, three colors, 6" x 12" (15 x 30 cm). The Louvre, Paris.

Six Figures (fig.11–43) is a study of male and female half- and quarter-length figures. Notice how the heads, topped with hats, all convey a sense of quiet, but strong, movement. Though these are only sketches, the forms of the figures are well defined.

When composing his paintings Watteau often chose figures and poses from his pages of life studies to include on the canvas. The vitality and spontaneity of the sketches are captured again in paint and embody the spirit of the French Rococo.

• How do Copley's and Stuart's portraits of European Americans demonstrate their sitters' desire for realism? (The relatively sober images of the new inhabitants of the young nation are more closely tied to stately Baroque art than are those in effusive Rococo works.)

Performing Arts Connection

The Gamut of Love, Antoine Watteau

Antoine Watteau merged the fantasy of the stage and the reality of everyday life into his art. *The Gamut of Love* describes upper-class life, which included playful courting of lovers, the ballet and pastoral masques during which the wealthy dressed in costumes and acted out scenes closely related to the theater. What role does music play in Watteau's depiction of the stages of love? What is it that connects the man and woman? (They both create the poetic music that symbolizes their interaction.)

• Have students contemplate the words of the great eighteenth-century French ballet master Jean-George Noverre: "A ballet is a picture, or rather a series of pictures;... the stage, as it were, the canvas on which the composer expresses his ideas; the choice of the music, scenery and costumes are his colors; the composer is the painter." Ask how Noverre's thoughts correspond to the fanciful paintings that Antoine Watteau and François Boucher made for their wealthy patrons.

Evaluate

Ask the class who the audience was for the lighthearted Rococo paintings. Where would the pleasure-seeking Parisians have hung these sorts of works? Can students imagine the elegant rooms and fancy boudoirs of the ladies and gentlemen who literally imitated the characters in these scenes?

Ask students if artists in America followed in the French Rococo tradition. Why might the citizens of the young United States not have particularly cared to emulate the lavish images of the European aristocracy? What kind of government ruled France? America?

Reteach

Ask students to find in contemporary fashion advertisements the equivalent of the flamboyant Rococo and the grand but more serious Baroque manner.

• Do students agree with each other's choices?

• Would they prefer to graduate from high school or be married in clothing that has a Baroque or a Rococo flair? Have them explain their decisions.

Instruct students to compare the figures in Watteau's works (figs.11–41, 11–42) to those in paintings by John Singleton Copley (fig.11–54) and Gilbert Stuart (fig.11–56).

• Are all these people from the same social background?

Francois Boucher

(1703–1770)

Most of the artists who painted the delicate and pretty decorations popular with the French nobility are forgotten, but Francois Boucher is well represented in the world's museums. Boucher's friends compared his colors to "rose petals floating in milk." His pink-fleshed nudes were in great demand. Many of his paintings dealt with mythological figures such as Venus, Diana and countless nymphs and Muses. But, he cared little about mythology and used these subjects to express his basic purpose—the painting of beautiful women. One of his largest works is *Pastoral Scene* (fig.11–44). It was probably painted for Louis XV or Madame de Pompadour, mistress to the King and patron of Boucher. It typifies the nobility's fascination with rural life in an ideal form. Instead of doing hard and dirty work, the shepherds and shepherdesses are shown in intimate conversation. The setting is romantic and idealized. The fountains and a mill house surrounded by feathery trees and backed by swirling clouds are perfectly pretty. The gorgeously costumed people are just as ideal. The pink skins and tiny delicate hands and feet are typical of the French Rococo paintings of figures. Several years after the painting was finished, it was reproduced in the form of a tapestry.

Jean-Baptiste-Simeon Chardin

(1699–1779)

While Watteau and Boucher were glorifying the earthly pleasures of the French aristocracy, Jean-Baptiste-Simeon Chardin drew on his lower middle-class background for painting subjects. Chardin used objects found in every kitchen and instilled a quiet dignity in them. His still lifes of common cooking utensils and kitchen objects were simple and strong in composition (fig.11–45). The triangular composition used so often by previous artists was used by Chardin to achieve a unified and powerful effect.

Chardin also painted servants and household workers in monumental form, giving them simple dignity and stature. How powerful Chardin's simple forms are as they are placed against a neutral and solid background. His genre subjects were the exact opposite of the typical Rococo paintings of flamboyance and delicate grace. They symbolize the power in the common people who will shortly take con-

11–44 How accurate is this view of eighteenth-century French rural life?
Francois Boucher, *Pastoral Scene*, 1748. Oil on canvas, 116 1/4" x 133" (295 x 338 cm). The J. Paul Getty Museum, Malibu.

11–45 This arrangement of common objects in a pyramidal composition gives them substance and importance. Jean-Baptiste-Simeon Chardin, *Still Life with Plums*, 1758. Oil on canvas, 16" x 19 3/4" (41 x 50 cm). The Frick Collection, New York.

trol of the government from the pleasure-seeking aristocracy.

Chardin's figures were as powerful as his still lifes. He often used nurses, servants and children as subjects. *The Attentive Nurse* (fig.11–46) is genre painting at its best. Heavy kitchen furniture, a delightful still life of ordinary items, and a charcoal heater on the floor are used for props. And what important task is the nurse performing? She is cracking a soft-boiled egg just removed from the pan. To paint such a person performing such a routine task with love and care adds importance to it. Chardin was interested in getting the common people to realize their importance and worth to society. He abandoned the painting of silky textures for the coarse homespuns of the lower classes. Instead of delicate wrinkles, his materials drape easily into heavy folds. The solidness, heaviness and simplicity of his subjects contrast directly with the frailness, delicacy and swirling of his contemporaries and their Rococo delights.

11–46 Chardin painted very different subjects than his contemporaries. Compare this genre scene to Boucher's *Pastoral Scene.* Jean-Baptiste-Simeon Chardin, *The Attentive Nurse*, 1738. Oil on canvas, 18" x 14 1/2" (46 x 37 cm). National Gallery of Art, Washington DC, Samuel H. Kress Collection.

Higher-Order Thinking Skills

1 Oddly enough, the French nobility were fascinated with what they perceived as the lives of everyday people, with whom they had very little, if any, contact. Ask the class what Chardin's *The Attentive Nurse* (fig.11–46) might have meant to a rich French nobleman or noble-woman.

2 The genre painting of Vermeer and Chardin made the ordinary events of daily life seem very noble and important without being overly dramatic. Ask students to make a list of genre subjects from their own experience and environment and discuss how one of them could be depicted so that it takes on new meaning and significance. Ask if such ideas could be used to make sketches.

Contextual Information

Canaletto

Canaletto's father, Bernardo Canal, was a well-known scene painter for the theater. Canaletto learned his trade from his father and began his career by painting scenes in the theater before he was 20.

By the age of 25, Canaletto had signed his first painting commission. Many of the canvases he painted were for wealthy English visitors to Venice, which is why so many of his paintings are now located in England.

11–47 What features of this ceiling reflect Tiepolo's Venetian background?
Giovanni Battista Tiepolo, Interior, *Residenz Palace*, 1751–1752. Fresco. Würzburg, Germany.

Giovanni Battista Tiepolo

(1696–1770)

In Italy, only Venice continued to produce artists who could rival those of France and keep Baroque splendor alive. The finest eighteenth-century painter in Venice was Giovanni Battista Tiepolo. He did not confine his work to Venice, but fulfilled commissions in northern Italy, Germany and Spain. Tiepolo's greatest achievements were his decorative ceiling frescoes. He was probably influenced by the Baroque ceiling painters of Rome. His ceiling frescoes covered enormous surfaces, but the feeling was light and airy, not heavy and dramatic. Figures float freely and lightly in vast expanses of sky.

Leaving Venice in 1750, Tiepolo took his two sons with him to Germany to work at the Residenz Palace of the Bishop of Würzburg. The hall ceiling in *Residenz Palace*, like other frescoes by Tiepolo, is a feast for the eyes rather than a vehicle for some profound message (fig.11–47). Swirling forms, joyous color and unbelievable perspectives create a painting that seems to dissolve the architecture and continue the view up to the sky. Saints, gods and heroes of various times prance through the heavens in one of the most sumptuous ceiling decorations ever painted.

Because of Germany's damp climate and harsh winters, the fresco technique could not be used year round. Tiepolo spent those cold months working on canvases with his oils. While in Würzburg, he

1707
Mt. Fuji erupts for the last time, Japan

1727
First Brazilian coffee cultivated

1751
Ben Franklin uses the Iroquois League as model for his Albany Plan of Union

World Cultural Timeline

1720
China conquers Tibet

1735
Antonio de Ulloa discovers platinum, South America

Multicultural Connection

The Iroquois League

Ask students if they are familiar with the connection between the Albany Plan of Union and the Iroquois League. If not, have them research how Franklin used the league as his model. The practicality and serious purpose of Franklin and the Colonists make it easy to understand why they would not have been interested in the frivolity of the European Rococo. Ask students to consider the contrast Franklin must have seen between life in the Colonies and the French courts he visited while soliciting support for the American cause.

painted the huge *Adoration of the Magi* as an altarpiece (fig.2–64). His free and slashing brushstrokes are combined with vibrant colors and a mastery of drawing to produce a startling composition. Tiepolo has made this humble event into a spectacular production. Numerous figures are crowded into the vertical format. Fabrics of various materials, from the rich silks of the kings to the coarse homespuns of the shepherds, are skillfully rendered. The clothes billow and fall effortlessly. They reflect the strong light that holds the composition together. Shadow and light are handled with surety and ease. The high-keyed emphasis naturally is placed on Mary and the Christ Child. The strong light, contrasting darker values, quivering dark lines, and flecks of light scattered throughout characterize the sparkling and joyous work of Tiepolo.

Antonio Canaletto
(1697–1768)

A new style of painting called ***view painting*** emerged in Venice early in the eighteenth century. Giovanni Antonio Canal, called Canaletto, depicted city views with incredible accuracy. Specializing in views of Venice, he sold dozens of them to the wealthy travelers. The perspective of Canaletto is very precise in many of his works. He probably made use of a camera obscura to project the correct lines and angles. In addition to his views of Venice, he painted realistic views of many of the capitals of Europe. His accuracy and detail were so carefully painted that in Warsaw, for example, the central core of the city was rebuilt after Nazi bombings according to Canaletto's painting.

Works like *The Basin of San Marco on Ascension Day* (fig.11–48) are historically important because they provide an exact picture of places as they appeared in the eighteenth century. The Grand Canal is choked with various types of gondolas and boats in celebration of the religious feast of the Ascension. The great landmarks of Venetian architecture are accurately detailed. Note the Doge's Palace in front of St. Mark's Basilica and the library on the left with the huge campanile behind it. All the buildings seen here are still in use. The huge Doge's state barge is tied up at its mooring in front of the palace. A viewer tends to be overcome by the profusion of detail (fig.11–b). Yet Canaletto was very conscious of design elements. He placed the movable parts of the composition—the figures and boats—in just the right places to provide scale, visual movement, contrast and pattern.

11–48 Many of Canaletto's landscapes were bought as souvenirs by wealthy travelers from other parts of Europe.
Antonio Canaletto, *The Basin of San Marco on Ascension Day,* about 1740. Oil on canvas. The Royal Collection, St. James' Palace, London.

Contextual Information

Wren

Christopher Wren was originally an astronomer and mathematician. When he decided to become an architect, he studied books and went to France to draw buildings and meet leading architects.

He once drew a master plan for London. Although it was never used, his plans for 52 churches were employed after the 1666 fire. In fact, Wren was named to the royal commission to rebuild the city.

Hogarth

Hogarth ignored a ready market for portraits and instead illustrated common activities and problems of the wealthy. His work amused the middle class, who could afford to buy his prints.

Hogarth is the first English artist of international stature. Before Hogarth, no seventeenth-century English artist had been as successful with wealthy patrons as the Flemish van Dyck and several other painters from continental Europe. This may have been due in part to the fact that the ruling Stuarts had close dynastic ties and long-term cultural links with the Continent.

The Great Fire

The Great Fire of London, which took place in 1666, was so catastrophic that its story has become a part of history.

On September 2, 1666, a fire started in Pudding Lane, in the house of the king's baker. From here, it quickly spread through the city's closely packed, wooden buildings. Everything burned in its wake.

Some efforts were made to contain the fire, but the tightly built-up area of old timber structures burned like dry tinder. The Great Fire raged from September 2 to September 5. It decimated four-fifths of the structures that had stood within the city walls. The riverside with its warehouses of wood and its flammable stocks suffered particularly severely. The old cathedral was a complete ruin.

Contemporary Print of the Great Fire of London in 1666.

The problem of rebuilding was tackled with great will. The right man in the right place at the right time was the architect Christopher Wren. To this day Wren's spires and domes help give London its characteristic look.

11–49 This cathedral was constructed after the previous one was destroyed during the Great Fire of London in 1666.
Christopher Wren. West facade, *St. Paul's Cathedral,* 1675–1710. London.

Christopher Wren
(1632–1723)

In seventeenth-century England, several architects began to make important contributions to the art scene. Christopher Wren, the great English architect of the late seventeenth century and early eighteenth century, left his mark on London by virtue of the forces of nature.

The disastrous London fire leveled great portions of the city in 1666. Wren was instrumental in designing many of the major buildings that replaced those that were destroyed. His most important structure is *St. Paul's Cathedral* (fig.11–49). St. Paul's Cathedral has a basically Gothic, longitudinal floor plan (Latin cross) with a very large choir. At the center of the exterior facade, two stories of paired Corinthian columns are topped with a decorated pediment, all of which stand forward like a French-styled pavilion. The corner towers are derived from Borromini's Church of Sant' Agnese and even have similar concave features. The beautiful dome is second in size to

Interdisciplinary Connection

Music and theater: Check your local events calendar for music, art or theater events that might tie in with Baroque and Rococo art in Europe. Check with college and university music departments for other performances or traveling orchestras.

11–50 Hogarth was arrested while making sketches for this painting. Why were the French unhappy with him?
William Hogarth, *O, The Roast Beef of Old England*, 1748. Oil on canvas, 31" x 37 1/2" (79 x 95 cm). Tate Gallery, London.

Higher-Order Thinking Skills

Hogarth's work has been very important to modern editorial cartoonists. To understand his work, one has to be very informed about life in his time. Provide newspapers in which students can find editorial cartoons and create a display that comments on current events. Ask what symbols and news stories one has to know in order to be able to interpret the cartoons correctly.

St. Peter's. The dome is vertical in feeling and stands on a high, columned drum over the crossing. The dome has been copied many times in Europe and the United States, as in the Capitol in Washington.

Although Wren drew on many sources for the design of St. Paul's, his finished work is a powerful Baroque statement. The interior is not as elaborate as Italian Baroque churches, but has a restrained and simple elegance more in keeping with Anglican Protestantism. Wren's use of circles, arches and framing to emphasize certain elements creates a Classic feeling.

William Hogarth

(1697–1764)

We have seen little of English painting to this point. We have observed painters from the continent, such as Holbein and van Dyck, move to England and serve as court painters. In the eighteenth century, however, painting in England comes into its own. The real founder of the British school of painting was William Hogarth. His satiric wit emerged in most of his work. He painted many portraits and argued long and loud that English painters were equal to those on the continent. However, his fame was established by several series of narrative paintings. These works, or "morality plays," came in sets of engravings for mass distribution to the common people. They dealt with such topics as problems in marriage, the ruinous life of an English rogue, the distressing life of a harlot, political corruption, and the results of alcohol abuse. In all of these series, he criticized society and the upper class's lack of morals. His work was naturally popular with the lower classes. His caustic wit knifed deeply into the heart of London society.

Hogarth's scathing satire can be felt in the painting *O, The Roast Beef of Old England* (fig.11–50), in which he attacks England's traditional enemy, France. The scene occurs before the gate of Calais in France—a gate built by the English. A huge side of beef is being delivered to an English eating house. The size seems so tremendous to the starving Frenchmen that they stumble about in disbelief and stare as if it was a mammoth gold nugget. As a barb to Catholic clergy, the Protestant Hogarth shows the priest as the only overfed person among his starving French countrymen. Near the left border, Hogarth is sketching the scene. Actually, he was arrested while sketching here and was imprisoned briefly as a spy. When he returned to England, he made this painting to get back at the French in his own way.

Contextual Information

Gainsborough

England's industrial revolution in the eighteenth century brought wealth to some middle-class merchants who could then afford to commission art. Gainsborough took advantage of this situation by painting popular full-length portraits of wealthy families and the royals.

Reynolds

Reynolds recognized that people liked their portraits to be improvements on reality, and his popularity for flattering his clients earned him a vast amount of money. He became an excellent businessman who carefully scheduled his appointments. Because of his friendships with wealthy people, his Classical style and his talent, he was elected president of the Royal Academy.

Sir Joshua Reynolds

(1723–1792)

Unlike Hogarth, who stayed at home in England, Sir Joshua Reynolds traveled in Europe. While living in Rome, he absorbed the influences of Renaissance and classical painting and architecture. He returned to England and, in 1768, helped to establish and become president of the Royal Academy of Arts, based on the example of the French school. Here, he lectured on his theories of art, which he based on his own intensive studies of European art.

He received a tremendous number of portrait commissions. He soon needed assistants to stretch the huge canvases and start the background work. Often his figures were placed in Classical settings to enhance their nobility, creating an artificial feeling. In the painting *Lady Sarah Bunbury Sacrificing to the Graces* (fig.11–51), the contemporary woman seems to be living in past times. The huge size of his portraits and the grand settings he devised would often flatter the subjects, making them seem more important than they actually were.

1750
Indonesian dyeing technique makes multicolored batik fabrics possible

1782
Bangkok established as seat of Thai monarchy

World Cultural Timeline

1780
The Bengal Gazette, **first newspaper in India, begins publication**

1795
First theater for Bengali plays opens, Calcutta, India

11–51 What classical influences do you find here?
Sir Joshua Reynolds, *Lady Sarah Bunbury Sacrificing to the Graces,* 1765. Oil on canvas, 93 3/4" x 59 3/4" (238 x 152 cm). The Art Institute of Chicago, W. W. Kimball Collection. 1922.

Multicultural Connection

Batik

Batik, a method of wax-resist textile dyeing, originated in Southeast Asia. This technique has been used for about a thousand years on the island of Java to produce elaborately patterned textiles. *Batik* is a Javanese word derived from *titik,* meaning "drop."

The basic method of using woodblock wax-resist techniques was introduced to Java in the twelfth century by the Indians who came to settle there and through early trading links. During the thirteenth century, batik was prac-

ticed only by the women of the sultan's family and the courts in the royal areas of central Java. Certain patterns were allowed only for court use or were used to identify particular families.

The Javanese invented a tool, the tjanting (pronounced chánting), that enabled them to produce extremely fine lines and details and bold, exotic patterns. The designs were of both geometric shapes and shapes derived from natural forms. Stylized designs of mythical birds and dragons, suggesting Indian and Chinese religious influence, were also used.

In batik, the areas of the fabric that are not to be dyed are drawn with the tjanting, which provides a reservoir for the melted wax. The fabric is then

Thomas Gainsborough
(1727–1788)

Although he would rather have painted landscapes, Thomas Gainsborough became one of England's finest portrait artists. He often would include large areas of open landscape as backgrounds for his subjects. His patrons were getting a bonus, almost two paintings in one.

Before the invention of photography, marriage portraits were often painted. The double portrait of young Squire William Hallett and his wife Elizabeth, called *The Morning Walk* (fig.11–52), is probably Gainsborough's finest. Obviously influenced by the outdoor portraits of van Dyck, Gainsborough's figures walk with their dog through a park. Feathery trees seem to move ever so slightly in the breeze. Carefully controlling the light and dark values, the artist skillfully places the light faces against dark foliage and balances them with splashes of light in other areas. Gainsborough's loose brushstrokes masterfully catch the glint of light on rustling fabrics. Great care is taken to paint the faces accurately, but the rest of the surface shimmers with flashing brushstrokes. Gainsborough's tendency to elongate the figures slightly always made his subjects seem regal and elegant. His success can be counted in over one thousand portraits that he painted.

After his reputation as a portrait artist was established, Gainsborough reserved some time for his favorite landscape painting. Only a few of the hundreds he did were sold; the others he stored away or gave to friends. He was living in London and relied on his memory for many of the scenes such as *Wooded Landscape with Peasant Resting* (fig.11–53). In his studio, he would often arrange miniature landscapes of broccoli stalks, moss, rocks and other materials to simulate nature and would paint from them. To establish scale or set the center of interest, he often included figures like farmers and farm children. Even though they were not accepted by contemporary London society, Gainsborough's landscapes greatly influenced later generations of English painters who made landscape painting the dominant subject matter.

11–53
Gainsborough advanced the idea that nature should not just be a backdrop for human activity, but could be a subject itself. Thomas Gainsborough, *Wooded Landscape with Peasant Resting*, 1750. Oil on canvas, 24 4/5" x 30 3/5" (63 x 78 cm). Tate Gallery, London.

11–52
Gainsborough's love of landscape painting is apparent in this double portrait. Thomas Gainsborough, *The Morning Walk*, 1785. Oil on canvas, 91 3/4" x 70 1/2" (233 x 179 cm). National Gallery, London.

Contextual Information

American Artists in the Eighteenth Century

Artists in early eighteenth-century America were frustrated at not having much professional support, because there were so few other artists who could earn a living from their art. They were beset by the high cost of materials and the perception that they were little better than sign painters and therefore unnecessary in the new country. If wealthy Americans wanted paintings, they bought European art whose value they knew.

Copley

Most American artists left the Colonies for Europe as soon as they could raise the necessary funds. Copley's situation was different, however. His work sold so well that he felt that he could not take the time off for a trip to learn about the latest in European styles. Finally, though, at the age of 36 and just as the American Revolution was beginning to affect the ability of his clients to buy his work, he left to study in Rome and later settled in London. In 1779 he became a full member of the Royal Academy. However, by 1815 his work had gone out of favor, and he died in debt.

Mrs. Richard Yates

Ask students if they think Mrs. Yates was financially well-off. How might her childhood have differed from her husband's? Unlike boys who were educated in the academics, daughters of wealthy families learned only enough math and reading to run a household. Most of their learning centered on the needle arts, music, drawing and painting. These accomplishments were designed to

John Singleton Copley
(1738–1815)

Americans during the eighteenth century were struggling to establish their cities and farmsteads in a land that was new and challenging. They had neither the time for the frivolity of the French Rococo nor sufficient wealth to support artists of the stature of Gainsborough or Reynolds. Several fine American artists, however, did emerge and some made an impact both here and in Europe.

The early works of John Singleton Copley, such as his portrait of *Paul Revere* (fig.11–54), were competent and often forceful. While Copley lacked formal training, he had considerable natural talent. He developed his own style after carefully studying the paintings of the European artists who were working in America. Intuitively aware of color, light and form, he produced excellent portraits that penetrated the personalities of his sitters.

The portrait of Paul Revere shows the famous silversmith and patriot in a moment of concentration. He holds one of his pitchers in his left hand. With his engraving tools handy, he seems to be wondering what type of design to work into the metal. A strong light is used to model the figure, which is placed before a solid, dark background. The work is a serious study of the man. The composition is strong; the edges are hard; and the figure is solid. All these qualities were different from those found in English and French painting of the same time. Copley went to Europe in 1775 to study with Reynolds and other European artists. Although his technical skills increased, his later work lost this fresh American approach. It became softer and more English in character.

Benjamin West
(1738–1820)

Born in the Commonwealth of Pennsylvania, Benjamin West left America in 1759, lived and painted in Rome for three years, and finally settled in London. He never returned to his native land. He became an outstanding portrait and historical painter in England. His style and work really belong in the study of English art. Adept at painting huge battle scenes, he was historical painter to King George III. He became president of the Royal Academy of Arts when Sir Joshua Reynolds died.

While in Europe, West came under the influence of Poussin. West used Poussin's grand conception of historical painting in *The Death of General Wolfe* (fig.11–55). Wolfe had died ten years earlier dur-

11–54 The artist did not have formal training when he painted this portrait, but he studied the works of others intently. He later went to Europe and studied with Reynolds.
John Singleton Copley, *Paul Revere*, 1768–1770. Oil on canvas, 35" x 28 1/4" (89 x 72 cm). Museum of Fine Arts, Boston, gift of Joseph W., William B., and Edward H. R. Revere.

ing the siege of Quebec in the French and Indian War. Sentiments in England about this event were strong. West decided to clothe his figures in contemporary dress and use realistic locations, but present them in an "heroic" way, like Poussin. The participants in previous historical paintings had been put in classical Roman togas and armor. West made them seem real and current. He endowed the scene with Baroque light and pathos. The work became a model for American historical paintings in the nineteenth century.

make them attractive and entertaining wives, and showed the world that their husbands earned enough money to allow them to engage in leisure pursuits.

• Ask students how they feel about the differences in the education that boys and girls received in the Colonies.

Is there still a division today in how the two sexes are treated in certain activities? What about in military academies, in automotive or homemaking classes or on sports teams?

11–55 **Expatriate artist, West, painted American historical events from his studio in London.**
Benjamin West, *The Death of General Wolfe*, 1770. Oil on canvas, 60 3/5" x 83 4/5" (154 x 213 cm). National Gallery of Canada, Ottawa.

11–56 **Stuart went to England to study with American Benjamin West.**
Gilbert Stuart, *Mrs. Richard Yates*, 1793–1794. Oil on canvas, 30 1/4" x 24 3/4" (77 x 63 cm). National Gallery of Art, Washington DC, Andrew W. Mellon Collection.

Gilbert Stuart

(1755–1828)

The most inventive of early American painters was Gilbert Stuart. He arrived in London in 1775, a penniless young student. After studying with Benjamin West for a time, he exhibited a portrait of a man on ice skates that became the sensation of the Royal Academy show in 1782. With his name established, he accepted many portrait commissions at prices exceeded only by Reynolds and Gainsborough. Handling his income poorly, however, he returned to America in debt. He spent the rest of his life painting the heroes of the new Republic, including the first president, George Washington.

He did not like to flatter his subjects, but painted them as he saw them. Most Americans liked this approach. Patrons such as *Mrs. Richard Yates* (fig.11–56) wanted to see themselves as they really were. Stuart's brushstrokes were strong and sure. His use of color, especially in the skin tones, was innovative. He used almost every color to portray the living quality of flesh.

Higher-Order Thinking Skills

Challenge the class to find characteristics about Copley's, West's and Stuart's paintings that indicate that they are American and not European. Ask what problems faced American artists and how they solved them.

Contextual Information

Joshua Johnson

Art historians look in many places for data about artists. The Baltimore city directories turned out to be one source of information about Joshua Johnson. In 1820 he is listed as a limner. In the December 19, 1798, Baltimore newspaper *Intelligencer*, he advertised himself as a "self-taught genius," assuring possible clients that he could paint a perfect likeness.

Lesson 11.5 Review Answers

1 *Pastoral Scene* is a romantic and idealized depiction of the nobility's fascination with an ideal rural life. The shepherds and shepherdesses depicted here do not seem to be familiar with hard work, but are gorgeously costumed with pink skin and tiny delicate feet and hands.

2 Chardin's peasants have dignity and stature rather than the flamboyance and delicate grace of Boucher's pink-skinned peasants. Chardin's peasants symbolize the power of the common people. The coarse, homespun clothes of Chardin's figures are draped in heavy folds which contrast with the delicate, pastel fabrics of Boucher's pretend peasants.

3 View paintings of Venice

4 Gainsborough painted his subject's faces accurately, but used loose brushstrokes on the rest of the surface. He often elongated the bodies. Copley's portraits were more serious, hard-edged studies of solid figures.

5 George Washington

6 Joshua Johnson

Chapter Review Answers

Review

1 Michelangelo designed the dome, Bernini designed the monumental piazza in front of St. Peter's, and Maderno added a nave to Michelangelo's building plan and designed the facade.

2 La Tour utilized strong tenebrism (contrast of light and dark) and realism in *Magdalen*, which is reminiscent of the work of Caravaggio.

Early African American Crafts

In African societies, art served both religious and social purposes. When Africans were transplanted to America as slaves, they lost their society and, with it, their reason for creating their ritual masks and sculptures. A common avenue of creativity open to African-Americans was in the handcrafting of necessary articles.

African-Americans continued to use materials that had been available to them in Africa: wood, metal, natural fibers and clay. The African artist also assimilated European techniques and ideas. Many of the handwoven bedspreads, quilts and coverlets that have survived from the early years of our country, for example, were created by African-American women.

Silversmithing was a responsible trade in the North as well as the South. Craftsmanship offered the slave both a way of earning freedom and a means of self-support afterward. Charleston and New Orleans were particularly famous centers for wrought-ironwork, which featured elaborate patterns of grapes and other fruits and flowers. Much of this work was done by African-Americans.

Joshua Johnson
(c. 1770–1825)

Little is known about Joshua Johnson, the first African-American artist to gain prominence as an artist in America. A self-taught artist, Johnson lived most of his life in Baltimore, where he became a recognized portrait painter of wealthy members of slave-holding families. However, two of his portraits of African-American men have survived. *Portrait of a Man* (fig.11–57) is typical of the style of portraits painted in the United States at this time. The man is shown in three-quarter view with his eyes looking directly at the viewer. The pose is somewhat stiff, and the portrait reveals little of the sitter's personality. The portrait is neatly rendered, and has a flat quality that was typical of the work of **limners**. Early American limners were artists who, during the cold winter months, painted single or group portraits without the faces. When spring arrived, they would find patrons who wanted their faces filled in. Johnson paid great attention to details like lace and buttons in his works. He usually posed his subjects in front of a background of drapery or an idealized landscape framed by a window.

11–57 Johnson is believed to have migrated to the United States from the West Indies. He probably was a self-taught artist.
Joshua Johnson, *Portrait of a Man*, about 1805. Oil on canvas, 28" x 22" (71 x 56 cm). Bowdoin College Museum of Art, Brunswick, Maine. Hamlin Fund.

1 How does Boucher's *Pastoral Scene* demonstrate characteristics typical of Rococo art?

2 Compare Chardin's concept of a peasant woman in *The Attentive Nurse* with Boucher's shepherdess in *Pastoral Scene*.

3 What painting subject was Canaletto's specialty?

4 How is the painting style of John Singleton Copley in *Paul Revere* different from Thomas Gainsborough's in *The Morning Walk*?

5 Which hero of the American Revolution did Gilbert Stuart paint many times?

6 Who was the first African-American to gain prominence in America as an artist?

3 The Rococo substituted lighthearted gaiety, charm and wit for the grandeur of the Baroque. The Rococo art and architecture often seems lighter than the Baroque.

4 West painted his figures in a heroic style as did Poussin.

5 Both facades have curved, convoluted surfaces with protruding features. They also both have sculptural domes and towers.

Interpretation

1 There is clutter on the floor and chair. Some of the children appear happy with their gifts of candy and toys. Two children are making fun of the boy on the left who is crying. The grandmother reaches toward a little girl holding a doll.

2 Students might discuss van Ruisdael's *The Windmill at Wijk by Durstede* with its calm landscape and turbulent sky, or Hals' robust, vital *Portrait of a Man* or the joyful party depicted in *Yonker Ramp and His Sweetheart*.

3 No one knows what this couple is saying or singing, but it should be fun to speculate.

4 Bernini's life-size David is in the act of winding up to hurl the stone from his slingshot. He has shed his armor and drapery swirls around his legs. He stares at Goliath and bites his lip in concentration. Michelangelo's giant (4.8 m.) nude intently contemplates Goliath, sizing him up before the battle. His slingshot is draped over his shoulder. His weight rests on one leg in a classical Greek contrapposto pose.

Primary Source

William Hogarth

Artists rarely admit that they paint to earn money, but William Hogarth, son of a poor schoolmaster, was not too proud to say that he looked for subjects that would earn money to care for his family. He decided to paint moral scenes because that subject had been overlooked by other painters and would appeal to citizens who were critical of the richer classes. Hogarth made prints of his paintings both to point out the vices and foolish-

ness of London society and to support himself financially.

Here, he tells us why he rejected one type of subject matter in favor of another:

Why I Gave Up
Conversation Pieces

I then married [1729], and commenced to be a painter of small conversation pieces, from twelve to fifteen inches high. This having novelty, succeeded for a few years. But though it gave somewhat more scope to the fancy [than engraving],

was still but a less kind of drudgery; and as I could not bring myself to act like some of my brethren, and make it a sort of manufactory, to be carried on by the help of background and drapery painters; it was not sufficiently profitable to pay the expenses my family required.

I therefore turned my thoughts to a still more novel mode, viz., painting and engraving modern moral subjects, a field not broken up in any country and any age.

Chapter Review

Review

1 What part of Saint Peter's Cathedral in Rome did Michelangelo, Bernini and Maderno each design?
2 How does the style of La Tour's *Magdalen with the Smoking Flame* remind you of Caravaggio's paintings?
3 How did the Rococo style paintings and architecture differ from the Baroque?
4 In what way is Benjamin West's *The Death of General Wolfe* similar to Poussin's paintings?
5 How are the exteriors of the Benedictine Abbey at Melk and the facade of Sant' Agnese alike?

Interpretation

1 What details or family interactions in Jan Steen's *The Feast of St. Nicholas* might be present in a family home today?
2 Select one of Frans Hals' or van Ruisdael's paintings. Describe the mood of this painting. Name a song or piece of music that seems to go with this picture.
3 Write a short story about what is happening in Watteau's *The Gamut of Love*. What song are they singing or what is their conversation?
4 Compare the statues of *David* by Bernini, Michelangelo (fig.9–26) and Donatello (fig.9–7). At what point in the story did each artist show his David? Describe the motion, emotion, size and pose of each sculpture.

Other Tools for Learning

 Maps
1 Why would southern Germany align itself more with Italy and Northern Germany with Scandinavia and the Netherlands?
2 Why do you think eighteenth-century American painters did not study in Europe and were often self-taught?

 Timelines
1 Select an event from the non-European timelines which influenced Western art. Explain your choice.
2 Select an event in the timelines that has probably made the world a better place in which to live. Explain why you chose this event.

Electronic Research
CD-ROM drive: *Microsoft Art Gallery*
Videodisk player: *National Gallery of Art* Videodisk
1 Rubens painted other lions besides the ones in the *Lion Hunt* in this chapter. Find another lion painted by Rubens. Compare it to the ones in the 1616 *Lion Hunt*.
2 Describe Caravaggio's *Supper at Emmaus*. How has Caravaggio made this scene dramatic? Research this painting further in the *Microsoft Art Gallery's* Composition and Perspective Guided Tour. Describe the foreshortening in this painting.

Primary-Source Connection

Hogarth turned from wealthy patrons to the business of providing engravings for the lower classes. Have students research some examples of these engravings and explain why they would have been so appealing to the lower classes.

• Have students use the text, the primary-source selection and any additional information turned up in their research to write a brief character sketch of Hogarth. Have the class discuss what that they find appealing about him.

• Have students speculate about why we find the lives and personalities of artists so fascinating. Do we feel the same about famous musicians or authors?

Europe in 1600. For example, *Vermeer's Officer and Laughing Girl* has a world map which was probably developed as a result of European explorations in search of Chinese tea.
2 Many events here would seem to have made the world better. The Japanese living near Mt. Fuji should have rejoiced that it released its pressure in 1707 and has not erupted since. The introduction of opera in Mexico City in 1711 and the opening of the first theater for Bengali plays in 1795 in India have probably made both parts of the world culturally more enjoyable. Coffee drinkers around the world are thankful for the cultivation of the first Brazilian coffee in 1727.

Electronic Research
1 Many of the Lion Hunt scenes are similar to the one in this book. The version in the London National Gallery is an unfinished sketch for a large picture which was never painted. Bodies of horses, men and lions swirl in a violent fight with straight lances crossing through the composition.
2 Three men surround Christ at a table which recedes into the picture, leading the viewer into the painting. Jesus' raised hand is foreshortened, making it seem to come out to the viewer. The scene is dramatic, with strong contrasts of light and dark.

Donatello's slight youth has already killed Goliath, and stands in a graceful contrapposto with his left foot on Goliath's severed head. He holds a sword and wears a hat crowned with a laurel wreath.

 Maps
1 Geographically, southern Germany is closer to Italy and northern Germany is closer to Scandinavia and the Netherlands.
2 Because the boat trip across the Atlantic Ocean was long, dangerous and expensive.

Timelines
1 Encourage students to be creative in considering possible connections between Western art and the rest of the world. For example, the Japanese emperor's forbidding his subjects to leave Japan in 1637 possibly stopped the spread of Japanese culture to the rest of the world, causing Japanese art and culture to seem very novel to Europeans when Japan did resume contact with the West. The development of woodblock techniques in 1725 by the Japanese printmaker Okumura Maganobu later influenced European printmaking.

Students might consider the influences of the development of the coffee industry in Martinique in 1723, or the introduction of Chinese tea into

Activity 1: Learning from Rembrandt

Activity Objectives
Students should be able to:

• Describe the different kinds of print-making.

• Look at a print and identify which process was used to create it.

• Produce a print in accordance with available tools and materials.

Thinking Critically
This project provides a good framework to acquaint students with a medium/process that may not be familiar to them. Refer students to pages 34 and 35. Review the different kinds of print-making and discuss how each differs from the rest.

Preparation Ideas

• Find examples of Rembrandt's etchings, particularly his self-portraits—or ask students to bring in examples as part of their assignment.

• Locate an intaglio print, perhaps a "second." Allow students to touch it in order to get a sense of the texture and feel of the paper.

• Bring in different kinds of prints and ask students to identify the process used to make them.

Notes on Materials
If your school is not equipped with printmaking supplies and a press, there are a number of alternative ways to approach this activity.

• Students can use drypoint needles to scratch a drawing into the surface of a plastic plate.

• As a no-cost alternative, students can use any sharp object, such as a compass point, for a tool. Check with local manufacturers for free scraps of flat plastic, heavy-weight acetate or Plexiglas.

• Students can apply water-based ink to the surface of their "etched" plate with a roller and then press by hand onto suitable paper. The result is a print of the surface of the plate with etched areas appearing as white lines. Explain to students that a press would allow them to print ink that has been *pressed into* the lines.

Activity 1

Learning from Rembrandt

Materials
pencils
drawing paper
etching supplies

Take a look.
• Fig.11–32, Rembrandt van Rijn, *Self-Portrait*, about 1636. Dutch. Oil on panel.
• Fig.11–35, Rembrandt van Rijn, *Saint Jerome in an Italian Landscape*, 1651. Dutch. Etching and drypoint.
• Fig.11–33, Rembrandt van Rijn, *The Shooting Company of Captain Frans Banning Cocq (The Night Watch)*, 1642. Oil on canvas.
• Fig.11–36, Rembrandt van Rijn, *The Syndics of the Cloth Guild*, 1662. Oil on canvas.

Think about it. Examine the work of Rembrandt van Rijn. Known as the greatest of the Dutch painters, he was very prolific, creating thousands of pieces of art including paintings, drawings and prints. He created hundreds of self-portraits, many of them etchings and dry-points.
• What characteristics are common to both his prints and his paintings?
• Can you see a variation in his style as he develops?
• Notice his use of *chiaroscuro*, which gives his work a feeling of drama through strong lights and darks.

Do it. Create an etching or drypoint portrait or self-portrait.
• Begin by doing drawings of yourself or your selected subject in various types of lighting. Work in charcoal or a soft lead pencil to get a good range of light and dark values.
• Once you have selected the best drawing, use it as the basis for an intaglio print on a metal or plexiglass plate. You will want to do

some research into the methods and materials needed by working with your art teacher or visiting a local library.

Check it. Are the shadows in your drawing consistent with the implied light source?

Helpful Hint: When making an intaglio print, the image will be backwards from the way it looks on your plate. To preview how your print will look, hold the plate up to a mirror.

Activity 2

Light and Contrast

Materials
pencils
drawing paper for sketching
construction paper: white, yellow, gray, black
glue

Take a look.
• Fig.11–6, Artemisia Gentileschi, *Judith and Maidservant with the Head of Holofernes*, about 1625. Oil on canvas.

Think about it. Artemisia Gentileschi, a follower of Caravaggio, was one of the first women painters in Western art to make an important contribution to the art of her time. Her painting, *Judith and Maidservant with the Head of Holofernes*, does not dramatize the beheading itself. Rather, she chose to emphasize the forms of Judith and her servant through the use of deep shadows and strong highlights. This technique of exaggerating the strong contrasts of light and dark is called *tenebroso*.

Do it.
• Ask a friend to pose in a casual manner. Perhaps he/she can be relaxing, reading the newspaper or reading a book. (Using a large over-stuffed chair would add to the mood.)

• Using only the reading lamp or a spotlight for the source of light, sketch the model on 12" x 18" paper. Focus on the *shapes* of the lights and darks, not just the contours of the model.
• Using black, gray, white and yellow construction paper, create a cut-paper composition using your sketch as the base.

white = lightest values
yellow and/or gray paper = middle values.
black = darkest values

Check it. Evaluate your own work based on the following:
• effective use of lights and darks
• technical skill in cutting and gluing
• effort

Helpful Hint: Refer to the *tenebroso* effect in Gentileschi's painting as you develop your own composition.

Additional Activities
• Research Saskia, Rembrandt's beloved wife, and the influence she had on his life and his painting career.
• Study the three versions of *David* by Donatello (fig.9–7), Michelangelo (fig.9–26), and Bernini (fig.11–3). Compare and contrast the sculptures, considering each artist's style and the emphasis they placed on pose, movement, expression and emotion.
• Discuss in class the lives of artists: Rembrandt, Caravaggio and Artemisia Gentileschi to better explain why these Baroque painters worked in the style they did.

• Sometimes companies that sell printing supplies will gladly send someone to your class for a free demonstration of printmaking materials and techniques.

Classroom Management
If students are hesitant about doing a portrait, or don't see the point of printing the same image over and over again, organize your class into groups to design calendars. In a group of twelve, for instance, each student would contribute one month, making twelve prints so that each member of the group would have a complete calendar.

Tips

• A nearby college or university might have a printmaking department. Ask if you could bring your class in for a demonstration.

• The *Journal of the Print World* is a good resource for articles on the history of printmaking and materials.

Activity 2: Light and Contrast

Activity Objectives
Students should be able to:

• Develop their awareness of the effect of light, dark and contrast in art.

Erik E. Linder

Age 17
Perkiomen Valley High School
Graterford, Pennsylvania
Favorite kinds of art: anything
I've never done before
Favorite artists: anyone who can
draw well

Activity 2, Light and Contrast

My class assignment was to make a cut-paper likeness of a live, volunteer model, using only black,
gray, yellow and white colored paper. To create the
dramatic tones of light and dark, the classroom's
lighting was altered using a small portable light.

While I was studying the model and setting,
I became a little nervous and wondered whether I
would be able to complete the project without first
going insane, but after a few minutes of sketching
I began to understand the concept and everything
started to pull together. After I did my sketch I realized that even though I had simplified many of the
shadows, some shapes were still too complicated to
successfully cut out and paste down. Now that I had
something to work with I toned down the shapes
once more and began to cut them out.

On the subject of influences, I would have to say
that I really haven't studied any modern or classical
artists very heavily, and don't feel influenced by
any one person or style. On the other hand, I do draw
a lot of my creative energy from personal experiences,
certain types of music, and what I see other students
doing.

The thing that I like most about the artistic
process would have to be the problem solving that is
involved. With every project I've ever done I've
always run into new problems that require new and
creative solutions.

ERIK E. LINDER

Megan, 1994. Construction paper, 12" x 18" (30.5 x 45.7 cm).

**Megan Schook, seated under a bright light for contrast, poses as
model for the class activity.**

Teacher Spotlight
Susan Klinger
Art Teacher
Perkiomen Valley High School

Prior to doing this activity, my students completed a lesson on chiaroscuro, using a portrait photograph
to break a subject into its lights and
darks. Some worked from a magazine photograph, but several worked
from photographs of family and
friends. They used tracing paper to
break the photo into just black and
white, learning to use their artistic
judgment to alter and adjust the
image to create more interesting
shapes and a pleasing composition.
The final image was rendered in pen
and ink. As they approached the
"Light and Contrast" activity, I used
the first activity as an example in
encouraging them to draw the
shapes of the lights and darks, not
just the contours of the model.

Tips

• Whether you use one model or several, have students do a quick series of
small warm-up drawings to practice
getting the overall impact of light and
dark without being overconcerned
about detail.

• Another option is to have students
photograph the arranged environment
in black and white to study the effect of
strong lighting in another medium.
Photographs could be a work of art in
themselves or used as a basis for further
sketches.

Evaluation
You might try using a "reflection sheet"
for student self-evaluation. Students
would answer questions about their
experience and their final piece of work.
This helps students understand what
you look for when grading their work.
Questions could include:

• How would you evaluate the effort
you put into your work?

• What problems did you encounter in
producing your work and how did you
solve them?

• Did you develop an effective pattern
of lights and darks in your work?

• Is technical skill in cutting and
gluing evident in your work?

• Arrange a model/subject in a high-
contrast setting.

• Produce a collage based on their
discoveries.

Thinking Critically
Review with students the meaning
of *tenebroso*. Ask them to find other
examples in this chapter, such as
Caravaggio's *The Supper at Emmaus*
(fig.11–4) and Georges de la Tour's
Magdalen with the Smoking Flame
(fig.11–14). Ask students:

• How does the use of strong contrasts
affect the mood of these paintings?

• What is the difference between
tenebroso and chiaroscuro?

Preparation Ideas

• Gather props—such as an armchair,
textured pillows, a newspaper and
hats—for students to use in setting up
a series of studies in class.

Notes on Materials

• Have gooseneck lamps, flashlights
or other kinds of directional lighting to
focus on the subject(s).

Classroom Management

• Ask for a volunteer to pose for the
class and appoint one or two students
to use props and lights to arrange an
environment. Have students do a series
of sketches with different models in different arrangements. Elevate models on
a table or a platform or rearrange desks
and tables for easy viewing.

Chapter 12 Organizer

Chapter 12 Opener: Three Opposing Views

Days	8 Week	1 Semester	2 Semester
	1	1	1

Objectives

Define the late eighteenth and early nineteenth centuries as a time of rapid change in Western society.

Understand that Neoclassicism, Romanticism and Realism rejected the frivolity of the Baroque and Rococo era.

Locate the birth of the severe Neoclassic style in France.

Describe how the emotionally charged Romantic style was a reaction against the cool Neoclassical manner.

Comprehend how Realist artists strove to paint exactly what they perceived in the world around them.

Articulate that the development of photography as an art form began in the nineteenth century.

National Standards

4a Students differentiate among a variety of historical and cultural contexts in terms of characteristics and purposes of works of art.

5a Students identify intentions of those creating artworks, explore the implications of various purposes, and justify their analyses of purposes in particular works.

3c Students describe the origins of specific images and ideas and explain why they are of value in their artwork and in the work of others.

4c Students analyze relationships of works of art to one another in terms of history, aesthetics, and culture, justifying conclusions made in the analysis and using such conclusions to inform their own art making.

5b Students describe meanings of artworks by analyzing how specific works are created and how they relate to historical and cultural contexts.

5a Students identify intentions of those creating artworks, explore the implications of various purposes, and justify their analyses of purposes in particular works.

Teacher Edition References

Lesson 12.1 Neoclassicism

Special Feature: Jacques-Louis David 382–383	Contextual Info 383	HOTS 383
Remainder of Lesson 12.1 384–389 World Cultural Timeline 384 Lesson 12.1 Review 389	Contextual Info 384, 386, 388 HOTS 385, 387, 389 Interdisciplinary 387	Multicultural 384, 388 Performing Arts 389

Lesson 12.2 Romanticism

Special Feature: Francisco Goya 390–391	Contextual Info 392 HOTS 391	Cooperative 392
Remainder of Lesson 12.2 392–399 World Cultural Timeline 392 Lesson 12.2 Review 399	Contextual Info 394, 396, 398 HOTS 393, 395, 397, 399 Inquiry 396, 398	Multicultural 397 Performing Arts 393, 395

Lesson 12.3 Realism

Special Feature: Rosa Bonheur 400–401	HOTS 401	
Remainder of Lesson 12.3 402–409 World Cultural Timeline 402 Lesson 12.3 Review 409	Contextual Info 402, 404, 406, 408 HOTS 403, 405, 407, 409	Inquiry 404 Interdisciplinary 407, 408 Materials and Techniques 402

Lesson 12.4 Photography

Special Feature: Edward Steichen 410–411	Contextual Info 411	HOTS 411
Remainder of Lesson 12.4 412 Lesson 12.4 Review 412 Primary-Source 413	Chapter Review 412 Contextual Info 412	HOTS 413

Classroom Connections

National Standards

Studio Activity 1
Watercolor Action

1a Students apply media, techniques, and processes with sufficient skill, confidence, and sensitivity that their intentions are carried out in their artworks.
3d Students evaluate and defend the validity of sources for content and the manner in which subject matter, symbols, and images are used in the student's works and in significant works by others.

Studio Activity 2
Dueling Styles

6c Students synthesize the creative and analytical principles and techniques of the visual arts and selected other arts disciplines, the humanities, or the sciences.

Ancillaries

Slides: Eiffel, Eiffel Tower, 74a, 149; Houdon, *Bust of Voltaire*, 77b, 151

Teacher Edition References

Timeline: Three Opposing Views 381
Map: Three Opposing Views 381
Context 380
Art 381
Quote 381

Ancillaries

Slides: David, *Portrait of Mme. Recamier*, 76b, 150
Large Reproductions: David, *The Death of Marat*, 17

Slides: Houdon, *Bust of Voltaire*, 77b, 151; Vignon, Church of the Madeleine, Paris, 75a, 152; Chalgrin, Arc de Triomphe de l'Etoile, Paris, 76a, 153
Large Reproductions: Vigée-Lebrun, *Marie Antoinette with her Children*, 18

Slides: Eiffel, Eiffel Tower, 74a, 149; Delacroix, *Liberty Leading the People*, 77a, 154; Constable, *Stoke-by-Nayland*, 78a, 155; Turner, *Slave Ship*, 78b, 156; Cole, *Niagara Falls*, 79b, 157; Bingham, *Fur Traders Descending the Missouri*, 79a, 158; Nash, Royal Pavilion, Brighton, England, 80a, 159; Garnier, Exterior of Opera, 80b, 160
Overhead Transparencies: The Artist and the Sketchbook, 13

Slides: Courbet, *A Burial at Ornans*, 81a, 161; Corot, *Monte Pincio, Rome*, 81b, 162; Homer, *Breezing Up, (A Fair wind)*, 82a, 164; Daumier, *Painter at his Easel*, 82b, 163; Cameron, *Mrs. H. Duckworth*, 83b, 165 **Large Reproductions:** Courbet, *Interior of My Studio, a Real Allegory Summing Up Seven Years of My Life as an Artist*, 19

Slides: Muybridge, *Animal Locomotion: Toddler Walking*, 84b, 166

Schedule

One day to sketch. One to three days to paint. (To shorten the class time, have students sketch prior to the studio or complete their paintings outside of class.)

Preparation: Assign prior to class so students may do research. One day for presentation.

Materials

pencils, drawing paper (sketch book), watercolor paint, watercolor paper, brushes, containers of water

(presentation)

Other Resources

Books

Boime, Albert. *The Academy and French Painting of the 19th Century.* London: Phaidon, 1971.

Clark, T. J., *The Absolute Bourgeois: Artists and Politics in France, 1848–1851.* Princeton: Princeton University, 1982.

Eitner, Lorenz. *Neo-classicism and Romanticism: 1750–1850.* 2 vols. Part of *Sources and Documents in the History of Art.* Englewood Cliffs: Prentice Hall, 1970.

Hamilton, George Heard. *Painting and Sculpture in Europe: 1880–1940.* 3rd ed., New Haven: Yale University Press, 1992.

Hitchcock, Henry Russell. *Architecture: 19th and 20th Centuries.* 4th ed. New Haven: Yale University Press, 1992.

Holt, Elizabeth Gilmore, ed. *A Documentary History of Art: From the Classicists to the Impressionists.* Vol. II. New York: Anchor Books, 1966.

Hudson River and Its Painters. Metropolitan Museum of Art. 1987.

Nochlin, Linda. *Realism and Tradition in Art: 1848–1900.* Part of *Sources and Documents in the History of Art.* Englewood Cliffs: Prentice Hall, 1966.

Robertson, Priscilla. *An Experience of Women: Pattern and Change in Nineteenth Century Europe.* Philadelphia: Temple University Press, 1982.

Video

David: The Passing Show. RM/ARTS/BBC, 1986.

Delacroix, Crystal

Delacroix: The Restless Eye. RM/ARTS/BBC, 1986.

Gericault: Men and Wild Horses. RM/ARTS/BBC, 1982.

Turner at the Tate, Crystal

Goya: Museum Without Walls, Kartes, 1986.

Ingres: Slaves of Fashion. RM/ARTS/ BBC, 1982.

Music

Classic
Hayden—*Symphony No. 101 in D Major (Clock Symphony); Symphony in G Major, No. 94 (Surprise Symphony)*
Mozart—*Clarinet Quintet in a Major The Marriage of Figaro (Opera) (Overture and scene 1); The Magic Flute*

Romantic
Beethoven—*Symphony No. 3 in E Flat Major, Op.55 (Eroica)*
String Quartet No. 16, Op.135
Chopin—*Prelude No. 2 in A Minor Nocturne No. 17, Op. 62, No.1*
Mendelssohn—*Scherzo from A Midsummer Nights Dream*
Schubert—*Hedge Roses Symphony in B Minor (Unfinished)*
Schumann—*Carnaval*
Brahms—*Symphony No. 3 in F Major*
Verdi—*Otello (Opera)*
Puccini—*La Boheme (Opera)*

Introduce

The late eighteenth and early nineteenth centuries saw a time of swift and tremendous change in Western society. Three art movements heralded in the new age: Neoclassicism, which admired the ancient Classical period; Romanticism, a more emotionally evocative style; and Realism, whose proponents focused on direct life experiences as their subject matter. In the nineteenth century, photography also gained recognition as a fine art form.

Lessons at a Glance

12.1 *Neoclassicism*
In order to bestow a regal status on its artworks, Neoclassicism evoked the ancient Greek and Roman past as well as the Renaissance. Napoleon Bonaparte encouraged the use of the cool, dignified and imposing Neoclassic style to glorify his authority and the growing strength of France.

12.2 *Romanticism*
Romantic artists rebelled against the dictates and conventions of Neoclassicism and instead built a style that relied heavily on intense emotion and individuality.

12.3 *Realism*
Realism emerged in the late nineteenth century while Neoclassicism and Romanticism were still active. Realism's adherents relied on personal experience and observation to portray the world around them in as natural a manner as possible. Realist artists were often criticized for the ordinariness of their subjects, particularly those glorifying the working class and their simple life.

12.4 *Photography*
Fine art photography began in the nineteenth century. At the time, scientific advances and artistic interests combined to produce an entirely new and versatile medium.

Objectives

Students should be able to:

Define the late eighteenth and early nineteenth centuries as a time of rapid change in Western society.

Understand that Neoclassicism, Romanticism and Realism rejected the frivolity of the Baroque and Rococo era.

12 Three Opposing Views

12–a The concept of a skeletal iron tower caused an uproar when it was first proposed. Nothing like it had ever been built. Despite the protests, it was constructed at the extravagant cost of one million dollars! Alexandre-Gustave Eiffel. *Eiffel Tower,* 1889. Paris.

D URING THE LATE EIGHTEENTH and early nineteenth centuries, tremendous shifts took place in the Western world. Life's tempo was speeding up and, during this relatively short period, three very different styles dominated. These were Neoclassicism, Romanticism and Realism.

Neoclassicism had its base in France, which was ruled by the dictator Napoleon Bonaparte. Napoleon's taste in art was severe. He did not like the exuberance and frivolity of the Baroque and Rococo styles and favored the more Classical approach of ancient Greece and Rome. Napoleon's word on everything was law, and art was no exception. The reaction to Baroque and Rococo was not only confined to France, however, and a general desire for something less fussy was felt all over the Continent and as far away as America.

Neoclassicism had such a firm hold on the Western world that it seemed unlikely that anything would budge it. However, some artists, irritated with the restrictions of Classicism, started working in a more emotionally evocative way. This approach, called Romanticism, had a huge impact on all the arts.

Neoclassicism looked toward the past while Romanticism dwelt in the realm of the imagination. Artists who resisted these two movements focused on direct experience, painting what they saw, whether it was pleasant or unpleasant. These artists were the Realists. The nineteenth century also saw the development of photography as an art form.

12–b This painter, like all the Realist artists, studied and sketched the common, everyday world. Rosa Bonheur, *The Horse Fair,* detail (fig.12–31).

Locate the birth of the severe Neoclassic style in France.

Describe how the emotionally charged Romantic style was a reaction against the cool Neoclassical manner.

Comprehend how Realist artists strove to paint exactly what they perceived in the world around them.

Articulate that the development of photography as an art form began in the nineteenth century.

Teach

Timeline

Ask students to examine the timeline to see which countries participated in the new era of the late eighteenth and early nineteenth centuries. Did significant events occur only in Europe?

Context

Share with students that as Western society in general experienced dramatic changes in the late eighteenth and early nineteenth centuries, women too took on new roles as they pushed beyond the boundaries that had previously dictated their lives. Rosa Bonheur, the artist of *The Horse Fair* (figs.12–b, 12–31), was one of a growing numbers of professional female artists at the time.

• Direct students to read her biography on pages 400 and 401 and discuss what type of personality they think she might have had to be able to succeed in a male-dominated career.

• Next, have the class carefully analyze the way in which Jacques-Louis David depicts women in his painting *Oath of the Horatii* (fig.12–1). Do they seem

*Beauty, like truth, is relative to
the time when one lives and
to the individual who can grasp it.*
Gustave Courbet

*The development of different styles often
centered in France, but artists all over Europe
were exploring new forms of expression.*

12–c A renewed interest in classical ideas
and design gave rise to a Neoclassical style
in painting, sculpture and architecture.
Jacques-Louis David, *Oath of the Horatii*, detail
(fig.12–1).

				1851–1863	
1752		1834	1848	Walter, US Capitol	
Ben Franklin	1789	**Ingres appointed**	**Marx and Engels,**	1865	1877
invents the light-	**US Constitution**	**director of French**	***Communist***	**Abraham Lincoln**	**Edison invents**
ning conductor	**adopted**	**Academy, Rome**	***Manifesto***	**assassinated**	**phonograph**

Three Opposing Views

1770–1784	1804	1840–1865	1851	1876	1883
Jefferson,	**Napoleon crowned**	**Barry and Pugin,**	**Melville,** *Moby Dick*	**Twain,** *Tom Sawyer*	**Homer paints**
Monticello	**emperor**	**Westminster**		1876	**solitude of ocean,**
1784–1785	1814	**Palace**		**Alexander Graham**	**Maine**
David, *Oath of the*	**Goya,** *Third of May,*			**Bell invents**	
Horatii	1808			**telephone**	

strong and independent? What appears
to be the discrepancy between what
some women were actually accomplishing in Western society at the time and
the idealized vision of frail, compliant
behavior that David puts forth? In a
sense, Bonheur, both as a female artist
and in her realistic canvas, symbolizes
women's achievements, while David's
painting represents the more sedate,
socially acceptable behavior that was
expected of women.

Art

Have students decide if anything like
the *Eiffel Tower* (fig.12–a) had been
built during the Renaissance or Baroque
period. Direct them to scan through
Chapters 9, 10 and 11 for visual
reference.

• What about this structure is completely new?

• How has Alexandre-Gustave Eiffel
made his building look modern?

• What makes it appear so sleek and
have a strong vertical emphasis?

• Have students compare the use of
line in the Eiffel Tower to that in the
Renaissance architecture of the *Square
Court of the Louvre* (figs.10–c, 10–28).
Which is more restrained? Although
the structures are actually within easy
walking distance of each other in Paris,
France, how do they each evoke two
totally different eras?

Quote

After students read Gustave
Courbet's quote, ask them to contemplate what the standard of
beauty is today in American society.
Instruct them to glance through the
chapter and decide if the contemporary concept of beauty corresponds
to that of the late eighteenth and
early nineteenth centuries.

Map

Ask: "In what part of Europe did
Neoclassicism, Romanticism and
Realism primarily occur? Where had
the center of artistic activity been
in the previous Baroque and Rococo
era?"

Evaluate

Ask students if Neoclassicism and
Realism were similar in style. How
would they describe the differences
between the two as evident in David's
Neoclassical *Oath of the Horatii* and
Bonheur's Realist work *The Horse Fair*?

• Which one was more closely tied to
the observable world?

• Which style presents an idealized
view of humankind?

• Is it easier to appreciate Bonheur's
Realist painting or David's Neoclassical
piece?

• What in the works has influenced
students' decisions?

Reteach

Ask students how a woman artist
dedicated to changing the status of
females in Western society during the
late eighteenth century might have
painted the *Oath of the Horatii*. What
would have been the major difference
between her and David's interpretation?
   Have students role-play David
defending his Neoclassical painting
Oath of the Horatii as beautiful,
according to Courbet's definition in his
quote. How would David's argument
have differed from Bonheur's definition
of beauty for her Realist work *The
Horse Fair*? Which piece do students
think is more appealing and why?

Lesson 12.1

In order to bestow a regal status on its artworks, Neoclassicism evoked the ancient Greek and Roman past as well as the Renaissance. Napoleon Bonaparte encouraged the use of the cool, dignified and imposing Neoclassic style to glorify his authority and the growing strength of France.

Warm-up

Ask students to pretend that they are Napoleon Bonaparte and have conquered much of Western Europe. Would they want to celebrate their victories with commissions in the style of Antoine Watteau's *The Gamut of Love* (figs.11–41, 11–42)? Why or why not? Does this type of art seem to fit Bonaparte's personality as a mighty European leader? Share that the Neoclassical style, evident in the images throughout Lesson 12.1, reflected Napoleon's desire to be seen as an all-powerful ruler.

Objectives

Students should be able to:

Recognize the enormous power that Napoleon Bonaparte wielded and his far-reaching impact on European politics and culture.

Perceive how Classical references in Neoclassicism were meant to associate the style with prestigious ancient Greek and Roman art.

Vocabulary Definitions

allegorical Symbolic of truths or generalizations about human nature.

Teach

Criticism/Art History: Instruct students to compare David's *Oath of the Horatii* (figs.12–c, 12–1) to Gianlorenzo Bernini's *Ecstasy of Saint Theresa* (fig.11–2) and also the earlier Renaissance paintings *Battle of San Romano* (figs.9–b, 9–15) and *Christ in the House of Levi* (fig.9–45). Is David's painting closer in style to the Renaissance or later Baroque works? What earlier era did both Neoclassic and Italian Renaissance artists most admire? How do students think ancient Roman and Greek culture was viewed in the late eighteenth century? Did people admire the ancient past more than the recent Rococo

---

12.1 Neoclassicism

FROM 1775 TO 1815, the Western world was in turmoil. The American Colonies gained independence from England. France was under the dictatorship of Napoleon Bonaparte. Napoleon's fierce attacks on Europe eliminated many Baroque monarchies, dissolved the Holy Roman Empire, and almost conquered Russia and England.

Comparing himself to the Roman emperors, Napoleon preferred art that drew heavily on the Classical Roman styles. Neoclassicism became not only the dominant artistic style, but also a way of life. Furniture, dress, painting, sculpture, architecture and the crafts all relied on ancient Classicism for their motifs and forms. No-nonsense Neoclassicism was partly a reaction to the lighthearted nature of Rococo. Neoclassicism became the backbone of the academies and was the official force in art well into the nineteenth century.

In 1738, Pompeii and Herculaneum were uncovered. The discovery of artifacts from these cities, together with Napoleon's fascination with Roman history and styles, led to increased interest in Classical themes, history and design. Greek, Roman and Renaissance art was studied intensely. During the Neoclassical period, this studied aspect of art was given as much weight as individual expression.

Key Notes

- Neoclassicism arises in part from a rejection of the Rococo, but particularly from a renewed interest in Classical ideas and design.
- Napoleon Bonaparte uses the Neoclassical style to reinforce his image as all-powerful ruler.
- Neoclassicism becomes firmly embedded in the academies.

Vocabulary
allegorical

12–1 David was one of the few artists to successfully make the transition from the French monarchy to the republic to the empire.
Jacques-Louis David, *Oath of the Horatii*, 1784–1785. Oil on canvas, 11' x 14' (325 x 426 cm). The Louvre, Paris.

Jacques-Louis David
(1748–1825)
Jacques-Louis David was a man perfectly in step with the spirit of the times. He began painting under Louis XVI, but, after the king was guillotined, he embraced the Neoclassical style. He became the most important artist under Napoleon. Most other Rococo artists were unable to make this change to Neoclassicism.

David began by painting in the decorative style of Boucher, who was a distant relative. After traveling to Rome in 1775, his ideas changed. In Rome, he studied and drew the Classic sculptures with infinite detail, establishing a style that was clean, crisp and hard-edged. He would not tolerate any evidence of brushstrokes in his own work or that of his students. When he returned to Paris his *allegorical*

---

period? During Napoleon's time, people associated Classical culture with the honorable ideals of loyalty and patriotism.

Art History: Direct students to read the story that David illustrates in *Oath of the Horatii*. Which does he present as more important, love (symbolized by the forlorn women) or patriotism (represented by the stoic, arms-bearing men)? (To guide students, you might ask that if they had to choose who would be in the picture, would they prefer the stronger men or the weeping women?) Why might Napoleon, as supreme ruler, have liked this painting? As a military leader, would he have wanted people to choose love or patriotism for their country?

Criticism: Have students examine the Classical architecture David included in *Oath of the Horatii* and then find similarities in some American buildings (for example, figs.12–9 and 12–10).

- Ask the class why American architects might deliberately have alluded to the ancient past in their structures.

- Ask students if they would hark back to older styles or develop completely new ones if they were designing buildings for a new nation that was trying to establish itself as a world power?

paintings began to suggest the ideals of Classic republicanism. He used Greek and Roman subject matter to show parallels with contemporary French politics. His were among the first history paintings.

The Oath of Horatii (fig.12–1) is a huge painting that uses a Roman story to arouse passion for French unity. It is a story of conflict between love and patriotism. The Horatii brothers are chosen to defend Rome in battle against neighboring Alba. But, one of the Horatii sisters is engaged to an Alban, and a brother is married to an Alban. Yet, the three brothers take an oath on the raised swords held by their father to defend Rome. They appear rigid, manly and heroic and symbolize patriotism and loyalty. The grieving sisters on the far right embody love and sorrow. As in the Classic tradition, patriotism is the clear winner over love. This painting is a perfect example of the Neoclassical style. Every figure is painted with absolute clarity. Edges are hard and crisp. The austere figures against the plain, neutral background seem almost frozen in action on a dramatically lit stage.

After Napoleon assumed power, David painted some mammoth canvases glorifying the little emperor. *Napoleon in His Study* (fig.12–2) shows the leader alone. The details are meant to reveal aspects of his personality to the French people. The burnt-down candle and the clock set at 4:13 a.m. suggest that the emperor had been working all night in the service of the country. The figure is as solid and immobile as a statue. The lighting is sharply focused. Together Napoleon and David helped define the Neoclassic style.

12–2 This pose became a model for official portraits in Western art and many men's portraits show them in this stance although without Napolean's trademark hand-in-his-vest.
Jacques-Louis David, *Napoleon in His Study*, 1812. Oil on canvas, 80 1/4" x 49 1/4" (204 x 125 cm). National Gallery of Art, Washington, D.C., Samuel H. Kress Collection.

Contextual Information

Ingres

Ingres went to Rome because he did not approve of Napoleon and the changes he made to proclaim himself emperor. The painter returned to France after Napoleon died.

Ingres accepted the Greek philosophy of art imitating nature, but he thought that artists should organize nature in their paintings, leaving out what does not contribute to an orderly composition.

• Ingres was a great admirer of Raphael. Have students compare the *School of Athens* (fig.9–30) to the *Apotheosis of Homer* (fig.12–6).

History Painting

In 1745, the French government reinstated history painting as the highest rank of painting and set official fees so that artists received much more money for this type of work than for portraits. Even the curriculum at the Royal School was changed to provide art students with more ancient history classes. Within a few years, the "Grecian taste" became the accepted style all over Europe. Furniture, jewelry, fashions, hairstyles and fabrics were designed in the Greek style.

12–3 Note the difference between the hands of the figure in this study and the finished painting. How have they changed? Can you spot any other adjustments that the artist has made?
Jean-Auguste-Dominique Ingres, *Louis Bertin*, 1832. Pencil drawing, 46" x 37 1/2" (116.7 x 95.3 cm). The Louvre, Paris.

12–4 Ingres is noted for his crisp polished portraits which have an almost photographic quality.
Jean-Auguste-Dominique Ingres, *Louis Bertin*, 1832. Oil on canvas, 46" x 37 1/2" (117 x 95 cm). The Louvre, Paris.

Jean-Auguste-Dominique Ingres

(1780–1867)

David's best pupil and primary spokesperson for Neoclassicism and its rigid rules was Jean-Auguste-Dominique Ingres. A child prodigy, Ingres entered art school at eleven and began studying with David at seventeen. Following David's instruction, he never allowed his brushwork to show. However, his style was much softer and more sensitive to texture and flesh than David's style. Ingres considered himself a historical painter, yet most of his income came from his nude paintings and cool, Classic portraits. He was a marvelous draftsman. He drew his portraits first before he painted them. An excellent example of this process can be seen in Ingres' pencil drawing and finished painting of *Louis Bertin* (figs.12–3, 12–4).

In the Classic tradition, Ingres would draw figures in the nude to make absolutely sure all the proportions were correct. Then, he would add the clothing in intricate detail. *Scipio and His Son with the Envoys of Antiochus* (fig.12–5) is a pencil drawing of small size, but immense ability. Some places are shaded to appear almost finished, while other areas are barely outlined. The poses, attitudes and drawing technique are handled masterfully.

Ingres' cool, undramatic Classicism can be seen in the huge *Apotheosis of Homer* (fig.12–6).

1800
Canton, China, is most populous city in world

World Cultural Timeline

1811
Ruler Muhammad Ali modernizes Egypt by improving irrigation and establishing industry

1815
Mt. Tambora on Sumbawa in Indonesia erupts. Volcanic dust in the atmosphere lowers temperatures worldwide

1818
Katsushika Hokusai, Japanese landscape painter, at height of his creativity

Multicultural Connection

Hokusai

As seen in Chapter 11, page 348, Ukiyo-e prints began to be produced in the late seventeenth century, after Japan had entered a period of renewed stability. Katsushika Hokusai (1760–1849) is considered one of the greatest Japanese printmakers of this school. Hokusai lived most of his life in Edo (Tokyo), studied woodblock engraving at an early age, and changed his name and residence more than thirty times. Although Hokusai used traditional Japanese printmaking styles, he incorporated his unique imagination and emotional values into his work. Hokusai became the first Japanese printmaker to focus on landscapes. His most celebrated works are the thirty-six views of Mount Fuji (1823–1831), which show Japan's most famous natural feature from various viewpoints and in various weather conditions. Many nineteenth-century painters, such as Edgar Degas, Henri de Toulouse-Lautrec and Paul Gauguin, were influenced by the work of Katsushika Hokusai.

• Have students compare and discuss landscape paintings from other cultures of this period. (For an additional image by Hokusai see page 101, fig.4–41.)

• Mount Fuji, a volcano in Japan, appears in many works by Hokusai and other Japanese artists. Ask students why they think this image plays such an important part in Japanese art.

In front of an Ionic temple, the blind poet is crowned by the Muse of epic poetry. The *Iliad* is symbolized by the sword held by one of the female figures below him. The *Odyssey* is symbolized by the rudder held by the other female figure. Ingres included figures he considered Classical geniuses from various periods, such as Phidias, Pindar, Aeschylus and Apelles; Raphael, Leonardo, Fra Angelico and Poussin; Shakespeare and Molière. Ingres' use of famous figures in a Classic setting is similar to Raphael's work in *The School of Athens* (fig.9–30).

12–5 Ingres' drawings have a very sculptural effect, but retain their life and do not become stiff.
Jean-Auguste-Dominique Ingres, *Scipio and His Son with Envoys of Antiochus*, 1827. Pencil on paper, 9 1/2" x 14 1/2" (24 x 37 cm). Norton Simon Art Foundation, Pasadena, California.

12–6 An apotheosis is the glorification of an individual or an ideal.
Jean-Auguste-Dominique Ingres, *Apotheosis of Homer*, 1827. Oil on canvas, 12 1/2' x 16 4/5' (386 x 514 cm). The Louvre, Paris.

Higher-Order Thinking Skills

Neoclassical artists did drawings such as *Scipio and His Son with Envoys of Antiochus* (fig.12–5) to work out every detail of their paintings prior to starting the actual painting. Ask the class whether such detailed preparation helps to create a better painting or inhibits creativity and expressiveness. If students were going to commission a painting, which way would they want their artists to work? Why?

Contextual Information

Vigée-Lebrun

Elizabeth Vigée-Lebrun was one of the most prominent and highly paid portraitists of her time. Her personal friendship with the Queen, Marie Antoinette, was an important factor in her gaining admittance to the Academy. In fact, formal rules technically barred Vigée-Lebrun from admission because she was married to an art dealer (Jean Baptiste Pierre Lebrun).

At the time she applied, it was more acceptable for a woman to enter the Academy as a portraitist or as a pastel painter. Vigée-Lebrun desired to be admitted as a history painter, the most prestigious category. She provided a history painting as her acceptance piece. Although the category into which she was accepted was never actually stipulated, it is assumed that because the piece was accepted, the Academy tacitly agreed to her desired classification.

Vigée-Lebrun's continued success could be related to advice given her by the French artist Joseph Vernet when she was still a teenager. She says in her memoirs that he told her not to follow any particular style or school of painting, but to study only old Italian and Flemish paintings and, most of all, to draw from nature, "the greatest teacher."

Houdon

Houdon, like David, managed to escape imprisonment during the French Revolution. Admired by leading thinkers and politicians of the period in France, he sculpted Voltaire, Rousseau, Diderot and Napoleon. In 1785 he came to the United States to sculpt George Washington.

Elizabeth Vigée-Lebrun

(1755–1842)

One of the most successful of all women painters, Elizabeth Vigée-Lebrun studied first with her father. She became an excellent portrait painter before she was twenty. At twenty-four, she was called to Versailles to paint Marie Antoinette. She stayed to become Painter to the Queen, and was elected to the Academy in 1783.

When the Revolution broke out, she went to Italy, Vienna, Prague, Dresden, Moscow and London before returning to Paris. Her career was a series of international triumphs; she received commissions everywhere she went. She was constantly busy during her long life. Over eight hundred paintings have been identified as her work.

Her *Mme. de Stael as Corinn Playing a Lyre* (fig.12–7) was painted in 1789. It is typical of a period when she was using landscapes as backgrounds for her sitters. Vigée-Lebrun helped establish the simple, high-waisted dresses of the Empire style shown here, which replaced the elaborate gowns of the old monarchy. David was the instigator of this Classic style, but Vigée-Lebrun's portraits of prominent people wearing such dresses helped make the new style popular throughout Europe.

12–7 The artist was unusual for being both a highly successful woman artist and for successfully surviving the political turmoil of the French Revolution.
Elizabeth Vigée-Lebrun, *Mme. de Stael as Corinn Playing a Lyre*, 1789. Musée d'Art et d'Histoire, Geneva.

The Age of Enlightenment

Radical changes in art, politics and society were made between 1715 and 1789. This period is known as the Age of Enlightenment, when the scientific knowledge of Newton and social theories of Locke and Diderot were available to anyone who could read.

Vigée-Lebrun's coloring was softer than that of David and Ingres and her poses more inventive. She was not in sympathy with Napoleon and his Empire. Nor did she follow David and Ingres and their dogmatic approaches to painting. However, her beautifully drawn and painted portraits were typical of artists at the turn of the century. She was more successful than most in working through the turmoil of the times.

Sculpture

Jean Antoine Houdon

(1741–1828)

Sculpture had been so important in ancient Greece and Rome that it would seem logical for sculpture to be as important to the Neoclassic movement, but such was not the case. The best of several sculptors working during the turmoil in France was Jean Antoine Houdon. He started his work during the reign of Louis XIV. He managed to adjust to the changing political philosophies and remain unscathed.

Although Napoleon was not an admirer of Houdon, his work was greatly honored by the philosophers Voltaire and Rousseau. In fact, Houdon made excellent likenesses of each. His work is anatomically accurate. At the same time, he was able to capture the personality of the sitter. In France, he sculpted Benjamin Franklin and Thomas Jefferson. Through them, he was invited to the new country, the United States. In 1785, he carved the first president, George Washington, in marble.

Houdon's brilliant realism can be seen in his bust of Benjamin

Franklin (fig.12–8). Although the drapery has Classic overtones, the sparkle of Franklin's wit is superbly expressed in both eyes and mouth. Technically perfect, Houdon's work is charged with life and is not as somber as many Roman sculptures. His sculpture seems about ready to spring to life.

12–8 Houdon did an extensive series of sculptures of America's important early statesmen.
Jean Antoine Houdon, *Bust of Benjamin Franklin.* 1780. Marble, 24" x 24" (61 x 61 cm). The Nelson-Atkins Museum of Art, Kansas City, Missouri. Purchase: Nelson Trust, 38–8.

Contextual Information

Monticello

Jefferson's *Monticello* (fig.12–9) shows Palladio's influence, but Jefferson added his own inventions, such as doors that open as they are approached. Monticello suggested the Greek revival style that was being imitated in America. The Doric order, seen in the columns at Monticello, was thought to express Classical Greek architecture.

12–9 Jefferson's home became the basic example of the American Georgian style.
Thomas Jefferson. *Monticello*, 1770–1784. Charlottesville, Virginia.

with a flat dome over the central space. Its portico and white-painted Doric columns and trim, which stand out from the red brick surface, became characteristic of an American style called Georgian. The noble simplicity of such architecture appealed to America's growing middle classes.

Neoclassicism and its influence are evident in the *United States Capitol* (fig.12–10). The Capitol was begun as a Georgian structure and enlarged by Benjamin Latrobe (1764–1820). It was completed as a massive, super-scale structure when Thomas Walter added the cast-iron dome in 1863. Considering the many architects who worked on it, the building has a remarkable feeling of unity. The dome is raised on a high, columned drum. It has an internal diameter of slightly over 98 feet and rises 220 feet above the floor.

In Berlin, the columned *Brandenburg Gate* (fig.12–11), topped with a four-horse Roman chariot, was built by Karl Langhans (1781–1869) along the lines of some Greek gateways. The gate later stood between East and West Berlin as a symbol of a divided city, from the end of World War II until 1989, when the Berlin Wall was torn down. The Brandenburg Gate is now a symbol of unification as it straddles one of the major avenues that runs through Berlin.

Paris has many fine examples of Neoclassic architecture, but none is better than the *Church of the Madeleine* (fig.12–12), designed by Pierre Vignon (1763–1828). The colossal structure is designed as a Roman Corinthian temple. It took over thirty-five years to complete. The exterior follows Classic ideas completely, but the interior was altered to allow light and windows.

12–10 Each level of the building repeats some characteristics of the prior level, but with alterations that create a distinctive look.
Thomas U. Walter. *United States Capitol*, 1851–1863. Washington, DC.

Architecture

Baroque and Rococo architecture was exuberant. Neoclassic architects replaced the overworked surfaces of Rococo palaces and churches with Classic simplicity and balance. Twisting and curling lines were replaced by straight ones. Frills were eliminated almost completely. Not only Napoleon's France, but all the Continent and even America were ready for a change from Baroque flamboyance to Neoclassic refinement and order.

Besides being one of our early presidents and the author of the Declaration of Independence, Thomas Jefferson (1743–1826) was also an architect. He designed his own home at *Monticello* (fig.12–9) and the first buildings at the University of Virginia at Charlottesville. He was influenced by the Italian architect, Palladio, and the Roman structures he had seen in France. Monticello is a two-story structure built along Palladian lines

1819
Simon Bolívar defeats Spanish and enters Bogotá, Colombia

World Cultural Timeline

1820	1828	1850
The Hindu College founded, Calcutta, India	***The Cherokee Phoenix*, a weekly newspaper, begins its seven-year run**	**The Navajo learn silversmithing from the Mexicans**

ᏌᏇᎡᎩ ᎡᏣᎠ, ᏚᎢᎡᎡᎩ ᎤᎢᏞᏕ Ꭴ°-
ᏫᏛ ᎦᎠᎩ ᎧᎬᎡᎠᎬ ᎤᏋᎯᏓᎠ, ᎩᎦ
ᎦᎠᎩ ᏏᎴᎠᎬᏘᎡᏋ ᎤᎦᎡᎠᎡᎵᏂ ᏏᏐ

Multicultural Connection

Navajo Silversmithing

The Navajo were the first southwestern Native Americans to work silver in the late 1850s. Navajo silversmiths learned the art of making jewelry from Mexicans who came up the Rio Grande valley from the south. At that time, the Navajo traded their horses to Mexican silversmiths for silver ornaments and thereby became strongly influenced by Mexican designs, many of which originated in Spain.

Navajo jewelry is characterized by large turquoise stones and heavy metalwork. It is believed that turquoise has special spiritual properties. The Navajo are best known for their squash-blossom necklaces, which were inspired by an ornament on the seams of trousers worn by Spaniards. Other designs have been adapted from those of the Plains Indians. These include concha belts, which the Navajo fashioned after those worn by enemy tribesmen on the Great Plains.

Today, the art of silversmithing is still practiced, often with the same tools the Navajo once used. Silver jewelry is not only valued for its beauty and status, but also for the economic stability it provides. See page 141, fig. 4–110 for an example of Navajo silverwork.)

• Have students identify other cultures they have studied that valued jewelry ornamentation as a form of status.

12–11 Can you name at least three Classical architectural elements that are used on this monument?
Karl Langhans. *Brandenburg Gate*, 1788–1791. Berlin.

12–12 French Neoclassical architecture took a monumental turn. Some of the buildings designed were so huge they could not be built with existing technology!
Pierre Vignon. *Church of the Madeleine*, 1806–1843. Paris.

12–13 What Classical precedents do you know for this ceremonial arch?
J. F. Chalgrin. *Arc de Triomphe de l'Etoile*, 1806–1836. Paris.

The *Arc de Triomphe de l'Etoile* (Arch of Triumph of the Star) in Paris was one of Napoleon's numerous monuments (fig.12–13). Like Imperial Rome's triumphal arches, this ponderous structure by J. F. Chalgrin (1739–1811) towers over surrounding structures. Nearly a dozen boulevards lead into the huge circular area containing the arch. The structure contains the eternal flame that honors France's unknown soldiers, as well as a list of the campaigns and victories of Napoleon.

From Leningrad to Madrid, from Copenhagen to Athens, builders used the columns, arches, domes, pediments, simplicity, order and balance of Classic architecture to create impressive Neoclassic cityscapes.

Lesson 12.1 Review

1 What was the name of the official art style when Napoleon was in power?
2 Name two reasons artists became so interested in creating art that was reminiscent of ancient Rome during the late eighteenth and nineteenth centuries.
3 Who became the leading French artist during the French Revolution?
4 How was Ingres' painting style different from his teacher David's style.

5 Name the woman artist who was Marie Antoinette's principal portrait painter.
6 Name some of the buildings designed by Thomas Jefferson.
7 What style of art influenced the design of the United States Capitol?
8 List three early leaders of the United States that Houdon sculpted.

Lesson 12.2

Romantic artists rebelled against the dictates and conventions of Neoclassicism and instead built a style that relied heavily on intense emotion and individuality.

Warm-up

Ask students to define what the word *romantic* means to them. What emotions and actions do they associate with the term? Have them characterize someone who is the opposite of romantic. Challenge them to apply these qualities to the images in the chapter opener.

Objectives

Students should be able to:

Understand how Romantic artists, exasperated with the restrictions and maxims of Neoclassicism, developed an emotional style based on tales of the Middles Ages, Africa and the Orient.

Describe how color, emotion and passion were key to Romantic art.

Articulate Romanticism's expansion into Western Europe.

Vocabulary Definitions

nonrepresentational art See *nonobjective art.*

nonobjective art Art that has no recognizable subject matter such as trees, flowers or people. The actual subject matter might be color or the composition of the work itself.

12.2 Romanticism

THE NEOCLASSIC STYLE, begun as a protest against the Rococo style of the eighteenth-century aristocracy, was firmly entrenched in Europe. Neoclassic traditions were taught at the Paris and London academies. It did not look as if anything could budge Neoclassicism. However, some artists had had quite enough of working within the Classic restrictions of form and proportion. Their rebellious feelings erupted into a full-blown movement called Romanticism.

The name came from a widespread revival of interest in medieval stories like *King Arthur and the Knights of the Round Table* and *The Search for the Holy Grail*. These stories about great adventures and heroism were called romances and were written in French. Instead of focusing on ancient Greece and Rome as the source of all good design, the Romanticists explored the Middle Ages. They were also fascinated by Africa and the Orient. While Neoclassic painters had revered Raphael, Poussin and the ancient Romans, Romanticists admired Rubens and Rembrandt. It was individualism versus the system; emotionalism versus intellectualism; and rebellion against the academies.

Color, emotion, content and passion became key ideas in Romantic painting. They replaced the Neoclassic stress on line, intellect, form and judgment. The new emotionalism generated excitement in the arts throughout Europe. All artistic endeavor was affected by it. Romantic poets such as Wordsworth and Keats explored a new freedom in writing. In music, Romanticism was championed by Beethoven and Schubert, and Italian tragic-opera flourished.

Key Notes

- Romanticism is born as a reaction against the restrictions of Neoclassicism.
- The new style emphasizes emotion and individualism.
- Romanticism ignites excitement throughout Europe.

Vocabulary

nonrepresentational

Special Feature

Francisco Goya

(1746–1828)

No painter worked in a style farther from Neoclassical ideals than Francisco Goya of Spain. He visited Italy, but remained unimpressed by the Classic and Renaissance masterpieces. He had no time for the restrictions that David imposed on artists. In 1786, Goya was appointed painter to King Charles IV of Spain and became responsible for the official portraits of the royal family. After a severe illness in 1792, he became totally deaf. Goya bought a home outside Madrid, known as La Quinta del Sordo ("The House of the Deaf Man"). He appears to have been an isolated, pessimistic man, but he is without doubt the genius of Romantic painting and printmaking.

12–15 A clue to the meaning of this image lies in the name Los Caprichos, Spanish for caprices, eccentricities, whims or freakishness.
Francisco Goya, *The Sleep of Reason Produces Monsters*, from *Los Caprichos* (Plate 43), c. 1794–1799. Etching and aquatint, 5" x 8" (12.7 x 20.3 cm). The Hispanic Society of America, New York.

Teach

Criticism: Instruct students to study Francisco Goya's *Third of May, 1808* (fig.12–14) and describe the feelings of the man in the white shirt, one of the soldiers and a horrified onlooker.

- Is it easier to imagine what is going on in their hearts and minds than it is for those figures in David's *Oath of the Horatii* (figs.12–c, 12–1)?

- Have students compare the artists' use of color and composition.

- Ask which painting moves them most immediately. How would they characterize the difference between the way Neoclassic and Romantic artists portray emotions?

Art History: Have students read the stories behind David's *Oath of the Horatii* on page 383 and Goya's *Third of May, 1808* on page 391.

- What is the difference in the reason David painted his work (to stir up patriotism and loyalty among French citizens) and Goya's goals (as social protest about the inhumanity of human beings to one another).

- How does David's use of an ancient story as an allegory and Goya's description of a recent atrocity affect each painting's ability to accomplish its creator's aim?

Higher-Order Thinking Skills

Have students contrast Goya's treatment of the soldiers to that of the peasants. Ask whether work like this, which describes violent events, is comparable to contemporary news coverage. Does it help people to understand such events or does it evoke emotional responses? Is dealing with such events a good path for an artist to take?

One of Goya's most powerful and emotional works is the monumental *Third of May, 1808* (fig.12–14). It shows the slaughtering of Spanish rebels by French soldiers. Done in 1814, just after the French left the country, Goya's dramatic work could be termed a "social protest" painting. Goya painted the incredible inhumanity of human beings toward each other. It is not at all allegorical, like the Neoclassic paintings. Instead, it is an emotional portrayal of the event as the artist remembered it. Goya captured its ferocity and gave it a startling sense of immediacy. The insistence on depicting real emotions, even those from our darker side, is a particularly Romantic characteristic. Compare the brushstrokes, edges of color,

emotional feeling and sense of action with David's *The Oath of the Horatii.* The differences between Neoclassic and Romantic painting are readily apparent.

Goya could not always follow his internal dictates and paint what he wanted. As the royal portraitist, he had to paint the royal family. But, here, the Romantic impulse is also strongly evident. Although he paints them in very royal poses, he somehow manages to give us a good idea of what they were really like.

Goya also made several series of brilliant etchings on a variety of subjects such as war, folklore, the follies of society (fig.12–15) and bullfights. His range of expression was unmatched in his time. His powerful statements are awesome to behold.

12–14 How did Goya want you to respond to this painting?
Francisco Goya, *Third of May, 1808*, 1814. Oil on canvas, 8' 9" x 13 1/4" (2.7 x 4.1 m). Prado Museum, Madrid.

Evaluate

Ask students what they think Goya meant by his title *The Sleep of Reason Produces Monsters* (fig.12–15). How do his words align him with Romantic rather than Neoclassical artists? Which movement believed in the supremacy of the human intellect?

Reteach

Have students consider if the personality of Francisco Goya would have been similar to or different from that of Jacques-Louis David. Ask what in the artistic styles supports their conclusions.

• Ask students if they would rather live in the type of world portrayed by David or that of Goya. Why are they drawn either to David's calm or to Goya's charged emotional view? Have them discuss their decision.

12–16 Géricault was influenced by Michelangelo. Where do you see that influence in this painting? Theodore Géricault, *Raft of the "Medusa"*, 1818–1819. Oil on canvas, 16' 1" x 23' 6" (4.9 x 7.2 m). The Louvre, Paris.

Contextual Information

Géricault

Géricault's most celebrated work is the *Raft of the Medusa*. With this painting, French Romanticism was launched and Géricault claimed his place as the founder of that movement in France. It is interesting to note that although Géricault is viewed as an integral part of nineteenth-century French painting, he exhibited no more than three works in his lifetime.

Theodore Géricault

(1791–1824)

The lifestyle of Theodore Géricault was pure Romanticism. He had little concern for his personal safety, loved to travel, always stood up for the less fortunate, and dedicated himself to an emotional life. He was successful in getting a painting exhibited in the Salon of the Academy when only twenty-one, a high honor. He lived and worked in Rome for several years. There he was influenced only by Michelangelo's muscular and dynamic figures and not his Classical surroundings.

When he returned to Paris, he painted his only large canvas, *Raft of the "Medusa"* (fig.12–16). It clearly shows Michelangelo's influence and Géricault's Romantic spirit. A government ship, the *Medusa*, was wrecked on the way from France to Senegal in 1816. The captain abandoned ship first, along with his crew. The 149 passengers were crowded onto a raft to be towed by the lifeboat. The raft was eventually cut adrift. After suffering extreme starvation and thirst, only fifteen survivors made it to the African coast. It was a national scandal that shook the entire country.

Géricault, always interested in humanity's struggle with nature, jumped into the subject with great enthusiasm. He interviewed the survivors, read the newspaper accounts, and made sketches and paintings of corpses and bodies at the morgue. He even had himself lashed to the mast of a small ship in a storm so he could feel the movement of the swells and the wind. Everything was done to make the painting realistic and authentic, but Géricault's Romantic treatment took him beyond realism. *Raft of the Medusa* is built around two pyramids, one of dead, dying and tragic figures and the other of hope and struggle. (Later painters would reject such an obvious attempt at organization as being too Classical and orderly.) Atop the second pyramid, several men wave clothing, trying to signal a distant ship so small and far away it can barely be seen. But, the gunboat *Argos* finally came to the rescue. Storm clouds and high seas add to the feeling of futility and constant hope in France's first great Romantic painting. Today, Géricault is known as the founder of Romanticism in France.

1851
Australian gold rush

World Cultural Timeline

1853
First railway and telegraph lines in India

1854
International trade brings Japanese prints to worldwide audience

1857
First universities founded in India

Cooperative Learning

Review with the class Géricault's *Raft of the Medusa* (fig.12–16). Have students find a newspaper article that they feel would be effective as the subject of a painting and then work in pencil, paint, collage or other media to recreate the event. Allow the class to use the walls in the hall or bulletin-board space to work out how the individual works could most effectively be displayed together to enhance their artistic message and emphasize their narrative content. Students will have to work together to hear each other out and justify their choices. Take pictures of the final display and have students write reviews of the exhibit. This can be done casually within the classroom or as a major project.

Eugene Delacroix

(1798–1863)

After Géricault's untimely death, leadership of the Romantic movement passed on to Eugene Delacroix. He and Ingres were exact contemporaries and the leaders in their separate movements. He produced thousands of paintings, sketches and watercolors.

Liberty Leading the People (fig.12–17) was inspired by the 1830 insurrection in Paris. The allegorical figure of Liberty, holding a tricolored French flag, is leading the revolutionaries over the street barricades in Paris. While he glorifies the cause of the victorious revolt, he also shows the horror and violence of fighting. In keeping with his theatrical feelings, he placed two dead figures in the foreground and blended allegory with reality. The huge painting was later purchased by the French government.

Two years after showing the painting, Delacroix made a trip to Spain and Morocco that changed his life. He experienced a way of life so different that he used the subject matter from this trip for many years. He was the first major painter in modern times to visit the Islamic world. He returned to Paris with a trunk of sketches and a head full of exotic memories. He painted a series of tiger and lion hunts from sketches made of caged animals. They swirl with incredible activity and lush color.

Compare *The Lion Hunt* (fig.12–18) with Rubens' painting of a similar subject to see why the Romantic artists admired his work. Raging animals, frightened horses and furious hunters are knotted together in an interwoven composition. The eye travels in and out as it follows the curves and counter-curves of men and beasts. Only the triangular format lends solidity to the composition and keeps the wild design under control. The slashing brushstrokes, intense colors and value contrasts are fitting for such Romantic subject matter. They point the way directly into the twentieth century.

Delacroix used photography to make studies of some subjects. He became expert at using the newly invented cameras. He was also the subject for many photographs taken by his friends, who were among the world's first photographers.

12–18 How has the artist organized his composition?
Eugene Delacroix, *The Lion Hunt*, 1861. Oil on canvas, 30" x 38 1/2" (76 x 98 cm). The Art Institute of Chicago, Potter Palmer Collection, 1922.

12–17 Delacroix has placed his self-portrait within the crowd. He is the businessman with the gun.
Eugene Delacroix, *Liberty Leading the People*, 1830. Oil on canvas, about 8' 6" x 10' 8" (259 x 324 cm). The Louvre, Paris.

Higher-Order Thinking Skills

1 The personification of ideas and ideals dates back to ancient times. Ask if Delacroix' Liberty is a goddess. What characteristics does he want the viewer to attribute to her?

2 Ingres made exacting drawings before painting; Delacroix painted directly on the canvas with no preliminary sketches. The two artists were rivals, and Parisian art critics liked to compare the two very different painters to start controversy. Have students find similarities and differences between Ingres' *Apotheosis of Homer* (fig.12–6) and Delacroix' *Liberty Leading the People* (fig.12–17).

Performing Arts Connection

Romantic Ballet: Dances for the Heart

In the eighteenth century, ballet steps were similar to those of social ballroom dancing. However, as performers gained greater skill, the gulf between amateurs and professionals widened as more and more virtuosic movement was designed. Female dancers reigned supreme in the mysterious and exotic story lines of the Romantic ballets. To enhance their sylphlike characters, ballerinas wore gauzy, flowing costumes and danced on their toes. Evocative music, gas lighting and curtains, which separated the staged illusion from the audience, also increased the ethereal atmosphere.

• Beginning in the mid-seventeenth century, ballet was performed on a raised proscenium stage. Have students discuss how the audience's location in front of and slightly below the dancers might have affected changes in choreography from earlier court dancing, which had been viewed from above and in the round? Have volunteers devise a brief movement sequence for others to observe from these two vantage points. Have the class compare the results.

Contextual Information

Concurrent Styles

Despite the choice of many artists to paint in a Romantic style, art academies in England and France were committed to Classical themes, figures and historical scenes. However, some English artists rejected that approach and painted scenes of untamed nature and calm, atmospheric landscapes.

Turner

Turner became a wealthy man largely through his mass-produced etchings. His experimental, expressive canvases were begun after he had established a clientele among the new industrialists at his own gallery in London. (See Chapter 2, fig.2–60 for another example of Turner's work in oil.)

Constable

Constable's *The Hay Wain* (fig.12–19) was a great success in Paris in 1824. His great talent was the ability to convey the atmosphere of a scene, and, in fact, he studied meteorology in order to better understand climate and weather. Constable portrayed shifting clouds, changing light and adjustments in nature that occur with changes in the time of day, weather or the seasons.

• Ask students to describe the time of day and the season depicted in *The Hay Wain.*

John Constable

(1776–1837)

John Constable was among the first painters to paint outdoors. He made dozens of quick studies on paper. He tried to match, as closely as possible, oil colors with those of nature. He loved the English landscape and never left England to find subject matter. He once said: "… water escaping from mill dams, willows, old rotten planks, slimy posts and brickwork—I love such things." In *The Hay Wain* (fig.12–19), he shows his skill in painting huge trees, flat fields, the stream and clouds. A red hay wagon is pulled through the Stour River near a typical English farmhouse.

Constable was the first artist to paint water with such sparkling clarity and depth of shadow. He achieved this effect by adding touches of white to the canvas. While critics liked his painting generally, they often made fun of his added whites and even called them "Constable's snow." This criticism, based on a lack of knowledge of what the artist was trying to do, was the beginning of a rift between artists and the public.

12–20 Some of this painting was done with a palette knife and not a brush. John Constable, *Stoke-by-Nayland*, 1836. Oil on canvas, 50 1/2" x 66 1/2" (126 x 169 cm). The Art Institute of Chicago, Mr. and Mrs. W. W. Kimball Collection. 1922.

12–19 An artist's style often changes over time. Compare this painting to *Stoke-by-Nayland*. John Constable, *The Hay Wain*, 1821. Oil on canvas, 50 3/4" x 72 3/4" (129 x 185 cm). The National Gallery, London.

The Hay Wain was one of six huge paintings that Constable did of subjects close to his home. They were the first landscapes done in a size normally used for important historical subjects. His figures are small and belong to the environment.

In his later years, Constable abandoned his careful depiction of nature. He began to paint with a great vibrancy and force. *Stoke-by-Nayland* (fig.12–20) is a large studio painting with the immediacy and verve of an outdoor sketch. The colors are applied freely. The artist even mixed and spread some of them right on the canvas with his flexible palette knife. The loose and rapid strokes and the elimination of detail create a spontaneous effect. Since the critics could not understand the white flecks of light in *The Hay Wain*, imagine how they felt about the wildness of this painting. The visual elements are similar in these two works, but *Stoke-by-Nayland* shows the drastic change in Constable's technique.

12–21 The artist spent much of his early career exploring the effects of natural light.
Joseph Mallord Turner, *Sun Rising Through Vapour: Fisherman Cleaning and Selling Fish*, 1807. Oil on canvas, 52 3/4" x 70 1/5" (134 x 179 cm). The National Gallery, London.

Joseph Mallord William Turner

(1775–1851)

While Constable developed two styles, Turner developed three or more. Working in the traditional English landscape style, Turner was accepted into the Royal Academy at only twenty-four, in 1799. His contemporary, Constable, was not admitted until 1829. Turner's earliest works were all in watercolor, a medium he used all his life. He produced about 19,000 watercolor paintings. He made sketching and watercolor painting trips all over Europe. The paintings were set against backdrops of brilliantly colored, high-keyed skies of mist, sunset and sunrise. *Sun Rising Through Vapour* (fig.12–21) clearly shows Turner's interest in the effects of light.

His later works are incredible compositions of swirling color and light. Turner enjoyed painting the pure movement of masses of color without representational meaning

12–22 What are the subjects of this work?
Joseph Mallord William Turner, *Snow Storm: Steam-Boat off a Harbor's Mouth*, 1824. Oil on canvas, 36" x 48" (91 x 122 cm). Tate Gallery, London.

(**nonrepresentational**), although he usually had some subject in mind. Study *Snow Storm: Steam-Boat off a Harbor's Mouth* (fig.12–22) first without looking for a subject. Just enjoy the swirling fog, steam, color, water and movement. Violent action is achieved without portraying people or things. The colors and values swirl in a vortex that eventually centers on the mast of a ship. No one at that time knew anything

of nonrepresentational painting, so Turner added the representation of a ship. However, the painting would be just as strong without it. Color and movement are the real subject. His work of this period anticipates the Impressionist movement. When Claude Monet spent time in London in 1870, the work of Turner had a profound impact on him and, through him, on the rest of the Impressionists.

Contextual Information

Cole

Throughout his life Cole walked through forests and fields with his notebook, sketching and writing verses. He said: "To walk with nature as a poet is the necessary condition of a perfect artist."

Popular Engravings

Paintings were too expensive for most people, but many artists, like Bingham and Audubon, found that their popularity and income increased when they sold engravings of their paintings. Currier and Ives also printed copies of paintings during this period.

Thomas Cole

(1801–1848)

In America, Thomas Cole was the leader of a group of painters in New York and New England called the Hudson River School. They painted a landscape that would soon vanish as the population expanded. Thomas Cole was born in England and came to America at seventeen. He returned to England to study painting and came back to America to paint. Many of his paintings depicted Classic ruins, but most, such as *View on the Catskill, Early Autumn* (fig.12–23), were painted in the studio from a series of sketches of the countryside. Like his English contemporaries, he added small figures (fig.12–24) that seem to enhance the grandeur and immensity of the landscape. To Cole, rustic beauty and ideal settings were the essence of America. His Romantic approach was adopted by his fellow artists. Other men in the group, led by an adventuresome spirit, soon left New England for the Rockies and even South America.

12–23 Cole and other Americans tried to portray both the uniqueness of the American wild landscape and the civilization of its settled land.
Thomas Cole, *View on the Catskill, Early Autumn*, 1837. Oil on canvas, 39" x 63" (99 x 160 cm). The Metropolitan Museum of Art, New York, gift in memory of Jonathan Sturges by his children, 1895.

12–24 Compare the use of figures in this painting with the figures Constable added to his landscapes. How are they similar?
Thomas Cole, *View on the Catskill, Early Autumn*, detail.

Multicultural Connection

Native Americans in American Landscape Painting

Cole's wild landscapes of the East would soon become spoiled by the influx of inhabitants. By the late 1820s, western New York was no longer a wilderness. The opening of the Erie Canal in 1825 had brought increasing commerce and a flood of tourists to the area of Niagara Falls. By this time, the area was also devoid of any Native American encampments. Cole, a romantic interpreter of the American landscape, made sketches of Niagara Falls in the spring of 1829, just before leaving for Europe. His painting, *Distant View of Niagara Falls*, resulted. In it, he suppressed any evidence of commercial development in this area. In an attempt to portray the rustic beauty and ideal setting of America, Cole inserted two Indians on a foreground ledge. It wasn't until the historical paintings of the early nineteenth century that Indians were portrayed as savages.

• Have students research and analyze other paintings of this period in which images of Native Americans appear.

George Caleb Bingham

(1811–1879)

While Cole was content to work in his beautiful New England, George Caleb Bingham followed the American dream to the West. Even though he studied painting in Germany, he grew up by the Missouri River. Many of his paintings are based on events he saw happen there. The quiet moments and genial activity of pioneering, not the violence and hardship, are what set Bingham's brush in motion. Politicians asking for votes, Daniel Boone leading a band of pioneers, and the boat people of the rivers were his favorite subjects. In *Fur Traders Descending the Missouri* (fig.12–25), Bingham eliminates the dangers of this kind of life. He concentrates on the romance of drifting down a huge, quiet river in the early morning mist. The boat is loaded with a bale of furs for the market in St. Louis. The scene is idealized enough to make most viewers desire such work. A small black fox sits in the prow of the dugout canoe and visually balances the elegant composition. Bingham painted a Romanticist's view of the daily life of ordinary people who were part of the westward expansion. Bingham became a politician in later life and gave up most of his painting activity.

Other Americans worked with images of America in their own terms. John James Audubon (1788–1851), for instance, painted the animals and birds of America. His work was made into colored engravings that became very popular in English homes. America was beginning to develop its own painting tradition.

12–25 Compare this American genre scene to a European one such as Bruegel's *Return of the Hunters* (fig.10–13).
George Caleb Bingham, *Fur Traders Descending the Missouri*, 1845. Oil on canvas, 29 1/4" x 36 1/4" (74 x 92 cm). The Metropolitan Museum of Art, New York, Morris K. Jesup Fund, 1933.

Higher-Order Thinking Skills

Cole painted the New England landscape as an allegory for his young country. Many of his paintings were seen in Europe and were taken as the truth about what America was like. Ask the class what they think Cole is saying about America. If European tourists came to America after seeing his paintings, would they have found what Cole had presented?

Inquiry

Have students research some of John James Audubon's prints. His works are very popular, and many books have been published about him. His most well-known work, *The Birds of North America*, was published in four volumes between 1827 and 1838. Students should include in their research presentation a description of Audubon's technique, as well as an explanation of why he should be considered a Romantic artist.

Contextual Information

The Royal Pavilion

By the end of the eighteenth century, artists were becoming interested in the exotic designs and patterns on goods brought back to Europe by merchants and missionaries. For the *Royal Pavilion* (fig.12–26), John Nash certainly demonstrated this influence. For the dining room, he designed a domed ceiling painted like a spreading palm tree. To complete the effect of an Indian pavilion, he designed water-lily chandeliers suspended from the cast-iron claws of scaly dragons, lotus-blossom lamps and Oriental lacquerware.

The Eiffel Tower

Alexandre-Gustave Eiffel, known as the engineer of bridges all over Europe, was considered the father of iron and steel construction in France. At first, however, Parisians were not so pleased with his work, and they complained bitterly about the tower that marred the beauty of their city, calling Eiffel's construction the "junkman's Notre Dame." Writers and composers even signed petitions to protest its building. Nevertheless, two million visitors visited the tower in its first year.

Structural steel made a great difference in the construction of tall buildings such as the Eiffel Tower (fig.12–a). No longer were builders confined to stacking huge stones. Steel frameworks covered by facades of thin stone, brick or metal allowed a lighter-weight building and faster construction. Otis' invention in 1852 of the first elevator also made taller buildings practical. Structural steel and the elevator were to have far-reaching effects on architecture.

12–26 Compare this home to Jefferson's Monticello (fig.12–9). John Nash. *Royal Pavilion,* 1815–1818. Brighton, England.

Architecture

In architecture, England was the leader in Romanticism. English architects continued to worship the style of Palladio and to borrow ideas from his buildings. They borrowed from other times and cultures as well. No single architectural style developed. Instead, mood and individual taste were guiding principles in architecture.

One of the most fascinating structures built was the *Royal Pavilion* at Brighton (fig.12–26). It was designed by John Nash (1752–1835). Built on the south coast of England, it was to be the summer home for the prince regent, later King George IV. Using existing structures as a beginning, Nash added and enlarged them to produce an Oriental fantasy. He imitated Islamic domes and encased chimneys in minaret-like forms. Interior spaces are styled after Greek, Egyptian, Chinese and Gothic rooms. Still, the entire fun-filled structure has an overall unity even though it looks like it was transported to Brighton from India on some huge magic carpet.

After 1800, a revival of the Gothic style became very popular in England, basically because the English thought of it as *their* style. They wanted to be independent of Napoleon, Neoclassicism or anything recalling France. So when the *Houses of Parliament* were to be

expanded, Gothic was the unanimous choice (fig.12–27). Sir Charles Barry (1785–1860) and A. Welby Pugin (1812–1852) were chosen as architects. The gigantic public building has the lacy feeling and perpendicular line found in Gothic cathedrals. Its Gothic feeling is so authentic that it easily blends with the nearby Westminster Abbey, a true Gothic structure.

In France, the major building activity took place in Paris. And what activity it was! Great portions of the city were rebuilt, most of it under the direction of Georges Eugene Baron Haussman

(1809–1891). Along the boulevards radiating from the Arc de Triomphe, Haussman made all buildings similar in style and only six stories in height. This similarity, together with the planting of trees along the wide boulevards, gives Paris its familiar unity and striking beauty.

Several large structures stand above the six-story limit imposed by Haussman. Some were already existing, such as Notre Dame and the Church of the Madeleine, but others were new. The most striking of these new buildings was the *Opera* (fig.12–28). Designed by Charles Garnier (1825–1898), it was intended to be the central focus of the new Paris. The showy magnificence of the exterior was popular with the emerging industrial bourgeoisie. The interior is an incredible tribute to luxury and Baroque taste. The grand staircase cascades through a lobby space that is almost as large as the auditorium

12–27 What Gothic elements do you see here? Compare this building to the Town Hall of Louvain, Belgium.
Sir Charles Barry and A. Welby Pugin. *Houses of Parliament,* 1836–1860. London.

Inquiry

Consult an architect or the historical society to discover if there are structures in your area that were built between 1775 and 1875. If so, arrange for the class to visit and have students analyze the buildings to determine if they are Neoclassic or anti-Classic in character. Encourage students to learn something about the structures: architect, date of construction, original purpose, present use, building materials, other buildings by the same architect.

12–28 What architectural elements from earlier periods do you find here?
Charles Garnier. *Grand Staircase of the Opera*, 1861–1874. Interior view. Paris.

12–29 This is a predecessor to our shopping malls.
Giuseppe Mengoni. *Galleria Vittorio Emanuele*, 1861–1877. Milan.

Higher-Order Thinking Skills

The Eiffel Tower radically changed people's perspective. Before the tower provided the opportunity to see Paris from a great height, balloonists had been about the only people who had a real idea of what buildings or the countryside look like from the air. Artists incorporated that new information into their work. Today, satellites have again changed people's perspective, and that is reflected in contemporary art. Ask students to speculate about what the next major change of perspective will be.

itself. Colored marble columns, gigantic sculptures, elaborate light fixtures and decorative reliefs fill the space.

The Industrial Revolution made possible the use of cast iron in nineteenth-century architecture. Cast-iron frames held up the domes of the Royal Pavilion at Brighton. Since it could be formed in any required shape, it was used to make arches and spans that could leap across large spaces. However, cast iron was affected by intense heat, and many such buildings were later destroyed in fires. Among those remaining is the *Galleria Vittorio Emanuele*, a shopping arcade (fig.12–29). It was designed in Milan by Giuseppe Mengoni (1829–1877), built in England and reassembled in Milan. It is actually a glass-covered shopping street, an early relative of today's enclosed shopping malls. Four separate arcades fan out from a domed octagon. The dome tops a huge open space at the intersection.

A landmark familiar around the world is the *Eiffel Tower* (fig.12–a). Built by Alexandre-Gustave Eiffel (1832–1923) as the central feature of the Paris Exhibition of 1889, it towers 100 stories above the city. It rests on four pylons and four separate foundations. When it was completed, it was the tallest structure in the world. Still standing today, its elevators can hoist visitors to the very top to obtain a bird's-eye view of this great city.

Lesson 12.2 Review

1 How did the Romantic movement get its name?
2 Name two Romantic poets, two Romantic artists and two Romantic musicians.
3 Explain what is happening in Goya's *Third of May, 1808*. How is Napoleon connected to this story?
4 Describe some of the measures that Géricault took to ensure that his painting *Raft of the Medusa* would be authentic.
5 Which artist is now considered to be the founder of French Romanticism?
6 What new invention did Delacroix use to make studies for his paintings?
7 Describe the sky in Constable's *The Hay Wain*.
8 What was Turner most interested in painting in *Snow Storm: Steam-Boat off a Harbor's Mouth*?
9 Name the group of painters that was led by Thomas Cole.
10 During the early nineteenth century in England, why did a revival of the Gothic style become popular rather than Neoclassicism, as in Paris?
11 Which French architect is most responsible for designing the contemporary city of Paris?

Lesson 12.2 Review Answers

1 The term *Romanticism* came from a widespread revival of interest in medieval stories such as *King Arthur and the Knights of the Round Table* and *The Search for the Holy Grail*.
2 Possible answers include:
poets—Wordsworth, Keats, Shelley, Byron.
artists—Goya, Géricault, Delacroix, Turner, Cole, Bingham, Constable.
musicians—Beethoven, Schubert, Chopin, Wagner.
3 French soldiers are shooting Spanish rebels. Since Napoleon was the emperor of France, he was the chief commander of the French soldiers depicted in this painting.
4 Géricault interviewed the survivors, read newspaper accounts, and sketched and painted corpses at the morgue. He also had himself lashed to the mast of a ship in a storm so he could experience the ocean swells and the wind.
5 Theodore Géricault
6 Photography
7 The sky is dramatic with patches of fresh blue sky covered by white clouds which are darker on the left.
8 Color and movement
9 The Hudson River School
10 The English considered Gothic to be *their* style, as opposed to the Neoclassic style which was popular with the French. The English did not want to associate themselves with Napoleon or France.
11 Georges Eugene Baron Haussman

Lesson 12.3

Realism emerged in the late nineteenth century while Neoclassicism and Romanticism were still active. Realism's adherents relied on personal experience and observation to portray the world around them in as natural a manner as possible. Realist artists were often criticized for the ordinariness of their subjects, particularly those glorifying the working class and their simple life.

Warm-up

Ask students to define the difference between being a realist and being a romantic. Which personality tends to take the true situation into consideration more seriously? In art, would they prefer to see unblemished images of the world or a bit of fantasy that could provide a brief escape from the pressures of everyday life? Share that some nineteenth-century critics disliked the Realists for depicting society in an honest manner.

Objectives

Students should be able to:

Describe how Realism emerged during the first half of the nineteenth century while Neoclassicism and Romanticism were still evolving.

Learn that Realist artists painted only what they could see and experience themselves.

Discern the Realists' preference for portraying the everyday world in a natural way.

Teach

Criticism/Art History: Have students compare the compositions in Rosa Bonheur's *The Horse Fair* (figs.12–b, 12-31) and David's *Oath of the Horatii* (fig.12–c and fig.12–1). Which painting appears artificial and staged and which one captures the spontaneity of an actual event? Share that Realist artists rejected both the Classical models of Neoclassicism and the highly emotional character of Romanticism. Instead, they chose to depict as closely as possible the world in which they lived. In large part, this interest was affected by the monumental changes occurring in Western society and their resulting impact on developing urban centers and the daily lives of the middle and lower classes.

12.3 Realism

I N THE FIRST HALF of the nineteenth century, while Neoclassicists tried to recall the glories of Rome and Romanticists imagined great things, another style of painting was developing. The painters in this group were called Realists. They believed that only what they could see and experience themselves was worthy subject matter. Subjects had to be treated in as natural and realistic a way as possible. Gustave Courbet said that he could not paint angels because he had never seen any. Not surprisingly, the Realists admired the work of the seventeenth-century Dutch and Flemish. Painters such as Vermeer were rediscovered and brought to light.

However, the public had some strong views themselves on the work of the Realists. And they were not favorable. They did not understand the progressive Realist philosophy that glorified the working class. According to the critics, Realist painting lacked spirit and was, therefore, not art. They showed their disapproval by not accepting the Realists' work into the Academy. But, undaunted, the Realists organized a *Salon des Refuses*, or Exhibition of Refused Art. In 1863, they showed their work in a huge tent near the Academy.

Looking at the work today, we are neither shocked nor offended by the work. The Realists painted fact, not fiction. They painted what they saw: green foliage, blue sky, brown earth, common everyday scenes of people engaged in daily labor or conversation.

Key Notes

- Realism emerges as the third style of the early nineteenth century.
- The Realists emphasize the depiction of the common, everyday world.
- Realist paintings cause anger among critics. They are rejected by the academies.

Special Feature
Rosa Bonheur
(1822–1899)

The French painter Rosa Bonheur, an important Realist painter, was both independent and unconventional. In an age when girls' education was secondary to boys', she successfully persuaded her father to let her attend boarding school with her brothers.

She worked in sculpture as well as painting, but it was her paintings of animals that brought her fame. Animals were her favorite subject (fig.12–30). She studied them carefully, even going to slaughterhouses to get pieces she could dissect. She sketched endlessly at horse fairs and cattle markets. By wearing men's clothing, she was able to move about more freely without being harassed by attendants and spectators. She kept her hair short for the same reason. Her life was dedicated to painting, and she never married.

Art History: Direct students to read Rosa Bonheur's biography on pages 400 and 401. Ask how her life as a female artist varied from that of Elizabeth Vigée-Lebrun (pp. 386–387, 413). Have the class especially consider Vigée-Lebrun's perception of her artistic endeavors when she states: "The result is that after having devoted my youth to work, with a constancy and assiduity very rare in a woman, loving my art as much as my life, I can scarcely count four works (portraits included) with which I am really pleased." How did their personalities and the two distinct eras in which these women lived contribute to the differences in their subject matter, style and experiences?

Evaluate

Ask the class what outlook on life Neoclassic and Romantic artists might share that would differ from that of the Realists.

- Do the first two movements adhere to an accurate depiction of the ordinary life?

- How does this tendency vary from the Realists?

Ask students if Bonheur's *The Horse Fair* and *Sheep by the Sea* (fig.12–30) are so truthful that they can be viewed as documents of specific moments in time. Despite the fact that Realist artists strove to represent the observable world, what artistic choices did they

Rosa Bonheur became the first woman artist to receive the coveted cross of the French Legion of Honor in 1865.

The Horse Fair (fig.12–31) is the painting that won Rosa Bonheur international acclaim. Based on many sketches done outdoors, the painting is alive with movement and tension. The horses are seen during an exercise period as trainers move them around to relieve their nervousness. The modeling of the horses that dominate the canvas is superb, and they are seen from many angles. The horses are not racing thoroughbreds, but heavy work horses. A horse fair was a

common event in France at the time. Bonheur painted this scene of an annual horse fair in Paris realistically, without including a storytelling quality.

Sky and trees in this painting are treated naturally, but are kept subdued. The visual movement is strongly horizontal from left to right. The break in grouping in front of the white horses stops the movement from running out of the frame. Some of the animals are not properly broken and rear up, while others walk sedately and allow themselves to be led. The lighting is very dramatic, as is the bright white of the central horses. Bonheur was interested in light and handled it beautifully. However, she never

12–30 The artist visited England and the Scottish Highlands and studied the herds of sheep that roamed the area.
Rosa Bonheur, *Sheep by the Sea*, 1869. Oil on cradled panel, 12 3/4" x 18" (32 x 46 cm). The National Museum of Women in the Arts, gift of Wallace and Wilhelmina Holladay.

experimented with it as the Impressionists would in the years that followed.

The Horse Fair was shown in the Salon of 1853 and then exhibited in the major cities in England. It was even taken to Buckingham Palace at Queen Victoria's personal request so she could have a private viewing. Scenes of nature were particularly popular in England at this time. There was a general desire in England and the continent for realistic work like Rosa Bonheur's.

12–31 Although we seldom see them today, work horses like the gray dappled percheron team shown here were the power for farming before tractors were invented.
Rosa Bonheur, *The Horse Fair*, 1853. Oil on canvas, 8' x 16' 3" (2.5 x 5 m). The Metropolitan Museum of Art, New York, gift of Cornelius Vanderbilt, 1887.

Higher-Order Thinking Skills

Ask students what hints about Bonheur's feelings for animals they find in her paintings. If students were at the horse fair, which horse would they buy? Why?

make in composition and color that could influence our interpretation of their subject matter?

Reteach

Ask students if the gender of an artist could influence the way history is recorded. Do they think their answer always holds true? Direct students to choose from another artistic period an artwork that illustrates a historic event. Have them describe how an artist of the opposite sex might have depicted the scene.

Rosa Bonheur chose to dress in man's clothing (requiring a police permit to do so) in order to avoid being harassed at the horse fairs, cattle markets and slaughterhouses in which she found her subject matter. Similarly, female authors used male names: Mary Ann Evans (1819–1880) published under the pen name George Eliot, and Aurore Dupin (1804–1876) wrote as George Sand.

• What does this indicate about nineteenth-century readers' expectations of an author's gender?

• Although creative women at the time were beginning to come into their own, what limitations did women still apparently face?

• How might these facts have kept numerous women artists and writers from either pursuing their dreams or gaining recognition during their lifetime?

• Although the obstacles are not as obvious today, can students describe ways in which creative women still encounter discrimination?

Contextual Information

Corot

Corot traveled to Italy in 1825 and spent two years painting in and around Rome. Between 1827 and 1834 he traveled widely in France and went again to Italy for brief periods in 1834 and 1843. His journeys are recorded in small, fresh sketches called *pochades*.

Corot suggested in his notes that an artist should be guided by feelings. The artist should listen to advice but follow only what feels right. He said: "It is better to be nothing than [to be] an echo of other painters."

Millet

Millet's paintings became widely known when prints were made of them and placed in schools for students' moral education. His paintings of common activities showed peasants working hard, saying prayers of thanksgiving and gathering grain left by reapers. By continually seeing these images, it was expected that children would grow up to be hard and diligent workers.

12–32 Leaves that seem to flutter in the light are a hallmark of Corot's landscapes.
Jean-Baptiste-Camille Corot, *Seine and Old Bridge, Limay*, 1870. Oil on canvas, 16 1/4" x 26" (41 x 66 cm). Los Angeles County Museum of Art, Paul Rodman Mabury Collection.

12–33 Why is this called a realistic portrait?
Jean-Baptiste-Camille Corot, *Agostina*, 1866. Oil on canvas, 52 1/4" x 38 1/2" (133 x 98 cm). National Gallery of Art, Washington, DC, Chester Dale Collection.

Jean-Baptiste-Camille Corot

(1796–1875)

The fascination with painting real things in real light first appeared in the early work of Jean-Baptiste-Camille Corot of France. Corot was concerned with the clearness of the light and the harmony between humans and their environment. He painted this harmony in small sketches and larger works, often done on the spot. Notice the clarity of light and form in *View of Venice, The Piazzetta Seen from the Quai of the Esclavons*. Even the title is factual (fig.2–6). Corot painted what

he saw—not the pageantry of the city nor a Romantic impression of it in a misty sunrise. He simplified the detail to show what he absorbed at first glance. Corot painted patches of color in flat strokes and used only a few high-keyed, closely related colors. His limited palette helps emphasize the unity of the scene. The huge, high-keyed sky intensifies the clear light and contrasting shadow. Corot includes figures, but they are only part of the Piazzetta. They do not tell a story or emphasize an emotion. Corot treats the entire canvas in a detached way, as if he were taking a snapshot to send home.

Midstage in his career, Corot moved near the forest of Fontainebleau, near the village of Barbizon. He began painting dreamy landscapes of trees, rivers and summery scenes in grayish tones. His vivid light was changed to a purplish-gray haze. His sure, blocky strokes were changed to wispy, soft touches—a complete transformation. These poetic paintings were very popular in America where they sold as fast as Corot could paint them. Done in his studio from memory or imagination, they brought him great financial reward, even though they were not his best work. *Seine and Old Bridge at Limay* (fig.12–32) is from this period. Corot has included some structures in this work, although most include just trees, water, sky and, perhaps, a few small figures.

1869
Suez Canal begun

1898
The Capital University, later Peking University, founded, China

World Cultural Timeline

1872
Japan's first railroad opens from Tokyo to Yokohama

1895
Korean independence follows the Sino-Japanese War

Materials and Techniques

Corot used heavy brushstrokes and dense impasto (thick, heavy application of paint with a brush or knife) to create a tonal harmony in his work. Corot achieved this by mixing white lead with other hues. The result was a tangible, luminous atmosphere in each of the artist's works.

Later, toward the end of his career, Corot made another about-face. He returned to solid forms, but used the figure as his theme instead of the buildings and landscapes of Italy. Few artists in history have had the ability to handle the figure and landscape with equal ease. His figures have a solid feeling and are strongly three-dimensional. His use of light was both dramatic and real, indoors as well as out. *Agostina* (fig.12–33) is a realistic portrait—no flattery, drama, romanticizing or story-telling. Rather, a standing peasant girl stares off into space. Corot seems as detached from the model as the model is from her world at the moment.

Jean François Millet
(1814–1875)

Although born of a peasant family in Normandy, Jean François Millet settled with his wife and fourteen children in the town of Barbizon and worked there for twenty years. In his early career, he painted typical Classic subjects and models. Soon, his attachment to the soil emerged in his genre paintings of the peasants in France. He painted the common activities of sowing seed, harvesting, plowing and gleaning with complete understanding. He wished to present the farm workers as dignified people, much as Chardin had done with servants in Paris. His painting of *The Gleaners* (fig.12–34) is a powerful

treatment of simple workers and their daily tasks. Note how the three solid forms stand out in front of the sun-drenched background. Millet has subordinated the main harvesting activity in the bright glare. The design is simple, powerful and fitting for the subject. The light is strong and the shadows are deep. There is absolute realism in color, form and simplicity. He does not glorify or unnecessarily embellish the peasant women. He simply shows their hard, back-breaking labor as they pick over the field for any good grain the harvesting crew has left. The simple dignity of Millet's work had a direct influence on Vincent van Gogh's paintings.

Higher-Order Thinking Skills
Gleaning for grain that had been left behind during harvest was common until modern times. *The Gleaners* (fig.12–34) is a dignified presentation of hard work by simple people. Ask students what they would select as a contemporary topic that would portray modern hard work.

12–34 Gleaning was a regular part of the harvest until recent times. How would you characterize Millet's portrayal of these women?
Jean François Millet, *The Gleaners*, 1857. Oil on canvas, 32 1/2" x 43 1/2" (83 x 111 cm). Musée d'Orsay, Paris.

Contextual Information

Realism

While Neoclassicism and Romanticism describe ideal and sometimes utopian themes and styles, Realism describes artists' goals of portraying the people and world around them without ancient symbols or themes. As Daumier and Goya accomplished through painting, Balzac and Dickens provided social comments on real life through literature.

Daumier

Daumier was primarily self-taught; he learned by studying Classical sculpture and Dutch and Flemish painting in the Louvre. In addition to his 4000 lithographs, Daumier also produced 300 drawings and 200 paintings. Exceedingly prolific, he also sculpted, using his plaster and bronze sculptures as models for his drawings of people. Today, these sculptures are much sought after by art collectors.

Courbet

Courbet was from a family of wealthy landowners. He was born in Ornans and often returned there in search of subject matter. Sent to Paris in 1840 to study law, Courbet defied his parents' wishes and took up the study of art. In the 1850s and 1860s, Courbet led the life of the typical bohemian artist. He subscribed to radical political views and rejected the established world, which did not look kindly on his painting.

Honoré Daumier

(1808–1879)

The people of Paris knew Honoré Daumier as the greatest social caricaturist in their newspapers. In his four thousand lithographic drawings for the newspaper, he took pot shots at the Royalists, the Bonapartists, politicians of all types, judges and lawyers. He was briefly imprisoned for his biting satire, but he never tempered his brilliant caricatures.

After 1848, he began to paint. His realism featured artists, performers, musicians, circus workers, dancers, audiences and the common people in daily activities. He wanted to show the people of Paris how they looked to him. His painting technique was different from his lithographic drawings. However, some of the characteristics of his caricatures carried over into his paintings.

In *Advice to a Young Artist* (fig.12–35), the young man has brought a portfolio of his work for the older artist to see and criticize. Daumier's monumental forms are powerfully simple. A strong light from the left illuminates the figures and causes them to stand forward from the neutral background. In his earlier paintings, Daumier had used oil washes applied in a thin manner. Here, the paint is heavy and the texture is sure. The simplification of features enhances the solidity of the forms, as in Chardin's work.

Daumier's painting *The Third Class Carriage* (fig.12–36) is more in the breezy style of his caricatures, but still has a marvelous solidity. As in most of his work, Daumier deals with the public where he finds them—in their urban environment. His subjects did not pose for him in his studio. Daumier used grid lines to enlarge his smaller sketches onto the canvas. Because he used thin washes of muted color, the grid lines are often visible.

12–35 What do you think the artist is telling the student? Honoré Daumier, *Advice to a Young Artist*, after 1860. Oil on canvas, 16" x 13" (41 x 33 cm). National Gallery of Art, Washington, DC, gift of Duncan Phillips, 1941.

12–36 What clues do you find to the social and economic status of these people? Honoré Daumier, *The Third Class Carriage*, 1862. Oil on canvas, 26" x 35 1/2" (65 x 90 cm). The Metropolitan Museum of Art, New York, Bequest of Mrs. H. O. Havemayer Collection.

Daumier remained poor all his life. His friends persuaded him to have an exhibition of his work only a year before he died. Thus, he received a small amount of recognition while living. Blinded by overwork, Daumier simply could not paint the last year of his life.

Inquiry

After reading about Courbet's experience of holding his own one-artist show, students might enjoy exploring the world of the art gallery. If possible, they should interview a gallery owner to get a sense of what is required for an artist to hold a solo exhibition. How is a one-person show different from a group exhibition?

A different perspective might be gained by also interviewing a local artist and asking the same questions.

Gustave Courbet

(1819–1877)

The most effective spokesperson for Realism was Gustave Courbet. He is quoted as saying, "The art of painting should consist only in the representation of objects which the artist can see and touch." This was the credo of Realism. Courbet's paintings were of events or things that he had seen and knew well. He associated himself with the working class and their search for their rights in French society. A social activist, Courbet found himself in constant trouble because of his association with admitted Socialists.

In the Salon of 1850, Courbet exhibited *Burial at Ornans* (fig.12–37). This gigantic painting is a masterpiece of Realism. There is no aristocratic funeral here or visualized soul being transported to heaven. Compare this work with El Greco's *Burial of Count Orgaz* (fig.9–37). Courbet shows the people of his home town of Ornans attending the graveside funeral of a friend. Courbet depicts the pallbearers with the coffin, the priest reading the

Office of the Dead, the altar boys, the mayor standing by the dog, the grave digger kneeling next to the open grave, the mourning friends and the clergy. Ordinary people are painted doing ordinary things at a very sad time. The mood is somber. The figures and faces are solid and real. The crucifix reaches into the overcast sky, uniting it with the grouped figures below. The dog certainly adds to the common, everyday feeling of the painting. The painting was so large that Courbet could not back up from it in his studio to see the overall effect. Yet, it is amazingly unified. The simple dignity of the peasants is captured superbly.

At the 1855 Universal Exposition in Paris, works by Ingres and Delacroix were prominently displayed. The works of Courbet were rejected, including *Burial at Ornans*. Never one to stand still, Courbet, with the help of friends, built a special shed called the Pavilion of Realism. Here, he mounted an exhibition of his work alone. This became the first modern-day, one-artist exhibition.

12–37 Notice how the artist uses patches of white to carry your eye across the composition.
Gustave Courbet, *Burial at Ornans*, 1849–1850. Oil on canvas, 10' 3" x 21' 11" (315 x 668 cm). Musée d'Orsay, Paris.

Contextual Information

Homer

Winslow Homer was a solitary person who said he needed to be alone to paint. To get the peace he wanted, he put a sign on his studio door saying "Go away. I am out."

A stay in England from 1881 to 1882 resulted in a change in Homer's subject matter. During that time, he lived in a fishing village and became fascinated with the sea and fisherman. He began painting large-scale images of nature, particularly the sea. Upon his return to the United States, he took up residence at Prout's Neck on the coast of Maine. He spent his winters in Florida and the Bahamas, where he continued to focus his interest on the sea.

To study the fury of ocean storms at close range, he built a small one-room studio on wheels that he moved along the coast. One wall of this studio was glass so that he could paint in almost all kinds of weather.

Window in Time

Art as Documentation

Before the invention of the camera, visual records of important events were communicated worldwide by artists, whose illustrations appeared in popular magazines and periodicals. Beginning in the 1840s, these illustrated magazines provided artists with a very large audience.

Artist-reporters, or Special Artists, as they were called, worked on location, much the same way as news correspondents. The Special Artists had to have various talents. They had to be able to draw quickly on location. From everything that was happening, they had to know what was most important to capture. And, somehow, they had to be in the right place at the right time.

Winslow Homer, an american, was one of the artists who recorded the Civil War for *Harper's Weekly*, a leading periodical in the United States at the time. He did over 800 drawings of the Civil War for them, and continued illustrating for *Harper's Weekly* until 1874.

Special Artists were employed mainly to cover wars, which sold more copies of newspapers and periodicals than any other event. They spent their time traveling from one side of the world to the other, recording the tense conflicts that erupted into fighting. Special Artists often found themselves in danger when they covered wars. Their constant note-taking aroused the suspicion of citizens and officials. During the 1870–71 war between France and Germany, anyone found drawing, or with drawings on their person, was in a lot of danger. The risk was so great that artist William Simpson made his notes on cigarette papers, so that if he was caught they could either be swallowed or smoked.

Another difficulty Special Artists encountered was getting their material to their editor on time. They might have to travel up to ten miles on foot in the middle of the night or take long stagecoach journeys if they were in the American West.

For almost fifty years, the Special Artists were free from competition. Even after the invention of photography, the mechanics of taking a photograph were so cumbersome and demanded so much fragile equipment that the Special Artist was still in great demand. The South African Anglo-Boer War of 1899–1900 saw the introduction of faster film, which allowed the first action photographs. Even then, artists' drawings were still used.

By the time World War I started in 1914, photography was the preferred medium for press illustration. Nevertheless, artists—including some famous painters who fought in the war—recorded the events in drawings and prints.

As the twentieth century progressed, photography and, eventually, motion picture film and videotape became the principal means of recording newsworthy moments. Today, there are only rare occasions, such as closed courtroom proceedings, when we continue to rely solely on artists' sketches to provide us with a visual record of an event.

Winslow Homer, *Baggage Guard*, 1865. Lithographic crayon and pen and ink on paper mounted on board, 9" x 18 1/4" (23 x 46 cm). Museum of Art, Carnegie Institute, Pittsburgh, Andrew Carnegie Fund.

12-39 What compositional purpose does the ship in the distance serve? Winslow Homer, *Breezing Up (A Fair Wind)*, 1876. Oil on canvas, 24" x 38" (61 x 97 cm). National Gallery of Art, Washington, DC, gift of the W. L. and May T. Mellon Foundation.

12-38 What effect does the sunlight have on the sense of volume in this painting? Winslow Homer, *Croquet Scene*, 1866. Oil on canvas, 16" x 26" (41 x 66 cm). The Art Institute of Chicago, Friends of American Art Collection, 1942.

Winslow Homer

(1836–1910)

From an early age, Winslow Homer knew he had to become an artist. Mostly self-taught, he began his professional art career by making wood engravings as illustrations for *Harper's Weekly*. During the Civil War, he was a field illustrator for the magazine. When the war was over, Homer began painting. His training as a detailed wood engraver pushed him toward Realism with his oils. A trip to Europe, in 1866, gave direction to his painting. From Corot and Courbet, he learned about the use of color and light under careful value control in clear tones and the application of heavy paint to canvas.

In *Croquet Scene* (fig.12–38), Homer achieved marvelous clarity of light. He used the dazzling sunlight to generalize and flatten details. A sunny Sunday afternoon is frozen in time. The brilliant colors of the girls' dresses are locked in place against the variety of contrasting greens of grass and trees. Homer approached the painting of light and color in terms of black, white and gray values. His early paintings have the same flat shapes and

intense value contrasts as early Impressionist work.

Perhaps Homer's most popular painting is *Breezing Up (A Fair Wind)* (fig.12–39). Three boys are out sailing with a New England fisherman. Each is lost in his own thoughts as the small craft skips over the Atlantic. Perhaps they dream of captaining a larger vessel like the one in the distance that so beautifully balances the painting. Those who are interested in sports relate easily to Homer and his work.

About 1873, Homer became seriously interested in watercolor (fig.2–27). He used it first to make

sketches for his oils, but found that people liked them enough to purchase some of them. He spent time in England painting the sea, fishermen and their wives in oils and watercolor. He was relaxed with his watercolors. They were fresh, spontaneous and alive. Homer was the first American artist to think of his watercolors as completed statements and finished works. To him, they were not sketches or preliminary studies for oil paintings. His contribution to the use of this medium greatly influenced the development of American watercolor painting.

Contextual Information

The Gross Clinic

The Gross Clinic (fig.12–41) was denied admission to the art section of the 1876 Centennial Exposition in Philadelphia because men and women of "weak nerves" would see it. It was finally placed in the medical section of the exposition.

12–40 Eakins used photographs as references to help him get all the details in his many paintings of sports activities.
Thomas Eakins, *The Biglin Brothers Racing*, 1876. Oil on canvas, 24" x 38" (61 x 91 cm). National Gallery of Art, Washington, DC, gift of Mr. and Mrs. Cornelius Vanderbilt Whitney.

Thomas Eakins

(1844–1916)

A more influential artist than Homer, Thomas Eakins is one of the finest painters America has produced. He went to Europe after studying at the Pennsylvania Academy. He returned with a dedication to paint only realistic facts and not explore imagination and sentiment. He taught drawing classes at the Pennsylvania academy and was unwavering in his stress on realism and accuracy. This determination forced his resignation when he insisted that all students, females included, draw from nude male and female models.

While Homer was concerned with nature, Eakins was interested primarily in the figure. He painted many realistic portraits of friends and approached his subjects logically and with mathematical precision. His perspectives are accurate because they were measured and plotted mathematically before the painting began. Yet in spite of such a careful system of work, his paintings have a strength and a naturalness. With his superb sense of observation, Eakins reveals a grand joy in nature and humanity.

The Biglin Brothers Racing (fig.12–40) is a fine example of Eakins' outdoor painting. He shows his two friends poised at the start of a race, waiting for the gun to sound. His realism depicts sparkling water, deep shadows, bright sunlight and muscular tension. All are perfectly integrated to make a complete and unified statement. This convincing outdoor subject was painted in Eakins' studio from sketches, photographs and his incredible memory.

Eakins' most powerful painting (and perhaps his most controversial) is *The Gross Clinic* (fig.12–41), painted for the Jefferson Medical College in Philadelphia. Dr. Samuel Gross, scalpel in hand, turns away

Interdisciplinary Connection:

Sports: Eakins painted swimmers, baseball players, wrestlers, boxers and oarsmen in sculls. His accuracy in portraying sports figures was aided by his interest in photography, which he used in his detailed study of the human body in action. Eakins was the first American to take multiple-exposure photographs of a moving subject on a single piece of film, much like today's stop-action photography.

• Have students research Eakins' sports images to create a gallery of sports popular in the late nineteenth century. Discuss how nineteenth-century versions of the sports are different from those today. Compare equipment, clothing, techniques and other aspects.

from the beginning surgery to talk to the students. His noble portrait unites the students above with the operation below. Each face is a superb individual portrait, yet the grouping of surgeons forms a strong unit. The powerful natural light from a skylight creates intense value contrasts that focus the viewer's attention on the operation. The students are painted in dim obscurity in the background. Each part is handled with absolute realism. Yet Eakins instilled a sense of drama. The fierce concentration of the doctors creates tension. As a final realistic touch, at the left, the mother of the young man on the operating table hides her face in a gesture of intense grief.

The scene seems spontaneous, but was carefully calculated. Eakins arranged the figures and the light to create the most dramatic impact on the viewers. His fellow Philadelphians and most art critics did not like his work. They felt that the blood on Dr. Gross's hand was not necessary and made the painting too realistic and gruesome. Eakins had succeeded in his quest for realism, but his public did not appreciate his mastery. Winslow Homer and Thomas Eakins were the cornerstone of Realism in America.

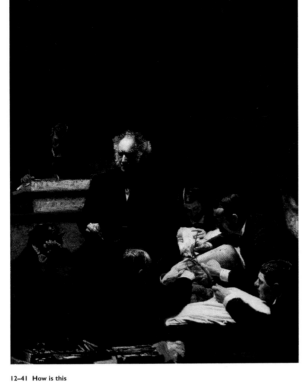

12–41 **How is this operating room different from a modern one?**
Thomas Eakins, *The Gross Clinic,* 1875. Oil on canvas, 96" x 78" (244 x 198 cm). Jefferson Medical College of Thomas Jefferson University, Philadelphia, PA.

Lesson 12.3 Review

1 What was the philosophy of the Realist artists concerning working-class people?
2 How large is Rosa Bonheur's *The Horse Fair*? Would it fit on the wall of your art classroom?
3 What were Corot's principal subjects after he began painting near Barbizon?
4 How was Millet trying to present the peasant women in *The Gleaners*?

5 During his lifetime, for what type of art was Daumier most famous?
6 What was Courbet's response to the rejection of his *Burial at Ornans* from the 1855 Universal Exposition in Paris?
7 Why did Thomas Eakins lose his job at the Pennsylvania Academy?

Lesson 12.3 Review Answers

1 The Realists glorified the working class. They painted everyday scenes of people working and interacting.
2 *The Horse Fair* is about 8′ x 6′ (2.5 x 5 m). It would probably fit on a wall in most classrooms.
3 Dreamy landscapes of trees, rivers and summery scenes
4 As dignified people—he shows their hard labor without glorifying them.
5 A caricaturist for the newspaper.
6 Courbet mounted his own exhibition in a shed which he and his friends built. They called it the Pavilion of Realism.

7 Because he stressed realism and accuracy, Eakins insisted that all his drawing students at the Pennsylvania Academy—both men and women—draw from nude male and female models. The school's administration did not share Eakins' dedication to realism—especially when it came to women drawing nudes—and forced his resignation.

Lesson 12.4

Fine art photography began in the nineteenth century. At the time, scientific advances and artistic interests combined to produce an entirely new and versatile medium.

Warm-up

Ask students who do not consider themselves artists if they have ever taken a photograph. Were they aware that they were making many artistic choices during the process? For instance, did they think about how to frame their subject, what objects to include, and how close or far away to be from the scene? Point out that in the nineteenth century, many people who had not acquired years of training could practice the new art form since photographic skills could be acquired relatively easily and without great expense.

Objectives

Students should be able to:

Perceive photography's roots in the camera obscura, an optical device of the sixteenth century.

Understand that the principles of the camera obscura were combined with the technological advances of photosensitive ground glass to produce the first photographs.

Comprehend how photographers and contemporary artists incorporated lessons from each other into their works.

Vocabulary Definitions

zoopraxiscope A photographic device invented by Eadweard Muybridge in the late 1870s which produced a series of images of a moving subject.

Teach

Criticism: Ask students if they believe cameras can lie. Or, do they consider photography an objective medium? Direct them to study Edward Steichen's *The Flatiron Building* (fig.12–43).

• Did the actual scene look exactly like the final image?

• How has Steichen created a highly evocative photograph?

12.4 Photography

PHOTOGRAPHY HAD ITS ROOTS in the *camera obscura* of the sixteenth century. When the principles of the camera obscura were combined with lithography (invented in 1798) to make a print from an image on photo sensitive ground glass, modern photography was born. After 1839, there were many people, including artists, who considered painting to be a dead art taken over by photography. Nevertheless, few early photographers thought in terms of art. They were satisfied to simply make portraits and take pictures.

The first creative photographers came from the ranks of painters, sculptors and draftsmen in Britain and France. Once photographers realized the extent of what their cameras could portray, they were on their way to creating a visual art of their own. The camera could capture the vitality of action, the beauty of form and, most particularly, the expressiveness of a situation.

The development of photography parallels the changes in painting to some degree. Realism, Impressionism and Expressionism are common to both fields. Painters learned from photographers and photographers took hints from painters. What one developed, the other soon used.

Key Notes

• Photography becomes a new art form.
• Photography and painting experience parallel developments and styles.
• Photography permits artists to freeze motion in order to study it in detail.

Vocabulary
zoopraxiscope

12–42 To what effect has Steichen used the principle of contrast in this photograph?
Edward Steichen, *J. Pierpont Morgan.* Courtesy of Southeby's, Inc.

Edward Steichen

(1879–1973)

Edward Steichen, an American, was one of the early photographers who thought of photography as an art form. Trained as a lithographer, Steichen decided to leave commercial illustration to become a fine artist.

Steichen began at an early age to appreciate the subtle qualities that could make photographs into art. He did not want to merely capture physical likenesses. Steichen also argued that photographers must not try to imitate painting, but must use their cameras to find their own ways of expressing themselves.

Steichen was also a noted portrait photographer. His well-known portrait of *J. Pierpont Morgan* (fig.12–42) is one of the few surviving portraits of the financier. Some years after taking the portrait, Steichen compared encountering Morgan's gaze to watching the oncoming headlights of an express train.

The Flatiron Building (fig.12–43) is a fine example of photography as art. Design and mood are balanced as if rendered with a brush. A variety of shapes loom amidst the rain-soaked air and streets. From the tree branches, which boldly flash across the scene, to the ghostly forms of the skyscraper and other buildings, Steichen's image is evocative and memorable. All the knowledge gained by the Realist painters about light, massing of tones, shapes connecting with each other, and the flattening of forms in the absence of light are explored in this one superb photograph.

• Have students consider his decisions in the length of time he exposed his film, what he kept in focus, what he left blurry, and what he chose to include in his final composition. (For instance, how would the impact of the photograph change if the first horse and carriage was farther down the street and therefore not silhouetted against the moody gray skyline?)

• Have students read on page 410 about Steichen's desire for photography to be an art form and not merely to imitate the observable world.

• Finally, ask if there are any purely objective art forms or if all media are affected by the way artists use them.

Art History: Ask students to compare Steichen's *The Flatiron Building* to Eadweard Muybridge's *Attitudes of Animals in Motion* (fig.12–45).

• Ask if they think Muybridge was more concerned about the artistic or the scientific capabilities of the new technology.

• Can the naked human eye freeze a moment in time for observation?

• What sort of impact could his split-second serial images have had on artists of the day? For example, how were Thomas Eakins (figs.12–40, 12–41) and the Impressionists (Chapter 13) greatly influenced by photography's ability to capture fleeting, spontaneous moments?

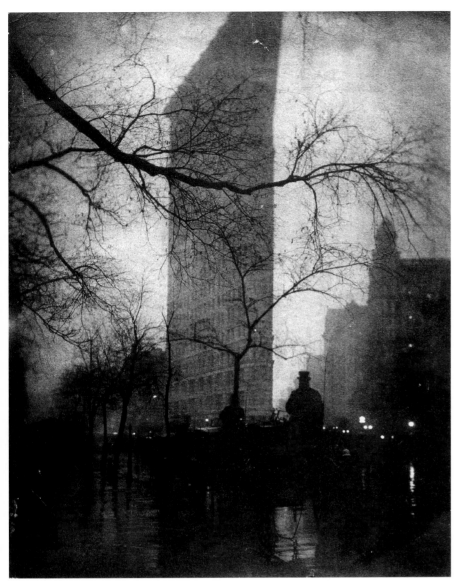

12–43 Principles of painting were also applied to photography to create works that were expressive.
Edward J. Steichen, *The Flatiron Building*, 1904. Photograph. The Metropolitan Museum of Art, New York, Alfred Stieglitz Collection, 1933.

Contextual Information

Steichen

Steichen practiced commercial photography in New York. He was chief photographer for *Vogue* and *Vanity Fair* magazines and was also in charge of the navy's combat photography during World War II.

Higher-Order Thinking Skills

Ask students to find a work that they have already studied to use for comparison to Steichen's photography. Have them explain the reasons for their choices.

Evaluate

Ask how the invention of photography revolutionized art and society.

• What effect did it have on artists and on ordinary citizens?

• Was the ability to create lifelike images now limited only to painters who had gone through years of academic training?

• How could painters use the medium to help them in their work?

Ask why some painters found photography an advantage while others felt the medium was threatening. How might these same issues affect contemporary painters' attitudes toward computer technology, which can produce and manipulate images in seconds?

Ask students to use images in Lesson 12.4 to defend the idea that what photographers specifically decide to leave out of their pictures can be just as important as what they choose to include.

Reteach

Have students examine a newspaper photograph of a war scene and then compare it to Goya's *Third of May, 1808* (fig.12–14). Ask which one is more accurate.

• Which one seems more artistic?

• Which medium more powerfully evokes their compassion?

• What are the limitations and advantages of each medium in being able to affect our emotions?

• Would students consider the newspaper image art or documentation?

• What sorts of choices might the photographer have made in snapping the picture?

• How would concern for an artistic composition, the communication of information, and persuasion have played into the photographer's decision?

Ask students if they have more photographic or more painted portraits of themselves. Starting in the nineteenth century, the relatively inexpensive photographic medium enabled the average people to acquire images. Previously, who throughout most of Western society had been the primary subjects and patrons of art?

Contextual Information

Early Photography

Photography became a practical tool for artists. At first, photographs substituted for long hours of posing and could be used for a quick-action pose. As the chemistry was improved, photographers could adjust lenses and developing solutions to achieve photographs that were admired by artists. This was the beginning of efforts to *make* photographs that were art rather than to *take* photographs that might be art. Matisse said that painting would "translate my emotions, my feelings and the reactions of my sensibility into colour and design, something that neither the most perfect camera, even in colours, nor the cinema can do."

Early Photographers

Edward Steichen followed the leadership of early photographers such as Henry Peach Robinson (1830–1901), Julia Margaret Cameron (1815–1879) (fig.12–44) and Oscar Rejlander (1818–1875) in thinking of photography as fine art.

The Realists and Romantics also were interested in photography as an aid in the study of action, form and light. In the late 1870s, Eadweard Muybridge (1830–1904) invented a device called a **zoopraxiscope**, which produced a series of images of a moving subject (fig.12–45). Thomas Eakins also worked on it. Artists could now actually see how muscles moved when humans or animals were in motion. They learned about movement and muscles under stress. For the first time in history, action could be caught and stopped for study. For example, it was now clear that, at some times in their movement, horses had all four hooves off the ground at the same time. Eakins devised a way to mount these images, which, when rotated, made the first moving picture.

The Realists made extensive use of photography to learn how things really looked. Courbet said that he considered the camera to be his sketchbook, a prime resource for his realistic paintings.

12–44 Cameron took up photography at the age of forty-eight.
Julia Margaret Cameron, *Ellen Terry at the Age of Sixteen*, 1863. Carbon print. The Metropolitan Museum of Art, New York, Alfred Stieglitz Collection, 1949.

12–45 Muybridge's sequential photographs of human and animal movements revolutionized artists' understanding of motion.
Eadweard Muybridge, *Attitudes of Animals in Motion*, 1878. Courtesy of Sotheby's, Inc.

Lesson 12.4 Review

1 Name an American photographer who considered photography to be an art.
2 What revolutionary techniques did Eakins use in his photography?
3 How did artists of the late nineteenth century use the camera as an aid to their painting?

Lesson 12.4 Review Answers

1 Edward Steichen
2 Eakins took multiple exposure photographs of a moving subject on a single piece of film. This technique was similar to contemporary stop-action photography.
3 Artists used the camera to study action, form and light. Photography allowed them to actually see how animal and human muscles moved. By capturing action on film, they could stop motion in order to study their subjects.

Chapter Review Answers

Review

1 Napoleon wished to compare himself to the Roman emperors.
2 Watteau's *The Gamut of Love* is like a theater set romanticizing the lives of his Parisian patrons. The scene is delicately lit with a shimmering surface of brushstrokes. Ingres' *Apotheosis of Homer* is cool, undramatic Classicism—almost the opposite of *The Gamut of Love* in feeling and mood.
3 They are very similar, both with swirling, twisting bodies of lions, men and horses. Although both are painted with visible brushstrokes, the forms in Rubens' painting are slightly more defined. Counting the lions is difficult—even when you have the advantage of looking at the originals—but it is fun to try.
4 El Greco's *Burial of Count Orgaz* is an imagined scene, dramatized and romanticized with saints and angels. The saints' robes are rich, sumptuous fabrics. Many of the bodies have been distorted. Courbet's *Burial at Ornans* is a real scene, neither romanticized nor dramatized, with real people in somber clothes doing ordinary things.

Interpret

1 David's painting stresses patriotism and love of country over love of family. A classical scene is idealized in the hard-edged clarity of Neoclassicism. Goya's dramatic painting is an emotional remembrance of an atrocity.

Primary Source

Elizabeth Vigée-Lebrun

Like many artists, past and present, Elizabeth Vigée-Lebrun found it necessary to paint portraits in order to earn a living. She traveled throughout Europe painting portraits of members of royal families, but she really wanted to paint the beautiful landscapes she saw on these travels. In this passage from her memoir, *Souvenirs*, she mentions this frustration.

"I bade adieu to the beautiful bay of Naples, the charming hills of Pausilippo and terrible Vesuvius with regret, and left for the third time to visit my dear Rome, and admire Raffaelle again in all his glory. When there, I undertook a great many portraits, which to tell the truth only partially satisfied me. I greatly regretted not having been able to employ my time, either at Naples or Rome, in painting pictures of subjects which inspired me. I had been named a member of all the Academies of Italy, which encouraged me to merit such flattering distinctions, and I was going to leave nothing in this lovely country which would add much to my reputation as an artist. These ideas were constantly on my mind—I have more than one sketch in my portfolio which could furnish the proof; but the want of money, as I had not one penny left of what I earned in France, and the natural weakness of my character, made me undertake engagements to the weary task of portrait painting. The result is that after having devoted my youth to work, with a constancy and assiduity very rare in a woman, loving my art as much as my life, I can scarcely count four works (portraits included) with which I am really pleased.

Many of the portraits which I took in Rome during my last stay there, however, procured me some gratification, amongst others, that of seeing again Mesdames de France, the aunts of Louis XVI, who at once asked me to take their portraits."

Chapter Review

Review

1 Why did Napoleon support art that was inspired by Classical Roman art?
2 Neoclassicism was a reaction to the Rococo style. Compare these two art styles in Ingres' *Apotheosis of Homer* and Watteau's *The Gamut of Love* (fig.11–42).
3 Compare Delacroix's and Rubens' *Lion Hunt* (fig.11–23). How are they alike? Try to count the lions in each.
4 Compare Courbet's *Burial at Ornans* with El Greco's *Burial of Count Orgaz* (fig.9–37). Which painting is of ordinary people?

Interpret

1 Compare Neoclassicist David's *Oath of the Horatii* to Romanticist Goya's *Third of May, 1808*. How does each artist view war?
2 Delacroix was artistically inspired by his trips to Spain and Morocco. If you could visit an exotic land to collect ideas for paintings, where would you go? Explain the reasons for your choice.
3 How would paintings like Bingham's *Fur Traders Descending the Missouri* encourage people to settle the western part of the United States?
4 Describe the scene in Homer's *Breezing Up (A Fair Wind)*. What sensations would the boys in the picture feel, smell and hear?

Other Tools for Learning

 Maps
Find three cities on the map in which famous buildings of the Romantic style are located. List the names of the buildings, their architects and the cities and countries in which they are located.

Timelines
Select one event from the 1800s that eventually led to a dramatic change in the way people live. Explain why you chose this event.

Electronic Research
Videodisc player: *Louvre Videodisc* (Disk 1: Painting, Drawing)
1 Study one of the paintings in this chapter such as Géricault's *Raft of the Medusa*, or David's *Napoleon in his Study* or *Oath of the Horatii* more carefully by looking at close-up details. What do you see in these close-up views that you had not noticed before?

CD-ROM drive: *Microsoft Art Gallery*
1 Discover more about Turner's revolutionary painting techniques. (Making Paintings Guided Tour)

Higher-Order Thinking Skills

Muybridge's photographs revolutionized the understanding of motion. We now use videotape and computers to better understand motion. Ask students to compare and contrast either videotape or computers with photography as ways to make artistic statements about motion.

Primary-Source Connection

Artists often wage personal battles between creating something that they know might sell and creating what they truly want, despite the possibility it will have little, if any, market value. Ask students how they would solve the dilemma that Vigée-Lebrun faced. How might her options have been different if she had been born two hundred years later?

David's work is smooth, and void of visible brushstrokes. Drawing and line are more important than color. The figures seem to be frozen in their poses. Goya's painting is alive with slashing brushstrokes, strong contrasts of colors and values, and a dramatic sense of action.
2 Students might pick Africa, Florida, California, Hawaii, Australia or any place that seems novel and romantic to them.
3 Bingham shows a romanticized view of the west. Floating down the river looks idyllic, not dangerous or difficult.
4 The boys probably taste salt spray as it hits their faces, and feel the cool breeze on their arms. They might be getting damp from the spray. They hear the splash of the waves against the boat. They are probably warm from the sun.

 Maps
1 Brighton, England: Royal Pavilion—John Nash
London, England: Houses of Parliament—Sir Charles Barry and A. Welby Pugin
Paris, France: Opera—Charles Garnier
Eiffel Tower: Alexandre-Gustave Eiffel
Milan, Italy: Galleria Vittorio Emanuele—Giuseppe Mengoni

 Timelines
1 There are many interesting choices. One possibility is the building of the Suez Canal which opened up parts of the Middle East to Western culture. It created a more efficient means of shipping oil to the West, providing much of the world with low-cost fuel.

Electronic Research
Videodisk Player: *National Gallery of Art* and *Louvre* videodisk
1 Students might notice the texture of the surface, the way edges are painted or objects too small to examine in detail in a photograph.

CD-ROM Drive: Microsoft Art Gallery
1 The Making Paintings Tour features Turner's *The Fighting Temeraire* in which he meticulously painted fine-lined ship rigging contrasted against an impasto of clouds reflecting sunlight.

Activity 1:
Watercolor Action

Activity Objectives
Students should be able to:

• Understand that watercolor is a medium that can be used for quick sketches, for adding color to a drawing, or as a medium for a major work of art.

• Make comparisons between the characteristics of watercolor and oil.

• Use personal experiences to bring meaning to their paintings.

• Develop an appreciation for the work of Winslow Homer and other watercolor artists.

Thinking Critically
Discuss students' personal style. Why do students personally respond more to one way of seeing than to another? What are their preferences as artists, but not necessarily as viewers?

Preparation Ideas

• Review figure drawing. Have students spend a class period doing gesture drawings of student models to sharpen skills with figure drawing before doing the on-site drawings.

• Before beginning the final study, students might do several watercolor exercises to reacquaint themselves with the special properties of watercolor. Remind students to layer colors to create effect rather than use less water to make colors dark.

Notes on Materials
Watercolor paints that come in semi-moist pans are great for easy transport, but students will be limited in their choice of color. If the budget allows, tube watercolors are preferable.

Classroom Management

• Organize a trip outdoors for students to sketch physical education classes. Decide where you're going; make up a list of materials students will need to take with them; and discuss ground rules before leaving the classroom.

Tips

• Have watercolor resource books on hand, such as *Understanding Transparent Watercolor* by Gerald Brommer, Davis Publications, Inc., 1993.

Activity 1

Watercolor Action

Materials
pencils
drawing paper (sketch book)
watercolor paint
watercolor paper
brushes
containers of water

Take a look.
• Fig.2–27, Winslow Homer, *After the Hunt*, 1892. Watercolor.
• Fig.12–38, Winslow Homer, *Croquet Scene*, 1866. Oil on canvas.
• Fig.12–39, Winslow Homer, *Breezing Up*, 1876. Oil on canvas.

Think about it. Compare the listed works by Winslow Homer. In each case, Homer has dealt with his subject in a realistic manner using strong value contrasts.
• In what ways are they similar? How are the paintings different?
• Notice that the watercolor painting has a sparkle to it that makes it look as if it were "lit from within." That quality is not evident in the more opaque medium of oils.

Do it.
• Choose a sport or activity that is part of your daily life.
• Take a sketch book "on site" to do drawings that capture people in motion. Consider the movement of individual figures as well as their relationship to each other.
• Record details, such as their clothing, props they may be using and the background. You may wish to take some photographs of the action to serve as a reference in the classroom.
• Develop a finished composition based on the sport or activity that you observed. Work this into a 11" x 14" watercolor painting.

Check it. Obtain feedback on your preliminary action sketches before starting to paint. See if others can tell what action you wish to portray by looking only at your figures (without clues provided by props or setting).

Helpful Hint: By using a gradual build-up of washes, you will create an image of color contrasts which will give your viewer the feeling of being there.

Activity 2

Dueling Styles

Take a look.
• Fig.12–14, Francisco Goya, *The Third of May, 1808*, 1814.
• Fig.2–19, Jean-Auguste-Dominique Ingres, *Thomas Church*, 1816.
• Fig.2–60, Joseph Mallord William Turner, *The Burning of the Houses of Parliament*, 1835.
• Fig.12–1, Jacques-Louis David, *Oath of the Horatii*, 1784–1785.
• Fig.12–7, Elizabeth Vigée-Lebrun, *Mme. de Stael as Corinn Playing a Lyre*, after 1808.
• Fig.12–17, Eugene Delacroix, *Liberty Leading the People*, 1830.
• Fig.12–22, Thomas Cole, *View on the Catskill, Early Autumn*, 1837.

Think about it. While the Neoclassic style grew out of a rebellion against the ornate styles of the eighteenth century, it soon became not only the accepted style, but dictated to artists the ways in which they should think. This, in turn, led to a new rebellion known as Romanticism.

Do it.
• Chart the differences between Neoclassicism and Romanticism.
• Consider styles, methods, emphases, techniques, influences, roots, philosophy and other features.

• Use the information to create a multimedia presentation of what you have learned. This could include a slide show, music, poetry and your own artwork.

Check it. As you work, discuss your ideas with other classmates to see what insights you can share that might broaden the scope of your presentations.

Helpful Hint: Ask your teacher or librarian for good sources of images to use in your presentation.

Additional Activities

• Many American buildings have been influenced by Neoclassic or Romantic styles. Photograph or sketch elements of architecture in your community that reflect these influences and arrange a photo essay.

• Research the Neoclassic architecture of Thomas Jefferson. Write a report tracing the roots of his style and include the works of Andrea Palladio and Robert Adam. List examples of Jefferson's work that still exist.

• Does Realism lean more toward Classicism or Romanticism, or can it go into both categories? Why do you think so? Choose a local landscape or cityscape as the subject of three drawings, each done in one of the three styles. As an artist, what style most fits your usual approach to your work? What new insights have you gained through this study?

• As a warm-up, show the video *Winslow Homer: The Nature of the Artist*, (VHS), National Gallery of Art.

Evaluation
Grading could be based on two categories listed on the board at the beginning of the project.

Compositional issues:

• Has the student considered both the foreground and the background?

• Has the student considered the relationship between the figures?

• Are details used to enhance the final work?

• Are the figures caught in action or do they appear to be stilted?

• Are the proportions of the figures accurate?

Technical issues:

• Is the watercolor overworked or does it appear to be fresh?

• Has the color remained transparent?

Activity 2:
Dueling Styles

Activity Objectives
Students should be able to:

• Understand the role played by the Neoclassicist movement in bringing an end to the popularity of Rococo.

• Investigate the importance and influences of past history, archaeologi-

Student Profile

Will Lee
Age 19
Aztec High School
Aztec, New Mexico
Activity I, Watercolor Action

My watercolor is about kids jumping off a bridge out on Ruins Road, near where I live. To me, it symbolizes the importance of the choices we make—especially as kids.

The main things I thought about during the creation of this picture were the composition and getting the figures to stand out against the background. Also, I was really trying to capture the drama of the storm approaching.

I haven't read a whole lot about art. There are always library books and art magazines in the classroom. I spend my spare time browsing through them and looking for ideas and new things to try. I'm developing my own style and learning to express my own thought and opinions. I think the thing I like most about art is the competition. It's fun to complete a piece and see how it stacks up with the rest of the class. I also enjoy competing locally and on the state level.

My advice for other students who enjoy creating art is to express your own ideas. If the idea is fresh, the artwork will be also.

Dave Pazniokas
Age 17
Mansfield High School
Mansfield, Massachusetts
Favorite kinds of art: watercolor, pencil
Favorite artists: Salvador Dali, M.C. Escher
Activity I, Watercolor Action

My painting is about finding new places with old friends.

What was your thought process when you were creating and developing your project?
To establish the background, then the foreground. I created the figures last in the area I would most like to be.

What do you enjoy most about the artistic process?
Being able to create something and have the final product look the way I intended it to look. Being able to create perspective to make it look three-dimensional.

What advice do you have for other students who enjoy creating art?
Try not to get frustrated and keep experimenting. You may find a style or media you excel in.

Follow the Leader, 1994. Watercolor, 11" x 14" (28 x 35.5 cm).

Searching for a Place, 1994. Watercolor, 11" x 14" (28 x 35.5 cm).

Teacher Spotlight
Suzy Goza
Art Teacher
Aztec High School

For this activity, we did lots of drawing in class. Using student models, we began with blind contour drawing and proceeded to timed poses (fifteen minutes being the longest). The kids were frustrated by on-site work. They didn't have the skills to quick-sketch and get enough information down on the page to work from. We compromised by drawing our figures in class and coming up with "on-site" backgrounds.

M. Susan Iovieno
Coordinator of Visual and Performing Arts
Mansfield Public Schools

We have a good supply of resources in my office/art library. I was able to give Dave historical information and visuals on Homer that were immediately at hand. Serendipity occurred when *School Arts* magazine for January 1995 arrived. In it was an article by an elementary instructor [Nancy Kremeier] who had used Winslow Homer's works to inspire storm-action paintings from her second graders. One might think this reference would be scorned by high-school students as being beneath them. Our students are taught that all work is worthy of respect and that something can be learned from any artist.

---

cal discoveries and fads on the culture of a country or region.

• Name the characteristics of Neoclassicism and Romanticism, important artists from each movement, some of their works and the characteristics of their style.

• Make a connection among the art, music and literature of the time period and discover how the era was affected by the political climate.

Thinking Critically

• Ask students how they would categorize their own school building or campus. Are there any prominent Classical or Romantic elements in the architecture? How about the details of its decoration?

• Ask students to evaluate their own style of art. Do they consider their work more Classical or Romantic? Why?

Preparation Ideas
There are many approaches that a student can take to study the differences between Neoclassicism and Romanticism. The research will become more meaningful if students can relate it to their personal interests. Some possibilities:

• Send students out on a weekend project to take photographs of neighborhood buildings that fall into one of the two categories. Students could then make a creative display of the results.

• Invite an architect to class to talk about how characteristics of these two

styles are finding their way back into some modern architecture.

Notes on Materials
Encourage multimedia presentations by asking students ahead of time if they will need a slide projector and screen, TV/VCR or other technical support. Your school media center or library may be able to work with you on preparation.

Classroom Management
As a two-group project, one group could work on Neoclassicism and the other on Romanticism. Within each group, individual students or subgroups could focus on painting, architecture or sculpture and make presentations to the rest of the class.

Chapter 13 Organizer

Days	**8 Week**	**1 Semester**	**2 Semester**
	1	1	1

Chapter 13 Opener: Impressionism and Post-Impressionism

Objectives	National Standards
Locate the heart of the avant-garde art world in France during the last quarter of the nineteenth century to the early twentieth century.	**4a** Students differentiate among a variety of historical and cultural contexts in terms of characteristics and purposes of works of art.
Understand how the Impressionists used light and color to describe pleasant, transitory scenes of middle-class life.	**5a** Students identify intentions of those creating artworks, explore the implications of various purposes, and justify their analyses of purposes in particular works.
Learn how the Post-Impressionists introduced composition and design to Impressionist color and light.	**2d** Students demonstrate the ability to compare two or more perspectives about the use of organizational principles and functions in artwork and to defend personal evaluations of these perspectives.
Comprehend how artists used personal styles to convey often desolate emotions and content, laying the foundation for the Expressionist movement.	**5d** Students correlate responses to works of visual art with various techniques for communicating meanings, ideas, attitudes, views, and intentions.

Lesson 13.1 Impressionism

Teacher Edition References

1	1	*Special Feature:* Claude Monet 418–419	Contextual Info 419, 420	HOTS 419
	2	Remainder of Lesson 13.1 420–429 World Cultural Timeline 426 Lesson 13.1 Review 429	Contextual Info 421, 422, 424, 426, 428 HOTS 423, 425, 427, 429 Cooperative 424	Interdisciplinary 427 Materials and Techniques 421, 4 Performing Arts 425, 427

Lesson 13.2 Post-Impressionism

1	1	*Special Feature:* Georges Seurat 430–431	Contextual Info 431 HOTS 431	Interdisciplinary 431
	2	Remainder of Lesson 13.2 432–439 World Cultural Timeline 434 Lesson 13.2 Review 439	Contextual Info 432, 434, 436, 438 HOTS 433, 435, 437, 439	Multicultural 434 Performing Arts 436

Lesson 13.3 Turn-of-the-Century Expressions

1	1	*Special Feature:* Edvard Munch 440–441	Contextual Info 441	HOTS 441
	1	Remainder of Lesson 13.3 442–444 Lesson 13.3 Review 444 Primary-Source 445 Chapter Review 445	Contextual Info 442, 444	HOTS 443

Classroom Connections

1	1	1	

	National Standards
Studio Activity 1 Still Life Pastel	**1a** Students apply media, techniques, and processes with sufficient skill, confidence, and sensitivity that their intentions are carried out in their artworks. **1b** Students conceive and create works of visual art that demonstrate an understanding of how the communication of their ideas relates to the media, techniques, and processes they use.
Studio Activity 2 Same Place Next Time	**1a** Students apply media, techniques, and processes with sufficient skill, confidence, and sensitivity that their intentions are carried out in their artworks. **1b** Students conceive and create works of visual art that demonstrate an understanding of how the communication of their ideas relates to the media, techniques, and processes they use.

Choose either Activity 1 or 2
Choose either Activity 1 or 2
Choose either Activity 1 or 2

Ancillaries

Ancillaries

Teacher Edition References

Slides: Gauguin, *The Day of the God (Mahana No Atua)*, 88a, 176

Timeline: Impressionism and Post-Impressionism 416
Map: Impressionism/ Post-Impressionism 417
Context 416
Art 417
Quote 417

Ancillaries

Slides: Monet, *Irises by the Pond*, 85b, 167

Slides: Pissarro, Place du Théâtre Français, 83a, 168; Degas, *Glass of Absinthe*, 84a, 169; Degas, *Rehearsal of a Ballet*, 86b, 170; Cassatt, *Mother and Child*, 87b, 171
Overhead Transparencies: The Influence of Japan, 14
Large Reproductions: Manet, *Luncheon on the Grass (Dejeuner sur l'Herbe)*, 20; Degas, *Little Fourteeen-Year-Old Dancer*, 21

Slides: Seurat, *Sunday Afternoon on the Island of La Grande Jatte*, 85a, 172; van Gogh, *Night Café*, 88b, 173
Large Reproductions: van Gogh, *Bedroom at Arles*, 22

Slides: Cézanne, *Mont Sainte-Victoire*, 86a, 174; Toulouse-Lautrec, *At the Moulin Rouge*, 87a, 175; Gauguin, *The Day of the God (Mahana No Atua)*, 88a, 176

Slides: Munch, *Street in Aasgaadstrand*, 89b, 177

Slides: Picasso, *The Old Guitarist*, 89a, 179; Rousseau, *Carnival Night*, 90b, 178

Schedule

Materials

This activity can be completed in one day.

vine charcoal, hard and soft pastels, pastel pencils for details, torchons, charcoal or watercolor paper, spray fixative, kneaded erasers, optional: masonite boards with bull clips, tracing paper

One drawing in class and next drawings outside of class.

select from materials listed in Activity 1 as needed

Other Resources

Books

A Day in the Country: Impressionism and the French Landscape. Holiday, 1984.

Degas. Metropolitan Museum of Art, 1988.

Edouard Manet: Painter of Modern Life. Metropolitan Museum of Art, 1983.

Farr, Denis. *Oxford History of Art Series. Vol.11: English Art 1870–1940.* London: Oxford University Press, 1979.

Hamilton, George Heard. *Painting and Sculpture in Europe: 1880–1940.* 3rd ed., New Haven: Yale University Press, 1992.

Harris, Ann S. *Women Artists: 1550–1950.* New York: Alfred A. Knopf Inc., 1977.

Hitchcock, Henry Russell, ed. *Architecture: 19th and 20th Centuries.* 4th ed. New Haven: Yale University Press, 1992.

Nochlin, Linda. *Impressionism and Post-Impressionism: 1874–1904.* Part of *Sources and Documents in the History of Art.* Englewood Cliffs: Prentice Hall, 1966.

Paul Gauguin: The Savage Dream. National Gallery of Art, 1988.

Rewald, John. *History of Impressionism.* 4th ed. New York: Harry N. Abrams Inc., 1990.

———. *Post-Impressionism From van Gogh to Gauguin.* 3rd. ed. New York: Harry N. Abrams Inc., 1990.

Rosenblum, Robert, and Janson, H. W. *19th Century Art.* New York: Harry N. Abrams Inc., 1984.

Videodiscs

In a Brilliant Light: van Gogh at Arles, Crystal
Musée d'Orsay, Crystal

Videos

A Sunday on the Island of La Grande Jatte - Georges Seurat, Crystal
Vincent: The Life and Death of Vincent van Gogh, Crystal
Degas, Crystal
Eduard Manet, Crystal
Toulouse-Lautrec, Crystal
Monet, Crystal
Mary Cassatt, Crystal
Seurat, Crystal
Cezanne, Crystal
Gauguin, Crystal

Music

Impressionistic Musical Examples
Debussy—*Prelude to the Afternooon of a Faun; La Mer*
la Falla—*Nights in the Gardens of Spain*
Respighi—*Fountains of Rome*

Introduce

During the last quarter of the nineteenth century, Impressionism revolutionized the Western European art world. For approximately fifteen glorious years, Impressionists created spontaneous, light-filled compositions that instantaneously caught the pleasures of middle-class life. The Post-Impressionists soon followed, reasserting more traditional concerns for design and composition. At the same time, various artists outside of France began to paint bleaker, more emotionally wrought scenes, paving the way for the later Expressionist movement.

Lessons at a Glance

13.1 *Impressionism*
Impressionism galvanized the Western European art world for fifteen brief but splendid years. The artists' short strokes of brilliant color captured fleeting moments of comfortable living. Although many contemporary critics derided Impressionism's portrayal of a scene's transitory qualities rather than its accurate description, the style's influence reverberated throughout Europe and Russia, and even across the ocean to the United States.

13.2 *Post-Impressionism*
Because Post-Impressionist artists were dissatisfied with Impressionism's casual compositions, they reintroduced form and structure into paintings that sometimes stressed vehement emotions. Post-Impressionism was not an organized and cohesive movement but rather one that encompassed numerous artists who shared common goals.

13.3 *Turn-of-the-Century Expressions*
While France remained a dominant force in Western art, artists from other European countries began to reflect a pessimistic view about contemporary urban society, eventually paving the way for the later Expressionist movement.

13 Impressionism and Post-Impressionism

I N THE SECOND HALF of the 1800s, a tremendous change in art occurred in France. A whole new style of painting developed called Impressionism. This new style revolutionized painting all over Europe. Since then, it has become one of the most popular and beloved stylistic periods in the history of Western art. Impressionists were interested in color and developed a fascination with the effect of light on color. Their goal was to create a spontaneous rendering, a quick, light-filled colorful impression of what was in front of them.

After about fifteen years, some artists wanted more than pure "instantaneity." The Post-Impressionists, as they were called, were still interested in light and color but also wanted to incorporate more traditional values of design and composition into their work.

During the late 1800s and early 1900s, Paris continued to be the art center of the world. Artists in other countries were also producing excellent work. Their styles often differed from the styles popular in Paris. These artists frequently focused on the bleak conditions they saw around them. They were at the forefront of the Expressionist movement.

A greater fluidity between styles had started to develop. Artists were becoming more individualistic and styles were beginning to evolve from one to the next more and more rapidly.

13–a Note the Japanese print on the wall behind Zola. Artists from this period found inspiration in the art of Japan.
Edouard Manet, *Emile Zola*, 1868. Oil on canvas, 57 1/4" x 45" (146 x 114 cm). Musée d'Orsay, Paris.

1863
Manet's *Luncheon on the Grass* refused by the Salon

1884–1886
Whistler, *Nocturne in Black and Gold: The Falling Rocket*
Seurat establishes pointillism technique

1891
Gauguin leaves for Tahiti

1893
First automobile (Benz)

1900
Freud's dream interpretation

1914
World War I begins

Impressionism and Post-Impressionism

1874
Degas, *Rehearsal on the Stage*

1889
van Gogh, *The Starry Night*

1892–1894
Monet, *Rouen Cathedral* series

1898
Pierre and Marie Curie discover radium and plutonium

1905
Einstein's theory of relativity

Objectives

Students should be able to:

Locate the heart of the avant-garde art world in France during the last quarter of the nineteenth century to the early twentieth century.

Understand how the Impressionists used light and color to describe pleasant, transitory scenes of middle-class life.

Learn how the Post-Impressionists introduced composition and design to Impressionist color and light.

Comprehend how artists used personal styles to convey often desolate emotions and content, laying the foundation for the Expressionist movement.

Teach

Timeline
Direct the students to plot on the timeline the life spans of the artists whose works are shown in the chapter opener. Ask if the art movements that each artist represents were consecutive or simultaneous. Explain that artists continued to work in their given style while other movements took over or sometimes evolved along with the new aesthetic approaches.

Context
Tell students to glance at the images in the chapter opener.

• Ask if these sorts of subjects, typical of Western European art during the late nineteenth century, were made for monarchs and religious leaders.

A work of art is *"a corner of nature seen through a temperament."*
Emil Zola

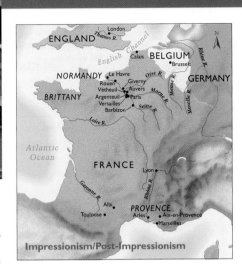

ENGLAND BELGIUM NORMANDY GERMANY BRITTANY FRANCE PROVENCE

Impressionism/Post-Impressionism

13–b Gauguin sometimes used Egyptian poses in his work. **What type of Egyptian art do these figures recall?** Paul Gauguin, *The Day of the God*, detail (fig.13–30).

Much of the activity of this period was focused around Paris, though many Impressionist artists found that the lighting in Southern France stimulated their work. Many were also fascinated with the reflection of light on water. Notice how many key towns are located along rivers or near the sea.

13–d The Impressionist movement derived its name from this painting. Claude Monet, *Impression: Sunrise*, 1872. Oil on canvas, 19" x 25 1/2" (49 x 65 cm). Musée Marmottan, Paris.

13–c European painters began to depict the anonymity and bleakness of contemporary urban life. In the late nineteenth century these artists planted the seeds of the Expressionist movement. Edvard Munch, *Girls on a Bridge*, detail (fig.13–32).

Quote

Instruct students to study Émile Zola's portrait (fig.13–a) after reading his quote. Have them guess at Zola's profession by reflecting on his words and the information that Edouard Manet provides in his painting. Since he has no easel but is surrounded by art, what might be Zola's connection to the art world? (He was a great supporter of Impressionism and wrote extensively about its artists and their work in his critical articles.)

Map

Ask in which country the Western European painting styles of the late nineteenth century thrived. Had the art center shifted from the previous era? After students review the map in Chapter 12, have them consider how radical Impression and Post-Impressionism must have looked in Paris, as compared to the more realistic Neoclassic and Romantic art of the earlier age.

Reteach

Instruct students to write an article as though they were art critics in the late nineteenth century. Have students compare Monet's *Impression: Sunrise* (fig.13–d) to Rosa Bonheur's *The Horse Fair* (figs.12–b, 12–31). Remind them that they are writing in the late 1880s and have never seen anything remotely like Monet's work.

• What are the major differences in the way the two artists have dealt with the composition, color and subject matter?

• Which painting do they believe more effectively communicates underlying sensations?

• Do they prefer the older Realist tradition or the new Impressionism style?

• Share with the class that Impressionist artists received little public praise during their lives. Have students conjecture why our appreciation of Impressionism has altered over the years.

• Ask what about their content informs students that art was no longer being dictated by powerful patrons.

Art

Have students examine Claude Monet's painting in fig.13–d without looking at the title.

• Ask how they would title the piece.

• Why do they think it was called *Impression: Sunrise* and how do the words relate to Monet's style?

• Can students detect small details or only the overall atmosphere of the scene?

• Does Monet rely most heavily on line, shape or color to convey the "impression" of the early-morning vista?

Evaluate

Ask students if ordinary people's lives in Western Europe were as proscribed by religion as they had been only a few centuries earlier. Ask how the subject matter of the artwork in Chapter 13 supports their answers.

• Ask the class if the art made just before and after the turn of the century shared a single style.

• How do the images in the chapter opener reveal the artists' distinct approaches to subject matter, emotion, color and composition?

• Had there been other periods in history where many important art movements occurred simultaneously within one country?

Lesson 13.1

Impressionism galvanized the Western European art world for fifteen brief but splendid years. The artists' short strokes of brilliant color captured fleeting moments of comfortable living. Although many contemporary critics derided Impressionism's portrayal of a scene's transitory qualities rather than its accurate description, the style's influence reverberated throughout Europe and Russia, and even across the ocean to the United States.

Warm-up

Hold up a single sheet of light-colored paper, preferably yellow or pink. Ask students if they think they are seeing one true color. Next have them examine the same sheet with the classroom lights dimmed, in direct sunlight, and then under a fluorescent lamp. Ask if the paper's color seemed to change in each circumstance. While Realist artists tended to portray the visible world as immutable, Impressionists painted the colors of objects as they appeared at a specific time of day and season of the year, thereby celebrating ever-changing nature.

Objectives

Students should be able to:

Discuss how Impressionism evolved from Realism's desire to reveal the world as it truly appeared.

Understand the Impressionists' unique use of color and light to capture the ephemeral essence of their scenes.

Describe Impressionism as the first revolutionary style to have originated in France since Gothic times, and its gradual influence in Europe, Russia and the United States.

Vocabulary Definitions

optical mixing (op-ti-kul) Technique used by Impressionist artists in which the viewer's eye blends juxtaposed dots of color from a distance.
broken color Painting technique (typical of Impressionism) that utilizes short touches of bright color, often complementary, placed side by side to create a vibrating effect.
series Many paintings exploring the same theme over a period of time.

13.1 Impressionism

ALL THE IMPRESSIONIST PAINTERS began as Realists. They were interested in natural colors and landscapes that they painted outdoors. Like Courbet and Corot, they painted people and things as solid, colored objects. But, they soon realized that the color of light had a tremendous effect on the color of objects. The color of the atmosphere at different times of the day changed the appearance of objects they were painting. Previous painters recorded the color of objects as they assumed them to be. The Impressionists painted color as they saw it—bright, glaring and high-keyed with colored light even penetrating the shadows. Sometimes, solid form was lost in the brilliance or mistiness of the light. The Impressionists wanted to express an immediate impression, not a detailed analysis. We all know what happens if we shut our eyes tightly and then quickly open them. That "one-second exposure" is what the Impressionists wanted to paint. Claude Monet described his goal in painting as "instantaneity."

The name Impressionism was first used in jest when Monet exhibited a work called *Impression: Sunrise* (fig.13–d) in an 1874 show. The painting's colored streaks and blobs on a pale blue ground represent what a person sees when taking a quick look at a sunrise over a harbor. Critics derisively called the works *impressions* and not paintings. The title stuck, although several Impressionists did not like it.

Impressionism was the first artistic revolution since the Renaissance and the first broad-based style to originate in France since Gothic times. It gradually built up a following throughout Europe, even in Russia. It was especially popular in the United States. Impressionism lasted about fifteen years before artists started following different directions.

Key Notes
- Impressionists revolutionize art by making light and color their subject matter.
- Artists seek to create an instant impression, not a detailed analysis.
- Impressionism originates in France and spreads throughout Europe and to America.

Vocabulary
optical mixing
broken color
series

Special Feature
Claude Monet
(1840–1926)

Claude Monet did not paint trees or fields, but simply the colors he saw—a little blue square, an oblong of pink, a streak of yellow or green dots. Monet took dabs of yellow and put them next to dabs of green and did not smear them together. Instead he let the viewer's eye blend them from a distance into a shimmering green. This technique, called *optical mixing* or the applying of *broken color*, was the basis for Impressionist theories of color and light.

Monet became the leading force in the Impressionist movement, bridging the span from the Realist world to the contemporary world of abstraction. Monet loved to work outdoors and to directly confront the environment he was painting. His early work reflects his training with the landscape painter Eugene Boudin, from whom he learned the fundamentals of Realist painting. But it also shows an early fascination with light. In *Argenteuil* (fig.13–1) Monet expressed this interest with a high-keyed palette, particularly in the large portion of

13–1 What elements does this seascape share with Jacob van Ruisdael's *The Mill at Wijk by Durstede* (fig.11–26)? Also look for their differences.
Claude Monet, *Argenteuil*, 1872. Oil on canvas, 19 3/4" x 25 1/2" (50 x 65 cm). National Gallery of Art, Washington, DC, Ailsa Mellon Bruce Collection.

Teach

Criticism: Ask students to imagine that they are a local meteorologist on TV. Quite unexpectedly, the station's art critic has become ill and they must now prepare a newscast about Claude Monet's paintings of *Rouen Cathedral* (figs.13–2, 13–3). Ask how their job and abiding interest in the changing weather affect their appreciation of the works. Have students read Monet's biography on pages 418 and 419 to help them prepare for their broadcast.

Evaluate

Ask students:

- What was more important to the Impressionists, the effects of color and light or the lifelike description of a scene?

- Why would Impressionists have been uninterested in depicting grand historical themes? Who and what were their subjects?

- If you were Claude Monet, how might your style and composition describing the Last Supper differ from Leonardo's earlier version (fig.9–23)? What effect might Monet's more momentary, less exacting view have had on the subject?

Reteach

Direct students to identify an issue that troubles them, possibly something regarding school or a world event. After they decide, instruct them to keep a journal in which they write down their thoughts about the topic at three different times each day for four days: when

13–2 What time of day do you think this painting portrays?
Claude Monet, *Rouen Cathedral: The Portal (in Sun)*, 1894. Oil on canvas,
39" x 26" (99 x 66 cm). The Metropolitan Museum of Art, New York, bequest
of Theodore M. Davis, 1915, Theodore M. Davis Collection.

13–3 Compare this work to fig.13–2 which depicts the same subject.
There are many paintings in this series.
Claude Monet, *Rouen Cathedral, West Facade, Morning Light* 1894. Oil on
canvas, 42" x 28" (107 x 72 cm). Musée d'Orsay, Paris.

sky and the reflecting water. He used flat patches of color in the foreground rather than trying to imitate the texture of the place. The heavy visual weight of the darker masses on the right is balanced by the single white sail on the left. By including such objects, Monet gave his seemingly unbalanced compositions a sense of stability.

But soon his work changed drastically. The flat brushstrokes of *Argenteuil* gave way to a shimmering effect in which the entire surface vibrated with color and light. There are no definite edges or contours to anything. The more Monet

painted outdoors, the more he realized that colors were constantly changing with the moving of the sun or the interruption of clouds or haze. To analyze these changes, he decided to paint a single subject at different times of the day, at different times of the year, under different light. This is what he did with the west facade of the *Rouen Cathedral* (figs.13–2, 13–3). Here was a heavy, massive surface, built and carved of stone. Yet, under Monet's skillful handling, one no longer sees the stone and carving, but only the light and color reflected from different surfaces.

Monet recorded these light and color changes on the church in more than thirty canvases.

Color and light became a new way of seeing. Monet stuck to the early credo of the Impressionist group: to depict visual sensations as experienced at a certain time and place.

they first wake up, just after lunch, and right before they go to sleep. At the end of four days, have students analyz e if their thinking about the issue was different at particular times of the day and if it changed over the course of the exercise.

• Do they have a different perspective from when they first began?

• Tell them to examine the two paintings of Rouen Cathedral to determine what Monet might have learned from conducting a similar experiment with his artwork. What might he have discovered about human vision by repeatedly painting the same subject? Explain that Impressionist art helps sensitize us to fact that nothing in life is truly static.

Higher-Order Thinking Skills

Ask students to compare the two paintings of Rouen Cathedral and speculate about the time of day, the season and the weather. What clues can they identify that led to their findings? For a bulletin board, photograph the same landscape many times over several seasons and times of day. Keep a journal of the dates, weather, times, and so forth. Ask students to speculate about the photographs and then confirm their opinions with your journal entries.

Contextual Information

Manet

Manet's paintings were accepted in Salon shows but were continually criticized. After Manet's death, Monet led a subscription effort to purchase Manet's *Olympia* for France. He raised over 19,000 francs to keep the painting from foreign collectors who were buying much of the Impressionist work at that time.

A Critic's Reaction to Impressionism

A *Le Figaro* critic described an 1876 exhibit of Impressionists' work as "a ruthless spectacle" and as "so-called paintings." He described the visitors to the gallery as "laughing in front" of the paintings done by "five or six lunatics." He continued: "…those self-styled artists give themselves the title of non-compromisers, impressionists; they take up canvas, paint, and brush, throw a few tones haphazardly and sign the whole thing."

Late Nineteenth Century Railway Stations in France

Railway stations all over France were covered with lightweight glass and iron sections and therefore looked somewhat like greenhouses. These glass-and-iron structures inspired awe and confidence in science and technology and continued to influence the architecture of the twentieth century.

France had one of the largest railroad systems in Europe in the late 1800s. Trains were extremely important at this time because they allowed people to travel inexpensively and quickly (55 mph) to the countryside, other cities in France and the seaside. Cities tried to outdo one

Edouard Manet

(1832–1883)

Monet's predecessor as unofficial leader of the Impressionist movement was Edouard Manet. Trained as a traditional painter, Manet was particularly attracted to the paintings and the brushwork of Diego Velazquez and Francisco Goya of Spain. Like them, Manet felt that the message of the artist was the brushstrokes and patches of paint on the canvas, not the subject matter that they represented. Manet wanted the viewer to look *at* his paintings and not through them like through some magic window. He wanted to make paintings that could be enjoyed for their color and arrangement and for the fact that they were paintings and not imitations of nature.

His early work had a flatness new to the world of painting. This flatness was difficult for his contemporaries to understand. In this flat approach to design, Manet was influenced by Japanese woodcuts that were popular imports in France. His *Gare Saint-Lazare* (fig.13–4), done in mid-career, has a flatness that is fascinating. Look at the young woman's face. It is too flatly painted if the viewer looks at it with Renaissance eyes. There are no dark shadows or depth, no chiaroscuro, no roundness of form. The light source is probably directly *behind* the artist, not to the side as in most previous paintings. No black was added to make the few shadows that exist in the painting. Form is achieved by changing color slightly or lightening a value here and there.

The format of the painting is like a snapshot of a young woman and girl at the train station (*gare* is French for station). The peculiar composition, with the vertical bars dominating, is fresh and startling. The little girl looks through the bars at a train that has passed by, leaving a cloud of steam in its wake. (Manet worked on the large canvas outdoors to capture the light-through-steam effect.) The woman on the left looks at the viewer with detached interest. She will soon drop her head and go on reading as her finger in the book's pages suggests. The appealing puppy in her lap sleeps in complete contentment.

All four sides of the canvas seem to have been "cropped," much as one would "crop" a snapshot. The candid, off-hand appearance is greatly enhanced by this device. The work's occasional unfinished look also contributes to this effect. Manet's work here is different from the Realism of Corot and vastly different from the Neoclassicism of David and Ingres.

13–4 The cropped, intimate look of a snapshot is coupled with the influence of Japanese prints to create a completely new look in painting.
Edouard Manet, *Gare Saint-Lazare*, 1873. Oil on canvas, 36 1/2" x 45 1/4" (93 x 114.5 cm). National Gallery of Art, Washington, DC, gift of Horace Havemeyer in memory of his mother, Louisine W. Havemeyer, 1956.

another in the size and style of their modern railroad stations. At Gare Saint-Lazare, the locale of Manet's painting of the same name (fig.13–4) and one of seven stations in Paris in the 1870s, a luxury hotel was attached to the station.

13–5 Compare Manet's technique in this scene to Frans Hals' technique in *Yonker Ramp and His Sweetheart* (fig.11–29). Edouard Manet, *The Waitress*, 1878. Oil on canvas, 38 1/2" x 30 1/4" (98 x 77 cm). The National Gallery, London.

Higher-Order Thinking Skills

1 Have students compare and contrast the scene in *The Waitress* (fig.13–5) to that in Hals' *Yonker Ramp and His Sweetheart* (fig.11–29).

2 Encourage students to discuss how Impressionism was in some ways more real than accurate, detailed depictions of the observable world. In what ways do dreams also sometimes seem more real than experiences in life itself? Although we normally consider what we see in our waking hours as real, the life inside our minds has its own truth, one that we experience more keenly with different senses.

Toward the end of his short life, Manet left the flat and even patches of color of his earlier work. He adopted the looser, longer strokes and vibrating color of the Impressionists. *The Waitress* (fig.13–5) was painted in Manet's studio. A real waitress at the Café de Bock in Paris posed for him. The arrangement of figures again produces a snapshot effect of an instantaneous glimpse into the café. It is almost as if the door were opened for a second and one looked quickly inside. Notice the directional brushwork in the material and on the hands and arms. Patterns of light values make the painting sparkle with light. The indefinite character of the people in the café and the band and the dancer on stage are truly impressions of the scene rather than a factual representation. Everything seems to quiver with excitement. Sparkling light transforms an everyday subject into a delightful event.

Materials and Techniques

In the second half of the nineteenth century, several new types of materials aided the work of the Impressionists. These included new colors and new kinds of paint; collapsible tin tubes for paint, which made painting outdoors much more convenient; and flat brushes, which allowed artists to apply paint in new ways.

Contextual Information

An Abundance of Artists

There were over 4000 full-time professional painters in or near Paris in the 1860s. In 1863, the Salon jury had to trim 5000 entries down to 2500. As a result, there was great competition among artists and gallery owners to attract favorable audiences. Paintings in galleries were hung from the floor to the ceiling, and even in dark corners.

Pissarro

Pissarro's home in Louveciennes was destroyed during the Franco-Prussian War; his paintings were destroyed, and he moved to England for a time to work with Monet. He became a teacher, and his students included Cézanne and Gauguin. By 1895, Pissarro's eyesight had deteriorated, and he had to give up painting out of doors. Many of his later works were done from windows in Paris.

Morisot

Morisot and Manet were friends, and she often asked his opinion of her work. One day she asked him to critique a painting of her mother and sister. He said it was very good except for one part. Then he took her brush and put a few strokes on the canvas; then he started on another area. He continued up the canvas, changing what Morisot had planned to enter in the Salon exhibition.

Part of Morisot's training included painting in the Louvre, visiting other museums and art colonies, and cultivating friendships with artists who were invited to her parents' home. Morisot's grandfather was Fragonard, and she studied with Corot, Manet and Renoir.

• Have students compare Morisot's paintings with those of her teachers and describe where in her work they see evidence of the teachers' instruction.

13–6 The artist is well known for his Paris street scenes. He captures a moment in time much as your eye would when quickly glancing out an upper-story window.
Camille Pissarro, *La Place du Théâtre Français*, 1898. Oil on canvas, 28 1/4" x 36 1/2" (72 x 93 cm). Los Angeles County Museum of Art, Mr. and Mrs. George Gard de Sylva Collection.

13–7 A close-up view of this painting makes the figures and objects dissolve into dabs and dashes of color
Camille Pissarro, *La Place du Théâtre Français*, detai.

Camille Pissarro

(1830–1903)

Although he was born in the West Indies, Camille Pissarro came to Paris when twenty-five, determined to be an artist. A good friend of the other Impressionists, he often bought their work to keep them from starving. He also let many of the young, struggling artists live on his property in the country and painted side by side with them. Pissarro was adept at capturing the feeling of a place through color and mood. The viewer can sense its atmosphere and even the time of year or day. His favorite subjects were scenes of the streets of Paris as viewed from second or third story windows.

13–8 This artist usually placed her subjects indoors in the direct sunlight of a window or terrace.
Berthe Morisot, *The Artist's Sister at a Window*, 1869. Oil on canvas, 21 3/4" x 18" (55 x 46 cm). National Gallery of Art, Washington, DC, Ailsa Mellon Bruce Collection.

In *Place du Théâtre Français* (fig.13–6), the viewer seems to be looking over Pissarro's shoulder, out the window and down onto the street below. The shimmering light and color of the hustle and bustle of a city street are felt immediately. People, horses and carriages appear to move as the tiny spots and dashes of color seem to melt and dissolve (fig.13–7). The viewer has to look through some leafless branches to see part of the scene. Pissarro often used this device to heighten the sense of movement and sparkle. Pissarro, like Monet, wanted to obtain an instantaneous sensation of the scene before him. He succeeded remarkably in his many refreshing and bright street scenes.

Berthe Morisot
(1841–1895)

A sister-in-law of Manet, Berthe Morisot worked and exhibited with the Impressionists, yet developed her own style. She posed for many of her friends and, in turn, painted many of them. *The Artist's Sister at a Window* (fig.13–8) expresses completely Morisot's philosophy of painting. The girl sitting by an open window, who seems to daydream while looking at her fan, creates a mood of loneliness. The application of color in flat patches reflects Manet's early influence on her work. Yet, Morisot was also influenced by her study of masterpieces of the Louvre and of Corot. Her design and composition are more solid than the off-hand, unposed look of many Impressionist works.

Crosscurrents with Japan

Following a long period of isolationism, in which Japan closed itself to foreign influence, Japan reopened trade relations with other nations in 1853.

By the 1860s, Japanese woodcuts became available in Paris and greatly influenced many of the French Impressionists. The beauty and economy of line in the prints caught the eye of the Impressionists and Post-Impressionists. The Japanese use of perspective and space was particularly appreciated. The woodcuts served as models for many of the formal qualities these artists were seeking to achieve in their own work.

In subject matter, Japanese *ukiyo-e* prints also were inspirational. *Ukiyo-e* was a style of genre painting that provided an informal glimpse of Japanese life. These casual scenes were just the type favored by European painters in the second half of the nineteenth century.

The Japanese themselves had been influenced in the seventeenth century by European prints which had made their way to Asia. So, when the French artists such as Manet (fig. 13–a), van Gogh, Cassatt and Gauguin started translating what they saw in Japanese prints into their own work, it was as much the result of a previous cross-fertilization as anything else. Borrowing from other traditions and producing something imaginatively new is an ongoing process in the arts.

Higher-Order Thinking Skills

1 White fabrics and objects are challenging to paint because using just a solid white does not convey any sense of the volume of the subject. Ask the class what colors and techniques Morisot used to convey the impression of her sister's white dress in *The Artist's Sister at a Window* (fig.13–8).

2 Instruct students to pretend that they are the Flemish Renaissance artist Jan van Eyck, who, through a time machine, has suddenly landed in a French art gallery in the late nineteenth century. How might he react to the Impressionist paintings shown in Lesson 13.1? Have students compare similarities and differences between *Arnolfini Wedding* (figs.10–b, 10–6) and the Impressionists' style, compositions, colors and subject matter. As van Eyck, are they excited or dismayed at Western art's progress over the centuries?

Contextual Information

Degas

Manet and Degas were both friends and rivals, and their artmaking processes were very different. Manet painted directly what he saw and used his instincts about what to eliminate. Degas carefully composed his canvases from drawings and notes. He drew on tracing paper, often layering one piece over another to correct or change poses of his subjects.

Absinthe

Absinthe was a popular drink in the nineteenth century. It was also the cause of death in many who drank it in quantity. It was then a legal drink but now is illegal because it is such a powerful narcotic.

Edgar Degas

(1834–1917)

Although Edgar Degas differed in many aspects from the Impressionists, he shared their interest in casual subjects and candid glimpses of people in action. He approached his work with intellectual curiosity. To achieve his desired instantaneity, he carefully considered design and the positioning of people and objects. Degas was a master of line and drawing and was reluctant to abandon it in favor of Impressionism's soft contours.

Degas was an excellent amateur photographer and worked with Eadweard Muybridge's and Thomas Eakins' studies of the human body and horses in motion. He applied their results to his own unique presentation of the figure in his painting.

Degas liked to paint in *series*; that is, many paintings exploring the same theme over a period of time. One subject that he explored in great detail and in hundreds of paintings, drawings and pastels was the ballet. He captured the instantaneous glimpse of figures in action. Degas explored the indoor, controlled lighting; the lighting often comes from below as in footlights. The views are often from peculiar vantage points, such as from wings, balcony boxes or from below the stage. All these features enhance Degas' candid glimpses of dancers working at their craft.

Rehearsal on the Stage (fig.13–9) is done in pastels. He was interested in the daily routine of practice and work—the constant search for perfection. The director is instructing his ballerinas while stagehands relax and watch. The softness of the costumes is contrasted with lines and edges on figures and in the background. Degas' soft blending of

13–9 Photography and the concepts of photographic composition strongly influenced Degas' work.
Edgar Degas, *The Rehearsal on the Stage*, 1874. Pastel over brush-and-ink drawing on paper, 20 3/4" x 28 1/4" (53 x 72 cm). The Metropolitan Museum of Art, New York, bequest of Mrs. H. O. Havemeyer, 1929. The H. O. Havemeyer Collection.

13–10 How does Degas make the viewer feel like a part of this scene?
Edgar Degas, *Carriage at the Races*, 1873. Oil on canvas, 14 1/2" x 22" (36.5 x 56 cm). 1931 Purchase Fund. Museum of Fine Arts, Boston.

Cooperative Learning

Group students (or have them group themselves based on their choices) and have them select a painting from another time period that they feel would lend itself well to the Impressionist style. Have students use tracing paper to transfer the image to paper or canvas, and then use acrylic, tempera, colored pencil or pastel to create the new Impressionist work. Help students identify what characteristic—such as color, brushstrokes or lighting—will be needed to make a truly Impressionist work.

Materials and Techniques

Degas experimented by first steaming pastels until they were soft. He then soaked them in different solutions until they could be used as paint. He even combined gouache, watercolor, ink, oil paint and pastels.

13–11 Trace the compositional path from the viewer to the center of interest.
Edgar Degas, *The Absinthe Drinker*, 1876. Oil on canvas, 36 1/4" x 26 3/4" (92 x 68 cm). Musée d'Orsay, Paris.

costume into background is an Impressionist technique for showing light bouncing off of form. However, as a line around a foot or down a leg suggests, Degas only uses softness to express action or to describe the material. His clustering of figures to one side or in one corner is balanced by open spaces and, perhaps, the careful placement of a separated figure or two. No matter how unbalanced or casual his groupings seem, they are always calculated to produce an asymmetric balance. This balance produces a feeling of immediacy and nonplanning. The medium of pastels is as much drawing as painting. It allowed Degas to convey the color and excitement of the ballet with more assurance than he could with oils.

Another theme that Degas covered completely in a series was racetrack activity. He treated the horses, jockeys, owners and crowds at the races with a marvelous sense of design. In *Carriage at the Races* (fig.13–10), which he painted outdoors, he used a carefully selected, high-keyed palette of pearly softness. Vibrating greens, pinks, yellows, blues and grays contrast with the crisp, darker tones of horses and the carriage. The combination definitely produces an outdoor feeling.

The carriage and the horses are placed off-center to add to the feeling of a momentary glimpse of the scene. They run out the bottom of the frame, as if cropped for some special effect. The composition is visually balanced by the partial carriage at the left edge.

While some artists saw the happy side of Parisian social life, Degas was not enchanted by what he saw. His *The Absinthe Drinker* (fig.13–11) shows a couple who have been sitting and drinking too long at their table. They no longer talk to each other but stare blankly at the activity in the café. At first, the painting has a snapshot quality and seems to lack formal composition. Yet, the more one looks, the more one realizes that everything works perfectly to attain that feeling. The zig-zag of the empty tables increases the sense of brooding and confusion. Diagonals slant in many directions. They even seem to extend forward from the picture plane, drawing the viewer into the scene. The milky green glass of absinthe becomes Degas' center of interest and the purpose for the painting.

Degas worked a great deal with pastels rather than oils. He was the first artist to exhibit them as finished works instead of preliminary sketches for paintings. As his eyesight weakened, he also spent much time working on sculptures because he enjoyed feeling the solidness of the forms and the action that they expressed. A multi-talented artist, he was a master of oils, pastels, pencil and sculpture.

Higher-Order Thinking Skills

Degas and other artists were intrigued by colored theater lights, a new technology in their time. At first, the lights were gas, which gave off a greenish glow. Later electric lights were (and still are) colored by the use of gels. Ask the class what evidence they can find of the impression of theater lights in *The Rehearsal on the Stage* (fig.13–9). What would change if the scene were illuminated by natural light?

Performing Arts Connection

Rehearsal on the Stage: Edgar Degas and the Ballet

Edgar Degas dared to illustrate the underlying truth of dance. Where the audience saw only graceful ballerinas, he divulged awkward behind-the-scenes moments. In *The Rehearsal on the Stage*, the five women on the left stretch, rest and stand about nonchalantly, unconcerned with how they might appear from our offstage vantage point. The presence of the unfinished scenery, two men lazily looking on, and the conductor's sweaty efforts compound the unglamorous, realistic view of the rehearsal process.

• Although performances often appear effortless, they require painstaking attention to detail, complex coordination of events and hours of practice to produce this illusion. Have the class list everything that they think is necessary to stage a ballet or musical. What would have to occur prior to the performance, behind the scenes and afterward? How many people would be involved to accomplish each task? (Note: Another example of a ballet scene painted by Degas can be found in Chapter 2, fig.2–59.)

Contextual Information
The Financial Side of Impressionism

The first exhibit of the *Société anonyme des artistes peintres, sculpteurs, graveurs etc.*, resulted in ridicule from critics and audiences. This lack of acceptance of the Impressionists contributed to their inability to make a successful living from their art. Except for those artists from wealthy and supportive families, the early Impressionists did not have money for food, rent or painting supplies. Because they could not afford to pay for models, they painted one another or themselves. Or they painted still lifes. Fortunately, some American collectors, who had been persuaded by Cassatt and a few art brokers, did buy Impressionists' work. Some art dealers gave or loaned money to artists. The Impressionists themselves often bought one another's paintings as each in turn had money or wanted to add to his or her collection. At one Impressionist auction, the artists had to buy back some of their work because the bids had been too low.

Renoir

Renoir liked to paint in the countryside around Paris, but during the Franco-Prussian War (1870–1871) he was told that he could not leave the city. He finally could not stand being confined further, so he marched down to city hall to see the official in charge. Quite by coincidence, the official had met Renoir previously and knew of his artistic reputation. He gave Renoir the necessary certificate to paint outside the city walls.

Much later Renoir's hands were badly affected by arthritis. When it severely hampered his movements, he continued to paint with a small piece of cloth placed in the hollow of his hand. His gnarled fingers gripped rather than held the brush. After a paralyzing stroke in 1910, Renoir was urged by his dealer to try sculpture with the help of an assistant, Richard Guino, who had studied with Maillol (*see* Chapter 14). As Guino worked from Renoir's drawings made for previous paintings, Renoir oversaw his work,

Pierre Auguste Renoir
(1841–1919)

Pierre Auguste Renoir's career stretched well into the twentieth century and progressed through several developmental stages. Throughout his career, he remained interested in painting women and the nude figure.

In his first period, he was interested in the bright, cheerful effects of light and air. For the 1877 Impressionist group exhibit (their third), Renoir painted the ambitious *Dance at the Moulin de la Galette Montmartre* (fig.13–12), which is the very essence of Impressionism. Renoir, always interested in painting people, depicts a Sunday afternoon outdoor dance in a popular district of Paris, the Montmartre. Beautiful people are enjoying conversation and dancing. The viewer is caught up in the effervescence that Renoir felt and painted. Flickering light filters through the trees and speckles the people with bits of sunshine. In this delightful interplay of light and shadow, Renoir uses no black paint, but all shadows are tinged with blue. The darker the value, the deeper the blue mixed with other colors.

During the first part of his career, Renoir painted portraits, still lifes, landscapes and figures in a fantastic surge of creativity. During his second phase, after restudying the great masters, Renoir gave up the transient effects of Impressionism. He painted solid, carefully defined

13–12 No black paint is used in this work even though many areas are understood as black.
Pierre Auguste Renoir, *Dance at the Moulin de la Galette Montmartre*, 1876. Oil on canvas, 51 1/2" x 69" (131 x 175 cm). Musée d'Orsay, Paris.

13–13 The long feathery brushstrokes used here are characteristic of Renoir's late work.
Pierre Auguste Renoir, *In the Meadow*, 1892. Oil on canvas, 32" x 25 1/2" (81 x 65 cm). The Metropolitan Museum of Art, bequest of Samuel A. Lewisohn.

1867
Diamonds discovered, Kimberley, South Africa

1881
Japanese women perform on stage for first time since development of *Kabuki* theater in 1600

1895
Cuba begins revolt against Spanish rule

World Cultural Timeline

1892
Electric clocks first used to time sports events, Japan

pointing with a stick to parts that needed to be changed.

• Because Renoir did not mold the clay for the sculptures, should they be considered his original work? How much of the work might have been collaborative, with Renoir and his assistant discussing the work together?

Cassatt

At the time of Cassatt's first visit to Paris, women were not admitted to the École des Beaux-Arts. She studied with two well-known painters, Charles Chaplin and Jean Léon Gérôme. However, she says that she learned the most from copying paintings by Correggio, Holbein and Velazquez.

Cassatt was known as an important artist in 1892, when a retrospective of

her work was shown in Paris. In 1893, she was asked to paint a mural for the World's Columbian Exposition Women's Building in Chicago. In 1904, Cassatt turned down a prize from the Pennsylvania Academy of Fine Arts. As a founding member of the Independent Exhibition, she felt that she must stick to their principle of entering only exhibitions in which there were no juries, medals or awards, because they felt that these would favor particular types of art to the exclusion of other good art.

• What are the good and bad points of art contests and awards?

• Are works that win prizes better than other works? Why? To whom?

13–14 Mothers and their children were a favorite subject for Cassatt.
Mary Cassatt, *Sleeping Baby*, about 1910. Pastel on paper, 25 1/2" x 20 1/2" (65 x 52 cm). Dallas Museum of Art, Munger Fund 1952.

Mary Cassatt
(1845–1926)

Mary Cassatt was born in Philadelphia. After studying art at the Pennsylvania Academy, she left for Paris in 1865 against the wishes of her parents. Here she was drawn to the work of the Impressionists, especially Degas'. In his solid design and superb draftsmanship she found the directions she wanted to take. Although influenced and helped by him, Cassatt never imitated him. She developed a style that combined the informal subject and composition of the Impressionists with her personal desire for precision and definition.

Mothers and children were Mary Cassatt's favorite subjects. She is unmatched in her ability to express, in both oils and pastels, the mutual love between the two. *Sleeping Baby* (fig.13–14), a delightful pastel, combines a seemingly casual glimpse into a nursery with a carefully designed composition. The center of interest is the tender touching of faces of the mother and her child. Arms, legs and darker values direct eye movement to this center. Like Degas, Cassatt used line along legs and arms to strengthen the design and to add solidity to the figures. Yet, the loose pastel strokes and high-keyed colors are features of the Impressionists with whom she exhibited.

Mary Cassatt was well respected among her peers in Paris, but was not recognized at home in Philadelphia, a dilemma which caused her to remain in Europe. But, she was tremendously influential in getting several American families to buy the paintings of her Impressionist friends. As a result, museums and private collections in the United States have superb collections of their work.

Higher-Order Thinking Skills

1 Have the class compare the use of color to portray light in *Dance at the Moulin de la Galette* (fig.13–12) and *The Rehearsal on the Stage* (fig.13–9).

2 Have students turn to fig.2–23 which is another example of Cassatt's favorite subject, mother and child. Ask them to analyze the work and provide three characteristics it shares with *Sleeping Baby*.

forms. In his third period, he tried to unite his first two by combining the formal balance and solidity of the traditional approaches with the shimmering effects of Impressionism. *In the Meadow* (fig.13–13) was painted during this time. The figures are placed carefully in a landscape. They are shaded to produce solid, rounded forms. Cool colors are used for shadows. Yet, the two figures blend softly into their surroundings. Edges on the two girls are nonexistent. Renoir has developed a soft, longish brushstroke that is characteristic of his later

work. Broken color and optical mixing are used with these strokes to create a soft, subtle and gently shimmering painting style.

In his fourth and final period, there is an exaggeration of this soft brushwork and the use of more intense colors, but the solidity remains. Whatever the period, joy never leaves Renoir's work. His fingers were crippled with arthritis at the end. Yet, Renoir still painted happy figures in sun-filled landscapes that in no way let one sense his pain.

Interdisciplinary Connection

History: Have students research the effects of the Franco-Prussian War in France and how the war might have affected the Impressionists, particularly Monet and Manet.

Performing Arts Connection

Popular Entertainment for the European Middle Class

The Industrial Revolution gave rise to the European middle class. Ask students to look at Renoir's *Dance at the Moulin de la Galette* to offer guesses at how these people spent their increased leisure time and money. Many enjoyed music and dance at outdoor cafes, parks, dance halls and popular theaters, and Renoir's flickering brushstrokes of sunlight and shadow catch the transitory nature of this active, carefree atmosphere.

• Have students identify movement in Impressionist artworks and also in musical compositions by Claude Debussy and Maurice Ravel. What adjectives describe the movement or action in both art forms?

Contextual Information

Whistler

Whistler won the case against Ruskin, but the cost of the trial bankrupted him. In 1879, he had to sell his house and paintings to pay his costs. He finally restored his fortune by the sale of prints.

• Have students find examples of prints that Whistler made during this period when he so desperately needed funds.

Rodin

Rodin was commissioned in 1891 to design a sculpture of Honoré de Balzac, a French writer. Originally, Rodin was going to make a portrait of Balzac. After seven years of research, he presented the full-body statue version at the Salon of 1898. People who admired Balzac were upset to see the rough handling, particularly since they could see the smoother, more lifelike handling in Rodin's *The Kiss* (1886) in the same exhibition. The Balzac sculpture became one of the first in which creative expression was more important than a truthful likeness. Some critics called Rodin's sculpture of Balzac a "nightmare," a "toad in a sack" and a "volcanic rock washed by the sea." The statue was returned to Rodin, and it took another 40 years before the plaster model was cast in bronze by a private group.

James Abbott McNeill Whistler

(1834–1903)

The American James Abbott McNeill Whistler moved to Paris in 1855 and four years later went to London, where he worked the rest of his life. Instead of adopting the broken color or the sunlit effects of Manet and Degas, Whistler often worked in grays and blacks. He blended his colors so carefully that he could obtain a wide range of hues and values with his limited palette. He was strongly influenced by Japanese prints and, for a while, included Oriental motifs and objects in his paintings.

By the late 1860s, Whistler returned to portraiture. He wanted to combine a realistic likeness of the sitter with an excellent sense of design. To this end, he looked to the simplification and stark arrangements of Degas and of the Japanese woodcut. An example is his best-known work, *Arrangement in Gray and Black No. 1: The Artist's Mother*, commonly known as *Whistler's Mother* (fig.13–15). The realistic portrait of the delicate woman is placed against a carefully designed background of vertical and horizontal rectangular shapes. The shapes, not the likeness, dominate the painting. Every item in the painting is an integral part of the design, including the draperies, the pictures on the wall, the floor and the placement of his mother's hands. He used the flat color areas of Manet, but not his brushwork. Instead, Whistler used thin glazes of color to build up his subtle grays. Even the title was selected to help the public see the painting as a design rather than a representational painting. Whistler often used titles that recall musical compositions, such as "arrangements," "symphonies," "harmonies" or "nocturnes."

In 1877, he exhibited *Nocturne in Black and Gold: The Falling Rocket* (fig.13–16). The painting caused a furor in London. The painting is an impressionistic view of skyrockets bursting in the English night. It swirls with muted colors and dark shadows, punctuated with vivid flecks of color. It is a symphony of color, tones, accents and dark passages. But the noted English art critic, John Ruskin, defender of traditional Realism, used his biting satire to remark that Whistler was "flinging a pot of paint in the public's face." Whistler could not let the challenge go and sued Ruskin for libel. During a lengthy trial, he struggled vainly to explain to judge and jury what he was trying to express in his painting. Whistler won the trial, but was awarded only one farthing in damages.

13–15 The composition of shapes is the subject, and the sitter is a part of the design.
James Abbott McNeill Whistler, *Arrangement in Gray and Black No. 1: The Artist's Mother*, 1871. Oil on canvas, 56 1/2" x 63 3/4" (144 x 162 cm). Musée d'Orsay, Paris.

13–16 The English art critic John Ruskin's criticism of this painting caused a lawsuit for libel.
James Abbott McNeill Whistler, *Nocturne in Black and Gold: The Falling Rocket*, 1874. Oil on panel, 23 1/2" x 18 1/2" (60 x 47 cm). The Detroit Institute of Arts.

Auguste Rodin

(1840–1917)

During the years of Impressionism, when color and light were all-important, Auguste Rodin burst on the scene with magnificent sculptural forms. He transformed the off-handedness and instantaneity of Impressionism into powerful, three-dimensional forms. Rodin's sculptures can be favorably considered with those of Donatello, Michelangelo and Bernini. Yet, they were so individual and personal that no followers imitated them.

Rodin's best works were cast in bronze, but were first formed with his hands in clay, plaster or wax. He loved the immediacy of these materials, which he could manipulate,

13–17 This is Rodin's best-known work.
Auguste Rodin, *The Thinker*, 1879–1889. Bronze, 28" (71 cm high). National Gallery of Art, Washington, DC, gift of Mrs. John W. Simpson.

push, stab and form. Impressionist paintings may seem unfinished, yet are complete. In the same way, Rodin often left his sculptures seemingly unfinished. He experimented with figures in action, accidental effects, and feelings of spontaneity and tension. Often the surfaces of his bronzes shimmer with light reflecting from his fingerprints and the rough surfaces.

Like the Impressionists, Rodin's work was not popular with critics and the public because it was not smooth, finished and beautiful. He planned a gigantic work, the *Gates of Hell* (which he never finished) that would have rivaled Michelangelo's Sistine Ceiling in the amount of effort expended. Models were made, but, because of frequent interruptions, he was never able to complete the task. His famous *The Thinker* (fig.13–17) was to be a small part of the entire monumental design.

Most of Rodin's works were never completed. Others were rejected by the patrons who had commissioned them. His *Monument to Balzac* (fig.13–18) was finally put in place in 1939, long after the artist's death. The sculpture of the French author is a massive form that is both powerful and expressive. Rodin wanted to show the author at the moment he conceived a new creative idea for a novel. Balzac (whom Rodin did not know) is shown wrapped in a long cloak and lost in thought. The huge

13–18 Rodin's sculptures were planned and formed in clay, plaster or wax, then cast in bronze.
Auguste Rodin, *Monument to Balzac*, 1897–98. Bronze, 110 3/4" (281 cm high). The Museum of Modern Art, New York. Presented in memory of Cort Valentin by his friends.

figure seems to be a mass of drapery with an unbelievably powerful head thrusting out of the folds. Again, the original concept was not appreciated by the patrons who wanted something more refined and traditional, but Rodin would not compromise his ideas. Viewed from below, the figure is overpowering. It is the summation of Rodin's sculptural expression.

Higher-Order Thinking Skills

Rodin is the sculptor of *The Thinker*, of which nine statues were cast. Each of these is considered an original. Explain that sculptures can be done in editions, just as prints are. Ask students if they feel that statues that are multiple originals are less valuable than, more valuable than, or of equal worth to those that are one of a kind. They should back up their positions with research.

Lesson 13.1 Review

1 From which style of art did Impressionism develop?
2 Which painting suggested the title Impressionism to the art critics?
3 Why did Monet paint so many versions of the Rouen Cathedral?
4 From what vantage point is the viewer looking at the *Place du Théâtré Français* in Pissarro's painting?
5 What medium did Degas use to draw *Rehearsal on the Stage*?
6 Which American woman Impressionist painted many pictures of mothers and children?
7 How are Rodin's sculptures similar to Impressionist paintings?

Lesson 13.1 Review Answers

1 Realism—All Impressionist painters began as Realists.
2 The Impressionist movement took its name from Monet's *Impression: Sunrise.*
3 Monet wanted to analyze the changes in colors as the sunlight changed during the day and from season to season.
4 The viewer seems to be looking over Pissarro's shoulder, out the window and down onto the street below.
5 *The Rehearsal on the Stage* was done in pastels.
6 Mothers and children were the favorite subjects of Mary Cassatt.
7 Rodin often left his completed sculptures appearing unfinished just as Impressionist paintings often do not seem completely finished. Fingerprints and rough surfaces on Rodin's bronzes reflect light, shimmering in a way that is similar to Impressionist paintings.

Lesson 13.2

Because Post-Impressionist artists were dissatisfied with Impressionism's casual compositions, they reintroduced form and structure into paintings that sometimes stressed vehement emotions. Post-Impressionism was not an organized and cohesive movement but rather one that encompassed numerous artists who shared common goals.

Warm-up

Have students carefully search for evidence of lines in George Seurat's painting *A Sunday on La Grande Jatte–1884* (fig.13–19). Ask them to come up with a name to describe the technique that Seurat invented. What geometric shape did he rely on for his pointillist style?

Objectives

Students should be able to:

Understand how the Post-Impressionists were indebted to their predecessors for unique ways of perceiving and expressing the visible world.

Identify how the new generation of artists broke away from the constraints of Impressionism and reinstated a strong sense of form and structure into their sometimes emotional works.

Discuss the characteristics of Post-Impressionism, which include expressionistic use of bold color, spontaneity, distortion of natural forms, geometric structuring, concern with painterly brushstrokes, personal insights and the continued interest in Impressionist light and color.

Vocabulary Definitions

pointillism A style of nineteenth-century French painting in which colors are systematically applied to canvas in small dots, producing a vibrant surface.
expressionists (ek-*spresh*-a-nists) Artists who try to communicate strong personal and emotional feelings to the viewer.

Teach

Criticism: Challenge students to pretend that they are the puppy in the lower right-hand corner of *A Sunday on La Grande Jatte–1884.*

13.2 Post-Impressionism

A
S THE NINETEENTH CENTURY came to an end, Impressionism had run its course as the new direction in art. The early goals of Impressionism had been abandoned and artists were exploring new aspects of the Impressionistic style. Artists who based their work on the color theory and techniques of Impressionism, but who developed their own unique styles, are loosely grouped together under the heading Post-Impressionists. They worked alongside many of the Impressionists, but they were no longer convinced by their instantaneous glimpses of nature and their seemingly unplanned canvases. They wanted to combine the color and light of Impressionism with the design and composition of traditional painting—much like Renoir's goals in his last period of work.

Two directions emerged among these artists. Cézanne and Seurat looked for permanence of form and concentrated on design. Van Gogh and Gauguin emphasized emotional and sensuous expression. The development of Impressionism had freed artists from traditional painting techniques and Renaissance concepts of space and form. Building on this new freedom, Post-Impressionism produced a variety of styles. It set the stage for the extreme range of individual expression that characterizes art in the twentieth century.

Key Notes

• Post-Impressionism combines the color and light theory of the Impressionists with the design and composition of traditional painting.
• Post-Impressionism produces a variety of unique styles.

Vocabulary

pointillism
expressionists

Special Feature

Georges Seurat

(1859–1891)

Color and light predominate in Seurat's paintings, but they are the very opposite of a quick "impression." Seurat went after a permanence of design. He used methodical and scientific techniques based on photography and the physics of light and color. Combining this knowledge with the techniques of the Impressionists, Seurat painted marvelously light-filled pictures. Before starting work on the final canvas, Seurat made many sketches in oils, charcoal and crayon to determine color, light, placement and shapes.

Seurat's largest and most impressive work, and a landmark in modern art, is *A Sunday on La Grande Jatte—1884* (fig.13–19). Seurat made forty preliminary studies for this painting. He placed each figure extremely carefully. The color was

---

13–19 Seurat's technique involves the placement of dots of color next to each other for the viewer's eye to mix. A similar technique is used today to create television and computer images.
Georges Seurat, *A Sunday on La Grande Jatte–1884*, 1884–1886. Oil on canvas, 81 1/2" x 121" (207.5 x 308 cm). The Art Institute of Chicago, Helen Birch Bartlett Memorial Collection.

• Do they think the picnicking people will move quickly out of their way as they romp along the riverbank?

• Then ask the class how long they think the figures have been in their positions. A moment? Hours?

• What element makes Seurat's work emit a timeless permanence? Have the class compare Seurat's solid composition to Monet's series of Rouen Cathedral (figs.13–2, 13–3)

Evaluate

Ask students to imagine that they are Post-Impressionist artists.

• Would they be upset if a critic lumped their art together with other painters in the same movement?

• Did all the Post-Impressionists share the same style? Have students cite images from Lesson 13.2 to support their conclusions.

• How do they feel when their individual efforts go unacknowledged but the group of which they are a part receives acclaim?

• Have they ever wanted to be judged apart from others and solely on their personal merits?

• How might this be applied to their own judgments about people? For instance, have they ever dismissed someone whom they do not know just because he or she is part of a group that they have previously formed a negative opinion about? Is this fair?

13–20 **Compare this seascape to Monet's** *Argenteuil.* **Consider color, brushstrokes, point of view.**
Georges Seurat, *Le Bec du Hoc at Grandchamp*, 1885. Oil on canvas, 21 1/2" x 25 1/2" (55 x 65 cm). Tate Gallery, London.

applied in tiny dots, each about the size of a pencil eraser. From a distance, the viewer's eyes visually mix these dots together to create the vast array of hues and values that make up the painting. For example, red dots placed next to yellow dots appear as an orange area. This technique, which is called *pointillism*, is similar to the placing of tessarae in a mosaic. Today, we see a similar technique to pointillism in the "dots" in halftones, TV images and color printing. The result of this technique in *La Grande Jatte* is a marvelously uniform surface that sparkles with light and color.

In the painting, the people of Paris, enjoying a Sunday afternoon in the park, are carefully arranged. They face either sideways or forward and are almost Egyptian in their formality. Seurat placed figures and landscape features according to a mathematical formula similar to one the Greeks used in their designs and compositions. As you can see, this work is definitely more solid than a fleeting glimpse.

Seurat painted a series of landscapes in the late 1880s, almost all of which included views of the sea. The flickering light of pointillism is especially appropriate in depicting sparkling water. In *Le Bec du Hoc at Grandchamp* (fig.13–20), a large cliff rises to break the far horizon. The view may look quite casual but Seurat always chose his subject matter with great care. Again, hundreds of thousands of points of color are applied to build up the surface and develop the final color range. Apparently Seurat walked around an area for a long time before he started making sketches and small painting studies of the final scene. He was looking for just the right view to fit his design formula.

Like the Impressionists, Seurat focused on color and light, but, as with the other members of the Post-Impressionist group, he went beyond these very specific interests. His method was highly scientific and the results much more solid than the instantaneity of Impressionism.

Contextual Information

Seurat

Seurat's reading of *The Scientific Theory of Color* (1881) by American physicist O. N. Rood was influential on his style. Rood's discoveries included the fact that colors mixed by one's eyes appeared stronger and more intense than printed mixed colors.

Higher-Order Thinking Skills

Seurat worked on a complex theory that he felt would help define how people see color. The idea of placing dots of colors close to each other so that the viewer's eye must mix them to perceive the intended color is still very much in use in printing and in video. Borrow a microscope or magnifying glass from the science department and have students examine printed photos and reproductions to see the small dots of color that make up the colors that they "read" in the image.

• Ask students to discuss the similarities and differences between these mechanical processes and Seurat's method of painting.

Reteach

Tell the class that most of the avant-garde artists at the turn of the century went unacknowledged during their lifetime and came to be appreciated only later.

• Ask how students would have felt if they had been these artists, knowing that although they were pursuing their passion, their achievements would probably remain unrecognized for years to come.

• How might this affect their attitude toward their artwork, their peers and the buying audience? Would fame after death be enough for them?

• Would public approval be vitally important to them as artists? Why or why not?

Interdisciplinary Connection

Social Science: Just as France continued to dominate the art scene in the late nineteenth and early twentieth centuries, its influence was also predominant in the development of costume. In the paintings of Impressionist artists, women were engaged in leisure activities or were onlookers or participants at sporting events. A subject's clothing can provide insights into his or her personality, wealth, religion, social status, occupation and nationality. Have the class examine the paintings of Monet, Morisot, Degas, Renoir, Cassatt, Whistler and Seurat. Ask how the women are dressed and what are they doing. What social classes do they depict?

Divide students into groups. Have each group select and research one of the following topics to support their interpretations:

1 What was the social and economic climate of the Western world during this period?
2 What outside factors helped to shape the characteristics of the forms taken by costume in the Western world?
3 How did the development of sports, theater and opera affect dress codes?
4 What effects did the Industrial Revolution have upon the textile industry?

Contextual Information
Cézanne

Cézanne spent his boyhood in Aix-en-Provence, where his father was a wealthy banker. Under family pressure, he trained as a lawyer in his hometown while also attending the local drawing academy. Cézanne later went to Paris to continue his study of art. Deeply hurt by rejections at the 1874 Impressionists' exhibition, Cézanne moved back to Aix-en-Provence. The small town, famous for its painters, had approximately 29,000 residents in 1880. Away from the busyness of the Paris art scene, Cézanne lost contact with people who would have helped make his work better known before his retrospectives in 1895 and 1898.

The writer and free-lance art critic Émile Zola had been a boyhood friend of Cézanne, and the artist introduced Zola to the Parisian Impressionists. Later in their lives, Zola grew impatient with Cézanne's lack of contact with the Paris art world. He did not see great changes in Cézanne's work and wrote a novel in which the artist (who is described as a person much like Cézanne) is called an "abortive" genius.

Paul Cézanne
(1839–1906)

Paul Cézanne was the leading painter of the late nineteenth century in France and one of the most influential artists in Western painting. Although he worked for a short while in Paris, he spent most of his life in relative seclusion in his hometown of Aix. His early work was Romantic, and he used Delacroix as his model. He applied his colors in juicy, thick passages. In the early 1870s, he met Pissarro and adopted the Impressionists' high-keyed palette. He exhibited with them at their first exhibition in 1874 and, again, at their third showing. All of his submissions to the Salon were rejected except one, in 1882. According to the standards of his time, he was a failure.

While the Impressionists used light to capture a fleeting moment, Cézanne's light seems permanent and all-encompassing. It illuminates colors and subjects, and shadows are often nonexistent. Cézanne did not want his paintings to imitate the realistic three-dimensionality of nature. He wanted them to remain as flat canvases with paint on them. Because he was concerned with the structure of the painting, he felt free to move objects and adjust relationships of color and form to produce the best design possible, even if it meant distortion. He discarded the traditional aerial and linear perspective and painted every part of the canvas with equal intensity—foreground, middle ground, background and sky. This led to compressing of space so that the canvas remained visually flat yet the colors seemed to indicate depth.

Near the town of Aix, the large mountain *Mont Sainte-Victoire* (fig.13–21) dominates the landscape. Cézanne painted the mountain often and explored his developing techniques and painting concepts.

In the version shown here, the mountain is in the background. Houses and trees fill the valley in front. Cézanne built up his painting by applying paint in flat, squarish patches or planes of color. Some of these planes may seem to be houses or trees, but were meant to be planes of color. The intensity of the colors remains strong throughout so that the sky seems as close to the viewer as the foreground. Colors and values are distributed over the picture plane to produce a visual balance. The whole painting reads as a mountain-dominated landscape. Yet it is built up of relatively equal, small, squarish, flat abstract planes of color that unify the composition.

Earlier in his life, Cézanne painted many portraits. His sitters often complained of extremely long sessions and many quit before the paintings were finished. Cézanne's approach to painting required hours

13–21 Cézanne creates a sense of perspective by overlapping planes of color.
Paul Cézanne, *Mont Sainte-Victoire*, 1904. Oil on canvas, 28″ x 35 1/4″ (71 x 89 cm). Philadelphia Museum of Art, George W. Elkins Collection.

13–22 Design of the painting was Cézanne's ultimate concern. Use the text to help you completely understand this design. Paul Cézanne, *Still Life with Apples and Peaches*, 1905. Oil on canvas, 32" x 39 1/2" (81 x 100 cm). National Gallery of Art, Washington, DC, gift of Eugene and Agnes Meyer.

of looking. He was intent on making sure of the placement of color and value and its relationship to the canvas. How different his approach was from the instantaneous approach of the Impressionists! When sitters would not tolerate the long hours of posing, Cézanne began working with still lifes. His patient and tedious working process often caused fruits to spoil before the painting was finished. He finally had to resort to using wax fruit and vegetables in his set-ups. His still lifes were carefully designed and made use of brilliant color.

Still Life with Apples and Peaches (fig.13–22) is an excellent example. At first glance, the painting appears to be a simple still life with fruit and a few ceramic pieces. However, like all of Cézanne's art, it is carefully designed. The rich colors glow from the canvas. The warm hues of the fruit contrast with the cool hues of the surroundings. Rather than add black to the peach color to create a feeling of form, Cézanne used flat patches of gradually changing color to produce roundness. This careful selection of adjacent colors made his painting process lengthy. The Impressionists had used color to dissolve form. Cézanne used patches of color to build up form. Blues are distributed throughout the painting as are touches of pink, yellow and orange.

Lines are either painted on the canvas or occur as breaks in value or color. Notice the lines of the cloth and table. Their many lines seem to flow diagonally from upper right to lower left. In order to balance that strong diagonal movement, Cézanne introduced counter movement from the lower right to the upper left in several lines and in the cloths. But more important, notice the slanting of the pitcher, the distortion of the bowl, and the arrangement of the fruit. All add to the counter movement and balance the design. Every brushstroke, color change and line has a purpose in the painting. The visual movement from object to object and the rhythm established with color and value accents produce a typical painting of perfect control, careful design and brilliant use of color. To Cézanne, the design of the painting was most important, not the imitation of the original still life. If distortion produced a better design, it was the artist's privilege, or even requirement, to distort.

Higher-Order Thinking Skills

Ask the class to compare *Mont Sainte-Victoire* (fig.13–21) to a landscape by Claude Lorraine. Ask students to state and explain their preference for one or the other. Explain that Cézanne painted Mont Sainte-Victoire many times over the years. Ask what advantages and disadvantages there might be in repeatedly portraying a subject.

Contextual Information

Lautrec

Lautrec began creating lithographs in 1894. His favorite subject matter for his art was the dance hall and the Paris night life of the 1890s. In 1897, Lautrec was commissioned by the Moulin Rouge cabaret to create his first poster. Thus he became the first artist to produce modern posters for commercial purposes. By means of lithography, he created dimension with the use of flat colors and line and brought this art form to a level of fine art. (See Chapter 2, fig.2–33 for another example of Lautrec's work in printmaking.)

• Discuss how posters are used today and their effectiveness in instructing or communicating a specific message.

• Have students compare Lautrec's prints with Ukiyo-e prints for subject matter as well as technique and composition. (See figs.2–48 and 4-e for examples of Ukiyo-e prints.)

Henri de Toulouse-Lautrec

(1864–1901)

Born in Albi to one of the noble families of France, Henri de Toulouse-Lautrec broke both legs when fourteen. Because they did not develop properly, his growth was stunted. Since he could not participate in his family's active social life, he went off to Paris to paint. He lived in the Montmartre area, Paris's theater district and artists' quarters. He spent much of his time in the cafés, cabarets and theaters. He drew caricatures and portraits with great skill. He liked to portray dancers and circus people, such as his dancer-friend *Jane Avril* (fig.13–23). In his quick, sketchy style, he was able to capture her character in a few rapidly applied lines. Lautrec created the same feeling of spontaneity in his paintings, although they often took a long time to finish. Thin washes of color are often used in combination with a sure, dark line which was an extension of his drawing technique.

Many of his paintings are of the night life of Paris, which he saw from "elbow height," as he himself

13–23 Notice how the artist has sketched some parts of this figure in greater detail than others. **Where has the artist placed his emphasis?** Henri de Toulouse-Lautrec, *Jane Avril*, 1892. Mounted on wood, 26 3/4" x 20 3/4" (68 x 53 cm). National Gallery of Art, Washington, DC, Chester Dale Collection.

said. *At the Moulin Rouge* (fig.13–24) reveals the influence of his friend Degas. The composition recalls *The Absinthe Drinker*. A group of his friends are clustered around a table in the cabaret. Lautrec and his much taller cousin can be seen crossing the canvas in the background. The diagonal table and the woman at the right seem to move forward from the picture

13–25 The artist designed many posters for the cafés and cabarets of Paris' theater district. Henri de Toulouse-Lautrec, *Moulin Rouge, La Goulue*, 1891. Poster. Indianapolis Museum of Art, Gift of the Gamboliers.

1904
African art begins to influence European artists

1917
Mexico adopts a new constitution

World Cultural Timeline

1912
First Japanese battleship built

1914
Panama Canal opens

Multicultural Connection

African Sculpture

Carved wooden sculptures were not made in all parts of Africa. They came mostly from the west and central parts of sub-Saharan Africa, the region south of the Sahara. People there found plenty of rainfall to grow crops and plenty of wood to build houses and cook food. As small settlements grew into villages and towns, art was created to be worn and displayed by leaders, to be used in dancing and ceremonies, and to honor the spirit world. Symbolic images were made for a specific, usually reli-

gious purpose. The use of stylized geometric forms and linear patterns later influenced the work of many artists in the early twentieth century. (See Chapter 4, pages 124–129, for more about African art.)

• Show examples of reliquary figures created by the Gabon cultures of the sub-Sahara. Ask what these art forms tell us about the beliefs and practices of these African cultures.

• Have students research the carved wooden sculptures made by the peoples of the Society, Austral, and Cook islands, which include Tahiti. What similarities do they see to the wooden sculptures of sub-Saharan Africa?

435

Higher-Order Thinking Skills

1 Have the class compare the lighting in the cabaret scene of *At the Moulin Rouge* (fig.13–24) to Degas' *The Rehearsal on the Stage* (fig.13–9).

2 Lautrec infuses *At the Moulin Rouge* with mood and feeling yet it is also superbly designed. Ask students to analyze the work in terms of movement, focus, color dominance, balance, shape and line.

plane. They bring the viewer into direct relationship with the scene. Lautrec's presentation of his lifestyle and social environment was as realistic as that of Daumier and just as biting in its social comment. He knew it well, and painted and drew it with gusto. He also lived it excessively, dying of alcoholism when only thirty-seven.

Lautrec was the first artist to produce modern posters for commercial purposes. His caricatures adorned advertisements for many of

the cafes and cabarets of the Montmartre (fig.13–25). Most of his prints of dancers were used to advertise their performances and were pasted on the kiosks of Paris. These kiosks were the billboards of the time. In the poster, notice Lautrec's use of strong, black line and flat areas of lighter color. Although he enjoyed painting, he did not consider his work worthy of display. At his early death, many fine works, not seen before by his friends, were found in his studio.

13–24 Toulouse-Lautrec was greatly influenced by Degas. This influence is evident in the strong diagonals and asymmetrical composition of the painting.
Henri de Toulouse-Lautrec, *At the Moulin Rouge*, 1892. Oil on canvas, 48 1/2" x 55 1/2" (123 x 141 cm). The Art Institute of Chicago, Helen Birch Bartlett Memorial Collection.

Contextual Information

Vincent van Gogh

During one of his voluntary stays in an asylum, in June of 1889, van Gogh painted *The Starry Night*. Approximately seven months later, he committed suicide. It is notable that many of the works by van Gogh with which we are most familiar were painted in the last two-and-a-half years of his life.

Vincent van Gogh

(1853–1890)

The first great Dutch painter since the seventeenth century, Vincent van Gogh did not start out as an artist. He worked for art dealers in The Hague, London and Paris. He also had a great love for humanity and was a language teacher in England, an evangelist in Brussels, and a missionary to coal miners in Belgium. At times, he was vital and exuberant while, at other times, depressed and melancholy. During several sieges of mental depression, he even admitted himself to sanitariums for help and rest. Van Gogh began painting when he was twenty-seven. He worked feverishly for only ten years before suicide ended his tragic life. Like Cézanne,

he was considered a failure. He sold only a single painting while he was alive. Yet today he is considered one of the world's more important artists. He left over eight hundred drawings and an equal number of paintings.

Van Gogh was very close to his brother, Theo, who was an art dealer in Paris. In his correspondence with Theo, van Gogh fully explained his reasons, techniques and feelings about each painting as he worked on it. These letters provide a fascinating insight into the creative processes of a deeply serious painter. Van Gogh spent most of his painting years in France, had few friends, and devoted himself fully to his painting.

His early work was traditional in

technique, dark in value and somber in color. But once he saw the work of the Impressionists, his colors brightened and his brushstrokes became visible. His paintings jumped alive with brilliant color and a textured surface never seen before. Rather than use the soft strokes of Renoir or the dots of Seurat, van Gogh jabbed at his canvas with vigorous strokes, applying paint in thick impasto.

Van Gogh was not satisfied with merely painting a scene or a person. He felt he had to say something about the subject or about himself and his own emotional involvement

13–27 Trace the motion of the brushstrokes to feel van Gogh's gesture with his brush.
Vincent van Gogh, *The Starry Night*, 1889. Oil on canvas, 29 1/4" x 36 1/2" (74 x 93 cm). The Museum of Modern Art, New York, Lillie P. Bliss Bequest.

Performing Arts Connection

Musical Paintings

Whistler, Mondrian and Kandinsky are just a few artists who produced works with musical connotations. Conversely, the famous popular song "Vincent" by Don McLean was inspired by the brilliant swirling stars that animate Vincent van Gogh's *The Starry Night*. There is also Stephen Sondheim's *Sunday in the Park with George*, which was inspired by Seurat's work.

• Have students individually or in small groups use a performing art to express a landscape. Have them formulate how they can abstractly communicate the scene's weather, light, sounds, atmosphere and movements. Ask them to stretch their imaginations to think of unusual vantage points, such as a view from the inside an erupting volcano, from above a far-off planet, or from the top of a tall tree in the rain forest.

13–26 Van Gogh was one of the few artists of his generation who carried on the tradition of portraiture.

Vincent van Gogh, *Portrait of a Peasant*, 1888. Oil on canvas, 25 1/2" x 21 1/4" (65 x 54 cm). The Norton Simon Art Foundation, Pasadena, CA.

with the subject. Artists who express their feelings and emotions through their work are called **expressionists**. Van Gogh began this movement, which was later given the logical title Expressionism.

In his portraits, van Gogh used radiant, vibrating colors to immortalize his subjects. As he said, he wanted to give them "something of the eternal which the halo used to symbolize." *Portrait of a Peasant* (fig.13–26) shows his late portrait style. Sizzling color is applied with choppy strokes to build up a textural surface. He used complementary colors (orange against blue, yellow against blue-violet, and red against green). The contrast of warm against cool creates a visual vibration that at first might seem shocking.

The Starry Night (fig.13–27) is the direct opposite of the cool and calculated paintings of Seurat, van Gogh's contemporary and friend. He tried to work in Seurat's pointillistic style for a time. However, the all-consuming passion of this painting is more in keeping with van

Gogh's character. It is planned and balanced, but at the same time it has a feeling of gushing spontaneity. It is as if the brush took control of the artist. Van Gogh turns the scene of a village at night, resting peacefully under the stars, into a writhing turmoil of activity. The stars not only glow in the dark sky, but move violently, perhaps noisily, as they churn through the universe. The writhing movement from left to right is halted by the moon. The moon lends stability to the sky and sends the viewer's eyes back into the picture. The snakelike vertical cypress tree also stabilizes the scene. At the same time it adds its own writhing movement. The jabbing brushstrokes across the town, trees and hills unify the entire surface. At times, the painting seems more like a textured tapestry than a painting on canvas. The curling rhythms indicate a rapidly done painting. Van Gogh probably produced it in a creative burst of activity. This provocative work forces the viewer to ask, "What is he trying to reveal about the night?"

Sidelight

Price of Art Today

Very few artists realize large sums of money for their art during their lifetime. Take, for example, the $54,000,000 recently paid for Vincent van Gogh's *Irises*. This is an extraordinary price, yet, ironically, van Gogh was able to sell only one painting in his lifetime. His brother, Theo, who was an art dealer, recognized the quality of the work, but not even he could persuade people to buy it. Had it not been for Theo's loans, van Gogh would have been in the poorhouse.

Paul Gauguin is another artist who never knew financial success, but whose work today commands huge prices. When Gauguin went to live in Tahiti, his lack of money was so dire that he was often ill and often nearly starved. The thin gloss of color on the canvases of this period are due to the fact that he could not afford sufficient materials to lay down a thicker base. Gauguin sent paintings back to France, but no one wanted to buy them, not even cheaply. Paul Gauguin's fortunes never improved, and he died poor at the age of fifty-five.

Some artists, however, do achieve recognition and financial success in their life, particularly the popular artists of the twentieth century. Picasso's work always sold well during his lifetime, even though it did not reach the prices that it does today. Contemporary American artist Jasper Johns has seen his works sold for over a million dollars.

Higher-Order Thinking Skills

1 Ask students to write their interpretation of van Gogh's attitude about the night in *The Starry Night* (fig.13–27) and then compare it to their own feelings about being outside at night. Ask what lines, shapes and colors they would use to convey their feelings.

2 Have students decide what music would evoke the atmosphere of van Gogh's *The Starry Night* and that of Seurat's *A Sunday on La Grande Jatte–1884* (fig.13–19).

• Ask which musical piece would be loud and which one calm and even-tempered. (To stimulate their thinking, you might play ballads and then jazz, or choral music against bombastic orchestral symphonies.)

• Discuss how and why the music they chose expresses the sensations in each painting.

3 Challenge students to detect the difference in the colored forms that the artists used to create their overall designs. (Seurat painted dots, and van Gogh used dashes.) Although both artists relied on repeated patterns to construct their compositions, do they convey the same effect?

• How does van Gogh visually communicate an awesome sense of motion and spirit?

• Ask students to guess what the two artists might have felt about each other's art.

• What might they have admired and what might they have disliked in the other's canvas?

• Which of the two paintings do students themselves find more appealing and why?

Contextual Information

Gauguin

Gauguin bought paintings by Cézanne, Sisley, Pissarro and Degas during the years when he was working as a stockbroker. When the stock market crashed in 1882, he thought it was a good time to leave the brokerage firm to paint. Later on, because he could not make a living as an artist, for his family's sake he moved to Denmark and tried being a salesman. His wife worked as a French teacher, but he was not able to make a living there either. For the rest of his life, Gauguin worked at odd jobs to pay for paint supplies.

Gauguin was part of a goup of artists called *synthetists*. The group was centered around Pont-Aven, a small village that rivaled Paris as a center for avant-garde art. They derived their art not from transcribing what they saw, but from a synthesis of impressions, including those from memory. They used brilliant colors outlined in black to express ideas, moods and emotions, and a complete rejection of naturalistic representation.

13–28 Gauguin searched art history for styles he felt he could meaningfully use in his work. Do you see any historical influences in this painting?
Paul Gauguin, *The Vision after the Sermon (Jacob Wrestling with the Angel)*, 1888. Oil on canvas, 28 3/4" x 36 1/4" (73 x 92 cm). The National Galleries of Scotland, Edinburgh.

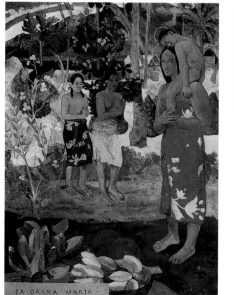

13–29 Gauguin rarely used lines, preferring to build his forms through color.
Paul Gauguin, *Ia Orana Maria*, 1891. Oil on canvas, 44 1/2" x 34 1/4" (113 x 87 cm). The Metropolitan Museum of Art, New York, bequest of Samuel A. Lewisohn.

Paul Gauguin

(1848–1903)

A very successful stockbroker, Paul Gauguin became intensely interested in painting in his late twenties. At first he painted for relaxation, but soon was accepted in the Salon show in 1876. He was drawn into the Impressionists' group, exhibited with them in 1879, and studied and painted with Pissarro. In 1883, he quit his job to paint. Within a few years he could no longer support his family. They soon left for his wife's homeland of Denmark. Convinced that European urban society was incurably sick, he began a long search for a better way of life. He lived in the villages of Brittany, a remote region of France, at several different times. He lived for a time in Arles with van Gogh. He traveled to the islands of Martinique and Tahiti and finally the Marquesas Islands in the South Seas, where he died in poverty.

In his painting, he rejected the formlessness of Impressionism, the traditional Western style of naturalism, and realistic portrayal. What was left for Paul Gauguin? He wanted to return to a primitive style of art with simple forms and symbolism rendered in a decorative and stylized way. Like Egyptian, medieval and Oriental artists, he outlined his shapes. He even used Egyptian poses in several of his paintings. He flattened form into decorative shapes and combined brilliant colors to express his feelings. His color combinations were innovative. He used purples with oranges, and bright blues with yellow greens.

The search for religious experience was important to Gauguin. In *The Vision after the Sermon (Jacob Wrestling with the Angel)*, he tried to show the simple, direct faith of the peasants of Brittany (fig.13–28). Shapes are flat, simplified and outlined. Modeling and perspective are minimal. Instead of natural colors, Gauguin used stained-glass colors to depict the trance-like rapture of the peasant women.

Gauguin hoped to find a simple and more meaningful lifestyle in Tahiti. Although he adopted native ways and took a native wife, he remained a sophisticated Parisian.

13–30 The artist sent his paintings to Paris to be sold so that he could support himself and continue to paint in Tahiti.
Paul Gauguin, *The Day of the Gods (Mahana No Atua)*, 1894. Oil on canvas, 26 3/4" x 36 3/4" (68 x 91 cm). The Art Institute of Chicago, Helen Birch Bartlett Memorial Collection, 1926.

His painting style and colors were already established in his Normandy paintings, and Tahitian influence on his work was very small. But, the natives and their colorful surroundings fill his canvases with a fascinating beauty.

One of his earliest Tahitian paintings is *Ia Orana Maria*, translated as "We Hail Thee Mary" (fig.13–29). A native woman and her son have haloes as if they are Tahitian versions of Mary and the Christ Child. Two women stand nearby in an attitude of worship. Their poses are copied from a photograph of a Javanese temple relief. Hidden in the colorful surroundings is a protective angel. Thus, Gauguin incorporates colorful and symbolic forms with a Tahitian setting to produce a unified painting. His symbolism is completely personal, distinct from the feelings and religious convictions of the Tahitian natives. Gauguin made this work to sell in Paris to support his stay in Tahiti.

In *The Day of the God* (fig.13–30), a young native mother and her two children are near the water while a huge image of a god towers over them. Almost as in an Egyptian register, a line of other natives perform their daily tasks in the background (fig.13–b). The water takes on a decorative pattern. Gauguin outlines brilliant colors in peculiar, flat shapes which are repeated in the sky. He has again combined Tahitian subject matter with his decorative symbolism and exotic colors to produce a handsome design.

Lesson 13.2 Review

1 What did Seurat do in preparation for painting *Sunday Afternoon on the Island of La Grande Jatte*? What technique did Seurat use to paint this picture? How large is *Sunday Afternoon on the Island of La Grande Jatte*?
2 Explain what concerned Cézanne so much in his paintings that he often would distort forms? What was he trying to achieve in his art?
3 What were some of Toulouse-Lautrec's favorite subjects to paint?
4 Describe the painted surface texture of Van Gogh's paintings.
5 Why is Van Gogh considered an *expressionist*?
6 How many paintings did Van Gogh sell in his lifetime? How much have his works sold for recently?
7 Why did Gauguin travel to Tahiti and the South Sea islands?
8 Describe Gauguin's painting style in *The Day of the God*.

Lesson 13.2 Review Answers

Lesson 13.3

While France remained a dominant force in Western art, artists from other European countries began to reflect a pessimistic view about contemporary urban society, eventually paving the way for the later Expressionist movement.

Warm-up

Instruct students to close their eyes and pretend that an imaginary problem is giving them a blinding headache and making them feel dizzy. Have them also strongly press a hand on either side of their temples, continuing with the pressure for a full minute. After releasing the tension and taking a few deep, long breaths, ask what colors and shapes they would use to describe their experience during the exercise. Instruct them to compare their visual descriptions to Edvard Munch's *The Cry* (fig.13–31). How does their imagined experience tell them that Munch's art expresses vastly different interests than those in the lighthearted Impressionist paintings?

Objectives

Students should be able to:

Understand that the seeds of Expressionism began in the Western European art of the late nineteenth and early twentieth centuries.

Discern that while France remained the Western art capital, vital experiments also occurred in other parts of the world.

Analyze the often despondent views of contemporary urban life described by a number of European artists.

Vocabulary Definitions

primitive The native arts of any culture, usually on a less sophisticated level than that of modern times; a culture before it adopts the ways of another. Also used to describe the art produced by untrained or naive artists.

13.3 Turn-of-the-Century Expressions

TOWARD THE END OF the nineteenth century and the beginning of the twentieth century, France dominated the art scene. There were, of course, some marvelous painters and sculptors in other countries. Their work often reflected the sterility and pessimism that many Europeans viewed as part of contemporary urban society. A number of artists followed in the footsteps of Goya, van Gogh and Gauguin by expressing their personal dissatisfaction with their cultural environment through painting.

The first seeds of the Expressionist movement which took hold in the early twentieth century can be found in the work of these artists.

Key Notes

- France continues to dominate the art scene in the late nineteenth and early twentieth centuries.
- A number of European painters express the bleakness of contemporary urban life and help trigger the beginnings of Expressionism.

Vocabulary

primitive

13–31 Munch tried to convey the sound of a cry in color and line. Was he successful? Edward Munch, *The Cry*, 1893. Oil and tempera on cardboard, 35 3/4" x 29" (91 x 74 cm). National Gallery, Oslo, Norway.

Special Feature

Edvard Munch

(1863–1944)

Edvard Munch learned about tragedy at an early age. When he was five, his mother died. Nine years later, his adored sister died from tuberculosis. These tragic events greatly affected his life and painting. He was obsessed with death, and it is featured continuously in his art. He borrowed some techniques from the Impressionists and Post-Impressionists, but his vision remained highly personal. He was concerned with death and dying, anxiety, loss and abandonment, and loneliness.

His first one-person show was in Berlin in 1892, and it was a total disaster. The subject matter of his paintings was too pessimistic and gloomy for most people. The exhibition caused an uproar and had to be closed after a week.

The Cry (fig.13–31) is Munch's most famous painting. It depicts a figure standing on a bridge. Her hands are on either side of her face. The scream coming out of her agonized mouth is as real as if we could hear it. She is turned away from the water and we do not know if her fright has been caused by something she saw in the water or by something she is looking at. Whatever it is, it is terrible. It is almost as if the sound waves coming out of her mouth turn into the fast flowing water. The figure is isolated at the bottom of the canvas. Behind her the river looks very ominous. This is a very disturbing painting. Even the sky is perturbed.

Teach

Criticism/ Art History: Ask students to compare the Impressionist paintings of everyday life in Lesson 13.1 to Edvard Munch's *The Cry* and Pablo Picasso's *The Old Guitarist* (fig.13–33).

- Do they think Munch and Picasso perceived the world in the same way the Impressionists did?

- Do students themselves hold one of these visions of the world?

- While the Impressionists were interested in outer, superficial activities, artists such as Munch and Picasso tended to use color and form to dig deep into the physiological realm of human experience.

Evaluate

Ask students why the artists in Lesson 13.3 are considered the initiators of the later Expressionist movement. How did their concerns differ from those of the Impressionists?

13–32 What mood do you feel from this work?
Edvard Munch, *Girls on a Bridge*, between 1904 and 1907. Oil on canvas, 31 1/2" x 27 1/4" (80 x 69 cm). Kimbell Art Museum, Fort Worth, Texas.

Many of Munch's works are infused with a feeling of imminent tragedy. The composition of strong diagonals and dark, foreboding shapes of *Girls on a Bridge* (fig.13–32) is characteristic of his work. The textured brushstrokes remind one of van Gogh, but the overall mood is typical of Munch's work. The faceless figures are unidentifiable and incapable of accepting one's pity or help as they stare into the dark depths of the river below (fig.13–d). Munch weaves a psychological drama, but makes no comment and offers no relief. At the time that Munch was emerging as a painter, Sigmund Freud was developing his theories of psychoanalysis. In a way, Munch was painting the states of mind Freud was studying. Clearly, *Girls on a Bridge* is more than a picture of people on a bridge, such as the Impressionists or Corot might paint. Munch was expressing his own feelings of gloom toward what he was seeing.

Contextual Information

Munch

After Munch's mother died, he was raised by his father, a shy physician who had withdrawn into depression that alternated with fits of rage. Munch himself was often sick as a child and felt utterly alone. He was later to paint this loneliness. He wrote that "illness, madness, and death were the black angels that kept watch over my cradle." He felt that emotional suffering was good for his art and wrote: "How much of my art I owe to suffering."

Munch was influenced by the expressive styles of Lautrec and van Gogh, and by Gauguin's use of simplified forms and nonrealistic, expressive, colors. To earn money quickly, Munch translated many of his paintings into woodcuts, etchings and lithographs.

Higher-Order Thinking Skills

Munch's *The Cry* is also sometimes titled *The Scream*. Ask students if they feel that the title makes a difference in the viewer's response to a work. Why? Have them find a work in the text that they would retitle and explain to the class the reasons for their choice.

Reteach

Many of the artists in Lesson 13.3 communicated their opinions about urban life in their paintings.

• Ask students to think of other artists throughout history who have functioned as social critics. You might clue them to Goya (figs.12–14, 12–15) or Daumier (figs.12–35, 12–36).

• Set up a panel in which students debate whether it is important for art to contain an underlying message or to focus solely on aesthetic elements of color, shape and form. Instruct them to site examples from the textbook to support their case.

Have students read the selections on Barbara Kruger, Jaune Quick-to-See Smith and Edward Kienholtz in Lesson 17.6. Ask what these contemporary artists have in common with Edvard Munch.

• How might these artists react to the content of his work? Do students think that any of these artists are satisfied with modern culture?

• Do students believe that art with social or political subjects makes it more exciting or detracts from its enjoyment?

Contextual Information

Picasso

At the age of 18, Picasso came to Paris with one hundred paintings to exhibit at Vollard's gallery. The exhibition was not a success because people did not understand his style. However, he found an audience with Germans who appreciated the avant-garde paintings before others did and accepted Picasso's Cubist paintings.

Paris in the Late Nineteenth Century

Paris at the end of the nineteenth century was in the midst of great changes. Large factories—the result of the Industrial Revolution—encouraged rural people to crowd into the city. Poor living conditions meant diseases such as TB, cholera, typhoid, typhus and diphtheria. Changes had to be made, and urban planning recreated the city with underground sewers, parks, public housing, gas, water and a trolley system.

Pablo Picasso

(1881–1974)

Pablo Picasso came to Paris from Spain as a young man in 1900. Like Munch and van Gogh, he was affected by the tragic mood that urban society was generating. His early work has been called his Blue Period because he painted beggars, derelicts and poor families with a predominately blue palette. The color fits the mood of the paintings. *The Old Guitarist* (fig.13–33) is composed entirely in blue tones. Sadness is expressed by the color, by the attitudes of the figures, and by the mysterious sea close by. Although Picasso's name weaves itself into the fabric of many aspects of twentieth-century art, his early work in Paris coincided with the beginnings of Expressionism.

13–33 What liberties has the artist taken with the figure to achieve the effect he wanted?
Pablo Picasso, *The Old Guitarist*, 1903. Oil on wood, 48" x 32" (123 x 82 cm). The Art Institute of Chicago, Helen Birch Bartlett Memorial Collection.

Window in Time

Art Theft of the Century

Boston, March 18, 1990. The early hours of the morning. While partygoers all over Boston are still celebrating St. Patrick's Day, one of the largest art heists of the century is taking place in Boston's Isabella Stewart Gardner Museum.

Although several guards are on duty during the hours the museum is open, few guards remain on the premises at night because an elaborate security system is in place. On this night, two overnight guards, one an art student and the other a musician, were on duty. One of the guards was patrolling the galleries while the other sat behind the security console at the Palace Road service entrance. At 1:24 a.m., the bell was rung at the house's Palace Road entrance.

Edouard Manet, *Chez Tortoni*. Isabella Stewart Gardner Museum, Boston

The outside TV camera that continuously scanned Palace Road and the side entrance showed two police officers ringing the bell. The guard at the desk pushed the outdoor speaker button and asked, "What's going on?"

"Boston Police," replied one of the men, adding that they had received a report of a disturbance in the outdoor compound. The museum gardens are surrounded by a high wall. The guard said he hadn't heard anything. The policeman then asked, "Any other guards on duty?"

"One," the watch desk guard replied. "He's upstairs doing rounds."

"Call him down and let us in," the policeman said. "We'll have to check out the garden compound."

This all seemed quite normal to the guard, and he did as the policeman said. The two men came in, and

the three of them chatted while they waited for the other guard to join them. But, once he had, the two bogus policemen spun the guards around and flung them against the wall. Quickly, they manacled the guards' hands and covered their eyes, ears and mouths with plastic tape. Then, they hustled them down the stairs to the basement and, taking them to opposite ends of a long corridor, handcuffed them to heating pipes and left them lying on the concrete floor.

The thieves were then free to do as they wanted. Clearly, they knew how the museum security was set up. Before starting the robbery, they turned around the video cameras taping them. They also broke open the security room, destroyed the videocassettes and switched off a central computer that recorded any movements in the gallery. However, they did not manage to turn the system off completely and some of their activities in the museum were taped. The theft was discovered when the morning personnel arrived and could not get in.

The thieves stole priceless works by Rembrandt, Vermeer, Flinck, Degas and Manet. The value of the stolen art was estimated at $200 million. However, the artworks are so famous that they can never be sold, traded or displayed in a private collection without instantly being recognized.

After the robbery, art experts predicted that the paintings would either be abandoned or anonymously returned. Gardner Museum officials take comfort in the knowledge that it usually takes a number of years to recover stolen art. They also know that the more famous the work, the higher the chance of recovery.

Higher-Order Thinking Skills

1 Ask how color conveys a mood in a painting. Have students find two works in the text that they feel use color effectively to convey a particular mood. Hold a discussion in which they explain their choices.

2 Have students imagine that they are art collectors at the end of the nineteenth century. Is there only one dominant style from which to choose, as had essentially been the case in earlier eras?

• Given the diversity of new individual approaches, which artists in Chapter 13 would they patronize?

• What is it about the artists' style and subject matter that attracts them? Direct students to try to convince each other of their opinions.

3 Have students consider what message about modern urban living that Edvard Munch expressed in *The Cry* (fig.13–31) and Pablo Picasso demonstrated in *The Old Guitarist* (fig.13–33).

• Do students think the two artists were content with society?

• What contributed to their opinions? How did the artists use color to greatly enhance their work's impact?

• Would the impact of Picasso's canvas change if he had painted it in pink, yellow or red, or if Munch had used rainbow colors in *The Cry*?

Contextual Information

Rousseau

Considered a "Sunday painter," Rousseau had a full-time job with a toll-collecting service for Paris, until 1893. After 22 years at the job, he retired at 49 with a small pension. By then, however, he had been exhibiting for eight years: he exhibited two paintings at the Salon of 1885. From 1901 to 1904, he was listed as a teacher at the Philotechnic Association, and he also taught art in his home.

Rousseau got ideas for his paintings from encyclopedias, children's books and botanical books. He invented some of the plants in his paintings and changed the proportion of others. He even painted more than 20 jungle scenes—all created while he was living in the city.

Lesson 13.3 Review Answers

1 France dominated the art scene toward the end of the nineteenth century through the advent of the twentieth century.
2 Munch's artwork portrayed scenes of death, dying, anxiety, loss, abandonment, and loneliness.
3 *The Cry* is Munch's most famous painting.
4 Picasso painted beggars, derelicts and poor families with a predominantly blue palette. The color fits the mood of the paintings. *The Tragedy* is from his blue period.
5 Because Rousseau had no formal art training, he developed a primitive style within his technical limitations.

Chapter Review Answers

Review

1 The Impressionists wanted to express an immediate impression, not a detailed analysis of objects, figures or landscapes. They were interested in portraying the effects of light and color.
2 Manet's paintings seem to be cropped with a candid, off hand appearance, as one would crop a snapshot. A slightly unfinished look and seemingly unposed arrangement also make the paintings seem like a momentary glance.

Henri Rousseau

(1844–1910)

A customs official of France, Henri Rousseau gave up his government job at middle age and took up painting. His goal was to paint the world around him with absolute realism, in the style of Ingres. Without any formal art training, this was impossible. Instead, he presents an enchanted world of forests and tropical jungles filled with exotic flowers, fantastic animals and an occasional person or two. Fellow artists admired his directness of vision, innocence of technique and his naive spirit. His *primitive* style was born of technical limitations, but produced paintings of great enchantment.

Rousseau painted in a new way—innocently and truthfully. Picasso and Gauguin called him the godfather of twentieth-century painting. In *The Sleeping Gypsy* (fig.13–34), he crafted a smooth surface with no visible brushstrokes, a technique not commonly used. The meaning of the work is mysterious and is not fully explained in the painting. The final interpretation is left to the viewer. The huge moonlit sky, simplified landscape elements, multicolored coat and the sniffing lion work together to create a sense of magical calm. Recently, it has been discovered that Rousseau used children's toys, purchased on sale at a Paris store, as models for the painting. He depicted them as realistically as he could.

The rhythmic beauty of his concepts was lost on the public. They considered him an untrained novice and laughed at his magical portrayals with outright indignation. In their derision, they overlooked the naive honesty and dreamlike expression of this delightful artist.

13–34 This painting is open to many interpretations. What story do you think the painting tells?
Henri Rousseau, *The Sleeping Gypsy*, 1897. Oil on canvas, 50 3/4" x 79" (129 x 201 cm). The Museum of Modern Art, New York, gift of Mrs. Simon Guggenheim.

Lesson 13.3 Review

1 As the twentieth century began, which country was the center of Western art?
2 What themes did Edward Munch paint?
3 What is Munch's most famous painting?
4 Why is Picasso's early work called his Blue Period? Name an example of a painting from his blue period.
5 Why did Henri Rousseau paint with an innocence of technique?

3 Renoir shows contemporary people enjoying themselves with light filtering through trees speckling the people with bits of sunshine. He was interested in color theory: using blues, not black, in the shadows.
4 Whistler was trying to combine a realistic likeness of his mother with an excellent design. He placed the woman in front of a background of vertical and horizontal rectangular shapes. He used flat areas of subtle grays in this asymmetrical composition with space on the left balancing the figure on the right.
5 Georges Seurat: pointillism, dots, sparkles, light, color, stiff, scientific.

Paul Cézanne: color, thick paint, distortion, compression of space, light, shadowless, squarish, flat, abstracted, planes of color.

Henri de Toulouse-Lautrec: nightlife, thin washes, dark lines, linear, dramatic lighting, caricatures.

Vincent van Gogh: impasto, brilliant color, expressionistic, textured surface.

Paul Gauguin: primitive, symbolism, simple forms, stylized, flattened form, decorative shape, brilliant color, Tahitian influence.

6 Van Gogh shows a peaceful village at night under a dark-blue sky filled with gold swirling stars. Wild brushstrokes cover the painting with a thick-textured impasto, creating a mood of passionate spontaneity.
7 In *The Sleeping Gypsy* a huge moonlit sky, simplified landscape elements, a multicolored coat and a sniffing lion create a sense of mystical charm. Rousseau used toys as models. The surfaces of his paintings are smooth.

James A. McNeill Whistler

James A. McNeill Whistler was an argumentative artist and disliked any criticism of his paintings or their titles. He rejected his friends' suggestion that he would earn more money if he simply gave his paintings names that indicated a real scene. He thought such a thing would be "a vulgar and meretricious trick." The following comments from Whistler's publication, *The Gentle Art of Making Enemies*, are his reply to these friends.

Cheyne Walk, London, May, 1878

Why should not I call my works "symphonies," "arrangements," "harmonies," and "nocturnes"? I know that many good people think my nomenclature funny and myself "eccentric." Yes, "eccentric" is the adjective they find for me.

The vast majority of English folk cannot and will not consider a picture as a picture, apart from any story which it may be supposed to tell.

As music is the poetry of sound, so is painting the poetry of sight, and the subject-matter has nothing to do with harmony of sound or of color.

Take the picture of my mother, exhibited at the Royal Academy as an *Arrangement in Grey and Black*, Now that is what it is. To me it is interesting as a picture of my mother; but what can or ought the public to care about the identity of the portrait?

Art should be independent of all clap-trap—should stand alone, and appeal to the artistic sense of eye or ear, without confounding this with emotions entirely foreign to it, as devotion, pity, love, patriotism, and the like. All these have no kind of concern with it; and that is why I insist on calling my works "arrangements" and "harmonies."

Primary-Source Connection

Have students read this excerpt from Whistler's book in conjunction with the description of his life and work on page 428. Then have them write a statement that Whistler might have made to the court, during his lawsuit against John Ruskin, in which he demonstrates why Ruskin should be found libelous. Do students agree with the court's decision? Why or why not?

Review

1 What were the Impressionists trying to achieve in their paintings?
2 What techniques did Manet use to make his paintings such as *Gare Saint-Lazare* and *The Waitress* seem like a snapshot or a view that was quickly glimpsed?
3 Explain why Renoir's *Dance at the Moulin de la Galette Montmartre* is a good example of Impressionism.
4 Describe the color and composition in Whistler's *Arrangement in Gray and Black No. 1: The Artist's Mother*. What was Whistler trying to achieve in this painting?
5 List four Post-Impressionist artists. After each one's name, write three adjectives to describe his style.
6 Describe the motion, the colors, the texture, the mood and the subject matter in van Gogh's *The Starry Night*. How large is it?
7 Describe a painting by Henri Rousseau. What did he use as his models? What is the texture of the painting surface? What is the subject?

Interpret

1 Select one of Degas' paintings; then describe how Degas directs the viewer's gaze through this composition, how he leads you into the painting and from one figure to the next. What do you think is the center of interest? What type of balance is this?
2 Explain the symbolism in Gauguin's *Ia Orana Maria*.
3 How are the composition and mood in Munch's

Girls on a Bridge similar to Degas' *The Absinthe Drinker*?

Other Tools for Learning

Maps
1 Find Arles and Paris on the map. Why do you think van Gogh might have moved from Paris to Arles?
2 Monet's *Impression: Sunrise* was painted at Le Havre. He painted the cathedral at Rouen, and he and Renoir painted at Argenteuil. What great river runs through all these towns?

Timelines
Select one event from the non-European cultural timelines and explain how this eventually affected the countries of North America.

Electronic Research
Videodisc player: *National Gallery of Art*
1 Look at an Impressionist painting, such as one of Monet's *Rouen Cathedral* series or his *Water Lilies*, either in an art gallery or on a video disk with close-up views. What does the surface of the painting look like close-up? What does the painting look like when you back away from it?

CD-ROM drive: *Microsoft Art Gallery*
1 To understand how Seurat created with pointillism, watch the animation sequence in the Making Paintings Guided Tour. Explain the pointillism technique.

Interpret

1 In *The Rehearsal on the Stage*, Degas clusters the figures in the left corner, asymmetrically balancing them with space on the right. He leads the viewer through the composition by overlapping figures, outstretched arms and pointing feet. The center of interest is the ballerina dancing on the left. Most of the figures look or point toward her.

In *Carriages at the Races* the visual center is the woman in the carriage in the foreground. The dark carriage contrasts with her light dress. The carriage and horses are off-center, creating a feeling of a momentary glimpse of the scene. Because the subjects bleed off the frame, the composition seems like a cropped photograph or a Japanese woodcut. This asymmetrical composition is visually balanced by the partial carriage on the left edge.

In *The Absinthe Drinker* the milky green glass of absinth is the focal point. The composition is asymmetrical with a cropped photo quality to it. Diagonal lines lead the viewer into the scene.
2 The native woman and her son are Tahitian versions of Mary and the Christ Child. Two women standing nearby are in a posture of worship similar to that in a Javanese temple relief. A protective angel is camouflaged in the colorful surroundings.
3 Both Degas and Munch expressed their feelings of gloom in their faceless female figures. Although Degas shows facial features in *The Absinthe Drinker*, the lady's face is blank—devoid of feeling. Strong diagonals lead the viewer through both compositions.

Maps
1 Arles is about three hundred miles south of Paris near the Mediterranean Sea. The weather is warmer and sunnier than in Paris.
2 The Seine River runs from Barbizon through Le Havre.

Timelines
1 Many topics are appropriate. The technology involved in using electric clocks to time sports events in Japan in 1892 developed into modern timing of athletic events. Cuba's revolt against Spanish rule in 1895 led to the United States declaring war on Spain in 1898 and the Spanish-American War. Not only did African art influence European artists, but later it affected American artists' work too. The 1910 Japanese annexation of Korea, together with Japan's increased aggressive military power, resulted in World War II and the deaths of thousands of North American soldiers. The opening of the Panama Canal in 1914 shortened the time needed for ships to travel from the Pacific coast to the Atlantic coast of the United States.

Electronic Research
1 Close-up views of Monet's *Water Lilies* and *Cathedral* are a mass of colorful brushstrokes. Only when the viewer backs away do the forms become recognizable.
2 Color was applied in small dots of primary colors. From a distance, these dots blend together, creating shades, tints, values and rounding objects. Only on close inspection are these individual dots of color visible.

Activity 1: Still Life Pastel

Activity Objectives
Students should be able to:

• Practice drawing from observation.

• Become familiar with pastels artwork by famous artists.

• Learn how to create a composition from a still-life setup.

• Use pastels to create an artwork.

Thinking Critically
Discuss well-known artists who worked in pastels, such as Paul Cézanne, Edgar Degas, Mary Cassatt and Auguste Renoir. Show students selected artworks of these artists, focusing on the composition, color blending, values, lines and other elements that make the work successful.

Preparation Ideas
Some useful references for these two pastel activities are:

Creevy, Bill. *The Pastel Book: Materials and Techniques for Today's Artist.* New York: Watson-Guptill Publications, 1991.

Dawson, Doug. *Capturing Light and Color with Pastels.* Cincinnati: North Light Books, 1991.

Martin, Judy. *The Encyclopedia of Pastel Techniques.* Philadelphia: Running Press Book Publishers, 1992.

Monnier, Genevieve. *Pastels.* New York: Rizzoli International Publications, Inc., 1984.

Roddon, Guy. *Pastel Painting Techniques.* Cincinnati: North Light Books, 1991.

Notes on Materials

• Use paper with a toothy surface, such as watercolor or charcoal paper, to allow for the buildup of layers.

• As an alternative to sketch pads, use individual sheets of paper secured to a clipboard or to masonite boards with bull clips. Have students hold the board vertically on their lap, which allows more students to obtain a better view at a closer range, and prevents pastel dust from building up on the work.

• Use tracing paper or other material to protect pastel painting from smudging when storing. Use spray fixatives only in a well-ventilated area.

• Provide tortillons, a paper stump rolled to a point, to blend small areas.

Activity 1

Still Life Pastel

Materials
vine charcoal
hard and soft pastels
pastel pencils for details
torchons
charcoal or watercolor paper
spray fixative
kneaded erasers
optional: masonite boards with bull clips, tracing paper

Take a look.
• Fig.13–22, Paul Cézanne, *Still Life With Apples and Peaches*, 1905. Oil on canvas.
• Fig.13–14, Mary Cassatt, *Sleeping Baby*, about 1910. Pastel on paper.
• Fig.13–9, Edgar Degas, *Rehearsal on the Stage*, 1874. Pastel on paper.

Think about it. Many well-known artists worked with pastels, among them Paul Cézanne, Edgar Degas, and Mary Cassatt. Study the color, line and composition in Cézanne's still life and the color blending in the pastels of Degas and Cassatt. Research other examples of pastel artwork and still lifes.

Do it.
• Choose interesting objects from your environment, ones that vary in shape, texture and color, to assemble for a still life.
• Do several practice sketches in vine charcoal before beginning your work in pastel. Draw one object at a time, concentrating on subtle details of that object; then draw thumbnail sketches of the still life to find a successful composition.
• Begin the still life with vine charcoal. Use white, black and gray hard pastels to outline the basic shapes. Draw lightly with hard pastels to build up color. Work with your teacher on the use of spray fixatives to seal the surface between layers.

• Change to soft pastels for the finishing layers.

Check it. Does your still life reflect your personal interpretation in your own style? Are the details and texture of the objects portrayed well?

Helpful Hint: Practice drawing loosely folded cloth, emphasizing the light and shadows.

Activity 2

Same Place Next Time

Materials
select from materials listed in Activity 1 as needed

Take a look.
• Fig.13–1, Claude Monet, *Argenteuil*, 1872. Oil on canvas.
• Fig.13–2, Claude Monet, *Rouen Cathedral*, 1894. Oil on canvas.
• Fig.13–3, Claude Monet, *Rouen Cathedral, West Facade, Sunlight*, 1894. Oil on canvas.

Think about it. Monet loved to work outdoors and to directly confront the environment he was painting. This was a departure from the artists of the past who might sketch outdoors but sought the comfort of their studios to do the actual painting.

Do it. Do a long-term study of the effect of light and atmosphere on a building.
• Find a building in your neighborhood that interests you. It can be a barn, a church or even a house on your block.
• Do a number of sketches of your building until you are very familiar with its structure, its details and its surroundings.
• Work in the medium of pastel, which will be easy to transport to the site and will allow you to reproduce the Impressionist color palette.

• Create these drawings at different times of the day: early morning, midday, late afternoon and even at sunset. Choose varying weather conditions as well. A bright sunny day, an overcast day, even a foggy day will each give you the opportunity to see your building in a different way.

Check it. Each time you do a new sketch, take a fresh look from another perspective. Though Monet painted the same subject many times, he would often sit in a new location and capture it from a different angle.

Helpful Hint: Using short strokes will create the shimmering effects of color so common in Impressionist work. Also, do not use black in your drawings, but, instead, search for color in the shadows of your building.

Additional Activities

• Analyze a still life by Cézanne and one by Renoir. Compare the similarities and differences in relation to: sensory qualities of each, the formal qualities of each, the technical qualities of each, and the expressive qualities of each.
• The dot patterns of Seurat's paintings use the same principle that modern printers used in recreating the color photography in this book. If you examine any color reproduction with a magnifying glass, you should only find four colors of ink—the three primary colors and black. Using these four colors of tempera paint, experiment with dot patterns to see if you can recreate a full-color image.

Classroom Management
Students should practice drawing from observation with pencil or vine charcoal to develop their drawing skills. Have them draw one object at a time, concentrating on subtle details of that object. It is also helpful to practice drawing loosely folded cloth, emphasizing the light and shadows.

Tips
In their future still-life assignments, students could experiment with more advanced pastel techniques, such as:

• *sgraffito*: etching into the pastel surface with an X-acto knife to create sharp lines or other textural design effects.

• *scrumbling*: layering veils of color with light, circular pastel strokes, using the side of the pastel crayon.

Evaluation

• Did each student create a personal interpretation of the still life in his or her own style?

• Is sensitivity to the surface quality of the objects and fabrics evident in the artwork?

• Did the student concentrate and put effort into seeing these objects through an artist's eyes?

• Did the individual grow artistically in his or her basic ability?

• Did he or she effectively blend and build up colors?

Student Profile

Rachel Miller

Age 17
Clarkstown High School North
New City, New York
Favorite kinds of art: painting, drawing and sculpture
Favorite artists: Salvador Dali, Henry Matisse, Edvard Munch
Activity 1, Still Life Pastel

This project is especially meaningful to me since I tend to work from my imagination. The still life gave me a lot of motivation—I wanted to do it, but I didn't rush myself to get it done.

While working, I didn't have an exact plan; I let the pastels simply flow. I wanted to make the piece appear sensitive, since the still life itself had a soft, fragile, warm glow. I wasn't looking for realism, it was more for a feeling, a tenderness that these objects did not emulate on their own, but one that I knew I could bring out. Every object is an art form and creates a certain kind of uniqueness.

Besides my own creative instincts, the history of art was another factor that influenced my piece. Not until a few years ago did I realize that I wanted to pursue the arts as a career. Henry Matisse had an enormous impact on me. He created his masterpieces from his heart, not with his eyes or his hands. In my opinion, his pieces became stronger as his sight weakened. They contained more expression, beauty and emotion. Copying an object directly may be beautiful, but if it has no emotion behind it, then it is not worth the paper on which it was created.

In the artistic process, I enjoy the thought-gathering. Simply thinking about the materials, style, and technique gives me the ability to expand my mind. When I brainstorm, I don't wonder how my piece will appear ultimately, rather I visualize constantly in my mind as an ongoing process. Anyone has an artistic license to create. I feel there are no limits in art. Exposing my mind to art is most important.

To other students interested in creating, I say, "Do it. What have you got to lose?" I believe in the importance of doing what you enjoy most and never settling for anything else. Even if I do not make it as a successful artist, I know I will continue creating art for my own personal pleasure. If you have a gift and you want to share it, take full advantage of it. As you continue to develop your talent, don't let criticism discourage you. The world needs more artists and thinkers. Express yourself, create, think and let your imagination flow.

Rachel Miller

Still Life with Wine Bottle, 1994. Pastel on charcoal paper, 12" x 18" (30.5 x 45.7 cm).

Activity 2: Same Place Next Time

Activity Objectives
Students should be able to:

• Learn what Impressionism means and how the name was coined.

• Gain skill in the technique of optical mixing as practiced by the Impressionists, as well as in the medium of pastel.

• Develop a knowledge of the color palette of the Impressionists.

Thinking Critically
Requiring students to work on-site over a sustained period of time will give them a real sense of what Monet must have experienced as he developed his own exploration of light at the Rouen Cathedral. This type of activity would be especially interesting for more advanced art students who are working on a portfolio. It will enable them to create a body of work that shows depth of idea and concept.

Preparation

• Find prints or photographs of Monet's *Rouen Cathedral* done at different times than the one in the text so that students can make comparisons.

Notes on Materials
See notes in Activity 1.

Teacher Spotlight

Barbara Levine
Art Department Chairperson
and Art Teacher
Clarkstown High School North

Students can bring in objects to add to the still life, but it is the teacher's responsibility to arrange interesting objects that vary in shape and texture. Sometimes I mix real fruit, such as a pineapple, with artificial. When Rachel Miller did the still life, I set up a continuous still life that could be seen from all sides. Students could choose the area they liked best and not be crowded by trying to see the objects from one position. That year, I added a stuffed animal for those who wished to draw that subject matter. It also helps to prop objects up at different levels before draping the surface with cloth. Cloths with patterned designs, like those in the still lifes by Henri Matisse, can add interest.

Classroom Management
This activity was designed as a homework assignment, with two drawings due per marking period, but it can be adapted to work in class. Take your class to an appropriate site within easy walking distance of your classroom. Go again at another time of year or on a day with significantly different weather than the first visit.

Tips
Find examples of optical mixing in the enlarged four-color dot patterns of contemporary color lithography. Perhaps a printer in your community has such examples available. Place it alongside a Monet or Seurat painting to help students understand some of the ideas and scientific approaches to Impressionism.

Evaluation

• Did the student show growth in his or her perception and ability over time?

• Was each sketch in his or her series clearly done at different times in different light conditions?

• Does his or her work demonstrate an understanding of Impressionistic color mixing and palette?

Chapter 14 Organizer

Days	8 Week	1 Semester	2 Semester	
	1	1	1	**Chapter 14 Opener: A Half-Century of "Isms"**

Objectives

Understand how many unique and exciting art styles existed simultaneously in the first half of the twentieth century.

Comprehend that the proliferation of Western avant-garde art movements reflects the mobility and self-searching attitude of its artists.

Explore the evidence of abstraction and Expressionism in the multiple styles that flourished after 1900.

National Standards

4c Students analyze relationships of works of art to one another in terms of history, aesthetics, and culture, justifying conclusions made in the analysis and using such conclusions to inform their own art making.

5a Students identify intentions of those creating artworks, explore the implications of various purposes, and justify their analyses of purposes in particular works.

2d Students demonstrate the ability to compare two or more perspectives about the use of organizational principles and functions in artwork and to defend personal evaluations of these perspectives.

Teacher Edition References

Lesson 14.1 Expressionism

1 / 1	*Special Feature:* Diego Rivera 450–451

Contextual Info 451   HOTS 451

2	Remainder of Lesson 14.1 452–463 World Cultural Timeline 452, 461 Lesson 14.1 Review 463

Contextual Info 452,454, 456, 458, 460, 462
HOTS 453, 455, 457, 459, 461, 463

Cooperative 453
Inquiry 452
Multicultural 452, 457, 461

Lesson 14.2 Abstract Art

1 / 1	*Special Feature:* Joseph Stella 464–465

Contextual Info 465   Interdisciplinary 465
HOTS 465

2	Remainder of Lesson 14.2 466–471 World Cultural Timeline 468 Lesson 14.2 Review 471

Contextual Info 466, 468, 470   Multicultural 467
HOTS 467, 469, 471   Performing Arts 466, 469

Lesson 14.3 Sculpture

1 / 1	*Special Feature:* Constantin Brancusi 472–473

Contextual Info 473   HOTS 473

1	Remainder of Lesson 14.3 474–475 Lesson 14.3 Review 475

Contextual Info 474   Inquiry 474
HOTS 475   Materials and Techniques 474

Lesson 14.4 Fantasy Art and Surrealism

1 / 1	*Special Feature:* Salvadore Dali 476–477

Contextual Info 477   HOTS 477

1	Remainder of Lesson 14.4 478–483 Lesson 14.4 Review 483

Contextual Info 478, 480, 482   Interdisciplinary 481
HOTS 479, 481, 483   Multicultural 482
Cooperative 480   Performing Arts 480, 483

Lesson 14.5 Photography

1 / 1	*Special Feature:* James Van Der Zee 484–485

HOTS 485

1	Remainder of Lesson 14.5 486–488 Lesson 14.5 Review 488

Chapter Review 489   Conservation 487
Contextual Info 486   Materials and Techniques 487
HOTS 487, 488

1	1	1	**Classroom Connections**

National Standards

Studio Activity 1
The Message on the Wall

1b Students conceive and create works of visual art that demonstrate an understanding of how the communication of their ideas relates to the media, techniques, and processes they use.

Studio Activity 2
Exploring Surrealism

1b Students conceive and create works of visual art that demonstrate an understanding of how the communication of their ideas relates to the media, techniques, and processes they use.
3b Students apply subjects, symbols, and ideas in their artworks and use the skills gained to solve problems in daily life.

Ancillaries

Slides: Picasso, *Les Demoiselles d'Avignon*, 92a, 187

Teacher Edition References

Timeline: A Half-Century of "Isms" 449
Map: A Half-Century of "Isms" 449
Context 448
Art 449
Quote 449

Ancillaries

Slides: Rivera, *Still Life*, 9b, 17

Slides: Roualt, *At the Circus: The Mad Clown*, 91b, 180; Kollwitz, *Self-Portrait*, 90a, 181; Modersohn-Becker, *Old Woman from the Poor House*, 92b, 182; Kirchner, *The Street*, 91a, 183; Marc, *Red Deer II*, 93b, 184; Orozco, *Zapata*, 94b, 185
Large Reproductions: Matisse, *Green Stripe (Madame Matisse)*, 23

Slides: Stella, *Brooklyn Bridge: Variation on an Old Theme*, 95b, 186

Slides: Picasso, *Les Demoiselles d'Avignon*, 92a, 187; Braque, *Musical Forms*, 96b, 188; Duchamp, *Nude Descending a Staircase*, 93a, 189
Overhead Transparencies: Steps to Abstraction, 15
Large Reproductions: Picasso, *The Family of Saltimbanques*, 24

Slides: Brancusi, *The Kiss*, 94a, 190

Slides: Barlach, *War Momument (Angel)*, 97b, 191; Giacometti, *Tall Figure*, 98b, 192

Slides: Dali, *Sacrament of the Last Supper*, 95a, 193

Slides: Chagall, *To My Betrothed*, 99b, 194; de Chirico, *Soothsayer's Recompense*, 100b, 195; Ernst, *The Sea*, 96a, 196; Magritte, *Time Transfixed*, 97a, 197; Oppenheim, *Object (Le Déjeuner en fourrurel)*, 98a, 198

Slides: Stieglitz, *The Steerage*, 99a, 199; Adams, *Face of Half Dome, Yosemite Valley*, 101b, 200; Weston, *Pepper*, 100a, 202; Weston, *Halved Cabbages*, 102b, 201

Schedule

A minimum of one day to draw and one day to paint.

This activity can be completed in one day.

Materials

paper or cloth, acrylic paint, house paint, paintbrushes of various sizes

magazines, scissors, 11" x 14" white paper, pencils, colored pencils, markers

Other Resources

Books

Andes, Dawn. *Art in Latin America.* New Haven: Yale University, 1989.
Arnason, H. H., and Wheeler, Daniel. *A History of Modern Art.* 3rd ed. Englewood Cliffs: Prentice Hall, 1986.
Barr Jr., Alfred H. *Cubism and Abstract Art.* Cambridge: Harvard University Press, 1986.
The Frescoes of Diego Rivera. Detroit Institute of Arts, 1986.
Helm, MacKinley, ed. *Modern Mexican Painters.* Salem, NH: Ayer Co., Publishers Inc., 1941.
Heyman, Therese Thau, Phillips, Sandra S., and Szarkowski, John. *Dorothea Lange.* San Francisco: Chronicle Books, 1994. Catalog.
Read, Herbert. *A Concise History of Modern Painting.* Part of *World of Art.* London: Thames and Hudson Inc., 1985.
Roditi, Edouard. *Dialogues.* San Francisco: Bedford Arts, Publisher, 1990.
Seldon, Rodman. *Conversations with Artists.* New York: Devin, 1957.

Videodisc

Picasso, Crystal
New Ways of Seeing: Picasso, Braque, and the Cubist Revolution, Crystal

Videos

The Cubist Epoch. Museum Without Walls, Kartes, 1986.
Picasso, Crystal
Kandinsky, Crystal
Joan Miro: Theatre of Dramas, Crystal
Matisse: Voyages, Crystal
The Frescos of Diego Rivera, Crystal

Music

Some Musical Examples from the First Half of the Twentieth Century
Schoenberg—*Pierrot Lunaire, Serannade, Opus 24*
Weber—*Variations for Piano, Opus 27*
Stravinsky—*Firebird; Petrouchka; The Rite of Spring*
Bartok—*Sonata for Two Pianos and Percussion*
Blich—*String Quartet No. 3*
Copeland—*Rodeo*
Berg—*Violin Concerto*

Introduce

The variety of early twentieth-century styles and the speed with which they emerged make easy chronological classification impossible. A myriad of artists explored abstract and expressionist tendencies, giving rise to a wealth of inventive movements that expressed a new age.

Lessons at a Glance

14.1 *Expressionism*
In the early twentieth century, artists in various Western European countries expressed deep emotions without regard to naturalism. While Expressionism did not catch on immediately in the United States, artists in Mexico found that bold colors and dynamic compositions aptly communicated the nation's revolutionary spirit after the fall of its dictator.

14.2 *Abstract Art*
Cubism, Futurism and De Stijl were three important early abstract movements that concentrated primarily on design.

14.3 *Sculpture*
In the early twentieth century, many sculptors for the first time dared to abandon strict representation in favor of innovative explorations of mass and space.

14.4 *Fantasy Art and Surrealism*
Fantasy art movements of the early twentieth century evolved from a long line of earlier traditions in which artists expressed the human imagination in visual form. The philosophies of Dada and Surrealism, two significant Fantasy movements, were originated by writers and then translated by artists into visual form.

14.5 *Photography*
In the first half of the twentieth century, photographers continued to focus on humanity and nature, even though painters and sculptors explored various modes of abstraction. Photographers interpreted the entire range of life's experiences—love, joy, tragedy, and so forth—in their strongly evocative pictures.

---

14   A Half-Century of "Isms"

FROM THE SEEDS OF Impressionism and Post-Impressionism grew a variety of styles that almost defy logical organization. Several styles flourished simultaneously. New art movements began and ended with amazing speed.

During the first half of this century, the two main movements in Europe were Expressionism and Abstract art. Expressionist artists sought to express their feelings in a strong way. They often focused on the stress and alienation of modern life. Abstract artists were more interested in design than in realistic imagery.

Two other major movements were Fantasy art and Surrealism. These movements focused on the power and mystery of the fantasy world. Often, these styles left the viewer with more questions than answers, much like our dreams do.

At this same time, photographers began experimenting in new directions. They used the camera to create beautiful interpretations of everyday life and the natural world.

14–a Many early twentieth-century artists were influenced by the art of Africa.
Pablo Picasso, *Les Demoiselles d'Avignon*, detail (fig.14–24).

14–b How does the photographer use space to bring this image to life?
Henri Cartier-Bresson, *Woman on a Stairway Talking to a Man with Cane.* Silver print. The Detroit Institute of Arts, Michigan State Council for the Arts Exhibition Fund.

Objectives

Students should be able to:

Understand how many unique and exciting art styles existed simultaneously in the first half of the twentieth century.

Comprehend that the proliferation of Western avant-garde art movements reflects the mobility and self-searching attitude of its artists.

Explore the evidence of abstraction and Expressionism in the multiple styles that flourished after 1900.

Teach

Timeline
Tell students to compare the styles of the artists listed along the timeline. Ask if there seems to be a logical continuity to their progression or if many vastly different approaches existed at once.

Context
Direct students to study the detail of Pablo Picasso's *Les Demoiselles d'Avignon* (fig.14–a). Ask what non-Western cultures they think might have influenced Picasso's painting. Does the woman's face look realistic? Tell students to glance through Chapter 4 (e.g., fig.4–79) to see if any of the objects are reminiscent of her face. Picasso, a

Expressionism to my way of thinking does not consist of the passion mirrored upon a human face or betrayed by a violent gesture. The whole arrangement of my picture is expressive.
— Henri Matisse

A Half-Century of "Isms"

NORTH AMERICA

Leningrad • Moscow • Weimar Dessau • Hannover Berlin • Utrecht Dresden • Cologne Strasbourg • Paris Munich • Ronchamp Venice • Avignon • Guernica • Athens •

EUROPE

Toronto • Lenox • Chicago • Buffalo • New York •

San Francisco •
Los Angeles •

Atlantic Ocean

Guadalajara • Mexico City •

Faster, easier modes of communication and transportation provide the means for art to bridge the Atlantic. New York plays a more important role as art schools develop in the United States.

14–c Expressionism does not connote a particular style. Artists such as Beckmann sought to express emotional states in their work. What emotions does this image evoke? Max Beckmann, *Baccarat*, detail (fig.14–17).

| 1900 First trial flight of Zeppelin | 1912 Duchamp uses "ready-made" objects displayed as art | 1917–1918 Stella, *Brooklyn Bridge* | 1922 Klee, *The Twittering Machine* | 1931 Dali, *The Persistence of Memory* | 1943–1945 Cartier-Bresson photographs for the Resistance |

A Half-Century of "Isms"

| 1907 Picasso, *Les Demoiselles d'Avignon* 1907 Triple Entente alliance between Britain, France and Russia | 1913 Boccioni, *Unique Forms of Continuity in Space* | 1917 Russian Revolution 1919 League of Nations | 1924 Miró signs Surrealist manifesto | 1939 World War II starts 1940 Discovery of penicillin | 1945 United Nations founded |

Joan Miró

Spanish-born artist living in France, avidly studied and collected masks and other objects from African civilizations.

Art

Instruct students to carefully describe the shapes in the mask/face of the female model in Picasso's *Les Demoiselles d'Avignon*. Next have them look at the entire painting (fig.14–24) to identify how Picasso used angular planes in the rest of the composition. What type of personality do these sharp-edged forms give the women? Ask students to explain how Picasso's style affects whether they would like to meet the people in the painting.

Evaluate

Have students compare Picasso's *Les Demoiselles d'Avignon* to *The Old Guitarist* (fig.13–33). Ask if Picasso painted the two canvases in the same style.

• Was it common for artists prior to the twentieth century to work in such vastly different modes? Starting in the twentieth century, many artists such as Picasso worked in various media and aesthetic phases.

• Ask students if it is more challenging to study artists whose approaches change over the years or those who develop in only a single manner.

• Do their own interests (such as in music, literature or fashion) change

Quote

After students read Henri Matisse's quote, have them examine figs.14–4, 14–5 and 14–6 to see how the art embodies his idea that "the whole arrangement of my picture is expressive." What advice or praise do students think Matisse might have offered Max Beckmann about his painting *Baccarat* (figs.14–c, 14–17)? While the two artists both used color and form expressively, how does their divergent content reflect separate outlooks on art's ultimate purpose? (Students can read more about Matisse on pages 452 and 453, and Beckmann on page 460.)

Map

Ask what non-European country began to play a significant role for the first time in the cutting-edge art movements of the early twentieth century.

over time or do students remain enthralled with only one style?

Reteach

Tell students to review the timeline and images in the chapter opener. Ask them if they believe that the artists illustrated here had been totally isolated in their hometowns or had been exposed to outside influences.

• What visual evidence supports the fact that they were aware of developments in other parts of the Western world?

• In contrast to the previous one hundred or so years, what advances in Western society made this mingling of influences possible?

• Could artists travel more easily?

• What technology now enabled images to cross national borders effortlessly? (photoreproduction)

• Do students feel that the massive amount of visual stimuli diluted the quality of early modern art or made it more exciting?

• How do they generally react to situations in which there are many new stimuli at once? Are they comfortable with confusion?

Lesson 14.1

In the early twentieth century, artists in various Western European countries expressed deep emotions without regard to naturalism. While Expressionism did not catch on immediately in the United States, artists in Mexico found that bold colors and dynamic compositions aptly communicated the nation's revolutionary spirit after the fall of its dictator.

Warm-up

Challenge students to "express" something vitally important about themselves in a nonverbal manner. What do they want to communicate and how can they do it most effectively?

Share with the class that many early twentieth-century artists found unusual ways of employing color, shape, line, composition and subject matter to express profound feelings in a visual fashion.

Objectives

Students should be able to:

Comprehend how the term *Expressionism* refers to an attitude of art rather than a specific style.

Describe how Expressionist artists in Western Europe and Mexico during the early twentieth century concentrated on communicating emotional states rather than naturalistic renderings of their scenes.

Vocabulary Definitions

avant-garde (ah-vant-*gard*) A style of twentieth-century art; also, any style of contemporary art in any period of time, being the newest form of visual expression and the farthest from the traditional ways of working.

nonobjective art Art that has no recognizable subject matter such as trees, flowers or people. The actual subject matter might be color or the composition of the work itself.

14.1 Expressionism

IT IS DIFFICULT TO GROUP ARTISTS according to style in the twentieth century. Each artist was trying to develop an individual style different from all other artists. But certain characteristics do group artists together for the sake of organization and study. The term *Expressionist art* refers to an attitude or philosophy of art rather than a style, because artists of many styles can be expressionistic in their work. The Expressionist artists working in the first half of the twentieth century were not interested in naturalism. They sought a means to express emotional states in their work as well as to portray the many stresses brought on by life in the modern world.

In France, there was Fauvism with its bold distortion, violent color and vigorous brushstrokes. In Germany, a number of solitary artists were setting the stage for the development of German Expressionism. Several Expressionist groups evolved in Germany. These included Die Brücke (The Bridge) and Der Blaue Reiter (The Blue Rider).

In America, artists after 1910, although familiar with Fauvism and German Expressionism, were very slow to adopt any part of the movements into their own work. Mexican artists, though, were spurred on by the fall of the dictator Porfirio Diaz. Their new freedom of expression developed into a national style "of the people" that typified the spirit of the Revolution. Combining simple, solid feeling of pre-Columbian figures and the powerful colors and forms of German Expressionism, artists decorated the walls and ceilings of Mexico City with vibrant murals.

Key Notes

- Expressionism is an attitude or philosophy of art rather than a particular style.
- Fauvism and German Expressionism dominate in Europe.
- In the Americas, Mexican artists develop their own style of Expressionism.

Vocabulary
avant-garde
nonobjective

14–3 Rivera has incorporated two different activities into one painting. Can you identify them? (The title gives a hint.) Diego Rivera, *The Making of a Fresco Showing the Building of a City*, detail.

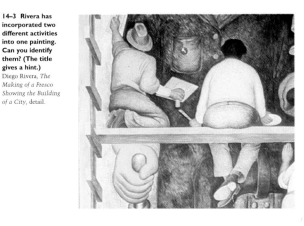

Special Feature
Diego Rivera
(1886–1957)

Diego Rivera was influenced by many styles, but ultimately achieved his own brilliant and personal expression. Rivera studied in Paris and knew Picasso and the rest of the artists in Paris creating the newest forms of visual expression (**avant-garde**). But, he returned to Mexico in 1921 to become actively involved in its politics.

Influenced by the simple, outlined forms of Gauguin and his own cultural heritage of Mayan and Aztec sculpture, Rivera developed a powerful and unique painting style. Rivera revived the fresco technique, which had not been used extensively for centuries, and put his ideas on public walls for all to see. *Liberation of the Peon* (fig.14–1) is a strong social protest against the inhumanity of the landowners toward those who worked for them. The figures are solid, bulky and rounded, much like those of Giotto. Folds in cloth are heavy and simple. Figures are shaded in the traditional way to create a feeling of roundness and dimension.

By the late 1920s, Rivera's murals were well-known in the United States. In the early 1930s, he was one of the most sought-after artists in this country. One of his numerous commissions was for a mural for the San Francisco Art Institute. *The Making of a Fresco Showing the Building of a City* (fig.14–2) was executed from April to June 1931. The mural's theme is the design and construction of a modern industrial city in the United States. The activities of workers and planners, both

---

Teach

Art History: Direct students to find connections between Diego Rivera's painting *Liberation of the Peon* (fig.14–1) and German Expressionist works by Paula Modersohn-Becker (fig. 14–10) and Käthe Kollwitz (fig.14–11).

- What theme and feelings do all the works share?

- Whom were they made for?

- How would students feel toward these artists if they were the dictators of the countries in which they lived?

- Would it be safe to tolerate this type of art? Have students use specific responses to the works to guide their answers.

Evaluate

Ask students if all the artists interested in Expressionism painted in a similar manner. What evidence can they find in the images in Lesson 14.2 to illustrate the variety of subject matter and aesthetic approaches? For example, were Matisse (figs.14–4, 14–5, 14–6) and Frida Kahlo (fig.14–21) expressing similar ideas? What societal factors might have contributed to their differences?

14–2 An artist of great talent, Rivera trained in Europe and brought the classical techniques of fresco back to Mexico.
Diego Rivera, *The Making of a Fresco Showing the Building of a City*, 1931. Fresco, 22'7" x 29'9" (688.3 x 906 m). San Francisco Art Institute.

above and below ground, are seen through a scaffold that supports a fresco painter (Rivera himself) and his assistants (fig.14–3). The giant helmeted worker in the background is the symbol of a technologically planned and worker-controlled industrial city. The worker is sovereign in this fresco. Rivera paints industry in an idealized setting where everyone works in harmony with each other.

Many ceilings and walls in major Mexican cities are covered with the powerful visual statements of Mexican Expressionists. These artists and their European counterparts embarked on a wide-ranging exploration of art as an expressive, emotional force.

14–1 Compare this fresco to some of those from the Italian Renaissance.
Diego Rivera, *Liberation of the Peon*, 1931. Fresco, 74" x 95" (188 x 241 cm). Philadelphia Museum of Art: Given by Mr. and Mrs. Herbert Cameron Morris.

Contextual Information

Rivera

Rivera thought that art should be simple, with a clear message that all people could understand, and he felt that painting on walls provided an accessible surface for his messages. Rivera's first mural was in encaustic, but it took too long to paint with the melted wax, so he switched to fresco. In his early frescoes, Rivera deeply scratched the outlines of his subjects in the wet plaster so that at least the outlines would last.

Rivera worked with Xavier Guerrero and experimented with various sand and lime mixtures for the plaster. They learned that sand from mines was freer from fungus than river sand. They mixed the mine sand with specially refined and filtered lime and used a cyanide wash to prevent fungus.

Most of Rivera's murals contain stories of Mexico's history. Evil is personified by Spaniards and capitalists; good by Indians and manual workers.

Higher-Order Thinking Skills

1 Instruct students to compare Rivera's *Liberation of the Peon* (fig.14–1) to Giotto's *Lamentation* (fig.8–43). Rivera was a communist who felt that art should serve the common people, incorporating their ethnic heritage. Many of his murals were controversial. Ask students to discuss or debate whether art should be controversial.

2 Ask students to compare Rivera's *Mother and Child* (fig.2–22) and his *Flower Day* (fig.3–21) to *Liberation of the Peon*. They should consider both style and subject matter. What makes all three unmistakably by the hand of Rivera?

Reteach

Ask students why expressionistic art can sometimes be more effective in relaying information than realistic art.

• Have they ever been more transported by images, smells, sounds or memories than by detailed descriptions of an event?

• Direct students to select a newspaper or history-book account of an occurrence that interests them and express their reactions to it in a visual manner. Do classmates understand each other's feelings solely by viewing the artworks and not by being told any additional information?

The Fauves

Between 1901 and 1906 in Paris, young artists were greatly impressed by the freedom, color and individual character of works by Cézanne, van Gogh and Gauguin. These artists filled their canvases with vigorous brushstrokes and raw, bright, hot colors that sizzled. One shocked critic described the art as the work of "wild beasts." The French word for wild beasts is Fauves, and the revolutionary artists accepted the title with pride; their work was thus called Fauvism.

Henri Matisse

(1869–1954)

While studying to become a lawyer, Henri Matisse felt the urge to paint—a feeling that completely changed his life. In the exhibition of 1905, Matisse exhibited several shocking works with the "wild beasts." He used intense colors and simplified complex subjects. This ability moved him into the forefront of Fauvism and he became spokesperson for the group. He wanted to express himself with simple color and shape rather than shading and perspective.

Six years after the Fauves exploded on the art scene, Matisse painted *The Red Studio* (fig.14–4), which summarizes his artistic goals. The dominant color of red is used for walls, floor and many of the pieces of furniture. Matisse creates a flattened effect, enhanced by the lack of shadow and value changes. On the wall are a number of his Fauvist paintings from the previous few years. Renaissance painting concepts are almost completely eliminated and a brilliant, personal quality emerges.

In his later years, Matisse experimented with collage—pinning and pasting brightly colored flat shapes on contrasting backgrounds. When confined to his bed by illness, he used his collage technique with powerful results. In 1950, he assembled one of his most beautiful collages, *Beasts of the Sea* (fig.14–5). He cut shapes directly from colored paper without first outlining them in pencil. From the hundreds of colored scraps strewn around his bed, this charming work emerged. It is a memory of a visit he made to the South Seas twenty years earlier. By looking carefully, as if into a lagoon, one can see simplified symbolic shapes that recall sea plants, coral, sea animals, fish, water, land and sky. Matisse arranged his cutouts like a series of small enameled panels. Instead of using pastel colors for water, sky and underwater forms, Matisse used vivid hues. These heightened colors, often contrasting and dissonant for greater impact, produce a visual excitement that a realistic representation of the underwater scene could not convey.

In 1943, Matisse became quite ill and was cared for by the Dominican nuns in the southern French village of Vence. To thank them for their help, he designed, financed and built them a wonderful chapel

14–4 In this picture of his studio, and in his other work, Matisse emphasized the idea that a painting of three-dimensional space still should remain true to the fact that a canvas is really two-dimensional.
Henri Matisse, *The Red Studio*, 1911. Oil on canvas, 71" x 86" (181 x 219 cm). The Museum of Modern Art, New York, Mrs. Simon Guggenheim Fund.

1900
The Boxers revolt against government, China

1908
Death of last Chinese Empress, Tzu-hsi

World Cultural Timeline

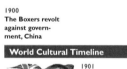

1901
Australia becomes independent country; commonwealth founded

1910
First Japanese airplane built

Multicultural Connection

Australian Art

Most people have little knowledge of or exposure to the art of Australia. The history of art on that continent involves two distinct traditions.

The first is the art of the aboriginal peoples. Rock paintings and rock engravings have been the primary means of visual expression for most of the native cultures (see Chapter 4, fig.4–67). Some of the paintings date to prehistoric times. Bark painting, sand drawings and the decoration of functional and religious objects are other art forms produced by the aborigines.

The development of European art in Australia began in 1788 with British colonization. In general, the European settlers followed the styles and movements that were current in Europe. Since the 1890s, painting has received considerable support in Australia; however, most artists study in London or Paris.

14–5 Matisse "drew" with his scissors in painted paper to create this memory of a visit to the ocean.
Henri Matisse, *Beasts of the Sea*, 1950. Paper on canvas (collage), 116 1/2" x 60 1/2" (296 x 154 cm). National Gallery of Art, Washington, DC, Ailsa Mellon Bruce Fund.

14–6 This chapel was a gift of thanks for care Matisse received when he was ill. The color from the windows changes as the sun moves and the weather changes.
Henri Matisse. *Chapel of the Rosary of the Dominican Nuns*, 1948–1951. Vence, France.

(fig.14–6). The chapel is white, inside and out. The only color comes from light entering through yellow, blue and green glass in the windows, casting ever-changing patterns on the floors and walls. The wall decorations are simple and linear, and are fired in black on the white tile. Matisse designed the altar, windows, wall decorations, crucifix, candelabra and even the vestments for the officiants. He provided a beautiful and uncomplicated environment for prayer and worship.

The extreme simplicity of Matisse's work is extraordinarily difficult to accomplish. The artist had a marvelous ability to look at a complex subject and then reduce it to its simplest elements using line and colored shapes. Of course, this is much more difficult to do than it looks, and few artists have ever done it as well as Matisse.

Contextual Information

Rouault

Rouault first took art lessons from his maternal grandfather and then served an apprenticeship as a stained glass painter. During this time (1890–1895), he restored medieval windows. Rouault's work represents an unusual combination for the twentieth century. His works appeal to modern taste, yet at the same time they make use of traditional Christian motifs.

Rouault was initially a member of the Fauves but when he became deeply concerned about the corrupt state of the world, he changed his subject matter to express the possibility of redemption through spiritual renewal.

Modersohn-Becker

Modersohn-Becker began taking drawing lessons at sixteen. From 1896 to 1898 she attended the Berlin School for Women Artists. She then moved to the artists' colony at Worpswede.

The artists at Worpswede rejected urban life preferring simple rural values. While at the colony she studied figure painting as well as graphic techniques.

Life at the colony proved somewhat confining for Modersohn-Becker. She left on her first trip to Paris in 1900 to expand her studies of modern art. In total she made four trips to Paris during which she visited museums and galleries and met other young artists.

She married Otto Modersohn in 1901 on one of her trips back to Worpswede. Eventually, she found the conflict between her domestic life and her creative life too difficult.

She left Modersohn in 1906 and moved to Paris. He followed her there and persuaded her to return to Worpswede in 1907. She died in November of that year.

Georges Rouault

(1871–1958)

A devout Catholic, Georges Rouault used his paintings to express his deep concern over the immoral conditions of poverty and war. Rouault's expression was personal and deeply rooted in his religious background and his fascination with medieval life. His early paintings were of various religious subjects, done in traditional styles. He also spent some time working in a stained-glass studio—an experience that helped shape his mature painting style. He met Matisse and, for a while, worked with the Fauves, enjoying their unrestrained use of color. But, by 1911, his work turned darker and more subjective as he expressed his indignation at the evils around him: prostitution, injustice, poverty and corruption. He became a marvelous printmaker during this time. He used many new technical devices in several series of prints that expressed his feelings.

Rouault's numerous depictions of Christ were often limited to tragic faces as his *Head of Christ* (fig.14–7) illustrates. While Matisse insisted that his entire composition expressed his feelings, Rouault felt that his "passion" was "mirrored upon a human face." Rouault's favorite impasto technique, broad brushstrokes and massive black lines, aids his personal expression. Since Grünewald, no artist had

14–8 Compare this painting to the stained glass *St. Denis and Jean-Clement* (fig.8–39) from the Cathedral of Chartres.
Georges Rouault, *The Old King*, 1937. Oil on canvas, 30" x 21" (77 x 54 cm). Museum of Art, Carnegie Institute, Pittsburgh.

expressed the tragedy, humility and suffering of Christ with such conviction and feeling. In such works, Rouault was leaning more toward German Expressionism than toward Fauvism.

Heavy black lines (like the lead in stained glass windows) are used to cage brilliant colors in *The Old King* (fig.14–8), one of Rouault's later works. This sorrowful monarch could be a figure from the Old Testament, like King David or Solomon. Glowing colors are separated by heavy lines. These lines also control eye movement and outline the half figure, separating it from the background. Rouault, using a technique vastly different from Impressionism, successfully combines his interest in medieval art and religious concepts with a personal, dynamic form of visual expression.

14–7 Do you see any similarities to medieval representations of Christ?
Georges Rouault, *Head of Christ*, not dated. Oil on panel, 23" x 19" (59 x 48 cm). Los Angeles County Museum of Art, bequest of David L. Loew in memory of his father Marcus Loew.

German Expressionism

The artists Paula Modersohn-Becker and Käthe Kollwitz set the stage for German Expressionism in their powerful and sympathetic studies of peasants and working-class people. Eventually, several groups emerged from the movement. Among these were Die Brücke and Der Blaue Reiter.

Paula Modersohn-Becker

(1876–1907)

Paula Modersohn-Becker was one of the most important German artists of her day. If Modersohn-Becker had not died at the age of 31, she would probably have become a dominant

14–10 The artist was influenced by Gauguin and van Gogh. What evidence of their influence do you see?
Paula Modersohn-Becker, *Old Peasant Woman Praying,* about 1905. Oil on canvas, 30" x 22 3/4" (76 X 58 cm). The Detroit Institute of Arts, gift of Robert H. Tannahill.

14–9 The artist died at the early age of thirty-one shortly after giving birth to a daughter. She painted this self-portrait the same year that she died.
Paula Modersohn-Becker, *Self-Portrait with Camellia Branch,* 1907. Oil on canvas, 24 1/2" x 12" (62 x 30 cm). Folkwang Museum, Essen.

figure in the Expressionist movement. She traveled often to France to see the work of Gauguin and van Gogh, introducing Gauguin's simplified forms, exotic color and use of line to Germany. These characteristics are evident in Modersohn-Becker's *Self-Portrait with Camellia Branch* (fig.14–9) done in 1907.

Old Peasant Woman Praying (fig.14–10) is a dramatic study of a German farm woman in an ancient attitude of worship. Although Modersohn-Becker's earlier work was more realistic, this portrait shows her personal feelings about such people. The painting reflects the influence of both Gauguin and van Gogh. Such features as yellow skin, heavy-lidded eyes, a prominent nose, and a melancholy look caused the Nazis to confiscate the work. The Nazis denounced this "ugly painting" in 1937 as "degenerate art." Most German Expressionistic paintings suffered a similar fate and were later sold by the government to collectors and museums outside the country.

Contextual Information

Kollwitz

While an art student, Kollwitz learned printmaking and became deeply influenced by the prints of Munch. She expressed her political beliefs in her work and knew that prints could be afforded by the middle class who shared those beliefs.

Kollwitz's father was a socialist who was active in the Social Democratic Workers Party. Kollwitz was encouraged by her parents in her depictions of the oppressed poor and in her anticapitalist convictions.

In 1929, Kollwitz became the first woman member of the Prussian Academy of the Arts in Berlin. However, in 1933, she was forced to resign by the government, which disagreed with her political views. (For another work by Kollwitz that depicts the oppressed poor, see Chapter 3, figure 3–14.)

Kirchner

Kirchner, like van Gogh, was emotional and sensitive and suffered from depression. In 1917, he had a breakdown and went to the seclusion of Switzerland to recover. Adding to his depression was the fact that his work was declared "degenerate" in 1937.

Nolde

Nolde was also declared a "degenerate" artist by the Nazis and forbidden to paint. He therefore hid his activities and painted small watercolors in secret. After World War II, he translated his covert work into large oil paintings.

14–12 Kollwitz did many self-portraits throughout her life. She never flinched from portraying her aging face or body.
Käthe Kollwitz, *Self-Portrait*, 1934. Charcoal and crayon on paper, 17" x 13 2/5" (43 x 34 cm). Los Angeles County Museum of Art.

Käthe Kollwitz

(1867–1945)

Käthe Kollwitz was one of the most powerfully emotional artists of this century. She worked in Berlin most of her life and was evacuated in the bombings of 1943. Her etchings, woodcuts, lithographs and drawings express her feelings about old age, hard work, war, motherhood and death. *Never Again War!* (fig.14–11) is a stirring example of this expression. She used the working-class people as her models even though she was married to a prominent Berlin doctor.

Her *Self-Portrait* (fig.14–12), one of many she did, was drawn with

14–11 Kollwitz created many posters to express the impact of World War I and its aftermath on Germany and her children. Like many other artists she felt war could not be allowed to happen again.
Käthe Kollwitz, *Never Again War!*, 1924. Lithograph. Courtesy Galerie St. Etienne, New York.

charcoal pencil when she was sixty-seven years old. The taut expression and lined features bear witness to a long and difficult life. The eyes and mouth are handled with special emphasis. The contrast of shadow and line is used effectively to produce a feeling of form and volume. Yet, the artist used very little detail, emphasizing instead the broad planes and the stark, powerful drama of the human face.

Die Brücke

(The Bridge)

A small brotherhood called Die Brücke (The Bridge) was formed in Dresden in 1905, the same year the colorful explosions of Fauvism were taking hold in France. The artists were ardent admirers of Munch, van Gogh and Gauguin. The group vehemently rejected academic training in art and all traditional forms of expression. They revived avid interest in the woodcut and other graphic means of expression. In their paintings and powerful and somber woodcuts, they emphasized violent color and distortion of features. They cried out against the economic and social conditions in Germany prior to World War I. They also studied African art in depth, especially the expressive masks and carvings, and tried to include some of those characteristics in their paintings. The group broke up in 1913, but in those few years exerted considerable influence on public taste.

Ernst Ludwig Kirchner

(1880–1938)

The early leader of Die Brücke was Ernst Ludwig Kirchner. He insisted that "art depends on inspiration and not on technique." In his early paintings, such as *The Street* (fig.14–13), he worked in flat color areas with bright hues and heavy black shapes. The tension and agitation of the street are expressed by sharp, angular shapes and vivid, acid colors. There is isolation and loneliness even in such crowded conditions.

Emil Nolde

(1867–1956)

Emil Nolde was a bit older than the rest of the members of Die Brücke and remained in the group for only two years. Like Rouault, he painted many religious themes, but his slashing brushstrokes and garish colors were not pleasing to the public. His grotesque faces in *Masks* (fig.14–14) show his interest in primitive cultures and his desire to relate them to his contemporary time. He used these faces to show personal contempt for immorality, greed, avarice, lust and hypocrisy as they appeared in his society.

14–13 What can you detect about who these people are and Kirchner's feelings about them? Ernst Ludwig Kirchner, *The Street*, 1913. Oil on canvas, 47 3/4" x 35 3/4" (121 x 91 cm). The Museum of Modern Art, New York.

14–14 There were many masks from non-Western cultures in museums and private collections. Nolde used some of them as a base upon which to comment about contemporary society. Emil Nolde, *Masks*, 1911. Oil on canvas, 28" x 30" (71 x 76 cm). The Nelson-Atkins Museum of Art, Kansas City, Missouri, gift of the Friends of Art.

Multicultural Connection

Charles White

In the 1930s, Charles White, who was influenced by the work of German artist Käthe Kollwitz, became recognized for his interpretations of African-American experiences. His earlier works had portrayed African Americans in massive, bold forms on murals reminiscent of the Mexican peasants of David Siqueiros and Diego Rivera. Although his focus on African-American working people during the reign of Abstract Expressionism caused him to be ignored by leading critics, he continued to focus on social themes and humanistic values for about forty years. In the late 1950s and early 1960s, White used his highly technical drawing skills and draftsmanship to address the issues of civil rights in a positive, humanistic approach. His aim was to relate the subject to his viewers and create an emotional response that would prompt political action. White believed that working primarily in black and white or sepia and white would sharpen the impact of his work. His medium was lithography, which he felt would reach more people, and his lithographs gained wide recognition in Europe. A major achievement for White took place in the early 1970s with his "Wanted Poster" series. Inspired by pre-Civil War posters advertising slave auctions and seeking runaway slaves, he used them as backgrounds for portraits of contemporary African Americans.

• Show examples of White's earlier and later works. Ask how are the works alike and different.

Contextual Information

"Degenerate art"

"Degenerate art" was a term used by Germans in the 1930s for art that did not reflect the ideas of the Nazis. German artists whose work was considered "degenerate" were forbidden to work, and people who sympathized with them were fired from their jobs. Hitler called modern art "political and cultural anarchy."

Kandinsky

While Kandinsky was a professor of law in Moscow, he saw an exhibition of French Impressionism. (One of the paintings in Monet's *Haystack* series was included among the exhibited works.) It so moved him that he quit his job and went to Munich to study painting.

One evening Kandinsky went into his studio and saw one of his paintings upside-down. This new viewpoint caused him to see it as an abstract painting and inspired a whole new way of painting. He wrote *Concerning the Spiritual in Art* in 1912, explaining his idea that the "pure" artist expresses "inner and essential" feelings.

The Bauhaus

The Bauhaus was started in 1919 in Weimar Germany as a school to teach a relationship between design and industrial production. Walter Gropius started the school, and many famous painters, including Kandinsky and Klee, taught there.

In 1925, the school moved into new buildings designed by Gropius, his staff and students in Dessau, Germany. In 1930, Gropius left to concentrate on his architectural practice, and Ludwig Mies van der Rohe took over. The Bauhaus moved to Berlin in 1932 but was closed down the following year by the Nazis. Many of the faculty came to the United States. One of them, Moholy-Nagy, founded the New

Der Blaue Reiter

(The Blue Rider)

Among the many other Expressionist groups spawned in Germany prior to World War I was a small, important group of artists who called themselves Der Blaue Reiter (The Blue Rider). Centered in Munich from 1911 to 1912, it included the German Franz Marc, and the Russian Wassily Kandinsky. They were not social revolutionaries, but were strong individual artists who exerted a powerful influence as twentieth-century art unfolded.

Franz Marc

(1880–1916)

While Franz Marc painted many kinds of subjects, his animal paintings are of major importance. Marc used brilliant color in a symbolic and arbitrary way. He combined color with shape and rhythm to dramatize the integration of all creatures in nature. There probably has never been a more joyful cow than the one cavorting in his work *The Yellow Cow* (fig.14–15). Placed into the rhythmic flow of an equally colorful landscape, the happy creature fills the picture with powerful

movement and an active shape. The movement of the animal seems to charge the environment with equal excitement. Marc's death during World War I cut short a very promising career.

14–15 Compare this cow to the cattle and bison painted on the cave walls at Lascaux. Franz Marc, *The Yellow Cow*, 1911. Oil on canvas, 55 1/2" x 74 1/2" (141 x 189 cm). Solomon R. Guggenheim Museum, New York.

Bauhaus, which became the Institute of Design in Chicago in 1937.

Bauhaus architects used new techniques and materials to create rational, functional and geometric buildings with no added decorations (for more about Bauhaus architecture see Chapter 16, page 528). Artists created furniture and light fixtures in the same way. The goal was function in the simplest, least decorative and most direct way.

Wassily Kandinsky

(1866–1944)

Wassily Kandinsky was born in
Moscow, but attended art school
in Munich. He is credited with
painting the first completely **nonobjective** painting about 1910. He
returned to Russia, but was soon
back in Germany, teaching at the
Bauhaus. (The Bauhaus was a
German art school where many
modern concepts of design originated.)

His early paintings were similar
in feeling to those of the Fauves,
with recognizable houses and trees
painted in vivid colors. The shapes
in *Study for Composition No. 2*
(fig.14–16) are already quite
abstract, but many forms are still
recognizable. Gradually, he simplified and abstracted these features
until only shape, color and line
were left. The subject matter was

not recognizable. He titled these
paintings with musical terminology
such as "Improvisation 9" or
"Composition No. 138." Kandinsky
explained that improvisations were
"unplanned and spontaneous
expressions of inner character, non-
material in nature."

Certain kinds of lines and various
colors had personal meaning to
Kandinsky. He wrote that to him
"blue is soft and round while yellow is sharp." He developed his
own personal language of color and
shape to express his feelings. His
later work was more geometric and
more carefully organized, but just as
nonobjective. His influence became
very strong in the Abstract
Expressionist movement following
World War II. Often, the colors
seem dissonant and slashing, as
sounds clash in the musical compositions of his friend Igor Stravinsky.

14–16 Kandinsky was also trained as a
musician. He titled his paintings with musical terminology.
Wassily Kandinsky, *Study for Composition No. 2*,
1909–1910. Oil on canvas, 51" x 38" (130 x 97 cm).
The Solomon R. Guggenheim Museum, New York.

Higher-Order Thinking Skills

Have students compare the cow in
The Yellow Cow (fig.14–15) to the
bulls of the *Bull Dance* fresco from
Knossos (fig.6–3). Ask what personality is attributed to the animals by
the artists.

Have students research the work of
Kandinsky. Suggest that they make a
point of discovering how he evolved
from a rather realistic painter to a
color-oriented Expressionist to an
Abstractionist. In the classroom, display examples of each phase of his
career for comparison and discussion.
Stravinsky's music would make an
appropriate accompaniment to this
visual study of Kandinsky's work.

Contextual Information

Beckmann

Beckmann started as a German Impressionist but then served as a medical orderly in World War I. Beckmann's fear and despair over Hitler's actions are shown in his work. The Nazis forced Beckmann to leave his teaching position and his home in Germany for Holland, where he was free to express his concerns in his art. He regarded painting as an ethical necessity to warn the world about sadism, cruelty and lust. The Nazis included his paintings in the infamous "degenerate" art exhibition.

Modigliani

Modigliani had a reputation for his artistic dress and wild lifestyle. The artist lived in poverty and was recklessly indifferent to the state of his health. Often in debt, he borrowed and begged money from friends.

Max Beckmann
(1884–1950)

Max Beckmann started out in the traditional mainstream of art, but after World War I he began painting his nightmarish expressions of decadence and the tragedy of the human condition. Beckmann painted humanity as puppet-like figures that have been dehumanized by social conditions. Bright, raw colors are outlined with hard black lines. Like many German artists of the time, Beckmann had to flee Nazi Germany when he was officially labeled "degenerate." His last three years were spent in the United States.

His symbolism and style are personal and often unexplainable. In *Baccarat* (fig.14–17), it is difficult to explain the man with the sword in an otherwise tranquil casino setting. Yet, most of his characters seem ominous and/or evil, which is part of Beckmann's symbolic vocabulary.

Amedeo Modigliani
(1884–1920)

Amedeo Modigliani was born in Italy, but spent most of his life painting in Paris. His early work was influenced by Toulouse-Lautrec. However, he soon developed a unique style based on the elongated distortion of African sculpture, the design and brushwork of Cézanne, the sketchy line and flat shapes of Matisse, and his innate Italian interest in portraiture. He was an excellent draftsman.

As *Gypsy Woman with Baby* (fig.14–18) shows, he was able to simplify human features into a dignified and simple statement. His style often recalls the Italian Mannerist distortion and elongation found in the work of El Greco. Although many outside influences can be found in Modigliani's work, his final expressions are completely unique in their design and emotional content.

14–18 Can you identify two sources of influence on Modigliani's painting?
Amedeo Modigliani, *Gypsy Woman with Baby*, 1919. Oil on canvas, 45 1/4" x 28 3/4" (115 x 73 cm). National Gallery of Art, Washington, DC, Chester Dale Collection.

14–17 Society after World War I was often characterized as decadent. Many artists commented on the degenerate self-centeredness and hinted at the dire consequences of such behavior.
Max Beckmann, *Baccarat*, 1947. Oil on canvas, 47" x 39" (119 x 100 cm). The Nelson-Atkins Museum of Art, Kansas City, Missouri, gift of the Friends of Art, 54-86.

14–19 The maguey plant is an important source of food, cloth, rope and other items for the desert people of Mexico.
José Clemente Orozco, *Mexican Landscape*, 1930. Oil on canvas, 30" x 37" (76 x 94 cm). Formerly at Los Angeles County Museum of Art, gift of Charles K. Feldman.

Expressionism in the Americas

Like Diego Rivera, other artists in Mexico combined expressionist techniques with social protest. Their works provided powerful political and social statements about the struggles of the common people, or *peons*, of Mexico.

José Clemente Orozco

(1883–1949)

Beginning with the fresco technique, José Clemente Orozco later used more modern materials to fill walls and ceilings in Guadalajara and other cities with his powerful statements. Orozco's murals are dramatic and political. They were often commissioned by revolutionary governments.

Mexican Landscape (fig.14–19) is a dramatic easel painting that features his powerful style. The forms are well rounded, like those of Rivera. However, they are painted with slashing brushstrokes and greater contrast of values, which create a more dramatic impact. Even this small canvas has the visual impact of a large mural because of the monumentality of the forms. The dominant feature is the huge maguey plant, which is a major source of food, drink, cloth, rope and other items for the desert people of Mexico. It seems as though these quiet, solitary figures are patiently waiting for more growth to sustain them a little longer. The background is treated with abstract shapes that place visual emphasis on the plant and the three human figures.

1910–17
Mexican civil war, Pancho Villa and Emiliano Zapata lead the military

1922
King Tut's tomb found

World Cultural Timeline

1918
Ottoman Empire collapses following WWI; Turkey forms

Multicultural Connection

Posada and the Mexican Civil War

In the days leading up to the Mexican Revolution, artists played an active role in stirring up discontent among the lower classes, who were oppressed by Porfirio Diaz, the dictator. José Guadalupe Posada is especially well-known for recording every aspect of the political and social scene in biting caricatures, which he produced and distributed on a daily basis. His portrayal of events in pre-revolutionary Mexico was vivid and generally wordless, insuring that even the illiterate would understand his satiric messages.

• Have students research and then discuss some of Posada's caricatures, including those he later made in support of Zapata and the revolutionary cause.

Contextual Information

Mexican Artists and Social Protest

In the twentieth century, Rivera, Orozco and Siqueiros were well-known artists who protested the actions by dictators that resulted in the suffering of Mexicans. All three created prints to present their ideas of social justice, mourning for the war dead, and the aspirations of the guerrillas.

Kahlo

Kahlo was 13 when she first saw Diego Rivera. He was painting a mural. When she was 15 and planning on a medical career, she was in a terrible bus-car accident, fracturing her pelvis, foot, and spine. While convalescing in bed, she began to paint.

Kahlo showed her first paintings to Rivera, who admired them. So did André Breton, who in 1938 arranged for an exhibition of her work in New York City. He billed her as a Surrealist, although she said she didn't paint dreams. She said she painted her own reality, which was based in Mexican colonial and folk art.

The Murals of East Los Angeles

Mural painting has had a long tradition in Mexico, going as far back as pre-Columbian times. Some of the greatest mural painting came out of the Mexican revolution when Diego Rivera, David Alfaro Siqueiros and José Clemente Orozco painted powerful political statements on walls in Mexican cities.

The tradition of Mexican mural painting continues on the walls of East Los Angeles. These murals have come about through the dedication of Judy Baca, a Mexican American. Hired by the city to teach art in a park in East Los Angeles, Baca made friends with the children and started studying the street life around her. As she looked at the graffiti-covered walls in the neighborhood, Baca realized that the community's history could be read on those walls. So, she formed a mural team and, for the first time in years, children from different neighborhoods and different gangs worked together. Through their murals, they expressed the issues and needs of the community as they saw them. The topics on the murals ranged from police brutality to drug abuse.

In 1976, Baca and her team started work on *The Great Wall of Los Angeles.* The longest mural in the world, this depiction of California's multicultural history from prehistoric to contemporary times runs over one-third of a mile along a flood control channel in the San Fernando Valley. The Great Wall was completed in 1983.

Judith F. Baca and others, section of *The Great Wall of Los Angeles.* SPARC.

14–20 The interior of the polyforum (not shown) contains a huge floor, ceiling and wall mural which portrays the struggle of the working class.
David Alfaro Siqueiros. Exterior, *Polyforum Cultural Siqueiros,* 1974. Acrylic enamel on asbestos-cement and steel, 50' (15 m) high. Mexico City.

David Alfaro Siqueiros

(1896–1974)

David Alfaro Siqueiros spent many years of his life in prison because of his revolutionary ideas and political connections. He worked with Rivera and Orozco on many mural projects. During the last twenty years of his life he was the only surviving member of the great triumvirate. Siqueiros designed murals of incredible dimension and powerful, emotional impact. The *Polyforum Cultural Siqueiros,* a huge structure in Mexico City, is home for many cultural arts (fig.14–20). The building is covered inside and out with mammoth murals of acrylic paint on asbestos-cement panels and sculptured steel. Its main feature is a gigantic floor, wall and ceiling mural of incredible complexity. The mural is called *The March of Humanity on Earth and Toward the Cosmos.* It is overpowering to the senses, especially when accompanied with programmed lighting and sound. The exterior is shaped like a dodecagon with over 12,000 square yards of painted surface. Each of its twelve huge facets contains a sculptured mural covering 300 square yards. Subject matter ranges from *Christ the Leader* (shown here) to *Atom as a Triumph of Peace over Destruction.* All are presented with vivid colors and surging lines. The work is a gigantic outdoor gallery for the people of Mexico.

Lesson 14.1 Review Answers

1 Picasso, Matisse, Gauguin, Mayan and Aztec cultures

2 A shocked critic described the brightly colored paintings as the work of "wild beasts" or, in French, *fauves.*

3 This collage of cut colored paper is nine feet tall, so it is taller than you are.

4 Heavy black lines surround brilliant colors in both *The Old King* and stained glass windows.

5 Käthe Kollwitz and Paula Modersohn-Becker

6 The members of the group Die Brücke were protesting the economic and social conditions in Germany before World War I. They drew inspiration from Munch, van Gogh, Gauguin, and African art, especially expressive masks and carvings. They rejected academic art training and all traditional forms of expression. In their paintings and woodcuts, they emphasized violent color and distortion of features.

7 Tension and agitation are expressed by sharp, angular shapes and bright, acid colors. There is isolation and loneliness in this crowded street.

8 Wassily Kandinsky

9 Toulouse-Lautrec, Cézanne, Matisse, El Greco, African art

10 To show that she was thinking about Rivera, Kahlo painted him on her forehead. The third eye on his head represents the master artist's ability to perceive more in life than people with only two eyes.

Frida Kahlo

(1907–1954)

Frida Kahlo was a self-taught artist who married Diego Rivera in 1929. Both artists were fiercely independent, and both worked feverishly at their painting. Kahlo painted works that often were psychologically mysterious, and she almost always worked with figures. Among her more than two hundred paintings are many self-portraits. In several, she showed her husband to be a powerful presence in her life. In *Diego y yo* (fig.14–21), to indicate that she was thinking about him, she painted him on her forehead. The third eye on his head is symbolic of the master artist's ability to perceive far more in life than other people. Kahlo's personal expressiveness, psychological intuition and artistic ability have placed her among Mexico's more able artists.

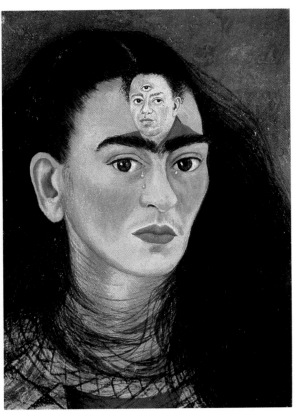

14–21 Kahlo created many paintings of her husband, Diego Rivera, and he remained a powerful influence in her life and work even after they were divorced.
Frida Kahlo, *Diego y yo*, 1940. Oil on masonite, 11 3/4" x 8 1/2" (30 x 22 cm). Courtesy, Mary Anne Martin/Fine Art, New York.

Lesson 14.1 Review

1 What were some of the artists and cultures that influenced Diego Rivera's art style?
2 How did Fauvism get its name?
3 What medium is Matisse's *Beasts of the Sea*?
4 What elements in Rouault's *The Old King* are similar to a stained-glass window?
5 Name two women German Expressionist artists.
6 What were some of the concerns of Die Brücke? From what artists did they draw their inspiration?

What art did they reject? What were some characteristics of the art of this group?
7 Describe the mood in Kirchner's *The Street*.
8 Which artist is recognized as having painted the first nonobjective painting?
9 Name three artists or cultures that influenced Modigliani's art.
10 Explain the symbolism in Kahlo's *Diego y yo*.

Higher-Order Thinking Skills

The Polyforum's powerful effect comes in part from the light and sound that accompany the artwork. Have students, either individually or in groups, select a painting to create light and sound for. Students can then discuss what they would create, or they can actually carry out the project.

Lesson 14.2

Cubism, Futurism and De Stijl were three important early abstract movements that concentrated primarily on design.

Warm-up

Organize students into pairs, with partners facing each other. Then have them place on top of their head a notebook with a blank page facing up. Tell them to slowly and carefully draw their partner while holding the notebook steady with one hand and drawing with a pencil in the other. After they are finished and have shared the results, ask students if their portraits are realistic. Do they look exactly like their partner? Although the pictures are based on real people, the compositions do not appear exactly lifelike. They are abstracted versions of what the students saw. Share with the class that some abstractionists made work based on the visible world, while others constructed compositions of entirely nonreferenced elements.

Objectives

Students should be able to:

Explain how abstractionists were mainly concerned with the design of their compositions rather than with the description of psychological states or realistic scenes.

Understand that Cubism, Futurism and De Stijl were significant abstract movements in Europe during the early decades of the twentieth century.

Vocabulary Definitions

simultaneity (*si*-mul-*ta*-nay-*i*-tee) The technique of depicting objects from separate vantage points in one work of art.

Teach

Criticism: Ask students to reflect on the warm-up exercise and decide whether Joseph Stella (fig.14–23) abstracted what he saw from life or whether he made up the composition completely in his head.

• Can students guess the subject of this work without looking at its title?

14.2 Abstract Art

EXPRESSIONIST ARTISTS were primarily concerned with the psychological and social drama of life. They expressed their feelings in symbolic and personal ways. Artists working with abstraction were mainly concerned with the design on the canvas and how the various parts related to each other. Twentieth-century painters explored many avenues of expression for varying lengths of time. In 1910, almost all who were so inclined tried their hands at Cubism. Futurism, dealing with dynamic energy, was another movement explored by writers and painters during the first decades of the twentieth century. In Holland, a nonrepresentational approach to art was called "De Stijl."

Cubism, Futurism and De Stijl were three important directions that abstract art took in the first half of the twentieth century.

Key Notes

• Abstract artists are interested in the design on the canvas and how the various parts relate to each other.

• Abstract art is explored in a variety of ways, including Cubism, Futurism and De Stijl.

Vocabulary

simultaneity

14–23 What characteristics of Futurism do you find in this painting of the famous amusement park?
Joseph Stella, *Battle of Lights, Coney Island, Mardi Gras*, 1913–14. Oil on canvas, 6'4" x 7'4" (195.2 x 215 cm). Yale University Art Gallery. Bequest of Dorothea Dreier to the Collection Société Anonyme.

Special Feature
Joseph Stella
(1880–1946)

Joseph Stella came from Italy to the United States at the age of twenty-five. He returned to his homeland when Futurism was in its developmental stages. Futurism was a branch of abstract art that emphasized the lines of force or dynamism of each object.

Stella brought this particular type of abstraction to his interpretations of New York. His painting of the *Brooklyn Bridge* (fig.14–22), the construction that had become a symbol of New York, is a visual song of praise to a structure that

---

• How has Stella evoked the sense of viewing the Coney Island scene from a spinning Ferris wheel or rollicking roller-coaster car?

• If Stella had used soft, rounded shapes, would his painting have conveyed the same sense of speed and motion?

• Have students find Stella's roots in Italian Futurism (figs.14–30, 14–31), which he had studied in his homeland before bringing a personal brand of the style to the United States.

Evaluate

Challenge students to prove with visual examples from Lesson 14.2 how the industrial age and technological advances affected the art of the early twentieth century.

Ask the class to defend dance, music and poetry as abstract art forms. Is this always the case or can these art forms sometimes be quite literal?

• Would they consider most literature and drama to be abstract or realistic?

• Which art form would they use to communicate a daydream, and which to relate a historical event?

was considered an industrial and engineering triumph. Towers, cables and beams of lights are all woven together with distant skyscrapers, tunnels and water. Together, they create a dynamic vision of interlocking space, light, form and color. Such glorification of industrialization is a positive expression of twentieth-century technology. It is the opposite of German Expressionism, which saw such mechanization as dehumanizing.

Like other abstract artists, Stella was concerned with the design on the canvas and how the various parts relate to one another. He often relied—as he does here—on a symmetrical balance on either side of a strong central axis to hold the composition together.

In *Battle of Lights, Coney Island, Mardi Gras, 1913–14* (fig.14–23), we are immediately struck by the energy of an amusement park filled with crowds of people. Stella's is not a literal depiction. Instead, he uses light, color and line to relate to the viewer the tumultuous nature of the scene.

As we have begun to learn, movements in art in the twentieth century follow neither a unified nor sequential path. The concept of abstraction, however, remains a vital force in art even today.

Contextual Information

Stella

Like other Futurists, Joseph Stella painted motion and modern technology, symbolized by the Brooklyn Bridge. The bridge was built largely by Italian laborers, who made up 75 percent of New York City's construction workers in 1897, and was a great source of pride to Italian Americans.

Stella described New York City as a "monstrous dream, chimeric reality, Oriental delight, Shakespearean nightmare, unheard of riches, frightful poverty. Gigantic jaw of irregular teeth, shiny black like a bulldozer, funereal gray, white and brilliant like a minaret in the sunlight, dull, cavernous black, like Wall Street after dark."

Higher-Order Thinking Skills

The Brooklyn Bridge is a symbol of New York. Ask the class what structure could serve as a symbol of your community. How could an artist portray it to convey its symbolic power? What colors could be used?

Reteach

Have students choose an image in Lesson 14.2 and describe what about the composition makes it abstract.

• What has the artist left out? Are these important details or has the artist provided the basics so that we quickly comprehend the essence of the scene?

• Direct students to follow the same process of abstraction with a newspaper or magazine photograph. Tell them to cut out and rearrange only the most vital segments so that the core of the scene is immediately understandable. Afterward, ask how thinking in abstract terms is different from working in a naturalistic manner. Which do they enjoy more and why?

Interdisciplinary Connection

Social Science: At the time that Stella painted the Brooklyn Bridge, there was serious debate about the large increase in immigration to America. Many of the "old" immigrants wanted to limit the number of people coming from poorer countries, including southern Italy and Eastern Europe.

Have students research the reasons these people were leaving Europe and the reasons for the objection to more immigrants. (With a limited number of apartments and jobs and nearly 12,000 immigrants arriving at Ellis Island every day, they were not welcomed by many Americans.)

Contextual Information

Les Demoiselles d'Avignon

Picasso began *Les Demoiselles d'Avignon* (fig.14–24) as an allegory. Originally, he was to have a man seated on the right, surrounded by fruit and women representing Vice. There was to be a man on the left holding a skull representing Virtue. In the finished painting, the head of the figure on the right resembles a mask from Itumba, in the area once known as the French Congo. The other head was influenced by a mask from the Ivory Coast.

Guernica

Picasso was commissioned to paint a mural for the Spanish government's pavilion at the 1937 World's Fair in Paris. Inspired by the destruction of Guernica, he began work on the huge canvas. He completed *Guernica* (fig.14–27) in two months and sent it to Paris.

After the fair was over, the painting was displayed at the Museum of Modern Art in New York City. Picasso insisted that it not be shown in Spain until that country ended Fascism. In 1981, *Guernica* was sent to Madrid, where it is now a prized symbol of Spanish heritage.

Cubism

Cubism was begun in 1907 by Pablo Picasso, who was joined shortly by his good friend Georges Braque. They used Paul Cézanne's ideas and his way of building up the surface with small squarish brushstrokes to launch a new way of seeing and painting the world. Like other abstract art, Cubism is primarily concerned with surface design, not emotion and personal feelings. What Picasso began in 1907 set the minds of artists on fire with ideas and possibilities undreamed of several years before.

Pablo Picasso

(1881–1974)

Pablo Picasso casts a long shadow across the art of the twentieth century. A creative innovator of ideas and techniques and a master of many styles, he was constantly searching and changing during his long lifetime. Born in Spain, and an excellent painter at nineteen, he moved to Paris to spend most of his years in France.

The beginning of Cubism burst onto the twentieth-century art scene with Picasso's painting *Les Demoiselles d'Avignon (The Maids of Avignon)* in 1907 (fig.14–24). Sketches reveal that Picasso at first included several other figures in the interior setting. As Picasso worked, he became aware of the relationships of shapes and colors to each other. These relationships became more important than the figures. For six months, he worked and reworked his design on the large canvas and never really finished it completely. What the viewer now sees are five fractured, nude figures and a small still life.

Picasso had been strongly impressed by his introduction to geometrical African masks. He overpainted the faces of two of the nudes with mask-like features, adding to the discordant quality of

14–24 This painting started the Cubist movement.
Pablo Picasso, *Les Demoiselles d'Avignon*, 1907. Oil on canvas, 95 1/4" x 93" (242 x 236 cm). The Museum of Modern Art, New York, acquired through the Lillie P. Bliss Bequest.

14–25 This Cubist portrait is a very different way for an artist to see his sitter. Can you find the sitter's features?
Pablo Picasso, *Daniel-Henry Kahnweiler*, 1910. Oil on canvas, 39 3/4" x 28 3/4" (101 x 73 cm). The Art Institute of Chicago, gift of Mrs. Gilbert W. Chapman.

Performing Arts Connection

Three Musicians, Pablo Picasso

In *Three Musicians* (fig.14–26), Pablo Picasso painted Pierrot, Harlequin and a veiled monk—all characters from the commedia dell'arte (an old form of Italian street theater)—in a shallow, stagelike setting. Ask how he visually indicates that music fills the air. In addition to the instruments and score, can students sense a tempo in Picasso's juxtaposing colors and angular shapes?

14–26 Without the credit information, it is hard to tell from the reproduction whether this work is painted or pasted.
Pablo Picasso, *Three Musicians*, 1921. Oil on canvas, 80" x 74" (204 x 188 cm). Philadelphia Museum of Art, the A.E. Gallatin Collection.

the work. These newly introduced, sharp angles caused him to rework the entire surface, repeating the angular features of the masks in the figures and the related background. This interplay of geometric shapes led to Cubism. Cubism was given its name by critics who saw the hard edges and geometric shapes and nothing else.

Although not considered a Cubist painting, *Demoiselles* is the painting that began the Cubist movement. The unlovely ladies of Avignon had started a revolution.

Picasso began to work with Georges Braque in developing true Cubism. Big, flat shapes were replaced by small, crisp facets and nearly monochromatic hues because bright hues would detract from the design. In Picasso's painting of the art dealer *Daniel-Henry Kahnweiler* (fig.14–25), the features are broken apart and reassembled in a new and unique way. Facial features, hands and still-life objects can be discerned, but they also seem to dissolve in a shattering pattern of translucent, geometric shapes.

After World War I, the work of Picasso changed radically as one style blended into many others. His wonderful *Three Musicians* (fig.14–25) is painted to look like colorful pieces cut into flat shapes and pasted onto a surface. Recognizable images emerge again in this work: a Pierrot and a Harlequin from Italian comedic theater and a Franciscan monk. The three are making music on a violin, a clarinet and a zither. This unlikely trio is thrust forward from a neutral background as the three happily play on their instruments. The color, shapes and textures create a pleasant and happy composition, locked together as tightly as a finished jigsaw puzzle.

Following a 1917 trip to Italy, where he saw many of the works of Giotto and Piero della Francesca,

Picasso developed a way of painting monumental figures in a rather Classic style. The lightning changes in his style after Cubism are too many to study here, but one work must be included. It is *Guernica* (fig.14–27), his most powerful painting and one of the most devastating social protest pictures ever composed.

Picasso painted *Guernica* as a commission for the Spanish government to exhibit at the Paris Exposition of 1937. The protest was against the massive bombing of the small Basque town of Guernica, which was a center of resistance in the ongoing civil war. By using flat, symbolic figures he was able to express extremes of suffering not possible in realistic representation. Actual destruction is shown only in a flaming building and some crumbling walls. A mother rushes screaming from a burning house, her arms flailing in the air. Agonized heads and arms reach out desperately from crumbling wreckage. At the left, a mother holds her dead child and shrieks toward the heavens. The bull, a Spanish symbol

14–27 Use the text to identify all of the elements of this painting that was created to protest the bombing of a small town.
Pablo Picasso, *Guernica*, 1937. Oil on canvas, 11 1/2' x 25 1/2' (3.5 x 7.8 m). Prado Museum, Madrid.

Higher-Order Thinking Skills

Guernica was prompted by the destruction of the town of the same name during the Spanish Civil War. Picasso was inspired by newspaper accounts of the event. (See an example of such a report in the primary-source selection on page 489.) Ask students to find a newspaper article whose subject they feel strongly about. Have them create sketches to show how they would convey the story in artwork.

Multicultural Connection

The Image of the Horse

When examining and interpreting works of art, we should realize that art can occasionally cross boundaries of culture and time to express different concepts through the use of similar forms. The horse in Picasso's *Guernica* expresses the agony, horror and suffering over the senseless slaughter of innocent people.

The *Horse of Selene* (Selene was the Greek goddess of the moon) was carved in marble about 435 BC for the east pediment of the Parthenon temple. This head of the Classical horse is part of the Elgin Marbles (see p.181), which were made to express devotion to the goddess Athena, to whom the Parthenon was dedicated.

In ancient China, a person's wealth was measured by the number of horses and chariots he had. During the Tang dynasty (618–906), sculptures and ceramics were made in the form of horses, and were glazed in red, yellow and green. Tang horses (fig.4–26) were buried with the wealthy as a symbol of their prosperity and loyalty to the emperor.

• Have students research how other images of horses have been used in art.

Contextual Information

The Armory Show

The 1913 Armory Show in New York was the first exhibition of modern French artists in America and was organized by American painters, including those of the Ash Can School (Henri, Glackens, Sloan, Luks and Shinn). The organizers were united in their opposition to the National Academy of Design, which had rejected their realistic paintings.

There were approximately 1600 works of art in the exhibition, including works by Goya, Delacroix, Courbet, Duchamp, Kandinsky and Brancusi. The exhibit traveled to Chicago and Boston, and it was estimated that over 250,000 people saw it.

One of the organizers, Walt Kuhn, said: "We want this show of ours to mark the starting point of the new spirit in art. . . . I feel that it will show its effect even further and make the big wheel turn over both hemispheres."

President Theodore Roosevelt, in response to his visit to the exhibit, wrote: "Take the picture which for some reason is called *A Naked man going down stairs* [sic]. There is in my bath-room a really good Navajo rug which, on any proper interpretation of the Cubist theory, is a far more satisfactory and decorative picture. Now if, for some inscrutable reason, it suited somebody to call this rug a picture of, say, *A well-dressed man going up a ladder*, the name would fit the facts just about as well as in the case of the Cubist picture of the *Naked man going down stairs*. From the standpoint of terminology each name would have

of human irrationality, surveys the scene of carnage. The screeching horse is perhaps symbolic of Spain's torment, yet it and other symbolism are never explained by the artist. The sun is mechanized with a light bulb, and textures simulate the newspaper articles that described the tragedy to a shocked world. A broken sword symbolizes the absolute defeat of the people. But, out of the handle of the sword a flower grows; hope is still alive. Pain, agony and chaos are everywhere, yet the design is solidly held together by a triangular composition. Picasso painted the enormous canvas in black, white and gray to

place the visual emphasis on the message as well as to develop a somber mood. *Guernica* combines Expressionism and Cubism in a mighty voice of protest. It is Picasso's most dramatic work.

Georges Braque

(1882–1963)

Georges Braque worked closely with Picasso in developing the vocabulary of Cubism. The two artists next began adding actual bits of real objects to their canvases: newspaper clippings, pieces of rope, bits of wallpaper and even sand. These pieces added a note of realism to the designed pictorial space. The result is called collage, from the French word *collé* for glue or paste.

14–28 How would you describe the space and perspective in this painting?
Georges Braque, *Still Life: The Table*, 1928. Oil on canvas, 32" x 51" (81 x 131 cm). National Gallery of Art, Washington, DC, Chester Dale Collection.

Following World War I, Braque worked on a series of figure paintings, but finally settled on the still life as his basic subject. Braque carefully structured his space. Using the fractured planes of Cubism, he abstracted from the setups to create beautiful designs. In *Still Life: The Table* (fig.14–28), he uses several typical Braque techniques. The table top is tilted forward. It becomes a background shape for the objects, which often seem about to slide off the inclined surface. The viewer sees each object from a separate vantage point, something a camera cannot do. One can see into the top of one bottle, but not into that of its neighboring flask. The viewer looks down on the dish with the apples. The wine glass is seen straight on and in perspective at the same time. This characteristic is called **simultaneity**. Notice how

1930
Mahatma Gandhi leads first significant act of passive resistance to British rule in India

1945
Arab League formed

World Cultural Timeline

1939
People's congress formed, Indonesia

whatever merit inheres in a rather cheap straining after effect; and from the standpoint of decorative value, of sincerity, and of artistic merit, the Navajo rug is infinitely ahead of the picture."

lines from the contour of one object can be found continuing in another place, causing the shapes and lines to weave a tight pattern over the surface. Colors and textures are brighter and more developed than in earlier Cubist paintings. Braque composed a sophisticated design based on simple objects.

Marcel Duchamp

(1887–1968)

Marcel Duchamp created what was probably the most controversial Cubist painting. His *Nude Descending a Staircase, No. 2* (fig.14–29) brought him quickly to the attention of the public. Along with other European and American artists, Duchamp exhibited his painting in the famous Armory Show in New York in 1913. It was America's first chance to see Cubism, Fauvism, Impressionism and Post-Impressionism in a single exhibition. The reaction was predictable. America's artists (even those who exhibited in the show) were appalled at how far they were behind the Europeans in their expression. America's public, used to seeing realistic representation, was absolutely irate. The general public was alienated by the artists and their new forms of communication.

Duchamp's painting was the primary target of critical attack. Calling it "an explosion in a shingle factory," one critic forever made the painting famous. Duchamp had fractured the movement of a figure as it descended the stairs, and the shapes *are* very shingle-like in their character. But, Duchamp presents not one image, but an entire series of movements, stopped in successive stages of action. The result is similar to stop-action or strobe-light photography. While viewers today understand that Duchamp was painting motion, the public in 1913 could not comprehend his form of art and, out of ignorance, laughed at the result.

14–29 Compare this painting to Muybridge's photographs of motion (fig.12–45).
Marcel Duchamp, *Nude Descending a Staircase, No. 2*, 1912. Oil on canvas, 58" x 35" (148 x 89 cm). Philadelphia Museum of Art, The Louise and Walter Arensberg Collection.

Contextual Information
The Futurists

Born in Italy, Futurism rejected traditional art. The Italian Futurists had to shake off the overwhelming presence of Italy's great artistic traditions from ancient Greece and Rome to the Renaissance and Baroque.

• Have students consider the words of the founder of the Futurist movement, Filippo Tommaso Martinetti: "A roaring automobile, which appears to run like a machine-gun is more beautiful than the *Victory of Samothrace.*"

Boccioni

Boccioni believed that objects have an emotional life of their own and react to their environment by "force lines." He advocated use of materials such as glass and electric lights and motors to create movement.

Futurism

During the first decades of the twentieth century, writers and avant-garde artists began an Italian movement called Futurism. As we have seen, Joseph Stella was influenced by this group.

Futurists were interested in the mechanized advancement of society and the destruction of all symbols of the past (museums, academies and large cities) because they held up progress. Thankfully, this phase of their program was not successful. Their favorite word was "dynamism." They wanted to show the "lines of force" that characterize various objects. The sense of movement generated in Duchamp's *Nude* was basic to Futurism.

Umberto Boccioni
(1882–1916)

The young leader of Italian Futurism, Umberto Boccioni, died in an accident during World War I, and the movement died with him. In *The Noise of the Street Penetrates the House* (fig.14–30), Boccioni combines the angular facets of Cubism with a tilting of planes to create a chaotic scene, filled with agitation and motion. People are working and children are playing as other people watch from balconies in a congested urban atmosphere of noise and confusing activity.

Boccioni's finest achievement, however, was in sculpture. His *Unique Forms of Continuity in Space* (fig.14–31) is a charging male figure caught in several aspects of walking at the same time. It is Duchamp's *Nude Descending a Staircase* in three dimensions. According to Boccioni, "motion and light destroy the materiality of bodies" and his sculpture goes about proving it. The forms seem to have been shaped by rushing air, whose currents seem to extend beyond the sculpture itself and to penetrate the form in other places. Solid forms and space are merging and interlocking, causing the negative volumes to be as important as the positive. In this respect, Boccioni's figure recalls Bernini's *David*, which interacts dynamically with its surrounding space. Yet, Boccioni's work combines abstract rather than representational forms to produce a human-like result in vibrant movement.

14–30 What activities can you identify here?
Umberto Boccioni, *The Noise of the Street Penetrates the House*, 1911. Oil on canvas, 39 1/2" x 39 1/2" (100 x 100 cm). Lower Saxony National Gallery, Hannover, Germany.

14–31 Figures in motion always intrigue sculptors. Can you think of another sculpture where motion plays an important part?
Umberto Boccioni, *Unique Forms of Continuity in Space*, 1913. Bronze, 43 3/4" (111 cm) high. Museum of Modern Art, New York, acquired through the Lillie P. Bliss Bequest.

De Stijl

(The Style)

A coldly intellectual approach to design was pioneered by another Dutch artist, Piet Mondrian. Mondrian led in the development of a nonrepresentational style, called *De Stijl*, Dutch for *The Style*. The basic precept of De Stijl was the complete reliance on design and the elimination of all feeling and emotion. It was the exact opposite of Expressionism.

Piet Mondrian

(1872–1944)

Coming from a tradition of Realistic painters (father and uncle), Mondrian rapidly changed styles from Realism to Impressionism, Post-Impressionism and Cubism. He was gradually flattening his natural forms and reducing them to linear patterns, as in *Tree* (fig.14–32). Natural color has been nearly eliminated as grays and blacks take over. Natural objects are reduced to lines.

Later, Mondrian restricted his design to vertical and horizontal black lines and his colors to the three primary hues (red, blue and yellow) plus black, white and gray. By doing this, all possibility of representation was eliminated. *Diagonal Composition* (fig.14–33) is one of about twenty of his paintings that are square and made to stand on one corner. It is an exercise in

14–33 The artist dispensed with images and focused on perfect relationships of color and line.
Piet Mondrian, Piet Mondrian, *Diagonal Composition*, 1921. Oil on canvas, 23 1/2" x 23 1/2" (60.1 x 60.1 cm). The Art Institute of Chicago, gift of Edgar Kaufmann, Jr.

visual balance; the three primary colors are distributed around an imaginary center point. There is no center of interest. The viewer's eye must see the whole design at one time. Every space is a different size; each line is a different thickness; and each "white" space is a different value of very light gray. The lines establish rhythms and the various values and hues create a sense of depth.

Careful calculations and mathematical precision are essential to such a dehumanizing style of art. "But, art," Mondrian said, "systematically eliminates the world of nature and man."

14–32 Mondrian searched to find the ideal linear essence of a tree. Was he successful?
Piet Mondrian, *Tree*, 1912. Oil on canvas, 37" x 27 1/2" (94 x 70 cm). Museum of Art, Carnegie Institute, Pittsburgh, Patrons Art Fund, 61.1.

Higher-Order Thinking Skills

1 Ask students to use photographs or their own drawings to analyze the essence of several natural forms, such as trees, shells and figures. If using photographs, students can place tracing paper over them to do their analysis.

2 *The Noise of the Street Penetrates the House* (fig.14–30) is meant to convey the impression one would receive upon opening the window in the midst of a bustling day in the city. It is as though the canvas is the window that has just been opened. Ask students if they ever have had the experience of opening a window and having all the noises of the outside world rush in. How does Boccioni convey that sensation in a visual manner?

Lesson 14.2 Review

1 Describe the bridge in Joseph Stella's *Brooklyn Bridge*. What type of compositional balance is in this painting?

2 What nationality was Pablo Picasso? In what country did he spend most of his adult life?

3 Describe the musicians in Picasso's *Three Musicians*. What instrument is each one playing?

4 What is the name of the technique perfected by Braque and Picasso where bits of real objects and paper were added to paintings?

5 Describe the simultaneity in Braque's *Still Life: Table*.

6 Explain why the 1913 New York Armory Show was important.

7 What is the main subject of Duchamp's *Nude Descending a Staircase*?

Lesson 14.2 Review Answers

1 It is a suspension bridge with towers, cables, beams of light, tunnels and skyscrapers in the background. This painting is symmetrically balanced on each side of a central axis.

2 Picasso was Spanish, but lived most of his life in France.

3 A Pierrot plays the clarinet in a black mask, a Harlequin holds a violin and is wearing a red-and-yellow, diamond-patterned suit, and a Franciscan monk plays a zither.

4 Collage

5 Each object can be seen from a separate vantage point. The viewer can see into the top of one bottle, but not into the nearby flask. The viewer looks down on the apple dish, but straight on at the wine glass.

6 The Armory Show combined Cubism, Fauvism, Impressionism and Post-Impressionism into one exhibition. It was many Americans' introduction to these art styles.

7 Motion

Lesson 14.3

In the early twentieth century, many sculptors for the first time dared to abandon strict representation in favor of innovative explorations of mass and space.

Warm-up

Have students guess Brancusi's subject in figs.14–34 and 14–36 without looking at their titles. Ask what visual information the artist has provided. Does learning their titles alter or enhance students' understanding of the sculptures? Have students defend their decision on whether knowing a work's title before looking at it limits or expands their ability to fully experience the piece. Do they feel titles are more important in abstract or realistic art?

Objectives

Students should be able to:

Describe how early modern sculptors pared down their forms to the bare essentials, leaving behind the age-old tradition of representation.

14.3 Sculpture

IN THE INNOVATIVE SPIRIT of early twentieth-century art, sculptors vigorously challenged traditional interpretations of mass and space. They became interested in reducing representational images to their elemental forms.

From their wide range of sculptural expression grew the varied trends of three-dimensional expression in the later part of the century.

Key Notes

* Sculptors challenge traditional interpretations of space and mass.
* Sculpted representations are reduced to their elemental forms.

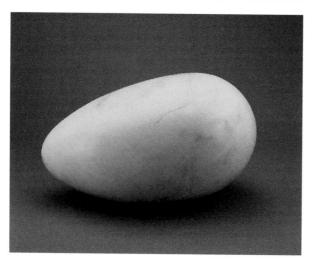

14–35 Brancusi reduced form to its essence. As he continued working, his art became more and more abstract.
Constantin Brancusi, *Sculpture for the Blind (The Beginning of the World)*, about 1916. Marble, 6 3/4" x 11 1/4" x 7" (17.14 x 28.27 x 17.78 cm). Philadelphia Museum of Art; The Louise and Walter Arensberg Collection.

Special Feature
Constantin Brancusi
(1876–1957)

Constantin Brancusi, one of the greatest sculptors of the century, was a Rumanian who came to Paris in 1904. He became involved with the Abstractionist movement and incorporated its theories into his sculpture. Brancusi wanted to reveal the essential shape hidden in everything we see.

Brancusi's limestone carving, *The Kiss* (fig.14–34), shows his interest in simplification and elimination of detail, a characteristic of African art that he admired. He cherished the basic upright shape of the block of stone. He considered it a strong and primitive form and carved as little as possible in it. There is just enough detail for the embracing lovers to be separately visible. Anonymous and innocent, they are an enduring symbol of love.

Many of his later works stressed simplicity so much that they became abstract pieces of art. These sculptures were either based on the oval egg form (fig.14–35) or soaring, vertical bird motifs. Brancusi was particularly interested in birds and the idea of flight. He was the first sculptor of abstract forms to completely eliminate normal representational reference and to emphasize the form itself.

Brancusi's *Bird in Space* (fig.14–36) is not a sculpture of a bird, but of the essence of flight made visible and touchable. He started with a bird standing at rest with its wings folded at its sides.

Teach

Aesthetics: Ask students to describe in as few words as possible a story about the beginning of the world. Afterward, ask them to count how many scenes they would need in order to illustrate their tale. Next ask them to imagine just a single image or object that could communicate the entire scenario in a split second. Direct them to Constantin Brancusi's sculpture in fig.14–35.

• Does this solitary egg communicate the idea well?

• How might Brancusi have reacted to the saying "a picture is worth a thousand words"?

Art History: Challenge students to write dialogue for a conversation between Michelangelo's sculpture *David* (fig.9–26) and Brancusi's two figures in *The Kiss* (fig.14–34).

• What would the image of David, carved in the beginning of the sixteenth century, want to ask the twentieth-century couple about their maker?

• What could the pair tell David about Brancusi's artistic interests that would help him understand early modern abstraction?

Contextual Information

Brancusi

Brancusi was born the son of peasants. He left home at the age of 11 and worked at odd jobs. At 18 he was apprenticed to a cabinetmaker in the provincial city of Craiova, Rumania. By 1898 he moved to Bucharest where he studied at the Academy of Fine Arts for four years.

Higher-Order Thinking Skills

Instruct the class to compare *Bird in Space* (fig.14–36) to photographs or videos of birds in flight.

Gradually, he refined the bird's shape until all its parts merged into a single vision of a bird about to soar into space. The high polish on the surface reflects surrounding space and objects and almost eliminates the form itself, uniting it with its environment.

Brancusi never really departed from working with the figure, and his themes were few, but he affected and influenced most of the major sculpture trends that followed him.

14–34 **Examine the various ways the sculptor has emphasized the closeness or unity of the two figures.**
Constantin Brancusi, *The Kiss*, 1912. Limestone, 22 3/4" (58 cm) high. Philadelphia Museum of Art, Louise and Walter Arensberg Collection.

14–36 **Brancusi wanted to express the essence of flight.**
Constantin Brancusi, *Bird in Space*, 1928. Bronze, 54" (137 cm). The Museum of Modern Art, New York.

Evaluate

Ask students to describe how both Brancusi's twentieth-century sculpture *The Kiss* and Michelangelo's *David* are both symbolic, even though the Italian Renaissance piece is far more realistic than the modern one.

• Which style do students believe more readily communicates its message?

• Do they understand the whole story behind David and Goliath and its larger political meaning in Florentine society as easily as they do the implications for eternal love represented by the two embracing figures?

Reteach

Ask students what the primary difference is between sculpture and painting. How does sculpture, as compared to two-dimensional art, deal with space and mass?

• Since sculpture by definition is three-dimensional, is it inherently more realistic than flat works that can convey only the illusion of depth and mass?

• Have students argue both sides of the concept and then examine the images in the lesson opener to determine which of their opinions holds true.

Contextual Information

Maillol

Originally Maillol was a textile designer but when his eyes became weak, he became a sculptor. He restricted his sculptures mainly to forms of southern French country women who served as his models. During the 1920s and 1930s, Maillol created book illustrations, including woodcut illustrations for a 1926 edition of Virgil's *Eclogues*.

Barlach

Barlach's work captured the frustration of Germans toward their government. His art was declared "degenerate" in 1938 by the Nazis.

Aristide Maillol

(1861–1944)

Starting his art career as a painter, Aristide Maillol soon felt more at home in three-dimensional art. He admired the simple strength of early Greek sculpture, and his female figures tend toward such Classicism. Sculptures such as his bronze *Summer* (fig.14–37) have a calm and self-sufficient sense of harmony that a bustling twentieth-century world cannot destroy. While his fellow Frenchman Rodin, had emphasized movement, Maillol emphasized a static balance and feeling of serenity in his full-formed figures.

Ernst Barlach

(1870–1938)

Ernst Barlach was a German Expressionist sculptor whose simple, strong style was the result of a visit to Russia and his contact with the peasants and their folk art. He carved in wood, but also cast bronzes such as *Frenzy (Der Berserker)* (fig.14–38) that expressed basic human emotions such as anger, fear, wrath and grief. The large forms are simply sculpted. Yet, they produce powerful works when combined with such elemental human traits. Often, the figure is locked to the base and not cut free from the block, which seems to add weight and substance to the finished form.

14–38 Folk art strongly influenced this sculptor's work. His forms are simplified but powerful. Ernst Barlach, *Frenzy (Der Berserker)*, 1910. Bronze, 21" x 27" (53 x 68 cm). The Nelson-Atkins Museum of Art, Kansas City, Missouri, gift of The Friends of Art, F65-18.

14–37 Maillol sculpted figures to represent all four seasons. Can you name an historical period that may have influenced him? Aristide Maillol, *Summer*, 1910. Bronze, 64 1/4" (163 cm) high. National Gallery of Art, Washington, DC, Ailsa Mellon Bruce Fund.

Materials and Techniques

Sculptors often cast more than one copy of a bronze. Of the edition of six numbered bronzes that Giacometti made of *Man Pointing* (fig.14–39), cast 1/6 belongs to the Museum of Modern Art, 2/6 to the Baltimore Museum of Art, 3/6 to the Tate Gallery, 4/6 to a private collection in London, 5/6 to the Des Moines Art Center, and 6/6 to a private collection in New York. The figures were cast at the Alexis Rudier foundry in Paris.

Inquiry

Some students might want to interview an artist who works with bronze. Have them inquire about the process of making casts and working with a foundry. They might also explore the advantages and disadvantages of working in this medium.

14–39 What emotions come to mind as you view this figure?
Alberto Giacometti, *Man Pointing*, 1947. Bronze, 70 1/2" (179 cm) high. The Museum of Modern Art, New York, gift of Mrs. John D. Rockefeller.

Alberto Giacometti

(1901–1966)

Alberto Giacometti was a Swiss sculptor who worked in Italy for several years before going to Paris. After 1934, he started to work on a series of figure sculptures. Their emaciated and elongated forms were first formed in plaster over a wire armature. The stick-thin figures, such as *Man Pointing* (fig.14–39), have come to be recognized as a powerful symbol of the loneliness and alienation of humanity in this century. The personal symbolism and expressive quality of his figures place Giacometti in the realm of Expressionism even though he was not formally associated with any of the groups or brotherhoods.

Higher-Order Thinking Skills

1 Have the class compare and contrast Maillol's sculpture to one from ancient Greece. Which one do students prefer? Why?

2 Maillol, Barlach and Giacometti each used the human figure as his subject. Have students compare and contrast the way each artist used the human form to convey an idea or emotion. What effect does each figure have on the viewer?

Lesson 14.3 Review

1 What was Brancusi trying to show in his sculpture?
2 What is the subject of Brancusi's *Bird in Space*?
3 Which historical art influenced Maillol's sculptures of female figures?
4 What did Giacometti's figure sculpture, such as *Man Pointing*, come to symbolize?
5 Name four early twentieth-century sculptors and an example of each one's work.

Lesson 14.3 Review Answers

1 Brancusi was trying to reveal the essential shape hidden in everything we see.
2 The essence of flight
3 Greek sculpture
4 The loneliness and alienation of humanity
5 Umberto Boccioni, *Unique Forms of Continuity in Space*; Constantin Brancusi, *The Kiss, Bird in Space*; Aristide Maillol, *Summer*; Ernst Barlach, *Frenzy*; Alberto Giacometti, *Man Pointing*; Meret Oppenheim, *Object*

Lesson 14.4

Fantasy art movements of the early twentieth century evolved from a long line of earlier traditions in which artists expressed the human imagination in visual form. The philosophies of Dada and Surrealism, two significant Fantasy movements, were originated by writers and then translated by artists into visual form.

Warm-up

Divide the class into small circles of five or six students. Have each student write a word on a sheet of paper and then toss the paper gently to the floor in the middle of the group. Instruct one person from each group to pick up the scraps and lay them one by one in a straight line. Ask if the resulting "sentences" make sense. What images or connotations do they suggest? Explain that Dadaists and Surrealists—who included poets, writers, performers and artists—often used chance elements, such as this technique, to create work that defied rational logic.

Objectives

Students should be able to:

Understand that modern Fantasy art stemmed from a lengthy history of artists who explored the seemingly illogical depths of the human psyche for their subject matter.

Describe how Fantasy artists incorporated chance elements, deliberately weird associations, and obscure personal symbolism into their work.

Examine how viewers are responsible for their own interpretations of Fantasy art.

Vocabulary Definitions

biomorphic shape (by-o-*mor*-fik) Artistic stylization suggested by organic forms.
assemblage (ah-*sem*-blij) A work of art composed of fragments of objects or materials originally intended for other purposes.

14.4 Fantasy Art and Surrealism

L IKE EXPRESSIONIST AND ABSTRACT ART, Fantasy art evolved from an earlier tradition. Greek mythology, the demons and monsters of the Middle Ages, the imagination of Bosch, the hideous nightmares of Goya, and even the personal symbolism of Munch were attempts to visualize the fantasy world of human imagination. In the twentieth century, many painters turned to psychological fantasy to express themselves. It was not long before groups such as the Dadaists and Surrealists were proclaiming their philosophies in paint and words.

The first Surrealist art exhibition took place in Paris in 1925. The exhibit featured artists such as Ernst, Arp, de Chirico, Klee and Picasso. Another painter who would form the heart of the Surrealist movement was Joan Miró. René Magritte and Salvador Dali would join in a few years. The work of these artists was called Surrealism because they were getting "beneath the realistic surface of life" or into a dream world of unreality. Early Surrealist work began with chance techniques such as rubbing a pencil over a paper placed on boards to see what the grain would suggest. Later, artists developed sophisticated presentations of logical or recognizable subject matter in very illogical situations or in weird associations. Much of later Surrealism developed around personal symbols that were unexplained by the artists. For example, Salvador Dali presents green giraffes that are fully ablaze and limp watches draped over a table, but he never tells the viewer what they mean.

Key Notes
• Fantasy art can be found in earlier traditions.
• Surrealists present recognizable subject matter in illogical situations.

> **Vocabulary**
> biomorphic
> assemblages

Special Feature
Salvador Dali

(1904–1989)
A Spaniard, Salvador Dali became the most famous Surrealist. His life itself was so thoroughly surrealistic—his wild actions, his weird utterances, his flamboyant clothing—that his integrity as an artist has often been questioned. However, the paintings talk for themselves. His personal painting style, influenced at first by Picasso and Miró, soon developed into a magical presentation of incredible draughtmanship and three-dimensional space.

The Persistence of Memory (fig.14–40), perhaps his best-known work, is a small painting of soft objects that represent things that are usually metallic and solid. Its technique recalls the Flemish art of the fifteenth century. He said that the idea came to him while eating soft cheese. The limp watches, gigantic ants and a partial face on a

14–40 Dali's surrealism relies on the placement of objects or people in unusual surroundings, either real or imagined, to convey the personal vision of the artist.
Salvador Dali, *The Persistence of Memory*, 1931. Oil on canvas, 9 1/2" x 13" (24 x 33 cm). The Museum of Modern Art, New York.

Teach

Criticism: Direct students to quietly examine Salvador Dali's *The Persistence of Memory* (fig.14–40) and list as many bizarre, unrealistic elements as they can find. Afterward, instruct them to close their eyes, go deep inside their imaginations, and then look again at Dali's painting. Now have them write down what they feel each element might mean.

• What visual clues guide their intuitive answers?

• Have classmates share their interpretations. Are any two alike?

• Share that Dali intentionally used mysterious personal symbols to force viewers to invent their own meanings for his paintings.

• Finish by asking students if they are comfortable examining Fantasy art, which can leave more questions than answers.

Aesthetics: Have students describe their visceral response to Dali's artwork (fig.14–40) and that of Giorgio de Chirico (fig.14–44), Paul Klee (fig.14–45), René Magritte (fig.14–50) and Meret Oppenheim (fig.14–51).

• Are their reactions to each artwork the same?

• Do they experience some as humorous and others as disturbing?

• How has each artist skewed logic to prompt their responses?

• Which piece do they find most appealing and why?

plain of immense depth are all startling objects, even today. The images are placed in a natural setting with the rocky cliffs of Spain in the background. These cliffs and other private symbolism occur often in Dali's work. Dali uses exacting realism in every part of his paintings because he claimed to "hate simplicity in all its forms," thus rejecting abstraction and any other simplified form of art.

Later in his life, Dali began painting religious subjects with his unique style and symbolism. *Sacrament of the Last Supper* (14–41) has many features similar to the deep-spaced *Persistence of Memory*, but the subject matter is entirely different. It, at first, recalls Leonardo's *Last Supper* in Milan. Upon closer examination, Christ's body is translucent, and a partial, symbolic torso is suspended in the air above the table. The floating segment of the dodecahedron (12-sided figure) is a symbol of the universe. The detail and painting techniques are wonders of craftsmanship. The composition is designed and carried out meticulously. The image, as in all Surrealist and Fantasy art, leaves the viewer with more questions than answers.

Dali's most famous religious painting is *Christ of St. John of the Cross* (fig.14–42). The viewer sees Christ from above. This viewpoint was used by Dali to exaggerate the weight of the body hanging from the cross. What else does this unusual perspective emphasize?

14–41 Compare this to Leonardo's *Last Supper* (fig.9–23). Which do you prefer? Why? Salvador Dali, *Sacrament of the Last Supper*, 1955. Oil on canvas, 65 3/4" x 105 1/4" (167 x 267 cm). National Gallery of Art, Washington, DC, Chester Dale Collection.

14–42 Dali has used three-point perspective in this painting. The vanishing point appears at the extreme bottom of the image. Salvador Dali, *Christ of St. John of the Cross*, 1951. Oil on canvas, 6'9" x 3'10" (204.8 x 115.9 cm). The St. Mungo Museum of Religious Life and Art, Glasgow, Scotland.

Contextual Information

Chagall

Unlike the artists who were his contemporaries and who expressed depression and the horror of war in their work, Chagall chose to paint a world of dreams and peaceful inter-actions. He described his father as "always full of love and in his way a poet. Through him I first sensed the existence of poetry. . . . I felt it in the nights, when I looked into the dark sky. Then I learned that there was also another world." The Hasidic religious world in which Chagall was raised encouraged a belief in other-world influences on this world. Angels spoke and affected human actions.

Chagall's friend, the poet Blaise Cendrars, invented the titles of many of Chagall's Parisian paintings. Since the second half of the twenti-eth century, artists have sometimes deliberately left their works untitled. Museums honor this and simply note on identifying labels and in catalogs that the work is untitled.

• Ask students how important titles are to works of art. Does it matter who gave the titles? In the past, museums gave titles to old works; would that make any difference to our appreciation?

Klee

Klee's early work included pencil landscape studies that showed an impressionist influence. He also pro-duced many black-and-white etch-ings early in his career, but a trip to North Africa in 1914 caused him to be (in his own words) "possessed by color." This brought on his mature style which was characterized by delicate color harmonies.

Klee also was a master draughts-man. The *Twittering Machine* is an example of his technique which he described as "taking a line for a walk."

Marc Chagall

(1887–1985)

Marc Chagall was born in Russia, but spent most of his life in France and the United States. He left his homeland for good after 1920 when the political climate no longer allowed personal expression and freedom of thought. Chagall's style is based somewhat on Cubism with its fractured planes, but his con-cepts and presentation are purely personal. His main subject is the Russia he remembered, a Russia of villages and fun-loving peasants, folklore and fairy tales. Reality is mixed with happy remembrances. The result is a delightfully personal style that has charmed viewers in countries around the globe. In *I and the Village* (fig.14–43), the cow dreams happily of a milkmaid. Lovers (one right side up, the other upside down) are on their way to the field. The village street has sev-eral upside-down houses, and a green-faced man holds a fantastic plant as he views the entire scene. Dreamlike memories, Jewish proverbs and Russian folk tales are woven to create a tapestry of Chagall's private thoughts.

The viewer need not be discour-aged by failing to understand the symbolism because Chagall himself said, "I do not understand them at all. They are not literature. They are only pictorial arrangements of images which obsess me." Chagall painted fantastic murals and ceilings, designed stage settings, produced lithographs and etchings, and created imaginative stained glass windows, all in his own personal style.

14–43 Dreams, memories, folklore and fairy tales all were part of Chagall's paintings.
Marc Chagall, *I and the Village*, 1911. Oil on canvas, 75 1/2" x 59 1/2" (192 x 151 cm). The Museum of Modern Art, New York, Mrs. Simon Guggenheim Fund.

14–44 What fea-tures in this paint-ing strike you as strange, or even disturbing?
Giorgio de Chirico, *The Mystery and Melancholy of a Street*, 1914. Oil on canvas, 34" x 28" (87 x 71 cm). Private Collection. Photo-graph courtesy Aquavella Galleries, Inc., New York. ©1996 Foundation Giorgio de Chirico/Licensed by VAGA, New York, NY.

A progressive skin and muscle disease forced Klee to change his style after 1935. His later work is broad and flat and utilizes thick lines and large areas of subdued color.

• Suggest that students research Klee's early style and compare it to his later, more well-known work. Often the work by which we best know an artist is rather different from previous or subse

quent styles in an artist's career. The early paintings of van Gogh and Mondrian also make interesting com-parisons to their later work.

Giorgio de Chirico

(1888–1978)

Giorgio de Chirico was an Italian artist, born in Greece, who studied in Athens and Munich before coming to Paris in 1911. He showed no interest at all in Impressionism, Cubism or Fauvism, but produced a series of disturbing cityscapes which are crisp, clean and altogether strange. Most of them, such as *The Mystery and Melancholy of a Street* (fig.14–44) have buildings of tremendous solidity that are lit from the side so that long shadows

are cast. Small figures produce a feeling of loneliness and despair. They appear to be the last beings left in the otherwise deserted city. Often, an unexplained shadow creeps in from the side, a shadow without an object to cast it. Vast spaces and large flat areas of little texture create a sensation of impending doom. De Chirico changed his style in later years to more traditional approaches and failed to live up to his early promise as an experimenter and leader in personal expression.

Paul Klee

(1879–1940)

Paul Klee was a Swiss-born artist who spent most of his life in Germany. He settled in Munich in 1911 and joined Der Blaue Reiter while working in near poverty. His small watercolors, etchings and drawings were done on his kitchen table while his wife gave piano lessons. He later taught at the Bauhaus and was a close friend of Kandinsky. Always interested in children's art, he developed a style that combined his personal wit with a childlike vision of the mysteries of life. He created poetic statements of a very personal nature.

Most of his work has a happy quality, such as *Twittering Machine* (fig.14–45), a delightful exercise in imagination. If the handle is cranked, perhaps bird sounds will be produced. Or, is Klee trying to tell viewers something about their insane urge to create machines to do everything—even to make mechanical bird sounds? Or, perhaps, machines can do everything, and humanity's trust in natural things is not valid. Klee supplies no answers. He only tickles the viewers' imaginations and sets them thinking—after they first smile a bit at his art and at themselves.

14–45 What do you think happens if you turn the crank? Paul Klee, *Twittering Machine*, 1922. Watercolor, pen and ink on oil transfer drawing on paper, mounted on cardboard, 25 1/4" x 19" (64 x 41 cm). The Museum of Modern Art, New York.

Freud and Art

The writings of Freud on the significance of dreams played a significant part in the art of the early twentieth century. Freud said that dreams were symbols of our most pressing desires and fears and that ideas flowed from our unconscious to our conscious minds if we let them. Artists found that Freud's theories fit their experiences because often ideas arise as the conscious mind is relaxed. In times past, artists spoke of being influenced by "muses"; now they accepted the idea that their subconscious minds held ideas and thoughts of how to express them.

Contextual Information

Duchamp

Duchamp thought that life was meaningless and that art had no value. He tried to destroy the preciousness that he felt had been given to art by museums, historians and critics. With Picabia and Man Ray, Duchamp became a leader of the Dada movement in New York.

Dada

During World War I, a group of artists and writers gathered in Zurich to organize a protest against the complete degradation of European society as well as the monstrous destruction of such a war. Their protest took the form of nonsense poetry. They snipped words from pages and dropped them on the table. From these random arrangements, they created poems. The name Dada originated from this nonsense attitude toward conventional language. Their anti-art doctrines spread across Europe and America. Artists used their personal styles to create spur-of-the-moment works, but the message was the same: All European culture was decadent and devoid of meaning. The Dada movement created chaos in the art world, among the public, and even in its own ranks. Members joined and left hurriedly and could not get along well with each other for any great length of time.

Jean (Hans) Arp

(1887–1966)

Jean (Hans) Arp was born in Strasbourg, a city which at times was German (his name was Hans) and at times French (his name was Jean). He made collages by cutting bits of paper and floating them to the floor. Then, he made their accidental arrangement permanent by gluing them to a sheet of paper. Such unplanned work was a protest against both the design quality and the emotional expression of previous styles of art. He began cutting random bits of wood with a band saw, gluing them together, and adding paint to create relief sculptures. Some sculptures suggested visual images, such as *Birds in an Aquarium* (fig.14–46). His **biomorphic** (stylized and organic) shapes and scenes are often whimsical.

14–46 Arp believed that accidental and intuitive compositions were as good as those planned according to rules and conventions.
Jean (Hans) Arp, *Birds in an Aquarium*, 1920. Painted wood relief, 9 3/4" x 7 3/4" (25 x 20 cm). The Museum of Modern Art, New York.

Max Ernst

(1891–1976)

Max Ernst was a German artist who made extensive use of collage techniques. He also worked with oils. He was associated with the Dada movement in his earlier years, but spent much of his life in the United States working with the elements of Surrealism. His painting *La Mer* *(The Sea)* (fig.14–47) allows one to view the sea and shore confrontation through Ernst's own eyes and inner vision. Sand, water and waves can be seen—or can they? Is that a sun and clouds above or a ball floating on water? Ernst presents a seascape of his own making, seen with unconventional eyes.

Cooperative Learning

Form students into groups to create short lists (perhaps five items) of everyday objects and of textures and patterns, one item per strip of paper. Students then put the strips of paper into boxes: objects into one box and patterns and textures into another. Each group member draws one paper from the objects box and one from the patterns/textures box. Each group then collaborates on how to combine the things they have picked from the boxes to create surreal objects. They can draw, trace or paint, or use any other form.

Performing Arts Connection

Dada

Dada (1916–1924) grew out of European and American artists' response to the incomprehensible devastation resulting from World War I. Disillusioned with rational thinking, Dadaists created deliberately nonsensical works that relied on chance, paradox and disorder to reveal the inconsistency and foolishness of conventional society. Dada artists randomly incorporated found materials from the trash, manufactured objects, illustrations and other mundane items to construct new, disturbing art that puzzled and frequently alienated observers. In Dada, the literal act of making the work was considered a performance and as important as the final product itself. Dada was not limited to visual artists but included poets, writers and philosophers who "performed" in word-association poetry readings, mad theatrical dramas or cabarets, and nonsense lectures.

Kurt Schwitters

(1887–1948)

Kurt Schwitters was a scavenger who gathered junk items from everywhere to include in his art. The German artist glued these objects to a ground and added some paint to make images, or **assemblages**, that were partly three-dimensional. Works such as *Construction for Noble Ladies* (fig.14–48) might contain ticket stubs, candy wrappers, announcements, bits of broken toys, wheels, boards and assorted trash. Schwitters became the ultimate Dada master. He recycled the refuse from a society he was demeaning into works of art for that same society to see. Viewers were of course disgusted at the sight of it, but the message was delivered.

14–48 Why do you think this work is called an assemblage?
Kurt Schwitters, *Construction for Noble Ladies*, 1919. Mixed-media assemblage of wood, metal and paint, 40 1/2" x 33" (103 x 84 cm). Los Angeles County Museum of Art.

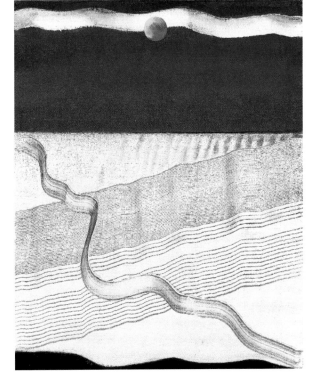

14–47 Do you see this as a seascape with the usual elements of sand, wind and water?
Max Ernst, *La Mer*, 1925. Oil on canvas, 16 1/4" x 12 1/2" (41 x 32 cm). Los Angeles County Museum of Art, Mr. and Mrs. William Preston Harrison Collection.

Higher-Order Thinking Skills

Collage is a medium that is unique to modern times. It is related to modern printing technology, which has created such a tremendous supply of images and words from which to choose. Over a specified period of time, such as two or three days, ask students to save paper they would ordinarily discard—graded papers, lists, junk mail, newspapers and magazines. Have them create collages that are a "paper trail" of a typical day.

After they have completed their collages ask students to discuss their processes of choosing items. Did they have more than enough items or not enough items from which to choose? Was it difficult to decide what to choose? Did the project make them more aware of certain elements in their day that they previously had not had occasion to carefully examine?

Interdisciplinary Connection

Literature: During the late 1800s, literature also took on themes of fantasy, surrealism and subtle satire. Danish writer Hans Christian Andersen (1805–1875) wrote fairy tales for children. Traveling throughout Europe, Asia and Africa, he wrote more than 150 stories. Among his famous tales of fantasy are "The Ugly Duckling," "The Emperor's New Clothes," and "The Little Mermaid." His stories have been translated into many languages and have been used as a basis for plays, films and visual arts.

Lewis Carroll (1832–1898)—British author, photographer, and mathematician—is best known for his fantasy children's classics *Alice's Adventures in Wonderland* (1865), and *Through the Looking Glass* (1871). The works, which were first illustrated by Sir John Tenniel, describe a child's dream adventures.

• Show students illustrations from some of these classics. Divide students into groups and have them read sections from these classics and interpret and discuss the illustrations. Have students report their findings to the class.

Contextual Information

Miró

Miró's automatic drawings contained personalized symbols that he used over and over again. He created a special group of them, abstracting the circles, stars, ladders, trees and animals into biomorphic and organic forms. His paintings, like Klee's, appear deceptively like children's drawings of insects and figures. Miró (unlike children, who do not consciously simplify or distort their drawings) simplified and distorted figures to create an unreal appearance.

The Surrealists' View of the World

Many artists were deeply disillusioned by World War I. Millions of dead and psychologically wounded veterans showed that human nature continued to be irrational and self-centered and that nothing on earth could be counted on to remain stable. The existential writings of Sartre seemed to be true.

Freud's theories of the levels of consciousness helped to explore these irrational acts against reason. When artists created works that could not be understood easily, some critics looked for explanations in what they felt to be aspects of the artist's subconscious.

Surrealists used images to provoke their audiences to think beyond the rational. Jungian psychology encouraged artists to explore cultural mythology as a repository of symbols and ideas for images. Surrealist paintings, movies, novels and poetry became dreamlike explorations of mysterious inner feelings and visions. Paintings were interpretations of dreams, and dreams contained elements of the artists' frustration, guilt, and aspirations. To view art became a way of seeing the artists' inner world—and sometimes their nightmares.

14–49 Miró developed a very personal symbolism for his painting, prints and tapestries.
Joan Miró, *Women at Sunrise*, 1946. Oil on canvas, 15" x 24" (38 x 61 cm). The Nelson-Atkins Museum of Art, Kansas City, Missouri, gift of the Friends of Art, 56-120.

Surrealism

As steam ran out of the Dada movement, its members began to work in varying styles and to proclaim different messages. In the rather peaceful years following the war, other movements would replace Dada, with Surrealism being the first and most direct descendant. André Breton was the instigator of Surrealism in 1924. A writer, not an artist, Breton followed the Dada philosophy of allowing things to happen naturally in his work rather than putting words together in a logical way. His emphasis on a dream world, word association games and unconscious writing was carried into the visual world of Surrealist painters and sculptors. We already have seen how Salvador Dali put his fantastic ideas and dreams on canvas. Now, we will look at three other artists who were part of the Surrealist movement.

14–50 Magritte is a popular artist. Perhaps this is because his paintings, though puzzling, often bring a smile to our faces.
René Magritte, *Time Transfixed*, 1938. Oil on canvas, 57 1/2" x 38 1/4" (146 x 97 cm). Art Institute of Chicago, Joseph Winterbotham Fund.

Oppenheim

Meret Oppenheim was one of the early Surrealists: she was invited by Giacometti and Arp to exhibit with them in 1933. Her transformed objects differed from other Surrealists' art because they were actually made into strange objects rather than paintings of combinations of real objects.

Multicultural Connection

The Influence of Ancient Persia

Ancient Persia (Iran) was well known for its miniature paintings and illuminated manuscripts, which reached their height during the late fifteenth and early sixteenth centuries. Persian miniature paintings illustrate historic and romantic stories and poems that accompany the manuscripts. Battles, hunting scenes, and illustrations to literature are among the predominant themes. Landscapes feature detailed, idealized settings accompanied by human and whimsical animal forms. Courtly scenes include many figures—sometimes in unusual, unrealistic poses—surrounded by complex geometric or floral designs. The complex com-

Joan Miró
(1893–1983)

Joan Miró charms the viewer with his Spanish wit and delightful menagerie of impossible animals and people. He uses black lines and flat shapes of red, yellow, blue, black and white that often seem cut from paper and glued to the canvas. In *Women at Sunrise* (fig.14–49), the shapes are suggestive of people, animals and a rising sun. At other times, his shapes and lines are purely abstract and suggest nothing. His biomorphic shapes seem to float on a soft background. When they overlap, they become transparent or create another shape.

In his later years, Miró also turned to abstract sculpture, using plastic and ceramic as his media. He also worked extensively with fibers, creating huge woven tapestry murals that repeat the colors, shapes and lines of his paintings. His joyful expressions of life are contagious. Viewers of his work in any media are caught up in his zest for living and his clever sense of humor.

René Magritte
(1898–1967)

René Magritte was a Belgian artist who developed his own witty style of Surrealism based on absurd combinations of realistically painted objects. These juxtapositions both amuse and puzzle the viewer. In *Time Transfixed* (fig.14–50), a partially realistic scene of a crisp, clean and detailed room is combined with a steaming train emerging from the fireplace. Each element is distinct, but, as in Dali's art, the total work raises more questions than answers. Often, Surrealist artists themselves do not know their motives for such improbable combinations.

Meret Oppenheim
(b.1913)

Meret Oppenheim exhibited the ultimate in Surrealist imaging by wrapping a cup, saucer and teaspoon with fur—recognizable objects in irrational combinations. She simply titled her controversial work *Object* (fig.14–51).

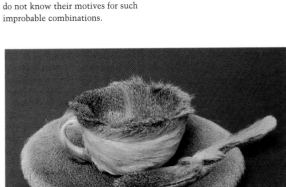

14–51 An ordinary object or grouping presented in an unusual way makes us stop and look carefully.
Meret Oppenheim, *Object*, 1936. Fur-covered cup, saucer and spoon, overall height 3" (7 cm). Museum of Modern Art, New York, Purchase.

Lesson 14.4 Review

1 Define Surrealism. List five surrealistic artists.
2 What nationality was Marc Chagall? Describe the subject of *I and the Village*.
3 In de Chirico's *The Mystery and Melancholy of a Street*, how does he create a feeling of impending doom, loneliness and despair?
4 What was Dada?
5 Describe the women in Miró's *Women at Sunrise*.
6 What unrelated objects does Magritte combine in *Time Transfixed*, and Oppenheim combine in *Object*?

positions of the figures and their surroundings are arranged to make flat patterns of color. Gold and silver colors are used decoratively as well as forde-picting sky, mountains and water. The paintings are further embellished with arabesques. In this art form, the Persians imaginatively linked historical facts and mythological fiction. They gave priority to legends, ancient folk beliefs, and art for arts sake over factual history and reality.

• Explain to students that the early history of Iran is told in the country's national epic poem, the *Shah Namah*, or *Book of Kings*, written around 1000 AD by the Persian poet Firdausi. Have students compare and contrast various illustrations from this epic with the work of Miró, Klee and Chagall.

Performing Arts Connection
Diaghilev and the Arts

Sergei Diaghilev, a genius in collaboration, brought the most avant-garde arts to Paris from his native Russia in 1906. During his career, he worked with Picasso, Matisse, Gris, Balla, Derain, Gabo, Rouault, de Chirico, Miró, Utrillo and Goncharnova. Many of these artists created costumes and sets for his Ballets Russes performances. Stravinsky, Satie and Ravel composed memorable scores for Diaghilev, and both Nijinsky and Balanchine danced with his famous troupe.

Higher-Order Thinking Skills

Miró used shapes to tell stories and to comment on things. Invite students to offer their interpretation of *Women at Sunrise* (fig.14–49) by creating a story or play that gives personalities to the characters, develops a plot or sequence of action, and comes to a conclusion.

Lesson 14.4 Review Answers

1 Surrealism is a twentieth-century art style in which artists combine normally unrelated objects and situations. Scenes are often dream-like or set in unnatural surroundings. Some Surrealist artists are Joan Miró, Rene Magritte, Meret Oppenheim, Salvador Dali, Marc Chagall, Giorgio de Chirico, Paul Klee, Jean Arp and Max Ernst.
2 Marc Chagall was born in Russia but lived most of his life in France and the United States. In *I and the Village*, he remembers his Russian village home where the cow dreams of a milkmaid. A pair of lovers with the woman upside down are on their way to the field. There is a row of houses with two houses upside down. A large green-faced man holds a plant and looks at the cow.
3 Small figures seem to be the last beings left in a deserted city. Vast spaces, unexplained shadows and large flat areas create a sensation of impending doom.
4 Dada was an art movement that rejected conventional art. Dada artists believed that all European culture was decadent and devoid of meaning. These artists created art spontaneously.
5 Women are suggested in the painting by yellow and green rounded shapes with red eyes and red and black lines.
6 Magritte combines a fireplace and a steam engine. Oppenheim covers a cup, saucer and teaspoon with fur.

Lesson 14.5

In the first half of the twentieth century, photographers continued to focus on humanity and nature, even though painters and sculptors explored various modes of abstraction. Photographers interpreted the entire range of life's experiences—love, joy, tragedy, and so forth—in their strongly evocative pictures.

Warm-up

Ask students to list all the places where they see photographs in daily life. Have them glance through magazines and find examples of photographs as social documents, artistic compositions and persuasive communication tools. Share that the scope of photography's influence greatly increased with the advent of photograph-based magazines such as *Life, Time* and *National Geographic*. Their huge circulations exposed photography to thousands who might not otherwise have seen any art.

Objectives

Students should be able to:

Understand that photographers in the early decades of the twentieth century concentrated on a broad range of human experiences for their subject matter.

Describe how travel, two world wars, and the emergence of photograph-based publications influenced the medium.

14.5 Photography

WHILE PAINTERS WERE EXPERIMENTING in all directions, photographers attempted to keep pace, although they were limited by what the camera could do. While painters explored abstraction, photographers continued to work with humanity and nature. The public (which did not understand abstraction) became increasingly appreciative of photographers. Travel in foreign countries, two world wars and the publication of magazines like *Look, Life* and *National Geographic* gave photographers plenty of opportunity for reportage, an area in which they excelled. Henri Cartier-Bresson became one of the finest reportage photographers.

Creative photographers searched for ways to interpret the everyday life of humanity—human relationships, ugliness, poverty, tragedy, sympathy, love, joy and the entire range of human emotion. The work of Edward Steichen and Alfred Stieglitz dominated the American scene. Other noteworthy American photographers of the period were Ansel Adams, Dorothea Lange, Edward Weston and the great social documentarian James Van Der Zee.

Key Notes

- While painters work in many stylistic directions, photographers are bound by the limits of the camera and darkroom techniques.
- Two world wars, increased world travel, and the publication of photograph-based magazines provide many opportunities for photo reportage.
- Creative photographers interpret the human condition.

14–53 What clues can you find in this photograph that would help you date it?
James Van Der Zee, *Couple in Raccoon Coats*, 1932. Photograph.

Special Feature

James Van Der Zee

(1886–1983)

Twelve-year-old James Van Der Zee was handed a simple box camera as a prize for selling twenty packets of perfume. He quickly became adept at using his camera and soon graduated to much more complex cameras.

A native of Lenox, Massachusetts, Van Der Zee lived most of his life in Harlem, New York. By 1915, he had opened a portrait studio in Harlem and started producing the enormous range of photographs depicting life in Harlem. He photographed the leading political, religious and cultural figures of the African-American community. He also recorded community events and celebrations. These included weddings, dinners and funerals. There are numerous images of the

---

Teach

Art History/Criticism: Have students examine figs.14–52, 14–53, 14–54 and 14–57. Ask what these photographs tell us about life in the first decades of the twentieth century.

- What feelings do they evoke?

- How do the photographers prompt particular emotions?

- Direct students to consider not just the theme, but also the photographers' choice of composition, distance from their subjects, and the objects that have been included or left out. Share that many photographers of the time became concerned with interpreting a wide range of human experiences in the modern world, including joy, pain, happiness and devastation.

Art History/Criticism: Ask students if Renaissance royal and religious leaders would have commissioned the type of photography in Lesson 14.5 if such art had been available.

- How did modern photography's subjects and audiences differ from those of the distant past?

- Why might themes concerning humanity not have suited earlier powerful leaders?

14–52 Why do you think this photograph is titled *Future Expectations?*
James Van Der Zee, *Future Expectations,* about 1915. Photograph.

latter which date from 1919 to 1920, the years of the great influenza epidemic. These photographs emphasize the dignity, pride and beauty of his subjects and represent our most important photographic archive of African-American life in Harlem.

A favorite technique of Van Der Zee's was to produce photographs that give us not only a physical record of the sitters, but also include a symbolic vision of their hopes and aspirations. *Future Expectations* (fig.14–52), taken about 1915, is one of those pictures. The young bridal couple is depicted with great and loving detail. The bouquet, the veil, the scalloped hem of the bride's dress, her shoes and the groom's starched white shirt are striking. Around the couple are the symbols of the home they desire. The living room with its fireplace represents the household of their dreams. Van Der Zee even places at their feet the daughter they hope to have.

Not all of Van Der Zee's photographs were so symbolic. *Couple in Raccoon Coats* (fig.14–53) is a fine example of his "straight" style. But, whether "straight" or more manipulated, his photographs record the life's work of the first great African-American photographer. They also provide an invaluable record of life in Harlem, especially during the period of the Harlem Renaissance (1919–1929), when all of the arts flourished there. Finally, the Van Der Zee archive illustrates how photography blossomed in the twentieth century and attained an important stature among the visual arts.

Higher-Order Thinking Skills

Ask students to plan a photograph that includes symbols for their future. Their plan can be drawn, written or made into a collage.

• Challenge students to cite painters in Chapter 14 (for example, Diego Rivera, Paula Modersohn-Becker, Käthe Kollwitz and Pablo Picasso) who also created art with social significance.

• Was Renaissance painting or the socially oriented art of the twentieth century more concerned with the lives of ordinary people?

• Was anyone or anything glorified in modern photography?

Evaluate

Ask students how the content of modern photography was different from earlier subject matter. Previously, much fine art photography had followed painting styles of the day. In the first part of the twentieth century, photographers focused on socially relevant themes or translated real-life objects and landscapes into startlingly beautiful abstractions. Ask students if they feel that these are worthy subjects for art. Have them defend their opinion in a class or group discussion.

Reteach

Have students consider why the public is generally more receptive to photography than to abstract art.

• Which one seems to require more effort to become comfortable with?

• Why might some people feel it easier to accept pictures of recognizable things?

• Ask students if the images they have at home, or ones they make themselves, tend to adhere closely to reality or if they explore realms outside the strictly observable world.

• What are the benefits of each style?

Contextual Information

Stieglitz

Stieglitz went to Germany from New York in 1886 to study mechanical engineering. He said that while walking in Berlin he saw in a store window a camera that seemed to be waiting for him. He quickly learned the technical instructions for developing images and became increasingly more interested in photography than in engineering.

Stieglitz returned to America in 1890 and found many amateur photo clubs and societies in New York City. He joined the Society of Amateur Photographers and became editor of *The American Amateur Photographer*. In this magazine, he urged readers to try new techniques and to use the pure, unretouched image as art rather than adjusting lights, shadows, focal lengths and lenses to create an image that looked like a painting. An advocate of "straight" photography, Stieglitz worked chiefly outdoors with rapid exposures.

Cartier-Bresson

Cartier-Bresson is known as a "legend" in photography because of his influence on so many modern photographers. When asked how he was able to achieve great compositions in his unposed photographs, he said that "there is one moment at which the elements in motion are in balance. Photography must seize upon this moment."

Group f.64

In 1932, a group of photographers influenced by Weston's straight photography formed a society that they called "Group f.64" because they set their lenses at small apertures to show greater details. Included in this group were Ansel Adams, Imogen Cunningham, John Paul Edwards, Edward Weston and Sonia Noskowiak.

Dorothea Lange did not exhibit with Group f.64 because her work was not made for the exclusive use of art but was documentary work for the Farm Security Administration (FSA). However, she was friends with many of the group's members.

Lange was disabled from childhood polio and said: "When I was working . . . with people who were strangers to me, being disabled gave me an immense advantage. People are kinder to you. It puts you on a different level than if you go into a situation whole and secure."

Photography Accepted as Art

The acceptance of photographs as "art" was achieved during the 1930s. Then the Museum of Modern Art in New York, the Art Institute of Chicago, and the Oakland Art Gallery opened departments of photography and galleries to exhibit photographs.

Window in Time

Curating Photographs

What better way to understand what a curator of photography does than to talk to one. Deborah Martin Kao is the assistant curator of photographs at the Fogg Art Museum, one of the art museums at Harvard University in Cambridge, Massachusetts. Here she explains the different types of exhibits that showcase photography.

Q: *How do you select the core of photographs that make up an exhibit?*

A: There are essentially three ways. Some exhibits are based on works of art that come out of the permanent collection. This kind of exhibit often depends on the strengths of the collection. Here at the Fogg, the strength is in twentieth-century American photography. We have a lot of documentary photography, so if we decided to do, say, a thematic exhibition based on photographers who had worked in the 1930s, that would be an example of a show coming from the strengths of an existing collection.

Another kind of show relies on borrowing works from other collections in many different locations. For instance, suppose a museum wants to mount a retrospective on a single artist, looking at all the works that artist did over a thirty- or forty-year period. The museum may have a handful of these works in its permanent collection. To complete the exhibit, the curator contacts other museums, commercial galleries or private collectors which may be willing to loan the needed works. This kind of show requires two or three years of research. Grants have to be written to obtain funding.

The third way a show can come about is when artists or experts send in suggestions. They might suggest they put on their own show, or they might want to collaborate with you. A great many suggestions come to a curator.

Deborah Martin Kao, assistant curator of photographs, Fogg Art Museum, Harvard University.

Q: *What steps do you follow for a show to be accepted?*

A: The concept is only the beginning. Once you have that, you have to sell your idea to the place where you want your show to be installed. Even if you're working in a museum, you have to present your idea. If I have an idea for a show, I write a proposal, just as I would if I were a freelancer. Then, I submit it to the director of the museum and all the other curators in the other departments.

Q: *What happens after the idea has been approved?*

A: A lot of planning! You really need to plan, even for a show that's an internal show. At an active institution like the Fogg, you need to plan a year or two in advance. First, a time slot for the show has to be found in the exhibition calendar. Six months before a show goes up, the date of the show must be set, and the title must be finalized. Four months before the show goes up, the publications department needs a list of objects. Then, using a scale model of the gallery, you cut up pieces of paper that are proportionate to the size of the objects. By laying out the works on a kind of architect's plan, you can experiment with their placement. Photographs can be placed in different-size cases instead of just being hung on the walls.

We think of photographs as being flat works on paper, but in fact you can put photographic emulsion on any material. You can even have photographic sculptures.

These are just some of the many challenges a curator of photographs must tackle. Additionally, a photography curator must always keep in mind the fragile nature of the medium, which is extremely sensitive to heat and direct light. Assistant Curator Deborah Martin Kao can attest to the variety of factors that must be juggled in caring for and exhibiting a collection of photographs.

Alfred Stieglitz

(1864–1946)

Alfred Stieglitz was a "straight" photographer, intent on recording whatever he saw around him directly, without resorting to special effects like double-exposure or double-printing. Yet, these "straight" photographs have an underlying composition of forms. Form, shape and meaning are all reflected in his best-known photograph, *The Steerage* (fig.14–54). Stieglitz captured this moment while sailing to Europe in 1907. The scene of passengers in the steerage section of the ship fascinated him. He described the scene later as "a picture based on related shapes and deepest human feelings." The drama of the people below the deck in steerage, separated from the observers on the upper deck by the white gangway, continues to affect viewers today.

Henri Cartier-Bresson

(b.1908)

Henri Cartier-Bresson has become one of the most influential photo-journalists of his time. He has traveled around the world covering wars, occupations of countries, and the people affected by these events. His photographs are pictures that tell stories, allowing viewers to see and experience events throughout Europe and the United States.

Woman on a Stairway Talking to a Man with Cane (fig.14–b) is an excellent example of the human quality in his work. As carefully constructed as a fine painting, it has superb contrasts, aerial perspective, balance, and the touch of human interest that sparks it to life.

14–54 Stieglitz regarded this as his finest photograph.
Alfred Stieglitz, *The Steerage*, 1907. Photograph. Courtesy George Eastman House.

Edward Weston

(1886–1958)

Edward Weston focused on the form of ordinary objects. In his tightly composed photographs, he captured the beauty in organic forms. In *Pepper* (fig.14–55), he transforms a common vegetable into a composition of flowing lines and textured surfaces.

14–55 Weston did a series of ordinary vegetables photographed as monumental sculptural forms.
Edward Weston, *Pepper*. Photograph. Courtesy Sotheby's, Inc.

Higher-Order Thinking Skills

1 While *The Steerage* (fig.14–54) is a powerful image, it is also a well-composed work of art. Have students identify the shapes and repetitions. They may use tracing paper or black, white and gray paper to analyze the composition.

2 Ask students to consider the circumstances under which Cartier-Bresson caught the unposed image in fig.14–b. What do they imagine transpired before the scene was photographed?

Materials and Techniques

The invention of a small, lightweight 35mm roll-film camera is the single most important development in professional photography equipment in the twentieth century. The Leica was introduced in 1925: it was the first commercially successful camera to combine instantaneous exposure, fast film advance and a high level of image definition under a variety of lighting conditions.

• Ask students to consider whether it would have been possible for Cartier-Bresson to have developed his approach to photography if this invention had not been available to him.

Conservation Note

Photographs are extremely sensitive to their environment. Excessive heat and humidity cause rapid deterioration. The ideal conditions for storage are temperatures below 70° Fahrenheit and relative humidity at about 45 percent. Direct sunlight and fluorescent lighting are extremely harmful to photographs.

• Ask students if they can recall any very old photographs they have seen. What was their condition?

• Have students visit (if available) a local photography collection (fine art or historical) and ask the curator to describe the particular problems attendant to the preservation of that collection.

Higher-Order Thinking Skills

The theme of mother and child is one that has often been repeated throughout the history of art. Have students select two images of mother and child from other periods and compare them to Lange's *Migrant Mother, Nipomo Valley* (fig.14–57).

Lesson 14.5 Review Answers

1 Cartier-Bresson was a photojournalist who tried to capture the moment of intense action or emotion that reveals the inner meaning of the event—the decisive moment.

2 The orderly, well-dressed, first-class passengers contrast with the distorted, huddled masses of steerage passengers below, symbolizing the separation between the rich and the poor.

3 The American wilderness, particularly Yosemite National Park in California

4 The careworn face of the mother with her children makes a powerful statement about migrant workers' desperate situation at the time. The woman looks hungry, worried and tired, but Lange focused on the woman's pride, strength and spirit. Soon after this photograph was printed in a San Francisco newspaper, food was rushed to feed the starving workers in her camp.

Chapter Review Answers

Review

14–56 During his lifetime, Adams was the foremost nature photographer in the United States. Ansel Adams, *Mt. Williamson from Manzazar*, 1944. Photograph. Courtesy of the Ansel Adams Publishing Rights Trust.

14–57 This image has become an icon of the Great Depression of the 1930s. Dorothea Lange, *Migrant Mother, Nipomo Valley*, 1936. Gelatin silver print. Dorothea Lange Collection, Oakland Museum, Oakland, CA.

Ansel Adams
(1902–1984)

Like the nineteenth-century landscape painters in America, Ansel Adams found an emotional response in the American wilderness. San Franciscan by birth, Ansel Adams used his camera to capture the grandeur of the mountains of the West (fig.14–56), especially in Yosemite National Park. Adams was a master of photographic technology. To record the smallest detail in sharp focus, Adams used the smallest opening for his lens. His black-and-white prints have dramatic contrasts of lights and darks that he achieved by using different-colored filters.

Dorothea Lange
(1895–1965)

Dorothea Lange ranks as one of the finest documentary photographers in America. During the Great Depression in the 1930s, Lange was hired by the United States government to photograph the plight of migrant workers in California. Her photographs were intended to inform the public and the government about the sad conditions of migrant families and the programs set up to serve them. Of the photographs she took for this assignment, the best-known is *Migrant Mother, Nipomo Valley* (fig.14–57). The worried, careworn face of the mother, the baby on her lap, and the two children who cling to their mother while turning from the camera provide a powerful statement and social documentary about the workers' desperate situation.

Lesson 14.5 Review

1 What type of photographer was Henri Cartier-Bresson?
2 Describe the contrasts in Stieglitz's *The Steerage*.
3 Where did Ansel Adams take many of his most famous photographs?

4 Describe the emotions in Dorothea Lange's *Migrant Mother, Nipomo Valley*. How did this photograph affect a change in people's lives?

1

artist	nationality	style	famous work	description
Rivera	Mexican	Expressionist	*Liberation of the Peasant*	simplified forms
Matisse	French	Fauve	*The Red Studio, Beast of the Sea*	bright, intense color simple, flat shapes collage
Rouault	French	Fauve	*The Old King*	stained glass, heavy lines, religious
Modersohn-Becker	German	Expressionist	*Old Peasant Woman Praying*	expressive use of color, simplified form
Kollwitz	German	Expressionist	*Never Again War!*	powerful emotion, working-class people
Kirchner	German	Expressionist	*The Street*	isolation, loneliness, bright colors
Nolde	German	Expressionist	*Masks*	slashing strokes, garish color, primitive cultures
Marc	German	Expressionist	*The Yellow Cow*	animals, symbolic, brilliant color
Kandinsky	Russian	Abstract, Expr.	*Open Green, Compositions*	nonobjective, spontaneous, bright color
Beckmann	German	Expressionist	*Baccarat*	nightmarish, bright, raw color, black lines
Modigliani	Italian	Expressionist	*Gypsy Woman with Baby*	elongated figures, sketchy lines, flat shapes
Orozco	Mexican	Expressionist	*Mexican Landscape*	dramatic, political slashing brushstrokes
Siqueiros	Mexican	Expressionist	*exterior of Polyform*	political murals
Kahlo	Mexican	Expressionist	*Diego y yo*	symbolic, pain, psychological
Stella	Italian-American	Abstract	*Brooklyn Bridge*	celebration of construction
Picasso	Spanish	Cubism	*Les Demoiselles d'Avignon*	fractured view, African art
Braque	French	Cubism	*Still Life on the Table*	collage, simultaneity
Duchamp	French	Cubism	*Nude Descending a Staircase*	motion, overlapping shapes
Boccioni	Italian	Futurist	*Noise of Street Penetrates House*	motion, cubism
Mondrian	Dutch	De Stijl	*Lozenge in Red, Yellow and Blue*	precise style, geometric rectangles, primary colors

Primary Source

Guernica: An Eyewitness Account

The bombings and killings at the Basque town of Guernica, Spain, by Germans at the command of the Spanish government, were recorded by newspaper reporters as well as by Pablo Picasso (fig.14–27). Noel Monks, the reporter of this passage, describes the aftermath of the bombing of Guernica:

"We'd eaten our first course of beans and were waiting for our bully beef when a government official, tears streaming down his face, burst into the dismal dining room crying, 'Guernica is destroyed. The Germans bombed and bombed and bombed.'

I was the first correspondent to reach Guernica, and was immediately pressed into service by some Basque soldiers collecting charred bodies that the flames had passed over. Some of the soldiers were sobbing like children. There were flames and smoke and grit, and the smell of burning human flesh was nauseating. Houses were collapsing into the inferno.

In the Plaza, surrounded almost by a wall of fire, were about a hundred refugees. They were wailing and weeping and rocking to and fro. One middle-aged man spoke English. He told me, 'At four, before the market closed, many aeroplanes came. They dropped bombs. Some came low and shot bullets into the streets.'"

Pablo Picasso, *Guernica*, detail (fig.14–27).

Chapter Review

Review

1 Make a chart describing the painters in this chapter. Write the artists' names in a column on the left. Across the top, make column headings for nationality, style, most famous work and a one- or two-word description of his or her art.
2 What technique did Rivera use to paint many of his murals? Name an artist from the past who also used this technique to paint murals.
3 How did Matisse emphasize the flatness of the picture plane in his *Red Studio*?
4 Describe the African influence in Picasso's *Les Demoiselles d'Avignon*. What features in this painting did Picasso develop into Cubism in later paintings?
5 List six American photographers from the early twentieth century. Describe one of these artists' photographs.

Interpret

1 Describe how Orozco's art is similar to Rivera's.
2 For what event was Picasso commissioned to paint *Guernica*? What is happening in this painting? Explain three of the symbols in *Guernica*. How large is this work?

3 Explain how Miró's style of Surrealism is different from Magritte's.
4 No one really knows what Dali's *The Persistence of Memory* means. Write a short story based on this painting.
5 Draw a typical Arp shape. Explain his technique for arranging these shapes.

Other Tools for Learning

Maps
Locate on the map the cities where Diego Rivera studied and where he worked. Do the same for Wassily Kandinsky.

Timelines
Describe how one of the events in the cultural timelines relates to a piece of art in this book.

Electronic Research
Videodisc player: *National Gallery of Art*
1 Find examples of Matisse's art. Describe one of his works such as *La Negresse*.
2 Compare Brancusi's sculptures with Giacometti's.

2 Rivera often used fresco like Michelangelo, Raphael, Giotto, Fra Angelico and Massacio.
3 He did not paint in shadows or value changes.
4 Picasso painted African masks over the faces of three of the nudes. He repeated the angular features of the masks in the figures and background. This interplay of geometric shapes led to Cubism.
5 James Van der Zee—*Future Expectations, Couple in Raccoon Coats*
Henri Cartier-Bresson—*Woman on a Stairway Talking to a Man with Cane*
Alfred Stieglitz—*The Steerage*
Edward Weston—*Pepper*
Ansel Adams—*Mt. Williamson from Manazar*
Dorothea Lange—*Migrant Mother, Nipomo Valley*

Interpret

1 Both artists painted large political murals filled with well-rounded figures, and both drew inspiration from their Mexican heritage.
2 Picasso painted *Guernica* for the Spanish government's exhibit at the Paris Exposition of 1937. Destruction of the town is shown by a flaming building and crumbling walls. The bull is a Spanish symbol of human irrationality. The screeching horse represents Spain's torment. The sun is a light bulb. The textures represent the newspapers that first reported this tragedy to the world. The broken sword symbolizes the defeat of the people. The flower growing out of the sword means that hope is still alive. *Guernica* is 11.48' x 25.46' (3.5 x 7.76 m).

Primary-Source Connection

Ask students how this eyewitness report aids their understanding of Picasso's painting. Why is it considered a primary source? (It is an immediate, direct account of the devastation that inspired the painting.)

3 Although both artists paint Surrealist dream-like compositions, Miró makes no attempt to make his abstract figures and settings realistic. Magritte's elements are distinct or realistic until the viewer begins to look more carefully at how objects are combined and placed in unbelievable settings. The total work raises more questions than answers.
5 Arp's shapes are often shaped like amoebas. He would drop bits of paper onto the floor and glue these accidental arrangements to paper.

Maps
Rivera studied in Paris and worked in Mexico City. Kandinsky studied in Munich and worked for a while in Moscow, later moving to Germany.

Timelines
Rivera and Orozco painted the political upheaval from the Mexican civil war in paintings such as Orozco's *Mexican Landscape* and Rivera's *Liberation of the Peasant*.

When King Tut's tomb was found in 1922, the burial mask of King Tut was discovered.

Electronic Research
1 *La Negresse* is a cut paper composition of brilliant flower shapes and a black dancer inspired by Josephine Baker, a popular American entertainer in Paris in the 1920s.
2 Giacometti's thin, lonely bronze figures contrast with Brancusi's usually heftier pieces which represent the essence of their subject.

Activity 1:
The Message on
the Wall

Activity Objectives
Students should be able to:

• Understand the definitions of Expressionism and Social Realism.

• Relate individual work to a whole finished piece.

• Work cooperatively.

• Expand their understanding of artistic expression in the form of murals.

Thinking Critically
Review the listed artwork with students (and any other examples you may find), and for each one ask:

• What is the topic and the mood of each image?

• What message do you think the artist is trying to convey?

• What elements of design contribute to the power of the visual image?

Preparation Ideas

• If the mural is to be displayed publicly or painted directly on a wall, be sure you secure permission from all necessary authorities, who may want to see a cartoon (sketch or painting) or participate in the topic selection from several proposals.

• Once the selection is made, prepare a timeline for completion, gather the materials, and set up a work schedule.

Notes on Materials

• Acrylic paints and house paint are the best materials to use. Quarts of intense colors of house paint can be purchased and then mixed with a light neutral or white for an extended value range.

• Have plenty of large brushes of varying widths and shapes on hand.

Classroom Management

• Ask students to list on the board possible topics for a mural. Ideas can spring from a number of sources, such as school and community history or events, scenes from great literature, or images of people in need of help today, such as victims of natural disasters, war or oppression.

Activity 1

The Message on
the Wall

Materials
paper or cloth
acrylic paint
house paint
paintbrushes of various sizes

Take a look.
• Fig.3–21, Diego Rivera, *Flower Day*, 1925.
• Fig.14–1, Diego Rivera, *Liberation of the Peon*, 1931.
• Fig.14–19, José Clemente Orozco, *Mexican Landscape*, 1930.
• Fig.14–20, David Alfaro Siqueiros. Exterior, *Polyforum Cultural Siqueiros*, 1974.

Think about it. Social Realism is often closely allied with the labor movements and revolutions of the twentieth century. This art is often involved in controversy because of its emphasis on content and political beliefs. Diego Rivera's idealization of Lenin in the mural he was painting for Rockefeller Center in New York City so upset owner, John D. Rockefeller, that he locked Rivera out of the building and had the mural destroyed.

Do it. Create a mural which portrays some aspect of student life in this or another culture. Emphasize the way that society sees students as well as your own feelings. Are teenagers eager young contributors? Avid scholars? Dangerous revolutionaries? Economic burdens?
• Work with classmates to sketch out ideas on paper until the group agrees on the topic and general presentation. Do a "final" line drawing sketch.
• Enlarge the cartoon to full size. The mural can be painted on paper, cloth or directly on the wall. If working on a wall, grid both the wall and the cartoon. Block in the large shapes within each grid box on the wall.

• Paint the large shapes, paying careful attention to color and values.
• Add the details.
• Finish the mural with a varnish to protect it.

Check it. Throughout the project, check that your scene, your choice of colors and your design works with those of your classmates.

Helpful Hint: Murals are meant to be read by the casual observer. Use characteristic poses, clothing, settings and colors to make your message clear to your viewer.

Activity 2

Exploring Surrealism

Materials
magazines
scissors
11" x 14" white paper
pencils
colored pencils
markers

Take a look.
• Fig.14–40, Salvador Dali, *The Persistence of Memory*, 1931. Oil on canvas.
• Fig.14–50, René Magritte, *Time Transfixed*, 1939. Oil on canvas.

Think about it. Surrealism is often the result of juxtaposing realistic portrayals of unrelated objects or objects in an imaginary or out-of-context environment. Surrealist artists stretched for associations between things that ordinarily have no relationship to each other.

Do it. Try making such visual associations yourself as follows.
• From magazines and other sources, clip various types of images (objects, people, plants, landscape).
• Put these images into a box and select five random choices.
• Draw these images in an environment that makes the relationships between them puzzling to the viewer.

Check it. Are your images realistically drawn? What unlikely elements or relationships make your composition surreal?

Helpful Hint: Surrealist writers and artists played a game called "Exquisite Corpse." Try this warmup exercise of juxtaposing random objects and concepts. Fold or cover a sheet of paper so participants cannot see each other's work. The first person draws a head, the second a torso, the third legs and feet. People, animals and imaginary creatures are all fair game.

Additional Activities

• "Facet Cubism" used flat geometric planes, much like the facets of a cut gem. Make a drawing of an apple or pear, using only triangles of various sizes and shapes to indicate the changes in light and form. You could do this as a line drawing, tempera painting or collage of different values of the same color.

• Study and analyze *Guernica* by Picasso and *Third of May, 1808* by Goya (fig.12–14). Both are powerful social statements, resulting from events that occurred during the artists' lives. Compare and contrast the content, style, use of color, purpose, size, visual impact, symbolism and your personal reaction to each work.

• Ask students to express why they prefer one topic over another. Identify which topic holds the strongest meaning for students. If students agree on the topic but have opposing ideas, divide the students into groups and let each discover ways to portray their view.

• Allow a planning stage for the submission of sketches to be included in the mural. Pin individual sketches to a bulletin board and help students discover how to work them together into a unified image. Or, work in reverse, with students sketching to fit a preorganized structure, perhaps in panels or according to the progression of images or events in a topic.

• Next have students sketch the image to size onto paper or cloth (to be hung on the wall) or directly onto the wall to

be painted. Work out a plan with students for the painting of the mural (top to bottom? left to right? dark colors first?). Problem-solve in advance; assign tasks; and set firm timelines.

Evaluation
Each student is responsible for some portion of the mural and receives a grade for it, along with a group grade for combined work.

Activity 2:
Exploring Surrealism

Activity Objectives
Students should be able to:

• Explain what makes an artwork surrealistic.

Student Profile

Andrew Lee

Age 15
West Potomac High School
Alexandria, Virginia
Favorite artists: Stephen Platt,
Julie Bell, Tsukasa Hojo
Activity 2, Exploring Surrealism

Out of all my art projects, this one about
Surrealism is one of the bigger projects that I've
dealt with. It means a great deal to me because
I had enough time to put an ample amount of
energy into my work. It also allowed me to express
my feelings that I wouldn't be able to represent or
state in another assignment.

The thought process was fairly critical. After I
had chosen my pictures, I had a tough time placing
them on the illustration board. The positioning of
the elements can become an important factor to
the outcome. That was something I learned from
the work of Magritte.

Some advice I would like to give to other students who enjoy creating art is not only to do your
best, also to carry out the extreme of your idea or
theme. Then people can feel what you were trying
to say and your work can be outstanding.

Freedom of Flight, 1994. Colored pencil,
15" x 20" (38 x 50.8 cm).

Anita Tam

Age 16
West Potomac High School
Alexandria, Virginia
Favorite artists: Lafarge, Copley
Activity 2, Exploring Surrealism

*Another student working on the
same assignment came up with a playful solution:*
My art project is of sentimental value to me
because it portrays two of my favorite things at
once (cats and flowers) and it is the product of
much time, effort and creativity. When I was
developing my project, I wanted to combine color
with a contrasting background and make my subject matter stand out. The thing I enjoy most about
the artistic process is the reward of seeing my
work come to life after spending a significant
amount of time enhancing all the little details.

Curiosity, 1994. Colored pencil,
15" x 20" (38 x 50.8 cm).

Teacher Spotlight
Melanie Mobley
Art Teacher
West Potomac High School

Surrealism is a very appealing subject
for high school art students. It
employs both the recognizable and
the dream-like qualities that interest
them. I have found this particular
lesson to be very effective when
used in the early part of the school
year.

There is an excellent success rate
among my students with this project, which leads the way for them to
feel comfortable in trying new techniques presented to them later in
class. They also appreciate the individualism that this activity fosters.
The Surrealism project is a natural
for group discussion and critique
since it requires the artists to explain
what they were trying to visualize.
This further serves as an opportunity
for new students to become part of
the group and to have their particular skills and interests understood by
the rest of the class.

Allowing students the choice in
using their own drawings, photographs or a combination of the two
further enhances the students' confidence. Students who feel more
comfortable rendering from a visual
reference will work as enthusiasti-
cally as those who prefer working
strictly from imagination.

• Produce a work that incorporates
surrealistic elements.

Thinking Critically
Have students review the work by Dali
and Magritte, and ask them:

• What makes this work surrealistic?
How does the artist create a magical,
mystical or dreamlike feeling?

• What visual elements does the artist
use to make unrelated images work
together in this painting?

Preparation Ideas

• Find slides, art books or other
resources with surrealistic images. Have
students research and bring in examples
of the work of different surrealistic
artists, such as Ernst, Arp, de Chirico,

Klee and Picasso, in addition to Dali
and Magritte.

Notes on Materials

• Collect (or have students collect)
images and sort them into categories
such as animals, inanimate objects,
tools, land/nature, people, clothing, food,
vehicles, sports, etc. Put each collection
of images into a separate box for random
selection of subject matter.

• If you wish to get away from magazine images, collect (or have students
collect) a variety of three-dimensional
objects. Use them to set up a miniature
environment as a launching pad for
sketches, from which students could
draw selected objects and make up the
setting for them.

Tips

• To generate mood, ask students to
close their eyes and recall a dream
they've had. Ask them to picture what
they saw or experienced, especially
peculiar images or events that didn't
make sense. Invite them to recreate the
dream image or invent a new one as if
they were dreaming.

Evaluation

• Does the student's work demonstrate an understanding of the concept
of Surrealism?

• Does the student effectively use
unrelated images to create a visually
fresh or surprising artwork?

• Does the work show skillful use of
color and strong composition?

Chapter 15 Organizer

Chapter 15 Opener: American Art 1900–1950

Objectives

Discover how art from the first part of the twentieth century embodied the enormous energy and life that permeated America.

Articulate the divergent but simultaneous explorations of Abstraction and Realism in the United States, despite the lack of strong public support.

National Standards

4b Students describe the function and explore the meaning of specific art objects within varied cultures, times and places.

4d Students analyze and interpret artworks for relationships among form, context, purposes, and critical models, showing understanding of the work of critics, historians, aestheticians, and artists.

Teacher Edition References

Lesson 15.1 The Early Years

Special Feature: George Bellows 494–495	HOTS 495	
Remainder of Lesson 15.1 496–501 World Cultural Timeline 498 Lesson 15.1 Review 501	Contextual Info 496, 498, 500 HOTS 497, 499, 501	Coooperative 500 Interdisciplinary 496

Lesson 15.2 The Influence of Abstraction

Special Feature: Georgia O'Keeffe 502–503	Contextual Info 503	HOTS 503
Remainder of Lesson 15.2 503–507 World Cultural Timeline 505 Lesson 15.2 Review 507	Contextual Info 504, 506 HOTS 505, 507	Performing Arts 505, 507

Lesson 15.3 The American Scene

Special Feature: Thomas Hart Benton 508–509	Contextual Info 509	HOTS 509
Remainder of Lesson 15.3 510–513 World Cultural Timeline 510 Lesson 15.3 Review 513	Contextual Info 510, 512 HOTS 511, 513 Inquiry 512 Multicultural 511	Performing Arts 510

Lesson 15.4 Social Realism

Special Feature: Jacob Lawrence 514–515	Contextual Info 515 HOTS 515	Collaborative 515 Interdisciplinary 515
Remainder of Lesson World Cultural Timeline 518 Lesson 15.4 Review 518 Primary-Source 519 Chapter Review 519	Contextual Info 516 HOTS 517, 518	Performing Arts 517

Classroom Connections

National Standards

Studio Activity 1
Depicting City Life

1a Students apply media, techniques, and processes with sufficient skill, confidence, and sensitivity that their intentions are carried out in their artworks.
1b Students conceive and create works of visual art that demonstrate an understanding of how the communication of their ideas relates to the media, techniques, and processes they use.

Studio Activity 2
Balancing Act

1a Students apply media, techniques, and processes with sufficient skill, confidence, and sensitivity that their intentions are carried out in their artworks.
1b Students conceive and create works of visual art that demonstrate an understanding of how the communication of their ideas relates to the media, techniques, and processes they use.

Choose either Activity 1 or 2
Choose either Activity 1 or 2
Choose either Activity 1 or 2

Ancillaries

Slides: Davis, *Lucky Strike*, 106b, 213
Hopper, *Nighthawks*, 106a, 211

Teacher Edition References

Timeline: American Art
1900–1950 492
Map: American Art 1900–1950 492
Context 492
Art 493
Quote 493

Ancillaries

Slides: Bellows, *Cliff Dwellers*, 101a, 203

Slides: Bannister, *Newspaper Boy*, 102a, 204;
Audubon, *Bay-Winged Bunting, Male*, 103b, 205;
Henri, *Blind Singer*, 104b, 206

Overhead Transparencies: Two Artists, Two Media, One Subject, 20
Large Reproductions: O'Keeffe, *Cow's Skull with Calico Roses*, 25

Slides: Sheeler, *American Landscape*, 105b, 207;
Gorky, *The Liver is the Cock's Comb*, 103a, 208;
Davis, *Lucky Strike*, 106b, 213

Slides: Wood, *American Gothic*, 104a, 209;
Kuhn, *The Blue Clown*, 105a, 210;
Hopper, *Nighthawks*, 106a, 211;
Bierstadt, *The Last of the Buffalos*, 107a, 212
Large Reproductions: Remington, *A Dash for the Timber*, 26

Slides: Lawrence, *Subway Acrobats*, 107b, 214
Overhead Transparencies: Two Views of America, 16

Slides: Shahn, *Miner's Wives*, 108b, 215;
Tooker, *Waiting Room*, 109b, 216

Schedule

One day to sketch. Two days to paint.
Students could make sketches and
photographs prior to class.

Materials

11" x 14" white paper (or larger),
tempera or acrylic paints, brushes,
surface for mixing paint,
containers of water

Introduce assignment before the
studio so students may bring
in objects.

wooden sticks, wire (assorted gauges),
fishing line or string, poster, bristol
and railroad board (assorted colors),
heavy-weight white paper, scissors,
mat knife, pencils, markers, straight
edge, glue, templates (optional),
colored pencils, watercolors (optional)

Other Resources

Books

Baigell, Matthew. *Dictionary of American Art*. New York: HarperCollins, 1980.

Benton, Thomas Hart. *An Artist in America*. 4th ed. University of Missouri Press, 1983.

Berry, Michael. *Georgia O'Keeffe*. New York: Chelsea House Publishers, 1988.

Brown, Milton W. *American Painting From the Armory Show to the Depression*. Princeton: Princeton University Press, 1970.

————. *American Art: Painting, Sculpture, Architecture, Decorative Arts, Photography*. Englewood Cliffs: Prentice Hall, 1979.

Cederholm, Theresa Dickason. *Afro-American Artists: A Bio-Bibliographical Directory*. Boston: Trustees of the Boston Public Library, 1973.

Diamonstein, Barbaralee, ed. *The Art World*. NY: Artnews Books, 1977.

Doezema, Marianne. *American Realism and the Industrial Age*. Part of *Theme in Art*. Cleveland: Cleveland Museum of Art, 1981.

Driskell, David C., et al. *Harlem Renaissance: Art of Black America*. New York: Harry N. Abrams Inc., 1987.

George Bellows: Portrait of an American Artist. Smithsonian Institution Press, 1982.

Hayes, Margaret Calder. *Three Alexander Calders*. NY: Universe Publishing, 1987.

Hunter, Sam, and Jacobus, John. *American Art of the 20th Century: Painting, Sculpture and Architecture*. Rev. ed. New York: Harry N. Abrams Inc., 1974.

McCoubrey, John W., ed. *American Art 1700–1960*. Part of *Sources and Documents in the History of Art*. Englewood Cliffs: Prentice Hall, 1965.

Opitz, Glenn B., and Collins, Jim, Rev. ed. Women *Artists in America: 18th Century to the Present (1790–1980)*. Poughkeepsie: Apollo Book, 1980.

Rose, Barbara, ed. *American Art Since 1900: A Documentary Survey*. New York: Praeger Publishers, 1968.

Rubenstein, Charlotte Streifer. *American Women Artists*. Boston: G. K. Hall, 1982.

Wilmerding, John. *American Art*. Pelican History of Art Series. Baltimore: Penguin USA, 1976.

Wheat, Ellen Harkins. *Jacob Lawrence, American Painter*. Seattle: University of Washington Press, 1990.

Videos

Jacob Lawrence: The Glory of Expression, Crystal

Isabel Bishop, Crystal

Georgia O'Keeffe, Crystal

Frederick Remington: The Truth of Other Days, Crystal

African American Art Past and Present, NASCO

Introduce

America was a hotbed of artistic activity in the first half of the twentieth century. A small group of dedicated artists forged a distinctive American Abstract style despite the public's lack of interest. Realists fared little better with the masses, who preferred a more decorative tradition to these artists' often harsh depictions of daily living.

Lessons at a Glance

15.1 *The Early Years*
American artists in the first half of the twentieth century reflected the staggering array of changes that infiltrated everyday life. Their paintings, which depicted both realistic and idealized visions of urban and country existence, continued an artistic tradition that had originated in the late nineteenth century.

15.2 *The Influence of Abstraction*
Although Abstract artists in America received little public acclaim, they forged a strong avant-garde style founded on European traditions.

15.3 *The American Scene*
Although the American art establishment swung toward Abstraction after the Armory Show of 1913, certain artists continued to work in a Realist vein. They strove to depict American scenes in a unique style that shunned European precedents.

15.4 *Social Realism*
American Social Realist art reflected the effects of the Great Depression of the 1930s and the imminent threat of outside totalitarian, socialist and communist governments. The Social Realists rejected the Abstract art then fashionable, as well as the Regionalists' portrayal of life far from the troubles of urban centers. Instead, in order to try to bring about social reform on a governmental level, the Social Realists described the hardships of ordinary citizens.

15 American Art 1900–1950

15–a The life of the city and the pulse of jazz vibrate through Davis' paintings. He used letters and words for their design quality and not their meanings.
Stuart Davis, *Something on the Eight Ball*, 1954. Oil on canvas, 56" x 44 4/5" (142 x 114 cm). Philadelphia Museum of Art. Purchased: Adele Haas Turner and Beatrice Pastorius Turner Memorial Fund. ©1996 Stuart Davis/Licensed by VAGA, New York, NY

AMERICA CHARGED INTO the first half of this century with a dynamic force, full of ideas and discoveries. It was a period of emerging brilliance for the young country. At the same time, the country experienced the Great Depression, two world wars and the harsh conditions of urbanization. The American art of this period reflects the highs and lows of these opposing forces, as well as influences from European Abstract and Expressionistic art.

American artists of the late 1800s also influenced the artists at the turn of the century. Some of the most important new artists were Realists who were part of the Ash Can School. Instead of painting romantic landscapes or portraits, these artists painted slums and other shocking scenes of everyday life.

At the same time, Abstract art from Europe captured the imagination of the American art world. It eventually received the support of the galleries and museums and went on to become the most important art movement after 1950.

The American public, on the other hand, desired a more decorative style of art. They had a difficult time supporting the artists of this period, except for the American Scene painters whose art attempted to capture the vastness, beauty and positive character of the country.

Although Abstraction would become the dominant force in the art of this period, many American artists continued to paint realistically. A group which formed after the Great Depression, called the Social Realists, depicted the dehumanizing aspects of urbanization, industrialization and the injustices of large bureaucratic institutions.

1903
Wright Brothers successfully fly a powered airplane

1912
The *Titanic* sinks

1920
Women's suffrage enacted in the United States

1928
Demuth, *I Saw the Figure Five in Gold*
1928
Mickey Mouse films

1935
Radar equipment in use
1936
Lange, *Migrant Mother*

1937
Disney's first full-length animation (*Snow White*)
1942
Hopper, *Nighthawks*

American Art 1900–1950

1908
Bellows (26) is youngest member elected to National Academy of Design

1913
The Armory Show changes American art, New York
1920
Babe Ruth sold to the Yankees for $125,000

1929
Stock Market crash
1932
Huxley, *Brave New World*

1945
The US drops atomic bombs on Hiroshima and Nagasaki

Objectives

Students should be able to:

Discover how art from the first part of the twentieth century embodied the enormous energy and life that permeated America.

Articulate the divergent but simultaneous explorations of Abstraction and Realism in the United States, despite the lack of strong public support.

Teach

Timeline

The years 1900–1950 brought tremendous changes in American technology and culture. Ask students to look at the images in the chapter opener and speculate about how the works might have been affected by the events listed on the timeline. Ask what other historical events or technological inventions of this period might have had an impact on American art.

Context

Direct students to find a similarity between the subject matter in Hopper's *Nighthawks* (figs.15–b, 15–25) and George Bellows' *Cliff Dwellers* (fig.15–1).

• How might the characters in these paintings feel?

• Do their lives appear filled with joy and serenity, or stress and depression?

• Since both Bellows and Hopper were interested in conveying experiences of ordinary citizens, what deductions can students make about life for many urban people in the first part of the

> In general it can be said
> that a nation's art is greatest
> when it most reflects the
> character of its people.
>
> Edward Hopper

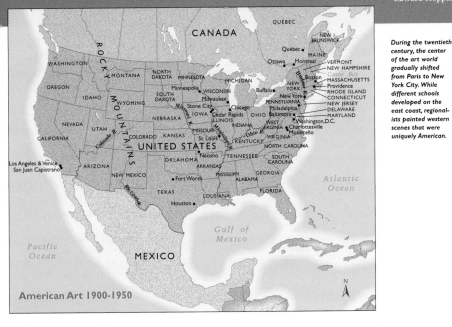

During the twentieth century, the center of the art world gradually shifted from Paris to New York City. While different schools developed on the east coast, regionalists painted western scenes that were uniquely American.

American Art 1900–1950

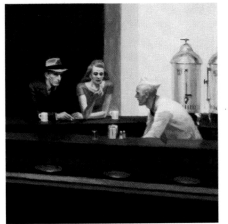

15–b Despite the growing influence of Abstract art, many American artists continued to favor Realism.
Edward Hopper, *Nighthawks*, detail (fig.15–25).

15–c Many of Calder's works in wire are three-dimensional drawings which convey tremendous personality.
Alexander Calder, *Sow*, 1928. Wire construction, 17" (43 cm) long. The Museum of Modern Art, New York, gift of the artist.

Quote

Direct students to glance at figs.15–c and 15–25 without looking at the names of the artists. Afterward, ask them to read the quote and decide which of the paintings was created by Edward Hopper, based on the sentiments of his statement. What kind of "character" or personality did Hopper present for America in *Nighthawks*? Would students choose these sorts of people and activities to symbolize the nation's character today? How might an increasing sensitivity to multicultural issues in recent decades affect their subjects and styles?

Map

Direct students to think about the size and variety of the land of North America. How could its expansiveness have affected the diversity of art styles that flourished here after the turn of the century? Which part of the United States was most likely to have been influenced by European art?

the first half of the twentieth century. Is there only a single trend in culture today? How does art, fashion, food and music reflect multiple, simultaneous interests?

• Ask students how American artists working in Abstraction and those exploring Realism might have felt toward Classical Greek and Roman art (as seen in the Chapter 6 opener and in lessons 6.2 and 6.3). What about their work supports students' conjectures?

• Have students discuss how something can be learned from the past, even if we do not emulate or necessarily approve of it. For instance, what important lessons can be learned from African-American slavery or the Holocaust?

Reteach

Ask students how Davis, who was an avid lover of jazz, might have reacted to music videos if he were alive today. What about his painting *Something on the Eight Ball* supports their answers?

twentieth century? Is the situation dramatically changed today?

• Share with students that many Realist artists delved into the mundane occurrences of human existence to reveal the depleting aspects of modern life.

Art

Tell the class that although Stuart Davis' *Something on the Eight Ball* (fig.15–a) is largely abstract, each ele-ment derives from the observable world.

• What evidence of America's modern environment can they detect in the painting?

• Where would Davis have seen large writing in public?

• How has he evoked billboards and flashing electric signs?

• Although it is difficult to make out the specific words and their meaning, Davis uses individual letters as dynamic elements in his composition; they push against and mingle with one another as though vying for space in a crowded city street.

How does Davis use color to evoke the energy of the American urban culture? Are his hues soothing? Their bold juxtaposition parallels the rhythms and syncopation of modern urban jazz music, which Davis listened to while painting.

Evaluate

• Ask students if a single style dominated the American art scene during

Lesson 15.1

American artists in the first half of the twentieth century reflected the staggering array of changes that infiltrated everyday life. Their paintings, which depicted both realistic and idealized visions of urban and country existence, continued an artistic tradition that had originated in the late nineteenth century.

Warm-up

Challenge students to imagine living in a period wracked with monumental and relentless change. What might be the effects of rapidly developing technology (which could be used for good or for destruction), two world wars, and a staggering economic depression on art? Would they as artists be interested in continuing to paint portraits of wealthy individuals or paintings that glorified their nation's past? What subjects might they want to turn to instead? Afterward, share that Lesson 15.1 considers some of the concerns that American artists began to explore in their abruptly changing culture.

Objectives

Students should be able to:

Understand how American Realists built on the tradition of nineteenth-century art.

Discuss how modern American artists responded to the enormous political, scientific and economic changes occurring in the United States.

Learn that Realist painters frequently depicted disturbing realities of urban life.

15.1 The Early Years

AMERICA UNDERWENT TREMENDOUS CHANGE in the first half of the twentieth century. Scientific discoveries would change everyone's lifestyle, two world wars would be fought, and a depression would stagger the country. American artists were bound to reflect these changes.

Several artists were concluding their life's work as the twentieth century dawned, and they formed the springboard for the new era in painting. John Singer Sargent was a master portrait painter and watercolorist. George Inness created gentle landscapes in contrast to Albert Bierstadt, who painted dramatic pictures of the Rockies.

Several African-American artists created works that equaled or surpassed their better-known contemporaries. Among these artists were Henry Tanner (who studied under Thomas Eakins), Edward Mitchell Bannister and the sculptor Edmonia Lewis.

And, then, there were the Expressionist painters who tried to communicate their feelings about American life. Their realistic paintings of crowded city streets and ragged people created disturbing social statements. Critics derisively dubbed this style "The Ashcan School."

Key Notes

- The foundation laid by artists in the late nineteenth century provides a basis for American art of the new century.
- Young American artists keep pace with the great changes taking place in the first part of the twentieth century.
- An expressive Realism is used to describe America's growing urban centers and their inhabitants.

Special Feature

George Bellows

(1882–1925)

At the age of twenty-six, George Bellows became the youngest member ever elected to the National Academy of Design. He was a prize student of Robert Henri, the leader of the Ashcan School. Bellows was an exceptional athlete who loved to draw. His interest in sports led him to paint several boxing scenes of bouts in New York's private clubs. But, he also loved to paint the unbelievable clutter and congestion of New York's East Side slums where thousands of immigrants shouted in languages he could not understand. He painted scenes of naked boys swimming in the East River, dock workers, smoky saloons and huge horses.

15–2 The lines of the bodies create the impact that dominates this composition.
George Bellows, *Stag at Sharkey's*. Oil on canvas, 36″ x 48″ (91 x 122 cm). The Cleveland Museum of Art, Hinman B. Hurlbut Collection.

Teach

Aesthetics/Art History: Have students discuss what images come to mind for a painting entitled *Cliff Dwellers*. Who or what might the inhabitants be and in what type of environment would they live? Afterward, direct students to examine George Bellows' work of that title (fig.15–1).

- What do students think Bellows was implying with his title about the plight of the urban underclass?

- What new title can they come up with that would also convey the sense of crowded desperation?

- Ask students to read about the painting on page 495 and then, based on their examination of the painting, decide if they like it. Does Bellows successfully communicate his message? Are they moved by his theme? Do they enjoy his style and composition even if they may not care for the subject matter?

Art History: Ask students to find the common theme in George Bellows' *Cliff Dwellers*, Edward Mitchell Bannister's *Newspaper Boy* (fig.15–6) and Henry O. Tanner's *The Banjo Lesson* (fig.15–9).

- What social and economic circumstances do the people in these paintings share?

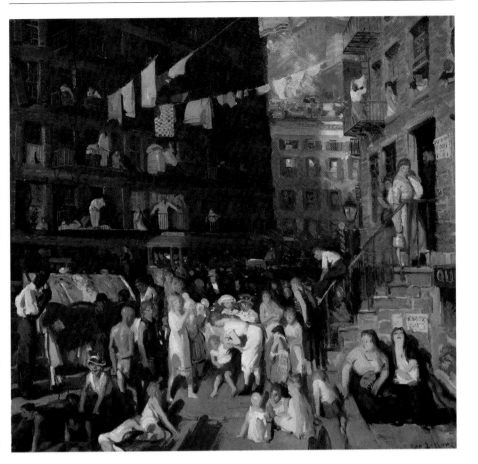

Cliff Dwellers (fig.15–1) is a clever title for a painting of the tenement dwellers of New York City. Bellows took the mass confusion of elements and organized a simple composition of darks and lights, eliminating much of the detail of the actual scene. The stark highlighting throws the some figures and parts of buildings into sharp relief. The activity in the painting is intense and varied yet is handled with care and compassion. Bellows felt keenly the confusion and needs of these people.

Bellows' best-known work is *Stag at Sharkey's* (fig.15–2). The painting is enormously powerful. A fight is in progress at one of the boxing clubs of which Bellows was so fond. The men are caught in action. Some areas of the canvas, like the foremost fighter's right glove, seem unfinished. This accentuates the implied motion of the moment captured by Bellows. As with the *Cliff Dwellers*, the artist makes use of sharp light and dark contrasts. The motion and force of the scene is balanced by the stable triangular formation of the three figures that

15–1 How has Bellows organized this chaotic scene to make it successful as a work of art?
George Bellows, *Cliff Dwellers*, 1913. Oil on canvas, 39 1/3" x 41 1/3" (100 x 105 cm). Los Angeles County Museum of Art, Los Angeles County Funds.

Bellows has created to anchor the composition. The painting is so "real" we feel as if we are one of the dark spectators. This is a shocking and startlingly raw painting in the Realist tradition.

Because Bellows never went abroad, he was not touched by the art movements flourishing in Europe. Bellows is regarded by many as the quintessential American artist.

• Why do students think many of these sorts of paintings were not immediately well received by critics of the day?

• What type of art do students think people preferred to hang in their homes?

• Does this art seem disturbing to them today? Why or why not? Why might we have become immune to images of hardship? For instance, how might the number of tragedies today and the way in which they are reported decrease our sensitivity to painful visual images?

Evaluate

How is Bellows' view of America different from that of Eakins and Homer? Ask students to explain how contemporary events can influence the art of the age.

Reteach

Provide students with copies of immigration charts for the first few decades of the twentieth century.

• Ask how many people arrived in the United States each year.

• Did most immigrants settle in the country or in major urban centers?

• In *Cliff Dwellers*, what kind of life does Bellows describe for many of these people?

• Next, provide students with more recent immigration charts. If they were composing a painting, how could they reflect the environments in which these more recent immigrants live? What visual elements could they include in their compositions to indicate the countries from which recent arrivals have come?

Higher-Order Thinking Skills

Ask students to imagine that they are part of the crowd in *Stag at Sharkey's* (fig.15–2). Have them describe what they see and hear.

Contextual Information

Sargent

Renowned for his great portraits, Sargent decided in 1907 that he was tired of his profession. Having produced nearly four hundred portraits, he did not abandon painting completely but spent the last twenty-five years of his life focusing on landscape and genre subjects.

Bierstadt

Bierstadt attained national recognition in the 1860s as a painter of large-scale landscapes, and his works were sought avidly by wealthy collectors. At the peak of his career, about 1870, Bierstadt was acclaimed internationally. His works commanded the highest prices ever paid for American paintings. However, in the late 1880s he fell into disfavor. For an exhibition of American painting at the Paris Exposition, a jury of New York City artists rejected *The Last of the Buffalo* (p.512).

John Singer Sargent

(1856–1925)

Another famous American artist, John Singer Sargent, was painting during the life and times of George Bellows. However, John Singer Sargent had begun painting much earlier than Bellows and his work followed a different tradition. Sargent was born in Europe of American parents and worked both in this country and Europe. He was a master portrait painter.

Although many of his portraits were more formally arranged, his *Daughters of Edward D. Boit* (fig.15–3) is a masterful portrait painting of the four girls. Sargent painted the daughters of his artist friend with the fluid brushstrokes that characterize his portraits. Sargent was influenced by Velazquez in technique, color and the casual arrangement of his figures. Notice the large blue and white Japanese vases and the magnificent use of shadow and light that Sargent always handled with great ease. His flashy style and elegant portraits earned him many wealthy clients on two continents.

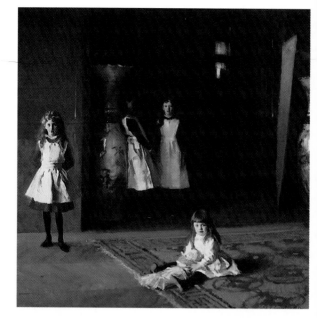

15–3 Sargent was influenced by Velazquez. Compare this portrait to Velazquez' *Las Meninas*.

John Singer Sargent, *Daughters of Edward D. Boit*, 1882. Oil on canvas, 87" x 87" (221 x 221 cm). Museum of Fine Arts, Boston, gift of the daughters of Edward D. Boit in memory of their father.

15–5 The popularity of Bierstadt's paintings helped make the Rocky Mountains a prime tourist destination.

Albert Bierstadt, *The Rocky Mountains*, Lander's Peak, 1863. Oil on canvas, 73 1/4" x 120 4/5" (186 x 307 cm). The Metropolitan Museum of Art, New York, Rogers Fund, 1907.

Interdisciplinary Connection

Social Science: Students may want to investigate the means of transportation used by Bierstadt and others to make their way to the panoramic scenes of the American West. Diaries and other first hand accounts will yield interesting details.

15–4 **Notice how the artist is more concerned with the general effect of the landscape rather than the specific details.**
George Inness, *The Home of the Heron*, 1893. Oil on canvas, 30" x 45 7/16" (76 x 115 cm). The Art Institute of Chicago, Edward B. Butler Collection, 1911.

George Inness

(1825–1894)

George Inness admired the work of the Hudson River School painters when he was only a boy. Inness also went to Europe to study and was influenced by the landscapes of Corot, Courbet, Constable and Turner. His gentle landscapes reflect his quiet personality. Inness' landscapes were faithful to nature. The general effect of a place was always more important to him than the specific details. *The Home of the Heron* (fig.15–4) is typical of the gentle moods he created. The muted colors and values of all are massed together to produce a definite feeling of place and time, without the need for specific details.

Albert Bierstadt

(1830–1902)

Albert Bierstadt was born and trained in Europe, and his paintings often reflected his interest in the Alps and other European locales. His landscapes of the American Rockies were so dramatic that they seemed to have been staged especially for his dramatic lighting. Bierstadt accompanied surveying expeditions to the Rocky Mountains and made numerous sketches and photographs. His large paintings, like *The Rocky Mountains, Lander's Peak* (fig.15–5), were composed from such sketches and painted in his New York studio. He romanticized the West to look the way easterners wanted it to look. His mountains were higher and more craggy, the gorges deeper, the reflections sharper, the waterfalls higher and the dramatic light sharper and clearer. Many critics claimed that he made the West look like the Swiss Alps with buffalo and Indians. He adds crowds of Indians and horses to the vast panorama and even shows his camera at the lower left. Such scenes soon drew people from the canyons of New York City to the new and glorious canyons of western America.

Thinking Like an Art Historian

Art historians tackle the problems of studying art in numerous and quite varied ways. The information, analysis or insights they offer contribute to a more complete picture of a work of art and the artist.

For instance, there are many ways in which an art historian might study a work of art such as Sargent's *Daughters of Edward D. Boit* (fig.15–3). A scholar interested in portraiture might study the history of portraiture from the Renaissance through the late twentieth century. In that case Sargent's work might be chosen to represent portraiture at the end of the nineteenth century. Another scholar might focus on just nineteenth century portraits. Yet another may only be concerned with Sargent's portraits and would study the *Daughters of Edward D. Boit* to better understand its place in Sargent's entire body of portrait work.

An art historian with different interests could research and analyze the depiction of children in art. Another might look at Sargent's work as part of a study on the history of oil painting. Or the research might be narrower in scope and study only Sargent's use of oil. A Velasquez expert might be interested in the influence of that artist on later generations, as Sargent's painting is an excellent example of this influence. The goal of all these approaches is to better understand works of art and their creators.

Higher-Order Thinking Skills

Have the class reconstruct the family and life of the daughters of Edward D. Boit (fig.15–3). Ask what they do every day. What is their routine? Do they go to school? Have students write a description of one day in the Boit daughters' life in 1882.

Contextual Information

African-American Artists

Americans in the late nineteenth and early twentieth centuries seldom purchased art by African-American artists. At that time, people wealthy enough to buy art purchased European old masters of known quality and value.

Nineteenth-century African-American art students found only a few college or art academy programs available to them. When they completed their schooling, they found Europe a more welcoming place than America had been. Tanner and Lewis spent their adult lives in Europe.

Bannister

Born in New Brunswick, Canada, Edward Mitchell Bannister began drawing as a child. In one of his first jobs, he learned photography. Bannister enrolled in art classes at the Lowell Institute and studied sculpture, but he was largely self-taught. By the 1870s, his work showed the influence of William Morris Hunt, one of the most important American painters in the Barbizon school. Both of their works were shown at various Boston exhibitions.

In 1871, Bannister moved to Rhode Island and became friends with the art community there. He later became a founder of the Providence Art Club, which formed the nucleus of what would become the Rhode Island School of Design.

Tanner

Henry O. Tanner studied at the Pennsylvania Academy with Thomas Eakins, who encouraged him to go to Paris. After he graduated, Tanner tried to sell his paintings, but in spite of his obvious talent, few people purchased his paintings. With the financial assistance of his parents and friends, he left in 1891 to study in Paris. Although Tanner lived in Paris the rest of his life, he was elected an associate member of the National Academy of Design in New York in 1909.

Edward Mitchell Bannister

(1828–1901)

The African-American painter Edward Mitchell Bannister was born in New Brunswick and later moved to Providence, Rhode Island. One of the founders of the Providence Art Club, his landscapes and seascapes were widely exhibited in his lifetime. Bannister also painted genre scenes. *Newspaper Boy* (fig.15–6) has a refreshing immediacy that causes the viewer to wonder about the life of the thoughtful young boy who sold newspapers more than 100 years ago.

Edmonia Lewis

(ca. 1844–1909)

Born in Ohio of a Chippewa mother and an African-American father, Edmonia Lewis was the first African American, male or female, to receive international recognition as a sculptor. In addition to portrait busts, she sculpted studies of ethnic women. Lewis once commented: "I have a strong sympathy for all women who have struggled and suffered." She was referring specifically to her marble sculpture, *Hagar* (fig.15–7). The quiet strength of the figure reinforces Lewis' statement. Hagar is an Old Testament figure who was banished with her son, Ishmael, to the desert.

15–6 Notice how the figure has been brought to the very front and to the edges of the picture plane.
Edward Mitchell Bannister, *Newspaper Boy*, 1869. Oil on canvas, 30" x 25" (76 x 63 cm). National Museum of American Art, gift of Mr. and Mrs. Norman B. Robbins.

15–7 Lewis was orphaned during her teens. She attended Oberlin College, perhaps on an Abolitionist scholarship.
Edmonia Lewis, *Hagar*, 1875. Marble, 52 5/8" x 15 1/4" x 17" (134 x 39 x 43 cm). National Museum of American Art, gift of Delta Sigma Theta Sorority, Inc., 1983.95.178.

World Cultural Timeline

1907	1911	1921
New Zealand becomes self-governing	Sun Yat-sen overthrows ruling Manchu dynasty	Chinese Communist Party forms in Mongolia
	1911	1921
	China unifies under democratic government	Japan's first census counts 77 million people

15–8 When Tanner initially decided to study art, he found it difficult to obtain art lessons because he was African-American. Finally, he did enroll in the Pennsylvania Academy of Fine Arts where he studied under Thomas Eakins.
Henry O. Tanner, *Angels Appearing Before the Shepherds*, about 1910. Oil on canvas. National Museum of American Art, gift of Mr. and Mrs. Norman B. Robbins.

Henry O. Tanner

(1859–1937)

The son of a distinguished minister, Henry Tanner often emphasized Bible stories in his paintings. At the Pennsylvania Academy of the Fine Arts in Philadelphia, he studied under Thomas Eakins, who became a strong influence on his work. Tanner went to Europe to study and work, and spent many years painting in Paris. In 1895, Tanner won an honorable mention for one of his paintings of a religious subject. His was the only American work to be so honored. Tanner continued to paint religious subjects with great frequency. Many of these works were given a very personal interpretation as in *Angels Appearing Before the Shepherds* (fig.15–8). The artist's vision of a host of angels appearing to shepherds in a landscape is extraordinary.

Genre themes were also important subjects for Tanner. *The Banjo Lesson* (fig.15–9) is a simple scene of African-American life. The figures are rendered realistically, without sentimentality, as one generation passes on knowledge to another. Tanner was the most honored of all African-American artists, here and abroad, and he was a powerful influence on others who worked with him.

15–9 What sounds might you associate with this scene?
Henry O. Tanner, *The Banjo Lesson*, 1893. Oil on canvas, 48" x 35" (123 x 89 cm). Hampton University Museum, Hampton, Virginia.

Higher-Order Thinking Skills

Ask students if Edmonia Lewis' *Hagar* (fig.15–7) is similar to the socially oriented themes of Bellows, Banister and Tanner.

- How is her work different?

- How does Lewis communicate the plight of women in Western society?

- Is she as explicit as the male painters or does she rely on traditional symbolism?

- Although Lewis uses a biblical theme, is her message as clear as the more documentary-type paintings?

Contextual Information

Henri

Robert Henri studied at the Pennsylvania Academy of Fine Art with Thomas Anshutz, a pupil of Thomas Eakins. He then went to Paris, where he learned the academic style of the École des Beaux-Arts, experimented with Impressionism, and was influenced by the work of Velazquez, Hals, Manet and Whistler.

Henri was appointed a judge in the 1907 National Academy of Design exhibition, but two of his own paintings were hung at the #2 level (meaning above or below the preferred eye level). He withdrew his paintings and, with Glackens and Sloan, planned an independent show.

American Art Academies

Samuel F. B. Morse was the first president of the National Academy of Design, founded in 1826 in New York City. With rooms for study and exhibition halls for annual shows, the academy's purpose was to provide a school for young artists. Morse had studied in London in the Classical manner, and that was the style advocated by the academy.

The early nineteenth century saw the growth of art academies in America. They included the American Academy of Fine Art and the National Academy of Design in New York City, the Pennsylvania Academy of Fine Art in Philadelphia, and the Boston Athenaeum.

The Art Students League School in New York was founded in the late 1870s by students unhappy with Classical and rigid training at the National Academy. Later, other schools grew up around charismatic teachers such as Chase, Henri and Hofman.

Realism in American Writing

Like the painters of the Ashcan School, who introduced a new realism into American painting, a new group of authors began to write books that were distinctly American in subject and realistic in tone. One of the first writers to establish this new realism was Theodore Dreiser. His first novel, *Sister Carrie*, was published in the United States in 1900 to mixed reviews and substantial opposition. Dreiser wrote straight-on about life in Chicago and New York, including its poverty, and exposed society's materialism. His characters were not heroic, nor did the novel follow conventional morality in which the bad were punished and the good rewarded.

Other writers who wrote objectively about American life included Sinclair Lewis and Upton Sinclair. Sinclair Lewis wrote of middle-class hypocrisy and conformity in his novels *Babbit* and *Main Street*. Upton Sinclair hit America in its stomach as well as its conscience by exposing the unsanitary conditions in the meat-packing industry in the nonfiction book *The Jungle*.

With characters drawn from everyday life, these writers set out to describe American life, what it was and what it was becoming; and, in so doing, raising questions about what it should be.

Robert Henri
(1865–1929)

In 1908, eight of Philadelphia's illustrators banded together to put on an exhibition of their paintings. Calling themselves *The Eight*, these Expressionist painters tried to communicate their feelings about American life in the crowded cities. Robert Henri, who pronounced his name "Hen-rye" to be as American as possible, became the leader of The Eight. They presented paintings of crowds, slums, clogged streets, ragged children, sports events, clowns and sunny afternoons. Critics jeeringly called them "The Ashcan School" because their realism became expressions of poverty and ugliness. America had always favored Realism, but such visual social statements were disturbing.

Henri's studio became a regular meeting place for The Eight as well as other young and aspiring artists whom he encouraged and helped. He urged them to paint the city and its people as they saw them and as they felt about what they saw. He encouraged his students to paint in their own way and to expand the tradition of American Realism begun by Eakins.

Henri's own style used broad brushstrokes in a direct way, much in the manner of Manet, Goya and Hals. *Snow in New York* (fig.15-10) is one of many snow-clogged cityscapes that he painted in his broad, freely brushed style. It is moody and clearly reflects Henri's knowledge and feeling about New York in winter. It is not the joyful snow scene of calendar painters, but the cold, everyday, hard-working reality of urban winters.

15–10 What devices has the artist used to create this rather gloomy feeling of winter?
Robert Henri, *Snow in New York*, 1902. Oil on canvas, 31 4/5" x 25 1/2" (81 x 65 cm). National Gallery of Art, Washington, DC, Chester Dale Collection.

Cooperative Learning

Have students research paintings of each of The Eight. Have them photocopy a representative painting by each to form an impromptu exhibition by the group. Divide the students into two groups and ask them to write critiques of the show. One group should voice approval of the works. The other group should take the role of those who were critical of the group and coined the term "The Ashcan School."

15–11 Compare this painting to Renoir's
***Moulin de la Galette* (fig.13–12).**
John Sloan, *Renganeschi's Saturday Night*, 1912.
Oil on canvas, 26 4/5" x 31 4/5" (67 x 81 cm). The
Art Institute of Chicago, gift of Mrs. John E.
Jenkins, 1926.

John Sloan

(1871–1951)

John Sloan was one of the most talented among The Eight. Sloan believed that a work of art need not have beautiful subject matter to be valid. To Sloan, the beauty of a painting was in the work itself, not in the subject. Sloan enjoyed painting any city scene and set up his easel in any street. People sitting on the steps, women drying their hair on a rooftop, or a woman hanging out her Monday's washing on a line could all become subject matter for Sloan's creative mind. *Renganeschi's Saturday Night* (fig.15–11) is simply a scene in an urban restaurant, rapidly brushed on canvas by an observant artist. No academic artist of the time would consider this appropriate subject matter, but Sloan filled the room with joy and delight. Sloan understood life in the city and fully enjoyed the people and their daily activities.

Lesson 15.1 Review

1 What were some scenes that George Bellows painted?
2 Describe the girls in Sargent's *Daughters of Edward D. Boit*. What are they wearing?
3 What subjects did Inness usually paint? Describe the mood in his painting *Home of the Heron*.
4 Describe the scene in Tanner's *Banjo Lesson*. What is the setting?
5 What was "The Ashcan School?" How did it get its name? Name two artists that were members of this group.
6 What was John Sloan's favorite subject to paint?

Lesson 15.1 Review Answers

1 Boxing scenes in New York's private clubs, New York slums, boys swimming in the East River, dock workers, saloons, horses
2 The three standing girls are wearing white pinafores over their dark dresses. They all have on dark stockings and shoes and their long hair is pulled back. The youngest child sits on a rug in a white dress holding a doll.
3 Inness usually painted realistic landscapes with gentle moods as in *Home of the Heron.*
4 A child sits on a man's lap learning to play a banjo. This setting is a humble home with cooking utensils in the foreground and a table in the background.
5 "The Ashcan School" was a label given to eight Philadelphia Expressionist painters who joined together to exhibit their paintings. The critics gave them this name because these artists portrayed poverty and the ugliness of America's slums in a disturbingly realistic manner. These artists called themselves "The Eight."
6 Any city scene

Lesson 15.2

Although Abstract artists in America received little public acclaim, they forged a strong avant-garde style founded on European traditions.

Warm-up

Ask students how they feel about an artist's right to pursue his or her interests regardless of public opinion. What would they say to encourage the development of the Abstract artists whose work is shown in Lesson 15.2? How might students use the ideals on which the United States was founded and the importance of freedom of expression in a democracy as part of their argument? Explain to students that American artists in the early decades of the twentieth century were often misunderstood, harshly criticized, or ignored by a public who desired more recognizable themes.

Objectives

Students should be able to:

Explain the long-term impact of the European modern art exhibited at the 1913 Armory Show in New York City.

Understand how Abstract artists in the United States relied on one another for encouragement because they received scant critical or public support.

Vocabulary Definitions

mobile (*mow*-beel) A balanced construction with moving parts, suspended from above, and moving freely in the air currents. May be set in motion by a motor. Invented by Alexander Calder in 1932.
stabile (*stay*-bile) A standing sculpture with moveable parts.

Teach

Criticism: Direct students to compare Georgia O'Keeffe's *From the Plains I* (fig.15–12) to the abstract European art of Cubism, Futurism and De Stijl (Lesson 14.2).

• Have half the class pretend to be European art critics of the day and write a review that finds fault with O'Keeffe's American work. How is her subject vastly different from the urban-inspired subjects of the European artists?

15.2 The Influence of Abstraction

F THE ASHCAN EIGHT HAD PROBLEMS being accepted by Americans, the small group of Abstract painters had an even greater struggle. But, Abstraction persisted. In America, there was one stronghold for the young experimenters—the studio of the master photographer Alfred Stieglitz. He admired the work of Cézanne, Rodin, Brancusi and Picasso and encouraged young American Abstractionists, such as Georgia O'Keeffe and John Marin, by showing their work in his New York studio.

The 1913 New York Armory Show opened American eyes to the European art scene. American artists realized they either had to change direction or be left out. Following World War I, American artists flocked to France to study and to work. Gradually, Abstraction became an important element in American art, even though it was not yet fully accepted by the public. The American public made little attempt to understand the language and meaning of the Abstractionists. Thus, the artists worked in isolation, receiving encouragement from each other and from a small, but growing, number of patrons, museums and galleries.

Key Notes

• New York Armory Show convinces American artists that they have to change direction.
• Despite the ridicule of the public, the Abstractionists forge a new path in American art.

Vocabulary

mobiles
stabiles

Special Feature
Georgia O'Keeffe
(1887–1986)

Born and raised on a large farm in Wisconsin, Georgia O'Keeffe was an American pioneer of Abstraction. Unlike other ground-breaking artists, her training and influences were entirely American.

O'Keeffe first drew and painted representationally, but this work did not satisfy her and she began making abstract drawings of landforms from memory. She mailed some of these charcoal drawings to a friend with express instructions not to show them to anyone else. The friend took them to Alfred Stieglitz, the famous photographer, who was running an avant-garde gallery in New York. Stieglitz loved

15–12 O'Keeffe did not study in Europe, but invented her own variety of American Abstraction based on natural forms.
Georgia O'Keeffe, *From the Plains I*, 1953. Oil on canvas, 48" x 84 1/4" (122 x 214 cm). McNay Art Institute, San Antonio, Texas.

• Ask the other half of the class to write essays from the role of O'Keeffe, describing her decision to use Abstraction to portray a uniquely American image.

Art History/Criticism: Ask students to ponder how American artists who had not traveled abroad might have learned about European avant-garde art. Based on the images in Lesson 15.2, how do students think these artists reacted to seeing paintings by the Impressionists (Lesson 13.1), Post-Impressionists (Lesson 13.2), Fauves (Lesson 14.1) and Cubists (Lesson 14.2) in the 1913 New York City Armory Show?

• How does the work of American artists after this period reflect direct influences of these styles?

• Do students think art critics and the public shared the artists' enthusiasm?

• Tell the class that reviewers called the modern European art poor, degrading, comic and humiliating. What kind of climate do students think this created for American artists dedicated to Abstraction? Do students themselves thrive in an environment of adversity or support?

them and showed them in an exhibition with two other artists. When O'Keeffe heard about this, she rushed down to New York to confront Stieglitz and make him take down the drawings. However, Stieglitz managed to persuade her to leave them up. Eight years later, they were married.

O'Keeffe's early subjects were gigantic close-up paintings of flowers or flower parts. She said, "I'll make them big like the huge buildings going up. People will be startled; they'll have to look at them." She moved in closer and closer to blown-up images of flowers until the vibrating center of a flower was sometimes all there was on her canvas. Nature's abstract forms always pleased her and, when Stieglitz died in 1946, she settled permanently in her beloved desert landscape of New Mexico.

From the Plains I (fig.15–12) is a powerful and dramatic work that captures the austere and quiet vastness of the plains. The yellow, red and orange hues add a hot and savage feeling to a flat land. In this painting, there is no monumental mountain to break the horizon; the horizon line itself becomes monumental.

O'Keeffe always took her forms from nature, no matter how abstractly she depicted them. The 1923 charcoal drawing, *Alligator Pears in a Basket* (fig.15–13), is one of these fluid, organic images derived from nature. The deliberate ambiguity of the composition makes us want to look very carefully at the image. A close look reveals subtle shadings of grays and blacks. The grays are so luscious they seem almost to be colors. O'Keeffe often worked with an element of surprise in order to shock the viewer into seeing differently.

In this drawing, the two thick charcoal lines ringing the fruit give us two different views of the pears.

Georgia O'Keeffe was one of the American artists who chose not to go to Europe to learn about abstraction. Her abstract paintings are a purely American invention.

15–13 How has the artist made full use of her medium?
Georgia O'Keeffe, *Alligator Pears in a Basket*, 1923. Charcoal drawing, 24" x 18" (61 x 46 cm). National Museum of Women in the Arts, gift of Wallace and Wilhelmina Holladay.

Contextual Information

Marin

Marin studied briefly at both the Pennsylvania Academy and the Art Students League. In 1905 he went to Europe, and in Paris he met Steichen, who introduced him to Stieglitz. Stieglitz exhibited Marin's work, and, as he did with many other struggling artists, he supported Marin financially.

Modern Salons

The home of Gertrude Stein became a salon for American and European artists to meet and discuss art. Matisse and Duchamp came there often, as did many writers, actors, dealers and dancers.

In America, Mabel Dodge and Walter and Louise Arensberg in New York City had salons for artists in the decade after the Armory Show.

Demuth

Demuth was from Lancaster, Pennsylvania, and studied at the Pennsylvania Academy of Fine Art. He was in Paris between 1912 and 1914 and there met Picasso, Matisse, Gris and Duchamp and became involved with Cubists, Fauves and Futurists. He returned to America in 1915 and became part of the group of artists who met at the Arensbergs'.

Sheeler

Sheeler left Philadelphia for New York City in 1919 because "anything stimulating and conducive to work was happening in New York." In New York, he did fashion photographs for *Vanity Fair* and *Vogue*. He was commissioned to photograph the Ford Motor plant near Detroit and used the photographs of the facility as the basis of a series of paintings, drawings and lithographs.

15–14 How do color and line create a sense of motion here?
John Marin, *Singer Building*, 1921. Watercolor on paper, 26 1/3" x 21 1/4" (67 x 54 cm). Philadelphia Museum of Art; The Alfred Stieglitz Collection.

15–15 Based on a poem by William Carlos Williams, this painting recalls a fire engine tearing through the city on a dark, wet night. How does the artist convey this image in abstract terms?
Charles Demuth, *The Figure Five in Gold*, 1928. Oil on composition board, 35 4/5" x 29 1/2" (91 x 75 cm). The Metropolitan Museum of Art, New York, Alfred Stieglitz Collection, 1949.

John Marin

(1870–1953)

John Marin studied to be an architect. However, after a trip to Europe, where he worked with Whistler, he turned to painting. Like Georgia O'Keeffe, Marin exhibited in Alfred Stieglitz's gallery. He was among the first Americans to experiment with Abstract art. His paintings have a Cubist feeling, in which soft lines break up the larger shapes. Much of his work, such as *Singer Building* (fig.15–14), explores cityscapes. He later concentrated on Maine landscapes and seascapes. He often painted in watercolor so he could work quickly in his own personal shorthand style, which expressed a sense of agitation and excitement. His paintings explode with color and line. They have a dynamic geometry that seems in constant motion. He said once that he could see and feel the "warring of great and small buildings in the city...and hear the sound of their strife." He once compared his brisk painting style to a golf game—the fewer strokes, the better. Although his paintings seem quickly done, they were carefully thought out before his brush first touched paper.

Charles Demuth

(1883–1935)

Charles Demuth was born in Pennsylvania. After studying in Philadelphia, he went to Paris. His early works were mostly Cubist watercolors of delicate, beautifully drawn houses, landscapes, grain elevators, acrobats and circus performers. Later, he painted in oils and worked on a series that he called "posters," although they were not meant to be actual posters. One was *The Figure Five in Gold* (fig.15–15), based on a poem written by his friend William Carlos Williams. Both the poem and the painting recall a shrieking fire engine tearing through the darkened city streets on a wet night. "Bill" and "Carlo" (for the name of the poet) appear in the Cubist design along with the roaring number five. The painting became Demuth's best-known work.

Charles Sheeler

(1883–1965)

After going through several phases and styles, Charles Sheeler found himself close to the thinking and design of the great and cool Renaissance designers, such as Raphael and Piero della Francesca. Instead of people, however, Sheeler used machinery, buildings and man-ufactured products as his subject because he enjoyed their geometric lines and solid structure. His intense interest in photography led him to believe that light is the great designer.

His carefully composed paintings combine the structure of abstraction with a realistic presentation of subject matter. *City Interior* (fig.15–16) is precisely put together and free of emotion. It combines interlocking darks and lights, verticals and horizontals, and lines and shapes. Sheeler painted the cities and the industrial scene with precision and careful attention to design and detail.

15–16 Renaissance design and concerns with realism are coupled here with industrial subjects for a very twentieth-century look.
Charles Sheeler, *City Interior*, 1936. Oil on fiberboard, 22" x 27" (56 x 69 cm). Worcester Art Museum, Massachusetts.

World Cultural Timeline

1921
First modern Chinese hospital founded, Peking

1926
Women gain right to run for political office, India

1931
First trans-African railway completed from Angola to Mozambique

1938
Oil discovered, Saudi Arabia

Performing Arts Connection

American Modern Dance

America's early modern dance pioneers abandoned the Classical ballet tradition in favor of movement that expressed their own unique spirits. Isadora Duncan poured out spontaneous, passionate, personal emotion rather than the representation of a character's feelings or actions. Ruth St. Denis called upon the mysteries of the Orient, while her partner and husband, Ted Shawn, turned to American folk material for inspiration.

In the second generation of modern dance, Martha Graham created a radical, austere movement vocabulary that conveyed stories rooted in the American experience as well as in the universal sentiments embodied by ancient Greek myths.

Contextual Information

Gorky

Arshile Gorky was deeply influenced by the work of Miró, Arp and Chilean Surrealist Roberto Matta, who had moved to the United States in 1939. Gorky's work was based on automatism (unconscious and uncensored movements on canvas).

Davis

Stuart Davis was born in Philadelphia, where his father was art director of *The Press* newspaper, which employed Sloan, Luks, Shinn and Glackens. He entered Henri's school at age 16 and exhibited five watercolors in the Armory Show.

Calder

A 1929 art critic said of Calder's work: "If this artist isn't crazy, he's drunk—or was when he did these things. We'll never hear from him again."

One of Calder's problems was how to combine art and the machines that moved his early mobiles so that viewers weren't conscious of the machines. Eventually he designed the mobiles to move with the wind.

Discussion

A number of years ago, an airport was given a large Calder mobile. The mobile was repainted in the colors of the local high school, and weights were added to the highest shapes to pull them lower so that the mobile would be shorter and allow an advertising display unit underneath it. (Later, the airport rehung and repainted the mobile after many people, including Calder, strenuously objected.)

• What do you think about making changes to a work of art? Once a work is sold, is the owner free to do with it what he or she wishes?

The Armory Show

Although art critics called the 1913 Armory Show "pathological" and

15–17 The title is not a clue to the meaning of this abstract work. It is up to you to make your own interpretation. Arshile Gorky, *The Liver Is the Cock's Comb*, 1944. Oil on canvas, 71 3/5" x 97 3/5" (182 x 248 cm). Albright-Knox Art Gallery, Buffalo, gift of Seymour H. Knox.

Arshile Gorky

(1904–1948)

Gorky came to America from Armenia when he was sixteen. He became the pioneer of an American artistic revolution later called *Abstract Expressionism*. His major contribution was in developing a unique style of abstraction based on his personal feelings and inner thoughts. Some of his works are based on the abstracting of representational objects. However, the shapes are so personal that they cannot often be recognized. The viewer is forced to look at the work without recognizable symbols. The shapes, lines and colors in *The Liver Is the Cock's Comb* (fig.15–17) are organic, not geometric. They appear to be floating and turning in congested space. They seem almost human, but soon the resemblance vanishes. Only shapes, lines and colors remain. This sensation comes and goes, leaving the viewer with ambiguous feelings. Each viewer must interpret the result in his or her own way. Gorky does not provide a clue, nor does the title help. His titles are personal. Perhaps they had meaning to Gorky when he finished the work.

Stuart Davis

(1894–1964)

Stuart Davis was a student of Robert Henri and exhibited several Realistic paintings (and even sold one) in the Armory Show. But, once he was exposed to Cubism, Fauvism and the rest of European experimentation, he turned from Realism to Abstraction. The abstract style he developed formed the bridge between European Cubism and American Abstract Expressionism later in the century. From a series of experiments in color and shape, Davis finally developed a style of hard-edge abstraction that was clean, colorful and personal. It sizzled with life and a jazz beat. His works often reflected the words, numbers, shapes and colors of urban life and advertising. Works such as *Something on the Eight Ball* (fig.15–a) are bright, joyful and carefully composed.

Like Matisse and Mondrian, Davis had the rare ability to reduce the complexities of his urban environment to rhythmic and electric designs. His unique paintings have the appearance of flat cutouts of brightly colored paper, of interlocking strips overlaid with parts of words and numbers. Davis' titles, like those of Arshile Gorky, are personal and are not literal references to the paintings. Each work is to be enjoyed as seen and not for hidden meaning. Davis worked with his powerful abstractions well into the second half of the twentieth century.

"hideous," viewers packed the rooms of the Post-Impressionists and Futurists so that one reporter said that it was "almost impossible" to see the paintings. At the start of the show, the admission fee was twenty-five cents; because of the crush of people, it was raised to one dollar, and still they crowded in.

Because of the show, the art world was "turned upside-down" as the value of American art plummeted and modern European paintings soared in value.

The show was a definite financial success for the organizers (earning $30,000 in sales the first week), but they were not thrilled when the final records revealed that an overwhelming number of sales were of European art rather than of their own work, which comprised half the exhibit. As a result, many members of the Association of American Painters and Sculptors, who sponsored the exhibit, resigned.

Alexander Calder

(1898–1976)

American sculptors during the first half of the twentieth century worked mostly in traditional ways and media, but with ever-increasing interest in simplifying the figure. Several, including Alexander Calder, began to work with new materials and in new ways.

Calder was among the first Americans to begin working with abstract forms in space. He moved to Paris in 1926 and began creating an imaginative menagerie of animals from wire and scraps of other materials. *Sow* (fig.15–c) and other three-dimensional, linear animals and circus performers are like whimsical drawings in space.

The light and airy feeling of his space drawings was carried into more technical constructions called *mobiles*. Calder's mobiles hung suspended from a single point. *Lobster Trap and Fish Tails* (fig.15–18) is a buoyant assemblage of shapes that is balanced so carefully that a single breath of air sets the sculpture in motion. It was constructed so that every movement produces a change in the visual configuration—with the possibilities being endless. Although this sculpture has a suggested subject matter, most of his mobiles were completely nonobjective. Calder also produced many standing sculptures that he called *stabiles*, such as the steel *Black Widow* (fig.15–19).

15–18 Every slight motion of the air changes the configuration of this sculpture. Alexander Calder, *Lobster Trap and Fish Tails*, 1939. Painted steel wire and sheet aluminum, about 101" x 115" (257 x 292 cm). The Museum of Modern Art, New York.

15–19 Why do you think Calder called this a *stabile*? Alexander Calder, *Black Widow*, 1959. Painted sheet steel, 7' 9" (2.34 m) high. The Museum of Modern Art, New York, Mrs. Simon Guggenheim Fund.

Lesson 15.2 Review

1 How did Alfred Stieglitz encourage American Abstractionists during the first part of the twentieth century?
2 Describe the mood of the landscape in Georgia O'Keeffe's *On the Plain I*.
3 How does Marin's *Singer Building* resemble Cubism?
4 What inspired Charles Demuth to paint *I Saw the Figure Five in Gold*?
5 What style did Arshile Gorky develop?
6 From what medium is Alexander Calder's *Sow* made?
7 What type of sculpture is Calder's *Lobster Trap and Fish Tails*?

Performing Arts Connection

Something on the Eight Ball, Stuart Davis

One day, while speaking with some friends who were jazz musicians, Stuart Davis accidentally switched the usual phrase "behind the eight ball" to "something on the eight ball." When this got a laugh, Davis decided to use it as the title of his painting. Although the work makes no specific reference to jazz, the juxtaposition of images and contrasting colors suggests a visual rhythm similar to the musical form and also reflects Davis' love of modern jazz, which he listened to while painting.

• Play the music of jazz musicians of Davis' time—Earl Hines, Duke Ellington, Louis Armstrong, Count Basie, Charlie Parker, Lester Young—while students view Davis' artwork. Have students discuss the existence of rhythm, contrast and tempo in both formats.

Lesson 15.3

Although the American art establishment swung toward Abstraction after the Armory Show of 1913, certain artists continued to work in a Realist vein. They strove to depict American scenes in a unique style that shunned European precedents.

Warm-up

Ask students to guess what subjects an artist who is categorized as a Regionalist might describe. What does the word *region* mean and how could it relate this to type of art?

Objectives

Students should be able to:

Comprehend how Realist painters of the American Scene depicted hard-working people in urban and country settings.

Learn that the American Scene painters from the Midwest, who became known as Regionalists, developed a truly American style that did not rely on European art for inspiration.

15.3 The American Scene

THE AMERICAN ART ESTABLISHMENT made a giant swing from Realism to Abstraction following the Armory Show in 1913. However, many American artists continued to work with Realism. Because they painted the farmlands and the cities of America in a realistic way, these artists, such as Edward Hopper and Walt Kuhn, were called American Scene painters. Each had an individual style, but the message was the same: America is vast, beautiful, abundant, lonely, crowded and full of honest, hard-working people.

Another group of American Scene painters from the Midwest became known as Regionalists because they limited their subject matter to the regions in which they lived. Grant Wood painted images of rural Iowa. Thomas Hart Benton painted his native Missouri. Although they developed independent styles, the Regionalists were trying to develop an art that was truly American. These artists did not want to look to Europe for inspiration.

Key Notes

- Many American artists continue to work in Realist style.
- American Scene artists paint American farmlands and cities.
- Regionalists, a group of midwestern American Scene artists, limit their subject matter to the regions in which they live.

Special Feature

Thomas Hart Benton

(1889–1975)

Benton was the leader of the Regionalists. Born in Neosho, Missouri, Benton was the son of a United States congressman and the grandnephew of a famous senator. His childhood and adolescence were filled with talk of the forces that were shaping the Midwest. So, it is no wonder that Benton limited his subject matter to the history and activities of typical midwestern farmers. These were the subjects he knew best. Sunburned farmers, sturdy horses and furrowed fields attracted him, not the people of Paris or New York. He tried all the avant-garde

15–21 What are the arts of the West?
Thomas Hart Benton, *Arts of the West*, 1932. Tempera, 8' x 13' (2.4 x 3.9 m). New Britain Museum of American Art, Connecticut. ©1996 T.H. Benton and R.P. Benton Testamentarry Trusts/Licensed by VAGA, New York, NY

Teach

Art History/Criticism: After students examine figs.15–20 and 15–21, ask where in the United States they think Thomas Hart Benton came from.

- Had the American West ever been the subject of cutting-edge art before this time?

- Do they think Edward Hopper (figs.15–b, 15–25) lived in the same part of the country?

- What is it that both these artists wanted to reveal about American life?

- Were they interested in grand events and famous people?

- How do their colors, compositions and styles communicate the character of the people and places they depict?

Criticism: Instruct students to write a dialogue for one of the characters in Benton's *Arts of the West* (fig.15-21). As this character, have students describe how Benton has captured the specific flavor of the Midwest and why they believe his style of distorting figures and melding numerous individual scenes together is a good way of describing the kind of lives they led. How can their character's personal experience of cowboy and farm life support their statements?

15–20 **Why would Americans, especially Kentuckians, have found this work appealing?** Thomas Hart Benton, *The Kentuckian*, 1954. Oil on canvas, 36 3/5" x 20 2/3" (93 x 52 cm). Los Angeles County Museum of Art, gift of Burt Lancaster. ©1996 T.H. Benton and R.P. Benton Testamentarry Trusts/Licensed by VAGA, New York, NY

styles, but ultimately felt comfortable only with his own brand of Realism.

The Kentuckian (fig.15–20) illustrates the type of historical subject he loved to paint. There is a slight distortion of humans, plant life and nature. However, the strongly lit forms, deep shadows and simplified design create a realistic image. The style is personal and unique. The large figure appears determined and ready to face whatever difficulties may lie ahead.

To preserve American history, Benton conceived a huge program of public mural art. The sixty-four murals would provide a complete pictorial history of the United States. Benton actually completed sixteen of these panels. In *Arts of the West* (fig.15–21), Benton wanted to present a great deal of information. The various landscapes are jammed. There is so much happening in this panel that it could easily be chaotic. Instead, it all fits together and is perfectly balanced.

Benton was a critic of modern trends in art. He forged an American art that was based on the history and folklore of the United States.

Evaluate

Ask students if the Regionalists looked to Europe for inspiration. What in Benton's artwork supports their answers?

Reteach

Have students decide what subjects and styles they would use if they were to work in a Regionalist style today. How would they visually translate the distinct characteristics of their own surroundings?

Share with the class what Benton wrote about *Arts of the West*: "The real subject is what an individual has known and felt about things encountered in a real world of real people and actual doings." Have students use examples from the painting itself to describe how Benton used a nonnaturalistic style to convey real experiences.

Higher-Order Thinking Skills

Instruct students to compare and contrast Benton's mural to one from another time. The class can construct a chronology of murals and their characteristics.

Contextual Information

Benton

In 1930, Benton began a mural for the New School for Social Research in New York City. (This was at the same time that José Clemente Orozco was painting a series of murals there.) He then painted a mural for Indiana's building at the 1933 Chicago World's Fair. Later he painted murals for the then-new Missouri capital building.

Before he painted his murals, Benton made clay models of the figures and landscapes; he had learned this approach from his study of Tintoretto and El Greco.

Social realists criticized Benton's paintings because they lacked a strong message for political change. Thirty years later, Benton said ". . . we were all in revolt against the unhappy effects which the Armory Show of 1913 had had on American painting. We believed that only by turning the formative processes of art back again to meaningful subject matter, in our cases specifically American subject matter, could we expect to get [this revolution]."

The Kentuckian

The Kentuckian was commissioned by Paramount Pictures in conjunction with a film it made by the same name. The film starred Burt Lancaster, whose features are easily recognizable in the face of the painting's central figure. Lancaster later owned the painting and gave it as a gift to the Los Angeles County Museum of Art.

15–22 Compare Rubens' *Castle of Steen* (fig.11–24), which was his farm, to this picture of American midwestern farming.
Grant Wood, *Stone City, Iowa*, 1930. Oil on wood panel, 30 1/3" x 40" (77 x 102 cm). Joslyn Art Museum, Omaha, Nebraska. ©1996 Estate of Grant Wood/Licensed by VAGA, New York, NY

Contextual Information

Hopper

Hopper studied with Henri at the New York School of Art between 1900 and 1906. He worked as a commercial artist and painted in his free time, frequently using his wife as his model. Hopper painted many scenes without people (fig.1–a) and others that show buildings with people who are not interacting with one another.

The Regionalists

After World War I, interest in modern art quieted down. There was a revival of interest in American history and American heroes, partly because the country became isolationist and did not want to be drawn into another war. The Regionalists centered their attention on their own geographic area and rebelled against big-city filth, Surrealism, Cubism and the elitism of academies and the large art museums. The general public liked the Regionalists' paintings and found themselves and their land portrayed in sensitive ways. In fact, a writer in a 1934 issue of *Time* announced that there was a new kind of art originating in the Midwest, developed in reaction to that "crazy parade" of "deliberately unintelligible" art that included Cubism, Dadaism, Futurism and Surrealism.

Grant Wood

(1892–1941)

Like Thomas Hart Benton, Grant Wood was a Regionalist. Wood was born on a small farm in rural Iowa and at an early age moved to Cedar Rapids. In his trips to Europe, Wood became interested in the exquisite detail of the early Flemish masters. His paintings, such as *Stone City, Iowa* (fig.15–22), reflect this fascination with detail. However, Wood used his midwestern imagination to produce trees and hills that are smoothly rounded and expertly trimmed to perfection. His work is painstakingly designed, drawn and painted to present a clean and crisp world of farmers, farms, countryside and people—an idealized American Scene. An icon of American culture, *American Gothic* (fig.15–23) is Wood's best-known work. The simple plainness of this farming couple conveys the austerity of rural American life at this time and leaves a lasting impression on the viewer.

15–23 This couple has become symbolic of America's midwestern farmers and the life they created.
Grant Wood, *American Gothic*, 1930. Oil on beaver board, 29" x 24" (76 x 63 cm). The Art Institute of Chicago, Friends of the American Art Collection, 1930. ©Estate of Grant Wood/Licensed by VAGA, New York, NY

1946	1947	1948
Jordan becomes independent	India becomes fully independent from Britain	South Africa officially adopts apartheid policy

World Cultural Timeline

1947		1948
Dead Sea Scrolls found		The Crazy Horse Memorial dedicated to all Native Americans, Black Hills, South Dakota

Multicultural Connection

Crazy Horse

Crazy Horse (1849?–1877) was an Oglala Sioux chief, and he became the leader of a band of Oglala and Cheyenne that resisted confinement to reservations. He joined up with Sitting Bull in 1875 in an attempt to prevent the occupation of the Black Hills of South Dakota by white settlers. In 1876, he defeated General Custer at the Battle of Little Big Horn. In 1877, Crazy Horse was forced to surrender to U.S. troops in Nebraska and was killed in a scuffle with his captors.

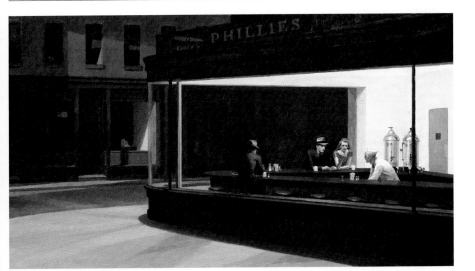

15–25 What does Hopper say here about life in American cities?
Edward Hopper, *Nighthawks*, 1942. Oil on canvas, 30" x 60" (76 x 152 cm). The Art Institute of Chicago, Friends of American Art Collection.

15–24 Although he was one of the organizers of the Armory Show, Kuhn stayed with his realistic painting style.
Walt Kuhn, *The Blue Clown*, 1931. Oil on canvas, 30" x 25" (76 x 64 cm). Purchase Collection of Whitney Museum of American Art, New York.

Walt Kuhn
(1880–1949)

Walt Kuhn was one of the American Scene painters. Although he was one of the organizers of the Armory Show, he could not change his painting style to adapt to the modern Abstractionism. He worked realistically, painting dramatic studies of clowns and circus performers. He had worked in circuses himself and painted his subjects with knowledge and compassion. He would catch his models, like *The Blue Clown* (fig.15–24), in off-duty moments and in moods of reflection. He was able to portray their sense of dignity and pride, of sadness and loneliness. He also captured the continuing sense of drama in which they lived and worked.

Edward Hopper
(1882–1967)

Another painter of the American Scene, Edward Hopper was one of Robert Henri's most talented pupils. He even sold a painting at the Armory Show. However, despite a trip to Europe and the increasing importance of Abstractionism in America, Hopper continued to work at his own brand of Realism. He was acutely sensitive to human emotions. He painted America from the inside out, concentrating on its feelings rather than the visibly evident. He closely observed the sadness of cheap hotel rooms, empty diners, cool nights, lonely people and cheerless houses. *Nighthawks* (fig.15–25) is a powerful and dramatic portrayal of loneliness of life in the big cities. His strong light is always garish and piercing. The subjects look exposed, as though they were put under a glaring spotlight. Hopper traveled from place to place and made mental notes of what he saw. He later put them together to visually express his feelings on American life.

Performing Arts Connection

The Greatest Show on Earth: The American Circus

A Scottish performer and horseman named John Bill Ricketts introduced the first modern circus to the United States in 1793. Phineas Taylor Barnum opened his in 1871 and made the circus the mammoth show it is today—multiple rings, sideshows of people with special physical traits and abilities, a menagerie of exotic animals from all over the world, and a midway or fairground alley for the selling of souvenirs and food, and for games and entertainment.

Contextual Information

Bierstadt

In 1858, Bierstadt joined an expedition to map a route to the Pacific, but he went only as far as the Rockies. He sketched scenes of the Rocky Mountains, rivers and Native Americans, and from these sketches, he made very large paintings when he returned to New York. He charged admission to see these paintings, thereby earning enough to travel frequently to Europe.

Remington

Remington had no formal art training before he left New York to see the West at age 19. By the late 1880s, he was earning money from selling his sketches to popular magazines and writing stories about cowboys and the Native Americans. He illustrated these stories with his sketches.

Window in Time

Romanticizing the West

And ever I am leaving the city more and more, and withdrawing into the wilderness. I must walk toward Oregon, and not toward Europe. And that way the nation is moving. We go westward as into the future, with a spirit of enterprise and adventure....The West is but another name for the Wild; and in Wildness is the preservation of the World.

–Henry David Thoreau,
Walking

The West—unspoiled, untamed, uncivilized—held Americans' imagination with a magnetic attraction. Like Thoreau, Americans saw the West and its untouched wilderness as a source of strength and truth. Nature was a reflection of both the grandeur and possibility inherent in America. The West was a state of mind as much as it was a landscape.

Images of the West have remained fixed in American lore in great part because of works by artists and writers. However, often these images are not completely accurate.

Artists such as Albert Bierstadt and Thomas Moran depicted the West in a romantic light. They wanted to show the grandeur and magnificence of what they saw, but without any harsh realities. The huge canvases were intended to be dramatic and spectacular; like the myth of the West, they were larger than life.

The Old West had largely vanished by the time Frederic Remington began to paint. Essentially, Remington created his own West, bigger and purer than what he saw. His works, which are charged with a sense of drama and excitement, are a pure celebration of the country and men who lived and worked upon it.

Both Remington and fellow artist Charles Russell transformed the cowboy from a ranch laborer who spent a lonely, monotonous life into a glamorous figure. Their cowboys are the embodiment of youthful freedom. Perhaps the cowboy, more than any other image, evokes the romantic spirit and freedom we associate with the West. He stood for the essence, not the reality, of the West.

Western American art is largely fantasy, yet in fantasy there is much truth. The works are a record of the feelings, attitudes, hopes and aspirations that objective sources cannot possibly convey. They are a vision of a better world called the West—a world of imagination and possibility.

Albert Bierstadt, *The Last of the Buffalo*, Oil on canvas, 71 1/4" x 119 1/4" (181 x 303 cm). In the collection of The Corcoran Gallery of Art, gift of Mrs. Albert Bierstadt.

Inquiry

By the early twentieth century, most Native Americans had been removed from their land, and many had been killed by disease, armies or settlers. Have students research the plight of Native Americans in the nineteenth century and find what factors and events dramatically changed their way of life.

Frederic Remington

(1861–1906)

Although he worked earlier in the century than the American Scene painters, Frederic Remington depicted life in the western part of the United States. He was a painter and sculptor of the great westward expansion. Although known primarily for his paintings, Remington began sculpting in bronze about 1895 and produced many fine pieces before he died in 1906. Sculptures such as *The Outlaw* (fig.15–26) show his supreme knowledge of horses, cowboys and their movement, based on countless hours of sketching and painting. Remington's work was traditional in concept because of its realism. The action and subject matter were strictly American to the point of nostalgia.

15–26 Whom do you think the outlaw is?
Frederic Remington, *The Outlaw*, 1906. Bronze, 22 2/3" (57.5 cm) high. Los Angeles County Museum of Art, William Randolph Hearst Collection.

Lesson 15.3 Review

1 Name two American Regionalists and the region or part of the country that they painted.
2 What subject did Walt Kuhn usually paint?
3 Describe how Hopper conveys a sense of loneliness in a city in his painting *Nighthawks*.
4 What is Grant Wood's most famous painting? Have you seen a parody of this?
5 What region of the United States provided Frederic Remington subjects to paint and sculpt?

Lesson 15.3 Review Answers

1 Possible answers include:

Thomas Hart Benton	Missouri and the Midwest
Grant Wood	Iowa
Edward Hopper*	Northeast
Frederic Remington*	West

*Not regionalists in the strictest sense, but American artists who focused their attention on one part of the country.

2 Clowns and circus performers
3 The large open spaces suggest emptiness and loneliness. The strong light is garish and piercing, making the people look exposed—as if they were under a glaring spotlight. The people do not seem to connect with each other emotionally.
4 *American Gothic*—Most students will have seen cartoons and ads based on this American icon of a Midwest farm couple.
5 The West

Lesson 15.4

American Social Realist art reflected the effects of the Great Depression of the 1930s and the imminent threat of outside totalitarian, socialist and communist governments. The Social Realists rejected the Abstract art then fashionable, as well as the Regionalists' portrayal of life far from the troubles of urban centers. Instead, in order to try to bring about social reform on a governmental level, the Social Realists described the hardships of ordinary citizens.

Warm-up

Have the class list adjectives that describe the experience of living in contemporary American society. Ask if their words seem to correlate to what Jacob Lawrence evokes in figs.15–28 and 15–27. Share that Social Realist artists strove to express the difficulties of urban life.

Objectives

Students should be able to:

Cite the cultural circumstances that turned the Social Realists away from Abstraction and toward an art that reflected the dehumanization of industrial and urban life.

Describe how the artists developed independent styles but shared a common desire to express the problems of average American people in the hopes of instigating governmental change.

Teach

Aesthetics/Art History: Have students study Lawrence's paintings *One of the Largest Race Riots Occurred in East St. Louis* (fig.15–28) and *Juke Box* (fig.15–27) and read the information about them on pages 514 and 515. Ask how Lawrence's style describes African-American life at the time. Then direct students to compare his work to Edmonia Lewis' *Hagar* (fig.15–7).

• What is the difference in the way Lewis, an artist from mixed descent, expresses her experience? (Students may wish to reread page 498 for specific information.)

• Do students feel that both artists are equally successful in communicating their points of view?

15.4 Social Realism

D
URING AND IMMEDIATELY FOLLOWING the Great Depression of the early 1930s, the United States experienced a period of mass unemployment, hard times and near social panic. Outside influences, such as totalitarianism, socialism and communism cast threatening shadows over the country.

In reaction to this difficult time, many American artists rejected Abstraction, which had become increasingly fashionable. They also dismissed the Realism of Benton and Wood, who lived away from the cities' problems. Instead, these Social Realists attacked the dehumanization of industrial and urban life. They tried to use their art to influence the course of government. Their work often focused on ordinary people and the many injustices imposed on them by an uncaring society.

Led at first by Ben Shahn and Reginald Marsh, the banner of Social Realism was later picked up by artists like Jacob Lawrence and George Tooker. These artists communicated their ideas and feelings about American society in different styles, but the messages still got across. They believed that painting must describe and express the people and their lives, problems and times. This belief sums up the aesthetic philosophy of the Social Realists.

Key Notes

• The hard times brought on by the Great Depression of the 1930s are often depicted by American artists of the period.
• Many American artists reject both Abstraction and the Realism of the Regionalists.
• Social Realism shows the dehumanization of urban life.

15–28 Written statements accompany each of the sixty panels in this series. Lawrence combed history books and newspapers in order to select exactly the right statement for each scene.
Jacob Lawrence, *One of the Largest Race Riots Occurred in East St. Louis*, panel 52 from *The Migration of the Negro*, 1940–1941. Tempera and gesso on composition board, 12" x 18" (30 x 46 cm). The Museum of Modern Art, New York, gift of Mrs. David M. Levy.

Special Feature

Jacob Lawrence

(b.1917)

In the 1920s, Harlem experienced a cultural flowering known as the Harlem Renaissance. Many of the greatest African-American writers, musicians, poets and artists lived in Harlem or took their inspiration from it. When Jacob Lawrence arrived in Harlem about 1930, the greatest surge of the Harlem Renaissance had passed. But, enough stimulus remained to help turn the child of a poor family into one of the most significant American artists of his time.

Lawrence studied art at the government-sponsored Harlem Art Workshop from 1932 to 1934. By the age of twenty-one, he had already made a name for himself as an artist. His tempera paintings of the Haitian general Toussaint L'Ouverture were shown in an exhibit of African-American artists. After this exhibition, Lawrence began several series of paintings about the heritage of his people and their struggle for equality. His angular, hard-edge style was appropriate for the themes that would dominate his work. He painted the experiences of African Americans: their hardships in the ghettos, the violence that greeted their move from the South to the North, the civil rights movement.

Juke Box (fig.15–27), like most of his paintings, tells a story. A lonely woman leans against the juke box, listening sadly to its music. Is she remembering better times? Why is she alone in such a large room? Is she enjoying the

---

• Why does one artwork appeal to them more than the other in terms of style?

Art History/Criticism: Instruct students to imagine being a politician who has just walked into an exhibition of the images in Lesson 15.4. As an elected official, how will they respond to the reporters waiting outside to interview them?

• Do they feel that the work raises good points?

• Can they disagree with the art's message but admire its technique?

• Why do they or do they not feel moved to try to accomplish something on the governmental level for the average people whose lives the artists depicted?

Evaluate

Ask students how Social Realists might have responded to Rococo art (Lesson 11.5).

• What might Social Realists have criticized about Rococo style and content? Were both movements politically potent?

• Whom did the Social Realists hope to influence with their work?

• Although the late eighteenth-century Rococo art was meant to please the aristocracy, how could these images have become inflammatory if they had gotten into the hands of the repressed underclass?

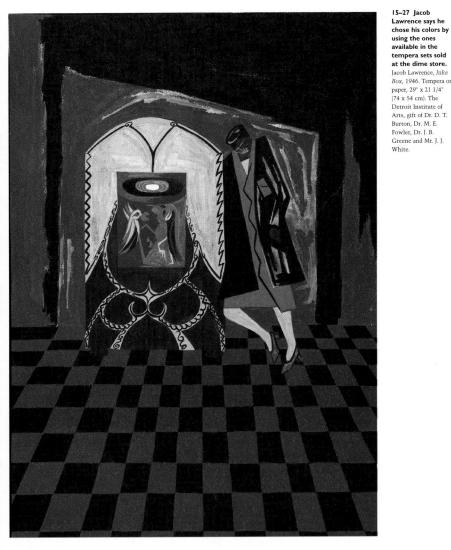

music? Why aren't others? All the answers to such questions could be narratives that Lawrence allows the viewer to imagine.

In the early 1940s, Lawrence created a sixty-panel series called *The Migration of the Negro* that dealt with the oppression of African Americans. *One of the Largest Race Riots Occurred in East St. Louis* (fig.15–28) is one of the best-known panels from that series. The race riot is not depicted realistically. Instead, Lawrence gives us a stylized and perfectly balanced dance of almost abstract shapes, which only make the work more chilling. The painting universalizes the hatred, lifting it above a more specific clash of individuals. The painting is dominated by the clenched fist holding the knife. This extremely moving and beautifully rendered painting is a searing example of Social Realism.

Contextual Information

Lawrence

Lawrence received his early art training at the Harlem Art Workshop. When he was young, he walked 60 blocks to see paintings and read art books at the Metropolitan Museum of Art. With the "Migration" series, Lawrence received recognition in the art world; twenty-six of the paintings were featured in color in the November 1941 issue of *Fortune* magazine. Lawrence's art dealer introduced him to the most well-known artists in New York City, including Shahn and Davis.

Higher-Order Thinking Skills

Jacob Lawrence collected quotes, sayings and newspaper articles to provide the text for his series works. Although they came from different sources, he put the written material together to form a story line. Have students collect their own materials from a variety of sources to create a story line. They may then do illustrations for their stories

• Do subjects that have the ability to ignite social unrest affect a viewer's enjoyment of the work? Is this necessarily a good or bad occurrence?

Reteach

Ask the class what kinds of connections they can make between art that tells a story, such as works by Jacob Lawrence (figs.15–27 and 15–28), and journalistic newspaper, radio or television reports.

• What are the similarities and differences in terms of point of view and depth?

• How do both fine art and journalism alter the way in which information is understood?

• Have students read Jacob Lawrence's statement about his art on page 519.

• Do they agree or disagree with the last paragraph, even though his style is not purely naturalistic?

• How might Lawrence's abstracted realism convey "the things I have experienced" more clearly than a strictly representational technique?

Cooperative Learning

As a teenager, Jacob Lawrence took advantage of classes and workshops offered in his Harlem community to learn about art. Have students investigate the opportunities that exist in your community to learn about art. Have

them consider the schools, the community and the media to create a guide to art opportunities in your area. The guide can be displayed or reproduced and distributed.

Interdisciplinary Connection

History: Have students research the race riots of East St. Louis. Can they find any photographs that document the riots? If they can, have them compare and contrast the photos and Lawrence's painting.

Contextual Information

Depression Era Federal Art Programs

In 1933, there were approximately 10,000 unemployed American artists. As a remedy, George Biddle proposed a program of government patronage for the arts to President Franklin Delano Roosevelt. He reminded Roosevelt of how Mexico had sponsored artists to express the ideals of the country by painting murals on schools and government buildings. Biddle said that young American artists would be "eager" to express American ideals if they were given government support. In fact, "they would be contributing to and expressing in living monuments the social ideals that you are struggling to achieve."

A pilot program sponsored by the Public Works of Art Project (PWAP) employed over 3,700 artists during the winter of 1933–34 to make 15,633 works of art. The following year, two government programs started. One was the Treasury Section of Painting and Sculpture, which lasted nine years and selected artists, on the basis of their ability as revealed in competitions for the commissions, to decorate federal buildings. The other project was the Works Progress Administration/Federal Art Program (WPA/FAP), which lasted from 1935 to 1943. It provided a small salary for any artist who could demonstrate any level of professional training.

Some complaints came from those who thought that the images were "un-American," in "poor taste" and of "communist influences," but most of the murals, prints and paintings that recorded lives of Americans at work, church and play were well liked and still exist in public buildings around the United States.

Art and Social Protest

Throughout his life, Ben Shahn was involved with political and moral issues, like those raised in the trial of Nicola Sacco and Bartolomeo Vanzetti.

Sacco and Vanzetti were Italian-American anarchists who had been charged with the robbery and murder of a paymaster and a guard in 1920. Evidence presented at the trial was far from conclusive, but still resulted in convictions. Their fate had been determined by the presiding judge, Webster Thayer. Thayer was highly biased against foreigners and anarchists and openly displayed his biases during the trial. The trial also took place during a period of national fear of anarchists and Communists.

The verdict was appealed, but in 1927 Sacco and Vanzetti were finally executed in the electric chair. The question of their guilt or innocence has never been resolved. The controversy over whether they were executed solely because of their political beliefs still remains.

Shahn did many works of the Sacco and Vanzetti trials, until as late as 1952, incurring the wrath of those who wanted the trials forgotten. His detractors said that what he was doing was not art. But, Shahn rejected art for art's sake and his willingness to comment on the life and social issues of his time never abated. As far as he was concerned, art and political action were perfectly compatible.

Ben Shahn, *The Passion of Sacco and Vanzetti*, 1931–1932. Tempera on canvas, 84 1/2" x 48" (215 x 122 cm). Collection of Whitney Museum of American Art, gift of Edith and Milton Lowenthal. ©1996 Estate of Ben Shahn/Licensed by VAGA, New York, NY

Ben Shahn
(1898–1969)

Ben Shahn grew up in a Brooklyn slum, studied art in Paris, and was the early leader of Social Realism. He hated injustice in any form. Through his art, he criticized and commented on the judicial system, racial injustice, and the plights of migratory workers and miners. His eloquent voice was heard and seen by millions. His work as a photographer, muralist and printmaker during America's rebuilding years gave him a variety of media with which to communicate.

Handball (fig.15–29) does not simply show American young people playing games. Instead, the painting indicates the tragedy of unemployment and the waste of human resources. The men have no choice but to spend their time idly. Shahn was a master at using empty space to symbolize loneliness. He could have treated this subject as an active, fun-filled sport. But the viewer feels at once that this was not his intention.

15–29 This artist worked as an apprentice for Diego Rivera and also used paintings and murals to comment on social conditions.
Ben Shahn, *Handball*, 1939. Tempera on paper over composition board, 22 1/2" x 31 1/2" (57 x 80 cm). The Museum of Modern Art, New York, Abby Aldrich Rockefeller Fund. ©Estate of Ben Shahn/Licensed by VAGA, New York, NY

15–31 For forty years, Bishop commuted every day from her suburban home to her studio in Manhattan. From the large picture window in her studio in Union Square, she observed the crowds on the streets below. Isabel Bishop, *On the Street*, about 1932. Oil on canvas, 14" x 26" (35 x 66 cm). Midtown Payson Galleries, New York City.

Reginald Marsh

(1898–1954)

Reginald Marsh painted the people of the streets during the 1930s. His subjects included crowds in the tenements, on the steps, in the streets, and at parks, beaches and theaters. His sketchy style, somewhat like Daumier's, was the result of numerous pen-and-ink sketches he made for newspaper cartoons. *The Bowery* (fig.15–30) captures the crowded living conditions and the congestion of life in parts of New York in the 1930s. Marsh's use of color, values and swirling movement creates a feeling of agitation and restlessness, even if his figures are relaxed and sleeping. The softness of his edges is drastically different from the harder edges of Shahn and Lawrence.

Isabel Bishop

(b.1902)

Although she was excited by the artists of the Armory Show, Isabel Bishop would not give up her Realistic style. She painted the workers, shoppers, derelicts and passersby outside her studio on Union Square in New York.

Bishop's paintings have a lively sense of movement that mirrors the constant flux and rhythm of people moving along crowded city streets. In paintings like *On the Street* (fig.15–31), she also captures the loneliness of the crowds. The well-dressed women look down, not around them, as they cut through the congested street. The light on the women further isolates them from the men on the fringes.

15–30 Remember that this was painted in 1930. What do you think these men are talking about? Reginald Marsh, *The Bowery*, 1930. Oil on canvas, 48" x 36" (122 x 91 cm). The Metropolitan Museum of Art, New York. Arthur H. Hearn Fund, 1932.

Performing Arts Connection

American Theater in the 1930s

During the 1930s, social theories and politics began to exert a major influence on contemporary theater in America. Many playwrights portrayed the lives and struggles of ordinary citizens. Actors, influenced by the methods of the Russian teacher Konstantin Stanislavsky delved deep into their own experiences to bring a sense of reality to their roles. Acting and story lines came together to communicate recognizable people in real-life situations.

Broadway Musical Theater

Early popular music in America had its roots in music hall, vaudeville, variety, and musical comedy traditions. In the twentieth century, American musicals flourished. Composers and lyricists such as George Gershwin, Ira Gershwin, Jerome Kern, Cole Porter, Richard Rodgers, Lorenz Hart and Oscar Hammerstein crafted memorable shows in which plots were linked together with song and dance.

• Play selections from both a musical and an opera, and have students examine the differences between the two forms. Discuss how the music, lyrics and action move the plot along in each. Is there a difference in the way characters are developed? Ask students to explain which they would rather compose, an opera or a musical.

Higher-Order Thinking Skills

Many groups of Social Realist painters issued statements or manifestos about the relationship of art and society. Based on the evidence in the paintings in the text, how did these artists see society and government? Write a statement you think they would accept.

Lesson 15.4 Review Answers

1 Social Realists attacked the dehumanization of industrial and urban life. They tried to influence the course of government with their art to correct injustices imposed on ordinary people by an uncaring society. Some American Social Realist artists were: Ben Shahn, Reginald Marsh, Jacob Lawrence
2 The Harlem Renaissance was a rebirth of the arts in Harlem in the 1920s and 1930s. Jacob Lawrence was one visual artist who was involved in this movement.
3 African-American experiences
4 *Handball* indicates the tragedy of unemployment and the waste of human resources as the men kill time instead of being productive.
5 Tooker repeated the same figure three times. This repetition and the bleak architectural setting intensify the scene's mood of hopelessness.

Chapter Review Answers

Review

1 If students justify their decisions, variations in this ranking are appropriate.

Most Realistic to Most Abstract

fig.	Artist	Title
fig.15–16	Sheeler	*City Interior*
fig.15–5	Bierstadt	*The Rocky Mountains*
fig.15–26	Remington	*The Outlaw*
fig.15–3	Sargent	*Daughters of Edward D. Boit*
fig.15–4	Inness	*Home of Heron*
fig.15–29	Shahn	*Handball*
fig.15–6	Bannister	*Newspaper Boy*
fig.15–11	Sloan	*Renganeschi's Saturday Night*
fig.15–30	Marsh	*The Bowery*
fig.15–31	Bishop	*On the Street*
fig.15–1	Bellows	*Cliff Dwellers*
fig.15–2	Bellows	*Stag at Sharkey's*
fig.15–9	Tanner	*The Banjo Lesson*
fig.15–10	Henri	*Snow in New York*

fig.	Artist	Title
fig.15–7	Lewis	*Hagar*
fig.15–21	Benton	*Arts of the West*
fig.15–22	Wood	*Stone City, Iowa*
fig.15–23	Wood	*American Gothic*
fig.15–20	Benton	*The Kentuckian*
fig.15–24	Kuhn	*The Blue Clown*
fig.15–25	Hopper	*Nighthawks*
fig.15–32	Tooker	*Government Bureau*
fig.15–13	O'Keeffe	*Alligator Pears*
fig.15–c	Calder	*Sow*
fig.15–8	Tanner	*Angels Appearing*
fig.15–28	Lawrence	*One of the Largest Race Riots*
fig.15–27	Lawrence	*Juke Box*
fig.15–14	Marin	*Singer Building*
fig.15–19	Calder	*Black Widow*
fig.15–15	Demuth	*The Figure Five in Gold*
fig.15–12	O'Keeffe	*From the Plains I*
fig.15–a	Davis	*Something on the Eight Ball*
fig.15–17	Gorky	*The Liver Is the Cock's Comb*

2 Benton made his subject huge compared to the other forms in the picture. He lit him strongly with deep shadows. The viewer looks up at the figure.

3

fig.	Artist	Title
fig.14–2	Rivera	*The Making of a Fresco*
fig.14–13	Kirchner	*The Street*
fig.14–22	Stella	*Brooklyn Bridge*
fig.14–23	Stella	*Battle of Lights*
fig.14–30	Boccioni	*Noise of Street Penetrates House*
fig.14–44	de Chirico	*The Mystery and Melancholy of a Street*
fig.15–1	Bellows	*Cliff Dwellers*
fig.15–10	Henri	*Snow in New York*
fig.15–14	Marin	*Singer Building*
fig.15–16	Sheeler	*City Interior*
fig.15–25	Hopper	*Nighthawks*
fig.15–28	Lawrence	*One of the Largest Race Riots*
fig.15–29	Shahn	*Handball*

George Tooker

(b.1920)

Along with Jacob Lawrence, George Tooker carried the banner of Social Realism into the post-World War II period. He painted the decline in the quality of life in the growing cities by emphasizing chilling loneliness and alienation. A prison-like environment seems to engulf city-dwellers in their subways, stations, offices and governmental agencies. In his *Government Bureau* (fig.15–32), he shows the plight of a depersonalized humanity confronting a faceless bureaucracy. The same male figure is repeated three times. This repetition and the bleak architectural setting intensify the scene's impact and eerie feeling of hopelessness.

Government Bureau is the stark, almost chilling, summation of the dehumanizing of urban society that the Social Realists sought to portray.

15–32 What does this painting tell you about the relationship of the individual and the bureaucracy?
George Tooker, *Government Bureau*, 1956. Egg tempera on gesso panel, 19 1/3" x 29 1/2" (49 x 75 cm). The Metropolitan Museum of Art, New York, George A. Hearn Fund, 1956.

1948
Israel created as Jewish homeland

1949
Indonesia becomes independent from the Dutch

World Cultural Timeline

1948
Mahatma Gandhi assassinated

1949
People's Republic of China established; all China now Communist

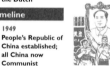

Lesson 15.4 Review

1 Name five American Social Realist artists. What were they trying to achieve in their art?
2 What was the Harlem Renaissance? Name an artist that was involved with this movement.
3 What subjects did Jacob Lawrence paint?
4 In addition to teenagers playing, what are some of the messages in Ben Shahn's *Handball*?
5 Describe how George Tooker depersonalized people in his *Government Bureau*.

Primary Source

Jacob Lawrence: A Philosophy of Art

Jacob Lawrence consistently painted scenes from the African-American experience because he wanted his people to know their history. In this statement, which was solicited by the Whitney Museum after it acquired a painting by Lawrence, the artist describes his philosophy of art:

"Painting is a way of expressing one's thoughts and feelings. I feel that I am more articulate in painting than in any other form of expression, therefore I am always striving to perfect this particular form of art so as to reach a greater degree of articulation.

For me a painting should have three things: universality, clarity and strength. Universality so that it may be understood by all men. Clarity and strength so that it may be aesthetically good. It is necessary in creating a painting to find out as much as possible about one's subject, thereby freeing oneself of having to strive for a superficial depth.

It is more important that an artist study life than study the technique of painting exclusively. Technique will come with the desire to make oneself understood. It is more important for the artist to develop a philosophy and clarity of thought.

My pictures express my life and experience. I paint the things I know about and the things I have experienced. The things I have experienced extend into my national, racial and class group. So I paint the American scene."

Chapter Review

Review

1 List the ten pieces of art that you liked best in this chapter. Rank them from most realistic to most abstract with one being the most realistic and ten the most abstract.
2 How has Benton made *The Kentuckian* heroic?
3 List the street and city scenes and the artists who painted them in chapters 14 and 15.
4 Which do you think is the most emotional? Which is the least emotional or impersonal?

Interpret

1 How did Bierstadt romanticize the American West? What effect did this have on the westward migration?
2 Compare Sheeler's cityscape to George Bellow's *Cliff Dwellers*. What was each artist most interested in portraying?
3 Compare Gorky's *The Liver Is the Cock's Comb* to Davis' *Something on the Eight Ball*. How are they alike? How are they different? Which is hard? Which is soft? Which is larger? Describe their colors.

Other Tools for Learning

 Maps
Find the regions on a map that Grant Wood, Frederic Remington and George Bellows painted.

 Timelines
1 Select an event on the cultural timeline that a Social Realist would have approved. Explain why you chose this event.
2 List several events in the timelines which contributed to the sense of loneliness and alienation found in much of the art of the first half of the twentieth century.

 Electronic Research
Videodisc player: *National Gallery of Art*
1 Look at Calder's sculpture in the lobby of the National Gallery in Washington, DC. Describe its size in relation to people and in relation to the space it occupies.

---

fig.15–30   Marsh   *The Bowery*
fig.15–31   Bishop   *On the Street*

4 Good candidates for the most emotional would be Boccioni's *The Noise of the Street Penetrates the House* or Marsh's *The Bowery*. Students might select Sheeler's *City Interior* or de Chirico's *The Mystery and Melancholy of the Street* as the least emotional.

Interpret

1 Bierstadt made his mountains higher, gorges deeper, reflections sharper, waterfalls higher and light clearer than they were in reality. These paintings lured people from the eastern cities to the West which they expected to be as beautiful as Bierstadt depicted.
2 Bellows was most interested in the people in the city. He felt the needs and confusion of the city dwellers. Sheeler was interested in the machinery and buildings in the city instead of the people. He enjoyed the city's geometric lines and solid structures.
3 Both *The Liver Is the Cock's Comb* and *Something on the Eight Ball* are Abstract Expressionism artworks. Gorky's painting has soft-edged organic shapes with blended colors. Davis' painting is full of bright, primary colors, and hard-edged shapes and words. *The Liver Is the Cock's Comb* is the larger of the two.

Timelines

1 The Social Realists would approve of any of the events which gave groups of people more freedom. This would include countries becoming self-governing, such as New Zealand in 1907, India in 1947 and Indonesia in 1949. Some Social Realists would have approved of the formation of the Chinese Communist Party in 1921 since they believed that communism could provide a better standard of living for the impoverished masses. They would also have supported the right of women to run for political office in India.
2 Some events that contributed to a sense of loneliness and alienation in art are:
The atomic bombing of Hiroshima and Nagasaki made the world aware of the powerful destructive forces available, and the possibility of completely destroying human civilization.
With the Stock Market crash in 1929, the United States joined the world in a severe economic depression
The assassination of India's Mahatma Gandhi in 1948.

Maps
Grant Wood painted the Midwest, Frederic Remington painted and sculpted the West, and George Bellows painted the state of New York.

Electronic Research
1 The huge red mobile fills the ceiling of the lobby, and makes the people seem very small in comparison.

Primary-Source Connection

Ask students to consider how they best express their own thoughts and feelings. Instruct students to write a brief statement that explains their special means of expression. (Forms of expression might include any of the fine arts or performing arts, language arts or sports.)

Multicultural Connection

Art and the People's Republic of China

Under the Chinese communist regime and the leadership of Mao Ze-dong, painting and the decorative arts served political purposes. Themes in painting praised the reconstruction of Chinese society under communist socialism. Folk arts, never held in high esteem during dynastic China, were honored. Weavings, basketry and jewelry, along with traditional ceramics, lacquer and jade, became important exports.

Activity 1: Depicting City Life

Activity Objectives

Students should be able to:

• Distinguish between painting styles, verbalizing differences in use of color, space, line, etc.

• Demonstrate their understanding of style by producing artwork that uses characteristic elements.

• Portray a scene with a lot of activity, energy and diverse elements.

• Successfully choose a color palette to enhance their design, and mix effective colors.

Thinking Critically

Review with students the art listed in "Take a look." Encourage discussion of their opinions by asking:

• How would you describe the style or mood of each painting?

• What elements of style or technique make each artist's work unique?

• Which elements would you like to use in a painting of your own? Why?

Preparation Ideas

As a warm-up (or alternative activity), find an interesting location near the school. Take students and sketch pads outdoors. Have the groups take turns posing while the others do rapid sketches of their positions and movements.

Notes on Materials

If you have access to photography equipment and a darkroom, you might want to organize a photographic field trip to take photographs to be used later for sketches. (See Teacher Spotlight.)

Tips

Preliminary ideas for paintings can be explored by having students use color magazine photos to do collage studies.

Evaluation

• Is the student's choice of subject a "scene with a lot of activity, energy and diverse elements," per the objectives?

• Does the finished work show the use and development of a unique style?

• Has the student appropriately used color to generate a mood?

Activity 1

Depicting City Life

Materials
11" x 14" white paper (or larger)
tempera or acrylic paints
brushes
surface for mixing paint
containers of water

Take a look.
• Fig.15–10, Robert Henri, *Snow in New York*, 1902.
• Fig.15–1, George Bellows, *Cliff Dwellers*, 1913.
• Fig.15–16, Charles Sheeler, *City Interior*, 1936.

Think about it. Much of the artwork in this chapter represents the artists' views of city life. Some capture a realistic likeness while others aim to reflect an impression of crowds of people, linear buildings and the bustle of activity. Choose an artist you would like to emulate, and identify what makes his/her style unique; for example: use of color, brushstrokes, details, composition and emphasis.

Do it.
• Choose an active place in your community among buildings, such as a shopping mall, an outdoor restaurant or other gathering place.
• Do several drawings or take photographs as references. Carefully work out the values in your sketches.
• Use tempera or acrylic paint to create a painting in the style of your choice.

Check it. Name the elements in each of your paintings that resemble the work of the artist being emulated. What makes your work uniquely your own?

Helpful Hint: Step back from your painting occasionally to consider how it looks from a distance.

Activity 2

Balancing Act

Materials
wooden sticks
wire (assorted gauges),
fishing line or string
poster, bristol and railroad board (assorted colors)
heavy-weight white paper
scissors, mat knife
pencils, markers
straight edge
glue
templates (optional)
colored pencils, watercolors (optional)

Take a look.
• Fig.15–18, Alexander Calder, *Lobster Trap and Fish Tails*, 1939.

Think about it. Alexander Calder worked with abstract forms in space called *mobiles*, the beginning of kinetic art. Look at his artwork listed above. How would you describe the shapes he uses and their relationship to each other?

Do it.
• Choose something you enjoy as a theme for your mobile; e.g., sports, music, animals, calligraphy, geometry, food, nature.
• Bring in objects or images related to your theme. Sketch these objects and plan how they will interact in a mobile. You may want to repeat some images or shapes. Plan what colors to use.
• Use wooden sticks or stiff wire (coat-hanger weight) as a base and attach string, wire or fishing line to build the structure that will support your objects.
• Draw your objects on heavy-weight poster board or paper. Cut them out and attach them to your frame.
• Hang your mobile or have a friend hold it up for you. Adjust the position of objects and/or lengths of string until everything balances.

Check it. Is your mobile balanced both physically and visually? If not, what adjustments can you make to the weight or design to improve visual balance and keep it moving smoothly?

Helpful Hint: If you hang your objects with fishing line, which is virtually transparent, your images will stand out more clearly, as if suspended in mid-air.

Additional Activities

• With wire as his medium, Alexander Calder explored drawing in space (see *Sow,* fig.15–c). The concepts are similar to contour drawing— smooth, fluid line, carefully observed relationships and emphasis on those features unique to the subject. Likewise, his approach mimics gesture drawing—capturing the character of a motion or gesture. Use heavy gauge, soft aluminum wire to create a sculpture of a figure or animal that is a drawing in space. Preliminary sketches will help you decide how to go about this work.

• If there are murals in your library, post office or school done during the thirties and forties, find out who painted them and in what medium. Write a description of them, explaining subject matter, symbolism and style. You can film, videotape or photograph details and parts to prepare a visual presentation.

Activity 2: Balancing Act

Activity Objectives

Students should be able to:

• Identify a unique form of sculpture.

• Appreciate the work that goes into creating mobiles.

• Create a design in space by translating two-dimensional ideas to three-dimensional space.

• Explore the balancing of objects, both visually and physically.

• Produce a successful mobile.

Thinking Critically

Ask the students to reorganize a famous sculpture or painting into parts and visualize it as a mobile. Ask them:

• How would the *Mona Lisa* look? The Statue of Liberty?

• What do the terms *kinetic art* and *mobile* mean? What is a stabile?

• Why do you suppose mobiles were not invented before the twentieth century?

• What materials do you think would be appropriate for making a mobile?

• What specific skills do you think Alexander Calder needed to create his mobiles?

Emily Susanna Morikawa

Strath Haven High School
Wallingford, Pennsylvania
Favorite kinds of art:
Impressionism, Genre painting
Favorite artists: Monet, Edward
Hopper, Manet, O'Keeffe
Activity 1, Depicting City Life

My project is an image of a restaurant window in a nearby town, Media. It represents a project of hard work. I had been unfamiliar with acrylics and had little experience with window reflections, so the project proved to be a challenge for me.

In our class we use photography as a quick sketch method. Photography is an effective way to get an accurate portrayal of the subject without interference from passing people or vehicles. For example, with some subjects that are in motion you don't get the opportunity to do even quick sketches because of their movement.

The thought process behind this work was that I wanted it to look as the photo did. It was very difficult working with the reflections and with the usage of color. I was hoping to develop a finished piece that looked realistic.

I have visited many museums in my life. My mother was an art major in school, so as a child I accompanied her on museum trips. I have seen many different techniques and subject matter—it teaches me how to handle different projects. I've seen how art has evolved and changed through time. It taught me that no matter how different one artist's style is from another, it is still unique and a piece of original work.

My advice to students who also enjoy creating art is to remain patient when you're having problems. Sometimes assignments are harder than others and mean more thinking and planning behind it. Many times during this piece, I almost gave up because it never looked right. My teacher helped me throughout it all the time, pushing me to work harder, and always demanding more from me that I thought I possessed. Usually I quit when it's not easy the first time, but I'm very proud of myself for following through this time, even when it got rough.

Emily Morikawa

Emily photographed the reflection in a storefront window to use as the foundation for her painting.
Reflections, 1994. Acrylic, 19 1/2" x 15" [49.5 x 38.5 cm].

Teacher Spotlight

James M. Ellis, Ed.D.

Chair, Visual and Performing Arts
Strath Haven High School

I use photography as a sketching tool with my students. We use this method of collecting images because it is so immediate and quick. It cuts the frustration level of students when they are working out of the classroom at sites where the everyday movement of people, animals and vehicles makes sketch books and pencil too slow for recording the images they wish to capture for later use. Since some of the tools my students use to render works are computers, scanners and manipulative software, the notion of camera as sketch gatherer is highly compatible with these technical processes.

It should be noted that this method is used to gather images and details of the subject and not necessarily to make photos that will be completely reproduced in the studio at a later date. Of course, the usual kinds of drawing on site are used when appropriate and when time permits, but I have found the camera sketch a very serviceable and real-world addition to today's art student's repertoire.

abstract and its parts may be simple or complex. Students should do several thumbnail sketches before constructing their mobile.

• Discuss what kinds of shapes and sizes would work better in a mobile. Encourage bold, graphic design. Point out that a silhouette alone will probably not be sufficient unless it's fairly distinctive. Discuss how students might best combine a cut edge with lines or colors within a shape.

Evaluation

• How much thought went into the theme and selection of objects?

• Are the objects/images designed and drawn well?

• How does the mobile hold together as a whole? Does it balance?

• In presenting the finished work, can the student articulate personal and artistic choices in creating the mobile?

Preparation Ideas

Encourage students to choose themes that tell something about themselves. Allow them to spend time drawing out their interests, help them find examples of ways to represent certain themes. A vegetarian might choose favorite vegetables, selecting shapes, colors and designs that work together well. You may want to have students bring in objects related to their theme and have a drawing session before beginning work on the mobile.

Notes on Materials

• Have a selection of several weights and colors of paper or boards on hand; e.g., 90 lb. to 120 lb. paper, bristol board, railroad board, etc.

• Have colored pencils and watercolors available for students who wish to focus more attention on the details and decoration of each object.

Classroom Management

• Students will need a lot of room in this project. If possible, set up large tables with materials, about eight students per table.

• When it's time to suspend the mobiles, set up students in pairs. One can hold the other's mobile while adjustments are made to balance it.

Tips

• Students may consider forms found in nature as a foundation for the mobile. The mobile may be representational or

Chapter 16 Organizer

Days	8 Week	I Semester	2 Semester

Chapter 16 Opener: Twentieth-Century Architecture

(1 | 1 | 1)

Objectives

Explain how Modernist architects abandoned brick and wood, preferring to use steel, reinforced concrete and huge expanses of glass in their towering, boxlike edifices.

Understand that Post-Modern buildings merged multiple styles at once to produce fascinating and often amusing visual experiences.

National Standards

5a Students identify intentions of those creating artworks, explore the implications of various purposes, and justify their analyses of purposes in particular works.

5d Students correlate responses to works of visual art with various techniques for communicating meanings, ideas, attitudes, views, and intentions.

Lesson 16.1 Modernism in Architecture

(1 | 1)

Teacher Edition References

Special Feature:
Ludwig Mies van der Rohe 524–525

HOTS 525

(1)

Remainder of Lesson 16.1 526–535
World Cultural Timeline 528
Lesson 16.1 Review 535

Contextual Info 526, 528, 530, 532, 534
HOTS 527, 529, 531, 533, 535
Inquiry 526, 531

Interdisciplinary 527, 532
Materials and Techniques 530
Multicultural 529, 533
Performing Arts 528, 534

Lesson 16.2 Post-Modernism

(1 | 1)

Special Feature:
Michael Graves 536–537

Contextual Info 537

HOTS 537

(1)

Remainder of Lesson 16.2 537–544
World Cultural Timeline 538, 542
Primary-Source 545
Lesson 16.2 Review 544
Chapter Review 545

Contextual Info 538, 542
HOTS 539, 540, 541, 543, 544

Cooperative 540, 542
Inquiry 539

Classroom Connections

(1 | 1 | 1)

National Standards

Studio Activity I
Harmony Inside and Out

1b Students conceive and create works of visual art that demonstrate an understanding of how the communication of their ideas relates to the media, techniques, and processes they use.
3b Students apply subjects, symbols, and ideas in their artworks and use the skills gained to solve problems in daily life.

Studio Activity 2
Model Community

1b Students conceive and create works of visual art that demonstrate an understanding of how the communication of their ideas relates to the media, techniques, and processes they use.
3b Students apply subjects, symbols, and ideas in their artworks and use the skills gained to solve problems in daily life.

Choose either Activity 1 or 2
Choose either Activity 1 or 2
Choose either Activity 1 or 2

Other Resources

Books

Jencks, Charles. *Modern Movements in Architecture.* Baltimore: Penguin USA, 1987.

Murphy, Wendy Buehr. *Frank Lloyd Wright.* Part of *Genius.* Englewood Cliffs, NJ: Silver Burdett Press, 1990.

Norwich, John J., ed. *Great Architecture of the World.* (Da Capo Quality Paperback Ser.). New York: Da Capo Press, 1991.

Stern, Robert. *New Directions in American Architecture.* Part of *New Directions in Architecture.* Rev. ed. New York: George Braziller Inc., 1969.

Thorne-Thomsen, Kathleen. *Frank Lloyd Wright for Kids.* Chicago, IL: Chicago Review Press Inc., 1994.

Whitford, Frank. *Bauhaus.* London: Thames and Hudson Inc., 1984.

CD-Rom

The Ultimate Frank Lloyd Wright: America's Architect, Crystal

Videos

Buckminster Fuller, Crystal
Frank Lloyd Wright: The Mike Wallace Interviews, Crystal
Le Corbusier, Crystal

Ancillaries

Slides: Wright, Robie House, Chicago, 110a, 219; Piano and Rogers, Centre National d'Art et de Culture Georges Pompidou, Paris, 115a, 226
Large Reproductions:
Lin, Vietnam Memorial, 27

Teacher Edition References

Timeline: Twentieth-Century Architecture 522
Context 522
Art 522
Quote 523

Ancillaries

Slides: Mies van der Rohe, Seagram Building, NYC, 108a, 217

Slides: Sullivan, Carson Pirie Scott Department Store, Chicago, 109a, 218;
Wright, Robie House, Chicago, 110a, 219;
Rietveld, Schroder House, Utrecht, Holland, 111a, 220;
Le Corbusier, Villa Savoye, Poissy, France, 112a, 221;
Le Corbusier, Unite d'Habitation, 110b, 222;
Skidmore, Owens, and Merrill, John Hancock Center, 111b, 223;
Wright, Guggenheim Musuem, New York, 113a, 224;
Saarinen, Dulles International Airport, Washington, DC, 114a, 225;
Piano and Rogers, Centre National d'Art et de Culture Georges Pompidou, Paris, 115a, 226
Large Reproductions: Pei, *Interior of East Building, National Gallery of Art,* 28

Slides: Venturi and Rauch, Fire Station, 112b, 227
Overhead Transparencies: Modern and Post-Modern at Home, 17

Schedule	**Materials**
Two days for a small sculpture. Larger sculptures will take longer.	newsprint for preliminary sketches, #3 or 4H pencils, erasers, 12" x 18" drawing paper suitable for watercolor and washes, water containers, assortment of round brushes (#2, #7, #10), pen and ink (optional)
Minimum of one day to plan and one day to build the model.	scissors, ruler, pencil, lightweight cardboard, glue, tape

Introduce

Modern architectural invention paralleled twentieth-century breakthroughs in science and technology. Initially, streamlined geometric structures of steel and glass punctuated the urban skyline. Eventually, the style was eclipsed by Post-Modernism, which simultaneously incorporated divergent influences in less austere and often whimsical manners.

Lessons at a Glance

16.1 *Modernism in Architecture*
Modern architecture first flourished in America, which was less entrenched in past traditions than Europe. Steel-framed structures—with gridlike patterns of vertical and horizontal beams—soared upward, punctuating the urban horizon.

16.2 *Post-Modernism*
Post-Modern architects grew tired of the geometric rigidity and impersonality of the earlier period. Instead, they embraced an endless variety of references, mixing history, popular expression, decoration and metaphor.

Objectives

Students should be able to:

Explain how Modernist architects abandoned brick and wood, preferring to use steel, reinforced concrete and huge expanses of glass in their towering, boxlike edifices.

Understand that Post-Modern buildings merged multiple styles at once to produce fascinating and often amusing visual experiences.

Teach

Timeline

Instruct students to compare the timeline for Chapter 16 to the timelines in Chapters 14 and 15. Have them explain how historic events during this period reflect the new age of Modernism. Ask how twentieth-century architecture correlates to the avant-garde painting and sculpture of the time.

16 Twentieth-Century Architecture

N EW IDEAS, NEW TECHNOLOGY, scientific breakthroughs and an extraordinary outpouring of energy marked the 1900s. And, nowhere was the new dynamism better showcased than in architecture. Heavy structures of wood and stone were replaced by the modern invention of steel skyscrapers.

The new form of architecture, called Modernism, completely changed the way cities looked. The tallest structures traditionally had been church spires; the higher they soared the closer worshipers were to God. These structures were overshadowed now by taller secular buildings that were higher than anyone had ever imagined. They pierced the sky and, with it, our notions of space.

Modern architects abandoned brick and wood for steel, reinforced concrete and huge expanses of glass. Theirs was an unadorned style of architecture that sought weightlessness in all of its structures.

By the 1960s and 1970s, architects had grown tired of the pure line and impersonality of Modernism. They wanted something more vibrant and less box-like, without as many rules. Post-Modernism, the style of today, combines many styles often in clever and humorous ways. For example, Walt Disney imagery may be mixed with Doric columns. Post-Modernists take the whole environment into account when designing new structures, making this style of architecture much more personal.

16–a Using walls of windows, Wright allowed exterior space to flow into the interior space of this home. He designed many of the house's small details, such as the colored leaded glass.
Frank Lloyd Wright. *Robie House*, detail (fig.16–4).

				1980 Lech Walesa heads Solidarity Movement in Poland	
1909 Wright initiates revolutionary style of modern architecture	1928 Gropius, Bauhaus 1940 Hemingway, *For Whom the Bell Tolls*	1955 Le Corbusier, Notre-Dame-du-Haut	1961 Yuri Gagarin first man to orbit Earth	1982 First artificial heart transplant	1986 Hole in ozone layer detected over Antarctica

Twentieth-Century Architecture

1909 Ford begins assembly-line auto manufacture 1918 Daylight saving time introduced in the US	1947 Flying saucers reported in the US 1947 Jackie Robinson (Brooklyn Dodgers) breaks racial barrier in sports	1959 Wright, Guggenheim Museum	1967 Buckminster Fuller, geodesic dome 1978 First personal computer	1985 Burgee and Johnson, AT&T Corporate Headquarters	1990 Break-up of the Soviet Union 1994 Construction of the Chunnel

Context

Have students research when the space race was at its height in the United States. If they had been architects asked to design a building epitomizing the age of space exploration, what would their structure look like?

• How would their proposal visually express the rapid scientific advances that enabled the United States to move forward in this arena?

• What shapes and colors would they incorporate? How would the building interact with the space around it?

Direct students to examine the California Aerospace Museum (figs.16–d, 16–32), designed by Frank Gehry & Associates.

• How does it relate to their plans?

• If they were to borrow certain elements from Gehry's building for their own design, which would they incorporate and why?

• Discuss how this building and modern architecture in general typify the overall spirit of technological advances in Western society.

Art

Ask students what formal element—color, shape or line—appears to be most significant in the Georges Pompidou National Center of Art and Culture (fig.16–c).

• Are all the lines created by the metal gridwork necessary?

"Less is more." Or is "Less a bore."

16–b This library is located across the street from the famous Mission of San Juan Capistrano. By incorporating elements of the Spanish mission style, it adheres to the Post-Modern intention of taking the surrounding environment into account when designing a new structure.
Michael Graves, *Public Library of San Juan Capistrano*, 1983. San Juan Capistrano, California.

16–d This architect has sought to convey the purpose of this building in a witty and appealing manner.
Frank O. Gehry & Associates. *California Aerospace Museum*, detail (fig.16–32).

16–c This museum and culture center sports its insides on its outsides. Does that appeal to you?
Renzo Piano and Richard Rogers. *Georges Pompidou National Center of Art and Culture*, 1977. Paris. (See fig.16–18.)

Quote

Divide the class into pairs and have each partner choose one of the quotes. Challenge students to debate each other about their choice by role-playing one of the architects represented in the chapter opener. Instruct them to support their argument by citing features of their building. Afterward, have them switch quotes to see if they can understand both sides of the issue.

• How do they influence the direction in which your eyes travel when looking at the building?

• Would the structure have the same sense of verticality if the exterior were a plain, solid wall?

• When in history have architects placed support elements on the outside of their buildings? (Direct students to reexamine Gothic architecture in Lesson 8.2.)

• What are the visual similarities and differences between Gothic churches and France's modern cultural center?

• How might their ultimate purposes have affected the variations in design?

Evaluate

Ask students if Post-Modernism consists of one set style. How does its variety affect many city landscapes? If they were the mayor of a major city, would they want one consistent style or would they allow multiple styles in their urban center? How do the images in the chapter opener influence their decision?

Reteach

Have students pretend that they are creatures from another planet who are touring the California Aerospace Museum. Ask how their responses might be different from that of humans who have never traveled through outer space. Afterward, ask students if all buildings should reflect their purpose. Can they cite examples from their own neighborhood to back up their position?

Question students if it is easier or more difficult for them to study and evaluate architecture than two-dimensional art. What about the two media makes them different?

• Why is the experience with a painting, drawing or photography unlike one with architecture?

• How do architecture's function, its relationship to people, and its interaction with the environment as well as its size, scale and materials impact their answer?

Lesson 16.1

Modern architecture first flourished in America, which was less entrenched in past traditions than Europe. Steel-framed structures—with gridlike patterns of vertical and horizontal beams—soared upward, punctuating the urban horizon.

Warm-up

Share with students that since prehistoric times, humans have turned to their environment for building resources. Ask them what the materials in today's buildings reflect about contemporary urban society.

• What kind of technology is necessary in order for these structures to be built?

• How might the materials vary in a forest or a desert?

• What if students lived on Venus or an imaginary island?

• Is it important for building materials to come from one's surroundings or is it equally valid for them to be artificially fabricated or imported from elsewhere?

Objectives

Students should be able to:

Understand how the invention of steel and metal-frame construction encouraged the development of the modern skyscraper.

Identify Modernism's clean, simple style, in which function prevailed over decoration.

Vocabulary Definitions

cantilever (*kan*-tl-ee-ver) A horizontal projection, canopy, balcony or beam balanced and supported with a fulcrum.
geodesic (jee-oh-*des*-ik) A form of geometry (solid) which forms the basis for structures built of interlocking polygons.

16.1 Modernism in Architecture

THE BIRTH OF MODERN ARCHITECTURE has much to do with breaking from the past. At the start of the twentieth century, there was a surge in construction, particularly in America. European cities had developed over centuries, while American cities underwent enormous growth and development in less than a century. Wood and stone had been the major building materials, and cast iron had been used to some degree, but these materials had severe limitations. New industries demanded a new type of architecture. Using the technology of steel and metal-frame construction, American architects developed the skyscraper, which dramatically changed the skylines and urban landscapes of Europe and America.

The steel frame, composed of vertical and horizontal beams riveted together, created a structure that was incredibly solid, rigid and strong. The structure was held together by the tensile strength of the steel instead of the enormous weight of stone. In such steel-frame structures, the walls do not have to bear the weight of the floors above. Instead, the steel became the primary support. Traditional arches and post-and-lintel elements were no longer needed. Buildings took on a gridlike appearance that echoed the supporting rectangular steel structure. The invention of high-speed elevators made it possible for skyscrapers to reach into the sky.

Architectural Modernism was based on the use of new technology and new man-made materials. Modern architects would embrace new technology and make efficient use of steel, concrete and glass construction. Lines were to be clean, without ornamentation and decoration. Function became a primary concern.

Key Notes

• Modern architecture makes a complete break with the past.
• Modernism relies on the new technology of steel and metal-frame construction.
• The lines of buildings are clean, and function becomes a primary concern.

> **Vocabulary**
> cantilevered
> geodesic

6–1 Although Mies van der Rohe worked with a number of building types, his most influential contribution was to the modern evolution of the skyscraper.
Ludwig Mies van der Rohe. *Lakeshore Drive Apartments,* 1951. Chicago.

Special Feature
Ludwig Mies van der Rohe

(1866–1969)
Like many German architects and artists, Ludwig Mies van der Rohe left Germany in the thirties because of Hitler's closed attitude toward modern art. He settled in Chicago as a practicing architect. Mies was a modest man who once said of his ambitions as an architect that he did not want to be interesting, he wanted to be good. Mies had a great impact on the Modern movement in the United States. The visual artist Mies was most closely linked to was Mondrian.

Mies designed many building complexes in and around Chicago, but among his best known are the *Lakeshore Drive Apartments* (fig.16–1), constructed in 1951. The two buildings comprise two severely elegant slabs set at right angles to each other to allow the most light to strike each apartment. Mies' simplified forms usually have slight detailing on windows and employ dark colors for the metal parts. The windows here, for example, may all seem alike. However, every fourth metal division is a bit wider, adding a sense of subtle rhythm to the surface.

Mies was very attracted to skyscrapers, and his skyscraper designs of the postwar period were the most influential of the Modernist period. Together with Philip Johnson, who was mainly responsible for the interiors, Mies designed the *Seagram Building* (fig.16–2) in New York City (1954–58). The exterior of the thirty-eight-story building is made of bronze-finished steel and amber glass.

Teach

Criticism: Ask students to imagine being a resident in Ludwig Mies van der Rohe's Lakeshore Drive Apartments (fig.16–1) or an employee at the Seagram Building (fig.16–2). As tenants, they are to explain to an American from the early 1800s why they enjoy living or working in these buildings. They might explain what about them is appealing: their scale, material, soundness of structure, incorporation of natural light, relationship to the environment, and sense of visual design. How might people from the past century respond to their claims?

Art History/Criticism: Challenge students to think of themselves as wealthy industrialists searching for an architect to build them an impressive yet functional corporate headquarters. First have them list their needs for the structure. Remind them to take disability access as well as function, material, environment and aesthetics into account. Next have them study the images in Lesson 16.1 to select an architect with whom they would like to work. To help them make their decision, have students consider how the existing example by their chosen designer demonstrates that he will be able to satisfy their requirements. Finally, ask them what kind of relationship they will want with the architect. Do they want the project to be a collaboration or would they prefer to list their desires and then leave the architect completely alone?

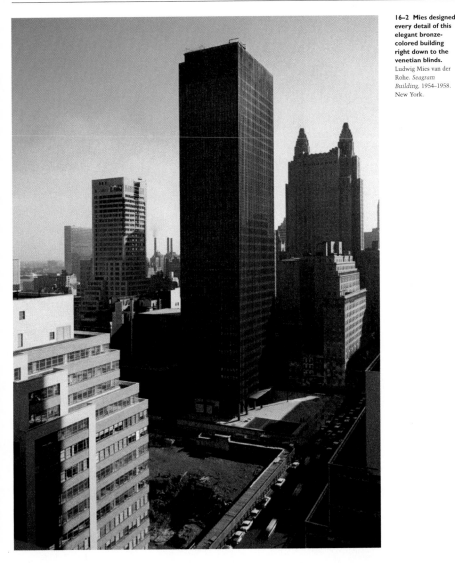

16–2 **Mies designed every detail of this elegant bronze-colored building right down to the venetian blinds.** Ludwig Mies van der Rohe. *Seagram Building,* 1954–1958. New York.

The rectangular building is set on a block-long plaza. Steel stilts support the building and give the bottom level an airiness that alleviates the solid form above. A pink granite pavement and lateral pools with fountains lead to a canopy and three sets of revolving doors. A visitor entering the bronze and glass-walled lobby is struck by its great simplicity and beauty. The Seagram Building is the perfect embodiment of modernism and of Mies' dictum, "Less is more."

Higher-Order Thinking Skills

Mies' buildings are often characterized as being "classic modern." Have students investigate the similarities and differences between modern and ancient Classicism by comparing one of Mies' buildings to one from ancient Classical times.

Evaluate

Ask students if great royal, religious or military leaders would be satisfied with the Modernist architectural style. Does its simplicity convey the same sense of grandeur and pomp and circumstance as, for example, Versailles (fig.11–c and p.344) or St. Peters (fig.11–7)? How do the images in Lesson 16.1 indicate who or what is glorified in Modernist architecture?

Reteach

Ask students to pretend that they are Thomas Jefferson, who spent nearly all of his adult life designing Monticello (fig.12–9). Instruct them to write an architectural review of Mies van der Rohe's style as seen in figs.16–1 and 16–2.

• How might Jefferson have felt about Mies' ambition to have his buildings be good rather than interesting?

• As ordinary citizens today, what do students think is interesting or perplexing about Mies' structures?

Ask students to imagine being the architect about to build one of the buildings in Lesson 16.1.

• What kind of relationship will they have with the person paying for the building, with the construction people, with its interior designers and with the landscapers?

• Have students consider how architecture, unlike most traditional two-dimensional art, requires interaction and input from many different sources.

Contextual Information

The Kaufmann House

Frank Lloyd Wright made all design decisions, and his clients could only hope for small compromises. For instance, Wright was not tall and frequently designed homes with low ceilings. The Kaufmanns wanted higher ceilings. The only compromise Wright made was to have higher ceilings in the guest house that was built up the hill and behind the Kaufmanns' main house.

The Kaufmanns were told to use furniture of Wright's design even if it was uncomfortable. (Wright admitted that his own furniture made him "black and blue," but he continued to specify it over ready-made furniture.) Instead they used their own collection of old dining-room chairs, much to the disgust of Wright.

Louis Sullivan

(1856–1924)

To find the beginnings of Modernism, we must go back to Louis Sullivan, who was one of the earliest architects to use steel construction. Sullivan believed that "form follows function." His most revolutionary work was the *Carson Pirie Scott Department Store* (fig.16–3), built in Chicago in 1901. The grid pattern of steel structure is very evident, with large windows used on all ten upper floors. The traditional heavy cornice and heavy window detail were eliminated. All ornamentation was eliminated except over the front doors at the rounded corner. Its stark simplicity heralded the beginning of modern architecture in America. America's developments would influence the entire world.

16–3 Unlike other buildings constructed at the same time, this store has decorative detail only over the front doors.
Louis Sullivan. *Carson Pirie Scott Department Store*, 1899–1901; enlarged 1899–1904. Chicago.

16–5 This famous house is popularly known as "Falling Water" because it is built over a waterfall. The sound of the falls can be heard throughout the house.
Frank Lloyd Wright. *Kaufmann House*, 1936. Bear Run, Pennsylvania.

Inquiry

The architectural and building professions are tied very closely to economic growth and recession. Have students research the economic growth of the country for the past ten years and compare that information to the number of houses built in those years.

Frank Lloyd Wright

(1867–1959)
Originally a student of Louis
Sullivan, Frank Lloyd Wright was
an individual genius. He developed
his own style and disregarded conventional construction. His primary
concern was to develop a compatible relationship between the structure and its location so that the
building would seem to grow out of
its environment. One of his earliest
revolutionary designs was for the
Robie House in Chicago, built in
1909 (fig.16–4). Wright disregarded
the traditional plan of enclosed
rooms with doors. Instead, he
allowed one room to flow into
another space, separated only by
partial walls. He let exterior space
flow into interior space (fig.16–a).
Roofs here are **cantilevered** and
seem to float without supports as
they reach out from the cubic forms
of the house. There is an overall
horizontal feeling to the homes he
built. They rest comfortably on
their sites. Wright had been favorably impressed by the design of the
Japanese Pavilion at the Chicago

16–4 Wright was very impressed by
Japanese designs he saw at the Chicago
World's Fair. What evidence of that
influence do you see?
Frank Lloyd Wright. *Robie House*, 1909. Chicago.

*Pennsylvania Railroad Station, 1906, New York
(33rd Street and Eighth Avenue).*

World's Fair in 1893. The simplicity
of forms, the horizontal lines, and
the honest use of materials in the
Robie House reflect the Japanese
influence.

In 1936, Wright designed and
built one of the most original living
spaces—the *Kaufmann House* at
Bear Run, near Pittsburgh, Pennsylvania (fig.16–5). Cantilevered
terraces stretch out over a stream
and waterfall. These terraces echo
the form and color of the natural
rock terraces below. Stone, wood,
color, shape, form and line are used
by Wright in a perfect marriage of
structure and site.

Great Buildings Lost

One of the greatest architectural blunders was committed
in 1963, when the beautiful
Pennsylvania Railroad Station
in New York City was torn
down.

The station, designed by
McKim, Mead & White and
completed in 1910, had been
built in the grand American
Neoclassical style. Scores of
immense granite columns lined
the perimeter of the site. From
the center rose a massive near-
replica of the ancient Roman
Baths of Caracalla. In here were
the ticket counters and the
main waiting room of the
station. At the west end of the
waiting room was a multi-
vaulted steel-and-glass concourse with stairs leading from
the concourse down to the
train tracks.

Once the building had been
demolished, the remaining railroad station was confined to a
basement concourse. All the
beauty of the old building was
gone. Train passengers hurried
to get out of the station as
quickly as possible. What had
been lost was much more than
just a building, for public
spaces affect us in very important ways. Anyone passing
through the old Penn Station
could not fail to respond to its
graceful and dignified monumentality or to feel a sense of
pride in its existence.

The loss of this great building, however, did have a positive effect. Its demolition
helped spur the beginning of
the architectural preservation
movement. Today a building
of such architectural importance probably would not be
demolished.

Higher-Order Thinking Skills

Wright has had a pervasive influence
on twentieth-century housing. Ask
the class to find buildings in your
community that reflect Wright's
ideas. Students should support their
choices by references to Wright's
work.

Interdisciplinary Connection

Business: Often major businesses
and corporations own art collections.
Thomas S. Monaghan, owner of
Domino's Pizza, Inc., was attracted at
the age of 12, to the designs of Frank
Lloyd Wright. Monaghan assembled
a major collection of Wright's designs
and furnishings and established The
National Center for the Study of Frank
Lloyd Wright in Ann Arbor, Michigan.
The Domino's Pizza World Headquarters
is designed after the prairie style of
Wright.

• Have students research the collections of other well-known business
families. The Rockefellers, for example,
were instrumental in establishing the
Museum of Modern Art in New York.
(Kress, Getty, Frick and Huntington are
other examples.)

Contextual Information

The Bauhaus School

Gropius directed the Bauhaus School of Art, Applied Arts, and Architecture. The school stressed the use of engineering principles in combination with experimentation and functional and economical design to create architecture and objects that linked humans with the new technical world. Students were encouraged to use their imagination to create design that was free of ornamentation and any nonfunctional shapes, staying honest to the materials. Architecture was to be created by an integration of all the arts.

Bauhaus students worked on mass-produced items to learn how to improve and simplify them. They made prototype models by hand. They learned the characteristics of objects made by hand and studied how these characteristics could be kept when production methods were changed. The goal at the Bauhaus was "to eliminate every drawback of the machine without sacrificing any one of its real advantages. We aimed at realizing standards of excellence, not creating transient novelties."

Schröder House

Gerrit Rietveld's Schröder House (fig.16–6) exemplifies the clean, functional geometric forms advocated by the Dutch De Stijl designers and architects who were led by Mondrian.

• Have students compare Wright's Robie and Kaufmann houses with the Schröder House.

Gerrit Rietveld

(1888–1964)

Many Europeans were influenced by Frank Lloyd Wright and the exciting new ideas he brought to building. A Dutchman, Gerrit Rietveld combined the influence of Wright and a working relationship with the painter Mondrian to create a distinctive modern look in his architecture. The *Schröder House* in Utrecht (fig.16–6), built in the first quarter of the twentieth century, still has great appeal today. Its crisp lines and multiple surfaces look like a Mondrian work in three dimensions.

Walter Gropius

(1883–1969)

and the International Style

After World War I, a style of architecture emerged in Germany, Holland and France called the

16–6 Can you see why this building might be considered a three-dimensional Mondrian painting? Gerrit Rietveld. *Schröder House*, 1924. Utrecht, The Netherlands.

International Style. It was the forerunner of contemporary architecture and the mass production building techniques of today. As a style, it nearly eliminated all ornamentation and avoided the use of natural materials, like wood or stone. Architects sought to produce a structure that appeared light in weight but did not have traditional architectural mass. To achieve the light appearance, flat surfaces and thin walls, they turned to glass. The result was a boxlike structure of steel, reinforced concrete and glass. The new buildings enclosed space instead of creating masses.

Walter Gropius was an early practitioner of the International Style and a powerful influence on twentieth-century art and architecture. In 1919, Gropius headed the Bauhaus. Great teachers from many countries came to the Bauhaus, where they stressed theories of the International Style. The Bauhaus taught more than just architecture. It also stressed the industrial and mechanical art processes as they related to painting, sculpture, crafts, printmaking and other art forms. Students of the Bauhaus influenced art and architecture in many countries for many years.

In 1925, Gropius moved the school from Weimar to Dessau and designed the new buildings himself. The main building (fig.16–7) is a huge glass box with flat planes of concrete and glass. Such gigantic walls of glass were used in construction until the 1970s when the energy crisis caused second thoughts. Less window space would make buildings more energy-efficient. Thus, much architecture of the 1980s used smaller windows and larger areas of masonry or concrete.

16–7 Glass walls were a hallmark of the International Style. Walter Gropius. *Bauhaus*, 1928. Dessau, Germany.

1920
Turkey established

1930
Uruguay wins first World Cup Soccer title

World Cultural Timeline

1921
Iraq established

1932
Saudi Arabia established

Performing Arts Connection

The Bauhaus, Walter Gropius

In 1919, artists, craftspeople and architects in Weimar, Germany, formed a multidisciplinary alliance committed to creating "the building of the future." The Bauhaus workshops were laboratories for experiments in glass, metal, furniture design and weaving that emphasized purity of form and function. Many of the Bauhaus artists also created sets and costumes for the avant-garde theater of the day.

Le Corbusier

(Charles-Edouard Jenneret)
(1887–1965)

Le Corbusier was a Swiss-born architect who grew up on the International Style. One of his earliest buildings, a residence called the *Savoye House* (fig.16–8), clearly shows the simplicity and sense of weightlessness that was possible with concrete and glass.

But Corbusier was one of the first to deviate from modern architectural principles. The concept of *Notre-Dame-du-Haut* (1955) was completely new (fig.16–9). Built on a hilltop near Ronchamp, France, the pilgrimage chapel abandons every aspect of the International Style. Using his favorite construction material, reinforced concrete, he formed an organic sculpture, not a shoe-box building. The floor plan is even irregular. The walls slope, slant and bend while the roof flares, curves and twists as if alive. Wedge-shaped windows are irregular and

of different sizes. Light floods hidden chapels from recessed skylights. Around every interior turn there seems to be a surprise. Built for worship by a small number of townspeople, the interior holds about fifty people. However, the outdoor seating area can accommodate over ten thousand religious travelers.

16–9 Reinforced concrete makes the organic forms of this chapel possible.
Le Corbusier. *Notre-Dame-du-Haut*, 1950–54. Ronchamp, France.

16–8 Views of the sky and surrounding countryside are visible from everywhere in this house. The main (upper) level of the house includes a central open courtyard.
Le Corbusier. *Savoye House*, 1929–1930. Poissy-sur-Seine, France.

Higher-Order Thinking Skills

Ask students to speculate about what it would be like to go to school in the Bauhaus building. How does it compare to their present school?

Multicultural Connection

Native American Architecture

Sometimes, the materials available for architecture dictate the way people manipulate shape, form, space and aesthetics so that structures fit their functions. Native Americans of the subarctic regions of Manitoba and eastern Saskatchewan were heavily dependent upon the bark of the white birch. The importance of birch bark in this area compares with that of bison rawhide in the Plains; it supplied material for wigwam coverings and was

used for other survival needs. Archaeologists have found that sewn birch bark was used for roofing, cache covers, house partitions and small and large containers for at least the last 2,000 years. (For more about Native American architecture see Chapter 4, page 138.)

• Have students research the winter snow houses (igloos) built by the Canadian Inuit and interpret the relationship of form and function in this type of architecture.

Contextual Information

Saarinen

Eero Saarinen's interest in manipulating materials so that his buildings look like huge sculptures was dependent on the use of reinforced concrete. Even the supporting Y-shaped piers, information desk and stairways at the TWA Terminal are sculptural.

Saarinen's father was a successful Finnish architect who came to the United States to become director of Cranbrook Academy in Michigan. Eero studied sculpture in Paris and then architecture at Yale. The result of these two pursuits was that Saarinen was successful in combining his love of sculpture with his architectural designs.

Wright

Wright had an international reputation by the late 1930s, and he received awards and honors from across the world. However, his own country, particularly the architectural profession, was much slower to offer official recognition. The Gold Medal of the American Institute of Architects (an organization Wright never joined) was presented to Wright in 1949, when he was 80 years old. He opened his acceptance speech with: "It's about time!"

Wallace K. Harrison

(1895–1981)

Under the influence of the International Style, American cities (mainly New York, Philadelphia and Chicago at first) became the settings for towering skyscrapers. Wallace K. Harrison's skyscraper was the first that had a simple shaft without changes or set-backs from top to bottom. The *Secretariat Building* of the United Nations in New York (1947–1950) was designed by a firm of architects under Harrison's direction. The building (fig.16–10) has a grid of glass and steel on the wide sides and unbroken marble panels on the ends. All service units, such as elevator machinery, water towers and air-conditioning equipment, are on the roof. These units are hidden from view by the structure's extended walls.

Frank Lloyd Wright

(1867–1959)

Frank Lloyd Wright continued to exert a strong influence on architecture into the second half of the twentieth century. We have seen his work from the earliest part of the century, when he was helping give birth to Modernism. Like other great artists, Wright's work evolved throughout his life. Even at the height of Modernism in the 1950s, he continued to do ground-breaking work. The plan of the *Solomon R. Guggenheim Museum* in New York (fig.16–11) is based on a circle. Inside, the gallery unfolds like a spiral. The museum was completed only after much battling with officials. It was acclaimed only after tremendous initial criticism upon its opening.

16–11 The interior of this museum is a continuous spiral with no clear delineation of levels. Frank Lloyd Wright. *Solomon R. Guggenheim Museum,* 1956–1959. New York.

Skidmore, Owings and Merrill

(b.1939)

Gordon Bunshaft was the chief designer for the architectural firm Skidmore, Owings and Merrill. Bunshaft was responsible for the next architectural development: the all-glass exterior of the *Lever House* (1951–52) in New York (fig.16–12). Like Gothic architecture, the design seems to defy gravity. The reflective glass tower and the two-story horizontal unit are supported by pylons above the street level. Foot traffic circulates from the pylons into a partially shaded open court. The structure itself occupies only about half of the total site, leaving room for the pleasant court. The court and space for foot traffic eliminate the feeling of congestion and crowdedness found in many urban streets. Sheathed in green-tinted glass, the Lever House reflects clouds, sky, sun and the surrounding environment. It was so successful in appearance and function that it became the model for hundreds of glass and metal skyscrapers (including Mies van der Rohe's Seagram Building) built around the world during the following quarter of a century.

16–10 The service equipment for this building is placed on the roof where it was out of the way. In the late 1940s and early 1950s, this was a new idea in architecture. Wallace K. Harrison. *United Nations Secretariat Building,* 1947–1950. New York.

Materials and Techniques

Wright was responsible for a number of innovations in architectural design and construction. Very early in his career, he designed the first office building (Larkin Building, Buffalo, 1904, now demolished) that incorporated air conditioning, double-glass windows, all-glass doors and metal furniture.

16–13 What connections do you see between the form of this terminal and its function?
Eero Saarinen. *Trans World Airlines Terminal, John F. Kennedy International Airport*, 1962. New York.

16–12 Bunshaft developed a way to create a building with an all-glass exterior. Lever House influenced architecture for years—until the cost of energy became too high.
Gordon Bunshaft and Skidmore, Owings and Merrill. *Lever House*, 1951–1952. New York.

Eero Saarinen

(1910–1961)

Eero Saarinen was involved in the construction of many beautiful structures. But his design of several air terminals alone would be enough to make him important. Before Saarinen, airport facilities failed to equal in quality and design the advances made in the aircraft themselves. Saarinen's sculptured, organic structures were the exception. They almost seem capable of flight themselves. The *Trans World Airlines Terminal* (fig.16–13) in New York (1962) has curves that flow like air currents and suggest cloud shapes in their sculptural contours.

His magnificent terminal for *Dulles International Airport* (fig.16–14) outside Washington, DC, (1962) makes use of mobile lounges to get passengers to planes. In the structure, there is nothing left of traditional building design. Sixteen

pairs of slanting concrete pillars support the enormous, hammock-shaped roof, which tilts to one side. No interior supports mar the vast enclosed space. With great window walls, the roof seems suspended from the sky. The entire building has a floating appearance. Both the Dulles and TWA air terminals are dynamic structures, perfectly

16–14 In designing this terminal, Saarinen also solved practical problems such as transporting passengers directly to the plane through mobile lounges.
Eero Saarinen. *Dulles International Airport Terminal Building*, 1962. Washington, DC.

Higher-Order Thinking Skills

Instruct students to compare Lever House (fig.16–12) to Chartres Cathedral (fig.8–15), where glass also played an important role. Ask how the role of glass is similar and different in these two buildings. Students should consider practical and aesthetic concerns, as well as the "meaning" of the glass in each building.

Inquiry

If possible, have students visit a local architectural firm to ascertain the types of buildings that the firm specializes in. They might also ask questions about the education and training of the firm's architects, the tools and materials of the profession, the process of designing and building a structure, and the challenges of finding and working with clients. Have students list several local buildings that the firm has designed and to follow up by visiting one or more of those buildings.

16–15 The reflecting pools mirror the rhythm of the vaulted roof and help to create an oasis for art. Louis I. Kahn. *Kimbell Art Museum*, 1966–1972. Fort Worth, Texas.

16–16 The geodesic dome, made of inexpensive materials which can be taken apart and reconstructed, is the signature structure of Buckminster Fuller. R. Buckminster Fuller. *United States Pavilion, Expo 67*, 1967. Montreal, Canada.

Contextual Information

Fuller

R. Buckminster Fuller was a philosopher, a poet, an architect and an engineer. He was a twentieth-century "Renaissance" man who thought that architecture could solve most of the world's problems. His earlier inventions included the Dymaxion house, an inexpensive, prefabricated, factory-assembled enclosure that was suspended from a central pole. Fuller claimed that he came up with the idea for the geodesic dome by studying dandelions.

Kahn

Louis Kahn's favorite building was the Baths of Caracalla in Rome, and it was his goal to create "very archaic looking buildings" with the solid chunky walls and long barrel vaults of ancient Roman architecture.

Kahn built very few important buildings until he was in his fifties, but his ideas and philosophy were passed on to his Yale students whose buildings are all over the world. Kahn liked to use concrete and was concerned about how sunlight and shadows affected the appearance of every part of his buildings. He used the "servant" space (duct work, air conditioning, etc.) to create large towers and arches, but the people who had to work in the buildings hated the small awkward spaces left for their work areas.

The Pompidou Center

The Georges Pompidou National Center of Art and Culture, which opened in 1977, is known as the "Beaubourg." Every utility is fully exposed: pipes, ducts and tubes are brightly color-coded according to

Louis I. Kahn

(1901–1974)

Louis I. Kahn was an admirer of Le Corbusier and studied his work intensively. However, Kahn devised his own original solutions to architectural problems and had a strong influence on his contemporaries. One of his finest designs (and also his last) was the *Kimbell Art Museum* (fig.16–15) in Fort Worth, Texas (1972). The main entrance, shown here, is a tree-filled patio flanked by two open arched vaults and reflecting pools. Vaults are used to roof the entire structure. They provide a powerful sense of unity throughout. Natural light is admitted through long slits located in the vaults. The light is diffused inside by a series of baffles (adjustable panels that deflect light). The baffles provide superior lighting for the paintings. Designed to hold works of art, the structure is a work of art itself.

R. Buckminster Fuller

(1895–1983)

R. Buckminster Fuller sought to make use of inexpensive, easily manufactured materials in his constructions. Fuller is best known for his **geodesic** dome, like the innovative *United States Pavilion* at Expo 67 in Montreal (fig.16–16). Geodesic refers to a form of solid geometry that is the basis for structures built of interlocking polygons. Much of the dome in Montreal was destroyed by a fire. Originally it was a bubble 170 feet high and 258 feet in diameter. Thick struts, joined with knot joints, carried the weight and held up an inner net on which 2000 acrylic caps were mounted. The interior climate was controlled by motors at the joints which reacted automatically to sunlight. The motors shifted blinds and controlled the ventilating system.

their function. In the building are art galleries; a center for industrial design; a public library; science, music and conference rooms; research facilities and a restaurant.

Interdisciplinary Connection

Science: Challenge students to locate a drawing of a recently discovered class of carbon molecules called fullerenes, which possess some of the same qualities of stability and symmetry as the shapes that Buckminster Fuller used.

Moshe Safdie
(b.1938)

Working mostly in his native Israel, Moshe Safdie has created some of the most unique and practical urban dwelling units yet conceived. Safdie created the dramatic structure called *Habitat* (fig.16–17) for Expo 67 in Montreal. Habitat was a new concept in housing. Mass-produced, precast, one-piece concrete units (each a complete apartment) were transported to the sight. They were then stacked like gigantic building blocks by huge cranes. The units came in different sizes and different interior arrangements. Therefore, the uniformity of usual apartments was avoided. Each floor has a play area for children. It is remarkable how much this contemporary structure resembles the earliest towns of Mesopotamia or the early pueblos of the Southwestern United States.

16–17 Each apartment is a ready-made module that can be stacked in a number of ways. Safdie has been very inventive in his efforts to design workable urban housing.
Moshe Safdie. *Habitat*, 1967. Montreal, Canada.

Renzo Piano
(b.1937)
and Richard Rogers
(b.1933)

The talk of the town—and the world—when it was built in the 1970s, the *Georges Pompidou National Center of Art and Culture* (fig.16–c) in Paris is the creation of Renzo Piano and Richard Rogers. It turns the functional style on its head by turning it inside out. A five-story escalator dominates the exterior along with the innards of the mechanical systems of the building (fig. 16–18). Glass walls enclose the open expanse of gallery and office space. The building still adheres to Modernist ideas, but with a visually sensational twist.

16–18 The exterior placement and lively coloring of the mechanical systems of this building suprise the viewer. They also make the viewer realize the amount of equipment, normally hidden, that is required to make a large building function.
Renzo Piano and Richard Rogers. *Georges Pompidou National Center of Art and Culture*. exterior section, (See fig.16–c).

Higher-Order Thinking Skills

Ask students to discuss the advantages and disadvantages of living and working in geodesic-dome structures. Students can sketch floor plans to visualize the placement of furniture, access routes (doors and halls) and windows in both rectangular and circular spaces.

Multicultural Connection
Nomadic Architecture

Architectural structures are designed and built for a variety of purposes, and in a variety of forms. They are built to glorify both people and their gods, to record historical information, to serve as fortifications and shelters, and to be used for rituals and ceremonies. They express themes that define where and how we live.

Some nomadic peoples in Iran and Afghanistan use long strips of woven cloth to cover the frames of their traditional yurt (tent). These woven strips, called kilims, are decorated with geometric patterns, the Tree of Life, eyes, hands, birds, animals and other symbolic images. The roaming lifestyle of these people did not permit the accumulation of material possessions. Thus, the yurt not only protected them from the elements and was conducive to their lifestyle, but was decorative as well.

Contextual Information

Pei

I. M. Pei was born in Canton, China, and came to the United States to enter M.I.T. at the age of 21. He received his architecture degree at Harvard when Gropius was teaching there.

• Challenge students to look at Pei's architecture to find any influence of Gropius' teaching. Have them describe what they find. (building materials, clean lines, no decoration, white surface)

Philip Johnson
(b.1906)
and John Burgee
(b.1933)

As the principles of an architectural firm, Philip Johnson and John Burgee were responsible for some of the most advanced thinking in major projects in the country. Instead of simply designing glass boxes, they used different solutions for different clients. *Pennzoil Place* (fig.16–19) in Houston (1976) is a dramatic example of this new direction. The two towers are separated by a ten-foot space and their tops are tapered at forty-five degrees. The glass wedge at the bottom provides

a gigantic lobby that is well-lighted, but climatically controlled. The ten-foot slit of air space between the towers changes as one moves around the building to view it. The dark color, together with the unique shapes, produce a daring new outline on the Houston skyline. Pennzoil Place is like a gigantic minimal sculpture.

Another Johnson and Burgee masterpiece is the towering *I.D.S. Center* (fig.16–20) in Minneapolis (1972). Again, the usual box form was avoided. The glass shaft rises like a molded sculpture above the city. The vertical setbacks alter the regularity of the surface and add

dramatic shadows and sharp contrasts. The glass-and-steel-covered courtyard allows light to enter the pedestrian levels and brings the outdoors inside all during the year, even in coldest winter.

16–20 Compare this building to Lever House.
Philip Johnson/John Burgee. *I.D.S. Center*, 1972. Minneapolis, Minnesota.

16–19 What effect do you think reflective glass buildings of this size might have on the surrounding buildings and streets at the height of summer in Houston?
Philip Johnson/John Burgee. *Pennzoil Place*, 1976. Houston, Texas.

16–22 This pyramid, like the one in Washington, DC, at the National Gallery of Art, lets light in and helps define the extensive underground space that has been added to the museum.
I. M. Pei. *Addition to the Louvre*, 1988. Paris.

Performing Arts Connection

Playing a Facade: The Sound of Architecture

Have students "map" the rhythms of architectural facades by placing blank music paper over images of buildings and drawing notes that follow their contours. Have them begin with a simple symmetrical structure such as the *East Building of the National Gallery of Art* (fig.16–21). Then have students progress to more complex facades, like

Le Corbusier's *Notre-Dame-du-Haut* (fig.16–9), R. Buckminster Fuller's *United States Pavilion at Expo 67* (fig.16–16) or any others that catch their fancy. Have students hum their facade "tunes" and examine if there are any parallels between what they see and what they hear.

I. M. Pei

(b.1917)

I. M. Pei has designed many hotels and government structures in America. One of his most dramatic buildings is the *East Building of the National Gallery* (fig.16–21) in Washington, DC (1978). Built to house part of the nation's great collection of art as well as a huge research library, the building occupies a wedge-shaped site on the Mall in Washington. The white marble structure shows a completely different face in each direction. One wall has no windows. Other walls have all windows. The huge pie-shaped section on the right rises like a white sliver when viewed from certain angles.

The solid, faceted planes do not prepare one for the marvelous open spaces inside. A mammoth skylight allows natural light to flood the interior. From various angles, one can look out at the wide vistas of the Mall and government buildings. The interior space is enhanced by sculptures and paintings prepared specifically by the artists for the spaces where they are located.

The sculptural forms in the foreground of the photograph are part of a fountain of twenty-four jets and a skylight system for the underground

concourse. The concourse connects the East Building with the older structure of the National Gallery. The architecture is a perfect relationship between the form of the structure and its intended function.

Pei was also commissioned to design an addition to the Louvre Museum (fig.16–22) in France. Based on the pyramid shape, the building, like Frank Lloyd Wright's Guggenheim Museum, was greeted with dismay and criticism when it was first built. Gradually the French have grown to appreciate the

16–21 Would you be surprised to learn that the inside of this building is flooded with natural light?
I. M. Pei. *East Building, National Gallery of Art.* 1978. Exterior view. Washington DC.

structure. Today, the Parisians are proud of this modern landmark in their city.

Pei has remained a Modernist throughout his career. His most current work continues to reflect the basic tenets of the movement and is clear proof of the enduring importance of this style even as other architectural trends evolve.

Lesson 16.1 Review

1 What technology did twentieth-century architects use to design and build skyscrapers?
2 Which Chicago building marked the beginning of modern architecture in the United States? When was this built?
3 Define *cantilevered*. Give an example of a cantilevered feature in architecture.
4 Name two buildings whose design was influenced by Mondrian?
5 What material did Le Corbusier use to construct Notre-Dame-du-Haut? How does this building vary from International Style structures?
6 Who designed the Guggenheim Museum in New York City? How is it different from the buildings surrounding it?
7 Describe the exterior of the Lever House in New York. Who designed this building?
8 How does the design of both Transworld Airlines Terminal in New York City and Dulles International Airport suggest their use or connection with flight? Who designed these buildings?
9 How is the Pompidou Center in Paris turned inside out?

Lesson 16.1 Review Answers

1 Steel and metal frame construction
2 Carson Pirie Scott Department Store, 1901
3 A horizontal projection, such as a canopy, balcony or beam, is cantilevered if it is secured at only one point. It is balanced on a fulcrum. Frank Lloyd Wright created cantilevered roofs in the Robie House in Chicago so that they seem to float without supports. In the Kaufmann House at Bear Run, Pennsylvania, Wright cantilevered terraces over a stream and waterfall.
4 Rietveld's Schröder House in Utrecht and Mies van der Rohe's Lakeshore Apartments
5 Le Corbusier used reinforced concrete to construct Notre-Dame-du-Haut which is organic in shape with rounded forms rather than an International-style box shape.
6 Frank Lloyd Wright designed the Guggenheim Museum, which is a cylinder surrounded by traditional rectangular buildings.
7 All-glass exterior. Gordon Bunshaft was the chief designer for the architectural firm of Skidmore, Owings and Merill who built the Lever House.
8 Eero Saarinen designed both of these terminals which have the look of being capable of flight themselves. The Trans World Airline terminal has curves that flow like air currents and sculpturally suggest cloud shapes. The Dulles terminal appears to float with huge windows and a roof that seems suspended from the sky.
9 A five-story elevator is placed on the outside of the building along with the mechanical systems which are usually concealed in traditional buildings.

Lesson 16.2

Post-Modern architects grew tired of the geometric rigidity and impersonality of the earlier period. Instead, they embraced an endless variety of references, mixing history, popular expression, decoration and metaphor.

Warm-up

Ask students to guess—without looking at the caption—what function the building in fig.16–25 was created for. What about its architectural elements, color and location indicates that the site is not a science or high-tech communications plant? What industry might be associated with the enormous fanciful swans and shells that sit on top of a colorful facade? After students examine the caption, ask them what other decorative elements they might have added or substituted to express the character of the Disney World hotel. Share that Michael Graves' wit, vibrancy and symbolism exemplify the Post-Modern movement.

Objectives

Students should be able to:

Explain that Post-Modernism rejected the steel and glass-box ideal of the previous generation.

Understand how Post-Modern architects did not confine themselves to one particular style but were deliberately eclectic in their approach.

16.2 Post-Modernism

I N THE 1960S AND 1970S, a reaction to Modernism's pure line and uncluttered space set in. A new architectural surge called Post-Modernism emerged. Post-Modern architects shunned the glass-box ideal and began treating materials and ideals with daring and personal conviction. Post-Modern architects wanted a more vibrant and eclectic form, turning to symbolism and historical periods like Classicism. However, the new architectural style still retained its modern elements, particularly its wit, abstraction and irony.

The Modernists concentrated on function and technology. Their designs were mostly hard-edged and impersonal, and depended on right-angle geometry. Post-Modernism, on the other hand, has no fixed rules and goes for a mixture of history, popular expression, decoration and metaphor. The Post-Modernists consider the site of a building. They strive to design buildings that work in harmony with the site and its direct and indirect environment. They consider how the building will relate to the history that shaped the locale. They listen carefully to the client's specific needs.

Modernist dogma has flown out of the window to be replaced by the eclectic designs of architects like Venturi, Jahn, Johnson, Burgee and Graves.

Key Notes

- In the 1960s and 1970s, there is a reaction to the impersonality and purity of Modernism.
- Post-Modernism embraces history, symbolism, vivid ornamentation and eclecticism.

16–25 Are you surprised to learn that this is a hotel complex? Why is it appropriate for its setting?
Michael Graves. *Walt Disney World Swan Hotel,* 1989. Orlando, Florida.

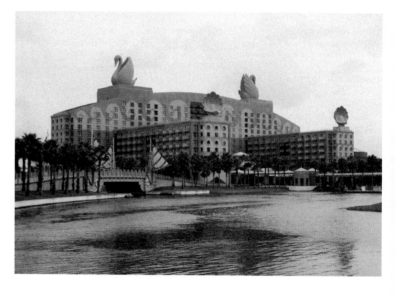

Special Feature
Michael Graves

(b.1934)

One of the leaders of Post-Modernism in the United States is Michael Graves. No other Post-Modernist architect has understood as much about Classical forms as Graves, or used them to create such strange and powerful new forms. Graves has often said that he designs as if he were a child, and the *Public Services Building* in Portland, Oregon, bears this out (fig.16–23). The Public Services Building (1980–83) is considered by many architects to be the first important monument to Post-Modernism.

On first look, the building resembles a child's colorful construction. It comprises simple blocks and very simplified classic forms. Graves also pays no heed to the usual scale rela-

Teach

Art History/Criticism: Instruct students to identify the Classical elements that Graves incorporates into his structures (figs.16–23, 16–24, 16–25). (The biographical sketch on pages 536 and 537 will help them if they need assistance.) Have students imagine being Classical architects from ancient Greece and Rome (see Chapter 6) on a visit to contemporary America. Ask them to describe their reactions to Graves' work.

- Are they impressed or appalled at his selection and alteration of the Classical elements?

- How do their own ancient buildings support their responses to his buildings?

Aesthetics/Criticism: Have students describe how the images in Lesson 16.2 reveal Post-Modernism's diverse approaches and yet also reflect each architect's personal conviction and daring.

- Which building do they find most outrageous and why?

- Why would they or would they not want to live or work in the structure?

16–23 Post-Modern architects often use a variety of historical styles, materials and colors on a single building.
Michael Graves. *Public Services Building*, 1980–1983. Portland, Oregon.

16–24 This buiding is located in Southern California. What impact has the climate had on its design?
Michael Graves, *Public Library of San Juan Capistrano*, Courtyard, detail of fig.16–b.

Contextual Information

Public Services Building

Grave's Public Services Building (fig.16–23) has been a controversial structure. It has been called a "jukebox," "dangerous," "a marzipan monstrosity," and "better fit for Las Vegas." Despite this criticism, Graves received the Honor Award for Design from the American Institute of Architects for this building.

Higher-Order Thinking Skills

Ask students to select a Classical building to compare to one of Michael Graves' buildings. Their writings or discussions should include their reasons for their choices.

tionships, yet produces a marvelously sophisticated design. Graves won the commission over pure Modernists. When the purists managed to get his sculpture of civic virtue removed from over the entrance, it was restored due to popular demand.

The construction begins as a three-storied stepped base and is surmounted by twelve stories filled with a grid of small windows. In the center of the main facade are huge mirror-glass windows. The massive windows are surrounded by a gigantic maroon-colored twentieth-century version of classical elements. The design is topped by an enormous keystone. The Portland building is a civic building that

embodies the dignity of the past in a completely original and present way.

The *Public Library of San Juan Capistrano*, California, is another example of Michael Graves's particular style of architecture (fig.16–b). Guidelines set by the town ordinance required new architecture to follow the indigenous Spanish mission style. As you can see, the guidelines have been perfectly carried out, but with a Post-Modern touch.

The organization of the building around a courtyard (fig.16–24) fits the Spanish style and allows light from the courtyard to filter into the rooms. At the heart of the complex, the courtyard is also a very restful

place to read. The courtyard includes a stream of water that issues from the upper levels of the building. The idea here is that water, like reading, provides nourishment.

For visitors to Disney World, a familiar sight is the *Walt Disney World Swan Hotel* (fig.16–25) and its companion, *the Dolphin Hotel*. With these buildings, Graves continues to adhere to classic forms, but he embellishes them—inside and out—with an abundance of color and exuberant decoration. The humor and liveliness of these hotels delight the viewer and certainly are in keeping with the atmosphere of the nearby theme park.

Evaluate

Ask students if Modernism or Post-Modernism had stricter rules and aesthetic principles. Instruct students to use the images in lessons 16.1 and 16.2 to defend their judgment.

Have students cite specifically how Michael Graves' work illustrates his conviction that he designs as if he were a child. (Have them review the information on pages 536 and 537, if necessary.)

• Ask if his style would be appropriate for all types of commissions.

• Ask students what type of public or private building they would hire Graves for and for what type they would hire another architect.

• If they were Graves, what type of commission might they refuse and why?

Reteach

Ask students to consider how Graves' incorporation of Classical architectural elements affects the status of his buildings. Are students impressed with his visual quotes of the past and the manner in which he makes something completely new with them, or do they think it degrades the quality of the older style? Have students debate the issue.

Contextual Information
Venturi

Venturi studied architecture at Princeton and worked in the offices of Saarinen and Kahn before establishing his own firm in Philadelphia. Although he studied with Kahn, Venturi developed a theory that architecture should use ideas from everyday environment, such as from fast-food restaurants, Las Vegas neon signs, and advertisements. Indeed, Venturi and his wife, Denise Scott Brown, use decorative aspects of pop and commercial design.

16–26 Venturi believes it is important to study the everyday architecture of the United States.
Venturi, Scott Brown and Associates, Inc., *Best Products Company Catalog Showroom*, 1978. McNay Art Museum.

Robert Venturi
(b.1925)
Denise Scott Brown
(b.1931)

Proclaiming that "Less is a bore," Robert Venturi is the architect who actually led the way to the Post-Modern movement. In his book *Complexity and Contradiction in Architecture* (1966), Venturi points out that much of the great architecture of the past was not simple and classic, but elaborate and complex. Many architects agreed with Venturi, and the premiere position of Modernism began to erode.

Throughout his career, Venturi has been an avant-garde designer and thinker. In partnership with his wife, Denise Scott Brown, he fostered the notion that the commonplace, or vernacular, architecture of the United States may be as important to study as the great cathedrals of medieval Europe and monuments of ancient Greece and Rome.

16–27 Many were surprised to learn that the commission for this addition to the National Gallery of London was won by Venturi. Previously, Venturi had few major commissions, although his theory and writings were very influential.
Venturi, Scott Brown, Rauch and Associates, Inc., *Sainsbury Wing, National Gallery*, 1991, London.

Although criticized for their views, Venturi and Scott Brown have succeeded in bringing these ideas to their commissions. A store they designed for the *Best Products Company* (fig.16–26) has a plain, long, rectangular facade that faces a conventional asphalt parking lot. However, the facade is punctuated by giant, colorful flowers.

Despite their influential writings, it was not until 1986 that Venturi and Scott Brown, with their partner,

John Rauch, won a major commission. It was the contract for the *Sainsbury Wing*, an addition to London's National Gallery (fig.16–27). The building is positioned on one of the world's best-known urban spaces, Trafalgar Square. The extension to England's greatest museum brought tremendous public scrutiny. It is noteworthy for its restrained, yet distinctive, appearance. The serene galleries, which house the museum's Early Renaissance collection, are filled with abundant—but indirect—natural light. The architectural elements, modern echoes of Brunelleschi, are strong and simple. They provide a most appropriate setting for the collection.

1958
First Chinese TV station begins broadcasting

1969
Navajo Community College, the first tribally established college, opens in Arizona

World Cultural Timeline

1964
160 mph train begins running in Japan

1970
First Chinese space satellite

Window in Time

Architectural Preservation

In the rush to embrace the new, buildings of historical importance and beauty have been torn down indiscriminately. Cities the world over saw and lost architecture of all styles. As look-alike skyscrapers replaced existing buildings, cities quickly lost their individual character. Today, however, the emphasis is on architectural preservation and restoration.

Architectural preservation takes several forms. In cities that once had a strong manufacturing base, old factories have been converted into shopping areas and restaurants. Projects like the Nicollet Mall in Minneapolis preserve existing architecture and often incorporate some new structures in the process.

A remarkable example of preservation is the recently restored *El Capitan Theater* in Los Angeles. El Capitan is one of the few remaining ornate movie theaters that were built in the 1930s. The theater, part of a six-floor office building, stands just across Hollywood Boulevard from the more famous Mann's Chinese Theater. El Capitan was originally designed for live performances in 1926 by G. Albert Lansburgh. In typical twenties style, it was a combination of Spanish Baroque, Moorish and East Indian elements.

El Capitan Theater, Los Angeles, view of marquis.

In 1941, El Capitan was renamed the Paramount and converted into a motion-picture house. During this conversion, much of the original architecture was concealed with dropped ceilings and corrugated plaster. In the process, balcony boxes and a pair of Baroque columns were removed.

However, in 1984, Pacific Theaters, Paramount's operator, and Buena Vista Pictures, the distribution arm of Disney, recognized the theater's potential. Despite its location in a rundown neighborhood, an $8.65 million restoration was carried out by architects Fields & Devereaux. The architects consulted with organizations as diverse as the National Parks Service, the Community Redevelopment Agency and local homeowner associations.

Careful restoration and preservation has returned the El Capitan to its original form. Three curtains conceal the El Capitan's 42- by 20-foot screen and they open and close for each film. A new THX-certified sound system blares "Hooray for Hollywood" between performances. Once in this theater, all the old magic of going to the movies returns.

The Helmsley Palace Hotel complex (1980) in New York City had to work with another kind of problem. The Villard House, an 1882 townhouse and designated historical landmark, stood on the site needed for the new complex. Because the Villard House could not be moved or destroyed, the architects incorporated the house into their master plan. Entrance to the luxury 1050-room hotel-apartment tower is now through the elegant historic house. The bronze and glass tower forms a dramatic backdrop for the Villard House. Although nearly 100 years separates the two constructions, each is enhanced by the other.

El Capitan Theater, Los Angeles, view of lobby.

Higher-Order Thinking Skills

Historic preservation and restoration often places people on opposite sides of issues relating to development and modernization. Ask students if they feel that old buildings should be preserved. Why? Have the class create guidelines for making decisions about restoration or demolition.

Inquiry

The National Historic Preservation Act of 1966 was a landmark piece of legislation in the historic preservation movement. Many important historic buildings had been demolished during the early 1960s. The outcry against this thoughtless destruction reached its peak with the demolition of Pennsylvania Station in New York City. (See sidelight on page 527).

The National Historic Preservation Act created a National Register of Historic Places. The properties on this list are considered important historically and are protected by law from destruction and random alteration. In general, a property must be more than fifty years old to appear on the register, although it is possible to include a newer structure if it receives an exemption because of its importance.

Ask students to determine if any local buildings are on the register. (If no local buildings appear on it, have students research important buildings in the state to determine if they are on the register.) In the process of their investigation students should ascertain why the buildings were placed on the register.

Contextual Information

Johnson

Philip Johnson became an architect relatively late in life, at 37 years of age. Prior to practicing architecture, he had been a critic, an author and the director of the architecture department at the Museum of Modern Art in New York. It was Johnson who organized the first American visits of Mies van der Rohe and Le Corbusier. Independently wealthy, Johnson in 1930 commissioned Mies to design his New York City apartment.

The *AT&T Corporate Headquarters* (fig.16–28) was criticized as "lollipop modern" and praised for its use of a traditional design. Its exterior is a return to stone (pink granite), and it has a broken-pediment top similar to eighteenth-century Chippendale furniture.

Philip Johnson
(b.1906)
John Burgee
(b.1933)

Both Johnson and his partner, John Burgee, have maintained their influence through many decades of twentieth-century architecture right into the Post-Modern era. In New York City, their *AT&T Corporate Headquarters* (now Sony) is a thirty-seven-story pink granite building, topped with a distinctive broken pediment (fig.16–28). The latter has been referred to by critics as "Chippendale" because they believed it was reminiscent of the famous early American furniture

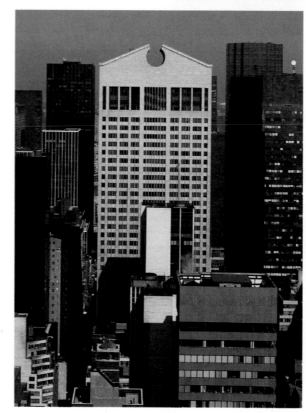

16–29 Why was the reference to Gothic architecture such an appropriate choice for this building?
John Burgee Architects with Philip Johnson. *PPG Place*, 1984. Pittsburgh.

style. The entrance to the building is through a six-story arch and colonnaded base. The ceiling of the monumental lobby is one hundred feet high.

PPG Place (fig.16–29) in Pittsburgh is a Gothic-styled tower in glass. The design is an appropriate reflection of the company's principal product—glass—and its longevity in the industry. The task of adapting monolithic stone construction to glass was carried off with style and success. All of Johnson and Burgee's buildings reflect something about their clients. At the same time, the buildings are an individualized approach to architectural excellence.

16–28 The distinctive profile of the top of this building makes it recognizable from many miles away.
John Burgee Architects with Philip Johnson. *AT&T Corporate Headquarters*, 1985. New York.

Cooperative Learning

Divide students into small groups and assign each group a historical architectural period. Review the examples in this chapter and discuss the historical influences seen in many of these buildings. Ask each group to come up with ideas about how their assigned period could be the next important influence in contemporary architecture. Remind students to consider that historical ideas are often incorporated with contemporary ideas. Groups can draw or describe their ideas and make a case for their predictions.

Helmut Jahn

(b.1940)

Helmut Jahn is responsible for constructing the most dynamic terminal to be found at Chicago's O'Hare International Airport. Large glassed spaces bring light and provide a sense of constant movement to the *United Airlines Terminal* (fig.16–30). The long route from gateway to baggage claim is made less boring by walkways with cheerful blinking neon lights and pleasant chiming sounds. The lights and sounds are activated by the movement of passersby.

Jahn also has designed several skyscrapers in major American cities. In New York, *750 Lexington Avenue* (fig.16–31) is distinctive for its combination of forms stacked one upon the other. There is no doubt that eclecticism is one of the few constants in Post-Modern architecture.

16–31 Do you find the variation in form in this building appealing? Or do you prefer the regularity of the Seagram Building and the Lever House?
Helmut Jahn, *750 Lexington Avenue*, 1989. New York.

16–30 Neon light sculpture and sound, which are activated by passersby, make the journey from airplane to baggage claim rather enjoyable.
Helmut Jahn. *United Airlines Terminal*, 1987. O'Hare International Airport, Chicago.

Higher-Order Thinking Skills

Ask students if murals and sequences of colored lights like those that Jahn did for O'Hare International Airport (fig.16–30) would be a good addition to the halls of their school. Have students defend their opinions.

Contextual Information

Gehry

Frank Gehry worked in his father's hardware store as a teenager and brought home shavings and pieces of wood that he and his grandmother used to build futuristic cities. Eventually, his college ceramics instructor encouraged him to enter the architecture program. Because of his use of shapes and space, much of Gehry's architecture can be described as large outdoor sculpture.

The Temporary Contemporary

The Museum of Contemporary Art in Los Angeles has another facility besides the building designed by Isozaki. The Temporary Contemporary was opened in the fall of 1983 as an interim exhibition space while the new museum was being designed and built. The temporary space originally had been a hardware store, warehouse and, finally, a parking garage. It was Frank O. Gehry who designed the temporary space. The people of Los Angeles were so taken with it, that the museum made the decision to release the space through the year 2038, thus making it somewhat more than temporary (though it still retains its name, The Temporary Contemporary).

Frank O. Gehry

(b.1929)

Frank O. Gehry and Associates of Venice, California, design buildings to capture the essence of their purpose, yet they also convey a certain wittiness. Gehry's *California Aerospace Museum* (fig.16–32) certainly reflects the building's function. Angles and planes barely seem to contain the dynamic action that

the word *aerospace* implies (fig. 16–d). Its interior spaces are contained and intimate, but the overall structure is bursting with energy.

A more recent commission of Gehry's, the *Frederick R. Weisman Museum* (fig.16–33), places all of its expressive emphasis on its stainless steel facade. The remainder of the building is strictly rectangular in shape and offers an ideal space in which to exhibit works of art.

16–32 How does the form of this building express its purpose?
Frank O. Gehry & Associates. *California Aerospace Museum*, 1984. Los Angeles.

16–33 Gehry has designed the main body of this building to be an ordinary rectangle. Why do you think this form would be preferred by the museum's curators?
Frank O. Gehry & Associates. *Frederick R. Weisman Museum*, 1993. University of Minnesota, Minneapolis.

1975 First Indian space satellite	1979 Japanese Maglev test train sets speed record at 321.2 mph	1984 Bishop Desmond Tutu of South Africa receives Nobel Peace Prize

World Cultural Timeline

1976 Aboriginal Land Rights Act gives greater rights to native Australians	1979 Egyptian-Israeli peace accord signed	1997 Hong Kong reverts from a British to a Chinese territory

Cooperative Learning

Divide the class into two groups and have each student in one group imagine being an architect from Lesson 16.2 whose style he or she particularly likes. Ask students to submit quickly sketched Post-Modern designs for a new twenty-first-century school. Have the second group act as the jury committee.

• What considerations will they take into account in choosing a winner?

• How will each architect's proposed style, scale, materials and relationship to the environment affect their opinions?

• You may wish to have the entire class build a scale model of the selected building and present it to the principal and other school officials for feedback. What objections or observations did these officials make that had not previously occurred to students?

Arata Isozaki

(b.1931)

Headquartered in Tokyo, the firm of Arata Isozaki and Associates has designed buildings in Asia, Europe and North America. The *Museum of Contemporary Art* in Los Angeles (fig.16–34) was Isozaki's first major job outside of Japan. Situated on a narrow site in downtown Los Angeles, the commission was difficult. The requirements of the client and neighboring commercial buildings almost proved the project's undoing. However, Isozaki solved his site problem by clustering the galleries around a sunken courtyard. Solid geometric forms are relieved by French curves. These contrasting elements entice the eye to roam continuously across the structure and absorb its detail.

C.A.D.

Computer-Aided Design

Everything that people make, whether it be a building, an automobile or a picture, has to be designed. Today, many designs are completed with the help of computer programs called CAD, or computer-aided design. Computers speed up the design process by enabling designers to try out many more ideas than before, all on the screen. CAD can

Screen from a CAD perspective

16–34 **Difficulties with neighbors in surrounding buildings led Isozaki to organize the museum galleries around a sunken courtyard. This design prevented the building from making a noticeable impact on the area and kept its neighbors happy.**
Arata Isozaki and Associates. *Museum of Contemporary Art*. 1986. Los Angeles.

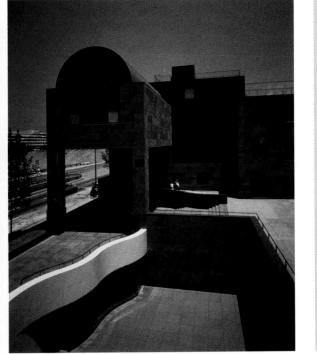

also quickly find answers to problems that once took a long time to solve.

CAD programs on desktop computers have replaced the drawing board completely in many industries. One software program can produce full-color or black-and-white graphics in seconds. Another allows three-dimensional models to be constructed on the computer screen and rotated in any direction so that all sides can be seen. A program can also plot the way in which heat or electricity will flow through a structure. The computer can calculate the amount of material needed for construction and how much it will cost to make.

An architect can draw a single plan and elevation of a building and the computer will carry out calculations to produce different elevations from the same set of measurements. For something like a house or bridge, it can calculate stresses and work out whether the design is strong enough. A designer can also zoom in on a section of a design, such as the floor plan of a house, to work more closely on part of it. CAD has cut down immeasurably on the time that used to be needed to produce any design, as well as on the error factor.

Higher-Order Thinking Skills

Isozaki's design for the Museum of Contemporary Art in Los Angeles had to meet the requirements of the client and its neighbors. Ask students whether neighbors, either commercial or residential, should have a say in the design of new structures.

Higher-Order Thinking Skills

As an effort to keep new structures from overshadowing existing buildings and important monuments, some communities, such as Washington, DC, have restrictions on the height of new buildings. Such laws have a side effect of raising rents because the amount of available space in desirable areas becomes limited. Ask students whether the aesthetics of the community as a whole should be allowed to override choices for the individual builder.

Lesson 16.2 Review Answers

1 The International Style was focused on function and technology with buildings that were hard-edged, impersonal and emphasized right angles. Post-Modern architecture has no fixed rules and mixes history, popular expression, decoration, metaphor and ecological considerations.

2 The Public Services Building in Portland, Oregon

3 Mies van der Rohe's buildings reflected the International Style—glass and steel boxes with minimal decoration and no humor or reference to classical Greek and Roman architecture. Graves' buildings display a sense of humor, elements completely out of traditional scale, and include classical architectural features.

The Public Services Building in Portland resembles a colorful toy construction with simple blocks and classic forms. A three-story base supports a twelve-story grid of small windows. Huge mirror-glass windows surrounded by a gigantic maroon-colored twentieth-century adaptation of classical elements are in the center of the main facade. An enormous keystone tops the design.

The Public Library of San Juan Capistrano, California is in the Spanish mission style. The buildings surround a courtyard with a stream of water issuing from the upper levels of the structure.

The Walt Disney World Swan and Dolphin Hotels adhere to classic forms but are filled inside and out with color, exuberant decoration (such as massive swans) and humor.

Cesar Pelli

(b.1926)

Cesar Pelli was born in Argentina and immigrated to the United States in 1952. He has had a long and active career. Somewhat critical of the overuse of eclecticism in Post-Modern construction, Pelli believes in the importance of placing a building sensitively into its environment.

One of his more prominent commissions is the *World Financial Center* (fig.16–35) in Battery Park City. Located at the tip of Manhattan Island, the towers instantly became an integral part of the city's skyline. Relying on the simple elements of glass and granite, Pelli has created a classically harmonious series of towers. The stepped set-backs and variously shaped copper tops that crown each building give the work its Post-Modern flavor.

Throughout his career, Pelli has focused on city buildings. Pelli's long-standing interest in the urban environment made him a logical candidate for the design of a quintessential urban construction: one of the tallest buildings in the world.

Cesar Pelli has executed designs for an eighty-eight-story building in Malaysia (fig.16–36). But, at the same time, there are plans being made in China to begin construction of a 125-story building. It seems that the quest to build extraordinarily tall buildings is never-ending.

The technology that propels us from the twentieth century into the twenty-first century makes possible all types and forms of buildings. Perhaps this helps account for the diversity of our architecture. For how long will this variety continue? When will events, ideas or inventions help change the course of architecture once again?

16–36 A rendering of a building design is generally made to give the client a better sense of how a completed building will look.
Cesar Pelli. *Model for Kuala Lumpur City Center,* to be completed in 1996.

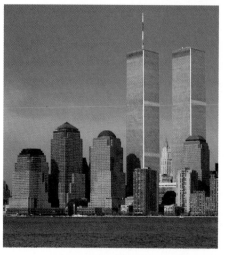

16–35 What makes this a Post-Modern rather than a Modern building?
Cesar Pelli. *World Financial Center,* 1988. New York.

Lesson 16.2 Review

1 How is Post-Modern architecture different from the International Style?

2 What building is recognized by most architects as the first Post-Modern building?

3 Describe one building built by Michael Graves. How is it different from anything built by Mies van der Rohe?

4 Who designed the Sainsbury Wing of London's National Gallery?

5 How did Helmut Jahn build a sense of dynamism into the terminal he designed in Chicago's O'Hare Airport?

4 Robert Venturi, Denise Scott Brown and John Rauch

5 In the long passages from the gateways to the baggage claim areas Jahn added blinking neon lights and chiming sounds activated by the movement of people walking by.

Chapter Review Answers

Review

1 Mies van der Rohe simplified forms so that they were clean, minimal and efficient design. He eliminated extraneous details.

Examples of less is more may be visualized in clothes. Picture a plain, black dress in contrast to a lace one. Or consider car designs. Less would be the aerodynamically designed smooth rounded bodies of contemporary cars and more might be the fringe and decoration of 1950s automobiles.

2 Wright was striving to develop a compatible relationship between the structure and its location so that the building would seem to grow out of its environment.

3 The house at Kaufmann House is cantilevered over a waterfall which is included in most photographs of the house.

4 In steel-frame buildings the walls do not bear the weight of the floors above as in traditional stone buildings. Instead, steel becomes the primary support. Traditional arches and post and lintel elements are no longer needed. The structure is held together by the tensile strength of steel instead of the enormous weight of stone.

Primary Source

Frank Lloyd Wright and the Critics

Now regarded as a great landmark of twentieth-century architecture, Frank Lloyd Wright's Solomon R. Guggenheim Museum in New York City was initially met with tremendous criticism.

Here we have an excerpt from an article written in 1960 by critic James Marston Fitch, just after the museum opened:

Frank Lloyd Wright, Solomon R. Guggenheim Museum, detail.

"Seen from the outside, the great exploding spiral is a powerful landmark; within, it appears as a magnificent vessel for containing the crowds, displaying them to far greater advantage than does the dress circle at La Scala or the grand staircase at the Paris Opera. But, it does not display painting or sculpture to equal advantage. On the contrary, with perverse if not malicious skill, Wright's museum dwarfs the art it might have been expected to magnify. He has set the individual pieces afloat in a vortex, a whirlpool, an interior volume of absolutely overpowering movement. He has taken unfair advantage of the artists: of poor dead Kandinsky, with his intersecting circles and delicate pastels; of elegant, modest Brancusi; of gay Miró. He has reduced them all to the level of lonely little shepherd boys, piping away in competition with Lohengrin. Michelangelo himself would be unsafe in Wright's museum."

Chapter Review

Review

1 Explain what Mies van der Rohe meant by "Less is more." Can you think of an example of an object that is not a building to illustrate this principle?
2 What was Frank Lloyd Wright trying to achieve in his architecture?
3 Why do you think Wright's Kaufmann House at Bear Run, Pennsylvania, is often called Falling Water?
4 How are the load-bearing characteristics of steel-frame construction different from traditional stone-building methods?
5 How does Wright's Robie House echo the prairie landscape surrounding Chicago?
6 Post-Modern architects make a point of building structures that are in harmony with their surroundings. Which Post-Modern building discussed in this chapter do you think best accomplishes this goal?

Interpret

1 How are Mies van der Rohe's Lakeshore Drive Apartments in Chicago like Mondrian's "Lozenge in Red, Yellow, and Blue"?
2 Which architect said "Less is a bore" and which said "Less is more"? Name a building to illustrate each slogan. Explain which building you like better.

3 Which architect was one of the first to stress form follows function? What does this slogan mean? Select an ordinary household object and explain how its form is related to its function.

Other Tools for Learning

 Timelines
1 Select an event from the timelines near the date when you were born. Why do you think this event was included on this timeline?
2 Which event on these timelines do you think will have the most impact on people in the twenty-first century?
3 Find several events in this chapter's timelines that made the world a smaller place. How do you think this bringing people closer together affected the architecture of this time period?

 Electronic Research
Look at I. M. Pei's East Building of the National Gallery on that gallery's video-disc. Describe the feeling of the interior space in the lobby.

---

5 There is a low, flat horizontal feeling to the house, especially in the roof lines, that echoes the flat prairie.
6 A favorite will probably be one of Graves' hotels at Disney World since they reflect the fun-loving entertainment center in which they are set, but a case could be made for any of the Post-Modern buildings in the chapter.

Interpret

1 Both are based on grids with simplified shapes. Both artists were seeking perfect, simplified design free from superfluous elements.
2 Robert Venturi, one of the designers of the Sainsbury Wing of London's National Gallery, said "less is a bore," and Mies van der Rohe, designer of Chicago's Lakeshore Drive Apartments,

said "less is more." Any Post-Modern building could illustrate less is a bore with its inclusion of classical details, color and humor. Students might be attracted to the clean, smooth design of International Style architecture which exemplifies less is more.
3 Louis Sullivan said "form follows function" which means first the function of the building or how it will be used should be considered, and then the building can be designed around these needs.

A chair may be beautiful to look at (its form), but it should be comfortable to sit in (its function). Spoons, forks, cups, clocks and wastebaskets are interesting to analyze for form and function.

Primary-Source Connection

Have students discuss the difficulties of bringing an innovative architectural idea to fruition. They might consider the particular problems that an architect like Wright encountered. Remind them that architects must find ways to convince their prospective clients to pay for the construction of their design. In most cases, the architect also must present the design to municipal review boards for approval.

Timelines
1 Students will probably select an event such as Bishop Tutu's receiving the Nobel Peace Prize for his efforts in eliminating South Africa's apartheid policy or the first artificial heart implant in 1985 which marked a step in a long procession of medical developments leading to the possibility of a better quality of life for many people.
2 Hopefully it will be one leading to peace. The 1994 break-up of the Soviet Union will politically change large portions of the world, but the invention of the personal computer in 1978 could eventually be an important link in building communication between all people of the world.
3 The Chinese and Indian space satellites in 1970 and 1975 helped join these populations with the rest of world. High speed trains brought people together. Whenever people experienced architecture and ideas of a different culture, they often incorporated these ideas into their buildings and art. With increases in communication there were greater architectural similarities as people could see what others were doing. Western architects such as Frank Lloyd Wright were influenced by Asian architecture, and International Style buildings were constructed all over the world.

Electronic Research
The lobby is huge to handle the large numbers of people that pass through it each day. Elevators lead up into the upper reaches of the space. Large windows flood light on the specially designed art—Calder's enormous mobile suspended from the ceiling, a Miro tapestry on the wall, and various sculptures on the floor.

Activity 1:
Harmony Inside and Out

Activity Objectives
Students should be able to:

• Become familiar with the work of Frank Lloyd Wright.

• Learn about design elements in architecture.

• Understand the meaning of "form follows function."

• Distinguish the line/style/form of the interior of a building and incorporate these elements into furniture design.

Thinking Critically
Ask for a discussion or report in response to the following:

• Discuss how architects as well as painters have tendencies toward Classicism or Romanticism and the role architects can play in determining building styles.

• Explain the concept of "form follows function." Is this concept applicable to other areas in art and design? If so, how?

To bring relevance to this exploration, ask students about their homes:

• Describe the exterior of your home. Do you think the architecture of your home is a good "marriage with nature"? Why or why not?

• Describe the interior of your home, specifically the furniture. What style is it? What are the characteristics and salient features of this style?

• If you could reorganize a particular room in your home, which room would it be? What is the size of this room? Would you suggest any renovations? Describe how the furniture would look in this room, including color, pattern or design (if any), as well as line and form.

Preparation Ideas
Collect books, slides and magazines on architectural design. Find examples of buildings reflecting designs found in nature.

Tips
Invite an architect and an environmentalist to talk to the students. Ask the guests to address environmental vs. building issues.

Activity 1
Harmony Inside and Out

Materials
newsprint for preliminary sketches
#3 or 4H pencils
erasers
12" x 18" drawing paper suitable for watercolor and washes
water containers
assortment of round brushes (#2, #7, #10)
pen and ink (optional)

Take a look.
• Fig.16–5, Frank Lloyd Wright. *Kaufmann House*, 1936.

Think about it. Frank Lloyd Wright believed in developing a compatible relationship between a structure and its location, so the building seemed to grow out of its environment. Just as the exterior of buildings are often in harmony with nature, so too the interior and its furnishings can complement and be in harmony with the building's exterior.

• Consult copies of architectural magazines that provide interior views of buildings.

• How would you describe the furniture?

• Is the interior and its components a perfect marriage with the exterior? Why or why not?

Do it. After studying Frank Lloyd Wright's Falling Water, design furniture for a particular room in the house. Use watercolors to add color. If you are planning an intricate pattern you may want to use colored pencils.

Check it. Compare your final drawings with the actual furniture Frank Lloyd Wright made for Falling Water. Your design solutions will be different, but do they foster the architect's philosophy?

Helpful Hint: Research different furniture styles throughout history. Where is this furniture housed?

Activity 2
Model Community

Materials
scissors
ruler
pencil
lightweight cardboard
glue
tape

Take a look. Review the buildings shown in this chapter—notice the environment surrounding each one. What is the function of each building? How do the activities in each building contribute to and rely upon the city that surrounds it?

Think about it. Work with other students to design a model community, building or architectural complex. Take time to consider the following questions (write down your answers):

• Where would it be located (city, state)?

• What is its function or purpose?

• What year does your structure represent (present, past or future)?

• What are the components of your structure? Is there more than one building, parks, patios, archways or sidewalks?

• How large will your structure be (both real-life size and model scale)?

• What will you name it?

Do it.

• Decide on a scale for your project. Architects commonly use 1/8" = 1 foot, but you need to consider what is most practical for your project. The scale for a town square composed of one- or two-story buildings would not be appropriate for a skyscraper.

• Measure out a ground plan on a cardboard base. Consider vehicular and pedestrian traffic, use of land and landscaping.

• Decide who is responsible for the construction of each component. Plan how to work together to keep your structures harmonious with one another.

• Cut the basic structures from cardboard, measuring to scale each time. Start with basic, solid shapes, then cut away parts you don't want and/or add strips of cardboard to build up shapes in layers.

Check it. What kind of information do you need to produce accurate models? What information needs to be shared among people working together on the same project?

Helpful Hint: If possible, visit a university architectural department or an architect's studio to see how architectural models look before you begin your own design; or refer to a book on architectural design or model building.

Additional Activities

• Examine forms that are found in nature. Simplify and abstract these forms. Create several stencils based on your abstract forms. Using acrylic paint, stencil a wall, fabric, paper, or even a piece of furniture.

• Take your sketchbook or camera on an architectural tour of your community. Sketch or photograph architectural details (window treatments, doorways, cornices, pediments, columns, rooflines, domes). Prepare a display of your findings and label each item with a few sentences telling: 1) name and/or location of the example; 2) the architectural influence that is evident (Greek, Classicism, French Renaissance, for example).

Activity 2:
Model Community

Activity Objectives
Students should be able to:

• Work cooperatively in the design and construction of a model community, building or architectural complex.

• Consider how the design and construction of a building impacts the environment.

• Study and evaluate buildings in their environment.

Thinking Critically
A well-developed stage of thinking, investigation and planning is essential to the success of this project. Review "Think about it" questions with students and guide them in the development of a workable plan.

Preparation Ideas
A useful book to have on hand for reference is *Design with Nature*, by Ian L. McHarg, Doubleday, 1971.

Notes on Materials
For more professional results in the use of cardboard for the models, inquire at an art-supply store for modeling cardboard used by architects. A low-cost alternative is corrugated cardboard, available free in the form of discarded boxes. Professional cardboard can be cut with scissors, whereas corrugated cardboard may require X-acto or matt knives for cutting. If using the latter, be sure to review safety precautions.

Student Profile

David Michael Goodman

Clarkstown High School North
New City, New York
Activity 2, Model Community

I felt overwhelmed as I gazed at the slope of the land situated beside Bebe Lake. I strolled along the bank of the lake, trying to find the best spot to build my house. I concluded that I had two options. The first was to build on the flat, level side. I pictured an ordinary-type house overlooking the panoramic views of the lake. My second option was to attempt to construct the house on the side of a steep incline of about 24 feet. I chose to design the house on the incline because it was a more challenging task and would call for a totally innovative design.

I positioned the entrance to the home in the rear of the house because I wanted the house to be focused on the lake. In the design of the interior, I chose to use walls of transparent glass to provide views of the lake from any room of the house. In the front, I chose to use glass blocks and translucent glass. The field of architecture has always fascinated me. Ever since I was a young boy, I enjoyed building and drafting. Back then, I used blocks, Lego and Lincoln Logs. As I matured, my constructions developed into more complex and realistic structures. I plan to attend Cornell University next fall to study architecture. There I will form a foundation for a career as an architect. I can't wait to get started!

David M. Goodman

Lakeside Studio House, 1994. Corrugated cardboard, wire, chipboard, 25" x 45" (63.5 x 114 cm).

Jacob Meanley

Bakersfield High School
Bakersfield, California
Activity 1, Harmony Inside and Out

I was to draw furniture that fit the character of Frank Lloyd Wright's house over the waterfall. It was interesting to go through the process of modeling furniture after nature. I tried to keep in mind the way water flows downwards in a waterfall. I tried to incorporate the roundness and downward lines of a waterfall into the furniture.

Most people complain that they're terrible in art and can only draw stick figures. But I believe that everyone is good in at least one aspect of art. Whether it be coloring or just critiquing, it's still all part of art and its process.

Jacob Meanley

Waterfall Furniture, 1994. Colored pencil, 12" x 18" (30.5 x 45.7 cm).

Classroom Management

• Have the class design and build a model city. This can be an ongoing project that calls on students' knowledge of history, geography, engineering, drawing and math.

• Have students work in small groups to plan their project. Have one person record the particulars about their community (size, name, purpose), and make a list of who will be responsible for which structures.

• If the building of a model is too grand in scope for your class, students can learn a great deal by discussing and drawing up plans for a community without actually building a three-dimensional structure.

Tips

• To bring personal relevance to the impact of effective urban planning, use the following article as the basis for a class discussion: "15 Ways to Fix the Suburbs," Newsweek, May 15, 1995. Ask students how they might redesign their own neighborhood.

• Invite an urban planner to speak to your class about his or her job and to bring sketches or examples of model community projects.

Evaluation

If a community environment has been designed and built (as opposed to a single building), have the students allowed for:

Teacher Spotlight

Barbara Levine
Art Department Chairperson and Art Teacher
Clarkstown High School North

This fall, when David Goodman was applying to college to study architecture, he approached me for assistance in selecting artwork for his portfolio. Since my son-in-law, Paul, is an architect, I suggested that David bring his artwork to my house so the three of us could view and discuss David's work. Paul brought his professional portfolio to give David an idea of how an architectural portfolio should look.

We selected artwork for David's portfolio that showed strong design capabilities. It helped that David had spent the previous summer taking a workshop which introduced him to architecture—planning, drafting and building of small three-dimensional structures. He had several good works to choose from. David modeled his portfolio after Paul's professional portfolio. He matted photographs of his three-dimensional architectural structures along with color Xerox copies of his general artwork in a bound portfolio case. The presentation was very effective, showing a promising architect in the making.

Kathy Kalson
Teacher of Fine Arts
Bakersfield High School

To be truthful, on this project I didn't do much. I simply gave the book to two of my students and invited them to participate as an independent study. They were asked to read the chapter and complete the assignment as homework in a short amount of time. Bless those boys. Jacob's came in a little rough. I sent him back to refine and utilize colored pencil. You see his results.

• open spaces, parks and playgrounds?

• amenities, shopping and activities within walking distance of dwellings?

• sidewalks to encourage walking?

• public transportation?

• housing for mixed-income residents?

Chapter 17 Organizer

Objectives

Identify New York City as the center of Western art after World War II.

Comprehend the individual styles of the various abstract and representational movements that span the second half of the twentieth century.

Discuss how artists' diverse concerns and aesthetic responses in the last decades of the century reflect the complexity of Western society.

National Standards

4a Students differentiate among a variety of historical and cultural contexts in terms of characteristics and purposes of works of art.

3a Students reflect on how artworks differ visually, spatially, temporally, and functionally, and describe how these are related to history and culture.

4d Students analyze and interpret artworks for relationships among form, context, purposes, and critical models, showing understanding of the work of critics, historians, aestheticians, and artists.

Teacher Edition References

Lesson 17.1 Abstract Expressionism

Special Feature: Willem de Kooning 550–551	Contextual Info 551	HOTS 551
Remainder of Lesson 17.1 552–555 World Cultural Timeline 552 Lesson 17.1 Review 555	Contextual Info 552 HOTS 553, 555	Multicultural 553

Lesson 17.2 Pop Art and Op Art

Special Feature: Claes Oldenburg 556–557	Contextual Info 557	HOTS 557
Remainder of Lesson 17.2 558–563 World Cultural Timeline 558 Lesson 17.2 Review 563	Contextual Info 558, 560, 562 HOTS 559, 561, 563 Cooperative 563	Interdisciplinary 562 Materials and Techniques 558 Performing Arts 562

Lesson 17.3 Color Field Painting

Special Feature: Helen Frankenthaler 564–565	Contextual Info 565 HOTS 565	Conservation 565
Remainder of Lesson 17.3 566–569 World Cultural Timeline 566 Lesson 17.3 Review 569	Contextual Info 566, 568 HOTS 567, 569	Performing Arts 566

Lesson 17.4 New Realism

Special Feature: Chuck Close 570–571	Contextual Info 571	
Remainder of Lesson 17.4 572–57 Lesson 17.4 Review 573	Contextual Info 572	HOTS 573

Lesson 17.5 Sculpture

Special Feature: Isamu Noguchi 574–575	Contextual Info 575	HOTS 575
Remainder of Lesson 17.5 576–577 Lesson 17.5 Review 577	Contextual Info 576	HOTS 577

Ancillaries

Slides: Lichtenstein, *We Rose Up Slowly*, 118b, 235;
Moore, *Sheep Piece*, Hertfordshire, England, 124a, 248
Overhead Transparencies:
Design: Traditional and Modern, 19

Teacher Edition References

Timeline: Art from the Fifties to the Present 548
Context 549
Art 549
Quote 549

Ancillaries

Slides: de Kooning, *Door to the River*, 113b, 228

Slides: Motherwell, *Elegy to the Spanish Republic No. 34*, 116a, 229;
Hofmann, *Flowering Swamp*, 114b, 230;
Pollock, *Number 1, 1948*, 115b, 231;
Krasner, *Rising Green*, 116b, 232;
Rothko, *Blue, Orange, Red*, 117a, 233

Slides: Oldenburg, *Giant Loaf of Raisin Bread, Sliced*, 117b, 234

Slides: Lichtenstein, *We Rose Up Slowly*, 118b, 235;
Johns, *Numbers in Color*, 118a, 236;
Warhol, 100 Cans, 119a, 237;
Vasarely, *Vega-Kontosh-Va*, 120a, 238;
Riley, *Drift #2*, 119b, 239
Large Reproductions: Rauschenburg, *The Bed*, 29

Slides: Frankenthaler, *White Sage*, 120b, 240

Slides: Albers, *Homage to the Square: Glow*, 121a, 241; Louis, *Faces*, 121b, 242

Slides: Close, *Phil*, 122b, 243

Slides: Rosenquist, *Nomad*, 122a, 244;
Estes, *Drugstore*, 123a, 245;
Hanson, *Hard Hat Construction Worker*, 123b, 246

Slides: Noguchi, *Lunar Landscape*, 124b, 247

Slides: Moore, *Sheep Piece*, Hertfordshire, England, 124a, 248;
Hepworth, *Figure for Landscape*, 125b, 249

Other Resources

Books

Arnason, H. H. *A History of Modern Art.* 3rd ed. Englewood Cliffs: Prentice Hall, 1986.

Lippard, L. R. *Pop Art.* New York: Thames and Hudson, 1985.

Lynton, Norbert. *The Story of Modern Art.* 2nd ed. Englewood Cliffs, NJ: Prentice Hall, 1989.

Mahsun, Carol A., ed. *Pop Art: The Critical Dialogue.* Ann Arbor: University of Michigan Press, 1988.

McShine, Kynaston. *Andy Warhol: A Retrospective.* New York: Museum of Modern Art, 1991.

Meisel, Louis K. *Photorealism.* New York: Harry N. Abrams Inc., 1989.

Motherwell, Robert, ed. *The Dada Painters and Poets: An Anthology.* 2nd ed. Cambridge: Harvard University Press, 1989.

Nadeau, Maurice. *History of Surrealism.* Cambridge: Harvard University Press, 1989.

Norris, Christopher, and Benjamin, Andrew. *What Is Deconstruction?* New York: St. Martin's Press Inc., 1989.

Pincus-Witten, Robert. *Postminimalism into Maximalism: American Art, 1966–1986.* Ann Arbor: University of Michigan Press, 1987.

Red Grooms Talks About Dali Salad. Minneapolis Institute of Arts, 1987.

Seldon, Rodman. *Conversations with Artists.* New York: Devin, 1957.

Walker, John Albert. *Glossary of Art, Architecture and Design Since 1945:* 3rd ed. Chicago: G.K. Hall, 1992.

Video

Abstract Expressionism, Crystal
Christo's Islands, Maysles. 1983.
Christo's Running Fence. Maysles, 1978.
Jackson Pollock, Crystal
The Mystery of Henry Moore. CBC Enterprises, 1985.
The Real World of Andrew Wyeth. RM/ARTS, 1980.
Roy Lichtenstein Reflections, Crystal
Warhol, Crystal
Willem de Kooning, Crystal

Chapter 17 Organizer

			Lesson 17.6 New Directions	Teacher Edition References	
	1	1	*Special Feature:* Christo and Jeanne Claude 578–579	Contextual Info 579	HOTS 579
		1	Remainder of Lesson 17.6 580–586 World Cultural Timeline 580 Lesson 17.6 Review 586 Primary-Source 587 Chapter Review 587	Contextual Info 580, 582, 584 HOTS 581, 583, 585, 586	Cooperative 584

1	1	1	Classroom Connections

	National Standards
Studio Activity 1 Sculpting with Cloth	**1a** Students apply media, techniques, and processes with sufficient skill, confidence, and sensitivity that their intentions are carried out in their artworks. **1b** Students conceive and create works of visual art that demonstrate an understanding of how the communication of their ideas relates to the media, techniques, and processes they use.
Studio Activity 2 Mimic the Masters	**1a** Students apply media, techniques, and processes with sufficient skill, confidence, and sensitivity that their intentions are carried out in their artworks. **1b** Students conceive and create works of visual art that demonstrate an understanding of how the communication of their ideas relates to the media, techniques, and processes they use.

Choose either Activity 1 or 2

Choose either Activity 1 or 2

Choose either Activity 1 or 2

Ancillaries

Overhead Transparencies: Art on Site, 18

Slides: Kienholtz, *The Wait*, 125a, 250
Large Reproductions: Quick-to-See Smith, *Rainbow*, 30

Schedule	Materials
one day to design sculpture and cut cloth. Another day to begin stitching together. With only two studio periods, students will finish it outside of class.	newsprint, pencils, tape, cloth, vinyl (various colors), needles, thread, foam rubber pillow filling
This activity can be completed in one day	tempera paints/paper or acrylic paints/canvas, brushes, water containers

Introduce

The advent of Abstract Expressionism after World War II shifted the focus of Western art to New York City. Soon after, a rapid succession of styles emerged, some exploring Abstraction (like the Op Art and Color Field movements), while others (such as Pop and, later, New Realism) returned to immediately recognizable images for their subject matter. Sculptors in the second half of the twentieth century also became more inventive in their use of materials, techniques and treatment of space. The astounding diversity of work in the final decades raises important questions about art as well as society itself.

Lessons at a Glance

17.1 *Abstract Expressionism*
Starting in the late 1940s, Abstract Expressionists dominated the American scene. The devastation of World War II, as well as the art of the European artists who had fled to the United States, influenced the artists' highly personal styles. Abstract Expressionists looked inward instead of out and communicated a sense of spontaneity and emotion through shape, color and line.

17.2 *Pop Art and Op Art*
While Pop Art and Op Art were highly divergent movements, both developed clean, hard-edged, cool styles in response to the passionate emotionalism of Abstract Expressionism. Pop artists culled mass, or "popular," culture for their subject matter and transposed it into the high-art realm, while Op artists relied on science to create the illusion of motion on flat canvases.

17.3 *Color Field Painting*
Color Field Painting developed in the 1960s and 1970s. The artist's flat areas of color contained none of the emotional painterly brushwork of the Abstract Expressionists. The enormous scale in which some of the artists worked created huge environments that engulfed the viewer.

17.4 *New Realism*
A revival in realistic art began in the 1970s, originating in California and spreading throughout the country. The New Realists' various depictions of daily life often functioned as visual metaphors.

17.5 *Sculpture*
Sculptors in the second half of the twentieth century explored a wide variety of materials, scales and techniques to create innovative three-dimensional works that reflected the diversity of modern and contemporary art.

17.6 *New Directions*
Since the 1960s, art has taken off in virtually innumerable ways. Artists have broken the confines of exhibition spaces, recruited viewers as active participants in their work, and tried almost every new technology as part of the art-making process.

17 Art from the Fifties to the Present

A T THE END OF WORLD WAR II, a dramatic shift in the art world occurred. Abstract Expressionism took New York and the Western world by storm. It was a breath of fresh air with an impact so tremendous that all eyes turned to New York, the new leader of the art world.

In the rapid pace of the post-war world, some artists tired of the emotionalism of Abstract Expressionism. These artists startled the art world with Pop Art and Op Art. Pop Art took its images from the popular culture. Op Art used scientific approaches to create motion on the canvas.

Styles began to change with greater and greater speed. In the late 1960s and into the 1970s, Color Field artists created serene paintings that relied solely on large areas of flat color. Realism reemerged in the 1970s. Like Pop artists, New Realists portrayed contemporary American life. The second half of the 1900s was also a very dynamic time for sculptors. They became much bolder and more inventive in their use of materials and space.

Diversity is the key to late-1900s art. An extraordinary array of materials, forms, interactions, juxtapositions, statements and environments has captured the imagination of many contemporary artists. As we move into the twenty-first century, we should continue to ask questions about what art is and about how we can better understand it.

17–a This Pop artist took his inspiration from the Sunday comics and oversimulated the ben-day printing dots used to print the comics.
Roy Lichtenstein, *Masterpiece*, detail (fig.17–14).

1950 Pollock, *Lavender Mist*
1962 Warhol, *100 Cans*
1968 Martin Luther King assassinated
1980 CNN offers round-the-clock news coverage
1980 Grooms, *Ruckus Rodeo*
1984 Geraldine Ferraro is first woman vice-presidential candidate in the US
1986 Nuclear accident at Chernobyl

Art from the Fifties to the Present

1951 Double-helix DNA proposed
1965 Vasarely originates Op Art
1969 First manned landing on the moon
1972–1976 Christo, *Running Fence*
1973 Vietnam War ends
1982 Alice Walker, *The Color Purple*
1989 Demolition of the Berlin Wall
1990 Violeta Barrios de Chamorro elected president of Nicaragua

Objectives

Students should be able to:

Identify New York City as the center of Western art after World War II.

Comprehend the individual styles of the various abstract and representational movements that span the second half of the twentieth century.

Discuss how artists' diverse concerns and aesthetic responses in the last decades of the century reflect the complexity of Western society.

Teach

Timeline
After students examine the timeline, have them identify events from the year of their birth (or a parent's birth)

Each age finds its own technique.
— Jackson Pollock

17–b
Contemporary art is often very difficult to capture with still photography. How would the experience of viewing this work of art in person differ from seeing this color image of the piece?
Jennifer Bartlett, *Spiral: An Ordinary Evening in New Haven*, 1989. Oil on canvas, tables, painted wood and steel, 108" x 192" (274 x 487 cm). Paula Cooper, Inc., New York.

17–d Many of Moore's wonderful sculptures are dramatically different when viewed from all four sides. Notice the size of the sheep in the pasture compared to the sculpture.
Henry Moore, *Sheep Piece*, 1972. Bronze, 223 1/2" (568 cm) long. Hertfordshire, England. Courtesy of the artist.

17–c Research for this project uncovered so many women of distinction that Chicago tripled the number of guests. Originally, Chicago conceived the work as a dinner attended by thirteen famous women.
Judy Chicago, *The Dinner Party*, 1979. Ceramic with handwoven cloth, each side 82' long (25 m). Through the Flower, Albuquerque, New Mexico.

Quote

Ask students how they think Jackson Pollock's comment applies to the images in the chapter opener. How does each piece reflect the tenor of the decade in which it was made? What do the differences in style from one period to the next indicate about the speed at which modern and contemporary art has progressed?

Evaluate

Ask students if art in the second half of the twentieth century has advanced in a strictly linear fashion. If they were to draw a family tree of styles, would there be only a main trunk or many branches, leaves and flowers?

• Do they find the great number of styles exciting or confusing?

• What questions can students pose that will help them become clearer about the artworks?

• Have the class share their findings and ask students if they feel comfortable with the often open-ended, unanswerable quality of contemporary art. Why or why not? What might increase their ease with its frequently ambiguous nature?

Reteach

Have students work in pairs, with one partner pretending to be an art dealer who represents the artists in the chapter opener.

• What would they say to sell these pieces to skeptical, potential buyers who know little about art or twentieth-century culture?

• How can they convince the buyers of the artist's importance and the significance of the work?

• What reservations does the prospective client have?

• What information would make the client want to acquire the work?

• Have students switch roles. Afterward, discuss if and how taking a look at both sides of the issue helped the class gain a better understanding of the art.

up to the present that they consider significant influences on modern culture. Ask if any of these occurrences have affected art.

Context

Have students research the social and political climate of American culture during the late 1960s and early 1970s. Ask what particular events helped shape the revolutionary temperament of the times.

• How does Judy Chicago's *The Dinner Party* (fig.17–c) reflect the far-reaching impact of the women's movement on public life as well as art? (Direct students to page 580 for specific information on Chicago's work.)

• How did the collaborative nature of her project enhance its political message?

Art

Instruct students to compare Roy Lichtenstein's *Masterpiece* (figs.17–a, 17–14) to an actual comic-book illustration.

• What is similar about the two media and what has Lichtenstein changed?

• Although Lichtenstein imitates the ben-day dots of commercial printing, how has he also introduced abstraction?

• How complex and detailed are the images? How many colors does he use? Does Lichtenstein establish a strong sense of depth?

• Although his figures are recognizable, are they very lifelike?

• For a challenge, have students choose an existing comic-book image and alter it to correspond to Lichtenstein's style.

Lesson 17.1

Abstract Expressionists

Starting in the late 1940s, Abstract Expressionists dominated the American scene. The devastation of World War II, as well as the art of the European artists who had fled to the United States, influenced the artists' highly personal styles. Abstract Expressionists looked inward instead of out and communicated a sense of spontaneity and emotion through shape, color and line.

Warm-up

Ask students to examine the images in Lesson 17.1 and ask why the term "Action Painting" is an appropriate name for Abstract Expressionism. What does the term indicate about the manner and speed in which the works were made? How does this process differ from Northern Renaissance (Chapter 10) or Dutch seventeenth-century art (Lesson 11.3)?

Objectives

Students should be able to:

Recognize the birth of Abstract Expressionism, America's first truly original avant-garde art movement.

Perceive the differences in individual approaches despite the artists' similar aims.

Comprehend the impact of Abstract Expression on Western art.

Vocabulary Definitions

drip painting Technique developed by Jackson Pollock in which he walked over a canvas with a can of paint, dripping and spilling paint about the canvas.

Teach

Criticism: Ask students to examine Willem de Kooning's paintings in figs.17–1 and 17–2. Ask how a house painter might feel about this work. What impact do students think de Kooning's own stint at painting houses had on his style, brushstrokes and the scale of the canvases? If de Kooning had been a jeweler, how might his painting style have developed? (Direct students to pages 550 and 551 for information on de Kooning's life and art.)

17.1 Abstract Expressionism

WITH POWERFUL AND DYNAMIC FURY, a movement called *Abstract Expressionism* exploded in New York following World War II. Abstract Expressionism got its title because it was abstract (emphasizing shape, color and/or line with no recognizable subject matter) and expressive (stressing emotions and individual feelings more than design and form). Partly as a reaction to the times they lived in, artists turned against reason. The New York artists wanted to hold on to their humanity in the face of the insanity they perceived around them. To do this, they looked inward instead of out. Their work had a spontaneous and very fresh feel to it. It was meant to be grasped intuitively by the viewer rather than reasoned out.

The style found its roots in Kandinsky and the more recent works of Gorky. Artists from Europe, fleeing Hitler's Germany and other totalitarian regimes, settled in New York and began teaching. They and their students were the instigators of Abstract Expressionism, or *Action Painting* as it was often called. However, artists went off in individual directions and developed personal styles and techniques. Based on the freedom of individual expression, the movement soon spread from New York to the rest of the Western world. The movement lasted about fifteen years, but during that time it revolutionized the art world. America had become the art leader of the world and remains so today.

Key Notes

- Abstract Expressionism explodes in New York following World War II.
- Based on individual expression, Abstract Expressionism stresses emotions and feelings more than design and form.
- Abstract Expressionism revolutionizes painting, and America takes over as leader of the art world.

Vocabulary
drip painting

17–2 Why is the term "Action Painting" appropriate for this work?
Willem de Kooning, *Woman I*, 1950–1952. Approx. 6' 4" x 4' 10" (193 x 147 cm). Collection, The Museum of Modern Art, New York, Purchase.

Special Feature
Willem de Kooning
(b. 1904)

Willem de Kooning came to the United States from Amsterdam in 1926. Hoping to become a magazine illustrator, he found himself churning out commercial art for whoever would hire him. In the depression, he actually worked for a while as a house-painter. This experience led him to use large house-painting brushes and enamel paint in the creation of his large sprawling canvases.

After painting realistically for many years, he leapt into Abstract Expressionism with great enthusiasm and became one of its leading exponents. His slashing brush covered large canvases with color and tremendous action that became his nonobjective subject matter. His huge paintings were often frantic and violent. These features are evident in the slashing quality of the brushwork. Nothing flows easily with de Kooning. It is all crabbed and leaping, drawing in and opening out, and deliberately crude. But, at the same time, he makes abstraction appear very natural, as though there is nothing complicated about it. It's as real in his hands as going to a baseball game or taking a train ride. Because the emphasis is on the act of painting as part of the subject matter, such work was called Action Painting.

The apparent spontaneity of de Kooning's work was often the result of many days of work. In *Easter Monday* (fig.17–1), de Kooning used newspaper transfers and oils as the media of the nonobjective work.

Evaluate

Ask students if it is easier to make art look spontaneous or meticulously accurate. Do artists who aim for a spontaneous appearance paint without a preconception of what they want or how they will approach their artwork?

- What about de Kooning's work indicates the depth of technical skill necessary to create pieces with such emotional intensity?

Ask students if the Abstract Expressionists shared a similar visual style. How do the images in Lesson 17.1 demonstrate that these artists all explored expression and emotion through color, shape and line, yet each developed his or her own individual manner?

As a prompt, direct students to compare Pollock's painting (fig.17–3) to Lee Krasner's (fig.17–7). While the two were intimately aware of each other's work, each pursued a separate course of Abstract Expressionism, adding to the richness of the overall movement as well as inspiring one another.

17–1 De Kooning received a traditional education in art, and classic principles of composition provide the structure for his free brushwork and spontaneous colors. Willem de Kooning, *Easter Monday*, 1956. Oil and newspaper transfer, 96" x 74" (244 x 188 cm). The Metropolitan Museum of Art, New York, Rogers Fund.

The painting is perhaps coincidentally strewn with E's. De Kooning often used letters of the alphabet as part of his huge swinging-motion paintings.

De Kooning was one of the prophets of the new style, but at the same time he was still very interested in the figure. His famous series of *Woman* paintings was inspired in part by advertising billboards.

Woman I (fig.17–2) is an excitement-packed painting slashed out at top speed. Amid the interplay of colors and brushstrokes, the overall shape of the body is recognizable. There is an emphasis on the face with its wide, rather leering grin. Like other Action Paintings, the image constantly comes into and out of focus. This is a violent and tremendously expressive painting.

Contextual Information

De Kooning

De Kooning worked for two years on *Woman I* (fig.17–2), although he didn't work on it continuously. He had put it away, but after an art historian saw it and commented on it, de Kooning reworked it. He had begun the work with the canvas attached to the wall. He cut off a portion along the right side and then later restored it with an aluminum painted band.

• Have students compare *Woman I* with *Les Demoiselles d'Avignon* (fig.14–24). Ask in what ways the artists made similar changes to reality. Have students describe the differences in the way paint was applied.

Higher-Order Thinking Skills

Arshile Gorky was a strong influence on many Abstract Expressionist painters, including de Kooning. Ask the class what traces of Gorky's influence they can find in de Kooning's work.

Reteach

Challenge students to imagine that they are curators of an Abstract Expressionist exhibition.

• Ask how they would respond to visitors who claim that their children could make art like de Kooning's or Jackson Pollock's.

• Have students use the images in the text to affirm the integrity of the artwork, artistic skill, and importance of the style to the history of art. (For instance, had this style ever been practiced in America before? Why is it important? How did artists take European abstract art into account but derive a totally new American style from these precedents? How are their works unlike children's scribblings? Could a child really create such complete but spontaneous-looking canvases?)

Contextual Information

The Abstract Expressionists Exhibited

In 1951, the Museum of Modern Art (MOMA) gave an exhibition called "Abstract Painting and Sculpture in America"; it was the first exhibition of the Abstract Expressionists. In 1958–59, the museum circulated through Europe a show of the "irascible eight"; it included work by Pollock, Kline, Rothko, Newman, de Kooning, Hofmann, Motherwell, Gottlieb and Reinhardt.

Pollock

Soon after Siqueiros opened his "experimental workshop" in New York City in 1936, Pollock joined it and began to investigate the use of spray guns, airbrushes, and a variety of synthetic paints and lacquers. He also experimented with the idea of "controlled accident." By 1949, critics of Pollock's paintings varied in their opinions, calling his work "degenerate" pictures, "as unpalatable as yesterday's macaroni," and a "shining new phenomenon of American art." A *Time* magazine reporter called Pollock "Jack the Dripper." Of his own style, Pollock said: "I continue to get further away from the usual painter's tools such as easel, palette, brushes, and the like. I prefer sticks, trowels, knives, and dripping fluid paint or a heavy impasto with sand, broken glass, and other foreign matter added." He felt that one of his goals was to get "in" his paintings by moving paint onto the canvas from all sides, like Native American sand painters.

• Have students research Pollock's life and work to learn how he developed from a traditional figure painter to an action painter. It will be insightful for them to learn of his solid training in art and then follow his evolving personal direction. They will be interested to find that Pollock studied under Thomas Hart Benton.

17–3 Pollock was influenced by Rubens and Orozco. What evidence of that influence do you find?
Jackson Pollock, *No. 1, 1950 (Lavender Mist)*. Oil enamel and aluminum on canvas, 87" x 118" (221 x 299 cm). National Gallery of Art, Washington, Ailsa Mellon Bruce Fund.

Jackson Pollock

(1912–1956)

In 1946, after going through realistic and abstract periods, Jackson Pollock began his series of **drip paintings**. His new working technique completely freed him from the use of traditional brushes and opened the door to Abstract Expressionism. Laying his canvas on the floor of the studio so he could walk on it, he literally put himself into his work. With a can of paint in his hand, he moved about the canvas, freely dripping, spilling and throwing the color with apparent abandon. Pollock's paintings were not haphazard. He was the force behind the paint's movement.

While he could not control the paint, he completely engaged himself in releasing both his own creativity and the possibilities within the paint. The final work can thus be viewed as an interchange between the "will" of the paint and the inner forces of the artist.

Pollock's *No. 1, 1950 (Lavender Mist)* is a complex interweaving of color and line that produces an overall web of fascinating texture (fig.17–3). Pollock intended this work to be flat in appearance, as if all the color were right on the picture plane. However, overlapping lines of various values and colors add a sense of shallow depth. Some lines seem to be floating above others. The thicker, darker lines create a feeling of rhythm. Perhaps without being aware of it, Pollock was determining the flow of paint. The unanticipated depth and rhythm suggest the ways in which Pollock's subconscious interacted with the flow of paint.

World Cultural Timeline

1912
African National Congress established to promote welfare of Blacks, South Africa

1916
Hipólito Irigoyen elected president of Argentina and starts compulsory pensions, the regulation of working hours and improved factory conditions

1917
Ras Tafari (Haile Selassie) becomes ruler of Ethiopia, greatly modernizing the country

1934
Henry Puyi becomes last emperor of China

Robert Motherwell
(1915–1991)

Robert Motherwell did not use the slurred brushstrokes of de Kooning. Instead, he kept a firm clarity to the outline of his freely formed shapes. Usually his paintings have flatly painted, delicate hues. The white backgrounds and powerful, bold black shapes intensify these delicate hues. *Elegy to the Spanish Republic* (fig.17–4) is part of a series of paintings Motherwell began in 1949. The paintings reflect the horror and destruction of the Spanish Civil War. The brooding black shapes suggest a mood of anguish and a sense of doom. Usually, his gigantic canvases were laid flat on the floor. Like Pollock, Motherwell walked on them during the designing and painting process.

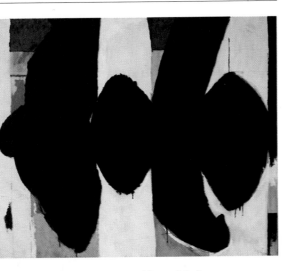

17–4 The spontaneity of the brushwork gives no hint that the artist actually made many small studies prior to painting the large canvases in this series. Robert Motherwell, *Elegy to the Spanish Republic*, 1953–1954. 80" x 100" (203 x 254 cm). Albright-Knox Art Gallery, Buffalo, New York. Gift of Seymour H. Knox, 1957. ©1996 Deadalus Foundation/Licensed by VAGA, New York, NY

17–5 Can you detect images here that have been abstracted in both color and form? Hans Hofmann, *Flowering Swamp*, 1957. Oil on wood, 48" x 36" (122 x 91 cm). Hirshhorn Museum and Sculpture Garden, Smithsonian Institution, Washington DC.

Hans Hofmann
(1880–1966)

Hans Hofmann came to New York from Germany and Paris to become one of America's most influential art teachers. He is best known for his canvases of heavily applied, brilliant color that seem to have some magical intensity. In *Flowering Swamp*, Hofmann painted several colored rectangles that seem to float over the background of softly brushed, but heavily built-up colors. *Flowering Swamp* (fig.17–5) is suggestive of water and flowers. However, the two rectangles immediately dismiss any idea of reality. They belong to Hofmann's brand of abstraction. Most of his work does not have representational aspects. While de Kooning's canvases are often violent, Hofmann's often have a sense of serenity and visual balance.

Multicultural Connection
Sand Painting

Pollock's painting technique has been compared to Native American sand painting. The function and meaning of sand paintings, however is quite different from Pollock's work.

Created by medicine men as part of a variety of healing ceremonies, Navajo sand paintings are intended to have magical effects. The paintings, which use colors from the earth (red and brown from wood charcoal; white from limestone), are made from sandstone, ground minerals and pollen. A medicine man draws complex, symbolic pictures of heroes or heroines from an ancient story or the Holy People. He incorporates symbols for north, south, east and west, and makes designs specific to an illness. The paintings range from small to as large as 20 feet in diameter and often require the work of many men and most of the day to complete. When the healing ceremony is completed, the sacred paintings are scattered to the wind and become part of the earth once again.

Contextual Information

The Working Methods of Abstract Expressionists

As Abstract Expressionist artists studied the writings of Freud and Jung, they were motivated to express their inner feelings in symbols and lines that were not imitations of the world around them, but interpretations of their fantasy worlds.

New materials, such as plastics, magnesium, Plexiglas and acrylic paints, also became forces for change in the appearance of art and the ways in which media are applied. New techniques, such as arc welding and airbrush painting, inspired artists to experiment with new ways to create.

Kline

Kline was interested in translating lines of the city streets, rail lines and bridges into paint. In the late 1950s, he enlarged his brushstrokes into abstract designs. Not the only artist then to limit his colors to black and white, he was joined by Motherwell, Newman, de Kooning and Pollock.

Krasner

Krasner was the only woman in the first generation of Abstract Expressionists. She decided to become a painter in her teens and later studied at Cooper Union School of Design, the Art Students League and the National Academy of Design in New York City. Krasner worked in the Works Progress Agency (WPA) as assistant to muralist Max Spivak, a Social Realist painter of cityscapes and factory scenes.

In discussing the nearly total male domination of Abstract Expressionism, Krasner said: "It is quite clear that I didn't fit into it. . . . I was not accepted . . . there was no room for a woman. When I was a student at the Hofmann school, Hofmann said to me one day, 'This is so good,' referring to what was on my easel, 'you would not know it was done by a woman.' He thought he was paying me the highest possible compliment. So it shows a state of mind that existed at this particular time."

Franz Kline

(1910–1962)

In his early work, Franz Kline painted the buildings and people of New York in a representational style. Then, in 1949, he began to refine his style to a vigorous, slashing form of abstraction. At first, his forms were derived from urban structures. But soon he expressed himself freely without relying on representative subject matter.

In works like *Meryon* (fig.17–6), he found he needed larger-sized canvases and less color to project his images of the energy of the city and contemporary life. He began using gigantic slashes of black and white. He liked to tack unstretched canvas to a wall or to the floor and use large house-painting brushes to apply house-paint in powerful and energetic vertical and horizontal strokes.

Lee Krasner

(1908–1984)

Lee Krasner was a powerful influence in the development of Abstract Expressionism, although she maintained her independence on the fringes of the movement. She progressed through realism and small abstractions. Eventually, she turned to much larger-sized canvases to fully contain her expressions. With each occasional change in style, she seemed to produce stronger statements. In 1954, she was working on her brilliant collages, such as *Shattered Light*. In creating these collages, she was actually tearing up old paintings to create dynamic new images. The resulting surfaces are rich in texture, color, movement and overall unity. They are noisy and joyous, and unique personal expressions. She was married to Jackson Pollock until his tragic death in an auto accident in 1956.

Mark Rothko

(1903–1970)

Born in Russia, Mark Rothko was an early Abstractionist. He first worked somewhat in the style of Arshile Gorky. He soon developed a style based on soft edges and blending colors. His expression was not the harsh and slashing furor of Kline or de Kooning, but a subtle and serene expression of a hushed and brooding mood. As his work became more simplified, the sizes of his canvases became larger. The color became less contrasting and less intense. He limited his large rectan-

17–6 By limiting his palette to black and white in the series to which this work belongs, this artist wanted to convey the energy of contemporary city life.
Franz Kline, *Meryon*, 1960. Oil on canvas, 93" x 77" (236 x 195 cm). The Tate Gallery, London.

17–7 The artist's collages consist of torn-up canvases. Old images are used to create new images.
Lee Krasner. *Shattered Light*, 1954. Collage, 34" x 48" (86 x 122 cm). Courtesy of the artist.

gular shapes to only two or three, as in *Blue, Orange, Red* (fig.17–8). The hazy edges give the feeling of shapes floating and vibrating in and out of the background color. When standing in front of a huge Rothko canvas, one almost has the feeling of floating along with the shapes. This sensation would be explored by the Color Field painters of the 1960s. His final works were done mostly in grays and blacks. Color, so important earlier, was completely abandoned.

Richard Diebenkorn

(b. 1922–1994)

Richard Diebenkorn was part of the second generation of Abstract Expressionists. Many of these painters turned from complete reliance on abstraction to representational subjects and figurative painting, but with expressive overtones. Diebenkorn combined reality with the expressive power and technique of the Abstract Expressionists. He developed a personal expression that relied on design, but was still emotional in feeling. *Cityscape I* (fig.17–9) shows the influence of Abstract Expressionism in the brushstrokes and reliance on flat shapes. However, the design is structured and not accidental or undisciplined. The muted colors are arranged in flat planes with soft edges. Often figures were included in his work. They also were treated as soft-edged planes rather than rounded forms.

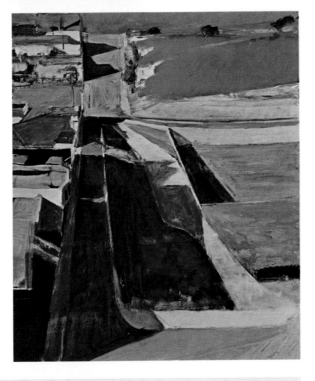

17–8 Compare this painting to Gorky's *The Liver Is the Cock's Comb.* Mark Rothko, *Blue, Orange, Red,* 1961. Oil on canvas, 90" x 81" (229 x 206 cm). Hirshhorn Museum and Sculpture Garden, Smithsonian Institution, Washington DC, gift of Joseph H. Hirshhorn Foundation, 1966.

17–9 Identify the artist's (and viewer's) vantage point here. Richard Diebenkorn, *Cityscape I,* 1963. Oil on canvas, 60 1/4" x 50 3/4" (153 x 129 cm). San Francisco Museum of Modern Art.

Lesson 17.1 Review

1 Explain what the term abstract expressionism means.
2 Why did so many European artists move to New York City during the late 1930s and early 1940s? What style did these artists begin in the United States?
3 List six abstract expressionists. After each artist's name, write three words or short phrases to describe his or her art.
4 Why was de Kooning known as an Action Painter?
5 Describe Jackson Pollock's drip painting method.

Lesson 17.1 Review Answers

1 Abstract expressionism refers to art that is abstract; that is, it emphasizes shape, color and/or line with no recognizable subject matter, and is expressive, stressing emotions more than design and form.
2 European artists were fleeing Hitler's Germany and other totalitarian regimes. They introduced Abstract Expressionism to the United States.
3 Willem de Kooning—women, slashing brushstrokes, tremendous action, frantic, violent, Action Painting, deliberately crude, apparent spontaneity
Jackson Pollock—Action Painting, drip painting, movement, web of texture
Robert Motherwell—clearly outlined forms, free-form shapes, delicate hues, flat, white backgrounds, bold shapes
Hans Hofmann—heavily applied paint, brilliant colors, serenity, visual balance
Franz Kline—gigantic slashes, black and white, powerful, energetic
Lee Krasner—brilliant-colored collages, rich texture, movement and overall unity, noisy, joyous
Mark Rothko—soft edges, blended color, limited color, simplified forms, serene expression, brooding mood
Richard Diebenkorn—some representational subjects, structured design, flat shapes
4 In de Kooning's art, the act of painting became an important part of the subject matter.
5 Pollock placed his canvas on the floor, and carrying a can of paint, he moved about the canvas, dripping, spilling and throwing colors with apparent abandon.

Lesson 17.2

While Pop Art and Op Art were highly divergent movements, both developed clean, hard-edged, cool styles in response to the passionate emotionalism of Abstract Expressionism. Pop artists culled mass, or "popular," culture for their subject matter and transposed it into the high-art realm, while Op artists relied on science to create the illusion of motion on flat canvases.

Warm-up

Ask students to bring in advertising images of ordinary commodities from magazines and newspapers. Display the images around the room and challenge students to articulate ways in which they could use these items as subject matter for art.

• What would students do to the compositions to translate them from commercial to fine art images?

• How do they feel about using such mundane elements as the focus of their compositions?

• Share with students that Pop artists' detached presentation of images selected from the public, or "popular," realm was initially shocking, as compared to the animated work of the earlier Abstract Expressionists.

Objectives

Students should be able to:

Identify mass culture as the subject matter of Pop Art.

Recognize that the detached, hard-edged style of both Pop Art and Op Art was a reaction to the seemingly undisciplined and visceral qualities of Abstract Expressionism.

Understand that Op artists were fascinated with optical illusions and strove to create the sensations of visual movement on two-dimensional surfaces.

Vocabulary Definitions

soft sculpture Sculpture made with fabric and stuffed with soft material.
combine painting Technique developed by Robert Rauschenberg in which artworks are made by fastening objects to abstract canvases, mixing reality with abstraction.

17.2 Pop Art and Op Art

ABSTRACT EXPRESSIONISM held firm sway for fifteen years. But, in the early sixties, a group of artists burst on the scene. Their subjects were Coke bottles, beer and soup cans, comic strip characters and hamburgers. Because these things were so common, or popular, their movement was labeled *Pop Art.* Pop Art was not really a style because the artists were working in so many different ways. Rather, it was an attitude toward art and toward genre subjects that were reminders of supermarkets, movies, television and the comics. Pop Art answered the undisciplined emotions of Abstract Expressionism with hard edges, almost no brushstrokes in many styles, and extremely careful preparation and drawing. Pop Art expressed an impersonal attitude toward the work and subject and had a lot to do with the artists' frustration with the art establishment. It incorporated a delightful sense of wit, satire and humor.

Many artists have been fascinated by visual illusions, and some have played tricks on the viewer's eyes. But, twentieth-century *Op Art* (*Optical Art*) makes use of scientific principles to create the sensation of movement on the picture plane. There are no focal points or traditional centers of interest in an Op Art work. The overall organization creates the proper effect. Sometimes, color makes the eye detect movement, and at other times, lines or shapes do. Op Art is carefully calculated and meticulously presented.

Key Notes
• Pop Art and Op Art are both reactions to the subjective emotionalism of Abstract Expressionism.
• Pop Art uses everyday objects and references as its subject matter.
• Op Art uses scientific principles to create illusions of movement.

Vocabulary
soft sculpture
combine painting

Special Feature
Claes Oldenburg
(b.1929)

The son of a Swedish diplomat, Oldenburg grew up in Chicago. In the 1950s, he moved to Manhattan and began using found materials to make sculptures and drawings of the objects he saw around him (fig.17–10). To help the viewer see the manufactured environment with new eyes, Oldenburg worked with various sculpture media. He enlarged ordinary household objects, such as a three-way electrical plug, to enormous size. He also developed the technique of *soft sculpture*, which added a surrealistic effect to his work.

Shoestring Potatoes Spilling from a Bag (fig.17–11) is made from painted canvas stuffed with soft kapok. The entire "sculpture" is soft to the touch. It sags humorously as it hangs limply from the ceiling. It would be startling in its soft form if it were actual size, but

17–10 How many everyday objects can you identify in this installation of Oldenburg's work? Claes Oldenburg, *Installation of One-Man Show*, exhibit at Green Gallery, New York, September 24–October 20, 1962.

Teach

Art History/Criticism: Have students glance at figs.17–11 and 17–15. Ask to whom these artworks might have appealed. Have students imagine being a fine art enthusiast in the early 1960s. Would they have readily embraced these images? Why or why not?

• Had anything like these ever been created in art history?

• What precedents did Pop Art have in terms of subject matter, style, size and meaning? For instance, how are these images similar to and vastly different from Northern Renaissance (Chapter 10) and seventeenth-century Dutch art (Lesson 11.3)?

• Now ask students to think about how ordinary people with no knowledge of art would react to these images. Would they see them as appealing? Puzzling? Offensive? How can the images support their answers?

Criticism: Tell students to stare quietly at Bridget Riley's *Fall* (fig.17–17), Victor Vasarely's *Vega-Kontosh-Va* (fig.17–18) and Richard Anuskiewicz *Iridescence* (fig.17–19) for a full three to four minutes. Have them note what happens to their eyes. Are they aware of the sensations in their entire bodies as they become lost in the images? Afterward, ask them to express this feeling with their torsos and arms. Next, challenge students to defend Op Art as realistic rather than abstract. Although the

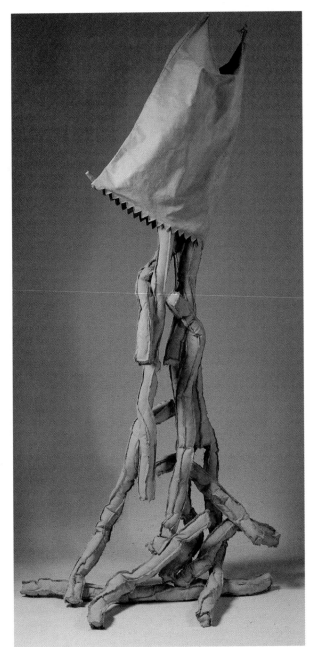

Oldenburg has enlarged it to nearly 10 feet high.

Oldenburg enjoys designing ordinary forms, like combs, trowels and typewriter erasers, and producing them as monumental-sized sculptures located in outdoor and indoor settings. There is also a great sense of humor in these sculptures. Yet, the viewer is forced to ask some questions. Do people make too much of commercialism and industrialism? Are these manufactured objects the real heroes of the twentieth century?

In 1965, Oldenburg started his "monument" proposals. A single object was to be enlarged to a gigantic scale and installed at a specific site. These objects include a huge baseball mitt, the head of a geometric mouse and a clothespin.

Oldenburg illustrates how Pop Art injected surprise, curiosity and humor into the art of the second half of the twentieth century.

17–11 Among the many everyday objects that Oldenburg has enlarged into giant sculptures are a clothespin, a baseball bat and a tube of lipstick.
Claes Oldenburg, *Shoestring Potatoes Spilling from a Bag*. Painted canvas, kapok, glue and acrylic, 107 3/4" x 46" x 42 1/8" (274 x 117 x 107 cm). Walker Art Center, Minneapolis, gift of the T. B. Walker Foundation, 1966.

Contextual Information
Oldenburg

Claes Oldenburg was sometimes referred to as "Pope of Pop." Born in Sweden, he majored in literature at Yale, taking his first art classes in his senior year. In 1962, he started making soft sculpture of cloth, foam rubber, kapok, plastic and vinyl. Influenced by Surrealism in size and materials and the incongruity of soft and hard, Oldenburg designed huge sculpture: a clothespin now in Philadelphia, a baseball bat in Chicago, a spoon with a cherry in Minneapolis, and a tube of lipstick on a tank in New Haven.

Higher-Order Thinking Skills

Ask students to determine what they think would be an appropriate subject for an Oldenburg sculpture for their school. Where would it be located? What materials would the artist use? How would the community receive it? How can a community be educated to understand what might be controversial art in public places?

paintings are constructed of colored forms on two-dimensional surfaces, what aspect of them appears real? Could the artists create the illusion of motion without the strict repetition in their designs?

Evaluate

Ask where Pop artists looked for their subject matter. If Pop artists were to cull Western culture today, what new media would be available to them that correspond to the magazines, billboards and comic strips that they used in the 1960s?

• How might high-tech computers, CD players and interactive disks influence their subjects and styles?

• If Andy Warhol's Campbell's soup cans (fig.17–15) epitomized the 1960s, what one commercial object might symbolize the present day?

• Ask students to cite examples in Lesson 17.2 to explain how Op artists created the illusion of movement in their paintings.

Reteach

Ask students to name past art styles that might appeal to Pop artists and then those that might appeal to Op artists.

• What about the subject matter or message of the previous styles might these later artists find interesting?

• Would Op artists perhaps be enchanted by Islamic art (Lesson 7.3)?

• How might Pop artists react to the American Social Realists (Lesson 15.4) or early twentieth-century photography (Lesson 14.5)?

Contextual Information

Lichtenstein

In the 1950s, Roy Lichtenstein worked in an Abstract Expressionist style but then wanted to get closer to cultural images. He started painting Disney-like characters and other common objects in the 1960s. He used an opaque projector to enlarge images directly onto his canvas. He then painted dots through stencils to replicate the ben-day process.

In 1960, Lichtenstein began teaching at Rutgers University and working with Allan Kaprow, who encouraged him to explore the comic-book image. Lichtenstein started with images on bubble-gum wrappers and comic books and moved to adventure images and drawings in yellow pages and mail-order catalogs. His first one-man show, in 1960, was sold out.

Robert Rauschenberg

(b.1925)

Robert Rauschenberg acted as the bridge between Abstract Expressionism and Pop Art when he fastened such mundane objects as license plates, street signs and men's clothes to his abstract canvases. He called them **combine paintings**. Like Picasso and Braque, he mixes reality with abstraction. Rauschenberg, however, uses the entire object, not simply scraps. He combines everything imaginable (silkscreen images, prints, objects, painting, stuffed birds and automobile tires) to create the visual sensation he desires. That sensation is often difficult for the public to comprehend. We are not used to looking at such a chaotic mixture of materials. Titles like *First Landing Jump* (fig.17–12) probably do not help either. But the artist makes the viewer look at ordinary things in a different context. The viewer is used to seeing tires on automobiles, not in "paintings." Pop artists want the viewer to see the commercial environment in a new way. By juxtaposing usually unrelated materials, Rauschenberg has succeeded.

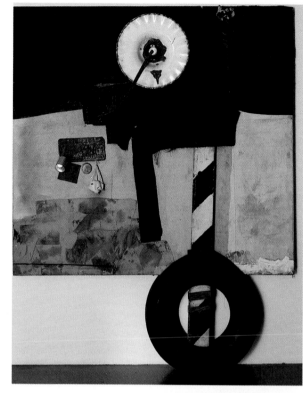

17–12 The challenge in works like this is to try to see everyday objects as shapes with color disassociated from their usual context. Robert Rauschenberg, *First Landing Jump*, 1961. Combine painting: tire, khaki shirt, license plate, leather straps, mirror, iron street light reflector, live blue light bulb, electric cable, steel spring, tin cans, various pieces of cloth, and oil paint on composition board, 89 1/4" x 81" (227 x 206 cm). The Museum of Modern Art, New York, gift of Philip Johnson. ©1996 Robert Rauschenberg/Licensed by VAGA, New York, NY

1949
Mao Zedong becomes leader of Communist China

World Cultural Timeline

1953
Tenzing Norgay reaches summit of Mount Everest

1966
Indira Gandhi becomes India's first woman prime minister

Materials and Techniques

To create the dots on his paintings, Lichtenstein first used a stiff brush and an aluminum plate in which he had drilled holes. In 1961, he put paper with the outlined image over door screening and rubbed the surface. During 1963, he experimented with various perforated metals as stencils.

17–14 Many of Lichtenstein's works poke fun at accepted ideas or trendy fashions of art. What is his message in this one?
Roy Lichtenstein, *Masterpiece*, 1962. Oil on canvas, 54 1/4" x 54 1/4" (138 x 138 cm). Collection of Leo Castelli Gallery, New York.

Jasper Johns

(b.1930)

Jasper Johns uses many Abstract Expressionist painting techniques, but his subject matter is as common as the American flag, targets, numbers, beer cans, flashlights and maps of the United States. Johns presents things that are often looked at, but seldom seen in detail. In *Numbers in Color* (fig.17–13), he shows numbers. He forces the viewers to look at common things that they often overlook. The complementary colors of blue and orange cry out for recognition as they seem to vibrate forward from and backward into the canvas. The overall effect is one of texture and pattern, but within that context, the individual numbers are the subject matter.

Roy Lichtenstein

(b.1923)

Roy Lichtenstein became one of the stars of Pop Art. Like other Pop artists, he wanted to play on the slick, multiple images of commercial art, its mechanical techniques and its glossy colors. Lichtenstein makes giant cartoon-like paintings. He even simulates the ben-day printing dots used to color the Sunday comics (fig.17–a). Paintings like *Masterpiece* (fig.17–14) look like they are cut from the comic page, but try to imagine this one 54 inches high. Often, he pokes gentle fun at the melodrama of the comics and the national fascination with them. Some of his works have verbal messages. His slick, machine-like style has remained the same for years. It is fun and art at the same time. His art brought Abstract Expressionism to an abrupt halt.

17–13 Johns' use of color and subject keeps your eye constantly moving over the surface with no one place to focus or rest.
Jasper Johns, *Numbers in Color*, 1959. Encaustic paint on newspaper and canvas, 66 1/4" x 49 1/4" (168 x 125 cm). Albright-Knox Art Gallery, Buffalo, New York, gift of Seymour H. Knox. ©1996 Jasper Johns/Licensed by VAGA, New York, NY

Higher-Order Thinking Skills

Borrow a magnifier or microscope to enable students to see the many small dots that make up a printed color image. Have students compare one of Lichtenstein's works to a frame from a comic strip. Ask why the Lichtenstein is considered art and the comic is not necessarily considered to be so. Can cartoons be art?

Contextual Information

Warhol

During the 1950s, Andy Warhol worked as an advertising illustrator, painting images of designer shoes and stationery. He began painting for himself in 1962, when he exhibited stenciled pictures of multiple dollar bills, soup cans (fig.2–34 and 17–15) and Coca-Cola bottles. His studio was called "The Factory."

Warhol made a six-hour film, *Sleep*, of a man sleeping, and an eight-hour film of the Empire State Building shot from the same angle the whole time.

Segal

After World War II, Segal attended New York University and majored in art education. He was unable to find a job when he graduated, so he built his own farm buildings, raised chickens, sold eggs, and painted in his attic. He later made his plaster sculptures in converted chicken coops.

Segal said that Hopper's paintings, as well as sculpture by Egyptians, Greeks, Michelangelo and Rodin, inspired him and that "I find myself bumping into the history of art that I love when I work."

Happenings

From the late 1950s to the early 1970s, artists experimented with happenings, which were lively, chaotic performances that suggested the confusing quality of daily life. In happenings, artists leveled the differences among performers (ordinary people executing everyday activities), objects (refuse from the urban environment) and the audience. They freely intermingled all these

Andy Warhol

(1928–1987)

Andy Warhol and Pop Art go hand in hand; it is hard to imagine one without the other. He zeroes in on American mass production and its boring repetitions. The consumer goes into the supermarket and sees hundreds of cans of Campbell's soup. The product is instantly recognized and found in nearly every market and home in the country. Warhol painted *100 Cans* (fig.17–15) in a boring, unexciting way—just the way they are lined up on the market shelves. He even used the mechanical silkscreen process to apply paint to canvas, and had other people do the work. This is how impersonal he became with the medium. Warhol's depictions of Campbell's cans also include a series of paintings of huge, individual soup cans. They hung in the same gallery in a row to simulate the supermarket experience. Warhol is also known for his images of Marilyn Monroe and other personalities. He created the images by using the same printmaking process he used for the cans.

17–15 One soup can may be boring, but 100 of them present patterns to find. Do you find yourself reading the labels to try to find one that is different?
Andy Warhol, *100 Cans*, 1962. Oil on canvas, 71 3/4" x 52" (182 x 132 cm). Albright-Knox Art Gallery, Buffalo, New York, gift of Seymour H. Knox.

George Segal

(b.1924)

George Segal was concerned with everyday sculptural subjects the same as Claes Oldenburg. However, he uses a different medium and subjects. He uses plaster to form people in everyday activities. Segal dips surgical gauze in plaster and wraps it around the person posing for him. Each section of the fast-drying plaster is cut off as soon as it dries. The parts are assembled to make a hollow cast of the person. The ghostly white figures in *Walk, Don't Walk* (fig.17–16) are startlingly real, especially when placed in a setting with real props, such as the street sign. There is nothing amazing or dramatic about the figures or their poses. They are simply realistic slices of American life—people going about their everyday jobs and routines.

17–16 Segal placed his subjects in real-world settings. He often looked for props in junkyards.
George Segal, *Walk, Don't Walk*, 1976. Plaster, cement, painted wood and electric light, 105" x 71 3/4" x 71 3/4" (267 x 182 x 182 cm). Whitney Museum of American Art, New York. ©1996 George Segal/Licensed by VAGA, New York, NY

elements. Filmmakers, musicians and poets, as well as painters and sculptors such as Jim Dine, Claes Oldenburg and George Segal, experimented with this new, revolutionary art form.

Higher-Order Thinking Skills

Have students create their own Pop work by repeating an image of a common item or product. Photocopying, cutting out and gluing, and then coloring can speed up the process. Have students discuss what had to be done to the work to make it visually interesting.

Contextual Information

Riley

Riley studied Seurat's theory of pointillism and initially worked in black and white, turning to color in 1966. She was in the first exhibition of the Op Art movement, "The Responsive Eye," which opened at the Museum of Modern Art in 1965 with a reproduction of Riley's *Current* (1964) on the cover of the catalog. Her work was given great praise from the beginning.

Vasarely

Op Art grew out of investigations of Gestalt psychologists in the 1920s and the research of Victor Vasarely in Paris in the 1940s and 1950s. It is based on the physiology of the eye and the brain's ability to respond to color and pattern; there is no association with the visual world.

Vasarely was a major pioneer of Op Art. He trained in Budapest, went to Paris in 1930, and worked as a graphic designer. In 1947, he began producing completely abstract paintings that explored optical effects. He published his theories in the *Yellow Manifesto* of 1955 and described his work as the creation of mechanistic, standardized shapes and colors.

Bridget Riley

(b.1931)

Instead of using the common, everyday images found in Pop Art, Bridget Riley worked on pure Op Art paintings in England for many years. She created surfaces that seem to undulate before the viewer's eyes. If the viewer gazes steadily in one place, shifts eye movement, or moves the work a bit, the image itself will move. Works such as *Fall* (fig.17–17) are capable of producing a dizzy sensation in some viewers. Riley's surfaces seem to wriggle and the viewer cannot make the sensation stop, especially when confronting the work in its actual size.

Victor Vasarely

(b.1908)

Victor Vasarely is the Hungarian-born leader of the Op Art movement in America. He works with geometric shapes and brilliant colors. His works, which he does not wish to call paintings, play tricks with the viewer's eyes. His surfaces seem to bulge in or out in either subtle or unbelievably abrupt bubbles. To achieve such effects, he changes the size of shapes or the width of lines and strips, as in *Vega-Kontosh-Va* (fig.17–18). Vasarely uses thin layers of oil paint and crisp, hard edges to produce his effects. He creates fantastic illusions of optical space and depth. His experiments formed the basis for an illusionistic movement in art

at the beginning of the 1980s. A museum in Aix-en-Provence, France, was built to hold his huge paintings, most of which are over twenty feet high. The effect of rooms filled with such gigantic images is overpowering for many viewers.

Richard Anuskiewicz

(1930)

Richard Anuskiewicz was another American leader in the Op Art movement. His paintings (fig.17–19) are carefully constructed with line and color to produce sensations of the same shape both advancing and receding. The placement of lines, shapes and colors is incredibly exact. His work is brilliant, balanced and optically stimulating.

17–17 Op images like this one can seem to move and can also produce sensations of colors even though they are painted in black and white only. Bridget Riley, *Fall*, 1963. Acrylic emulsion on hardboard, 55 1/2" x 55 1/2" (141 x 141 cm). The Tate Gallery, London.

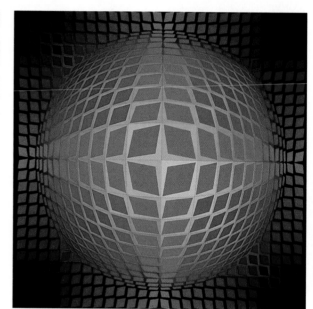

17–18 What design principles are at work here to make your eye interpret this as a three-dimensional form? Victor Vasarely, *Vega-Kontosh-Va*, 1971. Tempera on panel, 25 1/2" x 25 1/2" (65 x 65 cm). Los Angeles County Museum of Art, gift of Mr. and Mrs. Donald Winston.

Interdisciplinary Inquiry

Science: Have students research information on the physiology of the eye and the research of Vasarely. Some might interview a local ophthalmologist for information about the eye. Encourage students to discover why this type of art is so difficult to look at for long periods of time.

Performing Arts Connection

Less Is More

Beginning in the 1970s, many individuals in all the arts searched for the very essence of their medium. The polyrhythms of composer Steven Reich closely paralleled the undulating paintings of Op artist Bridget Riley and the repetitive, abstract choreography of Laura Dean. In every arena, artists inserted minute variations into their repetitive compositions in order to establish subtle, barely discernible nuances that produced a mesmerizing effect.

17–20 Although this piece is flat, the viewer's eye insists on reading it as a three-dimensional form.
Ron Davis, *Plane Sawtooth*, 1970. Polyester resin and fiberglass, 59 3/4" x 140 1/4" (152 x 356 cm). Albright-Knox Art Gallery, Buffalo, New York, gift of Seymour H. Knox.

17–19 Why do these colors seem to shift and glow?
Richard Anuskiewicz, *Iridescence*, 1965. Acrylic on canvas, 59 3/4" x 59 3/4" (152 x 152 cm). Albright-Knox Art Gallery, Buffalo, New York, gift of Seymour H. Knox. ©1996 Richard Anuszkiewicz/Licensed by VAGA, New York, NY

Ron Davis
(b.1937)

To create his optical works, Ron Davis began using contemporary materials like acrylics or polyester resins with fiberglass. He fused colors to the rear surface of fiberglass to create astonishing works of optical illusion. *Plane Sawtooth* (fig.17–20) is absolutely flat, not three-dimensional. It is cut from a sheet of fiberglass. Its unframed, irregular shape, when placed on the wall, adds dramatically to the illusion of three-dimensionality. Even when the viewer gets close to the wall, it is difficult to visually flatten out the illusion because it is so convincing. Some parts seem shadowed while others are transparent. The viewer's eyes, accustomed to looking at three-dimensional objects, cannot separate the illusion from reality.

Lesson 17.2 Review

1 How did the Pop Art movement get its name? List some of the leaders in this movement.
2 What is Op Art? How did Op Art artists create a sense of movement within their paintings?
3 Select an Op Art painting to stare at for a full minute. Describe your feelings at the end of the minute.
4 How many times larger than life is Oldenburg's *Falling Shoestring Potatoes*?
5 In Jasper John's paintings, what is he encouraging the viewer to notice? In *Numbers in Color*, what means does he use to focus our attention on his subject?
6 What do most of Roy Lichtenstein's paintings resemble? How are they different from his source of inspiration?
7 What was the underlying message in Warhol's *100 Cans*? What means did he use to apply the paint to his canvases?
8 Describe the method that Segal used to produce the figures in *Walk, Don't Walk*. What are the people doing in this sculpture?

Higher-Order Thinking Skills

Bridget Riley learned a lot about Georges Seurat and even copied one of his paintings to learn how he applied his paint. Ask the class what they think she learned.

Cooperative Learning

Pair up students and have one member of each pair take on the role of a Pop artist and the other take on that of an Op artist. Have them work to convince the other of the importance of their style and its potential impact on future generations. Suggest that they use both the similarities in the two styles (e.g., clean, hard-edged forms) and their differences (e.g., subject matter) to boost their arguments.

Lesson 17.2 Review Answers

1 The subjects of this art—Coke bottles, soup cans, comic-strip characters and hamburgers—were drawn from popular culture, hence, this movement was labeled *Pop Art*. Some of the leaders of the Pop Art movement were Claes Oldenburg, Robert Rauschenberg, Jasper Johns, Roy Lichtenstein, Andy Warhol and George Segal.
2 Op Art is short for Optical Art, a style in which a sense of movement is created by the use of scientific principles and optical illusions.
3 Staring at Bridget Riley's *Fall*, for example, could make one feel dizzy after a full minute.
4 *Falling Shoestring Potatoes* is five to six times larger than life.

5 In Jasper Johns' paintings, he encourages the viewer to notice common things that they often overlook. In *Numbers in Color*, he uses complementary colors of blue and orange that seem to vibrate on the canvas, calling attention to the numbers.
6 Lichtenstein's paintings resemble comics, but they are much larger than ordinary newspaper comics.
7 Warhol was calling attention to American mass production and its boring repetitions. He applied paint to canvas using a mechanical silk-screen process.
8 Segal wrapped people in gauze strips soaked in plaster. In *Walk, Don't Walk*, the people are standing by a traffic signal waiting to cross the street.

Lesson 17.3

Color Field Painting developed in the 1960s and 1970s. The artist's flat areas of color contained none of the emotional painterly brushwork of the Abstract Expressionists. The enormous scale in which some of the artists worked created huge environments that engulfed the viewer.

Warm-up

Ask students to close their eyes and imagine floating in cool shallow pools of water. What colors come to mind that could describe this experience? Have them glance at the Color Field paintings in Lesson 17.3 and discuss how their imaginings relate to these artworks.

Objectives

Students should be able to:

Explain that Color Field painters relied solely on flat, unarticulated fields of color.

Describe how large canvases and unpainted spaces provided entry into the compositions.

Vocabulary Definitions

stain painting The technique used by Helen Frankenthaler in which she stained her unprimed canvases with thinned paint.

shaped canvas A canvas in other shapes besides the traditional rectangle.

Teach

Aesthetics/Criticism: Instruct students to measure out the dimensions (7′ 2″ x 9′ 9″) of Helen Frankenthaler's *Mountains and Sea* (fig.17–21) on the classroom wall. Have students look at the image in the textbook and then its real scale on the wall to determine how the painting's size dramatically affects it. (If possible, a visit to a local museum to view similar artwork would be quite helpful.) Ask how Frankenthaler draws us into her space. Standing up close, would the viewer be able to see anything beyond the edges of the canvas? And what about the plain, unpainted portions of her work? Are they inviting empty spots for us to jump into? Ask students if they enjoy this work. Why do they find it more appealing than, less appealing than, or equally appealing as Op Art?

17.3 Color Field Painting

DURING THE SIXTIES AND SEVENTIES, a style called *Color Field Painting* developed into a very important area of art. This style owed much to Mark Rothko's large, flat color statements. It relied solely on flat fields of color. Color Field Painting had none of the emotionalism and slashing brushwork of Abstract Expressionism. The work produced was very cool, very serene and very beautiful. Color Field Painting was often minutely planned. However, artists also worked with improvisation and accidental happenings. Color Field Painting has also been labeled *Post-Painterly Abstraction*, *Classical Abstraction* and *Hard-Edge Painting*.

After World War II, many painters started working on a larger scale until their canvases were almost mural size. When huge paintings hang on the walls of museums or other public spaces, they become an important aspect of the interior environment. They draw the viewer into active visual participation with the work. Artists then began opening up space in the work itself by leaving large portions painted white or as natural canvas. This space became active open space to which the viewer could abandon himself or herself. Some artists designed three or four canvases to work together on three or four walls, acting as a total environment. This style is sometimes called *Enlarged Field Painting*.

Key Notes
• Color Field Painting relies solely on flat fields of color.
• Enlarged field painting opens up space in works by leaving portions painted white or as natural canvas.

Vocabulary
stain painting
shaped canvas

Special Feature

Helen Frankenthaler

b. 1928

Helen Frankenthaler is one of the major contributors to Color Field Painting, particularly to Enlarged Field Painting.

Many of her huge abstract paintings were painted on unprimed canvas that was stapled to the floor to make it taut. She works in a spontaneous way, pouring and spreading, pushing and flowing the stains and paints onto the canvas. What starts at the top may end up being a side or the bottom of the work. Part of the unstretched canvas may be cut off to change the shape or the dimensions. Working in such a spontaneous way is difficult for many artists, but Frankenthaler achieves wonderful results with it.

Mountains and Sea (fig.17–21) is the most famous of Frankenthaler's works. It is an important work because, with this painting, the

17–21 Cover the red shape or the gray stripe. What happens to the painting? Is it complete without either or both of those areas?
Helen Frankenthaler, *Mountains and Sea*, 1952. Oil on canvas, 7′2″ x 9′9″ (218.4 x 297 cm). Collection of the artist, on loan to the National Gallery of Art, Washington DC.

Evaluate

Ask students to study the images in Lesson 17.3 to try to decide which ones were perhaps stimulated by real-life subjects.

• Although the images are abstract, what about the ones students have chosen appear to have stemmed from the observable world?

• Which artists seem concerned only with the formal qualities of line, shape, color and composition? Are the titles of the works helpful?

Reteach

Have students try to determine how Frankenthaler painted *Mountains and Sea*, keeping in mind its enormous size and the fluidity of her pigment. Ask how she might have accomplished it without using an easel or small paint brushes. Students can refer to pages 564 and 565 to check their answers.

Ask students how they might connect Color Field Painting to earlier abstract movements. For instance, what lessons does it draw from Abstract Expressionism? What European forerunners does it have? In what ways is the style different from anything that had come before?

artist begins to use the technique of **stain painting**. It forced other artists to think about and use color in a very new way. Frankenthaler made this painting after returning from a trip to Nova Scotia. On her trip, Frankenthaler was struck by the juxtaposition of mountains right beside the ocean. The painting is abstract. Nevertheless, the image does convey a sense of mass adjacent to the horizontal blue line of the ocean. The painting was not received with much enthusiasm. Priced at around a hundred dollars, it failed to sell.

The Bay (fig.17–22) is composed of an irregular blue shape looming over a field of green and gray. The blues were painted first in various horizontal gestures. The layering of different blues gives the blue shape its billowy effect. According to Frankenthaler, she had painted the blues and then left them to dry. When she came back, she added the green and thought it was done. Later that day, she put in the gray and the red dot and decided it was done. This question of whether a work is done plays an important part in her work.

Mountains and Sea and *The Bay* are both very powerful representations of Color Field Painting, particularly Enlarged Field Painting.

17–22 Color Field painters generally avoid any sense of paint texture in their work.
Helen Frankenthaler, *The Bay*, 1963. Acrylic on canvas, 80 3/4" x 81 3/4" (205.1 x 207.7 cm). The Detroit Institute of Arts, gift of Dr. and Mrs. Hilbert H. DeLawter.

Contextual Information
Frankenthaler
Frankenthaler invented the "soak-stain" technique. For her first works in 1952, she poured turpentine-thinned oil paint on unprimed canvas. She switched to acrylic paint in 1963 to obtain a more saturated color and slower absorption time so that she could push the paint and let it flow over the canvas.

• Have students compare Frankenthaler's and Pollock's paintings. In what ways is their work similar?

Higher-Order Thinking Skills

Tell your students to pretend that they are the director of a major museum that owns a Frankenthaler painting in need of conservation. They also have the opportunity to purchase a new work of art that would be a significant addition to the museum's collection. The budget will not allow them to do both. Which would they choose, conservation or purchase? Why?

Conservation Note

Stain painting does not have any barrier between the paint and the canvas. Because ingredients in oil paints eat away at fabrics, the care of Frankenthaler's paintings presents many problems for the conservation department at museums that own her works. Much time and money are needed to preserve the paintings so that they do not deteriorate.

Contextual Information

Albers

At 31, Joseph Albers enrolled at the Bauhaus and proved to be one of the most gifted students. He was asked to become a junior member of the staff in 1923. He was made the workshop master of the stained-glass workshop and taught a preliminary course in which students experimented with materials such as paper to learn about construction. He was famous for projects such as sculpture made of used razor blades and wooden matches and sculpture made of cut and folded paper.

Joseph Albers

(1888–1976)

Joseph Albers became the teacher of many Color Field painters when he came to America from Germany in 1933. Albers began a long series of studies based on the interaction of color. Using the square as a motif, he demonstrated the qualities of color and how they interact when placed next to each other or near other colors. *Homage to the Square: Glow* (fig.17–23) illustrates the format and design of his experiments with color. In most of his works, the squares are placed as they are here. However, with different colors and combinations, the visual results vary. Here, the intensity of the central hue causes that square to come forward and float over the others. Albers published his fascinating studies in a book titled *Interaction of Color* in which he defines his research and explains his findings.

Barnett Newman

(1905–1970)

Barnett Newman was part of a movement to produce art totally without any visual or geometrical associations. His color fields are often huge and might be separated by a single, wide or narrow line of contrasting or similar hue. Because he wanted to reduce the content of the painting to virtually nothing, his work was called *Minimal Art*. It has also been called *Cool Art* because of its nonemotional quality and its characteristic precision. It is the direct opposite of the hot and emotional Abstract Expressionism.

17–23 Especially over the last 200 years, many artists like Josef Albers have developed theories about color and the ways that colors interact. Albers taught at the Bauhaus in Germany before he immigrated to the United States. Joseph Albers, *Homage to the Square: Glow*, 1966. Oil on fiberboard, 48" x 48" (122 x 122 cm). Hirshhorn Museum and Sculpture Garden, Smithsonian Institution, Washington DC.

Newman's *Adam* (fig.17–24) is a large canvas of two elements. A dark-valued reddish-brown color field is divided by bright red lines. The painting has no specific or hidden meanings. It is the most minimal statement that Newman could make at the time. He wanted the viewer to look at the work and see *it*. He did not want the viewer to see any suggestive subject matter or

geometrical organization. Perhaps the work would make the viewer think inwardly, much as the Oriental priest who looks at a blank wall and meditates.

Artists like Ad Reinhardt out-minimalized Newman later. Reinhardt painted a solid canvas of only black. He painted it so smoothly that no brushstrokes would show—the ultimate minimal statement.

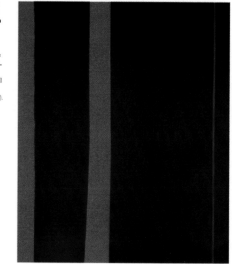

17–24 These huge canvases force the viewer to see them and be a part of them. There is no hidden message, just the experience of being with them. Barnett Newman, *Adam*, 1951–1952. Oil on canvas, 95 3/4" x 79 1/2" (243 x 202 cm). The Tate Gallery, London.

1972
China's isolationism ends with Richard Nixon's visit

1975
The Vietnam Conflict ends and North and South Vietnam reunite

World Cultural Timeline

1973
American Indian movement political protest at Wounded Knee

1979
Mother Teresa of Calcutta receives Nobel Peace Prize

Performing Arts Connection

John Cage's Minimalist Music

For composer John Cage, a minimalist definition of music is sound heard over time. For him, everyday noise could be the basis of art. In 1952, Cage composed a piece that lasts 4 minutes and 33 seconds. For the total performance of the piece, the pianist came out on stage, lifted the lid of the keyboard, and sat at the instrument without playing it. The random sounds from the audience constituted the work of art.

• What would be different and similar about each performance of John Cage's composition?

17–26 Many of
Kelly's beautiful
abstract shapes
began as part of
sketches of
everyday objects
such as shadows,
doors and windows.
Ellsworth Kelly, *Blue
Curve III*, 1972. Oil on
canvas, 67 3/4" x
166 1/2" (172 x 423
cm). Los Angeles
County Museum of
Art.

17–25 Noland
used very thin
pigment to stain
his canvases.
Kenneth Noland.
Song, 1958. Oil on
canvas, 69" x 69"
(175 x 175 cm).
Gift of the Friends of
the Whitney Museum
of American Art,
New York. ©1996 Ken
Noland/Licensed by
VAGA, New York, NY

Kenneth Noland

(b.1924)

Kenneth Noland studied with
Albers and continued the Color
Field emphasis on the canvas over
subject matter or design. He started
painting concentric circles on
unprimed canvas, which caused a
staining process and made the circles seem to pulsate and float.
He then moved to gigantic, inverted
chevrons of bright colors. Each
chevron is made up of several
stripes placed against a darkly
painted canvas. At first, they were
symmetrical, as in *Song* (fig.17–25).
But soon he moved the point of the
chevron to one side or the other.
More recently, he has painted huge
canvases of horizontal stripes of flat
color. The stripes float against vast
white fields, producing the effect of
flat landscapes. He was also one of
the first artists to work on **shaped
canvases**. Instead of using the rectangular shape, he worked with
canvases shaped like diamonds and
triangles.

Ellsworth Kelly

(b.1923)

Ellsworth Kelly works with pure
colors and geometric shapes. Some
of his designs have only two intense
colors and several large flat shapes.
Large is an apt word because often
his simple designs are mural-sized—

over 9 feet high and about 20 feet
wide. Kelly studied in Paris with
the Constructionists, artists who
worked abstractly with basic geometric shapes. He often uses acrylic
paints to attain the hard, perfect
edges of his shapes. Such precision
is essential to the concept and
style of Hard-Edge painting. It is
possible only with the use of masking tape and thinned pigments.

Blue Curve III (fig.17–26) is part
of a series of works based on shaped
canvases and curved shapes. The
edge of the intense blue color
appears to bulge forward from the
diamond-shaped frame. But, in
reality, it is perfectly flat.

Higher-Order Thinking Skills

In a natural or architectural setting,
Ellsworth Kelly often finds a beautiful shape that forms the basis of a
work. Ask students to find a photograph of a common thing or place.
Have them select a beautiful shape
from the photograph and sketch it.
Next, they are to add appropriate
color for the shape and enlarge it to
the biggest size that your classroom
can accommodate. Put the shapes
on the wall one at a time and discuss how they influence students'
perception of the room or hall.

Contextual Information

Louis

After first seeing Frankenthaler's work, Morris Louis destroyed his paintings. Even after that, he was so critical of his own paintings that he frequently destroyed them.

Louis worked with diluted paint poured on unprimed canvas, layer upon layer. One writer said that on one occasion Louis diluted two tubes of color in six gallons of thinner. When it was poured on the canvas, the thinner left a ring around the paint.

Louis put his canvases on a frame, slanted them against the wall of his dining room, and poured the paint across the canvas. By angling the frame, he determined the direction of the flow. On some paintings, he overlaid many colors; on others he poured the thinned paint in parallel stripes.

• Compare Louis' paintings with Frankenthaler's. How were they different? (Frankenthaler related frequently to landscapes and required the full canvas to make the composition; Louis sometimes used only the edges or middle portions. Frankenthaler used acrylic paint; Louis used oil.)

17–27 By overlapping and repeating this common shape and varying the color, Frank Stella invites your eye to follow him through the design and complete the forms. Although the protractor is the only shape used, other shapes are implied. Can you find them? Frank Stella, *Protractor Variation*, 1969. Fluorescent-alkyd on canvas, 120" x 240 1/4" (305 x 610 cm). Los Angeles County Museum of Art.

Frank Stella

(b.1936)

Frank Stella carried the shaped canvas still further. His geometric designs make use of the unframed edges as part of the painting. In *Protractor Variation* (fig.17–27), the interior lines and shapes repeat the curved and flat edges of the canvas itself. Unlike other Color Field painters, Stella used colors that are extremely varied. His protractor series often combines fluorescent paints and metallic colors that are visually jarring. The colors are carefully chosen to cause visual movement. What appear to be white lines are really narrow negative areas of unpainted canvas between the brightly painted shapes. During an earlier period of his development, Stella used these unpainted lines against a solid color field as the main element of the painting.

Adolph Gottlieb

(1903–1974)

Adolph Gottlieb was an Abstract Expressionist whose work became larger and larger. He developed a set of visual symbols in his art. He evolved a way of combining two opposite shapes: a disk and a ragged-edged form. The disk, often a soft-edged roundish shape, is calm and geometric. The ragged shape breaks out of any containment. People have labeled the shapes "bursts" and "blasts." The roundish shapes always float over the irregular ones. Although Gottlieb did not mind other readings of his powerful work, he only wanted to make the two opposite shapes work together as a unit. *Orb* (fig.17–28) illustrates these two visual symbols. The soft edges of the round shape were made by staining the raw canvas. They create a pulsating sensation of forward and backward movement. The powerful black shapes are reminders of Kline's slashing black strokes. However, by combining them with the round shapes, Gottlieb has produced a completely different and personal statement.

Sam Francis

(b.1923)

Sam Francis pours freely applied thin colors onto the canvas. The colors spread, stain and overlap, creating luminous transparent layers. In earlier works, such as *Basel Mural* (fig.17–29), the shapes are clustered in the top part of the gigantic canvas. In later works, the vivid color blobs are arranged around the edges of the canvas and almost slip out of sight. In both arrangements, the white area acts as a powerful, sparkling, positive area

17–28 Notice how the powerful black strokes compare with the softness of the circles. Adolph Gottlieb. *Orb*, 1964. Oil on canvas, 90" x 60" (228.5 x 152.5 cm). Dallas Museum of Art.

of vibrant space. The drips, blobs, lines, stains and bright colors add to the intensity of the unpainted areas. The unpainted areas seem to be space through which one can move. Some of these works by Francis are enormous, over thirty-two feet wide. They enwrap the viewer in sparkling white space.

17–29 The dripping paints, cut-off edges of shapes and open areas of white negative space create a sense of movement in and out of the picture plane as if the artist has given us only a part of a larger subject. Sam Francis, *Basel Mural*, 1956–58. Oil on canvas, 156 3/4" x 236 1/4" (398 x 600 cm). The Norton Simon Art Foundation, Pasadena, CA.

17–30 Controlling layers of transparency on a huge surface requires a lot of practice and the willingness to take risks to see the idea through. Morris Louis, *Point of Tranquility*, 1958. Synthetic polymer on canvas, 101 1/2" x 135" (258 x 343 cm). Hirshhorn Museum and Sculpture Garden, Smithsonian Institution, Washington DC.

Morris Louis

(1912–1962)

Morris Louis based his images on the physical movement of color across unprimed canvas. First, he poured diluted acrylic paint on the canvas. Then, he tilted the canvas and let the paint run until it produced superimposed veils of color. Sometimes, the shapes were linear, running from top to bottom. Others, such as in *Point of Tranquility* (fig.17–30), spread in different directions. The overlapping, transparent shapes create a feeling of depth on the huge flat surfaces. Although the work is spontaneous and unplanned, the working process is delicate and careful. Such a gigantic surface required special care in the application of each color. The tilting of the canvas to spread the paint had to be controlled, stopped and shifted to another angle until the supply of color was even. Colors had to run to a satisfactory shape and location. *Point of Tranquility* is a soft, gentle explosion of color. Colors seem to float like colored smoke in the white space of the canvas. It is a painting done completely without a brushstroke.

Lesson 17.3 Review

1 How do the Color Field painters cause viewers to notice their paintings and then to react with them?

2 Why is Barnett Newman's art described as minimal art and cool art?

3 What is the point in minimal art such as Barnett Newman's *Adam*? What is the artist trying to get the viewer to see?

4 Who was one of the first artists to paint on shaped canvases? Which artist use shaped canvases even more extensively?

5 How does Ellsworth Kelly make the hard edges in his paintings such as *Blue Curve III*?

6 How many protractors can you count in Stella's *Protractor Variation*?

7 What was Adolph Gottlieb's design concern as he painted the different shapes in *Orb*?

8 Would either Frank Stella's *Protractor Variation* or Sam Francis' *Basel Mural* fit on your bedroom wall?

Lesson 17.3 Review Answers

1 Color Field paintings are so large that they fill the viewer's field of vision or environment, drawing the viewer into active visual participation in the work. By leaving portions of the canvas neutral or white, the artist opens up space in the work in which the viewer can abandon him or herself. Some artists put three and four huge canvases together creating total environments.

2 Since he reduced the content of his painting to virtually nothing, Newman's work is called Minimal Art. It has also been called Cool Art because of its nonemotional quality and its characteristic precision.

3 Newman wanted the viewer to look at the art and see only the art itself. He did not want the viewer to see any suggestive subject matter or geometrical organization.

4 Kenneth Noland was one of the first contemporary artists to paint on shaped canvas. Frank Stella used shaped canvases even more extensively than Noland.

5 Kelly uses masking tape and thinned pigments to create hard edges.

6 The answer is approximately sixteen, but the number is not important. This question should encourage students to look carefully at this painting.

7 Gottlieb wanted to make the two opposite shapes work together as a unit.

8 Since each painting is about 10' x 20', it would probably be too large for most students' rooms.

Lesson 17.4

A revival in realistic art began in the 1970s, originating in California and spreading throughout the country. The New Realists' various depictions of daily life often functioned as visual metaphors.

Warm-up

Ask students to quickly look at the images in Lesson 17.4, not looking at the captions. Which do they believe are paintings and which appear to be photographs? After checking their answers, were they surprised at how accurately painters can represent the visible world? Why would some artists want to do this?

Objectives

Students should be able to:

Understand that Realism reemerged as an important movement in the 1970s.

Describe how New Realism reflects the high energy and variety of contemporary American society.

Teach

Ask students to closely examine Chuck Close's portraits in figs.17–31 and 17–32.

• What tool do they think helped Close capture such an exacting likeness of this man?

• Does Close hide the fact that he relies on a camera? How is the influence of photography evident in the study and in the final work?

• Ask students how knowing that Close wants to translate photographic information into paint affects the way they feel about his work.

• Would they have been more or less impressed if they had been unaware of the technical device he used?

17.4 New Realism

AMERICAN INTEREST IN REALISTIC ART never really disappeared from the scene. In the seventies, a revival began in California and spread rapidly throughout the country. The movement goes by various names like *Super-Realism, Photo-Realism, New Realism* and *Hyper-Realism*. Artists used commercial art techniques of airbrush, photography, spray or anything else that might help to produce realistic images. New Realism was based on genre art and the Pop paintings of the fifties. It led directly into the illusionistic paintings of the early eighties that astound the viewer with mind-boggling illusions of reality.

These works are rich in imagery and often function as visual metaphors. Familiar images often are juxtaposed in unusual and sometimes perplexing ways. Subjects are treated with cool, intellectual approaches and, in this way, differ from the Realism of the nineteenth century. New Realism reflects the high energy and variety of contemporary life in America.

Key Notes
• New Realism is based on the Pop Art of the fifties.
• A tremendous variety of images and metaphors reflect contemporary American life.

Special Feature
Chuck Close
(b.1940)
The ultimate research tool of the New Realists is the camera. One of the pioneers of the use of photography as a source of imagery is Chuck Close. Close started gaining attention in the late sixties with his gargantuan, photographically realistic black-and-white portraits of himself and his friends. Like other Realist artists, Close wants to make a very objective rendering of his subjects. He has said that his main objective is to translate photographic information into paint information.

He depicts only the human figure. Usually, the portraits are head and shoulder views seen frontally against a uniform background. These are completely dispassionate studies and do not in any way reflect the inner qualities of the subjects. Close gives equal attention to every physical characteristic. Instead of seeing the sitter's personality, we become very aware of how the artist has presented us with a gigantic illusion.

17–31 How does this compare to the acrylic painting of the same subject?
Chuck Close, *Mark, unfinished*, 1978. Watercolor, 53 1/2" x 40 1/2" (136 x 103 cm). Pace Wildenstein, New York.

Evaluate

Ask students if New Realist artists were concerned with the underlying emotion of their subject matter. What might the impersonal aura of their paintings reflect about contemporary urban society?

Ask students if artists before the advent of New Realism had ever used optical devices to create their work.

• Do they believe that artists should or should not rely on aids such as cameras, computers, video recorders and printing devices? Why?

• If students use a calculator in a math class, do they consider this a justifiable tool for learning or a means of shortcutting the process? Why is their opinion the same or different regarding art?

17–32 Would you want Chuck Close to do your portrait? Why or why not? Chuck Close, *Mark*, 1979. Acrylic on canvas, 9' x 7' (274 x 213 cm). Pace WIldenstein, New York.

Contextual Information

Close

Close uses a grid to enlarge the photographs for his paintings. After graphing both the photo and the canvas in exact proportions, he then transfers the information 1/4 inch at a time, matching the values in each section and even replicating any out-of-focus areas. The paintings take between three and six months to complete.

From a distance, the portraits appear to be giant blowups of photographs. Up close, they break down into fields of dots and marks.

Two paintings of the same person, Mark, give a good idea of how his technique works. *Mark,*

unfinished (fig.17–31) makes use of a mechanistic dot and square technique. It is a gridded image composed of horizontal bands of variegated color.

Mark, (fig.17–32) is a much more factual, realistic painting. This head resembles the way we look under

harsh fluorescent light. Pores, hairs, wrinkles and blemishes are nakedly displayed.

Close's work is representative of New Realism. His paintings are both perfect reproduction as well as gigantic illusion.

Reteach

Ask students if Chuck Close was the first to use optical devices in creating his artwork. What tool did Vermeer use (Lesson 11.3, pages 354–355) and what modern equipment influenced the Impressionists (Lesson 13.1)?

Have students identify how New Realism revealed something new to them about both painting and photography. Which images in Lesson 17.4 led them to these realizations and why?

Contextual Information

Estes

Estes works from several photographs, combining them into a more complex image. He presents wide-angle views and images inside windows, whereas a viewer would see only a reflection in a narrow angle. Estes moves the viewer's eye around the canvas with placement of shadows, tone, colors and shapes. Unlike a photograph, in which objects beyond the focal point are out of focus, Estes' works bring everything into sharp focus.

17–33 Andrew Wyeth's father was a painter and illustrator, and his son Jamie is also an artist. The family tradition in the arts may have given Andrew the self-confidence to follow his own interest and to use traditional techniques such as egg tempera.
Andrew Wyeth, *Christina's World*, 1948. Tempera on gesso panel, 32 1/4" x 47 3/4" (82 x 121 cm). The Museum of Modern Art, New York.

Andrew Wyeth

(b.1917)

Andrew Wyeth has painted in his own realistic way throughout the various isms and developments of twentieth-century art. His work is a continuation of the American Scene painting and portrays the natural environment of Pennsylvania and Maine. In addition to the natural landscape, he also paints portraits of his neighbors. Wyeth works in a natural and easy style, while using the exacting medium of egg tempera. From energetic and emotional sketches, he works to a finished product that seems absolutely real. Yet, the works are based on abstract structuring and design.

In paintings such as *Christina's World* (fig.17–33), he painted in the vast spaces and background first. Then, he added the figure over it. The girl was a crippled neighbor of Wyeth's. Her family's farm, shown in the painting, is next to his in Maine. The painting, like many of Wyeth's works, is a realistic presentation that also creates a mood. He is able to capture a moment in time

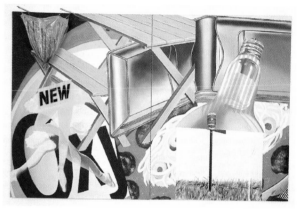

17–34 Use the text to help you find all of the images in this painting.
James Rosenquist, *Nomad*, 1963. Oil on canvas with plastic and wood, 84 1/4" x 209 1/2" (214 x 532 cm). Albright-Knox Gallery, Buffalo, New York, gift of Seymour H. Knox. ©1996 James Rosenquist/Licensed by VAGA, New York, NY

and a feeling of place, enriched by a touch of the universal experience with life, people and place. He raises commonplace subjects to levels of importance and dignity with immense skill.

James Rosenquist

(b.1933)

James Rosenquist worked as a billboard painter. In the sixties, he began to create king-sized paintings on canvas of billboard proportions. He uses many techniques of commercial and industrial artists, and he mimics the advertising style of art. His work has the feeling of Pop Art in its common subjects, but he combines many such images into one framework. In *Nomad* (fig.17–34), the viewer can see (from left to right) part of a detergent box, two pairs of ballerinas' legs, a redwood picnic table and bench, a gigantic billfold, spaghetti with meatballs and olives, part of a light bulb, a microphone and a patch of grass with a stake in it. He has also included a real plastic trash bag and a pile of sticks he used to mix his paints. Imagine watching a dozen television commercials or zipping by several advertising billboards. The work creates the same kind of impression.

17–36 These sculptures seem so real that passersby often try to interact with them by speaking to them or asking them questions!
Duane Hanson, *Self-Portrait with Model,* 1979. Polyester and fiber glass, life-size. Courtesy of the artist.

Richard Estes

(b.1936)

Richard Estes is a master of the urban scene. His buildings, windows and vehicles sparkle with the brilliance and clarity of a rainwashed day. People are generally absent or an insignificant part of the scene. They are not needed because the shine and reflection of chrome and glass surfaces produce plenty of life and interest. Estes works directly from photographs and slides. Colors, shadows, values and reflections are painstakingly reproduced. As in *Drugstore* (fig.17–35), the result is a cool, impassionate look at the city. *Drugstore* is a matter-of-fact photographic representation of a place. Estes' attitude is derived from Pop Art, but his technique and style are much more sophisticated.

17–35 Estes is particularly interested in reflections. What reflective surfaces do you find in this painting? Can you detect how the illusion of reflection was created?
Richard Estes, *Drugstore,* 1970. Oil on canvas, 59 3/4" x 44 1/2" (152 x 113 cm). The Art Institute of Chicago. ©1996 Richard Estes/Licensed by VAGA, New York, NY

Duane Hanson

(b.1925)

Duane Hanson produces life-size, colored models of people that are dressed and surrounded with actual things. The result is so lifelike that viewers often gape and giggle in disbelief and amusement. His three-dimensional New Realism is flawless and almost frightening at times. Hanson makes plaster casts of people, then creates polyester and fiberglass models from the casts. The models are tinted in natural colors. He works with ordinary people and even himself. In *Self-Portrait with Model* (fig.17–36), he surrounds the realistic sculptures with props that heighten the reality even more. His people and arrangements appear so real and ordinary that some viewers walk right past Hanson's work without realizing they are sculptures, not living people—the ultimate compliment to a Super-Realist artist.

Higher-Order Thinking Skills

Place a highly reflective object, such as a coffee pot, where students can carefully observe the reflections in it. Have them write about not only what they see but also what happens to the image because of the shape of the reflector. Then have them look at Richard Estes' painting (fig. 17–35) to see how he dealt with painting reflections. Hold a discussion of students' findings.

Lesson 17.4 Review

1 Give several names for the extremely realistic art movement that began in the 1970s. List a few artists involved in this movement.
2 How does Chuck Close use photography in his work? What is he trying to achieve in his painting?

3 How does James Rosenquist's *Nomad* differ from Andy Warhol's style of Pop Art?
4 Describe how Duane Hanson creates his sculptures. How are his sculptures like and different from George Segal's?

Lesson 17.4 Review Answers

1 Super-Realism, Photo-Realism, New Realism and Hyper-Realism. Artists involved in this movement include Duane Hanson, Richard Estes, Chuck Close and James Rosenquist.
2 Close uses photography as a source of images. He has stated that his main objective is to translate photographic information into paint information.
3 Warhol focused on one popular image or icon; Rosenquist combines many of these images so that the viewer has the feeling of seeing many commercials at once.

4 Hanson makes plaster casts of people, then creates polyester and fiber glass models from the casts. He tints these models in natural colors so that his sculptures seem real. Segal wraps people in plaster too, but he leaves his sculptures as white plaster gauze, so his creations do not appear as life-like as Hanson's.

Lesson 17.5

Sculptors in the second half of the twentieth century explored a wide variety of materials, scales and techniques to create innovative three-dimensional works that reflected the diversity of modern and contemporary art.

Warm-up

Ask students to list the sculpture materials with which they are most familiar. Previous to the modern era, what were the primary media? What materials do sculptors use today in addition to wood and marble? Why had artists not previously incorporated steel, Plexiglas, epoxy, leather, wire, plastic, fabrics and rubber?

Objectives

Students should be able to:

Discuss how sculptors after mid-century used a broad range of new materials, styles and techniques.

Teach

Art History/Criticism: Ask students to imagine being the Italian Renaissance artist Michelangelo (Lesson 9.2) visiting Isamu Noguchi's studio.

• What questions might Michelangelo ask Noguchi about *Great Rock of Inner Seeking* (fig.17–37)?

• What would he want to know about Noguchi's technique, expression of his subject, and choice of materials?

• Do students think Michelangelo would understand and appreciate Noguchi's art? What about the two artists' styles and interests supports their decision?

17.5 Sculpture

DURING THE SECOND HALF of the twentieth century, sculpture took gigantic steps in the use of new materials, techniques, concepts and directions. The direction of its development is even more varied than that of painting. Contemporary sculpture reflects the excitement and innovative work of artists using these new techniques and materials. The scale of sculpture in the second half of the twentieth century assumed great significance. In addition, there was the development of open sculpture. Open sculpture does not divide or enclose space in any fixed way.

New industrial materials and techniques helped the change in attitude toward sculpture. Many modern sculptors, such as David Smith, worked in factories to learn their skills in metalworking. An endless variety of materials have been used in sculpture: steel, Plexiglas, epoxy, fired clay, leather, wire, plastic, fabrics and rubber.

It is the variety, scale and openness of late-twentieth-century sculpture that makes it elude strict definition.

Key Notes

• New materials and techniques have given sculpture new direction in the second half of the twentieth century.

• Variety and scope of sculpture has made it difficult to strictly define.

Special Feature

Isamu Noguchi

(1904–1988)

Isamu Noguchi produced an amazing variety of sculptures in various materials. Born of Japanese-American parents, he spent his early years in Japan and then two years working with Brancusi in Paris. He later studied in China and Japan and worked in London and Mexico. His international background led to works of international feeling and acceptance. Noguchi was able to use the best modern tradition of Europe without losing himself or fixating on any single style.

During the 1940s, Noguchi emerged as a prominent stone

17–38 The sculpture garden is an example of "sited sculpture." The piece was designed specifically for this site. Isamu Noguchi. *Sculpture Garden*, Beinecke Rare Book and Manuscript Library at Yale University.

Evaluate

Ask if modern sculptors tried to represent reality exactly in their artwork. What types of subject matter have they explored and how have they manipulated materials in new ways to express abstract ideas?

Reteach

Ask students to describe what Renaissance artists might have felt about the flexibility that contemporary sculptors have in terms of style, subject and media.

17–37 Compare this sculpture to Brancusi's *Bird in Space* and *The Kiss.*
Isamu Noguchi, *Great Rock of Inner Seeking*, 1975. Granite, 143 3/4" (365 cm) high. National Gallery of Art, Washington, DC.

carver. *Great Rock of Inner Seeking* (fig.17–37) is carved from granite and weighs eight and one-half tons. Like much of his work, it has a primeval feeling. It seems closely related to traditional Japanese garden art and Zen Buddhist contemplation. Some of the textures were made naturally, some by the drill that severed the stone from its parent mass, and some by Noguchi. The cooperative effort is a magnificent and powerful form, exciting in its simplicity and solemn and quiet in its implications.

Noguchi has also designed some environmental spaces. He designed Detroit's Civic Center Plaza and the Sculpture Garden at Jerusalem's Museum of Art, as well as children's playgrounds and stage sets. His sculpture courtyard, or "garden," for the Beinecke Rare Book and Manuscript Library at Yale University (fig.17–38) is a sunken court, closed in by four glass walls, that can be seen either from above or from the rooms level with it. Looking down on it, the viewer sees a marble plaza on which a pyramid, a circle and a diamond are placed. There is a great sense of unity among the three huge forms. The classic simplicity and purity of the forms is striking.

The exploration of pure form and its translation into modern terms and the creation of unified sculptural spaces are Noguchi's contribution to sculpture of the late twentieth century.

Contextual Information
Noguchi

Noguchi studied and worked with Brancusi in the late 1920s; in the 1930s, he worked with Giacometti and experimented with Social Realism and Surrealism. Toward the end of the 1950s, Noguchi developed the combination of rough and smooth surfaces in his sculptures. His philosophy of art included doing as little as possible to the form to draw out the "soul" of the material. Simple shapes with only small areas of tool work became his trademark.

Higher-Order Thinking Skills

Have students select a site at their school or in their community that would be good for a sculpture or garden like Noguchi's. Ask how they would utilize the space. Students can then use simple geometric or organic forms to design several solutions for the space. Have students discuss, write about or draw their preferences.

Contextual Information

Smith

David Smith was a descendant of a Decatur, Indiana, blacksmith. He worked in automobile and locomotive factories, where he assembled and welded metal parts. Smith studied painting at the Art Students League but turned to sculpture after seeing Cubist assemblage sculpture by Picasso and Julio Gonzalez.

Nevelson

Nevelson studied at the Art Students League between 1929 and 1930 and then studied with Hans Hofmann in Germany. By 1932, she was in New York City working with Ben Shahn and Diego Rivera as part of a WPA project.

Of the color black, Nevelson said: "I fell in love with black, it contained all color. It wasn't a negation of color. It was acceptance. Because black encompasses all colors. Black is the most aristocratic color of all. The only aristocratic color. For me this is the ultimate. There is no [other] color that will give you the feeling of totality. Of peace. Of greatness. Of quietness. Of excitement."

Henry Moore

(1898–1986)

Almost all Henry Moore's abstracted works are based on the various forms of the human figure (fig.3–9). His early work was only slightly abstracted. In his later years, his forms became rounded and simplified.

Sheep Piece (figs.17–d, 17–39) is a monumental bronze work of two interacting forms. The forms could be two sheep huddling against a storm. Moore placed this casting in a sheep pasture, where it seems to belong. However, the powerful, smooth, rounded forms would be just as comfortable in front of a skyscraper or in the courtyard of a museum. Moore produced a tremendous body of work that is universally appealing. Its placement in locations around the world has made Moore's work easily recognizable.

17–39 How is this view of the sculpture different from the view seen in fig.17–d?
Henry Moore, *Sheep Piece*, 1972. Bronze, 223 1/2" (568 cm) long. Hertfordshire, England.

17–40 Imagine what this group sculpture would look like if you were standing in the arrangement.
Barbara Hepworth, *Assembly of Sea Forms*, 1972. White marble, tallest form 42 1/2" (108 cm) high. The Norton Simon Art Foundation, Pasadena, CA.

17–42 The space that it encloses is also a part of this sculpture.
David Smith, *Cubi XII*, 1963. Stainless steel, 109 5/8" x 49 1/4" x 32 1/4" (278 x 125 x 82cm). Hirshhorn Museum and Sculpture Garden, Smithsonian Institution, Washington DC. Gift of Joseph H. Hirshhorn, 1972. ©1996 Estate of David Smith/Licensed by VAGA, New York, NY

17–41 Identify the various shapes and trace how Nevelson uses their repetition to lead your eye around on the wall.
Louise Nevelson, *Homage to the World*, 1966. Wood, 107 1/2" (273 cm) high. The Detroit Institute of Arts.

Barbara Hepworth

(1903–1975)

Like Henry Moore, Barbara Hepworth was another English sculptor who worked with simplified forms. She created works in wood, bronze or marble. In *Assembly of Sea Forms* (fig.17–40), she used the traditional material of marble. However, she produced a contemporary effect by grouping the pieces to make the completed arrangement. The arrangement may be changed again and again, always producing another complete effect. When a viewer walks around the group, the relationships between each part and the whole change also. In this work, Hepworth has carved marble into the essence of sea forms: rocks, caves, eroded forms, pebbles and cliffs. The simplified units relate perfectly to each other in form and color. They unite to produce a marvelous group sculpture.

Louise Nevelson

(1900–1988)

Louise Nevelson experimented in the forties with all media. By the fifties, she found that her best expression was in wood. She filled boxes with found scraps, boards and pieces of old Victorian houses and arranged them in various configurations. Some were small and some huge, such as *Homage to the World* (fig.17–41). By painting everything a flat black, she unified the many different parts of the work. (Later, she painted them white and even gold.) This gigantic assemblage is an environmental sculpture that occupies two walls of a room.

In later years, Nevelson created an entire chapel of wood, painted white, inside a skyscraper in Manhattan. The chapel is a total environment of benches, walls, altar and vestments. She continued to work with wood into the seventies. But she also added Cor-Ten steel, lucite and aluminum to her list of materials. She produced gigantic outdoor as well as indoor works. A square in New York City is named

for her and contains seven mammoth steel sculptures, up to 70 feet high. It is an exterior environmental group of huge proportions.

David Smith

(1906–1965)

David Smith was one of the first American sculptors to weld steel into sculptural forms. He learned to work with metals by working in a locomotive plant and automobile factory. In the late fifties and early sixties, he developed a series of powerful images based on cubes. He welded cubes of various sizes and proportions from stainless steel. The hollow forms were assembled in a variety of combinations and burnished to produce a slightly textured surface. These reflective planes on his geometric structures pleased him because "the surfaces were lightened and unified with the atmosphere." He titled the twenty-eight-piece series *Cubi*. The illustration is *Cubi XII* (fig.17–42). Smith was in a highly productive period of his life when he died in an automobile accident.

Lesson 17.5 Review

1 Where is Isamu Noguchi's *Great Rock of Inner Seeking*? What is its mood or feeling? Of what Asian cultures is the viewer reminded?
2 Write three words that come to mind as you view Henry Moore's *Sheep Piece*. What nationality is Moore?
3 What is unusual about Barbara Hepworth's *Assembly of Sea Forms*?
4 How did Louise Nevelson create unity in her sculpture *Homage to the World*?
5 With what medium did David Smith create? Where did he learn to use these materials? Write a sentence describing *Cubi XII*.

Lesson 17.6

Since the 1960s, art has taken off in virtually innumerable ways. Artists have broken the confines of exhibition spaces, recruited viewers as active participants in their work, and tried almost every new technology as part of the art-making process.

Warm-up

Direct students to take objects from their pockets and book bags and to construct an interesting arrangement with the objects. Challenge students to take into consideration materials, textures and scale, and what they would like the work to mean. After viewing each other's constructions, ask students if there is any reason why their pieces could not be considered art. Share that many contemporary artists incorporate an endless variety of techniques and media to express a vast array of ideas and interests. The quality of any art should be judged on the integrity with which it was made and its ability to communicate. Good art does not necessarily have to be pleasing but rather should compel us to think in new or deeper ways.

Objectives

Students should be able to:

Comprehend how art from the 1960s to the present defies simple categorization.

Understand that the intermingling of art and technology has paved the way for fresh and exciting creative endeavors.

Teach

Art History/Criticism: Ask students to categorize each of the following as either sculpture or painting: *Running Fence* (fig.17–43), *The Umbrellas: Japan —USA* (fig.17–44), *Mirrored Room #2* (fig.17–45), *Untitled* (fig.17–46), *Ruckus Rodeo* (fig.17–48), *The Wait* (fig.17–52) and *Spiral: An Ordinary Evening in New Haven* (fig.17–b).

• Do any of the pieces fit easily into one category or the other?

• How have contemporary artists collapsed the barriers that previously delineated one medium from another?

17.6 New Directions

T IS EXTREMELY HARD TO DEFINE ART from the 1960s to the present. So many of the new directions are a far cry from the sculptures, paintings or photographs of the past. The variety of work and the experimental attitude of the artists defy easy classification.

In *Kinetic Art*, sculptors work with materials and motors to create pieces that literally move. Artists use light, sound, computers and electricity to bring their art to life. Videotapes, cinematography and animated film are the language of a new form called *intermedia*.

Artists also devise environments in which spectators participate. When they employ moving equipment to gouge designs in the western deserts, build circular jetties into lakes, or rearrange the ground into mounds, the result is known as *Earth Art*. Still other artists rely on words, diagrams or ideas to communicate concepts that they have in mind, but never intend to carry out. Since there is no finished object, their work is called *Concept Art*.

Artists also use laser beams, span huge valleys with curtains, spray plate glass, and organize mammoth ceramic projects. Finally, there are those who combine technology and art to examine ever-new avenues of expression. In truth, diversity is the only aspect that can be said to unite the many trends of recent decades.

Key Notes

• Art from the 1960s to the present day is so varied it defies classification.

• Kinetic art, intermedia, earth art, conceptual art and computer art are some of its expressions.

• The combination of technology and art opens up new vistas for artists.

Special Feature
Christo and Jeanne Claude
(both b.1935)

Christo (Javacheff) was born in Bulgaria and lives in New York City with his wife, Jeanne Claude. Together, they have draped unusual objects in several parts of the world. The Christos take something familiar and wrap or curtain it. While wrapping something familiar might sound pretty ordinary, it becomes distinctly astonishing when you think of surrounding anything as large as eleven islands in Miami's Biscayne Bay in pink plastic. Christo and Jeanne Claude have wrapped a bridge (the Pont Neuf in

17–43 What do fences and walls do to your experience of landscape?
Christo and Jeanne Claude, *Running Fence*, 1972–1976. Nylon and cable, 18' (5.5 m) high, 24 1/2 miles (39 km) long. Sonoma and Marin Counties, California. Courtesy of the artists.

• What new terms can students think of that would be appropriate for these examples? Installation art, environmental art and performance art are just a few of the names that have been devised for them.

Criticism: Divide the class into small groups. Have students select an image from Lesson 17.6 that puzzles them. Direct each student in turn to ask his or her group a few questions about the art. Group members should brainstorm possible answers to the inquiries. Encourage wild thinking and strong imagination, reminding students that their thoughts are valid as long as they are based on careful observation of the work itself. Afterward, ask the class if

they are comfortable with the often numerous possible interpretations of contemporary art.

• Is it easy for them to accept its open-ended nature?

• Can the brainstorming technique and exploration of multiple meanings be applied to other subjects in school?

• How could they use the process in math, science, history, language arts and physical education?

Paris), buildings (the German Reichstag), and one million square feet of the Australian coast.

In 1976, they completed *Running Fence* (fig.17–43), a 24 1/2-mile nylon curtain that snaked across California's Marin and Sonoma counties. The piece took four years to complete and, as in all their art, the Christos collaborated with public officials, scientists, environmentalists, artists, townspeople, farmers, construction workers, engineers, clothmakers and seamstresses. How do you feel about a project that cost three million dollars to assemble and was dismantled after several days? The Christos believe that their art is an event that is much more than the final installation. They begin a project with the initial idea, then sell drawings of the project to raise funds for it, and

finally coordinate thousands of workers and various equipment to construct the piece itself.

In 1991, the Christos completed their most ambitious endeavor, *The Umbrellas: Japan–USA* (fig.17–44), involving huge areas in both countries. In the United States, the Christos carefully plotted 1760 six-meter-tall yellow umbrellas on grasslands and rolling hills along 17 1/2 miles of Interstate 5, about an hour north of Los Angeles. In Japan, the Christos zigzagged 1340 blue umbrellas for 11 1/2 miles through small towns and farm country just outside of Tokyo. Can you imagine suddenly coming upon one of these sites unexpectedly? The sheer drama of the Christos' installation caused millions of viewers to appreciate their environment in new ways.

17–44 Different colors or new objects in unusual contexts cause us to experience our environment in a different way.
Christo and Jeanne Claude, *The Umbrellas: Japan–USA*. 1984–1991. Fabric, aluminum, paint, steel and concrete. Height including base 19'8 1/4" (6 m), diameter of umbrellas 28' 5" (8.66 m).

Contextual Information

Christo and Jeanne Claude

Christo and Jeanne Claude's umbrellas in Japan were placed close together, reflecting the population density of that nation. The umbrellas were blue, for the water that fertilizes the rice fields. In California, they were yellow and spaced far apart, spread across rolling hills of yellow and brown grass.

Higher-Order Thinking Skills

Christo creates a sense of mystery when he wraps an object. Have the class use muslin or brown paper and string or masking tape to wrap ordinary objects and then create a display of them. Discuss whether there are hints of what is within. Use a display or trophy case to put the show out where others can see it and the class can observe reactions and hear comments. What do other students and teachers say about the wrapped show? Have the class devise a way to explain the show to the school.

Evaluate

Ask students to cite specific artworks in Lesson 17.6 to demonstrate how some contemporary artists reject the past, while others use it as a touchstone. Have students propose what art of the twenty-third century might look like. How do they think it will relate to the present day and what will it abandon in terms of styles, subjects, media and techniques?

Reteach

Have students review the images in Lesson 17.6 and examine recent art periodicals for the latest art trends.

- Ask which artists they think are revolutionary. Why? Will the work still seem radical in the future?

- Why is it that the Impressionists (Lesson 13.1), Caravaggio (Lesson 11.1) and Jackson Pollock (fig.17–3) no longer strike us as shocking but were initially to the public at the time? Can we know today what will be significant in generations to come?

- Do attitudes about art ever change over time so that styles that were once dismissed come into vogue at a later period? Share that this has happened throughout art history. Why might this be true? What does it indicate about human taste and the stability of history?

Share with the class that some critics believe that contemporary art is a mere footnote in art history as compared to Italian Renaissance painting or Classical Greek sculpture. Have students

role-play the artists in Lesson 17.6 and defend the long-term importance of their work, what impact it will have on future generations, and its relevance to modern culture. Afterward, ask students if this exercise affected their attitude toward contemporary art.

- Do they understand it more clearly or have a deeper appreciation of the artist's struggle, intent, technique or style?

- What would they like to say to the artist if they were having a conversation over lunch?

Contextual Information

Chicago

Judy Chicago said: "I tried to challenge society's conception of what it is to be a woman. Fundamental to my work was an attempt to challenge the values of the society. If my needs, values, and interest differed from male artists' . . . it was up to me to help develop a community that was relevant to me and other women artists."

In *The Dinner Party* (fig.17–c), Chicago presented her version of the Last Supper, with places for 39 distinguished women, including Queen Hatshepsut of Egypt, Georgia O'Keeffe, Virginia Woolf, Isadora Duncan and Katharine Hepburn. The plates sit on handmade place mats made by over 100 needleworkers. Both the hand-painted plates and place mats are typical of what was considered by many to be "women's work," not "fine art."

• Why would pottery painting or needlework not be considered "fine art"?

Lucas Samaras

(b.1936)

Lucas Samaras has a strong interest in constructing environments, and his *Mirrored Room #2* (fig.17–45) is a prime example. What would it feel like to walk through the door into this many-mirrored space? Where does the floor begin and the tables, walls and ceiling end? The sparkling reflections fragment our vision and trick our senses. There is a sensation of being suspended in space. Samaras integrates the art with outside space by placing mirrors along its exterior that reflect and blend with the surrounding environment.

Dan Flavin

(b.1933)

Instead of paint and canvas, Dan Flavin uses fluorescent lights as his medium. He forms fluorescent lights into abstract geometric shapes, which he then mounts on the walls, floors or ceilings of his environments. Flavin's *Untitled* (fig.17–46) is a two-wall arrangement of circular tubes. The soft, warm light creates an inviting space for us to enter. Light sculptures such as these are best viewed in a darkened environment to sense the original glowing character envisioned by the artist.

17–46 During the 1960s, many artists began experimenting with lighting as a medium. Flavin has continued to explore the limitations and possibilities of light art.
Dan Flavin, *Untitled*, 1975. Daylight, warm fluorescent light, wall #1: 11 3/4" x 96" (30 x 244 cm); wall #2: 33 3/4" x 96" (86 x 244 cm). Leo Castelli Gallery, New York.

17–45 The artist mounted mirrors on a wooden framework. When a spectator moves into the mirrored environment, there is a sensation of being suspended in space.
Lucas Samaras, *Mirrored Room #2*, 1966. Wood and mirror, 96" x 119 1/4" x 96" (2.44 x 3.03 x 2.44 m). Pace Gallery, New York.

Judy Chicago

(b.1939)

Judy Chicago works in many directions with her art, but is always involved in advancing the cause of women's rights. Her monumental work of 1979 is a gigantic triangular table arrangement called *The Dinner Party* (fig.17–c). Each of the thirty-nine place settings, designed in glazed ceramic and set on an embroidered, handwoven cloth, represents a great, often unrecognized woman in Western history. The ceramic-tile floor below holds the names of 999 additional heroines.

1989 Tian'anmen Square student uprising, China

1995 Sons of Ramses II tombs found in Egypt

World Cultural Timeline

1992 South Africa votes to end apartheid

1994 Israeli-Jordanian peace accord signed
1994 Nelson Mandela elected president of South Africa

Chicago worked in the tradition of women's communal sewing bees, conceiving of the project herself and then relying on the assistance of many volunteers and employees to complete her ambitious task.

Earlier, Chicago painted *Reincarnation Triptych*, three paintings that express the dynamic characteristics of women whose lives are important to her. For *Virginia Woolf* (fig.17–47), Chicago sprayed acrylic paint over stencils to produce the resulting pattern. She added a forty-word statement about Woolf around the border. Chicago's ideas, based upon her personal philosophy of life, are as expressionistic as they are stimulating. Her art defies easy categorization.

17–47 The artist makes a point in all her work of educating the viewer about the role of women in history and art.
Judy Chicago, *Virginia Woolf*. Sprayed acrylic on canvas. 59 3/4" x 59 3/4" (152 x 152 cm). Through the Flower, Albuquerque, New Mexico.

Sidelight

Censorship and the Arts

In general, artists should be able to make any kind of work they like. This is called artistic freedom, and any restrictions on the Constitutionally protected right of free expression amount to censorship. However, when a federal agency or any public commission funds artists whose work may be considered offensive by the viewing public, problems arise.

Nudity is often considered offensive, as in the case of Tom Otterness's 1991 sculpture, *The New World*, commissioned by the General Services Administration (GSA) for a new Los Angeles courthouse and federal building. Otterness's 300-foot-long pergola included a few nude figures. The central statue was a nude baby girl holding a globe. Once the sculpture was installed, there were protests from judges who work

John Ahearn, Corey. Bronze, formerly in front of the 44th Precinct in the Bronx. Lifesize.

in the building. Two offending sections of the piece were removed and put in storage. However, the censorship resulted in widespread press attention, and the GSA agreed to reinstall the pieces.

John Ahearn's sculptures, however, have not been as fortunate. In 1991, three life-size painted bronze figures were put on pedestals in front of the 44th Precinct Police Headquarters in the Bronx. The statues were funded by the New York City percent-for-art program, which puts aside about one percent of any money for a new public building for the buying of artworks. Using neighborhood people as models, Ahearn depicted a girl on roller skates, a basketball player with a boom box, and a squatting teen wearing a hooded sweatshirt and holding a pit bull. The work underwent a community review and was approved. However, once the sculptures were in place, community residents complained that pit bulls and boom boxes are negative stereotypes. Ahearn voluntarily removed his sculptures and the works are currently in storage.

Higher-Order Thinking Skills

1 *The Dinner Party* was extremely controversial when it was shown in 1979. Ask students to imagine that they are curators at a museum and have an opportunity to book a controversial show, including works such as *The Dinner Party*, that they feel has artistic merit. What objections might the community raise? What ramifications might there be for the museum? For the artistic community? Would they book the show or not? Why?

2 Ask students who would be the focus of their art today and what the message would be if they created an installation piece like Chicago's *The Dinner Party*. What materials, style and techniques would they use? Could recent technology be useful? Finally, have students discuss whether politics and art should mix. Why do they think that the interweaving of the two either enhances or dilutes the work?

Contextual Information

Graves

Graves learned to make dioramas and animal models for her father's museum in Massachusetts. In Florence, Italy, to get a break from art museums, she visited a natural history museum where she discovered the wax life-size models of human bodies created by eighteenth-century anatomist Clemente Susini. Back in the U.S., Graves began to make wax-covered camels, using steel, burlap, polyurethane, animal skin and oil paint over wax.

Ruckus Rodeo

Ruckus Rodeo was created on commission for the Modern Art Museum of Fort Worth, Texas. It is Grooms' interpretation of an annual event in Fort Worth: the stock show and rodeo.

Grooms captures the colorful, lively and rather noisy atmosphere of the rodeo through exaggeration and the clever manipulation of detail. Everyone has heard of the Texas longhorn: Grooms creates a 16-foot-tall yellow bull with 6-foot-long horns!

Ruckus Rodeo is 50 feet in length. It includes the just-mentioned bull, bucking broncos (fig.17–48), cowboys and cowgirls, clowns and crowds of cheering fans.

17–48 Grooms fills entire rooms with papier-mâché figures and objects painted in vivid, sometimes clashing colors.
Red Grooms, *Ruckus Rodeo*, 1980. Sculpture wire, celastic, acrylic, canvas and burlap, 174" x 606" x 294" (442 x 1539 x 747 cm). Commissioned by the Modern Art Museum of Fort Worth. Museum purchase with funds from the National Endowment for the Arts and the Benjamin J. Tillar Memorial Trust.

Red Grooms

(b.1937)

Red Grooms works like no other living artist, although he was an abstract expressionist in his early years. He calls his papier-mâché environments "sculpto-pictoramas," and these colorful installations completely engulf us as we walk through them. Grooms combines sculpture, construction and painting to produce pieces that overflow with detail, exaggerated perspective, verbal and visual puns, and cartoonlike figures. Can you sense the roar and excitement of the crowd inside *Ruckus Rodeo* (fig.17–48)? Grooms spends an average of four months on each project, with some taking up to a year to complete. The artist also makes films, watercolors, prints, oils, drawings, bronzes and mechanized constructions.

Nancy Graves

(b.1940)

As a child, Nancy Graves wandered behind the scenes in Massachusetts' Berkshire Museum, where her father was on staff. She was particularly fascinated by the laboratories that created dioramas and taxidermy habitats. "Later the process of transformation became integral to my own...process...where art and the natural sciences are merged."

Her work *II-11-94* (fig.17–49) is a melding of science and the natural world. The huge starfish and flower dance together at the base, while manufactured items help complete the Z-like form. There are bits of grating and machine parts. A bulging cone of an old-fashioned hand juicer echoes the huge blue blossom below. Graves interjects nature once again with her translucent glass swirl that carries our glance up and out, as though translating the wind into visible form. Her delicate balance of shape, color and texture establishes an overall lyrical quality that defies the actual weight of the metal sculpture. With the exception of the handblown glass, Graves casts all her natural and manufactured objects in bronze.

New Frontiers

In recent years, artists have investigated an astounding multitude of concerns and styles. It is difficult, if not impossible, to identify all of the diverse trends, let alone to predict which ones will be considered important in the future. Artists are currently redefining Abstraction, Realism and Expressionism. They are challenging age-old traditions, exploring global politics and personal beliefs, and also examining the impact of ever-advancing technology on the modern world.

The question of why art has exploded in all these directions at once is both interesting and perplexing. Is this unbridled creativity an outgrowth of the endless possibilities emerging from current technology? Is art simply reflecting the revolutionary spirit that is changing the way people all over the world think, work and communicate? On the other hand, perhaps we are witnessing the storm that will soon give way to a more discernible future. Undoubtedly, artists' knowledge of the past and current experiences of new frontiers greatly enrich their many and diverse expressions.

It is vitally important to approach contemporary art with a sense of inquiry. What is this? How was it made? What does it mean to me? Did the artist perhaps have a different intention? Often, today's artists are concerned not with creating something pretty, but rather with having us consider what we see and what we believe.

Barbara Kruger

(b.1945)

What could be more innocent than a picture of Dick and Jane from the children's reading book that Barbara Kruger uses in *Untitled* (fig.17–50)? Look at Jane's adoring admiration of Dick's bulging preadolescent biceps.

17–49 Can you distinguish the bits of grating and machine parts that Graves has used in this work? How has she integrated these manufactured parts with the fragile beauty of glass? Nancy Graves, *II-11-94*, 1994. Bronze and glass, 19" x 7" x 11" (48 x 18 x 28 cm). Knoedler and Company, New York. ©1996 Nancy Graves/Licensed by VAGA, New York, NY

17–50 Words are an integral part of the images that this artist creates. Do you think the words provide you with more information about the piece, or do they raise questions in your mind? Barbara Kruger, *Untitled (We Don't Need Another Hero)*, 1987. Photographic silkscreen/vinyl. Mary Boone Gallery, New York.

But how do Kruger's carefully chosen words, borrowed from Tina Turner's popular song for the movie *Mad Max*, put another possible spin on the piece? Whose voice is making this statement? Does the work's meaning change if you hear the sentence said by a man or a woman? Do the words contradict the stereotypical images of boys and girls usually seen in society?

Kruger typically prints ambiguous statements over familiar imagery as a means of questioning the anonymous authoritarian voice in countless media and advertising campaigns. But her seemingly amusing juxtapositions are also alarming. They jolt us into recognizing how easily we accept these seductive messages, which make us want, buy or believe in nearly anything without so much as a second thought. Perhaps Kruger's skill at criticizing the media's ability to manipulate an unthinking public comes from her early success at *Mademoiselle* magazine, where she worked as chief designer when she was only twenty-two.

Higher-Order Thinking Skills

Have students compare Red Grooms' work (fig.17–48) to that of Frederic Remington (fig.15–26). Which do they prefer?

Contextual Information

Jaune Quick-to-See Smith

When Jaune Quick-to-See Smith was young, she went with her horse-trader father on long trips through the Montana mountains and frequently sketched the horses. In spite of her talent, she was not encouraged to be an artist, but she continued to paint the animals and nature in her environment. As a way of finding support and encouragement, Smith joined the Grey Canyon Artists, a Native American art organization. Her work combines traditional Native American images and symbols with contemporary images.

Window in Time

Computers and Art

The amazing range of things that computers can do has not been lost on artists. In recent years a whole new computer art form has developed. The origins of computer art can be traced back to 1952 when Ben F. Laposky, in the United States, used an analogic computer and a cathode tube oscillograph for the composition of his *Electronic Abstractions*. In 1956 he followed this up with the creation of a colored electronic image.

Since that time computer art has expanded considerably. In 1993 an International Festival of the Image was put on in Rochester, New York, as part of Montage '93. To reach a broad audience, sixteen group and solo exhibitions were placed in diverse locations, such as a shopping mall and the inner city, to show how art using new technologies can touch different audiences.

The artists involved tackled all kinds of subjects and used the computer in very different ways. Artist Alan Rath gave a riveting account of the *Challenger* space shuttle disaster. A sequence of black-and-white still images on seven monitors traced the development of the Apollo space program up to the 1986 shuttle launch. With flashing LED signs, bouncing ping-pong balls and intermittently blinking lights, Rath evoked the deadly explosion. At the same time, recorded phrases from the media coverage of the disaster were played, such as "technology triumphed," "What went wrong?" and "felt every one of them were my sons and daughter."

Esther Parada, another artist in the festival, began her two-dimensional exhibit with a turn-of-the-century photograph of a Spanish monument in Cuba and her own photographic portraits made in Latin America. Then she scanned, digitized and electronically overlaid the images with text about the European conquest of the Western Hemisphere. Presented as large, color ink-jet prints, her composites attained a great sense of spatial depth through their rich tonal values and the layering of images and typography. The message she was attempting to convey was that cultural identity comes about as a result of similar layering.

In an exhibition of her work at the Julie Saul Gallery in Manhattan, also in 1993, Penelope Umbrico showed yet a different use of the computer. Trained as a painter, Umbrico now uses photography almost exclusively. Umbrico began by photographing ordinary household objects either in blurred motion or out of focus, against a color background. She then scanned the images into a computer and manipulated them until she achieved wildly colorful abstractions. These abstractions were then turned into color prints. *Untitled (computer drawings)* is made up of 196 color prints, each approximately 8 1/2" by 6 1/2". The individual images are amoeba-like blobs, which Umbrico produced by cutting each photograph in half, then rejoining its pieces in a new orientation so as to create a new shape.

Incredible sleight-of-hand is also made possible by the computer. This was very ably demonstrated in

Richard W. Maile's *Birth of Elvis*, shown at the Siggraph '90 exhibition in Dallas in August 1990. He presented a digital image based on a reproduction of Botticelli's *The Birth of Venus*, but instead of the figure of Venus, Maile substituted a digitally integrated image of Elvis Presley.

Penelope Umbrico, Exhibition Installation, March 27–May 1, 1993. Julie Saul Gallery, New York.

Cooperative Learning

To create a private collection that spans many centuries, have each student develop a list of at least ten works from the text that he or she especially likes. To accompany the list, students should provide a journal that details the order of acquisition, why the work was acquired, what the basis is for the collection and what commonalities the works have. The journal should then be given to another student who is to act as a docent for the collection and develop a tour of the collection to present to the class, explaining the works and interpreting the owner's motives and interests.

Jaune Quick-to-See Smith

(b.1940)

Jaune Quick-to-See Smith deliberately uses references to her own Salish, Shoshone and French Cree descent to fight centuries of misconceptions and misrepresentations about the first inhabitants of North America. Her art captures the stinging reality of the discrimination and hardships that many Native Americans have experienced in the United States.

Smith's *I See Red: Ten Little Indians* (fig.17–51) recalls the popular children's nursery rhyme of the same name. Yet, the inclusion of only four figures alludes to the appalling death rate of young native children during her growing-up years. "By all odds, I should not be here today. In 1940, when I was born, one in ten children survived."

Smith writes the rhyme in Salish across notebook paper and a chalkboard, confronting the mistaken belief that native peoples had no written language. At the same time, the classroom image refers to the efforts of government and missionary schools earlier in this century to erase Native American children's sense of heritage. The children were severely punished for speaking their tribal tongues or honoring ancient customs.

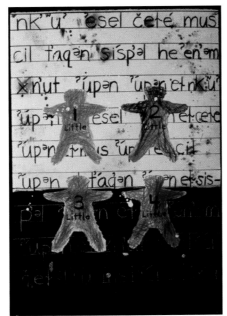

17–51 What does the phrase "Ten Little Indians" mean to you? Read the text for a better understanding of the artist's intent.
Jaune Quick-to-See Smith, *I See Red: Ten Little Indians*, 1992. Mixed media, collage on paper. 41 1/2" x 29 1/2" (105.5 x 75 cm). Steinbaum Krauss Gallery, New York.

Edward Kienholz

(1927–1994)

Edward Kienholz used the three-dimensional space of his stage-like environments to draw us into his shockingly personal dramas. What is the "wait" that he refers to in the title (fig.17–52)? Can you guess how this old woman feels? Where are the friends and family whose pictures she has gathered on the tabletop? The trinkets held in the woman's glass-jar necklace are remembrances from the past. In her last days, she clings to the cat for connection with another living being.

Kienholz learned carpentry, plumbing and engineering as a young boy on his family's farm in Washington State, and worked with his hands throughout his life. Kienholz included real objects in his constructed environments to create poignant scenes. Despite their departure from exact reality, they communicate their emotions quite strongly.

17–52 What is this woman waiting for?
Edward Kienholz, *The Wait*, 1964–65. Tableau, 80" x 148" x 78" (203 x 376 x 198 cm). Collection of Whitney Museum of American Art, New York, gift of the Howard and Jean Lipman Foundation, Inc.

Higher-Order Thinking Skills

Smith uses art to address social wrongs. Ask the class to discuss or write about whether art is obligated to deal with social issues. Is art that does so more or less noble or "good" than art that strives for the beautiful?

Performing Arts Connection

Performance Art: Many Arts in One

As early as the 1970s, Performance artists invented an entirely new art form that combines visual art, theater, dance, music, poetry and ritual. Today, Performance Art often continues to be highly personal and political. It varies as widely as its practitioners, who might incorporate anything from the latest technology to ancient ceremonies in their efforts to expand the previous boundaries of art.

Lesson 17.6 Review Answers

1 *Running Fence* was a 38.5 kilometer nylon curtain that snaked across California's Marin and Sonoma counties. *The Umbrellas: Japan—USA* had 1760, seven-meter-tall yellow umbrellas along 30 kilometers of Interstate 5 near Los Angeles, and 1340 blue umbrellas for 220 kilometers outside of Tokyo. Some students may think these projects are fun, crazy ideas. Others may be concerned about the environment and wonder who paid for the work.

2 Chicago recognizes great women who often are not mentioned in Western history. She is supporting the feminist cause of recognizing the contributions of women.

3 Grooms creates papier-mâché environments or sculpto-pictoramas using sculpture, construction and painting.

4 What is it? How was it made? What does it mean to me? Did the artist have a different intention?

5 Smith's *Ten Little Indians* recalls the children's nursery rhyme, but there are only four figures included because of the high death rate among young Native American children when the artist was a child. Smith wrote the rhyme in Salish across notebook paper and a chalkboard to confront the mistaken belief that native peoples had no

Joseph Beuys

(1921–1986)

Joseph Beuys decided to dedicate himself to the future of humanity after being shot down as a Nazi pilot in a remote region of Crimea and, subsequently, being saved by Tartars. Beuys' primary outlet became his socially motivated Performance Art. Performance Art is a form similar to theater, but the artist becomes an integral and active ingredient in the work itself. A great deal of Performance Art's impact comes from its shock value, expressed by irreverent humor, incongruity or explicit sexuality.

In *How to Explain Pictures to the Dead Hare*, Beuys covered his head with honey and gold leaf in order to resemble a sculpture. Then, he cradled a dead rabbit in his arms while

17–53 This image documents an event in which the artist spent one week with a coyote in a New York art gallery. Why might the artist have taken this action? Compare your ideas with the reason given in the text. Joseph Beuys, *I Like America and America Likes Me*, 1974. Performance at Rene Block Gallery, NY, May 23–25, 1974. Courtesy Ronald Feldman Fine Arts, New York.

discussing a painting with the creature. Beuys felt that "a hare comprehends more than many human beings with their stubborn rationalism."

In 1974, Beuys spent a week with a coyote in a New York art gallery (fig.17–53) in order to draw attention to how the animal, which is held sacred by a number of Native American tribes, was being persecuted by white society. He hoped that this event would help heal the rift between two opposing cultures within a single nation.

Jennifer Bartlett

(b.1941)

What happens when nature and the human-made world collide? In *Spiral: An Ordinary Evening in New Haven* (fig.17–b), Jennifer Bartlett explodes the backyard scene, sending birds, fish, tables, pots and chairs flying in all directions. But, do the bright hot flames singe even a single object? For all its destructive potential, Bartlett's fire generates enormous energy without so much as causing a single burn. Her title makes us wonder why she says there is anything "ordinary" about this evening event.

How might it feel to wander among the huge three-dimensional cones and red hexagon tables on the floor that imitate the painted images? Bartlett includes us in her work by encroaching on our own physical space. Since we share the stage with the installation, our entire bodies and not just our minds fully engage in the experience. Bartlett has been surrounding viewers with her investigations of simple, single themes since the 1970s. Her works are always based on recognizable elements. However, the repetition and manipulation of particular images infuse an abstract component into her final pieces.

Lesson 17.6 Review

1 Describe one of the Christos' projects. How do you feel about this creation?

2 Describe Judy Chicago's *The Dinner Party*. What cause does the artist support in this art?

3 What type of art does Red Grooms create? Name some materials he uses in his art.

4 What are some questions the viewer should consider when approaching contemporary art?

5 What are some of the symbols and messages in Jaune Quick-to-See Smith's *I See Red: Ten Little Indians*?

6 Explain what you think *The Wait* means in Edward Kienholz's environment? What are some clues to the woman's feelings?

7 What event in Joseph Beuys' life motivated him to be concerned about the future of humanity?

8 Do you see any similarities in themes shared by some of the art in this New Frontiers section?

written language. The classroom image refers to the efforts of schools in the early twentieth century to erase Native American children's sense of heritage.

6 The woman is probably waiting for death to join her family and friends. The trinkets in the woman's glass-jar necklace are remembrances from the past. She clings to the cat to connect with another living being.

7 Beuys was shot down as a Nazi pilot in a remote region of the Crimea and saved by the Tartars.

8 The art in the New Frontiers section of this lesson scrutinizes society, looking at apparently common ordinary scenes and pointing out the absurdity, injustice and loneliness in them. These artists take familiar images and layer them with social messages.

Chapter Review Answers

Review

1 Both paintings have the rapid brushstrokes, soft edges and flat shapes of Abstract Expressionism, but Diebenkorn's design is structured and not accidental or undisciplined. Diebenkorn relies on recognizable subject matter that is not found in Hofmann's *Flowering Swamp*. Diebenkorn's painting conveys a sense of calm in the empty, open spaces. Hofmann's painting has a sense of serenity and visual balance.

2 Like Picasso and Braque, Rauschenberg mixed reality with abstraction, but used entire objects, not just scraps.

3 The painted areas look like Abstract Expressionism. The real objects are more like Pop Art.

Primary Source

"...I wanted to be an artist."

In order to appreciate some forms of contemporary art, it is helpful to hear what artists have to say about their work. Artists speak about their intent, events and people that influenced their art, their relationship with their culture, and why they have selected a particular style, theme or technique.

Other artists refuse to discuss their intentions saying that what you see is what you see and each work's meaning is unique to the viewer.

Jennifer Bartlett:
"I always told everyone I wanted to be an artist. I want to move people. I'd like to be a strong, heartbreaking artist."

Jackson Pollock:
"Most of the paint I use is liquid, flowing...the brushes are used more as sticks and do not touch the surface...I'm able to be more free...and move about...with greater ease...it seems to be possible to control the flow of paint to a greater extent...I deny the accident...I have a general notion of what I'm about and what the results will be...I approach

painting in the same sense one approaches drawing, that is it's direct..."

Jaune Quick-to-See Smith:
"I knew I was an artist before I knew the word or the meaning. As a child, I lived on several reservations in very remote places. I didn't have store-bought toys so I entertained myself with whatever was at hand such as rocks, ferns, and dirt. In the woods or field I blotted out a world I didn't know how to deal with and created a small world I could manage."

Primary-Source Connection

Ask students to read the comments by the three artists and then discuss what the advantages and disadvantages are of reading the artists' thoughts about their work.

Chapter Review

Review

1 Compare the brushstrokes and design in Diebenkorn's *Cityscape I* with Hofmann's *Flowering Swamp*. What is the mood of each?

2 How are Picasso's and Braque's collages like Rauschenberg's combine paintings? How are they different?

3 Study Robert Rauschenberg's *First Landing Jump*. What looks like abstract expressionism? What seems more like Pop Art?

4 How are the sculptures of George Segal and Claus Oldenburg alike?

5 Helen Frankenthaler was a friend of Jackson Pollock. What are the differences and similarities in their methods of painting?

6 What are some other terms for Color Field Painting? Which term do you think describes this style best? Explain why.

7 Jackson Pollock studied with both Thomas Hart Benton and Hans Hofmann. Which artist do you think was more influential to his mature painting style?

Interpret

1 Rank the art movements—Abstract Expressionism, Pop Art, Op Art and Color Field Painting—from most emotional to least emotional. (You might want to refer to the chart on page 67).

2 Analyze *Christina's World* by Andrew Wyeth. What is the subject? What medium did he use? Describe the colors, contrasts, and textures. What is the mood? What is the center of interest? Is the balance symmetrical or asymmetrical? How does the artist direct your eye through the picture? Explain why you like or dislike this painting.

3 Compare Richard Estes' *Drugstore* with Edward Hopper's *Nighthawks*. What is the mood in each? How does each artist see the city? Which is more realistic?

4 Which artist in this chapter do you think creates the most realistic art? Use an example of this artist's work in your explanation of your choice.

Other Tools for Learning

Timelines
Consider how familiar you are with the international events on the timelines in this chapter. Do you think your counterparts 100 years ago would have been equally aware of events across the globe? Why or why not?

Electronic Research
Videodisc player: *National Gallery of Art*
1 After looking at several works by Henry Moore or David Smith, describe several characteristics that are found in most of the artist's sculptures.

Students may relate to the wistful pose of the girl and the realism of the grass and barn.

3 Estes paints a cool, impassionate view of the city, almost like a photograph. Hopper portrays lonely isolation with people that do not connect with each other. Hopper sees the dark shadows and empty spaces. Estes shows a light, clear, busy and bright city. Estes style is more realistic.

4 Hanson, Estes, Wyeth or Close would be valid choices.

Timelines

A century ago, news was carried by newspapers, telegraphs, word of mouth, books, magazines and posters. Television and radio had not been invented, so instantaneous images of events and people were not broadcast into homes. Students might have had a better understanding of history, but there was no way they could have been immediately aware of important events. They would not have had the vivid, moving images to introduce them to people in the news that we have today. Unless a famous person visited their town, they would have had to rely on black-and-white photographs to know what people in the news looked like.

Communication with Europe and America was nonexistent in some parts of the world.

Electronic Research

Henry Moore's work is usually simplified, smooth and rounded human or animal forms which often have openings enclosing space. David Smith's art is usually comprised of hard-edged minimalistic forms.

---

4 Both artists were concerned with common, everyday subjects.

5 Both artists worked on huge canvases which they walked on to paint. They both worked very spontaneously. However, Frankenthaler poured and spread her thin pigments staining the canvas, while Pollock threw and dripped his paints creating an overall web of texture.

6 Post-Painterly Abstraction, Classical Abstraction, Hard-Edge Painting

7 Hans Hofmann

Interpret

1 Most emotional: Abstract Expressionism, Pop Art, Op Art. Least emotional: Color Field Painting (A valid argument may be made that large areas of intense color can be very emotional.)

2 The subject is Wyeth's crippled neighbor, Christina, in a field near her

family's weathered Maine farm. Wyeth painted this piece in tempera on a gesso panel using warm, muted colors. The gold tones in the grass contrast with the pale blue of the sky and the light pink of Christina's dress. The fine brushstrokes of each blade of grass form an overall mass of texture that contrasts with the smooth sky and Christina's rounded form. The mood is quiet and peaceful with a feeling of loneliness or longing. The center of interest, the girl, is placed slightly off center, creating an asymmetrical composition. The viewer's eye is led from the girl's outstretched leg, along the curve of her body. She faces the farmhouse, directing the viewer's gaze toward it. Ruts also lead toward the farmhouse. A circular pattern in the grass helps keep the eye traveling through the composition.

Activity 1: Sculpting with Cloth

Activity Objectives

Students should be able to:

• Appreciate Oldenburg's vision and thought process when making soft sculpture.

• Look at common objects in a different light.

• Appreciate that art can express a sense of humor.

• Convert ideas and two-dimensional drawings into a successful soft sculpture.

Thinking Critically

Encourage group discussion or request a report in response to the following:

• Discuss the Pop Art movement in the twentieth century. Identify examples that show how Realism has persisted, but has done so with experimentation, individuality and imagination in the forefront of many new studio art concepts.

• What constitutes art? When does a paint palette become a work of art instead of a precast ordinary object?

• Discuss humor and satire in art. Cite examples.

Preparation Ideas

• You may want students to select one object, such as the artist's palette, to be produced as soft sculpture. This approach offers more control, allowing you to predict what kinds, colors and amount of cloth will be needed to produce a specific result. If students are allowed free reign to choose their object, you may ask that they bring in their own material.

• Another approach is to select potential objects for the students to choose from and to bring these in for sketches and planning. Part of the assignment could be for students to figure out how much material they will need, to research what will work best (velour? terry cloth? vinyl?), and to plan colors.

Notes on Materials

• Make a list of what fabric you will need and visit a fabric store that has a selection of inexpensive remnants. If your budget is tight, put out a general appeal to parents for any cloth they might be able to donate.

Activity 1

Sculpting with Cloth

Materials
newsprint
pencils
tape
cloth, vinyl (various colors)
needles
thread
foam rubber pillow filling

Take a look.
• Fig.17–10, Claes Oldenburg. *Installation of One-Man Show,* 1970.
• Fig.17–11, Claes Oldenburg. *Shoestring Potatoes Spilling from a Bag.*

Think about it. Change, innovation, and a quest for personal expression have led artists to create art in new and extremely diverse directions. Study the works of contemporary artist Claes Oldenburg, who views the manufactured world around us with a unique and imaginative perspective.

Do it. Design a large soft sculpture using vinyl material, cloth, and foam rubber pillow filling. For example, you might wish to create an artist's palette. The curved palette, exaggerated in size, would include a large hole for the thumb, with large cloth circles sewn onto the vinyl representing the paint colors.
• Select the object you wish to sculpt. Do a few rough sketches from more than one angle to consider how it will look three-dimensionally.
• Draw the object on newsprint at the size you wish to produce it. (In sewing, this is called making a pattern.) If there are pieces in different colors to be added, draw these also. Draw each side of your object to size.

• Fit the pieces together, perhaps holding them together with tape to see if it works. Make any adjustments.
• Lay each piece of the pattern on selected cloth and cut. Sew the pieces together and stuff with foam rubber filling.

Check it.
Is your finished sculpture recognizable as the object you selected? Have you sewn your work together such that the stitches are not distracting? Does your work look "finished"?

Helpful Hint: Choose a common, everyday object and see if you can enlarge it at least ten times its actual size. Have the object in front of you as you work, if possible, so you are working from observations, not memory.

Activity 2

Mimic the Masters

Materials
tempera paints/paper
or acrylic paints/canvas
brushes
water containers

Take a look.
• Fig.17–3, Jackson Pollock. *No. 1, 1950 (Lavender Mist).*
• Fig.17–13, Roy Lichtenstein. *Masterpiece,* 1962.
• Fig.17–14, Andy Warhol. *100 Cans,* 1962.
• Fig.17–21, Helen Frankenthaler. *The Bay,* 1963.
• Fig.17–26, Frank Stella. *Protractor Variation,* 1969.
• Fig.17–29, Morris Louis. *Point of Tranquility,* 1958.

Think about it. Review the work of contemporary artists listed above. Which style do you find most interesting? Why?

Do it. Make a tempera or acrylic painting in the style of one of the following artists (or others of your

choice). Use your own design, but work in that artist's style.
• Jackson Pollock: drip painting
• Roy Lichtenstein: current, simple comic style and colored dots
• Andy Warhol: repetition of forms using stencils
• Helen Frankenthaler or Morris Louis: flowing shapes
• Frank Stella: symmetrical designs created with a protractor

Check it.
Pair up with a friend and ask him or her to identify what aspects of style you've adopted and from which artist. Then do the same in response to your friend's work.

Helpful Hints:
Choose as your subject an object that has special meaning for you.

Additional Activities

• Compare the realistic sculpture of Duane Hanson to the monumental abstract works by sculptor Henry Moore. Are they both appealing to you? Explain your reactions. Consider the approach each artist has taken.
• Do a silkscreen self-portrait in the style of Pop artist Andy Warhol.
• Imagine yourself a young Renaissance artist who drops into a contemporary gallery in New York, London, Los Angeles or Paris. If you were a student of Raphael's, how would you feel? Which artists might you enjoy? With what aspects of twentieth century art could you identify? What types of art would be very disturbing to you? Explain why. Could you ever become comfortable in the twentieth century? Why or why not?

• When students are fitting together their newsprint patterns, have available the type of removable tape used by graphic designers, to allow students to assemble and take apart their pattern pieces without tearing the paper.

Classroom Management

• If working with a controlled project, such as the artist's palette, distribute equal amounts of cloth and materials to students for individual work.

• You might want to set up a central supply area or a couple of work areas with shared supplies of scissors, thread, needles and foam rubber pillow filling.

Tips

Contact community art galleries for the names of working artists. Invite them to a panel discussion about their directions in contemporary art.

Evaluation

• Did the student select an appropriate object?

• Did preliminary drawings show careful observation and an active thought process?

• Did the student successfully convert his/her sketches to a three-dimensional pattern?

• Is the final object well designed? Were colors well chosen? Does the stitching/stuffing of the sculpture have a neat and "finished" look?

Student Profile

Chris Byrd

Age 18
Lake Highlands High School
Dallas, Texas
Favorite kinds of art: Cubism,
Abstract
Favorite artists: Max Weber,
Juan Gris
Activity 2, Mimic the Masters

I have a fondness for guitars and the music they produce, because I play and enjoy listening to it. From my earlier work progressed to cubism and contemporary styles, using Lichtenstein. The dots and the lines gave this piece more energy and excitement similar to the music. I like this piece because the dots and the lines have created an extension of my cubistic style.

In addition to Picasso, Max Weber has also influenced my work. I tried to separate parts of my art and put them back together in different ways. Weber used patterns in his backgrounds as well as Lichtenstein.

I enjoy distorting the objects, and pushing them to their limits. I also enjoy experimenting and exploring with different media to create many different textures on one surface.

Some advice I have for other students is explore and create with many media, styles and techniques to express themselves.

Christina Vicki Ramirez

Age 18
Eastwood High School
El Paso, Texas
Favorite kind of art: Surrealism
Favorite artist: Salvador Dali
Activity 1, Sculpting with Cloth

My project is a soft sculpture of a tennis shoe. I decided to make a tennis shoe, particularly a Converse type tennis shoe, because Converse tennis shoes are so classic. I decided to try and capture that feeling I get when I wear them. I love shoes and think Converse are the one type of shoe that ties everyone together. It doesn't matter what race, sex or any other quality; everyone looks good in them.

My favorite part about the artistic process is the creative process. The area open to the imagination is so vast. You can do anything you want to and there's always going to be someone who likes it. My best advice for other students would be to follow what you want to do because in art nothing is ever right or wrong. It's all up to you.

Christina Vicki Ramirez

Tres Guitars, 1994. Oil, 40 1/2" x 32" (103 x 81 cm).

Christina's Shoe, 1994. Fabric and foam stuffing, about 30" x 15" (76 x 38 cm).

Activity 2: Mimic the Masters

Activity Objectives

Students should be able to:

• Discuss the distinctive styles and concepts of twentieth-century painting.

• Select a particular style they respond to and be able to articulate why.

• Produce a painting in the style of an artist of their choice.

Thinking Critically

Once students identify which artist's style to work with, ask them to:

• Write the elements of art (line, shape, form, texture, space, color, value) on the board.

• Write the principles (balance, unity, enphasis, contrast, pattern, rhythm, movement).

• Use these terms in verbalizing why and how they chose to imitate an artist's work.

Preparation Ideas

Find slides or ask students to research other examples of the work of the six artists listed in this activity. Use the images for a group discussion of the style of each artist.

Classroom Management

• One way to approach this project is to focus on an in-depth investigation of just one artist. For instance, a lesson on Lichtenstein could include research on the use of dots to make color halftones,

Teacher Spotlight

Marsha Hogue
Art Department Chair
Lake Highlands High School

Before we began creating any of the sketches, designs or ideas, we looked at examples of a wide variety of the work of each artist. They were not limited to just the examples in the current text. In this way, some stretched the concepts presented in their artwork to reflect some of the artist's work that appealed to them. Also, they were not confined to a particular media or size of paper, or told to recreate a particular image or style as you see it. I really wanted this to be their inquiry about an artist and his/her varied styles, techniques and use of media. Some students used Prismacolors, oil pastels, acrylic paint, or collage, or a combination of these.

Paula Turner
Art Department Head
Eastwood High School

We had a great time one Saturday morning in the basement at La Barata fabric store, selecting fabric for the projects. If we had had more time, I would have spent a week on sewing skills, both by hand and by machine.

or the history of the cartoon and comic strip. Divide the class into small groups to collect, share and critique possible cartoon strips to reproduce in a painting.

• This activity is ideal for small-group work. Write the names of several artists on the board. Have the class choose which artists to investigate. Each group could focus on a different artist, working together to research the artist's work. You might ask each group to make a presentation to the class before beginning individual paintings.

Evaluation

• Can the student use the terms of elements and principles to verbalize why and how he or she chose to imitate an artist's work?

• Has the student created an original work of art that incorporates the distinctive style of the chosen artist?

Reference

John Frederick Peto,
Job Lot Cheap
(Still Life with Books),
detail, after 1900.
Oil on canvas, 30" x
40" (76 x 101.7 cm).
San Francisco Art
Museums.

Map of Today's World

The best way to see what the world looks like is to look at a globe. The problem of accurately depicting the earth on a flat surface has challenged map-makers for centuries. This map, called a Robinson projection, is designed to show the earth in one piece, while maintaining the shape of the land and size relationships as much as possible. However, any world map has distortions.

This map is also called a *political* map, showing the names and boundaries of countries as they existed at the time of its creation. Political maps, of necessity, change every year as new countries develop. Some of the maps in this book are *physical*, showing where mountain ranges and rivers exist, while some maps combine both physical and political features.

Key to Abbreviations

ALB.	**Albania**
AUS.	**Austria**
B.–H.	**Bosnia–Hercegovina**
BELG.	**Belgium**
CRO.	**Croatia**
CZ REP.	**Czech Republic**
EQ. GUINEA	**Equatorial Guinea**
HUNG.	**Hungary**
LEB.	**Lebanon**
LITH.	**Lithuania**
LUX.	**Luxembourg**
MAC.	**Macedonia**
NETH.	**Netherlands**
RUS.	**Russia**
SLOV.	**Slovenia**
SLVK.	**Slovakia**
SWITZ.	**Switzerland**
YUGO.	**Yugoslavia**

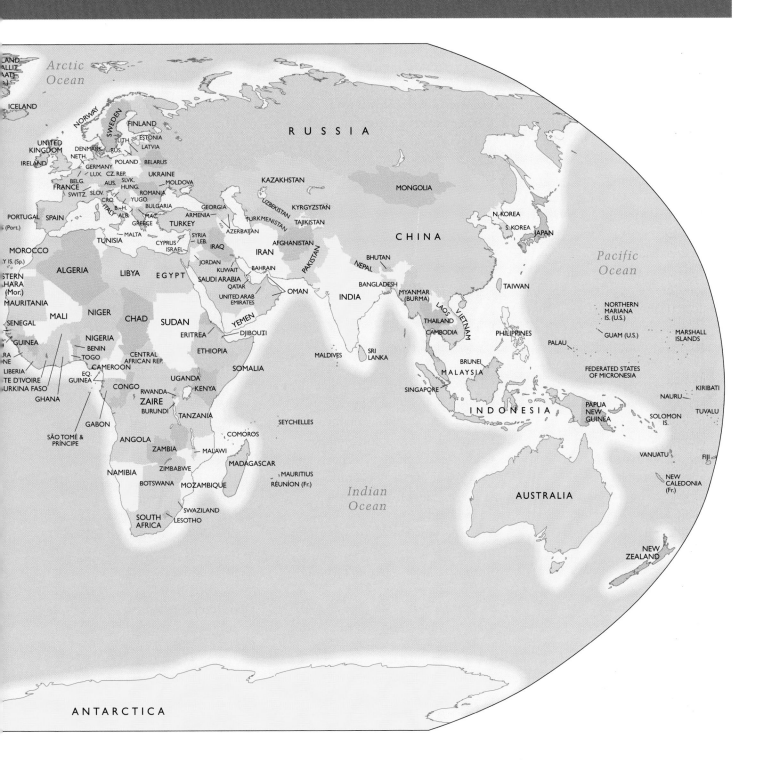

Arctic
Ocean

ICELAND

LAND
ALLIT
ATI
a)

NORWAY
SWEDEN
FINLAND

UNITED
KINGDOM
IRELAND
DENMARK
NETH.
LITH. ESTONIA
LATVIA
RUS.
POLAND BELARUS
GERMANY
BELG. LUX. CZ. REP.
FRANCE
SWITZ. SLOV.
AUS.
SLVK.
HUNG.
UKRAINE
MOLDOVA
ROMANIA
YUGO.
CRO.
B.-H.
ITALY
ALB.
MAC.
GREECE
BULGARIA
MALTA
GEORGIA
ARMENIA
AZERBAIJAN
TURKEY
CYPRUS
ISRAEL
SYRIA
LEB.
IRAQ
JORDAN
KUWAIT
BAHRAIN
QATAR
UNITED ARAB
EMIRATES

RUSSIA

KAZAKHSTAN

UZBEKISTAN
KYRGYZSTAN
TURKMENISTAN
TAJIKISTAN

MONGOLIA

CHINA

N. KOREA
S. KOREA
JAPAN

TAIWAN

PORTUGAL SPAIN
(Port.)

MOROCCO
Y IS. (Sp.)

STERN
HARA
(Mor.)

TUNISIA

ALGERIA
LIBYA
EGYPT

MAURITANIA

MALI
NIGER
CHAD
SUDAN

SENEGAL

GUINEA

RA
NE

LIBERIA
TE D'IVOIRE
URKINA FASO
GHANA

NIGERIA
BENIN
TOGO
EQ.
GUINEA
CAMEROON
CENTRAL
AFRICAN REP.
GABON

SÃO TOMÉ &
PRÍNCIPE

AFGHANISTAN

IRAN

PAKISTAN

BHUTAN
NEPAL

BANGLADESH

INDIA

OMAN

SAUDI ARABIA

YEMEN

DJIBOUTI

ERITREA

ETHIOPIA

SOMALIA

UGANDA
KENYA

CONGO
RWANDA
ZAIRE
BURUNDI
TANZANIA

ANGOLA
ZAMBIA
MALAWI
ZIMBABWE
MOZAMBIQUE
NAMIBIA
BOTSWANA
SWAZILAND
SOUTH
AFRICA
LESOTHO

MADAGASCAR

COMOROS

SEYCHELLES

MAURITIUS
RÉUNÍON (Fr.)

MALDIVES

SRI
LANKA

MYANMAR
(BURMA)
LAOS
THAILAND
VIETNAM
CAMBODIA

PHILIPPINES

MALAYSIA
BRUNEI
SINGAPORE

INDONESIA

Pacific
Ocean

NORTHERN
MARIANA
IS. (U.S.)

GUAM (U.S.)

PALAU

MARSHALL
ISLANDS

FEDERATED STATES
OF MICRONESIA

NAURU

KIRIBATI

PAPUA
NEW
GUINEA
SOLOMON
IS.

TUVALU

VANUATU

FIJI

NEW
CALEDONIA
(Fr.)

Indian
Ocean

AUSTRALIA

NEW
ZEALAND

ANTARCTICA

Pronunciation Guide for Artists' Names

Italicized syllables are accented.

Abramovitz, Max ah-*bram*-oh-vits
Adams, Ansel *ad*-ams, *an*-sull
Aeschylus *ess*-kul-luss
Aguilar, Rosalie ah-*gwee*-lar,
  rose-ah-lee
Alberti al-*bair*-tee
Angelico, Fra an-*jay*-lee-co, frah
Anuskiewicz, Richard an-*nu*-
  skah-vich
Anguissola, Sofanisba ahng-gwee-
  soh-lah, soh-fahn-*eez*-bah
Areogun *are*-ee-oh-gun
Arp, Jean (Hans) arp, zhahn (hahns)

Baciccio, Giovanni Battista
  bah-*chee*-chee-oh, jo-*vahn*-ee
  bah-*tee*-stah
Barlach, Ernst *bahr*-lock, airnst
Bellini, Giovanni bel-*lee*-nee,
  jo-*vahn*-nee
Bernini, Gianlorenzo bair-*nee*-nee,
  jahn-low-*rens*-oh
Beuys, Joseph boyss, *yo*-zef
Bierstadt, Albert *beer*-staht
Boccioni, Umberto bot-cho-nee,
  oom-*bair*-toe
Bologna, Giovanni boh-*loh*-nyah,
  jo-*vahn*-nee
Bonheur, Rosa bon-*err*
Boromini, Francesco bore-oh-*mee*-
  nee, fran-*chess*-co
Bosch, Hieronymus bosh, heer-*ahn*-
  ni-mus
Botero, Fernando boh-*tay*-roh,
  fair-*nahn*-doh
Botticelli, Sandro bot-tee-*chel*-lee,
  sand-ro
Boucher, Francois boo-*shay*,
  fran-*swah*
Brancusi, Constantin bran-*coo*-zee,
  con-stan-tin
Braque, Georges brahk, zhorzh
Bruegel, Pieter *brue*-gl, *pee*-ter
Brunelleschi, Filippo brew-nell-*less*-
  key, fee-*leep*-poh
Buonarroti, Michelangelo bwoh-na-
  roh-tee, mee-kel-*an*-jay-loh
Burgee, John bur-*ghee*

Campin, Robert cahm-*peh*, roh-*bair*
Canaletto, Antonio can-ah-*let*-toe,
  an-*toe*-nee-oh
Caravaggio car-ah-*vah*-jyoh
Cartier Bresson, Henri car-*tyay*
  bre-*sohn*, ahn-*ree*
Cassatt, Mary cah-*saht*
Cellini, Benvenuto chel-*lee*-nee,
  ben-vay-*noo*-toe
Cézanne, Paul say-*zahn*
Chagall, Marc sha-*gahl*
Chalgrin, J. F. shal-*gren*
Chardin, Jean Baptiste-Simeon
  shar-*da*, zhahn bah-*teest*-see-
  may-*on*
Chirico, Giorgio de *key*-ree-coh,
  jor-jyoh day
Christo *kriss*-toe
Claude Lorrain (Claude Gellée,
  zhuh-*lay*) klohd loh-*ren*
Clouet, Jean *cloo*-eh, zhahn
Copley, John Singleton *kop*-lee
Corbusier, Le kore-boo-zee-*ay*, leh
Corot, Jean-Baptiste-Camille
  ko-*roh*, zhahn-bah-*teest*-kah-
  mee-yuh
Courbet, Gustave koor-*bay*,
  goo-*stahv*
Cranach, Lucas crah-*nak* (soft),
  loo-kahs

Dali, Salvador *dah*-lee, *sahl*-vah-
  door
Daumier, Honoré doe-mee-*ay*,
  on-noh-*ray*
David, Jacques-Louis dah-*veed*,
  zjahk-loo-*ee*
Degas, Edgar day-*gah*, ed-*gahr*
Delacroix, Eugene dul-la-*krwah*,
  oo-*zhen*
DeKooning, Willem deh-*koon*-ing,
  vil-em
Demuth, Charles *day*-mooth,
Devereaux *dev*-er-roh
Diebenkorn, Richard *dee*-ben-korn
Donatello doe-nah-*tell*-oh
Duccio *doo*-chyoh
Duchamp, Marcel doo-*shahn*,
  mar-*sell*
Dürer, Albrecht *dur*-er, *ahl*-brecht

Eakins, Thomas *ay*-kins
Eiffel, Alexandre-Gustave *ee*-fel,
  al-ex-*andr*- goo-*stahv*
El Greco (Domenikos
  Theotocopoulos, thay-oh-toe-*coe*-
  poo-loss, doe-*may*-nee-coss)
  el *greh*-koh
Ernst, Max airnst
Estes, Richard *ess*-tess
van Eyck, Hubert fahn *ike*,
  hoo-bert
van Eyck, Jan fahn *ike*, yahn
Exekias ek-*sek*-ee-uhs

Fischer, Johann Michael *fish*-er,
  yoh-hahn
Flavin, Dan *flay*-vin
Fouquet, Jean foo-*kay*, zhahn
Fragonard, Jean-Honore fra-go-*nahr*,
  zhahn-oh-no-*reh*
Frankenthaler, Helen frank-en-
  thal-er

Garnier, Charles gahr-*nyay*, sharl
Gauguin, Paul go-*gen*
Gaulli, Giovanni Battista Francesco
  gah-*ool*-lee, jo-*vah*-nee bah-*tees*-
  tah fran-*chess*-koh
Gentile da Fabriano jen-*tee*-lay da
  fah-bree-*ah*-no
Gentileschi, Artemisia jen-teel-*ess*-
  key, ar-tay-*mee*-zee-ah
Gericault, Theodore *zhay*-ree-koh
  tay-oh-dor
Ghiberti, Lorenzo ghee-*bair*-tee,
  loh-*ren*-zoh
Giacometti, Alberto zhah-co-*met*-
  ee, al-*bair*-toe
Giotto *jot*-toe
Gislebertus geez-ul-*bair*-tuhs
Giorgione da Castelfranco jor-*joh*-
  nay dah cah-stell-*frank*-oh
van Gogh, Vincent vahn *go*,
  vin-sent
Gorky, Arshile *gor*-kee, *ar*-shil
Gottlieb, Adolph *got*-leeb, *ay*-dolf
Goujon, Jean goo-*zhahn*, zhahn
Goya, Francisco *goy*-ah, fran-*sis*-co
Gropius, Walter *grow*-pee-us
Grünewald, Mathias *groon*-eh-valt,
  mah-*tee*-ahs

Hals, Frans hahls, frahns
Hardouin-Mansart, Jules *are*-doo-ehn-mahn-sar zjool
Haussmann, Georges Eugene ohs-*mahn*, zjorzj oo-*zjehn*
Hasegawa Tohaku hah-seh-*gah*-wah, toe-*hah*-coo
Henri, Robert *hen*-rye
Herrera, Juan de er-*ray*-rah, wahn day
Hiroshige, Ando hear-oh-shee-gay, ahn-doe
Hokusai, Katsushika, ho-k'-sy, kaht-soo-she-ka
Holbein, Hans *hole*-bine, hahns
Houdon, Jean Antoine oo-*don*, zhahn an-*twahn*

Iktinus *ick*-tih-nus
Imhotep im-*hoh*-tep
Ingres, Jean-Auguste-Dominique aingr, zhahn-oh-*goost*-doh-min-*eek*
Isozaki, Arata ee-soh-zah-kee, ah-rah-tah

Jahn, Helmut yahn

Kallikrates kal-i-*crate*-ees
Kandinsky, Wassily kan-*dins*-key, *vahs*-i-lee
Kashani, Maqsud kah-shanee, mock-sud
Kienholz, Edward *keen*-hohlts
Kirchner, Ernst Ludwig *kear*-kner, airnst *lood*-vig
Klee, Paul clay
Klimt, Gustav klimt, *goo*-stahf
Kollwitz, Käthe *kahl*-vits, *kay*-teh
Ku K'ai-chih goo kai-juh

Lachaise, Gaston la-*shez*, ga-*ston*
Lange, Dorothea lang, dor-uh-*thee*-uh
Langhans, Karl *lahng*-hahns
La Tour, George de la-*toor*, zjorzj duh
Le Brun, Charles luh-*brun*, sharl
Leonardo da Vinci lay-oh-*nar*-doh dah *vin*-chee
Lescot, Pierre les-*koh*, pee-*air*

Leyster, Judith *lie*-stir, *you*-deet (jew-*dith*)
Lichtenstein, Roy *lick*-ten-stine
Lippi, Filippo *lip*-pee, fi-*lip*-po
Lysippus lie-*sip*-us

Ma Yuan ma you-an
Maderno, Carlo mah-*dair*-noh
Magritte, René mah-*greet*, ren-*ay*
Maillol, Aristide mah-*yahl*, ah-riss-*teed*
Manet, Edouard ma-*nay*, eh-doo-*are*
Mantegna, Andrea man-*ten*-ya, ahn-*dray*-ah
Marin, John *mar*-in
Martinez, Maria and Julian mar-*tee*-nez, *who*-lee-ahn
Martini, Simone mar-*tee*-nee, see-*moh*-nay
Masaccio ma-*zaht*-choh
Matisse, Henri mah-*teess*, ahn-*ree*
Medici, Lorenzo de *meh*-di-chee, loh-*ren*-zo day
Michelangelo mee-kel-*an*-jay-loh
Mies van der Rohe, Ludwig mees van der *roe*, *lood*-vig
Millet, Jean Francois mee-*lay*, zhahn fran-*swah*
Miro, Joan mee-*roh*, joe-on
Modersohn-Becker, Paula *moh*-der-sohn *bek*-ker
Modigliani, Amedeo moh-dee-lee-*ah*-nee, ah-may-*day*-oh
Mondrian, Piet *mohn*-dree-ahn, pate
Monet, Claude moh-*nay*, kload
Montenegro, Roberto mohn-tay-*nay*-groh, roh-*bair*-toe
Morisot, Berthe moh-ree-*zoh*, bairt
Mukhuba, Nelson muck-who-bah
Munch, Edvard moonk, *ed*-vard
Murillo, Bartholome Esteban moo-*ree*-yoh, bar-toh-loh-*may* *ess*-tay-bahn
Muybridge, Eadweard *my*-brij, *ed*-wurd

Niccolo dell' Arca *Knee*-Ko-lo dell *ar*-ka
Noguchi, Isamu noh-goo-chee, ees-sah-moo
Nolde, Emil *nohl*-deh, eh *meel*

Oeben, Jean Francois *ur*-buhn, zhahn frahn-swar
Oldenburg, Claes *old*-en-berg, klahss
Oppenheim, Meret *ahp*-uhn-hym, meh-*ray*
Orozco, José Clemente oh-*ross*-coh, ho-*say* cleh-*men*-tay

Palladio, Andrea pah-*lah*-dee-oh, an-*dray*-ah
Panini, Giovanni Paolo pah-*nee*-nee, jo-*vah*-nee *pah*-oh-loh
Peale, Raphaelle peel, *rah*-fay-ell
Pei, I.M. pay
Pelli, Cesar *pel*-lee, *say*-zar
Perrault, Claude pear-oh, klohd
Phidias *fid*-ee-us
Picasso, Pablo pee-*kahs*-oh, *pah*-blo
Pissarro, Camille pee-*sahr*-oh, cah-*meal*
Pollock, Jackson *poll*-lock
Poussin, Nicholas poo-*sahn*, *nick*-oh-lahs
Prandtauer, Jacob *pran*-tower, *yahk*-ob
Pugin, A. Welby *pyu*-jin

Raggi, Antonio *rah*-jee, an-*toe*-nee-oh
Raphael rah-fah-*ell*
Rauschenberg, Robert *rau*-shen-berg
Rembrandt van Rijn *rem*-brant van rhine
Renoir, Pierre Auguste ren-*wahr*, pee-*air* oh-*gust*
Riemenschneider, Tilman *reem*-en-shny-dr, *till*-mahn
Rietveld, Gerrit *reet*-velt, *gair*-it
Rivera, Diego ree-*vay*-rah, dee-*ay*-goh
Rodin, Auguste roh-*dan*, oh-*gust*
Rosenquist, James *roh*-zen-kwist
Rosso, Fiorentino *rohss*-soh, fyor-en-*tee*-noh
Rouault, Georges roo-*oh*, zjorzj
Rousseau, Henri roo-*soh*, ahn-*ree*
Rubens, Peter Paul *roo*-bens
Rude, Francoise rood, fran-*swahz*
Ruisdael, Jacob van *rwees*-dahl, *yah*-cob van
Ruysch, Rachel royss, rah-kel

Saarinen, Eero *sahr*-in-en, *air*-oh
Safdie, Moshe *sahf*-dee, *moh*-shuh
Samaras, Lucas sah-*mah*-ras,
   loo-kus
Schwitters, Kurt *schvit*-urs, kort
Seurat, Georges suh-*rah*, zjorzj
Shen Chou sun-joe
Siqueiros, David Alfaro see-*kayr*-
   ohss, *day*-vid al-*far*-oh
Sluter, Claus *sloo*-tr, *klows*
Staël, Nicholas de stahl, nee koh
   lah duh
Steen, Jan stain, yahn
Steichen, Edward *sty*-ken
Stieglitz, Alfred *stee*-glits
Suger, Abbot soo-*gay*, *a*-but

Tao Chi dow-jee
Tiepolo, Giovanni Battista tee-*eh*-
   po-lo, jo-*vah*-nee bah-*tees*-tah

Tintoretto (Jacopo Robusti)
   tin-toe-*ret*-toe, (*yah*-coe-poe
   roe-*booss*-tee)
Titian (Titiano Vecelli) tish-un
   (tee-tsee-*ah*-noh vay-*chell*-ee)
Toledo, Juan Bautista de toe-*lay*-
   doe, wahn baw-*tees*-tah day
Toulouse-Lautrec, Henri de
   too-*looz* low-*trek*, ahn-*ree* duh

Uccello, Paolo oo-*chell*-loh,
   pah-oh-loh

van Dyck, Anthony fahn *dike*,
   an-toe-nee
Vasarely, Victor va-sah-*rell*-ee
Vasari, Giorgio va-*sah*-ree, *jor*-jyoh
Vau, Louis le voh, loo-*ee* le

Velazquez, Diego vay-*lass*-kess,
   dee-*aye*-goh
Vermeer, Jan fare-*meer*, yahn
Veronese (Paolo Caliari) vay-roe-
   nay-zay, (*pah*-oh-loh kal-ee-
   are-ee)
Vigée-Lebrun, Elizabeth vee-*zhay*
   luh-*brun*, uh-*lee*-zah-bet
Vignon, Pierre vee-*nyon*, pee-*air*
Villon Jacques vee-*yohn*, zhahk
Warhol, Andy *war*-hall
Watteau, Antoine wah-*toh*,
   an-*twahn_*
Webster, Elon web ster, eh-lon
van der Weyden, Rogier van der
   vay-den, roh-*jair*
Wright, Frank Lloyd rite, loid
Wyeth, Andrew *why*-eth

Zimmerman, Dominikus *tsim*-ur-
   mahn, doe-*min*-ih-kus
Zurbaran, Francisco de *zoor*-bah-
   ran, fran-*sis*-coe day

Pronunciation Guide for Places and Terms

Acropolis ah-*krahp*-uh-lis
Abu Simbel *ah*-boo *sim*-bul
Aegean a-*jee*-un
Aix eks
Altamira ahl-tah-*mee*-rah
Amboise am-*bwahz*
Amiens *ah*-mee-en
Angkor Thom *ang*-kore tahm
Angkor Wat *ang*-kore wot
Arc de Triomphe de I'Etoile
  ark duh *tree*-omf duh leh-*twahl*
Arezzo ah-*retz*-oh
Argenteuil ahr-zhahn-*toy*
Ashurnasirpal ash-er-*naz*-er-pahl
Asuka ah-soo-*kah*
Avignon ah-veen-*yohn*

Baalbek *bal*-beck
Babylonia ba-bi-*loh*-nyah
Barbizon bahr-bih-*zon*
Baroque ba-*rohk*
Basel *bah*-zel
Bayeux bah-*yuh*
Beijing bay-*zhing*
Benin ben-*een*
Bokhara boh-*cahr*-ah
Bologna boh-*loh*-nyah
Borobodur bor-oh-boh-*duhr*
Breda *bray*-dah
Bruges brooszh
Byzantine *biz*-ahn-teen

Calais cal-*ay*
Casale cah-*sah*-lay
Chambord shan-*boar*
Chartres shartr
Chateau sha-*toe*
Chateaux sha-*toe*
Chenonceaux shen-ahn-*soh*
Cheops *kee*-ahps
Cheyenne shy *an*
Chichen Itza *chee*-chen *eet*-zah
Colmar *coal*-mahr
Cologne coh-*lone*
Colosseum kahl-uh-*see*-uhm
Constantinople *kahn*-stan-tin-
  oh-pul
Cordova kor-*doh*-vah
Cyclades sick-*la*-dees

Dada *dah*-dah
Deir el Bahari dayr el bah-*hah*-ree
Der Blaue Reiter dehr *blah*-way
  right-er
De Stijl deh *sty*-ul
Die Brücke dee *broock*-eh
Dijon dee-*zjohn*
Doge *dojh* (soft)

Eiffel *y*-ful (Eng: *eye*-ful)
El Castillo el cas-*tee*-yoh
El Escorial el eh-skor-ee-*ahl*
Epidauros ehp-eh-*dor*-us
Euphrates you-*fray*-tees

Flemalle fleh-*mahl*
Fontainebleau fohn-ten-*bloh*

Gare Saint Lazare gahr sen lah-*zahr*
Ghent gent (hard g)
Giverny *zhee*-ver-nay
Giza *gee*-zah (hard g)
Gudea goo-*dee*-ah
Guernica *gwer*-ni-ka
Guilin *gwee*-lun

Haarlem *har*-lem
Hagia Sophia *hah*-zhee-ah
  soh-*fee*-ah
Han dynasty hahn
Heliopolis hee-lee-*ahp*-oh-liss
Herculaneum her-cue-*lay*-nee-um
Holofernes hoe-loh-*fer*-nays
Hue hway

Ife *ee*-fay
Il Gesu ill *jay*-soo
Invalides in-vah-*leed*
Isenheim *iss*-en-hime
Isfahan *iss*-fah-hahn

Jericho *jer*-eh-ko
Jerusalem jeh-*roo*-suh-lem

Kamakura kah-mah-*koo*-rah
Karnak *kahr*-nack
Kiev key-*eff*
Knossos *no*-sohs
Kyoto *kyoh*-toh

La Grande Jatte lah grahnd zhaht
Lascaux lass-*ko*
Las Meninas lahs men-*een*-yahss
Le Havre luh hahv
Leiden *lye*-den
Les Demoiselles d'Avignon
  lay *dem*-wah-zell dah-veen-*yohn*
Loire River lwahr
Louvain loo-*van*
Louvre loovr

Madeleine mah-duh-*lin*
Maesta mah-aye-*stah*
Magi *may*-jie
Mamallapuram mah-mah-lah-
  poor-um
Mantua *man*-too-ah
Masada mah-*sah*-dah
Medici *meh*-di-chee
Mesopotamia mess-oh-poh-*tay*-
  mee-ah
Minoan min-*noh*-uhn
Mohenjo-daro moh-hen-jo-*dah*-roh
Monte Alban *mohn*-tay ahl-*bahn*
Monticello mohn-ti-*chell*-oh
Montmartre mon *martr*
Montreux mahn-*truh*
Mont Sainte Victoire mohn sen
  vik-*twahr*
Moulin de la Galette moo-*lahn*
  duh lah gah-*lett*
Moulin Rouge moo-*lahn* roozjh
Mughal *mo*-gull
Mycenae my-*see*-nee

Nanzenji nan-*sen*-jee
Nara *nah*-rah
Navajo *nah*-vah-hoh
Naxos *nahx*-ohs
Nevers neh-*vair*
Nijo nee-jo
Nineveh *nin*-eh-vuh
Notre Dame noh-*trah* dahm
Nuremberg *noor*-em-burg

Oaxaca wah-*hah*-cah
Osaka oh-*sah*-kah

Padua *pa*-doo-ah
Paestum pie-*aye*-stum
Pagan *pah*-gahn
Palazzo Ducale pah-*laht*-zoh
    doo-*kahl*-eh
Palazzo Vecchio pah-*laht*-zoh
    veh-key-oh
Pantheon *pan*-thee-on
Parthenon *par*-then-on
Penang pen-*ang*
Persepolis per-*seh*-poh-lis
Piazza della Signoria pee-*aht*-zah
    del-lah *seen*-yor-*ee*-ah
Piazza Navona pee-*aht*-zah nah-
    voh-nah
Pieta pee-aye-*tah*
Pisa *pee*-sah
Poitiers pwah-*tyay*
Pompeii pahm-*pay*-ee
Port en Bessin port ahn bes-*ehn*
Poseidon poh-*sigh*-dun
Prado Museum *prah*-doh

Qing Dynasty ching

Ravenna rah-*ven*-ah
Reims reemz
Renaissance *ren*-eh-*sahnss*
Rijksmuseum *rikes*-myoo-zee-um
Rococo roh-*koh*-koh
Romanesque *ro*-mahn-esk
Ronchamp roh-*shahn*
Rouen roo-*ahn*

St. Apollinare in Classe saint
    ah-pahl-in-*ahr*-ay in *klahss*-eh
Sainte Chapelle sant shah-*pell*
St. Denis sahn duh-*nee*
Sakkara (Saqqara) sah-*kahr*-ah
Salisbury *sals*-burr-ee
Samothrace *sam*-oh-thrace
San Francesco san fran-*chess*-coh
San Rocco san *rock*-oh
San Lorenzo san loh-*ren*-zoh
Santa Maria del Carmine *san*-tah
    mah-*ree*-ah *del* cahr-*mee*-nay
Santa Maria della Grazie *san*-tah
    mah-*ree*-ah del-lah *graht*-see-eh
San Vitale san vih-*tahl*-ay
San Zavier del Bac san *hahv*-yair
    del bahk
Sawankhaloke kiln sah-*wahnk*-ah-
    lock kill
Schoenbrun *show*-en-broon
Scythia *sith*-ee-ah
Segovia seh-*goh*-vee-ah
Seine River sen
Seto *see*-toe
Seville seh-*vee*-yah
Sforza *sfort*-sah
Shekwan *shek*-wahn
Shoshone shoh-*shoh*-nee
Siena see-*en*-ah
Staffelstein *stah*-fell-stine
Stanza della Segnatura *stahn*-zah
    del-la seg-nah-*too*-rah
Sumer *soo*-mur
Sumeria soo-*mair*-ee-uh
Sutton Hoo *suht*-uhn hoo

Tabriz tah-*breeze*
Taj Mahal tazh mah-*hahl*
Tenochtitlan teh-*nok*-tit-lahn
Teotihuacan *tay*-oh-tee-*wah*-kan
Thebes theebs
Tigris *ty*-gris
Todai-ji toe-dah-ee jee
Toledo toe-*lay*-doe
Topkapi *top*-cap-ee
Torgau *tohr*-gow
Toulouse too-*looz*
Tuilleries *twill*-er-ee

Uffizi Gallery oo-*feet*-see
Ur er
Urbino oor-*bee*-noh

Vendome vehn-*dome*
Versailles vehr-*sigh*
Vesuvius vuh-*soo*-vee-uhs
Vetheuil veh-*twahl*
Vezelay *ves*-eh-lay
Vicenza vee-*chen*-zah
Vierzehnheiligen *fear*-tsayn-*high*-
    li-gen

Wijk by Durstede vike by
    duhr-sted-eh
Worms vhorms
Würzburg *virts*-burg

Xian *chee*-an

Yosemite yoh-*sem*-i-tee

Zaire zy-*ear*
Zhou dynasty jo
Zwiefalten *tswee*-fahl-ten

Glossary

Correct pronunciation of difficult words is Indicated.

Italics indicate emphasis or accent in pronunciation.

abbey A complex of buildings comprised of a monastery and a church.

aborigine (a-bor-*ij*-i-nee) Indigenous or native inhabitants as differentiated from an invading or colonizing people.

abrade To scrape or rub off.

Abstract Expressionism A twentieth-century painting style that features large-scale works and expression of feelings through slashing, active brushstrokes.

abstraction (ab-*strak*-shun) A work of art that emphasizes design and a simplified or systematic investigation of forms. The subject matter may be recognized or may be completely transformed into shape, color and/or line.

acropolis The citadel of a Greek city; its highest point, containing temples and public buildings.

acrylic paint (a-*krill*-ik) A mixture of pigments that can adhere to almost any surface.

adobe (a *doh* bee) A clay brick made of sun-dried earth used as a building material. Any structure made of adobe bricks.

aerial perspective A method of creating the illusion of distance by representing objects further away with less clarity of contour and in diminished color. Also called **atmospheric perspective**.

aesthetic (es-*thet*-ik) Pertaining to the philosophically pleasing, beautiful and emotional nature of man; also, a pattern of thinking so oriented.

aesthetics (es-*thet*-iks) The description and explanation of artistic phenomena and aesthetic experience by means of psychology, sociology, ethnology or history.

agora (ah-*go*-rah) Greek word for assembly; the square or marketplace that was the center of public life in an ancient Greek city.

aisle (*eye*-l) The long, narrow space on each side of the nave of a church, usually between a row of columns and the outer wall. Often referred to as "side aisles."

alabaster A fine-grained gypsum or calcite (like marble), often white and translucent (though sometimes delicately tinted), used for sculpture and architectural columns.

allegorical Symbolic of truths or generalizations about human nature.

altar A structure on which to place or sacrifice offerings to a deity.

altarpiece A painted and/or sculpted work of art that stands above or at the back of the altar. It usually represents visual symbols of the Mass or depicts the saint to whom the chapel is dedicated, and may contain scenes from his or her life. See **retable** and **reredos**.

ambulatory (*am*-byoo-lah-tor-ee) Any passageway around a central space. A place for walking around the apse of a church, often a continuation of the side aisles; also, a covered walkway around a cloister.

Amida (ah-*me*-dah) The Buddha of the Western Paradise, particularly popular in eleventh-century Japan. Pictured with short curly hair, elongated ear lobes, long arms and an urna on his forehead.

amphitheatre (*am*-fi-*the*-a-ter) A double theater or closed arena, such as the Roman Colosseum; an elliptical or circular space surrounded by rising tiers of seats.

amphora (am-*for*-ah) A storage jar having an egg-shaped body, a foot and two handles, each attached at the neck and shoulders of the jar.

Anasazi (ah-nah-*sah*-zee) "The Ancient Ones"; early pueblo-dwelling peoples of the plateaus of the American Southwest.

anatomy The structure of the human body (or of animals or plants).

Andean (an-*dee*-an) Region of the Andes mountains of western South America and the mountain-oriented highland culture of indigenous people there.

Angkor (ong-*kore*) Ancient Khmer temple complex in Northwest Cambodia and center of the ancient Khmer kingdoms from the tenth to thirteenth centuries.

animal style Artistic practice of making objects in the shape of, or with motifs based on, animals; specifically refers to a tradition of art among the nomads of Eastern Europe and Central and Northern Asia.

animism The religious or spiritual attribution of conscious life to natural objects; the belief in the existence of spirits separable from bodies.

anthropomorphic (an-thro-po-*more*-fik) Refers to giving human characteristics to non-human objects or beings. Many Egyptian and Brahmanic gods were animals in the form of humans.

Apache (ah-*patch*-ee) Tribe of Native Americans inhabiting the American Southwest, artistically distinguished by their coiled basketry, large beaded women's collars and decorated fine leatherwork.

Apollo (ah-*pall*-oh) Greek god of the sun, prophecy, music, medicine and poetry; artistically significant as a model of physical beauty, dignity and serenity.

apostle (ah-*pos*-ell) In Christian usage, refers to the twelve followers of Christ who spread his teachings throughout the Mediterranean world. The apostles of Buddha are known as "lohan."

apse A large semi-circular (or polygonal) area at the choir end of a church. Usually contains the altar. May also be found at the ends of transepts or at the ends of smaller chapels.

aqueduct (*ak*-wah-dukt) An artificial channel for carrying water from a distance.

arabesque (ar-uh-besk) Intricate and fanciful surface decoration generally based on geometric patterns and using combinations of flowering vines, tendrils, etc.

arcade A series of arches and their supports (columns). When placed against a wall and used mainly as decoration, the result is called a "blind arcade."

arch An architectural construction (semi-circular or pointed) built of wedge-shaped blocks (voussoirs) to span an opening and usually supported by columns or piers. A corbeled arch is made by overlapping layers of stones, each one projecting slightly farther over the opening than the one below it. A building dependent upon arches for its structure is said to be "arculated."

archaeology Unearthing and study of evidences from past cultures which have been hidden from human eyes for centuries.

archaic (ar-*kay*-ik) Referring to the early phase of an artistic development; specifically applies to the span of ancient Greek art prior to the Classical period.

architecture (ar-ki-tek-choor) The art and science of designing and erecting buildings.

architrave (arch-i-trave) The main horizontal beam at the bottom of an entablature, resting on the capitals of columns. Often made of several lintels to stretch the length of the building.

archivolt (ar-ki-volt) The concentric moldings above the arched openings in Romanesque and Gothic churches, often decorated with sculpture; also, the underside of an arch.

Art Nouveau (art new-voh) Abstract style in European and American arts from the 1880s to 1930s characterized by the use of undulating waves or flames, flower stalks and flowing lines.

artifact Object, usually simple, that reveals human workmanship and modification.

artisan (ar-ti-zen) A person manually skilled in making a particular product; a craftsperson.

artist An individual who professes and practices the manipulation of materials in executing the concepts of his or her imagination. One who reflects the aesthetics and technology of his or her era and a cultural "editor" of the environment.

Ashanti (ah-shahn-tee) A people and former kingdom of West Africa, artistically significant in their use of highly stylized and simplified fertility dolls as well as their mud-built houses with foundations ornamented with curvilinear patterns.

Asoka (ah-show-kah) First Indian Emperor and Buddhist enthusiast responsible for the origins of Buddhist art, 274–236 BC.

assemblage (ah-sem-blij) A work of art composed of fragments of objects or materials originally intended for other purposes.

Asuka (ah-skah) Early Japanese capital city and name of the first Buddhist cultural period there (538–645), artistically significant for importation of Korean and Chinese sculpture and architecture.

atlantes (at-lan-teez) Supports or columns in the form of carved male figures.

atrium (ay-tree-um) The inner court of a Roman house, open to the sky. Also, the enclosed (but open to the sky) courtyard in front of the main doors of a basilica or church.

Attic Pertaining to Attica, a region of Greece, and the artistic style developed there in pre-Classical times; also, the story above the main colonnade of a building.

Avaloketisvara (ah-vah-lok-eh-tesh-vah-rah) The merciful Bodhisattva of Buddhism, manifested in Chinese culture as Guan Yin, the Goddess of Mercy; known to the Japanese as *Kannon*.

avant-garde (ah-vant-gard) A style of twentieth-century art; also, any style of contemporary art in any period of time, being the newest form of visual expression and the farthest from the traditional ways of working.

axial (ak-si-ell) Describing a building plan that has a strong emphasis along one direction.

Ayuthaya (ah-you-tee-ah) Early Thai kingdom, founded 1350, artistically distinguished by its free mixing of Burmese, Khmer and Ceylonese styles.

Aztec People and kingdom of ancient central Mexico, noted for their advanced civilization before their conquest by Cortés in 1521, artistically distinguished by their large temple-oriented cities.

azulejos (ah-jew-lay-os) Glazed pottery tiles, usually painted in bright colors and floral or other patterns, used in Spanish, Portuguese and Hispanic architecture.

balance A principle of design that refers to the visual equalization of elements in a work of art. There are three kinds of balance: symmetrical (formal); asymmetrical (informal); and radial.

baldachin (bal-dah-cheen) A fixed canopy of wood, stone, fabric, etc., over an altar, throne or doorway. Sometimes portable, as when it is over a movable statue during a parade or procession.

balustrade A row of short pillars or columns topped by a railing.

Bamara (bah-mar-ah) A tribe of west Africa, particularly in Mali.

Ban Chiang (bahn cheng) Site of prehistoric burial grounds in northeast Thailand believed to be the oldest remains yet discovered of Bronze Age civilization. Distinguished by a fine grade of earthenware with very thin hand-built walls and curvilinear slip decoration.

baptistry (bap-ti-stree) An area in which the Sacrament of Baptism is administered, either within an area of a church or as a separate building.

Baroque (bar-oak) A period and style of European art (seventeenth century) which emphasized color and light. Work was characteristically exuberant, large, filled with swirling lines, and required emotional involvement; also refers to any highly ornate style.

barrel vault A semi-cylindrical ceiling spanning an open room, such as in Romanesque churches.

basketry The art of making wickerwork objects by methods of plaiting stalks, cane, rushes, etc.

basket weave Technique of forming a fabric wherein double threads are interlaced to produce a checkered pattern, similar to that of a woven basket.

bas-relief (bah ree-leef) A low, partially-round sculpture that emerges from a flat panel.

basilica (bah-sill-ee-ka) Roman civic building of rectangular form in which the ground plan was divided into nave, side aisles and apse, and was approached through a narthex. In Christian architecture, a church building similar in shape was the major worship form from the third to eighth centuries.

batik (bah-teek) A coloring or dyeing process using a wax stencil to protect design areas from coloration by dyeing of cloth or paper.

battlements Parapets built on top of walls with indentations for defense or decoration.

Bauhaus (bow-hows) A German art school, begun in 1918, that stressed science and technology as major resources for art and architecture. Many modern concepts of design were originated at the Bauhaus which affect contemporary artistic ideas.

bay A rectangular division (compartment) or a building, marked off by consecutive pairs of piers, columns or other supports. Large stained glass windows were put into the bays of Gothic cathedrals. The size of Chinese and Japanese temples is measured in terms of the number of bays along the facade.

bema (bee-mah) The raised sanctuary or chancel space in an early Christian or Eastern Orthodox church. In a synagogue, the elevated pulpit from which scripture is read.

Benin (beh-neen) A people and former kingdom of Nigeria, artistically distinguished by their fine-quality bronze castings of the sixteenth and seventeenth centuries.

Bible The collection of sacred writings of the Christian religion that includes Old and New Testaments, or that of the Jewish faith which contains only the Old Testament.

biomorphic shape (by-o-*mor*-fik) Artistic stylization suggested by organic forms.

bishop A spiritual overseer of a number of churches in a diocese of Greek, Roman Catholic and Anglican Church organizations. See **cathedral**.

blue-and-white A general term for the underglaze cobalt-decorated porcelain ware produced in China beginning in the Yuan dynasty. Cobalt produces the blue color, often of various intensities depending upon quality and thickness, and the white is the color of the kaolin body itself. Also, any pottery which seems to duplicate the style of such Chinese ware.

Bodhisattva (bode-he-*saht*-vah) A Buddhist saint, one who has compassionately refrained from entering eternal enlightenment (nirvana) in order to minister to the needs of mortals.

bond Pattern of alternating the directions of individual bricks or stones in a masonry wall.

Borobudor (bore-u-beh-*door)* An Indonesian stupa with ten levels.

Brahma (*brah*-mah) The Indian creator-god of the Hindu trinity; the ultimate basis of all existence; the universal self.

Brahmanism (*brah*-mahn-izm) Orthodox Indian religion adhering to the pantheon of the Vedas, stressing the pre-eminence of Siva, Indra and Vishnu as well as the practice of sacrifices and ceremonies.

broken color The effect produced from the application of optical mixing.

Buddha (*boo*-dah) Gautama Siddhartha, founder of Buddhism, c.563–483 BC; also any Buddhist sage who has achieved enlightenment in accordance with the teachings of Gautama.

Buddhism (*boo*-dizm) Religious belief based on the teachings of Gautama Buddha that suffering is inherent in life and that one can be liberated from it by mental and moral self-purification. Hinayana Buddhism stresses individualistic faith and a simple iconography. Mahayana Buddhism evolved in the second century under the teachings of Nagayana, stressing a complex understanding of the five eons of time, the four levels of creation, and the role of saints or Bodhisattvas.

burnish To polish leather-hard clay with a smooth object, rubbing to seal the porous surface of the clay; also, any such rubbing on any material.

buttress A massive support built against a wall to receive the lateral thrust (pressure) exerted by a vault, roof or arch. See **Flying Buttress**.

caliph (*kay*-liff) Title of an Islamic ruler, functioning in both religious and secular affairs.

calligraphy (kah-*lig*-ra-fee) The art of beautiful writing or printing; fine lettering of elegance, often thought in the West as being similar to the grace of Oriental writing.

campanile (camp-uh-*neel*-ee) A bell-tower either attached to a church or freestanding nearby.

campo santo A cemetery, from the Italian word for "holy field."

camera obscura (ob-*skyoor*-ah) A box with a small opening on one side through which an image was transferred in reverse onto the opposite wall of the box; similar to a modern camera.

cancello (can-*chell*-oh) A latticed screen or grille separating the choir from the nave.

candi (*john*-dee) Javanese commemorative structure, temple or shrine.

canopy (*kan*-ah-pee) An ornamental, roof-like covering placed above a statue, tomb, niche or altar.

cantilever (*kan*-tl-ee-ver) A horizontal projection, canopy, balcony or beam balanced and supported with a fulcrum.

canvas Surface of woven linen or other fiber on which an artist applies paint, and the most common ground or support for an oil painting; also, any painting executed on such material.

capital The top element of a column, pier or pilaster, usually ornamented with stylized leaves, volutes, animal or human forms. The entablature rests on capitals in Doric, Ionic and Corinthian orders.

caricature (*kar*-i-ki-choor) A drawing, painting or sculpture of a person that exaggerates selected characteristics of the subject, such as a prominent chin or large eyes. Often humorous.

cartoon A full-scale drawing from which a painting or fresco is made. Also, a simplified humorous drawing.

carving The subtractive process of sculpture in which parts of a block are cut or chiseled away, leaving the finished work.

caryatid (care-ee-*ah*-tid) A support or column in the form of a human figure, usually female. See **atlantes**.

casting A method of reproducing a three-dimensional object by pouring a hardening liquid or molten metal into a mold bearing its impression.

castle A fortified habitation, primarily used for defense, composed of a central dungeon, or keep, and outer defense works.

catacombs (*kat*-i-komz) Underground burial places made up of passageways and niches for holding the sarcophagi. Some catacombs contained chapels and meeting rooms of the early Christians.

cathedra The chair or throne of a bishop.

cathedral The main church of a diocese, containing the cathedra, or bishop's chair. See **bishop**.

celadon (*sell*-a-don) Pottery glaze characterized by a pale-green to bluish-green color, derived from iron, popularly used during the Sung dynasty in China and later in Korea and Thailand; also, ware covered with such a glaze.

cella (*sell*-ah) The main rectangular room of a temple containing the image of a god, goddess or cult deity.

centaur (*sen*-tor) A creature of Greek mythology with the head and torso of a man and the body and legs of a horse.

center of interest The area of a work of art toward which all visual movement is directed. It is the visual focal point of the work.

centering A wooden framework to support a stone arch or vault during construction.

ceramics Objects made of clay and fired in a kiln; also, the art of producing such objects.

chaitaya (*chah-ee*-tee-ah) A Buddhist sanctuary.

chakra (*shak*-rah) Iconographic wheel symbolizing the first sermon of Buddha and the progression of the law.

Chan (john) Buddhist sect emphasizing contemplation and meditation, self-discipline and the teaching that the Buddha is inherent in all things. Known in Japan as Zen.

chancel (*chan*-sell) The space kept for clergy and the choir in a church, between the nave and the apse. It is usually separated from the nave by steps, a railing or a screen.

Cha-no-yu (cha-*know*-you) The "way tea"; a prescribed ceremony for appreciating the process of making and drinking tea, connected with Zen meditation. This ceremony has inspired the creation of utensils and art objects to be used and appreciated during the tea-making process.

château (sha-*toh*) A French castle or large country house. (plural=châteaux)

Chavin (chow-*veen*) The mother culture of Andean cultures, dating from about 500 BC, centered in the Peruvian highlands.

chedis (*jay*-dee) A tiered, pointed, spire-like Thai pagoda.

cherub One of an order of angelic beings, often visualized in European art as a winged child.

Cheyenne (shy-*enn*) A tribe of North American natives of the north central plains that created unique silverwork in 1870s; this tribe is also noted for its fine leatherwork.

chiaroscuro (key-ah-ross-*kyoo*-roh) A technique for modeling forms in painting by which the lighted parts seem to emerge from surrounding dark areas. Strong contrast of dark and light values in painting.

Chilkat (*chill*-cat) A band of Tlingit Indians of southern Alaska, artistically unique in their woven, twined and plaited blankets in symbolic bear and other animal patterns.

Chimu (*chee*-moo) An urbanist culture of Andean peoples, reaching a zenith of creative activity about 1200, noted for their heavy adobe architecture on terraced sites, their use of interlocking fish designs, and stirrup pottery vessels in representations of birds and humans.

Chinoiserie (chee-nwa-*sree*) Style of European arts and crafts growing from a fanciful and idealized concept of "exotic" China based on travelers' accounts and isolated objects of Chinese art.

choir (kwire) The part of the church in which the service is sung, usually the apse; also, a group of trained singers.

Chola (*cho*-la) Dynasty of Indian rulers powerful from 846–1279, artistically distinguished by excellent graceful bronze castings, mostly notably of the Nataraja.

chops In Chinese art, the signature seal of the artist stamped on the work.

Churrigueresque (chur-*ig*-er-esk) Extravagantly ornamented architecture of Baroque Spain and the Hispanic world characterized by abundant and indiscriminate use of decorative motifs, twisted columns and complex ornamentation.

cityscape A work of art that shows views of city streets, plazas, courtyards, buildings and activities taking place in the urban environment.

cire perdue (sear per-*dew*) Method of casting molten metal into a cavity originally filled with a wax model. The resulting casting is an exact replica of the wax original.

Classical Relating to form regarded as having reached its greatest standard of excellence before modern times, i.e., Classical Greek or Classical Inca architecture.

Classical Abstraction Another name for Color Field Painting.

Classicism The practice of using stylistic elements and/or myths derived from the Greek Classical period.

clay Fine-grained earth, chiefly composed of aluminum silicate and formed by natural water deposition which is plastic, easily formed, and becomes hard and brittle upon treatment by high heat (firing).

clerestory (*clear*-story) The upper section of a wall (windowed or open) used for fighting and ventilation; also, the upper story of the nave of a church building.

cloisonné (kloy-soh-*nay*) Technique for setting colored glass, stones or enamel between thin strips of metal on a metal surface.

cloister (*kloy*-ster) A covered walkway or ambulatory around an open court or garden. Usually, a colonnade faces the garden, allowing light to enter.

Cochise Culture (ko-*cheese*) Ancient Southwest Native American society noted for unfired clay pottery.

codex (*ko*-decks) A manuscript in book form, often with pages arranged in an accordion-fold, as distinguished from a scroll.

coelanoglyph (koh-eh-*lan*-oh-gliff) A low-relief carving set into a flat panel, below the surface as distinguished from a bas-relief.

coffer In architecture, a square, rectangular or polygonal recess in a ceiling to reduce the weight of the structure.

coiling To build up with concentric rings.

Colima (ko-*lee*-ma) Culture of Western Mexico, artistically distinguished by superior free-hand molded clay vessels in animal and human forms, some with stirrup handles.

collage A technique in which the artist glues materials such as paper, cloth or found materials to some type of ground.

colonnade A series of columns, usually supporting lintels or arches.

color An element of design that identifies natural and manufactured things as being red, yellow, blue, orange, etc.

Color Field Painting A style of painting that relies solely on flat fields of color.

column (*kol*-um) An upright post, bearing the load of the upper part of a building. It consists of a base, a shaft and a capital. An engaged column is half a column, attached to a wall, and non-weight bearing.

combine Painting Technique developed by Robert Rauschenberg in which artworks are made by fastening objects to abstract canvases, mixing reality with abstraction.

Commanche (ko-*man*-she) Native American tribe of western Texas and New Mexico, artistically distinguished by its tipis, leather boots, clothing and elaborate beadwork.

complementary colors Any two colors that are located opposite each other on a color wheel. When mixed together they will tend to subdue the intensities and produce a grayed hue. When placed side by side, they produce optical vibrations.

composition The ordered arrangement of the elements (colors, shapes, lines, etc.) in a work of art, usually according to the principles of design.

computer art Artwork created on computer screens with computer software programs and printed on computer printers.

concept art A style of art in which the artist expresses the idea concept of a proposed work of art in verbal or diagram form. The actual work will probably not be carried out.

Confucianism (kun-*few*-shun-izm) System of social interaction based on the teachings of Confucius (551–479 BC) who preached reforms of Chinese society during the Zhou dynasty. Stresses order and loyalty; personal virtue; devotion to family and to the spirits of ancestors and justice.

connoisseur (kon-i-soor) A person with expert knowledge or training; a person of informed and discriminating taste.

contemporary art Refers to the art of today; the methods, styles and techniques of artists living now.

content The subject matter in a painting or other work of art.

contour (*kon*-toor) A single line or lines that define the outer and often the inner edges and surfaces of objects or figures.

contrapposto (kon-tra-*pohs*-toh) Technique of sculpting a human figure in a pose that shows the weight of the body in balance. With weight on one leg, the shoulders and hips counterbalance each other in a natural way so that the figure does not fall over. Developed in the late Greek period.

contrast A principle of design that refers to differences in values, colors, textures and other elements to achieve emphasis and interest.

Cool Art Another name for Minimal Art.

cool colors The hues on one side of the color wheel which contain blue and green.

Coptic Native of Egypt; descended from ancient Egyptians.

corbel (*kore*-bell) An overlapping arrangement of stones, each layer projecting a bit beyond the row beneath it; also, a bracket of stone, wood or brick projecting from the face of a wall which may support a cornice or arch.

Corinthian (koh-*rin*-the-en) One of the Classical styles of architecture of ancient Greece (fourth century BC) that features tall, slender columns topped with ornate capitals decorated with stylized acanthus leaves.

cornice (*kor*-niss) Any projecting ornamental molding along the top of a building, wall, arch, etc.; also, the topmost projecting part of an entablature in a Classical Greek building.

course Rows of stones or bricks that form a horizontal layer of a wall.

crafts Works of art that generally have a utilitarian purpose, including ceramics, macramé, leatherwork, metals, weaving, fabrics, jewelry, furniture, basketry, etc.

craftsperson One who fabricates useful and well-designed objects of quality, durability and function. **Craftsmanship** implies the skillful practice of this process.

crenelations (*kren*-i-lay-shens) Indentations or notches such as in battlements.

cromlech (*krom*-lek) A circle of monoliths, usually enclosing a type of altar.

crossing The area of a church where the transept intersects the nave. Sometimes a dome or tower is built over this area, further emphasizing it as the focal area of the worship space.

crucifix (*kroo*-sih-fiks) A representation of a cross with the figure of Christ's crucifixion placed on it.

cruciform (*kroo*-sih-form) In the shape of a cross; usually a floorplan of building in such an arrangement.

crypt (kript) A vaulted space below ground level, usually beneath the raised choir or apse of a church, or under a temple or shrine.

Cubism (*kyoo*-biz-em) A style of art in which the subject is broken apart and reassembled in an abstract form, emphasizing geometric shapes.

cult figures Figures of religious devotion or ritualistic value.

cult magic Mystic practices of a system of religious beliefs and rituals.

culture Elements that add to the aesthetic aspects of life, enriching it with beauty and enjoyment; also, a society or civilization marked by distinctive concepts, habits, skills, implements and art forms.

cupola (*coop*-oh-lah) A rounded convex roof on a circular base; a dome of small size.

curtain wall A wall that carries no weight other than its own; a nonstructural panel set between weightbearing pillars in a building.

dagob (duh-*gobb*) A small stupa-like architectural form which symbolically represents the commemorative function of the Buddhist stupa.

dais (*day*-ahs) A raised platform, usually at one end of a long room.

Dao See **Taoism**.

Dayak (*die*-yak) Coastal and Highland people of Borneo, known for their bold graphic designs in painting and carving.

Delftware Blue-and-white faience pottery made in the Dutch city of Delft, inspired by Ming porcelain, which reached a peak in quality and production between 1650 and 1750; also, a term generally applied to any such European-produced blue-and-white china.

descriptive perspective shows more important objects larger than less important objects.

Deva Raja (day-va *rah*-jah) A god-king; the concept in Javanese and Southeast Asian culture that the ruler is an earlier counterpart of a divine being, usually Siva or Buddha.

diaper (*die*-uh-per) Decorative unit or motif, often abstract or symbolic, repeated to create intricate surface decoration.

Dibutsu (*die*-boot-sue) Japanese name for Buddha.

Ding Zhou (ding jshoo) Region of Henan and Hebei provinces of China, producing non-Imperial pottery, especially during the Song dynasty, decorated with typical dark brown free-flowing floral designs; also the pottery made there.

diocese. See **bishop**.

diptych (*dip*-tik) A pair of wood, ivory or metal panels (large or small) usually hinged together, with painting or carving on the inside surfaces. Usually placed over an altar.

distort To deform or stretch something out of its normal shape.

Doge (*doe*-jshay) Italian word for the chief magistrate in the former republics of Venice and Genoa.

dolmen A grouping of huge, uncut stones, set on end and covered with a large single stone, apparently used by Neolithic peoples as a burial altar.

dome A hemispherical or beehive-shaped vault or ceiling over a circular opening. May be elevated further by placement on a drum. If placed over a square opening, the transition to a round shape is made by use of pendentives in the four corners.

Doric The earliest of the classical style of ancient Greek architecture, characterized by sturdy columns that have no base and are terminated by simple, undecorated capitals.

dormer A window placed vertically in a sloping roof, and with a roof of its own.

dragon Legendary animal usually represented as a monstrous winged and scaly serpent or lizard with a crested head and enormous claws. Symbolic to the Chinese of Imperial power.

Dravidian The people, language and culture of much of South India, often regarded as the native people of the subcontinent.

dress To prepare stone for architectural purposes by carving or decorating.

drip painting Technique developed by Jackson Pollock in which he walked over a canvas with a can of paint, dripping and spilling paint about the canvas.

drolleries (*drole*-er-ees) The marginal designs, usually whimsical or fanciful, found on medieval European manuscripts.

drum The cylindrical wall supporting a dome; also, one of several sections composing the shaft of a column.

Dvaravati (dvar-ah-*vaht*-tee) The earliest known period of Thai Buddhist culture and art, flourished in the sixth to eleventh centuries.

earth art Artworks which involve the natural environment and in which spectators participate.

earth works Large formations of moved earth, excavated by artists in the surface of the earth and best viewed from a high vantage point.

earthenware Vessels of a coarse nature made from clay fired at a low temperature. Commonly left unglazed.

easel painting Any kind of painting done in a studio (on an easel) which can be transported from place to place.

eclecticism (e-*klek*-ti-*siz*-em) The practice of using compositional elements or artistic styles derived from a variety of sources.

edge A linear separation between two color areas; also, the outer contour of a shape or form.

Edo (ay-doe) Japanese capital city (Tokyo) and name often given to the rule of the Tokugawa shogunate (1615–1867), significant as a period when Japan essentially closed itself to the outside world.

egg tempera See **tempera**.

element The graphic devices with which the artist works, such as line, shape, color, texture, etc.

elevation The external faces of a building; also, a side or front view of a structure, painted or drawn to reveal each story with equal detail.

ellipse (ih-*lips*) A curved line that is drawn to produce an oval shape with specific geometric proportions.

elongated Stretched out lengthwise; drawn in a way as to exaggerate height or length.

embroider (em-*broy*-der) To ornament textiles with stitching of colored thread or other fine material.

emphasis (*em*-fah-sis) A principle of design by which the artist or designer may use opposing sizes, shapes, contrasting colors or other means to place greater attention on certain areas, objects or feelings in a work of art.

enamel Powdered colored glass that is fused by heating to a ceramic or metal ground; a work of art created by this method. Overglaze enamels are applied over previous glazes.

encaustic (en-*koz*-tik) A method of painting on a ground, with colors dissolved in hot wax; also, a work of art produced by this technique.

engaged To be partially set into a larger mass; not fully freestanding.

engaged column See **column**.

engraving The process of incising lines into a surface to create an image; also, a print made by inking such an incised surface.

Enlarged Field Painting Style of painting which uses large-scale canvases designed to draw the viewer into active visual participation with the work.

entablature (en-*tab*-li-*choor*) The upper part of an architectural order, being the part placed above the columns, usually consisting of architrave, frieze and cornice.

entasis (*en*-tah-sis) The subtle convex swelling of a Classical Greek column shaft.

epistle (i-*pis*-el) A message; in Christian usage, one of the letters of the apostles that make up twenty-one books of the Biblical New Testament.

espadaña (es-pah-*dahn*-ya) A gable wall on the facade of a building in which the curved top extends above the roof line; characteristic of Spanish and Hispanic architecture.

etching A technique in which a metal plate is incised by acid through needle-thin scratches in a waxed coating. The image is inked and printed on paper; also, the print made by this process.

Eucharist (*you*-cah-rist) From the Greek word for *thanksgiving*: the Sacrament of the Lord's Supper. Also, the consecrated bread and wine used in this sacrament; also, the sacrament itself.

Evangelists (i-*van*-je-lists) The four writers of the Gospels in the New Testament: Matthew, Mark, Luke and John; frequently visualized by their respective symbols of an angel, a lion, a bull and an eagle.

export ware Objects made expressly for the tastes of a foreign market; in ceramics, shapes and designs may be made to order which are alien to the native aesthetics of the producing craftspersons.

Expressionism (ex-*spresh*-a-*niz*-em) Style of art begun in Germany early in the twentieth century. The artists working in this style sought to communicate strong personal and emotional feelings to the viewer.

expressionists (ex-*spresh*-a-nists) Any style of art in which the artist tries to communicate strong personal and emotional feelings to the viewer.

eye level A horizontally drawn line that is even in height with the viewer's eye. In perspective drawing and painting, it can be the actual distant horizon line, but it can also be drawn in a close-up still life.

facade (fah-*sahd*) The front of a building.

faience (fay-*ahns*) Opaque low-firing colored ceramic glaze; also, earthenware decorated with such glaze.

famille rose (fa-*meal* rose) Chinese porcelain decorated in the Qing dynasty under European influence, using a mixture of opaque whites to paint scenery of court life, birds, flowers, etc.

famille verte (fah-*meal vehr*d) Chinese porcelain developed in the Qing dynasty, decorated with overglaze enamels, principally greens and weaker reds and yellows.

fan vault A complex vault with radiating ribs, characteristic of late English Gothic (perpendicular) architecture.

Fates, Three In Greek and Roman mythology, the goddesses Clotho, Lachesis and Atropos, who were believed to have the ability to determine the course of human life.

Fauvism (*foe*-vism) A style of painting which used brilliant colors for expressive purposes in France of the early twentieth century.

feldspathic Crystalline silica-based minerals used in the formulation of high firing ceramic glazes.

ferroconcrete See **reinforced concrete**.

fertility The capability to produce abundantly; the successful breeding and reproduction of the species.

fête galante (fet gah-*lahnt)* Elegant entertainment.

fetish An object to which magical powers are ascribed; a good luck charm.

field The area in which a design, decoration or painting is applied.

filigree (*fill*-i-gree) Ornamental openwork of thinly hammered ribbons of metal; the process of making such openwork; also, any delicate design resembling delicate work.

finger weaving Technique of forming fibers, rushes, cornhusks and bark into fabric by twining, braiding without a loom.

flamboyant Decoration or style characterized by waving curves suggesting flames; also, any ornate style in a flashy or resplendent style. Specifically, a decorative architectural style of mid-thirteenth century Europe stressing curving tracery in flame-like patterns.

flash-firing Method of firing coarse pottery in an open pit with highly combustible fuel, much like a bonfire.

Flemish Characteristic of Flanders (Belgium); usually refers to the culture of this area from the fourteenth to seventeenth centuries.

flint A very hard quartz or silica stone.

fluting The shallow, rounded, concave, vertical grooves in the shaft of a column.

flying buttress A supportive structure consisting of a tower buttress and a flying arch which spans the side aisles and supports the upper wall of the nave of a Gothic church.

folk art Objects made by untrained artists with a combined goal of being functional and pleasing to the eye.

foreshortening A method of drawing or painting an object or person that is not parallel to the picture plane so that it seems to recede in space, giving the illusion of three dimensions. Parts get smaller as they recede in space.

forge To shape metal by hammering heated pieces with directed blows of a mallet or other driving tool.

form An element of design that is three-dimensional and encloses volume, such as a cube, sphere, pyramid, cylinder. Also, in metalworking, to shape metal with hammered strokes.

Formalism Stylization based on traditionally accepted forms.

format The shape, size and general composition of a work of art or publication.

fortress church A strongly fortified worship building in which Christianity faced military threats from local opponents.

forum A central gathering place for the people of a town, particularly of ancient Rome. A place for judicial and public business.

Franciscan A member of the monastic order founded in 1209 by Francis of Assisi; peaceful proselytizers of native coastal Indians who built missions—each a day's walk apart along the southern California coast—as stations for their work in the late eighteenth century

friar A brother or member of one of four Mendicant Roman Catholic Orders—Franciscan, Augustinian, Dominican and Carmelite.

free form Not having prescribed geometric proportions.

fresco A method of painting in which pigments suspended in water are applied to a thin layer of wet plaster so that the plaster absorbs the color and the painting becomes part of the wall.

frieze (freeze) Any horizontal band, decorated with moldings or patterns, either painted or carved, usually at the upper end of a wall; specifically in Greek architecture, the middle layer (plain or carved) of an entablature.

frontal A pose in figure drawing or sculpture in which figures face forward.

Fu-nan (foo-nahn) Ancient Southeast Asian empire (c. 100–525), typified by their worship of Harihara, their early sculpture of Buddha and Vishnu, and their use of canals to drain the rice lands of Cambodia.

Futurism (fyoo-cha-riz-em) A style of painting and sculpture that emerged in Italy, early twentieth century. Futurism emphasized the machine-like quality of "modern" living.

gable A shaped piece of a wall, generally triangular, at the end of a ridged roof; called a pediment in Classical Greek architecture.

gallery A story over the aisle and open to the nave through an arcade in Christian church architecture. Also, a contemporary commercial enterprise that exhibits works of art for sale.

gamelon (gam-eh-lahn) A Javanese orchestra incorporating bronze gongs, wooden xylophone-like chimes, drums and wind instruments. Used to accompany puppet and human theatrical performances.

Gandhara (gahn-dar-ah) School of earliest Buddhist sculpture in the Indian province of Bactria distinguished by the use of Hellenistic and Persian anatomical representation. Also known as the Indo-Greek or Greco-Buddhist School.

Ganges civilization (gan-jeez) Society of the Indo-Gangetic plains of northern India from about 1500 BC, noteworthy for the evolution of the Vedic writings fundamental to Brahmanic religion.

Gautama (gow-tah-mah) The historical Buddha, Sakyamuni. See **Buddhism**.

genre (zhahn-ra) Referring to the common, ordinary; also, a type of localized art.

genre painting The representation of acts and/or scenes from everyday life.

geodesic (jee-oh-des-ik) A form of geometry (solid) which forms the basis for structures built of interlocking polygons.

geometric Referring to mechanical, human-made shapes such as squares, zigzags, circles, spirals, checkerboard patterns, bands, etc.; also, a period of ancient history when decorative motifs of such patterns were commonly used on pottery (i.e., Geometric Greek pottery).

gesso (jess-oh) A mixture of finely ground plaster and glue that is often spread on a surface prior to painting.

gilding A covering of gold leaf over inexpensive or perishable materials.

glaze In pottery, the thin coating of minerals which provides the glassy coloring and waterproof gloss for the final ware. In painting, a transparent mixture of a small amount of color dissolved in a large amount of the vehicle (such as linseed oil mixed with turpentine in oil painting) that changes the hues of previously painted surfaces.

gopura (go-poor-uh) Elaborate, pyramidal, tapered gateway towers typical of South Indian Hindu temple architecture.

gospel In Christian usage, the story of Christ's life and teaching, as found in the writings of the first four books of the New Testament.

Gothic A style of art in Europe of the twelfth–fifteenth centuries, emphasizing religious architecture and typified by pointed arches, spires and verticality.

gouache (gwash) Any opaque water-soluble paint or opaque watercolor.

Great Pueblo An era of Southwestern Native American culture (1050–1300) marked by large communities of multi-storied buildings and the first appearance of polychrome painted pottery in the region.

Great Wall A massive fortification built during the Qin dynasty of China to keep out the nomads of Mongolia and Manchuria.

Greco-Buddhist See **Gandhara**.

Greek cross A cross with four arms of equal length.

grid-iron A design consisting of a network, i.e., a street pattern or the regular divisions of a decorative surface.

groin (groyn) The sharp edge formed by two intersecting vaults.

groined vault A vault formed by the intersection (at right angles) of two barrel vaults of equal size so that the groins form a diagonal cross.

ground (grownd) The surface on which a painting is made.

Guan Yin (gwahn yin) The Chinese Buddhist goddess of mercy, an interpretation of the Indian Bodhisattva Avaloketisvara. A compassionate goddess, benevolent to children and protective of sailors.

guilds (gilds) Independent associations of artisan-manufacturers and bankers in Renaissance Florence. The Italian word is *arti*, from which the word *art* comes.

Gupta (goop-tah) The ruling dynasty (320–600) synonymous with the golden age of Indian art, artistically significant for its Indianization of Buddhist images, the evolution of Mahayana Buddhist iconography and the digging of early cave temples (Chaitya).

gypsum (jip-some) A white, calcium-sulphate mineral, useful as a painting pigment.

Haida (high-dah) Coastal Indians of British Columbia, artistically known for their symbolic and abstract wood carvings, totem poles and plank houses.

halo The circle of light shown around the head of a saint or of a holy person; also used to identify the divinity of a god. Also known as a nimbus.

Han (han[d]) The second longest Chinese dynasty (206 BC–221 AD), divisible into a number of phases. Artistically typified by aristocratic tomb art; sophisticated silk, lacquer, glazed ceramics; and clay models of architecture and daily-use objects.

handbuilt (hand-bilt) Ceramic objects formed without the use of a potter's wheel, typically using slabs or coils of clay to construct vessels.

Haniwa (*hahn*-ee-wah) The late Neolithic culture of the Japanese Tumulus Age (300–700), named for the sculptured cylinder-like clay guardian figures typically found at burial sites of the period; also, the sculptures of humans, architecture and animals made during the period.

Hanuman (*hahn*-oo-*mahn*) The mythological king of the monkeys in the *Ramayana*, responsible for Rama's successful recovery of his kingdom.

Hard-Edge Painting A style of art in which the artist uses crisp, clean edges and applies the values and colors so they are even and flat.

harmika (har-*meek*-ah) The small railed balcony surmounting the dome of a stupa.

hatching The use of parallel lines to create shading. When lines are overlapped at angles to each other, the technique is called crosshatching.

Heian (*hey*-on) The long-lived Japanese dynasty (794–1185) named for the new capital city at Kyoto. The later phase (894–1185) is known as the Fujiwara period. The Heian dynasty is significant for the establishment of Amida Buddhist sects, aristocratic refinement at court and the flowering of the arts.

Hellenistic An era of Mediterranean culture influenced by the Greek world following the conquest of Alexander the Great.

heraldic (heh-*ral*-dik) Relating to coats of arms and family crests or emblems.

hieroglyphs (high-row-*gliffs*) Characters in the picture-writing system of many ancient cultures that use pictures or symbols representing sounds, words or ideas.

Hindu (*hin*-doo) The dominant religion of India, acknowledging a pantheon of earth spirits, the foremost of which are Brahma (the creator), Vishnu (the Preserver) and Siva (the Destroyer).

Hispanic (hiss-*pan*-ick) Pertaining to Spain or its people throughout the world.

Hohokam (ho-*ho*-kahm) An ancient Southwestern American culture (100–1400) that developed from contacts with Mexico, typified by their use of irrigation canals, and artistically marked by red-on-buff pottery, the use of copper, and fine textiles and stonework.

Hopi (*ho*-pee) A pueblo-dwelling people of the Shoshone group of Arizona, considered the finest Native American weavers. Their pottery of ancient times was decorated with abstract stylized animals. Modern distinction is in repoussé silverwork and turquoise and shell settings.

horizon line (hor-*ize*-on) The division between earth and sky, as seen by an observer.

Hours, Book of A book for private devotions, containing the prayers for the seven canonical hours of the Roman Catholic Church. Often executed in illuminated manuscript form.

Huaxtec (*wahx*-tec) The war-like culture of Northern Veracruz which peaked between 600 and 900 but survived through Aztec times. Artistically noted for miniature and large sculptures of human and anthropomorphic gods.

hue (hyoo) The attribute of a color that gives it its name. The spectrum is usually divided into six basic hues: violet, blue, green, yellow, orange and red.

humanism The renewed interest at the beginning of the Italian Renaissance in the art and literature of antiquity. Also, any concern with the study of humanity and its writings and activities.

hydria (*heye*-dree-ah) A large jug used to carry water.

hypostyle (*hip*-oh-stile) A building having a roof or ceiling supported by rows of columns; used to describe a hall constructed of many columns; also, a row of columns.

Iban (*eh*-bahn) A tribe of coastal rice farmers in Northern Borneo, artistically distinguished by their stilted communal longhouses, finger weaving and fine basketry.

Iberia (eye-*beer*-ee-ah) The European peninsula composed of the Spanish, Portuguese and Basque peoples.

Ibibo (*ee*-bee-bo) An African tribe of the Nigeria region, artistically noted for their ritual wooden masks.

Ica (*ee*-ka) The coastal people of Southern Peru, noted for their thin polychromatic pottery in the tradition of the Nazca culture, 1200–1500.

icon (*eye*-kon) A religious image or likeness; in the Eastern Orthodox religion, usually a panel painting of a saint or of Christ.

iconoclasm (eye-*kon*-oh-klasm) Destruction of images or icons; historical examples include the Iconoclastic Controversy (eighth–ninth centuries), the Protestant purges (sixteenth–seventeenth centuries), the Tang repression (845) and the Japanese persecution of Christians (1580–1640).

iconography (eye-kon-*ah*-gra-fee) The system of symbolic elements in a work of art; the system of symbols traditionally used to identify a deity, illustrated by pictures or other visual representations; also, the study of symbols and their meanings.

iconostasis (eye-kon-*ah*-stah-sis) A decorated screen (often of icons) in Eastern Orthodox churches, separating the main part of the church from the sanctuary.

idealization The representation of objects or people in a stylized and perfected way, often following a preconceived model. Greek and Indian gods idealized human forms.

idiom (*id*-eum) A style or design peculiar to a specific place or time.

idol (*eye*-dul) A representation or symbol of a deity used as an object of worship.

Ife (*ee*-fay) The African civilization of the Nigerian coast, flourishing 1200-1500.

ikebana (ee-kay-*bahn*-ah) Japanese art of flower arranging, using flowers and other organized objects to depict mood and movement.

illumination (i-*loo*-mi-*nay*-shun) Colored illustrations, often containing gold and silver, that decorated manuscripts in medieval times in Europe.

imari (ee-*mar*-ee) Porcelain produced in the Azita region of Kyushu Island, Japan, decorated with underglaze blue and overglaze red enamels. Often gilded.

impasto (im-*pass*-toe) A thick, heavy application of paint, with either brush or knife.

imperial art (im-*peer*-i-al) Objects of beauty and high value produced by workers hired by a ruler or the court; usually the finest products become the property of the crown for use at court or as royal gifts.

impress To push into; in ceramics, patterns are made in soft or leather-hard clay by pressing with textured tools, stamps or chops.

Impressionism (im-*presh*-ah-*niz*-em) A style of painting begun in France about 1875. It stresses a candid glimpse of the subject, spontaneity and an emphasis on the momentary effects of light on color.

Inca (*ing*-kah) An ancient imperialist Peruvian culture (1200–1532) unifying many local cultures of the Andes and ruled by a king (inca). Artistically noted for their encouragement of native traditions and their expert construction of fortified cities.

incise (in-*size*) To cut into a surface with a sharp tool.

Indo-Greek See **Gandhara**.

Indra (*in*-druh) King of the Vedic gods of India, personification of the Aryan warrior, and the god of thunder and the atmosphere.

Indus Valley civilization A sophisticated early civilization of Northern India and Pakistan, probably influenced by Mesopotamian cultures, flourishing about 4000–1500 BC; distinguished by their water-worship, grid-iron pattern streets and early bronze casting.

inlay To set one material into recessed areas of another substance; to decorate with such insertions.

intaglio (in-*tahl*-ee-oh) A printmaking technique in which ink is transferred from areas beneath the surface (etched, engraved or scratched) onto paper, resulting in a print.

intensity (in-*ten*-si-tee) The strength, brightness or purity of a color. The more intense the color, the less it is weakened with admixtures of neutrals or its complementary color.

intermedia (*in*-ter-*meed*-ee-ah) An art form that uses videotapes, cinematography and animated film.

Ionic (eye-*ahn*-ik) A Classical Greek style of architecture characterized by slender columns with fluted shafts and capitals, decorated with scroll-like devices (volutes).

Iroquois (*eer*-oh-coy) The native people of Northeastern America whose hunting and fishing economy produced significant carved-bone tools; masks; carved, painted, wooden weaponry; and bark canoes.

Islam (is-*lahm*) A religious faith based on belief in Allah as the sole deity as revealed to the prophet Mohammed (570–632); also, the civilization based on that Arabic faith.

ivory (*eye*-vah-ree) A hard, white dentine substance of the tusk of elephant, hippopotamus, walrus and narwhal; also, an article made of that substance, usually by carving.

jade (jayd) Highly valued opaque-to-translucent stone, usually nephrite or jadite; known to the Chinese as *Yu*; also, a carved object made of such material.

Jain (jayn) The Indian religion following the teachings of Vardhamana Mahavira (sixth century BC), based on a doctrine of peace, harmony and non-violence.

Jalisco (hah-*lees*-ko) An ancient culture of West Mexico more attuned to Peruvian and Hohokam influences than other Mexican cultures. Thrived 100–300. Artistically known for ceramic figures of natural proportion in brown and gray clay.

jamb (jam) The upright piece, forming the side of a doorway or window frame. In Romanesque and Gothic cathedrals, the jambs were the location for tall, sculptural figures.

Jesuit (*jeh*-zoo-it) A member of the Roman Catholic "Society of Jesus," founded by Loyola in 1534, and responsible for much of the spread of Christianity in the post-Reformation period.

Jesus (*jeez*-us) Christian Son of God and Savior of the world (4 BC–30 AD) whose teachings stressed peaceful co-existence, salvation based on His dying for humanity's sins, and a resurrection to eternal life. Also known as The Christ.

jewelry (*joo*-el-ree) Objects of precious materials, usually metals and gems, worn for personal adornment.

Jomon (jo-*mahn*) Neolithic hunting society of prehistoric Japan (7000–200 BC), artistically typified by rope-designed pottery and clay fertility dolls.

Judaism (*joo*-day-iz-em) The Jewish religion, characterized by belief in one God and by a religious life in accordance with scriptures and rabbinic traditions; the Hebrew culture.

Judeo-Christian (*joo*-day-oh) Culture originating with Biblical Abraham and continuing through the periods of prophecy into the Christian era; the common culture shared by Christians and Jews and their heritage of religious and societal values.

jun (chun) Chinese celadon ware and kiln site in Henan Province, typified by glazes of lavender and greenish blue, frequently splashed and suffused with purple and crimson, produced by copper which has been reduced in firing.

kabuki (kah-*boo*-kee) Popular Japanese drama, both tragic and comic, involving highly costumed male actors.

kachina (kah-*chee*-nah) Small dolls or figures made by Pueblo Indians which represent the gods and are used to teach religion.

Kamakura (kah-mah-*koo*-rah) The military government in Japan (1192–1338) with a capital city at Kamakura, whose arts reflect military austerity and the growth of Buddhist salvation sects.

Kannon (*kan*-on) Japanese equivalent of the Bodhisattva Avaloketisvara and the Chinese Guan Yin. The goddess of mercy.

Karen (*kar*-en) Tribal hill people of Tibeto-Burman stock living in North Thailand, Laos and Burma, noted for their embroidered clothing and handicrafts.

keep The massive central tower of a castle and the final point of defense; also, a tower-like fortress.

Kenyah (*ken*-yah) The tribal people of Borneo, artistically noted for fine basketry.

keystone The topmost stone in an arch, and the last stone to be placed in the construction of the arch; the stone that balances the gravitational forces pulling on the arch.

Khmer (kmair) The ancient kingdom and people of Cambodia, emerging as a distinct cultural group in the sixth century, climaxing in the twelfth century with the construction of huge god-king temple complexes at Angkor and Angkor Thom.

kiln (kill) An oven capable of controlled high temperatures in which clay objects are fired or baked; also, the complex of a pottery-producing site, including workshops, studios and firing chambers.

kinetic art (ki-*net*-ik) Any three-dimensional art that contains moving parts and can be set in motion either by air currents or some type of motor. Also may refer to art in which changing light patterns are controlled by electronic switches.

Kiowa (*ky*-oh-wah) A nomadic tribe of the Oklahoma region noted for fine leather garments ornamented with beadwork.

kiva (*kee*-vah) A subterranean chamber ceremonially used by Southwestern Native Americans as a worship center; kivas were square in early phases of Pueblo culture and round during the Great Pueblo era. Roofs are low and slightly domed.

Koran (koh-*rahn*) The sacred writings as revealed by Allah to Mohammed, and the foundation of the Islamic faith.

kore (*kor*-ay) A female figure, a clothed sculpture in archaic Greek art.

krater (*kray*-ter) A tall, wide-mouthed vase, usually of earthenware, in ancient Greece and Rome. It had two handles and was used for mixing water and wine. **kraton** (kray-*tahn*) An Islamic royal palace complex.

kris (kreese) An Islamic dagger with a wavy blade, held with a decorated pistol-grip handle. Commonly associated with Southeast Asia and Javanese arts.

Krishna (*krish*-nah) A Hindu god and incarnation of Vishnu, the Preserver.

kufic script (*koo*-fik) An early Arabian writing form, used in the region south of Babylon.

kutani (koo-*tah*-nee) Kiln site and name of Japanese seventeenth-century porcelain richly decorated in overglaze enamels in patterns of birds, plants, landscapes and textiles.

kylix (*ky*-lix) An ancient Greek, two-handled, shallow wine cup, often with a stem and foot.

lacquer (*lack*-er) A durable natural resin which, when applied in many thin layers over a base of clay, wood, cloth or basketry, forms a tough and permanent object. Objects so made are called lacquer or lacquerware.

landscape A work of art that shows the features of the natural environment (trees, lakes, mountains, etc.).

lantern A small dome, usually with windows around its drum, built atop a larger dome or on a roof to allow light to enter the structure.

Lao (lau) The hill tribe people of Indo-China, noted artistically for colorful patchwork stitchery and heavy silver jewelry.

Latin cross A cross in which the vertical member is longer than the horizontal one.

leather-hard The stage in the drying process of a clay object when designs are carved and impressed, handles and other appliqués added and coatings of colored clay slips applied.

limners Early American artists who painted portraits without faces and later found patrons who wanted their faces filled in.

line An element of design that may be two-dimensional (pencil on paper), three-dimensional (wire) or implied (the edge of a shape or form).

linear perspective (*lin*-ee-ar) A system of drawing or painting to give the illusion of depth on a flat surface. All parallel lines receding into the distance are drawn to one or more imaginary vanishing points on the horizon in such a work.

linocut (*lin*-oh-cut) A relief print made by cutting a design into a block of linoleum and applying ink to the surface.

lintel (*lin*-tl) Horizontal structural member that spans an opening between two walls or posts.

lithography (li-*thog*-ra-fee) A printmaking process in which a flat stone, previously marked with a greasy substance (either a special ink or crayon) that will retain the ink, is charged with ink, placed against paper and run through a press, producing a print known as a lithograph.

live rock Stone carved where it is found in nature; rock still in its original location.

local color The color of an object seen in white (or natural) light and free from reflected colors and shadow.

Lokeshvara (low-kesh-*vahr*-ah) The Khmer equivalent of the compassionate Bodhisattva Avaloketisvara (See **Guan Yin** and **Kannon**). Depicted with a turban and four arms that carry a lotus, a rosary, a flask and a book.

longhouse Communal dwelling for an entire tribe in Borneo. The front half of the structure is a common verandah, and the back half is divided into individual dwellings for each family.

Long Shan (loong shahn) The Neolithic Chinese culture (c. 3000–1600 BC) of Gansu province, artistically typified by thin black pottery made with a potter's wheel and burnished by hand.

loom A frame or device in which yarn or other threadlike material is woven into fabric by the crossing of threads, called weft, over and under stationary warp threads.

lost-wax process See **cire perdue**.

lotus A variety of water lily popular in Egyptian, Hindu and Buddhist iconography as a symbol of purity.

low relief A surface that has only slight variations between the highest and lowest parts. Bas-relief is sculpture of low relief on a wall, and a coelanoglyph is a sculpture of low relief carved into a wall surface.

lunette (loo-*net*) A semi-circular area, such as the space at the end of a vaulted room or over a door, niche or window. When it is over the portal (main door) of a church, it is called a tympanum.

lustre (*luss*-ter) An iridescent metallic ceramic glaze or surface on glass; this effect may be created intentionally or may occur when pieces are buried in certain soils for long periods of time.

Madonna Mary, the mother of Jesus Christ.

madrasah (mah-*drahs*-ah) A style of mosque using an enclosed courtyard, but open to the sky.

maesta (my-*ays*-tah) An altarpiece with a central panel representing the enthroned Madonna adored by saints. From the Italian word for "majesty."

Mahayana (mah-hah-*yan*-ah) See **Buddhism**.

majolica (mah-*yall*-ikah) Earthenware with an opaque, low-fired, tin, enamel glaze, ornamented with colors of mineral oxides.

Manchu (*mahn*-chew) See **Qing**.

mandala (*mahn*-dahl-uh) A mystical geometric design symbolizing a supernatural understanding of the universe. Called a *mandara* in Japan.

mandorla An almond-shaped outline enclosing the full figure of a person endowed with divine light, usually Christ.

Mannerism A style and period of European art (sixteenth century) notable for its deliberate reaction against the balance of High Renaissance art. It is characterized by subjective expression, distortion of the figure, peculiar placement of figures in the composition, exaggerated perspective view and a crisp and harsh treatment of light and shadow.

Maori (*mou*-ree) Native peoples of New Zealand, artistically distinguished by totemic carvings, shellwork and finely-plaited house walls.

mask A covering worn over the face, often ascribed with supernatural powers, worn during rituals in animistic societies.

masonry (*may*-son-ree) Stone or brick-work in architecture; also, the pattern of bricks laid vertically or horizontally by courses to build up a wall.

mass The physical bulk, weight and density of a three-dimensional object; also, the celebration of the Eucharist in a Christian Church.

mastaba (mah-*stah*-bah) A rectangular Egyptian tomb of mud brick and masonry with sloping sides and a flat top used to cover the burial chamber.

mat (matt) A dull or non-reflecting surface. Also, a cardboard frame surrounding a print, drawing, watercolor or photograph.

Mauryan (*moo*-ree-un) An early Indian kingdom, founded by Chandragupta Maurya about 322 BC, uniting India for the first time. Artistically distinguished by the evolution of the stupa and the Ashokan pillar.

mausoleum (*maw*-sa-*lee*-um) A magnificent and stately tomb.

Maya (*my*-uh) An ancient Classical civilization of Eastern Mexico and the Yucatan (300–800), artistically distinguished by colored frescoes, excellent weavings, iconographic sculpture and boldly illustrated codices.

medallion (mi-*dal*-yen) A tablet or panel in a wall or window bearing a figure in relief; a portrait or a symmetrical ornament.

medium A material used by an artist and often implying the technique of using that material. The plural is **media**. Also, the solvent which suspends pigments in a paint.

megalithic Consisting of huge undressed stones, usually arranged by prehistoric peoples.

megaron (*meg*-a-rahn) In Minoan and Mycenaean culture, a large rectangular space with a hearth at the center and four columns supporting the roof. The main hall or room in palaces or houses of these early Greek cultures.

Meiji (may-jee) The Japanese era (1868–1912) of enthusiastic learning from the West.

mei-ping (may-ping) Shape of a tall Chinese vase typified by a gently tapering body toward a broad shoulder and a short narrow neck.

Melanesia (mel-ahn-*ee*-shah) The cultural area of the South Pacific, east of Fiji, artistically distinguished by painted wooden images, totemism and the tribal arts of New Guinea.

menhir (*men*-eer) A single, upright, undressed monolith, usually of prehistoric origin.

Meo (meow) The hill tribe people of Northern Thailand, Laos and Burma, artistically noted for their fine embroidery and heavy textured silverwork.

Meso-America The cultural areas of Central America and Mexico.

metallurgy (*met*-al-ur-gee) The science and technology of working with metals.

metope (*met*-oh-pee) The carved or plain areas between the triglyphs in the frieze of a Doric building.

Micronesia (my-crow-*nee*-shah) Islands of the Pacific north of the Equator and east of the Philippines where colorful weavings are produced.

minaret (min-a ret) A tall, slender tower attached to a mosque from which the muezzin (crier) calls people to prayer.

Ming dynasty The Chinese dynasty (1368–1644), significant for its achievements in foreign trade, scholarship and the arts (particularly in porcelain)

miniature (*min*-ee-a-*choor*) A small painting executed with great detail; a small portrait, picture or decorative letter on an illuminated manuscript.

Minimal Art Usually a wood or metal sculpture (but also a painting) using flat areas or planes in what seems a simple, geometric composition. Also, any non-representational art form using very simplified forms and colors.

mishima (mih-*shee*-mah) A Korean technique of applying colored slip into textured or etched surfaces of leather-hard pottery, developed during the twelfth century. Resulting decorative patterns are exposed after the excess slip is scraped away and the piece is glazed and fired.

Mission Indians (*mish*-en) Native tribes of Southern California who were served by the missions of San Diego, San Gabriel and San Fernando, noted for their soft-coiled baskets and fine featherwork.

Mission Style An architectural tradition of the Southwest United States, inspired by Franciscan-built churches and dormitories, typified by thick white adobe walls, arcaded or pillared verandahs, curvilinear gable walls and unglazed red tile roofing.

mixed media A two-dimensional art technique that uses more than one medium, for example, a crayon and watercolor work.

Mixtec (*mix*-teck) An ancient Mexican culture in the Puebla and Oaxaca region, flowering in the sixth-seventh centuries, but contemporary with Toltec and Aztec peoples. Significant artistically for their immense pyramid at Cholula and their fine manuscripts painted on animal skins.

mobile (*mow*-beel) A balanced construction with moving parts, suspended from above, and moving freely in the air currents. May be set in motion by a motor. Invented by Alexander Calder in 1932.

Mochica (moh-*cheek*-ah) A coastal South American culture noted for fine pottery and adobe pyramidal temples (500 BC–900 AD).

modeling (*mod*-al-ing) The forming of a three-dimensional form in a soft substance such as clay or wax. Also, the effect of light falling on a three-dimensional form, delineating its form by means of shadow and light. Also, representing this three-dimensionality of forms in a painting by means of light and dark values.

Mogollon Culture (moh-*gull*-on) The first ancient American culture of the Southwest to produce fired clay objects, from about 200 BC–1400 AD; influential on later Pueblo cultures.

Mohammed (moh-*hahm*-ed) The prophet and founder of the Islamic faith who lived in Arabia (570–632).

mold The hollow form into which molten materials (gold, lead, plaster, etc.) are poured to create a cast sculpture.

molding An ornamental strip that gives variety to the surface by creating light and shadow.

Momoyama (mo-mo-*yahm*-ah) The exuberant and vital Japanese shogunate (1573–1615) which was the pinnacle of the Samurai culture, Zen-inspired arts and political unification. The era characterized by castle construction and use of feudal armament.

monastery (*mohn*-i-*ster*-ee) Living quarters for monks.

Mongol See **Yuan**.

monochromatic (*mohn*-ah-kro-*mat*-ik) One color; refers to colors formed by changing the values of a single hue by adding the neutrals (black, white and gray).

monolith (*mohn*-oh-*lith*) A large single block of stone used in architecture or sculpture; also, a structure made of such large stones.

monotype (*mohn*-oh-tipe) Any of several printmaking techniques where the image printed is unique and not able to be reproduced.

montage (mohn-*tazh*) A composition composed of several pictures, usually pasted together; also, a painting that has that appearance.

Monte Alban (*mohn-tay ahl*-bahn) A classical Mexican civilization (200-500) of Zapotec origins, artistically distinct for burial urns in the form of gods; also, the sacred urban and necropolis center of many later Mexican civilizations.

monumental (*mohn*-you-*men*-tal) A work of art that is huge in size, often displayed in public squares. By extension, it refers to the quality of a work of art that may be small in actual size, but has the characteristics and feeling of a huge work.

Moorish Referring to the Moors, the Islamic rulers of Spain (710–1492), particularly their architecture, typified by the use of arches, stucco, tile roofing and polychromatic majolica.

mosaic (mo-*zay*-ik) A work of art consisting of pieces of colored marble or glass (tesserae) embedded in a layer of adhesive material.

mosque (mosk) An Islamic temple or place of worship.

mother-of-pearl The hard, pearly, iridescent substance forming the inner layer of a mollusk shell, used in inlay work in jewelry and furniture.

motif (mo-*teef*) The main subject or idea of a work of art, such as landscape or still life; also, the two- or three-dimensional configuration repeated in a pattern.

mound builders Early Native Americans of the Middle West and Southeast who formed large earthen burial mounds and fortifications thus creating the first earth works in America (100–1000).

movement A principle of design referring to the arrangement of parts in a work of art to create a slow-to-fast movement of one's eye through the work. Also, a style, school or artistic thought and practice, i.e., the Impressionist movement.

Mudéjar (*mood*-ay-yar) The style of Moorish architecture.

mudra (*moo*-druh) A ritual gesture which grew out of a simple gesture of the Buddha, symbolizing mystical power or action in mime or dance.

muezzin (moo-*zeen*) See **minaret**.

Mughal (*moh*-gull) The Islamic empire in India, which was founded by Baber in 1526 and flourished until 1857. Also spelled Mongul.

mullion (*mull*-yen) A vertical member separating two areas of a window.

mummification (*mum*-i-*fi*-kay-shun) The embalming of a dead body in preparation for burial as done by the ancient Egyptians.

mural (*myoor*-ul) A painting on a wall, usually large in format.

Muromachi (mur-oh-*motch*-ee) The Japanese shogunate (1338–1578) whose capital city was Kyoto, characterized aesthetically by the growth of Zen-related concepts of simplicity, restraint, subtlety, and artforms such as ikebana, sumi-e and the cha-no-yu.

Muses (*myoos*-ez) The nine sister-goddesses of Classical Greek mythology who presided over learning and the arts. There were Muses for epic poetry, history, love poetry, music, tragedy, sacred song, dance, comedy and astronomy.

Muslim (*muz*-lim) A believer in the Islamic faith.

mysticism (*miss*-ti-*siz*-um) A spiritual discipline of communion and unity with the divine, often achieved through meditation or trance-like contemplation.

Nabis (nah-*bee*) A small group of French artists who painted (1889–1899) in a style of flat, bold colors and were unconcerned with naturalism.

Naga (*nah*-gah) A divine serpent in Hindu mythology representing water spirits, guardians of cisterns and sacred water; a favorite motif in Thai, Indian and Southeast Asian Hindu art.

Nandi (*nahn*-dee) The mythological bull upon which Siva rides; hence, a symbol of Siva's fertility and reincarnation powers.

Nara (*nah*-rah) The city associated with the early Buddhist Japanese era (646–794), subdivided into the Hakuho (646–710) and the Tempyo (710–794). The period is artistically significant for its Chinese-style architecture, iconographic Buddhist sculpture in the Tang style, and the inculcation of Confucian and Buddhist ideals.

narthex A porch or vestibule, sometimes enclosed, preceding the main entrance of a church.

Nataraja (nah-tah-*rah*-jah) The "Lord of the Dance" aspect of Siva who dances the Nataraj in the frenetic art of eternal reincarnation; a popular motif in Hindu sculpture.

naturalism (*nach*-er-i-*liz*-em) The suggestion, in a work of art, of the direct observation of a scene or of a figure; also, an Italian Renaissance concept of interest in the world of nature including exploration of it scientifically.

Navajo (*nah*-vah-ho) A tribe of Native American Indians, related to the Pueblo group of the American Southwest, artistically noted for their unpainted pottery, use of the true loom in weaving outstanding blankets and rugs, and excellent hammered silverwork.

nave The central section of a church where the congregation assembles. In a basilican plan, the space extends from the main entrance to the apse or the crossing. The nave is usually flanked by side aisles.

Nayarit Mexican culture of Western coastal Mexico, artistically distinguished by the creation of ceramic figures of exaggerated features.

Nazca The coastal culture of Peru, noted for thin polychrome pottery produced from 100–1200.

necropolis (neh-*crop*-oh-liss) A cemetery of an ancient city.

negative space The area around the objects in a painting, sometimes called the background.

Neoclassicism (*nee*-oh-*klass*-i-*siz*-em) A style of art in nineteenth-century France that was a reaction to Baroque. This style was derived from the art and culture of ancient Greece and Rome and imitated this period's architecture and fascination for order and simplicity. Also, any revival of Classical ideas in the arts..

Nestorian (nest-*or*-ee-an) A sect of Christianity following the teaching of Nestorius (d. 451) who believed that the divine and human aspects of Christ are separate.

neutral A color not associated with any hue, such as black, white and gray; a neutralized color made by combining complementary colors to produce a grayish hue.

Nevers (neh-*vehr*) The center of French faience manufacture, originally established by Italian potters about 1565, typified by large plates decorated with engraving-like scenes and rich borders.

N'gere (nn-jerry) The tribal people of Nigeria, noted artistically for ritual masks.

niche (nitch) A recess in a wall, usually intended to hold a statue.

nimbus See **halo**.

Noh (no) Classical Japanese drama, originating in the fourteenth century and derived from temple dances; the stylized presentation by two richly costumed actors performing against no scenery.

Nok Ancient Nigerian civilization of about 500 BC, noted for its large sculptural figures.

nonobjective art Art that has no recognizable subject matter such as trees, flowers or people. The actual subject matter might be color or the composition of the work itself.

nonrepresentational art See **nonobjective art.**

obelisk (ob-eh-lisk) A tapering four-sided shaft of stone (usually one piece) topped by a pyramidal form, typical of Egyptian art. Sometimes called "Cleopatra's Needles."

Oceania (o-shee-*ahn*-ee-ah) Geographic region comprising the islands of the Pacific, artistically characterized by totemic and mystic sculptures of perishable materials, the general use of bright colors and fetishes.

oculus (*ah*-cue-lus) A circular opening in a wall or in the top of a dome, from the Latin for "eye."

odalisque (oh-dah-lisk) Any reclining female figure used as the subject for a painting or sculpture, from the French for "harem slave."

oil paint An opaque mixture of pigments dissolved in linseed oil using turpentine as a solvent; applied to a gessoed panel or canvas ground.

Olmec (*ohl*-mek) The mother culture of ancient Mexico (2000 BC-700 AD), centered in the Gulf coastal area, noted for the construction of the sacred city of Monte Alban and for the buildings and sculptures at La Venta.

Oneida (oh-*ny*-dah) An Iroquois tribe that moved to the Wisconsin area (1822-1827) where they became noted for fine silverwork.

Op Art A style of art that confuses the visual senses by generating optical vibrations or ambiguous or undulating spatial relationships.

optical mixing (*op*-ti-kul) Technique used by Impressionist artists in which the viewer's eye blends juxtaposed dots of color from a distance.

oracle bone (*or*-ah-kul) Large, usually flat, mammal bones or tortoise shells upon which prehistoric Chinese shamans drew picture messages. When heated, the bones cracked, revealing the response of the mystic forces, and were interpreted by the shamans who were acting as the voice of god, or oracle.

order An architectural system based on the prescribed style of column and entablature, such as the Greek Doric, Ionic and Corinthian. Also, the organization of the parts of a work of art.

overglaze Design or color applied onto a piece of ceramic after it has been glaze fired, usually made permanent by firing to a low temperature.

overlapping planes A perspective technique involving the placement in a flat composition of one object in front of another, thus creating an illusion of depth.

Paekche (*pahk*-shay) An ancient kingdom of Southwestern Korea (18 BC-663 AD) noted for its adoption and promotion of Buddhism and associated Chinese-style aristocratic arts.

pagoda (pah-*go*-dah) A circular or octagonal structure built to preserve relics, commemorate unusual acts of devotion, act as an omen of good fortune or as a water tower. Based on the Indian stupa, the form was modified when introduced to China in the third century, and again when introduced into Japan in the sixth century. Usually built of an odd number of stories.

painterly style or **painterly quality** A technique of painting in which forms are depicted by patches of color rather than by hard and precise edges. Brushstrokes are left visible as part of the surface of the painting.

painting A picture or other image composed of applied colors; the art or occupation of producing such works.

painting knife A small, shaped blade made expressly for applying paint to canvas, creating a textural surface.

palette (*pal*-it) A board or flat surface on which a painter places (and mixes) the supply of paint to be used. Also, the typical group of colors that a particular artist (or school of art) uses.

palette knife A small spatula used for mixing colors on the palette and for cleaning paints from the palette. It may be used as a painting knife.

palisade A raised earthen embankment held in place by closely set posts which act as a retaining wall.

Palladian (peh-*lay*-dee-en) An architectural style based on Renaissance motifs revived and altered by Andrea Palladio (1518-1580) which typify the buildings of Georgian England and British colonies in Asia and America.

Pallava (*pau*-lah-vah) A Southeast Indian kingdom that flourishing about 600-750, artistically distinguished by its rock-cut freestanding temples.

Pantheon Greek for "all the gods"; therefore, a temple dedicated to all the gods. Specifically, the round-domed structure built in Rome in 25 AD.

Paracas (pah-*rock*-us) An ancient culture of the south coast Peru, noted for excellent thin sculptural pottery, often in human form.

Paracas (pah-*rock*-us) **Necropolis** An ancient Peruvian culture named for burial mounds. This culture yielded weavings of superb quality.

paradigm (*pair*-ah-dime) An exceptional example or outstanding object, representative of an entire group of similar pieces.

parchment The treated skin of a lamb or goat, processed to make a smooth, flexible surface for manuscript writing and illumination.

Passion (*pash*-un) The suffering of Jesus Christ during the last week of His earthly life.

pastel A chalky, colored crayon. Also, a chalky, light-valued color.

patina (pah-*tee*-nah) The thin surface coloration on an old object or metal sculpture resulting from natural oxidation or from the careful treatment by heat, chemicals or polishing agents.

pattern A principle of design in which combinations of lines, colors and shapes are used to show real or imaginary things. Pattern may also be achieved by repeating a shape, line or color.

pavilions (pah-*vill*-yens) Protrusions of central entrance and corner sections from the facade of a building.

pediment The triangular area over the entablature in Classical Greek architecture, formed by the ends of a sloping roof and the cornice.

pendentive (*pen*-den-tiv) A triangular piece of vaulting springing from the corner of a rectangular area to support a round or polygonal dome. Usually four pendentives spring from the four corners of a crossing to support the dome.

Pentateuch (*pen*-tah-took) The first five books of the Old Testament containing early history and law of Judeo-Christian culture.

permutation (*per*-myoo-*tay*-shun) The complete change in the nature of a constituent mineral in a ceramic glaze during the firing process.

perspective The representation of three-dimensional objects and space on a flat surface to produce the same impression of distance and relative size as that received by the human eye. **Aerial** or **atmospheric perspective** creates the illusion of distance by muting color and blurring detail as objects get farther away. **Descriptive perspective** shows more important objects larger than less important objects. **Linear perspective** employs sets of parallel lines moving closer together in the distance until they merge as an imaginary vanishing point on the horizon. Overlapping planes create distance by placing objects in front of other objects. **Worm's eye perspective** creates a feeling of majesty and distance by looking up at subject matter from a low point in the composition.

petroglyph (*pet*-row-glif) A carving on rock, usually of a stylized image or message in such images.

phoenix (*fee*-niks) A legendary bird which rises in youthful reincarnation from its own ashes of destruction. Regarded by the Chinese as the emperor of all birds and as an emblem of beauty.

photography (fa-*tog*-ra-fee) The art or process of producing images on photo-sensitive paper.

Photo-Realism A revival of realistic art that occurred in the 1970s.

pictograph (*pik*-ta-graf) A drawing or painting stylizing or simplifying a real image; picture-writing, thus the basis of hieroglyphics and ideographs.

picture plane The flat surface which the artist uses as a starting point for a painting. It is not the paper or canvas itself, but an imaginary flat plane that the artist uses as a visual reference, and which is at the same level or depth as the surface itself.

pier (peer) A massive vertical masonry pillar that supports an arch, vault or other kind of roof. Also used under pendentives to support a dome. A square area in a Gothic church marked by a pier at each corner is known as a "bay."

pieta (pee-ay-*tah*) The scene of Mary holding and mourning over the body of the dead Christ, her son. From the Italian word for "pity."

pigment A dry powder that supplies the coloring agent for paint, crayons, chalk and ink.

pilaster (pih-*las*-ter) A rectangular engaged column, sometimes decorative, but at other times used to buttress a wall.

pillar Any vertical architectural member, such as a column, pier or pilaster.

Plains Indians Semi-nomadic horsemen of the Western Mississippi basin, including the Blackfoot, Crow, Sioux, Cheyenne, Arapaho, Kiowa and Comanche tribes. Artistically significant for excellent leatherwork, bone and horn carving, and symbolically decorated rawhide tipis.

plane A flat surface that can be measured by length and width (two dimensions).

plastic The quality that describes material that can be shaped or manipulated, such as clay or wax; flexibility. Also, the three-dimensional quality (roundness) of an artwork. Also, any of a number of synthetic materials with various physical characteristics.

Plateresque (pla-ter-*esk*) A rich, ornate style of decoration resembling overdecorated silverwork, typical of the Spanish Baroque era.

plaza A public square or assembly space.

plinth The base of a building, column, pedestal or wall which is usually marked on top by a molding.

pointillism (*point*-till-iz-em) A style of nineteenth-century French painting in which colors are systematically applied to canvas in small dots, producing a vibrant surface.

polychrome (*pol*-ee-*krom*) Several colors rather than one (monochrome).

Polynesia (pahl-ee-*nee*-zha) A scattered island group of the East Pacific with an artistic tradition characterized by the use of perishable materials and shells, and by large mystic sculptures in wood and stone.

polyptych (pah-*lip*-tik) An altarpiece or devotional painting consisting of more than three panels joined together.

Pomo (*poh*-moh) A Native American tribe of central coastal California, regarded as the finest basketmakers in the world, although their other arts are not highly developed. Typical of their baskets are fine, water-tight weaving, and ornamentation with polychromatic feather work.

Pop Art A style of art in the 1950s that used popular, mass-media symbols (such as a Coke bottle) as subject matter, treating them in both serious and satirical ways.

porcelain (*por*-sell-in) Fine white clay, made primarily of kaolin; also, an object of such clay which is hard, translucent, sonorous, non-porous and, usually, very thin. Porcelain may be decorated with mineral colorants under the glaze or with overglaze enamels.

portal A door or gate, usually of importance or large in size. In Gothic cathedrals, there were usually three portals in the main facade.

portico (*por*-tih-ko) A porch with a roof, supported by columns and usually having an entablature and a pediment.

portrait The image of a person's face, made of any sculptural material or any two-dimensional medium.

positive design A pattern or image created by painting or carving.

positive space The objects in a work of art as opposed to the background or space around the objects.

post and lintel The oldest and simplest way of building an opening: two vertical members (posts) support a horizontal beam (lintel) above them, creating a covered space. The structure can be part of a wall or can be freestanding.

poster A form of graphic art, created for the purpose of making a public announcement.

Post-Impressionism The style of late nineteenth-century French art that immediately followed the Impressionists. Paul Cézanne was a leader of this style which stressed more substantial subjects than those of the Impressionists, and a conscious effort to design the surface of the painting.

Post-Painterly Abstraction Another name for Color Field Painting.

potter's wheel A weighted horizontal disc that revolves on a vertical spindle, upon which clay is symmetrically shaped by a potter as the wheel spins.

pottery Ceramic ware made from clay that is shaped while moist and soft, and made hard and brittle by firing; also, coarser ware so made.

prang A tiered, rounded spire, used in Thai architecture.

pre-Columbian The culture of Meso-America and South America prior to the European colonization period initiated by Columbus' voyage of 1492.

primary colors The hues from which all other spectrum colors can be made: red, yellow and blue (in painting): red, green and blue (in light waves).

primitive The native arts of any culture, usually on a less sophisticated level than that of modern times; a culture before it adopts the ways of another. Also used to describe the art produced by untrained or naive artists.

print A multiple impression made from a master plate or block, produced and printed by the artist (or under his/her supervision).

printmaking The art of producing prints.

proofs The trial prints produced by a printmaker prior to making the final edition (completed set of prints).

proportion (prah-*por*-shen) A comparative size relationship between several objects or between parts of a single object or person. In figure drawing and painting, the correct relationship between the size of head and body.

prototype An original model on which other similar objects are patterned; the first in a series; a piece which inspires future creations.

Pueblo (*pweb*-lo) A communal dwelling consisting of groups of continuous flat-roofed stone or adobe houses; the Native American culture of the Southwestern United States typified by its use of such dwellings, and artistically noted for its excellent slip-painted pottery, loom-woven clothing and blankets, and kachinas.

pylon (*pie*-lahn) The huge entrance structure for an Egyptian freestanding temple, formed by a pair of square tapering piers with a flat top and no connecting lintel. From the Greek word for "gateway." Also, significant pillars in contemporary architecture.

qibla (*kee*-blah) A niche in the inner wall of a mosque, facing toward Mecca.

Qin (chin) A short-lived Chinese dynasty (221–206 BC) responsible for the unification of China, artistically noted for the standardization of Chinese writing and the unification of the Great Wall.

Qing (ching) The final dynastic era of China (1644–1911) also known as the Manchu named for the foreign ruling family. Artistically responsible for few innovations in the major arts, although new forms of ceramic decoration evolved and production of trade goods expanded as a result of contacts with European traders.

quatrefoil (*kwa*-trah-foyl) A four-lobed form used for ornamentation.

Quetzalcoatl (kwet-sah-*kwah*-tel) A Meso-American god representing the dual forces of nature as a bird (sky) and serpent (earth) combination. Called the Feathered Serpent.

radial balance A design based on a circle with features radiating from a central point.

Rama (*rah*-mah) The king and hero of the Ramayana epic and one of the incarnations of Vishnu (the Preserver).

Ramayana (rah-mah-*yah*-nah) The Hindu epic tale of King Rama and his wife Sita, which teaches morality and worthy human behavior. Known in Thailand as the *Ramakien*.

Ravana (rah-*vah*-nah) A mythological demon-king, depicted with multiple heads and arms in Hindu iconography.

realism A mid-nineteenth-century style of art based on the belief that the subject matter should be shown true to life, without any stylization or idealization. By extension it can refer to realistically painted work of any time.

reduction (re-*duk*-shun) The stage in the firing process of glazed ceramics that results in insufficient oxygen for combustion, causing chemical changes in the oxides in clay and glaze.

Regency (*re*-jen-see) The period during which George, Prince of Wales, ruled England in the stead of his father (1811–1820), typified artistically by a taste for exotic Indian and Chinese motifs in art and architecture.

register (*rej*-i-ster) One of a series of horizontal bands placed one above the other, usually a format for painting. Commonly used in Egyptian tomb painting, medieval church sculpture, Aztec codices and manuscript illumination.

reinforced concrete Building material composed of concrete with rods or webs of steel embedded in it; ferroconcrete.

relief (re-*leef*) A sculptural surface which is not freestanding, but projects from a background of which it is a part. High relief or low relief describes the amount of the projection. See **bas-relief**.

reliquary (*reh*-li-kweh-ree) A container for religious relics.

reliquary figures are carved guardians that stand above basket receptacles for ancestral remains.

Renaissance A revival or rebirth of cultural awareness and learning: specifically in Europe, a period of time (about 1400–1600) following the middle ages that featured an emphasis on human beings and their environment, on science and on philosophy, all of which directed the interest back to the culture of ancient Greece and Rome.

rendering The careful and complete drawing or painting of an object, place or person to make it appear realistic.

repoussé (ree-*pooh*-say) The technique of hammering or pressing sheet metal from the reverse side to raise up a shaped or ornamented pattern; a piece of metalwork so made.

representational (*rep*-re-zen-*tay*-shun-ul) Any artistic style in which objects or figures are easily identified.

reredos (*reer*-dahs) An ornamental facing or screen of stone or wood covering the wall at the back of an altar; a hanging of velvet or silk for the same purpose.

resin (*rez*-in) A tree gum substance used to waterproof unglazed fired pottery by rubbing it into the porous surface.

retable (ree-*tay*-bull) A large ornamental wall behind an altar with shelves or frames enclosing decorated panels.

rhythm (*rith*-em) A principle of design that indicates a type of movement in an artwork or design, often by repeated shapes, lines or colors.

rib A slender projecting arch, used as support in Romanesque and Gothic vaults. In late Gothic architecture, the ribs are often ornamental as well as structural, forming lace-like patterns.

ribbed vault A vault constructed of a system of self-supporting ribs and a web of thinner material, filling the spaces between the ribs.

ritual (*rich*-oo-al) A formal procedure or act in a religious observance.

rococo (roh-*koh*-koh) A late Baroque style (about 1715–1775) that can be described as pretty, private and, often, erotic and effete; also, any such elaborate or overdone phase in any culture.

Romanesque A style of architecture, painting or sculpture popular in the eleventh and twelfth centuries.

Romanticism (ro-*man*-ti-*siz*-em) A style of art that emphasizes the personal, emotional and dramatic aspects of exotic, literary and historical subject matter. Specifically, a European style from the mid-eighteenth century onward.

rosary (*ro*-zeh-ree) A string of beads used as a memory aid in the recitation of prayers in any religion; specifically refers to a series of prayers to the Virgin Mary aided by such a device.

rosette (ro-*zet*) A circular decorative element, suggestive of a flattened rose.

rose window A circular window with stone tracery radiating from the center and a characteristic feature of Gothic church architecture.

rotunda (ro-*tun*-dah) A round building or interior hall, topped by a dome.

roundel A circular decorative element.

rustication (russ-tee-*kay*-shun) A surface of massive stonework, having a rough contour with deep joints, with a resultant appearance of strength and solidity.

salon (sah-*lon*) A reception room. Also, an exhibition of the works of living artists and, specifically, the annual exhibition of French art in Paris.

samurai (*sah*-moo-ry) A member of the feudal warrior class of medieval Japan.

sanctuary (*sangk*-choo-er-ee) A sacred or holy place, usually enclosed within a temple or church building, often housing an altar and other worship aids.

sarcophagus (sar-*koff*-ah-gus) A stone coffin, often elaborately carved.

saturation (*sach*-ah-*ray*-shun) Also called intensity. The measure of the brilliance and purity of a color. Saturation decreases as the hue is neutralized.

scale The relative size of an object when compared to others of its kind, to its environment or to humans.

school Artists who have a similar philosophy and style or who work under a common influence.

script Written or printed lettering.

sculpture (*skulp*-cher) A three-dimensional work of art.

Scytho-Parthians (*sith*-oh-*par*-thee-uns) Ancient nomadic peoples of Southeast Europe and Central Asia before 100 BC, artistically significant for their development of the "animal style."

secondary colors Orange, green and violet: hues produced by the mixing of equal parts of two primary colors.

section (*sek*-shun) A diagram of a building, showing how it would look if it were cut open on a vertical plane.

secular (*sek*-yew-lar) Non-religious.

self-portrait A portrait of the artist created by the artist.

sepia (*see*-pee-ah) A warm dark-brown color.

sepulchre (*sep*-uhl-ker) A place of burial; a tomb.

serape (sehr-*ah*-pee) A blanket-like shawl worn in Hispanic cultures.

seraph (*sehr*-ahf) An angel; a celestial being.

series Many paintings exploring the same theme over a period of time.

serigraphy (seh-*rig*-raff-ee) A form of printmaking using stencils attached to a porous screen of silk through which the ink is forced. Also called silk screen printing.

serpentine (*sir*-pen-teen) A mineral with a dull green color, composed of magnesium silicate, usually with a mottled appearance closely resembling jade; also, a winding, snake-like line or design.

sfumato (sfoo-*mah*-toh) A slight blurring of the edges of figures and objects in a painting, creating a hazy feeling and aerial perspective.

sgraffito (skrah-*fee*-toh) The process of scratching lines into the surface of a work of art to expose the surface underneath.

shade A low-valued color, made by adding black to a hue.

shading Graduated variations in value, often used in painting to give a feeling of volume, form and depth.

shaft The main part of a column, between the base and the capital, which may be plain, fluted or twisted.

Shailendra (shy-*lynn*-druh) The Buddhist kingdom of ancient central Java (700–850) artistically noted for the construction of the ten-layered cosmic mountain stupa at Borobudor.

shaman (*shah*-mun) A priest who uses magic to cure the sick, predict the future or control nature.

Shang The Bronze-age culture in northern China (about 1600–1027 BC), artistically distinguished by their fine ritual containers made by the cire-perdue process.

shape An element of design that is an enclosed space, having only two dimensions. Shapes can be geometric (triangular, square, etc.) or organic (free form, with curving and irregular outlines).

shaped canvases Canvases in other shapes besides the traditional rectangle.

Shingon (*shin*-gon) A sect of Japanese Buddhism, and the major esoteric philosophy of Japan.

Shinto (*shin*-to) The native religion of Japan, marked by veneration of nature spirits.

shogun (*show*-gun) A generalissimo; military rulers who controlled Japan beginning with the Kamakura era, leaving the Emperor as a figurehead.

Shoshone (show-*show*-nee) A Native American tribe of the Central Basin; a basketmaking group of nomadic seed-gatherers.

side aisle The arcaded walkways on either side of the nave of a Christian church.

sikhara (*sick*-ah-rah) The tall curved roof of an Indian sanctuary.

silk screen See **serigraphy**.

simultaneity (*si*-mul-*ta*-nay-i-tee) The technique of depicting objects from separate vantage points in one work of art.

sinicization (sin-uh-siz-*ay*-shun) The process of acquiring Chinese culture.

Sioux (soo) Native Americans of the Plains, living in tipis and artistically noted for colored and beaded leatherwork, silversmithing and quillwork.

Sita (*see*-tah) The legendary wife of the epic-king, Rama.

Siva (*shee*-vah) The third member of the Hindu trinity and controller of great destructive and procreative powers. Also known as Bhairava (The Frightful); Nataraja (Master of the Dance); and Vinadhara (Master of the Arts). Represented with one of two wives (Parvati or Uma); with Nandi (the bull upon which he rides); as a man with a third eye; or as a phallic symbol known as a *lings* (which looks like a fire hydrant).

Six Dynasties An era of political turmoil in China (256–589) during which various dynasties ruled parts of China, and Buddhism from India became well established, especially in the sculpture of the Northern Wei (about 400–550).

sketch A quick drawing that catches the immediate feeling of action or the impression of a place or situation.

slip A thin mixture of clay and water, used both as a clay glue and as a paint on leather-hard ware.

soft sculpture (*skulp*-cher) Sculpture made with fabric and stuffed with soft material.

Song (sung) The Chinese dynasty (960–1127 in the North, continuing until 1279 in the South) during which Chinese aesthetics reached a zenith of sophistication, notably in architecture, painting and ceramics.

space An element of design that indicates areas in a painting (positive and negative); also, the feeling of depth in a two-dimensional work of art.

spandrel A space between two arches and a horizontal molding or cornice above them.

spectrum Bands of colored light, created when white light is passed through a prism; the full range of color.

sphinx (sfinks) A creature of Egyptian art with the body of a lion and the head of a man. In Greek mythology, a monster with the winged body of a lion and the head of a woman.

sprigging The attaching of pre-formed, leather-hard clay ornaments to a larger form; these ornaments are usually plant forms, human or animal bas-reliefs, or geometric bands.

squash blossom (skwash *bloss*-um) A popular motif among Southwestern Native American silversmiths, resembling an open trumpet-like flower and representing abundance.

Sri Vijaya (sree vih-*jih*-ah) An ancient Hindu-Buddhist kingdom of Southeast Asia (eighth–thirteenth centuries) stretching from Java to Southern Thailand, significant for early bronze images and as a Buddhist monastic center.

stabile (*stay*-bile) A standing sculpture with moveable parts.

stain painting The technique used by Helen Frankenthaler in which she stained her canvases with paint.

statue (*stach*-oo) A freestanding sculpture.

stele (*stee*-lee) An upright slab, bearing sculptured or painted designs or inscriptions. From the Greek for "standing block."

stencil (*sten*-sill) A method of producing images by cutting openings in a mask of paper, wax or other material so that paint or dye may go through the openings to the material beneath. Used in serigraphy, batik and ceramic decoration.

step pyramid A solid stone structure built of six huge steps and used as a tomb for an Egyptian Pharaoh.

still life A group of inanimate objects arranged to be painted or drawn; also, a painting or drawing of such an arrangement.

stirrup handle A hollow, loop-like handle resembling in shape the inverted U-shaped metal holder for a horseman's foot. Common in pre-Columbian pottery.

stoa (*stow*-ah) A large porch or covered colonnade in Greek architecture, used for a meeting place, walkway or place for small businesses and offices.

structure (*struk*-cher) The compositional relationships in a work of art; also, a building.

stucco (*stuk*-oh) Any of several types of plaster used for decorative cornices, moldings or ceilings; also, a cement coating for the exterior of a building.

stupa (*stew*-pah) A reliquary structure based on the Vedic funerary mound which represents the Buddhist cosmic mountain and commemorates sacred places, events or people (especially Buddha and Buddhist monks).

stupa-temple A Burmese modification of the Buddhist monument, incorporating a worship space underneath the bell-shaped stupa.

style (stile) The distinctive characteristics contained in the works of art of a person, period of time or geographic location.

stylization (*stile*-i-*zay*-shun) The simplification or generalization of forms found in nature to present a personal and more decorative feeling in a work of art or lettering.

stylobate (*sty*-low-bayt) The immediate foundation for a row of columns, often set on a foundation.

subject That which is represented in a work of art.

subtractive sculpture Sculpture formed by cutting away excess material from a block, leaving the finished work.

Sui (swee) A short-lived Chinese dynasty (581–618) during which Buddhist art and architecture evolved into a more Chinese and less Indian style.

Sukothai (*soo*-koh-ty) An early Thai kingdom (1238–1349) during which national architectural and sculptural styles became established; the golden age of Thai Buddhist sculpture and ceramics.

sultan A local Muslim sovereign; a ruler of both secular and Islamic aspects of society.

sumi-e (*soo*-mee-ay) Japanese black ink painting on white paper in the Chinese style.

Super-Realism A twentieth-century style of painting that emphasizes photographic realism. Many times the objects are greatly enlarged, yet keep their photographic appearance.

support The material in a painting upon which the work is done (canvas, panels, paper, etc.).

Surrealism (seh-*ree*-a-*liz*-um) A style of twentieth-century art in which artists combine normally unrelated objects and situations. Scenes are often dreamlike or set in unnatural surroundings.

Sutra (*soo*-trah) Buddhist scripture.

symbol A form, image, sign or subject representing a meaning other than its outward appearance.

symmetry (*sim*-i-tree) A formally balanced composition.

tabard A tunic with open sides.

Tang (tang) Classical Chinese dynasty (618–906) typified by a cosmopolitan character which encouraged the growth of new ideas. Artistically significant for the development of the pagoda form, glazed and unglazed tomb figures and other pottery masterpieces; the final Chinese influence on Buddhist sculpture and sophisticated ink paintings.

Tao (*dah*-oh) The Chinese philosophy regarding the relationships of nature and its forces, based on the teachings of Lao zi in the sixth century BC; means "The Way"; Taoism.

tapestry (*tap*-i-stree) A wall hanging of textile fabric painted, embroidered or woven with colorful ornamental designs or scenes.

tapestry weave A plain or basketweave fabric in which the weft threads are compressed so as to completely cover all warp threads.

Tarascan (tah-*rass*-kan) A culture of West Mexico that maintained independence during the reign of the Aztecs, significant for its claywork.

tatami (tah-*tah*-mee) Rice-straw flooring mats, 36" x 72", about 2" thick, used in Japan.

tattoo An indelible mark or design fixed upon the body by production of sores or insertion of pigment under the skin. From the Tahitian word *tatu* for "a mark."

technology (tek-*nahl*-oh-gee) The understanding and systematic use of materials, tools and processes.

tempera A water-based paint in which egg yolk is used as a vehicle. Some commercially made paints are called tempera, but are actually gouache.

tenebrism A late-sixteenth-century Italian painting technique which exaggerated strong contrasts of light and dark. (tenebroso in Italian)

Teotihuacan (tee-oh-*tee*-hwah-kahn) A classic Mexican civilization (about 350–850) and sacred city of temple pyramids, typified by the use of colored frescoes of gods, symbols and human subjects.

terra cotta Baked earth-red clay, used in ceramics and sculpture. Often glazed, it is used in both architectural decoration and tableware.

tessera (*tess*-ah-rah); pl. tesserae (*tess*-ah-ree) Bits of colored glass or stone used in making mosaics.

texture (*teks*-chur) The element of design that refers to the quality of a surface, both tactile and visual.

Thai (ty) Ancient and contemporary people of the Chao Phaya basin, emerging as a culturally distinct group in the thirteenth century, artistically distinguished by their Buddhist architecture, sculpture and mosaics.

therianthropic (theer-ee-an-*throp*-ic) The combination of human and animal forms into one being, such as a centaur or sphinx.

theriomorphic (theer-ee-ah-*mor*-fik) Having the form of an animal, such as a god taking the form of a jaguar or falcon.

thrust A strong, continued pressure, as the outward force exerted by an arch or vault that must be counterbalanced by buttressing.

thunderbird A mythological bird of North American Indian culture, responsible for thunder, lightning and rain; depicted in a stylized geometric pattern with outstretched wings.

Tiahuanaco (tee-a-*wan*-ah-ko) The Andean culture that united the region's various cultures (about 900–1200).

Ting A Chinese three-legged vessel made of clay, lacquer or bronze for ceremonial purposes.

tint A light value of a hue made by adding white to the original color.

tipi (*tee*-pee) A conical, rawhide dwelling consisting of groups of buffalo hides stretched over a framework of poles, its base diameter ranging from 12 to 30 feet. Characteristic dwelling of the Plains Indians of America.

tokonoma (toh-koh-*noh*-mah) An alcove in a Japanese interior, wherein are placed single objects of beauty for appreciation.

Toltec (*toll*-teck) A war-like people of semi-nomadic origin who unified northern Mexico about 947. Their capital at Tula is characterized by a temple with a pyramidal base and columns of atlantes.

tondo A round-shaped painting.

tone The modification of a color (hue) through the addition of neutrals.

Torah Jewish religious literature.

torii (*tore*-ee) The freestanding gateway at the entrance to a Japanese Shinto temple, consisting of two upright posts supporting a curved lintel, with a straight crosspiece below.

totem (*toe*-tem) An animal or natural object which symbolizes a clan or family. **totem pole** A tall post or pillar carved with the heredity marks, emblems or badges of a tribe or clan, functioning as a type of family tree.

Totonac (toe-*toe*-nack) The classic Mexican civilization of Veracruz (100–1000) typified artistically by the great religious pyramid temple center of El Tajin and light-hearted terra-cotta sculpture.

tracery Ornamental stonework in a decorative pattern with a lace-like effect; a decorative interlacing of lines suggestive of such stonework.

transept The part of a cross-shaped church at right angles to the long nave, usually with one arm on each side of the crossing.

transitional (tran-zish-en-l) A style of art in which influences and tastes are changing from an established practice to a distinctly different form.

transmutation (*tranz*-myoo-*tay*-shun) The conversion of one element into another; a process in the firing of some specialized ceramic glazes.

trefoil (*tree*-foyl) A three-lobed form or ornamentation.

triforium (try-*for*-ee-um) An arcade, often blind, below the clerestory of the nave in a Gothic church.

triglyph (*try*-glif) A group of three vertical ridges alternating with a plain metope in the frieze of a Doric Greek building.

triptych (*trip*-tik) An altarpiece consisting of three panels joined together. Often, the two outer panels are hinged to close over the central panel.

triumphal arch (try-*um*-fal) A monument built to commemorate a great victory with an open vaulted passageway through it. Also, in the Christian church, the large arched opening that separates the chancel (apse) from the nave of the church.

trompe-l'oeil (tromp loy) A type of painting that is so realistic (in form, color, size and lighting) that the viewer may be convinced that it is the actual subject and not a painting. From the French for "fool the eye."

true arch A round arch that actually supports the weight of a wall as opposed to a blind arch which is a surface motif in a wall.

truss An assemblage of structural members forming a rigid framework under a roof; also used in bridge design.

turret A small tower, which may be functional or ornamental, at the outside angle of a larger structure.

twining To wind or twist.

tympanum (*tim*-pa-num) A carved or decorated space over the door and under the arch of a Romanesque or Gothic church facade.

ukiyo-e (oo-key-*oh*-eh) Japanese pictures of the "floating world" pleasure district of Edo. These were first made in paint, but were more commonly produced in editions of polychrome woodcuts. They are the unique creation of the Edo period.

unity A principle of design that relates to the sense of oneness or wholeness in a work of art.

urna (*urn*-ah) The third eye of Buddha, iconographically depicted as a curl of hair on the forehead.

ushnisha (ush-*neesh*-ah) The knot of hair at the crown of Buddha's head or a bulge in the back of his skull which symbolically represents his wisdom.

value (*val*-yoo) An element of design that relates to the lightness and darkness of a color or tone.

vanishing point An imaginary point or points at eye level, toward which parallel lines recede and where they will eventually meet in perspective drawing and painting.

vault (vawlt) An arched roof or covering made of brick stone or concrete. A barrel vault or tunnel vault is semi-circular. A corbeled vault is made by having each course protrude a little beyond the course below it until the two sides meet. See **groined vault**.

Vedas (*vay*-dahs) Sacred writings of Hindu philosophy, including the hymns to nature (Sanhitas); ethical and moral writings (Brahmanas); treatises on metaphysics (Aranyatas); and the quest for truth (Upanisads). Formulated during the centuries before 600 BC giving the name "Vedic Era" to the previous millennium.

vehicle (*ve*-i-kull) The binding agent in paint that holds the pigment together and forms a film that adheres to the support or ground.

velarium An awning at the top of the Colosseum in Rome that protected spectators from sun and rain.

vellum A fine parchment made from calfskin and used for writing, manuscript illumination and book binding.

view painting An eighteenth-century style of painting depicting city views with incredible accuracy.

Vishnu (*veesh*-noo) The preserver god of the Hindu trinity, often incarnated as the mild and benevolent Krishna.

volute (voh-*loot*) A spiral ornament, resembling a rolled scroll.

voussoir (voo-*swahr*) A wedge-shaped stone block used in the construction of an arch.

walkabout An initiation ritual for Australian aborigines entering adulthood involving survival skills against nature.

ware A general term for pottery, particularly pottery made for export or sale; by extension, anything made for sale or barter.

warm color A hue in the red to yellow range in the spectrum.

wash A thin transparent layer of paint; also, a thinned mixture of solvent and paint.

wat (wot) A Thai or Laotian temple; a Khmer pagoda.

watercolor Any paint that uses water as a medium, including acrylic, gouache, casein, tempera and transparent watercolor. In a more restricted sense, a paint which has gum arabic as a vehicle and water as a medium (called transparent watercolor or aquarelle). Also, a painting done with this paint.

wattle-and-daub (dawb) A building technique for filling in walls between structural members using a fabrication of poles interwoven with slender branches, reeds, etc., and imbedded with mud.

Wayang Style (*wy*-yong) Indonesian painting of figures which duplicates the flat side views of local shadow puppets; also, relief carving in a form similar to the wooden puppets of local plays. While this style originated in the Hindu-Javanese kingdoms, the plays (Wayang) are part of the Islamic culture as well.

web The thin masonry surface between the ribs of a vault.

Wei (way) Name of a number of dynastic eras in China between 220 and 535, controlling various regions of the country, artistically distinguished by early Buddhist sculptures in the Gandharan style.

westwork The western facade of a medieval European church that includes the main entrance and usually several towers.

wheel-thrown Ceramic objects made by forming clay on a spinning disc, producing a symmetrical round form. See **potter's wheel**.

woodcut A relief print made by cutting a design into the flat surface of a block of wood and applying ink only to the raised surface.

wood engraving A relief print made from a design cut into the end grain of a hardwood block and applying ink only to the raised surface.

Xia (*she*-ah) An ancient Chinese culture (1500–1200 BC) typified by the evolution of oracle bones on which pictographic symbols were inscribed as messages to the gods; also spelled Hsia.

Yamato (ya-*mah*-toh) The cultural area of old Japan, being the plain where Nara, Kyoto and Osaka are located.

yamato-e (ya-*mah*-toh-ay) Japanese style painting, an indigenous response to Chinese brush painting, typified by Japanese genre subjects in a delicate linear style.

Yang Shao (yang show) A Neolithic culture of central China (about 7000–1600 BC), typified artistically by handbuilt terra-cotta pottery with impressed designs or slip-painted spiral motifs.

Yaqui (*yah*-kee) A tribe of Uto-Aztec Indians of Sonora, Mexico.

Yayoi (*yah*-yoy) An agricultural society in pre-historic Japan (200 BC–300 AD) typified artistically by thin-walled, footed pottery.

Yuan (*you*-un) The Mongol dynasty of Chinese history which controlled all of China (1279–1368), artistically significant for the development of blue-and-white porcelain, an infusion of Central Asian culture and a revival of Tang artistic practices.

Zapotec (za-*poh*-tek) Ancient Mexican people in the Valley of Oaxaca (wah-*hah*-kah) (about 200–1000) centered at Monte Alban, typified by their architecture of stuccoed and painted temples and pyramids.

Zen A Buddhist sect emphasizing contemplation and meditation, self-discipline, and that the Buddha is inherent in all things. More commonly known by the Japanese spelling (Zen), it originated in China as Chan.

Zhou (zhoh) Chinese dynasty (1111–256 BC) typified artistically by elaborate cast bronze ritual vessels and sophisticated jade carving; Chou.

ziggurat (*zig*-oo-rat) The high temple platform, built of mud brick, of Sumerian and Assyrian architecture. Usually built in the form of a truncated stepped pyramid with ramp-like stairways leading to the sanctuary at the top.

zoopraxiscope A photographic device invented by Eadweard Muybridge in the late 1870s which produced a series of images of a moving subject.

Zuni (*zoo*-nee) A tribe of Southwestern Native Americans, artistically distinguished as the finest of Pueblo silversmiths and typified by their use of turquoise.

Bibliography

Further Reading

There are literally hundreds of books on the shelves of libraries and bookstores that offer both general and detailed information about art and art history. Some are technical while others feature many pictures; some are written for art specialists, others for the general public. The authors found the following books useful, but by all means explore school, university (if accessible) and public libraries for more information.

General Reference

Boorstin, Daniel J. *Creators: A History of Heroes of the Imagination.* New York: Random House Inc., 1992.

Carey, John, ed. *Eyewitness to History.* New York: Avon, 1990.

Chapman, Laura. *A World of Images.* Worcester, MA: Davis Publications, Inc., 1992.

———. *Art: Images and Ideas.* Worcester, MA: Davis Publications, Inc., 1992.

Chilvers, Ian. *The Concise Oxford Dictionary of Art and Artists.* New York: Oxford University Press, 1990.

Cooke, Jean, et al. *History's Timeline.* London: Grisewood and Dempsey, 1981.

Cunningham, Lawrence, and Reich, John. *Culture and Values: A Survey of the Western Humanities.* 2 vols. New York: Holt, Rinehart and Winston Inc., 1982.

de la Croix, Horst, and Tansey, Richard G. *Gardner's Art through the Ages.* 10th ed. Orlando: Harcourt Brace Jovanovich, 1995.

The Dictionary of Art. Jane Shoaf Turner, Ed. 34 vols. New York: Grove's Dictionaries, Inc., 1996

Fine, Elsa H. *Women and Art: A History of Women Painters and Sculptors from the Renaissance to the Twentieth Century.* Montclair, NJ: Allanheld and Schram, 1978.

Finn, David. *How to Look at Sculpture.* New York: Harry N. Abrams Inc., 1989.

Fleming, William. *Arts and Ideas.* 8th ed. Orlando: Harcourt Brace Jovanovich, 1991.

Fletcher, Banister. *A History of Architecture.* Ed. J.C. Palmes, 18th ed., rev. New York: Macmillan, 1975.

Friedenthal, Richard, trans., et al. *Letters of the Great Artists.* Vol. 1, *From Ghiberti to Gainsborough.* Vol. 2, *From Blake to Pollock.* London: Thames and Hudson Inc., 1963.

Goldwater, Robert, and Treves, Marco. *Artists on Art: From the Fourteenth to the Twentieth Century.* New York: Pantheon Books, 1974.

Grun, Bernard. *The Timetables of History: A Horizontal Linkage of People and Events.* Updated ed. New York: Touchstone, 1987.

Harris, Ann S. *Women Artists, 1550–1950.* New York: Alfred A. Knopf Inc., 1977.

Hartt, Frederick. *History of Art: Painting, Sculpture, Architecture.* 3rd ed. New York: Harry N. Abrams Inc., 1989.

Hobbs, Jack A., and Duncan, Robert L. *Arts, Ideas and Civilization.* Englewood Cliffs, NJ: Prentice Hall, 1989.

Hobbs, Jack and Salome, Richard A. *The Visual Experience.* 2nd ed. Worcester, MA: Davis Publications, Inc., 1995.

Holt, Elizabeth G. *A Documentary History of Art: The Middle Ages and The Renaissance* , vol I: *Michelangelo and The Mannerist–The Baroque and The Eighteenth Century,* vol II, 2nd ed. Princeton: Princeton University Press, 1983.

———, ed. *Impressionist: Art and Architecture in the Nineteenth Century.* Vol. 3 of *Documentary History of Art.* New Haven: Yale University Press, 1986.

Honour, Hugh, and Fleming, John. *The Visual Arts: A History.* 3rd ed. Englewood Cliffs, NJ: Prentice Hall, 1991.

Jacobus, Lee A. *Humanities.* New York: McGraw-Hill Inc., 1986.

Janson, H. W. with contributions by Anthony F. Janson. *The History of Art.* New York: Harry N. Abrams Inc., 1995.

Murray, Peter, and Murray, Linda. *A Dictionary of Art and Artists.* 5th ed. London: Penguin, 1984.

Phipps, Richard, and Wink, Richard. *Invitation to the Gallery: An Introduction to Art Appreciation.* Carmel, IA: Brown and Benchmark, 1987.

Piper, David, ed. *Random House Dictionary of Art and Artists.* New York: Fodor's Travel Publications Inc., 1990.

Read, Herbert, and Stangos, Nikos, eds. *The Thames and Hudson Dictionary of Art and Artists.* Rev. ed. London: Thames and Hudson, Inc. Inc., 1988.

Slatkin, Wendy. *The Voices of Women Artists.* Englewood Cliffs, NJ: Prentice Hall, 1993.

———. *Women Artists in History.* 2nd ed. Englewood Cliffs, NJ: Prentice Hall, 1989.

Vidal-Naquet, Pierre. *The Harper Atlas of World History.* New York: Harper and Row, 1987.

Prehistoric Art, Mesopotamia and Egypt

Aldred, C. *Akhenaten and Nefertiti.* New York: Brooklyn Museum/Viking Press, 1973.

———. *Art of Ancient Egypt.* 3 vols. New York: Trans-Atlantic Publications Inc., 1974.

———. *Development of Ancient Egyptian Art from 3200 to 1315 BC.* New York: Trans-Atlantic Publications Inc., 1975.

Amiet, P. *Art of the Ancient Near East.* New York: Harry N. Abrams Inc., 1980.

Childe, V. G. *The Dawn of European Civilization.* 6th ed. New York: Alfred A. Knopf Inc., 1958.

El Mahdy, Christine, ed. *The World of the Pharaohs: A Complete Guide to Ancient Egypt.* London: Thames and Hudson Inc., 1989.

Frankfort, H. *The Art and Architecture of the Ancient Orient.* 4th rev. New Haven: Yale University Press, 1992.

Grand, P. M. *Prehistoric Art: Paleolithic Painting and Sculpture.* Greenwich: New York Graphic Society, 1967.

Graziosi, P. *Paleolithic Art.* New York: McGraw-Hill Inc., 1960.

Groenewegen-Frankfort, H. A., and Ashmole, B. *Art of the Ancient World.* Englewood Cliffs, NJ: Prentice Hall, 1971.

Leroi-Gourhan, A. *Treasures of Prehistoric Art.* New York: Harry N. Abrams Inc., 1967.

Lloyd, Seton, Müller, H. W., and Martin, R. *Ancient Architecture: Mesopotamia, Egypt, Greece.* New York: Harry N. Abrams Inc., 1974.

Mekhitarian, A. *Egyptian Painting.* New York: Rizzoli International Publications Inc., 1977.

Mellaart, J. *Earliest Civilizations of the Near East.* New York: McGraw-Hill Inc., 1965.

——. *The Neolithic of the Near East.* New York: Scribner, 1975.

Michalowski, K. *Art of Ancient Egypt.* New York: Harry N. Abrams Inc., 1985.

Moortgat, A. *The Art of Ancient Mesopotamia.* New York: Phaidon, 1969.

Poulsen, V. *Egyptian Art.* Greenwich: New York Graphic Society, 1968.

Powell, T. G. E. *Prehistoric Art.* New York: Praeger Publishers, 1966.

Sandars, N. K. *Prehistoric Art in Europe.* New Haven: Yale University Press, 1992.

Smith, W. S., and Simpson, W. K. *The Art and Architecture of Ancient Egypt.* New Haven: Yale University Press, 1992.

Strommenger, E., and Hirmer, M. *Five Thousand Years of the Art of Mesopotamia.* New York: Harry N. Abrams Inc., 1964.

Thom, A. *Megalithic Sites in Britain.* Oxford: Clarendon Press, 1967.

Wainwright, Geoffrey. *The Henge Monuments: Ceremony and Society in Prehistoric Britain.* London: Thames and Hudson Inc., 1990.

Wolff, Walther. *The Origins of Western Art: Egypt, Mesopotamia, the Aegean.* New York: Universe Publishing, 1989.

Ancient Greece and Rome

Adam, S. *The Technique of Greek Sculpture in the Archaic and Classical Periods.* New York: Thames and Hudson Inc., 1967.

Andreae, B. *The Art of Rome.* New York: Harry N. Abrams Inc., 1977.

Banti, L. *Etruscan Cities and Their Culture.* Berkeley: University of California, 1973.

Boardman, John. *Greek Art.* Rev. ed. New York: Thames and Hudson Inc., 1985.

Boethius, A. *Etruscan and Early Roman Architecture.* 2nd integrated ed., rev. New Haven: Yale University Press, 1992.

Brendel, O. J. *Etruscan Art.* Harmondsworth, NY: Penguin USA, 1978.

Brilliant, R. *Arts of the Ancient Greeks.* New York: McGraw-Hill Inc., 1973.

——. *Roman Art from the Republic to Constantine.* New York: Phaidon, 1974.

Bulfinch, Thomas. *The Age of Fable.* Reprint of 1855 ed. Irvine: Reprint Services, 1989.

Carpenter, R. *The Architects of the Parthenon.* Baltimore: Penguin USA, 1970.

Charbonneaux, J., Martin, R., and Villard, F. *Classical Greek Art.* New York: George Braziller Inc., 1973.

Christ, Karl, and Holme, Christopher, trans. *The Romans.* Berkeley, CA: University of California Press, 1984.

Coolidge, Olivia. *Trojan War.* Boston: Houghton Mifflin Co., 1990.

Hamilton, Edith. *Mythology: Timeless Tales of Gods and Heros.* New York: New American Library, 1989.

Hampe, R., and Simon, E. *The Birth of Greek Art from the Myceanean to the Archaic Period.* New York: Oxford University Press, 1981.

Hood, S. *The Arts in Prehistoric Greece.* Harmondsworth, NY: Penguin USA, 1978.

——. *The Minoans: The Story of Bronze Age Crete.* New York: Praeger Publishers, 1981.

Kleiner, Diana E. E. *Roman Sculpture.* New Haven: Yale University Press, 1992.

Lawrence, A. W. *Greek and Roman Sculpture.* New York: Harper and Row, 1972.

——. *Greek Architecture.* 4th ed., rev. New York: Penguin USA, 1983.

MacDonald, W. L. *The Architecture of the Roman Empire.* New Haven: Yale University Press, 1982.

MacKendrick, Paul. *The Greek Stones Speak: The Story of Archaeology in Greek Lands.* New York: W.W. Norton, 1983

Martin, Roland. *Greek Architecture: Architecture of Crete, Greece, and the Greek World.* New York: Electa/Rizzoli International Publications Inc., 1988.

Mayani, Zacharie. *The Etruscans Begin to Speak.* New York: Simon and Schuster, 1962.

Nash, E. *Pictorial Dictionary of Ancient Rome.* 2 vols., 2nd ed., rev. New York: Hacker, 1980

Papaioannou, Kostas. *The Art of Greece.* New York: Harry N. Abrams Inc., 1989.

Perowne, S. *The Archaeology of Greece and the Aegean.* New York: Viking, 1974.

Pollitt, J. J. *The Art of Rome and Late Antiquity: Sources and Documents.* Englewood Cliffs, NJ: Prentice Hall, 1966.

Renfrew, C. *The Emergence of Civilization: The Cyclades and the Aegean in the Third Millennium BC.* London: Methuen, 1972.

Richardson, E. *The Etruscans: Their Art and Civilization.* Chicago: University of Chicago Press, 1964.

Richter, G. M. A. *A Handbook of Greek Art.* 9th ed. New York: DaCapo, 1987.

——. *The Sculpture and Sculptors of the Greeks.* 4th ed., rev. New Haven: Yale University Press, 1970.

Sprenger, M., Bartolini, G., Hirmer, M., and Hirmer, A. *The Etruscans, Their History, Art, and Architecture.* New York: Harry N. Abrams Inc., 1983.

Stewart, Andrew. *Greek Sculpture: An Exploration,* 2 vols. New Haven: Yale University Press, 1990.

Strong, Donald, and Ling, Roger. *Roman Art.* 2nd rev. ed. New Haven: Yale University Press, 1992.

Veyne, Paul et al eds. *A History of Private Life.* Vol. 1: *From Pagan Rome to Byzantium.* Trans. Arthur Goldhammer. Cambridge: Harvard University Press, 1987.

Ward-Perkins, John B. *Roman Architecture.* New York: Rizzoli International Publications Inc., 1988.

——. *Roman Imperial Architecture.* New Haven: Yale University Press, 1992.

Early Christian, Byzantine Art and Early Medieval Art

Arnold, Bruce. *Irish Art: A Concise History.* Rev. ed. London: Thames and Hudson Inc., 1989.

Beckwith, J. *The Art of Constantinople: An Introduction to Byzantine Art.* 2nd ed. New York: Phaidon, 1968.

——. *Early Christian and Byzantine Art.* 2nd ed. New Haven: Yale University Press, 1992.

Dodwell, C. R. *Painting in Europe, 800–1200.* New Haven: Yale University Press, 1992.

Grabar, A. *The Beginnings of Christian Art, 200–395.* London: Thames and Hudson Inc., 1967.

——. *Early Christian Art.* New York: George Braziller Inc., 1971.

——. *The Golden Age of Justinian, from the Death of Theodosius to the Rise of Islam.* New York: George Braziller Inc., 1971.

Krautheimer, R. *Early Christian and Byzantine Architecture*. 4th ed. New Haven: Yale University Press 1984.

MacDonald, William L. *Early Christian and Byzantine Architecture*. New York: George Braziller, 1963.

Mango, C. Ed. *The Art of the Byzantine Empire, 312–1453: Sources and Documents*. Toronto: University of Toronto Press, 1986.

———. *Byzantine Architecture*. New York: Rizzoli International Publications Inc., 1985.

Marzials, Sir Frank, trans. *Memoirs of the Crusades*. London: Dent and Sons, 1955.

Mathews, T. J. *Byzantine Churches of Istanbul: A Photographic Survey*. University Park: Pennsylvania State University Press, 1976.

Mayer, Hans Eberhard. *The Crusades*. New York: Oxford University Press, 1993.

McEvedy, Colin. *The New Penguin Atlas of Medieval History*. London: Penguin, 1992.

Megaw, Ruth, and Megaw, Vincent. *Celtic Art: From Its Beginnings to the Book of Kells*. London: Thames and Hudson Inc., 1989.

Milburn, Robert L. P. *Early Christian Art and Architecture*. Berkeley: University of California Press, 1991.

Nordenfalk, C. *Early Medieval Book Illumination*. Geneva/New York: Skira/Rizzoli International Publications Inc., 1988.

Runciman, S. *Byzantine Style and Civilization*. Baltimore: Penguin USA, 1975.

Snyder, James. *Medieval Art: Painting, Sculpture, Architecture, Fourth to Fourteenth Century*. New York: Harry N. Abrams Inc., 1989.

Weitzmann, K. *Byzantine Book Illumination and Ivories*. London: Vriorum Reprints, 1980.

———. *Late Antique and Early Christian Book Illumination*. New York: George Braziller Inc., 1977.

White Jr., Lynn. *Medieval Technology and Social Change*. London: Oxford University Press, 1964.

Zarnecki, G. *Art of the Medieval World: Architecture, Sculpture, Painting, The Sacred Arts*. Englewood Cliffs, NJ: Prentice Hall, 1976.

Romanesque and Gothic

Aries, Philippe, and Duby, Georges, gen. eds. *A History of Private Life: Revelations of the Medieval World*. Cambridge, MA: Belknap Press, 1988.

Bowie, T., ed. *The Sketchbook of Villard de Honnecourt*. 3rd ed. Bloomington: Indiana University Press, 1968.

Cennini, C. D. *The Craftsman's Handbook (Il Libro dell'Arte)*. New York: Dover Publications Inc., 1933.

Cole, B. *Giotto and Florentine Painting, 1280–1375*. New York: HarperCollins, 1977.

Conant, K. J. *Carolingian and Romanesque Architecture, 800–1200*. 4th ed. New Haven: Yale University Press, 1992.

Erlande-Brandenburg, Alain. *Gothic Art*. New York: Harry N. Abrams Inc., 1989.

Frankl, P. *Gothic Architecture*. Baltimore: Penguin USA, 1962.

Gies, Joseph, and Gies, Frances. *Life in a Medieval Castle*. New York: Harper and Row, 1979.

———. *Life in a Medieval City*. New York: Harper Perennial, 1981.

Grabar, Oleg. *The Formation of Islamic Art*. New Haven: Yale University Press, 1987.

Kubach, H. E. *Romanesque Architecture*. New York: Rizzoli International Publications Inc., 1988.

Martindale, A. *Gothic Art*. New York: Praeger Publishers, 1967.

Von Simson, Otto Georg. *The Gothic Cathedral: Origins of Gothic Architecture and the Medieval Concept of Order*. 3rd enl. ed. Princeton: Princeton University Press, 1988.

White, J. *Art and Architecture in Italy, 1250–1400*. 2nd ed. New Haven: Yale University Press, 1992.

Renaissance Art

Andres, Glenn, et al. *The Art of Florence*. 2 vols. New York: Abbeville Publishing Group, 1989.

Avery, C. *Florentine Renaissance Sculpture*. Trafalgar Square Publishing, 1989.

Baxandall, Michael. *Painting and Experience in Fifteenth-Century Italy: A Primer in the Social History of Pictorial Style*. 2nd ed. New York: Oxford University Press, 1988.

Beck, James. *Italian Renaissance Painting*. New York: HarperCollins, 1981.

Benesch, O. *The Art of the Renaissance in Northern Europe*. Rev. ed. London: Phaidon, 1965.

Blunt, Anthony. *Art and Architecture in France, 1500–1700*. 4th ed. New Haven: Yale University Press, 1992.

Bull, George, trans. *Lives of the Artists*. Vol. 1. New York: Viking Penguin, 1988.

Cole, B. *Masaccio and the Art of Early Renaissance Florence*. Bloomington: Indiana University Press, 1980.

Cutler, C. D. *Northern Painting: From Pucelle to Bruegel*. New York: Holt, Rinehart and Winston, Inc., 1968.

Earls, Irene. *Renaissance Art: A Topical Dictionary*. New York: Greenwood Publishing Group Inc., 1987.

Freedberg, S. J. *Painting in Italy: 1500–1600*. 3rd ed. New Haven: Yale University Press, 1992.

Friedlander, M. J. *Early Netherlandish Painting*. 14 vols. New York: Praeger Publishers, 1967–1973.

———. *From Van Eyck to Bruegel: Early Netherlandish Painting*. Ithaca: Cornell University Press, 1981

Gilbert, Creighton. *History of Renaissance Art throughout Europe: Painting, Sculpture, Architecture*. New York: Harry N. Abrams Inc., 1973.

Hartt, Frederick. *History of Italian Renaissance Art: Painting, Sculpting, Architecture*. 4th ed. Ed. David G. Wilkins. New York: Harry N, Abrams Inc., 1994.

Hibbard, H. *Michelangelo*. 2nd ed. New York: HarperCollins, 1985.

Hills, Paul. *The Light of Early Italian Painting*. New Haven: Yale University Press, 1990.

Murray, Peter. *Renaissance Architecture*. New York: Rizzoli International Publications Inc., 1982.

Panofsky, E. *Early Netherlandish Painting*. 2 vols. New York: HarperCollins, 1971.

Seymour Jr., Charles. *Sculpture in Italy, 1400–1500*. New Haven: Yale University Press, 1992.

Shearman, J. K. G. *Mannerism*. New York: Viking Penguin, 1978.

Snyder, J. *Northern Renaissance Art: Painting, Sculpture, the Graphic Arts from 1350 to 1575*. New York: Harry N. Abrams Inc., 1985.

Symonds, John Addington. Trans. *The Life of Benvenuto Cellini*. Oxford: Phaidon Press, 1995.

Vasari, G. *The Lives of the Most Eminant Painters, Sculptors and Architects.* 10 vols. Reprint of 1915 ed. New York: AMS Press.

Waterhouse, E. K. *Painting in Britain, 1530–1790.* 4th ed. New Haven: Yale University Press, 1992.

Baroque and Rococo Art

Bazin, Germain. *Baroque and Rococo.* New York: Thames and Hudson Inc., 1992.

Gaunt, W. *The Great Century of British Painting: Hogarth to Turner.* London: Phaidon, 1971.

Gerson, H., and Ter Kuile, E. H. *Art and Architecture in Belgium, 1600–1800.* Baltimore: Penguin USA, 1978.

Held, J., and Posner, D. *Seventeenth and Eighteenth Century: Baroque Painting, Sculpture, Architecture.* Ed. H.W. Janson. Englewood Cliffs, NJ: Prentice Hall, 1972.

Hempel, E. *Baroque Art and Architecture in Central Europe.* Baltimore: Penguin USA, 1977.

Kalnein, W. Graf, and Levey, M. *Art and Architecture of the Eighteenth Century in France.* Harmondsworth, NY: Penguin USA, 1972.

Levey, M. *Rococo to Revolution: Major Trends in Eighteenth Century Painting.* New York: Oxford University Press, 1977.

Nash, J. M. *The Age of Rembrandt and Vermeer: Dutch Painting in the Seventeenth Century.* New York: Holt, Rinehart and Winston, Inc., 1972.

Rosenberg, J. *Rembrandt, Life and Work.* Rev. ed. Ithaca, NY: Cornell University Press, 1980.

———, Slive, S., and Ter Kuile, E. H. *Dutch Art and Architecture, 1600–1800.* 3rd ed. New Haven: Yale University Press, 1992.

Stechow, W. *Dutch Landscape Painting of the Seventeenth Century.* Ithaca, NY: Cornell University Press, 1981.

Waterhouse, Ellis. *The Dictionary of Sixteenth and Seventeenth Century British Painters.* Woodbridge, England: Antique Collectors' Club, 1988.

Wittkower, R. *Art and Architecture in Italy, 1600–1750.* 3rd ed. New Haven: Yale University Press, 1992.

Nineteenth Century Art

Brown, M. W. *American Art to 1900.* New York: Harry N. Abrams Inc., 1977.

Clark, T. J. *The Painting of Modern Life: Paris in the Art of Manet and His Followers.* Princeton: Princeton University Press, 1986.

Driskell, D. C. *Two Centuries of Black American Art.* California: Los Angeles County Museum of Art/New York: Alfred A. Knopf Inc., 1976.

Harris, Neil. *The Artist in American Society: The Formative Years, 1790–1860.* Chicago: University of Chicago Press, 1982.

Herbert, Robert L. *Impressionism—Art, Leisure and Parisian Society.* New Haven: Yale University Press, 1988.

Holt, Elizabeth G., ed. *Impressionist: Art and Architecture in the Nineteenth Century.* Vol. 3 of *Documentary History of Art.* New Haven,: Yale University Press, 1986.

Honour, H. *Neoclassicism.* Baltimore: Penguin USA, 1968.

———. *Romanticism.* New York: Harper and Row, 1979.

Janson, H. W. *Nineteenth Century Sculpture.* New York: Harry N. Abrams Inc., 1985.

Nochlin, L. *Realism.* Baltimore: Viking Penguin USA, 1972.

Novotny, F. *Painting and Sculpture in Europe, 1780–1880.* New Haven: Yale University Press, 1992.

Rosenblum, R., and Janson, H. W. *Nineteenth-Century Art.* Englewood Cliffs, NJ: Prentice Hall, 1983.

Wilmerding, J. *American Art.* Baltimore: Penguin USA, 1976.

Twentieth Century Art

Ades, Dawn. *Art in Latin America: The Modern Era, 1820–1980.* New Haven: Yale University Press, 1989.

Arnason, H. H. *History of Modern Art: Painting, Sculpture, Architecture, Photography.* 3rd rev. and enl. ed. New York: Harry N. Abrams Inc., 1986.

Baker, Kenneth. *Minimalism: Art of Circumstance.* New York: Abbeville Publishing Group, 1989.

Beardsley, John, and Livingston, Jane. *Hispanic Art in the United States: Thirty Contemporary Painters and Sculptors.* Houston: Museum of Fine Arts/New York: Abbeville Publishing Group, 1987.

Braun, Emily, ed. *Italian Art in the Twentieth Century.* Munich: Prestel-Verlag, 1989.

Brown, Milton W. *The Story of the Armory Show.* New York: Abbeville Publishing Group, 1988.

Campbell, Mary Schmidt; Driskell, David C.; Levering, David Lewis; and Ryan, Deborah Willis. *Harlem Renaissance: Art of Black America.* New York: Studio Museum, Harlem/Harry N. Abrams Inc., 1987.

Celant, Germano. *Un-Expressionism: Art Beyond the Post-Modern Era.* New York: Rizzoli International Publications Inc., 1988.

Crane, Diana. *The Transformation of the Avant-Garde: The New York Art World, 1940–1985.* Chicago: University of Chicago Press, 1989.

Doty, R., ed. *Contemporary Black Artists in America.* New York: Whitney Museum of Art, 1971.

Dube, W. D. *The Expressionists.* New York: Thames and Hudson, 1985.

Geldzahler, H. *American Painting in the Twentieth Century.* New York: Metropolitan Museum of Art, 1965.

Godfrey, T. *The New Image: Painting in the 1980s.* New York: Abbeville Publishing Group, 1986.

Goldberg, Rose Lee. *Performance Art: From Futurism to the Present.* Rev. and enl. ed. New York: Harry N. Abrams Inc., 1988.

Golding, John. *Cubism: A History and Analysis, 1907–1914.* 3rd. ed. Cambridge: Harvard University Press, 1988.

Green, Chris. *Cubism and Its Enemies: Modern Movements and Reaction in French Art, 1916–1928.* New Haven: Yale University Press, 1987.

Hammacher, A. M. *Modern Sculpture: Tradition and Innovation.* New York: Harry N. Abrams Inc., 1988.

Herbert, R. L., ed. *Modern Artists on Art.* Englewood Cliffs, NJ: Prentice Hall, 1965.

Hunter, S., and Jacobus, J. *American Art of the Twentieth Century: Painting, Sculpture, Architecture.* Englewood Cliffs, NJ: Prentice Hall, 1974

Jaffe, H. L. C. *De Stijl, 1917–1931: Visions of Utopia.* New York: Abbeville Publishing Group, 1982.

Jencks, Charles. *Post-Modernism: The New Classicism in Art and Architecture.* New York: Rizzoli International Publications Inc., 1987.

Leymarie, Jean. *Fauves and Fauvism.* New York: Rizzoli International Publications Inc., 1987.

Lippard, L. R. *Pop Art.* New York: Thames and Hudson, 1985.

Lynton, Norbert. *The Story of Modern Art.* 2nd ed. Englewood Cliffs, NJ: Prentice Hall, 1989.

Mahsun, Carol A., ed. *Pop Art: The Critical Dialogue.* Ann Arbor: University of Michigan Press, 1988.

McShine, Kynaston. *Andy Warhol: A Retrospective.* New York: Museum of Modern Art, 1991.

Meisel, Louis K. *Photorealism.* New York: Harry N. Abrams Inc., 1989.

Motherwell, Robert, ed. *The Dada Painters and Poets: An Anthology.* 2nd ed. Cambridge: Harvard University Press, 1989.

Nadeau, Maurice. *History of Surrealism.* Cambridge: Harvard University Press, 1989.

Norris, Christopher, and Benjamin, Andrew. *What Is Deconstruction?* New York: St. Martin's Press Inc., 1989.

Pincus-Witten, Robert. *Postminimalism into Maximalism: American Art, 1966–1986.* Ann Arbor: University of Michigan Press, 1987.

Rosenblum, R. *Cubism and Twentieth-Century Art.* Rev. ed. New York: Harry N. Abrams Inc., 1976.

Rubin, W., ed. *Pablo Picasso, A Retrospective.* Greenwich: New York Graphic Society for the Museum of Modern Art, NY, 1980.

Shikes, Ralph E. *The Indignant Eye.* Boston: Beacon Press, 1969.

Twentieth Century Architecture

Cole, D. *From Tipi to Skyscraper: A History of Women in Architecture.* Cambridge: MIT Press, 1978.

Hitchcock, H. R. *Architecture: Nineteenth and Twentieth Centuries.* 2nd ed. Baltimore: Penguin USA, 1971.

Klotz, Heinrich. *History of Postmodern Architecture.* Cambridge: MIT Press, 1988.

Pevsner, Nikolaus, Sir. *A History of Building Types.* London: Thames and Hudson Inc., 1987.

———. *The Sources of Modern Architecture and Design.* New York: Oxford University Press, 1968

Scully, Vincent. *Architecture.* London: Harvill, 1991.

———. *Modern Architecture.* Rev. ed. New York: Braziller, 1974.

Trachtenberg, M, and Hyman, I. *Architecture: From Prehistory to Post-Modernism.* New York: Harry N. Abrams Inc., 1985.

Photography

Buckland, Gail. *Fox Talbot and the Invention of Photography.* Boston: David R. Godine Publisher, Inc., 1980.

Daval, J. L. *Photography: History of an Art.* Skira/Rizzoli International Publications Inc., 1982.

Gernsheim, H., and Gernsheim, A. *The History of Photography from the Camera Obscura to the Beginning of the Modern Era.* 2nd ed. New York: McGraw-Hill, 1969.

Greenough, Sarah, et al. *On the Art of Fixing a Shadow: One Hundred and Fifty Years of Photography.* Washington, DC: National Gallery of Art/Chicago: Art Institute of Chicago, 1991.

Jeffrey, Ian. *Photography: A Concise History.* New York: Thames and Hudson, 1982.

Newhall, Beaumont. *The History of Photography from 1839 to the Present Day.* 5th rev. ed. New York: Museum of Modern Art, 1982.

Phillips, Christopher, ed. *Photography in the Modern Era: European Documents and Critical Writings, 1913–1940.* New York: Metropolitan Museum of Art, 1989

Rosenblum, Naomi. *The History of Women Photographers.* New York: Abbeville Publishing Group, 1994.

Szarkowski, John. *Photography Now.* New York: Museum of Modern Art, 1990.

Nonwestern Art and Cultures

Barrow, Terrence. *An Illustrated Guide To Maori Art.* Honolulu: University of Hawaii Press, 1984.

———.*The Art of Tahiti and the Neighbouring Society, Austral and Cook Islands.* New York: Thames and Hudson Inc., 1979.

Ben-Amos, Paula. *The Art of Benin.* Thames and Hudson Inc., 1980.

Braun, Barbara. *Pre-Columbian Art and the Post-Columbian World: Ancient American Sources of Modern Art.* New York Harry N. Abrams Inc., 1993.

Chanda, Jacqueline. *African Arts and Cultures.* Worcester, MA: Davis Publications, Inc., 1993.

Corbin, George A. *Native Arts of North America, Africa, and the South Pacific: An Introduction.* Harper & Row, 1988.

Courtney-Clarke, Margaret. *African Canvas: The Art of West African Women.* New York: Rizzoli International Publications Inc., 1990.

Creswell, K. A. C. *A Short Account of Early Muslim Architecture.* Rev. and enl. ed. Aldershot, England: Scolar, 1968.

D'Alleva, Anne. *Native American Arts and Cultures.* Worcester, MA: Davis Publications, Inc., 1993.

Exploring the Visual Art of Oceania: Australia, Melanasis, Micronesia, and Polynesia. Honolulu: University of Hawaii Press, 1979.

Goodwin, Godfrey. *A History of Ottoman Architecture.* New York: Thames and Hudson Inc., 1992.

Guidoni, Enrico. *Primitive Architecture.* New York: Rizzoli International Publications Inc., 1987.

Heyden, D. and Gendrop, P. *Pre-Columbian Architecture of Mesoamerica.* New York: Rizzoli International Publications Inc., 1988.

Hoag, John D. *Islamic Architecture.* New York: Rizzoli International Publications Inc., 1987.

Hutt, Julia. *Understanding Far Eastern Art: A Complete Guide to the Arts of China, Japan, and Korea.* New York: Dutton, 1987.

Myth of Primitivism: Perspectives on Art, The. New York: Routledge, 1991.

National Museum of African Art. *The Art of West African Kingdoms.* Washington D.C.: Smithsonian Institution Press, 1987.

Thomas, Nicholas. *Oceanic Art.* London: Thames and Hudson Inc., 1995.

Thorp, Robert L. *Son of Heaven: Imperial Arts of China.* Seattle: Son of Heaven Press, 1988.

Sabloff, Jeremy A. *The Cities of Ancient Mexico.* New York: Thames and Hudson Inc., 1989.

Individual Artists/ Museum Catalogues

Many books on individual artists and museum catalogues from various specialized exhibitions can be found. Museum libraries and bookstores are well stocked with such publications.

Electronic Media

CD-ROM Disks

American Visions

Ancient Egyptian Art: The Brooklyn Museum. Digital Collections, Inc.

A Passion for Art: Corbis

Art Gallery: The Collection of the National Gallery, London. Microsoft Corporation.

Ancient Lands. Microsoft Corporation.

Encarta: The Complete Multimedia Encyclopedia. Microsoft Corporation.

The Great Buildings Collection. Van Nostrand Reinhold.

Great Paintings: Renaissance to Impressionism—The Frick Collection. Digital Collections, Inc.

Masterworks of Japanese Painting: The Etsulo and Joe Price Collection: Digital Collections, Inc.

Tate Gallery: ATTICA Cybernetics

The New Grolier Multimedia Encyclopedia. Grolier Electronic Publishing.

Perseus 1.0. Yale University Press.

Videodiscs

American Art from the National Gallery of Art. National Gallery of Art.

Art of the Western World Series. The Annenberg/CPB Project.

A Day in the Country: Impressionism and the French Landscape. Comco Productions.

Dream Machine Series. Voyager Company.

The First Emperor of China. Voyager Company.

The Louvre Videodisc Series. Voyager Company.

Masterpieces of Italian Art Series. Crystal Productions.

Masterpieces of the Met. Metropolitan Museum of Art.

Musée d'Orsay.National Gallery of Art. Videodisc Publishing Inc.

New Ways of Seeing: Picasso, Braque and the Cubists. Home Vision.

Perseus 1.0. Yale University Press.

Regard for the Planet. Voyager Company.

Salamandre: Châteaux of the Loire. Voyager Company.

With Open Eyes: Images from the Art Institute of Chicago.

Videos

Abstract Expressionism. Crystal Productions.

American Art from the National Gallery of Art. National Gallery of Art.

Ancient Egypt. Time-Life Films.

Ancient Greece. BBC Television.

Art Appreciation. Crystal Productions.

Art of the Western World. The Annenberg/CPB Project.

At the Louvre with the Masters. Home Vision Cinema.

At the Met: Curators' Choice. NVC.

Centre Georges Pompidou: The Big Escalator. RM Arts.

Footloose in History. Crystal Productions.

Introduction to Sculpture. National Gallery of Art.

Light of the Gods. National Gallery of Art.

Masterpieces of British Art. Crystal Productions.

Masterpieces of Italian Art Series. Crystal Productions.

Masterpieces of the Met. Metropolitan Museum of Art.

Masters of Illusion. National Gallery of Art.

Masterworks of Painting. Crystal Productions.

The Mind's Eye. BBC Horizon.

National Gallery of Art. Videodisc Publishing Inc.

New World Visions: American Art and the Metropolitan Museum. WNET, BBC.

20th Century American Art. Crystal Productions.

Sources and Credits

Primary Source Citations

Ch. 1, page 15: Holt, Elizabeth G. *A Documentary History of Art: The Middle Ages & The Renaissance*, vol. I, expanded ed. Princeton: Princeton University Press, 1981. **Ch. 2, page 55**: Nevelson, Louise. *Dawns and Dusks: Taped Conversations with Diana MacKown*. New York: Helen Merill Ltd., 1976. **Ch. 3, page 73**: Goldwater, Robert, Marco Treves, eds. *Artists on Art*. New York: Pantheon, 1972. Shikes, Ralph E. *The Indignant Eye*. Boston: Beacon Press, 1969. **Ch. 4, page 143**: Fong, Wen. *Summer Mountains: The Timeless Landscape*. New York: The Metropolitan Museum of Art, 1975. **Ch. 6, page 201**: Alberti, Leon Battista. *Ten Books on Architecture*. New York: Transatlantic Arts [c.1966]. **Ch. 7, page 227**: Reprinted by permission of the publishers and the Loeb Classical Library from Procopius: *The Buildings*, vol. 7, translated by H.B. Dewing, Cambridge, Mass.: Harvard University Press, 1935. **Ch. 8, page 257**: Evans, Joan. *Monastic Life at Cluny 910-1157*. London: Archon Books, 1968. **Ch. 9, page 299**: Symonds, John Addington. *The Life of Michelangelo Buonarroti*. 3rd ed., 2 vols., New York: Scribners, 1899. **Ch. 10, page 327**: Holt, Elizabeth G. *A Documentary History of Art: The Middle Ages & The Renaissance*, vol. I, expanded ed. Princeton: Princeton University Press, 1981. **Ch. 11, page 377**: Ireland, John. *Hogarth Illustrated*, 3 vols., London: 1791-1798; 1805 edition. **Ch. 12, page 413**: Le Brun, Madame Vigeé. *Souvenirs*. New York: R. Worthington, 1879. **Ch. 13, page 445**: Whistler, J.A. McNeill. *The Gentle Art of Making Enemies*. New York: 1893. **Ch. 14, page 489**: Monks, Noel. *Eyewitness*. Frederick Muller, 1955. **Ch. 15, page 519**: Lawrence, Jacob. "Philosophy of Art," statement solicited by the Whitney Museum of American Art, to relate to the Lawrence painting *Depression* (1950), which they own, May 30, 1951. Whitney Museum Library, Jacob Lawrence Artist File. **Ch. 16, page 531**: Fitch Manes Marston. "Frank Lloyd Wright's War on the Fine Arts." *Horizon* volume 3 no.1, September 1960. **Ch. 17, page 587**: Goldwater, Marge et al. *Jennifer Bartlett* rev. ed. New York: Abbeville Press, 1990. O'Connor, Francis Valentine and Eugene Victor Thaw eds. *Jackson Pollock: A Catalogue Raisonné of Paintings, Drawings, and Other Works* vol 4. New Haven: Yale University Press, 1978. Jaune Quick-To-See Smith from an interview with Trinkett Clark, Curator of Twentieth-Century Art at The Chrysler Museum, Norfolk, VA for the *Parameters* brochure and exhibitiion, October 9, 1992.

Special Feature Artist Portraits and Icons

Ch. 9, page 262: Death Mask of Filippo Brunalleschi, 1446, clay, Museo dell'Opera del Duomo, Florence. **Ch. 9, page 276**: Leonardo da Vinci, Self-Portrait, drawing, Biblioteca Reale, Turin. **Ch. 9, page 288**: El Greco, *Portrait of a Man* (Self-Portrait), oil on canvas, 16" x 12" (40.6 x 30.5 cm), The Metropolitan Museum of Art, New York. **Ch. 10, page 304**: Robert Campin, Flower vase, detail of fig. 10-1, *Mérode Alterpiece*, about 1425-1426, oil on panel, 25" x 10" (64 x 27 cm), The Metropolitan Museum of Art, New York, The Cloisters Collection, 1956. (56. 70). **Ch. 10, page**

314: Albrecht Durer, *Self-Portrait as a Boy*, drawing, The Albertina Museum, Vienna. **Ch. 10, page 322**: Juan Bautista De Toledo, El Escorial, tower, c. 1563-1584, outside Madrid. **Ch. 11, page 332**: Gian Lorenzo Bernini, Self-Portrait, oil on canvas, Galleria Borghese, Rome. **Ch. 11, page 340**: Georges de La Tour, *Magdalen with a Smoking Flame*, detail of fig. 11-14, about 1630-1635, oil on canvas, 46" x 36 1/4" (117 x 92 cm), Los Angeles County Museum of Art, gift of the Ahmanson Foundation. **Ch. 11, page 360**: Diego Velazquez, *Las Meninas*, detail of fig. 11-37, self-portrait of Diego Velazquez, oil on canvas, 124 3/4" x 107 3/4" (317 x 274 cm), Prado Museum, Madrid. **Ch. 11, page 364**: Rosalba Carriera, *Antoine Watteau*, oil on canvas, Museo Civico, Treviso, Italy. **Ch. 12, page 382**: Jacques Louis David, Self-Portrait, oil on canvas, Uffizi Gallery, Florence. **Ch. 12, page 390**: Francisco Goya, Self-Portrait, 1815, oil on canvas, Prado Museum, Madrid. **Ch. 12, page 400**: Anna Elizabeth Klumpke, *Rosa Bonheur*, 1869, oil on canvas, 46 1/8" x 38 5/8" (117.2 x 98.1 cm), The Metropolitan Museum of Art, New York, Gift of the artist in memory of Rosa Bonheur, 1922. **Ch. 12, page 410**: Edward J. Steichen, Self-Portrait, photograph, National Portrait Gallery, Washington, DC. **Ch. 13, page 418**: Claude Monet, photograph, Caisse Nationale des Monuments Historiques et des Sites, Paris. **Ch. 13, page 430**: Laurent, *Georges Seurat*, 1883, conté crayon, 15 1/4" x 11 1/2" (38.75 x 29.25 cm), Département des Arts Graphiques, Paris. **Ch. 13, page 440**: Edward Munch, *Self-Portrait with Female Mask*, 1892, oil on wood, 27 1/2" x 17 1/2" (70 x 44.5 cm), Munch Museum, Oslo. **Ch. 14, page 450**: Juley, Peter A., Diego Rivera, photograph, Peter A. Juley & Son Collection, National Museum of American Art , Washington, DC. **Ch. 14, page 464**: Stella, Joseph, Self-Portrait, 1920's, drawing, Philadelphia Museum of Art: Alice Newton Osborne Fund, Katharine Levin Farrell Fund, Margretta S. Hinchman Fund, Joseph E. Temple Fund and funds contributed by J. R. Massey and Marion Stroud Swingle. **Ch. 14, page 472**: Constantin Brancusi, photograph. **Ch. 14, page 476**: Juley, Peter A., Salvadore Dali, photograph, Peter A. Juley & Son Collection, National Museum of American Art, Washington, DC. **Ch. 14, page 484**: Van Der Zee with Violin, 1931, photograph. **Ch. 15, page 494**: Bellows, George Wesley, Self-Portrait, lithograph, 10 1/2" x 7 7/8 " (26.7 x 20 cm), National Portrait Gallery, Washington, DC. **Ch. 15, page 502**: Georgia O'Keeffe, photograph. **Ch. 15, page 508**: Thomas Hart Benton, photograph. **Ch. 15, page 514**: Jacob Lawrence, photograph, Francine Seders Gallery Ltd. **Ch. 16, page 524**: Mies van der Rohe, photograph, Courtesy of Illinois Institute of Technology. **Ch. 16, page 536**: Michael Graves, photograph. **Ch. 17, page 550**: Portrait of W. de Kooning, photograph, Collection of the Center for Creative Photography, Tuscon, AZ. **Ch. 17, page 556**: Robert Mapplethorpe, Claes Oldenburg , 1989, photograph, Courtesy PaceWildenstein, photograph. **Ch. 17, page 564**: Arkatov, J., Helen Frankenthaler, photograph. **Ch. 17, page 570**: Close, Chuck, Self-Portrait, oil on canvas, 100 x 84 " (254 x 213 cm), Courtesy PaceWildenstein. **Ch. 17, p. 574**: Isamu Noguchi, photograph, Isamu Noguchi Foundation, Inc., Long Island City, NY. **Ch. 17, page 578**: Christo and Jeanne-Claude in front of the Reichstag, Berlin 1991, photograph.

Photo Credits

Peter Accettola, 2-29; The Albertina Museum, Vienna, 10.IC.2, 10-15; Albright-Knox Art Gallery, Buffalo, New York, 2-52, 15-17, 17-4, 17-13, 17-15, 17-20, 17-34; Alinari/Art Resource, NY, 6-29, 8-43, 12-16; American Museum of Natural History, 4-89; Courtesy Amon Carter Musuem, Ft. Worth, 14-54; Courtesy of the Ansel Adams Publishing Rights Trust, 14-56; Archiv Cameraphoto Venizia/Art Resource, NY, 9-34; James Arkatov,17.IC.3; ©ARS, Scala/Art Resource, NY, 13-31; Museum of Art and Archaeology, University of Missouri, Columbia, 5T-b; Art Institute of Chicago, 11-51, 12-18, 12-20, 12-38, 13-19, 13-c, 13-30, 14-25, 14-33, 15-4, 15-11, 15-25, 15-b, 17-35; Art Resource, NY, 8-13, 6-b, 6-d, 7-33, 8-26, 10-16, 12-a, 16-13; Baltimore Museum of Art, 1-6; Bettmann, 8T-d, 11.WT.2, 13T-4, 16T-3, 16T-4, 17T-2, 17T-5, 17T-6; Tom Bernard, 16-26; Michael Bodycomb, 2-d, 8-44, 8-d; Mary Boone Gallery, New York, 17-50; David L. Ryan/The Boston Globe, 14.SL; Bowdoin College Museum of Art, Brunswick, ME, 11-57; Bridgeman/Art Resource, NY, 9T-2, 11T-6, 13-b, 14-30; British Library, London, 7-28, 7-29; British Museum, 1-9, 2-3, 2-42, 4-2, 4-6, 4-35, 4-82, 4-c, 5-10, 5-11, 5-13, 5-16, 5-22, 5-29, 5-30, 6-14, 6-15, 6-40, 7.IC.1, 7-1, 7-2, 7-30, 7-34; British Tourist Authority, 8-33; Gerald F. Brommer, 4-57; The Brooklyn Museum, 4-110, 4-86, 4-93; Courtesy Malcolm Brown Gallery, Cleveland, 2-32; Brown Brothers, Sterling, PA, 15T-1; Suzanne Brown Gallery, Scottsdale, AZ, 4-101; Bryn Mawr College Archives, 1-11; Dan Budnik, 4-16; Hillel Burger, Peabody Museum, Harvard University, 2-40, 2-43, 2-58, 3-3, 4-60, 4-61, 4-62, 4-100, 4-60, 4-61, 4-62, 4-5; Michele Burgess, 2-66, 11T-8, 15T-4; Kimberly Burnham, 4-47; Cameraphoto/Art Resource, NY, 9-45; Camerique/H. A. Roberts, 11.WT.1; Museo e Gallerie di Capodimonte, Naples, 9-40; Richard Carafelli, 2-9, 17-3; Casimir, 8-23; Leo Castelli, Inc., 17-14, 17-a; ©Judy Chicago, 1973,17-47; © Christo, 17-43; Courtesy Circle Fine Arts Corporation, Chicago, IL, 3-10; ©The City of Oakland, The Oakland Museum, 14-57; Geoffrey Clements, 1-a, 3-8, 17-25; Cleveland Museum of Art, 2-21, 2-30, 4-8, 4-28, 4-43, 15-2; ©Stuart Cohen, 11-7; Paula Cooper, Inc., NY, 17-b; In the collection of the Corcoran Gallery of Art, 15.WT; Cranbrook Institute of Science, 4-112; Culver Pictures Inc., 11.SL.1, 11T-b, 12T-3, 12T-5, 12T-6, 13T-2, 14T-5, 15T-c, 15T-d, 17T-3; Daitokuji, Kyoto, Japan, 2-14; Dallas Museum of Art, 13-14, 17-28; Friedmar Damm, 3-20, 8-29, 12-11; Bevan Davies, courtesy of Pace Wildenstein, 17-31; Bob Davis, 4-33; The Detroit Institute of Arts, 3-e, 14-10, 6-33, 11-6, 13-16, 14-b, 15-27, 17-22, 17-41; Mark Downey, 4-52, 4-55; Dumbarton Oaks, Washington, DC, 4-87, 4-88; Karen Durlach, 3-4, 3-d, 4-90; Timothy Eagan, 4-40; Ecole des Beaux-Arts, Paris, 6.SL.2; John Elk Photography, 4-22; Bonnie Elliott, SP.17.6; Lorene Emerson, National Gallery of Art, Washington, DC,11-22; Foto Marburg/Art Resource, NY, 7-31; Fratelli Alinari/Art Resource, NY, 6-32; Fratelli Fabri, Milan/Art Resource, NY, 10.WT.2; Freer Gallery of Art, Smithsonian Institution, Washington, DC, 4.PS.1, 4-27a, 4-27b, 4-30, 4-37, 4-41; Robert Frerck, 6T-2, 1-14, 4-94; © The Frick Collection, New York, 2-62, 10-21, 10-a, 11-45; Isabella Stewart Gardner Museum, Boston, 13.WT; Gemaldegalerie, Staatliche Museen, Berlin-Dahlem,

Index

Acknowledgments

My grateful thanks to the many artists and their representatives who provided both permission and illustration of their works, including Christo and Jeanne-Claude, Chuck Close, Judy Chicago, Duane Hanson, and Bridget Riley. PaceWildenstein, Julie Saul and Mary Boone Galleries in New York provided gratis materials for this book. Dr. Henri Dorra gave permission to use several of his excellent diagrams which add to the book's clarity.

Many museums were helpful in providing photographic materials and documentary information for which I am grateful. They include The Metropolitan Museum of Art, New York, National Gallery, Washington, The Museum of Modern Art, New York, The Nelson-Atkins Museum of Art, Kansas City, Museum of Fine Arts, Boston, Kimbell Art Museum, Fort Worth, Texas, Peabody Museum, Harvard University, Art Institute of Chicago, Philadelphia Art Museum, Detroit Institute of Arts and Los Angeles County Museum of Art. Also the following photo suppliers: Art Resource, New York, Derin Tanyol, Saskia Ltd., Bettmann, Culver Pictures, Oliver Radford, Cambridge, MA, embassy of Zimbabwe, Consulate General of Japan, Boston and International Society for Informational Education, Tokyo.

I would like to thank the following teachers for editorial consultation: Merceda Saffron, West Springfield High School, Springfield VA, Kaye Passmore, Notre Dame Academy, Worcester, MA, Sandi Hammonds, Woodson High School, Fairfax, VA, Sallye Mahan-Cox, Robinson Secondary School, Fairfax, VA, Roger Tomhave, Art Curriculum Specialist, Fairfax County Public Schools, Fairfax, VA, Virginia Fitzpatrick, Moore College of Art, Philadelphia, PA, and Trinket Doty, McLane High School, Fairfax, VA.

I express my special thanks to those who went out of their way to help, encourage, and express interest in the book as it developed. To Dave Kohl who supplied many visuals and the basic text for Chapter 4. His knowledge and friendship are deeply appreciated. To Davis Publications, who for so long have supported art education and who eagerly and consistently supported this project from its initial stages to this third edition. To Gerald Stashak and Wyatt Wade who have always supported my efforts in working with Davis Publications. To Helen Ronan who worked mightily on this third edition, and whose insight, editorship and perseverance were vital in this evolving process of revision and publication. Thanks also to Douglass Scott, WGBH Design, for superb workmanship and a very positive approach to this project.

And to my wife, Georgia, whose patience, understanding, and constant help in many ways are most appreciated.

I thank you all!

Gerald F. Brommer

Studio City, California
December, 1995

Managing Editor: Wyatt Wade
Associate Editor: Helen Ronan
Production Editors: Nancy Bedau,
    Nancy Burnett
Production: Steven Vogelsang
Copyeditor: Janet Stone
Contributing Editors: Carol Marshall,
    Abby Remer
Photo Research: Ewa Moncure
Editorial Assistance: Jane Boland

Design: Douglass Scott,
Cathleen Damplo, WGBH Design

Editorial Consultants:

Trinket Doty
McLane High School, Fairfax, VA

Virginia Fitzpatrick
Moore College of Art, Philadelphia, PA

Sandi Hammonds
Woodson High School, Fairfax, VA

Sallye Mahan-Cox
Robinson Secondary School, Fairfax, VA

Kaye Passmore
Notre Dame Academy, Worcester, MA

Merceda Saffron
West Springfield High School, Springfield, VA

Roger Tomhave, Art Curriculum Specialist
Fairfax County Public Schools, VA

Front Cover: *Funerary Mask of Tutankhamun*, 1352 B.C., 18th Dynasty. Gold, lapis, cloisonné, quartz. 21 1/4" (54 cm) tall. Thebes. Cairo Museum, Egypt. Photo by Fred J. Maroon.
Back Cover: *Funerary Mask of Tutankhamun*. Photo by Giraudon/Art Resource, New York.

Jacob Lawrence,
*Library Series–
Schomburg*, 1986.
Gouache on paper,
30" x 22".
Courtesy of the
artist and Francine
Seders Gallery,
Seattle.

Text Resources

Contextual Information

Multicultural Connections

General: Religious art from other cultures 250, Cacao Bean 324, The Image of the Horse 467

African: The Kingdom of Nubia 180, The Kingdom of Ghana 215, The Mali Empire 224, The Zimbabwe Culture 234, Ife Bronzes 238, Kilwa 280, The Kongo Kingdom 310, African Printmaking Techniques 317, Slave Trade 318

African-American: Charles White 457

Australian: Australian Art 452

Cambodian: The Temple of Angkor Wat 224

Chinese: Confucius 180-181, The Invention of Paper 188-189, Calligraphy 220, Art of the People's Republic of China 519

Indian: The Stupa of Sanchi 195

Islamic: The Thousand and One Nights 273

Japanese: The Tea Ceremony 272, Raku-ware 284, Kabuki 292, Hokusai 384

Mexican: Posada and the Mexican Civil War 461

Middle Eastern: Nomadic Architecture 533, The Influence of Ancient Persia 482

Native American: The Mound Builders 194, The Anasazi 244, Navajo Silversmithing 388, Native Americans in American Landscape Painting 396, Crazy Horse 511, Native American Architecture 529, Sand Painting 553

Pre-Columbian: The Olmec Civilization 176, Earliest Calendar in Mexico 188, Mesoamerican Ballgames 214, Chocolate 245, The Inca Empire 248

Primary-Source Connections

15, 55, 73, 143, 169, 201, 227, 257, 299, 327, 377, 413, 445, 489, 519, 545, 587

Conservation Notes

109, 186, 196, 216, 245, 487, 565

Cooperative Learning

15, 63, 140, 183, 224, 243, 293, 325, 392, 500, 540, 542

Inquiry

13, 37, 64, 134, 140, 236, 252, 264, 269, 291, 397, 398, 404, 424, 452, 474, 480, 512, 526, 531, 539, 563, 584

Materials and Techniques

22, 28, 31, 34, 50, 52, 80, 84, 97, 254, 271, 307, 308, 316, 402, 421, 424, 474, 487, 530

Artists and Their Works

Art Materials

Media

Media \ Chapter	1		2		3		4		5		6		7	
Activity	1	2	1	2	1	2	1	2	1	2	1	2	1	2
acrylic			●											
cardboard					●				●					
cellophane														
charcoal														
charcoal, vine													●	
clay, modeling							●		●					
clay, plasticine														
clay, terra cotta											●			
cloth: cotton, wool														
cloth: burlap, muslin														
colored pencil					●									
Conté crayon														
felt-tip markers		●		●										
felt-tip markers, fine	●	●			●									●
house paint														
pastels/pastel pencils														
pen and ink														
pencils	●				●						●	●		●
plaster of Paris												●		
prismacolor			●											
rock									●					
scrap metal									●					
string (or fishing line)														
tempera			●		●	●								●
vinyl														
watercolor			●									●		
wire									●					
wood									●					

Paper/Surfaces

Paper/Surfaces \ Chapter	1		2		3		4		5		6		7	
Activity	1	2	1	2	1	2	1	2	1	2	1	2	1	2
bristol board														
canvas														
chipboard														
construction paper														
drawing, white														
4 x 6														●
6 x 9														●
8 1/2 x 11						●								
11 x 14			●	●	●									
12 x 18			●								●	●		
15 x 22			●									●		
18 x 24			●									●		
embroidery transfer														
Kraft paper								●						
newsprint														
poster board 12 x 18		●												
poster board 18 x 24		●												
railroad board														
sketchbook														
strips	●													
tracing paper														
watercolor paper														

● = required, ● = optional

Tools

Chapter		1		2		3		4		5		6		7	
Activity		1	2	1	2	1	2	1	2	1	2	1	2	1	2
brushes				●		●	●		●					●	
clay tools								●							
drawing board													●		
embroidery floss															
eraser		●													
etching tools															
glue, white			●		●										
glue, clear									●						
kneaded erasers													●		●
mat knife															
needles, sewing															
needles, embroidery															
paint mixing trays				●		●	●								
ruler/straight edge		●				●						●			
scissors		●	●		●	●			●						
tape			●		●										
templates															
torchons															
water/container				●		●	●	●				●		●	

Other

Chapter		1		2		3		4		5		6		7	
Activity		1	2	1	2	1	2	1	2	1	2	1	2	1	2
brown paper bags									●						
bucket														●	
buttons									●						
clips, bull															
felt									●						
foam rubber filling															
found objects		●													
embroidery hoops															
iron/board															
magazines			●		●										
masonite boards															
mirrors									●			●			
newspaper								●				●		●	
paper clips														●	
photographs												●			
plastic, bags								●				●			
plastic, cloth								●				●			
spray bottle								●				●			
spray fixative															
Styrofoam platter												●			
terry-cloth towel												●			
thread															
toothpicks									●						
wooden sticks															
yarn									●						

● = required, ● = optional

8		9		10		11		12		13		14		15		16		17	
1	2	1	2	1	2	1	2	1	2	1	2	1	2	1	2	1	2	1	2
			●					●				●		●		●			●
			●																
●																			
																●			
						●													
	●						●								●		●		
										●	●								
	●														●				
																		●	
●																			
			●											●					
															●		●		
●	●												●		●		●		
																●	●	●	
															●				
										●	●								
			●					●						●		●			●
										●	●								
																●			
																		●	
●																			
●																			
												●							
										●	●								
			●																
			●																
										●	●								
																●		●	
															●				
															●				

Art Suppliers

Distributors, Manufacturers General

American Art Clay Co., Inc.
Armada Art Inc.
Art Extension Press
Art Supplies Wholesale
Barry Art Supplies
Dick Blick Co.
Chaselle, Inc.
Cheap Joe's Art Stuff
Co-op Artists Mat'l.
J.L. Hammett
Martin/F. Weber Co.
Nasco Arts and Crafts
S & S Worldwide
Sax Arts & Crafts
Triarco Arts & Crafts, Inc.
United Art & Education
    Supply
Utrecht Mfg. Corp.
Vanguard Crafts, Inc.
R.B. Walter Art & Craft Materials

Adhesives, Fixatives

Glue, Paste, Rubber Cement
American Art Clay Co., Inc.
American Tombow, Inc.
Binney & Smith Inc.
Borden, Inc.
Crown Art Products Co. Inc.
Koh-I-Noor
Pentel of America
Scratch-Art Co., Inc.

Calligraphy Supplies

Bee Paper Co., Inc.
Empire Berol USA
Hunt Manufacturing Co.
Koh-I-Noor
Pen, Ink
Sakura of America, Inc.
Scratch Art Co., Inc.
Sign and Art System
Staedtler, Inc.

Ceramics

Clay & Glazes
American Art Clay Co., Inc.
Amherst Potters Supply
A.R.T. Studio Clay Company
Bailey Ceramic Supply
Continental Clay
Creative Paperclay Co., Inc.
Georgies Ceramic & Clay Co.
Laguna Clay Company
Mile Hi Ceramics Inc.
Minnesota Clay Co. USA
Montoya/MAS Int'l., Inc.
Sargent Art Inc.
Texas Pottery Supply

Kilns
American Art Clay Co., Inc.
Amherst Potters Supply
A.R.T. Studio Clay Co.
Bailey Ceramic Supply
Contemporary Kiln, Inc.
Continental Clay Co.
Georgies Ceramic & Clay Co.
Laguna Clay Company
Mile Hi Ceramics
Minnesota Clay Co. USA
Montoya/MAS Int'l.
Paragon Industries, Inc.
Skutt Ceramic Products, Inc.
Texas Pottery Supply
West Coast Kiln and Supply

Kiln Venting Systems
American Art Clay Co., Inc.
Amherst Potters Supply
A.R.T. Studio Clay Company
Bailey Ceramic Supply
Continental Clay Co.
Georgies Ceramic & Clay Co.
Laguna Clay Company
Mile Hi Ceramics
Minnesota Clay Co. USA
Edward Orton Jr. Ceramic Foundation
Paragon Industries, Inc.
Skutt Ceramic Products, Inc.
Texas Pottery Supply
Vent-A-Kiln Corporation

Tool & Supplies
American Art Clay Co., Inc.
Amherst Potters Supply
A.R.T. Studio Clay Company

Bailey Ceramic Supply
Continental Clay Co.
Debcor, Inc.
Duralite, Inc.
Falcon Co.
Georgies Ceramic & Clay Co.
Kemper Enterprises, Inc.
Laguna Clay Company
Mile Hi Ceramics, Inc.
Minnesota Clay Co. USA
Montoya/MAS, Int'l.
Edward Orton Jr. Ceramic Foundation
Texas Pottery Supply
West Coast Kiln and Supply

Color Wheels

Crescent Cardboard Co.
Crystal Productions
M. Grumbacher, Inc.
Nita Leland Studio

Cutters, Knives and Scissors

Binney & Smith Co. Inc.
Fiskars Manufacturing Corp.
Russell Harrington Cutlery
Hunt Manufacturing Co.
Quartet Manufacturing Co.

Drawing Supplies

Boards
Ampersand Art Supply
Bee Paper Co., Inc.
Crescent Cardboard Co.
M. Grumbacher, Inc.
Koh-I-Noor
Quartet Manufacturing Co.
Scratch Art Company
Strathmore Paper

Crayons
Binney & Smith Inc.
Empire Berol USA
General Pencil Co.
Lyra/William Bruce Co.
Sakura of America, Inc.
Sargent Art, Inc.
Scratch Art Co. Inc.

Ink
Graphic Chemical & Ink Co.
Hunt Manufacturing Co.
Koh-I-Noor

Markers
American Tombow, Inc.
Binney & Smith Inc.
Empire Berol USA
General Pencil Co.
Koh-I-Noor
Lyra/William Bruce Co.
Quartet Manufacturing Co.
Rock Paint
Sakura of America, Inc.
Sargent Art, Inc.
Sign and Art System
Staedtler

Paper & Pads
Bee Paper Co., Inc.
Bemiss-Jason Corporation
Crescent Cardboard Co.
M. Grumbacher, Inc.
Hunt Manufacturing Co.
Pacon Corporation
Scratch Art Co., Inc.
Strathmore Paper Co.

Pastels/Chalk
Binney & Smith Inc.
Empire Berol USA
General Pencil Co.
M. Grumbacher, Inc.
Hunt Manufacturing Co.
Koh-I-Noor
Lyra/William Bruce Co.
Quartet Manufacturing Co.
Sakura of America, Inc.
Sargent Art, Inc.

Pencils (Charcoal & Colored)
American Tombow, Inc.
Binney & Smith Inc.
Empire Berol USA
General Pencil Co.
M. Grumbacher, Inc.
Hunt Manufacturing Co.

Koh-I-Noor
Lyra/William Bruce Co.
Sargent Art Inc.
Staedtler, Inc.

Pens
American Tombow, Inc.
Empire Berol USA
General Pencil Co.
Hunt Manufacturing Co.

Koh-I-Noor
Lyra/William Bruce Co.
Sakura of America, Inc.
Scratch Art Co., Inc.
Staedtler, Inc.

Fabrics

Burlap, Felt, Silk
Bemiss-Jason Corporation
Chicago Canvas & Supply
DEKA/Decart, Inc.
Rupert, Gibbon & Spider
Silkpaint Corporation
Testfabrics, Inc.

Painting and Dyeing Supplies

General
Binney & Smith Inc.
Chicago Canvas & Supply
Crown Arts Products Co.
DEKA/Decart, Inc.
Farquhar International
　　Limited
Flex Flo Dispenser/Lamp Products
M. Grumbacher, Inc.
PRO Chemical & Dye Inc.
Silkpaint Corp.
Siphon Art Products

Silkpainting
Crown Arts Products Co.
DEKA/Decart, Inc.
PRO Chemical & Dye Inc.
Rupert, Gibbon & Spider
Silkpaint Corporation

Painting Supplies

Brushes, Cleaners
Binney & Smith Inc.
Empire Berol USA
General Pencil Co.
M. Grumbacher, Inc.
Koh-I-Noor

Marsel Co.
Norchem Industries Inc.
Sargent Art, Inc.

Canvas & Supplies
Chicago Canvas & Supply
Crown Arts Products Co.
Eldon Enterprises
M. Grumbacher, Inc.
Stretchmaster

Easels
Bemiss-Jason Corp.
Quartet Manufacturing Co.

Paints
(Acrylics, Oils, Tempera, Watercolor)
Binney & Smith Inc.
Chroma Acrylics, Inc.
Colorations
DEKA/Decart, Inc.
Empire Berol USA
M. Grumbacher, Inc.
Hunt Manufacturing Co.
Koh-I-Noor
Laguna Clay Company
Nova Color Artists' Acrylic Paint
PRO Chemical & Dye, Inc.
Quartet Manufacturing Co.
Rock Paint
Sargent Art, Inc.
Siphon Art Products

Palettes
Bee Paper Co., Inc.
Bemiss-Jason Corp.
Empire Berol USA
M. Grumbacher, Inc.

Paper

Watercolor, Construction,
Tissue, Tracing, Transfer, etc.
Bee Paper Co., Inc.
Bemiss-Jason Corporation
Crescent Cardboard Co.
M. Grumbacher, Inc.
Hunt Manufacturing Co.
Saral Paper Co.
Scratch Art Co., Inc.
Strathmore Paper

Papermaking & Marbling Supplies
Basic Crafts Co.
Bemiss-Jason Corporation
DEKA/Decart, Inc.
The Famport Company
Gold's Artworks, Inc.
Hunt Manufacturing Co.
Welsh Products, Inc.

Photographic Supplies

D'Ing Products

Printmaking

Blockprinting, Presses, Tools, Supplies

Bemiss–Jason Corporation
DEKA/Decart, Inc.
Graphic Chemical & Ink Co.
Hunt Manufacturing Co.
Jiffy Foam, Inc.
Rembrandt Graphic Arts
Rock Paint
Scratch Art Co., Inc.

Etching, Press, Tools, Supplies

American Art Clay Co., Inc.
Graphic Chemical & Ink Co.
Hunt Manufacturing Co.
Rembrandt Graphic Arts

Sculpture Supplies

American Art Clay Co., Inc.
Bailey Ceramic Supply
Bemiss-Jason Corporation
Binney & Smith Inc.
Continental Clay Co.
Creative Paperclay Co., Inc.
Jiffy Foam, Inc.
Kemper Enterprises Inc.
Laguna Clay Company
Mile Hi Ceramics, Inc.
Minnesota Clay Co. USA
Montoya/MAS International, Inc.
Sierra Hills Stone
Stewarts of CA, Inc.
Texas Pottery Supply
West Coast Kiln and Supply

Yarns, Fibers, Plastic Lace, Weaving Supplies

Bemiss-Jason Corporation
Phyllis Damon Associates
DEKA/Decart, Inc.
Good Wood Ltd.
Harrisville Designs, Inc.
School Products Co., Inc.

Directory of Suppliers

A

American Art Clay Co., Inc. 4717 West 16th St., Indianapolis, IN 46222
American Tombow, Inc, 4467-C Park Dr., Atlanta, GA 30329
Amherst Potters Supply Inc., 47 East St., Hadley, MA 01035
Ampersand Art Supply, 1500 East Fourth St., Austin, TX 78702
Armada Art Inc., 290 Nye Ave., Irvington, NJ 07111
Art Extension Press, P.O. Box 389, Westport, CT 06881
A.R.T. Studio Clay Company, 1555 Louis Ave., Elk Grove Village, IL 60007
Art Supplies Wholesale, 4 Enon St., Rte. 1A, Beverly, MA 01915

B

Bailey Ceramic Supply, 62-68 Tenbroeck Ave, Kingston, NY 12401
Barry Art Supply, 126 N. Orange Ave., Sarasota, FL 34236
Basic Crafts Co., 1201 Broadway, New York, NY 10001
Bee Paper Co., Inc., P.O. Box 2366, Wayne, NJ 07470
Bemiss-Jason Corp., Dept. SA, P.O. Box 699, Neenah, WI 54957
Binney & Smith Inc., 1100 Church Lane, Easton, PA 18042
Dick Blick Co., P.O. Box 1267, Galesburg, IL 61402
Borden, Inc., 180 E. Broad St., 13th Floor, Columbus, OH 43215

C

Chaselle, Inc., 9645 Gerwig Lane, Columbia, MD 21046
Cheap Joe's Art Stuff, 300A Industrial Park, Boone, NC 28607
Chicago Canvas & Supply,3719 W. Lawrence, Chicago, IL 60625
Chroma Acrylics, Inc., 205 Bucky Dr., Lititz, PA 17543
Colorations, 30799 Pinetree Rd., Suite 232, Cleveland, OH 44124
Contemporary Kiln, Inc., 26-O Commercial Blvd., Novato, CA 94949
Continental Clay Co., 1101 Stinson Blvd. NE, Minneapolis, MN 55413
Co-op Artists' Materials, P.O. Box 53097, Atlanta, GA 30355
Creative Paperclay Co., Inc.1800 S. Robertson Blvd., #907, Los Angeles, CA 90035

Crescent Cardboard Co., 100 W. Willow Rd., Wheeling, IL 60090
Crown Arts Products Co., 90 Dayton Ave., Passaic, NJ 07055
Crystal Productions, 1812 Johns Dr., P.O. Box 2159, Glenview, IL 60025

D,E

D'Ing Products, P.O. Box 24272, 5695 Cherokee Rd., Lyndhurst, OH 44124
Phyllis Damon Associates, Box 224, Wellesley Hills, MA 02181
Debcor, Inc., 513 W. Taft Dr., South Holland, IL 60473
DEKA/Decart, Inc., Box 309, Morrisville, VT 05661
Duralite,Inc., 15 School St., Riverton, CT 06065
Eldon Enterprises, P.O. Box 355, Huron, OH 44839
Empire Berol USA, 105 Westpark Drive, Brentwood, TN 37024-2248

F,G

Falcon Company, 770 Cole Ranch Rd., Encinitas, CA 92024
The Famport Company, 145 Windsor Ave., Rockville Centre, NY 11570-5910
Farquhar International Limited, 937 Dillingham Rd., Pickering, Ontario, Canada, L1W 1Z7
Fiskars Manufacturing Corp, 7811 W. Stewart Ave., Wausau, WI 54401
Flex Flo Dispenser/Lamp Products, P.O. Box 771, Jamestown, NY 14702
General Pencil Co., Box 5311, Redwood City, CA 94063
Georgies Ceramic & Clay Co., 756 NE Lombard, Portland, OR 97211
Gold's Artworks, Inc., 2100 N. Pine St., Lumberton, NC 28358
Good Wood Ltd., Rt.2, Box 447A, Bethel, VT 05032
Graphic Chemical & Ink Co, P.O. Box 27, Villa Park, IL 60181
M Grumbacher, Inc., 100 North St., P.O. Box 68, Cranbury, NJ 08804-0068

H,I,J

J.L. Hammett, P.O. Box 9057, Braintree, MA 02184
Russell Harrington Cutlery, 44 Green River St., Southbridge, MA 01550
Harrisville Designs, Center Village, P.O. Box 806, Harrisville, NH 03450
Hunt Mfg. Co., 230 South Broad St., Philadelphia, PA 19102
Jiffy Foam, Inc., 221 Third St., Newport, RI 02840

K,L,M

Kemper Enterprises, 13595 12th St., Chino, CA 91710

Koh-I-Noor, 100 North St., Bloomsburg, NJ 08804

Laguna Clay Company, 14400 Lomitas Ave., City of Industry, CA 91746

Nita Leland Studio, P.O. Box 3137, Dayton, OH 45401-3137

Lyra/William Bruce Co.,P.O. Box 1027, Willowgrove, PA 19090

Marsel Co., P.O. Box 382, Hartsdale, NY 10530

Martin/F. Weber Co., 2727 Southampton Rd., Southampton, PA 19154

Mile Hi Ceramics Inc., 77 Lipan St., Denver, CO 80223-1540

Minnesota Clay, 8001 Grand Ave., South, Bloomington, MN 55420

Montoya/MAS International, Inc., 435 Southern Blvd., W. Palm Beach, FL 33405

N,O

Nasco Arts and Crafts, 901 Janesville Ave., Ft. Atkinson, WI 53538-0901

Norchem Industries Inc., P.O. Box 659, Benton City, WA 99320

Nova Color Artists' Acrylic Paint, 5894 Blackwelder St., Culver City, CA 90232

Orton Ceramic Foundation, 6991 Old 3C Highway, Westerville, OH 43082

P,Q,R

Pacon Corp, P.O. Box 2397, Appleton, WI 54913-2397

Paragon Industries, Inc., 2011 South Town East Blvd., Mesquite, TX 75149-1122

PRO Chemical & Dye Inc., P.O. Box 14, Somerset, MA 02726

Quartet Manufacturing, Inc., 5700 Old Orchard Rd., Skokie, IL 60077

Rembrandt Graphic Arts, P.O. Box 130, Rosemont, NJ 08556

Rock Paint,P.O. Box 482, Milton, WI 53583

Rupert, Gibbon & Spider, P.O. Box 425, Healdsburg, CA 95448

S

S & S Worldwide, P.O Box 513, Colchester, CT 06415

Sakura of America, Inc., 30780 San Clemente St., Haywood, CA 94544

Saral Paper, 322 West 57th St., Suite #30-T, New York, NY 10019

Sargent Art, Inc., 100 E. Diamond Ave., P.O. Box 218, Hazleton, PA 18201

Sax Arts & Crafts, P.O. Box 51710, New Berlin, WI 53151

School Products Co, Inc. 1201 Broadway, New York, NY 10001

Scratch Art Co., Inc., P.O. Box 303, Avon, MA 02322

Sierra Hills Stone, P.O. Box 572, Angels Camp, CA 95222

Sign and Art System, P.O. Box 434, Greensboro, NC, 27402

Siphon Art Products, P.O. Box 150710, San Rafeal, CA 94915

Silkpaint Corporation, P.O. Box 18, Waldron, MO 64092

Skutt Ceramic Products, Inc., 2618 SE Steele St., Portland, OR 97202

Staedtler, Inc., 21900 Plummer St., Chatsworth, CA 91311

Strathmore Paper Co., S. Broad St., Westfleld, MA 01085

Stewarts of CA, Inc., 16055 Heron Ave., La Miranda, CA 90638

T,U

Testfabrics, P.O. Box 420, 200 Blackford Ave., Middlesex, NJ 08846

Texas Pottery Supply, P.O. Box 161305, 801 D Airway Drive, Ft. Worth, TX 76106

Triarco Arts & Crafts, Inc., 14650 28th Ave., N., Plymouth, MN 55447

United Art & Education Supply, P.O. Box 9219, Ft. Wayne, IN 46899

Utrecht Mfg., Corp, 111 Fourth Ave., New York, NY 10003

V,W,X,Y,Z

Vanguard Crafts, Inc., 1081 E. 48th St., Brooklyn, NY 11234

Vent-A-Kiln Corporation, 621 Hertel Ave., Buffalo, NY 14207

R.B. Walter Art & Craft Materials, P.O. Box 51795, New Berlin, WI 53151

Welsh Products, Inc., Box 845., Benicia, CA 94510

West Coast Kiln and Supply, 10003 Custer, Lucerne Valley, CA 92356

Safety in the Classroom

The secondary art program utilizes all kinds of specialized equipment, materials and tools. Precautions must be taken to insure that working with art materials does not lead to student illness or injury. **Failure to take necessary precautions may result in litigation if students become ill or are injured in the art room.** While restrictions are necessary, the teacher should be assured that nontoxic materials can usually be substituted for toxic ones with little or no extra cost, and good classroom management will prevent accidents.

Under the art material labeling law passed by Congress in October, 1988, every manufacturer, distributor, retailer and some purchasers (schools) have a legal responsibility to comply with this law. The law amended the Federal Hazardous Substances Act to require art and craft materials manufacturers to evaluate their products for their ability to cause chronic illness and to place labels on those that do.

CP, AP, and HL. What do they mean? The Art and Craft Materials Institute, Inc. has sponsored a certification program for art materials, certifying that these products are nontoxic and meet standards of quality and performance.

CP (Certified Product) are nontoxic, even if *ingested, inhaled* or *absorbed*, and meet or exceed specific quality standards of material, workmanship, working qualities and color.

AP (Approved Products) are nontoxic, even if *ingested, inhaled* or *absorbed*. Some nontoxic products bear the **HL (Health Label)** seal with the wording, "Nontoxic," "No Health Labeling Required." Products requiring cautions bear the HL label with appropriate cautionary and safe use instructions.

Teachers should check with their school administrators to determine if the state board of education has prepared a document concerning art and craft materials that cannot be used in the classroom, and listed products that may be used in all grade levels. If no list is locally available, contact The Art and Craft Materials Institute, Inc., 715 Boylston Street, Boston, MA, 02116 for a list of art products bearing the CP, AP, or HL/Nontoxic Seal.

In addition to determining that only nontoxic media are available in the classroom, the teacher is responsible for instruction in how to use all tools and equipment correctly and safely.

Make sure that the artroom has accident preventing items such as the following:

• Signs on or near all work areas and equipment where injury might occur if students are careless, or should have instruction prior to use of the equipment.

• Protective equipment such as safety glasses, respiratory masks and gloves.

• A first aid kit containing antiseptics, bandages and compresses.

• Adequate ventilation to exhaust fumes from kilns, dust and procedures such as melting wax for batik.

• Safety storage cabinets and safety cans for flammable liquids. It is preferable not to keep them in the classroom.

• Self-closing waste cans for saturated rags.

• Soap and water wash-up facilities.

• Lock cabinets for hazardous tools and equipment.

• Rules posted beside all machines.

Precautions the teacher may take:

• Always demonstrate the use of hand and power tools and machines.

• During demonstrations, caution students concerning any potential hazards related to incorrect use of equipment.

• Give safety tests before permitting students to use tools and machines, and keep the tests on file.

• Establish a safety zone around all hazardous equipment.

• Establish a dress code for safety indicating rules about clothing, jewelry and hair in order to prevent accidents.

• Establish a code of behavior conducive to the safety of individuals and their classmates, and enforce it.

• Keep aisles and exits clear.

• Be aware of any special problems among students such as allergy, epilepsy, fainting or handicap.

Some "Do Nots" for the Safety Conscious Art Teacher:

• Do not absent yourself from the art room when pupils are present.

• Do not ignore irresponsible behavior and immature actions in the art room.

• Do not make the use of all tools and machines compulsory.

• Do not permit students to work in the art room without supervision.

• Do not permit pupils that you believe to be accident prone to use power equipment. Check on the eligibility of some mainstreamed students to use power tools.

Teachers should demonstrate constant concern for safety in the art room, and teach by example to help students accept responsibility for accident prevention. For a thorough discussion of health and safety hazards associated with specific media and procedures see *Safety in the Artroom* by Charles Qualley, 1986.

Richard Salome, 1995

Multicultural Art Education

The racial and ethnic mix of the American population has changed dramatically in the past decade, with nearly one in every four Americans claiming African, Asian, Hispanic or Native American ancestry.

Multicultural art education is not just for minority students. It provides a new perspective for everyone to understand that a democratic culture is ever-changing. A multicultural curriculum recognizes the role played by the indigenous peoples of this continent as well as its immigrants.

Multicultural art education can benefit students from all cultural groups equally. The visual arts provide an obvious connection across cultures and with past civilizations. For students more concerned with "becoming an American" than learning about their cultural heritage, the opportunity to access information about their cultural identity may be a source of discomfort. For multicultural education to succeed, teachers must perceive it as dealing with the contributions of all peoples regardless of color or cultural background. A major challenge for the teacher is the identification of art experiences that can create a common ground among students of various cultures. (Richard Salome, 1995)

Discovering Art History provides many opportunities for creating this common ground. Though it is primarily a survey of Western art, every chapter of the book has a multicultural element. The first two chapters introduce the student to art appreciation by utilizing works of art from around the world. The third chapter deals with cross-cultural influences. Chapter four is a broad survey of art outside of the Western tradition. Chapters five through seventeen take an in-depth look at the art of the Western world. Integrated into these thirteen chapters are world cultural timelines. These timelines allow students to see the world events that coincided with the art and history in each chapter. The classroom connection activities sometimes incorporate a multicultural component. For example, while studying tapestries of the Middle Ages and making one themselves, students will see how their peers in New City, New York made a tapestry entitled *Diversity*. The project helped the New City students explore the wide diversity of cultures at their school.

In this Teacher's Edition you will find a multitude of ways to make multicultural and cross-cultural connections. Questions and suggested discussion topics throughout the book allow students to consider and compare their own cultural heritage with the life and art of long ago. There also is ample opportunity to have them compare those seemingly distant times with contemporary American life. For instance, interesting connections are made between medieval pilgrimage routes in Europe and the arrival of British settlers in North America, as well as the assistance they received from Native Americans. Students also are asked to consider the types of sites to which Americans make pilgrimages today.

These connections make the art being studied come alive with meaning and relevance to the life of the student while also assisting them to more fully comprehend and appreciate the greatest works of art in the Western tradition.

Special Needs

iscovering Art History is easily adaptable to those students with special needs. Making this material accessible will undoubtedly bolster these students' performance in other academic areas such as history, geography, art appreciation etc., while also enhancing their own studio art sensibilities. Regardless of functioning level or degree of disturbance, most artists can successfully incorporate art historical influences provided there is sufficient motivation to drive these connections.

The key to developing this critical motivation lies in introducing the material as part of an individualized intervention. In keeping with the national mainstreaming and inclusion initiatives (now known as IDEA), instructional strategies must be adopted toward the special child's individual learning styles and preferences. Because most students with developmental disabilities, sensory deficits or emotional difficulties are egocentric, learning styles begin with "the self." Material which reflects a child's own thoughts, feelings, memories, culture or gender orientation, will decrease the incidence of indifference, boredom and resistance. As the student begins to identify with the content of artists' work through the ages, there comes a willingness to take risks and entertain ideas that are not so obviously relevant to life in the special education classroom, institution or the streets.

Promoting self identification and personal relevance can be accomplished by addressing several domains of the student's functioning. These domains operate on different psychological and cognitive levels and are mutually enriching and reinforcing.

The first involves **universality.** Art is a universal language that relies upon "illusions" or symbols that cut deeper than cultural orientation and academic capacities. The artworks studied in this volume draw upon those psychological forces which authors E. Gombrich and E. Dissanayake have described as being biologically significant—meaning that all the world's peoples share pre-programmed responses to certain visual forms or schemes.

The mentally retarded child is just as apt to "connect the dots" as he/she might form visual constellations of the night skies and landscapes. The same retarded child might stack cubes or rings to form architectural structures—it need only to be pointed out that such child-like stacking is the very same process used in some of the world's great building systems, such as the pueblos of the Southwest, the Hindu temples of India and Han house models of ancient China. Such elemental processes can be introduced on a sliding scale of conceptual simplicity or complexity without diluting the content and without condescending to the special needs child. Two-dimensional forms such as the circle is another example of a compelling form that is universal to all art making. The circle resonates from its many beginnings: the mother's face or breast, the blazing sun, a drop of water. Whether studying a Greek drinking cup (fig. 1-4), Kollwitz's self-portraits (fig. 14-12), Rouault's *Head of Christ* (fig. 14-7) or the Taj Mahal (fig. 4-24), the primal form of the mandala is engaged. Drawing upon its power is archetypal, unconscious and automatic.

The second domain involves the human forces that derive from **power and aggression.** One cannot escape their ubiquitousness in our culture – they predominate on every personal and soci-etal level. With students for whom aggression is a way of life, art forms that exercise these impulses are often a motivational factor. During studio activities, students may be drawn to the Easter Island figures (fig. 4-60), Malanggen masks (fig. 4-61) or Sepick figures of New Guinea (fig. 4-65) for their life-essence and power. Sexuality also is a constant in life and art. It can be easily seen and grasped in the macho power of Rodin's sculptures, Lautrec's decadent night life, or the primal sensuality of Gauguin's native women. Often artworks propose antidotes for sexual or aggressive action. For example, anger and sensuality are transcended in the repose of the Buddha. By introducing such work to immature or disturbed students, the art teacher demonstrates how powerful emotions and impulses can be safely channeled through symbolic means. The material is both alluring and relevant, hence promoting critical motivation to engage a range of art historical content.

The third domain is that of **culture**, which includes one's own family heritage, peer or other group identification. While family background is a most obvious resource to draw upon, other more discrete cultures might exert a more powerful effect upon relevance and motivation. Most students, regardless of handicap, embrace popular teen culture. Images which reflect Pop-photo realism such as Warhol's soup cans and Duane Hanson's slice-of-life sculptures are readily accessible images. Physically handicapped students may relate to Lautrec and his life struggles. Those with emotional instabilities might be drawn to van Gogh or Munch, while females seem taken with Frida Kahlo. Special education initiatives require that content goes to where the child is currently functioning. Once reached, the teacher attempts to broaden their frame of reference as Lowenfeld (1982) counseled—increasing adaptation and normalization until the student can entertain not just self-specific material but that of a more generalized nature as well.

The final domain is tied to the special child's **developmental level**—issues which impact upon those with mental retardation, and certain visually impaired or autistic students. For students with these and other conditions, the capacity for grade level responses is greatly diminished. Art historical material must be geared to their level, again, without diluting the integrity of the material or student. Artists and artistic styles can be introduced which are reminiscent of the child's own work, such as the mentally retarded child whose figures resemble that of Klee or Miro. Activities which cover a range of figurative styles, from Kandinsky to the X-ray bark paintings of Australian Aborigines allow for different influences to be engaged. By sliding along the developmental art historical scale, students of disparate abilities may connect with important influences while at the same time, achieve a kind of parity within the classroom with their "normal" peers. It communicates that each child can contribute to the class' body of knowledge.

The organizational structure of *Discovering Art History* is designed to accommodate a very flexible program for all student levels. Students with special needs can focus on the chapter openers which present an overview of the period under study. A brief opening text along with a map, timeline and images provide the student with a direct and simple means of learning about the key periods of Western art. By tailoring art history to the individual needs of the student, we provide what is most valuable in education—an atmosphere which looks beyond differences toward mutual respect, empathy and inclusiveness that not only enriches the education of those with special needs, but that of all children.

David R. Henley, 1995

The National Visual Arts Standards

Visual Arts

I n grades 9–12, students extend their study of the visual arts. They continue to use a wide range of subject matter, symbols, meaningful images, and visual expressions. They grow more sophisticated in their employment of the visual arts to reflect their feelings and emotions and continue to expand their abilities to evaluate the merits of their efforts. These standards provide a framework for that study in a way that promotes the maturing students' thinking, working, communicating, reasoning, and investigating skills. The standards also provide for their growing familiarity with the ideas, concepts, issues, dilemmas, and knowledge important in the visual arts. As students gain this knowledge and these skills, they gain in the ability to apply knowledge and skills in the visual arts to their widening personal worlds.

The visual arts range from the folk arts, drawing, and painting, to sculpture and design, from architecture to film and video—and any of these can be used to help students meet the educational goals embodied in these standards. For example, graphic design (or any other field within the visual arts) can be used as the basis for creative activity, historical and cultural investigations, or analysis throughout the standards. The visual arts involve varied tools, techniques, and processes—all of which also provide opportunities for working toward the standards. It is the responsibility of practitioners to choose from among the array of possibilities offered by the visual arts to accomplish specific educational objectives in specific circumstances.

Grades 9–12 Standards

1. Content Standard: Understanding and applying media, techniques and processes

Achievement Standard, Proficient:
a. Students apply media, techniques, and processes with sufficient skill, confidence, and sensitivity that their intentions are carried out in their artworks

b. Students conceive and create works of visual art that demonstrate an understanding of how the communication of their ideas relates to the media, techniques, and processes they use

Achievement Standard, Advanced:
c. Students communicate ideas regularly at a high level of effectiveness in at least one visual arts medium

d. Students initiate, define, and solve challenging visual arts problems independently using intellectual skills such as analysis, synthesis, and evaluation

2. Content Standard: Using knowledge of structures and functions

Achievement Standard, Proficient:
a. Students demonstrate the ability to form and defend judgments about the characteristics and structures to accomplish commercial, personal, communal, or other purposes of art

b. Students evaluate the effectiveness of artworks in terms of organizational structures and functions

c. Students create artworks that use organizational principles and functions to solve specific visual arts problems

Achievement Standard, Advanced:
d. Students demonstrate the ability to compare two or more perspectives about the use of organizational principles and functions in artwork and to defend personal evaluations of these perspectives

e. Students create multiple solutions to specific visual arts problems that demonstrate competence in producing effective relationships between structural choices and artistic functions

3. Content Standard: Choosing and evaluating a range of subject matter, symbols, and ideas

Achievement Standard, Proficient:
a. Students reflect on how artworks differ visually, spatially, temporally, and functionally, and describe how these are related to history and culture

b. Students apply subjects, symbols, and ideas in their artworks and use the skills gained to solve problems in daily life

Achievement Standard, Advanced:
c. Students describe the origins of specific images and ideas and explain why they are of value in their artwork and in the work of others

d. Students evaluate and defend the validity of sources for content and the manner in which subject matter, symbols, and images are used in the student's works and in significant works by others

To meet the standards, students must learn vocabularies and concepts associated with various types of work in the visual arts. As they develop greater fluency in communication in visual, oral, and written form, they must exhibit greater artistic competence through all of these avenues.

In grades 9–12, students develop deeper and more profound works of visual art that reflect the maturation of their creative and problem-solving skills. Students understand the multifaceted interplay of different media, styles, forms, techniques, and processes in the creation of their work.

Students develop increasing abilities to pose insightful questions about contexts, processes, and criteria for evaluation. They use these questions to examine works in light of various analytical methods and to express sophisticated ideas about visual relationships using precise terminology. They can evaluate artistic character and aesthetic qualities in works of art, nature, and human-made environments. They can reflect on the nature of human involvement in art as a viewer, creator, and participant.

Students understand the relationships among art forms and between their own work and that of others. They are able to relate understandings about the historical and cultural contexts of art to situations in contemporary life. They have a broad and in-depth understanding of the meaning and import of the visual world in which they live.

4. Content Standard: Understanding the visual arts in relation to history and cultures

Achievement Standard, Proficient:
a. Students differentiate among a variety of historical and cultural contexts in terms of characteristics and purposes of works of art

b. Students describe the function and explore the meaning of specific art objects within varied cultures, times and places

c. Students analyze relationships of works of art to one another in terms of history, aesthetics, and culture, justifying conclusions made in the analysis and using such conclusions to inform their own art making

Achievement Standard, Advanced:
d. Students analyze and interpret artworks for relationships among form, context, purposes, and critical models, showing understanding of the work of critics, historians, aestheticians, and artists

e. Students analyze common characteristics of visual arts evident across time and among cultural/ethnic groups to formulate analyses, evaluations, and interpretations of meaning

5. Content Standard: Reflecting upon and assessing the characteristics and merits of their work and the work of others

Achievement Standard, Proficient:
a. Students identify intentions of those creating artworks, explore the implications of various purposes, and justify their analyses of purposes in particular works

b. Students describe meanings of artworks by analyzing how specific works are created and how they relate to historical and cultural contexts

c. Students reflect analytically on various interpretations as a means for understanding and evaluating works of visual art

Achievement Standard, Advanced:
d. Students correlate responses to works of visual art with various techniques for communicating meanings, ideas, attitudes, views, and intentions

6. Content Standard: Making connections between visual arts and other disciplines

Achievement Standard, Proficient:
a. Students compare the materials, technologies, media, and processes of the visual arts with those of other arts disciplines as they are used in creation and types of analysis

b. Students compare characteristics of visual arts within a particular historical period or style with ideas, or themes in the humanities or sciences

Achievement Standard, Advanced:
c. Students synthesize the creative and analytical principles and techniques of the visual arts and selected other arts disciplines, the humanities, or the sciences

Excerpted from *The National Visual Arts Standards* published by the National Art Education Association, 1994.